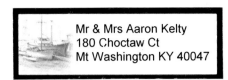
A HISTORY OF THE

DESCENDANTS

OF

ABRAHAM BRENEMAN

Born in Lancaster County, Pennsylvania, December 3, 1744, and settled near Edom, Rockingham County, Virginia, in 1770, or soon after

AND

A COMPLETE GENEALOGICAL REGISTER

WITH

BIOGRAPHIES OF MANY OF HIS DESCENDANTS FROM THE EARLIEST AVAILABLE RECORDS TO THE PRESENT TIME, GIVING DATES IN THREE CENTURIES

By

CHARLES D. BRENEMAN

D1607540

PUBLISHED BY THE AUTHOR
ELIDA, OHIO
Copyright, 1939

Lindale Mennonite Church built in 1898 on the ground that ABRAHAM BRENNEMAN donated "during his lifetime" for a public burying ground.

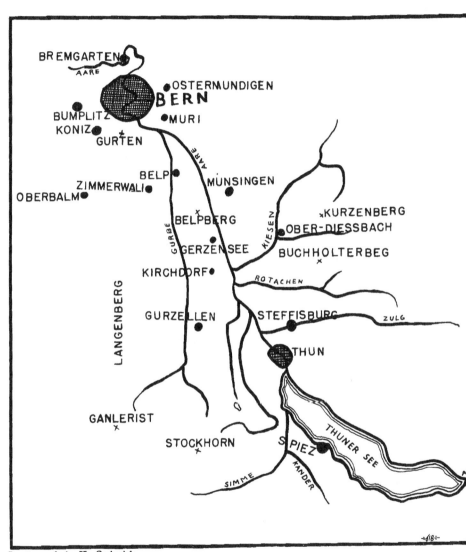

Courtesy of A H. Gerberich

The Aare Valley, Switzerland.
The Original home of the Bronnimans.

DEDICATION

To the immense number of descendants of
ABRAHAM BRENEMAN who have gone
to their reward, to the generation living at
this present time, to the future generations to
come, and especially to Mrs Martha Angeline
Belsh, of Cairo, Ohio, the last surviving
granddaughter of the father of this large family, this book is affectionately dedicated

PREFACE

From my earliest recollection, the kinsfolk who visited in our home at various periods had a fascination that somehow gripped me, and certain incidents associated with these visits left impressions on my memory, which were never forgotten. Especially was this true when the kinsfolk came from a distance. I was ever interested in learning how these folks lived and did things away from where we were at home, and as my parents were both inclined to rehearse and speak of the active life of their kin, it always made a marked impression on me. Frequently father and mother would narrate incidents of their kin in Virginia and elsewhere, and I would pay the closest attention to them. It seemed there was born in me an inherent inclination for the study of kinship. As I grew to manhood, the press of material things and an active life along other lines dulled this inclination for a period of years and this inclination lay dormant until I grew older when it again broke out with increased fervor.

In my early life my mother came into possession of the Funk and Heatwole family histories, of which noble families she was a descendant. Later in life the writer also came to own a copy of the Geil history, which was a later record of his kin on his mother's side. Over these histories I spent many pleasant hours looking up family connections until I had them pretty well fixed in my mind. Then again, soon after the year 1900 my Aunt Barbara Breneman of near Edom, Va., gave to my mother a short history of my father's ancestry, which she in turn gave to the writer. This soon resulted in a growing desire to study the history of the Breneman family. Not until in 1929 did the fervor break out to the extent that I made an effort to bring my inclinations to a reality. While considering these purposes, the historian finds himself facing the fact that he is nearing the sunset of life, when, in many instances, fluency and polish in writing have ceased, at least to some extent. However, I have given points and dates, and if in the future some of the more cultured relatives wish to add spice and fluency, they can do so. Hence we hope that coming generations will continue these genealogies by beginning where this history leaves off, so that as it grows in numbers, it may also grow in interest. This history should have been written long ago, but it appears that no one would undertake the task. While many were thoroughly efficient, no one was willing to do this important work.

Collecting the material and writing this history has required more time and work than had been anticipated, but this delay has resulted in a fuller and more complete history than would have been possible if we had finished it sooner as had been originally planned. It is the conviction of the author that the work will be more satisfactory and enduring than if it had been prepared more hurriedly and less accurately.

v

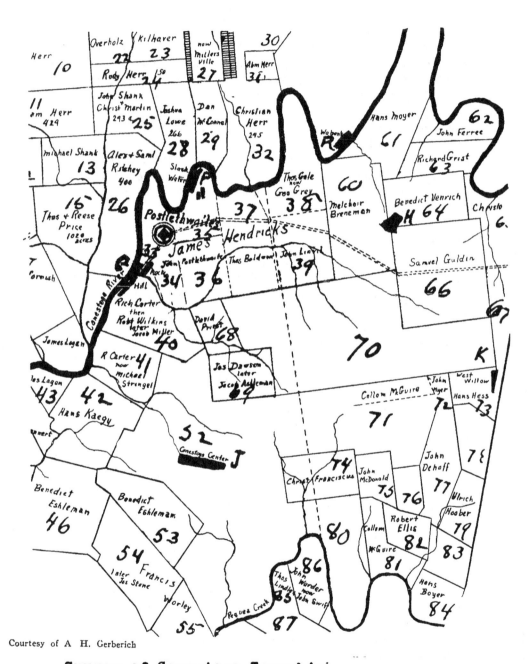

Courtesy of A. H. Gerberich

Survey of Conestoga Township,
made in 1716-1718. The dark spot "H" touching
Melchior Brenimans land indicates the Village of
New Danville. Four miles south of Lancaster Pa.

EXPRESSION OF APPRECIATION

In a few words we should like in sending forth this volume to pay a special tribute to those who have so generously and willingly assisted in gathering data, without which this work could not have been written.

Above all we are grateful to Prof Albert H Gerberich, of Carlisle, Pa., who since July, 1929, has faithfully and wholeheartedly co-operated with me in this great task, without whose assistance much of the material of this work would not be as complete as it now is Prof. Gerberich in 1938 (from the same press that this history will be printed) placed on the market the general history of the Brenneman Family of America as well as much data that he has gathered from Switzerland and Germany of our former ancestors in those countries prior to their coming to America

We also owe special gratitude to the late Mrs. Frances Algers, of Broadway, Va ; Mrs Belle Burkholder, of Dale Enterprise, Va , S B. Wenger, of South English, Ia.: Mrs Effie C. Sharps, of Dayton, Va , Anthony A Brenneman, of Waurika, Okla., Mrs H. A Wine, of Waynesboro, Va ; Mrs. Santa Houff Cline, of Waynesboro, Va ; Oren B Theiss, Jr, of Louisville, Ky ; Leroy Hargesheimer, of Louisville, Ky , Oren R. Brannaman, of Cloverdale, Ind ; Mrs Augusta Bruffey, of Searcy, Ark ; and Jacob A Brenneman, of Elida, O Besides these there are many who for their efficient work are to be commended and to whom many thanks are due for their assistance in looking up certain lineages in their immediate v cinity for the benefit of this history.

The writer points with pride to this fact that, although many of these families have been separated for more than one hundred years, in a very great majority of cases the Breneman descendants were exceedingly prompt in reporting their family records and were anxious for the publicat.on of the work.

There were some, however, who answered only after continued reminders. Then again, a very few could not be stirred up to sufficient interest to respond; hence the missing links in these families It is taken for granted that these would not appreciate the history if donated to them Then there were some who had been separated from their friends so long that they have been lost track of and could not be solicited for their records Indeed these are to be pitied, and for these cases I am not responsible The writer desires that the relatives realize this fact and that he left no means untried to locate every member of the family. He feels that he has done his best to find everyone connected with the family tree.

In securing the information of these aged ancestors and their descendants, it was necessary to interview grandfathers and grandmothers, examine family Bibles, old documents, public records and inscriptions found in the old cemeteries, etc. Since much of the information came in crude form, it was necessary to rearrange and compile it until the manuscript could be understood The author does not expect that this work could do other than create some mistakes, yet all this was a small task compared with the letter writing to so many nooks and corners for the information needed Some of the answers were so mixed up and badly written that they were often very difficult to analyze. It is to be wondered whether one in a thousand of the readers of this history will pause for a moment and consider the amount of work connected with the search for the material of this vast relationship

The historian commenced the gathering of material for this work in July, 1929, and has donated his time ever since until its completion He has borne his own expense for the gathering of data, and if the expense of publication of the work will be compensated by the sale of books, the writer will feel that he has done only his duty Therefore it is to be expected that the Brenneman descendants will be liberal and prompt in purchasing books and helping defray the expense of publication

It was with difficulty that all these available points were obtained, and yet since the completion, I accept the results with a feeling of satisfaction that the history of our noble ancestors and their descendants has been recorded.

In concluding this work the writer hopes that his efforts may not have been in vain, and that the work may receive your hearty approval and support

Sincerely your servant,

The Author

A BRIEF SKETCH

The biography of the author of this history can be summed up very briefly He was born near Singers Glen, Rockingham Co, Va, April 27, 1866, and moved with his parents to Morgan Co, Mo, in the spring of 1870 Here they resided until Oct., 1880, when they moved to near Elida, Allen Co, Ohio He has spent the remainder of his life in this vicinity

His father passed away in Mar., 1882, before the writer was sixteen years of age, and being the oldest of a family of five children, was made responsible by the help of a noble and devoted mother for providing for the family The writer's education consequently was limited, and no one more fully realizes than he his inability of producing a work equivalent to the efforts of those who are up to date writers for the press and the public

So, Kind Reader, I hope you will pardon all mistakes, errors, and omissions found within this history with the full assurance of the writer that they were not done intentionally. The writer may have done many unwise things during his life, but let us hope that he has done at least one wise thing in collecting and writing this history, and preserving the genealogy of the family for the future generations.

He has been a farmer most of his life. He is a member of the Mennonite Church He has served on the Executive Board of the Ohio Mennonite Sunday School Conference for nearly twenty-five years, and for eight years he was a member of the District Mission Board. For twenty years he was trustee for the Salem and Central Mennonite churches. He was also on various committees.

Sincerely your humble servant,

Charles D Breneman

Elida, Ohio

THE NAME

About the origin of the name, there are various theories.

(1) One of the likely theories is the word "Brenneman" means "the man from the BRENNER," a pass on the Tyrolean Alps, between Austria and Italy.

(2) Some say it signifies a distiller.

(3) Some say it originated from the burning of a man at the stake during the Reformation.

(4) Possibly the most likely origin was given by Dr. H. Turler, at one time archivist at Bern, Switzerland, to the late Senator Horace L. Holdeman of Marietta, Pa., who was a descendant of Melchior Breniman, the pioneer. Dr. Turler stated that it took its name from the hamlet of BRENDI, near Bern, Switzerland, where as early as 1479 there were numerous families found by the name of BRENDIMANN (later changed to BRÖNNIMANN) to designate the inhabitants of the place. The place BRENDI is now called BRONNI From the records at Bern, we learn that our forefather, Melchior BRÖNNIMANN, the exile born in 1631, subscribed his name as here shown His sons Melchior, Jr., and Christian, after coming to America, chose to use an abbreviated form of the different forms of spelling the name in their native land (Brendimann and Bronnimann) In 1737, as shown by the record of wills in the courts of Lancaster County, Pa., we find that Melchior, Jr, the Pioneer, endorsed his will as here shown, "Breniman" In the records of the same court we find that his brother Christian signed his will in 1757 "Branaman" On Mar. 21, 1786, Melchior Breniman, Jr., youngest son of Melchior the Pioneer subscribed to his will thus "Melchor Brenneman."

By referring to the public records of Rockingham and Augusta counties in the Shenandoah Valley of Virginia, we find that the name was almost unanimously signed "Branaman" between the years 1770 and 1815. After this time the sentiment was to choose other ways of spelling the name, but all are variations of the original name John J. Wenger of Harrisonburg, Va, a great-grandson of Abraham Breneman, the progenitor of the descendants shown in this history, found by examining the records of deeds for Rockingham County for the years 1806 and 1808 that his name was written "Abram Branaman" (while the inscription on his stone which was replaced by a new one in 1914 by his grandson David C. Brenneman shows the "E" instead of the "A"). From authentic documents we learn that the first set of children all signed their names "Branaman" while of the second set of children, Henry, Christian, John, Jacob, and David later in life signed their names "Brenneman." Melchior, the oldest son from the first set of children, on May 15, 1813, signed a legal document, as shown above, "Branaman" a copy of which is still in the possession of the writer of this history, he being a great-grandson of Melchior. Hence since the last 100 years, community influences have brought about various ways of signing the name and the writer of this history, desiring to conform to the peculiar wishes of each family, is following the choice of the head of each tribe in this volume.

MEMORIAL

From the Archives at Bern, Switzerland, we learn that Melchior Bronnimann the Exile, was born in Switzerland, about 1631-32, and his home was at Ober-Deissbach, on the north slope of the Buchhalterberg Prof. Gerberich in his research found that the Bronnimann family was established in Canton Bern, Switzerland, as far back as 1479, part cularly in the neighborhood of Belp and in the Aare Valley. From this point as a center, the various families seem to have scattered abroad. It will be seen that the family was an old and respected one, though it had its ups and downs like most families had

In this work we are interested particularly in its h·story from the time of its flight into Germany However, it is necessary that we understand the facts underlying the flight of our ancestors from Switzerland and hear the circumstances attending upon it From the very beg nning of the Reformation, there were re-ligious leaders among the Protestants who did not believe in infant baptism and were convinced that the Scriptures taught that the ceremony should be postponed till riper years, when the candidate could recognize the spiritual significance of the act, the washing away of sin In Holland and Switzerland there arose impor-tant congregations of these so-called Anabaptists. In the latter country the co-operation of Anabaptists w.th the great reformer Zwingli assisted greatly in the establishment of Protestantism. They later separated from him when he made it manifest that he intended to set up a state church Throughout the sixteenth and seventeenth centuries, the Anabaptists (frequently called Mennonites from Menno Simons, their leader 'in Holland and Germany) suffered continuous per-secutions in Switzerland. In addition to their insistence upon adult baptism and their opposition to a state church, their refusal to take oaths or bear arms had made them objects of condemnation Many were executed by drowning, burn-ing, and beheading, down to the martyr bishop, Hans Landis in 1614. Others were sold to neighboring countries as galley-slaves The mildest sentence was exile and confiscation of property, forbidding them to return to Switzerland on pain of death. Melchior Bronnimann, being an adherent to this faith and refusing to abjure his Mennonite belief, was warned, and finally punished by imprisonment in the castle of Thun in the year 1659 We next hear of his flight to (the Palati-nate) Greisheim, twenty miles northwest of the city of Worms in Germany in the year 1671 The flight was unquestionably due to the severe government mandate of 1670, wh.ch caused exiles to leave Switzerland for Germany in large numbers, for a short period of religious toleration. The Thirty Years War had so completely wasted the land that the rulers were quite willing for a time to waive religious orthodoxy in search for a people that would restore their wasted lands and repeople their towns. However, this period of freedom from persecu-tion did not last long until they exper.enced the same fate as did their brethren in other parts of Europe during the last half of the sixteenth and the first half of the seventeenth centuries. The established church tried to turn them from their faith, and when unsuccessful, it persuaded the government to lock them up in prisons or put them to death. It was during this period that the many battles fought between the French and Germans in the time of Louis XIV, the Palatinate was made the battlefield of struggle. Many of these nonresistant Christians were driven out of the country by the French and German armies. Many of them fled to the lowlands of the Rhine where they could not have existed had it not been their rescue with money, food, and clothing. Others found their way to America

The sacrifice that Melchior and his wife made for the ideal of religious liberty should not be lightly passed over by us, their descendants   Their lives should stand out before us on the page of history as lives of purest heroism. They should be an ever-living inspiration to their thousands upon thousands of descendants, particularly in this age when the nobility of self-abnegation is as misunderstood and undervalued as it was in their day. Because they feared God and chose to part with life sooner than to put aside the ideals they cherished, we their descendants enjoy the freedom and happiness of a new world today. The Almighty has powerfully blessed their seed and has truly "led the blind by the way they knew not" to a land of promise removed from the scenes of their suffering and captivity. Because Melchior Bronnimann stood like a rock while the flood of terror and bigotry swirled around him, and because his wife stood at his side with unflinching loyalty, we are able to say with pride that our ancestors participated in the founding of the American nation. While Melchior never returned from Greisheim to his native land, his sons Melchior and Christian came to America from his adopted home.

Melchior Breniman, Jr, son of Melchior the Exile, according to tradition was born in 1665 and the place of his birth was Canton Bern in Switzerland. Like his father he learned the weavers' trade. He was a young man of great energy and intense religious convictions and became a preacher in the Mennonite Church, serving various communities of refugees in Rhein-Hessen and the Pfalz. He and his brother Christian were the first of the family to emigrate to America, caused by the renewed persecutions of his people by the Elector Palatine, after Louis XIV had overrun the land of his adoption in South Germany. They came here that they might find safety and freedom of conscience for themselves and for their families   Prof Gerberich says that he pursued the occupation of farming, weaving, and preaching, while M. G. Weaver, in his book "Mennonites of Lancaster Conference," lists him as a Mennonite bishop. At once after arriving in America he arranged to provide a home for his family and soon purchased land in Strasburg Township, Chester County, Pa., which is that portion of now Conestoga Township, Lancaster Co. (the latter county not being formed or taken from Chester County until 1729). Melchior Breniman's name appears with that of his brother Christian in J. S Mombert's "History of Lancaster County," page 423 "with those who purchased land in the county in 1710," and also among the "Swiss settlement," in same history, page 416, for the years 1715-16-17. The late J C Burkholder of Harrisburg, Pa, under date of Sept. 14, 1929, states that Melchior came to America about 1713 and located on 500 acres of land which is now Conestoga Twp., Lancaster Co, Pa   He also states that one-half of the ground on which the Stone Mennonite Church south of New Danville, Pa, stands, was taken from his farm   (Here we again quote Prof. Albert H. Gerberich) Melchior is first assessed in the year 1718, four shillings and six pence, before this he may have resided a few years with the Mennonite community in Germantown where he had many friends, and where his brother was located for many years   But in 1717 we have the date that he acquired land in Conestoga Township from the following: From the minute books of the board of property of Feb 8, 1717, we find this statement· "Agreed with Martin Kendig and Hans Herr for 5000 acres of land to be taken in several parcels about Conestoga and Pequea Creek at the usual quit rent of one English shilling, to be paid annually at Chester on the first day of March yearly from the first survey. It being for several of their countrymen that are lately arrived." The warrant for this land is signed Sept 22, 1717, to different individuals by the Penns. Among whom were Melchior Breniman and Hans Burkholder who received adjoining tracts in the allotment   Melchior Brenimann (which is from this on known as

Melchior the Pioneer) received a title for 500 acres   Horace Haldeman, a descendant of Melchior the Pioneer, made a research of the holdings of his ancestor in 1874 and found that in addition to the above-named tract he owned one farm of 200 acres, one of 90 acres, one of 125 acres and another of 700 acres that he purchased from the Indian trader Pierre Bezillion on Dec 3, 1728, located on the Susquehanna, which later came in possession of his son Christian. The original plantation in the Conestoga region which was his home place was situated just northwest of the land granted to the original Pequea colony in 1709-1710   The village of New Danville is built on part of Melchior's holdings, which extended from the Conestoga and Mill Creek (4 miles south of Lancaster city) to the stone church on the other side of New Danville   Melchior the Pioneer had children as follows Christopher, Christian, John, Adam, Catherine who married John Steiner, and Melchior, Jr , who seems to have been born from a second wife whose name was Elizabeth   So far as known the last named son was the only child born to him in America   Melchior the Pioneer died Jan 20, 1737   His will was probated April 2, 1737, in the Lancaster courthouse, and was written in High Dutch language, in will book X, 2-28   He had in his life time transferred most of his property to his several children   A few of the items of his will read as follows· "It is my will that my plantation be valued at 160 acres   Item, it is my will that my wife have a third part of all my personal estate and the use and profit of my plantation until my youngest son Melchior Breniman shall marry and after the marriage of my son Melchior my said wife shall have out of the profits of my plantation four pounds a year during the rest of her natural life   Item, it is my will that before any division be made of my personal estate my son Melchior shall first take out of the same the weavers loom and tackle, my Bible, and my chest   Item, if my son Melchior shall die without lawful issue then it is my will that my sons Adam and Christian shall be heirs to my plantation and land "   Under date of Dec 1, 1937, Rev Ira D Landis of Lititz, Pa , a descendant of Melchior states as follows "Hans Burkholder and Melchior Brenimann had selected their burying ground along their line fence, consequently the road between their tracts went around their God's acre   Later the stone Mennonite Church, called the New Danville Church, was built at the same location and half of the ground was taken from each of the above tracts, the road curving west around same then slightly eastward when it again follows its former course   Melchior the Pioneer was buried in this the present church cemetery at New Danville, Pa

*   *   *   *   *

Melchior Breniman, Jr , youngest son of Melchior the Pioneer was born on the old homestead of his father's farm in Aug , 1718, near New Danville, Lancaster Co , Pa , and died at the same place Apr 19, 1794   He long survived his elder brothers, all of whom died thirty years or more before him   He married Anne Good (1722-1800) daughter of Jacob Good of Conestoga, who was a son of Peter Good an immigrant to Lancaster Co , in 1715   Melchior, Jr , and wife had 13 children of whom 11 survived them Peter, Melchior, Abraham. Isaac, Margaret, Rudolph, David, Elizabeth, Jacob, Eve. Ann, John, and Henry   The parents are buried at New Danville Mennonite Church   Melchior, Jr , was a prosperous farmer and left his children well established in life at his death   His will which was rather lengthy was written in 1786, and for some reason his son Abraham was not mentioned, which has given the idea that Melchior and son Abraham were at variance, but this may not have been the case as he may have given him his portion earlier as was often the custom at that period. His mother gave Abraham his full portion in her will before her death.

xii

FAMILY CHARACTERISTICS

The older generations of the Breneman family were rather a large portly build of folks, with an iron will that gave them the sturdy characteristics that have been handed down to the present generation. They were rather of a heavy set build, in height usually ranging from 5 ft. 8 in., to 6 ft. and over, and many weighing over 200 pounds Large feet and hands were very common among them.

Those of us living in the present age should pause and revere our noble ancestors to whom we owe a debt of gratitude and respect, when we listen to the experiences related by our forebears of the privations they endured, battling with sickness, and even premature death, because of a lack of proper medical aid, and facilities of caring for their sick.

The first they did after obtaining a grant for a home was to clear a patch of ground where they might build a log cabin usually covered with clapboards put on without nails (for they had no nails) This was called "home." Every member of the family that could work helped to clear the ground of trees that they might plant some seeds and raise some food to live on; these were the good old days when there were no "bums or loafers," but everyone that could work did their part to make this the greatest land in the whole wide universe and to make it a fit place to raise our future generations. They traveled over dangerous paths, made long trips on horseback and often by foot that they might bring a few necessities that they could not provide at home. This was long before the railroads were built. They cut their grain with sickles, plowing their ground with wooden moldboard plows. The boys wore homespun trousers; the girls wore worsted dresses that their mothers had spun the flax or thread to weave the goods from. Yet they were always happy. Their diet was usually alternated in this way, mush and milk for supper, and milk and mush for breakfast.

Now, dear reader or kinsman, pause and think of your hard-working Christian ancestors; some, especially the ungodly, perhaps seldom if ever, entertain a thought of thankfulness to their noble progenitors who cared for them, much less to the God who created them

* * * * *

ABRAHAM BRENEMAN whose immediate ancestors were written of in the foregoing memorial, and who was the progenitor of the thousands of descendants who have been recorded in this volume, was born Dec. 3, 1744, on the ancestral plantation, near New Danville, Lancaster County, Pa. He was the third child of Melchior Breniman, Jr., and Anna Good. Abraham was reared and grew to manhood on the old homestead where he received his training which in after years proved to be a valuable asset to him in guiding his future career.

Abraham soon after having grown to manhood in Lancaster County, married Marie Reiff of Pennsylvania. They seem to have lived in Lancaster County for a few years after which they moved to near Edom, Rockingham Co, Va, about 1770 or soon after. Here he purchased a tract of land on Linvilles Creek of at least 800 acres. During the Civil War the courthouse was burned at Harrisonburg, Va, and many of the valuable records were destroyed, among these were the copies of deeds and wills of our ancestor, consequently we will be obliged to be deprived of entering copies of these valuable documents in this history. Abraham Breneman was a hard working tiller of the soil, with a determined will to build a home for his family. He braved the ravages of wild beasts and savage Indians He endured all the inconveniences of pioneer life that we might enjoy the fruits of his labors and privations in later years Long before the present school system he provided more than the ordinary education for his family.

xiii

He had sixteen children born to him, fourteen of which grew to maturity, and became the foundation for thousands of homes in every part of the United States, and some in foreign countries. He was the ancestor of 111 grandchildren

It has invariably been said that these descendants are a hard-working folk, honest, industrious, economical, and are usually classed among the influential citizens of the community in which they chance to reside They are a God-fearing people, conscientious, devoted family, and are respected as such.

The older generations were mostly farmers, many of them being large land-holders Of the later generations we have nearly every walk of life represented ministers of the Gospel, doctors, teachers, lawyers, judges, bankers, and many holding places of trust, etc ; in fact they are devoted to any occupation they choose for their vocation in life, and this accounts for their usually succeeding in their undertakings.

In presenting this work to the Brenneman family, we do so in a plain common way asking no honor to ourselves but only a duty We only present the history of a plain, industrious, thrifty, upright, Christian people. We present the history of an ancestry which were a Christian and law-abiding people We sincerely hope that their posterity may think their lives worthy of imitation. May we never forsake the virtues of the fathers and bring shame and reproach upon an honored name, but may we look forward and upward, submitting ourselves to the will of the Lord, and finally all have our names written in the great book of eternal life. With this hope we present this work to the relatives and public

Very sincerely yours,

The Author

ALIENS UNDER THE ENGLISH GOVERNMENT

The disadvantage under which the unnaturalized were placed is very well stated by an entry which appears in the minute book of the board of property under date of September 22, 1717, in Pennsylvania The entry is as follows· "Martin Kendig and Hans Herr and Hans Funk with several of the Palatines, their countrymen having applied to purchase land near Conestoga and Pequea Creek to accommodate those of them who have lately arrived in this province, who are their relations, friends and acquaintances and whom they assure the board are honest and conscientious people Their request being considered and the circumstances of those people in relation to their holdings of lands in the dominion of Great Britain were asked, if they understood the disadvantage they were under by their being born aliens, that therefore their children could not inherit, nor they themselves convey to others the lands they purchased according to the laws of England which may in such case be extended hither They answered they were informed thereof before. however inasmuch as they removed themselves and families into this province they were notwithstanding the said disadvantage willing to purchase lands for their own dwelling. It was further said by the commission-ers that it was their business to sell and dispose of the proprietors' lands to such as would purchase it, yet at the same time they were willing to let them know as they are aliens the danger that might ensue if not in time prevented, also that some years ago a law was enacted by the late Queen Anne for enabling divers aliens particularly named therein to hold and enjoy lands in this province and that the like advantage might probably be obtained for those amongst themselves that were of good report if a petition were preferred to this present assembly, when they sit to do business With this advice they seemed pleased and desired to be informed when such a sitting of the assembly would be that they might prefer a petition to them for such a law as is above mentioned "

Petitions for the above privilege were sent to the assembly, but this was just the time, it will be remembered when Governor Keith was especially alarmed at the German immigration, and it appears that no attention was paid to the demands of the Petitioners. Keith was followed by Gordon who was more liberal, and it was under Governor Gordon's administration that the Mennonites of Lancaster County were finally permitted to become British subjects and thereby acquire the right to "sell and bequeath" their lands, before naturalization had been granted them. But for various reasons this bill was discussed at times and did not become a law until 1729, until they had proved themselves to be of good character and well behaved and showed themselves honest and inclined to industry.

Because of this we can justly say out of honorable self-respect of our forebears that they were loyal to, but would not be a burden to the government under which they lived.

TRADITION versus FACTS

Tradition is ever an unsafe guide Captain John R. Brenneman of Philadelphia, b. Mar. 5, 1842, relates the following to his nephew, the Rev. George Elmer Brenneman, D D., of Pittsburgh, Pa. The information given us is that Melchior Brenneman, who was of the landed estate class of Bavaria, Germany, and who was possessed of an estate of 36,000 acres was on the losing side of one of the movements in the Thirty Years War. He fled to Switzerland where he died and was buried near Lake Constance The Thirty Years War was from 1618-1648. It was his three grandsons who came to America, by the kindly offer and solicitation of William Penn, and were possessed of landed estates in Lancaster County, Pa., Melchior and Christian coming in 1709 and Christopher in 1719 Captain Brenneman moreover related that the Brenneman family employed and sent the Attorney General, who served under President Johnson, to go to Germany and lay claim to the ancestral estate This was easily done, but the inheritance was cut off by the fact that the estate was confiscated by the government. This statement can not be confirmed but if it is true then Melchior the Exile that was born near Bern, Switzerland, in 1631 or 1632, and became the refugee was the son of the Melchior of Bavaria.

Another tradition that many still well remember was this, and came from what seemed to be an unquestionable source, that we were the descendants of Christian Brenemann, who had come to America between 1709 and 1713, and had settled near Germantown, Pa This statement had been handed down from the grandsons of the first pioneers that landed in America. But after a more complete investigation we found that his brother, Melchior Brenemann, who came over at the same time left a will that was probated April 2, 1737, in the Courts of Lancaster Co., Pa , that recorded the names of his children, those of which he had not already transferred lands to in his lifetime, were given their allotments. In this instrument he wills his old homestead of 160 acres to his youngest son Melchior, Jr , (1718-1794) There is also a document on record, signed by Melchior, Jr., bearing date of 1793 (one year before the latter's death) as a voucher for the genuineness of the signature of his father, saying that he had often seen his father write his name when he was a boy.

Hence since this Melchior, Jr , was the father of Abraham Breneman our progenitor, we accept the established fact that we are the descendants of Melchior Brenimann the Pioneer that had settled in Conestoga, Lancaster Co., Pa , soon after arriving in America

EXPLANATION

Directions.—First, pay no attention to pages; use numbers instead. Turn to index and find the family you desire to look up. There may be many individuals having the same name, but by looking whom they married, you will know when you have the person you desire. Then turn to the number following the name and follow this number forward or backward and you can trace every one in that particular family. For example, **No. 1180 Third Generation,** Barbara Brannaman and Peter Baker. You now turn to this number and find that Barbara Brannaman was the second child of Daniel Brannaman who is No. 7, he being the sixth child of Abraham Breneman who is No. 1 in this history.

Tombstones of Abraham Breneman and Wife Marie.

Henry Breneman, born Nov. 1, 1791

THREE GENERATIONS

Daniel Brenneman, born June 8, 1834
Timothy H. Brenneman, born Sept. 20, 1860
Jesse L. Brenneman, born Aug. 26, 1886

H. A. Munaw, M.D.

DESCENDANTS OF ABRAHAM BRENEMAN

1. First Generation.

3) Abraham Breneman, third son of Melchior and Anna Good Breneman, was born in Lancaster Co , Pa , Dec. 3, 1744, m. Marie Reiff of Lancaster Co., Pa , b July 29, 1746, died in Rockingham Co , Va , Mar. 29, 1788. He married afterwards Magdalena Shank, daughter of Adam and Magdalena (Eyeman) Shank, b. Jan. 22, 1769, d May 31, 1851. She is supposed to have been buried in Fairfield Co., Ohio

Abraham moved with his first wife near to Edom, Rockingham Co., Va., and settled on Linville Creek about 1770 where he lived until his death Mar 8, 1815, at the age of 70 y 3 m 5 d He was the father of 16 children and 111 grandchildren.

He owned in a single tract, about 800 acres of land on Linville Creek The copy of his deeds and will were destroyed during the Civil War when the armies of Sheridan made their raid through the Shenandoah Valley and the courthouse at Harrisonburg was destroyed by fire The records were so badly burned that they could not be read

He donated the ground for the Breneman's cemetery a short distance north of Edom, which became the most used for burial purposes of the early settlers of the community for many years In 1898 a church was built on the ground and was named the Lindale Church, and the cemetery is now known by that name In 1826 a church was built on another part of the estate that had belonged to him in his lifetime, and was named the Breneman's Church, and a cemetery was laid out there and goes by the name of the Breneman's cemetery.

Abraham Breneman, the progenitor of this large family that will be recorded in this history, has been described by his youngest son David Breneman of Cairo, Ohio, as being a tall, slender man, smooth shaved, and of a robust constitution and highly respected by the church of his choice, and by his neighbors as well That he was a pillar in the church is shown by the fact that there were regular church services held at his residence (in the early days they had no church houses) Some of the ministers who officiated in the services were Abraham Neiswander, Peter Burkholder, Frederick Rhodes (who was a son-in-law) and Henry Shank, whose wife was a sister to Abraham's first wife.

It is said that he was often seen leading a funeral procession with the corpse of a child resting on the saddle before him He died of camp fever which he contracted by coming in contact with the soldiers who had just returned from the War of 1812 He and his first wife are buried in the Lindale cemetery He and both of his wives were Mennonites

1 Magdalena Breneman, b. Dec 6, 1770 No. 2.
2 Elizabeth Breneman, b Feb 22, 1773 No. 3.
3. Melchior Breneman, b May 11, 1775 No. 4
4 Frances Breneman, b Oct 18, 1777. No. 5
5 Anna Barbara Breneman, b Jan 13, 1780. No 6
6 Daniel Breneman, b. Mar 24, 1782 No. 7.
7 Abraham Breneman, Jr , b Apr. 10, 1785 No. 8.
8 Eve Margaret Breneman, b Mar 22, 1788, d in infancy.

(From second wife)
9 Henry Breneman, Nov. 1, 1791 No. 9.
10. Christian Breneman, b July 17, 1793. No. 10

1

11 John Breneman, b ————, 1795 No. 11
12. Jacob Breneman, b Oct 6, 1796 No 12
13 Mary Breneman, b about 1798 No 13.
14 Susan Breneman, b Nov 18, 1799, d Aug 18, 1807 No 13a
15 Catherine Breneman, b Feb 2, 1802 No 14
16 David Breneman, b May 14, 1805 No 15

No. 2. Second Generation. 1.

1) Magdalena Breneman, b Dec 6, 1770, near Edom, Va , d Aug 20, 1851,
aged 80 y 6 m 14 d , m Frederick Rhodes, b June 13, 1769, d June 21, 1847 Both
were buried in the Early cemetery near Pleasant Valley, Rockingham Co., Va
He was a minister in the Mennonite Church, of which they were both members.
They lived on a 500-acre farm, which they had purchased about six miles south
of Harrisonburg, Va After their death their son, John Rhodes, became the owner
of the farm that his father had owned Before his death he divided up the farm
among his children, and most of the farms still belong to some of the heirs The
descendants of Magdalena and Frederick Rhodes are very numerous as will be
seen by the number of records in this history

1 Anthony Rhodes, b Mar 21, 1789 No 16
2 Elizabeth Rhodes, b Dec 17, 1792 No 17
3 Frances Rhodes, b ————— No 18
4 Frederick Rhodes, b ————— No 19
5 John Rhodes, b Feb 2, 1800 No 20
6 Samuel Rhodes, b ————, 1806 No 21

No. 3. Second Generation. 1.

2) Elizabeth Breneman, b. Feb 22, 1773 near Edom, Va , d. May, 1815, m
Michael Miller, b in 1765, in York Co , Pa He was the son of Samuel and Magdalena Wiley Miller, and a brother of Christian Miller of York Co , Pa Michael
moved with his father to Virginia in 1782, where his father purchased the old
Miller homestead of 215 acres two miles west of Harrisonburg, Va , in that year
It was here that Michael and Elizabeth lived and died Here they reared their
family of seven children

1 Frances Miller, b ————, 1794 No 22
2 Marie Miller, b ————, 1801 No 23.
3 Nancy Miller, b July 30, 1803 No. 24
4 Magdalena Miller, b. Dec. 19, 1805. No 25
5 Barbara Miller, b ————, 1807 No 26.
6 Elizabeth Miller, b Aug. 21, 1808 No 27
7 Michael Miller Jr , b ————— No 28

No. 4. Second Generation. 1.

3) Melchior Breneman, b May 11, 1775, near Edom, Rockingham Co , Va ,
d April 22, 1828 He married Elizabeth Burkholder, b Sept 29, 1777, d Sept 28,
1831 She was the daughter of Peter and Margaret (Huber) Burkholder of near
Dale Enterprise, Rockingham Co , Va This Peter Burkholder was born in 1748
in Switzerland, the son of Christian Burkholder who had made plans to immigrate
to America in 1755 but died in March of that year before he got started His
widow, however, carried out his plans and came to this country with her six
children, landing in Lancaster Co , Pa , in July of the same year Melchior and
Elizabeth were farmers They belonged to the Mennonite Church, in which church
Melchior was a deacon

Melchior purchased 560 acres of his father's old homestead near Edom, Va ,
where they reared their family of two sons and two daughters, who controlled the

2

sole ownership after his death. He was interested in the education of his descendants as will be seen by the fact that he with his sons Abraham and Peter, by the assistance of his half-brother, Christian Breneman, were the most influential promoters in the building of the Breneman's Church house on the part of the farm that later became the possession of his son Peter. This church was built in 1826 for the double purpose of holding church services and also day school during the weekdays as this was before the present free school system was in effect. This church building was in continuous use until in 1919, when it was removed, because the worshipers had settled nearer to the location of the Lindale Church, that had been built in 1898 on the grounds of the original cemetery Melchior and his companion are both buried in the Lindale cemetery

   1 Abraham Breneman, b ————————. No 30.
   2. Peter Breneman, b. July 26, 1803 No. 29.
   3. Daniel Breneman, b. Dec 7, 1805, died young
   4. Elizabeth Breneman, b ————, 1818 No. 31
   5. Anna Breneman, b ————————. No 32.

No. 5. Second Generation. 1.

4) Frances Breneman, b Oct 18, 1777, near Edom, Rockingham, Co., Va. She died in Pendleton Co, on April 21, 1837, and was buried in Mossy Creek cemetery in Augusta Co, Va She married John Landes, b Aug. 1, 1778, in York Co, Pa After the death of his wife Frances, his oldest son, Samuel Landes, took his father with them to Putnamville, Ind, in 1837, where he died Feb. 4, 1846 He is buried at Greencastle, Ind They were married on July 8, 1800, in Virginia. Farmers

   1 Samuel Landes, b June 10, 1801 No 1172.
   2 John Landes. b April 1, 1803 No 1173
   3 Abraham Landes, b ——————— No 1174
   4 Susanna Landes, b. ——————. No 1175.
   5 Nancy Landes, b —————— No. 1176
   6 Hannah Landes, b —————— No 1177.
   7 Christian Landes, b April 5, 1814 No 1178
   8 Catherine Landes, b —————— No 1178½
   9 Henry Landes, b ————, 1819 No 1179

No. 6. Second Generation. 1.

5) Anna Barbara Breneman, b Jan 13, 1780, near Edom, Va, d. Mar 25, 1845. buried in Rockingham Co, Va, m Jacob Hildebrand, b Feb. 17, 1782, d Feb 14, 1862, buried at Hildebrand Church in Augusta Co, Va Farmers Mennonites They lived about five miles north of Waynesboro, Va He had a large tract of land in his possession Later in life he gave his son, the late Bishop Jacob Hildebrand, his home place.

   1 Henry Hildebrand, b Dec 28, 1808 No 33
   2 Magdalena Hildebrand, b Dec 2, 1810 No 34
   3 Anna Hildebrand. b Aug 12, 1813, d Nov. 16, 1879, unmarried.
   4 Jacob Hildebrand, Jr, b Nov 17, 1816. No. 35

No. 7. Second Generation. 1.

6) Daniel Breneman, b Mar 24, 1782, near Edom, Rockingham Co, Va, d. in 1870 in Putnam Co, Ind, m Anna Magdalena Burkholder, b ————, 1780. daughter of Peter and Magdalena Huber Burkholder, of near Dale Enterprise, Rockingham Co, Va. She died in 1865 at the age of 85 years, both are buried at Cloverdale, Ind They were married in Virginia and lived there until 1820, after which they moved to near Danville, Ohio. where they were farmers They lived

3

for a number of years north of Danville, but because of the malarious location, they moved south of Danville a few miles where they lived until they could no longer care for themselves After this their son Jacob took them to his home at Cloverdale, Ind , and cared for them the remaining days of their life In their younger days they were Mennonites, but later they united with the Methodist Church Daniel was possessed with a very enthusiastic disposition religiously, and it is said that he held family devotion all of his life Some of his descendants are possessed with a rare gift of music in many ways

    1 Abraham Brannaman, b ————————, d at the age of 12 years
    2 Barbara Brannaman, b Nov 25, 1806 No 1180
    3 Susan Brannaman, b ————, 1809 No 1181
    4 Ann Brannaman, b Feb 10, 1814 No 1182
    5 Jacob Brannaman, b Sept 6, 1816 No 1183
    6 Betsy Brenneman, b ————, 1819 No 1184
    7 Lydia Brannaman, b Oct 14, 1821 No 1185
    8 Julia Brannaman, b May 8, 1826 No 1186
    9 Mary Brannaman, b ———————— No 1187

No. 8. Second Generation. 1.

7) Abraham Breneman, Jr , b April 10, 1785, near Edom, Va , d in 1843 in Augusta Co , Va , m Elizabeth Hartman, b ————, 1797, in Virginia She died in April, 1872 Both were buried in the Mount Solon cemetery Augusta Co , Va Farmer United Brethren Church They lived near Mt Solon, Va , and owned a farm of 200 acres of land where they reared their family He died rather young of gangrene, which came from an infection of his limb But he chose death rather than to have his limb removed

    1 Sallie Brenaman, b ———————— No 36
    2 Mary Brenaman, b Nov 13, 1824 No 37
    3 Samuel H Brenaman, b ————, 1826 No 38
    4 Catherine Brenaman, b June 15, 1829. No. 39
    5 Malinda Brenaman, b July 3, 1832 No 40
    6 Elizabeth Brenaman, b May 19, 1836 No 41

No. 9. Second Generation. 1.

9) Henry Breneman, b Nov 1, 1791, near Edom, Va d Aug 24, 1866, in Fairfield Co , O , on Aug 8, 1815, m Barbara Beery, b Aug 3, 1797 in Rockingham Co., Va., daughter of George and Susan (Funk) Beery. They moved to near Bremen, O , in 1816, and all of his children were born in Fairfield Co Barbara died Mar. 28, 1838, of small pox He married Esther Good Oct 6, 1840 She died Oct 27, 1841, at the age of 33 years and some days Henry married third wife, Anna Rhodehefer, July 27, 1843 She died Aug 17, 1859.

Henry was baptized and received into the Mennonite Church when 22 years of age In the spring of 1816 he immigrated with his bride of a few months to Rush Creek Twp , Fairfield Co , O , where he was one of the pioneers He prospered there and his success influenced others of his relatives to come out from Virginia and join him He acquired and kept in cultivation two farms in addition to conducting a grist mill and a saw mill So great was the demand for his "Super-Fine-Flour" that he had to run his grist mill day and night, his sons, John and George, taking their turns as millers

In 1838 small pox visited the Rush Creek settlement, and among the victims were a ten-year-old son of Henry, and then two days later his wife They were buried in a cemetery at Sugar Hill near Bremen, O Henry himself lies buried in the Pleasant Hill cemetery near Bremen, O

4

His grandson, Timothy H. Brenneman, of Goshen, Ind, says of his grandfather that he was a fine old gentleman This was the unanimous verdict of his neighbors He was a good reader, and he often read to his family out of a mammoth volume of the "Martyrs' Mirror," a German classic, published at Ephrata, Pa, in 1814 His son, Daniel, fell heir to the old book, which was destroyed by fire in 1894 Henry was also a good footman, having twice made the round trip over the mountains between Fairfield Co, O, and Rockingham Co, Va, his boyhood home He was a loyal Mennonite, and his children continued in that faith.

1 John M Brenneman, b May 28, 1816 No 42
2 Susanna Brenneman, b Oct 19, 1818 No 43
3 George Brenneman, b May 11, 1821 No 44
4 Anna Brenneman, b May 18, 1824. No 45
5 Catherine Brenneman, b Sept 4, 1826 No 46
6 Abraham Brenneman, b June 8, 1829, died of small pox, Mar 26, 1838
7 Henry B Brenneman, b Aug. 12, 1831 No. 47.
8 Daniel Brenneman, b June 8, 1834 No 48.

(From second Marriage)
9 Magdalena Brenneman, b Sept 25, 1841. No 49.

No. 10. Second Generation. 1.

10) Christian Breneman, b July 17, 1793, near Edom, Rockingham Co, Va, d Dec 9, 1859 He married Anna Shank, b May 10, 1795, of Virginia She died Jan 17, 1867 Both are buried in the Lindale cemetery near Edom, Va Farmers Mennonites.

Christian Breneman was a strong supporter of building the Breneman's Church on a part of the ancestral estate He owned and lived on 248 acres of his father's homestead He was a farmer all his life A portion of his will is still preserved in the court house at Harrisonburg, Va, the document being partly burned in the destruction of the old building by the Union troops in the Civil War He reared a large family of children, who became the heads of large families

1 Frances Breneman, b about 1818 or 1819. No 50
2 Esther Breneman, b May 11, 1822 No. 51
3 Magdalena Breneman, b ————, 1823. No. 52
4 Henry Breneman, b ————, d. at 21 y. of age
5 Martin L Breneman, b Feb 29, 1826. No. 53
6 Lydia Breneman, b Nov 10, 1827 No. 54.
7 Joel Breneman, b ————, d young.
8 Michael Breneman, b. ————, d. young
9 Hannah Breneman, b April 9, 1834 No 55
10 David C Breneman, b May 10, 1836 No 56
11 Rebecca Breneman, b ————, 1838 No 57
12 Christian Breneman Jr, b ————, d young

No. 11. Second Generation. 1.

11) John Breneman, b ————, 1795, near Edom, Va, d April 10, 1867, in Allen Co, O, m Elizabeth Stemen, b June 10, 1800, in Virginia. She died in Virginia leaving one daughter He then married Elizabeth Beery, b. Feb. 10, 1797. She died (no date) in Virginia leaving two sons He afterwards married Nancy Grove of Virginia, b Sept 11, 1800 John and his last wife are buried in the Salem cemetery near Elida, O He was a farmer near Edom, Va, in the early part of his life, but in 1831 he moved to Fairfield Co, O, where his last seven

children were born, the first four having been born in Virginia. In 1854 he moved with his family to near Elida, Allen Co, O., where he purchased a farm of 160 acres, on which he lived and died. It is said that he owned considerable land besides his home farm. He with all his companions were Mennonites.

    1. Magdalena Brenneman, b. Sept. 30, 1818, in Virginia. No. 58.

(From second wife)

    2. Isaac Brenneman, b. May 12, 1825, in Virginia No. 59.

    3 David Brenneman, b Sept 13, 1826, in Virginia. No 60

(From third wife)

    4. Lydia Brenneman, b. Dec. 29, 1829, in Virginia No. 61.

    5. Noah Brenneman, b. Oct. 31, 1831, in Ohio No 62.

    6. Martin G. Brenneman, b. Aug. 3, 1833, in Ohio. No 63.

    7. Elizabeth Brenneman, b. Feb. 9, 1835, in Ohio. No. 64.

    8 John G. Brenneman, b April 2, 1837, in Ohio No. 65.

    9. Henry Brenneman, b Aug 6, 1839, in Ohio No. 66

    10. Nancy Brenneman, b. Sept. 3, 1841, in Ohio. No. 67.

    11. George Brenneman, b. Mar. 30, 1843, in Ohio. No 68.

No. 12. Second Generation. 1.

    12) Jacob Breneman, b. Oct 7, 1796, near Edom, Va, d. near Elida, O., Jan 1, 1865. He married Mary Beery, b. Nov. 20, 1802, near Edom, Va. She died in October, 1832, in Fairfield Co., O., and is buried in Mt. Tabor cemetery in that county. He married Caroline Ogden, born in Hardy Co., Va., July 12, 1819. Jacob and his first wife were Mennonites; his second wife was a Methodist. In early life he lived near Edom, Va., but in the fall of 1828 he moved with his family to Fairfield Co, O., where he lived until in 1853 He then moved with his family to a farm he purchased from a Mr Stuckey about one mile from Elida, Allen Co., O., where he lived and died His widow survived him for thirty-five years. His son, David, remained on the farm of 160 acres and cared for his mother until her death. The farm was sold by quitclaim deed to his son, David, and is still in the hands of the heirs at the present time (1939). His second wife, Caroline, died Oct. 4, 1900. Both Jacob and his second wife are buried in the Salem cemetery near Elida, O.

    1. John L. Brenneman, b. Oct. 24, 1821, in Virginia No. 69.

    2. Abraham Brenneman, b June 21, 1823, in Virginia No. 70.

    3. Barbara Brenneman, b June 17, 1824, in Virginia. No. 71.

    4. Isaac Brenneman, b. Sept. 25, 1825, in Virginia. No 72.

    5. Elizabeth Brenneman, b. Aug. 29, 1828, in Ohio

    6. Joseph Brenneman, b. Sept. 5, 1830, in Ohio.

    7. Anna Brenneman, b. Sept. 25, 1831, in Ohio

    8. Mary Brenneman, b. Oct 18, 1832, in Ohio.

      (The last four died in infancy)

(From second wife)

    9. Catherine Brenneman, b. Mar. 8, 1838. No 73

    10 David Brenneman, b. Nov 28, 1840 No 74

    11. Jacob R. Brenneman, b. May 18, 1843. No. 75.

    12. Rebecca Brenneman, b. Jan. 2, 1847. No. 76.

    13. Sarah Ann Brenneman, b Nov. 10, 1849 No. 77.

    14. William Franklin Brenneman, b April 30, 1852 No. 78.

    15. Noah E. Brenneman, b. Nov. 8, 1855. No 79.

    16. Charles B. Brenneman, b July 12, 1862 No. 79½.

No. 13. Second Generation. 1.

13) Mary Breneman, b about 1798 near Edom, Rockingham Co., Va., m. Joseph Beery, b. near Edom, Va., Aug. 8, 1798. They moved from Virginia to near Bremen, Fairfield Co., O., soon after marriage, where their children were born. Farmers Mennonites, at Bremen, O. Joseph died April 15, 1841 Mary died ——————. Both were buried in the Pleasant Hill cemetery near Bremen, O

1. Catherine Beery, b July 5, 1821 No 80.
2 Abraham Beery, b Oct 2, 1824 No 81.
3 Joseph Beery, b Nov 18, 1827, d April 20, 1831
4 Magdalena Beery, b Dec 4, 1832 No. 82.
5. John Beery, b Nov 8, 1837. No 83

No. 14. Second Generation. 1.

15) Catherine Breneman, b Feb 2, 1802, near Edom, Va., died Mar. 7, 1865, in Champaign Co., O., m —————— Frank of Virginia In the "Herald of Truth" of April, 1865, we find that she lived in Champaign Co., O., that she had been a widow for several years, that she had three brothers and a sister left, and that she seems to have had no children, at least none are mentioned. She belonged to the Baptist Church for thirty-three years.

No. 15. Second Generation. 1.

16) David Breneman, b May 14, 1805, near Edom, Rockingham Co., Va., d Sept 4, 1892, m Catherine Moyer, b Jan 15, 1809, near Edom, Va She died Sept 19, 1878. Both died near and were buried in the cemetery adjoining their farm at Cairo, O After their marriage they lived near Edom, Va., their native home until in the fall of 1843 they moved to Fairfield Co., O., where they lived for 18 months Then they moved to the 80-acre farm he purchased just outside the limits of Cairo, Allen Co., O., where they spent the remaining days of their lives Eight children were born to them in Virginia, and one in Fairfield Co., O The remaining three were born in Allen Co That David Breneman was a fine old man is the statement that a number of his old neighbors made to the writer long after death They were members of the Christian Church

1 Daniel Brenneman, b July 29, 1829, in Virginia No 84.
2 Abraham Brenneman, b Feb 22, 1831, in Virginia No 85
3. Elizabeth Brenneman, b Mar 21, 1833, in Virginia. No. 86
4 Samuel C Brenneman, b April 4, 1835, in Virginia No 87.
5 Rebecca Brenneman, b Mar 7, 1837, in Virginia No. 88
6 Mary Catherine Brenneman, b Nov 19, 1838, in Virginia. No. 89.
7 Sarah Ellen Brenneman, b Nov 1, 1840, in Virginia. No. 90
8 Lydia Frances Brenneman, b Dec 13, 1842, in Virginia No 91
9 David D Brenneman, b April 4, 1844, in Fairfield Co., O No 92
10 John H Brenneman, b Aug 24, 1848, in Allen Co., O No 93.
11. Jacob Peter Brenneman, b July 8, 1849, in Allen Co., O No 94
12 Martha Angeline Brenneman, b Feb 27, 1852 No 95

No. 16. Third Generation. 2.

1) Anthony Rhodes, b Mar 21, 1789, near Pleasant Valley, Rockingham Co., Va., d May 4, 1877 He married Elizabeth Showalter, b ——————, d —————— They lived in early life in Botetourt Co., Va., but later moved to Rockingham Co., near Mt. Clinton, Va., where they died and were buried at the Bank cemetery They were Mennonites, he being a deacon in the church

1 Frances Rhodes, b —————— No 208

2. Sallie Rhodes, b. —————. No. 209.
3 Maggie Rhodes, b. —————. No. 210.
4 Frederick A. Rhodes, b. Feb. 22, 1819. No. 211.
5. Henry A. Rhodes, b. —————. No. 212.
6 John Rhodes, b. —————. No. 213.
7. ————— Rhodes, b. —————, m and lived in Botetourt Co., Va.
8 Esther Rhodes, b. —————. Unmarried.

No. 17. Third Generation. 2.

2) Elizabeth Rhodes, b Dec 17, 1792, near Pleasant Valley, Va , d Jan. 14, 1875, m. Samuel Weaver, b Sept 12, 1790, d Mar. 13, 1857 They lived on a farm of 134 acres which they purchased of Joseph Frank in May, 1829 This farm lies about two and one-half miles west of Harrisonburg, Va , near the Weaver's Church, and is still in possession of his grandson, Elias Brunk. They were Mennonites and are buried in the Weaver cemetery Mr Weaver was a wagon maker in connection with his farming operations

1 John Weaver, b July 25, 1818 No. 215.
2 Magdalene Weaver, b —————, 1823 No 216
3 Frederick Weaver, b Feb 14. 1820. No 217
4 Frances Weaver, b April 28, 1825 No 218
5 Anna Weaver, b ————— No 219
6. Betty Weaver, b —————, died young.
7. Samuel Weaver, Jr , b. —————, died young.
8 Joseph Weaver, b June 21, 1831 No 220
9. Mary (Polly) Weaver, b Aug 23, 1833. No. 221.
10 David H Weaver, b Aug 14, 1837 No. 222.
11 Sarah Weaver, b Feb 3, 1839 No 223

No. 18. Third Generation. 2.

3) Frances Rhodes, b —————, near Pleasant Valley, Va , m Joseph Fry, b —————. They lived near Mt Sidney, Va They were farmers and Mennonites and were buried in the Salem cemetery, in Augusta Co , Va No further record could be found of them.

1 Magdalene Fry, b. —————. No. 224.
2. Frederick Fry, b. —————.

No. 19. Third Generation. 2.

4) Frederick Rhodes, Jr., b —————, near Pleasant Valley, Va , m Kate Stover, b ————— They were farmers near Mt. Sidney, Augusta Co , Va. They were buried in Parnassas cemetery.

1 John F. Rhodes, b Oct 13, 1837 No 225
2. Maggie Rhodes, b —————. No. 226
3 Kate Rhodes b. —————. No. 227.
4. Sallie Rhodes, b. —————. No 228.

No. 20. Third Generation. 2.

5) John Rhodes, b Feb. 2, 1800, near Pleasant Valley, Va , m Franie Bowman, b. March 1811, m Nov. 19, 1829. They lived on the 500-acre farm of his father, Frederick Rhodes, six miles south of Harrisonburg, Va , and after the death of his father became the owner of the land, which is at this writing (1937) mostly owned by his descendants They were Mennonites and were buried in the Early cemetery.

1. Sallie Rhodes, b. Oct. 26, 1830. No. 229.
2. Frederick Rhodes, b. Sept. 19, 1832. No. 230.

8

3. Magdalena Rhodes, b Feb. 20, 1835 No 231
4 David Rhodes, b May 26, 1837 No 232.
5 Catherine Rhodes, b. Aug. 15, 1840. No. 233.
6. Elizabeth Rhodes, b Sept 20, 1843, single.
7 John Rhodes, b Mar 6, 1846. No 234
8 Fanny Rhodes, b Oct 12, 1850. No. 235.

No. 21. Third Generation. 2.

6) Samuel Rhodes, b ————, 1806, near Pleasant Valley, Va., m Anna
Rhodes, b ————, 1809, daughter of Henry Rhodes. Samuel died in ————,
1841. His wife died ————, 1861 They owned a large farm near Pleasant Valley, south of Harrisonburg, Va They were Mennonites and were buried in the
Early cemetery.
1 Elizabeth Rhodes, b Feb. 13, 1830 No 236
2 Magdalena Rhodes, b Oct. 9, 1831. No. 237
3. Susie Rhodes, b Sept 25, 1834. No. 238
4 Frances Rhodes, b. Feb. 26, 1839 No 239
5 Frederick S Rhodes, b April 27, 1833. No 240.
6 Henry L Rhodes, b May 10, 1825 No 241
7 Samuel Rhodes, Jr , b. ————, d. single.

No. 22. Third Generation. 3.

1) Frances Miller, b ————, 1794, near Harrisonburg, Va , m Jacob Shank,
b ————, son of Henry and Magdalena Reiff Shank The Shanks lived on
Frances' parents' old homestead of 215 acres during her life She was buried in
the Shank graveyard a short distance south of the building Jacob was buried in
the new cemetery near the Weaver's Church, the new burying ground being a
part of the Miller farm, also Mennonites
1 Henry Shank, b June 14, 1817 No 626.
2 Jacob Shank, Jr , b May 12, 1819 No. 677.
3 John Shank, b Sept 22, 1821. No 745.
4 Anna Shank, b Sept. 15, 1824 No 800.
5 Samuel Shank, b July —, 1827, d Aug 21, 1831.
6 Michael Shank, b July 15, 1829. No 809.

No. 23. Third Generation. 3.

2) Marie Miller, b Jan 1, 1801, near Harrisonburg, Va., d. Nov. 14, 1884, m ,
in 1824, John Freed, b ————, 1801, d March, 1862 Both were buried in Forest
Rose cemetery, east of Lancaster, O They lived in Virginia until in 1832 when
they moved on a one-horse dandy wagon to Fairfield Co , O., and settled 5 miles
northeast of Lancaster on a farm of 980 acres which remained in the hands of
their descendants until 1914 Marie Freed was considered a very intelligent woman,
a great admirer of art, and had in her possession a wonderful collection of china-
ware and other things She was a great reader, especially of religious books, and
she was fond of music, both instrumental and vocal She could almost quote the
Bible by heart and she spent much time in prayer. John Freed was a kindly
father, and he, too, was a devoted religious worker in the River Brethren Church
of which they were both loyal members
1 Abraham Freed, b Aug 25, 1825 No. 893

No. 24. Third Generation. 3.

3) Nancy Miller, b July 30, 1803, near Harrisonburg, Va , d July 17, 1867, m.
Daniel Showalter, b. Jan 1, 1802, d. June 1, 1889. They lived near Broadway,
Rockingham Co., Va , on their farm of 112 acres The farm is still in the hands

9

of his grandson, Howard Showalter, who lives on it at this time (1936) They were Mennonites, he being a minister of the gospel. They were buried at the Trissels Church, near Broadway, Va

1 Frances Showalter, b Feb. 12, 1828 No 917.
2 Elizabeth Showalter, b. Jan 7, 1826 No 1159.
3 Anna Showalter, b Aug 17, 1824. No. 952
4 Sallie Showalter, b. —————. No. 972.
5. John D Showalter, b April 12, 1829 No 975.
6. Michael Showalter, b. Feb 15, 1831 No. 1037.
7. Daniel Showalter, b. Dec 21, 1839. No 1319.
8. Joseph Showalter, b June 5, 1833 No. 1334

No. 25. Third Generation. 3.

4) Magdalena Miller, b Dec 19, 1805, near Harrisonburg, Va., d Dec. 9, 1865, m. Abraham Beery, b Dec 25, 1803 He died May 17, 1849 She married for a second husband, Rev Samuel Shank, Sr All were Mennonites. Abraham Beery and wife lived near Edom, Va , and both were buried in the Lindale cemetery one mile north of Edom Farmers.

(Children were all from first marriage)

1 Jacob T. Beery, b Sept 7, 1826 No 1054
2 Elizabeth Beery, b June 7, 1828 No 1057
3 Lydia Beery, b Nov 25, 1829 No 1059
4 John H Beery, b Aug 20, 1831, twin No 1062
5 Michael Beery, b Aug 20, 1831, twin No 1066
6 Annie Beery, b Dec 21, 1833 No 1070
7 Abraham Beery, Jr , b April 25, 1836 No 1077
8 Sallie Beery, b Oct 25, 1839 No 1082
9 Fanny Beery, b Sept 7, 1842, unmarried.
10 Barbara Beery, b Sept. 16, 1844 No 1089
11 Mary M Beery, b Dec 16, 1846 No 1090

No. 26. Third Generation. 3.

5) Barbara Miller, b ————, 1807, near Harrisonburg, Va , d March —, 1861, m John B Keagy, b Oct 28, 1802 They moved from Rockingham Co to Augusta Co about 1830 Here they reared their family on the farm located on Naked Creek.

1. Michael Keagy, b Nov 22, 1831, d Sept 22, 1865, single No 1188
2 Rudolph Keagy, b Nov 30, 1833. No 1189.
3. John Keagy, b. June 22, 1836, d Mar 10, 1855
4 Elizabeth Keagy, b Mar 26, 1838, d April 6, 1838
5. Susanna Keagy, b May 18, 1839 No. 1207.
6 Isaac Keagy, b May 25, 1841, d June 11, 1861
7. Jacob Keagy, b May 21, 1844 No 1230
8. Anna Keagy, b. Mar 9, 1847 No 1231
9 Mary Keagy, b May 15, 1849, d July 19, 1869, single

No. 27. Third Generation. 3.

6) Elizabeth Miller, b Aug 21, 1808, near Harrisonburg, Va , d Oct 9, 1881, m. David Eversole, b April 10, 1802, d Jan 25, 1881 Soon after marriage they moved from Rockingham Co , Va , to Fairfield Co , O , where they lived until they died It was here they reared their large family on the farm They were buried in the Forest Rose cemetery near Lancaster, O

1 Mariah Eversole, b Aug 13, 1830. No 1233

2 Henry Eversole, b Oct 2, 1831. No 1309.

3 Jacob Eversole, b June 29, 1833. No. 1244.

4. Elizabeth Eversole, b. Dec 20, 1835, d 1853.

5 David Eversole, Jr, b Mar 12, 1838 No 1260.

6 Lydia Eversole, b Aug 1, 1840 No 1270

7. Susan Eversole, b. July 25, 1841, d Dec 15, 1879.

8 Emmanuel Eversole, b Dec 28, 1842 No. 1289.

9 John P Eversole, b Feb 10, 1845 No 1290.

10 Nancy Eversole, b Sept 13, 1847 No. 1291

11 Martha Eversole, b Dec 27, 1850 No 1301.

No. 28. Third Generation. 3.

7) Michael Miller, Jr, b ——————, near Harrisonburg, Va, m. Mrs. Mary Fauly (nee Stoneburner), of Loudoun Co, Va about 1835. They lived in Fairfield Co, O They were buried in Mt Tabor cemetery, east of Lancaster, O. Evangelical

1. Marie A Miller, b —————— No 1306

2 Mary Elizabeth Miller, b Feb 22, 1839 No. 1307.

3 Michael C Miller, b ————————— No 1308.

4 John E Miller, b Oct 14, 1844 No 1313

5. Abram Miller, b ——————, d at 5 or 6 years.

6 David E Miller, b —————— No 1314

7 Frank P Miller, b March 2, 1853 No 1318

No. 29. Third Generation. 4.

2) Peter Breneman, b. July 26, 1803, near Edom, Rockingham Co., Va., d. April 17, 1864, m Frances Good, b March 20, 1811, d March 9, 1849. She was a daughter of Rev Daniel and Magdalena Witmer Good He later married Mary Funk, b June 11, 1813, d Oct 24, 1882, daughter of Christian and Susan (Geil) Funk All were Mennonites, and were buried in the Lindale cemetery near Edom, Va Peter acquired and lived on 200 acres of the ancestral farm that had belonged to his father and formerly to his grandfather, Abraham Breneman. The Breneman's Church, that had been built in 1826, and removed in 1919, stood on this farm The old Breneman's cemetery is still in use and is being kept in order. Mr Breneman was an up-to-date farmer and business man. He was very influential in the community in which he lived, and by the time of the Civil War he had become rather wealthy As he was conscientious on the question of war, he spent most of his wealth by paying fines to keep his sons out of the service

1 John Breneman, b Oct 30, 1830 No. 96

2 Magdalena Breneman, b Mar 22, 1833 No 99.

3 Lydia Breneman, b Nov. 26, 1835 No 111.

4 Daniel Breneman, b Oct 14, 1837, d May 10, 1862.

5. Melchiah Breneman, b Oct 13, 1839. No. 161.

6 Peter Breneman, Jr, b May 6, 1845. No. 173.

7 Elizabeth Breneman, b Dec 8, 1847 No. 184.

(Children from second wife)

8 David W Breneman, b Oct. 24, 1850 No. 185

9 Susanna Breneman, b Jan. 19, 1856. No. 199.

No. 30. Third Generation. 4.

1) Abraham Breneman, b ————————, d ——————, near Edom, Rockingham Co, Va, m Hannah Furry, b ——————, 1802 Abraham, like his brother Peter, acquired 200 acres of his father's farm that had formerly belonged to his

grandfather, Abraham Breneman, in his lifetime, until in 1850 he sold this farm to a Mr Shaver, and purchased a farm in Brocks Gap This land is now in the hands (1936) of Jack Turner and Charles Shoemaker Abraham was a highly respected and successful business man, his advice being much sought after in his home community where he lived They were Mennonites They are said to be buried in the Breneman's cemetery

1 Jacob Breneman, b Jan 29, 1824 No 1364
2 Daniel Breneman, b Mar —, 1826 No 1370
3 Elizabeth Breneman, b Mar 5, 1830 No 1376
4 Sophiah Breneman, b April 2, 1840 No 1377
5 Anna Breneman, b 1832 No. 1378
6 Abraham Breneman, Jr , b Mar. 3, 1835 No 1379
7 Mary Breneman, b —————— No 1380
8 John Breneman, b Dec. 6, 1827, d Nov 19, 1846

No. 31. Third Generation. 4.

4) Elizabeth Breneman, b ——, 1818, d 1901 She was born near Edom, Va , m Emmanuel Grove, b ————. They lived on a farm of 75 acres near Edom, Va , that she had inherited from her father's estate, until during the Civil War when her sons took them to Darke Co , Ohio, where they lived until their death They were buried in Darke Co , O

1 Emmanuel Grove, Jr , b ————, 1838 No 1414
2 David Grove, b Mar 23, 1837 No 1415

No. 32. Third Generation. 4.

No 5) Anna Breneman, b ————, d ———— She was born near Edom, Va , m Reuben Amick, ———— Anna Breneman was a daughter of Melchior Breneman, and she inherited 75 acres of the old homestead where they lived until in later years they moved away to parts unknown to the friends of the present, and every effort has been made but with no success as to their location Mrs Elizabeth Breneman Long of Virginia, her niece, says that they had several children

No. 33. Third Generation. 6.

1) Henry Hildebrand, b Dec 28, 1808, near Waynesboro, Va , d in Hamilton Co , Ind , m (1st) Esther Billhyner, b July 29, 1810 She died Mar 10, 1865. M (2nd) Emma Clarkson, b Oct 1, 1834, d Feb 1871 M. (3rd) Sarah Crisswell (nee Beck), b Jan 27, 1827, d in 1893 All were buried at Cicero cemetery, Hamilton Co . Ind

(Issue from second wife)

1 Ira Hildebrand, b June 17, 1868 No. 1554
2 Son, stillborn

No. 34. Third Generation. 6.

2) Magdalena Hildebrand, b Dec 2, 1810, near Waynesboro, Va , d in Rockingham Co , Va , Oct 6, 1898, m David Rhodes, b June 3, 1810, d Oct 6, 1859, in Rockingham Co , Va , where they had lived all their married life Farmers Mennonites, of which faith he was a minister in the Middle District

1 Jacob A Rhodes, b. Oct 17, 1831. No. 1555
2. Henry E Rhodes, b Dec 30, 1833 No 1561
3 Samuel Rhodes, b May 19, 1836, d Aug 4, 1858
4 Peter S Rhodes, b. Nov 25, 1838 No 1570
5. David Rhodes, Jr , b. Dec 6, 1840, d. Jan. 1, **1841.**
6. John L Rhodes, b Jan. 1, 1842. No. 1582.
7 Daniel H Rhodes, b June 5, 1844 No 1587.

8 Joseph W Rhodes, b Oct 9, 1846. No 1588
9 Gabriel D Rhodes, b Nov 23, 1848, d. Nov 22, 1870
10 Noah Rhodes, b Mar 3, 1851, d June 7, 1852, twin
11 Seth Rhodes, b Mar 3, 1851, d same day, twin
12 Levi C. Rhodes, b Nov 23, 1853 No 1589.

No. 35. Third Generation. 6.

4) Jacob Hildebrand, Jr , b Nov. 17, 1816, about five miles north of Waynesboro, Va , d Feb 15, 1899, m Magdalena Gochenour, b. Jan. 22, 1814, d. Feb. 15, 1899. Both husband and wife passed away on the same day and were buried in the Hildebrand cemetery in Augusta Co., Va. Mennonites. He was a very able bishop in Augusta Co , Va He was a farmer and acquired his father's large farm about five miles north of Waynesboro, Va.
  1. Frances Hildebrand, b. Sept. 14, 1841. No. 1590
  2. Samuel Hildebrand, b. Jan 11, 1845 No 1613.
  3. Jacob L. Hildebrand, b Aug. 11, 1848 No. 1619
  4 Magdalena Hildebrand, b Oct. 16, 1853 No 1649.
  5 Mary Hildebrand, b Aug 5, 1856 No 1653.

No. 36. Third Generation. 8.

1) Sallie Brenaman, b ————————, d —————————, m. John Walton, b ——————— They lived in Augusta Co , Va
  1 Samuel Walton, b ——————. No 1830.
  2. Mary Walton, b —————— No 1831.
  3 Catherine Walton, b —————— No 1832.
  4 George W Walton, b. Nov 24, 1857 No. 1833.

No. 37. Third Generation. 8.

2) Mary Brenaman, b Nov 13, 1824, near Mt. Solon, Augusta Co., Va., d. Mar 19, 1901, m George L. Obaugh, b July 24, 1822 Mary was buried at Mt. Solon, Va., but Mr Obaugh was buried at Afton, Tenn.
  1. Samuel Harrison Obaugh, b ——————— No. 1834.
  2. Sarah Obaugh, b. ——————— No 1835.
  3. James A Obaugh, b Mar. 26, 1854 No 1836
  4 William Albert Obaugh, b. Dec 24, 1856. No. 1837.

No. 38. Third Generation. 8.

3) Samuel H Brenaman, b ———————, 1826, in Augusta Co , Va , d. Oct. 11, 1883, m Elizabeth Neff, b in 1828, in Rockingham Co , Va , d May 20, 1900, in Augusta Co , Va Both were buried in Mt. Zion cemetery.
  1 J Neff Brenaman, b. Jan 1854, d July, 1922, unmarried.
  2 Watson Brenaman, b ———————, 1858 No 1842
  3 Bettie Brenaman, b Sept 29, 1857, twin No 1843
  4 Ella Brenaman, b. Sept. 29, 1857, twin, d. in infancy.
  5 J Lee Brenaman, b. ———————, 1862, d in 1921, single.
  6 Robert C Brenaman, b. ———————, 1864, d 1921, single
  7 Buena Brenaman, b Feb 23, 1865. No. 1847.
  8 Margaret Brenaman, b Sept 7, 1867. No 1850.
  9. Samuel H Brenaman, Jr , b Nov. 30, 1869. No. 1852.
  10 Charles L. Brenaman, b ———————, 1873 No 1853.

No. 39. Third Generation. 8.

4) Catherine Brenaman, b June 15, 1829, in Augusta Co., Va , d. May 13, 1901, m Robert Thuma, b Feb 15, 1829 He was killed in the Civil War June 9, 1862.

13

He was buried at Silver Creek cemetery, Jamestown, Ohio Methodists. In 1866 she married John Crum of Saratoga, Ind. She with her second husband were buried at Saratoga, Ind.

1. John Abraham Thuma, b Dec 16, 1851. No. 1855.
2. Thomas Newton Thuma, b. Dec 29, 1853. No. 1861.
3. Fannie Elizabeth Thuma, b ————, 1860 No 1864.
4. Sallie Florence Crum, b. Sept. 14, 1868. No 1872.
   (Last child from second husband)

No. 40. Third Generation. 8.

5) Malinda Brenaman, b. July 3, 1832, in Augusta Co., Va., d Dec. 2, 1915, in Van Wert Co, O, m. William Kiracofe, July 28, 1850, b. May 10, 1827, in Augusta Co., Va He died in Van Wert Co., O, Dec. 5, 1901 He was a minister in the United Brethren Church They moved to Allen Co, O, in 1857, and located near Elida. They later moved to Van Wert Co, O, where they both died and were buried in the cemetery at Wren, O.

1. Margaret Elizabeth Kiracofe, b. April 12, 1851 No. 1876
2. Sarah Jane Kiracofe, b. Nov. 12, 1852. No. 1900.
3. John Luther Kiracofe, b Feb 18, 1854. No. 1904.
4 Mary Catherine Kiracofe, b. Nov 18, 1856, d Oct 24, 1862
5. Samuel Henry Kiracofe, b April 2, 1859. No. 1915
6 Alenor Malinda Kiracofe, b Sept. 24, 1861 No. 1918.
7. Charles William Kiracofe, b. Dec 7, 1865 No. 1920
8 Newton Irvin Kiracofe, b. May 24, 1867 No 1927
9 Lockey Ann Kiracofe, b. Feb. 22, 1870 No 1933.
10. James Stewart Kiracofe, b. Nov. 23, 1873 No. 1934.

No. 41. Third Generation. 8.

6) Elizabeth Brenaman, b. May 19, 1836, at Mt Solon, Va, m. William Woodell, b. ————, d July 18, 1887. Address: Mt. Solon, Va He was constable, sheriff, sale crier and farmer. Mr Woodell was buried at Emmanuel cemetery, Augusta Co, Va. Later the family moved to Cuba, Ill., where Elizabeth died Sept. 22, 1920, and was buried in Cuba, Ill, cemetery. United Brethren.

1. Elizabeth Ann Woodell, b Oct. 19, 1853 No. 3509.
2 Steward Irvin Woodell, b. Dec. 28, 1855 No. 3522.
3. Margaret Jane Woodell, b. Apr. 11, 1857. No. 3523.
4. John Baldwin Woodell, b. Feb. 18, 1861. No. 3536.
5. Mary Catherine Woodell, b. Nov. 22, 1863. No 3541.
6. William Howard Lee Woodell, b Aug. 4, 1866. No. 3542.
7. James Harrison Clark Woodell, b Sept 11, 1869. No. 3547
8. Virginia Ida Bell Woodell, b. Mar. 2, 1874. No. 3548

No. 42. Third Generation. 9.

1) John M Brenneman, b near Bremen. O., May 28, 1816, d near Elida, O, Oct. 3, 1895, m in June, 1837, Sophiah Good, daughter of Joseph and Magdalena Campell Good She was born Mar 23, 1815, in Virginia. Mrs Brenneman died Feb 27, 1883. Both were buried in the Salem cemetery near Elida, O. They owned and lived on their farm of 174 acres located in Sugar Creek Twp., Allen Co., O., where they died. John M Brenneman with his wife united with the Mennonite Church in Fairfield Co, O Soon after their marriage in April, 1844, he was chosen to the ministry of the gospel in the Mennonite Church in Fairfield Co. Since his education was very limited, he took about two years of schooling in the public school together with his older children In the fall of 1848 he moved to

Franklin Co , O , where he resided a little over six years While living in Franklin Co , he was ordained to the office of bishop in 1849 In the spring of 1855 he moved with his family to Allen Co , O., where he resided until his death.

The great purpose and concern of his life was the welfare of the Church, which he loved, and the salvation of souls He was much concerned especially for the spiritual welfare of his children and grandchildren. He devoted very little of his time to looking after his temporal affairs, but left these mostly in the care of his eldest son, Joseph.

His disposition was to look on the dark, rather than on the bright side of things, to the serious, rather than to the enjoyable or glad aspect of things.

From the time of his ordination he entered upon his work with great vigor, and soon rose to prominence, his services being called for in many different congregations Being of an aggressive type, he was one of the early advocates of Sunday schools, English preaching, evening meetings, etc. He himself could speak fluently in both the German and English languages. It was through his influence that the "Herald of Truth," the official church paper of the Mennonite Church was promoted by John F Funk of Chicago, Ill , in 1864. In 1867 the permanent home of the Publishing House was moved to Elkhart, Ind From the beginning of the publication John M Brenneman was a regular contributor and writer for the church organ He wrote several books of which "Plain Teachings" was considered the choice of his writings

In his official capacity in his home congregation he was very stern, and inclined to be rather radical on some questions in his early life. This attitude resulted in a serious loss in many of the descendants of the older brethren of his congregation, but in his later life he was one of the most congenial advisers the writer ever worked with.

About twenty years before his death he became afflicted with a form of paralytic affection, which gradually grew worse on him until he could no longer serve in his capacity as leader in the church work For several years he rarely attended services On the morning before his death he requested to have sung the hymn, "Abide with Me, Fast Falls the Eventide." His funeral was held from the Salem Church with John F. Funk of Elkhart, Ind , in charge The sermon was preached from the text of his own selection, Deut 5·29.

1 Joseph Brenneman, b April 13, 1838. No 2340
2 Susanna Brenneman, b Nov 5, 1839 No 2382
3 Lydia Brenneman, b April 21, 1841 No 2385.
4 Anna Brenneman, b April 1, 1842 No 2426
5 Henry A. Brenneman, b Sept. 7, 1844 No 2427
6 Moses Brenneman, b May 4, 1846 No 2428
7 Manassa Brenneman, b Dec 12, 1847, d Feb 12, 1848
8 Catherine Brenneman, b. Dec 10, 1849 No 2441
9 Levi Brenneman, b July 27, 1851 No 2452
10 George Brenneman, b Mar 1, 1853, d May 15, 1853.
11 Elizabeth Brenneman, b May 5, 1854, d. Nov 12, 1857.
12 Magdalena Brenneman, b June 30, 1857. No 2453

No. 43. Third Generation. 9.

2) Susanna Brenneman, born near Bremen, Fairfield Co , O , d. in Tennessee, Oct 4, 1908, m. Henry Shenk, b. June 14, 1817, near Harrisonburg, Va., d April 19, 1876, near Elida, O Both were buried in the Salem cemetery near Elida, O They were related. See number 626 M in 1840 They lived in Fairfield Co , O., until in 1855 when they moved on their farm two and one half miles west of Elida where they lived until his death, the widow living there for many years after being

15

left alone. In her old age she went to live with her daughter Lydia Powell near Knoxville, Tenn., where she died.

1. Jacob Shenk, b. June 25, 1841, d. Oct. 1, 1842
2. Anna Shenk, b Aug 4, 1843, d Oct 5, 1851.
3 Henry Shenk, Jr., b. Nov 15, 1845, d June 21, 1847
4. John M. Shenk, b. Jan 19, 1848   No 627.
5 Andrew Shenk, b. Aug 20, 1850   No. 644
6 Daniel Shenk, b Sept 27, 1853   No. 652
7. Catherine Shenk, b. Oct 30, 1856.   No 664
8 Lydia Shenk, b April 7, 1859   No. 667
9 Abraham P. Shenk, b Feb 15, 1862   No. 670.

No. 44. Third Generation. 9.

3) George Brenneman, b near Bremen, O, May 11, 1821, d. in Putnam Co., O, May 13, 1889, m. Anna Burkholder, b Mar 20, 1819, d Mar. 26, 1896. Both were buried in the Salem cemetery near Elida, O. Mennonites   Miller and farmer. He was ordained to the ministry in Fairfield Co, O., in the fall of 1852. He attended day school after he was ordained   He moved to Putnam Co, from Allen Co., just across the county line, in the spring of 1853   He was ordained to the office of bishop for the Pike and Salem congregations near Elida, Allen Co, O, which office he filled with credit until his death   Like his brother, John M. Brenneman, his services were frequently called for in the different congregations in Ohio and Indiana, serving on several important committees, as well as going as far east as Pennsylvania for baptismal services, and ordinations   Bishop John N Durr, of Martinsburg, Pa, says of him, that he was received into the church, ordained to the ministry, and later ordained as bishop in less than two years time

Unlike his brother, John M, he was inclined to look on the cheerful side of things, always lively and talkative, rather slow to accept charges against his brethren, yet when duty demanded he could rebuke in a kindly way that usually reached his members and brought about a reconciliation.

It was during the latter part of his life that these congregations began to grow in numbers so that it became necessary to build new church houses at both the Salem and Pike places of worship.

1. Elizabeth Brenneman, b Dec 4, 1841, d Feb 4, 1842.
2 Catherine Brenneman, b Mar. 20, 1843   No 2462
3 Lydia Brenneman, b Feb. 17, 1845   No 2466
4 Nancy Brenneman, b Mar. 6, 1847.   No 2469
5. Henry Brenneman, b April 7, 1851   No 2475.
6 Sarah Brenneman, b Sept. 25, 1853.   No 2488
7. Samuel Brenneman, b July 26, 1857   No. 2500.
8 George G Brenneman, Jr, b Sept 14, 1862.   No. 2504.

No. 45. Third Generation. 9.

4) Anna Brenneman, b May 18, 1824, near Bremen, O., d. near Elida, O, Nov. 28, 1910, m Oct. 3, 1845, John Huber, b May 1, 1822. He died May 16, 1875   Both were buried at the Salem cemetery near Elida, O   After marriage they lived in Fairfield Co, O., until 1852 when they moved to Putnam Co., O., where they lived until after his death several years, when she came near to Elida to live with her son Jacob Huber until her death   Mennonites   Farmers

1. Jacob B Huber, b Dec 1, 1844   No 2511
2 Elizabeth Huber, b Sept 10, 1846, d Feb 25, 1870   Mennonite, teacher
3. Henry Huber, b. Mar 10, 1849.   No 2538
4 Barbara Huber, b June 24, 1851.   No. 2551.

5 George Huber, b. Sept 24, 1853. No. 2554.

6 Matilda Huber, b June 16, 1858. No 2555.

7. Daniel Huber, b. Feb. 21, 1861, d Jan. 27, 1865.

8. Susanna Huber, b July 29, 1864, d April 14, 1865.

9 Amos Huber, b. Feb 20, 1867, d Nov. 17, 1869, twin.

10. Emma Huber, b Feb 20, 1867, twin. No 2556

No. 46. Third Generation. 9.

5) Catherine Brenneman, b Sept 4, 1826, near Bremen, O., d. Sept. 6, 1874, m. George Mumaw, b April 10, 1818, in Westmoreland Co., Pa., m. Nov. 9, 1845. He died 1886 They lived in Holmes Co, O Farmers. Mennonites.

1. Susan Mumaw, b Mar 15, 1847 No 2557.

2 Henry A. Mumaw, b Jan 27, 1850 No 2587.

3. Amos Mumaw, b. June 27, 1852 No. 2590.

4 Rachael Mumaw, b May 21, 1856, unmarried.

5. Fannie Mumaw, b. Feb 19, 1859, d. Apr. 10, 1930.

6 John Mumaw, b. Jan 30, 1862 No 2602.

7. Mary A Mumaw, b Jan 22, 1865, single, d May 28, 1893, at Lakeside Hospital, Cleveland, O

8 Infant died at the age of eight days

No. 47. Third Generation. 9.

6) Henry B Brenneman, b near Bremen, O, Aug. 12. 1831, d at Elkhart, Ind. Sept 15, 1887, m Matilda Blosser, b Aug 15, 1856, d Sept. 15, 1895. They never had any children of their own, but he was a great friend of children. His later years he spent working in the Mennonite Publishing House at Elkhart, Ind. He edited the "Words of Cheer" for some years—a weekly especially for children Mennonites Buried at Elkhart, Ind.

No. 48. Third Generation. 9.

7) Daniel Brenneman, b. near Bremen, O, June 8, 1834, d at Goshen, Ind, Sept. 10, 1919 He m Susanna Keagy of New Market, Va, Mar. 22, 1857. She was born May 18, 1839, d Mar 28, 1908 Both were buried at Oak Ridge cemetery, Goshen, Ind He was a minister in the Mennonite Brethren of Christ Church of Goshen, Ind. They were closely related. For his biography turn to No. 1207, where his descendants will be found in consecutive order following the line of his companion that first entered the family register, which closes at No 1232.

1 Mary M Brenneman, b April 24, 1859 No. 1208

2 Timothy H. Brenneman, b Sept 20, 1860 No. 1209.

3 John S Brenneman, b May 4, 1862 No 1214.

4 Josiah Brenneman, b June 28, 1864. No 1215.

5 Rhody K. Brenneman, b July 17, 1866. No 1220.

6 Martha A. Brenneman, b July 29, 1868 No 1222

7. Naomi S. Brenneman, b Sept 1, 1870 No. 1226.

8. Daniel J. Brenneman, b May 19, 1873 No 1227

9. Phoeba P. Brenneman, b Aug. 31, 1875 No. 1228.

10 Mahlon M Brenneman, b. Nov 12, 1877. No 1229.

No. 49. Third Generation. 9.

9) Magdalena Brenneman, b Sept 25, 1841, near Bremen, Fairfield Co., O, d. July 10, 1910, m. John Funk, b Nov 6, 1840, d Oct. 29, 1922 Both were buried at Oneida, Kans. Farmers Christian Church Address was Oneida, Kans.

1. Henry B. Funk, b. Oct. 21, 1861, d. Nov. 10, 1861.

2. Abraham L. Funk, b. Oct 22, 1863. No 2607.

3. Elizabeth Ann Funk, b. July 23, 1865. No. 2608.
4. Lydia H. Funk, b. Mar. 7, 1868. No. 2610.
5. Sarah C. Funk, b. Jan. 22, 1870, single.
6. James E. Funk, b. April 30, 1872 No 2613.
7. Eva Odel Funk, b. Feb. 28, 1874 No 2614.
8. Fred W. Funk b. Aug. 22, 1878 No 2615.
9. Roy L. Funk, b. ——————, d. at birth.

No. 50. Third Generation. 10.

1) Frances Breneman, b. about 1818 or 1819, near Edom, Va., died ————
——, m. Christian Funk Sept. 3, 1833, b. near Broadway, Va., Jan 16, 1812. Mennonites. Farmers. Address was Rushville, Va.
1. Anna Funk, b. Sept. 30, 1838. No. 2616.
2. Susan Funk, b. Jan. 11, 1842. No. 2623.
3. Samuel C. Funk, b. Oct. 20, 1845. No. 2632.
4. Esther E. Funk, b. Jan. 2, 1848. No. 2638.
5. Martin D Funk, b. Aug 14, 1851 No. 2639.
6. Abraham B. Funk, b Dec 12, 1853 No. 2643.
7. James N. Funk, b. May 21, 1856 No 2644

No. 51. Third Generation. 10.

2) Esther Breneman, b. May 11, 1822, near Edom, Va., d. Nov. 22, 1896, in Allen Co, Ind., m. Lewis B Ridenour, Oct. 10, 1848, of Rockingham Co., Va. He was born July 28, 1822, d in Indiana Nov. 20, 1878. Both were buried near Monroeville, Ind. In ——————— they moved to near Monroeville, Ind, where they purchased a farm of 640 acres and they lived there until they died. The farm is still (1937) in the hands of some of the descendants. Mennonites.
1. Ann Elizabeth Ridenour, b Feb. 10, 1850. No. 2647.
2. Adam Pierce Ridenour, b. Mar. 3, 1853. No. 2648.
3. Lydia Margaret Ridenour, b ———————, 1856 No. 2652.
4. Ephream B Ridenour, b Nov 14, 1858. No. 2653.
5. Catherine Esther Ridenour, b. April 11, 1861. No. 2654.
6. Sarah Ridenour, b June 29, 1863 No 2655.

No. 52. Third Generation. 10.

3) Magdalena Breneman, b ———————, 1823, near Edom, Rockingham Co., Va., d ———————, m Oct. 26, 1843, Christian Brunk, b Feb. 13, 1823, d. Dec. 3, 1906. Buried in the Lindale cemetery Mennonites. Mr. Brunk was ordained to the ministry, July 24, 1859 He lived near Edom, Va.
1. Michael E. Brunk, b. Oct. 4, 1844 No. 2663.
2. Annie E. Brunk, b. July 15, 1846. No. 2674
3. Susanna C. Brunk, b April 30, 1848, d. Dec. 16, 1862.
4. Joseph H. Brunk, b. Feb. 23, 1851 No. 2693.
5. Noah C. Brunk, b Dec. 30, 1852 No. 2695.
6. Fannie R. Brunk, b. April 29, 1855. No. 2696.
7. John M. Brunk, b. May 3, 1858, d. Oct. 13, 1862.
8. Ben D. Brunk, b. Aug. 1, 1860, d. Oct. 7, 1862.
9. Frank T. Brunk, b. Sept 18, 1862. No. 2697.

No. 53. Third Generation. 10.

5) Martin L. Breneman, b. Feb. 9, 1826, near Edom, Va, d. Jan 24, 1898, in Polo, Mo., m Susanna Beery, Nov. 2, 1848 She was born Jan. 26, 1828, in Virginia, d. Jan 13, 1898, in Polo, Mo. Both were taken back to Virginia and buried in the Lindale cemetery near their old home. They lived near Edom, Va., where their

children were all born except the youngest one, who was born in Missouri. On April 12, 1868, they located at Morton, Ray Co., Mo. There being no Mennonite Church there, of which they were members, they in the same year united with the Brethren Church at Oak Grove, five miles northwest of Polo, Mo. In 1880 he was elected to the office of deacon, where they lived devoted Christian lives. A year or two before their death they sold the farm and moved to Polo where they both died eleven days apart, aged 72 and 70 years.

1. John Simon Brenneman, b Mar 17, 1850, d. Jan. 25, 1852.
2. Anthony A. Brenneman, b. Feb 14, 1852. No. 2698.
3. Jacob H. Brenneman, b. Mar. 29, 1854 No 2706.
4. Fannie A. Brenneman, b. Sept. 4, 1856 No. 2720.
5. Virginia M Brenneman, b. Oct 13, 1858. No. 2725.
6. Hettie C. Brenneman, b Oct. 4. 1860. No. 2735.
7. Martin D. Brenneman, b. Mar. 21, 1863. No. 2737.
8. Emma S Brenneman, b Feb 16, 1865. No 2739.
9. Minnie H. Brenneman, b May 6, 1867. No. 2742.
10. Mary E Brenneman, b. Sept. 5, 1869. No 2744.

No. 54. Third Generation. 10.

6) Lydia Breneman, b Nov. 1827, near Edom, Rockingham Co., Va., d. Mar. 4, 1903, m Isaac Wenger in 1848, b. Mar. 28, 1823, d Mar. 28, 1906. Mennonites. Farmers. Both were buried in the Lindale cemetery near Edom, Va. Address was Linville, Va Of Mr. Wenger it is said by those that knew him that he was an expert business manager, and yet never in a hurry, neither did he hurry any of his employes, of which he had many, nor did he have trouble with anyone. It is said that he owned 1600 acres of land on Linville Creek, Rockingham Co., Va., including two large flouring mills, all of which he himself superintended in his easy-going way.

1. Anna Wenger, b. July 1, 1849. No 2745.
2. Joseph Wenger, b Oct. 28, 1850. No. 2746.
3. Jacob C. Wenger, b Jan. 19, 1853. No 2752.
4. Henry H. Wenger, b Feb. 14. 1856. No. 2753.
5. Barbara Wenger, b. Oct. 17, 1858, d. Oct 17, 1896, single.
6 Isaac B. Wenger, b Oct 10, 1860. No. 2754.
7. David Wenger, b. Apr. 20, 1863. No. 2755.
8 Minnie C. Wenger, b. Mar. 12, 1865. No. 2756.
9. John J. Wenger, b Nov. 16, 1866. No. 2761.
10. William H. Wenger, b. Aug. 25, 1869. No. 2762.

No. 55. Third Generation. 10.

9) Hannah Breneman, b. April 9, 1834, near Edom, Rockingham Co., Va., d. May, 1919, m. Jacob Wenger, Mar. 13, 1853, b. June 4, 1829, d. July 22, 1879. Soon after marriage they settled on a farm one-half mile east of Greenmount, Va., and six miles northwest of Harrisonburg, Va He and his wife had both been reared on the farm, and were acquainted with the problems of farm life, as well as with the thrift and industry required in order to make farming a success. Both had acquired only a limited education as was common with rural folks of their day. Address was Greenmount, Va Mennonites.

1. Christian Wenger, b. Mar. 6, 1854, d. Nov. 13, 1863.
2 Barbara Wenger, b. May 17, 1855. No. 2772.
3 Solomon B. Wenger, b. Jan. 7, 1857. No. 2775.
4. Anna Wenger, b. Oct. 7, 1858. No. 2779.
5. Lydia Wenger, b. May 10, 1860. No. 2782.

6. Adam Wenger, b. Feb 9, 1862. No. 2783
7. Timothy Wenger, b Feb. 18, 1864 No 2784.
8. Amos D. Wenger, b Nov. 25, 1867. No 2787.
9. Samuel M. Wenger, b. Sept. 5, 1870, d. Feb. 23, 1893.
10. Magdalena Wenger, b. Oct. 24, 1872 No. 2792.
11. Catherine E. (Katie) Wenger, b. Mar 25, 1875 No 2794.

No. 56. Third Generation. 10.

10) David Christian Breneman, b. near Edom, Rockingham Co, Va., May 10, 1836, d. Feb. 1915, m Frances Good, b. April 15, 1834, d. Mar. 22, 1915, near Newton, Kans, and was buried in the Pennsylvania Mennonite cemetery near there. Unfortunately for David he provided a home for his wife in the fall of 1882 near Edom, Va, and then left her. After spending some time in the vicinity of Cairo and Elida, O., he went farther west, spending much of his time in Missouri and Kansas He was twice married after deserting his wife, but both of his later marriages proved to be failures, as neither of his last wives would remain with him About a year or so before his death he returned to his native home in Virginia After his return to his former home, he erected an iron fence around the Lindale cemetery and replaced his grandfather's tombstone with a new one. He also put up a tombstone for himself and changed the spelling of his name from the original custom of his ancestor to the custom of his relatives in the West. He was a successful financier and business man. He was buried in the Lindale cemetery near Edom, Va., near where he was born.

1. David C Brenneman, b. May 25, 1856, d Jan. 9, 1863.
2. Henry Tilman Brenneman, b Sept 8, 1858 No. 2795.
3 Jessie P. Brenneman, b. Oct 11, 1860 No 2803.
4 Fannie Brenneman, b ——————— No 2808.
5. Infant Brenneman, b ——————, died young
6. David S. Brenneman, b Sept. 9, 1867, d June 15, 1882.
7. Lydia E. Brenneman, b. Dec. 6, 1869 No 2809.
8 George Brenneman, b ———, 1871. No 2812
9. Joseph W. Brenneman, b ———, 1873 No 2813
10 Annie Brenneman, b. July 15, 1875. No. 2816.
11. Jennie Brenneman, b Sept. 22, 1879 No. 2817.

Note.—The above mother went to live with her children in Kansas the later part of her life.

No. 57. Third Generation. 10.

11) Rebecca Breneman, born ———, 1838, near Edom Va., d. Feb. ———, 1904. She married Henry Geil of Virginia for his second wife in 1869. He was born Dec. 1, 1831, and died Nov 19, 1904. Farmer. Mennonites. Dayton, Va.
No issue.

No. 58. Third Generation. 11.

1) Magdalena Brenneman, b. Sept. 30, 1818, near Edom, Va., d. Aug. 4, 1890, m. George Blosser, b. Jan 2, 1813, d Mar. 23, 1898. They lived near Allentown, Allen Co, O., and were buried in the Allentown cemetery. Farmer.

1. Elizabeth Blosser, b. Dec. 21, 1837. No. 2818.
2. Mary Blosser, b. Oct 19, 1839. No. 2819.
3. John Blosser, b. Aug. 21, 1841. No. 2820.
4. David Blosser, b April 27, 1843. No. 2821.
5. George Blosser, b. June 22, 1845. No. 2822.
6. Rebecca Blosser, b. Nov 4, 1847, d. Sept. 1925, single.
7. Henry Blosser, b. Oct 1, 1849. No. 2827.

8 Samuel Blosser, b. Nov. 11, 1851, d. 1862, single.
9 Lewis Blosser, b Oct. 9, 1853. No 2834.
10. Martin Blosser, b Dec 6, 1855. No. 2835.
11. Nancy Blosser, b. Mar. 22, 1858. No. 2837.
12. Lydia Blosser, b. Oct. 30, 1860 No. 2840.
13. Isaac Blosser, b. Feb. 24, 1866, d. —————————, single.

No. 59. Third Generation. 11.

2) Isaac Brenneman, b. May 12, 1825, near Edom, Rockingham Co., Va., d. Aug. 27, 1885, m. Elizabeth Huber of Fairfield Co , O., May 15, 1853. She was born April 28, 1825, d Jan. 5, 1873 Farmers. Mennonites. Both were buried in the Salem cemetery near Elida, O Before marriage he came to Allen Co., O., and entered 160 acres of land in Marion Township, where he started in the woods to clear up a home for his family. He was rather short in stature and stoop-shouldered. The writer would feel that he had not done justice without saying that he was one of the most willing souls to do a favor for any one in need of help. He was kind-hearted, sociable, and honest with all—the good qualities that go to make a man happy, and also all who came in contact with him Their address was Elida, Ohio.
  1. Infant died at birth.
  2. Benjamin Brenneman, b. Sept 27, 1855 No. 2841.
  3 Nancy E Brenneman, b. Mar. 16, 1858 No. 2845.
  4 John I. Brenneman, b. Feb 12, 1860. No. 2846
  5. Susanna H. Brenneman, b July 12, 1867. No. 2847.

No. 60. Third Generation. 11.

3) David Brenneman, b Sept 13, 1826, near Edom, Rockingham Co., Va , d. Feb. 16, 1875, at his home near Delphos, O , m. Leah Stemen, April 5, 1849. of Fairfield Co , O. She was born June 29, 1831; d. Aug. 24, 1907. Both were buried in the Salem cemetery near Elida, O. Mennonites. Farmers.

Mr. Brenneman entered 160 acres of government land in Section 33 of Marion Twp , Allen Co., O., in 1852 He settled for it at a government office at Ft. Defiance, O., at $1 25 per acre. He made the trip on a canal boat from Delphos to Defiance on the Miami and Erie Canal. This was under Martin Van Buren's administration. He was an easy-going successful farmer, and was held in high esteem by his neighbors and friends.
  1. Lydia Brenneman, b. April 14, 1850. No. 2848.
  2 Catherine Brenneman, b July 2, 1852 She was an invalid for many years. Single. D. April 16, 1920.
  3 Elizabeth Brenneman, b. July 3, 1854, d. —————————. No. 2855.
  4 Samuel S Brenneman, b. July 5, 1859 No. 2859.
  5. Ezra Brenneman, b. Nov. 10, 1882, d. Jan. 25, 1863.

No. 61. Third Generation. 11.

4) Lydia Brenneman, b Dec. 29, 1829, near Edom, Va , d. Jan. 2, 1908. On Feb. 24, 1853 she married Nicholis Stemen of Fairfield Co., O , b. Jan. 11, 1829, d. Feb. 17, 1896 They lived near Pickerington, O., all their lives. Mennonites. Farmers. Address was Pickerington, O.
  1. John Stemen, b. Feb 28, 1854 No 2862.
  2. Nancy Stemen, b. June 6, 1855. No. 2863
  3. Lewis Stemen, b. Mar. 21, 1862. No. 2864.
  4. William Stemen, b. Oct 4, 1864 No 2865.
  5. Emma Stemen, b. Jan. 26, 1868. No. 2866.

21

No. 62. Third Generation. 11.

5) Noah Brenneman, b. Oct 31, 1831 in Fairfield Co. O. d Mar. 14, 1914, m. (1st) Diana Humes of Allen Co, O, d. May 31, 1851. She and her child were buried in the Pfiefer cemetery, three miles east of Elida On Nov. 28, 1857, he married (2nd) Catherine Stemen of Fairfield Co, O., b. May 3, 1838. She died later in Dec., 1886. He married (3rd) Lydia Hoover who died later, on Mar. 22, 1891, he married (4th) Elizabeth Boyer Rife, of Mummasburg, Pa Mr. Brenneman was a minister in the Mennonite Church.

    1. Nancy E Brenneman, b ————, d May 13, 1851

(Second marriage)

    2. Henry Brenneman, b. Mar 7, 1859 No 2867
    3 Malinda Brenneman, b. June 28, 1862 No. 2869
    4. James Brenneman, b June 4, 1867
    5. William Brenneman, b June 13, 1874, d in the Philippine Islands during the Spanish American War.

No. 63. Third Generation. 11.

6) Martin G Brenneman, b. in Fairfield Co, O., Aug. 3, 1833, d. Mar. 19, 1919, m. Anna Hunsaker in 1856, b. Sept. 30, 1837, d June 8, 1912. He owned and lived on a 90-acre farm just across the line from the Salem Mennonite cemetery near Elida, O., and was for many years in charge of the cemetery which he cared for to his credit, for it was always kept in the best of condition by him. He was a Mennonite

    1. Nancy Jane Brenneman, b April 26, 1858 No. 2876
    2. Mary Brenneman. b May 12, 1860 No 2888
    3 John H. Brenneman. b June 12, 1862 No 2904.
    4. Matilda Brenneman, b May 25, 1864, d July 3, 1888.
    5. Lydia Brenneman, b Mar 13, 1867 No. 2910.
    6. Sarah Elizabeth Brenneman, b Sept 24, 1872. No 2913.

No. 64. Third Generation. 11.

7) Elizabeth Brenneman, b in Fairfield Co, O, Feb. 9, 1835, m. Samuel Diller, Mar. 16, 1856. He was born ————, 1839, in Fairfield Co, died in ————, 1911. They lived in Allen Co., two miles east of Elida, O Mennonites. Buried in the Salem cemetery.

    1. John B. Diller. b. Dec. 16, 1856. No. 2914.
    2. Lydia Diller, b. May 31, 1858, d Dec. 24, 1858
    3. Nancy Diller, b. Jan. 7, 1860, d. Dec. 2, 1872.
    4. George Diller, b Mar. 23, 1862 No. 2922.
    5. Barbara Diller, b. Jan. 28, 1864. No. 2924.
    6. Henry B. Diller, b. April 21, 1866. No 2931.
    7. Samuel S. Diller, b. July 2, 1868. No 2932
    8. William Diller, b. May 31, 1870. No. 2933.
    9. Andrew Diller, b. May 1, 1873. No. 2938.

No. 65. Third Generation. 11.

8) John G. Brenneman, b. April 21, 1837 in Fairfield Co., O., d. in Allen Co., O., June 6, 1917, m. Mary N. Laman, Sept. 20, 1860, b. ————, 1844, d. ————, 1917. Both were buried in the Salem cemetery near Elida, O. Mr. Brenneman was a Mennonite. They lived on the farm four miles west of Elida. He was a careful farmer and business man

    1. Wm. Henry Brenneman, b. Jan. 10, 1862. No. 2939.
    2. John Frank Brenneman, b. Oct. 6, 1863. No. 2941.

3. Benoni S. Brenneman, b. Dec 6, 1864   No. 2944.
4. George W. Brenneman, b. Oct. 6, 1866. No. 2945.
5. Charles Brenneman, b. Mar. 10, 1868, d. Sept. 16, 1870.
6. Nancy Brenneman, b. Dec. 14, 1869. No. 2947.
7. Daniel L. Brenneman, b. Jan. 1, 1871. No. 2949.
8. Samuel S. Brenneman, b. Oct. 2, 1874. No. 2952.
9. A. Margaret Brenneman, b June 10, 1877. No. 2957.
10. James A. Brenneman, b April 29, 1879. No. 2958.
11. Osie Brenneman, b. Nov 22, 1884. No. 2959.

No. 66. Third Generation. 11.

9) Henry Christian Brenneman, b Aug. 6, 1839, in Fairfield Co., O., d. in his home northwest of Norborne, Mo , Dec. 5, 1921, m. Dec. 15, 1870, Elizabeth Witcher of Ray Co., Mo., b. Dec. 24, 1849, d. Mar. 1, 1927.

Mr. Brenneman was a successful farmer and stock raiser in Carroll Co., Mo. Of him it is said that he was honest and kind, and, of his gentlemanly qualities, all who came in contact with him readily testify He was a devout Christian who showed his faith by his works. He was a member of the Church of Christ. They were buried in the Liberty Church cemetery near Norborne, Mo.

1. Maude May Brenneman, b. Sept. 23, 1873. No. 2961
2. John Ernest Brenneman, b. May 31, 1876. No 2964.
3. Berthy Viola Brenneman, b. Feb 4, 1870. No. 2967.
4 Leona Anna Brenneman, b. May 12, 1880. No 2969.
5. William Henry Brenneman, b Jan. 13, 1887, d. Aug. 4, 1888.
6. Elma Elizabeth Brenneman, b. Jan. 19, 1891. No. 2970.

No. 67. Third Generation. 11.

10) Nancy Brenneman, b Sept. 3, 1841, in Fairfield Co., O., d. Mar. 13, 1932, at her home near Elida, O. She married David Culp, June 20, 1861, b. Oct. 10, 1838, in Fairfield Co., O., d. at their home near Elida, O., Sept. 20, 1911. Mennonites. They purchased the old homestead of her father, John Brenneman, about one and a half miles northeast of Elida, O , where they both died. Buried in the Salem cemetery near Elida.

1. John B. Culp, b. June 11, 1862. No 2971.
2. Elizabeth A Culp, b June 30, 1864, d. Oct. 10, 1880.
3. Emma J. Culp, b Oct. 8, 1866. No. 2977.
4. Nancy C Culp, b Feb 10, 1869. No 2978
5. Malinda A. Culp, b Aug 26, 1871. No. 2986.
6. Christian L. Culp, b. Nov. 14, 1873   No. 2991.
7. Ellen M. Culp, b. Dec 11, 1875, d. Sept. 26, 1884.
8 Cora Mae Culp, b May 22, 1878. No. 2993.
9. Martha M. Culp, b Mar. 13, 1881. No 2996.
10 Sarah E. Culp, b Sept. 9, 1883. No. 2997.
11. Lena F. Culp, b. Oct. 22, 1886, single.

No. 68. Third Generation. 11.

11) George Brenneman, b. Mar. 30, 1843, in Fairfield Co., O., d. at his home in Van Wert Co., O., April 20, 1926 He married Sarah E. Doner Oct. 3, 1872; b. Aug. 8, 1854, d Aug. 14, 1907. He afterwards married Elizabeth Fishpaugh.

(Children from first marriage)
1. Ollie M. Brenneman, b. Aug. 1, 1873. No. 3000.
2. Orpha A. Brenneman, b. Oct. 31, 1875. No 3001.
3. David William Brenneman, b. April 15, 1878. No. 3005.

4. Loy S. Brenneman, b. Feb. 8, 1880. No. 3008.
5. Oscar E. Brenneman, b. April 27, 1885. No. 3010.
6. Harold D Brenneman, b Aug. 13, 1890 No. 3011.

No. 69. Third Generation. 12.

1) John L. Brenneman, b Oct. 24, 1821, not far from Edom, Va, died in Allen Co., O, Sept 4, 1911, m. Elizabeth Keller, Oct 16, 1845, born June 6, 1828, d. Feb. 27, 1886 Mennonites Mr Brenneman moved with his parents from Virginia to Fairfield Co, O., in 1828 After marriage he moved in June to the farm he still owned at his death near Elida, Ohio John L was a very careful and exact farmer; everything had to be done in its proper order and time. His farm of 160 acres, located in Marion Twp, was a model farm and well improved with good substantial buildings Everything had to be kept tidy and clean, even the fence corners and the roadside. A few hours before he died he had been digging plantain along the roadside He came to the house and complained to his companion of being tired and in a short time passed away. On Jan 5, 1893, he married Mrs. Elizabeth J. Breneman (nee Shank), mother of the writer of this History, for his second wife. (C D B)

(Eleven children from his first wife)
1. Mary Brenneman, b. Dec 13, 1847, d. from a fall Feb. 22, 1852.
2 Sarah E Brenneman, b. May 21, 1850. No 3012
3. Jacob D. Brenneman, b. Mar 5, 1852 No. 3024.
4 George J Brenneman, b April 7, 1854 No 3025.
5 Lewis B Brenneman, b. July 10, 1856. No 3037
6 Caroline E Brenneman, b. May 1, 1858 No 3044
7. Barbara Brenneman, b Feb 24, 1861 No. 3045
8 Lydia F Brenneman, b Aug 16, 1863 No 3050
9 Elizabeth M. Brenneman, b Jan 5, 1865 No 3051
10 Nancy C. Brenneman, b May 7, 1867 No 3055
11 Abraham J Brenneman, b July 21, 1870 No 3056

No. 70. Third Generation. 12.

2) Abraham Brenneman, b June 21, 1823, near Edom, Va, d July 26, 1912, in Lancaster, O, at his home. He married Oct 15, 1851, Nancy Cable, b. July 17, 1831. He was a merchant at 141 West Wheeling St, Lancaster, O English Lutherans
1. Frank P. Brenneman, b Aug. 9, 1854 No. 3063.
2 Charles Clinton Brenneman, b Feb 2, 1858, dealer in real Estate etc., and died single Feb. 1901.

No. 71. Third Generation. 12.

3) Barbara Brenneman, b June 17, 1824, near Edom, Va, d at Bronson, Mich., Feb. 28, 1904, m. John Keller, b. in Berks Co., Pa., Dec 15, 1825, d. in Mich, May 7, 1899. They were married in Fairfield Co, O, Sept 23, 1845. Mennonites. Farmers. They settled in Hocking Co, O., until in 1847 they moved to Allen Co., O and in 1866 to Bronson Co, Mich., where they lived until death. Children were all born in Ohio except Lydia F who was born in Michigan.
1. Jacob B Keller, b Oct 27, 1846 No. 3064.
2. Abraham Keller, b Jan 12, 1850. No 3068.
3. Mary C. Keller, b. Jan. 29, 1851 No 3069.
4. Isaac Keller, b. May 24, 1852 No 3074
5. Caroline Keller, b. Aug. 21, 1855. No. 3077.
6. George W. Keller, b Jan. 31, 1858 No 3078.

7. Sarah A. Keller, b. April 25, 1859. No 3081.

8. Nancy J. Keller, b. July 7, 1860. No. 3084.

9. Elizabeth Keller, b. Jan. 20, 1862, d. Feb 17, 1862.

10. Joseph H. Keller, b April 25, 1863. No. 3090.

11. Rebecca Keller, b. Jan. 5, 1865. No. 3091.

12. Lydia F. Keller, b. Feb. 9, 1867. No 3093.

No. 72. Third Generation. 12.

4) Isaac Brenneman, b. Sept 25, 1825, near Edom Va., m. Mary J. Dean in Fairfield Co , O., Oct 28, 1852 She was born Mar. 3, 1833. Methodists. Farmers. Address, Kirksville, Mo. They moved from Ohio to Adair Co., Mo., in 1867.

1. Eliza Alice Brenneman, b. Sept. 17, 1853.

2. Mary Elizabeth Brenneman, b. April 15, 1855. No. 3094.

3. Emma A. Brenneman, b. May 20, 1858.

4. George D Brenneman, b. July 19, 1860 No. 3095.

5. Samuel S. Brenneman, b. Oct. 21, 1863. No. 3096.

No. 73. Third Generation. 12.

9) Catherine Brenneman, b Mar 8, 1838, in Fairfield Co., O., d. July 10, 1907, m. (1st) Abraham Friesner, b Jan 9, 1826, d Dec 31, 1870. She married (2nd) George W. Keckler, b July 24, 1851 He died in 1914 and was buried at Pleasant Hill cemetery near Sturgis, Mich. With her first husband she moved to Branch Co , Mich , where they lived until his death Farmer Methodists.

1. Emma Ellis, b ————, 1857. No. 3097.

2. Louise I Stemen, b Oct. 10, 1859, d Aug 28, 1883.

(The above were born out of wedlock)

3. Caroline Friesner, b. Oct 3, 1864. No 3098.

4 Jacob Friesner, b. Sept 24, 1865 No. 3099.

5. Daniel Friesner, b Feb 26, 1867. No 3101

6. Lydia Ann Friesner, b July 3, 1869 No 3110

7. David Keckler, b ————————. No. 3111.

8. Mary Keckler, b ————————. No. 3112.

9. Myrtle Keckler, b ————————. No. 3113.

10 Barbara M Keckler, b. Aug. 23, 1880. No. 3114.

No. 74. Third Generation. 12.

10) David Brenneman, b. Nov 28, 1840, in Fairfield Co , O., d. April 2, 1919, m Phoeba Ann Lutz, b Dec 15, 1846, in Fairfield Co., O , d. in 1924. David came with his parents to the farm just west of Elida, Allen Co , O , where they lived until their death. David enlisted in Company A, One Hundred Eighteenth Regiment Ohio Volunteers Infantry, in which he served until the close of the Civil War. He was discharged June 20, 1865. After his marriage he purchased his father's farm where they lived until their death. Methodists. They were laid to rest in the Greenlawn Mausoleum just south of Elida, O.

1. Laura A. Brenneman, b. Oct 10, 1867. No. 3117.

2. Irvin E. Brenneman, b. Sept. 28, 1869. No. 3123.

3. Sarah E Brenneman, b July 19, 1871. No. 3124.

4 Stephen A. Brenneman, b Nov 8, 1873. No. 3127.

No. 75. Third Generation. 12.

11) Jacob R. Brenneman, b. May 18, 1843, in Fairfield Co., O. He came with his parents to Allen Co , in 1853. He was married to Elizabeth Stemen of Allen Co , O. She was born ——————, and died ——————. He was a merchant in

Elida for many years, where they lived and died Both are buried in their mausoleum in Greenlawn cemetery near Elida, O. He was a Civil War veteran.

They had no children.

No. 76. Third Generation. 12.

12) Rebecca Brenneman, born in Fairfield Co, O., Jan. 2, 1847, d. Jan. 15, 1923, at Bronson, Mich., m. Daniel F. Beery Dec. 22, 1864, b. in Hocking Co., O., and later of Allen Co. He was born April 27, 1842, and died Mar. 19, 1911, at Bronson, Mich. After marriage they moved to Bronson, Mich , where they lived until their death and where they were buried.

1. Caroline Beery, b. Mar. 12, 1866 No 3130
2. Sarah A. Beery, b Nov. 6, 1867, d Sept. 20, 1868.
3. Abraham Beery, b. April 19. 1869 No. 3138.
4. Catherine Beery, b. Aug 28, 1870, d Mar. 8, 1871
5. William F Beery, b Jan 5, 1872 No 3139
6 Barbara Beery, b July 31, 1873, d Mar. 9, 1879.
7. Jacob Beery, b Nov. 6, 1875.
8. Harvey F. Beery, b. Mar. 5, 1878. No 3143
9. Matilda Beery, b. April 13, 1880 No. 3145
10 Elizabeth Beery, b. May 9, 1882. No 3151.
11 Arthur Beery, b. April 4, 1885. No 3153.
12 Irvin Beery, b. Feb. 6, 1889. No. 3154.

No. 77. Third Generation. 12.

13) Sarah Ann Brenneman, b Nov 10, 1849, in Fairfield Co., O., d. in Van Wert Co, O , May 24, 1937, m Thomas Wisher of Allen Co, O. They lived near Grover Hill, Van Wert Co, O , which was their address. Farmers. Christian Church

1 Fanny Stemen, b ————, 1870 No. 3155
2. James Wisher, b. ————, 1874 No 3160
3. Charles Wisher, b. ————, 1876 No. 3162
4. William Wisher, b. ————, 1878. No. 3170.
5 Daisy Wisher, b. Sept 28, 1880. No. 3171.
6. Jennie Wisher, b. Jan. 15, 1883 No 3177.
7 Elsie Wisher, b. ————. No. 3181.
8 Mary Wisher, b. ————. No. 3182.
9 David Wisher, b. ————.

No. 78. Third Generation. 12.

14) Franklin Brenneman, b April 30, 1852, in Fairfield Co., O , d in Allen Co., Sept. 11, 1885, m. Emma Sawmiller Nov. 25, 1875. She was born Sept. 8, 1857, and died in Washington, D C., July 23, 1932. Both were buried in the Salem cemetery near Elida, Ohio. He was a section hand on the Pennsylvania Railroad. United Brethren

1. Edna Lee Brenneman, b. Sept 20, 1881. No. 3184.

No. 79. Third Generation. 12.

15) Noah Eversole Brenneman, b in Allen Co., O., Nov. 8, 1853, d. Feb. 21, 1937 in same county, m Elizabeth E. Humphry, b. Jan. 1, 1856 They were married Sept. 20, 1877. After their marriage they moved on a farm in the northwestern part of Sugar Creek Twp , Allen Co , where they lived until their children were all born. In 1892 they purchased a small home one-half mile east of Elida where they spent the remaining days of their life. He was township trustee of

German (now American) Twp., for many years. Burial in Greenlawn cemetery near Elida, O. United Brethren Church.

1. William J. Brenneman, b. April 10, 1878. No. 3186.
2. Merlin Brenneman, b. Nov. 14, 1879. No. 3188.
3. Abner Brenneman, b. June 12, 1882. No. 3191.
4. Cloyd Brenneman, b. April 12, 1885, d. Aug. 20, 1890.

No. 79½. Third Generation. 12.

16) Charles B. Brenneman, b. near Elida, O. July 12, 1862, d. at Toledo, O., Mar. 20, 1931, m. Rosetta Loomis of Port Clinton, O. on Mar. 24, 1888, b. Dec. 28, 1857, and d. at Burr Oak, Mich., Feb. 21, 1924. Both were buried near Bronson, Michigan. Mr. Brenneman was railroad worker.

1. Infant daughter, b. Feb. 17, 1889, died at birth.
2. Bessie Caroline Brenneman, b. Oct. 12, 1890, at Rodney, Mich., died April 11, 1903 at Grand Rapids, Mich.
3. Myrtle Leona Brenneman, b. Aug. 7, 1893. No. 3192.
4. Lee Jacob Brenneman, b Mar. 12, 1895. No. 3193.
   (The last two named were born at Cedar Springs, Mich.)

No. 80. Third Generation. 13.

1) Catherine Beery, b July 5, 1821, d. Sept. 25, 1888, m. Jacob Funk, June 20, 1850. They lived near Bremen, O. Mennonites.

1. Jacob Funk, Jr., b May 8, 1852, d. July 17, 1857.
2. Mary M Funk, b July 5, 1855. No. 3194.
3. Matilda Funk, b. Nov. 16, 1857, d. June 11, 1858.
4. Rebecca Funk, b. Aug. 24, 1859. No. 3195.
5. Noah Funk, b. April 23, 1862. No report.
6. Joseph Funk, b. Sept 14, 1864, d Aug. 23, 1895.
7. Elizabeth Funk, b. Sept. 14, 1864. Twin. No. 3196.

No. 81. Third Generation. 13.

2) Abraham Beery, b. Oct 2, 1824, d May 14, 1901. He married Mary Beery in Oct. 1844. She was born in Perry Co., in 1824. Mr. Beery and wife were near relatives. Mr. Beery was born in Fairfield Co., O., near Bremen. After his wife's death he married for his second wife another Mary Beery that was a near relative to his first wife. His children were from his first wife. Mennonites. Farmers. Bremen, Ohio.

1. Elizabeth Beery, b. May 7, 1846, died in infancy.
2. Jacob Beery, b. Dec. 6, 1847, died in infancy.
3. Mary Beery, b. April 6, 1849. No. 3197.
4. Nancy Beery, b. Aug. 29, 1851, died in infancy.
5. Magdalena Beery, b Apr. 22, 1853, d. Apr. 23, 1879.
6. Lydia Beery, b. Nov. 29, 1855. No. 3199.
7. Sarah E. Beery, b. April 25, 1861. No. 3200.
8. Noah Beery, b. April 19, 1864, d. Sept. 1, 1865.

No. 82. Third Generation. 13.

4) Magdalena Beery, b. Dec. 4, 1832, near Bremen, O., d. Oct. 11, 1894, m. Christian C. Beery of near Singers Glen, Va , Aug. 8, 1831. They were married in Ohio, Aug. 30, 1855. Mr. Beery was a minister in the Mennonite Church from 1870 to the date of his death caused by apoplexy at Caledonia, Mich. Farmer at Caledonia, Mich. He died June 29, 1900. Buried in Michigan.

1. John W. Beery, b. July 15, 1856. No 3208.
2. Abraham H. Beery, b. Mar. 25, 1858. No. 3209.

3. Mary C. Beery, b. Mar 23, 1861. No. 3210.
4 Susan Beery, b. Feb. 20, 1863, died in infancy.
5. Lydia Beery, b July 13, 1864 No. 3212.
6. Matilda Beery, b. Nov. 24, 1866, died in infancy.
7. Henry B. Beery, b. Sept. 3, 1868, d Dec 12, 1905.
8. Malinda M. Beery, b Jan 24, 1871. No. 3213.
9. Lewis G Beery, b Jan. 25, 1875, died in infancy.

No. 83. Third Generation. 13.

5) John Beery, b. Nov 8, 1837, d Mar. 23, 1858, m. Lydia Foreman, b. Mar. 6, 1838, d. Sept 3, 1907. They lived near Bremen, O Mr. Beery was buried in Bremen, O, and Mrs Beery in Perry Co, O.

1. George W Beery, b Oct 27, 1857 No 3275

No. 84. Third Generation. 15.

1) Daniel F Brenneman, b July 29, 1829, near Edom, Va., d near Delphos, O., Feb. 8, 1865, m. Catherine Myers Both were buried in the Wesley Cemetery near Cairo, O Address was Delphos, O, near which they lived at time of their death.

1 Libby Brenneman, b ——————
2. David Brenneman, b ——————
3 George N Brenneman, b. Sept. 9, 1863, d. Feb 11, 1865

Libby and David later went to Arizona where they were living at the time of the settling of their grandfather's estate in 1892 and 1895, which is shown by the settlement of the estate by Jacob Brenneman, Executor.

No. 85. Third Generation. 15.

2) Abraham Brenneman, b Feb. 22, 1831, near Edom, Rockingham Co, Va, d in Allen Co, O, Aug 16, 1927 He married Eliza Ward, b. July 18, 1835, and d Mar. 10, 1927. In the fall of 1843 Abraham came with his parents to Fairfield Co, O. and about eighteen months later they moved to near Cairo, O., near which location he lived the rest of his life After marriage he with his wife settled on a farm just north of Cairo, where they lived until Mar 1878, when he purchased a farm of 250 acres a few miles southwest of Cairo where he lived until his death. He was always a prosperous farmer; his business qualities were very outstanding; his influence was very marked in his home community and church. He was one of the wealthiest men in Allen Co Realizing not very long before his death that his time was drawing near, he settled up his vast estate with his children, and after his death there were only about ten thousand dollars in United States bonds to be disposed of by his son, William C, who was made the executor of his remaining estate He owned 918 acres of land at one time They were members of the Christian Church at Cairo, Ohio. Both he and his wife and several of his family that died single were laid away in the family mausoleum that he had built several years prior to his death in the Cairo cemetery

1 Henrietta Brenneman, b Oct. 24, 1858, d. Oct. 20, 1887.
2. William C. Brenneman, b. Nov. 20, 1860. No. 3214.
3. Mary Brenneman, b. Feb. 2, 1863. No. 3216.
4. David W. Brenneman, b. Mar. 31, 1865, d. Oct. 15, 1868
5 Sarah A. Brenneman, b. July 20, 1867. No 3220.
6. Abraham P. Brenneman, b. Mar. 7, 1870, d. Oct. 15, 1871.
7. Benton Brenneman, b Aug. 19, 1872. No. 3221.
8. Frank Brenneman, b Dec. 23, 1874. No 3225.

No. 86. Third Generation. 15.

3) Elizabeth Ann Brenneman. b. Mar. 21, 1833, in Va , m. George Freet, b ――――――. They lived in Mich.

1. Ella Freet, b. ――――――.
2 Henrietta Freet, b. ――――――.
3. Ida Freet, b ――――――.

No. 87. Third Generation. 15.

4) Samuel C Brenneman, b April 4, 1834, in Rockingham Co , Va., d. in Mo. Mar 9, 1915, m Catherine Ward of Allen Co., O , b. Oct. 20, 1839, and d. Oct. 16, 1895, in Ohio. Both were buried in the Wesley Chapel cemetery near Cairo, O Farmer

1 George Brenneman, b Jan. 10, 1859 No 3230.
2 Lewis Brenneman, b Feb. 9, 1861 No 3232.
3 Mary Brenneman, b. July 27, 1864 No. 3233.
4 Jacob Brenneman, b. Dec 7, 1871, d. Sept 18, 1892.

No. 88. Third Generation. 15.

5) Rebecca Brenneman, b Mar 7, 1837, near Edom, Rockingham Co , Va., d. in Allen Co , O , April 20, 1910. She was buried at Cairo, O, Christian Church. She married William Ward, b Oct 23, 1837. He died in Kansas, May, 1918. He was buried near Ellis, Kans Rebecca reared her family near Elida, O.

1. Jacob Ward, b Dec. 15, 1859. No 3237.
2 Alice Ward. b April 28, 1861, d Nov. 4, 1864.
3 Benjamin F. Ward, b Nov. 4, 1864 No 3243
4 Hugh O Ward, b Mar. 10, 1866. No. 3245.
5 Charles M. Ward, b Sept 19, 1867, d Oct 10, 1871.
6 Frank C. Ward, b June 1, 1873. No. 3247.
7. Olive Ward, b. Nov. 2, 1876, d Jan. 2, 1877.

No. 89. Third Generation. 15.

6) Mary Catherine Brenneman, b Nov 19, 1838, near Edom, Va., m. Samuel Meyers, b. ――――, 1838, d Sept 12, 1864. She died Oct. 6, 1920. They were married Nov. 20, 1857. They lived in Paulding Co , O. Farmers. Samuel W. Meyers was wounded in the Civil War and died from the effects of the wound.

1. Mary C Meyers, b. ――――, 1858. No. 3248.
2 Jennie Meyers, b May 25, 1860. No 3249.
3 Charles Meyers, b. Nov. 8, 1862 No 3250.
4. Emma Meyers, b. Oct 12, 1864 No 3251.

No. 90. Third Generation. 15.

7) Sarah Ellen Brenneman. b Nov. 1, 1840, near Edom, Va , d. Dec. 10, 1919, near Bucklin, O., m Joseph Grubb. b. ――――――, d. May 28, 1917. They lived near Bucklin, O. Farmers. They had no children

No. 91. Third Generation. 15.

8) Lydia Frances Brenneman, b Dec 13, 1842, near Edom, Va., d. Dec. 10, 1922. She came with her parents from Virginia in 1843. She married Samuel Whisler of Virginia and soon afterwards they settled in Va., near Broadway. He died Mar 20, 1930. Both were buried in Va.

They had no children

No. 92. Third Generation. 15.

9) David D Brenneman, b. Apr. 4, 1844, in Fairfield Co., O. In 1845 his parents brought him to near Cairo, Allen Co , O , where he remained all his life

He died Sept. 22, 1927. He married (1st) Eliza Middlestedder, b. Dec. 10, 1848, d. June 4, 1894; (2nd) Mary Sherry of Elida, b. in 1868 and d. 1896. On June 29, 1897, he married Anna Klingman, b Mar. 23, 1859. Buried in the Cairo cemetery.

1. George Theodore Brenneman, b. Oct. 21, 1868, d. Mar. 29, 1869.
2. Ora Brenneman, b. Mar. 26, 1870 No. 3252.
3. Amos Sylvester Brenneman, b. Nov. 10, 1872. No. 3254.

(From second wife)
4. Dean David Brenneman, b. Jan. 31, 1896.

No. 93. Third Generation. 15.

10) John H. Brenneman, b. Aug. 24, 1846, near Cairo, O., d. July 20, 1920, m. Susan Frances Haruff, d. Dec. 1, 1907. They owned and lived on an 80-acre farm just west of Cairo. Address was Cairo, O. Buried in the Cairo cemetery.

1. Jessie Austin Brenneman, b. July 3, 1883. No 3256
2. Esta Rebecca Brenneman, b. Nov. 28, 1884 No. 3257
3. James Sheldon Brenneman, b Aug 31, 1886 No. 3258.
4. Mattie Orpha Brenneman, b June 3, 1888. No 3259.
5. Paul Otis Brenneman, b Mar. 27, 1896.
6. Charles Sherman Brenneman, b Apr. 28, 1898. No. 3261.
7. Cleo May Brenneman, b. May 1, 1902, d Sept. 18, 1903.
8. Oscar Harold Brenneman, b. Feb. 12, 1904. No. 3261½.
9. Margaret Cecilia Brenneman, b. July 11, 1906.

No. 94. Third Generation. 15.

11) Jacob Peter Brenneman, b July 8, 1849, near Cairo, O., d. May 19, 1926, m. Sicily Blackburn, b. Mar. 2, 1856, d. Feb, 1929 They lived and died at Buckland, O, where they were buried He was a school teacher for many years and later in life was a derrick builder. Christian Church.

1. Ethel Brenneman, b. Sept. 16, 1875. No. 3262.

No. 95. Third Generation. 15.

12) Martha Angeline Brenneman, b. Feb 27, 1852, near Cairo. O., m. Harmon Belch, b. Oct 2, 1850, d. Oct 25, 1892. At this date (Nov. 3, 1938) she is still living on the old homestead just outside the corporation line of the village of Cairo, and is the last living grandchild of Abraham Breneman, the progenitor of the vast throng of descendants of this family history. Burial place in the adjoining cemetery at Cairo, Ohio.

1. Minnie Elva Belch, b. Mar. 24, 1874 No. 3263.

No. 96. Fourth Generation. 29.

1) John Breneman, b. near Edom, Rockingham Co., Va, Oct. 30, 1830, d. Jan. 27, 1864. He was reared on his father's farm one mile north of Greenmount. The Breneman's Church was built on this same farm in 1826 by the Funks, Shanks, Swanks, and Brenemans of the vicinities of Linville, Singers Glen, Greenmount, and the Brush, for the double purpose of having church services on regular occasions and for holding public school during a part of the year. There were no public schools at that time in the state of Virginia. It was at this place where he received his early school training. Early in life he went in the water swimming while overheated, developed white swelling in his knee, and became a cripple for life. Because of this affliction his father gave him a special course of training in school. He became master of seven languages, after which he took up the profession of teaching for several years. He also served as Clerk for the Commissioners of Revenue of Rockingham Co, Va. Bishop Lewis J. Heatwole of Va. says that he attended school under him in 1862 and that he was the most sociable

and most loving teacher that he ever attended school under. He married Barbara Brunk of Rockingham Co., Va. She was born Nov. 5, 1836. They were only permitted to live together a few years because of his early death. She died Dec. 3, 1905. She never married again after his death. They were Mennonites, and were both buried in Lindale cemetery near the place of his birth.

There was one daughter from this union.

1. Elizabeth Frances Breneman, b. May 5, 1863. No. 97.

No. 97. Fifth Generation. 96.

1) Elizabeth Frances Breneman, b. May 5, 1863, d. May 2, 1934, m. Jacob Alger, b. April 17, 1857, d. May 22, 1912. Farmers. Mennonites. Buried at the Zion Church.

1 Barbara Alger, b. Sept. 7, 1881. Single A teacher.

2 John H. Alger, b. Mar. 7, 1893 No 98

3 Verdie E. Alger, b Aug. 5, 1900. Single A teacher.

No. 98. Sixth Generation. 97.

2) John H. Alger, b. Mar. 7, 1893, near Broadway, Va., m Anna C. Hostetler, b. June 21, 1897. Farmers, Mennonites. Address: Broadway, Va. Deacon.

1. John Paul Alger, b. July 4, 1922

2. Robert S. Alger, b Aug. 2, 1923.

3. Ralph J. Alger, b. Nov. 2, 1924.

4. Nelson E. Alger, b Jan. 17, 1928

5 Elizabeth Catherine Alger, b June 23, 1929.

6. Mildred Frances Alger, b Nov. 11, 1930.

No. 99. Fourth Generation. 29.

2) Magdalena Breneman, b. Mar. 22, 1833, d. April 15, 1879, m. James Ritchie, b. May 12, 1832, d. Dec. 30, 1909. Farmer.

1. Sallie Frances Ritchie, b. July 14, 1858 No. 100.

2. Peter B. Ritchie, b. Nov. 9, 1860, d. Dec. 8, 1909. Single.

3. Charles E. Ritchie, b. June 2, 1863. No. 101.

4. John Franklin Ritchie, b. May 12, 1866. No. 102.

5. William G. Ritchie, b. Mar 30, 1873 No. 103.

No. 100. Fifth Generation. 99.

1) Sallie Frances Ritchie, b. July 14, 1858, in Rockingham Co., Va., d. at Noblesville, Ind., Mar. 28, 1916. She married Joseph H. Roudabush of Va., b. May 20, 1857. They lived at Noblesville, Ind Farmer. Christian Church. Address: Noblesville, Ind.

1. Luther Newton Roudabush, b July 4, 1885. No. 104.

2 Ida Belle Roudabush, b. Sept. 3, 1886. No. 105.

3. Earl Robert Roudabush, b July 29, 1889. No. 106.

4. Claude Franklin Roudabush, b. June 27, 1891. No. 107.

5. Mary Alice Roudabush, b. July 10, 1908 No. 108.

No. 101. Fifth Generation. 99.

3) Charles E. Ritchie, b June 2, 1863, in Va., m. Sept. 9, 1886, Mary C. Swartz, b Mar. 3, 1859. Address· Mt Clinton, Va , No issue.

No. 102. Fifth Generation. 99.

4) John Franklin Ritchie, b May 12, 1866, in Va , m. Mary E. Liskey, b. Nov. 25, 1858, d. July 13, 1897. Address: Harrisonburg, Va., R. 6.

1. Maggie V. Ritchie, b. May 9, 1889. No. 102¼.

2. Elsie P. Ritchie, b. Sept. 24, 1890. No. 102½.
3. Ollie M. Ritchie, b. July 13, 1895.

No. 102¼. Sixth Generation. 102.
1) Maggie V. Ritchie, b May 9, 1889, in Va , m. William Simmers, b. in 1863 in Va. They live in Missouri. No issue.

No. 102½. Sixth Generation. 102.
2) Elsie P. Ritchie, b Sept. 24, 1890, in Va , m. Samuel Wenger, b Dec. 10, 1884. No children.

No. 103. Fifth Generation. 99.
5) William G Ritchie, b. Mar. 30, 1873, in Rockingham Co , Va., m Grace J Walton, Mar. 15, 1906 She was born Nov 24, 1878 Farmers Christian Church. Address: Commiskey, Ind.
1. Loraine Harrell Ritchie, b Jan. 5, 1898 No 109
2. Wilma Pearl Ritchie, b June 30, 1902 No 110.
3. Ronald Ritchie, b Sept 26, 1907.
4. Howard Ritchie, b. June 16, 1913.

No. 104. Sixth Generation. 100.
1) Luther Newton Roudabush, b. July 4, 1885, m. Goldie Maud Depry, b , Dec. 6, 1885. Address· Noblesville, Ind.
1. Walter Earl Roudabush, b. July 27, 1911
2. Agnes Lucille Roudabush, b. Sept. 29, 1916.
3. Joseph Charles Roudabush, b. June 5, 1915, d in infancy.

No. 105. Sixth Generation. 100.
2) Ida Belle Roudabush, b Sept 3, 1886, m Vernon Cleo Metsker, b Nov. 22, 1882 They live in Indiana.
1. Robert Moxey Metsker, b April 2, 1916.
2 Richard Aldine Metsker, b Mar. 16, 1920

No. 106. Sixth Generation. 100.
3) Earl Robert Roudabush, b July 29, 1889, m Mary E. J. Wiseman, b. Nov. 7, 1895 Address Noblesville, Ind.
1. Julia Bernice Roudabush, b. April 24, 1915
2. Ruby Ellen Roudabush, b Oct 4, 1916.

No. 107. Sixth Generation. 100.
4) Claude Franklin Roudabush, b. June 27, 1891, m Carrie May Revis, b. Feb. 24, 1895. Address· Noblesville, Ind.
1. John Franklin Roudabush, b Jan. 6, 1915, d Jan 9, 1915.
2. Mabel Frances Roudabush, b. Sept. 2, 1916
3 Joseph William Roudabush, b Mar. 29, 1919.
4. Donald Eugene Roudabush, b May 23, 1924.
5 Martha Ann Roudabush, b. Dec. 20, 1927.

No. 108. Sixth Generation. 100.
5) Mary Alice Roudabush, b July 10, 1894, m Raymond Carl Gatewood, b. July 18, 1894. Address Noblesville, Ind
1. Joseph Carl Gatewood, b Aug 5, 1917
2 Gertrude May Gatewood, b Oct 21, 1919

No. 109. Sixth Generation. 103.
1) Loraine Harrell Ritchie, b Jan 5, 1898, m Elizabeth Cave, b. Aug. 28, 1894 Married Aug 17, 1923 Address Commiskey, Ind

No. 110. Sixth Generation. 103.

2) Wilma Pearl Ritchie, b. June 30, 1902, m. Lester J. Southerlan, b. April 25, 1898. Address: Commiskey, Ind.

1. Jaunita (Waneta) Southerlan, b. Jan 3, 1921.
2. Lawrence Southerlan, b. April 19, 1922.
3. Isabella B. Southerlan, b. Aug 20, 1927.

No. 111. Fourth Generation. 29.

3) Lydia Breneman, b Nov 26, 1835, d. Jan. 1, 1894, m. Abraham Hupp. b. Dec. 4, 1826. He died Jan 1, 1864 She married (2nd) David Secrist, b. July 30, 1835. d. Sept. 30, 1916. She was born near Edom, Va., and they lived there their entire life.

1. Fannie Hupp, b. Nov. 6, 1854. No. 112.
2. Virginia F. Hupp, b Jan 11, 1857, d Mar. 23, 1864.
3. Alvaretta F Hupp, b Oct 24, 1858 No. 118
4. Marietta B Hupp, b Nov. 10, 1860. No. 125.
5. Charles B Hupp, b Nov. 11, 1862. No 130.

(From second marriage)

6 Laura J. Secrist, b. Feb. 20, 1866. No 141.
7 Minnie R. Secrist, b. May 15, 1868. No 147.
8. Franklin M. Secrist, b Feb 3, 1871. No 150.
9. Bertie S. Secrist, b. July 20, 1873 No. 154.
10 Isadora B Secrist, b. Oct 10, 1875. Single.
11. Zona D. Secrist, b June 10, 1899. No. 160.

No. 112. Fifth Generation. 111.

1) Fannie M. Hupp, b. Nov 6, 1854, d Jan 20, 1924, m. Benjamin Henkel, b April 27, 1855, d Feb 14, 1934 Address Harrisonburg, Va., R 1. Church of the Brethren Farmers.

1. William J. Henkel, b. June 26, 1879. No. 113.
2 Mertie E Henkel, b. Feb 18, 1886, died May 10, 1887.
3 Homer C. Henkel, b Aug 1888. No 114.
4. Elmer M. Henkel, b Feb 5, 1894 No 115

No. 113. Sixth Generation. 112.

1) William J. Henkel, b June 26, 1879, m Bertie A. Whistler, b May 22, 1882. Married Dec. 24, 1901 Farmers. Address: Greenmount, Va. Brethren. Related. No. 1084.

1. Roy Carlton Henkel, b. July 12, 1903. No. 116.
2 Ralph W Henkel, b. April 13, 1907. No. 117.

No. 114. Sixth Generation. 112.

3) Homer C. Henkel, b. Aug. 18, 1888, m July 18, 1911, Lula Edna Whisler, b. Dec. 10. 1895 Address· Harrisonburg, Va , R. 4. Church of Brethren.

1. Charles L. Henkel, b. Sept. 10, 1915.
2. Harry Lee Henkel, b Nov. 24, 1934, d. Dec. 4, 1934.

No. 115. Sixth Generation. 112.

4) Elmer M. Henkel, b. Feb 5, 1894. He died Jan. 21, 1919, m. Ruth G. Landes, b. ————. No issue.

No. 116. Seventh Generation. 113.

1) Roy C. Henkel, b. July 12, 1903, m. Mar. 31, 1926, Fleta Whetzel.
1. Anna Lou Henkel, b. Nov. 10, 1930.

No. 117. Seventh Generation. 113.

2) Ralph W. Henkel, b. April 13, 1907, m. Sept. 21, 1926, Frances Miller.
1. Helen V. Henkel, b. Nov. 21, 1927.
2. Phyllis M. Henkel, b Mar. 31, 1929.

No. 118. Fifth Generation. 111.

3) Alvaretta F. Hupp, b Oct. 24, 1858, near Edom, Va , d. July 24, 1896. She married Silas Shaver, b. Aug. 7, 1862. He died May 7, 1925. Farmers. Church of Brethren. Address: Mathias, Va.
    1. Frank Shaver, b. Feb. 22, 1884, in Rockingham Co., Va., d. June, 1908, from coming in contact with an electric wire.
    2 William Shaver, b. Aug. 13, 1885. No. 119
    3. Lillie Shaver, b. Dec. 3, 1886. No. 120.
    4 John Shaver, b. July 1, 1889 No. 122
    5. Jacob Shaver, b. April 17, 1892 No. 123.
    6. Bertha Shaver, b. May 29, 1894. No 124.

No. 119. Sixth Generation. 118.

2) William Shaver, b Aug 13, 1885, in Rockingham Co , Va , m. Rhoda Smith ——————. Address. Meyerstown, Pa , R 1 Mrs. Smith was a member of the U. B Church.
    1. Ivan Gilbert Shaver, b Sept. 3, 1913
    2. Vada Mae Shaver, b April 23, 1915.
    3. Vergil Berlin Shaver, b. Sept. 4, 1921.
    4 Elmer Franklin Shaver, b Jan 9, 1925.

No. 120. Sixth Generation. 118.

3) Lillian Shaver, b. Dec. 3. 1886, in Rockingham Co , Va., m. Aug. 17, 1908, Walter A. Gronondyke, b July 27, 18— Address: Muncie, Ind., R. 8. Church of the Brethren.
    1. Odessa Mae Gronondyke, b. Oct. 7, 1908.
    2. Robert Elmer Gronondyke, b. April 3, 1911. No. 121
    3. Florence Arabelle Gronondyke, b. Nov. 20, 1921.

No. 121. Seventh Generation. 120.

2) Robert Elmer Gronondyke, b. April 3, 1911, m. Mar. 23, 1929, Priscilla Snyder. Address: Muncie, Ind.
    1. Robert Keith Gronondyke, b. May 15, 1930.

No. 122. Sixth Generation. 118.

4) John Shaver, b. July 1, 1889, in Rockingham Co., Va , m. Pearlie Caplinger. Address: Hershey, Pa. Mennonites.
    1. Jason Hays Shaver, b. Feb. 3, 1915.
    2. Leatha Pauline Shaver, b. Aug. 13, 1919.
    3. Velma Shaver, b. June 24, 1921.
    4. Irene Shaver, b. Sept. 11, 1925.
    5. Norman Walter Shaver, b. Nov. 29, 1926.

No. 123. Sixth Generation. 118.

5) Jacob Shaver, b. April 17, 1892, in Rockingham Co., Va., m. Jan. 1, 1922, Mae Mathias. Address: Mathias, Va.
    1. Nena Gay Shaver, b. Feb. 14, 1924.
    2. William Shaver, b. Sept. ——, 1930.

No. 124. Sixth Generation. 118.

6) Bertha Shaver, b. May 29, 1894, in Rockingham Co, Va., m. Jan. 1, 1921, Kenney Miller. Address: Genoa, Va. Mrs. Miller was a member of the U. B. Church.

No. 125. Fifth Generation. 111.

4) Marietta B. Hupp, b. Nov. 10, 1860, in Rockingham Co., Va., m. Isaac S. Davis, b. May 1, 1853, d. Nov. 19, 1912. Address: Broadway, Va. United Brethren.
1. Charles Witmer Davis, b. Feb. 14, 1883. No. 126.
2. Emma Florence Davis, b. Mar. 14, 1881. No. 127.

No. 126. Sixth Generation. 125.

1) Charles Witmer Davis, b. Feb. 14, 1883, m. Aug. 20, 1909, Fanny Fitwater. Address: Broadway, Va.
1. Ivan Witmer Davis, b. June 27, 1910.
2. Stanley Isaac Davis, b. Oct. 10, 1913.

No. 127. Sixth Generation. 125.

2) Emma Florence Davis, b Mar. 14, 1881, m. Dec. 29, 1901, Charles Runion, b. Jan. 26, 1877. Address: Martinsburg, W. Va.
1. Edna Barbara Runion, b. Feb. 24, 1903. No. 128.
2. Lena Dodd Runion, b. Dec. 4, 1905. No 129.
3. Virginia Garnett Runion, b. Dec. 25, 1917.

No. 128. Seventh Generation. 127.

1) Edna Barbara Runion, b. Feb. 24, 1903, m. Harry Fries.
1. Harry Fries, Jr., b Jan. 27, 1924.

No. 129. Seventh Generation. 127.

2) Lena Dodd Runion, b. Dec. 4, 1905, m Hugh Stilwell, b. ——————.
1. Bruce Stilwell, b. April 13, 1925.
2. Charles Melvin Stilwell, b. Mar. 19, 1927.

No. 130. Fifth Generation. 111.

5) Charles B. Hupp, b. Nov. 11, 1862, in Rockingham Co., Va., m. Aug. 3, 1882, Hannah Dove, b. Sept. 30, 1865. Address: Criders, Va. Church of the Brethren
1. Mary Etta Hupp, b. July 30, 1884. Single.
2. Nora Halena Hupp, b. May 22, 1886. No. 131.
3. Raleigh Melvin Hupp, b. Mar. 22, 1889. No. 132.
4. Effie Lydia Hupp, b. Oct. 30, 1891. Single.
5. Charles Abraham Hupp, b. Oct. 26, 1893. No. 133.
6. Joseph Leonas Hupp, b. Nov 23, 1895. No. 134.
7. William Franklin Hupp, b July 19, 1898 No. 135.
8. Hannah Susan Hupp, b. Dec. 10, 1900. No. 136.
9. Minnie Bliss Hupp, b. Mar. 4, 1903. No. 137.
10. Myrtle Rachel Hupp, b. Oct. 4, 1905. No. 138.
11. Samuel DeWitt Hupp, b. Dec. 11, 1909. No. 139.

No. 131. Sixth Generation. 130.

2) Nora Halena Hupp, b. May 22, 1886, in Va., m. Benjamin Emler Lantz, b. July 1, 1887. Church of the Brethren. Address: Criders, Va.
1 Jay Elmer Lantz, b. Jan. 13, 1910. No. 140.
2. Melvin Dove Lantz, b. Mar. 30, 1914.
3. Ivan Charles Lantz, b. June 15, 1916.
4. Raymond Olen Lantz, b. Dec. 19, 1917.

5. Layman Guy Lantz, b. Dec. 19, 1917. Twins.

6. Goldie Virginia Lantz, b Aug. 1, 1921.

No. 132. Sixth Generation. 130.

3) Raleigh Melvin Hupp, b. Mar 22, 1889, in Va , d. May 4, 1936, m. Bessie Jane Mitchell, b. Dec. 27, 1890 Address Criders, Va. Church of the Brethren.

1. Loy Breneman Hupp, b. May 15, 1922

2. Nellie Grace Hupp, b Dec. 4, 1924.

3 Roy Lamon Hupp, b. May 26, 1926.

No. 133. Sixth Generation. 130.

5) Charles Abraham Hupp, b. Oct 26, 1893, in Rockingham Co., Va., m. Lula Vernal Crider, b. Sept. 16, 1898 Address. Bergton, Va Church of the Brethren

1. Vita May Hupp, b Oct 2, 1917.

2. Elmer Guy Hupp, b. May 8, 1919.

3. Mary Ruth Hupp, b Oct 12, 1922.

4 Charles Dorman Hupp, b. Sept 24, 1924.

5. Stella Florence Hupp, b Dec. 1, 1926

6 Magdalena Grace Hupp, b. May 18, 1928.

No. 134. Sixth Generation. 130.

6) Joseph Leonas Hupp, b Nov 23, 1895, in Va., m. Minnie Stultz, b. Jan 14, 1903. Address: Bergton, Va Church of the Brethren.

1. Wanda Helen Hupp, b July 25, 1927.

2. Cletus Howard Hupp, b Mar. 30, 1929.

No. 135. Sixth Generation. 130.

7) William Franklin Hupp, b July 19, 1898, in Va., m Gussie Jane Shike, b Dec. 1, 1896. Address. Bergton, Va Church of the Brethren.

1. Alma Jane Hupp, b. Jan. 13, 1925

2. Franklin Dove Hupp, b May 21, 1928.

No. 136. Sixth Generation. 130.

8) Hannah Susan Hupp, b Dec. 10, 1900, in Va , m. Irvin Lorenza Crider, b. Sept. 2, 1902 Address: Peru, W. Va Church of the Brethren.

1. Margie Arline Crider, b. Sept. 6, 1922

2. Dorman Wayne Crider, b. May 29, 1924

3. Nina Dove Crider, b. Mar. 1, 1926.

4 Narland Mayberry Crider, b. Oct. 13, 1928.

No. 137. Sixth Generation. 130.

9) Minnie Bliss Hupp, b Mar. 4, 1903, in Va., m Elmer Lee Comlis, b. Feb 1, 1903. Address: Ft. Seybert, W. Va. Church of the Brethren.

1. Velma Nadiene Comlis, b. Feb. 13, 1924.

2. Lena Grace Comlis, b. July 17, 1926.

3. Ralph Lee Comlis, b. Jan. 26, 1929.

No. 138. Sixth Generation. 130.

10) Myrtle Rachel Hupp, b. Oct. 4, 1905, in Va., m. Jacob Clarence Lantz, b Oct 7, 1900. Address: Criders, Va. Church of the Brethren.

1. Violet Grace Lantz, b. May 16, 1928.

No. 139. Sixth Generation. 130.

11) Samuel DeWitt Hupp, b. Dec. 11, 1909, in Va., m. Ina Marie Dove, b Nov. 28, 1914 Address: Bergton, Va.

1. Virginia Hupp, b. July 29, 1929, died same day.

No. 140. Seventh Generation. 131.

1) Jay Elmer Lantz, b Jan 13, 1900. m Bliss Viola Fried, b. May 14, 1903.

1. Ray Granville Lantz, b. Dec. 14, 1929

No. 141. Fifth Generation. 111.

6) Laura J. Secrist, b Feb. 20, 1866, in Rockingham Co., Va., d. Mar. 19, 1914, m. Samuel Ritchie, b. April 28, 1861, d. Oct. 15, 1912. Church of the Brethren.

1 Rosa Ritchie, b. Aug. 30, 1886. No. 142.

2. William Ritchie, b. Mar. 13, 1889. No. 143.

3. David Ritchie, b. June 18, 1890. No. 144.

4. Minnie Ritchie, b. Oct. 23, 1894. No. 145.

5. Mary Ritchie, b July 31, 1902. Single.

No. 142. Sixth Generation. 141.

1) Rosa Ritchie, b. Aug 30, 1886, in Va, m. Luther Ritchie, b. July 15, 1880.

1. Raymon Ritchie, b. Dec. 23, 1910.

2 Ruth Ritchie, b Feb 19, 1917.

No. 143. Sixth Generation. 141.

2) William Ritchie, b. Mar. 13 1889, in Va., m. Ida Sevier, b. Jan. 3, 1889.

1. Ivan Ritchie, b. Oct. 16, 1914.

2. Otis Ritchie, b Nov. 4, 1916.

3 Mallie Ritchie, b July 6, 1918

4. Melvie Ritchie, b Aug. 3, 1920.

5 Truman Ritchie, b Oct. 11, 1922.

6 Clara Ritchie, b. Nov. 3, 1924.

7. Orpha Ritchie, b July 1, 1927.

No. 144. Sixth Generation. 141.

3) David Ritchie, b June 18, 1890, in Rockingham Co., Va., m. Ama Frances Brunk, b. Jan. 17, 1896 Address: 130 S. Scott St., Lima, O. Church of the Brethren.

1. Laura Isola Ritchie, b. Sept. 29, 1913

2. Howard William Ritchie, b. Dec. 27, 1919.

No. 145. Sixth Generation. 141.

4) Minnie Ritchie, b. Oct. 23, 1891, m. Levi A. Dove, b. Mar. 8, 1891. Church of the Brethren.

1 Ina Marie Dove, b Nov. 28, 1914. No. 146.

2. Laney R. Dove, b. Nov. 12, 1915.

3. Dean A Dove, b. Oct. 8, 1917, d. Oct. 11, 1918.

No. 146. Seventh Generation. 145.

1) Ina Marie Dove, b Nov 28, 1914, m. Samuel DeWitt Hupp, b. Dec. 11, 1909. Refer to No. 139 (related).

No. 147. Fifth Generation. 111.

7) Minnie R. Secrist, b. May 15, 1868, in Rockingham Co., Va., m. Samuel Dove, b. Aug. 29, 1866. Mr. Dove died Mar. 23, 1918. Address: Bergton, Va. Church of the Brethren.

1. Wilmer F. Dove, b Mar. 12, 1888. No. 148.

2. David F. Dove, b. May 4, 1890 No 149.

3. Grace V. Dove, b Oct. 12, 1896. Single. Teacher.

No. 148. Sixth Generation. 147.

1) Wilmer F. Dove, b. Mar. 12, 1888, m. Sept. 10, 1911, Mary A. Crider, b. April 20, 1891.

1. Wilma A. Dove, b. Aug. 25, 1916.
2 Neva A. Dove, b. Oct. 8, 1918.
3. Alda Grace Dove, b. April 27, 1921.

No. 149. Sixth Generation. 147.

2) David F. Dove, b. May 4, 1890, m Emma B. Smith, b. May 5, 1888, d. Feb. 20, 1928. They were married April 22, 1912.

1. Iola A. Dove, b. Aug. 3, 1913.
2. Leota G. Dove, b. July 18, 1915.
3. Conrad L. Dove, b. April 20, 1918, d. Dec. 15, 1925.
4. Glen L. Dove, b. Jan. 16, 1920.
5. Stella G Dove, b. Mar. 14, 1922.
6. Lottie May Dove, b. Feb. 6, 1928, d. same day, twin.
7. Berlin F. Dove, b. Feb. 6, 1928.

No. 150. Fifth Generation. 111.

8) Franklin M. Secrist, b. Feb. 3, 1871, in Rockingham Co., Va., m. Rachel Dove, b. Dec. 23, 1869. Address: Criders, Va. Church of the Brethren.

1. Lory E. Secrist, b. July 31, 1892. No. 151.
2. Arthur E. Secrist, b. Jan. 4, 1896.
3. Ida D. Secrist, b. Dec. 1, 1897.
4. Ransom V. Secrist, b. April 13, 1902. No. 152.
5. Casper R. Secrist, b. June 1, 1905. No. 153.

No. 151. Sixth Generation. 150.

1) Lory E. Secrist, b. July 31, 1892, m. Eva Munggole, b. April 8, 1906.

No. 152. Sixth Generation. 150.

4) Ransom V. Secrist, b. April 13, 1902, m. Ola Fink, b. Dec. 25, 1900.

1. Edna I. Secrist, b. June 26, 1926.
2. James M. Secrist, b. July 29, 1928.

No. 153. Sixth Generation. 150.

5) Casper R. Secrist, b. June 1, 1905, m. Dracie L. Fink, b. Oct. 30, 1903.

1. Waldo F. Secrist, b. July 17, 1925.
2. Monroe H. Secrist, b. July 12, 1927.
3. Allen W. Secrist, b. May 3, 1929.

No. 154. Fifth Generation. 111.

9) Bertie S. Secrist, b. July 20, 1873, in Rockingham Co, Va., m. June 4, 1893, James H. Turner, b. Mar. 26, 1871. Address Broadway, Va., R. 3. Farmer. Mennonites. He is a minister. They live near Cootes Store.

1. Dora E. Turner, b. Jan 3, 1895. No. 155.
2. Rosa A. Turner, b. Oct. 17, 1896. No. 156.
3. James E. Turner, b. Aug. 23, 1900. No 157
4. Kate L. Turner, b. Mar. 17, 1904. Single.
5. Benjamin W. Turner, b. Nov. 8, 1905. No. 158.
6. David R. Turner, b. Mar. 23, 1907. No. 159.
7. Franklin R. Turner, b. Feb. 11, 1911.
8. Mae S. Turner, b. Dec. 15, 1912. No. 3706.

No. 155. Sixth Generation. 154.

1) Dora E. Turner, b. Jan. 3, 1895, m. Samuel C. Gladwell, b. Jan. 2, 1890. Mrs. Gladwell is a Mennonite; Mr. Gladwell is a Methodist.

1. John L. Gladwell, b. Dec. 14, 1910.
2. Ralph L. Gladwell, b. Feb. 20, 1922.

No. 156. Sixth Generation. 154.

2) Rosa A. Turner, b. Oct. 17, 1896, m. Olen S. Lantz, b. June 23, 1895. Mennonites.

1. Guy W. Lantz, b. June 7, 1917.
2. Turner R. Lantz, b. Feb 23, 1919

No. 157. Sixth Generation. 154.

3) James E Turner, b. Aug. 23, 1900, m Beatrice Shickle, b. Jan. 17, 1903. Mr. Turner is a Mennonite, Mrs. Turner is a United Brethren.

1. Vivian June Turner, b. June 21, 1921.

No. 158. Sixth Generation. 154.

5) Benjamin W. Turner, b. Nov. 8, 1905, m. Mabel Turner, b. Dec. 5, 1907. Mr. Turner is a Mennonite, Mrs. Turner is a member of the Church of the Brethren.

1. Janet Louise Turner, b. May 10, 1925.

No. 159. Sixth Generation. 154.

6) David R. Turner, b. Mar. 23, 1907, in Rockingham Co., Va., m Leila Propst, b April 6, 1908. Mr Turner is a Mennonite and Mrs. Turner, a Methodist.

No. 160. Sixth Generation. 111.

11) Zona D. Secrist, daughter of Isadora Secrist, was born June 10, 1899. She m. Elbert L. Dove, b. April 2, 1903. Address: Bergton, Va. Church of the Brethren.

No. 161. Fourth Generation. 29.

5) Melchiah Breneman, son of Peter Breneman and Frances (Good) Breneman, was born Oct. 13, 1839, near Edom, Rockingham Co., Va. He grew to manhood on his father's farm one mile north of Greenmount. On Dec. 24, 1863 he was married to Elizabeth Jane Shank, daughter of David Shank and Rebecca (Funk) Shank, of near Harrisonburg, Va. Elizabeth was born April 24, 1841. Near the beginning of the Civil War he was drafted into the service of the Southern army as a cavalryman. He served there for over three years. During that time he had three horses shot out from under him, each time making his escape. About sunset of the day before the battle of Gettysburg he received a bullet in his left side, lodging near his heart, which he carried to his grave. About eight months before the close of the war he decided to desert the service, and together with Abraham Good, George Brunk, Simon Cooper, they equipped themselves with a horse, wagon, and with some provisions and placed their wives on them and started over the mountains. The men walking after night and resting during the day until they had crossed the line into the union territory where they separated, A. P. Good and wife and George Brunk and wife going to Fairfield Co., O., and Simon Cooper and wife going to Muncie, Ind., while Melchior and wife went to Lancaster Co., Pa. After the close of the rebellion, he again returned to their native home in Virginia where they remained until in February of 1870, when he moved with his family to Morgan Co., Mo. Here he again settled on the farm and became a farmer, which was his former vocation. On Sept 25, 1875, he was ordained to the office of deacon to serve the Mt. Zion Mennonite Church at Mt. Zion, Mo.,

which place he filled until Oct., 1880. He then moved with his family to Allen Co., O., where he served the Salem congregation in the same capacity until his death on Mar. 27, 1882. His companion was buried by his side on July 4, 1913, in the Salem cemetery near Elida, Ohio.

In his duties as a deacon he was possessed with the rare quality of almost always being able to restore an amiable settlement and conditions of peace between such as were at variance with each other, himself being of a mild and patient disposition. He was the father of three sons and two daughters.

1. Charles David Breneman, b. April 27, 1866 No. 162
2. Rebecca Frances Breneman, b. Feb 16, 1870. No. 163.
3. George Gabriel Breneman, b Sept 25, 1871. No 164.
4. John Peter Breneman, b. Sept. 7, 1876 No 165.
5. Mary Magdalena Breneman, b. Nov 21, 1878, d Aug 6, 1901. Single.

No. 162. Fifth Generation. 161.

1) Charles David Breneman, b April 27, 1866, in Rockingham Co., Va , near Singers Glen, m. Mary C. Brenneman, b. Oct. 29, 1867, in Wayne Co , O They were married Dec 4, 1886, by Rev Daniel Brower. Farmer until 1936. Mennonite. Elida, O. Burial ground at Salem Church near Elida, O.

1. Christian B. Breneman, b. Jan. 30, 1888 No 166.
2. Lillie Elizabeth Breneman, b. Feb. 19, 1889. No. 167.
3. Alvin Melchiah Breneman, b Jan 31, 1893 No. 168.
4. Ruth Irene Breneman, b Jan 23, 1896. No 169.
5. George Arthur Breneman, b. Feb. 8, 1898. No. 170.
6. Naomi Esther Breneman, b. Jan 26, 1901. No 171.

No. 163. Fifth Generation. 161.

2) Rebecca Frances Breneman, b Feb 16, 1870, in Va , m. Feb. 19, 1907, John I. Brenneman, b. Feb. 12, 1859, in Ohio Address: Elida, O. Farmer. Mennonites. They reared two children whom they got from the Orphans' Home at West Liberty, O.

1. Ralph Moore, b. May 25, 1907.
2. Mary Fry, b. Oct. 29, 1913.

No. 164. Fifth Generation. 161.

3) George Gabriel Breneman, b Sept 25, 1871, in Mo , m Armilda Bunch, b. April 20, 1877, in Mo. They were married Dec 28, 1898, at Purcell, Mo. She died Mar. 16, 1904 and was buried at Purcell, Mo. He married (2nd wife) Mrs. Zadie Main (nee Newman), b. June 14, 1883, at Carthage, Mo. She died in California. George died April 30, 1936. He and his last wife are buried at Gutter City, Calif. One child from each union

1. Fern J Breneman, b Sept. 9, 1900, at Purcell, Mo. No. 164¼.
2. Doris Mae Breneman, b. April 10, 1911, at Marysville, Calif. (Doris is teaching school at Santa Cruz, Calif. 1937, '38, '39).

No. 164¼. Sixth Generation. 164.

1) Fern J. Brenneman, b Sept. 9, 1900, at Purcell, Mo. m. Oct. 15, 1937, at San Francisco, Calif., John Hamilton Bell, b Jan 6. 1901, at New York City, N. Y. Address: 707 Stocton St , San Francisco, Calif. Methodists.

No. 165. Fifth Generation. 161.

4) John Peter Breneman, b. Sept. 7, 1876, in Mo , m. Fanny Good, b. June 15, 1881, in Morgan Co , Mo. John died July 9, 1933, at his home in Hesston, Kans.

Fanny died at the hospital at La Junta, Colo, April 9, 1936. Clerk. Address: Hesston, Kans. No children.

No. 166. Sixth Generation. 162.

1) Christian B. Breneman, b. Jan. 30, 1888, in Allen Co, O., m. Rose E. Berry, b. April 23, 1892, in Virginia. Farmers Elida, Ohio. Mennonites. They were married Apr. 20, 1911.
1. Lois Irene Breneman, b. Mar. 25, 1912.
2. Edna Elizabeth Breneman, b. June 26, 1913.
3. Mary Ethel Breneman, b Dec 10, 1914
4. Emma Lucille Breneman, b. April 26, 1916.
5. Eunice Virginia Breneman, b. Sept 14, 1917. No. 166¼.
6. Charles Andrew Breneman, b. Dec. 16, 1919.
7. Clark David Breneman, b July 3, 1922
8. Helen Frances Breneman, b Oct 4, 1925.
9. Daughter (Stillborn) Sept. 5, 1930
10. Ruth Ann Breneman, b. Nov. 2, 1934

No. 166¼. Seventh Generation. 166.

5) Eunice Virginia Breneman, b Sept 14, 1917, near Elida, O, m Feb. 27, 1937, Louis Shenk, b June 30, 1915 Address: Elida, Ohio. Laborer. Mennonites.
1 Jerome Louis Shenk, b. Oct. 30, 1938.

No. 167. Sixth Generation. 162.

2) Lillie Elizabeth Breneman, b Feb. 19, 1889, near Elida, O, m. Dec 25, 1910, Allen L Steiner, b Aug. 10, 1890, near Orrville, O. Address: 313 E. Oak St, Orrville, O Manager of Royal Body Co Mennonites.
1. Eda Mae Steiner, b. Dec. 1, 1911. No. 172.
2 Lloyd Emerson Steiner, b Apr 1, 1914 No 172¼.
3 Irene Elizabeth Steiner, b Dec. 8, 1919.
4. Dale Jay Steiner, b. June 8, 1921.

No. 168. Sixth Generation. 162.

3) Alvin Melchiah Breneman, b. Jan 31, 1893, near Elida, O, m. May 23, 1922, Mabel Kauffman, b Apr. 5, 1888, near West Liberty, O. Address: Lima, O., R 4. Farmer. Mennonites
1. Doris Evelyn Breneman, b Dec 22, 1923
2. Beulah Pearl Breneman, b. Nov. 3, 1926.

No. 169. Sixth Generation. 162.

4) Ruth Irene Breneman, b Jan. 23, 1896, near Elida, O., m. Feb. 26, 1920, Glen W Yoder, b Nov. 27, 1895, near Orrville, O. Address: Cor. Pike and Elm St., Orrville, O. Carpenter. Mennonites.
1. Charles Robert Yoder, b Mar. 28, 1921
2. Richard Johnathan Yoder, b May 17, 1925.

No. 170. Sixth Generation. 162.

5) George Arthur Breneman, b Feb 8, 1898, near Elida, O, m. June 25, 1918, Mabel Martin, b. Sept 11, 1896, near Orrville, O. Address: 1018 Spink St., Wooster, Ohio Insurance salesman. Mennonites.
1. June Irene Breneman, b. June 13, 1919.
2. George Martin Breneman, b. July 2, 1922.
3. Edwin J. Breneman, b. Sept. 29, 1927.

No. 171. Sixth Generation. 162.

6) Naomi Esther Breneman, b. Jan. 26, 1901, near Elida, O., m. July 14, 1923, Henry David Ross, b. Mar. 23, 1901, near Elida, O. Address: Belle Ave., Orrville, O. Mennonites. Superintendent of Smucker's Apple Butter and Preserve Factory at Orrville, O.

    1. Robert Rex Ross, b. Aug. 4, 1925.

    2. Carolyn Louise Ross, b. Mar. 23, 1930.

No. 172. Seventh Generation. 167.

1) Eda Mae Steiner, b. Dec. 1, 1911, near Orrville, O., m. Dec. 25, 1930. Earl Ott, b. Nov. 28, 1907, near Orrville, O. Address· 227 E Bowman St., Wooster, O. Electrician. German Reformed Church.

    1. Joanne Elizabeth Ott, b. July 30, 1936.

No. 172¼. Seventh Generation. 167.

2) Lloyd Emerson Steiner. b. Apr 1, 1914, near Orrville, O , m. June 18, 1935, Pauline Douglas, b. June 18, 1911, in Orrville, O. Address. 216 E Water St., Orrville, O. Methodists. Foreman Royal Body Company.

No. 173. Fourth Generation. 29.

6) Peter Breneman, b. May 6, 1843, near Edom, Va , d. Mar. 13, 1901, at Brooklyn, Ia , m. Sept. 1, 1870, Barbara Neiswander, b Nov. 29, 1848. d. Feb. 17, 1930, at Brooklyn, Ia Laborer. Mr. Breneman was a Mennonite and Mrs Breneman a Dunkard. They moved from Virginia to Iowa in 1885.

    1. Emma Frances Breneman b. Feb. 26, 1872. No. 174.

    2. Mary Magdalena Breneman, b Mar. 10, 1873 No 175.

    3. Edward Samuel Breneman, b. Nov 10, 1875. No 176

    4. Susanna Katherine Breneman, b. Dec. 8, 1878. No 177.

    5. John Peter Breneman, b. May 25, 1881, single, at Brooklyn, Ia.

    6. William Wate Breneman. b. Aug 15, 1882, d. Sept. 13, 1882.

    7. Oscar Charles Breneman, b Oct. 5, 1883, single, at Brooklyn, Ia.

    8 Frank Breneman, b May 30, 1889 at 1247 Fairmount Ave , Council Bluffs, Ia. No. 3649

No. 174. Fifth Generation. 173.

1) Emma Frances Breneman. b. Feb. 26, 1872, in Va , m. John O'Halleran, b. ——————. Address: Thayer, Ia. Congregational Church.

    1. Ethel Laverne O'Halleran, b. July 3, 1896. No. 178.

    2. Waneta Gertrude O'Halleran, b. June 20, 1899, d. Sept., 1899.

    3 Robert Charles O'Halleran, b. Feb 12, 1902 No. 179.

    4. Donald James O'Halleran, b. July 26, 1906 Single. Address: Happy, Tex.

No. 175. Fifth Generation. 173.

2) Mary Magdalena Breneman, b. Mar. 10, 1873, in Va , m. William Fry, b. ——————, d. June, 1901. She married (2nd) Jacob R. Gwin in Nov. 1903, b. Aug. 18, 1854, d. Oct. 8, 1937 Address: Gilman, Ia. (was Victor, Ia). Congregational.

    1. Paul Raymond Fry, b. June 28, 1896 No 180.

    2 Esther Marie Fry, b. Dec. 11, 1899 No. 181.

    3. Clarence Edward Gwin, b. Aug. 2, 1904, d. Jan. 5, 1931.

    4. Arnold Gwin, b. Mar. 19, 1906. No. 175½.

    5. Margaret Gwin, b. Aug. 29, 1911. No. 175¾.

No. 175½. Sixth Generation. 175.

4) Arnold Gwin, b. Mar. 19, 1906, m. in April, 1931, Marie Mullen. Address: Guernsey, Ia. Farmer.

1. Wayne Arnold Gwin, b. Oct 26, 1931.
2. Marilyn Jean Gwin, b. April 22, 1933.
3. Wendell Raymond Gwin, b. Aug. 25, 1934.

No. 175¾. Sixth Generation. 175.

5) Margaret Gwin, b. Aug. 29, 1911, m Mar. 29, 1934, Clinton E. Reedy. Address: 924 Lafayette St., Waterloo, Ia. Service station manager.

No. 176. Fifth Generation. 173.

3) Edward Samuel Breneman, b. Nov. 10, 1875, in Rockingham Co., Va., m. Eve May Wheeler, b. July 14, 1883. They were married Jan. 22, 1902. Address: Brooklyn, R. 4, Ia. Farmer. Church of the Brethren.

1. Belva Lucile Breneman, b Nov 24, 1902 No. 182.
2. Everett Wheeler Breneman, b Oct 15, 1904. No. 182¼.
3. Grace Hannah Breneman, b. May 14, 1907. No. 182¾.
4. Lawrence Edward Breneman, b. May 23, 1910. No. 182½.
5. Alvin Samuel Breneman, b Feb 6, 1914. No. 3623.
6. Eva Barbara Breneman, b. Feb 28, 1918.
7. Ethel May Breneman, b. Sept. 13, 1920.

No. 177. Fifth Generation. 173.

4) Susanna Katherine Breneman, b. Dec. 8, 1878, in Va., m. in Oct., 1900, George Bucknam. Address 1247 Fairmount Ave, Council Bluffs, Ia. Congregational.

1. Frederick James Bucknam, b. Jan 1, 1902. No. 183.
2 Margarie Louise Bucknam, b. Jan 29, 1905. No. 3651.
3. Edith Barbara Bucknam, b July 2, 1908. No. 3652
4. Bruce Bucknam, b. Oct. 7, 1911. No. 3650.

No. 178. Sixth Generation. 174.

1) Ethel Laverne O'Halleran, b. July 3, 1896, d Mar. 6, 1924, m. Roland Bohnsack, in Dec., 1922.

1. Ellan Barbara Bohnsack, b. Feb. 16, 1924

No. 179. Sixth Generation. 174.

3) Robert Charles O'Halleran, b. Feb. 12, 1902, m. Eva Beery in May, 1929. Address: Thayer, Ia

No. 180. Sixth Generation. 175.

1) Paul Raymond Fry, b. June 28, 1896, in Iowa, m. Cecilia Keenan in Aug., 1927. Address: Marshalltown, Ia., Box 66. Bookkeeper.

No. 181. Sixth Generation. 175.

2) Esther Marie Fry, b. Dec. 11, 1899, in Ia., m Henry E. Stahl, in June, 1923. Address: Gilman, Ia. (was Malcon, Ia.).

1. Loraine Marie Stahl, b. July 30, 1924.
2. Howard Heney Stahl, b. Feb 23, 1926, d. Mar. 20, 1930.
3. Margaret Mary Stahl, b. Sept. 25, 1928, d. Mar. 11, 1930.
4. Lyle Edward Stahl, b. Aug. 5, 1930.
5. Keith Dale Stahl, b. Oct. 7, 1933.
6. Norman Richard Stahl, b. Oct. 24, 1935.

No. 182. Sixth Generation. 176.
1) Belva Lucile Breneman, b. Nov. 24, 1902, m. Aug. 31, 1924, W. F. Willett, b April 24, 1900. Address. Brooklyn, Ia.
1. Robert Laverne Willett, b. Sept. 3, 1926.
2. Ralph Emerson Willett, b. Jan. 25, 1931.

No. 182¼. Sixth Generation. 176.
2) Everett W. Breneman, b Oct. 15, 1904, in Iowa, m. Aug. 14, 1931, Aletha Whitford. Address: Epworth, Ia.
1 Darrell Eugene Breneman, b. July 22, 1932
2. Don Charles Breneman, b. June 24, 1937.

No. 182½. Sixth Generation. 176.
4) Lawrence Edward Breneman, b. May 23, 1910, in Ia., m. Feb 18, 1933, Dora Ladd. Address: Chelsea, Ia.
1. Faye Elaine Breneman, b May 22, 1936

No. 182¾. Sixth Generation. 175.
3) Grace Hannah Breneman, b May 14, 1907, in Ia , m. Feb 18, 1933, H. D. Little. Address 1545 Lawrence St , Eugene. Oreg
1. Larry Breneman Little, b Mar. 11, 1935.

No. 183. Sixth Generation. 177.
1) Frederick James Bucknam, b. Jan. 1. 1902. in Ia., m. in Mar., 1928, Doris Rosch. Address: 1247 Fairmount Ave., Council Bluffs, Ia.
1. Barbara Alice Bucknam, b. April 20, 1932 (adopted).

No. 184. Fourth Generation. 29.
7) Elizabeth Breneman, b. Dec. 8, 1847, in Rockingham Co., Va., m. John Y. Long, b. in 1825 in Va., d. in Dec , 1902. Address· Harrisonburg, Va., R. 4. Farmer. Church of the Brethren. Mrs. Long is still well and hearty at this date (Feb. 15, 1939). No children.

No. 185. Fourth Generation. 29.
8) David W. Breneman, b. Oct 24, 1850, in Rockingham Co , Va., d. April 9, 1925, m. Mary Ellen Andes, b. Nov. 19, 1851, d. May 30, 1923. Both were buried in the Sterling cemetery, Loudoun Co., Va.

David Breneman was a very successful business man. He at one time owned and operated over thirteen hundred acres of land in Virginia. He was an earnest church worker and Sunday-school superintendent. It is said of him that regardless of how much lacked in his pastor's salary he always made up the shortage. He was reared on his father's farm near Edom, Rockingham Co , and lived there until some years before his death. He sold his interests there and bought land in Loudoun Co., Va., where they died. Address was Ryan, Loudoun Co., Va.
1. William Eli Peter Breneman, b. Aug. 18, 1872. No. 186.
2. Sallie Isabella Breneman, b May 16, 1874. No. 187.
3. Eugene Walter Breneman, b. Mar. 19, 1876, single, Ryan, Va.
4. Marion David Breneman, b. Feb. 3, 1878, single. Salisbury, Md.
5. Paul Douglas Breneman, b. Jan. 31. 1880. No. 188.
6. Abraham Otterbein Breneman, b. Mar. 21, 1882. No. 189.
7. Jacob Irvin Breneman, b. Aug. 9, 1883. No. 190.
8. Stella Queen Breneman, b. May 19, 1886. No. 191.
9. Nora King Breneman, b. Sept. 25, 1891. No 192.
10 John Burtner Breneman, b May 22, 1894 No 193
11. Mary Christian Breneman, b. Sept. 13, 1897. No. 194¼.

No. 186. Fifth Generation. 185.

1) William Eli Breneman, b. Aug. 18, 1872, in Rockingham Co, Va, m. Jan. 19, 1897, Rhoda Ella Chandler, b. Mar 10, 1869, d. Aug. 22, 1927. Address: Ashburn, Va., Farmer. Burial at Sterling cemetery, Loudoun Co, Va. United Brethren.

    1. Neoma A Breneman, b. Mar. 22, 1901, d. Jan. 16, 1902.

    2. Lone Eve Breneman, b. Feb. 14, 1904. No. 194

    3. Abraham A. Breneman, b Apr. 27, 1905, d. Aug. 28, 1905.

No. 187. Fifth Generation. 185.

2) Sallie Isabelle Breneman, b. May 16, 1874, Rockingham Co, Va., m. Jan. 20, 1897, Joseph H. Foley, b. Feb. 17, 1874, d. June 16, 1930. Buried in Sterling cemetery, Loudoun Co., Va. Address. Ryan, Va. United Brethren. No issue.

No. 188. Fifth Generation. 185.

5) Paul Douglas Breneman, b. Jan. 31, 1874, Rockingham Co., Va., m. Dec. 24, 1903, Edith Luveonie Crawn, b May 29, 1880, in Augusta Co., Va. Mr. Breneman is a United Brethren and Mrs Breneman is a Methodist. Farmers. Address: Ryan, Va.

    1 Eve Magdalene Breneman, b May 4, 1905. No 3448.

    2. May Alberta Breneman, b. Dec 5, 1907. No. 195.

    3 Sylvia Pauline Breneman, b June 12, 1914.

No. 189. Fifth Generation. 185.

6) Abraham Otterbein Breneman, b Mar. 21, 1882, Augusta Co, Va., m. Oct. 27, 1903, Sallie Rebecca Wampler, b. July 13, 1883. They live at 133 W. Dewey Ave., Youngstown, O. Church of the Brethren.

    1. Fern Long Breneman, b Jan 9, 1905. No. 196.

    2 Carrie Isabelle Breneman, b. May 3, 1904. No. 197.

    3 Rebe Irene Breneman, b Nov 8, 1908. No 198

    4 Ashby Otterbein Breneman, b Aug 6, 1917, at Weyers Cave, Va.

No. 190. Fifth Generation. 185.

7) Jacob Irvin Breneman, b Aug 9, 1883, Augusta Co., Va., m. Nov. 16, 1909, Bertha Cornelia Carpenter, b. Dec. 12, 1878, in Rockingham Co., Va. Mr. Breneman is a United Brethren, and Mrs. Breneman is a German Reformed. Address: 1001 Monroe St., N. W., Washington, D. C

    1. Irvin Carpenter Breneman, b. Oct 22, 1915, in Loudoun Co, Va.

No. 191. Fifth Generation. 185.

8) Stella Queen Breneman, b. May 19, 1886, Augusta Co., Va., m. Feb. 4, 1906, William W. Crawn, b. May 30, 1882. Address: Ryan, Va.

    1. Mary Elizabeth Crawn, b Oct 31, 1906 No 3449

    2 Ruby Louise Crawn, b April 25, 1908 No. 3450.

    3. Marion David Crawn, b. Feb. 17, 1917.)

    4. Martha Isabelle Crawn, b. Feb 17, 1917.)

No. 192. Fifth Generation. 185.

9) Nora King Breneman, b. Sept. 25, 1891, Augusta Co., Va., m. Dec. 27, 1913, Thomas Putnam Mayhugh, b. June 23, 1891, in Loudoun Co., Va. Mrs. Breneman is a United Brethren. Address: Herndon, Va, R 1.

    1. Alvie Thomas Mayhugh, b. Oct. 24, 1915, d at birth.

    2. Russell Alfred Mayhugh, b. April 5, 1917. Twin.

    3. Mary Jane Mayhugh, b. April 5, 1917. Twin, died at birth.

No. 193. Fifth Generation. 185.

10) John Burtner Breneman, b. May 22, 1894, in Rockingham Co, Va., m. Aug. 13, 1912, Lucy McCutcheon in Rockville, Md Address: 3619 O St., N. W., Washington, D. C. Mr. Breneman was a member of the Baptist Church.

1. Ellen Elizabeth Breneman, b June 5, 1913.
2. Margaret Burtner Breneman, b Mar 2, 1915.

Both children were born in Fairfax Co., Va.

No. 194. Sixth Generation. 186.

2) Lone Eve Breneman, b. Feb. 14, 1904, m Dec. 27, 1926, to John Wesley Marple, b. Oct. 11, 1900. Mrs. Marple is a United Brethren.

No. 194¼. Fifth Generation. 185.

11) Mary Christian Breneman, b Sept 13, 1897, m Nov. 26, 1930. William Anthony Gillispie, b. April 5, 1889. He died Dec. 4, 1936. Address: Washington, D. C. Presbyterian.

No. 195. Sixth Generation. 188.

2) May Alberta Breneman, b. Dec. 5, 1907, in Augusta Co, Va., m. June 17, 1927, George Wm. Haines, b Dec. 13, 1902, in Loudoun Co, Va. Methodists.

1. George Douglas Haines, b. Oct. 20, 1928
2. Wilma Jean Haines, b. July 27, 1930.
3. Allan Thomas Haines, b. Feb 6, 1935.
4 Shirley Irene Haines, b. June 3, 1937.

No. 196. Sixth Generation. 189.

1) Fern Long Breneman, b. Jan. 9, 1905, at Weyers Cave, Va., m. June 18, 1925, Joseph Welsh, b. Jan. 8, 1902, in Mahoning Co., O. Address: 1024 Oakhill Ave., Youngstown, O.

1. Edward Lawrence Welsh, b April 17, 1926.
2. Joseph Wallace Welsh, b. May 27, 1927.

No. 197. Sixth Generation. 189.

2) Carrie Isabelle Breneman, b May 3, 1904, at Weyers Cave, Va., m April 18, 1923 Ernest Ralph Morris, b April 15, 1902, at Port Republic, Va. Address: Staunton, Va.

1. Calvin Ralph Morris, b. April 12, 1924, at Youngstown, O.
2. Alvin Olen Morris, b. April 12, 1924 Twins.
3. Harold Howard Morris, b. Dec. 22, 1925, d. in infancy.
4. Ernest Rudolph Morris, b. Aug. 20, 1928, in Ohio.
5. Joseph Breneman Morris, b. Dec. 2, 1929, in Ohio.
6. Billy Dean Morris, b. May 26, 1931, d Aug. 21, 1931. Billy was buried at Mt. Olive cemetery, Rockingham Co, Va.

No. 198. Sixth Generation. 189.

3) Reba Irene Breneman, b. Nov. 8, 1908, at Ryan, Va., m. Nov. 24, 1927, Russel Harry Guy, b. Aug. 16, 1903, at Lisbon, O.

1. Nellie Irene Guy, b. Aug. 20, 1928, at Youngstown, O.

No. 199. Fourth Generation. 29.

9) Susanna Breneman, b. Jan. 19, 1856, near Edom, Rockingham Co., Va., d. April 30, 1917, m. Abraham Fulk, b. Feb. 16, 1854, d. Sept. 27, 1899. Farmers. Mennonites.

1. Josiah Franklin Fulk, b. Aug. 6, 1879. No. 200.
2. Anna Belle Fulk, b. April 25, 1883. No. 201.

3. Charles Elmer Fulk, b Sept 16, 1881, d. June 3, 1893.
4. David I Fulk, b. Sept 4, 1885. No. 202.
5. Harden Crawford Fulk, b. Dec. 15, 1886, d Jan. 30, 1890.
6. Effie Frances Fulk, b. April 4, 1889. No. 203.
7. Mary Catherine Fulk, b. May 18, 1891, d. June 9, 1893.
8. Ada Susan Fulk, b. Sept 11, 1892. No. 204.
9. John Edward Fulk, b May 19, 1896. No. 205.
10. Warden Holmes Fulk, b. Nov. 4, 1894, d. Mar. 25, 1895.
11. Lesta Pearl Fulk, b. Mar. 25, 1898. No. 206.
12. Abraham Breneman Fulk, b Dec. 17, 1900. No. 207.

No. 200. Fifth Generation. 199.
1) Josiah Franklin Fulk, b Aug 6, 1879, in Rockingham Co., Va., m. Emma May, b. May 3, 1869. Address· Singers Glen, Va. No issue.

No. 201. Fifth Generation. 199.
2) Anna Belle Fulk, b April 25, 1883, in Rockingham Co., Va., m. Walter O. Burkhoider, b. Nov. 20, 1875, in Rockingham Co, Va They were married Feb. 1, 1911 Farmers. Mennonites. Address: Dale Enterprise, Va.
1. Hazel E. Burkholder, b. Jan. 26, 1914
2. Warren S. Burkholder, b. Sept. 7, 1918.
3. Walter O. Burkholder, Jr., b. Aug. 7, 1920, d. Oct. 5, 1920.
4. Vivian C. Burkholder, b Jan 22, 1923.

No. 202. Fifth Generation. 199.
4) David I Fulk. b. Sept. 4, 1885, in Va., m. May B Hopkins, b. Mar. 17, 1886, in Va. Address: Linville Depot, Va.
1. Helen V. Fulk, b. Oct. 2, 1911.
2. Herman A. Fulk, b. Oct. 2, 1913.
3. Howard D. Fulk, b. Sept. 9, 1915.

No. 203. Fifth Generation. 199.
6) Effie Frances Fulk, b. April 4, 1889, in Rockingham Co, Va, m Ollie O. Warner, b Nov. 16, 1895. Address· Ralston, Va.
1 Neva C. Warner, b. July 4, 1922.

No. 204. Fifth Generation. 199.
8) Ada Susan Fulk, b. Sept 11, 1892, in Rockingham Co., Va., m. Robert Shiflett, b. Dec. 9, 1888. Address· Harrisonburg, Va.
1. Harold F. Shiflett, b. June 20, 1913. No. 204¼.
2. John B. Shiflett, b. June 29, 1915.
3. Goldie E Shiflett, b. Sept. 11, 1917.
4. Dora F. Shiflett, b. Aug 29, 1920

No. 204¼. Sixth Generation. 204.
1) Harold F. Shiflett, b. June 20, 1913, in Rockingham Co., Va, m. Feb. 20, 1936, Edith Kittrell Bell, b. July 11, 1911. Address. Washington, D. C.

No. 205. Fifth Generation. 199.
9) John Edward Fulk, b. May 19, 1896, in Rockingham Co., Va., m. Beulah Warner, b Feb 13, 1899. Insurance agent at Harrisonburg, Va. Presbyterians.

No. 206. Fifth Generation. 199.
11) Lesta Pearl Fulk, b. Mar 25, 1898, in Rockingham Co., Va, m. Byrl C. Skelton, b. Nov. 7, 1901. Address: Washington, D. C.

1 Betty Rose Skelton, b. June 7, 1925.
2. Dora Mae Skelton, b. Oct. 22, 1926.
3. Adabelle Frances Skelton, b Mar 9, 1931.
4 Cecil Byers Skelton, b. Oct. 9, 1932.

No. 207. Fifth Generation. 199.

12) Abraham Breneman Fulk, b Dec 17, 1900, in Rockingham Co., Va., m. Martha Susan Howes, b July 23, 1907 Address· Washington, D. C.
1 Catherine Elizabeth Fulk, b April 10, 1925, d. April 17, 1925.
2 Nancy Ellen Fulk, b. Sept 5, 1936.

No. 208. Fourth Generation. 15.

1) Frances Rhodes, b about 1813, in Va m William Meyers, b ——————, in Va.
1. William Meyers, b ——————, d at 20 years.
2 John Meyers, b ——————, d at 4 years
3. Ward Meyers, b ——————.
4 Frank Meyers, b. ——————.
5 Charles Meyers, b ——————
6 Clifford Meyers, b. ——————
7. George Meyers. b. ——————
8 Bertie Meyers, b ——————

No. 209. Fourth Generation. 16.

2) Sallie Rhodes. b. about 1815, in Va , m Rush Meyers, b ——————. Address: Mt Clinton, Va. N. F. R

No. 210. Fourth Generation. 16.

3) Maggie Rhodes, b about 1817, m ———— Owen, b. ——————.
1 Fannie Owen. b ——————
2 Betty Owen, b ——————.

No. 211. Fourth Generation. 16.

4) Frederick A. Rhodes, b Feb 22, 1819. in Rockingham Co., Va , d. Feb 12, 1900, m. Magdalena Heatwole, b Jan 20, 1820. She died Mar. 12, 1898 They lived near Rushville, Va Farmers Mennonites Mr Rhodes was a deacon Both were buried at the Bank Church.
1 Elizabeth Rhodes, b Sept 30, 1841 No 242.
2. Margaret Rhodes, b Oct. 14. 1843 No. 246.
3. Fannie Rhodes, b. Mar 5, 1846. No. 249
4 Mary V. Rhodes, b May 31, 1848 No 251
5 William Rhodes, b Nov 3, 1853 No. 252
6. Josiah Rhodes, b. Mar. 10. 1856, d. ——————.
7. Reuben Rhodes, b May 26, 1858. No. 254.

No. 212. Fourth Generation. 16.

5) Henry A. Rhodes. b. about 1822 in Va., m April 3, 1851, Mary Frank, b. Mar. 13. 1832, d. Jan. 6, 1885 Address: Hinton, Va.
1. Sarah E. Rhodes, b. Oct. 20, 1852. d. Dec. 9, 1853.
2. Timothy E. Rhodes, b. Feb 17. 1854. No. 255.
3. James W. Rhodes, b. Feb 27, 1856 No. 256.
4 Franklin R. Rhodes, b April 25. 1858. No. 257.
5 Barbara A. Rhodes, b. Oct. 14. 1860 No 258.
6. John H. Rhodes, b. Dec. 7, 1862. No. 259.

7 Virginia A Rhodes, b Dec 3, 1865 No 260
8 Joseph A Rhodes, b Nov 4, 1867, d. Nov. 13, 1871.
9 Mary M Rhodes, b Dec 18, 1870 No 261
10 Isadora Rhodes, b Mar. 7, 1873.

No. 213. Fourth Generation. 16.

6) John Rhodes, b about 1824, in Rockingham Co , Va., m. Sarah Kerns, b.

1 Charles Rhodes, b. ————————
2 Taylor Rhodes, b —————————.
3 Rush Rhodes, b ——————————
4. James Rhodes, b —————————.
5 Alice Rhodes, b ——————————
6 Sallie Rhodes, b —————————

No. 215. Fourth Generation. 17.

1) John Weaver, b July 25, 1818, in Rockingham Co., Va., and d. April 8, 1877, m Magdalena Heatwole, b Nov 12, 1825, in Va , d June 22, 1880. Mennonites. Mr Weaver was a minister of the gospel Address Spring Creek, Va

1 Sem Weaver, b Feb 15, 1847 No 262
2 Solomon Weaver, b Mar 12, 1849 No. 269.
3 Elizabeth Weaver, b July 11, 1851, d. Aug 9, 1867.
4 Nancy Weaver, b June 5, 1853 No 270
5 Reuben Weaver, b Mar 2, 1856 No 276
6 Jacob Weaver, b Dec 24, 1857. No 277
7 Frances Weaver, b Oct 23, 1861 No 278
8 John Weaver, b April 20, 1865, d Mar 24, 1868

No. 216. Fourth Generation. 17.

2) Magdalena Weaver, b about 1823, and d in 1853, m. Jacob Brunk, b Dec. 13, 1821 Mennonites No issue

No. 217. Fourth Generation. 17.

3) Frederick Weaver, b Feb 14, 1820, in Rockingham Co., Va , d Oct. 18, 1851, m. Susan Heatwole, b July 16, 1822, in Va Farmers Mennonites. Address: Dale Enterprise, Va.

1 Elizabeth Weaver, b Oct 30, 1842, d single
2 Margaret Weaver, b Mar 26, 1844 No 280.
3 Frances Weaver, b Nov. 13, 1845 No 286
4 Abraham D Weaver, b. Nov 3, 1847 No 290
5 Jacob D Weaver, b Mar 1, 1850, d Mar 13, 1852.
6 Susanna Weaver, b Jan 25, 1852. No 298

No. 218. Fourth Generation. 17.

4) Frances Weaver, b Apr 28, 1825, in Rockingham Co., Va , m. Nov. 11, 1847, Samuel Coffman of Greenbrier Co , Va He was born June 2, 1822, d. Aug. 28, 1894. They were both Mennonites He was ordained to the ministry and soon after- wards to the office of bishop, which place he filled for 42 years. Their children were all born at Dale Enterprise, Va

1 John S Coffman, b Oct 16, 1848 No 312
2 Jacob B Coffman, b July 28, 1850 No 319
3 Lizzie Coffman, b Feb 9, 1852 No 322
4 Anna M Coffman, b Oct 12, 1855 No 323
5 Mary A Coffman, b Feb 19, 1857 No 340

6 Joseph W Coffman, b Feb 19, 1857, twin No. 347

7 Daniel H. Coffman, b April 4, 1859 No 352

8. David A. Coffman, b Apr 14, 1861, d Jan 18, 1868

9 Sarah C Coffman, b Mar 29, 1863 No 361

10 Fannie V. Coffman, b Oct 30, 1865 No 362

11 Rebecca S Coffman, b Mar 24, 1868 No. 363

No. 219. Fourth Generation. 17.

5) Anna Weaver, b ——————, d Mar 19, 1889, m. Jan. 13, 1842, John Brunk, b Aug 31, 1819. d Jan 7, 1896 Shoemaker and farmer. Mennonites Address Dale Enterprise, Va

1 Samuel Brunk, b Jan 8, 1843 No 372

2 Christian H Brunk, b Nov 8, 1845 No 373

3 Frederick W. Brunk, b Dec 31, 1847 No 374

4 Martin W Brunk, b Apr 14, 1851 No 375

5 Elizabeth Brunk, b Mar 22, 1854. No. 376

6 Elias Brunk, b June 2, 1856 No 377.

7 Jacob Brunk, b. Feb 20, 1862, d. May 21, 1863

8 John Brunk, b Mar. 3, 1864 No 378.

No. 220. Fourth Generation. 17.

8) Joseph Weaver, b June 21, 1831, in Rockingham Co, Va., d. in Jasper Co., Mo., July 11, 1911. He married Mary Shank, b ——————, d. Feb. 22, 1856, in Virginia He married afterwards Susanna Shank, daughter of David and Rebecca Funk Shank, b Sept 26, 1837, in Rockingham Co, Va. She died Feb. 7, 1910. Both were buried in the Weaver cemetery near Oronogo, Mo All were Mennonites Mr Weaver was for many years a minister of the Mennonite Church in Jasper Co, Mo He was a successful business man, and his counsel was much in demand in his home community He was a farmer by occupation.

1 Susanna Weaver, b. Aug 18, 1853 No. 379

2 Betsy Weaver, b. Mar. 7, 1855 No 380

(From second wife)

3 John M Weaver, b July 11, 1858 No 381

4 David S Weaver, b July 17, 1860 No 385

5 Benjamin F Weaver, b May 29, 1862 No 389

6 Jeremiah J Weaver, b Sept 3, 1864 No 391

7. Mary V Weaver, b July 28, 1866 No 398

8. William H. Weaver, b Aug. 31, 1868 No 402

9 Charles A Weaver, b Dec 20, 1870 No 403.

10. Ernest G Weaver, b. Mar 13, 1873, d Jan 7, 1874

11. Jesse E Weaver, b Dec 4, 1874 No 407

12 Alice R Weaver, b Feb 10, 1877 No 408

13 Jonas Weaver, b Mar. 20, 1880 No 409

14 Nellie Weaver, b Nov 21, 1883, d Sept 19, 1884

No. 221. Fourth Generation. 17.

9) Mary (Polly) Weaver, b Aug 23, 1833, in Rockingham Co. Va., d July 6, 1921, m George Brunk of Va, b Jan 29, 1831, d Aug. 17, 1905 Both died at the home of their son, Samuel C Brunk, near Elida, O, and were buried in the Salem cemetery near Elida They lived near Broadway, Va., where they reared their family Farmers. Mennonites He was a minister. In their declining years they settled in Allen Co, O, where several of their children had settled and lived with their son until their death.

1 Elizabeth E Brunk, b May 8, 1854   No 410.
2 Samuel C Brunk, b. Feb 1, 1857 No 411.
3 Perry E. Brunk, b Jan 19, 1858 No 412
4 Franklin B Brunk, b Jan 28, 1860. No. 413
5 Frances W. Brunk, b. Sept. 3, 1861 No 414.
6 John J Brunk, b Nov. 24, 1862. No 415.
7 Anna Brunk, b Feb 26, 1864, d July 12, 1866.
8 Lydia W Brunk, b Sept 20, 1866 No 416
9 Christian Brunk, b Mar 20, 1868 No. 417.
10 Mary C Brunk, b June 1, 1870. No. 418.

No. 222. Fourth Generation. 17.

10) David H Weaver, b Aug 14, 1837, d. Mar. 5, 1907, m. Bettie Kiester, b Oct 21, 1836, d April 11. 1900 They were buried at the Bank Church on Dry River in Rockingham Co , Va
1 Sarah F Weaver, b Dec. 21, 1856 No 472
2 Etta E Weaver, b ————————-. No 473.
3 Wm Clifford Weaver, b Oct 26, 1867. No. 475.
4 Mary Weaver, b Mar 2, 1874 No 474
5 Martin D Weaver, b ————————   N. F. R.

No. 223. Fourth Generation. 17.

11) Sarah Weaver, b Feb 3, 1839, near Harrisonburg, Va , m. Nov. 8, 1866, James William Sharps, b May 20, 1843, in Barber Co , W. Va. She died Nov 9, 1918 He died Dec 4, 1916 They were buried at Weavers Church, near Harrisonburg, Va
1 Jacob Sharps, b Nov 11, 1867 No 477
2 John Sharps, b Mar. 27, 1870 No 480
3 Betty Sharps, b Jan 25. 1872 No 481
4 William Sharps. b Sept 5, 1873 No 485
5 Mary M. Sharps. b Feb 28, 1878 No. 488
6 Joseph Sharps, b. Jan 31, 1875.

No. 224. Fourth Generation. 18.

1) Maggie Fry, b ————————-, in Augusta Co , Va , m. Feb. 14, 1867, Ashbury Menefee Hamrick, b Jan 26, 1832

No. 225. Fourth Generation. 19.

1) John F. Rhodes, b Oct 13, 1837, in Rockingham Co , Va., d Mar 24, 1906, m July 13, 1862, Mary Catherine Cox, b Mar 26, 1841, d. Mar 28, 1922. They lived in Virginia Both were buried at Spades Church in Rockingham Co. United Brethren
1. Robert A Rhodes, b. April 20, 1861. No 490
2 Charles E Rhodes, b. Aug 31, 1864. No 491
3. William B Rhodes, b Feb 6, 1866. No. 492
4 Minnie B. Rhodes, b Nov 2, 1867 No 494
5 Frances Catherine Rhodes, b Sept. 11, 1869 No 498.
6 John Adam Rhodes, b July 19, 1871 No. 499
7 Lula Ann Rhodes, b May 30, 1873 No. 500
8 Hettie Jane Rhodes, b Oct 1, 1875 No 501
9 George Henry Rhodes, b Mar. 13, 1878 No. 502
10 Homer Winfield Rhodes, b Dec 7, 1880 No. 503.
11. Odie Lena Rhodes, b. Dec 25, 1881 No. 504.
12 Walter Hamilton Rhodes, b Nov. 16, 1883 No. 505.

No. 226. Fourth Generation. 19.

2) Maggie Rhodes, b ————————, m George Bauserman, b ————————.
They lived at Mt Clinton, Va. No issue

No. 227. Fourth Generation. 19.

3) Kate Rhodes, b ————————, m George Wilson, b ———————— They
lived in Augusta Co, Va No children

No. 228. Fourth Generation. 19.

4) Sallie Rhodes, b ————————, in Virginia, m Tilden Whitmer, b
————————. They lived in Augusta Co., Va They had three children
1 Otho Whitmer, b. ————————
2. Bradford Whitmer, b ————————, d ————————.
3. ———— ————

No. 229. Fourth Generation. 20.

1) Sallie Rhodes, b Oct 28, 1830, in Va, m Peter Shoemaker, b ————————.
d. ————————; m. (2nd) Frederick Rhodes
1. Sarah Shumaker, b. ———— No 506
2. John Shumaker, b ———— No. 507
3. Bettie Shumaker, b ———— No 508
4 David E Shumaker, b ————. No 509

No. 230. Fourth Generation. 20.

2) Frederick Rhodes, b Sept. 19, 1832, in Va., m. Bettie Huffman, b ————
————. Address Harrisonburg, Va
1. Edd Rhodes, b ———— No 510
2. Etta Rhodes, b ———— No 511.
3 Lucy Rhodes, b ————————

No. 231. Fourth Generation. 20.

3) Magdalena Rhodes, b Feb 20, 1835, in Va, d Aug 16, 1900, m Abraham
D. Heatwole, b Nov 11, 1829, in Va, d Aug 28, 1913. Farmers. Mennonites
They lived at Pleasant Valley
1. Frances Heatwole, b May 30, 1853 No 512
2 Hugh Heatwole, b Mar. 3, 1855 No 524
3 Elizabeth Heatwole, b Dec 31, 1858 No 528
4 Margaret Heatwole, b April 27, 1862 No. 535.
5. John A. Heatwole, b July 12, 1866. No. 541.
6. Charles E Heatwole, b Mar. 26, 1874. No. 545.
7. Sallie Heatwole, b Jan. 27, 1878 No. 548.

No. 232. Fourth Generation. 20.

4) David Edward Rhodes, b. May 26, 1837, in Va., d. July 16, 1917, m Fannie
Lineweaver, b June 30, 1845, d Mar 30, 1887, m Feb 28, 1867, near New Rection,
Va. Farmers Mennonites He was a deacon Address. Rockingham, Va
Buried in Early's cemetery
1. Elizabeth Catherine Rhodes, b. Jan. 31, 1868, d. April 4, 1870.
2. John Henry Rhodes, b June 15, 1869. No 553
3. Mary Frances Rhodes, b Apr 10, 1871. No 556
4. Annie E Rhodes, b. Sept 11, 1875, d. May 10, 1881.
5. Jacob William Rhodes, b Mar 25, 1878, single, address: Ottawa, Ill
6. David Edward Rhodes, Jr, b. Oct. 11, 1881, d. same day.

David Edward Rhodes married (2nd) Margaret Driver, widow of John A. Driver.

No. 233. Fourth Generation. 20.

5) Catherine Rhodes, b. Aug 15, 1840, in Va She died Nov. 15, 1878, m. Gideon Wenger, b Mar. 1, 1843, in Va

1 John Daniel Wenger, b June 1, 1869, d Jan. 1, 1879.

2. Elizabeth Frances Wenger, b. Aug 15, 1870 No. 560.

3. Sarah Luella Wenger, b. Feb. 22, 1872 No 561.

4 Rhodes Solomon Wenger, b Feb 6, 1874 No. 562.

5. Marvin Cleophas Wenger, b. Apr. 6, 1876 No. 563.

6 Catherine Anna Wenger, b. Oct. 27, 1878, d. Nov. 2, 1887.

No. 234. Fourth Generation. 20.

7) John Rhodes, b Mar 6, 1846, in Va , m Amanda Whitsel, b. —————.

1 Samuel Rhodes, b. —————. No. 564

2. Sudie Rhodes, b. —————. No. 565

3 Gertrude Rhodes, b ————, 1877 No 566

4 Bessie Rhodes, b ————— No 567

5 John E Rhodes, b ————— No. 568.

6 Alice Rhodes, b. ————— No 569.

7. Frederick Rhodes, b Feb 23, 1887. No 570

8 Glen Rhodes, b. —————. No 571.

9 Howard E Rhodes, b ————— No 571½.

No. 235. Fourth Generation. 20.

8) Fannie Rhodes, b Oct 12, 1850, in Va m Calvin Pence, b. —————
They lived in Rockingham Co , Va.

1 Edd Pence, b ————— No 572

No. 236. Fourth Generation. 21.

1) Elizabeth Rhodes, b Feb 13, 1830, in Va , m Peter O. Heatwole, b. July 12, 1827 They lived on Muddy Creek, Rockingham Co., Va. Mennonites.

1. Annie M Heatwole, b April 24, 1850 No. 573.

2. Simon H Heatwole, b Nov 5, 1857 No 582

3 Samuel Heatwole, b Dec 27, 1853, d Dec. 1, 1857.

4 Mary E Heatwole, b Mar. 28, 1896 No. 584

5 Johnathan B Heatwole, b. Aug 6, 1858 No 588.

6 Peter R Heatwole, b April 25, 1860

7 Conrad S. Heatwole, b Aug 29, 1862 No 590

8 DeWitt A. Heatwole, b Nov 12, 1865 No. 592

9 Elizabeth Heatwole, b Nov 24, 1869 No 593

No. 237. Fourth Generation. 21.

2) Magdalena Rhodes, b Oct 9, 1831, in Va , d. Dec. 18, 1894, m. in 1853 Peter Blosser, b Dec 31, 1831, d Nov 23, 1904 Farmers. Mennonites Deacon. Buried in Weaver cemetery, Harrisonburg, Va.

1 Samuel H Blosser, b Oct 3, 1855 No 2066.

2. Annie F. Blosser, b June 7, 1857 No. 2098.

3 Margaret S Blosser, b Nov 9, 1858 No. 2103.

4. Elizabeth E. Blosser, b April 20, 1860.

5 Daniel A Blosser, b. —————.

6. Lydia C Blosser, b. —————, 1866, d —————, 1872.

7 Mary M. Blosser, b Dec 6, 1867 No 2104.

8 Emma L Blosser, b Jan 27, 1873 No. 2106.

No. 238. Fourth Generation. 21.

3) Susie Rhodes, b. Sept. 25, 1834, in Va , m Jacob Early, b ——————

1 Sarah Ann Early, b —————— No 2113

2. Fannie Early, b. —————.

3 David Early, b. ————— No. 2118

4 Joseph Early, b ————— No. 2123

5 Lucy Early, b ————— No 2124.

6 Charles Early, b ————— No. 2126

No. 239. Fourth Generation. 21.

4) Frances Rhodes, b Feb 26, 1839, in Va , d Dec 26, 1904, m in 1867, Samuel Early, b Oct. 15, 1843, d Aug 29, 1914

1 Bettie F. Early, b July 11, 1868, died June 24, 1926

2. Sallie M. Early, b. July 6, 1872 No 2128

3 Frank W. Early, b May 31, 1876 No 2133

4. J. Roy Early, b Mar. 13, 1879 Twin No 2136

5 Octavio V Early, b Mar 13, 1879. Twin No 2140

No. 240. Fourth Generation. 21.

5) Frederick S. Rhodes, b April 27, 1833, near Pleasant Valley, Va , d Sept. 12, 1893. He married (1st) Elizabeth Whitmer, (2nd) Oct 11, 1866, Catherine Swartz, b. Dec. 22, 1836, d Aug 30, 1897. Farmers Mennonites. Address: Hinton, Va.

1. John Samuel Rhodes, b. Aug. 26, 1857. No. 2141.

2 Lucy Ellen Rhodes, b. June 3, 1859 No 2142

(Second Marriage)

3 Rebecca Ann Rhodes, b. Dec 4, 1867 No 594

4 Mary Agnes Rhodes, b May 23, 1870. No. 595.

5. William E. Rhodes, b Mar. 25, 1873 No 596

6. Alfred Henry Rhodes, b Aug 26, 1875 No. 597.

No. 241. Fourth Generation. 21.

6) Henry L Rhodes, b. May 10, 1825, in Rockingham Co , Va., m Margaret Heatwole, b. Mar 19, 1830, same as above Address Dale Enterprise, Va. Farmer. Mennonites.

1 Mary E Rhodes, b. April 2, 1851 No 598

2 David Rhodes, b. ————— d May 16, 1859

3. Susanna Rhodes, b —————, d Mar 24, 1873.

4 Priscilla F Rhodes, b ————— d June 25, 1864

5. Rebecca Rhodes, b. Feb 4, 1857. No 606

6 William H. Rhodes, b Nov. 7, 1861. No 611

7. Lydia A. Rhodes, b. Jan. 30, 1864. No 614.

No. 242. Fifth Generation. 211.

1) Elizabeth Rhodes, b Sept 30, 1841, in Rockingham Co., Va., m Christian Shank of Singers Glen, Rockingham Co , May 26, 1862 Farmers. Mennonites Deacon.

1. Magdalena M Shank, b. Aug. 27, 1863 No 243

2. Emmer R Shank, b. Aug 6, 1865 No 244

3 Frederick A. Shank, b. June 18, 1870 No. 245

No. 243. Sixth Generation. 242.

1) Magdalena M Shank, b Aug 27, 1863, in Va , m. Rev. Samuel Rice, b Jan. 4, 1857. They were married Aug 23, 1881 He was a minister in the United

Brethren Church for some years, but more recently joined the Lutheran Church and is now preaching for them Address Lemoyne, Pa.

1. Ward B Rice, b. Aug 13, 1885
2 James E. Rice, b Feb 5, 1887.
3 Paul B. Rice, b July 17, 1890.
4 Statton L. Rice, b Feb 26, 1893
5 Joseph E. Rice, b April 20, 1897.
6. Ruel K Rice, b. Oct. 12, 1899.
7. Frederick Rice, b. April 17, 1904.

No. 244. Sixth Generation. 242.

2) Emmer R Shank, b Aug 6, 1865, in Rockingham Co , Va., m. June 8, 1897, Theressa Beery, b. Oct 9, 1871. Mr Shank is a graduate of Bridgewater College of Virginia, and of the Wittemburg College of Springfield, Ill. He was principal of the Belmont public school of Roanoke, Va , for a number of years. He then continued his studies at the Virginia University. After this he took the position of professor of mathematics in the University School for Boys at Memphis, Tenn He has since returned to his farm near Singers Glen, Va., but was later elected prinpal of schools at Singers Glen, Va Lutheran No issue reported.

No. 245. Sixth Generation. 242.

3) Frederick A Shank, b June 18, 1870, in Rockingham Co., Va., m. Dec. 8, 1891, Gertrude Mitchell, b June 8, 1871, in same place. Address: Timberville, Va. Miller by trade Mr Shank is a Methodist and Mrs. Shank a Christian.

1. Gracelle B. Shank, b Mar. 9, 1893.
2 Catherine E Shank, b. Aug 22, 1900
3 Fuda G Shank, b Feb. 18, 1907

No. 246. Fifth Generation. 211.

2) Margaret J Rhodes, b Oct 14, 1843, in Rockingham Co., Va , m. Aug. 14, 1867, John A Driver, b Nov 8, 1841. d Feb. 14, 1879. Farmers. She was a Mennonite Address Hinton, Va

1 Savilla F Driver, b. Sept 29, 1868 No 247.
2. Laura A Driver, b Oct 2, 1870 No 248
3 Mary E Driver, b Oct. 4, 1873, single.
4 John S Driver, b Dec 23, 1876, d Jan. 1, 1882.

No. 247. Sixth Generation. 246.

1) Savilla F. Driver, b Sept 29, 1868, near Hinton, Va., m. Nov. 13, 1890, Daniel R Martin. Address Waynesboro, Va Farmers. Mennonites

1. Jacob Leander Martin, b Nov 10, 1891 No. 1027.
2 Bertha V Martin, b Nov 6, 1893, single.
3 Minnie M Martin, b Oct 2, 1895, d June 21, 1911.
4 John D. Martin, b Mar 29, 1898 No 1028.
5. William H Martin, b June 20, 1900 No. 1029.
6 Marie E Martin, b July 21, 1902. No 1030
7. Fannie R. Martin, b Oct 31, 1904 No. 1031
8 Margaret C Martin, b Nov 29, 1906, d Feb. 6, 1910.
9 Daniel R Martin, b June 16, 1910.
10 Ralph L. Martin, b May 30, 1913.

No. 248. Sixth Generation. 245.

2) Annie Laura Driver, b Oct 2, 1870, near Hinton, Va , m Jan. 15, 1890, George F. Etter, b Mar 3, 1868, at Dayton, O Farmer and undertaker Mennonites Address: Stuarts Draft, Va.

1. Charles N. Etter, b. Nov. 23, 1893   No 1032.
2 Earle D. Etter, b Dec 13, 1896   No 1033.
3 George I Etter, b. May 5, 1904   No 1034.

No. 249. Fifth Generation. 211.

3) Fannie Rhodes, b. Mar 5, 1846, near Rushville, Va , m. Sept. 12, 1867, Joseph N Driver, b Mar 14, 1845, near Timberville, Va. He died Aug. 9, 1890. Mr. Driver was ordained a minister of the Mennonite Church at the Trissels Church in Rockingham Co. in 1869. He was a very able speaker and pillar in the church He was ordained to the office of bishop in Augusta Co , at the Springdale Church May 12, 1888 He died Aug 9, 1890

1 Mary M Driver, b Dec 25, 1868, single
2 Frederick A Driver, b Aug 3, 1870 No 250
3. Elizabeth C. Driver, b Mar 24, 1874, d Mar 7, 1878
4 Sallie F Driver, b Oct 10, 1876, d Jan 13, 1881
5 Lewis D Driver, b June 11, 1879, d Jan 29, 1889.
6. Joseph R Driver, b June 17, 1884. No 1035
7. Daniel W. Driver, b Sept 29, 1888 No 1036

No. 250. Sixth Generation. 249.

2) Frederick A Driver, b. Aug 3, 1870, in Va , m April 5, 1906, Daisy Kiracofe On Aug 6, 1905, Frederick was ordained deacon in the Mennonite Church at the Springdale Church State dairy inspector Address Waynesboro, Augusta Co , Va

1 Frances Elizabeth Driver, b April 11, 1909
2 Thelma Margaret Driver, b Mar 1, 1912

No. 251. Fifth Generation. 211.

4) Mary Virginia Rhodes, b May 31, 1848, in Rockingham Co., Va , m Feb. 2, 1870, Henry Brenneman of Allen Co , O , b Sept. 7, 1844, in Fairfield Co , O. Mr. Brenneman was instantly killed by lightning Aug. 28, 1878. Farmer, near Elida, O Mennonites.

1 Timothy H. Brenneman, b July 14, 1871
Dr Timothy H Brenneman graduated in medicine at the University of Virginia He practiced his profession at Virginia Beach, Va In Dec., 1904, he went to New York City to assist in performing a surgical operation, and on account of a slight wound on his hand he contracted blood poison from which he died Jan. 28, 1905 Unmarried Mennonite

Mrs. Mary Virginia (nee Rhodes) Brenneman m. (2nd) Samuel Shank, b. Jan 16, 1828, d April 30, 1901 She married (3rd) Perry X Heatwole, b. July 21, 1850, she died Nov. 10, 1925.

No. 252. Fifth Generation. 211.

5) William Rhodes, b. Nov 3, 1853, in Rockingham Co , Va , m. in 1877 Jennie Barger of Augusta Co , Va Photographer, at Newport News, Va.

1. Pearl Rhodes, b ——————. No 253.

No. 253. Sixth Generation. 252.

1) Pearl Rhodes, b ——————, m Menno Sharps, b —————— Address· Funkstown, Md

1 Virginia Sharps, b ———, 1905
2 —————— ———, b July 24, 1907

No. 254. Fifth Generation. 211.

7) Reuben S Rhodes, b May 26, 1858, in Rockingham Co., Va., m. Maggie Rhodes, daughter of Peter Rhodes, Sept. 5, 1878, b. —————, d. ————. Address: Dayton, Va.

1 Raleigh D. Rhodes, b. Mar 7, 1880
2. Emmer F. Rhodes, b Oct 21, 1881
3 Lewis J. Rhodes, b. Oct. 14, 1883.
4. Elsie V. Rhodes, b Oct. 14, 1885
5. Annie M. Rhodes, b Oct 31, 1888
6 Webster C Rhodes, b Mar 8, 1890.
7 Ida B. Rhodes, b July 24, 1892.
8. Paul T. Rhodes, b. July 28, 1894.
9. Nettie E. Rhodes, b. Jan. 19, 1897.
10 Peter R Rhodes, b Feb. 13, 1899
11 John H. Rhodes, b April 6, 1901
12 Mary F Rhodes, b. Oct 12, 1903

No. 255. Fifth Generation. 212.

2) Timothy E Rhodes, b. Feb 17, 1854, in Va , m. Dec. 6, 1879, Laura Jones, b ————— Address. Harrisonburg, Va.

No. 256. Fifth Generation. 212.

3) James W Rhodes, b Feb 27, 1856, in Va , m Oct 26, 1880, Lucy M. Bowers Address· Hinton, Va

No. 257. Fifth Generation. 212.

4) Franklin R Rhodes, b. April 25, 1858, in Va , m Feb 26, 1880, Bettie F. Long, b. ————— Address· Chrisman, Ill.

No. 258. Fifth Generation. 212.

5) Barbara A. Rhodes, b Oct 14, 1860, in Va., m. Feb. 28, 1889, Robert L. Detrick, b —————. Address. North River, Va Farmer U B. Church.

1 Elsie Florence Detrick, b Jan 3, 1891.

No. 259. Fifth Generation. 212.

6) John H. Rhodes, b Dec 7, 1862, in Va , m May 22, 1889, Minnie V. Weller, b ————— Clerk United Brethren Address Lilly, W Va

1 Lester W. Rhodes, b Feb 25, 1890

No. 260. Fifth Generation. 212.

7) Virginia A Rhodes, b Dec. 3, 1865, in Rockingham Co., Va., m. Jan. 17, 1889, Conrad S. Heatwole, b Aug 29, 1862 Farmer Address Dayton, Va Mennonites.

1. LaRue Z. Heatwole, b Jan 20, 1890. No. 591.

No. 261. Fifth Generation. 212.

9) Mary M Rhodes, b. Dec 18, 1870, in Va m ————— —————. Address: Hinton, Va

No. 262. Fifth Generation. 215.

1) Sem S Weaver, b Feb 15, 1847, in Va , m Dec 10, 1868, Mary Lehman, b Feb 27, 1852, d. July 24, 1890 Mr Weaver was a wagonmaker by trade Address· Mt Clinton, Va. Mennonites. He was ordained to the ministry at the Bank Church, Aug 18, 1878, in Rockingham Co , Va

1 Elizabeth L Weaver, b. Nov. 17, 1869 No. 263.
2 Mary M Weaver, b Dec 23, 1871, d. Dec 1, 1881

3 John A. Weaver, b. July 9, 1873. No 264
4 Lydia C. Weaver, b. July 8, 1875 No 265.
5. Nancy B. Weaver, b. July 15, 1876, d Oct. 18, 1892.
6 Annie R. Weaver, b Dec. 8, 1877. No 266
7. Sarah R Weaver, b. Dec 6, 1879
8. Emma V Weaver, b Jan 18, 1881 No 267.
9 Martin D Weaver, b. Mar 13, 1882, d Jan 12, 1883
10 Sadie S. Weaver, b April 5, 1884 No 268
11 Oliver S. Weaver, b Jan 21, 1888, d Mar 21, 1892

No. 263. Sixth Generation. 262.

1) Elizabeth L. Weaver, b Nov 17, 1869, in Rockingham Co, Va, m Oct. 10, 1897, D. H. Andrews, b April 20, 1874 Address Mt. Clinton, Va. Farmer Mennonite.
1 Mary E Andrews, b Feb 21, 1899, d Feb 28, 1899.
2 Anna C Andrews, b Oct 19, 1902
3. Vada C Andrews, b Dec 8. 1903
4 Ruth M. Andrews, b Feb 19, 1906

No. 264. Sixth Generation. 262.

3) John A Weaver, b July 9, 1873, in Rockingham Co, Va, m May 25, 1897, Lillian S Messick, b Dec 1, 1872 Address Mt Clinton, Va, Tombstone cutter Mennonite
1 Charles D Weaver, b May 27, 1900
2 Edna Marie Weaver, b Aug 3, 1906

No. 255. Sixth Generation. 262.

4) Lydia C Weaver, b July 8, 1875. in Rockingham Co., Va, m Aug 13, 1899, Jacob F Heatwole, b Feb 18, 1875 Address Dale Enterprise, Va Farmer. Mennonite
1. Sadie R Heatwole, b Feb 21, 1901
2. Almeta P Heatwole, b. May 29, 1903
3 Margaret L. Heatwole, b May 1, 1905
4 Lucile F Heatwole, b. Feb 7, 1907

No. 265. Sixth Generation. 262.

6) Annie Rebecca Weaver, b. Dec 8, 1877, near Mt Clinton, Va., m Sept. 7, 1905, Perry J Swope. Address Dale Enterprise, Va Farmer. Mennonites
1. Lelia C. Swope, b July 1, 1906.

No. 267. Sixth Generation. 262.

8) Emma V Weaver, b Jan 18, 1881. near Mt Clinton, Va., m Jan 25, 1900, John R Wenger, b ————, 1879 Address Dayton, Va Farmers Mennonites
1 Lena Wenger, b. June 12, 1901.
2. Alma Wenger, b. June 28, 1903.
3 Reuben S Wenger, b Dec 4, 1906

No. 268. Sixth Generation. 262.

10) Sadie S Weaver, b. April 5, 1884, near Mt. Clinton, Va, m April ——, 1906, John L Rhodes Address Mt Clinton, Va Farmer

No. 269. Fifth Generation. 215.

2) Solomon Weaver, b Mar 12, 1849, in Rockingham Co, Va, d July 11, 1889, m in 1879, Susan Sandy. Address· Spring Creek, Va Tinner by trade Mennonites
1 Floria Weaver. b June 4, 1884, d Nov 29, 1896

4) Nancy Weaver, b June 5, 1853, near Spring Creek, Va., d. Oct. 11, 1917, m. Abram B. Burkholder, b Jan 4, 1850, in Rockingham Co., Va., d. —————— Farmer. Mennonites. He was ordained to the ministry at the Bank Church, July 15, 1877. Address: Harrisonburg, Va.

    1. Maggie F. Burkholder, b. April 9, 1872. No. 271.
    2. John D. Burkholder, b. Aug 10, 1873. No. 272.
    3. Reuben S. Burkholder, b Sept 11, 1876. No. 273.
    4. Mary E Burkholder, b Aug 6, 1878, d. Aug 31, 1894.
    5. Joseph A Burkholder, b Jan. 6, 1882 No 274.
    6. Nannie E. Burkholder, b Nov. 24, 1883 No. 275.
    7. Perry A Burkholder, b. Aug. 12, 1886 No. 991
    8. Emmanuel J Burkholder, b May 23, 1891. No. 3609.
    9. Amos H Burkholder, b. July 31, 1893 No. 3610.
   10 Ella D Burkholder, b. April 4, 1897. No 3611.

No. 271. Sixth Generation. 270.

1) Maggie F Burkholder, b April 9, 1872, near Harrisonburg, Va., d. May 9, 1934, m. in 1891, Emmanuel J Swope Address Harrisonburg, Va, R. 1 Farmer Mennonites

    1. Ira B. Swope, b June 23, 1892. No. 3625
    2. Mary E. Swope, b. Dec 3, 1893 No. 3626
    3. John A Swope, b Sept. 11, 1896 No 3627.
    4 Oliver D. Swope, b Aug 21, 1898. No. 3628
    5 Herman F. Swope, b. Dec. 12, 1900. No. 3629.
    6 Nannie E Swope, b Jan. 6, 1902 No. 3630
    7 Joseph W Swope, b Feb 29, 1904. No. 3631
    8. Paul S. Swope, b Apr 24, 1905 No. 3632.
    9. Emmanuel J. Swope, b. June 24, 1907 No. 3633.
   10 Roy Daniel Swope, b May 21, 1911, d Sept 25, 1915.
   11 Cleo James Swope, b. Aug. 17, 1915. Address· North Lima, Ohio
   12 Margaret Frances Swope, b Mar 7, 1918 Address North Lima, Ohio

No. 272. Sixth Generation. 270.

2) John D Burkholder, b Aug 10, 1873, near Harrisonburg, Va., m. Nov 13, 1895, Dora Humbert, New Hope, Va, b Nov. 10, 1878, d. July 14, 1935 Address Harrisonburg, Va Osteopathic physician. Mennonites

    1 Bertha C. Burkholder, b Sept. 11, 1896 No. 3620.
    2 Nellie A Burkholder, b May 2, 1898 No 3627
    3 Lena G. Burkholder, b Dec. 12, 1900 No 3628.
    4 John D. Burkholder, Jr, b Jan 25, 1906 No. 928.

No. 273. Sixth Generation. 270.

3) Reuben S Burkholder, b Sept 11, 1876, near Harrisonburg, Va., m. Oct 28, 1904, Effie V Grove, b Aug 1, 1881 Address· Waynesboro, Va Real estate dealer Mennonites

    1 Oren G Burkholder, b Mar. 27, 1906
    2. Lettie E Burkholder, b June 15, 1908 No 3617
    3. Ray A. Burkholder, b April 9, 1912. No. 3618
    4 Nelson R Burkholder, b Nov 6, 1915 No 3619

No. 274. Sixth Generation. 270.

5) Joseph A. Burkholder, b Jan 6, 1882, near Harrisonburg, Va, m. May 13, 1903, Fannie Showalter, b Jan. 4, 1884 Address North Lima, O. Real estate dealer Mennonites Related. For family see mother's line, No. 998.

No. 275. Sixth Generation. 270.

6) Nannie C Burkholder, b Nov 24, 1883, near Harrisonburg, Va, m June 1, 1905, Daniel W Good, b April 1, 1884. Address Sterling, Ill Farmer Mennonites.

1. Esther C Good, b Dec 12, 1906 No 3612
2 Lloyd D. Good, b Dec 3, 1912 No 3613
3. Edna E Good, b Oct 23, 1916

No. 276. Fifth Generation. 215.

5) Reuben Weaver, b Mar 2, 1856, in Rockinghan Co, Va (mute), m Lucy M. McCammick in 1888 (mute), Baptist In early life he became afflicted with a severe attack of brain fever, which later took the form of a prolonged abscess in the ears and in time left him with the total loss of hearing He was placed in care of the institute for the blind, deaf and mute, at Staunton, Va, where he became a mechanic For a long time he held the important position of superintendent of the department of carpentering at the institution where he received his training

1 Owen G Weaver, b Mar 27, 1906

No. 277. Fifth Generation. 215.

6) Jacob Weaver, b Dec 24, 1857, in Rockingham Co, Va, m Nov 18, 1880, Mary C Heatwole, who d Feb 3, 1898 He married Nov. 14, 1900, Mrs Maud Miller, b April 2, 1872 Address Spring Creek, Va Farmer Mennonites

1 Isa F Weaver, b Sept 11, 1892, d April 18, 1893.
2 William Weaver, b June 16, 1894, d next day

(From second marriage)

3. Magdalena F. Weaver, b Nov. 6, 1902.
4. John R Weaver, b July 3, 1903

No. 278. Fifth Generation. 215.

7) Frances Weaver, b Oct 23, 1861, in Rockingham Co, Va, m Aug. 6, 1880, Charles G. Shank, b Feb 25, 1857 Address· Dale Enterprise, Va. Farmer. Mennonites

1 Reuben D. Shank, b. Mar 29, 1882, d April 5, 1882.
2 Effie C. Shank, b. April 27, 1883 No 279
3. Nannie E. Shank, b Oct. 18, 1884 No 876
4 Elmer D Shank, b. June 21, 1886 No 877
5. Joseph Shank, b. Dec. 1, 1887, d Dec 18, 1887.
6 Infant son, b. Feb 1889, d same day
7. Infant son, b June 25, 1890, d next day
8 Maggie Shank, b July 24, 1891, single
9 Lewis W Shank, b June 17, 1893 No 877½
10 Emmanuel J. Shank, b. May 9, 1895 Twin No 878.
11. Samuel A Shank, b May 9, 1895 Twin No 879.
12 Infant son, b Feb 14, 1898, d. next day
13 John W Shank, b Mar 27, 1899. No 880.
14 Mary R Shank, b Feb 21, 1902, single

No. 279. Sixth Generation. 278.

2) Effie C Shank, b April 27, 1883, in Rockingham Co, Va, m Dec 6, 1906, William Sharps, b Sept 5, 1874 Address Harrisonburg, Va. Farmer Mennonites Related Come in two ways For family see No. 873

No. 280. Fifth Generation. 217.

2) Margaret Weaver, b. Mar 26, 1844, in Rockingham Co., Va., m. Oct. 3, 1867, Manassas Heatwole, b ——————, d Nov. 25, 1890. Address: Dayton, Va Farmer. Mennonites

1. Elizabeth Heatwole, b Nov. 20, 1860, d. Aug. 19, 1888.
2. Annie F Heatwole, b. July 13, 1870 No 281.
3 Abram D. Heatwole, b June 27, 1872. No. 282.
4 John G. Heatwole, b Feb 18, 1875. No 283.
5. Jacob F Heatwole, b Feb 18, 1875 Twins. No 284
6. Mary V Heatwole, b July 29, 1877. No. 285
7. Rebecca Heatwole, b Dec. 14, 1879.
8 Sophiah M. Heatwole, b Feb 5, 1883.
9 Lewis A. Heatwole, b July 25, 1885, d. May 5, 1892.

No. 281. Sixth Generation. 280.

2) Annie F Heatwole, b July 13, 1870, in Va, d. Aug 28, 1900, m. Oct 13, 1891, Daniel P. Wenger, b. April 16, 1870.

1 Lena C Wenger, b. May 20, 1893
2 William A Wenger, b Nov 21, 1894
3 Marie E Wenger, b. Aug. 30, 1896

No. 282. Sixth Generation. 280.

3) Abram D Heatwole, b June 27, 1872, in Va., m. Lydia Heatwole, April 12 1894. Address Dayton, Va Farmer. Mennonites.

1 Owen B Heatwole, b July 30, 1895
2 Anna E Heatwole, b. Sept 11, 1897.
3 Mary N Heatwole, b Feb 22, 1900
4. Pauline N Heatwole, b Aug 16, 1902, d. Oct. 23, 1902.
5 Peter E. Heatwole, b. Oct 14, 1903.
6 Edith V Heatwole, b Jan. 4, 1907.

No. 283. Sixth Generation. 280.

4) John G. Heatwole, b Feb 18, 1875, in Va., twin, m. Jan. 19, 1899, Fannie Suter, b. Mar 24, 1875, in Va Address· Harrisonburg, Va Farmer. Mennonite.

1 Annie M Heatwole, b Jan. 3, 1900
2. Guy J Heatwole, b Jan 9, 1901.
3 Marion S. Heatwole, b. Sept. 2, 1902, d. Oct. 25, 1903.
4 Katie B Heatwole, b Jan 18, 1904.
5 John F Heatwole, b. Mar. —— 1905.

No. 284. Sixth Generation. 280.

5) Jacob F Heatwole, b Feb 18, 1875, in Va, twin, m Aug 13, 1900, Lydia Weaver, b ————————— Address Harrisonburg, Va Farmer. Mennonites.

1 Sadie R Heatwole, b Feb 21, 1901.
2 Almeta P Heatwole, b May 29, 1903
3 Margaret L Heatwole, b May 1, 1905
4 Lucile F. Heatwole, b Feb 7, 1907

No. 285. Sixth Generation. 280.

6) Mary V Heatwole, b July 29, 1877, in Va, m April 16, 1899, Jacob Wenger, b ———————— Address Harrisonburg, Va. Farmer. Mennonites

1 Nellie M. Wenger, b Apr 1, 1900, d Jan 8, 1905
2 Vada C Wenger, b. Nov. 27, 1901
3 Lewis J Wenger, b May 6, 1903
4 Della R Wenger, b Aug. 10, 1907

No. 286. Fifth Generation. 217.

3) Frances Weaver, b. Nov 13, 1845, in Va, m Oct 6, 1867, Peter S Hartman, b Nov. 29, 1846, in Va. Address. Dale Enterprise, Va Farmer Mennonites

1 Jacob D. Hartman, b Nov 23, 1870. No. 287.

2. Elizabeth S Hartman, b June 7, 1874 No 288

3. Daniel M. Hartman, b Nov. 23, 1877, d Sept 19, 1880

4 Mary M. Hartman, b April 5, 1880 No. 289.

5 Sarah F. Hartman, b April 21, 1885, d Oct 17, 1890.

No. 287. Sixth Generation. 286.

1) Jacob D. Hartman, b. Nov 23, 1870, in Va., m. Aug. 9, 1891, Eurie F Showalter, b. Oct. 30, 1869 Address Dale Enterprise, Va Farmers Mennonites

1 Walter E. Hartman, b June 19, 1895. No 1151.

2. Wilmer C. Hartman, b April 8, 1897. No 1152.

3. Daniel J. Hartman, b Mar. 4, 1899. No 1153

No. 288. Sixth Generation. 286.

2) Elizabeth S Hartman, b June 7, 1874, in Va, m July 21, 1891, William H Rhodes, b. Nov 7, 1861. Address Harrisonburg, Va. Farmer and carpenter Mennonites

1. Ward A. Rhodes, b Aug 2, 1892

2. P. Alfred Rhodes, b. April 1, 1894.

3. Fannie B Rhodes, b. Aug. 21, 1896

No. 289. Sixth Generation. 286.

4) Mary M Hartman, b April 5, 1880, in Va, d Jan 23, 1938, m John E Heatwole, Oct 13, 1896 Mennonites Address Harrisonburg, Va Farmer and poultryman. Buried Weaver's cemetery

1. Ethel F. Heatwole, b. Nov 11, 1897.

2. Grace P. Heatwole, b Dec 13, 1899

No. 290. Fifth Generation. 217.

4) Abraham D Weaver, b Nov 3, 1847, in Rockingham Co, Va, m June 23, 1872, Rebecca Shank, b Jan 3, 1853 near Harrisonburg, Va. She died Feb 10, 1914. Mr. Weaver later married Mrs Barbara Powel, of Elida, O., where he lived until his death. He was taken back to Virginia for burial Address. Dale Enterprise, Va Farmer. Mennonite Related to No 681

1. Walter S Weaver, b Aug 18, 1873 No 291

2 Otho B Weaver, b Jan 17. 1875 No 292

3 Rawley Jacob Weaver, b Oct 13, 1877 No. 293.

4 John W. Weaver, b July 5, 1881. No 294

5. Lena V. Weaver, b. Sept 24, 1883 No. 295

6. Ward D. Weaver, b Oct 23, 1888. No 296.

7 Annie M Weaver, b May 13, 1891 No 297

No. 291. Sixth Generation. 290.

1) Walter S Weaver, b Aug 18. 1873, in Rockingham Co, Va, m Aug 10, 1899. Marie E Alfred Address Lynchburg, Va Merchant Christians

1 Meredith A Weaver, b Nov —, 1901.

No. 292. Sixth Generation. 290.

2) Otho B Weaver, b Jan 17, 1875, in Rockingham Co, Va, died June 4, 1914, m Jan. 16, 1896, Alice Swartz, b Nov 27, 1877 Address Mt Clinton, Va Farmer. Mennonites.

1. Wade Hampton Weaver, b Oct 27, 1896. No 736

2. Fleta Pearl Weaver, b. July 31, 1899. No. 737.
3 Raymond A. Weaver, b Feb 9, 1901. No. 738.
4 Marvin David Weaver, b Sept 21, 1904 No 739

No. 293. Sixth Generation. 290.

3) Rawley Jacob Weaver, b Oct. 13, 1877, in Va., m. Nov. 19, 1899, Sallie A. Heatwole, b. Nov. 17, 1881 Address· Dayton, Va. Farmer. Mennonite.
1 Marion R Weaver, b Oct. 1, 1900 No. 740.
2 Carl Henry Weaver, b Oct 9, 1903.
3 Della P Weaver, b. April 3, 1906 No 741.
4 Mabel H Weaver, b Feb 17, 1910
5. Ruth M. Weaver, b Oct. 6, 1914 No. 3667.
6 Rolland J Weaver, b. Aug. 24, 1920.

No. 294. Sixth Generation. 290.

4) John W Weaver, b July 5, 1881, in Rockingham Co., Va., d. at Goshen, Ind , Dec 24, 1917. m April 17, 1904, Orilla Bickel, b Sept. 29, 1883. They lived at Goshen, Ind
1 William Ray Weaver, b Dec 17, 1906

No. 295. Sixth Generation. 290.

5) Lena Virginia Weaver, b Sept 24, 1883, in Va., m. Sept 25, 1901, Leonard Houston Jones, b. Sept 2, 1877. Address: Hinton, Va. Miller by trade. Mennonite
1 Irene M Jones, b Aug 2, 1902. No 742.
2 Edna Rebecca Jones, b. Sept. 2, 1906 No. 743.
3 Vada Anna Jones, b Aug 14, 1909. No. 744
4 Virginia Weaver Jones, b June 20, 1921.

No. 296. Sixth Generation. 290.

6) Ward D. Weaver, b Oct 23, 1888, in Va , m. Ollie Mae Shuler, b Oct. 24, 1894 Express agent
1 Mae R Weaver, b. Oct. 4, 1913.

No. 297. Sixth Generation. 290.

7) Annie M. Weaver, b. May 13, 1891, in Rockingham Co., Va., m. Feb 25, 1915, Rhodes Homer Driver, b Aug 5, 1890, d Feb. 24, 1936, in Virginia. Farmer. Mennonites
1 Harold Weaver Driver, b Jan 7, 1916.
2 Reba Virginia Driver, b Oct 11, 1917
3. Edith Rebecca Driver, b. Mar. 25, 1920.
4 Gladys Anna Driver, b. Sept 14, 1921.
5 Brownie Marie Driver, b Mar 9, 1928

No. 298. Fifth Generation. 217.

6) Susanna C Weaver, b. Jan. 25, 1852, in Rockingham Co., Va., m. Nov. 17, 1873, Solomon D Heatwole, b July 21, 1853, in Va. Address: Dayton, Va. Farmer Mennonite.
1 Emma F. Heatwole, b Nov 13, 1874 No 299
2. Joseph H. Heatwole, b Sept. 4, 1876 No 302
3 Walter J Heatwole, b Oct 28, 1878 No. 304
4 Hettie D Heatwole, b Nov. 29, 1880 No 306
5 William H Heatwole, b Nov 23, 1882 No 308
6 Lydia S Heatwole, b Feb 3, 1885. No 309.

7. Calvin J. Heatwole, b. May 5, 1887. No. 310.

8. Mary C. Heatwole, b Jan. 7, 1891. No. 311.

No. 299. Sixth Generation. 298.

1) Emma F. Heatwole, b Nov. 13, 1874, near Dayton, Va , m Jan. 16, 1902, Daniel Wenger, as his second wife Address Harrisonburg, Va Farmer. Mennonite.

1. Oliver Boyd Wenger, b Feb 2, 1903 No 300

2. Anna Susan Wenger, b. Oct 24, 1904

3 Edna R. Wenger, b July 24, 1906

4. Addie M. Wenger, b Feb 24, 1910

No. 300. Seventh Generation. 299.

1) Oliver Boyd Wenger, b Feb 2, 1903, near Harrisonburg, Va., m May 6. 1924, Goldie Heatwole, b July 16, 1904 Address. Harrisonburg, Va. Janitor Mennonite

1. Sheldon Leroy Wenger, b April 5, 1925

2. Helen Frances Wenger, b June 2, 1929

No. 302. Sixth Generation. 298.

2) Joseph H. Heatwole, b Sept 4, 1876, near Dayton, Va., m Mar 2, 1902, Emma C. Brenneman, b Nov 17, 1880, d Mar 27, 1914. Joseph married (2nd) Nov. 12, 1918, Effie Brenneman, b May 27, 1883 Address Elida, O Farmer Mennonite

(Issue from first wife)

1. Orpha Heatwole, b Sept. 26, 1902. No 2376¼

2. Susanna Heatwole. b Mar 14, 1904 No 303

3 Warren Heatwole, b. June 15, 1906

4 Milton Heatwole, b. June 30, 1908

5 John Heatwole, b. Sept 14, 1910.

6 Mary Heatwole, b Dec 13, 1912 No 325½.

7 Mark Heatwole, b July 8, 1915 No. 2377

No. 303. Seventh Generation. 302.

2) Susanna Heatwole, b Mar 14, 1904, near Elida, O , m Elmo F. Showalter. b Mar. 14, 1904. in Va Address Roscoe, Calif (Ellwood) Manufacturer Mennonites.

1 Bruce Showalter, b Dec 24, 1925, d Sept. 6, 1937

2 Carol Wayne Showalter, b. Aug 30, 1929

3. June Elaine Showalter, b Dec 19, 1931.

No. 304. Sixth Generation. 298.

3) Walter J. Heatwole, b Oct 28, 1878, near Dayton, Va , m. Nora Harlan. b. May 21, 1881 Address Dayton, Va Farmer Mennonite

1. Ada P. Heatwole, b Oct 9, 1902

2. Pauline S. Heatwole, b Nov 22, 1903. No 305.

3 Edna H. Heatwole, b Jan 8, 1907.

4 Naoma M Heatwole, b Nov 26, 1912 No 3666

No. 305. Seventh Generation. 304.

2) Pauline S Heatwole, b Nov 22, 1903, near Dayton, Va , m. Sept 21, 1926. Mahlon L Blosser. b Jan 16. 1904 Address Harrisonburg. Va . Star Route Farmer

1. Glendon Lee Blosser, b. Dec. 14, 1930.

2 Glennys Marie Blosser, b. Dec. 14, 1930 Twins.

No. 306. Sixth Generation. 298.

4) Hettie D Heatwole, b Nov 29, 1880, near Dayton, Va., m. Jan. 11, 1900, John A Rhodes, b Sept 3, 1873 Address Hinton, Va Miller by trade

1. Ressie R. Rhodes, b Feb 26, 1902 No. 307.
2 Annie E. Rhodes, b. Nov 19, 1908.

No. 307. Seventh Generation. 306.

1) Ressie R. Rhodes, b Feb. 26, 1902, in Va, m Dec 24, 1926, Frank D Heatwole, b. in 1905 Address Hinton, Va Shopwork.

1. Raymond R Heatwole, b. Nov 19, 1927.

No. 308. Sixth Generation. 298.

5) William E Heatwole, b Nov 23, 1882, near Dayton, Va., m. Oct. 1, 1908, Dora Powel, Elida, O, b. June 6, 1888 Address Elida, O Farmer. Mennonites

1. Virgil Heatwole, b Nov 27, 1909
2. Alma Heatwole, b Sept 15, 1911
3 Raymond Heatwole, b. July 10, 1913.
4. Grace Heatwole, b Aug 26, 1916.
5 Lewis Heatwole, b. Aug. 29, 1918.
6. Vernon Heatwole, b. June 15, 1927

No. 309. Sixth Generation. 298.

6) Lydia S. Heatwole, b Feb 3, 1885, near Dayton, Va., m. Sept. 7, 1907, Q H. Riddle, b Mar. 2, 1871 Address Harrisonburg, Va. Farmer.

1 Raymond Riddle, b. Sept. 10, 1908
2. Katherine V Riddle, b Feb. 15, 1911.
3. Cleta I. Riddle, b Feb 19, 1913.
4 Goldie E. Riddle, b. Aug. 29, 1914
5 Margie J. Riddle, b Aug 2, 1916.
6 Mamie S Riddle, b Sept 14, 1918

No. 310. Sixth Generation. 298.

7) Calvin T. Heatwole, b. May 5, 1887, near Dayton, Va., m Nov. 6, 1913, Effie R Barnhart, b Feb 4, 1890. Address Dayton, Va. Farmer.

1. Lola V Heatwole, b Jan. 1, 1915.
2 Wilma M. Heatwole, b Sept 5, 1922

No. 311. Sixth Generation. 298.

8) Mary C. Heatwole, b. Jan 7, 1891, near Dayton, Va, m. Feb. 11, 1913, Earl Showalter, b Mar 31, 1890 Address: La Junta, Colo. Farmer. Mennonite minister.

1 Carl E. Showalter, b Nov 29, 1913.
2. Richard M. Showalter, b. June 15, 1918.
3 Earl Showalter, Jr., b Dec. 9, 1923.

No. 312. Fifth Generation. 218.

1) John S Coffman, b at Dale Enterprise, Rockingham Co, Va, Oct 16, 1848, d July 22, 1899, in Elkhart, Ind He was married to Elizabeth Heatwole, Nov 11, 1869, b July 31, 1845, and d Sept. 5, 1919 Both were buried at Prairie Street cemetery

J. S Coffman gave his heart to God in his youth, uniting with the Mennonite Church by baptism, July 4, 1861, at a time when the Civil War was raging. The southern confederacy was gradually forcing able-bodied men over sixteen years of age into the service

Because of conscientious convictions he, with others, became a refugee and made his way to the states of Maryland and Pennsylvania, where he remained for two years, when he returned to his home in Virginia.

On July 18, 1875, he was ordained to the ministry. His early life was given to teaching singing schools and day schools, having acquired his knowledge by studying much at nights and spare moments It is said of him that after his marriage, being poor in earthly means but rich in purpose, he began homebuilding on a farm at the foot of Mole Hill in Rockingham Co, Va By hard work and economic methods they got along nicely He managed to work his farm, teach, study, and attend school J S Coffman, when encouraged to attend the Bridgewater Normal by Dr Bucher, exclaimed that much as he would like to, could not because his family had a first claim on him. He was assured that there would be a way out and that he should be present on Monday morning He was present and asked Dr Bucher for the use of his book on "Quackenboss Rhetoric" as he was short on means Dr Bucher at once assured him that he could have the use of any other volumes that he might need. In the meantime Dr Bucher learned of how he labored under difficulties, and when young Coffman asked how much he owed for the use of the books, Dr Bucher answered, "I take nothing for favors from a young man who gets his lessons on the plow handle while the horses are resting" The tears at once started over the cheeks of John And he never forgot this kindness, and after years showed his appreciation by writing him friendship letters In his last letter, among other questions, he asked, "What are you doing for the Lord's work"

On the day of his call to the ministry, he had not felt much conviction up to the time of the last prayer, when at once he received the token from the Lord that he was the chosen This was a great day for the Mennonite Church of America. He being the one chosen introduced the greatest evangelistic movement that had ever taken place in the Mennonite Church.

His first sermon was short and to the point and well delivered He avoided the time worn custom of preaching in a sing song style. He prepared his sermons well, which, in the beginning, caused some offense. But young Coffman became a leader in the church which gradually led others into a more systematic preparation of their sermons.

On June 17, 1879, he left the home of his youth for Elkhart, Ind, where he was to take a place on the editorial staff of the "Herald of Truth," and where he became a great stimulus to the success of the interests of the cause

Coffman had a very pleasing way of presenting his discourses and always made a lasting impression on his hearers and especially on the young people. When the revival spirit began to take hold of the church he at once said, "What are we doing for our young people?" Here was a large field open for harvest By nature Coffman filled the place by being filled with the Spirit of God Well built, nearly six feet tall, weighing one hundred and seventy pounds, graceful, neat, smooth shaven, with a clear winning gray eye, kind face, fluent speech, refined manner, and a great amount of "personal magnetism" He was fitted physically on the one hand, while his devoted, pious character with good common sense, the experience of a thorough conversion, and the outpouring of God's Spirit upon him for service fitted him on the other hand spiritually for the work to which he had been called

He was very successful in his evangelistic work Through his efforts hundreds of our brightest young people were saved to the church of their fathers.

Coffman never gathered much of this world's goods together, but he at one time said to the writer that he could not do efficient work for the Lord until he promised the Lord to be a poor preacher (financially) all his life which he carried out to the end.

He helped to promote a number of innovations in the church that have been monuments to the present day Among this number was the Elkhart Institute, the first church school of the church of his choice He supported the Mennonite Book and Tract Society from its beginning. He helped to introduce the Sunday School Conference into the Mennonite Church He, perhaps more than any other member, brought about a condition whereby the difference between the Old Mennonite Church and Amish Mennonite Church were forgotten and cast aside.

Coffman was often misunderstood by well meaning brethren but he had an exceptional way of getting the good feeling of even his opposers In his death the church lost a strong pillar and aggressive worker, but his labors are still going on At his funeral were ministers from Ohio, Indiana, Pennsylvania, and Illinois

While his funeral was being held at the church in Elkhart, Ind, an overflow service was held at the Elkhart Institute Hall, and at the same time a meeting was held at the Bank Church in Virginia He was the father of 5 sons and 2 daughters (Arranged by C. D Breneman.) He was buried at Elkhart, Ind.

1. William Perry Coffman, b. Jan. 13, 1871. No. 313.
2 Samuel Frederick Coffman, b June 11, 1872. No 314.
3 Jacob M Coffman, b Aug 18, 1873 No 315
4 Ansel V Coffman, b April 30, 1875. No 316
5 Fannie E Coffman, b. Jan 29, 1877. No 317
6 Daniel J. Coffman, b April 22, 1879, single
7 Anna B Coffman, b. Mar 12, 1881. No 318

No. 313. Sixth Generation. 312.

1) William Perry Coffman, born in Rockingham Co, Va, Jan 13, 1871, m Jan 9, 1895, to Lydia Hug of Elkhart, Ind, born Mar 19, 1869. Printer at Burbank, Calif
1 Esther Coffman, b Nov. 11, 1895, twin
2 Ethel Coffman, b Nov 11, 1895, twin
3 Mary Frances Coffman, b —————.

No. 314. Sixth Generation. 312.

2) Samuel Frederick Coffman, born in Rockingham Co, Va, June 11, 1872, m Nov 20, 1901, Ella Mann, b Jan 1, 1873 Address Vineland, Ont He is a minister and bishop in the Mennonite Church Like his father, Samuel is a very influential leader and is interested in educating the young people His services are much in demand as an instructor in Bible knowledge in many localities and especially in his home conference district His wife died Feb 9, 1935. Burial in Vineland cemetery
1. John Ezra Coffman, b Oct. 6, 1902
2 Magdalena Elizabeth Coffman, b July 6, 1904
3 David William Coffman, b Dec. 14, 1905. No 314½
4 Barbara Frances Coffman, b. April 3, 1907
5. Saloma Ellen Coffman, b Sept 24, 1910.

No. 314½. Seventh Generation. 314.

3) David William Coffman, b. Dec 14, 1905, in Ontario, Canada, m Sept. 6, 1931, Margery Grendalyn Chambers, b May 20, 1906, in Bedford, England. Address: Vineland, Ont.
1. Frederick William Coffman, b Sept. 5, 1933
2 David Lewis Coffman, b Aug 12, 1935.

No. 315. Sixth Generation. 312.

3) Jacob Manasseh Coffman, born Aug 18, 1873, in Va , m. July 1, 1900, Vesta DeCamp. Jacob died April 13, 1932 Address Elkhart, Ind , where he was a postal clerk No issue

No. 316. Sixth Generation. 312.

4) Ansel Victor Coffman, b. April 30, 1875, in Va , m. Sept. 16, 1906, Harriet Durham, b ————, 1880, d Mar 10, 1930 Address 1832 Grenshaw Blvd , Los Angeles, Calif Dentist Episcopal Church
1 Ezra Durham Coffman, b April 10, 1923

No. 317. Sixth Generation. 312.

5) Fannie Elizabeth Coffman. b Jan 29, 1877, in Va , m. Jacob C Landes Address: S Prairie St., Elkhart, Ind Salesman
1 Ruth Landes, b ————
2 John Landes, b ————.

No. 318. Sixth Generation. 312.

7) Anna Barbara Coffman. b Mar 12. 1881. in Ind , m Jacob B. Bontrager, b ———— Address Elkhart. Ind. Carpenter and real estate dealer Mennonite No issue.

No. 319. Fifth Generation. 218.

2) Jacob B. Coffman. b at Dale Enterprise, Va , July 28, 1850, d Feb. 23, 1930, m Oct 14, 1875, Sallie B Showalter, b Nov 2. 1855 Address Dayton, Va Brethren
1 Ernest Coffman, b April 22, 1881 No 320
2 S Frank Coffman, b Sept 23. 1883 No 321

No. 320. Sixth Generation. 319.

1) Ernest S. Coffman, b April 22, 1881, near Dayton, Va , m May 9, 1906, Bessie Phares, b Mar 2, 1885 Address 18 College St , Dayton, O Minister in Church of the Brethren
1 Leah Frances Coffman, b April 17, 1907
2 Ernest Ralph Coffman, b Jan 22, 1909

No. 321. Sixth Generation. 319.

2) S. Frank Coffman, b Sept. 23, 1883, near Dayton, Va , m. Maud Carter Address: Richmond, Va No. children

No. 322. Fifth Generation. 218.

3) Lizzie C. Coffman, born at Dale Enterprise, Va., m. Feb. 22, 1872, to John Wallis Minnich, b Mar. 30, 1839. She died ————; he died ————
1 Lillie F. Minnich, b. Jan. 6, 1873, died single
2 Wade H Minnich, b June 9, 1877. M but both are dead.
3 Charles L. B Minnich, b Nov 6, 1879, died single.

No. 323. Fifth Generation. 218.

4) Anna M. Coffman, born at Dale Enterprise, Va., Oct 12, 1855, d near Elida, O , Oct 22, 1931. She was married Oct 7, 1875, to John S Swartz, b May 13, 1854, in Va. Both were buried at the Salem Cemetery near Elida. O Address was Elida, Ohio. Mennonites.
1 Fannie H Swartz, b Dec. 9, 1876, d Feb. 1878
2 Samuel D. Swartz, b. Mar 3, 1878 No 324
3 Bertie A Swartz, b Sept. 16, 1879 No 325
4 C Sherman Swartz, b Aug 3, 1881 No 326

5. Ina K. Swartz, b. May 3, 1883. No 327.
6. J. Clyde Swartz, b. April 4, 1885. No 328
7 C. Josephine Swartz, b April 29, 1887, d Dec 15, 1889.
8 Anna V. Swartz, b April 3, 1889. No. 329.
9. Joseph A Swartz, b May 12, 1891, d. June 1, 1932.
10 Jacob B. Swartz, b. July 26, 1893 No 330
11 William S. Swartz, b Sept. 26, 1895. No 331.
12 Alden D Swartz, b Aug 9, 1899. No. 332.

No. 324. Sixth Generation. 323.
2) Samuel D Swartz, b Mar 3, 1878, in Va , m. Dec 24, 1902, Myrtie Wenger, b Oct 4, 1881, d Jan 1, 1921 He married (2nd) on Feb. 19, 1927, Clara Keene, b July 24, 1900 Address Phoenixville, Pa Farmer. Mennonite.
1 Mary E Swartz, b Dec 3, 1903 No. 333.
2 Paul D Swartz, b Dec 23, 1904 No 334
3 Jonas H Swartz, b Jan 19, 1906. No 335
4 Martha Swartz, b Oct 12, 1907, d in infancy
5 Fannie M Swartz, b Nov 17, 1908, d. April 21, 1929.
6 Chester S Swartz, b Nov 10, 1910
7 Ruth E Swartz, b Sept 16, 1913.
8 Anna C. Swartz, b. Feb 19, 1916
9 Laura E Swartz, b Sept 3, 1918
10 Beulah K Swartz, b April 1, 1919.
(From second marriage)
11 Charles Swartz, b. Aug. 17, 1927.
12 Edith Swartz, b Sept 28, 1928
13 Samuel Swartz, Jr., b. Sept. 22, 1930.
14 Ralph Swartz, b Nov. 4, 1932.
15 Mildred Rebecca Swartz, b June 10, 1936.

No. 325. Sixth Generation. 323.
3) Bertie A Swartz, b Sept 16, 1879, in Rockingham Co, Va , m Feb 23, 1905, to Jesse Leedy, b Feb 24, 1884, d Dec 8, 1906, m (2nd) Mar 29, 1910, to James Stalter, b Mar. 28, 1871, in O Address Lima, O , R 3. Salesman. Mennonites
1. Rowena Leedy, b July 24, 1906 No 336
2 S Frederick Stalter, b Mar. 25, 1911. No 325½.
3 Anna Mary Stalter, b Oct 14, 1912
4 Virginia Stalter, b Jan 28, 1916.
5 Miriam Stalter, b Sept 13, 1919.

No. 325½. Seventh Generation. 325.
2) S Fred Stalter, b Mar 25, 1911, near Elida, O , m Dec 25, 1935, to Mary Heatwole, b Dec 13, 1912 Address: Elida, O , R 1 Laborer. Mennonites
1 Carolyn Louise Stalter, b Aug 15, 1936
2 Shirley Ann Stalter, b Oct 19, 1938

No. 326. Sixth Generation. 323.
4) C Sherman Swartz, b Aug 3, 1881, in Rockingham Co., Va , m. April 21, 1909, to Lydia Stemen, b Sept 22, 1881, in O Address Elida, O R 1 Farmer and laborer Mennonites
1 Marion Swartz, b July 18, 1910, d Feb 4, 1921.
2 Samuel C Swartz, b May 17, 1912.
3 Irene Frances Swartz, b. Jan 15, 1914.

4 Bertha M. Swartz, b. Sept. 22, 1917
5. Charles S. Swartz, b June 2, 1919
6. Betty Jane Swartz, b. Nov. 19, 1922.

No. 327. Sixth Generation. 323.

5) Ina K Swartz, b May 3, 1883, in Va, m Jan 1, 1905, to Elmer J. Shank, b Jan. 18, 1884 Address· Elida, O , R 1. Truck gardener Mennonite.

1. Waneta M Shank, b. Aug. 20, 1905 No. 337.
2. Arvilla J Shank, b Dec. 19, 1907 No. 338
3 Isaac S. Shank, b. July 8, 1913. No 3691
4 Wilmer C Shank, b. Aug 30, 1916

No. 323. Sixth Generation. 323.

6) J Clyde Swartz, b April 4, 1885, in Rockingham Co , Va., m Aug 30, Anna Flisher, b Sept 22, 1884 Address Lima, O., R 4 Gardener. Mennonites.

1 Winona Swartz, b April 28, 1910
2 John Swartz, b Oct 17, 1911 No. 2416
3. Vernon Swartz, b Aug. 23, 1913.
4 Ernest Swartz, b Feb 21, 1916
5 Anna Karen Swartz, b June 12, 1917
6. Opal Swartz, b Dec 14, 1919
7. Willis A. Swartz, b Aug 24, 1924, d Feb —, 1925
8 Weldon E Swartz, b June 1, 1927

No. 329. Sixth Generation. 323.

8) Anna V Swartz, b April 3. 1889, in Va., m Aug 22, 1907, to Jacob A. Brenneman, b Sept 22. 1885, in Allen Co , O Farmer Mennonites Address· Elida, Ohio. R 1.

1 Edna I. Brenneman, b Aug 2, 1908 No 339
2 William O Brenneman, b. Dec 29, 1912 No 2497.
3. Freda E. Brenneman, b Feb 4, 1915 No 2498
4. Elizabeth G Brenneman, b. Jan 10, 1919

No. 330. Sixth Generation. 323.

10) Jacob B Swartz, b July 26, 1893, in Va , m Alice Lightfoot Address Flint, Mich Tool maker

1 Stanford S Swartz, b. Feb 14, 1917.
2 Marjorie L. Swartz, b June 24, 1919.
3. Anna Jean Swartz, b. July 21, 1920
4 Wilbur A. Swartz, b Aug 24, 1923
5 Evelyn Swartz, b. June 14, 1927
6. Virginia Swartz, b ————
7 Dorothy Swartz, b Oct 1, 1931.
8 Jay Junior Swartz, b Nov 17, 1932
9 Beverly Swartz, b Aug 17, 1934
10 Clifford Carl Swartz, b. June 10, 1936

No. 331. Sixth Generation. 323.

11) William S. Swartz, b Sept 26, 1896, in Rockingham Co , Va , m Dec 7, 1917, to Ruth Kimler, b Aug 24, 1898 Address Flint, Mich Tool maker and foreman Methodist

1 Betty L Swartz, b. Mar. 15, 1920
2 William W. Swartz, b. Oct 13, 1922
3 James J. Swartz, b. Oct 13, 1922 Twins

No. 332. Sixth Generation. 323.

12) Alden D Swartz, b Aug 9, 1899, in Rockingham Co, Va, m Nov. 10, 1930, Coyla Manzer, b. —————. Address Flint, Mich Tool inspection foreman

1. Alden Richard Swartz, b Mar 15, 1932
2 Lou Ann Swartz, b Aug 30, 1933
3. Robert Lavern Swartz, b. July 13, 1935.
4 Roger Coffman Swartz, b Sept 6, 1936

No. 333. Seventh Generation. 324.

1) Mary E Swartz, b Dec 3, 1903, in Allen Co, O, d July 26, 1928, m. Sept 22, 1926, to Lloyd Black, b Sept. 2, 1906
1 L Junior Black, b July 3, 1928.

No. 334. Seventh Generation. 324.

2) Paul D Swartz, b Dec 23, 1904, m Feb 22, 1927, Grace Bechtel, b. May 26, 1906 Address: Spring City, Pa Trucker Mennonite
1 Robert Swartz, b Nov 14, 1929

No. 335. Seventh Generation. 324.

3) Jonas H Swartz, b Jan 19, 1906, m June 28, 1930, to Dorothy Plank, b May 26, 1908 Address Phoenixville, Pa Knitter in hosiery mill Mennonite

No. 336. Seventh Generation. 325.

1) Rowena Leedy, b July 24, 1906, in Allen Co, O, m May 3, 1928, to Timothy H Brenneman, b Oct 7, 1905 Address Pehuajo, F. C. O, Buenos Aires, South America Mennonite Missionary to South America
1 Patricia Ann Brenneman, b Aug. 24, 1931.
2 Donald Leedy Brenneman, b. Feb 19, 1934.

No. 337. Seventh Generation. 327.

1) Waneta M. Shank, b Aug 20, 1905, m Aug 10, 1927, to William Huntsberger, b Mar. 4, 1903 Address Spring City, Pa. Farmer Mennonite.
1 June Claribell Huntsberger, b Mar 2, 1929
2 Ray Shank Huntsberger, b Aug. 6, 1934

No. 338. Seventh Generation. 327.

2) Arvilla J Shank, b Dec 19, 1907, m. Nov 14, 1929, to Amos Bechtel, b Oct 24, 1908 Address: Spring City, Pa Farmer Mennonites.
1 Marjorie Louise Bechtel, b Aug 3, 1932
2 Janet Marie Bechtel, b Sept 25, 1935.
3 Freda Mae Bechtel, b Jan 10, 1938

No. 339. Seventh Generation. 329.

1) Edna I Brenneman, b Aug 2, 1908, m June 11, 1927, Merle G Stemen, b Aug 28, 1904 Address Elida, O Laborer Mennonites
1 Dale A Stemen, b. Aug 24, 1928
2 Warren Lee Stemen, b. Sept 17, 1930
3 Mirian Elizabeth Stemen, b Mar 16, 1932
4 Anna Margaret Stemen, b June 13, 1934
5 John Jacob Stemen, b Jan 4, 1936

No. 340. Fifth Generation. 218.

5) Mary A Coffman, b Feb 19, 1857, at Dale Enterprise, Va, m Nov 11, 1875, to Lewis J Heatwole, b Dec 4, 1852 Mrs Heatwole died Nov 18, 1926 He died Feb 26, 1932 They lived for several years in Cass Co, Mo, but later re-

turned to their former home in Virginia, near Dale Enterprise. Mennonite. Lewis J. Heatwole was a minister and bishop in the Mennonite Church, and was an almanac calculator for many years, having been a deep student of astronomy. He is the author of the book, "Key to the Almanac and the Sidereal Heavens" He taught school for many years.

1 Verdie May Heatwole, b. Nov 21, 1876, died same day.
2. Fannie C Heatwole, b. Nov. 20, 1877. No. 341.
3. Nellie V. Heatwole, b July 29, 1879 No 342.
4 Bessie P. Heatwole, b July 7, 1881 No 343.
5 Justus B. Heatwole, b Mar 20, 1883, single
6 Anna L. Heatwole, b. Sept. 7, 1884, single
7 Elizabeth M. Heatwole, b Nov. 16, 1889 No 344.

No. 341. Sixth Generation. 340.
2) Fannie Catherine Heatwole, b. Nov. 20, 1877, m Oct. 27, 1912, to Charles M. Grove, b Mar 22, 1886 Address Stuarts Draft, Va Farmer Mennonite No issue

No. 342. Sixth Generation. 340.
3) Nellie Virginia Heatwole, b. July 29, 1879, m Aug 28, 1900, to Eugene C Suter, b April 6, 1877 Address: Harrisonburg, Va Farmer Mennonite.

1. Blanche V Suter, b Mar. 5, 1903 No 345
2 Mary E Suter, b. July 7, 1905
3. C. Justus Suter, b. July 3, 1907 No 346
4 James H. Suter, b May 17, 1910.
5 Grace E Suter, b Dec 18, 1919.

No. 343. Sixth Generation. 340.
4) Bessie Pearl Heatwole, b. July 7, 1881, m. Nov. 9, 1905, to Oscar E. Wenger, b. June 19, 1881. Address. Linville, Va U S Mail carrier Mennonites

1. Raymond H Wenger, b Feb 2, 1907.
2. Marvin D. Wenger, b Mar 23, 1911, died same day
3. Linden H. Wenger, b Dec. 26, 1912
4 Mildred G. Wenger, b Sept. 21, 1916
5. Edith V. Wenger, b. April 2, 1919.

No. 344. Sixth Generation. 340.
7) Elizabeth Maude Heatwole, b Nov. 16, 1889, m. June 2, 1921, Earl Grove, b. Jan. 26, 1897. Address· Dale Enterprise, Va Farmer. Mennonite

1. Virginia E. Grove, b. Oct. 1, 1922.

No. 345. Seventh Generation. 342.
1) Blanche V. Suter, b. Mar. 5, 1903, m. Nov. 29, 1928, to Amos Rhodes, b. Jan 21, 1902 Address: Harrisonburg, Va. Farmer.

No. 346. Seventh Generation. 342.
3) C Justus Suter, b July 3, 1907, m June 29, 1927, to Della Weaver, b April 3, 1906 Address· Dale Enterprise, Va Plumber. Mennonites

1 Glennys Marie Suter, b Sept 21, 1928, d. Oct 27, 1928
2 Dorothy Ann Suter, b. Mar. 5, 1930

No. 347. Fifth Generation. 218.
6) Joseph W Coffman, b Feb. 19, 1857, near Dale Enterprise, Va., m. Mar. 6, 1879, Sallie Heatwole, b. Dec 19, 1859 He died April 25, 1933. He was a minister of the Mennonite Church in Virginia. Address: Dayton, Va.

I. Homer W. Coffman, b. June 3, 1881. No. 348.

2 Mollie G Coffman, b Oct 3, 1883 No 350
3. Nellie F Coffman, b Dec 23, 1896, single

No. 348. Sixth Generation. 347.

1) Homer William Coffman, b June 3, 1881, m. Ella Swope, b Aug 20, 1882.
Address Dayton, Va Farmer Mennonites
  1 Robert J. Coffman, b Jan 19, 1908. No 349.
  2. Sarah E. Coffman, b Sept 24, 1909.
  3 Homer A Coffman, b Dec 22, 1911
  4. Samuel S Coffman, b Aug 10, 1914
  5. Paul E Coffman, b Jan 14, 1917.
  6 Naomi C. Coffman, b July 19, 1918
  7 David A Coffman, b Jan 9, 1921
  8 Phoebe F Coffman, b. Oct. 22, 1925.

No. 349. Seventh Generation. 348.

1) Robert Joseph Coffman, b Jan 19, 1908, m Dec 31, 1930, Arnelia Mary
Swartz, b ——————— Address Dayton, Va.

No. 350. Sixth Generation. 347.

2) Mollie Grace Coffman, b Oct 3, 1883, m. Melvin Jasper Heatwole, Jan. 22,
1903 He was born Dec 10, 1878 Address Dayton, Va. Farmer. Minister in the
Mennonite Church
  1. Lora F Heatwole, b Nov 3, 1903
  2 Joseph D Heatwole, b Jan 9, 1905. No. 351.
  3 Martha A Heatwole, b Feb 16, 1907.
  4 John C. Heatwole, b June 27, 1909, d June 24, 1911.
  5 Esther V Heatwole, b Oct 16, 1911
  6 Ina Grace Heatwole, b Mar 4, 1914
  7. Mark S Heatwole, b April 5, 1916
  8 Melvin J Heatwole, b April 26, 1918
  9 James W Heatwole, b Mar 9, 1920
  10. Hiram Z. Heatwole, b July 28, 1921
  11 Nancy O Heatwole, b Mar 23, 1923
  12 Stillborn, Oct 1, 1924

No. 351. Seventh Generation. 350.

2) Joseph D Heatwole, b Jan 9, 1905, m June 1, 1926, to Fannie Belle Shank,
b ——————. Address Bridgewater, Va Mennonites.
  1. Joseph D. Heatwole, Jr, b. July 14, 1927.
  2 Ruth V Heatwole, b Dec. 5, 1928
  3 Dwight S Heatwole, b June 24, 1930

No. 352. Fifth Generation. 218.

7) Daniel H. Coffman, b April 4, 1859, at Dale Enterprise, Va, m Sarah R.
Geyer, Feb. 11, 1883, b Feb 21, 1860 They moved from Virginia to Elkhart, Ind.
in 1888 where he is a retired carpenter and farmer. Mennonites, of which church
he is a deacon Address Goshen, Ind, R 8.
  1 Mattie S. Coffman, b Feb. 4, 1884. No. 353.
  2 Grover F. Coffman, b Jan 25, 1885 No 354
  3 Lizzie D Coffman, b Nov 16, 1886, single
  4 C Victor Coffman, b June 21, 1888 No 355.
  5 John W. Coffman, b July 5, 1890 No 356.
  6 Eva May Coffman, b Sept 21, 1892 No. 357.

7 Dorothy Coffman, b May 17, 1894 No 358
8 Anna F Coffman, b. Dec 22, 1895. No. 359.
9 Clara Coffman, b Feb 12, 1897, single
10 Mary Coffman, b Nov 4, 1898. No 360
11 Ruth Coffman, b. April 28, 1901, single

No. 353. Sixth Generation. 352.

1) Mattie S Coffman, b Feb 8, 1884, in Va, m Nov. 23, 1906, Thomas O. Eldridge, b Nov 8, 1878, d Mar 4, 1930 Address Goshen, Ind, R. 8
1 Chalmer Eldridge, b. July 22, 1907.
2 Murle Eldridge, b Oct 17, 1908.
3 Guy Eldridge, b June 10, 1912, d Mar. 7, 1930

No. 354. Sixth Generation. 352.

2) Grover F Coffman, b Jan 25, 1885, in Rockingham Co, Va. m June 19, 1915 to Mabel Pletcher, b Dec 27, 1888 Address Goshen, Ind Carpenter and builder.
1 Roy Willis Coffman, b Sept 28, 1918.

No. 355. Sixth Generation. 352.

4) Charles Victor Coffman, b June 21, 1888, m. Sept 13, 1919, Vinetta Garber, b May 5, 1894. Address Shipshewana, Ind Carpenter
1 John Elden Coffman, b Jan 20, 1921
2. Donald Victor Coffman, b Jan 15, 1922
3 Lois Evelin Coffman, b Oct 2, 1923

No. 356. Sixth Generation. 352.

5) John W Coffman, b July 5, 1890, m Mar 20, 1915, Margie Prough, b Dec 4, 1894 Address Wawaka, Ind Farmer
1 Ancil Clair Coffman, b Feb 17, 1916
2 Carol Nadine Coffman, b Sept 24, 1926

No. 357. Sixth Generation. 352.

6) Eva May Coffman, b Sept 21, 1892, m. Jan 17, 1914, to Paul Eaton, b Sept 11, 1894 Address Goshen, Ind Mechanic
1. Glenn E Eaton, b Nov 15, 1914
2 Harry A Eaton, b. Feb 17, 1916
3. James A Eaton, b Feb 17, 1916. Twins.
4 Esther Eaton, b Oct 23, 1921
5 Phillis Eaton, b Nov 23, 1927

No. 358. Sixth Generation. 352.

7) Dorothy Coffman, b. May 17, 1894, m Dec 22, 1918 to Earl Shoup, b Aug 28, 1884 Address. Middlebury, Ind Farmer.
1. Robert Shoup, b. Oct 14, 1919, d Oct 23, 1919
2 Dale Shoup, b Oct 2, 1920.
3. Darline Shoup, b July 7, 1922
4 Kittie Shoup, b May 27, 1924.
5 Thomas Shoup, b Feb. 3, 1928

No. 359. Sixth Generation. 352.

8) Anna F Coffman, b Dec. 22, 1895, married Mar. 20, 1914 to Orla E Kalb, b. —————. He died Nov 21, 1915. She married (2nd) Dec. 3, 1919, Noble Showalter. Farmer.
1. Ruby Fern Kalb, b July 14, 1915

(Second marriage)

2   Vesta C Showalter, b Feb 3, 1921.

No. 360. Sixth Generation. 352.

10) Mary Coffman, b Nov 4, 1898, m Mar 27, 1920, Perry Prough, b Aug. 7, 1895 Address Goshen, Ind , R 8.

1   Kathlene Prough, b Mar 14, 1921.
2   Earl Alfred Prough, b Sept. 5, 1922.
3   Grace Irene Prough, b. Jan 3. 1927.

No. 361. Fifth Generation. 218.

9) Sarah C Coffman, b Mar 29, 1863, at Dale Enterprise Va., m. Nov. 25, 1883, John Thomas Heatwole, b Mar 28, 1863, d —————. Her address· Dayton, Va Mennonite

1   Oliver W Heatwole, b Nov. 4, 1864 No 443
2   Stella E Heatwole, b Oct 22. 1886 No. 444
3   Mattie C Heatwole, b Sept 5. 1888 No 447.
4   John L Heatwole, b Sept 12. 1890 No 448
5   Paul V Heatwole, b Aug 15. 1892 No. 449
6   Joseph W Heatwole, b Mar 3. 1895 No 450
7   David Heatwole, b Apr 15, 1897, d in infancy
8   Nellie Heatwole, b Jan 26, 1898, d in infancy
9   Emery B Heatwole, b Jan. 16, 1899 No. 451.
10 Ruth F Heatwole, b May 19, 1902 No 452
11 Hazel E Heatwole, b Aug 1, 1904 No 453.
12 Jacob Heatwole. b May 11. 1909, d same day

No. 362. Fifth Generation. 218.

10) Fannie V Coffman, b Oct 30, 1865, at Dale Enterprise, Va., d Oct. 3, 1904 She married Mar 6, 1890, Abraham P. Shenk, b. Feb. 15, 1862, in Allen Co., O Address. Denbigh, Va , Mennonites

1   Samuel C. Shenk, b May 9, 1891 No. 671.
2   John M Shenk, b July 10, 1893, d May 21, 1894
3   Henry M Shenk, b. Aug 2, 1894. No 672
4   Mary C Shenk, b Aug 28, 1896.
5   Jacob A Shenk, b Feb 17, 1900. No 674
6   Phebe Shenk. b Jan 26, 1902 No. 675
7   Anna M Shenk, b Sept 26, 1903 No. 676

No. 363. Fifth Generation. 218.

11) Rebecca Coffman, b Mar 24, 1868. at Dale Enterprise, Va , m. Oct 19, 1888, Perry D Hartman, b Sept 30, 1866 Rebecca died Dec. 23, 1926 Address· Harrisonburg, Va Mennonites

1. Fannie E Hartman, b Aug 24, 1889, d Oct 26, 1889
2   Leanna C. Hartman, b Aug. 3, 1890 No 364.
3   William F Hartman, b Sept 22, 1892 No 366
4   Wilda F. Hartman, b Sept 22, 1892. Twins. No. 365
5. Mary M Hartman, b Mar. 8, 1894 No. 367
6   Daniel Hartman, b June 1, 1896, d Nov 30, 1903
7   Lewis Hartman, b June 18, 1898 No 368.
8   Jacob C Hartman, b Dec 21, 1899 No. 369.
9   Irene S Hartman, b Mar. 17, 1902. No 370.
10 Pauline R Hartman, b Mar 17, 1902, single
11 Dorothy Hartman, b Feb 22, 1904 No 371

No. 364. Sixth Generation. 363.

2) Leanna Catherine Hartman, b. Aug 3, 1890, m. —————, Peter Samuel Showalter, b April 14, 1887 Address Harrisonburg, Va Farmer. Mennonite.

1 Hubert D. Showalter, b Jan 13, 1918
2 Infant (Stillborn).
3. Roy Samuel Showalter, b. Feb 14, 1931

No. 365. Sixth Generation. 363.

3) Wilda Frances Hartman, b Sept 22, 1892, m. Dec. 2, 1915, Ira Asa Shenk, b July 27, 1890 Address Elida, O , R 2 Farmer Mennonite

1. Harold H Shenk, b. Sept. 4, 1917
2 Lorene F Shenk, b Nov 9, 1919.

No. 366. Sixth Generation. 363.

4) William Franklin Hartman, b Sept 22, 1892, m Nov. 15, 1916, Anna Marie Powell, b Sept 14, 1897 Address Delphos, O , R 2 Farmer and mechanic Mennonite.

▸ 1 Marvin D. Hartman, b. Aug 11, 1918.
2 Clara I Hartman, b June 26, 1921
3 Edwin S Hartman, b. May 31, 1926
4 Robert M. Hartman, b Nov. 15, 1928.

No. 367. Sixth Generation. 363.

5) Mary Magdalena Hartman, b Mar 8, 1895, m. Nov 11, 1915, Ward Augustus Rhodes, b Aug 2, 1892 Address Harrisonburg. Va Mennonites

1 Nellie V. Rhodes, b May 2, 1918.
2 Frank E Rhodes, b Nov 27, 1919
3. Elizabeth M Rhodes, b Aug 14, 1922
4 Floyd J. Rhodes, b July 18, 1924

No. 363. Sixth Generation. 363.

7) Lewis Samuel Hartman, b June 18, 1898, m Dec. 4, 1919, Grace Larue Good, b Mar 22, 1897 Address Harrisonburg, Va. Farmer Mennonite

1. 2 Twins, b Nov 3, 1920, d same day
3 Harold F. Hartman, b Dec 21, 1921
4. Ruth L. Hartman, b. Oct 29, 1923
5 Lewis P. Hartman, b Oct. 28, 1925
6 Paul S Hartman, b. Dec. 15, 1927

No. 369. Sixth Generation. 363.

8) Jacob Coffman Hartman, b. Dec 21, 1899, m. Feb. 8, 1922, Esther Ada Diller, b July 14, 1901 Address Delphos, O , R 2 Mennonites Butcher and laborer.

1 Melvin S Hartman, b Nov. 9, 1922.
2 Marion A. Hartman, b Jan 25, 1927
3. Beulah C. Hartman, b Dec 22, 1928
4 Bertha R. Hartman, b Nov 4, 1931.

No. 370. Sixth Generation. 363.

9) Irene Susan Hartman, b Mar 17, 1902, m Mar 4, 1925, J David Ramer, b. Nov 3, 1902 Address. Elida, O Salesman Mennonite Church, of which he is a deacon.

1. Milton D. Ramer, b. July 8, 1927.
2. Charlotte L Ramer, b. Feb. 4, 1929.
3. John R Ramer, b July 27, 1931.

No. 371. Sixth Generation. 363.

11) Dorothy Robena Hartman, b Feb 22, 1904, m Dec 20, 1929, Rudy Harold Diller, b Oct. 29, 1909 Address Harrisonburg, Va Truck driver Mennonite

1 Robert E Diller, b Mar. 19, 1931

No. 372. Fifth Generation. 219.

1) Samuel Brunk, b June 28, 1843, d ————————. He married Susan Hartman, April 21, 1864. She was born ————— She died Oct. 12, 1913. Farmer. Mennonite. Harrisonburg, Va.

1 Annie E Brunk, b July 9, 1866 No 1938

2 Sarah F. Brunk, b Jan. 8, 1869, d Aug 29, 1869

3 John D Brunk, b Mar 13, 1872 No 1939

4. Laura E Brunk, b. Oct 10, 1877 No. 1944.

5 Lessie S Brunk, b June 21, 1886, d June 3, 1889

No. 373. Fifth Generation. 219.

2) Christian H Brunk, b Nov 8, 1845, d May 7, 1921, m Mary E. Ralston, b Nov 16, 1850, d Oct 3, 1928 Harrisonburg, Va Clerk of county court. Mennonites Buried in Cooks Creek cemetery

1 Nora Bell Brunk, b Sept 15, 1874, d April 15, 1892.

2. Lillie A. Brunk, b Oct 20, 1875 No 785

3 Oliver C Brunk, b Sept. 13, 1878 No 787.

4 John N. Brunk, b July 21, 1881, d April 5, 1883

5. Talford R. Brunk, b Oct 28, 1891, d Jan 19, 1899.

6 Gracie M Brunk, b Jan 20, 1895, single.

No. 374. Fifth Generation. 219.

3) Frederick W. Brunk, b Dec 31, 1847, d Feb 8, 1921, m. July 25, 1871, Mary Kreider, b Mar 11, 1847, d Sept 29, 1899. Elkhart, Ind. Jeweler and optician Mennonites

1. Adeline V Brunk, b Sept 10, 1872. No 1945.

2 Verda E Brunk, b July 5, 1875 No 1946.

3 John K Brunk, b Dec 26, 1876 No 1947.

4 Anna B. Brunk, b Dec 9, 1878 No. 1949

5 Enos C. Brunk, b May 27, 1881, d Aug 9, 1902

6. Harry T. Brunk, b. Oct. 16, 1884, single.

Harry is a jeweler at 314 S 43rd St , Louisville, Ky

No. 375. Fifth Generation. 219.

4) Martin W. Brunk, b April 14, 1851, d ————————, m Nov 26, 1871, Mary V. Shank Both are dead Address Ladd, Va Farmer. Mennonite deacon.

1 Reuben J Brunk, b Mar 22, 1873, single

2 Ida C Brunk, b Aug 28, 1875 No 1951

3 Charles C Brunk, b Jan 14, 1879 No. 1952.

4 Waldo H Brunk, b Jan 30, 1881. No 1953

5. William M. Brunk, b. Feb 1, 1888 No 1954.

No. 376. Fifth Generation. 219.

5) Elizabeth Brunk, b. Mar. 22, 1854, m Oct 10, 1878, Martin B. Rhodes. Address: Dayton, Va. Farmer. Mennonite

1. Raleigh C. Rhodes, b Mar 28, 1880. No 1955

2 Ina Susan Rhodes, b Nov 15, 1885. No 1956.

3 Verna V. Rhodes, b. Jan 26, 1891 No. 1957.

4. Samuel L. Rhodes, b Jan 27, 1896. No. 1958.

No. 377. Fifth Generation. 219.

6) Elias Brunk, b July 2, 1856, m Dec 25, 1879, Elizabeth Heatwole, b April 19, 1857, d Feb. 17, 1928 Elias Brunk still lives on the farm that Elizabeth Rhodes and Samuel Weaver his grandparents lived on about two and one-half miles west of Harrisonburg, Va (1937) Address Dale Enterprise, Va Farmer. Mennonite deacon

1 Rufus E Brunk, b Mar 6, 1881. No 1049
2 Joseph A Brunk, b Sept 21, 1883 No 1051
3. John C Brunk, b Nov 16, 1885 No. 1052
4 Harry Brunk, b June 21, 1898 No 1053

No. 378. Fifth Generation. 219.

8) John Brunk, b. Mar. 3, 1864, m Oct 2, 1884, Phoeba Hess, b. ———————
Address Linville Depot, Va Blacksmith Mennonite.

1 Minnie F Brunk, b Sept. 24, 1885 No 1559
2 Anna J Brunk, b Aug 20, 1887 No 1960

No. 379. Fifth Generation. 220.

1) Susanna Weaver, b Aug 18, 1853, d Oct 1, 1929, m Mar 1875, to Isaac Smith Address Oronogo, Mo.

1 Joseph C Smith, b Mar 14, 1876
2 Florence Smith, b Sept 6, 1878 No 770
3 Arthur A Smith, b. July 20, 1881 No 774.
4 Clara B. Smith, b Aug 30, 1883 No 775
5 Olive H Smith, b Feb 14, 1886 No 776
6 Ethel A Smith, b June 14, 1889 No 777.
7 Edna C Smith, b Oct 2, 1892 No 778

No. 380. Fifth Generation. 220.

2) Elizabeth Weaver, b Mar 7, 1855, d Sept 30, 1930, m April 30, 1874, in Jasper Co, Mo, Albert D Hotchkiss. b April 28, 1847, d Aug 6, 1931 He was born in Homer, Cortland Co, N Y They lived in Iowa

1. Isadora B Hotchkiss, b. Feb 8, 1875. No 761.
2 Agnes M Hotchkiss, b May 4, 1879 No 766
3 Frank W Hotchkiss, b. Nov 9, 1885 No 768.
4 Leslie E Hotchkiss, b. May 24, 1888, d Sept 29, 1908

No. 381. Fifth Generation. 220.

3) John Medford Weaver, b July 11, 1858, d June 19, 1924, m Mar, 1882, to Frances Ellen Printz, b Feb 25, 1856 Address Oronogo, Mo Farmer Mennonites.

1. Mae Weaver, b. May 30, 1884 No 382
2 Harley C Weaver, b April 26, 1887 No 383.
3 Ida Pearl Weaver, b. Sept. 8, 1892. No. 384.

No. 382. Sixth Generation. 381.

1) Mae Weaver, b May 30, 1884, m Nov. 1912, to Alfred Avery, b June 28, 1882 Address Oronogo, Mo Driller and contractor Methodist.

1 Irene June Avery, b Feb. 26, 1914
2 Elsa Ernestine Avery, b. Dec. 11, 1916.
3 Estin Weaver Avery, b. Feb 6, 1919.

No. 383. Sixth Generation. 381.

2) Harley C. Weaver, b April 26, 1887, m Dec, 1912, to Mary C. Bartley, b April 8, 1894 Address Oronogo, Mo Farmer Congregational

1. Carl Russel Weaver, b Jan 2, 1914.
2 Kenneth Elwin Weaver, b. Jan. 1, 1916.
3. Marvin Eugene Weaver, b June 9, 1920

No. 3C4. Sixth Generation. 381.
3) Ida Pearl Weaver, b Sept 8, 1892, m Oct , 1915, to Albert T Woodward, b Aug 17, 1891. Address Oronogo, Mo Merchant. Methodists
1. Frances Emily Woodward, b. Jan 26, 1918
2 Evelyn Pearl Woodward, b Aug 9, 1922
3 Doris Elizabeth Woodward, b. Feb 4, 1928.

No. 385. Fifth Generation. 220.
4) David S. Weaver, b July 17, 1860, d May 5, 1929, m. Jan. 5, 1892, Barbara Diller, b Feb 17, 1866 Address La Junta, Colo Farmer. Mennonite The author would not feel that he had done his duty without mentioning his generous, devoted, Christian life. He had been blessed with much of the things of this world that are usually looked upon as making one rich, but in a generous Christian spirit he gave away his thousands in order to make others happy, and that the gospel could be carried to foreign countries as well as to his own native country.
1 Anna R. Weaver, b Nov 27, 1892. No 386.
2 Martin L Weaver, b July 15, 1894 No. 387.
3 Twin son, b July 27, 1894, d. same day.
4. Joseph A Weaver, b May 10, 1895, d. Mar. 29, 1897
5 Frances E. Weaver, b June 1, 1898. No. 388.
6 Paul E Weaver, b Dec 18, 1902 No. 790
7 Grace Weaver, b. Oct 7, 1906, d. Jan. 8, 1908

No. 336. Sixth Generation. 385.
1) Anna Rose Weaver, b Nov 27, 1892, m. April 20, 1924, to Silas Hertzler, b July 27, 1888 He is a teacher at Goshen College, Goshen, Ind. He holds a doctor's degree. Anna was a registered nurse Address· Goshen, Ind Mennonites.
1. Mary E Hertzler, b. July 20, 1925
2. Paul D. Hertzler, b. Sept 5, 1926
3. Ruth C. Hertzler, b Jan. 14, 1931
4 John Hertzler, b Mar 6, 1934, twin
5. Joanne Hertzler, b Mar 6, 1934, twin

No. 3£7. Sixth Generation. 385.
2) Martin L Weaver, b July 15, 1894, m April 20, 1924, Esther Pauline Berkey, b June 21, 1901
1. Carolyn J Weaver, b Dec 6, 1925
2. Glen E. Weaver, b Sept 6, 1930.

No. 383. Sixth Generation. 3£5.
5) Frances Ella Weaver, b June 1, 1898, m Feb 4, 1923, Ernest Grimm, b Mar. 9, 1899 Address La Junta, Colo Farmer. Mennonites.
1. Kieth Lyle Grimm, b Oct 27, 1924
2. Kathryn Marie Grimm, b. Oct. 4, 1926
3. Donald Everett Grimm, b. Oct 18, 1936

No. 3£9. Fifth Generation. 220.
5) Benjamin F. Weaver, b. May 29, 1862, d. Dec. 9, 1918, m. Aug. 16, 1884, Delilah C. Breneman, b. June 3, 1865. Address: Oronogo, Mo Farmer. Mennonite.
1. Willie A Weaver, b. April 8, 1886. No 390

No. 390. Sixth Generation. 389.

1) Willie A. Weaver, b. April 8, 1886, m. Nov. 20, 1910, Cora A. Wilson, b. April 13, 1891 Address Oronogo, Mo Farmer

No. 391. Fifth Generation. 220.

6) Jeremiah J. Weaver, b Aug 3, 1864, m Mar. 29, 1892, Mirah Diller, b. May 9, 1868. Address 1310 S 36 St , Kansas City, Kans Mennonites

1. Levi A Weaver, b Jan 7, 1893 No. 392
2 Isaiah R. Weaver, b Jan 17, 1895. No 393
3. George H. Weaver, b Sept. 13, 1896 No 394
4. Bertha S. Weaver, b Oct 29, 1898. No. 395
5. Ruth Weaver, b Feb 14, 1902, twin No 396
6. Ray Weaver, b Feb 14, 1902, twin No. 397.
7 John A. Weaver, b May 16, 1909

No. 392. Sixth Generation. 391.

1) Levi A Weaver, b Jan 7, 1893, m Dec 30, 1915, Martha Shenk, b. Nov 9, 1887. Address: 1108 S 37th St , Kansas City, Kans Cabinetmaker.

1 Mildred S. Weaver, b. Mar. 18, 1918
2. Allen J Weaver, b. Sept 7, 1920.
3 Anna P. Weaver, b April 22, 1924
4 Edith M Weaver, b Aug 8, 1927
5. Mary L. Weaver, b May 14, 1929

No. 393. Sixth Generation. 391.

2) Isaiah R Weaver, b Jan 17, 1895, m June, 1926, Mary M Jones, b. ——————— Address Blackwell, Okla Butcher No children

No. 394. Sixth Generation. 391.

3) George H Weaver, b Sept. 13, 1896, m. Sept 4, 1919, Cora E Zuercher, b. July 13, 1894

1. Arlene Weaver, b Dec 21, 1920
2. Vernon H. Weaver, b. Dec. 27, 1928

No. 395. Sixth Generation. 391.

4) Bertha S. Weaver, b Oct 29, 1898, m July 25, 1931, Theodore Steward Address· Phoenix, Ariz , R 6

No. 396. Sixth Generation. 391.

5) Ruth Weaver, b Feb. 14, 1902, m. June 23, 1923, Chris P. Stuckey Address: Newton, Kans.

1. Betty M. Stuckey, b Mar 17, 1924, d Sept 22, 1931.
2. Raymond Stuckey, b Sept , 1926, twin
3. Richard Stuckey, b. Sept., 1926, twin

No. 397. Sixth Generation. 391.

6) Ray Weaver, b Feb 14, 1902, m Mar , 1928, Leona Millian, b ——————. Address: 904 N. Main St , Blackwell, Okla.

1. Billie Ray Weaver, b. ———————
2. Jerry James Weaver, b ———————

No. 398. Fifth Generation. 391.

7) Mary Virginia Weaver, b July 28, 1866, m Mar. 13, 1889, Abraham Breneman, b. Jan. 27, 1869, d May 13, 1892 On Jan 18, 1905 she married Samuel E. Cockley, b Nov. 27, 1859, and d May 6, 1933 All were Mennonites. Abraham was buried in the Weaver cemetery, Oronogo, Mo Mary now lives with her daughters at Elkhart, Ind

1. Bessie E. Breneman, b Dec 13, 1889. No. 399.
2 Zaidee A. Breneman, b Jan 11, 1892. No 400
   (Second marriage)
3. Leona F. Cockley, b Feb 22, 1906 No. 401

No. 399. Sixth Generation. 398.
1) Bessie Ella Breneman, b Dec. 13, 1889, m June 23, 1912, Roy Ebersole, b. Aug. 29, 1885. Address 608 N. Lusher Ave., Elkhart, Ind. Laborer. Mennonite
1. Ethel Marie Ebersole, b Sept 20, 1913 No. 3657.
2. Lester Oneil Ebersole, b July 24, 1922

No. 400. Sixth Generation. 398.
2) Zaidee Alice Breneman, b Jan 11, 1892, m Feb. 11, 1912, Vernon E. Reiff, b. July 28, 1890. Address: 1625 Roys Ave , Elkhart, Ind. Merchant. Mennonites.
1. Gladys Virginia Reiff, b Feb. 27, 1913.
2. Marianna Maude Reiff, b Mar 19, 1916.

No. 401. Sixth Generation. 398.
3) Leona Fae Cockley, b Feb. 22, 1906, m Dec 24, 1930, Jason O. Miller, b. June 21, 1896. Mennonites Address. Elkhart, Ind , R. 4.
1. Marvin Jay Miller, b Oct 13, 1931
2 Mary Alice Miller, b Sept 16, 1933
3 Velda Fern Miller, b April 14, 1937

No. 402. Fifth Generation. 220.
8) William H Weaver, b Aug 31, 1868, m Nov 5, 1907, Clara I. Johnson, b. June 18, 1883 Address Twin Falls, Idaho Mennonite Brethren in Christ and Methodist. Hotel owner
1. Bessie M Weaver, b. Dec 6, 1909
2. Dorothy G. Weaver, b April 10, 1911
3. James A. Weaver, b July 26, 1913.
4 John W Weaver, b Feb 25, 1915

No. 403. Fifth Generation. 220.
9) Charles A. Weaver, b Dec 20, 1870, m Feb. 21, 1893, Mary C. Mishler, b. Mar. 1, 1867, d Dec. 23, 1895 Married (2nd) Mar 10, 1898, Sarah E Horning, b. Dec 26, 1870. Address· Alba, Mo Farmer Congregational.
1. Jennie B Weaver, b Sept 7. 1902 No 404
2. Lee a Weaver, b. Dec. 28, 1904. No. 405.
3. Rose Lucile Weaver, b Jan 7, 1907 No 406

No. 404. Sixth Generation. 403.
1) Jennie B Weaver, b Sept 7, 1902, m Sept 20, 1930, John Dix, b April 28, 1902 Address Joplin, Mo School teacher Congregational.

No. 405. Sixth Generation. 403.
2) Lee Arnold Weaver, b. Dec. 28, 1904, m Aug. 11, 1928, Iva Hodson, b. Nov. 24, 1905. Address: Alba, Mo Farmer. Congregational.
1 Charles David Weaver, b Dec 31, 1929
2 Evelyn Jewell Weaver, b Sept 28. 1933

No. 406. Sixth Generation. 403.
3) Rose Lucile Weaver, b Jan 7, 1907, m Mar 10, 1928, Walter Bennett, b. Mar 27, 1903 Address Alba, Mo Farmer Congregational.
1 Errol Eugene Bennett, b Feb , 1929, d Feb 5, 1929.
2 Lois Weaver Bennett, b Dec 16, 1931

No. 407. Fifth Generation. 220.

11) Jesse E Weaver, b Dec 4, 1874, m Aug 7, 1901, Mary E. Rohrer, b Jan. 21, 1873. Farmer and minister Address Oronogo, Mo Congregational Jesse E Weaver died Feb 25, 1933, at his home near Oronogo, Jasper Co., Mo He was born and lived all his life on the farm which his parents, the late preacher Joseph and Susanna Weaver, purchased after moving to this county from Virginia about 1869. As a young man he united with the Mennonite Church, of which his father was the pastor It was a thriving church until about 1896 when another minister moved into the community and influenced a number of the like faith to settle in the same congregation, soon after which differences of opinion arose and finally resulted in such strong dissensions that some of the original number withdrew, among which was the subject of this sketch Jesse being a strong leader was soon prevailed on to lead the one group together with many other folks of his community. He was soon licensed to preach by the Congregational Church, and had constantly been active in preaching the Word until the time of his death Through his influence a country church was built near his home in 1910, where he served for 23 years He also served as pastor of a church 25 miles from his home where he held services once a month, also at a schoolhouse 10 miles from his home where he preached once a month His patience, kindness, and Christian fortitude won for him many friends in the surround.ng community. He was called into many homes to speak words of comfort to the sick and dying In his last illness when delirious, he preached the Word of God and sang and quoted many spiritual songs.

In the 23 years of his pastorate he preached 517 funeral sermons In his passing the community lost a strong contender for the faith, and the church, a leader who will not soon be forgotten Funeral services were held Tuesday afternoon, Feb. 28, 1933, at the Tower of Light Church of which he had been pastor, where approximately 2000 persons had gathered to pay the last tribute of respect to one who spent a life of service among them.

1. Frank E. Weaver, b July 9, 1902
2 Harry A Weaver, b April 8, 1906. killed Nov 1, 1938, in truck accident
3 Dortha A. Weaver, b Mar. 11, 1910
4. Chester J Weaver, b Nov 9, 1911
5 Pauline L Weaver, b Jan 17, 1922.

No. 408. Fifth Generation. 220.

12) Alice R Weaver, b Feb 10, 1877, in Jasper Co, Mo, m Feb. 7, 1900, John R Driver, b Sept 9, 1871, d June 21, 1926, in Morgan Co., Mo Address Versailles, Mo. Farmer. Mennonites.

1. Ada S Driver, b. Dec 14, 1901, d June 13, 1914
2 Pearl M. Driver, b. Nov 15, 1903, d Dec 4, 1923
3. Mary A. Driver, b Oct 22, 1907 No 408½
4 Ruth E. Driver, b Jan 30, 1910, d June 12, 1922
5. Fannie M Driver, b Aug 12, 1922, d Jan 8, 1914
6. Gladys V. Driver, b. Sept 4, 1916 No 408¾.

No. 408½. Sixth Generation. 408.

3) Mary A. Driver, b Oct 21, 1907, in Morgan Co, Mo, m May 18, 1932, Leroy Gingerich, b Feb 16, 1908 Farmer Address Versailles, Mo Mrs Gingerich is a school teacher Mennonites Burial ground is at the Mt Zion Mennonite Church

No. 403¾. Sixth Generation. 403.

6) Gladys Viola Driver, b Sept 4, 1916, in Morgan Co., Mo , m. Carl Hilty, Dec. 24, 1934, at Versailles, Mo Mennonites They live in Iowa.

1. Twila Mae Hilty, b. Mar. 9, 1936.

No. 409. Fifth Generation. 220.

13) Jonas R. Weaver, b. Mar. 20, 1880, in Jasper Co., Mo., m. Dec. 24, 1902, Nannie A. Bare, b. Oct 25, 1876. Address· Oronogo, Mo. Farmer. Congregational

1 Harold M. Weaver, b Feb. 25, 1905. No. 3700.

2. Ralph J. Weaver, b. April 14, 1907.

3. Earl E. Weaver, b May 31, 1909.

4. Nellie M. Weaver, b. Mar. 11, 1911

5 Anna B. Weaver, b Nov. 23, 1915

No. 410. Fifth Generation. 221.

1) Elizabeth E Brunk, b May 8, 1854, near Broadway, Va , m. Dec. 28, 1873, Daniel P. Mason. b. —————— Address. Broadway, Va. Farmer. Mennonites.

1. Mary C Mason, b Dec 18, 1875 No 419

2. Emma C Mason, b June 11, 1877, single

3. Anna F. Mason, b. April 24, 1879 No 420.

4. Sarah M. Mason, b. Mar 7, 1881, d Nov 7, 1885.

5. Lydia R Mason, b. April 28, 1883 No 421.

6 Cora A. Mason, b. Feb 3, 1885, single

7 George M Mason, b Mar 6, 1889 No. 422

8 Perry D Mason, b —————— No 423

No. 411. Fifth Generation. 221.

2) Samuel C Brunk, b Feb 1, 1857, near Broadway, Va., m Anna Shank, daughter of Samuel and Sarah (Rhodes) Shank. She was born Jan. 1, 1857. Samuel died ——————, 1922 He was buried in the Salem cemetery near Elida, O Address Elida, O Farmer. Mennonites Deacon

1 Sarah Alice Brunk, b. June 18, 1879 No 424.

2. Timothy Brunk, b Jan 17, 1881. No 427.

3 Gabriel Brunk, b Mar. 4, 1883. No. 428.

4. Solomon M Brunk, b Sept 11, 1884 No 429

5 Emma C. Brunk, b. Nov. 13, 1886 No 430

6. Mary Brunk, b Mar 14, 1888, single

7 Anthony Brunk, b. Oct. 10, 1891, d. July 28, 1900.

8 Paul Brunk, b Feb. 9, 1897. No. 431.

9 Reuben Brunk, b. May 31, 1894. No. 432.

No. 412. Fifth Generation. 221.

3) Perry E. Brunk, b Jan 19, 1858, near Broadway, Va., d. Jan. —, 1930, near Elida, O., the place of his home, m Oct 30, 1881, Marie J. Powel, of Va , b Nov. 11, 1857, by Bishop George Brenneman She died June 17, 1938, at Detroit, Mich. Both are buried at the Pike Church near Elida, O , which was their address. Mennonites. Farmer On Apr. 30, 1889, he was ordained a deacon, and on May 21, 1905, he was ordained a minister at the Pike Church near Elida, O.

1. George L. Brunk, b. Dec 2, 1882. No. 435.

2. Andrew S. Brunk, b Aug. 13, 1884 No 437.

3. Mary E Brunk, b Mar 15, 1886 No. 438

4. Henry J. Brunk, b Jan 23, 1888. No. 439.

5. Elizabeth R. Brunk, b. Dec. 29, 1889. No. 440.

6. Clifford F. Brunk, b Oct 24, 1891. No 442¼
7 Lewis Brunk, b. June 15, 1894   No 441
8. Walter Brunk, b Sept 18, 1896, unm.
9. Lloyd C. Brunk, b. Oct 23, 1898 No. 442.

No. 413. Fifth Generation. 221.

4) Franklin B Brunk, b Jan 28, 1860, near Broadway, Va, m Jan 4, 1887, Elizabeth H. Eshelman, b. ————, d ————, m. (2nd) Mattie Eby Address· Maugansville, Md Mennonite
1. Joseph E Brunk, b Mar 7, 1888 No 454.
2. Mary Brunk, b Oct 12, 1889, d Nov 8, 1889
3. George Brunk, b Nov 17, 1890. No 455
4. Samuel H Brunk, b. May 7, 1892 No 456
5. Henry M. Brunk, b. ———— No 457
    (From second wife)
6. Fannie E. Brunk, b ———— No 458.
7. Christian Brunk, b ———— No 459

No. 414. Fifth Generation. 221.

5) Frances W. Brunk, b Sept 3, 1861, near Broadway, Va., m. Aug. 5, 1886, Otis Wilkins, b. Nov. 1, 1861, in Va. Address Elida, O Laborer Mennonites.
1. Lillian V. Wilkins, b Apr. 14, 1889 No 460.
2. Annie F. Wilkins, b Nov 5, 1891 No 461
3. Mary E Wilkins, b Dec 22, 1893. No 462.
4. Lydia Wilkins, b Apr. 22, 1898. No 463

No. 415. Fifth Generation. 221.

6) John J. Brunk, b Nov. 24, 1862, near Broadway, Va, d. Sept 9, 1900, m Lillie Carpenter of Va., b ————, d ————, m Mar. 12, 1891, Magdalena Wenger, b. Oct. 24, 1872, of Green Mountain, Va Address Green Mountain, Va. Farmer. Mennonites.
1. Aldine Brunk, b ————, 1887 No. 464
    (From second union)
2. Menno Jacob Brunk, b Oct 3, 1892, unmarried.
3. Kate Amanda Brunk, b. Oct 15, 1893, unmarried
4. Lewis Samuel Brunk, b Oct 30, 1895. No 2793.
5. Mary Edith Brunk, b. July 22, 1897
6. Anna Barbara Brunk, b. June 6, 1899, unmarried

No. 416. Fifth Generation. 221.

8) Lydia W. Brunk, b Sept 20, 1866, near Broadway, Va., m May 29, 1904, Hiram Hoover, b. Jan. 22, 1852, died July 28, 1930. Farmer. Mennonites. Elida, O. Lydia died July 9, 1935, in Ohio They are buried at Salem cemetery.
1. George W. Hoover, b July 18, 1905 No 465.
2. Mary V. Hoover, b Nov 1, 1909 No. 466

No. 417. Fifth Generation. 221.

9) Christian Brunk, b Mar. 20, 1868, near Broadway, Va, m Rebecca Landes, ————. Address Cowan, Va Farmer Mennonite
1. Nora Gertrude Brunk, b ———— No 467
2. William Edward Brunk, b. ————. No. 468
3. Ama Frances Brunk, b Jan 17, 1896 No 469.
4. Earl Franklin Brunk, b ———— No. 470.

84

10) Mary C. Brunk, b June 1, 1870, near Broadway, Va.; she d. ——————, m. Noah Holler of Va.

    1. Lula Holler, b —————— No 471.

No. 419. Sixth Generation. 410.

1) Mary Elizabeth Mason, b Dec 18, 1875, in Va., m John D. Moyer, b. ——————, d Nov. 31, 1931. Address Lebanon, Pa Mennonites.

    1. Benjamin Moyers, b ——————.
    2. Anna F. Moyers, b. ——————
    3. Lula Moyers, b. ——————.
    4. Infant d. at birth.
    5. Infant d. at birth

No. 420. Sixth Generation. 410.

3) Anna F. Mason, b. April 24, 1879, in Va., m. Hiram Weaver, b. ——————. Address: Harman, W. Va Mennonites Engaged in mission work

No. 421. Sixth Generation. 410.

5) Lydia Rebecca Mason, b. April 28, 1883, in Va., m. Dec. 27, 1903, Charles E. Van Pelt, b. Sept 22, 1883, m (2nd) John Petrue. She lives in Lima, O.

    1. Mary E. Van Pelt, b Oct. 7, 1904. No 779.
    2. David D. Van Pelt, b Mar 6, 1906, d. Jan 20, 1921.
    3. Icy P. Van Pelt, b Feb 4, 1908 No 780
    4. Tracy M. Van Pelt, b June 12, 1910. No 781.
    5. Infant died at birth

David lost his life while working at the locomotive works by the explosion of a furnace, Lima, O

No. 422. Sixth Generation. 410.

7) George M. Mason, b Mar 6, 1889, in Va, m Rosa Stayner. Address: Broadway, Va. Baker by trade Mennonites

    1. Harold Mason, b ——————.
    2. Raymond Mason, b. ——————.
    3. Bernice Mason, b. ——————

No. 423. Sixth Generation. 410.

8) Perry D Mason, b ——————, in Va, m Ressie Southerly, b ——————. Address: Broadway, Va. Laborer Mennonite.

    1. Owen Mason, b. ——————.
    2. Pauline Mason, b. ——————.
    3. Infant died at birth.
    4. Mary Mason, b ——————.

No. 424. Sixth Generation. 411.

1) Sarah Alice Brunk, b June 18, 1879, m. Benjamin F. Howard, b. Mar. 31, 1877, d. Aug. 4, 1905. Address. Elida, O. Farmer Mennonite. Burial in the Salem cemetery near Elida, O Alice married (2nd) John Hartman of Va.

    1. Clara Howard, b. ——————. No. 425.
    2. Raymond Howard, b. Nov 20, 1905 No 426.

No. 425. Seventh Generation. 424.

1) Clara Howard, b ——————, m Noah Good, b. ——————. Address: Elida, O. Farmer. Mennonites Have children.

No. 426. Seventh Generation. 424.

2) Raymond B. Howard, b. Nov 20, 1905, near Elida, O , d. April 2, 1937, in Va., m Anna M. Sharps Address: Woodstock, Va Chiropractor. Mennonites

No. 427. Sixth Generation. 411.

2) Timothy Brunk, b Jan 17, 1881, near Elida, O , m Thersa Carmean, b. July 19, 1883, near Elida, O Address: Elida, O Laborer U B. Church.
1. Cretora E. Brunk, b. Mar 16, 1906.
2. Chester A Brunk, b Mar 1, 1910.
3. Charles Clayton Brunk, b Apr 8, 1912 No 3589
4. Virgil Robert Brunk, b Nov. 9, 1919
5 Russell Wm. Brunk, b May 6, 1925.

No. 423. Sixth Generation. 411.

3) Gabriel Brunk, b. Mar. 4, 1883, near Elida, O , m. Oct. 16, 1904, Dora C. Mosier, b Aug 13, 1883, same place Address Elida, O Farmer. Mennonite. Minister.
1. Marie Agnes Brunk, b. ————————.
2. Rudy Brunk, b July 14, 1906 No. 433
3. Vera V. Brunk, b. Jan 3, 1910 No 782
4. Lois Brunk, b. Nov. 15, 1911 No 783.
5. Esther Brunk, b. Nov 21, 1913 No 784
6. Ida May Brunk, b Dec 22, 1915.
7. Mary Brunk, b. Feb 20, 1918.
8. Martha Brunk, b Feb 20, 1918
9. Dora Brunk, b. May 15, 1922.
10 Norman Brunk, b. July 22, 1924

No. 429. Sixth Generation. 411.

4) Solomon M. Brunk, b Sept 11, 1884, near Elida, O , m Nov 2, 1905, Mattie Stalter, b Nov 10, 1880 Address. Delphos, O , R 2. Farmer and carpenter. Mennonite. Deacon in the Pike congregation near Elida, O
1. Wilbur F. Brunk, b Nov. 25, 1906 No 434
2. Marie Brunk, b April 2, 1909.
3. Arthur S Brunk, b. Jan. 25, 1911 No. 3264
4. Lola Brunk, b Mar 1, 1918
5. Roy Brunk, b July 18, 1919.

No. 430. Sixth Generation. 411.

5) Emma C. Brunk, b Nov. 15, 1886, near Elida, O , m Dec. 10, 1908, Menno S. Shenk, b. Dec. 31, 1876 Address Elida, O , R 2 Carpenter Mennonites.
1. Laurel Shenk, b Feb 18, 1911.
2. Zela Shenk, b. Sept. 14, 1914

No. 431. Sixth Generation. 411.

8) Paul W Brunk, b Feb 9, 1897, near Elida, O , m. Feb 24, 1921, Minnie W. Good, b. Sept. 12, 1901 Address Royersford, Pa Farmer. Mennonite
1. Wilson S. Brunk, b. May 26, 1922
2. Beulah M Brunk, b July 19, 1924
3. Grace E Brunk, b. May 27, 1928
4. Melvin S Brunk, b April 24, 1933

No. 432. Sixth Generation. 411.

9) Reuben Brunk, b. May 31, 1894, near Elida, O., m. Apr 19, 1919, Leah Good, b. April 24, 1896 Address Elida, O , R 2 Farmer Mennonite

1. Lillian Brunk, b. April 10, 1920
2. Lawrence Brunk, b. Jan. 29, 1922.
3. Gladys Brunk, b Sept. 21, 1924.
4. Alice Brunk, b. April 7, 1926.
5. Miriam Brunk, b Nov. 22, 1927.
6. Kenneth Brunk, b. Dec. 17, 1929.
7. Margaret Brunk, b Sept. 3, 1931

No. 433. Seventh Generation. 428.

2) Rudy Brunk, b July 14, 1906, m Mar. 10, 1928, Emma S. Moore, b. May 20, 1908. Address: Lima, O , R 3. Huckster. Mennonite.
1. Waneta Brunk, b Jan 12, 1929
2. Wanda Virginia Brunk, b Jan. 3, 1936.

No. 434. Seventh Generation. 429.

1) Wilbur F. Brunk, b. Nov 25, 1906, near Elida, O., m. June 6, 1930, Florence Edna Diller, b. Nov. 23, 1902. Address Elida, O., R. 2. Farmer. Mennonite.
1. Leonard Samuel Brunk, b. April 14, 1931.
2. Herbert Franklin Brunk, b. May 18, 1936.

No. 435. Sixth Generation. 412.

1) George L. Brunk, b Dec. 2, 1882, near Elida, O., m June 14, 1905, Hazel Bechtel, b. July 24, 1886. Address· 621 W. Elm St , Lima, O. Dentist.
1. Carl Brunk, b Feb. 11, 1906. No. 436.
2. Wilford Brunk, b Mar 21, 1910 No. 3284
3. Ruth Brunk, b June 4, 1915

No. 436. Seventh Generation. 435.

1) Carl Brunk, b. Feb 11, 1906, m Jane Shinn, b. Aug. 25, 1909, d. July 22, 1932, buried in Woodlawn cemetery; m. (2nd) June, 1935, Lucille Metzger
1. Thomas George Brunk, b. July 21, 1932

No. 437. Sixth Generation. 412.

2) Andrew S. Brunk, b Aug 13, 1884, near Elida, O., m at La Junta, Colo., Gale Trust, b ———————. Address 2906 E Jefferson, Apt 2-B, Detroit, Mich. Physician and surgeon
1. Perry E. Brunk, b Dec 23, 1914

No. 438. Sixth Generation. 412.

3) Mary Etta Brunk, b Mar. 15, 1886, near Elida, O., m. David Edward Stuttsman, b Sept 15, 1881. Address· Elida, O., R. 2.
1. Miriam Stuttsman, b April 13, 1907
2 George Donald Stuttsman, b Sept. 29, 1911. No 438¼
3. Max Henry Stuttsman, b Nov 16, 1916.
4 Milton Stuttsman, b. Oct. 8, 1924

No. 438¼. Seventh Generation. 438.

2) George Donald Stuttsman, b Sept. 29, 1911, m. Carrol Coan, b ———————, 1914. Address: 423 Middlebury St , Elkhart, Ind.
1. Donald Edward Stuttsman, b April 7, 1931
2 Jack G. Stuttsman, b Sept 17, 1932.

No. 439. Sixth Generation. 412.

4) Henry J. Brunk, b. Jan 23, 1888, near Elida, O , m Esther Pearl Brenneman, b. Oct. 6, 1891. Address was Otto Lake, Mich Dentist Related; see No. 2946.
1. William H Brunk, b June 23, 1916.

No. 440. Sixth Generation. 412.

5) Elizabeth R Brunk, b Dec 29, 1889, near Elida, O , m. O. Glen Brenneman, b. April 15, 1892. Address Delphos, O Undertaker Presbyterians.

1. Jannette Brenneman, b June 13, 1913.
2. Wilma Brenneman, b June 1, 1925, d Sept 1, 1928

No. 441. Sixth Generation. 412.

7) Lewis P. Brunk, b June 15, 1894, near Elida, O., m. Bertha Red, b. ———————. Address: 1558 W High St , Lima, O. Dentist. U. B. Church.

1. Lewis T. Brunk, b. ———————.
2. Robert Brunk, b ———————

No. 442. Sixth Generation. 412.

9) Lloyd C. Brunk, b Oct 23, 1898, near Elida, O , m Fannie Foust, b ———————. Address· 433 South Manistigue, Detroit, Mich. Dentist.

1. Hazel Lucille Brunk, b April 27, 1920

No. 442¼. Sixth Generation. 412.

6) Clifford F. Brunk, b. Oct. 24, 1891, near Elida, O , m Aug. 20, 1938, Lydia Lehman, of Ft. Wayne, Ind , at the Congregational Church in Ft Wayne, Ind. They will reside in Detroit, Mich , where he is a member of the Brunk Bros. Hospital. Physician and surgeon.

No. 443. Sixth Generation. 361.

1) Oliver W. Heatwole, b Nov 11, 1884, m June 11, 1914, Edith L. Travis, b. April 21, 1894. Address. 905 Quackenbos St , N W , Washington, D. C District representative Oakland Motor Car Co Christian Church.

1. Henry T. Heatwole, b. Aug 9, 1915
2. Oliver W. Heatwole, Jr , b Aug. 23, 1918
3. Catherine V. Heatwole, b Jan. 23, 1921
4. Dorothy L. Heatwole, b April 13, 1926.
5. David S Heatwole, b. Mar 2, 1929

No. 444. Sixth Generation. 361.

2) Stella E Heatwole, b. Oct. 22, 1886, m. Feb 14, 1906, Emmer F. Rhodes, b. Oct. 21, 1881. Address: Dayton, Va. Mennonites R. F. D. mail carrier, farmer, and restaurant operator at Staunton, Va.

1. Sadie L. Rhodes, b Oct. 14, 1907. No. 445.
2. Charlie F. Rhodes, b Aug 12, 1909, d Mar 28, 1915.
3. Paul H. Rhodes, b. July 17, 1911 No 446.
4. Margaret V. Rhodes, b Feb 8, 1913
5. Minnie F. Rhodes, b Feb. 10, 1916
6. Hazel F. Rhodes, b May 31, 1917
7. Thomas R. Rhodes, b. April 24, 1919.
8. Emmer F. Rhodes, b. Sept 8, 1922.
9. Helen E Rhodes, b May 8, 1925
10. William J Rhodes, b. Aug 19, 1926.
11 Stella M Rhodes, b Dec 28, 1928
12 Stanley Everett Rhodes, b Oct 22, 1931

No. 445. Seventh Generation. 444.

1) Sadie L Rhodes, b. Oct. 14, 1907, m Mar. 27, 1929, Willie R Rhodes, b. ———————. Address· Dayton, Va Silk mill worker. Mennonites

1 Glen W Rhodes, b April 6, 1930

No. 446. Seventh Generation. 444.

3) Paul H. Rhodes, b July 17, 1911, m. Sept. 25, 1930, Katie P. Knisely, b. ——————— Address Dayton, Va Farmer. Mennonite

No. 447. Sixth Generation. 361.

3) Mattie C. Heatwole, b. Sept. 5, 1888, m. June 30, 1919, Miner E. Snyder, b. June 25, 1888. Store manager. Christian Church. Address: 907 Quackenbos St., N. W., Washington, D. C.

1. Jewell C. Snyder, b Sept 26, 1920.
2. Joseph E. Snyder, b Oct. 18, 1928, twin
3. Alfred E. Snyder, b Oct. 18, 1928, twin.

No. 448. Sixth Generation. 361.

4) John L. Heatwole, b Sept. 12, 1890, m Jan. 6, 1916, Bessie I. Deter, b. Oct. 8, 1894 Address: 53 Westover St., Clarendon, Va Christians.

1 Thomas Holmes Heatwole, b. Oct. 8, 1916.
2. Jean Minerva Heatwole, b Oct. 17, 1918, d Jan. 15, 1922.
3. John Lawrence Heatwole, b. Sept 13, 1920.
4. Janet Jacqueline Heatwole, b Sept 10, 1922
5. Norma Frances Heatwole, b Aug. 31, 1924
6. James Lowell Heatwole, b Sept 5, 1926.
7. Betty Ann Heatwole, b April 4, 1928.
8. Arnold Rockne Heatwole, b Mar 28, 1931.

No. 449. Sixth Generation. 361.

5) Paul V. Heatwole, b. Aug. 15, 1892, m. May 25, 1929, Loreen E. Hamilton, b. Oct. 21, 1905 Mr Heatwole is a member of the Baptist Church, and Mrs. Heatwole, of the Methodist Church Address 24 N Central Ave., Staunton, Va. Restaurant.

1. Son born Nov 9, 1930

No. 450. Sixth Generation. 361.

6) Joseph W Heatwole, b. Mar. 3, 1895, m. Marie ———————. They live in Washington, D. C No children.

No. 451. Sixth Generation. 361.

9) Emery B Heatwole, b Jan 10, 1899, m Oct 10, 1922, Ruby Myrtle Corbin, b. Jan. 29, 1900 Address: Berwyn, Md Produce dealer. Brethren.

1. Emery Boward Heatwole, b Sept. 10, 1928.

No. 452. Sixth Generation. 361.

10) Ruth F. Heatwole, b. May 19, 1902, m. Dec. 29, 1917, Lariston D. Hill, b ———————. Seventh Day Adventist Address 421 Idona Ave., Youngstown, O Streetcar conductor.

1. Jean L. Hill, b. June 22. 1918
2. Wendell Hill, b Jan. 14, 1920
3. Mary K. Hill, b Oct. 11, 1922
4. Theodore E. Hill, b. Aug. 26, 1925.

No. 453. Sixth Generation. 361.

11) Hazel E Heatwole, b. Aug 1, 1904, m. Dec. 27, 1922, George F. Wine, b Nov. 7, 1902. Address. Annville, Pa, R 3 Farmer. Methodist.

1. Norman F. Wine, b. Jan 27, 1923
2 Bonnie J. Wine, b. April 9, 1924.
3. June C. Wine, b. Oct. 17, 1925.
4. Romaine H. Wine, b Oct 25, 1928.

5. Charlotte C. Wine, b. May 5, 1930
6 Audrey Frances Wine, b Sept 20, 1931.

No. 454. Sixth Generation. 413.
1) Joseph E. Brunk, b. Mar 7, 1888, m. May 24, 1911, Alice Yoder, b. May 7, 1886. Address: Goshen, Ind. Mennonite.
1. Ivan W. Brunk, b July 29, 1915.
2. Milton Brunk, b Apr. —, 1920
3. Adella May Brunk, b. Nov. 12, 1922.
4 Dorothy Brunk, b Dec. 10, 1927, d Feb 10, 1934
5. Mabel Brunk, b. July 25, 1926

No. 455. Sixth Generation. 413.
3) George F. Brunk, b Nov. 17, 1890, m Annie Hollaway, b ——————. Address: Washington, D C Carpenter Mennonite, minister.
1 Harold Brunk, b. ——————
2 Marie Brunk, b. ——————
3 Irma Brunk, b ——————
4. Emily Brunk, b. ——————

No. 456. Sixth Generation. 413.
4) Samuel H. Brunk, b May 7, 1892, m Jan 3, 1915, Mollie Wenger, b Aug. 6, 1893. Address. Fentress, Va Mennonite, minister
1 Ida Mae Brunk, b Mar 14, 1916.
2 George Franklin Brunk, b Nov. 12, 1918
3. Daniel Wenger Brunk, b June 11, 1920
4 Edith Mattie Brunk, b. Mar 19, 1922
5 Samuel Henry Brunk, Jr, b Oct 31, 1926

No. 457. Sixth Generation. 413.
5) Henry M Brunk, b Jan. 30, 1895, m Nov. 8, 1916, Nora Kraus, b May 31, 1895. Address Hyattsville, Md Building Supply. Mennonites
1. Esther Brunk, b. Dec 3, 1917
2 Ellen Brunk, b. Feb 12, 1919
3 Ruth Brunk, b May 5, 1922
4. Alma Brunk, b. Oct. 24, 1924
5 H. Nelson Brunk, b Oct. 7, 1927.
6 Henry M. Brunk, Jr., b Sept. 2, 1929
7. Perry E Brunk, b. April 11, 1932.
8. Joseph Brunk, b. Sept 19, 1935.

No. 458. Sixth Generation. 413.
6) Fanny Brunk, b Apr. 14, 1901, m Dec 22, 1920, Benjamin Kornhaus, b Oct. 21, 1897 Address. Denbigh, Va Farmer. Mennonites
1. Glen Kornhaus, b Feb 7, 1922
2 Frank Kornhaus, b Mar. 3, 1925.
3 John Henry Kornhaus, b Mar. 22, 1927.
4 Leona Kornhaus, b Jan 29, 1931.
5 Benjamin Kornhaus, Jr, b. Feb. 2, 1932.
6 Annie Marie Kornhaus, b Oct 7, 1934

No. 459. Sixth Generation. 413.
7) Christian W. Brunk, b Aug 4, 1899, m Jeanette Leaky, b. ——————.
Address: Hyattsville, Md. Mennonites
1 Franklin M Brunk, b. ——————
2 Elsie Brunk, b ——————.

3. Charles Brunk, b. ————————
4 Martha Brunk, b. ——————————.
5. Robert Brunk, b ——————————.

No. 460. Sixth Generation. 414.

1) Lillie Wilkins, b. Apr 14, 1889, m Jan. 7, 1914, Irvin Good, b. June 10, 1887. Address: Lima, O., R. 3. Carpenter. Mennonites.

1. Otis James Good, b. Oct. 31, 1914.
2. Rosella Mae Good, b May 5, 1916.
3 Irvin Leroy Good, b. Mar. 21, 1919
4. George Thomas Good, b Oct. 23, 1924
5. Albert Franklin Good, b Oct 17, 1925, twin
6. Alberta Frances Good, b. Oct 17, 1925, twin
7. Nettie Jean Good, b. May 8, 1928

No. 461. Sixth Generation. 414.

2) Annie F Wilkins, b Nov. 5, 1891, m Dec 20, 1908, Isaac Miller, b. ——————————. Farmer Mechanic Address Lima, O., R. 3. Mennonites.

1. Wilber Miller, b. Feb 28, 1910, d Aug., 1912.
2. Berlin Miller, b Mar 30, 1912
3. Pauline Miller, b Aug 18, 1913
4. Velma Miller, b. Aug. 22, 1915.
5 Arnold Miller, b Feb 14, 1919.
6. Freda Miller, b. Jan. 30, 1922.
7 Geneva Miller, b Oct 24, 1924

No. 462. Sixth Generation. 414.

3) Mary E Wilkins, b Dec 22, 1893, d. Nov. 24, 1933, m. Feb. 21, 1917, Oscar Greider, b Nov 7, 1890 Address: Elida, O , R. 1. Huckster. Mennonites.

1 Beulah Greider, b Jan 27, 1919
2 Ella Greider, b. Mar 13, 1921.
3. Clara Greider, b. July 28, 1923

No. 463. Sixth Generation. 414.

4) Lydia Wilkins, b Apr 22, 1898, m Sept. 6, 1923, Carl Philips, b —————————— Address. Elida, O , R 1 Laborer. No children.

No. 464. Sixth Generation. 415.

1) Aldine C Brunk, b about 1887, m. Eva Harder, b. ——————————, Morgan Co , Mo. Address Dhamtari, Central Province, India Mennonites. Missionary to India No issue

No. 465. Sixth Generation. 416.

1) George W. Hoover, b. July 18, 1905, m Mildred Carr. Address: Elida, O
1. Son (stillborn)
2 Anna Mary Hoover, b Apr 19, 1930

No. 466. Sixth Generation. 416.

2) Mary V. Hoover, b. Nov 1, 1909, m Aug. 11, 1931, George Willis Ross, b Dec 7, 1907 Address Toledo, O., R 3 Laborer Mennonites

1 Reta Carolyn Ross, b May 6, 1934.
2. Elaine Marie Ross, b Aug 31, 1936

No. 467. Sixth Generation. 417.

1) Nora Gertrude Brunk, b. ——————————, m. Charles Spitzer, b. ——————————.

No. 468. Sixth Generation. 417.

2) William Edward Brunk, b ——————————, m. Ada Davis, b. ——————————.

No. 469. Sixth Generation. 417.

3) Ama Frances Brunk, b Jan 17, 1896, in Rockingham Co, Va., m. David Ritchie, b. Jan. 18, 1890, same place as above Address: Lima, O. Laborer. Church of the Brethren.

1. Laura Isola Ritchie, b Sept. 29, 1913.
2. Howard William Ritchie, b. Dec 27, 1919.

No. 470. Sixth Generation. 417.

4) Earl Franklin Brunk, b ————————, m Luela Emsweller, b ————————.

No. 471. Sixth Generation. 418.

1) Lula Holler, b. ————————, m. C. F Coffman, b ————————. Address: Geer, Va

No. 472. Fifth Generation. 222.

1) Sarah F. Weaver, b. Dec. 21, 1856, in Rockingham Co, Va, m Martin Heatwole, b. Mar 22, 1846, in Va. Address Mt Clinton, Va. Mennonite.

1. Oliver D. Heatwole b Sept 11, 1876, drowned in North River, Aug 2, 1883
2. Elizabeth N. Heatwole, b July 27, 1878
3. Rawley O Heatwole, b. Feb 11, 1881.
4. Emmer C. Heatwole, b Nov. 25, 1883
5. Addie D Heatwole, b Aug 21, 1885.
6. Effie R Heatwole, b Mar 28, 1888
7. Tracy E. Heatwole, b Dec 9, 1890
8 Weldon W Heatwole, b Apr 6, 1894
9 Fleta P. Heatwole, b Feb 10, 1897

No. 473. Fifth Generation. 222.

2) Elizabeth Etta Weaver, b ————————, in Rockingham Co, Va, m. Dec. 25, 1887, Martin B Miller, b ———————— Address Bridgewater, Va. Farmer. Church of the Brethren, minister

1 Lottie E. Miller, b. Mar 29, 1889.
2 Grace D Miller, b Oct 10, 1891
3 Wilette W Miller, b Aug 2, 1902
4. Martin D. Miller, b. Mar. 20, 1906.

No. 474. Fifth Generation. 222.

3) Mary M. Weaver, b Mar 2, 1874, in Va, m Jacob T Miller, b. Apr. 6, 1867. Address: Bridgewater, Va Farmer. Dunkard

1. Lessie M. Miller, b Feb 7, 1893.
2. Wayland W. Miller, b. Aug 17, 1895
3 Magdalene L Miller, b. Aug. 8, 1903

No. 475. Fifth Generation. 222.

4) Wm Clifford Weaver, b Oct 26, 1867, in Va., m Jan. 23, 1890, Lula V. ————————, b. May 14, 1872. Address Hinton, Va Farmer and carpenter. Methodist

1 Wilmer E Weaver, b Sept 21, 1891
2. Ollie G. Weaver, b Aug 29, 1893.
3 Ora David Weaver, b. July 4, 1895
4 Robert Leroy Weaver, b Jan 5, 1898
5 William Lloyd Weaver, b Mar. 14, 1900.
6 Clifford Carl Weaver, b. Dec 23, 1901
7 Ethel Virginia Weaver, b Jan. 17, 1906, d Aug. 11, 1929.
8. Garland Elmer Weaver, b Jan. 20, 1908.
9. Charlotte Roena Weaver, b Mar 3, 1910.

No. 477. Fifth Generation. 223.

1) Jacob S Sharps, b Nov. 11, 1867, near Harrisonburg, Va., m. April 15, 1890, H. Eliza Bowman Address. Harrisonburg, Va.

1. Lowell V. Sharps, b July 12, 1899. No. 478.
2. S. Frances Sharps, b Oct 9, 1904 No 479

No. 478. Sixth Generation. 477.

1) Lowell V Sharps, b July 12, 1899, in Va., m Lucele Della Kinzie, b. Mar. 7, 1900. Address High Point, N C

1 Lowell V. Sharps, Jr., b May 10, 1924
2 Donald K. Sharps, b. Oct 4, 1926.
3 Helen E Sharps, b Dec 21, 1931.

No. 479. Sixth Generation. 477.

2) S. Frances Sharps, b Oct 9, 1904, in Va , m. June 3, 1925, to Lloyd L. Meyers, b Apr. 14, 1906. Address Harrisonburg, Va.

1. Nelson L Meyers, b. Jan 27, 1927
2 Carroll E Meyers, b Oct 10, 1929
3 Duene Frances Meyers, b Oct. 26, 1931.

No. 480. Fifth Generation. 223.

2) John F. Sharps, b Mar 27, 1870, d Aug 14, 1931, m Mary A. Suter, Oct. 20, 1896, at Harrisonburg, Va Address Harrisonburg, Va Burial at Weavers Church

1. Ralph C Sharps, b June 21, 1898.
2 Jacob W Sharps, b Aug 15, 1895.
3 Edna P Sharps, b Sept 6, 1903
4 Roy E. Sharps, b. Sept. 12, 1907.

No. 481. Fifth Generation. 223.

3) Elizabeth F. Sharps, b ————————, d. Jan 7, 1932, m Jan. 3, 1903, John W Thompson. Address Harrisonburg, Va

1. Mary Anna Thompson, b. Oct 13, 1903, R. Nurse, single.
2. Paul E. Thompson, b July 13, 1905 No. 482.
3. Daniel M. Thompson, b Oct. 7, 1907. No. 483
4 Sarah F. Thompson, b. June 15, 1910. No. 484.
5. Edna Mae Thompson, b June 16, 1914

No. 482. Sixth Generation. 481.

2) Paul E Thompson, b July 13, 1905, near Harrisonburg, Va., m. Imogene Coffman, b Sept. 25, 1906, m April 15, 1927. at Orkney Springs, Va.

1 Robert E. Thompson, b. Aug. 11, 1929.

No. 483. Sixth Generation. 481.

3) Daniel M Thompson, b Oct 7, 1907, near Harrisonburg, Va., m. Aug. 2, 1930, Margaret S Bowman, b Nov 2, 1907 Address Harrisonburg, Va.

1. Doris E Thompson, b Apr 17, 1932

No. 484. Sixth Generation. 481.

4) Sarah F. Thompson, b June 15, 1910, near Harrisonburg, Va., m June 16, 1930, Walter Snyder, b. Nov 15, 1909 Address· Harrisonburg, Va.

1 Marvin Leo Snyder, b Aug 28, 1930

No. 485. Fifth Generation. 223.

4) William A. Sharps, b Sept. 5, 1873, in Rockingham Co., Va , m. Effie C. Shank, b. Apr 27, 1883, m Dec 6, 1906. Address: Dayton, Va., R. 2. Farmers Mennonite.

1. Anna M. Sharps, b Sept. 23, 1907 No 486
2. Joseph W. Sharps, b. Jan 11, 1909 No. 487
3. Harold L. Sharps, b. May 19, 1912

No. 486. Sixth Generation. 485.

1) Anna M. Sharps, b Sept 23, 1907, near Dayton, Va., m Nov. 6, 1929, Raymond Howard, b. Nov 20, 1905, in Allen Co, O , d in Virginia, Apr. 2, 1937. Address: Harrisonburg, Va Chiropractor Mennonite.

No. 487. Sixth Generation. 485.

2) Joseph W Sharps, b Jan 11, 1909, near Dayton, Va , m. Mar 11, 1930, Effie E. Wenger, b Nov. 9, 1911 Address. Dayton, Va.
1. Lois V Sharps, b Nov. 20, 1931.

No. 488. Fifth Generation. 223.

5) Mary M. Sharps, b Feb 28, 1878, in Rockingham Co , Va , m Sept. 20, 1899, Abram D Long, b. Feb 28, 1878, d. June 23, 1937, in Virginia where he lived Address. Harrisonburg, Va. Mennonite
1. Louis William Long, b Sept 12, 1900 No 489

No. 489. Sixth Generation. 488.

1) Louis William Long, b Sept 12, 1900, near Elida, O , m. April 17, 1920, Della Keyes, b Sept. 8, 1899 Address Hampton, Va.
1. Mabel Louise Long, b Mar 29, 1921.
2. Frances Lorine Long, b Dec 3, 1922
3. Esther May Long, b June 18, 1924.
4. Lewis W. Long, Jr., b. Jan 23, 1927
5. Dorothy Long, b Mar. 25, 1929
6. Joseph Edward Long, b Aug 10, 1932.

No. 490. Fifth Generation. 225.

1) Robert A Rhodes, b Apr 20, 1861, d Sept 13, 1928, m Estella Arthur They lived in California where he died They had four children

No. 491. Fifth Generation. 225.

2) Charles E. Rhodes, b Aug 3, 1864, d Sept 19, 1925, buried at Spades Church in Rockingham Co , Va , m Ida Greer.
1 Bessie Geyer Rhodes, b ——————.

No. 492. Fifth Generation. 225.

3) William Bradford Rhodes, b Feb. 6, 1866, in Va , d. in Calif , Sept 13, 1928, m. Fannie Greer. Carpenter. Methodists.
1. Eva Rhodes, b ——————. No. 493.

No. 493. Sixth Generation. 492.

1) Eva Rhodes, b. ——————, m —————— Orloff. One daughter, Ethel Rose Orloff, was born in 1918

No. 494. Fifth Generation. 225.

4) Minnie Belle Rhodes, b Nov 2, 1867, in Rockingham Co , Va., m George Shaver. Address. Harrisonburg, Va United Brethren.
1. W. Frank Shaver, b. ——————.
2. Perry Ernest Shaver, b Dec 22, 1892 No 495
3. Otho F. Shaver, b ——————. No. 496
4. Nina E Shaver, b. —————— No 497.
5 Paul O Shaver, b ——————

No. 495. Sixth Generation. 494.

2) Perry Ernest Shaver, b Dec 22, 1892, in Farquier Co, Va, m. Ediia V. Buckingham, Sept 2, 1922, at Philadelphia, Pa., b Jan 8, 1894. Address: 114 S. 57th St, Philadelphia, Pa Mechanical engineer. Methodists.

No. 495. Sixth Generation. 494.

3) Otho F Shaver, b ——————, in Va, m. (1st) Alma Bary, b —— ——; m. (2nd) Mary Mauck, b ——————. Address: Harrisonburg, Va.
    1 Otho Shaver, Jr, b. ——————
      (Second wife)
    2. Carl Shaver, b ——————
    3 Evelyn Shaver, b. ——————.
    4. Gilbert Shaver, b. ——————.
    5. Margaret Shaver, b. ——————.

No. 497. Sixth Generation. 494.

4) Nina E Shaver, b ——————, in Rockingham Co., Va, m. Ernes Neff, b ——————, d Nov 4, 1925. United Brethren Church.
    1 Frances Neff, b ——————.

No. 498. Fifth Generation. 225.

5) Frances Catherine Rhodes, b Sept. 11, 1869, in Va., m. in 1889 Emmet Erman. N. F R.

No. 499. Fifth Generation. 225.

6) John A Rhodes, b. July —, 1871, in Va, m Etta Baker. They have four children. Address: Harrisonburg, Va.

No. 500. Fifth Generation. 225.

7) Lula Ann Rhodes, b. May 30, 1873, in Rockingham Co., Va., m. Charles D. Evers. Address: Covington, Va.
    1. Orrville Evers, b. ——————.
    2. William Evers, b. ——————.
    3. Marie Evers, b ——————
    4. Charles Pane Evers, b. ——————.

No. 501. Fifth Generation. 225.

8) Hettie Jane Rhodes, b. Oct. 1, 1875, in Rockingham Co, Va., m. Walter Koouts. Address: Republic, Va She has one child dead, and two stepchildren, Douglas and Mabel.

No. 502. Fifth Generation. 225.

9) George Henry Rhodes, b Mar. 13, 1878, in Va., m. ——————, and lives in Spokane, Wash.
    1 Irene Virginia Rhodes, b ——————.

No. 503. Fifth Generation. 225.

10) Homer Whitefield Rhodes, b. Dec. 7, 1888, in Va, m Lula Beery, b. ——————. They live in Rockingham Co, Va
    1 Ernest Rhodes, b ——————.
    2 Alvin Rhodes, b ——————.

No. 504. Fifth Generation. 225.

11) Odie Lena Evelyn Rhodes, b. Dec. 25, 1881, in Va., m. John Ackers, b. ——————, d. —————— Address· Covington, Va Two children

12) Walter H Rhodes, b Dec 16, 1883, in Rockingham Co , Va , d June 26, 1928, m. Susie Beery. He was buried at the Weavers Church in Va
1. Thelma Catherine Rhodes, b --————————

No. 506. Fifth Generation. 229.

1) Sarah Shumaker, b ——————————, in Va , m Contento Neri, b ——————. Italian. Address: Atlanta, Ga.
1. Geribalda Neri, b. ——————.
2. Ward Neri, b ——————.

No. 507. Fifth Generation. 229.

2) John Shumaker, b ——————————, in Va , in Etta Sandy, b ——————— Address· Pleasant Valley, Va. No issue.

No. 508. Fifth Generation. 229.

3) Bettie Shumaker, b ——————————, in Va m. for second wife Calvin Pence, b. ——————————. No issue

No. 509. Fifth Generation. 229.

4) David E. Shumaker, b ——————————, in Va , m. Josephine Salser, b ——————————. Address: Atlanta, Ga. No children

No. 510. Fifth Generation. 230.

1) Edward Rhodes, b ——————————, d. ——————————, m Cora Pulse, b —————————— Address: Harrisonburg, Va They have four children

No. 511. Fifth Generation. 230.

2) Etta Rhodes, b. ——————————, in Va., m John Tutwiler. Address North River, Va. They have one child.

No. 512. Fifth Generation. 231.

1) Frances Heatwole, b. May 31, 1853, in Rockingham Co., Va , d Mar. 2, 1938, m Aug. 10, 1876, Daniel Wenger, b Apr 7, 1847, d June 10, 1893 He was buried in Pleasant Valley Cemetery Address Dayton, Va. Farmer Mennonites
1 Bettie F Wenger, b May 22, 1877. No 513.
2. Arthur S. Wenger, b Jan 5, 1879. No 514
3. Sarah M Wenger, b Aug 12, 1880. No 515
4. Emmanuel J. Wenger, b Jan 1, 1883 No. 518
5. Lydia A Wenger, b. Apr 25, 1886 No 519.
6. Mattie E. Wenger, b Aug 18, 1888. No 520.
7. Abraham D Wenger, b Jan. 9, 1891 No. 521.
8. Bertha E. Wenger, b Oct. 30, 1893, twin No. 522
9. Verdia A Wenger, b Oct 30, 1893, twin. No 523

No. 513. Sixth Generation. 512.

1) Bettie F Wenger, b May 22, 1877, near Dayton, Va , m Luther H. Coakley, b. May 25, 1874. Address Dayton, Va
1. Effie Frances Coakley, b May 15, 1914
2. Marion L. Coakley, b. Sept 28, 1915
3. Annie Virginia Coakley, b Oct 12, 1917

No. 514. Sixth Generation. 512.

2) Arthur S Wenger, b Jan 5, 1879, near Dayton, Va , m. Ada S Coffman, b. April 21, 1891, d Feb 16, 1920; m (2nd) Florence Knisely, Sept 25, 1921. Address· Dayton, Va Dunkard No children

No. 515. Sixth Generation. 512.

3) Sarah Magdalena Wenger, b Aug 12, 1880, near Dayton, Va., m. Dec. 4, 1902, Philip Knisely, at Dayton, Va Mennonite.

1. Emmanuel D Knisely, b Sept 8, 1903. No 516.
2 Martha Knisely, b. in 1904, d in 1904.
3. Artie L. Knisely, b. June 4, 1906.
4. Vernie Magdalena Knisely, b Nov. 18, 1907. No. 517.
5. Fannie Mae Knisely, b. Sept 15, 1909.
6. Herman Wilson Knisely, b July 29, 1911.
7. Irvin Daniel Knisely, b ————, 1913.
8 Reuben Wenger Knisely, b Feb 6, 1915
9. Della Mearl Knisely, b Jan 1, 1917, twin.
10. Delilah Pearl Knisely, b Jan. 1, 1917, twin.
11. Naomi Catherine Knisely, b Aug 6, 1920

No. 516. Seventh Generation. 515.

1) Emmanuel D. Knisely, b. Sept. 8, 1903, in Va., m. April 22, 1923, Bertha E. Christen. Address Mt Clinton, Va.

1. Harry Lee Knisely, b. Nov 9, 1923.
2. Ray Wilson Knisely, b. Aug 12, 1927
3. Lorene E Knisely, b Dec. 16, 1930

No. 517. Seventh Generation. 515.

4) Vernie Magdalena Knisely, b Nov 18, 1907, in Va., m Feb. 14, 1929, John S Burkholder, at Dayton, Va. Address Dayton, Va.

1 Sadie Lee Burkholder, b Jan. 1, 1930

No. 518. Sixth Generation. 512.

4) Emmanuel J. Wenger, b. Jan 1, 1883, in Rockingham Co., Va, m. Nov. 8, 1903, Nora Keyton Address: Blackstone, Va. Dunkards

1. Laura T. Wenger, b June 22, 1905, d July 18, 1906.
2. Emma V. Wenger, b June 1, 1907
3. Ira Wenger, b. ————, 1909
4. Leonard Wenger, b ————
5. Ruth Belle Wenger, b Aug. —, 1915
6 Arthur R Wenger, b. Aug 12, 1920.

No. 519. Sixth Generation. 512.

5) Lydia Ann Wenger, b April 25, 1886, in Rockingham Co., Va, m Nov. 19, 1908, Elam Eberly. Address: Orrville, O Farmer. Mennonites.

1. Barbara Frances Eberly, b Dec. 25, 1909 No 3701.
2 Emma Elizabeth Eberly, b Mar 16, 1911.
3. Walter Lloyd Eberly, b. Oct 21, 1912.
4 David Roy Eberly, b. Mar. 10, 1914. No. 3702.
5 Elsie Virginia Eberly, b. June 10, 1918
6. John Wenger Eberly, b Feb 19, 1920.
7. Mary Ellen Eberly, b Nov. 15, 1921.
8 Ruth Edna Eberly, b July 29, 1923, d Jan. 23, 1924.
9. Mabel Sarah Eberly, b. Feb. 13, 1925.
10. Eva Magdalena Eberly, b. July 30, 1927.
11. Benjamin Elam Eberly, b May 8, 1932.

No. 520. Sixth Generation. 512.

6) Mollie E. Wenger, b Aug 18, 1888, in Rockingham Co., Va., m. Aug. 5, 1908, at Orrville, O. William E Knisely Address: Crewe, Nottoway Co., Va.

1. Ralph O. Knisely, b. Aug 25, 1910
2 Frank Daniel Knisely, b June 19, 1912
3. Alice Grace Knisely, b. Dec. 27, 1913, d. Dec 31, 1913.
4. Dorothy Fern Knisely, b Sept 17, 1915.
5 Maud Ada Knisely, b Jan 12, 1918
6 Cleo Frances Knisely, b Mar 1, 1920.
7. Florence Ethel Knisely, b Mar 17, 1922.
8. Dwight Wm. Knisely, b. May 4, 1924.
9 Margaret Nell Knisely, b Nov 1, 1925
10 Paul Howard Knisely, b Mar 8, 1928.

No. 521. Sixth Generation. 512.

7) Abraham D Wenger, b Jan 9, 1891, in Rockingham Co, Va, m. Eva Harper, b July 14, 1894. Address Dayton, Va. Farmer and produce dealer. Mennonites
1. Emory Daniel Wenger, b. April 26, 1915.
2. Elizabeth Frances Wenger, b Mar 23, 1916
3. Artie Harper Wenger, b. Feb 16, 1919.
4. Ethel Lena Wenger, b Mar 9, 1921
5. Joseph Owen Wenger, b. May 29, 1923.
6. Ruth Virginia Wenger, b July 4, 1925
7. Warren Wilson Wenger, b. April 24, 1927
8. Dorothy Ellen Wenger, b June 25, 1929

No. 522. Sixth Generation. 512.

8) Berthy E Wenger, b. Oct 30, 1893, at Dayton, Va, m Feb 8, 1921, Elmer Martin, b. Feb 15, 1890, at Bowdil, O Address. Bowdil, O, R 2 Farmer. Mennonite
1 Abram D Martin, b. July 15, 1922
2. John Daniel Martin, b. Nov. 8, 1923.
3. Martha F Martin, b July 25, 1925.
4 Amos W. Martin, b Oct. 3, 1928.

No. 523. Sixth Generation. 512.

9) Verdia A. Wenger, b. Oct 30, 1893, at Dayton, Va., m. Nov., 1914, Frank E. Simmons. Address: Harrisonburg, Va., R 6 Bricklayer.
1. Blanche E. Simmons, b. Dec. 20, 1915
2. Daughter (stillborn).
3 Daughter (stillborn).
4. Paul A. Simmons, b. Jan. 2, 1918
5. Son (stillborn).
6 Owens Simmons, b July 5, 1922.
7. Beulah Simmons, b. Mar 4, 1925
8. Norma Simmons, b May 2, 1927.
9 Carl S. Simmons, b Mar, 1929

No. 524. Fifth Generation. 231.

2) Hugh A. Heatwole, b. Mar. 3, 1855, in Rockingham Co, Va., m. Aug 10, 1879, Laura Shank, b. Oct. 8, 1860, d. June 12, 1905.
1. Ward A. Heatwole, b. Feb. 25, 1884.
2. Howard H. Heatwole, b. Nov. 8, 1886 Separated from his wife
3. Wilmer H. Heatwole, b. July 28, 1891. No. 526.
Hugh A. Heatwole married second wife June 24, 1906, Laura V. Knicely, daughter of Lewis Knicely. Address: Harrisonburg, Va.

No. 525. Sixth Generation. 524.

2) Howard H. Heatwole, b Nov. 8, 1886, in Va , m Leoia Sandy, b. ————.

No. 526. Sixth Generation. 524.

3) Wilmer H. Heatwole, b. July 28, 1891, m. Hattie Knicely, daughter of his stepmother Address: Dayton, Va. They have five children.

1. Mildred Virginia Heatwole, b Feb 26, 1913. No. 3451.
2. Glen Heatwole, b Feb. 28, 1914 No 3452.
3 Hubert Alvin Heatwole, b. Aug. 24, 1915. No. 3453.
4. Dwight Everett Heatwole, b Dec. 1, 1921.
5 Wilmer Leroy Heatwole, b. Mar 27, 1929.

No. 523. Fifth Generation. 231.

3) Elizabeth E. Heatwole, b Dec. 31, 1858, near Pleasant Valley, Va., m. Algernon G. Tutwiler, b. Sept. 19, 1856 Address· Pleasant Valley, Va. Farmer. United Brethren.

1. Guernie A. Tutwiler, b May 13, 1880 No. 529.
2 Lucy M. Tutwiler, b. Feb 23, 1884. No 530
3 Charles E Tutwiler, b Jan 10, 1887. No. 532.
4 Florence L Tutwiler, b Aug 18, 1889. No 533.
5 Luther A. Tutwiler, b. Oct. 2, 1893. No 534.
6. Maud Irene Tutwiler, b ————. No 3597.

No. 529. Sixth Generation. 528.

1) Guernia A Tutwiler, b May 13, 1880, in Rockingham Co , Va , m Dec 23, 1902, Arthur Mouse Address: Clinton, Okla.

1. Harry F. Mouse, b Sept 15, 1905. No 529¼.
2. Lillian M. Mouse, b July 23, 1907. No 529½
3. Letha Mouse, b ————.
4. Lena Mouse, b ————
5. Roy Mouse, b. ————.
6. Lester Mouse, b. ————

No. 529¼. Seventh Generation. 529.

1) Harry F. Mouse, b. Sept 15, 1905, m. Pearl Mechum.

1. Harry Gene Mouse, b ————.
2. Marva Lee Mouse, b. ————.
3 Genevieve Mouse, b. ————

No. 529½. Seventh Generation. 529.

2) Lillian M. Mouse, b July 23, 1907, m (1st) Guy Flint, b ————, m (2nd) J H. L. Meyers, b. ————.

No. 530. Sixth Generation. 528.

2) Lucy M Tutwiler, b Feb. 23, 1884, in Rockingham Co., Va , m. Geordia T. Sandy, Dec. 26, 1905. Address· Mt Crawford, Va.

1 Myrtle E Sandy, b Dec. 7, 1906 No. 531.
2. Raleigh Albert Sandy, b. ————.
3. Evelyn Virginia Sandy, b ————.
4. Margaret Katherine Sandy, b ————. No. 531¼
5. Wilda Rosemary Sandy, b. ————.
6. Vernon G. Sandy, b ————.
7. William Leonard Sandy, b ————.

No. 531. Seventh Generation. 530.

1) Myrtle Elizabeth Sandy, b Dec 7, 1906, m Roger Lam Address· Mt Crawford, Va.

1 Lynwood Stanley Lam, b ————————
2 Ralph Sandy Lam, b ————————
4. Herbert Raleigh Lam, b ————————
3. Marvin Lee Lam, b. ————————.
5 Hazel Katherine Lam, b ————————

No. 531¼. Seventh Generation. 530.

4) Margaret Katherine Sandy, b ————————, m Ralph Gerald Sayre. Address: Mt. Crawford, Va

No. 532. Sixth Generation. 528.

3) Charles E. Tutwiler, b Jan 10, 1887, m Mabel Bowers, b ————————. Address· Harrisonburg, Va.

1 Charles Tutwiler, Jr., b ————————

No. 533. Sixth Generation. 528.

4) Florence L. Tutwiler, b. Aug 18, 1889, d at Oxford, N C, m Leonard Meyers, b. ———————— Address Oxford, N. C.

1 John Albert Meyers, b. ————————.

No. 534. Sixth Generation. 528.

5) Luther A Tutwiler, b Oct 2, 1893, m Blanche Dilliad Address Dayton, O

1. Bertha Pauline Tutwiler, b ————————.

No. 535. Fifth Generation. 231.

4) Margaret Heatwole, b April 27, 1862, near Pleasant Valley, Va, m. Rev. Silas D. Skelton, May 25, 1882 He was born Oct. 21, 1860 He was ordained to the ministry of the United Brethren Church in 1885 His preparation was received at the Shenandoah Institute at Dayton, Va He has been active in the ministry until the time that he was eligible to become retired Mr. Skelton made a tour of Europe about the year 1907 Mrs Skelton died Sept. 7, 1931, and was buried in the family cemetery at Berkley Springs, W. Va.

1 Pearl E Skelton, b Aug 14, 1883 No 536
2. Lule E Skelton, b. Feb 14, 1885, d. Mar. 14, 1885
3. Elbert E. Skelton, b Oct. 8, 1886, twin No. 537
4. Elsie A. Skelton, b Oct. 8, 1886, twin. No 538.
5. George W. Skelton, b Sept 30, 1889. No 539.
6 Annie M. Skelton, b. Mar 24, 1892, d. April 25, 1893
7. Harry A. Skelton, b. Feb 25, 1896 No 540

No. 536. Sixth Generation. 535.

1) Pearl E. Skelton, b Aug. 14, 1883, m July 2, 1906, Elmer H Haddox, b Oct. 13, 1881 Address: Berkley Springs, W. Va

1. Evelyn Catherine Haddox, b Aug. 8, 1908
2. Mary Frances Haddox, b July 17, 1915
3. Ruth Virginia Haddox, b Mar 19, 1917
4. Margaret Elizabeth Haddox, b Mar 1, 1923

No. 537. Sixth Generation. 535.

3) Elbert A Skelton, b. Oct 8, 1886, m June 16, 1909, Ella May Hisey Address. Front Royal, Va.

1 Maxwell Earl Skelton, b June 19, 1913

No. 538. Sixth Generation. 535.

4) Elsie A. Skelton, b Oct 8, 1886 (twin), m Mar. 14, 1912, Oscar David Louderback. Address: Winchester, Va

1 Wilda Eloise Louderback, b Sept. 21, 1913, d June 7, 1916.
2 Page Gordon Louderback, b. Aug 24, 1915.

No. 539. Sixth Generation. 535.

5) George W. Skelton, b. Sept. 30, 1889, m. Jessie Hisey, Dec. 20, 1908. Address. Penn Laird, Va

1 Emma Margaret Skelton, b Feb 25, 1910
2. Charles Douglas Skelton, b Feb 19, 1912
3. Jane O'Neill Skelton, b Aug 8, 1917
4. George William Skelton, b Nov. 13, 1920

No. 540. Sixth Generation. 535.

7) Harry A Skelton, b Feb 25, 1896, m. April 1, 1922, Lennis Vaughn Anderson. Address Front Royal, Va
1. Lennis Vaughn Skelton, b April 13, 1923

No. 541. Fifth Generation. 231.

5) John A Heatwole, b. July 12, 1866, near Pleasant Valley, Va. m. July 9, 1891, Leanna Showalter, b —————, in Va She died Oct 24, 1903, and was buried in the Early cemetery in Va He m. Oct. 5, 1916, at Orrville, O , Emma Good His children are all from his first marriage Address: Dalton, O , R. 1. Farmer Mennonites.

1 Ira A Heatwole, b. Nov. 1, 1892. No. 542
2 Isaac N. Heatwole, b. Aug 14, 1894. No 543
3. Irvin P Heatwole, b Oct 13, 1895, d Feb. 4, 1896
4 Ard A. Heatwole, b Feb. 15, 1899, d Jan. 23, 1900.
5 Gabriel H. Heatwole, b. Nov. 13, 1901. No. 544.

No. 542. Sixth Generation. 541.

1) Ira A. Heatwole, b Nov. 1, 1892, m Feb. 3, 1925, Anna Wenger, b. Jan. 9, 1894 Address: Harrisonburg, Va., R 5 Farmer. Mennonite.
1 John Vinson Heatwole, b Jan. 22, 1926.

No. 543. Sixth Generation. 541.

2) Isaac Nelson Heatwole, b. Aug 14, 1894 in Va., m. Nov. 2, 1922, May Beery, b. Feb 17, 1898 at the same place Address: Dayton, Va. Mennonites.

No. 544. Sixth Generation. 541.

5) Gabriel H Heatwole, b. Nov. 13, 1901, in Va , m Dec. 25, 1930 at Orrville, O., Ida Horst. She died Oct 9, 1931 Buried in the Martins cemetery near Orrville, O He m. (2nd) Mar. 23, 1933, Ada E Eberly, b. May 29, 1902 of Orrville, O Address: Dalton, O
1 Child stillborn.

(From second union)
2. Paul David Heatwole, b. June 24, 1934.
3. Mary Leana Heatwole, b. Aug. 24, 1935, d. Sept. 6, 1937.
4. Bertha Mae Heatwole, b. May 2, 1937.
5. Melvin Jay Heatwole, b Jan 2, 1939, triplet, d. Jan. 9, 1939.
6. Alvin Ray Heatwole, b Jan. 2, 1939, triplet, d Jan. 9, 1939.
7. Myron Ralph Heatwole, b. Jan. 2, 1939, triplet.

No. 545. Fifth Generation. 231.

6) Charles E. Heatwole, b. Mar. 26, 1874, near Pleasant Valley, Va., m. Fannie Belle Linaweaver, Dec. 24, 1893 She was born Sept. 24, 1875, in Va., d. Feb. 12, 1916, in Ohio. Charles m. (2nd) Magdalena Zimmerman, b. Nov 1, 1881, in Ind. Farmer. Mennonites.

(From first companion)
1. Elva Heatwole, b. Dec. 19, 1894. No. 546.
2. Vernie Heatwole, b June 13, 1896. No. 547.
3. Robert Heatwole, b. Oct 22, 1902, located in Orrville, O
   (From second wife)
4. Mark Heatwole, b Aug. 1, 1921.

Charles E. Heatwole died Apr. 7, 1937. He and his first wife are buried in the St Michael Lutheran cemetery near Marshallville, O.

No. 546. Sixth Generation. 545.

1) Elva Heatwole, b Dec 19, 1894, in Va, m. Guy Lang, b Sept 23, 1894 Address· Massillon, O.
1 Guy Lang, Jr., b. June 17, 1918

No. 547. Sixth Generation. 545.

2) Vernie Heatwole, b. June 13, 1896, in Va, m. Dent Stephon, b. Mar 18, 1892. Address: Orrville, O
1. Olen E. Stephon, b. Sept 7, 1917
2. Leonard W. Stephon, b. Feb. 4, 1924

No. 548. Fifth Generation. 231.

7) Sallie S. Heatwole, b Jan. 27, 1878, near Pleasant Valley, Va, m Dec 22, 1895, Noah H. Brenneman, of Elida, O, b July 20, 1873 Farmer Mennonites Address· Elida, O
1. Earl L. Brenneman, b Mar 22, 1898 No. 549
2. Ada V. Brenneman, b. Sept. 1, 1899. No 550.
3. Clarence Brenneman, b. Sept. 13, 1901 No. 551
4. Horace O. Brenneman, b. Feb 8, 1904. No 552.

No. 549. Sixth Generation. 548.

1) Earl L. Brenneman, b. Mar. 22, 1898, near Elida, O., m Aug 9, 1919, Viola Moore, b Nov. 5, 1892. Address. Lima, O, R 4 Mennonites Laborer
1. Ray Laverne Brenneman, b May 13, 1920.
2. Mayson Jay Brenneman, b Oct 26, 1925, triplet.
3. Malba Fae Brenneman, b. Oct 26, 1925, triplet.
4. Margaret May Brenneman, b Oct. 26, 1925, triplet. d Nov 2. 1929
5 Norma Louise Brenneman, b Nov 2, 1929.

No. 550. Sixth Generation. 548.

2) Ada V. Brenneman, b Sept. 1, 1899, near Elida, O, m Ira L Kriswell, b Feb 3, 1890, in Va, m Dec 21, 1916 Address. Cleveland, O Guard at state hospital.
1 George Robert Crisswell, b Jan 17, 1924.

No. 551. Sixth Generation. 548.

3) Clarence Brenneman, b Sept. 13, 1901, near Elida, O, m April 17, 1926, Mildred Seifred, b Feb. 7, 1907 Address Lima, O Works at Lima locomotive works.
1. Lula May Brenneman, b. Jan. 13, 1929.
2. Leonard Lee Brenneman, b. July 13, 1930.

No. 552. Sixth Generation. 548.

4) Horace Q. Brenneman, b Feb. 8, 1904, near Elida, O., m Nov. 11, 1928, Mildred Miller, b. Jan. 19, 1904. Address Cleveland, O Mechanical drawing.

No. 553. Fifth Generation. 232.

1) John Henry Rhodes, b June 16, 1869, in Va., m. Nov. 18, 1897, Emma Sarah Martin, b. April 8, 1870 Address. Rockingham, Va. Mennonites
1 David Michael Rhodes, b Sept 29, 1899. No. 554.
2 Mary Rebecca Rhodes, b. Sept 21, 1904. No 555.

No. 554. Sixth Generation. 553.

1) David Michael Rhodes, b Sept. 29, 1899, in Va., m. Nov. 16, 1920, Naomi Ruth Koogler, b. Oct. 18, 1900. Address Rockingham, Va. Farmer. Mennonite.
1. Frances Priscilla Rhodes, b. Aug 18, 1921.
2. Catherine Rebecca Rhodes, b Jan 16, 1924.
3. Ruth Rosella Rhodes, b Nov. 5, 1925.
4. John Irvin Rhodes, b. May 3, 1927
5. Noah Leland Rhodes, b. Feb 9, 1929.
6 Aaron Martin Rhodes, b Dec 15, 1930
7 Joseph Owen Rhodes, b April 24, 1932
8. Anna Sarah Rhodes, b. Oct. 5, 1933
9. Martha Naomi Rhodes, b Jan 14, 1935
10 Esther Elizabeth Rhodes, b May 1, 1936.

No. 555. Sixth Generation. 553.

2) Mary Rebecca Rhodes, b Sept 21, 1904, in Va., m. Sept 1, 1931, Roy DeWitt Burkholder, b. Feb 4, 1908. Address: Pleasant Valley, Va. Farmer.
1. Roy DeWitt Burkholder, Jr., b Aug. 21, 1933.
2 Oliver Ansel Burkholder, b. May 13, 1935.

No. 556. Fifth Generation. 232.

2) Mary F. Rhodes, b April 15, 1871, in Va , m Henry Edward Heatwole, b. Aug. 23, 1870. He was an architect with the Fravel Sash and Door Co., of Harrisonburg, Va. Mennonite. Address Harrisonburg, Va.
1. Dessie May Heatwole, b. July 18, 1896 No. 557.
2. Fanny B Heatwole, b. Jan. 4, 1899 No. 558.
3 Hazel M Heatwole, b. May 7, 1906 No. 559.

No. 557. Sixth Generation. 556.

1) Dessie May Heatwole, b July 18, 1896, in Va , m. Aug. 23, 1917, R R. Linhaus, b. Dec. 13, 1894. Address Dayton, Va.
1. Eveline Arline Linhaus, b. Oct. 3, 1918
2 Richard Lee Linhaus, b Nov. 24, 1922

No. 558. Sixth Generation. 556.

2) Fannie B. Heatwole, b Jan. 4, 1899, in Va , m June 7, 1921, Michael Showalter, b May 14, 1899. Address. Dayton, Va.
1 Edward H Showalter, b. June 2, 1922.
2 Marvin H. Showalter, b. Nov. 3, 1923.
3. Harry Showalter, b. Mar. 13, 1925, twin
4. Harold Showalter, b Mar. 13, 1925, twin.
5 Daniel P. Showalter, b April 22, 1927
6. Mary F. Showalter, b July 29, 1928
7. Michael R. Showalter, Jr , b. May 19, 1930, d Feb 1, 1931
8 John H. Showalter, b. Aug. 8, 1931

9. William H. Showalter, b. May 5, 1933.
10. Margaret E. Showalter, b Jan. 18, 1935.
11. Eunice M. Showalter, b. Oct. 25, 1936.

No. 559. Sixth Generation. 556.
3) Hazel M Heatwole, b May 7, 1906, in Va., m Jan 26, 1926, Paul E. Wenger, b Oct 8, 1904. Address: Harrisonburg, Va
1. Harry H Wenger, b Dec 3, 1927.
2 Raymond D. Wenger, b. Mar 5, 1930
3. Marion E. Wenger, b July 29, 1932
4. Arlene F. Wenger, b. Nov. 4, 1935.

No. 560. Fifth Generation. 233.
2) Elizabeth Frances Wenger, b Aug 15, 1870, in Va, m Albert Hemp They live in South Dakota and have two children.

No. 561. Fifth Generation. 233.
3) Sarah Luella Wenger, b Feb. 22, 1872, in Va, m Albert Long, b. ——————; married (2nd) ———— Cook. They live in South Dakota and have two children from first union and three children from second union.

No. 562. Fifth Generation. 233.
4) Rhodes Solomon Wenger, b Feb 8, 1874, in Va, m ——————

No. 563. Fifth Generation. 233.
5) Marvin Cleophas Wenger, b. April 6, 1876, in Va., m ——————

No. 564. Fifth Generation. 234.
1) Samuel Rhodes, b ——————, m. Mary Ella Yeakel, b. ——————. Address· Weyers Cave, Va. Barber.
1 Lottie May Rhodes, b ——————, m James Bennington.
2. Harry Rhodes, b ——————, single
3. Pearl Rhodes, b ——————, m Allen Mappan
4. May Rhodes, b ——————, m Hammit Mappan

No. 565. Fifth Generation. 234.
2) Sudie Rhodes, b ——————, m Peter Hanger, b. ——————. Address: Weyers Cave, Va. Bricklayer and plasterer
1. Edgar Hanger, b. ——————, m. Lucele Van Pelt
2. Margie Hanger, b ——————, m. Olin Davis.
3. Minor Hanger, b. ——————, m. Louise Davis
4. Ceciel Hanger, b ——————, m Olga Davis.
5. Leola Hanger, b ——————, m Reguald Parter
6. Mildred Hanger, b ——————
7. Marie Hanger, b. ——————.

No. 566. Fifth Generation. 234.
4) Mary Gertrude Rhodes, b ——————, 1877, d. May 20, 1921, m Lester E Holmes, b ——————. Bureau of Engraving, Washington, D C, which was their address. Burial at Spades cemetery
1. Perry Watson Holmes, b ——————, m Anna ——————. One child, Shirley Ann Holmes, b ——————

No. 567. Fifth Generation. 234.
5) Bessie Rhodes, b ——————, m. Nolan E Kemper, b. ——————. Attendant in Washington, D C, hospital. Burial at Spades cemetery.
1. Viola Catherine Kemper, b ——————, m. George D. Wetzel.

No. 568. Fifth Generation. 234.

3) John E. Rhodes, b ——————, m. Hassie Mines, b. ——————.
Farmer at North River, Va Burial lot at Spades cemetery No children.

No. 569. Fifth Generation. 234.

6) Alice Rhodes, b ——————, m Samuel Eaton, b ——————. Address: Harrisonburg, Va. Buyer of furs U. B. Church. Burial at Spades cemetery.
1. Melvin Eaton, b ——————, m Elsie Davis.
2. Russell Eaton, b ——————, m. Edna Cliff.
3 Pauline Eaton, b ——————, m Charles Morrison.

No. 570. Fifth Generation. 234.

7) Frederick A. Rhodes, b Feb 23, 1887, in Va, m May 12, 1914, Malnua White, b. July 26, 1891. Burial plot at Spades cemetery Barber. U. B. Church. Address: Rockingham, Va.
1. Elizabeth Amanda Rhodes, b Oct. 14, 1916
2. Doris Louise Rhodes, b. Dec. 27, 1924.
3. Evelyn Lucele Rhodes, b Sept 1, 1927.
4 Frederick A Rhodes, Jr, b. June 17, 1929.

No. 571. Fifth Generation. 234.

8) Glen Rhodes, b. ——————, m. Lillian Smith, b ——————, d. ——————, m. Ruth Baugher, b ——————. Employe at Navy Yard, Washington, D. C.
1. Vincent Rhodes, b ——————
2. Robert Rhodes, b ——————
3. Bernard Rhodes, b ——————
4 Virginia Rhodes, b ——————
(From second marriage)
5 Dorothy Rhodes, b ——————

No. 571½. Fifth Generation. 234.

9) Howard E. Rhodes, b. ——————, m (1st) Pearl Saylor, b ——————, d. ——————; m. (2nd) Daisy Williams, b. ——————. Employe at Navy Yard, machinist, Washington, D. C. Address: Cedar Hill, Washington, D C. Burial at Spades cemetery
1. Elmer Rhodes, b. ——————
(From second wife)
2. Shirley Rhodes, b. ——————.
3. Nancy Lee Rhodes, b. ——————

No. 572. Fifth Generation. 235.

1) Edward Pence, b. ——————, 1871, in Rockingham Co., Va, m. Cora Early, b. ——————. Lives in Harrisonburg, Va
1 Olive Pence, b ——————.

No. 573. Fifth Generation. 236.

1) Annie M. Heatwole, b. April 24, 1850, in Va., m. Frank Jones, b. Feb. 23, 1855. Address: Hinton, Va Farmer. She was a Mennonite and he was a U. B.
1. Fannie M Jones, b. Mar. 29, 1874. No. 774.
2. Minnie S. Jones, b Feb. 21, 1876 No. 775.
3. Leonard H Jones, b. Sept 2, 1877 No. 576.
4. John D. Jones, b Nov 21, 1879. No 577.
5. Mattie F. Jones, b. July 22, 1882 No 578
6. Etta M Jones, b. July 29, 1885 No. 579

7 Josie E. Jones, b Nov 18, 1891 No 580
8. Annie Jones, b. Feb 15, 1894. No 581.

No. 574. Sixth Generation. 573.
1) Fannie M Jones, b. Mar 29, 1874, near Hinton, Va., m June 14, 1896, Lewis Good, b Sept 15, 1875, in Va They live on his father's homestead at Mole Hill. Address Dayton, Va Mennonites Farmer and minister.
1 Grace Larue Good, b Mar. 22, 1897 No. 3454
2. Frank Rush Good, b. Dec. 16, 1899 No. 3455
3 Oliver Lewis Good, b Nov 25, 1903 No 3456.
4. Josie Irene Good, b Oct. 7, 1907 No. 3457.
5 Marion Samuel Good, b Feb 27, 1913 No 3458.

No. 575. Sixth Generation. 573.
2) Minnie S Jones, b Feb 21, 1876, in Va , m Mar 15, 1896, Amos Knisely, b Aug 17, 1872 Address. Hinton, Va Farmer. Mennonites
1. Tracy P. Knisely, b. Sept 10, 1898.
2. Louetta J. Knisely, b. May 5, 1900 No 3459.
3 DeWitt P. Knisely, b Aug. 15, 1902 No 3460
4. Leonard F Knisely, b Dec 13, 1904 No 3461
5. Lewis S. Knisely, b Aug 28, 1907 No. 3462
6 John R Knisely, b. Sept 18, 1909 No 3463.
7 Sallie M Knisely, b Aug. 6, 1913

No. 576. Sixth Generation. 573.
3) Leonard H. Jones, b. Sept 2, 1877, near Hinton, Va , m Sept 25, 1901, Lena Weaver, b Sept 24, 1883 Address Dale Enterprise, Va Farmer and minister. Mennonite Burial place at Weavers Church
1 Irene M Jones, b Aug. 12, 1902. No 3464
2 Edna R Jones, b. Sept 2, 1906 No 3465
3 Vada A Jones, b Aug. 14, 1909 No 3466
4 Virginia W. Jones, b June 20, 1921

No. 577. Sixth Generation. 573.
4) John D. Jones, b. Nov 21, 1882, near Hinton, Va , m Apr 24, 1907, Maude Hahn Address Hinton, Va. Farmer U B. Church

No. 578. Sixth Generation. 573.
5) Mattie F. Jones, b. July 22, 1882, near Hinton, Va m. Dec 27, 1906, Lewis J Rhodes, b Oct. 14, 1883. Address Dayton, Va Farmer. Mennonites
1 Alma M. Rhodes, b Dec 12, 1909 No. 3467.
2. Reuben F. Rhodes, b. July 14, 1913 No 3468
3 Warren J. Rhodes, b May 12, 1916
4. Lester P Rhodes, b Mar. 9, 1922, d. same day
5 Marion L. Rhodes, b. Dec 18, 1924.
6. Joseph D. Rhodes, b May 22, 1928

No. 579. Sixth Generation. 573.
6) Mary Etta Jones, b July 29, 1885, near Hinton, Va , m. Aug. 15, 1907, Daniel K Knisely, b. May 17, 1885 Farmer and undertaker Mennonites Burial at Pleasant View, Va. Address· Dayton, Va.
1 Pauline F. Knisely, b Jan 29, 1908 No 579¼
2. A. Marie Knisely, b. Oct. 15, 1909 No. 579½
3. Marvin J. Knisely, b. June 18, 1912.
4. Ethel G. Knisely, b. May 5, 1914.
5 Alice R. Knisely, b Apr 30, 1916, d Jan 31, 1920.

6. Reba C. Knisely, b. Jan. 31, 1918.
7 David F. Knisely, b Nov. 15, 1919.
8. Martha R. Knisely, b. Dec 31, 1920
9 Blanche V Knisely, b. Mar. 5, 1923.
10 Amos D. Knisely, b. June 25, 1925.
11 Louella J Knisely, b Nov 13, 1926
12 Howard E. Knisely, b Feb 13, 1931.

No. 579¼. Seventh Generation. 579.

1) Pauline F. Knisely, b Jan 29, 1908, m. Feb. 1, 1934, Amos Henry Horst, b May 7, 1908
    1 Joseph K. Horst, b Nov 12, 1934, d same day
    2 Ruth Elizabeth Horst, b Dec 15, 1935.

No. 579½. Seventh Generation. 579.

2) A. Marie Knisely, b Oct 15, 1909, m. Dec 4, 1930, Frank I. Rohrer, b Feb 14, 1905.
    1. Esther R. Rohrer, b Sept 2, 1931
    2 Paul D Rohrer, b Sept 11, 1932
    3 Lua M Rohrer, b. Sept 30, 1933
    4 Mattie L. Rohrer, b. Feb 4, 1935

No. 580. Sixth Generation. 573.

7) Josie E Jones, b Nov. 18, 1891, near Hinton, Va , m Dec. 31, 1912, Amos D Rohrer, b. Mar 22, 1892 Address Dayton, Va.
    1 Eva M Rohrer, b. June 11, 1914
    2 Blanche E Rohrer, b Feb 21, 1916
    3 Ruth V Rohrer, b Mar 24, 1917.
    4 Emory J Rohrer, b Sept. 17, 1918
    5 Anna C Rohrer, b July 31, 1920
    6 Mary F Rohrer, b June 5, 1922
    7. Naomi R Rohrer, b Sept 8, 1924
    8 Josie E Rohrer, b Feb 18, 1927
    9. Frederick H Rohrer, b June 30, 1928
    10 Lydia M Rohrer, b Aug 9, 1931
    11. Samuel R Rohrer, b Nov 9, 1934
    12 Hubert D Rohrer, b Oct 15, 1936

No. 581. Sixth Generation. 573.

8) Annie Elizabeth Jones, b Feb 15, 1894, in Va, m June 21, 1913, William Rhodes Rohrer, b April 19, 1894. Address Dayton, Va.
    1. Ruby Louise Rohrer, b. Sept 28, 1913 No. 581¼.
    2 Anna Evangeline Rohrer. b Oct 4, 1914
    3. Gilbert Jones Rohrer, b May 22, 1917
    4 Hazel Chaelena Rohrer, b July 6, 1919
    5. Frank William Rohrer, b July 8, 1921
    6 Grace Magdalena Rohrer, b Sept 13, 1923
    7 Alice Elizabeth Rohrer, b July 17, 1925
    8 Joseph Israel Rohrer, b Sept 23, 1927
    9. Ethel Marie Rohrer, b Sept 5, 1929
    10 Mary Evelyn Rohrer, b Dec 21, 1931
    11 Daniel Henry Rohrer, b Jan 13, 1934
    12 Annie Virginia Rohrer, b Dec 5, 1935

No. 581¼. Seventh Generation. 581.

1) Ruby Louise Rohrer, b Sept 28, 1913, in Va, m. Nov 15, 1934, Paul Titus Martin, b. Sept 12, 1910 Address New Holland, Pa.

1 Louise Virginia Martin, b Oct 3, 1936

No. 582. Fifth Generation. 236.

2) Simeon H Heatwole, b Nov 5, 1857, in Rockingham Co., Va., m. Nov. 29, 1876, Luella Showalter, b April 22, 1858, d July 26, 1892. Address Hinton, Va. Carpenter. United Brethren

1. Myrtle O. Heatwole, b Mar. 6, 1879
2. Infant son, b. Jan. 7, 1881, lived two days.
3. Roy S Heatwole, b. Sept. 28, 1882 No 583
4 E Walker Heatwole, b Sept 10, 1884
5. Isie Dorah Heatwole, b. Nov 26, 1886
6 Houck P. Heatwole, b. Dec. 1, 1891

Simeon married (2nd) Laura M. Zirkle Dec 26, 1895, born Oct 1, 1873

No. 583. Sixth Generation. 582.

3) Roy S Heatwole, b Sept. 28, 1882, near Hinton, Va, m April 3, 1907, Naoma Payne, of Harrisonburg, Va Address Roanoke, Va. Mechanic. United Brethren

No. 584. Fifth Generation. 236.

4) Mary E Heatwole, b Mar. 28, 1856, in Va., m Caleb W. Burkholder, Nov. 30, 1876. He was born Aug 7, 1857, and died Dec. 10, 1891 He was on a load of hay when the team ran away and he was thrown violently off the load to the ground receiving injuries from which he soon died Address: Harrisonburg, Va. Farmer. Mennonite.

1. Minnie M. Burkholder, b May 7, 1878 No 585
2. Effie A Burkholder, b Aug 8, 1879 No. 586
3 Oliver A. Burkholder, b June 16, 1884 No. 587
4 Andrew L Burkholder, b Nov. 30, 1889. No 3272

No. 585. Sixth Generation. 584.

1) Minnie M Burkholder, b May 7, 1878, near Harrisonburg, Va, m Oct. 20, 1906, Jacob Kiser, as his second wife He was born Feb 20, 1864, and died Dec. 3, 1931. Address Lily, Va Farmer. Mennonites No issue.

No. 586. Sixth Generation. 584.

2) Effie A. Burkholder, b Aug 8, 1879, near Harrisonburg, Va, m Nov. 28, 1899, Perry Robert Cline, b. Sept 20, 1872, d Jan. 21, 1935 Address· Harrisonburg, Va. Farmer. Mennonite and Presbyterian

1. Russell DeWitt Cline, b July 7, 1902 No. 3266
2. Emery Turner Cline, b. June 25, 1904 No 3267.
3. Mary Pearl Cline, b. May 28, 1908
4. Franklin Davis Cline, b Jan 24, 1915
5. Edward Marshall Cline, b Feb 9, 1919

No. 587. Sixth Generation. 584.

3) Oliver Atlee Burkholder, b June 16, 1884, d July 21, 1937, near Harrisonburg, Va, m Feb 20, 1907, Anna Grace Showalter, b Oct 18, 1884. She was daughter of Daniel P and Hettie E (Rohrer) Showalter Address· Dayton, Va. Farmer Mennonite

1 Roy DeWitt Burkholder, b Jan 24, 1908 No 3268
2. John Samuel Burkholder, b July 13, 1909 No 3269
3. Esther Larue Burkholder, b Mar 12, 1911 No 3270

4 Daniel Showalter Burkholder, b Dec 5, 1912
5. Paul Marvin Burkholder, b Jan. 5, 1915. No. 3271
6 Mary Elizabeth Burkholder, b Mar 20, 1917.
7. Nellie Grace Burkholder, b Feb. 20, 1919
8. Henry Lawrence Burkholder, b Jan 8, 1921
9. Frances Orpha Burkholder, b Dec 1, 1923.

No. 588. Fifth Generation. 236.

5) Johnathan B Heatwole, b. Aug 6, 1858, in Rockingham Co, Va., m. July 15, 1880, Lydia A. Rhodes Address. Dayton, Va Machinist. United Brethren.
1. Irvin O. Heatwole, b Sept 27, 1882
2. Franklin P Heatwole, b. Sept. 14, 1884
3. Ellis J Heatwole, b Nov 23, 1886.
4. Victor P. Heatwole, b June 7, 1889
5. Luther E. Heatwole, b July 15, 1892
6 Lula O Heatwole, b July 21, 1894
7. Kirkley R Heatwole, b Sept 6, 1896

No. 589. Fifth Generation. 236.

6) Peter R. Heatwole, b April 25, 1860, in Rockingham Co., Va., m. Jan. 25, 1894, Clara E. Simmers, b May 11, 1873 Address Hinton, Va. Farmer.
1 Howard Heatwole, b. Oct. 19, 1895
2. Samuel O Heatwole, b April 6, 1900, twin
3. Katherine E. Heatwole, b April 6, 1900, twin
4. Frank D. Heatwole, b Feb 14, 1905.

No. 590. Fifth Generation. 236.

7) Conrad S Heatwole, b Aug. 29, 1862, in Rockingham Co, Va, m. Jan. 17, 1889, Virginia Annie Rhodes, b Dec 3, 1865 Address· Dayton, Va Farmer. Mennonite.
1. Larue Z Heatwole, b Jan 20, 1890 No 591

No. 591. Sixth Generation. 590.

1) Larue Z. Heatwole, b Jan 20, 1890, in Rockingham Co, Va., m. Mar 3, 1909, Israel Showalter, of Va Address Dayton, Va Farmer. Mennonite.
1. Howard Showalter, b Mar 2, 1912
2. Warren Showalter, b Feb 28, 1913
3. Joseph Showalter, b Sept. 10, 1919
4. Claud Showalter, b April 16, 1920
5 Mark Showalter, b Sept 19, 1922
6. Mahlan Showalter, b Nov 7, 1923
7. Annice Showalter, b. Dec 17, 1925

No. 592. Fifth Generation. 236.

8) DeWitt A. Heatwole, b Nov 12, 1865, in Rockingham Co, Va, m. Dec. 17, 1889, Minnie L Brooks, b Mar 16, 1868 Address Staunton, Va. Miller Presbyterians No issue He died in California in 1936

No. 593. Fifth Generation. 236.

9) Elizabeth Heatwole, b Nov 24, 1869, in Rockingham Co, Va, m. Jacob Kiser as his first wife She died in the hospital at Richmond, Va.
1. Stella Kiser, b Nov. 18, 1889

No. 594. Fifth Generation. 240.

3) Rebecca Ann Rhodes, b Dec 4, 1867, in Va, m Dec. 25, 1889, Joseph G. Beery, b. Mar. 8, 1866 Address: Dayton, Va Farmer Mennonites.

1. Mary Florence Beery, b Oct 15, 1890. No. 1103.
2. Ward Edward Beery, b Jan. 13, 1892. No 1104.
3. Frank Henry Beery, b May 21, 1895. No. 1105.
4. Walter Rhodes Beery, b Aug 25, 1899 No 1106
5. Ada Catherine Beery, b. Feb. 14, 1904, single.

No. 595. Fifth Generation. 240.

4) Mary Agnes Rhodes, b May 23, 1870, in Va She died Jan. 4, 1936, m Sept. 2, 1897, John Albert Zepp He died Feb 25, 1925 Address Hinton, Va Lutherans
1. Ernest F G. Zepp, b Sept 17, 1899, killed by a wagon June 8, 1910
2. Bessie E. Zepp, b July 5, 1902 No 2150
3. Nellie Agnes Zepp, b Nov 23, 1905 No 2151

No. 596. Fifth Generation. 240.

5) William Edward Rhodes, b Mar 25, 1873, in Va, d Aug 27, 1913, m Feb. 11, 1900, Vesta V. Spitzer, b. Sept. 18, 1876 Mr Rhodes died of blood poison Mennonites. Address Hinton, Va Painter and paperhanger.
1. Percy S. Rhodes, b May 18, 1900 No 2152.
2. Vada M. Rhodes, b. Dec 19, 1902, single.
3 Harley E. Rhodes, b Dec. 2, 1907. No 2153.

No. 597. Fifth Generation. 240.

6) Alfred Henry Rhodes, b Aug 26, 1875, in Va., m Sept. 15, 1897, Mary M. Lahman, b Nov 24, 1878 Address Dayton, Va Farmer On April 9. 1913, they moved to Columbiana, O
1. Mary Naomi Rhodes, b. Mar. 16, 1899 No 2154
2 Minnie Susan Rhodes, b May 24. 1901 No 2155
3. Annie Catherine Rhodes, b Mar. 1, 1903 No. 2156
4. Fannie Rebecca Rhodes, b June 25, 1906 No 2157.
5 Jacob Henry Rhodes, b. Oct 5, 1908, d Apr, 1913.
6 Joseph Daniel Rhodes, b May 20, 1911, d April 13, 1919
7. Sarah Virginia Rhodes, b. May 10. 1916
8 John Reuben Rhodes, b July 18, 1918
9 Hannah Elizabeth Rhodes, b Aug 29, 1922
Jacob and Joseph died of scarlet fever and measles soon after their arrival to Ohio

No. 598. Fifth Generation. 241.

1) Mary E. Rhodes, b April 2, 1851, near Dale Enterprise, Va. April 11, 1872, she married Samuel M Burkholder. He was born near Harrisonburg, Va., May 16, 1849. He died July 5, 1929 He was a well-to-do farmer in the Shenandoah Valley of Va He was an active worker in the Mennonite Church, of which he was a deacon He was also much interested in family history Address· Dale Enterprise, Va.
1. Aldine C Burkholder, b April 2, 1873 No 599.
2. Walter C Burkholder, b Nov 20, 1875. No 600
3. Ada F. Burkholder, b Dec 13, 1877 No 601.
4 Ellis W. Burkholder, b July 3, 1880 No 603.
5 Lillie A. Burkholder, b April 27, 1883 No 605

No. 599. Sixth Generation. 598.

1) Aldine C Burkholder, b April 2, 1873, in Rockingham Co, Va., m Annie Mae Blanks, b Nov 3, 1889 Residence San Marcus, Tex Presbyterians Teacher.

1. Helen Burkholder, b April 13, 1910.
2. Aldine C. Burkholder, Jr., b June 25, 1920.

No. 600. Sixth Generation. 598.

2) Walter O. Burkholder, b. Nov 20, 1875, near Dale Enterprise, Va., m. Anna Belle Fulk, b. Apr. 25, 1883. They were married Feb 1, 1911. Address: Dale Enterprise, Va. Farmer. Mennonites.
1. Hazel E. Burkholder, b Jan 26, 1914.
2. Warren S. Burkholder, b. Sept. 7, 1918.
3. Walter O Burkholder, Jr , b. Aug 7, 1920, d Oct. 5, 1920.
4. Vivian C. Burkholder, b Jan 22, 1923.

No. 601. Sixth Generation. 593.

3) Ada F. Burkholder, b Dec 13, 1877, near Dale Enterprise, Va , m Dec. 20, 1900, John S. Click, b July 6, 1879 Address: Bridgewater, Va. Rural mail carrier. Presbyterians
1. Clara C. Click, b Mar. 4, 1902. No. 602.
2. Frank B Click, b Aug 2, 1912. No. 601½.

No. 601½. Seventh Generation. 601.

2) Frank B. Click, b Aug. 2, 1912, in Rockingham Co., Va , m. Evelyn Randolph. Address: Staunton, Va.

No. 602. Seventh Generation. 601.

1) Clara C. Click, b. Mar 4, 1902, in Rockingham Co , Va., m. Jan 9, 1920, Ernest L. O'Roark, b Dec. 2, 1896 She m (2nd) ——————— Lookritis.
1. Clara V. O'Roark, b Oct. 8, 1921
2 Ernest O'Roark, Jr , b. May 22, 1925.
3. Florence Lookritis, b. ——————

No. 603. Sixth Generation. 598.

4) Ellis W. Burkholder, b July 3, 1880, near Dale Enterprise, Va., m Mar. 25, 1902, Alice V. Heatwole, b. Dec. 6, 1883. Address· Dale Enterprise, Va. Orchardist and farmer Mennonite.
1. Raymond A Burkholder, b May 21, 1903. No. 604.
2. Harry W. Burkholder, b Nov 23, 1912
3 Mary G. Burkholder, b Oct. 4, 1914.

No. 604. Seventh Generation. 603.

1) Raymond A Burkholder, b May 21, 1903, near Dale Enterprise, Va., m. July 22, 1925, Elizabeth M Smith, b May 17, 1907 Address: Dale Enterprise, Va. Mechanic Presbyterians.
1. Lloyd H Burkholder, b. Jan. 25, 1927.
2. Yonne Elizabeth Burkholder, b July 4, 1928
3. Nancy Mary Burkholder, b ——————.
4. Joyce Burkholder, b ——————

No. 605. Sixth Generation. 598.

5) Lillie A. Burkholder, b. April 27, 1883, near Dale Enterprise, Va , m. Jan. 1, 1908, Simeon Brenneman, b Mar 4, 1879, near Elida, O. Farmer Mennonites Address: Elida, O., R. 1.
1. Edwin S. Brenneman, b. Dec. 9, 1908
2. Mary Evelyn Brenneman, b Mar. 11, 1913.
3. Robert E. Brenneman, b Jan. 28, 1915.

No. 606. Fifth Generation. 241.

5) Rebecca C. Rhodes, b. Feb. 4, 1857, near Dale Enterprise, Va , d July 13, 1922, in Va., m. Oct. 13, 1881, to Perry F. Shank, b Dec 25, 1858, in Rockingham Co. Va. He died June 15, 1927 Farmer. Mennonites Address: Dayton, Va.

1. Elvin M. Shank, b Jan. 1, 1883 No 607.
2 William J. Shank, b Nov. 21, 1884. No. 608.
3. Amos D Shank, b Feb 26, 1887 No 609
4. Owen R. Shank, b Feb 4, 1890, d May 13, 1903
5. Ada M. Shank, b June 9, 1894, d Oct 26, 1896
6. Paul T. Shank, b Jan 23, 1897 No 610.

No. 607. Sixth Generation. 606.

1) Elvin M. Shank, b Jan. 1, 1883, at Dayton, Va , m Dec. 31, 1908, Beulah W. Beery, b. Aug 17, 1889 Address· North River, Va Farmer.

1. Ray Franklin Shank, b Dec 27, 1914
2. Harry Wilson Shank, b Oct 9, 1917

No. 608. Sixth Generation. 606.

2) William J Shank, b Nov. 21, 1884, near Dayton, Va , m. Feb. 6, 1908, to Sadie Olive Barnhart, b Dec 4, 1886. Address Dayton, Va. Farmer Mennonites

1 Raymond B. Shank, b Mar 21, 1910
2. Ethel C Shank, b Mar 3, 1920
3. Naomi V Shank, b May 29, 1923

No. 609. Sixth Generation. 606.

3) Amos D. Shank, b Feb 26, 1887, near Dayton, Va , m Dec 29, 1910, Mary E. Beery, b Aug 21, 1890, at Goods Mill, Va . d Oct 14. ——. Address Dayton, Va. Miller and farmer Mennonite.

1. Ruth Virginia Shank, b. June 9, 1912
2 Cecil Daniel Shank, b Dec 14, 1915
3. Mabel Catherine Shank, b Dec. 18, 1916, died same day
4. Owen Edward Shank, b Feb 9, 1918
5 Alma Elizabeth Shank, b Aug. 15, 1919
6 Warren Franklin Shank, b Nov 18, 1920
7. Grace Lucille Shank, b May 5, 1923.
8 Nelson Beery Shank, b July 7, 1926.
9. Hensel Aaron Shank, b April 12, 1928.

No. 610. Sixth Generation. 606.

6) Paul T. Shank, b Jan 23, 1897, near Dayton, Va , m. Aug 27, 1919, to Annie Florence Heatwole, b Jan 3, 1893 Address· Dayton, Va. Farmer. Mennonites

1. Hazel Catherine Shank, b Mar 23, 1921
2. Mark Heatwole Shank, b. July 11, 1922
3. Perry Franklin Shank, b June 11, 1925
4. Mabel Elizabeth Shank, b May 14, 1928

No. 611. Fifth Generation. 241.

6) William H. Rhodes, b Nov 7, 1861, near Dale Enterprise, Va., m July 21, 1891, to Elizabeth E Hartman, b June 7, 1874 Address: Harrisonburg, Va Carpenter. Mennonites.

1. Ward Augustus Rhodes, b. Aug 2, 1892 No 612
2. Peter Alfred Rhodes, b. April 1, 1894, d. May 11, 1902
3. Fannie Belle Rhodes, b Aug 21, 1896 No 613

No. 612. Sixth Generation. 611.

1) Ward Augustus Rhodes, b Aug 2, 1892, near Harrisonburg, Va , m Nov. 11, 1915, Mary Magdalena Hartman, b Mar. 8, 1895. Address Harrisonburg, Va. Salesman for wholesale warehouse. Mennonite

1. Nellie Virginia Rhodes, b May 2, 1918.
2 Frank Edward Rhodes, b. Nov 27, 1919.
3. Elizabeth Margerite Rhodes, b Aug 14, 1922
4. Floyd Jacob Rhodes, b. July 18, 1924.

No. 613. Sixth Generation. 611.

3) Fannie Belle Rhodes, b Aug 21, 1896, near Harrisonburg, Va., m. Mar. 2, 1912, Kent N. Shank, b Jan 1, 1888 Address: Harrisonburg, Va. Farmer and dairyman Mennonite An adopted son, Lloyd DeWitt Shank, b. Sept 18, 1922.

No. 614. Fifth Generation. 241.

7) Lydia Ann Rhodes, b Jan 30, 1864, near Dale Enterprise, Va., m Mar. 4, 1886, to Israel H Rohrer, b Feb 17, 1860, near Leamon place, Lancaster Co., Pa He died at their home near Dayton, Va , Feb 24, 1931, buried near the Pleasant View Church Mennonites

1. Ava Myra Rohrer, b Feb 13, 1887 No 615
2 Henry Warren Rohrer, b Sept 18, 1888 No. 616
3 Maggie Edith Rohrer, b Aug 7, 1890 No 617
4 Amos Daniel Rohrer, b Mar 22, 1892 No 618.
5 William Rhodes Rohrer, b April 19, 1894 No 619.
6 Annie May Rohrer, b Mar 6, 1896 No 620
7 Ella Amelia Rohrer, b Mar 14, 1898. No. 621.
8 John Sanford Rohrer, b Oct 12, 1900 No 622
9 Mary Esther Rohrer, b Jan 26, 1903, single
10 Frank Israel Rohrer, b Feb 14, 1905 No 623
11 Mabel Rebecca Rohrer. b Mar 12, 1908 No 624

No. 615. Sixth Generation. 614.

1) Ava Myra Rohrer. b Feb 13, 1887, near Dayton, Va , m Jan. 14, 1914, to Amos Eberly, b July 30, 1888, near Orrville. O They lived near Orrville until 1926 when they moved to near Dayton, Va Address Dayton, Va.

1 Marion Israel Eberly, b May 17, 1915
2 Edwin Wayne Eberly, b Aug 27, 1917
3 Warren Rohrer Eberly, b Feb 21, 1920
4 Mark Rhodes Eberly, b April 22, 1923
5 Mary Esther Eberly, b Aug 17, 1926

No. 616. Sixth Generation. 614.

2) Henry Warren Rohrer, b Sept 18, 1888, near Dayton, Va , m July 28, 1908, to F Bertie Simmers, b. April 13, 1890 Address Dayton, Va Mennonites She was a daughter of Abraham and Margaret (Rhodes) Simmers

1 Arlene Simmers Rohrer, b Sept 16, 1908 No 625
2. Marvin Daniel Rohrer. b Aug 27, 1912
3 Edith Virginia Rohrer, b Mar 27, 1922
4. Warren Israel Rohrer, b Nov 23, 1926, twin
5 Willie David Rohrer, b Nov 23, 1926, twin

No. 617. Sixth Generation. 614.

3) Maggie Edith Rohrer, b Aug 7, 1890, near Dayton, Va m. Jan 31, 1923, Joseph C Koogler, b Sept , 1894, near Hinton, Va Address: Dayton, Va Mennonites

1 Paul Rohrer Koogler, b Nov 23, 1929

No. 618. Sixth Generation. 614.

4) Amos Daniel Rohrer, b Mar 22, 1892, near Dayton, Va., m Dec 31, 1912, Josie E. Jones, b. Nov. 18, 1891, near Dayton, Va Address· Dayton, Va Mennonites Related, come in two ways; for family refer to No. 580

No. 619. Sixth Generation. 614.

5) William Rhodes Rohrer, b April 19, 1894, near Dayton, Va , m. Annie E. Jones, b. Feb 15, 1894 Address. Dayton, Va. Mennonites. Related, come in two ways; for family reference see No 581

No. 620. Sixth Generation. 614.

6) Anna Mae Rohrer, b Mar 6, 1896, near Dayton, Va , m. Dec 31, 1918, to Paul T. Rhodes, b July 28, 1894, near Dayton, Va. Address. Dayton, Va Mennonites.

1. Miriam Esther Rhodes, b Oct 13, 1919
2. Lydia Virginia Rhodes, b May 20, 1922.
3. Norman Rohrer Rhodes, b Aug. 27, 1924.
4. Melva Rebecca Rhodes, b. Nov 17, 1926
5. Ida Ruth Rhodes, b. Sept. 26, 1928.
6. Frank Reuben Rhodes, b Sept 30, 1930.

No. 621. Sixth Generation. 614.

7) Ella Amelia Rohrer, b. Mar 14, 1898, near Dayton, Va., m. Oct. 16, 1919, Samuel L. Rhodes, b. Jan 27, 1896 Address· Dayton, Va Mennonites.

1. Anna Ruth Rhodes, b. May 14, 1920.
2. Roy Franklin Rhodes, b. June 12, 1922.
3. Wilda Mae Rhodes, b. Jan. 26, 1924.
4 Edwin Rohrer Rhodes, b. Feb 4, 1926
5. Marvin Brunk Rhodes, b Jan 6, 1928
6. Lena Frances Rhodes, b Jan. 15, 1930.
7. Betty Louise Rhodes, b. Jan 8, 1932.

No. 622. Sixth Generation. 614.

8) John Sanford Rohrer, b Oct 12, 1900, near Dayton, Va , m Jan 1, 1924, Zelda N Heatwole, b April 28, 1904, near Dayton, Va. She died suddenly Jan 4, 1931, at their home in Dayton. Buried near the Weavers Church

1. Glen Edwin Rohrer, b Dec 19, 1924
2. John Sanford Rohrer, Jr., b Sept 4, 1927

No. 623. Sixth Generation. 614.

10) Frank Israel Rohrer, b. Feb. 14, 1905, near Dayton, Va , m Dec. 14, 1930, Annie Marie Knisely, b Oct 15, 1909 Address· Dayton, Va Mennonites

1. Esther Rebecca Rohrer, b Sept 2, 1931.

No. 624. Sixth Generation. 614.

11) Mabel Rebecca Rohrer, b Mar 12, 1908, near Dayton, Va , m Feb 15, 1928, Russell D Cline, b. July 7, 1902 They live near Mt Clinton, which is their address Mennonite.

1. Glen Rohrer Cline, b. Aug. 17, 1929
2. Marie Elizabeth Cline, b Mar 2, 1931

No. 625. Seventh Generation. 616.

1) Arline Simmers Rohrer, b Sept. 16, 1908, in Va., m June 2, 1927, Oliver L. Good, b Nov. 25, 1903 Address Dayton, Va Mennonites

1. Eunice Arline Good, b. Mar. 1, 1928

2. Joseph Henry Good, b. Feb 13, 1930.

3. Alice Grace Good, b Jan 30, 1932.

No. 626. Fourth Generation. 22.

1) Henry Shenk, b. June 14, 1817, in Rockingham Co., Va., d. in Allen Co., O., April 19, 1876, m. Susanna Brenneman of Fairfield Co., O She was born Oct. 19, 1818, and died near Knoxville, Tenn., at the home of her daughter, Mrs. Lydia Powell, Oct. 4, 1908. Both were buried in the Salem Cemetery near Elida, O., where they had located in 1860 Their address was Elida, O They were closely related and their descendants will all be recorded under the father's name, as it is a large family.

1. Jacob Shenk, b. June 25, 1841, d Oct. 1, 1842

2. Anna Shenk, b. Aug 4, 1843, d Oct. 5, 1851.

3 Henry Shenk, b Nov. 15, 1845, d June 21, 1847

4. John M. Shenk, b Jan 19, 1848, d Dec 19, 1935 No. 627.

5. Andrew Shenk, b. June 20, 1850 No 644

6 Daniel Shenk, b. Sept. 27, 1853. No. 652.

7. Catherine Shenk, b. Oct 30, 1856. No 664.

8. Lydia Shenk, b April 7, 1859. No 667.

9 Abraham P. Shenk, b Feb 15, 1862 No 670

No. 627. Fifth Generation. 625.

4) John M Shenk, b Jan. 19, 1848, in Fairfield Co., O , d near Elida O., Dec. 19, 1935, m Dec 24, 1868, Frances Good of Elida, b —————, d. Oct. 10, 1917. J. M Shenk was ordained to the ministry at the Salem Church on ————— and to the office of bishop at the same place ————— for the Salem and Pike congregations While in the prime of life he did much traveling and evangelistic work He was a strong leader and had a strong influence over his followers, being possessed with a very devoted and spiritual nature, which made him very successful in his official capacity in the church of which he was a very zealous member He was also possessed with a strong will, which was the means of bringing upon him much grief in his own congregations in his declining years. Both he and his companion are buried in the Pike cemetery near Elida, O , which was his postoffice address.

1. Henry Shenk, b Feb 15, 1870, d. Mar. 16, 1870.

2 Abraham J Shenk, b Oct 23, 1871 No 628.

3. Amos M Shenk, b. Sept 3, 1873 No 629.

4. Simon G Shenk, b. Oct 5, 1875 No 633.

5. Moses B Shenk, b July 15, 1877 No. 637

6. Reuben J Shenk, b June 29, 1879 No. 638

7. John L. Shenk, b Aug. 21, 1881. No 639.

8. Levi J Shenk, b July 18, 1883. No 640

9. Daniel F Shenk, b. Oct 17, 1886 No. 641.

10. Rebecca S. Shenk, b. Oct 6, 1889 No. 642

11 Jacob B Shenk, b. Nov 3, 1892. No. 643

No. 628. Sixth Generation. 627.

2) Abraham J Shenk, b Oct 23, 1871, near Elida, O , m. Mar. 8, 1896, Malinda Good, of Knoxville, Tenn , b May 28, 1873. She died in Va , Jan. 6, 1935. Mr. Shenk died in Va.

1. Edith Shenk, b June 1, 1897, single.

2. Lillie S. Shenk, b June 13, 1899, twin

3 Lydia F Shenk, b June 13, 1899, twin No 3705.

4. Irvin H Shenk, b Aug. 31, 1901, d. Dec. 10, 1904.

5. Elsie R. Shenk, b July 31, 1903   No 3707
6. Ezra W. Shenk, b. July 10, 1915

No. 629. Sixth Generation. 627.

3) Amos M. Shenk, b. Sept 3, 1873, near Elida, O , m Mar. 6, 1898, Alice M. Hilty, b. May 17, 1871 Address· Nampa, Ida Farmer. Mennonites. Minister of the gospel.
1. J. David Shenk, b. Jan 29, 1899.
2. Ruth C. Shenk, b April 15, 1900. No 630.
3. Mark H. Shenk, b. Nov. 23, 1901. No. 631.
4. Samuel G. Shenk, b. Jan. 26, 1904 No 632
5. Fanny Elizabeth Shenk, b Aug 23, 1905
6. Timothy L. Shenk, b. July 27, 1907.
7. Esther R. Shenk, b. Dec. 27, 1908
8. Paul A Shenk, b. Aug 22, 1911.
9. Amos M. Shenk, Jr., b. July 10, 1914.

No. 630. Seventh Generation. 629.

2) Ruth C. Shenk, b. April 25, 1900, in Ohio, m. Nov. 11, 1918, George Carrico

No. 631. Seventh Generation. 629.

3) Mark H. Shenk, b. Nov. 23, 1901, m. Dec. 3, 1928, Ada Criffield

No. 632. Seventh Generation. 629.

4) Samuel G. Shenk, b Jan 26, 1904, married Eunice Nelson Dec. 16, 1925.

No. 633. Sixth Generation. 627.

4) Simon G. Shenk, b. Oct. 5, 1875, near Elida, O , m Mar. 1, 1896, Mary M Shank, b. Feb. 12, 1875 in Mo Address. Elida, O. Farmer. Mennonite. Simon G. was a minister in the Mennonite Church He was instantly killed by an approaching train May 8, 1934.
1. Stella R. Shenk, b April 29, 1897 No 634.
2. Ada E. Shenk, b. July 26, 1898 No. 635.
3. Ralph B. Shenk, b. Aug 10, 1902. No 635½.
4. Wilbur Shenk, b. Aug 19, 1905. No 3654
5. John Shenk, b. Nov. 4, 1906 No. 636.
6. Alma Shenk, b Jan. 20, 1912
7. Daniel Shenk, b. Aug 7, 1915, d. at two days.
8 Chester Shenk, b July 16, 1916, d Mar 24, 1922
9. Mary Shenk, b Nov. 27, 1917.

No. 634. Seventh Generation. 633.

1) Stella R. Shenk, b April 29, 1897, near Elida, O., m. Aug. 11, 1918, Clarence Auxberger, b. July 27, 1897. Address: Delphos, O , R. 2. Farmer. Mennonite.
1. Frederick Auxberger, b. April 27, 1921.
2. Donald Auxberger, b. Dec. 21, 1925.
3. Myron Auxberger, b. Aug 20, 1929.

No. 635. Seventh Generation. 633.

2) Ada E. Shenk, b. July 27, 1899, near Elida, O., m. April 17, 1926, Everett Kirkendall, b. April 6, 1906. Address Lima, O , R. 3 Farmer. Mennonites
1. Robert Kirkendall, b. May 7, 1927.
2. Richard Kirkendall, b Dec 29, 1929.

3. Darrell E. Kirkendall, b. Sept 17, 1932.
4. Helen Esther Kirkendall, b Nov. 13, 1934.

No. 635½. Seventh Generation. 633.
3) Ralph B. Shenk, b. Aug. 10, 1902, near Elida, O , m. Lucelle Layman, b. ――――.
1. David Lewis Shenk, b June 14, 1935.
2. Michael Edward Shenk, b. Dec. 8, 1936.

No. 636. Seventh Generation. 633.
5) John Shenk, b Nov 4, 1906, near Elida, O., m. Mary Margaret Morgan, b. April 20, 1911, near Elida, O. Address: Elida, O. Farmer. Methodists.
1. Bettie Jo Shenk, b June 28, 1933.

No. 637. Sixth Generation. 627.
5) Moses B. Shenk, b. July 15, 1877, near Elida, O , m. Jan. 1, 1908, Ellen M. Landes, b. April 11, 1883 Address Hesston, Kans. Cream gatherer. Mennonites.
1. Ruth F. Shenk, b. Nov. 8, 1908
2. Verda R. Shenk, b. Feb. 5, 1910
3. Mamie L Shenk, b July 29, 1912.
4. Anna M Shenk, b Mar. 18, 1914
5. Erma R. Shenk, b. April 28, 1917.
6. Mary E. Shenk, b. Oct. 24, 1919.
7. Paul J. Shenk, b July 18, 1921.
8. Grace I. Shenk, b Aug 7, 1925

No. 638. Sixth Generation. 627.
6) Reuben J. Shenk, b June 29, 1879, near Elida, O., m. Sept. 9, 1908, Myrtle Lutz, b. ――――, 1889, d. Aug. 20, 1931, at Nampa, Ida. Farmer in Idaho.
1. Grace Elizabeth Shenk, b. Sept. 28, 1909 No 638¼.
2. Mary Ellen Shenk, b. Aug. 17, 1915.
3 Marjorie Shenk, b Nov 17, 1921.

No. 638¼. Seventh Generation. 638.
1) Grace Elizabeth Shenk, b. Sept. 28, 1909, m. Oct. 15, 1929, Rollie S Brown. Address Nampa, Ida
1. Wallace Edwin Brown, b. Aug. 24, 1934.

No. 639. Sixth Generation. 627.
7) John L. Shenk, b Aug 21, 1881, near Elida, O., m. Alma Biddinger, Feb., 1903, near Spencerville, O Address: Philadelphia, Pa Music teacher.
1. Alma Jane Shenk, b ――――.
2. Marcella Shenk, b. ――――.

No. 640. Sixth Generation. 627.
8) Levi J. Shenk, b July 18, 1883, near Elida, O., m. Amanda M. Yoder, b. Dec. 9, 1883. They were married Nov. 28, 1908. Merchant. Newport News, Va. Mennonites.
1. Mabel R Shenk, b. Oct 13, 1909, d Nov. 26, 1912
2. Wilmer A. Shenk, b. June 1, 1911
3. Lester J. Shenk, b June 17, 1913.
4. Homer V. Shenk, b. Oct 14, 1915, d. Mar. 15, 1916.
5. Mary F. Shenk, b. Dec 22, 1916.
6. Margaret M. Shenk, b Feb. 15, 1919.
7 Mildred V Shenk, b Nov 14, 1920

8. John M. Shenk, b. July 27, 1923
9. Miriam G Shenk, b. Nov. 15, 1928

No. 641. Sixth Generation. 627.

9) Daniel F. Shenk, b Oct 17, 1886, near Elida, O , m Fannie Schraag, b. Oct. 12, 1884. Address Sheridan, Oreg. Mennonite minister and farmer.

1. Lloyd Shenk, b Sept. 6, 1911.
2. Kenneth Shenk, b. Dec 30, 1912
3. Ronald Shenk, b. June 20, 1918
4. Mildred Shenk, b. Aug 18, 1920

No. 642. Sixth Generation. 627.

10) Rebecca S Shenk, b Oct 6, 1889, near Elida, O , m Feb 24, 1923, Asa Hertzler, b Aug. 7, 1889 Address. Denbigh, Va. Farmer Mennonites

1. Virgil R Hertzler, b May 19, 1924, twin
2. Virginia M. Hertzler, b May 19, 1924, twin
3. Alvin S. Hertzler, b July 25, 1925.
4 Alice R. Hertzler, b. Aug 24, 1926
5. Amy L. Hertzler, b Jan. 9, 1928

No. 643. Sixth Generation. 627.

11) Jacob B Shenk, b Nov. 2, 1892, near Elida. O , m Laura King, b June 16, 1892. Address: La Junta, Colo Mennonites.

1. Irene E. Shenk, b. Jan 10, 1917.
2. Alice L Shenk, b June 24, 1919
3. Lois N. Shenk, b. Dec 6, 1920
4. Doris F. Shenk, b Jan 20, 1922
5. Laura A. Shenk, b Aug 7, 1923
6. Norma C. Shenk, b Dec 31, 1925
7 Jacob B. Shenk, b Feb 26, 1927
8. Robert N. Shenk, b Sept 10. 1928, d. Sept 23, 1928.

No. 644. Fifth Generation. 626.

5) Andrew Shenk, b Aug 20, 1850, in Hamilton Co , Ind., m Mar 24, 1872, Susan Good, b. July 7, 1850. Address Oronogo. Mo Farmer Mennonite Andrew was ordained to the ministry in the Pike Church near Elida, O., in 1890. About 1895 he moved to Oronogo, Mo , where he was ordained to the office of bishop in Sept., 1896 He died Nov 18, 1937, at his home near Oronogo, Mo.

1 Henry G. Shenk, b Feb 8, 1873 No 645.
2 Noah B. Shenk, b. Jan 2, 1874. No. 646
3. Perry J. Shenk, b Dec 19, 1876 No. 647
4. Gabriel D Shenk, b. Oct 9, 1878 No 648
5. Rhoda F. Shenk, b Nov. 8, 1880 No 649
6. Timothy C. Shenk, b Sept 10, 1883, d July 9, 1893.
7. Mary M Shenk, b. Nov 9, 1887, twin No 650.
8. Martha A. Shenk, b. Nov 9, 1887, twin No 651

No. 645. Sixth Generation. 644.

1) Henry G Shenk, b. Feb. 8, 1873, near Elida, O., m May 27, 1899, Rosella Golden. Address unknown His wife and children live in Lima, O.

1. Infant Shenk, b. and d. Mar 5, 1901.
2. Irene D. Shenk, b. Mar 17, 1903 No. 3593.
3. Paul C. Shenk, b. ————, 1907 No 3594.
4. Merl Shenk, b ————, 1911. No. 3595.

No. 646. Sixth Generation. 644.

2) Noah H Shenk, b. Jan 2, 1874, near Elida, O., d. in Neutral, Kans., June 23, 1923, m. Mary Mitchel. Noah was ordained in 1910. Address: Neutral, Kans Minister in the Mennonite Church Two children Henry and Clifford Shenk

No. 647. Sixth Generation. 644.

3) Perry J Shenk, b Dec. 19, 1876, near Elida, O., d. Sept. 28, 1937, m Jan. 1, 1900, Myrtle M. Anderson, of Oronogo, Mo Address. Oronogo, Mo. Mennonite. He was ordained a minister in Jasper Co., Mo., in 1910.
1. Alma Esther Shenk, b. Oct 10, 1900.
2. Wilbur E. Shenk, b. Oct 12, 1909.

No. 648. Sixth Generation. 644.

4) Gabriel D. Shenk, b Oct 9, 1878, near Elida, O., m. May 22, 1904, Luella M. Sharrer. Address: Sheridan, Oreg. Minister and bishop in Mennonite Church He was ordained minister in 1923 and bishop in 1925.
1. Bertha Shenk, b. ——————.
2. Wesley Shenk, b. ——————.
3. Vernon Shenk, b. ——————.
4. Mildred Shenk, b ——————.
5. Helen Shenk, b ——————
6. Jennella Shenk, b ——————.

No. 649. Sixth Generation. 644.

5) Rhoda F. Shenk, b Nov. 8, 1880, near Elida, O , m. Hiram Yoder.
1. Wayne Yoder, b. ——————.
2. Louise Yoder, b. ——————
3. Max Yoder, b. ——————.
4 Margaret Yoder, b. ——————
5 Jessie Yoder, b. ——————.
6. Robert Yoder, b. ——————

No. 650. Sixth Generation. 644.

7) Mary M Shenk, b Nov 9, 1887, near Elida, O , m Dec. 30, 1915, E. J. Berkey, b. Mar 16, 1874. Address. Oronogo, Mo. Farmer. Mennonite, minister.
1. Mabel C. Berkey, b Feb 4, 1920
2 Ruby L Berkey, b. Nov 26, 1921.
3. Bernice E. Berkey, b April 14, 1925.
4. Earl A Berkey, b. May 30, 1927, twin.
5 Elsie S Berkey, b. May 30, 1927, twin.
6. Janet E Berkey, b Sept 30, 1929

No. 651. Sixth Generation. 644.

8) Martha A Shenk, b Nov 9, 1887, near Elida, O , m. Levi A. Weaver, b. Jan. 7, 1893, m Dec 30, 1915 Address Oronogo, Mo. Related, see No. 392 for family.

No. 652. Fifth Generation. 626.

6) Daniel Shenk, b Sept 27, 1853, in Franklin Co, O , m. Dec. 9, 1875, Rachel Stemen, b Jan 16, 1852, in Allen Co , O , d. Feb. 19, 1890. She was buried in the Salem cemetery near Elida, O On Nov. 5, 1891, he married Matilda Hilty, b. Feb. 20, 1867. Daniel is a minister in the Mennonite Church. Address: Denbigh, Va.
1. Menno S. Shenk, b. Dec. 31, 1876. No 653.
2 Andrew S. Shenk, b. July 29, 1878 No. 654.
3 Emma J. Shenk, b. Aug 16, 1880. No. 655.

4 Jacob Shenk, b Nov. 19, 1882, d Aug, 1884.
5 Anna L. Shenk, b. Feb 9, 1885 No 659
  (From second wife)
6 Elizabeth Shenk, b. Sept 7, 1892
7. William H Shenk, b Oct 17, 1893
8 Daniel D. Shenk, b Dec. 23, 1894 No. 660.
9 Raymond J Shenk, b July 31, 1896. No 661
10 Susanna Shenk, b. Oct 16, 1898. No 662
11. Mary V. Shenk, b. Dec 2, 1900. No 3396
12. Alice Shenk, b Oct 25, 1902 No 663
13 Amos Shenk, b. April 30, 1905, single
14 John H Shenk, b April 19, 1910 No 3665

No. 653. Sixth Generation. 652.
1) Menno S Shenk, b Dec 31, 1876, near Elida, O, m. Dec. 10, 1908, Emma C. Brunk, b Nov 15, 1886 Address Elida, O Carpenter. Mennonites Related, see No. 430
1. Laural Shenk, b Feb. 18, 1911
2 Zela Shenk, b. Sept. 14, 1914.

No. 654. Sixth Generation. 652.
2) Andrew S. Shenk, b July 29, 1878, near Elida, O, m Oct 21, 1899, Rhoda E. Stemen, b Dec 31, 1879. Address: Elida, O Painter Mennonites
1 Menno Wilson Shenk, b Nov 16, 1900 No 2418
2. Carol W. Shenk, b. May 20, 1902 No 2419.
3. Oliver W Shenk, b. Nov 2, 1903 No 2420
4 Edgar Shenk, b July 28, 1906 No 2421
5 Rhoda Shenk, b June 24, 1908 No 2422
6 Margaret Shenk, b May 26, 1910 No 2423
7 Roland Shenk, b Dec 22, 1911
8. Louis Shenk, b June 30, 1915 No 166¼
9 Clayton Shenk, b Oct 14, 1917, d Aug 31, 1927

No. 655. Sixth Generation. 652.
3) Emma J Shenk, b Aug 16, 1880, near Elida, O, m. Mar. 1, 1901, John Stemen, b Dec. 24, 1879. Address: Elida, O. Painter. Mennonites.
1 Carl M Stemen, b. July 15, 1903 No. 656
2 Katherine Stemen, b July 15, 1903 No 657
3. Merle G. Stemen, b Aug 28, 1904 No. 658
4. Rowena Stemen, b Jan. 16, 1909 No 3584
5. Nina Stemen, b May 25, 1911 No 3585
6. Connie R. Stemen, b Oct 9, 1916, died
7. Carrie M. Stemen, b Oct 9, 1916, died.
8 Elva L. Stemen, b. Oct. 4, 1921.

No. 656. Seventh Generation. 655.
1) Carl Milton Stemen, b July 15, 1903, near Elida, O, m. Mar. 27, 1929, Bertha Nones, b. May 18, 1907 Address 999 Fisher Rd., Grosse Point, Mich Dental technician.
1. Kenneth Stemen, b. Dec. 5, 1933.

No. 657. Seventh Generation. 655.
2) Katherine Stemen, b July 15, 1903, near Elida, O, m Ellis Good, b. July 9, 1902, m. Nov 7, 1924. Address Logan, O Farmer Mennonite.
1. Wayne E Good, b Sept —, 1925, d ————, 1925

2. Marcella J. Good, b. Aug 25, 1926
3. Leota F. Good, b Oct. 10, 1928.
4. Wilma I. Good, b July 29, 1930.
5. Doris Janette Good, b Aug 20, 1932.
6. Evelyn Gertrude Good, b Aug 13, 1934.

No. 658. Seventh Generation. 655.

3) Merle G. Stemen, b Aug 28, 1904, near Elida, O., m. June 11, 1927, Edna I. Brenneman, b Aug 2, 1908 Address· Elida, O. Mennonites. Related, see No. 339 for family.

No. 659. Sixth Generation. 652.

5) Anna Lena Shenk, b Feb 9, 1885, near Elida, O., m Jan. 22, 1906, Henry Peter Hertzler, b. Oct 27, 1883. Address Denbigh, Va Farmer Mennonite Burial place in Warwick River Mennonite cemetery.
1 Arthur Virgil Hertzler, b Feb 9, 1907. No. 659¼.
2 Milford Raymond Hertzler, b Mar. 19, 1908. No. 659½.
3 Menno Simon Hertzler, b June 18, 1910, d. May 24, 1934
4 Lois Gertrude Hertzler, b April 15, 1913. No 659¾.
5. Anna Ruth Hertzler, b. Sept 10, 1915.
6 Henry William Hertzler, b April 4, 1917.
7. Oliver Wendel Hertzler, b. Sept. 26, 1918, twin
8 Oril Ola Hertzler, b. Sept. 26, 1918, twin.
9 Edith Grace Hertzler, b Feb 18, 1921
10. Dora May Hertzler, b May 30, 1923

No. 659¼. Seventh Generation. 659.

1) Arthur Virgil Hertzler, b Feb 9, 1907, near Denbigh, Va., m. Aug. 1, 1932, Edna Frances Brunk.
1. Robert Allen Hertzler, b Oct 15, 1933.

No. 659½. Seventh Generation. 659.

2) Milford Raymond Hertzler, b Mar 19, 1908, near Denbigh, Va., m. Oct. 5, 1933, Ada Ruth Hostetler.
1. James Rowland Hertzler, b. Jan. 30, 1934
2 Carolyn Grace Hertzler, b Jan. 22, 1937.

No. 659¾. Seventh Generation. 659.

4) Lois Gertrude Hertzler, b April 15, 1913, near Denbigh, Va., m. May 16, 1937, John Virgil Hostetler. Address. Denbigh, Va.
1. Marjorie Grace Hostetler, b. June 19, 1938.

No. 660. Sixth Generation. 652.

8) Daniel D Shenk, b Dec 23, 1894, near Denbigh, Va , m. Aug. 19, 1923, Nancy Boyer, b. Oct. 24, 1901. Address. Denbigh, Va Carpenter and farmer. Mennonites Burial place at Warwick River Mennonite Church.
1. Lois Virginia Shenk, b. Nov. 2, 1924.
2. Daniel Martin Shenk, b. Nov. 23, 1925, d. Dec. 7, 1925
3 David William Shenk, b. Oct. 10, 1926.
4 Paul Eugene Shenk, b Mar. 8, 1929.
5. Joseph Donald Shenk, b Dec. 8, 1930.
6. Elizabeth Ann Shenk, b. April 2, 1933
7. Nancy Alice Shenk, b. Oct. 25, 1935.
8. Lauretta Mae Shenk, b June 7, 1936

No. 661. Sixth Generation. 652.

9) Raymond J. Shenk, b. July 31, 1896, near Denbigh, Va., m. Aug. 27, 1924, Clara Wenger, b. Aug. 21, 1899. Address: Cottage City, Md. Carpenter. Minister in Mennonite Church.

1. Doris Jean Shenk, b. Jan 14, 1926
2. Raymond Jacob Shenk, b Mar 30, 1927
3. Harold Leon Shenk, b Dec 14, 1929.
4. Clarene Virginia Shenk, b. July 5, 1932

No. 662. Sixth Generation. 652.

10) Susanna Shenk, b Oct. 16, 1898, near Denbigh, Va , d. at Elverson, Pa , May 6, 1935, m. Dec. 10, 1924, Melvin Hertzler, b Mar 21, 1894. Address· Elverson, Pa Farmer. Mennonite

1. Daniel Levi Hertzler, b. Oct. 19, 1925.
2. Katherine Anna Hertzler, b. April 22, 1928
3 Truman Ray Hertzler, b Jan 30, 1930
4. Paul Melvin Hertzler, b. Sept 8, 1931.
5 Martha Carol Hertzler, b Dec 15, 1933

No. 663. Sixth Generation. 652.

12) Alice Shenk, b Oct 25, 1902, near Denbigh, Va , m Dec 28, 1926, J Paul Sauder, b July 23, 1902 For a number of years he taught science in high school He is associate editor of the "Missionary Messenger " In March, 1937, J. Paul Sauder was ordained to the ministry at (1407 Ida St) Tampa, Fla , to have charge of the mission at that place.

1 Joseph Paul Sauder, Jr , b April 7, 1929, twin
2. John Allen Sauder, b. April 7, 1929, twin.
3. William Richard Sauder, b May 24, 1932
4 Lydia Ann Sauder, b. May 24, 1934.

No. 664. Fifth Generation. 625.

7) Catherine Shenk, b Oct. 30, 1856, near Elida, O , d Aug 13, 1921, in Warwick Co., Va , m Dec. 3, 1876, Martin B Shank, b Sept. 7, 1854, in Rockingham Co , Va , d Mar 6, 1931, in Va Both were buried at the Warwick River Mennonite Church Address was Denbigh Va Farmer Mennonites.

1 Susanna Shank, b. —————, d. in 1903.
2. John M Shank, b. Oct. 12, 1880 No 665.
3 Perry F. Shank, b Dec. 15, 1882. No. 3392.
4. Clara R. Shank, b June 12, 1885. No. 666
5. Cora E. Shank, b Mar. 13, 1888. No 3394.
6. Lydia E. Shank, b Sept 5, 1891, single
7 Lewis D Shank, b. Mar 25, 1894. No 3395.

No. 665. Sixth Generation. 664.

2) John M Shank, b. Oct 12, 1880, near Elida, O , m Oct. 11, 1903, Mary May Miller. Address· Annville, Pa Mennonites

1. Paul Virgil Shank, b —————.
2. John Mark Shank, b —————. No 3397.
3. Naomi Ruth Shank, b —————. No. 3398
4 Ralph M Shank, b. ————— No 3399
5. Aaron Shank, b. —————.
6. Walter Shank, b —————
7. Gladys Shank, b —————.
8 Mary Louise Shank, b —————.

No. 666. Sixth Generation. 664.

4) Clara R. Shank, b. June 12, 1885, near Elida, O , m. Jan. 1, 1905, Walter Grove, b. April 25, 1880 Address· Washington, D. C. Mennonites.
1. Edna Ethel Grove, b. Mar 16, 1910.

No. 657. Fifth Generation. 626.

8) Lydia Shenk, b April 7, 1859, near Elida, O., m. May 20, 1889, Henry J. Powell, b. ——————, d. June 7, 1923, near Knoxville, Tenn. Address: Knoxville, Tenn. Farmer. Mennonite, and a deacon.
1. Lewis J. Powell, b. June 4, 1881. No. 668.
2. Mary S. Powell, b Feb. 19, 1883.
3. Verdie V. Powell, b. Oct 19, 1885
4. Walter A Powell, b Mar. 10, 1888. No. 669.
5. William H. Powell, b July 7, 1891, d June 27, 1894.
6. Andrew Powell, b Aug. 3, 1893, d. Dec 4, 1895
7. John V. Powell, b. May 15, 1895, d. Feb 7, 1898.
8 Daniel C Powell, b May 8, 1897, d

No. 668. Sixth Generation. 667.

1) Lewis J Powell, b June 4, 1881, near Elida, O , m. June 29, 1911, Ida E. Hertzler, b June 11, 1879 Address: South English, Ia. Hardware dealer. Mennonite
1. John S. Powell, b April 11, 1912.
2 Junior Powell, b Dec. 1, 1913
3 Mary Helen Powell, b. Aug 15, 1919

No. 669. Sixth Generation. 667.

4) Walter A Powell, b Mar 10, 1888, near Elida, O., m. Bessie Howard. Address: South English, Ia
1. Bernice Powell, b. ————.
2. Hazel Powell, b. ————.
3. Doris Powell, b ————

No. 670. Fifth Generation. 626.

9) Abraham P. Shenk, b Feb 15, 1862, near Elida, O., m. Mar. 6, 1890, Fannie V. Coffman, b. Oct 30, 1865, d Oct. 3, 1904 On Nov. 22, 1906, he m. Samantha Showalter, b Dec 6, 1871, in Rockingham Co., Va. Address: Denbigh, Va Mennonites
1. Samuel C Shenk, b. May 9, 1891 No. 671.
2. John M Shenk, b. July 10, 1893, d May 21, 1894
3. Henry M. Shenk, b. Aug 2, 1894 No 672
4. Mary C. Shenk, b Aug 28, 1896
5. Jacob A Shenk, b. Feb. 17, 1900 No 674
6. Phebe Shenk, b. Jan 26, 1902. No 675.
7 Anna M. Shenk, b Sept. 26, 1903 No 676.
   (From second marriage)
8. Martha May Shenk, b May 15, 1909 No 3400
9. Ezra Cornelius Shenk, b. Feb. 23, 1911 No 676½
10. George Abram Shenk, b May 22, 1913
11. Lydia Pearl Shenk, b. —— 14, 1915.

No. 671. Sixth Generation. 670.

1) Samuel C. Shenk, b May 9, 1891, m Icy P Shank, b. May 9, 1893, in Morgan Co., Mo. She died at Denbigh, Va , Feb 26, 1922 Mennonites. On Sept.

2, 1925, he m. (2nd) Retta Boyer Address. 19 Lee Ave, Takoma Park, Md. Produce merchant.
   1. Stanley Coffman Shenk, b. Mar. 30, 1919.
      (From second wife)
   2 Charles B. Shenk, b. Dec. 5, 1928.

No. 672. Sixth Generation. 670.

3) Henry M. Shenk, b. Aug. 2, 1894, near Elida, O, m. Dec. 6, 1917, Frankie D. Showalter, b Feb. 26, 1892, d Oct. 20, 1935 Related, see No. 1004 Address Denbigh, Va Mennonites
   1. Fannie V. Shenk, b Oct. 7, 1918 No. 3653.
   2 Mary E Shenk, b Mar. 1, 1921
   3 Ellen E Shenk, b Nov. 4, 1923
   4 Phebe F Shenk, b. July 14, 1926.
   5 Esther L. Shenk, b. Oct. 20, 1928.
   6 Henry M Shenk, Jr., b Feb 22, 1931, twin
   7 Helen M Shenk, b Feb. 22, 1931, twin

No. 674. Sixth Generation. 670.

5) Jacob A Shenk, b Feb. 17, 1900, m Dec 8, 1926, Lucy Wenger, b. Nov 4, 1902 Address: Harrisonburg, Va. Hatchery Mennonite
   1 Jacob Paul Shenk, b. Jan. 7, 1931.
   2 James A Shenk, b. Mar. 3, 1934.

No. 675. Sixth Generation. 670.

6) Phebe F Shenk, b Jan. 26, 1902, m Dec 6, 1922, Clyde Kraus, b June 5, 1900. Address Denbigh, Va Feed merchant at Denbigh Mennonites
   1. Clyde Norman Kraus, b Feb 20, 1924.
   2 Harry Lee Kraus, b Sept. 9, 1925.
   3. Lewis Jacob Kraus, b Nov. 3, 1926
   4 Vivian Frances Kraus, b July 20, 1931, d Aug. 14, 1931.

No. 676. Sixth Generation. 670.

7) Anna M. Shenk, b Sept 26, 1903, m Jason W. Brunk, April 15, 1922 He was born Aug. 12, 1897 Address. 4034 Georgia Ave, Washington, D. C. Produce merchant.
   1. Jason W. Brunk, Jr., b Nov. 10, 1923.
   2. Willis Coffman Brunk, b June 10, 1925
   3. Beatrice Virginia Brunk, b. Mar. 6, 1927.
   4. Mary Elizabeth Brunk, b. Dec. 6, 1936

No. 676½. Sixth Generation. 670.

9) Ezra Cornelius Shenk, b Feb 23, 1911, m April 20, 1933, Pauline Mast, b. Jan. 31, 1911. Address: Denbigh, Va. Farmer. Mennonite.
   1. Eleanor Grace Shenk, b Mar. 3, 1934.
   2. Carl Joseph Shenk, b. Sept. 22, 1936.

No. 677. Fourth Generation. 22.

2) Jacob Shank, b May 12, 1819, in Rockingham Co., Va., d Aug. 13, 1889. On Oct. 13, 1842, he married Barbara Beery, b April 29, 1824, d. Mar. 26, 1868 Jacob was buried at Weavers cemetery and Barbara was buried at Lindale cemetery. Address: Harrisonburg, Va. Farmer. Mennonite
   1. John Shank, b. July 3, 1843, drowned Mar. 1, 1845.
   2. Anna Shank, b. Oct 3, 1844. No 678
   3. Noah Shank, b. May 3, 1847, d Mar. 21, 1880, in Mo

4. Mary M. Shank, b. Dec 29, 1849. No. 679.
5. Rebecca Shank, b. Jan. 3, 1853. No 681.
6. Lydia Shank, b. July 2, 1856. No. 688.
7. Jacob Shank, Jr., b. Nov. 23, 1858. No. 689
8. Erasmus C. Shank, b. Jan. 2, 1861. No 729
9. Isaac S. Shank, b. Feb 24, 1863. No. 693
10. Amos H. Shank, b. May 3, 1865 No. 709.

No. 678. Fifth Generation. 677.

2) Anna Shank, b. Oct. 3, 1844, near Harrisonburg, Va., m. Jan. 25, 1865, George O. Roudabush.

1. Fannie B Roudabush, b Dec 16, 1866 in Va. No 678¼.

No. 678¼. Sixth Generation. 678.

1) Fannie B. Roudabush, b. Dec. 16, 1866, m Nov. 5, 1884, John R. Suter. Address: Harrisonburg, Va. Salesman Mennonites.

1. Marion Jasper Suter, b Sept 16, 1885, d Mar. 14, 1887.
2 John Early Suter, b Feb. 7, 1887. No 716.
3 Anna Mary Suter, b Aug 27, 1889 No. 717.
4 Lawrence E Suter, b. Dec 3, 1891. No. 718.
5 Homer R Suter, b Feb. 12, 1894 No 719.
6 Nettie E. Suter, b. Mar. 1, 1896
7. Jacob C Suter, b. Nov 28, 1898. No 720
8. Walter T. Suter, b. Aug 23, 1901. No. 721.
9 Robert D. Suter, b. May 24, 1904. No. 722.
10 Menno R. Suter, b. Mar. 16, 1907. No. 723.
11 Claude R. Suter, b. Mar 2, 1910

No. 679. Fifth Generation. 677.

4) Mary M. Shank, b. Dec 29, 1849, near Harrisonburg, Va., m. Nov. 26, 1867, Robert J. Mason. Address· Waynesboro, Va. Presbyterians.

1 William Shank Mason, b. Nov. 22, 1868, d. Nov. 30, 1868.
2. Nora V. Mason, b. Apr. 4, 1870, d. Oct. 22, 1872.
3. Irene Lydia Mason, b. June 23, 1883.
4. Robert L. Mason, b. July 24, 1886. No. 680.

No. 680. Sixth Generation. 679.

4) Robert L. Mason, b July 24, 1886, m. Jan. 4, 1914, Mary Ethel Morris, at San Marcus, Tex. Address 816 American National Bank Building, Roanoke, Va. Medical doctor.

1 Mary Ethel Mason, b. June 15, 1918 at Roanoke, Va.
2 Mildred Hope Mason, b April 1, 1922, as above.
3. Elizabeth Ann Mason, b. July 8, 1931, as above.

No. 681. Fifth Generation. 677.

5) Rebecca Shank, b Jan 3, 1847, near Harrisonburg, Va , m. Abram D. Weaver, b Nov 3, 1847, m June 23, 1872 Farmer Mennonites. Address: Dale Enterprise, Va Related, for family refer to No. 290

No. 688. Fifth Generation. 677.

6) Lydia Shank, b. July 2, 1856, near Harrisonburg, Va , d Sept 14, 1898, m Sept 25, 1879, William H Suters, b June 22, 1857.

1 Oscar Marion Suters, b June 21, 1880 No. 724
2 Jacob Ward Suter, b. Sept. 2, 1882. No. 725.
3 Claude David Suter, b Nov 19, 1885

4. Mary Edna Suter, b. May 16, 1888. No. 726.
5. Vada Pearl Suter, b. June 26, 1891. No. 728.
Claude D Suter, single   Address: Brunswick, Ga.

No. 689. Fifth Generation. 677.

7) Jacob Shank, Jr., b Nov 23, 18:8, in Va, m in 1878, Anna Vantrumpt of Mo   Address: Rockingham, Ray Co., Mo.
1. Nora Shank, b. ——————.
2. Milo Shank, b. ——————.
Both are married but have no further report

No. 693. Fifth Generation. 677.

9) Isaac S. Shank, b Feb 24, 1863 in Rockingham Co, Va, m April 12, 1883, Rebecca Smith, of Va She died —————— In ——————, 1885, he married Sophiah E Brenneman born May 24, 1864 in Wayne Co, O Isaac died Feb. 2, 1912, buried in the Salem cemetery near Elida, O, where they resided. Address Elida, O. Farmer Mennonites. Related.
1. Elmer J. Shank, b Jan 18, 1884. No 327
   (From second wife)
2. Susanna R Shank, b. Dec 2, 1886 No 695
3. Jacob B Shank, b. Aug. 13, 1888 No 696
4. Ira Asa Shank, b July 27, 1890 No 697.
5. Laura A. Shank, b June 8, 1892 No. 698.
6. Otho B Shank, b. April 22, 1894 No. 699
7. Ellen O. Shank, b July 10, 1896 No 700
8 Erasmus C Shank, b Feb. 11, 1898 No. 701
9. Effie M. Shank, b Nov 1, 1900. No 702.
10 Rhuda R Shank, b Sept 9. 1902, was killed instantly by a train Feb 19, 1925.
11. Noah Shank, b Jan. 14, 1905 No. 704
12 Timothy H. Shank, b. Oct 25, 1908, single, living at 1693 Shenandoah, Los Angeles, Calif.

No. 695. Sixth Generation. 693.

2) Susanna R Shenk, b Dec 2, 1886, near Elida, O, m May 24, 1908. Irvin O Diller, b April 2, 1884 Address. Elida, O, R 1. Farmer. Mennonite
1. Ira A Diller, b May 29, 1908. No 2917.
2 Clara A Diller, b. Aug. 18, 1910. No. 2918.
3 Ralph H Diller, b Nov. 24, 1914 No 2919
4 Martha E Diller, b Aug 24, 1922.

No. 696. Sixth Generation. 693.

3) Jacob B Shenk. b Aug 13, 1888, near Elida, O, m Barbara Culp, b Jan 29, 1894, at same place Address· Elida, O, R 1 Farmer and mechanic Mennonite
1. Merlin I Shenk. b May 6. 1913
2 Nellie C Shenk, b Aug 11, 1914
3 Rollin A Shenk, b Jan 6, 1917
4 Alice M Shenk, b Dec 14, 1918.
5 Warren G. Shenk, b July 4, 1921
6 Oral J Shenk, b April 18, 1924
7 Timothy L Shenk, b —————— 28, 1926
8 Cretora O. Shenk, b Feb. 21, 1928
9 Lester Eugene Shenk. b June 28, 1929, twin
10 Esther Genette Shenk, b June 28, 1929, twin

11. Edward Shenk, b. ————, 1933
12 Billy Arthur Shenk, b June 22, 1935.

No. 697. Sixth Generation. 693.

4) Ira Asa Shenk, b July 27, 1890, near Elida, O, m. Dec. 2, 1915, Wilda Frances Hartman, b Sept. 22, 1892 Address: Elida, O. Farmer. Mennonite.
1. Harold H. Shenk, b. Sept. 4, 1917.
2. Lorene F. Shenk, b. Nov. 9, 1919.

No. 698. Sixth Generation. 693.

5) Laura A. Shenk, b June 8, 1892, near Elida, O., m. April 30, 1913, Samuel J. Powell, b. Mar. 23, 1892 Address Elida, O, R 1. Farmer. Mennonite.
1. Mabel E. Powell, b. May 13, 1914
2. John K. Powell, b. Aug. 5, 1915. No. 2929.
3. Dorothy M Powell, b April 6, 1917 No. 3702
4. Betty M. Powell, b Nov 28, 1921, d. Jan 16, 1928
5. Samuel J. Powell, Jr., b. Feb. 23, 1923

No. 699. Sixth Generation. 693.

6) Otho B. Shenk, b. April 22, 1894, near Elida, O, m. Feb. 18, 1917, Hattie King, b Aug. 24, 1897 Address Elida, O, R 1 Farmer. Mennonite, minister.
1. Mark Shenk, b Dec 19, 1917.
2. Louelle Shenk, b May 6, 1923
3 Paul David Shenk, b July 10, 1932.

No. 700. Sixth Generation. 693.

7) Ellen I Shenk, b. July 10, 1896, near Elida, O, m. Sept. 20, 1921, Peter Strayman, b. Jan 31, 1892. Address Ottowa, O Druggist. Seventh Day Adventist.
1. George Elmer Strayman, b Feb. 1, 1925.
2 Marcell Louise Strayman, b Mar 9, 1929.
3 Russell Theo Strayman, b Sept. 6, 1930.

No. 701. Sixth Generation. 693.

8) Erasmus C. Shenk, b. Feb 11, 1898, near Elida, O., m. July 31, 1927, Florence Ehrnman, b July 24, 1901 Address: Elida, O., R. 1. Farmer.
1. Luella Irene Shenk, b June 8, 1928
2. Ruth Shenk, b Mar. 26, 1930

No. 702. Sixth Generation. 693.

9) Effie M. Shenk, b. Nov. 1, 1900, near Elida, O., m. Oct. 14, 1922, John Cusick, b Jan 3, 1893 Address Lima, O Railroad employe. No issue

No. 704. Sixth Generation. 693.

10) Noah Shenk, b Jan. 14, 1905, near Elida, O., m. July —, 1928, Frances Bessire, b. Sept. 1, 1907 Address: Elida, O, R 2. Farmer and teacher.
1 Patricia A. Shenk, b. Mar. 16, 1929.
2. Carolyn Gene Shenk, b Aug 3, 1930.
3 Constance Elaine Shenk, b Oct. 1, 1932.
4 Shirley Lou Shenk, b. Mar 18, 1934.
5 Kay Frances Shenk, b. Jan. 19, 1936.

No. 706. Sixth Generation. 693.

1) Elmer J Shank, b Jan 18, 1884, in Rockingham Co., Va., m. Jan. 1, 1905, Ina K Swartz, b May 3, 1883, in Va Address· Elida, O., R. 1. Truck farmer. Mennonite Related, for family see No. 327

127

No. 709. Fifth Generation. 677.

10) Amos H Shank, b. May 3, 1865, in Rockingham Co, Va, m July 12, 1883, Fannie C Knisely, b. May 5, 1864. Address: Dayton, Va Milling Buried at Weavers Church

1 Basil L Shank, b Nov. 11, 1883 No 710
2. Elsie B Shank, b Aug 20, 1885 No 711
3 Wilmer C Shank, b Mar 22, 1887 No 712
4 Claude M Shank, b. Aug 25, 1888 No. 713.
5 Della P Shank, b. July 18, 1891, d. Jan. 16, 1893.
6. Clifford O. Shank, b Mar 15, 1894 No 714

No. 710. Sixth Generation. 709.

1) Basil L. Shank, b. Nov. 11, 1883, near Harrisonburg, Va., m. Aug 28, 1924, Effie Irene Pratten of Detroit. Mich Address 14435 Prevert Ave, Detroit, Mich Real estate

1 June LeMay Shank, b April 2, 1926
2 Bruce Amos Shank, b Sept 16, 1928

No. 711. Sixth Generation. 709.

2) Elsie B Shank, b Aug 20, 1885, near Harrisonburg, Va, m Dec 25, 1906, Homer C Swope, b Jan 26, 1886 Address Dayton, Va Farmer No issue

No. 712. Sixth Generation. 709.

3) Wilmer O Shank, b Mar. 22, 1887, near Harrisonburg, Va, m Dec 24, 1912, Edna V. Baxter, born in Augusta Co, Va Address Emmitsburg, Md Miller by trade

1. Weldon B Shank, b. Dec. 7, 1913.
2. Odell J Shank, b April 12, 1915
3. Roscoe W. Shank, b Sept 5, 1920
4. Cleo B Shank, b Oct 23, 1927, twin
5 Leo L Shank, b Oct 23, 1927, twin

No. 713. Sixth Generation. 709.

4) Claude M Shank, b Aug. 25, 1888, near Harrisonburg, Va, m Oct 15, 1907, Jessie Hall, of Ft Wayne, Ind Address 1510 Oakland St, Ft. Wayne, Ind

1. Robert F. Shank, b May 4, 1908.
2 Kenneth M Shank b Jan. 1, 1910 No 715
3 Ralph H Shank, b Oct 26, 1911, killed in auto wreck, Sept 19, 1930
4. Leonard O Shank, b. Sept. 20, 1914.
5 Rolland Shank, b. Sept. 13, 1917.
6 Bettie V. Shank, b Aug 12, 1922

No. 714. Sixth Generation. 709.

6) Clifford O. Shank, b. Mar. 15, 1894, near Harrisonburg, Va, at Dayton. O Soldiers' Home, Co 7 Single

No. 715. Seventh Generation. 713.

2) Kenneth O Shank, b Jan 1, 1910, m Jan 18, 1930, Clementine Dewyel, b. Sept 3, 1911 Address Ft Wayne, Ind

No. 716. Seventh Generation. 678¼.

2) John Early Suter, b Feb 7, 1887, in Va., m Oct 7, 1907, N Pearl Blosser, b July 8, 1888 Address Harrisonburg, Va Mennonite Ordained minister Aug 11, 1907

1. Margaret G Suter, b Mar 12, 1911
2 Mary Ethel Suter, b July 7, 1912

128

3 Frances E Suter, b Jan 16, 1916
4. Daniel B Suter, b. April 25, 1920

No. 717. Seventh Generation. 678¼.

3) Anna Mary Suter, b Aug 27, 1889, in Va, m Jan 24, 1912, Lewis P Showalter, b Nov 8, 1890, ordained to the ministry on Jan 7, 1922, at the Lindale Church, near Edom, Va Address Broadway, Va Mennonites
1 John S Showalter, b May 14, 1914
2 Ruth F Showalter, b May 4, 1917
3 Lewis Menno Showalter, b Feb 24, 1921, d Aug 16, 1923
4 Marion E. Showalter, b. Oct 24, 1926

No. 718. Seventh Generation. 678¼.

4) Lawrence E. Suter, b. Dec. 3, 1891, in Va., m. Mar. 14, 1912, E Pearl Showalter, b July 31, 1890 Mennonites.
1 Helen L Suter, b Oct 15, 1912
2 Harold D Suter, b July 15, 1915
3 Dorothy F Suter, b April 20, 1918
4 J Richard Suter, b Mar 2, 1924

No. 719. Seventh Generation. 678¼.

5) Homer R Suter, b. Feb. 12, 1894, in Va., m. Feb 15, 1916, Orpha V Blosser, b. Jan. 18, 1893. Mennonites
1. Hazel M. Suter, b. Feb. 9, 1922
2 Katherine Suter, b Sept 24, 1928

No. 720. Seventh Generation. 678¼.

7) Jacob C Suter, b Nov 28, 1898, in Va., m Oct. 14, 1923, Mary F Shank, b. June 8, 1903. Mennonites
1 Doris Suter, b. Dec. 6, 1924
2 Eldon L Suter, b. April 13, 1927.
3 Raymond O Suter, b June 20, 1928

No. 721. Seventh Generation. 678¼.

8) Walter T. Suter, b. Aug 23, 1901, in Va, m Jan 6, 1927, Mary E Showalter, b Sept. 5, 1914 Mennonite
1. Glen W Suter, b. Oct. 2, 1927.

No. 722. Seventh Generation. 678¼.

9) Robert D Suter, b May 24, 1904, in Va, m Mar 30, 1931, Pauline O Painter, b. Oct 25, 1906. Presbyterians.
1 Robert Nolan Suter, b Feb 22, 1932.

No. 723. Seventh Generation. 678¼.

10) Menno R Suter, b. Mar. 16, 1907, in Va., m. April 19, 1930, C. Margaret Wenger, b. Feb 24, 1910. Mennonites.
1 Jared D Suter, b Mar 31, 1932

No. 724. Sixth Generation. 688.

1) Oscar M Suter, b June 21, 1880, m Goldie Edwards, of New Orleans, La Address New Orleans, La
1. Elaine Virginia Suter, b ————————

No. 725. Sixth Generation. 688.

2) Jacob Ward Suter, b Sept 2, 1882, in Va., m May Rodgers of Texas Address. Birmingham, Ala
1. Mary Ella Suter, b ————————.

129

2. Ward Rodgers Suter, b. ————————.
3. Robert Suter, b. ————————, d. ————————.
4. Sarah Helen Suter, b. ————————.

No. 726. Sixth Generation. 683.

4) Mary Edna Suter, b. May 16, 1888, in Va , d. 1933, m. Oct. 28, 1908, Ernest C. Liskey. Address: Harrisonburg, Va

1. Goldie Lee Liskey, b. Nov. 12, 1909. No 727
2. Ernest C Liskey, Jr., b July 24, 1911

No. 727. Seventh Generation. 726.

1) Goldie Lee Liskey, b Nov 12, 1909 in Va , m June 18, 1932, Robert Sullivan.

No. 728. Sixth Generation. 683.

5) Vada Pearl Suter, b. June 26, 1891, in Va , m Nov. 20, 1912, Jacob N Liskey Address· Rockingham, Va.

1. Jewett W. Liskey, b. Nov. 23, 1913, d June 16, 1932
2. Evelyn Virginia Liskey, b. Jan. 24, 1915.
3. Dorothy Edna Liskey, b. June 22, 1917

No. 729. Fifth Generation. 677.

8) Erasmus C. Shank, b. Jan. 2, 1861, in Rockingham Co , Va , m. Aug. 16, 1882, Ida C. Rhodes, b. Feb 24, 1862, d May 6, 1931 Address: Waynesboro, Va. Farmer. Mennonites. Minister in the Mennonite Church in Augusta Co., Va Burial in Springdale cemetery.

1 James Aaron Shank, b Feb 20, 1883, d. Feb 24, 1883.
2 Bertie Pearl Shank, b. Feb 24, 1884. No 730.
3 Ollie F. Shank, b Oct 4, 1886 No. 731
4. Joseph L. Shank, b Jan 11, 1889, d. Dec. 20, 1892.
5. Infant Son, b Jan. 10, 1892, d. same day.
6. Edna Mae Shank, b. Nov. 20, 1893. No 732.
7. Jacob Rhodes Shank, b. Oct. 8, 1895. No 733.
8. Anna M Shank, b Mar. 22, 1898, d. Dec. 27, 1906.
9. Eva Lee Shank, b. Jan. 17, 1901.
10. Erasmus Clayton Shank, b Mar. 5, 1904. No 734.
11 Russell M. Shank, b. Dec 17, 1906 No. 735.

No. 730. Sixth Generation. 729.

2) Bertie Pearl Shank, b. Feb. 24, 1884, in Va., d. Feb. 26, 1931, m. Sept. 13, 1911, Frank I. Wenger, b. Oct 18, 1883. Waynesboro, Va. Farmer Mennonites No issue.

No. 731. Sixth Generation. 729.

3) Ollie F. Shank, b. Oct. 4, 1886, in Augusta Co , Va., m May 19, 1909, Joseph Grabill, b. Mar 8, 1887. Address. Elkhart, Ind . R 6. Farmer. Mennonites

1. Mary Elnora Grabill, b. Dec 11, 1911.
2. Irvin Erasmus Grabill, b. Jan. 8, 1916.
3 Esther Virginia Grabill, b. Dec 1, 1925

No. 732. Sixth Generation. 729.

6) Edna May Shank, b. Nov 20, 1893, in Augusta Co , Va., m Dec. 30, 1914, Ira Showalter, b Oct 3, 1893. Farmers. Mennonites.

1 Marjorie K. Showalter, b. May 12. 1917.
2 Winford E Showalter, b May 24, 1919.
3. W. Milton Showalter, b Mar 13, 1923.
4 Lois B Showalter, b. Mar 18, 1926

5. Dorothy P. Showalter, b Sept. 29, 1927.
6. Leonard E. Showalter, b Mar. 12, 1929
7. Shirley R. Showalter, b. Jan. 5, 1931.

No. 733. Sixth Generation. 729.
7) Jacob Rhodes Shank, b. Oct. 8, 1895, in Augusta Co., Va., m. Dec 8, 1923, Ida Ferster, b. May 18, 1902, of Pa Farmer. Mennonites.
1. Clifford Clement Shank, b —— 23, 1924.
2 Lloyd Coffman Shank, b. Dec. 7, 1925
3. Clinton Wayne Shank, b. Apr. 14, 1927.
4. Cecil Orlen Shank, b. Nov 8, 1928.
5. Chester Stonald Shank, b. May 20, 1930.
6. John Witmer Shank, b. Feb 9, 1932.

No. 734. Sixth Generation. 729.
10) Erasmus C. Shank, Jr., b Mar. 5, 1904 in Augusta Co., Va , m. Dec 2, 1925, Mary Holsinger. Address: Waynesboro, Va. Farmer. Mennonite.
1. Lucille Holsinger Shank, b. May 11, 1927.
2 Elizabeth Beery Shank, b. July 15, 1931.

No. 735. Sixth Generation. 729.
11) Russell M. Shank, b. Dec 17, 1906, in Augusta Co., Va., m. Jan. 28, 1928, Marjorie Houff, b Aug 3, 1911 Address Waynesboro, Va Farmer. Mennonites.
1. Russell Mason Shank, b. July 6, 1932.

No. 736. Seventh Generation. 292.
1) Wade Hampton Weaver, b Oct 27, 1896, in Rockingham Co , Va., m. Tracie Arlington Weaver, b. Oct 29, 1893 Farmer. Presbyterians.
1. Virginia Alice Weaver, b Nov. 15, 1917.
2. Frances Lucille Weaver, b. Apr 10, 1919.
3. Wilmer Fultz Weaver, b June 6, 1921.
4. Madge Pauline Weaver, b. Nov. 4, 1923.
5. Ray Willard Weaver, b. Feb 18, 1925.
6 Ralph Otho Weaver, b July 7, 1927.
7. Harold David Weaver, b May 16, 1931.
8 Helen Louise Weaver, b. Sept 8, 1932.

No. 737. Seventh Generation. 292.
2) Fleta Pearl Weaver, b. July 31, 1899, Rockingham Co , Va., m. Sept 11, 1916, Elmer Elsworth, b. Nov 13, 1894. Presbyterians. Baker.
1. Ruth Irene Elsworth, b Nov. 16, 1917.
2 Elmer Elsworth, b. May 13, 1919.
3. Dorothy Lee Elsworth, b Aug. 30, 1921.
4 Phyllis Ann Elsworth, b. Mar. 29, 1930.

No. 738. Seventh Generation. 292.
3) Raymond Abraham Weaver, b Feb. 9, 1901, in Va , m. June 15, 1921, Maude Virginia Witmer, b Sept 21, 1901 Farmer Presbyterians.
1. Dorothy Elizabeth Weaver, b April 29, 1926.
2 Richard Wilson Weaver, b Sept. 9, 1932

No. 739. Seventh Generation. 292.
4) Marvin David Weaver, b. Sept 21, 1904, in Va., m June 10, 1925, Alice Lillian Liskey, b. Feb. 26, 1905. Bookkeeper. Presbyterians.
1 Lucille Mildred Weaver, b June 1, 1926.

No. 740. Seventh Generation. 293.

1) Marion R. Weaver, b. Oct. 1, 1900, in Va , m. Anna R Shank, b Dec. 15, 1901.

1. Winston O. Weaver, b. Nov 25, 1920

No. 741. Seventh Generation. 293.

3) Della P. Weaver, b. Apr. 3, 1906, in Va , m. June 29, 1927, C Justus Suter, b. July 3, 1907.

1 Glennys Marie Suter, b Sept 2, 1928, d Oct , 1928.

2. Dorothy Ann Suter, b. Mar 5, 1930

3 Donald Eugene Suter, b Apr 17, 1932

No. 742. Seventh Generation. 295.

1) Irene May Jones, b. Aug. 12, 1902, in Va., m. Jan. 26, 1922, Robert R Swartz, b. Jan 22, 1901. Mennonites. Farmers.

1 Dwight Franklin Swartz, b Jan. 14, 1924.

2 Mildred Elizabeth Swartz, b Dec 22, 1927

No. 743. Seventh Generation. 295.

2) Edna Rebecca Jones, b. Sept 2, 1906, in Va , m May 7, 1930, John Wenger Harman, b. Oct 14, 1907 Cabinet maker Mennonite.

1. Shirley Belle Harman, b. June 29, 1931.

2 Merlin David Harman, b ————————

No. 744. Seventh Generation. 295.

3) Vada Anna Jones, b. Aug. 14, 1909, in Va , m May 7, 1930, James Taft Shank, b. Oct. 6, 1908. Mr Shank is a Mennonite minister. Address: Mt. Crawford, Va.

1. James Leonard Shank, b Jan. 17, 1933.

No. 745. Fourth Generation. 22.

3) John Shank, b Sept. 22, 1819, in Rockingham Co , Va , d. Mar. 29, 1898, at Summum, Ill., m. Mary Branson, b Nov 18, 1824, d. Mar. 30, 1896. Both were buried at Ipava, Ill. Early in life they moved from Virginia to Summum, Ill , at which place he had a general store and was postmaster in connection with it. His son Chester was his partner in the later years of his life. He was married the second time after the death of the first wife, but we have been unable to learn who she was. After his sons grew to manhood they changed the spelling of the name to Schenk by which name they will be known in this history. He was one of the first settlers in Fulton Co., Ill.

(John Schenk's birth must be an error —The author)

1. Myron Schenk, b. 1850 No 746.

2 Frances Schenk, b 1853 No. 793.

3. Caroline Schenk, b. 1855. No. 796

4. Chester Schenk, b 1862 No 798

No. 746. Fifth Generation. 745.

1) Myron P. Schenk, b. 1850, d 1904, m Mary McLaren, b. 1852, d 1926 Physician at Summum, Ill Both were buried in Summum cemetery

1. Clark Schenk, b. 1873. No. 747.

2 Fannie Schenk, b 1876. No. 750.

3. Mae Schenk, b. Feb. 20, 1878 No 755

4. Belle Schenk, b 1881. No. 760.

No. 747. Sixth Generation. 746.

1) Myron Clark Schenk, b 1873, m. Martha Wilson, b 1875. Physician at Rushville, Ill.

1. Oliva D. Schenk, b. 1894 No. 748.
2. J. Paul Schenk, b 1897. No. 749.

No. 748. Seventh Generation. 747.

1) Oliva D. Schenk, b. 1894 in Ill., m. B. C Bradford
1. Paul Cullen Bradford, b. in 1923 or 1924.

No. 749. Seventh Generation. 747.

2) J. Paul Schenk, b. 1897, m. Gladys Greer.
1. Martha Jean Schenk, b. 1925.
2. Richard Greer Schenk, b 1928.

No. 750. Sixth Generation. 746.

2) Fannie Schenk, b. Sept., 1875, m June 30, 1894, Merritt Langston, b 1870, d. 1928. Physician. Methodist Peoria, Ill
1. Ruth Langston, b 1896. No. 751.
2. Merritt Langston, b. 1900. No. 752.
3. Fern Langston, b 1902. No. 753.
4. Russell Langston, b 1905. No. 754.
5 Mary Langston, b 1907.

No. 751. Seventh Generation. 750.

1) Ruth Langston, b in 1896, in Ill., m Clyde Eaton.
1. Clyde Eaton, Jr., b. ——————.
2. John Paul Eaton, b. 1925
3. Marvin Eaton, b. ——————.

No. 752. Seventh Generation. 750.

2) Merrett Langston, b. 1900, in Ill., m. Marjory Creviston.
1. Marjory Ann Langston, b. 1925.
2. Merritt Langston, b 1929

No. 753. Seventh Generation. 750.

3) Fern Langston, b 1902, in Ill., m. Ellis Dorman.
1. Robert Dorman, b. 1921
2. Jean Dorman, b 1925.
3. Dorothy Dorman, b. 1928.

No. 754. Seventh Generation. 750.

4) Russell Langston, b 1905, in Ill, m. Grace Lynch. No issue.

No. 755. Sixth Generation. 746.

3) Mae Schenck, b Feb. 20, 1878, in Ill., m Aug. 30, 1896, William J. Hartzell, b. May 14, 1877. Address 228 E. Duryea St, Peoria, Ill. Teacher. Congregational.
1. Harold G Hartzell, b. Dec 7, 1897 No 756.
2. Esther E. Hartzell, b Mar. 29, 1900 No. 757.
3. Lenore B. Hartzell, b. Feb 5, 1903. No 758.
4 Myron W. Hartzell, b Nov 18, 1908 No 759

No. 756. Seventh Generation. 755.

1) Harold G. Hartzell, b. Dec. 7, 1897, in Ill, m Mabel Deoble, b ——————
Address: Peoria Heights, Ill

1. Paul Hartzell, b. ——————.
2. Donald Hartzell, b. ——————.

No. 757. Seventh Generation. 755.
2) Esther C. Hartzell, b Mar. 29, 1900, in Ill., m A. A. Pugh. Address: Peoria Heights, Ill.
1. James Pugh, b ——————.
2. Thomas Pugh, b. ——————.
3. Nancy Pugh, b. ——————

No. 758. Seventh Generation. 755.
3) Lenore Hartzell, b. Feb 5, 1902, in Ill, m. Frank Piel. Address. Peoria Heights, Ill.
1. William Piel, b ——————.
2 Richard Piel, b. ——————.

No. 759. Seventh Generation. 755.
4) Myron W. Hartzell, b. Nov 18, 1908, in Ill, m. Ethelyn Tidebuck, b —————. Address: Peoria Heights, Ill

No. 760. Sixth Generation. 746.
4) Belle Schenk, b. ——————, 1881, in Ill, m. ——————, 1901, A. R Linebaugh, b. ——————, 1882. Address Havanna, Ill. Farmer
1. Alletha Linebaugh, b ——————, 1901, twin
2. Alberta Linebaugh, b ——————, 1901, twin. No. 791
3. Helen Linebaugh, b ——————, 1904. No 791¼
4. Frank Linebaugh, b. ——————, 1906
5. Marion Linebaugh, b. ——————, 1908
6 Evelyn Linebaugh, b ——————, 1910 No 792

No. 761. Sixth Generation. 380.
1) Isadora B Hotchkiss, b Feb 8, 1875, m Feb 6, 1895, Edward A Clark, b Dec. 23, 1865. Address Beldron, S Dak Farmer Congregational.
1. Harry Leroy Clark, b. Mar. 14, 1897 No 762
2. Avery Albert Clark, b Dec 21, 1898 No. 763.
3. Lula Madge Clark, b. July 25, 1904 No 764.
4. Clara Mae Clark, b. Mar 3, 1908 No 765

No. 762. Seventh Generation. 761.
1) Harry Leroy Clark, b Mar. 14, 1897, m Clara L. Neilson, Oct 30, 1920
1. Maurice Edward Clark, b. Sept. 27, 1921.
2. Deween Marle Clark, b July 19, 1925

No. 763. Seventh Generation. 761.
2) Avery Albert Clark, b Dec 21, 1898, m Mar. 17, 1923, Genevieve Schmidt
1. Marion Jean Clark, b. Nov 2, 1923.
2. Avis Alberta Clark, b May 28, 1925.
3 James William Clark, b Sept 19, 1926
4. Mary Lee Clark, b. Aug. 15, 1929
5. John Perry Clark, b Dec 18, 1930.

No. 764. Seventh Generation. 761.
3) Lula Madge Clark, b. July 25, 1904, m July 18, 1925, Hamilton Eugene Girard.
1. Beverly Madge Girard, b. Aug 5, 1926.
2. Eugene Hamilton Girard, b July 11, 1930

No. 765. Seventh Generation. 761.

4) Clara Mae Clark, b Mar 3, 1908, m. Sept. 20, 1924, Raymond G. Meyers
1. Monte Irvin Meyers, b. May 19, 1925.

No. 766. Sixth Generation. 380.

2) Agnes M Hotchkiss, b May 4, 1879, in Iowa, m. Dec. 7, 1898, John Wright, b. May 9, 1876, d May 13, 1924. Address: Granger, Ia. Rural mail carrier. Buried in the Lincoln cemetery.
1. Everett Allison Wright, b Feb. 19, 1900.
2. Ralph Albert Wright, b. May 24, 1903. No 767.

No. 767. Seventh Generation. 766.

2) Ralph Albert Wright, b. May 24, 1903, m. Edna Gifford   Address: 803 N. H St, Richmond, Ind.
1. Max Edward Wright, b. —————.

No. 768. Sixth Generation. 380.

3) Frank W. Hotchkiss, b. Nov. 9, 1885, m. Mar. 11, 1914, Pearl Roth, b Nov. 4, 1890. Address: Granger, Ia. Farmer   Christian Church.
1 Franklin R. Hotchkiss, b Jan. 24 1915.
2. Cheryl P. Hotchkiss, b. Feb. 12, 1918
3. Thelma M Hotchkiss, b Dec. 21, 1921.

No. 770. Sixth Generation. 379.

2) Florence May Smith, b Sept. 6, 1878, in Mo, m. June 22, 1897, George Marsailes Hoover, b May 4, 1874. Address· Superior, Ariz., Box 186. Mechanic Christ Church.
1. Carl E. Hoover, b. June 3, 1898.
2. Stella May Hoover, b. Mar. 1, 1903. No. 771.
3. Buford M Hoover, b May 4, 1905

No. 771. Seventh Generation. 379.

2) Stella May Hoover, b. Mar. 1, 1903, m in 1916 W. G Overly.
1. Edgar Grant Overly, b. Aug 1, 1921 (from first marriage)
On July 1, 1932, Mrs. Overly married W. G. Wallzie, living at Flagstaff, Ariz.

No. 772. Seventh Generation. 379.

1) Carl E Hoover, b. June 3, 1898, m. ———————. When last heard of was in Carthage, Mo. One son

No. 773. Seventh Generation. 379.

3) Buford M Hoover, b May 4, 1905, m. —————— Address: Glendale, Ariz, R 1 One son. No further report

No. 774. Sixth Generation. 379.

3) Arthur A Smith, b July 20, 1881, in Mo, m. Feb. 14, 1906, Cora F. Pearson, b 1875 Address· Mountain Grove, Mo. Farmer. Methodist. No issue.

No. 775. Sixth Generation. 379.

4) Clara B Smith, b Aug 30, 1883, in Mo, m Aug. 22, 1906, Elsworth S. Chambers, b. Jan 16, 1878, d Mar. 5, 1918 Address· 106 N. Walnut St, Commerce, Okla. Miner. Christian Church
1 Ruth Chambers, b. Jan. 13, 1908
2 Wayne Chambers, b. Feb 17, 1911.

No. 776. Sixth Generation. 379.

5) Olive Helen Smith, b Feb 14, 1886, m Feb 17, 1916, William Oscar Rudd, b Jan 2, 1882 Address 2531 Harvard Ave, Butte, Mont Housekeeper

No. 777. Sixth Generation. 379.

6) Ethel A Smith, b. June 14, 1889, in Mo., m ——————— Trigg. Address: 3677 Boise Ave , Venice, Calif.

No. 778. Sixth Generation. 379.

7) Edna C. Smith, b. Oct. 2, 1892, in Mo , m ——————— Pott Address: Toledo, O

No. 779. Seventh Generation. 421.

1) Mary E Van Pelt, b Oct 7, 1904, m Wilbur Alexander. Mrs Alexander is a nurse at the T. B Sanitarium of Springfield, O Church of Christ No children.

No. 780. Seventh Generation. 421.

3) Icy P Van Pelt, b Feb 4, 1908. m Francis English Address. Columbus Grove, O , R. 4. Church of Christ.

1 Infant son (stillborn), Dec , 1929
2 Elizabeth Genell English, b July 19, 1931
3 A daughter born Sept., 1934.

No. 781. Seventh Generation. 421.

4) Tracy M Van Pelt, b June 12, 1910, m Walter McClain Address Lima, O . R. 4. Church of Christ.

1 William Arthur McClain, b. June 11, 1929.
2 Donna Jean McClain, b. Oct. 13, 1930.
3. Mary Lou McClain, b Nov 14, 1931
4 Richard Clyde McClain, b. Aug 1, 1932

No. 782. Seventh Generation. 428.

3) Vera V. Brunk, b. Jan. 3, 1910, near Elida, O., m Dec. 22, 1934, Louis H Good, b Feb. 3, 1911, at South Boston, Va Address South Boston, Va. Mennonite.

1 Mary Ellen and Martha May born Dec 7, 1935; died same day.

No. 783. Seventh Generation. 428.

4) Lois Brunk, b Nov 15, 1911, near Elida, O , m. Feb 21, 1934, Paul Bare, b Sept. 26, 1910 Address Elida, O., R 2 Laborer Mennonite

1. Cretora Lois Bare, b. Feb 10, 1935.

No. 784. Seventh Generation. 428.

5) Esther Brunk, b Nov 21, 1913, near Elida, O , m Nov. 17, 1934, Merlin Good, b Aug 6, 1911. Address: Elida, O., R. 2.

1 Ruby Lucille Good, b. Feb. 20, 1936

No. 785. Sixth Generation. 375.

2) Lillie Anna Brunk, b Oct. 20, 1876, in Va , m June 1, 1904, Heishey H Weaver, b. July 30, 1877. Address: 254 Newman Ave , Harrisonburg, Va. Produce dealer Presbyterians Burial ground at Harrisonburg, Va

1 Mary Elizabeth Weaver, b. Oct 13, 1905 No 786
2 Charles Oliver Weaver, b Mar 21, 1911

No. 786. Seventh Generation. 785.

1) Mary Elizabeth Weaver, b. Oct. 13, 1905, in Va., m. ——————— Shields

No. 787. Sixth Generation. 375.

3) Oliver Curry Brunk, b. Sept 13, 1878, in Va , m Bernice Hall of Lynchburg, Va Physician in Richmond, Va.

1 Elizabeth Curry Brunk, b July 22, 1922

No. 788. Seventh Generation. 311.

1) Carl E Showalter, b Nov 29, 1913, m Nov 25, 1934, Ruby Yoder, of East Holbrook, Colo. Address, La Junta, Colo
1 Geraldine Showalter, b Sept, 1935

No. 790. Sixth Generation. 385.

6) Paul E Weaver, b Dec 12, 1902, m Apr 14, 1935, at La Junta, Colo, Jennie E Snyder Address: La Junta, Colo. Mennonites.

No. 791. Seventh Generation. 760.

2) Alberta Linebaugh, b ————, 1901, in Ill, m. Edward Platte, a ranger from Nebraska Mrs Platte was a school teacher before marriage.
1 Archie Stillman Platte, b ————, 1931
2 Mary Jane Platte, b Nov 22, 1934

No. 791¼. Seventh Generation. 760.

3) Helen Linebaugh, b 1904, in Ill, m Samuel Witzig Laborer Address Havannah, Ill
1 Beverly Ann Witzig, b Nov 10, 19—

No. 792. Seventh Generation. 760.

6) Evelyn Linebaugh, b 1910, m Robert C Seigrist Evelyn is a graduate beauty culturist
1 Leslie Eugene Seigrist, b. May 4, 1936

No. 793. Fifth Generation. 745.

2) Frances Schenk, b 1853, d 1892, m Luke Wilcox Clark, b 1841, d 1914 Physician. Buried at Rushville, Ill, which was their address.
1 John Wheeler Clark, b Mar 4, 1873 No 794
2 Myron Walter Clark, b Aug 7, 1876. Address Cartersville, Mo Single
3 Earl Wilcox Clark, Address. Cartersville, Mo. Single
4 Martin Homer Clark, b ——————— No 795.

No. 794. Sixth Generation. 793.

1 John Wheeler Clark, b Mar 4, 1873, at Rushville, Ill., m. June 12, 1917, Jessie Irene Rowden, b Aug 6, 1885 Address: Cartersville, Mo. Physician. No issue.

No. 795. Sixth Generation. 793.

4) Martin Homer Clark, b. ——————, Rushville, Ill, m Pearl Martin in 1917 Address Hall and Vine Sts, Cartersville, Mo
1 ————————————, failed to report

No. 796. Fifth Generation. 745.

3) Caroline Schenk, b Dec 31, 1856, at Summum, Ill, m. William L Russell, b. Oct. 13, 1851 at Ipava, Ill She died July 9, 1926 He died Feb. 19, 1921 Buried at Cartersville, Mo.
1 Raymond D Russell, b Sept 2, 1880 No 797.
2 Myron Russell, b —————— No 797½.
3 Kenneth Russell, b —————— No 797¾.

No. 797. Sixth Generation. 796.

1) Raymond D. Russell, b Sept 2, 1880, Ill., m Nov 16, 1902, Grace LaRue, b Sept. 9, 1881, at Ipava, Ill Address Chillicothe, Mo. Farmer Methodists
1 Mildred Marjorie Russell, b Nov 19, 1904, d Apr 16, 1913, buried at Chillicothe, Mo

No. 797½. Sixth Generation. 796.

2) Myron M. Russell, b July 12, 1888, at Ipava, Ill, m July, 1910, Katherine Robertson, b. Dec 31, 1888, at Tina, Mo. They live at Chillicothe, Mo No issue.

No. 797¾. Sixth Generation. 796.

3) Kenneth W Russell, b July 6, 1895, at Ipava, Ill Single Address. Chillicothe, Mo

No. 798. Fifth Generation. 745.

4) Chester Schenk, b Nov 28, 1862, d Mar. 6, 1924, buried at Astoria, Ill., m Lucelle Sweeny, b May 6, 1863 Address Summum, Ill Merchant and postmaster.

1. Anita Louise Schenk, b. July 12, 1892. No 799
2. Gladys Schenk, b. Dec 5, 1893, single.
3. Allen Melvin Schenk, b Sept. 4, 1899, d Dec. 18, 1905

Gladys Helen Schenk is a professor of music at Summum, Ill, where she is caring for her mother.

No. 799. Sixth Generation. 798.

1) Anita Louise Schenk, b July 12, 1892, at Summum, Ill, m Oct 2, 1921, William Kost, b. Aug 7, 1892 Address Astoria, Ill, where he is a druggist Methodists. Mr Kost was a first sergeant of the 123rd Field Artillery, 58th Brigade of the 33rd division during the World War He was in the medical department, and spent 18 months in the St Miehl Argonne Verdun, and was in the army of occupation in Germany.

1. William Robert Kost, b May 2, 1923

No. 800. Fourth Generation. 22.

4) Anna Shank, b Sept 15, 1824, near Edom, Va On Aug 17, 1843, she m John B Wenger, b Sept 16, 1820 Mr. Wenger died suddenly Mar. 31, 1883. Mrs. Wenger died at Harrisonburg, Va Mennonites

1 Elizabeth Wenger, b. Sept. 1, 1848 No. 801
2. John A. Wenger, b. Aug. 26, 1859 No 802
3 David H Wenger, b July 23, 1862, d Aug 20, 1890

No. 801. Fifth Generation. 800.

1) Elizabeth Wenger, b. Sept 1, 1848, in Va., m Dec. 24, 1872, Daniel J. Meyers, b. Mar. 19, 1850 Address Harrisonburg, Va Church of the Brethren

1. Anna R. Meyers, b July 3, 1874 No 803
2. John W. S. Meyers, b. May 28, 1876. No. 804.
3. Elizabeth S. Meyers, b. Nov 17, 1877 No. 805.
4 Samuel D. Meyers, b June 24, 1880, d Apr. 24, 1881.
5. Lydia M. Meyers, b Nov. 28, 1882. No 1017.
6. Isaac D. Meyers, b June 28, 1885 No 806.
7. Sallie C Meyers, b April 3, 1887. No 807
8 Minnie J. Meyers, b. June 8, 1889 No 1011

No. 802. Fifth Generation. 800.

2) John A. Wenger, b Aug. 26, 1859, near Harrisonburg, Va, m. Nov 18, 1880, Sallie R Driver, b Nov. 29, 1859 Address. Mt. Clinton, Va. Church of the Brethren.

1. Bettie A Wenger, b Jan 10, 1882 No 808
2. Savilla F. Wenger, b Jan 25, 1884 No 1023
3. John D. Wenger, b Feb. 5, 1886. No. 1024.
4. William N. Wenger, b. Mar. 24, 1888. No 1025.
5 Lydia S. Wenger, b Mar 14, 1890 No 1026.

No. 803. Sixth Generation. 801.

1) Anna R Meyers, b. July 3, 1874, near Harrisonburg, Va., m. Jan. 30, 1894, John W Showalter. Address. Linville Depot, Va. Farmer.

1. Clara Showalter, b. Feb 26, 1897. No. 1012.
2. Lillie Showalter, b. Mar. 30, 1899.
3. Isadora Showalter, b. Mar. 13, 1902.
4. Effie N. Showalter, b. Aug. 14, 1903.
5. John B. D. Showalter, b Dec. —, 1904.
6. Albert Meyers Showalter, b Feb. 10, 1907.
7. Howard Anthony Showalter, b Aug. 10, 1909.
8. Anna Rebecca Showalter, b July 6, 1911.
9. DeWitt Raymond Showalter, b May 26, 1913

No. 804. Sixth Generation. 801.

2) John W. S Meyers, b May 28, 1876, in Va, m. Oct 5, 1901, Annie E. Miller Address Harrisonburg, Va Farmer, near Garvers Church.

1. Elizabeth C. Meyers, b Oct 17, 1902. No. 1013.
2. Alvin P. Meyers, b. Oct. 5, 1904 No 1014.
3. Ralph M Meyers, b Aug 12, 1906 No. 1015.
4. Mary O Meyers, b Feb 25, 1909, d. July 25, 1909.
5. Daniel J. Meyers, b July 14, 1910.
6. Myrtle A Meyers, b Sept 22, 1912.
7. Harold A. Meyers, b Oct 26, 1914
8. Tressa Vae Meyers, b Aug 1, 1920
9. Annie Mae Meyers, b June 15, 1923.

All were born near Harrisonburg, Va, and all are members of the Church of the Brethren.

No. 805. Sixth Generation. 801.

3) Elizabeth S Meyers, b Nov 17, 1877, in Harrisonburg, Va, m June 30, 1900, S. D Zigler. who is a minister of the Church of the Brethren Address: Harrisonburg, Va

1. John M Zigler, b June 30, 1901, d Apr. 18, 1902
2. Earl M Zigler, b Jan 12, 1903 Teacher
3. Ruth Zigler, b June 26, 1905 No 1016.
4. Glen V Zigler, b April 1, 1907, d. Aug 21, 1907.
5. Grace M Zigler, b. July 22, 1908, R N
6. Leona M. Zigler, b Feb 24, 1910
7. Isaac M. Zigler, b Nov 28, 1915.
8. Alma M Zigler, b. July 18, 1919

No. 806. Sixth Generation. 801.

6) Isaac D Meyers, b June 28, 1885, near Harrisonburg, Va., m. Dec. 27, 1904, Isadora S Click Address: Dayton, Va. Brethren Church.

1. Lloyd Meyers, b. April 14, 1906 No 1018
2. Victor Jackson Meyers, b Dec 8, 1910. No. 1019.

No. 807. Sixth Generation. 801.

7) Sallie C. Meyers, b April 3, 1887, in Rockingham Co, Va, m. Dec. 2, 1903, Wade G. Flory, b. Nov. 6, 1881 Address: Dayton, Va. Farmer. Brethren.

1. Cleta Blanche Flory, b Oct 28, 1904. No. 1020.
2. Minnie Myers Flory, b Nov. 15, 1906 No. 1021.
3. Mabel Cathryn Flory, b. Mar 25, 1910 No 1022.
4. Charles Edward Flory, b. Oct. 4, 1913.
5. Arvetta Virginia Flory, b Nov 2, 1917.
6. Arlie Lee Flory, b. Oct 29, 1927.

No. 808. Sixth Generation. 802.

1) Bettie A. Wenger, b Jan. 10, 1882, near Harrisonburg, Va, m. Feb. 18, 1900, B. M. Hedrick. Address Bridgewater, Va.

1 M. Raymond Hedrick, b April 29, 1902.
2 John Randolph Hedrick, b. July 9, 1903
3. Esther Marion Hedrick, b July 16, 1906
4. Bayard M Hedrick, b July 29, 1916.

No. 809. Fourth Generation. 22.

5) Michael Shank, b July 15, 1829, near Harrisonburg, Va, d. June 26, 1905. On Aug. 31, ———, he was united in marriage to Lydia Beery. She was born near Edom, Va., Jan. 6, 1830 She died Mar. 13, 1884 She together with her daughter Abbie died, and others of the family were injured from the effects of gas fumes from the coal stove in their home. In 1885 he married Margaret Rhodes (nee Heatwole), she was born Mar. 13, 1830, and d July 7, 1892. He and his first two wives were Mennonites. On July 30, 1893, he married Sarah Miller, b. Jan. 1, 1855, and d. June 24, 1932. Address: Dale Enterprise, Va. Truck farmer Children are all from first marriage.

1. Fannie M. Shank, b. May 17, 1852. No 810
2. Hettie M. Shank, b. Aug 2, 1855. No. 822.
3 John W. Shank, b Oct. 27, 1854. No. 831.
4 Catherine Shank, b Dec 2, 1855. No. 848.
5. Charles G. Shank, b. Feb 25, 1857. No 872.
6 Laura Shank, b. Oct. 8, 1860. No 881
7. Abbie Shank, b Aug. 8, 1863, d. Mar. 24, 1884.
8 Jacob L Shank, b July 18, 1870 No 885.

No. 810. Fifth Generation. 809.

1) Fannie M. Shank, b. May 17, 1852, near Dale Enterprise, Va, m Jan. 5, 1875, J. C. McNett, b. Sept 28, 1847 Mrs McNett died Jan. 6, 1920 She was a Mennonite. Address: Harrisonburg, Va Burial at Pike Church cemetery

1. Laura V. McNett, b Sept. 22, 1876 No 811
2. Clara B. McNett, b. Dec. 12, 1877 No 812.
3 Luther M. McNett, b. Sept 10, 1879 No. 813.
4 Emma P. McNett, b. Sept 25, 1881 No 814
5. William C. McNett, b Feb. 12, 1883 No. 817.
6. Mattie J. McNett, b. April 29, 1885 No 819.
7. Arthur B. McNett, b. June 19, 1887, single, lives in Md.
8. Tracie K. McNett, b. June 14, 1891 No. 820
9. Elsie M. McNett, b. Feb. 18, 1893, T.N
10 Atlee F. McNett, b Jan 7, 1896 No 821

No. 811. Sixth Generation. 810.

1) Laura V. McNett, b Sept. 22, 1876, in Va., m Jan. 2, 1904, Scott Willis Address: Pittsburgh, Pa.

No. 812. Sixth Generation. 810.

2) Clara B. McNett, b. Dec. 12, 1877, in Va, m Nov. 25, 1902, Timothy D. Swartz, b. Aug 15, 1882 Address Harrisonburg, Va. Progressive Brethren minister, and carpenter.

1. Reva I. Swartz, b. Feb 3, 1906
2. Aldalene L. Swartz, b April 9, 1911.
3. Welby Swartz, b. April 19, 1915.

No. 813. Sixth Generation. 810.

3) Luther M. McNett, b. Sept. 10, 1879, in Rockingham Co., Va., m. Dec. 25, 1911, Mrs. Maud Miller. Employed by the White Mountain Creamery, New Bremen, O.

1. Atmer B. McNett, b. Jan. 12, 1913.
2. Betty Jane McNett, b. May 12, 1915, d. same day.
3. Virginia F. McNett, b. Oct. 9, 1917.
4. Lowell M. McNett, b June 10, 1919.
5. Richard L. McNett, b. Apr. 14, 1925.

No. 814. Sixth Generation. 810.

4) Emma P. McNett, b. Sept. 25, 1881, in Rockingham Co., Va., m. Nov. 18, 1900, Clark L Trobaugh, b. Nov. 30, 1878, d Jan 26, 1931. Address: Harrisonburg, Va.

1. Lillie F. Trobaugh, b. Oct. 10, 1901.
2. Maud B. Trobaugh, b Oct. 28, 1902. No. 815.
3. William J. Trobaugh, b. Mar. 21, 1904.
4. Lawrence A. Trobaugh, b May 1, 1905.
5. Mary E. Trobaugh, b. May 2, 1907 No. 816.
6. Edward A. Trobaugh, b July 17, 1908
7. Lloyd L. Trobaugh, b. Sept 15, 1911.
8. Pearl D Trobaugh, b Oct 13, 1912.
9. Calvin B. Trobaugh, b. Nov. 17, 1915.
10 Clark L Trobaugh, Jr , b Aug 21, 1920.

No. 815. Seventh Generation. 814.

2) Maud B Trobaugh, b Oct 28, 1902, in Rockingham Co, Va , m Nov. 15, 1923, Dewey Senger, b. Sept 21, 1898 Address: Harrisonburg, Va.

1 Celestine B. Senger, b. Oct. 16, 1924.
2. Norlyn Lee Senger, b July 21, 1927.
3 Betty Ann Senger, b Feb 21, 1930

No. 816. Seventh Generation. 814.

5) Mary E. Trobaugh, b. May 2, 1907, in Rockingham Co , Va., m Aug. 23, 1927, Elmer D Showalter. Address· Harrisonburg, Va.

No. 817. Sixth Generation. 810.

5) William C. McNett, b. Feb. 12, 1883, in Rockingham Co., Va., m. July 15, 1906, Olive I Snyder, b July 11, 1888 Address: Lima, O , R 8 Church of the Brethren

1. Lela McNett, b June 25, 1908 No 818.
2 Glenna McNett, b Aug 25, 1909
3 Ralph McNett, b. July 24, 1911.
4. Julia McNett, b. May 22, 1914
5. Robert McNett, b Feb. 13, 1917
6. Helen McNett, b May 11, 1919
7. John McNett, b. Aug. 2, 1921
8 Martha McNett, b Nov 18, 1922.
9. Dorothy McNett, b. Aug. 24, 1924.
10. Frances McNett, b. Feb. 20, 1926.
11. James McNett, b Aug. 26, 1927.
12. Betty June McNett, b. June 7, 1929
13. Maxine McNett, b. Nov. 11, 1930.
14 Barbara Ann McNett, b Jan 26, 1932.

No. 818. Seventh Generation. 817.

1) Lela J McNett, b June 25, 1908, near Lima, O , m. Oct 9, 1926, Russell E. McDorman, b Dec 31, 1902. Teacher in Public Schools Church of the Brethren. Beaver Dam, O.

1. Richard Eugene McDorman, b Aug 6, 1929.
2. Wilbur Russell McDorman, b Nov. 5, 1930

No. 819. Sixth Generation. 810.

6) Mattie J McNett, b Apr. 29, 1885, Rockingham Co., Va , m. ——————— Richardson Living in Washington, D C.

No. 820. Sixth Generation. 810.

8) Tracie K. McNett, b June 14, 1891, Rockingham Co , Va., m. William Black Living in Pittsburgh, Pa No children

No. 821. Sixth Generation. 810.

10) Atlee F. McNett, b Jan. 7, 1896, Rockingham Co , Va , m Jan 28, 1917, Frances E. Myers, b. Mar 17, 1897 Address Dayton, Va Farmer

1. Rowland M McNett, b. June 13, 1922
2 Mary L McNett, b. Feb. 16, 1924
3. Kathleen F McNett, b Jan 26, 1926, d Aug 2, 1927.
4 Glenna W. McNett, b. Feb 26, 1927.
5 Harold F. McNett, b Apr 10, 1928
6 Norman B McNett, b June 9, 1929

No. 822. Fifth Generation. 809.

2) Hettie M Shank, b Aug 2, 1853, near Dayton, Va., d. July 7, 1924 On April 17, 1873, she was united in marriage to David H Burkholder, b Jan. 16, 1852. He died Oct. 22, 1920 They lived near Harrisonburg, Va Mennonites Buried in Pike Church cemetery.

1 Annie C. Burkholder, b. Jan 11, 1874 No 823.
2. Martin L. Burkholder, b Feb. 21, 1875, twin No 825.
3 Jacob B Burkholder, b. Feb 21, 1875. twin, d in infancy.
4 Minnie F. Burkholder, b Mar 15, 1877 Mennonite
5. Sophia M. Burkholder, b Aug 30, 1879 No 826
6 Lydia M. Burkholder, b Apr 29, 1881 Single Mennonite
7. Emma L Burkholder, b July 9, 1883 No 828
8. Herman F. Burkholder, b. Apr 7, 1885. No 829.
9. Lewis A Burkholder, b. Nov. 24, 1889. No 830.

No. 823. Sixth Generation. 822.

1) Annie C Burkholder, b Jan 11, 1874, near Harrisonburg, Va , m Jan 10, 1906, Henry S. Alderfer, of Souderton, Pa He died Dec 31, 1912.

1. David H Alderfer, b. Sept 7, 1907 No 824.

No. 824. Seventh Generation. 823.

1) David H. Alderfer, b Sept 7, 1907, Souderton, Pa , m Mar 27, 1932, Mary L. Histand, b. Mar 26, 1906, Doylestown, Pa., R N. Mennonites. Employed by the Mennonite Publishing House at Scottdale, Pa.

1. Joseph Alderfer, b Jan. 3, 1934.
2. Frederick Alderfer, b. April 4, 1938

No. 825. Sixth Generation. 822.

2) Martin L. Burkholder, b Feb 21, 1875, near Harrisonburg, Va , m. Dec. 8, 1896, Etta M. Swartz, b June 22, 1872 She died Aug 13, 1921 Address· Harrisonburg, Va Farmer. Mennonites.

1. Clifford A. Burkholder, b Oct 31, 1897. No 3704
2. Marion D Burkholder, b June 18, 1899 No. 827
3 Paul F. Burkholder, b June 6, 1901
4 Esther R. Burkholder, b June 13, 1903.
5. Eva M Burkholder, b Aug 12, 1905.
6. Ruth L. Burkholder, b. Sept 22, 1907.
7. Herman L. Burkholder, b Aug 31, 1909
8. Irene C. Burkholder, b. Oct 28, 1911, twin.
9. Pauline E. Burkholder, b Oct 28, 1911, twin
10 Clayton B Burkholder, b Oct. 23, 1917.

No. 826. Sixth Generation. 822.

5) Sophia M. Burkholder, b Aug 30, 1879, near Harrisonburg, Va., m. Nov. 29, 1903, Otho O. Rhodes, b Apr 26, 1880. Address: Harrisonburg, Va Electrician. Mennonite

1. Mary E. Rhodes, b Aug 3, 1907.
2 Lloyd B. Rhodes, b. Apr 10, 1911
3. Clarence E. Rhodes, b. Sept. 3, 1916.
4. Gladys L. Rhodes, b. Nov. 14, 1918.

No. 827. Seventh Generation. 825.

2) Marion D. Burkholder, b June 18, 1899, near Harrisonburg, Va , m. June 2, 1927, E. C. Moyer, b Souderton, Pa , Aug. 19, 1896 Address Brentwood, Md. Carpenter Mennonites.

1. Ruth L Burkholder, b. Oct 12, 1928
2. David Burkholder, b. July 15, 1934.
3 Lois Arlene Burkholder, b July 23, 1936.

No. 828. Sixth Generation. 822.

7) Emma L. Burkholder, b July 9, 1883, near Harrisonburg, Va , m Oct. 20, 1907, Joseph E. Huber, b Dec 8, 1880 Address Delphos, O., R. 2. Carpenter. Mennonite

1 Gladys L Huber, b. Aug. 25, 1908
2 Hettie E. Huber, b. Apr 13, 1910, d Feb 16, 1931.
3. Aaron D Huber, b Jan 5, 1912
4. Dorothy M. Huber, b Nov 5, 1914
5. Martha F Huber, b —— 3, 1916
6 Daniel A Huber, b. ————, 1918
7 Ornan L Huber, b Apr. 10, 1922

No. 829. Sixth Generation. 822.

8) Herman F. Burkholder, b. Apr 7, 1885, near Harrisonburg, Va , m. June 29, 1915, Anna V Good, b Feb 13, 1891 Address Harrisonburg, Va Farmer Mennonite

1. Daniel J Burkholder, b May 6, 1916
2. Ruby B. Burkholder, b June 26, 1918.
3. Charles B. Burkholder, b Jan 9, 1921
4. William H. Burkholder, b Sept 20, 1923
5 Ralph J. Burkholder, b Nov 27, 1927
6 Franklin Burkholder, b ——————

No. 830. Sixth Generation. 822.

9) Lewis A. Burkholder, b. Nov 24, 1889, near Harrisonburg, Va , m Jan. 20, 1914, Laura R. Wenger, b Aug 23, 1889, near Edom, Va Address Denbigh, Va. Dairyman and poultryman Mennonites

1. James D Burkholder, b Oct 24, 1914
2 Nelson D. Burkholder, b Mar. 24, 1916
3. June E. Burkholder, b June 9, 1920
4. Frances B Burkholder, b Feb 21, 1925
5. Lewis A Burkholder, Jr, b Feb 8, 1927

No. 831. Fifth Generation. 809.

3) John W Shank, b Oct. 27, 1854, near Dayton, Va, d Mar. 10, 1920, m Oct 20, 1878, Hanna F Heatwole, July 4, 1824 Address: Dayton, Va Farmer Mennonites.

1. Sally E. Shank, b Jan 15, 1880 No 832
2 Irvin C Shank, b. Nov 7, 1881, d June 15, 1896
3. Clara K. Shank, b. Dec 7, 1883 No 836.
4 Bertha B Shank, b Oct 31, 1885. No 839
5 Kent M. Shank, b. Jan 1, 1888 No 842
6 Frank M. Shank, b Oct 9, 1890 No 843
7 Annie M. Shank, b Mar 18, 1893 No 844
8. Glenn W. Shank, b Dec. 8, 1895 No 845
9. Wade H Shank, b. Jan 21, 1898 No 846
10 Fannie I Shank, b June 12, 1900 No 847

No. 832. Sixth Generation. 831.

1) Sally E. Shank, b Jan 15, 1880, near Dayton, Va, m Dec. 23, 1900, Jacob D Kiser, b Nov. 22, 1880 Address Harrisonburg, Va Farmer. Mennonites

1 Josie I. Kiser, b Nov 7, 1903
2 Carl L Kiser, b Mar 12, 1905 No 833
3 Marvin T Kiser, b Mar 28, 1907. No 834
4 Ruby T Kiser, b Apr 16, 1909 No 835
5 Oren S. Kiser, b June 24, 1911
6 Oliver B. Kiser, b July 9, 1913
7. Della M Kiser, b Dec 24, 1915
8. Alvin J Kiser, b Feb 15, 1918
9 Grace E Kiser, b. Jan 16, 1920

No. 833. Seventh Generation. 832.

2) Carl L Kiser, b Mar 12, 1905, near Harrisonburg, Va., m May 18, 1927, Della R Wenger, b Aug 10, 1907 Address Harrisonburg, Va Farmer Mennonite

1. Gladys V. Kiser, b Nov 21, 1928
2 Raymond J Kiser, b Mar 6, 1930

No. 834. Seventh Generation. 832.

3) Marvin T Kiser, b Mar 28, 1907, near Harrisonburg, Va, m. Nov 20, 1928, Edna E. Campbell, b. Oct. 8, 1911 Address Waynesboro, Va Mennonites.

1 Roy D. Kiser, b Oct 12, 1930
2 Orvan H Kiser, b May 17, 1932

No. 835. Seventh Generation. 832.

4) Ruby T Kiser, b Apr 16, 1909, near Harrisonburg, Va., m. June 16, 1923, Sem W Swope, b Mar 27, 1908 Address Harrisonburg, Va Teacher Mennonite.

No. 836. Sixth Generation. 831.

3) Clara K Shank, b Dec 7, 1883, m in 1903, Enos Heatwole, b Sept 28, 1882 Address Dayton, Va Farmer Mennonite, deacon

1 Ralph T Heatwole, b Mar 11, 1904 No 837.

2. Vada F. Heatwole, b Oct 12, 1905
3 Della P. Heatwole, b Sept 6, 1907, d Mar. 9, 1920
4 Eli D. Heatwole, b Feb 14, 1910 No. 838.
5. Alice B. Heatwole, b June 14, 1912
6. Hanna M. Heatwole, b Aug 6, 1914
7. Catherine R. Heatwole, b. Mar. 5, 1916
8. David E. Heatwole, b Nov. 9, 1919.
9 Eunice I. Heatwole, b Apr 28, 1922
10 Nelson J. Heatwole, b Sept 24, 1928.

No. 837. Seventh Generation. 836.
1) Ralph T. Heatwole, b. Mar 11, 1904, near Dayton, Va., m. June 2, 1926, Vera Early. Address Dayton, Va. Farmer. Mennonite
1. Oren E Heatwole, b Mar. 23, 1927
2. Enos E Heatwole, b Dec 14, 1928
3. Daniel T Heatwole, b Dec 23, 1929
4. Ray W. Heatwole, b Nov —, 1931

No. 838. Seventh Generation. 836.
4) Eli D. Heatwole, b Feb 14, 1910, near Dayton, Va., m Nov. 25, 1931, Annie Rhodes Address Dayton, Va Farmer. Mennonites.

No. 839. Sixth Generation. 831.
4) Bertha B. Shank, b. Oct 31, 1885, near Dayton, Va, m. Oct 26, 1903, Joseph L. Knisely, b Nov 29, 1882 Address Dayton, Va. Farmer. Mennonites.
1. Eula M. Knisely, b. Jan 15, 1904. No 840.
2 Infant daughter, b Feb 15, 1904, d Feb 26, 1905
3 Katie P Knisely, b June 3, 1908 No 841.
4. Frank S. Knisely, b. Jan. 29, 1917.

No. 840. Seventh Generation. 839.
1) Eula M. Knisely, b Jan 15, 1904, near Dayton, Va., m Dec 24, 1924, Paul E Good Mennonites Minister and mission worker at Roaring, W. Va.
1. Emory J. Good, b. Feb 28, 1927.
2 Harly D. Good, b Apr 5, 1931

No. 841. Seventh Generation. 839.
3) Katie P. Knisely, b June 3, 1908, near Dayton, Va, m Sept. 25, 1930, Paul Rhodes Address: Dayton, Va Mennonite
1. Edith M. Rhodes, b. Apr. 26, 1931.
2. Willard F. Rhodes, b June 19, 1932, d Oct 4, 1932.

No. 842. Sixth Generation. 831.
5) Kent M Shank, b Jan 1, 1888, near Dayton, Va, m. Mar. 2, 1916, Fannie B. Rhodes, b Aug 21, 1896 Address Harrisonburg, Va. Farmer and dairyman. Mennonite
1 Lloyd D. Shank, b Sept 18, 1922 (adopted).

No. 843. Sixth Generation. 831.
6) Frank M. Shank, b Oct 9, 1880, near Dayton, Va., m. Aug. 27, 1914, Verna R. Shank, b. Feb 12. 1893, at Roseland, Nebr. Address: Hubbard, Oreg. Employed in dairy and poultry business Mennonite.
1 Beulah M. Shank, b Sept 16, 1915.
2 Ralph E. Shank, b. Dec 30, 1916.
3 Hazel E. Shank, b Nov 6, 1918.
4. William L Shank, b. Mar 15, 1921

5. Glenn E. Shank, b. Dec 26, 1924.
6. Lyle J. Shank, b. Nov. 25, 1927.
7. Belva M. Shank, b. Oct 21, 1932, twin.
8. Thelma F. Shank, b Oct. 21, 1932, twin.

No. 844. Sixth Generation. 831.

7) Anna M. Shank, b Mar 18, 1893, near Dayton, Va., m Jan 2, 1929, Olin Propst, b. Jan. 25, 1902. Address: Dayton, Va. Farmer. Mennonite.
1. Frances Mae Propst, b. Nov 16, 1929, d. Dec. 18, 1929
2. Eula C. Propst, b Dec. 25, 1930.

No. 845. Sixth Generation. 831.

8) Glenn W. Shank, b Dec 8, 1895, near Dayton, Va., m. Nov 23, 1921, Verna Hildebrand, b Jan 3, 1898 Address: Dayton, Va. Farmer and fruit grower. Mennonite.
1. Stanley G. Shank, b. Jan. 12, 1924.
2. Julia E. Shank, b. Dec 28, 1927.

No. 846. Sixth Generation. 831.

9) Wade H. Shank, b. Jan. 31, 1898, m. Vada R Swartz, b Sept 19, 1902; m. on Dec. 20, 1928. Address: Harrisonburg, Va Farmer. Mennonite
1. Orval M. Shank, b. Aug 14, 1929

No. 847. Sixth Generation. 831.

10) Fannie I. Shank, b June 12, 1900, near Dayton, Va, m. June 1, 1922, Ammon Heatwole, b. Oct. 30, 1903 Address Dayton, Va Farmer. Mennonite.
1. John P. Heatwole, b. June 20, 1924.
2. Geneva F. Heatwole, b. June 29, 1926
3. Hazel B. Heatwole, b. Apr 20, 1930.

No. 848. Fifth Generation. 809.

4) Catherine Shank, b Dec. 2, 1855, near Dayton, Va., d. July 17, 1932, m. Oct. 29, 1874, Martin A Lahman, b May 22, 1854. He died Oct. 8, 1904. She married Henry Blosser on May 6, 1914 Address· Harrisonburg, Va Children are all from first marriage.
1. Lydia F. Lahman, b. Aug. 8, 1875. No 849.
2. Ada B. Lahman, b. Jan. 7, 1877. No. 855.
3. Charles L. Lahman, b Sept 25, 1878, d. July 26, 1898.
4. Michael A. Lahman, b. Sept. 20, 1880. No 857.
5. John C. Lahman, b. Aug. 17, 1882. No. 860.
6. Joseph M. Lahman, b. Apr. 5, 1884. No. 861
7. Abbie C. Lahman, b. Mar. 8, 1886. No. 863
8. Emory A. Lahman, b Oct. 30, 1887, d Feb. 8, 1897
9. Hanna M. Lahman, b. Jan 31, 1890. No. 864
10. Ottie M. Lahman, b. Aug. 11, 1891 No. 866
11. Bayard E. Lahman, b Oct. 11, 1892. No. 867
12. Della P. Lahman, b. Dec. 15, 1893. No 868
13. Roy J. Lahman, b Dec 31, 1894. No 869
14. Isa D. Lahman, b. July 4, 1896 No. 870
15. Weaver C. Lahman, b. Dec 18, 1897 No. 871

No. 849. Sixth Generation. 848.

1) Lydia F. Lahman, b Aug 8, 1875, near Harrisonburg, Va., m. Feb 20, 1895, James H. Shank. Address: Mt Crawford, Va. Mennonite, deacon
1. Archie M. Shank, b May 3, 1896, d. Apr. 10, 1900.

2. Bertha K. Shank, b. Mar. 24, 1899. No. 850.
3. Lillie M. Shank, b. Mar. 1, 1901, d Mar. 20, 1901.
4. Mary F. Shank, b. July 19, 1902. No. 851.
5. Pearl E. Shank, b. Jan. 6, 1905. No. 852.
6. Fannie B. Shank, b Nov. 6, 1906. No 853
7. James T. Shank, b. Oct. 6, 1908. No 854.
8. Boyd L. Shank, b Aug 19, 1910.
9. Ada E. Shank, b. May 17, 1912, d. Jan. 8, 1915
10. Olive L. Shank, b. Jan. 22, 1915, d. Feb. 4, 1915
11. Annie G. Shank, b. Mar. 15, 1916.
12. Byard W. Shank, b. Feb 20, 1918

No. 850. Seventh Generation. 849.
2) Bertha K. Shank, b Mar. 24, 1899, m Feb. 12, 1919, Frank Beery, b. May 21, 1895. No issue

No. 851. Seventh Generation. 849.
4) Mary F. Shank, b July 19, 1902, m. Dec. 7, 1921, Walter Beery, b. Aug. 25, 1899. Address: Dayton, Va. Farmer. Mennonite
1. Lydia Ann Beery, b. July 5, 1923
2. Carrie V. Beery, b July 27, 1924
3. Vada M. Beery, b. Oct. 14, 1925.
4. Vera A. Beery, b. Sept 5, 1928.
5. Lois M. Beery, b Nov. 4, 1931

No. 852. Seventh Generation. 849.
5) Pearl E. Shank, b. Jan. 6, 1905, near Mt. Crawford, Va , m. Dec. 24, 1926, John Brenneman, b. Jan. 30, 1893 Address. Denbigh, Va Mechanic. Mennonites.
1. Bettie Jane Brenneman, b Feb 8, 1928
2. John Henry Brenneman, b. Oct. 22, 1929.
3. Bertha Frances Brenneman, b. Dec 14, 1932

No. 853. Seventh Generation. 849.
6) Fannie B. Shank, b Nov. 16, 1906, near Mt Crawford, Va , m. June 1, 1926, Joseph D. Heatwole. Address: Bridgewater, Va Farmer. Mennonite.
1. Joseph DeWitt Heatwole, b. July 14, 1927
2. Ruth V. Heatwole, b. Dec 5, 1928.
3. Dwight S. Heatwole b June 24, 1930.
4. Mary E Heatwole, b Sept 3, 1932

No. 854. Seventh Generation. 849.
7) James T. Shank, b. Oct. 6, 1908, near Mt. Crawford, Va., m. May 7, 1930, Vada A. Jones, b. Aug. 14, 1909. He was ordained to the ministry in the Mennonite Church Nov. 26, 1932. Address Mt Crawford, Va.
1. James L. Shank, b Jan 17, 1933
2 Charles F. Shank, b. Jan. 10, 1936

No. 855. Sixth Generation. 848.
2) Ada V. Lahman, b. Jan 7, 1877, near Mt. Crawford, Va., m. Jan. 9, 1902, Perry J. Blosser, b June 16, 1876 Address: South English, Ia. Farmer. Mennonite. Bishop at South English, Ia
1. Wilmer D. Blosser, b. April 24, 1903, d. Dec 27, 1918.
2. Abbie G. Blosser, b. Nov. 17, 1904.
3. Aquila G. Blosser, b. Mar. 28, 1906. No. 856.
4. A. Dwight Blosser, b. Sept. —, 1907.

5. Menno C. Blosser, b. May 4, 1909.
6. Oren D. Blosser, b. June 29, 1911 No 856½
7. Mary Kate Blosser, b Dec 25, 1913
8. Eugene E Blosser, b Mar 28, 1917
9. Amos L. Blosser, b Nov 19, 1920

No. 856. Seventh Generation. 855.
3) Aquila H. Blosser, b Mar 28, 1906, in Iowa, m. Oct 6, 1931, Mabel A.
Frey. Mennonite.

No. 856½. Seventh Generation. 855.
6) Oren D. Blosser, b June 29, 1911, in Iowa, m Dec , 1935, Emily Slabaugh.

No. 857. Sixth Generation. 848.
4) Michael A Lahman, b Sept 20, 1880, near Mt Crawford, Va , m Fannie
Baker, Oct. 31, 1900. Address Harrisonburg, Va Contractor. Brethren
1. Ruth O. Lahman, b Feb 27, 1902 No 858
2. Lloyd E. Lahman, b May 28, 1905. No 859
3. Mary G. Lahman, b Sept 14, 1907.
4. Hubert B. Lahman, b June 23, 1912 No 859½
5 Mervyl A. Lahman, b Nov 26, 1914

No. 858. Seventh Generation. 857.
1) Ruth O. Lahman, b Feb 27, 1902, in Va , m Clevis Apple, May 7, 1924
1 Dorris C. Apple, b May 27, 1925
2. Clevis O. Apple, Jr , b Mar 29, 1928

No. 859. Seventh Generation. 857.
2) Lloyd E. Lahman, b May 28, 1913, in Va , m Bernice Chapman, Sept. 9,
1925.
1. Nancy L. Lahman, b Feb 19, 1927
2. Lloyd C. Lahman, b Dec. 10, 1930.

No. 859½. Seventh Generation. 857.
4) Hubert B. Lahman, b June 23, 1912, in Va , m April 4, 1931, Mildred B
Coffman.

No. 860. Sixth Generation. 848.
5) John C. Lahman, b Aug 17, 1882, in Rockingham Co., Va., m Mar. 17,
1910, Isa Beery. On the morning of Nov 26, 1912, she lost her life when their
home was destroyed by fire at Denbigh, Va Her two children suffocated with
their mother at the same time John C. married Nov 27, 1913, Katie Y. Horst,
for his second wife. Address: Denbigh, Va. Farmer. Mennonites.
1. Isaac B. Lahman, b Dec 20, 1910, d Nov. 26, 1912.
2. David M. Lahman, b Jan. 29, 1912, d. Nov. 26, 1912.
    (From second wife)
3. Rhoda H. Lahman, b Sept 9, 1914
4. Lydia H. Lahman, b. Dec 31, 1915
5. John J Lahman, b April 7, 1917.
6. Mary C. Lahman, b May 27, 1919
7. Ada V. Lahman, b Aug 1, 1920
8. Amos W. Lahman, b Mar. 5, 1922
9. Ezra C. Lahman, b July 8, 1923
10. Mark A. Lahman, b. Sept 12, 1925.
11. Nathan E. Lahman, b. Jan. 29, 1927.
12. Anna P. Lahman, b Mar 2, 1929, d. same day.

No. 861. Sixth Generation. 848.

6) Joseph M. Lahman, b. April 5, 1884, in Rockingham Co., Va., m. Mamie Miller, Oct. 8, 1905. She died May 5, 1923. He died Aug. 17, 1923. Address: Dayton, Va.

1. Melvin Lahman, b. June 9, 1906.
2. Stella Lahman, b. April 19, 1908. No. 862
3. Paul Lahman, b. Jan. 16, 1912
4. Marshall Lahman, b. April 22, 1914.
5. Nelson Lahman, b. June 8, 1917
6. Margueritte Lahman, b Nov. 15, 1920.
7. Jennings Lahman, b April 11, 1923.

No. 862. Seventh Generation. 861.

2) Stella Lahman, b. April 19, 1908, m April 7, 1927, Millard Coakley. Address: Oaks, Pa.

No. 863. Sixth Generation. 848.

7) Abbie C. Lahman, b. Mar. 8, 1886, in Rockingham Co., Va., m. Nov. 4, 1908, Daniel Shank. Both died Feb 17, 1920, three hours apart with flu. Address: Linville, Va. Mennonites.

1. Velma M. Shank, b Oct. 8, 1910.
2. Naomi E. Shank, b. Feb 6, 1912
3. Pauline V Shank, b. Nov. 13, 1913
4. Emma C. Shank, b. June 16, 1915
5. Grace M. Shank, b. Feb 25, 1918
6 Aaron D. Shank, b. Nov 10, 1919

No. 864. Sixth Generation. 848.

9) Hannah M. Lahman, b Jan 31, 1890, in Rockingham Co., Va , m. Nov. 4, 1908, Joseph Brunk, b Sept 21, 1883 Address: Harrisonburg, Va. Farmer Mennonite.

1. Kathryn Brunk, b Mar. 6, 1910 No. 865.
2. Ruby F Brunk, b. Dec 12, 1911. No. 3391.
3. C Elias Brunk, b July 6, 1913.
4. Dwight L Brunk, b. June 21, 1918
5. Mildred I. Brunk, b. Aug 26, 1926

No. 865. Seventh Generation. 864.

1) Kathryn E. Brunk, b Mar 6, 1910, m. Kenneth Good, Aug. 2, 1932, b. Nov. 15, 1910.

1. Nolan Kenneth Good, b June 2, 1933.

No. 865. Sixth Generation. 848.

10) Ottie M Lahman, b Aug. 11, 1891, in Va., m. May 11, 1910, Luther Bowman. Address: Harrisonburg, Va. Farmer. Mennonites.

1. Infant born and died June 20, 1911.
2 Brownie M. Bowman, b. May 10, 1912.
3. Millard M. Bowman, b Sept 13, 1914
4. Durward L. Bowman, b. May 14, 1916
5. Roy S. Bowman, b. Dec. 17, 1917.
6. Howard A. Bowman, b Sept 1, 1919
7. Lelia A. Bowman, b. Aug. 2, 1921.
8. Vada F. Bowman, b. Aug. 16, 1923
9. Paul D Bowman, b. Aug. 23, 1925
10. Joseph A. Bowman, b Sept. 24, 1927
11. Infant born and buried Aug. 21, 1929

12. Wade M. Bowman, b. Dec. 15, 1930.
13. Linden Ray Bowman, b. Aug. 31, 1932.

No. 867. Sixth Generation. 848.

11) Bayard E. Lahman, b Oct. 11, 1892, in Rockingham Co., Va., m. May 3, 1916, Ethel Heatwole, b. Nov. 11, 1897 Address: Harrisonburg, Va. Farmer. Mennonites, he was a deacon.
1. Harold H. Lahman, b. Jan. 6, 1918.
2. Mildred I. Lahman, b. Mar. 2, 1920.
3. Doris A Lahman, b April 18, 1928.

No. 868. Sixth Generation. 848.

12) Della P. Lahman, b Dec. 16, 1893, in Rockingham Co., Va., m. July 14, 1914, Walter Hartman, b June 19, 1893. Address: Harrisonburg, Va. Truck farmer. Mennonites.
1. Floyd D. Hartman, b Jan. 21, 1915
2. Alta P. Hartman, b July 3, 1916
3. Roy D. Hartman, b. Nov. 3, 1917, d Nov. 12, 1917.
4 Ruby F Hartman, b July 19, 1929.

No. 869. Sixth Generation. 848.

13) Roy J. Lahman, b Dec 31, 1894, in Va., m. Dec. 13, 1916, Clarice Swartz, b. Oct. 11, 1894. Address: Bridgewater, Va Food dealer. Mennonites.
1. Reba A Lahman, b Dec 1, 1917.
2 Emory F. Lahman, b Dec. 10, 1918.
3. Alma E Lahman, b July 14, 1920
4. Wilda V. Lahman, b Aug. 9, 1922.
5. Marvin L Lahman, b. Sept 12, 1923.
6. John R. Lahman, b. June 6, 1925
7. Charles E. Lahman, b. Aug. 2, 1927.
8 Glen E. Lahman, b. Feb 2, 1929.
9. Welden E. Lahman, b July 3, 1931.

No. 870. Sixth Generation. 848.

14) Isa D. Lahman, b. July 4, 1896, in Va , m. Mar. 12, 1919, Emory Coakley, b. May 16, 1900. Address: Petersburg, Va.
1. Bernice C. Coakley, b. May 9, 1920.
2. Mary C. Coakley, b. Nov. 3, 1921.
3. Annie R. Coakley, b. Mar. 22, 1924.
4. Emory L. Coakley, b. April 11, 1927.
5. Dorothy V. Coakley, b. Feb. 9, 1930.

No. 871. Sixth Generation. 848.

15) Weaver C. Lahman, b. Dec 18, 1897, in Rockingham Co., Va., m. July 21, 1923, Nina Heatwole. Address: Dale Enterprise, Va.
1. Ruth V. Lahman, b. Jan. 24, 1924.
2. Wilbur C. Lahman, b. June 24, 1928.

No. 872. Fifth Generation. 809.

5) Charles G. Shank, b. Feb. 25, 1857, near Harrisonburg, Va., d. Dec. 5, 1905. On Aug. 6, 1880, he was united in marriage to Frances Weaver, b. Oct. 23, 1861. Address: Harrisonburg, Va. Mennonite. Burial in Weavers cemetery.
1. Reuben D. Shank, b. Mar. 29, 1882, d Apr. 5, 1882.
2. Effie C. Shank, b. April 27, 1883. No. 873.
3. Nannie E. Shank, b Oct. 8, 1884. No. 876.

4. Elmer D. Shank, b. June 21, 1886. No. 877.
5. Joseph Shank, b. Dec. 1, 1887, d. Dec. 18, 1887.
6. Infant son b. and d. in Feb, 1889.
7. Infant son b June 25, 1890, d. next day.
8. Maggie F. Shank, b. July 24, 1891.
9. Lewis W. Shank, b. June 17, 1893. No. 877½.
10. Emmanuel J. Shank, b May 9, 1895, twin No. 878.
11. Samuel A. Shank, b. May 9, 1895, twin. No. 879.
12. Infant son, b. Feb 14, 1898, d next day.
13. John W. Shank, b Mar. 27, 1899. No 880.
14 Mary R. Shank, b Feb. 21, 1902

No. 873. Sixth Generation. 872.

2) Effie C. Shank, b. April 27, 1883, near Harrisonburg, Va., m. Dec. 6, 1906, William Sharps, b. Sept. 5, 1873. Address Dayton, Va. Farmer. Mennonites.
1. Anna M. Sharps, b Sept. 23, 1907 No. 874.
2. Joseph W. Sharps, b. Jan 11, 1909. No 875.
3 Harold L. Sharps, b May 19, 1912.

No. 874. Seventh Generation. 873.

1) Anna M. Sharps, b Sept 23, 1907, near Dayton, Va., m. Nov. 6, 1929, Raymond Howard, b Nov. 20, 1905, d Apr. 2, 1937. Address: Harrisonburg, Va. Chiropractor. Mennonites For record see No. 486.

No. 875. Seventh Generation. 873.

2) Joseph W. Sharps, b Jan. 11, 1909, near Dayton, Va., m. Mar. 11, 1930, Effie E. Wenger, b. Nov. 9, 1911. Address. Dayton, Va. For record see No. 487.
1. Lois V Sharps, b Nov. 20, 1931
2. Polly Anna Sharps, b. Feb. 13, 1933.

No. 876. Sixth Generation. 872.

3) Nannie E Shank, b. Oct. 18, 1884, near Harrisonburg, Va., m. Sept. 12, 1923, Henry J. Bailey, b. Sept 24, 1882. Address: Cullom, Ill Farmer. Mennonites.

No. 877. Sixth Generation. 872.

4) Elmer D. Shank, b June 21, 1886, near Harrisonburg, Va., m. Ada Showalter, b May 18, 1887.
1. Arthur Shank, b Mar. —, 1910, d. Feb 4, 1911
2. Leta Shank, b. Jan. 9, 1914

No. 877½. Sixth Generation. 872.

9) Lewis W. Shank, b June 17, 1893, near Harrisonburg, Va., m. Dec. 13, 1914, Anna Hartman, b Mar. 3, 1890 Address Sterling, Ill.
1. Eldon C. Shank, b. Dec. 17, 1915.
2 James L. Shank, b. July 27, 1918
3. Carroll D. Shank, b Aug. 27, 1926

No. 878. Sixth Generation. 872.

10) Emmanuel J. Shank, b May 9, 1895, near Harrisonburg, Va., m. Sept. 11, 1918, May E. Frye, b Mar. 10, 1903. Address: Hinton, Va. Laborer in silk mills. Mennonite.
1. Frances L. Shank, b. Aug 19, 1919.
2. Kathleen V. Shank, b Feb. 8, 1921.
3. Esther Pearl Shank, b Aug. 13, 1922
4. Paulina B. Shank, b. Jan. 7, 1924

5. Alvin D. Shank, b June 16, 1925
6. Reba A. Shank, b. April 13, 1927.
7. Dorothy J. Shank, b. Sept 24, 1928
8. Anna Belle Shank, b. Mar , 1932, d May, 1932
9. Aravilla M. Shank, b. Jan 15, 1931

No. 879. Sixth Generation. 872.

11) Samuel A. Shank, b. May 9, 1895, near Harrisonburg, Va., m. Nov. 1, 1923, Ada Witmer, b Feb 21, 1893, of Lancaster Co , Pa. Address: Dayton, Va. Mennonites.
1. Charles W. Shank, b. Nov 23, 1924.
2. Enos Glendon Shank, b Sept. 18, 1926
3 Roxie M. Shank, b. Aug 1, 1928
4 Ruby V Shank, b Feb 27, 1931
5 Rhoda May Shank, b. May 23, 1932

No. 880. Sixth Generation. 872.

13) John W. Shank, b Mar 27, 1899, in Rockingham Co , Va , m. Aug. 31, 1920, Irene Hess, b. June 16, 1897 Address Harrisonburg, Va Silk throwing
1. Ralph W. Shank, b. May 19, 1921.
2. Janet M Shank, b Mar 26, 1928

No. 881. Fifth Generation. 809.

6) Laura Shank, b Oct 8, 1860, in Rockingham Co , Va , d June 12, 1905, m. Aug 10, 1879, Hugh A. Heatwole, of Pleasant Valley, Va. He was a blacksmith and auctioneer. She died June 12, 1905
1. Ward C. Heatwole, b Feb 25, 1884
2. Howard H. Heatwole, b Nov 8, 1886 No 882
3 Wilmer H Heatwole, b. July 28, 1891. No 883.

No. 882. Sixth Generation. 881.

2) Howard H Heatwole, b Nov. 8, 1886, at Edom, Va , m May 5, 1913, Leora F. Landis. He is a salesman and has no permanent address. No issue.

No. 883. Sixth Generation. 881.

3) Wilmer H. Heatwole, b. July 28, 1886, m Jan 7, 1912, Hattie B Knisely, of Pleasant Valley, Va., Dayton, Va Farmers.
1. Mildred V. Heatwole, b Feb 26, 1913 No. 884
2. Glen O. Heatwole, b Feb 28, 1914
3. Hubert A. Heatwole, b Aug 24, 1915.
4. Dwight E. Heatwole, b Dec 1, 1921.
5. W. Leroy Heatwole, b. Mar. 27, 1929.

No. 884. Seventh Generation. 883.

1) Mildred V. Heatwole, b Feb 26, 1913, at Pleasant Valley, Va., m May 30, 1930, Wade A. Kiracofe, of Hinton, Va Silk employe Methodists.
1. Lois Jean Kiracofe, b. Sept. 29, 1930.

No. 885. Fifth Generation. 809.

8) Jacob L Shank, b. July 18, 1870, near Dayton, Va , d Oct. 14, 1926. On Dec. 20, 1891, he was united in marriage to Fannie Good, b. Aug 1, 1866. Farmer and fruit grower. Address· Dayton, Va Mennonites
1. Ward D. Shank, b Dec. 28, 1892 No 886
2. Weldon M Shank, b. Aug. 17, 1894 No. 887
3. Daniel G. Shank, b July 30, 1896 No 888.
4. David C. Shank, b. June 21, 1898. d. June 28, ——.

5. Wilmer P. Shank, b. Sept 21, 1899. No. 889
6. Anna Ruth Shank, b. Oct 12, 1901 No. 890.
7. Mary F. Shank, b. June 8, 1903 No. 891.
8. Grace M. Shank, b. May 25, 1908 No. 892
9 Jacob L Shank, Jr., b July 2, 1912.

No. 886. Sixth Generation. 885.

1) Ward D. Shank, b Dec. 28, 1892, m. Jan. 28, 1915, to Agnes Landes, b. Jan. 19, 1892. Address Dixon, Ill Farmer. Mennonites.
1. Ralph D. Shank, b. Sept. 2, 1915.
2. Wilda V. Shank, b. Jan. 8, 1917.
3. Vada P. Shank, b Aug 13, 1918
4. Grace F. Shank, b. Sept 12, 1919
5. Raymond L. Shank, b. Mar 13, 1921.
6. Wilmer J. Shank, b Sept 22, 1922
7. Goldie F Shank, b Feb 10, 1925.

No. 887. Sixth Generation. 885.

2) Weldon M. Shank, b. Aug. 17, 1894, near Dayton, Va., m. Dec. 19, 1915, Edna Ebersole Address. Rock Falls, Ill. Farmer. Mennonites.
1. Wilma F. Shank, b. Jan. 7, 1917.

No. 888. Sixth Generation. 885.

3) Daniel G. Shank, b. July 30, 1896, near Dayton, Va., m. Feb. 28, 1916, Irene Heatwole, b April 17, 1898. Address· Harrisonburg, Va. Farmer. Mennonites.
1. Evelyn M. Shank, b Mar. 27, 1919.
2. Norma V. Shank, b Sept. 3, 1920.
3. Robert F. Shank, b. Oct. 12, 1922
4. Orwan C Shank, b. June 18, 1928.

No. 889. Sixth Generation. 885.

5) Wilmer P. Shank, b Sept 21, 1899, near Dayton, Va., m. Feb. 11, 1923, Mary V. Rhodes, b Jan. 13, 1903 Address: Mt Clinton, Va. Farmer. Mennonite
1. Mabel Lee Shank, b. Jan 2, 1924
2. Floyd C. Shank, b Feb. 26, 1925
3. Norman R Shank, b. Dec. 10, 1926
4 Gladys L. Shank, b Dec 2, 1928.
5 Raleigh C Shank, b June 10, 1931.

No. 890. Sixth Generation. 885.

6) Annie Ruth Shank, b Oct 12, 1901, near Dayton, Va., m. Nov. 25, 1920, Marion R Weaver, b. Oct 1, 1900 Address Penn Laird, Va. Creamery manager. Mennonites
1 Winston O Weaver, b Dec 15, 1921.

No. 891. Sixth Generation. 885.

7) Mary F Shank, b June 8, 1903, near Dayton, Va , m. Oct. 14, 1923, Jacob Suter, b. Nov. 28, 1899. Address Harrisonburg, Va Carpenter. Mennonites.
1 Doris Suter, b. Dec. 6, 1924
2. Eldon Suter, b. April 13, 1927.
3 Raymond Suter, b June 20, 1928.

No. 892. Sixth Generation. 885.

8) Grace M. Shank, b May 25, 1908, near Dayton, Va , m. June 30, 1931, Harman S. Campbell, b. Mar. 4, 1910 Address: Dayton, Va. Farmer Mennonite

1) Abraham Freed, b. Aug. 23, 1825, in Rockingham Co, Va, d. May 25, 1893, m. Oct. 10, 1847, Susan Harmon, b Jan —, 1830, d June 13, 1913, daughter of Frederick and Phoeba Harmon Abraham and Susan both died on the old homestead, near Lancaster, O., which he had inherited from his parents   Here they reared their entire family of 11 children. The farm remained in the family until 1914 when it was sold. They were buried in the Forest Rose cemetery near Lancaster, O. From the age of 14 years, Mr. Freed was always afflicted with white swelling in his limb, he was a patient sufferer, and was ever active in life's duties and employments. He was an ardent student of science and art, of which his became a master mind, his strongest inclinations were towards mathematics, geology, and botany. Prof. Freed's educational opportunities were very meager, as his only schooling was what he received in the common schools of his day, the only additional training that he received was three months at the Greenville Academy   He grew up with an unquenchable thirst for a knowledge of nature At the age of 18 years he began teaching school as a means of furthering his education in buying books, etc   In his botanical collection were all kinds of wild flowers, ferns, etc. His collection in geology consisted in minerals, shells, precious stones, Indian relics, stuffed birds, reptiles, lava from Mt. Vesuvius, etc. With his telescope he studied the stellar system, and with his microscope he studied insects, plant life, etc.

He taught for 15 years in the academy at Pleasantville, O. After he could no longer teach, he delivered many lectures always illustrating them with his own inventions and drawings   His services were in great demand on the lecture platform   His peculiar talent placed him in a class to himself, and for this reason his friends being so differently made up often failed to understand his silence, but his greatest pleasure was found in showing his visitors his collections that he had and answering any questions they might ask   When before students and professors, he was at his best and was a very fluent speaker.

Mr Freed was a kind husband and a true affectionate father. On Oct. 12, 1892, a few months before his death on the occasion of their first family reunion of their large family he had prepared a short talk for Mrs Freed and the family. In these remarks he showed his gratitude that so large a family had been spared except one. He also expressed his great joy that not one had gone astray. He said that we as parents have tried to impress the principles of right and justice and to live right and virtuous lives. He always respected the devoted Christian principles and lives of his father and mother, of his wife and children   He never sought to deter his family from following their own judgment on this subject He often attended church services   His sympathies were on the side of morality and virtue. He despised profanity and everything of a kindred character. At one time in delivering an oration he made these statements "We live in deeds, not years; in thought, not breaths, in feelings, not figures on a dial; we should count time by heart throbs, he lives most who thinks most, feels the noblest, acts the best "

A few days before his death he made this statement to a visiting minister, that "I love nature and nature's God " He never openly accepted Christ as his Saviour. Mrs Freed was a United Brethren

1 Clara S Freed, b. Mar 18, 1849 No 894.
2. John M. Freed, b Apr. 26, 1850, d Aug 28, 1877.
3. Mary E Freed, b Feb 28, 1853. No. 901.
4 Frances Elizabeth Freed, b Nov. 28, 1854 No. 909
5 Lydia Freed, b Jan. 1, 1858 No. 910
6. Ella M Freed, b. Aug 7, 1860. No. 911

7. Emma Pauline Freed, b Apr. 15, 1862. No. 912.
8. Etta Alice Freed, b. Mar. 25, 1864. No. 913.
9. Charles L. Freed, b. July 9, 1866. No. 914.
10. Alvah T. Freed, b. July 12, 1868. No. 915.
11. Stella B. Freed, b. May 13, 1870. No. 916.

No. 894. Fifth Generation. 893.

1) Clara B. Freed, b. Mar. 18, 1849, Fairfield Co., O., m. Dec. 24, 1866, Michael Krause. They moved to Illinois in 1867, and from there to Kansas in 1870. About 1905 they settled at Fairfax, Okla. Methodists.
1. Edith L. Krause, b. Mar. 27, 1868 No. 895.
2. Charles E. Krause, b. July 19, 1869. No. 896.
3. Mary M. Krause, b. Nov. 19, 1872. No. 897.
4. Delman F. Krause, b. Jan. 24, 1875. No. 898.
5. Frederick M. Krause, b. July 3, 1877. No. 899.
6. Leonard F. Krause, b. Mar. 4, 1879. No 900.

No. 895. Sixth Generation. 894.

1) Edith L Krause, b Mar 27, 1868, m. Mar. 23, 1891, Frank Jones. Farming near Fairfax, Okla.
1. Ethel Jones, b Nov. —, 1894.

No. 896. Sixth Generation. 894.

2) Charles E. Krause, b. July 19, 1869, m. June 24, 1894, Orpha Poor. They remained at Cedarville, Kan
1. Norma Krause, b. July —, 1899

No. 897. Sixth Generation. 894.

3) Mary M. Krause, b Nov. 19, 1872, m. Mar. 23, 1891, Lewis Krause. Living at Akron, Ind. Have issue N. F. R.

No. 898. Sixth Generation. 894.

4) Delman F. Krause, b. Jan. 24, 1875, m. Ada ——————.
1. Lloyd Krause, b. ——————, 1902.
2 Michael Krause, b ——————, 1905

No. 899. Sixth Generation. 894.

5) Frederick M. Krause, b. July 3, 1877, m. in 1902. When last heard from, he was farming at Dustin, Okla. At least three children.

No. 900. Sixth Generation. 894.

6) Leonard F. Krause, b. Mar. 4, 1879, m. July 12, 1900, ——————————.
They live at Fairfax, Okla.
1. Merle Krause, b. ——————.
2. Constance Krause, b. ——————
3. Ruth Krause, b. ——————.
4 Frederick Krause, b. ——————.

No. 901. Fifth Generation. 893.

3) Mary M. Freed, b. Feb 28, 1853, at Pleasantville, O., m. Jan 19, 1871, John Hempy, in Fairfield Co., O. After living for some time in Ind., they moved to near Bellefontaine, O , where they located. Their family have mostly settled near there.
1. Alva M. Hempy, b. Mar. 19, 1874. No. 902.
2. Myrtle M Hempy, b. Mar. 8, 1876. No. 903.
3 Frank P. Hempy, b Sept 29, 1878. No. 904.

4. Roy Hempy, b. Nov. 18, 1884 No 905.
5. Nellie E Hempy, b. Oct 16, 1886. No 906
6. Paul C Hempy, b. Dec. 1, 1888. No. 907.
7. Mary E Hempy, b Jan 27, 1892. No. 908

No. 902. Sixth Generation. 901.

1) Alva M. Hempy, b Mar. 19, 1874, at Huntington, Ind , d. ——————.
Road contractor. He was caught in a sand quarry and smothered to death. m.
Elizabeth Graybill, at Rushylvania, O., their address, where he resided. His
widow and son still operate the quarry
1. Helen Hempy, b Feb 2, 1901 No 3670
2. Myron G Hempy, b. Aug. 27, 1905 No 3671.

No. 903. Sixth Generation. 901.

2) Myrtle M. Hempy, b. Mar. 8, 1876, at Huntington, Ind , m Oct. 16, 1896,
John H Foltz They live on a farm near Springfield, O Their children are all
married
1. Fern P. Foltz, b Nov 17, 1897 m
2 Mary Z. Foltz, b Aug 17, 1902 m
3. Sue C. Foltz, b. Feb 28, 1905, m.
4. Ivy Foltz, b ——————
5 Omer Foltz, b ——————, m

No. 904. Sixth Generation. 901.

3) Frank P. Hempy, b Sept 29, 1878, near Bellefontaine, O , m Nov. 28,
1900, Goldie Richardson, d May 13, 1901, in Logan Co , O , on Oct 1, 1905, m.
Pearl Shuff in Huntington, Ind Address Waldo, O
1 Roy Hempy, b. ——————, d. ——————.
2 Charles Hempy, b ——————
3. Fern Hempy, b ——————.
4 Martha Hempy, b ——————.
5. Luella Hempy, b. ——————.
6 Eva Hempy, b. ——————
7. Flossie Hempy, b. ——————
8 Norma Hempy, b ——————
9. Frankie Hempy, b. ——————.
10 Delma Hempy, b. ——————.

No. 905. Sixth Generation. 901.

4) Roy Hempy, b. Nov. 18, 1884, near Bellefontaine, O., m July 3, 1905,
Nellie Parker. Mr. Hempy died in 1912 of blood poison. Mrs Hempy died two
years later of d·phtheria. Address was Bellefontaine, O
1 Forest P Hempy, b Jan. 14, 1906
2 Ferrell R Hempy, b Aug. 24, 1907.
3 Reed Hempy, b. ——————.
4 Robert Hempy, b ——————.
5 Ruth Hempy, b Dec 25, 1912 and was adopted by her father's Aunt Stella
    B Freed and Robert Rutter

No. 906. Sixth Generation. 901.

5) Nellie E Hempy, b Oct. 16, 1886, near Bellefontaine, O , m June 18,
1908, Curtis Peters Address. Lockbourne, O.
1 Loraine Peters, b ——————
2 Annie Peters, b ——————.
3. Jane Peters, b ——————

156

6) Paul C. Hempy, b. Dec. 1, 1888, near Bellefontaine, O. A World War veteran, m. ——————, and lives in Detroit, Mich.

1. Ada May Hempy, b ——————.
2. James Hempy, b ——————

No. 908. Sixth Generation. 901.

7) Mary E Hempy, b. Jan 27, 1892, in Hancock Co, O., m. William Ives. They lived for some time in Detroit, Mich., then moved to Columbus, O., where he died Mrs. Ives now lives in Springfield, O.

1 Willard Ives, b. ——————, a graduate of the Ohio State University.

No. 909. Fifth Generation. 893.

4) Frances Elizabeth Freed, b. Nov. 28, 1854, m. Charles R. Clement. Physician of Groveport. O. No issue.

No. 910. Fifth Generation. 893.

5) Lydia Freed, b Jan 1, 1858, d ——————, 1912, m Oct 13, 1881, Abram Good, of Bremen, O., who was teacher, farmer, and architect. He lived to be 82 years old. They lived in Columbus, O. Church of God.

1. Stella J. Good, b. Mar. 4, 1884. No. 3672.
2 Anna Good, b. Mar 8, 1886, d Mar 25, 1888
3 Harry Good, b. Apr. 29, 1890 No 3673.

No. 911. Fifth Generation. 893.

6) Ella M. Freed, b. Aug. 7, 1860, m. Jan. 24, 1889, James Spence, d. Jan. 27, 1937 Address: Delaware, O Burial at Delaware, O. Methodists.

1. Ralph Spence, b. Nov. 18, 1889 No 3674.
2 Pauline Spence, b. Apr 18, 1891. No 3675.
3 Anna M. Spence, b. Nov 22, 1893 No 3676.
4 Paul Spence, b Aug 29, 1895 No 3677

No. 912. Fifth Generation. 893.

7) Emma Pauline Freed, b. Apr. 15, 1862, near Lancaster, O., m. Dec. 24, 1889, Samuel Elmer Bunn, b Nov 22, 1863. Merchant. Reformed. Address: 344 Parkwood Ave, Springfield, O.

1 Mary H Bunn, b Oct. 16, 1891 No 3678
2 Lenora F. Bunn, b. Mar. 7, 1905. No. 3679

No. 913. Fifth Generation. 893.

8) Etta A Freed, b. Mar 25, 1864, d. June 28, 1936, m. May 22, 1899, Rev. H S Bailey They lived at 2895 Cor Entry Rd., Columbus, O.

1 Vivian Bailey, b Dec 9, 1894 No 3680.
2 Stanley Bailey, b Oct 17, 1896 No 3681.
3 Frances Bailey, b. Oct. 22, 1903 No 3682.

No. 914. Fifth Generation. 893.

9) Charles L. Freed, b July 9, 1866, near Lancaster, O., m. Feb., 1890, Ida Stewart Address Lancaster, O Fruit grower United Brethren.

1 Deceased

No. 915. Fifth Generation. 893.

10) Alva T Freed, b July 12, 1868, near Lancaster, O, m. Oct. 8, 1891, Myrtle Freed, daughter of Henry Freed, of Hancock Co, O. Address: Basil, O. Farmer and fine stock raiser.

1. Harold V. Freed, b Nov 1, 1895. No 3683.
2. Lois G. Freed, b. Jan 28, 1901. No. 3684.
3 Dorothy Freed, b. May 13, 1903. No. 3685.

No. 916. Fifth Generation. 893.

11) Stella B. Freed, b Mar. 13, 1870, near Lancaster, O , m. Jan. 14, 1914, Robert Rutter, b. Mar. 14, 1869 Address: 629 E. Wheeling St , Lancaster, O. Probation officer. Presbyterians.

1. Adopted daughter, Ruth Rutter, b Dec. 25, 1912.

No. 917. Fourth Generation. 24.

1) Frances Showalter, b. Feb 12, 1828, near Harrisonburg, Va., d. June 13, 1905. She married Daniel Brunk of near Broadway, Va., who was born Sept 20, 1824. Address: Dale Enterprise, Va. Mennonites.

1. David Brunk, b. Dec. 26, 1847. No. 918.
2. Jacob Brunk, b. Dec. 9, 1850, d in 1852
3. Solomon Brunk, b. Mar. 24, 1853, d. in 1855.
4. Simon Brunk, b. Mar. 3, 1855. No 924.
5. Nancy Brunk, b. Jan. 1, 1857. No 948
6. Mary Brunk, b. July 15, 1859. No 951.
7. Barbara Brunk, b Jan 2, 1862, d Mar 22, 1890, unmarried.

No. 918. Fifth Generation. 917.

1) David Brunk, b. Dec. 26, 1847, near Dale Enterprise, Va., m. Aug. 22, 1871, Elizabeth A. Hartman, granddaughter of Bishop Peter Burkholder Address: Harrisonburg, Va. Mennonites.

1. Emmanuel H. Brunk, b. Jan 19, 1873 No. 919
2. Frances Brunk, b Nov. 24, 1874, d Aug 28, 1879.
3. Timothy F. Brunk, b July 13, 1876 No. 920
4. Bettie M. Brunk, b Sept 14, 1878 No 921
5. Lydia S. Brunk, b. Mar. 3, 1881. No. 922.
6. Rosa V. Brunk, b Dec 18, 1882. No. 923
7. Daniel M. Brunk, b Mar. 16, 1888, d Aug. 27, 1891

No. 919. Sixth Generation. 918.

1) Emmanuel H. Brunk, b Jan. 19, 1873, near Harrisonburg, Va., m Sept. 15, 1896, Martha K. Martin, b. Oct. 25, 1877, of Washington Co., Md. Address Denbigh, Va. Gardener. Mennonite.

1. Jason W. Brunk, b. Aug. 12, 1897 No 939.
2. Mary E. Brunk, b. July 31, 1900, d. Aug. 7, 1904.
3. J. Irvin Brunk, b. Sept 2, 1905 No 940.
4. Herman E. Brunk, b. April 17, 1907. No. 941.
5. Homer Emmanuel Brunk, b Dec 14, 1913, d Mar. 24, 1916
6. Melvin Martin Brunk, b. April 27, 1915, d April 28, 1916.
7. Earl Douglas Brunk, b. Dec. 9, 1918

No. 920. Sixth Generation. 918.

3) Timothy F. Brunk, b. July 13, 1876, near Harrisonburg, Va., m Sept 6, 1900, Elizabeth N. Heatwole, b. July 28, 1878 Address: South English, Ia Farmer. Mennonites.

1. Lorene V. Brunk, b. Nov 25, 1902. No 942.
2. Leota F. Brunk, b. Mar. 19, 1904. No. 943.
3. Roy H. Brunk, b Jan. 17, 1910. No. 944
4. Tracie P. Brunk, b. May 2, 1912
5. Boyd A. Brunk, b. May 15, 1919.

No. 921. Sixth Generation. 918.

4) Bettie M. Brunk, b. Sept. 14, 1878, near Harrisonburg, Va , m. Henry B. Keener, b. Nov 3, 1882. Address: Harrisonburg, Va. Mennonite, minister

1. Mary E. Keener, b Sept. 16, 1906, R N
2. Catherine V. Keener, b. April 17, 1908.
3 Oliver M. Keener, b. Oct 30, 1910
4. Eunice E. Keener, b Feb 4, 1913

No. 922. Sixth Generation. 918.

5) Lydia S. Brunk, b Mar. 3, 1881, near Harrisonburg, Va., m. Ernest S. Harman, b. July 24, 1880, d. Dec. 18, 1930, at South Boston, Va. Buried at Weavers Church in Rockingham Co, Va Address: Houston, Halifax Co., Va. Farmer Mennonites

1 Howard D Harman, b Dec 6, 1905 No. 945
2. John W. Harman, b Oct. 14, 1907. No. 946
3 Seba F. Harman, b. May 7, 1909. No. 947.
4 Frank Timothy Harman, b July 2, 1912

No. 923. Sixth Generation. 918.

6) Rosa V. Brunk, b. Dec. 18, 1882, near Harrisonburg, Va, m. Nov. 23, 1904, Henry B. Weber, b Feb 18, 1879 Address· Maugansville, Md. Carpenter. Mennonites

1 Gertrude C. Weber, b Nov 14, 1906, d. same day.
2 Edna F. Weber, b Mar 30, 1908, d. June 8, 1908
3 Leonard D Weber, b. Aug. 30, 1911.

No. 924. Fifth Generation. 917.

4) Simon Brunk, b Mar. 3, 1855, near Harrisonburg, Va, m. Amanda Shank, b in Washington Co., Md. Address Rushville, Va. Farmer. Mennonites.

1. Perry S. Brunk, b. Aug 17, 1883. No 925
2 Katie F. Brunk, b Oct. 24, 1884. No 926.
3. Christian D. Brunk, b. Feb 4, 1885 No 930
4. Naomi E. Brunk, b. Aug 15, 1887 No. 929.
5 Mattie V. Brunk, b Jan 13, 1889 No 931
6 Anna M. Brunk, b Nov. 23, 1890, single, teacher.
7 Ira D. Brunk, b Nov. 10, 1892. No. 932.
8 Amos W. Brunk, b July 27, 1895. No. 933.
9. Nellie A. Brunk, b July 16, 1897. No. 934
10. Esther R. Brunk, b Aug. 31, 1901 No. 935
11. Ruth Marie Brunk, b June 1, 1903, single, teacher.

No. 925. Sixth Generation. 924.

1) Perry S. Brunk, b Aug. 17, 1883, in Washington Co., Md. m Mar. 22, 1905, Nannie V. Miller Address. Des Moines, Ia. Methodists

1. Katherine A. Brunk, b June 29, 1906. No. 936
2. Esther Marie Brunk, b Dec. 21, 1907 No. 937.
3. Laura Belle Brunk, b June 21, 1910 No 938.
4. Dorothy E. Brunk, b Aug 8, 1914
5 Virginia L Brunk, b Dec. 7, 1920

No. 926. Sixth Generation. 924.

2) Katie Frances Brunk, b Oct. 24, 1884, in Washington Co, Md., m. Sept 2, 1902, Michael Heatwole, b Feb 26, 1882 Address· Harrisonburg, Va. Mennonites

1 Goldie Fern Heatwole, b July 16, 1904. No. 927
2 Marjorie V Heatwole, b Oct 12, 1907. No. 928.
3 Reba K Heatwole, b May 6, 1914
4 William M. Heatwole, b. Mar 16, 1919

No. 927. Seventh Generation. 926.

1) Goldie F. Heatwole, b July 16, 1904, in Va., m May 6, 1924, Oliver R Wenger, son of Daniel P Wenger, near the New Rection Church, Rockingham Co., Va.

1. Sheldon L Wenger, b April 5, 1925
2. Helen F. Wenger, b. June 2, 1929

No. 928. Seventh Generation. 926.

2) Marjorie V. Heatwole, b Oct 12, 1907, in Va , m. June 3, 1930, John D Burkholder, Jr , son of Dr John D Burkholder, of Harrisonburg, Va Mennonites.

1. Nancy V. Burkholder, b Sept 27, 1931

No. 929. Sixth Generation. 924.

4) Naomi E Brunk, b Aug 15, 1887, in Rockingham Co , Va , m Goldie Adam Cline. Address: Palmyra, Pa Mennonites

1. Cecil Woodrow Cline, b Dec. 28, 1912
2. James Porter Cline, b July 2, 1914
3. Richard Brunk Cline, b Dec 22, 1918
4. Robert Sheldon Cline, b Nov. 23, 1921

No. 930. Sixth Generation. 924.

3) Christian D Brunk, b Feb 4, 1886, in Washington Co., Md , in Aug 10, 1918, Ida Legrand, at Sumtex, S. C Address Sumtex, S. C. Baptists.

1. Marjorie Louise Brunk, b Nov. 2, 1919
2. Virginia Caroline Brunk, b. Oct. 2, 1921.

No. 931. Sixth Generation. 924.

5) Mattie V Brunk, b Jan 13, 1889, in Rockingham Co , Va , m July 2, 1919, Edgar J Cline, b Jan 26, 1897. Address: Broadway, Va. Farmer and poultryman. Mennonites.

1. Mary Catherine Cline, b Dec. 23, 1920.
2. Pauline Virginia Cline, b. Mar. 3, 1922

No. 932. Sixth Generation. 924.

7) Ira David Brunk, b Nov 11, 1892, at Pleasant Valley, Va., single. He is blind He attended school at the Institute for Blind at Staunton, Va , where he stood at the head of his class, graduating at the age of 18 years. At the present time (1932) he is employed by a musical firm at South Boston, Va , selling and tuning pianos

No. 933. Sixth Generation. 924.

8) Amos W Brunk, b. July 27, 1895, near Pleasant Valley, Va , m July 27, 1923, Grace V. Vexling. They live at Prescott, Ia. Methodists.

1. James E. Vexling Brunk, b July 4, 1927.

No. 934. Sixth Generation. 924.

9) Nellie A. Brunk, b. July 16, 1897, at Pleasant Valley, Va., m. Daniel R Heatwole. They live at Palmyra, Pa.

1. Shirley Nell Heatwole, b Oct 1, 1923, d May, 1931
2 Daniel R. Heatwole, Jr , b. Mar. ———.
3. Nancy Ann Heatwole, b May ———.

No. 935. Sixth Generation. 924.

10) Eston R. Brunk, b Aug 31, 1901, at Pleasant Valley, Va , m Oct 13, 1929, Marian Frances Yates, Sumtex, S. C.

No. 936. Seventh Generation. 925.

1) Kathryn A. Brunk, b Jan. 29, 1906, at Powshick, Ia., m. Dec. 24, 1927, Howard I. Smith, b. Aug. 26, 1906, at Springfield, Ill. Address. Des Moines, Ia.

No. 937. Seventh Generation. 925.

2) Esther M. Brunk, b. Dec. 21, 1907, in Ia, m. Sept. 2, 1928, Carroll W. Hearlsman, b. Dec. 25, 1906, at Ottumwa, Ia. She was killed in an auto wreck April 2, 1932 They lived at Des Moines, Ia.

No. 938. Seventh Generation. 925.

3) Laura Belle Brunk, b June 21, 1910, in Ia., m. Aug. 6, 1929, Chester W Blair, b. Aug. 8, 1904, at Council Bluffs, Ia Address: Des Moines, Ia
1. Lauralyn L. Blair, b. May 18, 1930.

No. 939. Seventh Generation. 919.

1) Jason W Brunk, b Aug 12, 1897, m Mabel Shenk.

No. 940. Seventh Generation. 919.

3) Jacob Irvin Brunk, b Sept 2, 1905, m Ruth Smoker, b Dec. 15, 1908. Mr Brunk is employed by the Mennonite Publishing House, Scottdale, Pa. Mennonites.
1. Floyd Chester Brunk, b. Feb 3, 1930
2. Leota Marie Brunk, b. Nov 30, 1931

No. 941. Seventh Generation. 919.

4) Herman Elvin Brunk, b April 17, 1907, m Marcella Sims.

No. 942. Seventh Generation. 920.

1) Lorene V Brunk, b Nov. 25, 1902, m. Sept 6, 1923, Earl T Henderson, son of Thomas and Mary Henderson, of Frederick, Ia
1. Ansel Lee Henderson, b. Sept. 25, 1926.
2. Bettie Louise Henderson, b. Aug 24, 1931

No. 943. Seventh Generation. 920.

2) Leota F. Brunk, b Mar 19, 1904, m Feb 14, 1925, Roy A Moss, son of Frederick and Ellen Moss, of Unionville, Ia.
1. Joan A. Moss, b. Nov. 19, 1929.

No. 944. Seventh Generation. 920.

3) Roy H Brunk, b Jan. 17, 1910, m April 19, 1930, Anna Mae Faulkner, daughter of Ralph and Catherine Faulkner, of Chicago, Ill.

No. 945. Seventh Generation. 922.

1) Howard D Harmon, b Dec. 6, 1905, m. Aug 2, 1932, Virginia H Holsinger, b Nov, 1911, daughter of Marion and Ressie Hess Holsinger. Mennonites

No. 946. Seventh Generation. 922.

2) John W Harmon, b Oct 14, 1907, m. May 7, 1930, Edna Rebecca Jones, b. Sept. 2, 1906, daughter of Leonard and Lena (Weaver) Jones Mennonites
1 Shirley Belle Harmon, b June 29, 1931.

No. 947. Seventh Generation. 922.

3) Seba F Harmon, b May 7, 1909, m Mar 22, 1932, Menno S Brunk, b Aug. 9, 1909, son of George and Katie (Wenger) Brunk Mennonites
1. David Jones Brunk, b Nov 10, 1933
2. Marie Frances Brunk, b. Feb 20, 1936.

No. 948. Fifth Generation. 917.

5) Nancy Brunk, b. Jan. 1, 1857, near Dale Enterprise, Va , m. Mar. 27, 1877, Samuel J. Parrett. Farmer Mennonites Address Dale Enterprise, Va. Mrs Parrett died Nov. 30, 1889

1. Martin L. Parrett, b. May 9, 1878. No. 949
2. Mary F. Parrett, b. Oct 22, 1881. No 950.
3. Philip G. Parrett, b. Sept. 30, 1884.
4. Enos D. Parrett, b Aug. 25, 1888, d. Jan. 31, 1889.

No. 949. Sixth Generation. 948.

1) Martin L. Parrett, b May 9, 1878, m Oct 8, 1892, Margaret Catherine Brooks Address: Waynesboro, Va Farmer Mennonite and Presbyterian

1. V. Wallace Parrett, b. Oct 25, 1893
2 Ray Lyman Parrett, b Jan 12, 1896
3. Lola Elizabeth Parrett, b Aug 9, 1897 No 3477
4 Carl P. G Parrett, b Sept 20, 1912 No 3478

No. 950. Sixth Generation. 948.

2) Mary F. Parrett, b Oct. 22, 1881, m Apr 1, 1908, Herman T B Campbell, b. June 27, 1883. Farmer. All Mennonites Address: Waynesboro, Va , R 2 Burial at Springdale Church.

1. Raymond Ercil Campbell, b Aug. 12, 1908 No 3473.
2. Herman Samuel Campbell, b Mar 5, 1910 No 3474
3 Edna Elizabeth Campbell, b. Oct 7, 1911 No. 3475.
4 Thelma Frances Campbell, b Mar 1, 1913. No. 3476
5. Lester Boyd Campbell, b June 9, 1914.
6. Harold Parrett Campbell, b Feb 5, 1916

No. 951. Fifth Generation. 917.

6) Mary Brunk, b. July 15, 1859, near Harrisonburg, Va., m Henry Shubert, of Washington Co., Md Wheelwright. Address Hagerstown, Md. Mennonites
1 Lillie May Shubert, b. July 27, 1891.

No. 952. Fourth Generation. 24.

3) Anna Showalter, b Aug 17, 1824, near Broadway, Va , m. Sept 11, 1845, Jacob Trissell. She died Apr 20, 1882, Jacob died May 3, 1879 They lived near Harrisonburg, Va.

1. Elizabeth Trissell, b. July 3, 1846. No. 953.
2. Nancy Trissell, b. Jan. 31, 1849, d. Aug. 9, 1864.
3. Barbara Trissell, b. July 9, 1851. No 961
4. Daniel Trissell, b. Mar 31, 1853. No 962
5. Sallie Trissell, b. July 31, 1855. No 963
6. Joseph W. Trissell, b July 13, 1858. No 964
7. Hettie Trissell, b. June 21, 1861. No. 965
8. John N Trissell, b June 26, 1864 No. 969
9. Jacob Abraham Trissell, b. July 20, 1867. No 970
10. David Trissell Trissell, b Mar 21, —— No 971

No. 953. Fifth Generation. 952.

1) Elizabeth Trissell, b July 3, 1846, in Rockingham Co , Va, d June 21, 1929, m. Feb. 11, 1871, John Blosser, b July 3, 1849, and died May 3, 1930 Address: Harrisonburg, Va. Farmer. Mennonites.

1. Jacob Blosser, b Oct 18, 1872 No 954
2 Margaret Blosser, b. Mar. 13, 1875, single
3 Benjamin Blosser, b June 21, 1877 No 955

162

4. Joseph Blosser, b. June 30, 1879. No. 956.
5. Annie Blosser, b. Aug. 19, 1881 No. 957.
6. Elizabeth Blosser, b Sept. 16, 1883. No. 958.
7. Frances Blosser, b. July 16, 1886. No. 959.

No. 954. Sixth Generation. 953.

1) Jacob Blosser, b. Oct 18, 1872, in Rockingham Co., Va., m. Minerva Showalter, b. —————. Address Harrisonburg, Va.
1. Gurney Blosser, b. —————.
2. Mary Blosser, b. —————.
3. Abraham Blosser, b. —————.
4. Rachel Blosser, b —————.
5. Martha Blosser, b. —————.
6. Solomon Blosser, b. —————.

No. 955. Sixth Generation. 953.

3) Benjamin Blosser, b. June 21, 1877, in Rockingham Co., Va., m. Jerucia Head. Address: Harrisonburg, Va.
1 Paul Blosser, b. —————
2. Victor Blosser, b. —————.

No. 956. Sixth Generation. 953.

4) Joseph Blosser, b. June 30, 1879, in Rockingham Co., Va., m. Effie Whillbarger. Address: 536 S. High St., Harrisonburg, Va.
1. Harold Blosser, b. —————.
2. Chida Blosser, b. —————.

No. 957. Sixth Generation. 953.

5) Annie Blosser, b Aug. 19, 1881, in Rockingham Co., Va., m. William A. Showalter. Address: Harrisonburg, Va., R. 4. No issue.

No. 958. Sixth Generation. 953.

6) Elizabeth Blosser, b. Sept 16, 1883, in Rockingham Co., Va., m. John Philips, b. —————.
1. Grace Philips, b. —————.

No. 959. Sixth Generation. 953.

7) Frances Blosser, b. July 16, 1886, in Rockingham Co., Va., m. Frederick Philips, b. —————, d. —————, m. (2nd) Stillwell May, b. —————. Address: 140 C St., S. E., Washington, D. C.
1. James Philips, b. —————.
2. Frederick Philips, b —————.

No. 960. Fifth Generation. 952.

2) Nancy Trissell, b Jan. 31, 1849, in Va., d. Aug. 9, 1864. She never married Buried at Trissells cemetery in Rockingham Co., Va.

No. 961. Fifth Generation. 952.

3) Barbara Trissell, b. July 9, 1851, in Rockingham Co, Va., d. Feb. 17, 1926. She married Feb. 6, 1873, Noah Blosser, d. Aug. 15, 1920. Buried at Weavers Church. No issue.

No. 962. Fifth Generation. 952.

4) Daniel Trissell, b. Mar. 31, 1853, drowned near Steamboat Springs, Colo., on June 18, 1890. Single. Buried in the Weavers cemetery in Va.

No. 953. Fifth Generation. 952.

5) Sallie Trissell, b July 31, 1855, in Rockingham Co, Va, d Oct. 12, 1912. Single. Buried in Weavers cemetery

No. 964. Fifth Generation. 952.

6) Joseph Trissell, b July 13, 1858, in Rockingham Co., Va, m Nov. 12, 1883, Hannah Sanger. Living at Fruita, Colo They have two children, but not reported.

No. 955. Fifth Generation. 952.

7) Hettie Trissell, b June 21, 1861, in Rockingham Co, Va, m Dec 23, 1892, Perry B. Wenger.
1. Leota A Wenger, b Nov 11, 1893 No 966
2. Anna M. Wenger, b. Nov 2, 1895
3. Etta E. Wenger, b. April 25, 1897
4. Benjamin D. Wenger, b Oct 2, 1889. No. 967
5 Julia B Wenger, b Aug 25, 1901
6 Ella N. Wenger, b. Dec 8, 1903.
7 Trissell P. Wenger, b Mar 24, 1906 No. 968

No. 966. Sixth Generation. 965.

1) Leota A. Wenger, b Nov 11, 1893, m Mar 11, 1914, Weldon I Good.
1. Marie W. Good, b Nov. 4, 1914, d Oct 7, 1919.
2. Lorene W. Good, b. Jan 11, 1916, d same day.
3. Ada W. Good, b Mar 28, 1917
4. Alfred W. Good, b. Aug 29, 1918, d. Jan. 18, 1928
5 Alice W. Good, b Feb 17, 1921
6 Pauline M Good, b Aug 20, 1923, d Oct 23, 1923.
7. Bertha Lee Good, b Dec. 16, 1925.
8. Charlotte V. Good, b. Mar 29, 1928.
9 Rodney D. Good, b Nov. 10, 1932

No. 967. Sixth Generation. 965.

4) Benjamin D. Wenger, b Oct. 2, 1899, m. Oct 21, 1927, Ethel Edmonson.

No. 958. Sixth Generation. 965.

7) Trissell P. Wenger, b Mar 24, 1906, m Mary Gravite, Dec 22, 1926
1. Charles E Wenger, b Nov 3, 1927, d Nov 25, 1927.
2. Ruth E. Wenger, b. April 7, 1929.

No. 969. Fifth Generation. 952.

8) John N. Trissell, b. June 26, 1864, m. Lillie F. Trissell (nee Hess). She had been married to his younger brother, David, and after his death she married his brother as above shown. They reside near Harrisonburg, Va, their address. All Mennonites.
1. Gail Edith Trissell, b Mar 26, 1911.
2. Iva Marie Trissell, b April 3, 1913
3. Fern Culora Trissell, b. Nov 28, 1914
4. Rose Trilby Trissell, b. June 16, 1916
5. John Ward Trissell, b. Sept. 16, 1918
6. David Lloyd Trissell, b Mar. 25, 1920

No. 970. Fifth Generation. 952.

9) Jacob Abraham Trissell, b. July 20, 1867, d. on April 30, 1893. Single Buried in the Weavers cemetery near Harrisonburg, Va.

No. 971. Fifth Generation. 952.

10) David Trissell, b. Mar. 21, 1872, and d Sept. 18, 1902, m. Lillie F. Hess, Jan. 12. 1902. No children His widow later married his brother, John N Trissell

No. 972. Fourth Generation. 24.

4) Sallie Showalter, b —————————, near Broadway, Va., d. ——————, m. Abraham Shank, b. Oct. 19, 1829. He died June 22, 1901 Abraham was a prominent minister in the Mennonite Church. He was also ordained bishop, Sept. 5, 1875. Address was Broadway, Va.

    1. Nancy Shank, b Oct. 30, 1855. No. 973.

    2. Isabelle Shank, b. Sept 9, 1859 No 974

No. 973. Fifth Generation. 972.

1) Nancy Shank, b. Oct. 30, 1855, near Broadway, Va., m. Oct. 2, 1873, Reuben Rhodes. By accident Mr Rhodes has been blind for many years, but his devoted wife has been his constant helper Address was Broadway, Va. Mennonites.

    1. Miller D. Rhodes, b —————— No. 973¼.

No. 973¼. Sixth Generation. 973.

1) Miller D Rhodes, b —————————, near Broadway, Va , m. Nov. 19, 1885, Hannah R. Neff.

1 Nellie G Rhodes, b Nov 6, 1896

No. 974. Fifth Generation. 972.

2) Isabella Shank, b Sept. 9, 1859, near Broadway, Va., m Amos Martin, in 1882. Address: Cearfoss, Md

No. 975. Fourth Generation. 24.

5) John D. Showalter, b April 12, 1824, near Broadway, Va , d Jan. 18, 1904, m. in Oct., 1850, Elizabeth (Sallie) Driver, b. Oct. 13, 1825, d. May 8, 1895 Buried at the Weavers Church in Rockingham Co., Va. Address was Crisman, Va. Farmer and miller. Mennonites.

    1. Daniel P. Showalter, b Aug 24, 1851 No. 976

    2. Samuel J. Showalter, b July 25, 1853 No. 990.

    3. Jacob D. Showalter, b. Dec. 4, 1854. No. 997.

    4. Catherine Showalter, b April 1, 1856, d. Oct. 16, 1861.

    5. Cyrus B Showalter, b. Oct. 14, 1857. No. 1007.

    6. Eliza Showalter, b. June 27, 1861. d. Aug. 27, 1863.

    7. Nancy E. Showalter, b. Mar. 9, 1865. No. 1008.

    8 Sarah F Showalter, b Dec. 19, 1868, d. April 2, 1902.

No. 976. Fifth Generation. 975.

1) Daniel P. Showalter, b Aug. 24, 1851, near Broadway, Va., m. May 16, 1880, to Hettie E Rohrer, b. Feb. 26, 1858, in Lancaster Co , Pa. Address: Dayton, Va.

    1 Ida Elizabeth Showalter, b. April 20, 1881. No 977.

    2. John Rohrer Showalter, b. Feb 15, 1883. No 980.

    3. Anna Grace Showalter, b Oct. 18, 1884. No 981.

    4. Israel Rohrer Showalter, b July 2, 1886. No 984.

    5. Harry Rohrer Showalter, b. Aug. 13, 1889. No 985.

    6 Sarah Mabel Showalter, b. Oct. 18, 1891 No 986.

    7 Mary Amelia Showalter, b. April 9, 1894. No. 987.

    8. Daniel Rohrer Showalter, b May 26, 1897. No. 988.

    9. Michael Rohrer Showalter, b. May 14, 1899. No. 989.

No. 977. Sixth Generation. 976.

1) Ida Elizabeth Showalter, b Apr 20, 1881, near Crisman, Va., m. Dec. 21, 1904, to Joseph Roy Early, b. Mar. 13, 1879, near Dayton, Va. He was a son of Samuel and Frances Rhodes Early. He was a farmer and thresher. Dunkards.

1. Vera Marie Early, b Feb 5, 1906. No. 978.
2. Naomi Virginia Early, b. Dec. 9, 1908 No. 979.
3. Samuel Showalter Early, b. Sept. 7, 1912 No. 2139.
4 Byard Daniel Early, b. April 29, 1917.
5. Mary Orpha Early, b Oct. 24, 1919

No. 978. Seventh Generation. 977.

1) Vera Marie Early, b. Feb. 5, 1906, near Crisman, Va., m. June 2, 1926, to Ralph Frank Heatwole, b. Mar. 12, 1904 Farmer. Mennonites.

1. Owen Early Heatwole, b. Mar 23, 1927.
2. Enos Edward Heatwole, b. Dec 14, 1928
3. Daniel Percy Heatwole, b Dec. 23, 1929.
4. Roy Winford Heatwole, b. Nov. 22, 1931, d July 17, 1933.
5. Willard J. Heatwole, b Aug 22, 1933.

No. 979. Seventh Generation. 977.

2) Naomi Virginia Early, b. Dec. 9, 1908, near Dayton, Va., m. Dec. 2, 1930, to John J. Wenger, b. Jan. 16, 1909. Farmer. Mennonites.

1. Lloyd Edward Wenger, b. Sept. 10, 1931.
2. John E. Wenger, b July 2, 1933.

No. 980. Sixth Generation. 976.

2) John R. Showalter, b. Feb 15, 1883, near Crisman, Va , m Sept 14, 1910, Wilda G. Brunk. Mennonites Farmer.

1. Anna Elizabeth Showalter, b. Feb. 10, 1911.
2. Harry Brunk Showalter, b. Oct. 24, 1918.
3. Ruth Showalter, b Aug 13, 1913, d. same day
4. John Daniel Showalter, b. Dec. 13, 1914.
5. Maud Virginia Showalter, b. Feb 17, 1917.
6. Robert Joseph Showalter, b. July 1, 1919.
7. Wilda Grace Showalter, b. Nov. 18, 1921.
8. Gabriel Hugh Showalter, b. Mar. 13, 1923.
9. Martha Louise Showalter, b. April 21, 1925.

Three other children died in infancy and are buried at Pleasant View near Dayton, Va.

No. 981. Sixth Generation. 976.

3) Anna Grace Showalter, b Oct. 18, 1884, near Crisman, Va., m. Feb. 20, 1907, Oliver C. Burkholder, b. June 16, 1884, son of Caleb Burkholder. Farmer. Mennonite.

1. Roy DeWitt Burkholder, b. Jan. 24, 1908. No. 3268.
2. John Samuel Burkholder, b. July 13, 1909 No. 3269.
3. Ester Larue Burkholder, b. Mar. 12, 1911. No. 3270.
4. Daniel Showalter Burkholder, b. Dec. 5, 1912.
5. Paul Marvin Burkholder, b. Jan. 5, 1915. No. 3271.
6. Mary Elizabeth Burkholder, b. Mar. 12, 1917.
7. Nellie Grace Burkholder, b. Feb. 10, 1919.
8. Henry Lawrence Burkholder, b. Jan. 8, 1921.
9. Frances Orpha Burkholder, b. Dec. 1, 1923.

No. 984. Sixth Generation. 976.

4) Israel Rohrer Showalter, b July 2, 1886, near Crisman, Va, m. Mar. 3, 1909, Larue Z. Heatwole, b. Jan. 20, 1890, near Hinton, Va. Farmer. Mennonite.
1. Howard Heatwole Showalter, b. Mar. 2, 1912.
2. Warren Conrad Showalter, b. Feb. 28, 1913.
3. Joseph Daniel Showalter, b Sept. 10, 1918.
4. Claude Rhodes Showalter, b. April 16, 1920.
5. Mark Israel Showalter, b. Sept 19, 1922
6. Mahlon Franklin Showalter, b Nov. 7, 1923
7. Annie Marie Showalter, b. Dec 17, 1925.

No. 985. Sixth Generation. 976.

5) Harry Rohrer Showalter, b. Aug 13, 1889, near Crisman, Va, m Nov 24, 1914, Sadie Weaver, b. Aug 24, 1889, near Columbiana, O., daughter of David Weaver and Salome Blosser She died Dec 26, 1915. He married Aug. 19, 1920, Melisse Weaver, sister of his first wife She was born July 8, 1884 Buried in Mahoning Co, O.
1 Esther Virginia Showalter, b. Dec 18, 1915.
   (From second wife)
2 Infant daughter, b June 30, 1921, d July 2, 1921.
3 Elmer Weaver Showalter, b Feb 17, 1923.
4. Mary Agnes Showalter, b. June 30, 1924.
5 Joseph B. Showalter, b July 29, 1926, d Dec. 21, 1926.
6 Anna Ruth Showalter, b. July 18, 1928

No. 986. Sixth Generation. 976.

6) Sarah Mabel Showalter, b Oct 18, 1891, near Crisman, Va., m. Feb. 24, 1914, to Webster Clay Rhodes, b Mar. 8, 1890, near Dayton, Va. He was a son of Reuben S. Rhodes. Farmer. Mennonites.
1 Mark Showalter Rhodes, b Dec. 28, 1914.
2. Harry Wayne Rhodes, b. June 6, 1916.
3. Frank Webster Rhodes, b Mar. 21, 1918, d. Sept. 17, 1918.
4. Eber Ansel Rhodes, b July 18, 1919
5 Edith Virginia Rhodes, b Feb. 25, 1921.
6 Daniel Rohrer Rhodes, b. July 28, 1923, d May 23, 1924
7. Reuben Swope Rhodes, b Dec 11, 1924.
8 Duke Clement Rhodes, b Oct. 11, 1926.
9. Esther Magdalene Rhodes, b. July 6, 1928
10. John Clay Rhodes, b Aug. 30, 1930.
11 Ida Rosalene Rhodes, b Mar. 29, 1932.

No. 987. Sixth Generation. 976.

7) Mary Amelia Showalter, b April 9, 1894, near Crisman, Va., m. Feb. 11, 1919, Ward E Beery, b Jan 13, 1892, near Dayton, Va. Farmer. Mennonites.
1 Esther Ruth Beery, b Dec 16, 1919
2 David Showalter Beery, b. Jan. 12, 1921.
3 Mabel Rebecca Beery, b Nov. 12, 1922.
4 Joseph Galen Beery, b. Mar. 30, 1924, twin
5 Daniel Pierce Beery, b Mar 30, 1924, twin
6 Hettie Irene Beery, b. Nov. 25, 1925.
7. Emery Charles Beery, b May 10, 1927.
8 Wilda May Beery, b. Mar. 29, 1929.
9 Ada Marie Beery, b Feb 14, 1931.
10 Anna Grace Beery, b. July 17, 1932.

No. 988. Sixth Generation. 976.

8) Daniel R. Showalter, b. Mar. 26, 1897, near Crisman, Va, m. Dec 5, 1918, Anna Mary Koogler, b. Dec. 19, 1896, near Lily, Va. Farmer. Mennonites. She was a daughter of Ervine and Rebecca Wenger Koogler.

1. Justus Koogler Showalter, b. Sept. 25, 1920.
2. Samuel Christian Showalter, b. Dec. 23, 1922.
3. Ervin Gail Showalter, b. May 21, 1924.
4. Nathan Edwin Showalter, b. July 15, 1926.
5. Daniel Rohrer Showalter, b. April 8, 1929.
6. Rebecca Susan Showalter, b. April 25, 1930.

No. 989. Sixth Generation. 976.

9) Michael R. Showalter, b. May 14, 1899, near Dayton, Va., m. June 7, 1921, Fanny Belle Heatwole, b Jan 14, 1899, near Rockingham, Va Farmer. Mennonites. Michael not living, buried at Pleasant Valley.

1. Edward Heatwole Showalter, b June 2, 1922.
2. Marvin Heatwole Showalter, b. Nov. 3, 1923.
3 Harry H. Showalter, b Mar 3, 1925, twin.
4. Harold H. Showalter, b. Mar. 3, 1925, twin
5. Daniel Paul Showalter, b. Apr. 22, 1927.
6. Mary Frances Showalter, b July 29, 1928.
7. Michael R Showalter, b May 19, 1930, d Feb. 1, 1931
8. John Henry Showalter, b Aug 8, 1931.

No. 990. Fifth Generation. 975.

2) Samuel J Showalter, b. July 25, 1853, near Crisman, Va, d. in 1919, m Sept. 20, 1877, Sarah M. Good, b Nov. 22, 1863, daughter of Daniel J and Marie Heatwole Good, d Jan. 8, 1938 Address Waynesboro, Va Farmer Mennonites.

1. Mattie K. Showalter, b. July 21, 1888. No 991.
2. John D. Showalter, b Dec 24, 1889 No 992
3. Mary Edna Showalter, b. Feb 10, 1892 No 993
4. Lizzie F. Showalter, b June 22, 1894 No 994
5. Ada M. Showalter, b. Oct 9, 1896. No 995
6. Willie F. Showalter, b Oct. 10, 1899 No 996
7. Samuel J. Showalter, Jr., b Nov. 9, 1901
8. Marion G Showalter, b. June 4, 1905, d Aug. 27, 1907.

No. 991. Sixth Generation. 990.

1) Mattie K Showalter, b. July 21, 1888, m. Dec 22, 1915, Perry A Burkholder, b. Aug. 12, 1886. Address: Waynesboro, Va. Mennonites.

1. Sylvia Isabel Burkholder, b Nov. 14, 1919.
2. Merlia Abraham Burkholder, b. Sept. 15, 1924
3. Lyle Samuel Burkholder, b. Jan 1, 1927

No. 992. Sixth Generation. 990.

2) John D. Showalter, b Dec 24, 1889, m. Feb. 2, 1916, Mae Edna Houff, b. Dec. 4, 1888. Address Waynesboro, Va. Lutherans.

1. Adopted daughter, Mary Margaret, b Mar. 7, 1926

No. 993. Sixth Generation. 990.

3) Mary Edna Showalter, b. Feb. 10, 1892, m. Dec. 5, 1916, Orrville C Flory, b. July 14, 1892. Address: Stuarts Draft, Va. Mennonite and Brethren.

No. 994. Sixth Generation. 990.

4) Lizzie F. Showalter, b June 22, 1894, m Dec. 27, 1917, Carl Hartman, b April 8, 1897, near Harrisonburg, Va. Address: Waynesboro, Va. Mennonites.

1. Milford Dee Hartman, b. Dec. 21, 1918
2. Robert Showalter Hartman, b Sept. 16, 1921.
3 Sarah Frances Hartman, b Oct. 3, 1922.
4 Phyllis Amelia Hartman, b Feb. 5, 1924.
5 Mildred Good Hartman, b. Oct. 15, 1930.

No. 995. Sixth Generation. 990.

5) Ada M. Showalter, b. Oct. 9, 1896, m Nov. 14, 1917, Jacob L. Martin, b
Nov. 10, 1891. Address: Waynesboro, Va. Mennonites.
1. Winston K. Martin, b. Sept. 27, 1918
2. Resalia S. Martin, b Feb. 1, 1920
3. Jacob Grady Martin, b Oct 17, 1932.

No. 996. Sixth Generation. 990.

6) Willie F. Showalter, b Oct. 10, 1899, m. Aug. 4, 1920, Isaac Myers, b.
July 8, 1897. Address· Edom, Va. Mennonite and Brethren.
1. James Maxwell Myers, b. April 25, 1922, d. next day.
2. Helen Elizabeth Myers, b. April 18, 1924.
Note.—Samuel J. Showalter not married Address 6327 Green St., Chicago,
Illinois.

No. 997. Fifth Generation. 975.

3) Jacob D. Showalter, b. Dec. 4, 1854, near Broadway, Va., m Feb. 8, 1883,
Mary Heatwole, daughter of Joseph and Lydia Rhodes Heatwole. Address:
Dayton, Va. Farmer Mennonites
1. Fannie Showalter, b Jan. 4, 1884 No 998.
2. Margaret Showalter, b. Dec. 24, 1885. No 1001.
3. Maude Showalter, b Dec 5, 1887 No 1002
4 E. Pearl Showalter, b July 31, 1890 No. 1003.
5. Frankie Showalter, b Feb 26, 1892 No. 1004
6. Lydia Showalter, b April 30, 1894, d June —, 1896
7. John B. Showalter, b. Sept 2, 1896. No 1005
8. Rena N. Showalter, b. Sept 18, 1899. No 1006
9. Mary E Showalter, b. Feb 18, 1903, d Jan 25, 1905.
Note.—Lydia was buried at Weavers Church and Mary was buried at Pike
Church.

No. 998. Sixth Generation. 997.

1) Fannie Showalter, b. Jan. 4, 1884, m May 13, 1903, Joseph A. Burkholder,
b. Jan. 6, 1882, son of A. B. and Nancy Weaver Burkholder. They live near North
Lima, O.
1. Harry C. Burkholder, b Mar. 1, 1904 No. 999.
2. Elizabeth M. Burkholder, b. Nov. 20, 1905. No. 1000.
3. Wilmer J. A Burkholder, b. Aug 26, 1907, d. April 13, 1917.
4. Dee Howard Burkholder, b Aug. 15, 1909, d July 25, 1911.
5. Mary E. Burkholder, b. Mar. 3, 1911. No. 3615.
6. Joseph A. Burkholder, b Sept. 8, 1913. No 3616.
7. Virginia L. Burkholder, b. Dec 8, 1915
8. Frances M. Burkholder, b. Sept. 10, 1918.

No. 999. Seventh Generation. 998.

1) Harry C. Burkholder, b. Mar. 1, 1904, m. Goldie Stauffer Address Po-
land, O. Mennonites.
1. Ronald E. Burkholder, b. Feb: 8, 1928
2. Marilyn M Burkholder, b. May 20, 1931

No. 1000. Seventh Generation. 998.

2) Elizabeth M. Burkholder, b. Nov 20, 1905, m. Melvin Hostetler, b. Feb. 12, 1903. Address: 1419 N. Market St., Orrville, O. Mail carrier. Mennonites.
1. Wendell R. Hostetler, b. Oct. 25, 1928.
2. Janet Ann Hostetler, b. Aug. 6, 1934.
3. Judith Elizabeth Hostetler, b. June 16, 1938.

No. 1001. Sixth Generation. 997.

2) Margaret Showalter, b Dec. 24, 1885, m. Aug. 29, 1911, F. A. Conrad. Methodists
1. Jean Conrad, b Dec. 21, 1922.

No. 1002. Sixth Generation. 997.

3) Maude E. Showalter, b Dec. 5, 1887, m. Dec. 27, 1910, Daniel P. Showalter, son of Jacob W and Margaret Heatwole Showalter Address Dayton, Va. No children.

No. 1003. Sixth Generation. 997.

4) E. Pearl Showalter, b. July 31, 1890, m. Mar. 12, 1912, Lawrence Suter, son of John R. and Fannie (Roudabush) Suter. Address: Harrisonburg, Va , R 5. Mennonites
1. Helen Suter, b. Oct. 15, 1912
2. Harold Suter, b. July 15, 1915
3. Dorthy Suter, b. April 20, 1918
4. Richard Suter, b Mar. 22, 1925

No. 1004. Sixth Generation. 997.

5) Frankie D. Showalter, b. Feb. 26, 1892, m. Dec. 6, 1917, Henry M. Shenk, son of Abraham P and Fannie Coffman Shenk Frankie died Oct 20, 1935 Related, see No. 672. Address: Denbigh, Va. Mennonites
1. Fannie V. Shenk, b. Oct. 7, 1918
2. Mary E. Shenk, b. Mar. 1, 1921.
3. Ellen E. Shenk, b. Nov. 4, 1923
4. Phebe F. Shenk, b. July 14, 1926.
5. Esther L. Shenk, b. Oct. 20, 1928
6. Henry M. Shenk, b. Feb. 22, 1931, twin
7. Helen M. Shenk, b Feb. 22, 1931, twin.

No. 1005. Sixth Generation. 997.

7) John B. Showalter, b Sept. 2, 1886, m. July 2, 1927, Lucille Wasser. They live in Chicago, Ill Presbyterians
1. Dorothy Showalter, b. Dec. 31, 1927.

No. 1006. Sixth Generation. 997.

8) Rena N. Showalter, b. Sept. 18, 1899, m May 22, 1918, Claude F. Coakley, son of James and Anna Heatwole Coakley. Address Harrisonburg, Va
1. Claude F. Coakley, Jr., b April 30, 1919.
2. John R. Coakley, b. Jan. 10, 1922, d. Jan 20, 1930.
3. Roselie Coakley, b. Jan. 30, 1926.
John R. Coakley was buried at Natural Bridge, Va.

No. 1007. Fifth Generation. 975.

5) Cyrus B. Showalter, b. Oct 14, 1857, near Singers Glen, Va., d. Aug. 20, 1937, m. Nov. 13, 1883, Lydia Wenger, b. May 10, 1860, near Greenmount, Va. They moved to Kansas in 1910. Address: Convoy, Kans. Mennonites Farmer.
1. Edward W. Showalter, b Sept. 8, 1884 No. 1107.
2. Elizabeth O. Showalter, b. Dec. 17, 1885. No. 1108.

3. Hannah B. Showalter, b. Nov. 13, 1887. No. 1110.
4. Oliver B. Showalter, b Sept. 15, 1889. No. 1111.
5. Amos M Showalter, b. Dec. 15, 1891. No. 1112.
6. Ada May Showalter, b. Feb. 4, 1894. No. 1113.
7. John L. Showalter, b. April 23, 1896. No. 1114.
8. Nellie Kate Showalter, b. Mar. 20, 1898. No. 1115.
9. Clara M. Showalter, b. Nov. 1, 1900. No. 1116.
10. Laura Nannie Showalter, b. April 19, 1903.

No. 1008. Fifth Generation. 975.
7) Nancy E. Showalter, b. Mar. 9, 1865, m. Mar. 5, 1896, Robert H. Showalter, son of Michael and Emily Jane (Whisler) Showalter. Mennonites.
1. Sadie F. Showalter, b. April 3, 1897, single.
2. Clark R. Showalter, b. Nov 14, 1898. No. 1009.
3. Mary E. Showalter, b Sept. 5, 1904. No 1010.

No. 1009. Sixth Generation. 1008.
2) Clark R. Showalter, b. Nov. 14, 1898, m. Mar. 28, 1923, Minnie B. Eagle, b. Nov. 20, 1900, daughter of Adam and Lillie Foley Eagle
1. Robert E. Showalter, b. July 11, 1925.
2. Carl R. Showalter, b. Jan 4, 1930.

No. 1010. Sixth Generation. 1008.
3) Mary E. Showalter, b. Sept. 5, 1904, m Jan. 6, 1927, Walter Tracy Suter, b. Aug. 23, 1901, son of John R. and Fannie Roudabush Suter. Mennonites.
1. Glen W. Suter, b. Oct 2, 1927.

No. 1011. Sixth Generation. 801.
8) Minnie Jane Myers, b. June 8, 1889, m. Oct 6, 1909, Henry Edward Showalter, b. Mar. 24, 1886. Address: Bellrose, L. F , New York. Reformed Church.
1. Helen Virginia Showalter, b. Mar. 12, 1913.
2. Dorothy Lee Showalter, b. May 10, 1922.

No. 1012. Seventh Generation. 803.
1) Clara Elizabeth Showalter, b Feb. 26, 1897, m. June 5, 1917, Roy Wampler Diehl, b. Nov. 3, 1892. Address: Scotts Ford, Va.
1. Nelson Showalter Diehl, b. May 20, 1918.
2. May Virginia Diehl, b July 20, 1920.

No. 1013. Seventh Generation. 804.
1) Elizabeth C. Myers, b. Oct. 17, 1902, m. Dec. 30, 1925, Harold T. Acker, b. Oct. 20, 1904, at Mt. Clinton, Va. Farmer. Brethren.
1. Harold T. Acker, Jr., b. July 26, 1927.
2. Freda C. Acker, b. May 25, 1929
3. John W. Acker, b. Mar. 30, 1931.
4. James M. Acker, b. Mar. 26, 1933

No. 1014. Seventh Generation. 804.
2) Alvin P. Myers, b. Oct. 5, 1904, m. Jan. 23, 1932, Virginia Logan, b. May 11, 1905. Address· Harrisonburg, Va. Brethren. Miller by trade.

No. 1015. Seventh Generation. 804.
3) Ralph M. Myers, b. Aug. 12, 1906, m June 8, 1926, Beulah Landes, b. April 18, 1903. Farmer. Brethren.
1. Doris J. Myers, b. June 25, 1930.
2. Richard W. Myers, b. July 18, 1932.

No. 1016. Seventh Generation. 805.

3) Ruth M. Zigler, b. June 26, 1905, m Mar. 17, 1926, Everett M Bowman
1. Donald Victor Bowman, b. June 23, 1928.

No. 1017. Sixth Generation. 801.

5) Lydia M. Myers, b. Nov. 28, 1882, m. May 28, 1907, Hunter H. Saufley, b. Dec. 26, 1883, at Cross Keys, Va. Farmer.
1. Virginia Saufley, b. April 3, 1908.
2. Frenchie Arlette Saufley, b. Aug 28, 1909.
3. Gaylen Myers Saufley, b Feb 26, 1912.
4. Hinton Huffman Saufley, b. Mar. 30, 1914.
All born at Cross Keys, Va. Address. North River, Va

No. 1018. Seventh Generation. 806.

1) Lloyd Myers, b. April 14, 1906, m June 3, 1925, Frances Sharps. Address: Harrisonburg, Va Operates express truck from Harrisonburg to northern cities. Brethren.
1. Nelson L. Myers, b Jan 27, 1927.
2. Carroll Eugene Myers, b Oct 10, 1929
3. Duene Frances Myers, b Oct 26, 1931

No. 1019. Seventh Generation. 806.

2) Victor J. Myers, b. Dec. 8, 1910, m June 3, 1928, Margaret Landes, b Jan. 11, 1912. Brethren. Address· Dayton, Va.

No. 1020. Seventh Generation. 807.

1) Cleta B. Flory, b. Oct 28, 1904, m Dec. 24, 1928, Austin W Kirbey
1. William Paul Kirbey, b Dec 8, 1930

No. 1021. Seventh Generation. 807.

2) Minnie M. Flory, b. Nov. 15, 1906, m Feb. 10, 1924, Rufus O Driver
1. Cathryn Driver, b April 29, 1927

No. 1022. Seventh Generation. 807.

3) Mabel C Flory, b Mar 23, 1910, m Mar. 1, 1930, Charles W Farrer
1 Dorothy Jean Farrer, b Feb 22, 1931.

No. 1023. Sixth Generation. 802.

2) Savilla F. Wenger, b. Jan. 25, 1884, m Dec 18, 1912, Hiram L Hedrick, of Versailles, Mo He died near Royersford, Pa, Mar. 7, 1932.
1. Margaret L. Hedrick, b. Sept 22, 1913.
2. Evelyn W. Hedrick, b. Dec 22, 1916
3. Hiram Lee Hedrick, b. Sept. 6, 1918.

No. 1024. Sixth Generation. 802.

3) John D. Wenger, b. Feb 5, 1886, m Dec 25, 1909, Verdie Garber of Bridgewater, Va.
1. John Lynwood Wenger, b. June 27, 1913.
2. Ralph D Wenger, b. April 3, 1917

No. 1025. Sixth Generation. 802.

4) William Neff Wenger, b. Mar. 24, 1888, m Oct. 22, 1913, Ada Miller of Bridgewater, Va., at Washington, D C.
1. Byron M. Wenger, b Dec. 2, 1917
2. Lloyd M. Wenger, b. April 9, 1923.
3. Ada Marie Wenger, b Nov. 25, 1929.
4. Dorothy Virginia Wenger, b. Dec. 31, 1931

No. 1026. Sixth Generation. 802.

5) Lydia S. Wenger, b Mar. 14, 1890, m Clifford Heatwole, of near Lily, Va.
1. Warren W. Heatwole, b. ―――――――

No. 1027. Seventh Generation. 247.

1) Jacob L. Martin, b Nov 10, 1891, near Waynesboro, Va , m. Nov. 14,
1917, Ada M. Showalter, b. Oct. 9, 1896 Address. Waynesboro, Va. Mennonites.
1. Winston Keith Martin, b. Sept 27, 1918.
2. Rosalie Savilla Martin, b. Feb. 1, 1920
3. Jacob Grady Martin, b. Oct 17, 1932

No. 1028. Seventh Generation. 247.

4) John D. Martin, b Mar. 29, 1898, near Waynesboro, Va , m April 12,
1921, Mary A. Craigg, b. April 26, 1901 Address. Waynesboro, Va. Farmer.
Mennonites. Burial ground at Springdale Church.
1. Clinton Earl Martin, b Feb 12, 1922
2. Roy Daniel Martin, b. Nov. 19, 1924
3. Thelma Catherine Martin, b. Jan. 1, 1927
4 Mary Frances Martin, b Feb 6, 1933

No. 1029. Seventh Generation. 247.

5) William H. Martin, b. June 20, 1900, near Waynesboro, Va , m. Mar. 22,
1923, Florence Hershey Address: Wengers Mill, Pa. Farmer. Mennonite.
1. Hershey Leroy Martin, b May 15, 1923.
2. Gertrude Evelyn Martin, b. July 31, 1925.
3. Barbara Sue Martin, b. Mar. 31, 1927.
4. William Martin, Jr , b. Nov. 6, 1930.
5. Elener Jean Martin, b June 5, 1932

No. 1030. Seventh Generation. 247.

6) Marie E. Martin, b July 31, 1902, near Waynesboro, Va., m. Mar. 10, 1921,
Jason H. Weaver. Address: Waynesboro, Va. Hatchery. Mennonites.
1. Elwood Daniel Weaver, b. Dec. 25, 1921
2. Ralph Letcher Weaver, b. Jan. 7, 1924.
3. Jason H. Weaver, Jr , b June 15, 1926
4. Nancy Lee Weaver, b. Jan. 5, 1929.
5 Charlene Marie Weaver, b Nov 14, 1931, twin
6 Lorene Elizabeth Weaver, b. Nov 14, 1931, twin

No. 1031. Seventh Generation. 247.

7) Fannie Ruth Martin, b Oct. 31, 1904, near Waynesboro, Va., m. April 25,
1923, Elmer J. Heatwole, b June 20, 1902 Address Waynesboro, Va. Mechanic.
Mennonites.
1. Kenneth Martin Heatwole, b Jan 1, 1927.
2. Louise Frances Heatwole, b. Nov 14, 1929.

No. 1032. Seventh Generation. 248.

1) Charles Marvin Etter, b Nov. 23, 1893, near Stuarts Draft, Va., m. Aug.
12, 1924, Callie A. Withrow. Address: Waynesboro, Va. Undertaker. Methodists.
1. Patricia Etter, b Aug. 10, 1925.

No. 1033. Seventh Generation. 248.

2) Earl Driver Etter, b. Dec 13, 1896, near Stuarts Draft, Va , m. June 10,
1920, Lillian Gardner. Address: Waynesboro, Va. Miller by trade Methodists.
1. Earl Driver Etter, Jr , b Aug. 31, 1923.

No. 1034. Seventh Generation. 248.

3) George Irvin Etter, b. May 5, 1904, near Stuarts Draft, Va., m. Nov. 3, 1931, Hazel L Cash. Address Waynesboro, Va. Undertaker

No. 1035. Sixth Generation. 249.

6) Joseph R Driver, b. June 17, 1884, in Augusta Co., Va., m. Dec. 2, 1908, Lizzie Weaver, b. April 2, 1885, d. Feb 27, 1932, in Augusta Co., where they lived She was buried in the Springdale cemetery. Joseph Driver was ordained to the ministry in the Mennonite Church in Augusta Co, Va., Nov. 11, 1911, at the Springdale Church, and on Sept 23, 1932, was ordained bishop at the same place. Address: Waynesboro, Va.

1. Ruth Virginia Driver, b. July 3, 1910.
2. Martha Elizabeth Driver, b. Aug 2, 1912. No. 2791
3. Ruel Weaver Driver, b. Nov. 23, 1914
4. Mary Frances Driver, b. Feb 16, 1917. No 3648
5. Frederick A. Driver, b July 25, 1920
6 Joseph R Driver, b. Sept 8, 1923, d. Sept. 4, 1926
7. Naomi May Driver, b May 23, 1926.
8. David Hershey Driver, b. Oct 3, 1929.

No. 1036. Sixth Generation. 249.

7) Daniel W. Driver, b. Sept. 29, 1888, in Augusta Co, Va, m. May 8, 1913, Maud Shank, b. Mar. 26, 1892 On Aug 17, 1921, Mr. Driver was found unconscious about noon and remained in that condition until seven in the evening when he passed away. Farmer. Mennonites Waynesboro, Va.

1. Justus Shank Driver, b. June 10, 1914
2. Lois Elizabeth Driver, b. June 18, 1917, d. Aug 1, 1918.
3. Richard Nelson Driver, b Sept. 3, 1919.

No. 1037. Fourth Generation. 24.

6) Michael Showalter, b Feb 15, 1831, near Broadway, Va, m. Mar. 10, 1853, Elizabeth Shank, b Jan. 20, 1831, daughter of Bishop Samuel and Elizabeth (Funk) Shank. She died Jan 29, 1913, and he died Oct. 18, 1906. Farmers. Mennonites. Address was Harrisonburg, Va.

1. Moab H. Showalter, b Dec 15, 1855. No. 1038.
2. Susan V. Showalter, b. Oct. 15, 1856. No. 1126.
3. George B. Showalter, b Sept. 18, 1857. No. 1040.
4. Nettie Showalter, b. Nov. 17, 1859 No. 1041.
5. Mary C. Showalter, b. April 1, 1862. No. 1042.
6. Franklin B. Showalter, b. July 17, 1864. No. 1043.
7. Nancy V. Showalter, b May 6, 1867. No. 1044.
8. William C. Showalter, b. Oct. 30, 1869, twin. No. 1045.
9. Urie F. Showalter, b Oct. 30, 1869, twin. No 1150.
10. Laban M. Showalter, b. Sept. 2, 1872. No. 1047.
11. Walter L. Showalter, b Dec. 17, 1875 No. 1048.

No. 1038. Fifth Generation. 1037.

1) Moab H. Showalter, b. Dec. 15, 1855, near Harrisonburg, Va., m. Oct. 23, 1879, Anna Shank, b. May 27, 1862, in Maryland. She died Nov. 7, 1934. Farmer Mennonites. Address: Reid (near Hagerstown), Md.

1. Amanda C. Showalter, b. Nov. 27, 1880. No. 1117.
2. Alvah M. Showalter, b. Dec. 24, 1881. No. 1118.
3. Infant son, b. Oct. 30, 1883, d. same day.
4. Amos F. Showalter, b May 19, 1885. No. 1119

5. Bertie E. Showalter, b Feb. 13, 1887, single.
6. Emma B. Showalter, b. Sept. 21, 1889. No. 1122.
7. Martin W. Showalter, b. Feb. 4, 1892. No. 1123.
8. Minnie G. Showalter, b. Mar. 6, 1894. No. 1124.
9. Irvin F. Showalter, b. Dec. 21, 1895. No. 1125.

No. 1040. Fifth Generation. 1037.

3) George B. Showalter, b. Sept. 18, 1857, near Harrisonburg, Va., m. Oct. 30, 1884, Elizabeth E. Blosser, b. April 20, 1860. Mr. Showalter is an able minister in the Mennonite Church in Rockingham Co, Va. Farmer. Mennonites. Address: Broadway, Va.
1. Noah D. Showalter, b. Feb. 22, 1886. No. 1129.
2. Timothy M. Showalter, b. Dec. 19, 1887. No. 1131.
3. Louis P. Showalter, b. Nov. 8, 1890, twin. No 1132.
4. Paul P. Showalter, b. Nov. 8, 1890, twin. No. 1133.
5. Maggie F. Showalter, b. Sept. 6, 1892. No. 1134
6. Infant Showalter (stillborn).
7. Mark C. Showalter, b. Feb. 10, 1895 No. 1135
8. Luke C. Showalter, b June 8, 1898 No 1136.
9. Michael M. Showalter, b. May 17, 1900. No. 1137.
10. John A. Showalter, b. Aug 8, 1904, d. Apr. 1, 1906
11. Elizabeth H. Showalter, b. June 11, 1907.

No. 1041. Fifth Generation. 1037.

4) Nettie Showalter, b. Nov. 17, 1859, near Harrisonburg, Va. She was never married, but remained at home and cared for her parents until they died.

No. 1042. Fifth Generation. 1037.

5) Mary C. Showalter, b. April 1, 1862, near Harrisonburg, Va., d. Mar. 3, 1927, m. July 11, 1886, Daniel A. Blosser. Address: Harrisonburg, Va. Farmer. Mennonites.
1 N. Pearl Blosser, b. July 8, 1888 No. 1138.
2. Nannie E. Blosser, b. Jan. 15, 1890. No. 1139
3. Orpha V. Blosser, b. Jan. 18, 1893. No 1140.
4. Mary S. Blosser, b. April 18, 1897.
5. Daniel J. Blosser, b. Mar 9, 1899. No. 1141.
6. Michael O. Blosser, b. May 12, 1901. No. 1142.
7. Mahlon L. Blosser, b. Jan. 16, 1904. No. 1143.

No. 1043. Fifth Generation. 1037.

6) Franklin B. Showalter, b July 17, 1864, near Harrisonburg, Va., m. Nov. 15, 1887, Emma Bixler, b. April 11, 1864. Mr Showalter was an extensive farmer at Harrisonburg, Va. Later he lived in Ohio and Colorado after which he returned to near Harrisonburg, Va , but again in 1933 he migrated to Roscoe, Calif. Mennonites.
1. Earl E. Showalter, b. Mar. 31, 1890 No. 1144
2. Della V. Showalter, b. Oct. 2, 1894, single.
3. Elmo F. Showalter, b. Nov 27, 1898. No. 1145.

No. 1044. Fifth Generation. 1037.

7) Nancy V. Showalter, b. May 6, 1867, near Broadway, Va., m. Nov. 17, 1887, Jacob Snively Martin. Farmer. Mennonites. Mr. Martin was ordained to the ministry April 14, 1896. Mrs. Martin was paralyzed Dec. 1, 1931 and after a second stroke Oct 9, 1932, she passed away; aged 65 y. 5 m. 3 d. Address: Hinton, Va.

1. Nettie Alice Martin, b. April 17, 1889, d Jan 14, 1893.
2. Infant son (stillborn), Sept 4, 1890.
3. Mary Mabel Martin, b. Jan 4, 1892, d. Dec. 4, 1903
4. Fannie Elizabeth Martin, b. July 29, 1893.
5. John Paul Martin, b Sept 6, 1896 No 1044½
6 Ruth Showalter Martin, b Sept 20, 1899 She fell from a load of wheat June 24, 1911, when a prong from a fork penetrated through her brain from which she died July 26, 1911.
7. Carl Martin, b. May 11, 1898, d May 17, 1898
8. Ellwood Martin, b Aug 29, 1901, d Aug. 31, 1901

No. 1044½. Sixth Generation. 1044.

5) John Paul Martin, b. Sept. 6, 1895, m Dec. 31, 1916, Anna Katherine McDorman. Address: Hinton, Va.
1 Jacob Elburn Martin, b. June 2, 1923.
2. John Paul Martin, Jr, b. April 10, 1926.

No. 1045. Fifth Generation. 1037.

8) William C. Showalter, b. Oct 30, 1869, near Harrisonburg, Va, m. Dec. 28, 1892, Effie F. Bell Address Harrisonburg, Va Merchant. Mennonites.
1. Pauline Showalter, b. Oct. 18, 1893. No. 1146.
2. Roy S Showalter, b. Dec 20, 1896, d Feb 10, 1897
3 Ethel Showalter, b Oct 5, 1898 No 1147
4. Michael Showalter, b Nov 10, 1900
5. Harold Showalter, b April 29, 1902 No 1148
6 Morrison Showalter, b. Sept 28, 1903, d July 2, 1905.
7. Joseph Showalter, b. April 23, 1904 No 1149
8. Effie Showalter, b. Dec 24, 1906
9. Oliver Showalter, b. June 26, 1908
10 Doris Showalter, b Sept 24, 1910
11. W. C. Showalter, b Sept. 13, 1912.
12. Marguerite Clarince Showalter, b Sept 3, 1914
13 George Branner Showalter, b Sept 29, 1916.

No. 1047. Fifth Generation. 1037.

10) Laban M. Showalter, b. Sept. 2, 1872, near Harrisonburg, Va, m. Jan. 8, 1895, Bertie C. Liskey, b Nov 12, 1876 Address· Dayton, Va. Farmer. Mennonites. No issue.

No. 1048. Fifth Generation. 1037.

11) Walter L Showalter, b Dec 17, 1875, near Harrisonburg, Va, m. June 3, 1895, Nannie E. Horner, b Oct. 20, 1877. Address Harrisonburg, Va. Farmer and United Brethren minister.
1. Wilbur M. Showalter, b. June 20, 1896 No 1154
2. Mattie E Showalter, b Sept. 1, 1899. No. 1155.
3. Mary E Showalter, b. Dec. 8, 1901 No 1156
4. Walter R Showalter, b May 7, 1904 No 1157
5. Elmer D. Showalter, b July 16, 1908 No. 1158
6 Ruby N. Showalter, b. Jan. 17, 1913
7. Laban Michael Showalter, b May 31, 1917.
8. Howard Ellwood Showalter, b Sept. 23, 1921.

No. 1049. Sixth Generation. 377.

1) Elmer Rufus Brunk, b Mar. 6, 1881, m (1st) Maude Virginia Coffman, b. Oct. 29, 1887, d. Oct 7, 1909 She was a daughter of Albert and Sarah (Gar-

ber) Coffman He married (2nd) Nannie Elizabeth Blosser, daughter of David and Mary (Showalter) Blosser She was born Jan. 15, 1890.

1 Maude Virginia Brunk, b. Sept 28, 1909 No. 1050
  (From second wife)
2 Mary Elizabeth Brunk, b May 4, 1913
3 Evelyn Juanita Brunk, b Dec 2, 1921

No. 1050. Seventh Generation. 1049.

1) Maude Virginia Brunk. b Sept 28, 1909, m Wade Henry Good
1. Elmer Richard Good, b. Aug. 20, 1930.
2 Jean Brunk Good. b Sept 24, 1932.

No. 1051. Sixth Generation. 377.

2) Joseph Aaron Brunk, b Sept 21, 1883, m. Hannah Mary Lahman, b Jan. 31, 1890 Related; for fuller report see No 864.

No. 1052. Sixth Generation. 377.

3) John Claude Brunk, b Nov 16, 1885, m June 20, 1913, Inez Schrock, b Sept 17, 1888 They live at Chesterton, Ind Dairyman Mennonites

1 Barbara Brunk, b Oct 2, 1917
2 Jay Frank Brunk, b Mar 16, 1923

No. 1053. Sixth Generation. 377.

4) Harry Anthony Brunk, b June 21, 1898, m Lena Gertrude Burkholder, b Dec 12, 1900, daughter of John D and Isadora Humphrys Burkholder

1 James Robert Brunk, b May 25, 1926
2 David Christian Brunk, b Jan 5, 1929
3 Samuel Frederick Brunk, b Dec. 21, 1932

No. 1054. Fourth Generation. 25.

1) Jacob T Beery, b Sept 7, 1826, near Edom, Va , d. Nov. 29, 1854 Mennonite He married May 17, 1850, Isabelle A Atchison, b May 17, 1832 Methodist Farmer Buried at Edom, Va

1 George W. Beery, b Nov 6, 1851 No 1055
2 Benjamin F Beery. b Jan 17, 1854 No 1056.

No. 1055. Fifth Generation. 1054.

1) George W Beery, b Nov 6, 1851, near Edom, Va , m April 20, 1886, Bettie Franklin, b April 6, 1866 Address Coakley, Stafford Co , Va. Farmer. Baptists.

1 Kellog F Beery, b June 5, 1889, d May 17, 1890
2 Wm Gordon Beery, b May 13, 1891
3 Louis Franklin Beery, b Sept 28, 1897

No. 1056. Fifth Generation. 1054.

2) Benjamin F Beery, b Jan 17, 1854, at Edom, Va , m Sept 15, 1880, Sallie Poage, b Dec 24, 1859 Address Mt Clinton, Va. Farmer. Presbyterians Mr Beery for a few years had formed a partnership with his cousin A B. Driver and kept a general store at Mt Clinton. Va , but again went back to the farm

1 Susan Beery, b. and d. July 27, 1881.
2 Primrose Gatewood Beery, b Sept 23, 1884
3 Anna Isabelle Beery, b Feb 23, 1886
4 Jessie May Beery, b Nov 6, 1889
5 Susan Page Beery, b Aug 24, 1890.
6 Sallie Elizabeth Beery, b Sept 24, 1892
7 Mabel Grace Beery. b Nov 27, 1894, d Nov 29, 1894.

177

7

8 Turner Ashby Beery, b. Jan 2, 1897.

9 Margaret Cameron Beery, b May 20, 1899

10 Moffett Posage Beery, b Sept 26, 1901

No. 1057. Fourth Generation. 25.

2) Elizabeth Beery, b June 7, 1828, near Edom, Va, death and burial at Cooks Creek Church May 24, 1879, m April 11, 1850, Lewis Driver, b Mar 6, 1827, near Timberville, Va He was killed in a storm at Mt Clinton, Va, July 2, 1892 Farmer. Mennonites Address Mt Clinton, Va

1 Abraham B Driver, b Feb 2, 1851 No 1058

2. Infant son (stillborn), July 21, 1854

3 Infant son (stillborn), May 15, 1859

4 Margaret Jane Driver, b July 22, 1862, d Aug 10, 1863

No. 1058. Fifth Generation. 1057.

1) Abraham B Driver, b Feb 2, 1851, near Mt Clinton, Va, m Oct 12, 1875, Fannie Curry, b Mar 24, 1853 Address Harrisonburg, Va Merchant and farmer.

1 Rosa May Driver, b. Aug 25, 1876, died at six weeks of age

2 George Curry Driver, b. Jan 7, 1878.

3. Anna Madge Driver, b. July 11, 1881

4 Lewis Robert Driver, b. Mar 2, 1886.

5. James Glen Driver, b. Aug. 10, 1889.

6 Augustus Bernard Driver, b May 18, 1892.

7 Thomas A Blaine Driver, b Aug 6, 1895

No. 1059. Fourth Generation. 25.

3) Lydia Beery, b Nov 25, 1829, near Edom, Va, m Sept 16, 1852, Noah Keller, b. June 25, 1828, d Dec 12, 1877. They lived at Colfax, Fairfield Co, O. After the death of her husband she lived for some time at the old homestead with her daughter, but decided to sell the home, and with her daughter went to Blackshear, Ga., to live with her son Evangelical Association.

1 John W. Keller, b June 25, 1853. No. 1060.

2 Abram Beery Keller, b Oct 24, 1859, d Aug, 1860

3. Emma F Keller, b Mar 10, 1862 No 1061.

No. 1060. Fifth Generation. 1059.

1) John W Keller, b June 25, 1853, in Rockingham Co, Va, m July 9, 1879, Mollie L. Benedum, b Nov 28, 1855 She died Sept 10, 1883 Teacher Evangelical Address. Blackshear, Ga

1. Hardy F Keller, b June 12, 1879

2 Harry R Keller, b Oct 14, 1882, d Aug 25, 1883

No. 1061. Fifth Generation. 1059.

3) Emma F. Keller, b Mar 10, 1862, in Rockingham Co, Va, m. Oct 13, 1887, Homer V. Graham, b Dec 12, 1857 She lived with her mother near Colfax, O, but later moved to Blackshear, Ga Evangelical No issue

No. 1062. Fourth Generation. 25.

4) John H Beery, b Aug 20, 1831, near Edom, Va, d Sept 11, 1896, m in 1852 Delilah Neishwander, b May 5, 1830, near Edom, Va She died Nov. 23, 1904. They lived near Lima, O, since 1875, where they died on their homestead Both are buried in the Sugar Creek cemetery near Lima. **Farmer. Church of the** Brethren.

1. Newton C. Beery, b Jan 7, 1854 No 1063

2 Lydia E. Beery, b Mar 23, 1857 No 1065

3 Isaac N Beery, b Aug 10, 1860, d Dec 2, 1863
4 Benjamin F Beery, b Nov 2, 1863, d Jan. 5, 1864.

No. 1063. Fifth Generation. 1062.

1) Newton C Beery, b Jan 7, 1854, near Edom, Va., d April 9, 1932, m. Sept. 5, 1878, Elizabeth Herzog, b Feb. 20, 1858 He was a farmer until late in his life when he moved to Lima, O , where he lived until his death. Buried in the Woodlawn cemetery, Lima, O Address· Lima, O.

1 George W. Beery, b Sept 20, 1879 No 1064
2 Minerva Beery, b July 5, 1881, d Aug. 23, 1881
3 Delmar A. Beery, b Jan. 21, 1883 No. 1098.
4 Cora E Beery, b July 15, 1885 No 1099
5 Isaac N Beery, b Mar 1, 1888 No 1100
6 Ephraim Beery, b July 24, 1890 No 1101
7 Lydia E Beery, b May 12, 1893. No 1102

No. 1064. Sixth Generation. 1063.

1) George W Beery, b Sept 20, 1879, near Lima, O., m. Dec 25, 1901, Minnie Irvin Address Lima, O , R 5

1 Irvin A Beery, b Nov 18, 1902
2 Edith E. Beery, b Jan 18, 1904 No 1094
3 Robert Beery, b Dec 15, 1905, d July 19, 1913
4 Mary Beery, b Oct 17, 1907 No 1095
5 Ruth Beery, b Oct 25, 1909 No 1096
6 Paul Beery, b May 26, 1911.
7 Cora Eve Beery, b Mar 4 1913
8 Marguerite Beery, b Feb 10, 1917
9 George Beery, Jr , b Oct 29, 1918
10 Wilma Beery, b July 23, 1922
11 Earnest Beery, b Sept 11, 1924

No. 1065. Fifth Generation. 1052.

2) Lydia E Beery, b Mar 23, 1857, near Edom, Va , m Dec 23, 1882, Ami Miller Church of the Brethren Address Beaverdam, O Farmer No issue

No. 1066. Fourth Generation. 25.

5) Michael A Beery, b Aug 20, 1831 (twin to John), near Edom, Va., m. Sept 18, 1853, Sallie A Atchison b Feb 5, 1835 Address Sommerville, Va. Farmer Methodists Michael in 1862 volunteered in the Stafford Cavalry Co. A, 9th Regiment of the Confederate army He was in many skirmishes and battles, the seven days battle at Richmond, Gettysburg, and many others

1 Lillian I Beery, b Oct 25, 1854 No 1067
2 Edward T Beery, b Aug 6, 1866 No report

No. 1057. Fifth Generation. 1066.

1) Lillian I Beery, b Oct 25, 1854, in Rockingham Co , Va , m Mar 15, 1877, Benjamin S West, b Mar 15, 1829 Address Laural, Md Merchant Methodists

1 Elizabeth Lyle West, b Jan 20, 1878
2 Whedeen E West, b Dec 13, 1879, twin.
3 Pearl G West, b Dec 13, 1879, twin No 1068
4 Marian B West, b Jan 8, 1882
5 Ashby C West, b Jan 13, 1884
6 Frederick F West, b Oct 15, 1886
7 Pauline B West, b Aug 3, 1891, d Aug 16, 1892

The first four of these children were born in Stafford Co, Va, Ashby and Frederick in Prince Williams Co, Va

No. 1068. Sixth Generation. 1057.

3) Pearl G. West, b Dec 13, 1879, in Stafford Co, Va, m May 27, 1903, William H. Wells, b. April 5, 1867. Electrical engineer in Washington, D C Baptists.

1 Viola B. Wells, b. Mar 5, 1904

No. 1070. Fourth Generation. 25.

6) Annie Beery, b Dec. 21, 1833, near Edom, Va, d. Nov. 8, 1904, m Aug. 11, 1853, Jacob Driver, b Jan 25, 1830, near Timberville, Va, d Nov. 7, 1877 Address: Mt Clinton, Va Farmer. They were Mennonites, of which church he was an able minister

1. Fannie Driver, b May 31, 1854 No 1071
2. Lyda C Driver, b Sept 21, 1856 No 1073
3 Solomon P Driver, b Feb 28, 1859 No 1074
4. Mary M. Driver, b Nov 4, 1861, d Sept 20, 1876
5. Abraham D. Driver, b. Mar 13, 1864. No 1075
6 Joseph W. Driver, b. Jan 17, 1867, single
7. Annie E Driver, b Jan. 18, 1870
8. Jacob Lewis Driver, b May 10, 1873 No 1075½
9 Ida Belle Driver, b Jan 23, 1876 No. 1076

No. 1071. Fifth Generation. 1070.

1) Fannie Driver, b May 31, 1854, at Mt Clinton, Va, d Nov. 8, 1933, m Dec. 22, 1885, Noah Smith, b Oct 4, 1852 He died July 27, 1918 Farmer Mennonites. Address· Mt Clinton, Va

1. Daisy Belle Smith, b May 2, 1887 No 1072

No. 1072. Sixth Generation. 1071.

1) Daisy Belle Smith, b May 2, 1887, near Mt Clinton, Va, m Frederick Jackson. Address Purcellville, Va Baker Presbyterians No issue

No. 1073. Fifth Generation. 1070.

2) Lydia Catherine Driver, b Sept 21, 1856, near Mt Clinton, Va, known as Cassie Driver She, being an invalid, was never married. She died Mar 18, 1934 Mennonite

No. 1074. Fifth Generation. 1070.

3) Solomon P Driver, b Feb 28, 1859, at Mt Clinton, Va, m. May 5, 1897, Emma Wilson of Ada, O, b April 1, 1867 Address Lima, O Carpenter

1 John Z. Driver, b Aug 15, 1898
2 Anna Irene Driver, b May 3, 1901
Both are married, but the writer has made several attempts to get in touch with them, but has failed to do so

No. 1075. Fifth Generation. 1070.

5) Abraham D Driver, b Mar 13, 1864, near Mt Clinton, Va, m Aug 17, 1893, Lydia Kauffman, b Dec 22, 1870, near Versailles, Mo They lived for a number of years on the Kauffman homestead just south of the Mt Zion Mennonite Church in Morgan Co. Mo, near Versailles, Mo, but later moved to Hesston, Kans A few years later to their present address at La Junta, Colo Mennonites

1. Edith V Driver, b Oct 17, 1894 No 3581
2 David K Driver, b Mar 8, 1897 No 3582

3   Alice I Driver, b Apr 6, 1899   No 3583
4. Eunice F. Driver, b Feb 2, 1901, d June 20, 1901
5. Florence M Driver, b July 5, 1903, single
6. Harvey Allen Driver, b. Mar. 13, 1906. No 3606
7   Clarence Vernon Driver, b July 18, 1911, single

No. 1075¼. Fifth Generation. 1070.

7) Anna Elizabeth Driver, b Jan. 18, 1870, near Mt Clinton, Va , m Nov. 20, 1918, Benjamin F Beery, b Jan 17, 1854, d Nov. 18, 1923. Farmer. Presbyterians Address: Mt. Clinton, Va No children.

No. 1075½. Fifth Generation. 1070.

8) Jacob Lewis Driver, b May 10, 1873, near Mt. Clinton, Va., m in fall of 1905 Cassie Nunamaker of La Junta, Colo. She died. He later married Mrs. Fanny Yoder, of La Junta, Colo. Address La Junta, Colo , R 2. No children.

No. 1076. Fifth Generation. 1070.

9) Ida Belle Driver, b Jan 23, 1876, near Mt Clinton, Va , d Jan 2, 1937, at her home in Cairo, O On Nov. 9, 1898, she married Ira V. Miller, b. Mar. 4, 1872, near Cairo, O He died Dec 4, 1929. Both were buried at the East Side cemetery. Address: Cairo, O Farmer Lutherans Two adopted children.
1. Preston Waltz, b. ——————.
2. Margaret Armentrout, b ——————

No. 1077. Fourth Generation. 25.

7) Abraham Miller Beery, b April 25, 1836, near Edom, Va., d July 31, 1895, at Lancaster, O., m July 16, 1868, Louisa Bury (not Beery). She was born July 16, 1844. English Lutherans Merchant Address: Lancaster, O Mr. Beery went to Fairfield Co , O , before reaching the age of twenty-one years and worked a short time on the farm of his uncle Michael Miller In 1858 he entered the dry goods store of Mrs E A Beck as clerk, and remained in that position for nine years, with the exception of the time spent in the federal army He enlisted and served as Commissary Sergeant in the 61st O V I., and was present at the battles of Cedar Mountain, Bull Run No 2 He was discharged at Germantown, Oct 5, 1862, on account of physical disability In 1867 he commenced the dry goods business under the firm name of Beery Brown and Co. He six years later sold his interest to P Rising and remained with him and successor until February, 1882, when he formed a partnership under the firm name of Beery, Beck, and Obaugh, and began the clothing business which he continued for a number of years. In 1895 he was elected mayor of Lancaster City, but died after a few months of service He was a man respected and honored by all who knew him and his death at the age of fifty-nine was universally regretted
1. George Orman Beery, b June 26, 1869 No. 1078
2   Frank Edwin Beery, b. Oct 26, 1872 No 1079
3   Mary Louise Beery, b Dec 11, 1875 No 1080.
4   Abram Wilmot Beery, b Sept 15, 1881 No 1081

No. 1078. Fifth Generation. 1077.

1) George Orman Beery, b June 26, 1869, at Lancaster, O , m. Nov 11, 1896, Gabriella Smith, b Aug 1, 1872 Address Lancaster, O English Lutherans Physician Dr Beery graduated from the high school at Lancaster, after which he studied medicine and graduated from the Miami Medical College of Cincinnati, O , in 1891. He practiced medicine in Lancaster, O He is naturally a business man and is a factor in business circles of his home town

181

1. Frederick Webb Beery, b July 12, 1899, d Mar 29, 1900
2 Marian Beery, b. Feb 8, 1903 No 1971

No. 1079. Fifth Generation. 1077.

2) Frank Edwin Beery, b Oct 26, 1872, at Lancaster, O., tailor by trade, at 121 N Columbus Street, Lancaster, O Mr Beery served in Co I 4th Ohio Volunteer Infantry as a corporal during the war with Spain, which regiment, after being in camp at Chickamauga Park, was ordered to Porto Rico. He participated in several engagements, and remained there until the regiment was ordered home after the close of the war He married Mary Shaner He died in 1926 No children

No. 1080. Fifth Generation. 1077.

3) Mary Louise Beery, b Dec 11, 1875, at Lancaster, O , m Oct 29, 1902, George C Miller, b. Nov 28, 1863 English Lutherans Husband is an attorney Wife graduated from high school at Lancaster, O , and taught music for a few years before marriage Address Lancaster, O
1 Donald Clement Miller, b Oct 29, 1903. Is an attorney

No. 1081. Fifth Generation. 1077.

4) Abraham Wilmot Beery, b Sept 15, 1881, at Lancaster, O , d at Tonopah, Nebr., Feb 2, 1917 Single Clerk Graduated from high school at Lancaster English Lutheran

No. 1082. Fourth Generation. 25.

8) Sallie Beery, b Oct 25, 1839, near Edom, Va , m Nov 28, 1861, Jacob J Frank, b. June 30, 1841 Address was Stuarts Draft, Va Presbyterians Farmer
1 Virginia A Frank, b Aug 21, 1862
2 Susan M Frank, b June 29, 1864 No 1083
3 Charles M Frank, b Feb 9, 1866 No 1087
4 Louise Belle Frank, b April 1, 1869 No 1088
5 Mary E. Frank, b May 1, 1872
6 Jacob B Frank, b Mar 11, 1880

No. 1083. Fifth Generation. 1082.

2) Susan M Frank, b June 29, 1864, at Stuarts Draft, Va , m July, 1881, William F Whistler, b Dec 23, 1859 Address Singers Glen, Va Farmer U B Church
1. Bertie A. Whistler, b May 22, 1882 No 1084
2 Minnie F Whistler, b Jan 21, 1884 No 1083¼
3 Vernon G. Whistler, b April 30, 1886 No 1083½
4 Charles B Whistler, b May 25, 1890 No 1083¾
5 Jacob F. Whistler, b April 28, 1893 No 1083⅞
6 Lula Edna Whistler, b Dec 10, 1895 No 1086

No. 1083¼. Sixth Generation. 1083.

2) Minnie F Whistler, b Jan 21, 1884, near Singers Glen, Va , m John A Hopkins. Address· Linville, Va , R 2 Janitor U B and Church of the Brethren Burial place, Singers Glen, Va
1. William Howard Hopkins, b ————————
2. Clarence Franklin Hopkins, b ———————
3 Robert E Hopkins, b ——————
4. John Stanley Hopkins, b ——————
5. Raymond Hopkins, b —————————.
6 Eunice Marie Hopkins, b ———————
7 Marvin Richard Hopkins, b ———————.

No. 1083½. Sixth Generation. 1083.

3) Vernon G Whistler, b April 30, 1886, near Singers Glen, Va., m Anna D Mason Address Harrisonburg, Va Carpenter United Brethren. No children

No. 1083¾. Sixth Generation. 1083.

4) Charles B Whistler, b May 2ʒ, 1890, near Singers Glen, Va., m. Daisy Hopkins Address: Harrisonburg, Va., R 4 Carpenter. U B Church.
1 Charles B Whistler, Jr., b. Sept 9, 1917.

No. 1083⅞. Sixth Generation. 1083.

5) Jacob F Whistler, b April 28, 1893, near Singers Glen, Va., m Ida Good Address· Linville, Va Laborer
1. Frankie Whistler, b ———, 1929
2 Son, b. 1936, died in infancy

No. 1084. Sixth Generation. 1083.

1) Bertie A. Whistler, b May 22, 1882, near Singers Glen, Va., m Dec 24, 1901, William Henkel, b June 26, 1879 Farmer at Greenmount, Va. Brethren. Related, see No. 113.
1. Roy Carlton Henkel, b July 12, 1903. No. 116
2 Ralph W. Henkel, b April 13, 1907 No 117.

No. 1086. Sixth Generation. 1083.

6) Lula Edna Whistler, b Dec 10, 1895, near Singers Glen, Va , m Homer C. Henkel, b Aug 18, 1888 Address Harrisonburg, Va , R. 4. Church of the Brethren
1 Charles L Henkel, b Sept 10, 1915
2. Harry Lee Henkel, b Nov 24, 1934, d. Dec 4, 1934

No. 1087. Fifth Generation. 1082.

3) Charles Michael Frank, b Feb 9, 1866, Stuarts Draft, Va , m April 20, 1899, Jane G Christman, b Sept 9, 1876 Address Stuarts Draft, Va. Presbyterians Farmer.
1. James Christman Frank, b Oct 6, 1900
2 Robin Virginia Frank, b Sept 9, 1902.

No. 1088. Fifth Generation. 1082.

4) Louisa Bell Frank, b. April 1, 1869, at Stuarts Draft, Va., m April 25, 1886, John F Swank, b Aug 28, 1862 Address. Singers Glen, Va Farmer U. B. Church
1 Myrtle Elizabeth Swank, b Sept 8, 1887
2 Sallie Virginia Swank, b. June 21, 1890
3 Stella May Swank, b Mar 6, 1898.
4 Mary Loisa Swank, b Oct 16, 1899
5 Ethel Frank Swank, b Aug 21, 1901
6 Mabel Irene Swank, b ———.

No. 1089. Fourth Generation. 25.

10) Barbara A Beery, b Sept 16, 1844, near Edom, Va , d. Feb 18, 1914, at Forestburg, Tex , m Mar 6, 1863, John W Bowers, b Jan 23, 1844, in Berkley Co , W. Va He died April 23, 1909, at Forestburg, Tex. They are buried in Forestburg, Tex , cemetery Merchant and farmer Presbyterians
Mr and Mrs Bowers moved from Rockingham Co , Va , in 1866 to Scott Co., Mo , in 1868 They moved to Galveston, Tex , later to Bell Co , and still later by team and wagon they journeyed for several months without any particular destination in view, finally stopping for a time in Smith Co In 1873 they settled

near Forestburg, Montague Co In 1876 Mr. Bowers was elected and served two years as assessor of Montague Co, when on account of ill health in 1880 he entered into the mercantile business In 1883 they moved to Forestburg continuing the same business.

1 Annie Laura Bowers, b. Nov. 23, 1864. No 1523
2. John Hackett Bowers, b Oct 30, 1866 No 1525
3 Thomas Edward Bowers, b May 30, 1869 No. 1528
4. Mollie Virginia Bowers, b. Aug 20, 1871 No. 1530.
5. Ida Kate Bowers, b Nov 11, 1873, d Dec 25, 1874.
6 Minnie Frances Bowers, b Sept 28, 1876, single.
7. Joseph Richard Bowers, b. Jan 22, 1878 No 1534.
8 Pearl Elva Bowers, b July 31, 1880. No 1536
9. Robert Ashby Bowers, b. July 13, 1882 No 1539.
10 Edna Lee Bowers, b. July 13, 1885 No 1540

No. 1090. Fourth Generation. 25.

11) Mary Magdalene Beery, b Dec 16, 1846, near Edom, Va., d. May 31, 1911, m John H. Frank, b April 15, 1837 He died Aug 5, 1900; both are buried at Mt Clinton. Va Address Mt Clinton, Va Mrs Frank was a Mennonite

1. Laura B. Frank, b June 15, 1867. No. 1091.
2. Annie S Frank, b Mar. 13, 1869 No 1092
3. William H Frank, b Nov 23, 1871 No 1093.
4. Benjamin F. Frank, b. Mar. 23, 1874. No. 1962.
5 Edward B Frank, b Mar 7, 1876 No 1963
6 Alice M. Frank, b Sept 20, 1878, d Aug 2, 1881
7. Addie P Frank, b. July 11, 1881. No 1968
8. Bessie F. Frank, b July 3, 1884, d. July 26, 1931.
9 John S Frank, b. Jan 30, 1887 No 1969
10 Joseph C Frank, b Feb. 10, 1890. No 1970

No. 1091. Fifth Generation. 1090.

1) Laura Belle Frank, b June 15, 1867, near Mt Clinton, Va , m June 2, 1897, John W Daugherty, b Oct 28, 1858 Address Mt. Clinton, Va. Farmer. Presbyterians No children

No. 1092. Fifth Generation. 1090.

2) Annie Susan Frank, b May 13, 1869, near Mt Clinton, Va , m. Dec. 27, 1898, Edward L Krohn, b Dec 3, 1868 Address Pandora, O Farmer. Methodists

1 Frank G. Krohn, b Mar 17, 1900 No 1961

No. 1093. Fifth Generation. 1090.

3) William Henry Frank, b. Nov. 23, 1871, near Mt Clinton, Va., m Dec. 25, 1901, Lena Baldwin, b. Mar 23, 1882 Address Mt. Clinton, Va. Machinist U. B. Church.

1 Clarence Baldwin Frank, b Nov. 4, 1902 No 1966
2. Carl B. Frank, b April 28, 1905 No 1967.
3. Ray Frank, b ———— 23, 1910

No. 1094. Seventh Generation. 1054.

2) Edith E Beery, b. Jan 18, 1904, near Lima, O., m Aug 11, 1925, Robert T. Roush Farmer.

1 Russell Roush, b June 13, 1926.
2 Evelyn Roush, b Feb. 1, 1927.
3 Hazel Roush, b Aug 15, 1929
4 Raymond Roush, b Oct 9, 1932.

No. 1095. Seventh Generation. 1064.

4) Mary Beery, b. Oct 17, 1907, near Lima, O , m. Nov. 22, 1928, Eugene O'Dell.

No. 1096. Seventh Generation. 1064.

5) Ruth Beery, b Oct 25, 1909, near Lima, O , m Jan. 14, 1932, Ora C. Knecht Teacher

1 Gilbert Morris Knecht, b Feb. 19, 1933

No. 1097. Sixth Generation. 1063.

3) Delmar A. Beery, b Jan 21, 1883, near Lima, O., m Aug. 17, 1908, Carrie Elliott, b Nov 9, 1885, Beaverdam, O. Carpenter. Church of the Brethren.

1. Elizabeth C Beery, b Aug 20, 1911 No 1098.
2 Delmar E. Beery, b May 3, 1928.
Foster son taken at 10 months of age.
Carl L Beery, b Dec 31. 1923

No. 1098. Seventh Generation. 1097.

1) Elizabeth C Beery. b Aug 20, 1911, near Beaverdam, O., m. July 11, 1931, Lewis R Van Meter Address Bluffton, O Mrs Van Meter is a member of the Church of Christ. and Mi Van Meter is a Methodist Farmer.

1 Joan Lou Van Meter. b July 23. 1932

No. 1099. Sixth Generation. 1063.

4) Cora E Beery, b July 15, 1885, near Lima, O , m. Sept 4, 1907, Frederick H Fisher, b Oct 4. 1879 Mrs Fisher is a graduate nurse from the Lima Hospital, June 22, 1896. Address 600 W Elm St , Lima. O Real estate dealer No children Lutherans

No. 1100. Sixth Generation. 1063.

5) Isaac N Beery. b Mar 1, 1888, near Lima, O , m Nov. 1, 1913, Mary Ellen Pierce, b July 30, 1887, in Putnam Co , O. City fireman. Methodist. Address: 612 S Elizabeth St., Lima, O

1 Lydia Mae Beery, b April 18, 1914

No. 1101. Sixth Generation. 1063.

6) Ephraim Beery. b July 24, 1890, near Lima, O , m May 3, 1910, Lena M Baker, b July 3, 1891 Address 407 South Jackson St . Lima, O. City fireman Methodist

1. Frederick N Beery, b Jan 29, 1912
2 Frances Beery, b ———— 11, 1914
3. Marie Beery, b Aug 2, 1916
4 Virginia Beery, b Feb 20, 1919
5 Geraldine Beery, b. Nov. 20, 1920
6 Helen Beery, b May 4, 1924
7 Velma Beery, b Sept. 26, 1928
8 Gene Ray Beery. b Jan 11. 1931
9 Dorothy Mae Beery. b Feb 8, 1933

No. 1102. Sixth Generation. 1063.

7) Lydia E Beery, b May 12, 1893, near Lima, O , m. Feb. 26, 1914, Ray R. Murry. b May 16, 1889 Address Bellefontaine, O . R 4 Farmer Presbyterians.

1 Ellen Louise Murry, b Oct. 7, 1919

No. 1103. Sixth Generation. 594.

1) Mary Florence Beery. b Oct 15, 1890. near Dayton, Va , m Dec. 25, 1919, Calvin Simeon Heatwole. b July 21. 1895 Address Dayton, Va , R 2 Farmer. Mennonites

185

1. Harold Vernon Heatwole, b. Oct 26, 1920.
2 Anna Magdalena Heatwole, b Nov. 9, 1921.
3. Mary Rebecca Heatwole, b Mar 23, 1923.
4 Grace Elizabeth Heatwole, b. Mar. 15, 1924.
5 Paul Simon Heatwole, b Dec 12, 1925.
6 Joseph Newton Heatwole, b Feb 25, 1927.

No. 1104. Sixth Generation. 594.
2) Ward Edward Beery, b Jan 13, 1892, near Dayton, Va , m Feb 11, 1919, Mary Amelia Showalter, b Apr 9, 1894 Ten children Related, two ways, refer to No 987

No. 1105. Sixth Generation. 594.
3) Frank Henry Beery, b May 21, 1895, near Dayton, Va , m Feb 11, 1919, Bertha Katherine Shank, b Mar 24, 1899 Address Dayton, Va Farmer Mennonites

No. 1106. Sixth Generation. 594.
4) Walter Rhodes Beery, b Aug 25, 1899, near Dayton, Va , m. Dec 7, 1921, Mary Florence Shank, b July 19, 1902 Address Dayton, Va Poultryman Mennonites
  1 Lydia Ann Beery, b July 5, 1923
  2 Carrie Virginia Beery, b July 27, 1924
  3. Vada Mildred Beery, b Oct 16, 1925
  4. Vera Agnes Beery, b Sept 5, 1928
  5 Lois Miriam Beery, b Nov. 4, 1931

No. 1107. Sixth Generation. 1007.
1) Edward W Showalter, b Sept 8, 1884, in Rockingham Co, Va , m. April 27, 1921, Alvina Luers, b Mar 7, 1886 Address Keota, Ia Farmer Mennonites No children

No. 1108. Sixth Generation. 1007.
2) Elizabeth O Showalter, b Dec 17, 1885, in Rockingham Co, Va , m. June 23, 1908, Noah D Showalter, b Feb. 22, 1886 Address Sedalia, Mo. Farmer and abstracting Mennonites
  1 Esther E Showalter, b Oct 12, 1911 No 1109
  2 Oliver D Showalter, b April 6, 1914 No 3438
  3 George A Showalter, b Sept 20, 1915 No. 3439.
  4 Aaron C. Showalter, b Feb 5, 1917
  5 Edith L Showalter, b Aug. 17, 1918
  6. Elmer M. Showalter, b May 20, 1920
  7. Paul Showalter, b April 22, 1925
  8 Timothy Showalter, b Jan 5, 1927
  9. Omar Showalter, b Feb 14, 1928.

No. 1109. Seventh Generation. 1108.
1) Esther E Showalter, b Oct 12, 1911, in Rockingham Co, Va , m Ernest Antonia, in 1932 Address Catabo, Mindano Island, Philippine Islands Teacher in High School
  1 Ernest Antonia, b 1933

No. 1110. Sixth Generation. 1007.
3) Hannah E Showalter, b Nov 13, 1887, in Rockingham Co, Va , m Sept 30, 1913, George B Hilty, b Nov 7, 1884 Address Hammett, Ida Farmer Mennonites Burial place, Glenns Ferry, Ida
  1 Georgia Lois Hilty, b Sept 8, 1914
  2 Caroline Hilty, b Sept 26, 1916.

3. Almeta Joy Hilty, b Dec 20, 1920
4. Adelia Mae Hilty, b Aug 11, 1925, d Sept 5, 1930

No. 1111. Sixth Generation. 1007.

4) Oliver B Showalter, b Sept 15, 1889, in Rockingham Co , Va , m. Nov 10, 1917, Salome Yoder, b Aug 29, 1890 Bank cashier at Yoder, Reno Co., Kans Mennonites

1. Robert Showalter, b. Nov. 2, 1918.
2 Richard Showalter, b Feb 2, 1920
3. Russell Showalter, b Sept. 29, 1921.
4 Roberta Showalter, b April 3, 1926.
5 Ray Edward Showalter, b Nov 1, 1929

No. 1112. Sixth Generation. 1007.

5) Amos M Showalter, b Dec 15, 1891, in Rockingham Co , Va , m. Dorothy —————— Address· Harrisonburg, Va An adopted son.

No. 1113. Sixth Generation. 1007.

6) Ada M Showalter, b Feb 4, 1894, in Rockingham Co., Va., m. Feb. 9, 1916, John P Zimmerman, b Sept 29, 1891 Address· Conway, Kans. Farmer. Mennonite

1. Lester Jay Zimmerman, b. July 16, 1918
2 Clinton Dale Zimmerman, b Aug 3, 1924
3 Gladys Irene Zimmerman, b. Oct. 31, 1926.
4 Nellie Florence Zimmerman, b Dec 17, 1928

No. 1114. Sixth Generation. 1007.

7) John L Showalter, b April 23, 1896, in Rockingham Co , Va , m ——— Blough Address Davidsville, Pa

1 ————— Showalter, b ————.
2 ————— Showalter, b ————.

No. 1115. Sixth Generation. 1007.

8) Nellie K Showalter, b Mar 20, 1898, in Rockingham Co., Va , m. Sept 30, 1923, Silas J Horst, b Jan 11, 1893 Address South English, Ia Farmer. Mennonites and a minister at South English, Ia

1 Emery Glen Horst, b Mar 15, 1928.
2 Hazel Fern Horst, b May 15, 1932
The above children were adopted as babes

No. 1116. Sixth Generation. 1007.

9) Clara M Showalter, b Nov 1, 1900, in Rockingham Co , Va , m Feb 3, 1930, Henry Cooprider, b Nov 11, 1896 Farmer at McPherson, Kans Mennonites No children, but have taken two twin babies to raise
James Benny and Joice Betty, b. Feb 8, 1928

No. 1117. Sixth Generation. 1038.

1) Amanda C Showalter, b Nov 27, 1880, in Rockingham Co , Va , m. Abram N Baer, b Aug 7, 1879, in Washington Co , Md Address Hagerstown, Md., R 4

1 Alvah H Baer, b June 16, 1911 No 1120
2 Abram M Baer, b June 2, 1912.
3 Anna M Baer, b June 22, 1914, d same day
4 Bertha E Baer, b April 1, 1916
5 Martha K. Baer, b Oct 4, 1918, d Oct 18, 1918
6 Leonard P. Baer, b Jan 5, 1920
7 Ida M Baer, b July 21, 1921.

No. 1118. Sixth Generation. 1038.

2) Alvah M Showalter, b Dec 24, 1881, in Rockingham Co, Va, m. Nov. 28, 1905, Katie Shank, of Franklin Co, Pa Address Hagerstown, Md, R. 6

1. Infant, deceased Oct. 25, 1907.
2 Martha G. Showalter, b Feb 14, 1910.
3. Esther A. Showalter, b Sept 22, 1913.
4. Cora E Showalter, b Sept 11, 1915
5 Dortha M Showalter, b July 5, 1918
6 Roy M Showalter, b Nov 29, 1924

No. 1119. Sixth Generation. 1038.

4) Amos T. Showalter, b May 19, 188?, in Rockingham Co, Va, m Rhoda Shank, b. June 20, 1888, in Franklin Co, Pa Address Hagerstown, Md, R 6.

1. Preston M Showalter, b Nov. 21, 1909. No. 1121
2 Anna R Showalter, b. Feb. 13, 1911.
3 Naomi P Showalter, b Aug 16. 1912
4 Aden L Showalter, b. Mar 14, 1914
5 Ethel M Showalter, b Oct 3, 1915
6 Harvey M Showalter, b Mar 4, 191-, d Aug 15. 1917
7 Mary G. Showalter, b Jan 14, 1919
8. Paul D Showalter, b May 26, 1920
9 Mabel I Showalter, b. May 24, 1923.
10 Glen D Showalter, b Oct 12. 1930

No. 1120. Seventh Generation. 1117.

1) Alvah S Baer, b June 16, 1911, in Md, m Elizabeth Kuhns, b Aug 8, 1912 Address Hagerstown, Md, R 6

No. 1121. Seventh Generation. 1119.

1) Preston M Showalter, b Nov 21, 1909, in Md., m Florence Martin, b. Nov 11, 1909 Address Hagerstown, Md

1 Amos M. Showalter, b. July 8, 1931

No. 1122. Sixth Generation. 1038.

6) Emma B Showalter, b Sept 21, 1889, in Md, m Samuel Eby, b. Sept. 4, 1889. Address. Williamsport, Md, R 3 Minister Mennonite

1 Lewis V. Eby, b. Nov 30, 1915
2. Raymond M. Eby, b Sept. 7, 1917.
3 Carl S. Eby, b June 15, 1920
4 Marie V Eby, b. May 6, 1922.
5 Norman E Eby, b Jan 6, 1926
6 Dorothy M Eby, b. April 28, 1928

No. 1123. Sixth Generation. 1038.

7) Martin W Showalter, b Feb 4, 1892, in Md, m Katie Reiff, b Sept 25, 1896, in Franklin Co, Pa Address Hagerstown, Md, R 4

1 Laban R Showalter, b. Feb 11, 1917.
2 Clarence R Showalter, b Mar 13. 1921
3 Elmer M Showalter, b April 19, 1923.
4 Iva S Showalter, b July 21. 1924

No. 1124. Sixth Generation. 1038.

8) Minnie G. Showalter, b Mar 6, 1894, in Md, m Henry N. Hostetler, b Oct. 14, 1893, in Adams Co, Pa Address Hagerstown, Md

1 Menno H Hostetler, b Nov 23. 1916.
2. Anna G Hostetler, b Mar. 24, 1918.

3 Amos I Hostetler, b Nov 9, 1919
4 Mary A Hostetler, b. Oct. 5, 1921.
5. John M Hostetler, b Sept 2, 1924.
6 Ada R Hostetler, b Oct. 4, 1927.

No. 1125. Sixth Generation. 1038.

9) Irvin F. Showalter, b Dec 21, 1895, in Md., m. Fannie Miller, b Nov. 11, 1894 Address Maugansville, Md
1 Anna M Showalter, b. Aug 30, 1927
2. Pearl M Showalter, b Oct 3, 1930.
3 Irvin D Showalter, b Oct 18, 1932, twin
4. Stella Showalter, b. Oct. 18, 1932, twin, died next day.

No. 1126. Fifth Generation. 1037.

2) Susan V Showalter, b Oct 15, 1856, near Harrisonburg, Va., m. May 31, 1877, Perry X. Heatwole, b July 21, 1850 Susan died Dec 25, 1912. She for two years previous to her death had been taking treatment in North Carolina. During a fire which destroyed the hotel where she was lodging she was compelled to jump from a second story to save her life, which added injury to her delicate constitution Address Dayton, Va Mennonites
1. Walter D Heatwole, b. Jan 15, 1880. No. 1127.
2 William M Heatwole, b Feb 26, 1882 No 1128
3 Lena M Heatwole, b Oct 20, 1888, d Jan 10, 1893

No. 1127. Sixth Generation. 1126.

1) Walter D. Heatwole, b Jan 15, 1880, near Dayton, Va., m Jan 17, 1901, Zella E Heaton b Dec 3, 1880 United Brethren.
1. Walter D. Heatwole Jr., b Mar 30, 1914
2 Raymond W Heatwole, b Oct 25, 1918

No. 1128. Sixth Generation. 1126.

2) William M Heatwole, b Feb 26, 1882, near Dayton, Va., m. Sept. 2, 1903, Katie Frances Brunk, b Oct 24, 1884 Address Hinton, Va Farmer. Mennonites
1 Goldie F Heatwole, b July 16, 1904.
2 Marjorie V Heatwole, b Oct 12, 1907

No. 1129. Sixth Generation. 1040.

1) Noah Dan'el Showalter, b Feb 22. 1886, near Broadway, Va., m. June 23, 1908, Lizzie O. Showalter, b. Dec 17, 1885. Address: Sedalia, Mo. Abstract dealer Lives on farm First cousins, for family see the mother's line, No. 1108

No. 1131. Sixth Generation. 1040.

2) Timothy M Showalter, b Dec 19, 1887, near Broadway, Va., m April 10, 1910, Nancy Susan Snipe, b Feb 26, 1886 Address. Broadway, Va. Farmer and orchardist Mennonites Mr Showalter is a minister in Rockingham Co., Va.
1 Anna Belle Showalter, b Feb 7, 1911
2 Mary Magdalena Showalter, b Feb 22. 1912
3 Ada Elizabeth Showalter, b Aug 4, 1913.
4 Emma Frances Showalter, b Jan 8, 1915
5 Daniel Timothy Showalter, b May 25, 1916
6 Martha Susan Showalter, b April 15. 1918
7 Ida Ruth Showalter, b Aug. 27, 1919.
8 Grace Irene Showalter, b May 29, 1925

No. 1132. Sixth Generation. 1040.

3) Lewis Peter Showalter, b Nov 8, 1890, near Broadway, Va., m Jan 24, 1912, Anna Mary Suter, b Aug 25, 1889 Address Broadway, Va Farmer. Mennonite minister

1. John Suter Showalter, b. May 14, 1914
2. Ruth Frances Showalter, b. May 4, 1917.
3 Lewis Menno Showalter, b Feb. 24, 1921, d Aug. 16, 1923.
4 Marvin Earl Showalter, b Oct. 24, 1926.

No. 1133. Sixth Generation. 1040.

4) George Paul Showalter, b Nov 8, 1890, near Broadway, Va, m Nov. 22, 1917, Ruth Ellen Lesher, b Sept. 5, 1896. Address Broadway, Va Farmer Mennonites.

1. Margaret Ann Showalter, b Dec. 5, 1919.
2 Frances Ellen Showalter, b Dec 17, 1921
3 Alice Marie Showalter, b. Jan 20, 1925.
4. John Paul Showalter, b Feb 22, 1927.
5. Milton Lesher Showalter, b Feb 23, 1930

No. 1134. Sixth Generation. 1040.

5) Magdalena Frances Showalter, b Sept. 6, 1892, near Broadway, Va, m Jan. 17, 1932, Amos Brenneman, b Nov 6, 1885 Address Denbigh, Va Dairyman Mennonites Mrs Brenneman was a trained nurse at the La Junta, Colo, Mennonite Sanitarium

1. George H Brenneman, b Jan 21, 1934

No. 1135. Sixth Generation. 1040.

7) Mark Cephas Showalter, b Feb. 10, 1895, near Broadway, Va, m Dec. 11, 1919, Amanda E Hege, b Apr 5, 1891 Address Broadway, Va Farmer Mennonites

1. Mahlon Hege Showalter, b Jan 13, 1921
2 Henry Edwin Showalter, b Mar. 12, 1923
3 Melvin Eugene Showalter, b Feb 6, 1925
4. Anna Virginia Showalter, b. Dec 29, 1926.
5 Fannie Catherine Showalter, b Jan 8, 1929
6. Rhoda Elizabeth Showalter, b. Mar. 16, 1931.

No. 1136. Sixth Generation. 1040.

8) Luke C Showalter, b Jan 8, 1898, near Broadway, Va., m June 16, 1924, Lydia Kauffman, b April 12, 1892 Address Broadway, Va Farmer Mennonites

1. Kenneth Luke Showalter, b April 1, 1925.
2 Harold Kauffman Showalter, b July 3, 1926
3 Barbara Virginia Showalter, b July 21, 1928
4 Alta Mae Showalter, b Nov 29, 1930

No. 1137. Sixth Generation. 1040.

9) Michael Blosser Showalter, b May 17, 1900, near Broadway, Va, m Aug 30, 1922, Millie Ellen Emswiler, b Apr 11, 1900 Address: Needmore, W Va Carpenter and painter

1. Evelyn Marie Showalter, b July 23, 1923
2 Helen Louise Showalter, b Mar 13, 1929

No. 1138. Sixth Generation. 1042.

1) N. Pearl Blosser, b July 8, 1888, near Harrisonburg, Va, m Oct, 1897, J. Early Suter. Address Harrisonburg, Va Mennonite minister.

1. Margaret G Suter, b Mar. 12, 1911

2 Mary Ethel Suter, b. July 7, 1912
3. Frances E Suter, b. Jan 16, 1916.
4. Daniel B Suter, b. April 25, 1920.

No. 1139. Sixth Generation. 1042.
2) Nannie E. Blosser, b. Jan 15, 1890, near Harrisonburg, Va., m. Aug. 2, 1911, Elmer R. Brunk, b Mar 6, 1881 Address: Harrisonburg, Va.
1 Mary E Brunk, b May 4, 1913.
2 Evelyn J Brunk, b. Dec 2, 1921

No. 1140. Sixth Generation. 1042.
3) Orpha V. Blosser, b Jan 18, 1893, near Harrisonburg, Va., m Feb. 15, 1916, Homer R. Suter Address· Harrisonburg, Va.
1 Hazel M. Suter, b Feb 9, 1921
2 Katherine V Suter, b Sept 24, 1928

No. 1141. Sixth Generation. 1042.
5) Daniel J Blosser, b Mar 9, 1899, near Harrisonburg, Va., m Dec. 3, 1919, Grace F Heatwole, b ——————— Address: Harrisonburg, Va.
1 Sanford D Blosser, b Nov. 26, 1923
2 Thelma M Blosser, b Sept 26, 1927

No. 1142. Sixth Generation. 1042.
6) Michael O. Blosser, b May 12, 1901, near Harrisonburg, Va , m. Feb 21, 1931, Fannie M Good Address· Harrisonburg, Va.
1 Mildred Joyce Blosser, b Mar. 21, 1931.

No. 1143. Sixth Generation. 1042.
7) Mahlon L Blosser, b Jan. 16, 1904, near Harrisonburg, Va , m. Sept. 21, 1926, Pauline S. Heatwole Address Harrisonburg, Va.
1. Glendon Lee Blosser, b Dec 14, 1930, twin
2 Glenbys Marie Blosser, b Dec 14, 1930, twin.

No. 1144. Sixth Generation. 1043.
1) Earl E Showalter, b. Mar 31, 1890, near Harrisonburg, Va., m. Feb. 11, 1913, Mary C Heatwole, b Jan 7, 1891 Mennonites. He is a minister at La Junta, Colo Related. come in two ways For family refer to No. 311.

No. 1145. Sixth Generation. 1043.
3) Elmo F Showalter, b Nov 27, 1898, near Harrisonburg, Va , m. Susanna Heatwole, b Mar 14, 1904, near Elida, O. Address: Roscoe, Calif Manufacturer Mennonites
1 Bruce Ellwood Showalter, b Dec 24, 1925. Deceased
2 Carol Wayne Showalter, b. Aug 30, 1929.
3 June Elaine Showalter, b Dec 19, 1931.

No. 1146. Sixth Generation. 1045.
1) Pauline Showalter, b Oct 18, 1893, at Harrisonburg, Va , m. Dec. 28, 1919, John Lloyd White No children

No. 1147. Sixth Generation. 1045.
3) Mary Ethel Showalter, b Oct 5, 1898, at Harrisonburg, Va , m. Aug 27, 1921, Theron Jennings Rice Mr Rice died Mar 23, 1924
1 Theron Jennings Rice, Jr , b Aug 18, 1922

No. 1148. Sixth Generation. 1045.
5) Harold W Showalter, b Apr 29, 1902, at Harrisonburg, Va , m Aug 18, 1928. Marie North of Shelly, N C

No. 1149. Sixth Generation. 1045.

7) Joseph Wilmer Showalter, b. April 23, 1904, at Harrisonburg, Va., m. Kathryn Welsh, of McKeesport, Pa.

1. Diana Patricia Showalter, b. July 6, 1931.

No. 1150. Fifth Generation. 1037.

8) Eurie Frances Showalter, b Oct. 31, 1869, at Broadway, Va, was united in marriage Nov. 23, 1890, to Jacob D Hartman, at Dale Enterprise, Va Address Harrisonburg, Va

1. Walter Irvin Hartman, b. Jan. 19, 1893. No. 1151.
2. Wilmer Carl Hartman, b Apr 8, 1897 No. 1152
3 Daniel Jacob Hartman, b Mar 4, 1899 No 1153

No. 1151. Sixth Generation. 1150.

1) Walter Irvin Hartman, b Jan 19, 1893, near Harrisonburg. Va. m July 14, 1914, Della Pearl Lahman, b Dec 16, 1893.

1 Floyd DeWitt Hartman, b Jan 21, 1915
2. Alta Pearl Hartman, b July 2, 1916
3. Roy DeWitt Hartman, b July 2, 1917, died same day.
4 Ruby Frances Hartman, b July 19, 1928
5 Juanita Fern Hartman, b Nov. 27, 1932.

No. 1152. Sixth Generation. 1150.

2) Wilmer Carl Hartman, b Apr. 8, 1897, near Harrisonburg, Va, m Dec 27, 1917, Elizabeth F Showalter, b June 22, 1894 Address Waynesboro, Va

1 Milford D Hartman, b. Dec. 21, 1918.
2 Robert Showalter Hartman, b. Sept 15, 1921.
3 Sarah Frances Hartman, b Oct 3, 1922.
4. Phillis Amelia Hartman, b Feb 5, 1924
5 Mildred Good Hartman, b Oct. 15, 1930

No. 1153. Sixth Generation. 1150.

3) Daniel Jacob Hartman, b Mar 4, 1899, near Harrisonburg. Va., m Dec 23, 1919, Lena Pearl Good, b June 10, 1898 Address Harrisonburg, Va

1 Ralph Leroy Hartman, b June 1, 1921, d Dec 12, 1923
2. Dwight Wilson Hartman, b Mar 25, 1923
3 Geraldine Ann Hartman, b Oct. 1, 1924
4 Brownie Virgina Hartman, b Sept 24, 1925
5 Raymond Carroll Hartman, b. Oct. 27, 1927.
6 Evelyn Blanche Hartman, b Aug 6, 1929.
7 Reha John Hartman, b Mar. 5, 1932.
8. Ewell Daniel Hartman, b Mar 25, 1933

No. 1154. Sixth Generation. 1048.

1) Wilber Michael Showalter, b June 20, 1896, near Harrisonburg. Va. m Jan 16, 1922, Bonnie Hamilton, of Virginia Address Harrisonburg, Va

1 Wilbur Hamilton Showalter, b. Jan 16, 1923.

No. 1155. Sixth Generation. 1048.

2) Martha Elizabeth Showalter, b Sept 13, 1901, near Harrisonburg, Va, m Nov 12, 1932. John W Morrison

No. 1156. Sixth Generation. 1048.

3) Mary Esther Showalter, b Dec 8, 1901, near Harrisonburg, Va, m Emerson M Nelson Address· Harrisonburg, Va, R. 5

1 Nancy Lee Nelson, b Aug. 12, 1923

2 Dora Mae Nelson, b Jan 6, 1925
3 Emerson Mason Nelson, b. Oct. 1, 1927.
4. James Leroy Nelson, b Sept. 2, 1929
5 Ruby Virginia Nelson, b July 3, 1931.

No. 1157. Sixth Generation. 1048.

4) Walter Raymond Showalter, b May 7, 1904, near Harrisonburg, Va, m
July 27, 1930, Ottie Virginia Cox
1 Walter Raymond Showalter, Jr., b May 6, 1932

No. 1158. Sixth Generation. 1048.

5) Elmer David Showalter, b July 16, 1908, near Harrisonburg, Va, m Aug
23, 1927, Mary Elizabeth Trobaugh, of Virginia.

No. 1159. Fourth Generation. 24.

2) Elizabeth Showalter, b Jan 7, 1826, near Broadway, Va, m Samuel
Cline, b Aug. 17, 1821 Address was Goods Mill, Va Farmer Both were buried
at Mill Creek Cemetery in Rockingham Co, Va Church of the Brethren of
which Mr Cline was a minister
1 Michael Cline, b Sept 18, 1845 No 1160
2 Daniel Cline, b ————— No 1161
3 John Cline, b —————. No 3351.
4. Kate Cline, b Sept 26, 1848 No 1162
5 Lizzie Cline, b. Sept 22, 1859 No 1163
6 Samuel Cline, b. Nov 13, 1858. No 1164.
7 Frederick Cline, b Aug 19, 1852 No 1165
8 Annie Cline, b April 11, 1857 No 1166.
9. Jacob Cline, b Oct 13, 1861. No 1167
10. Sue Cline, b. April 18, 1864 No. 1168.
11 Joseph Cline, b Sept 29, 1866. No. 1169.

No. 1160. Fifth Generation. 1159.

1) Michael Cline, b Sept 18, 1845, in Rockingham Co., Va, m Sarah Good,
b. July 26, 1846 Mr Cline died 1906 Buried at Mill Creek cemetery
1 Mary Elizabeth Cline, b ————— No 1455
2 Lucy E Cline, b. —————. No. 1461.
3 Nannie N. Cline, b. —————, single.
4 Laura F Cline, b ————— No 1465
5 Thomas S Cline, b ————— No. 1466.
6 Charles D Cline, b. —————. No. 1467.
7. Emma Cline, b ————— No. 1468.
8 William E Cline, b ————— No 1470
9 John F. Cline, b —————, single
10 Hattie Cline, b ————— No. 1471.
11. Fleeta V. Cline, b ————— No 1473
12 Malvin Q Cline, b —————

No. 1161. Fifth Generation. 1159.

2) Daniel Cline, b —————, in Rockingham Co., Va., m. Ruth Showalter, b ————— Address was Versailles, Mo Farmer and stock raiser
Church of the Brethren, of which he was a minister Burial at Prairie View cemetery in Morgan Co, Mo
1 Walter Cline, b Aug 17, 1870 No 1451
2. John Samuel Cline, b. Oct 11, 1874 No 1452
3. Sophiah Kate Cline, b. Mar. 8, 1877. No. 1453.

No. 1162. Fifth Generation. 1159.

4) Nancy Catherine Cline, b Sept 26, 1848, in Rockingham Co, Va, d Apr. 23, 1924, same place She married Reuben T Lam, b Dec. 23, 1841 He died Oct 16, 1903, burial at Mill Creek cemetery

1 Annie E Lam, b. Aug 15, 1869 No 1441
2 Laura C. Lam, b July 22, 1872. No. 1445.
3. Joseph S. Lam, b. Feb 28, 1875
4 Ada S Lam, b Feb. 28, 1877 No 1448.
5 John W Lam, b Oct 8, 1879 No 1449
6 Thomas T. Lam, b Dec. 11, 1882.
7. Daniel Worthington Lam, b Jan 30, 1886, d. Dec 25, 1890
8. Sattie E Lam, b Jan 1, 1889 No 1450

No. 1163. Fifth Generation. 1159.

5) Lizzie C Cline, b Sept 22, 1859, in Rockingham Co, Va, d Dec 23, 1932 She married Oct. 19, 1880, David B Wampler, b Feb 12, 1858, he died Oct 16, 1907 Farmer Teacher Minister in Church of the Brethren Buried at Mill Creek cemetery. Address Penn Laird, Va

1 Nellie M Wampler, b Aug. 22, 1881 No 1474
2 Mamie E Wampler, b Feb 23, 1884 No. 1475
3 Letitia J Wampler, b Dec 19, 1886 No 1476.
4 Hattie Beatrice Wampler, b Oct 30, 1889, single
5 Leonard S. Wampler, b Mar 20, 1892 No 1478
6 Clinton I Wampler, b Jan 13, 1895 No 1479
7 Clarence S Wampler, b Feb 9, 1897 No 1480

No. 1164. Fifth Generation. 1159.

6) Samuel Cline, Jr, b Nov 13, 1858, in Rockingham Co, Va, d Apr 14, 1911, m. Fannie Harshbarger, b Apr 17, 1859, d Apr 14, 1912. Burial in Mill Creek cemetery Farmer Church of the Brethren

1. Florence Elizabeth Cline, b. Sept. 9, 1877. No 1481.
2 Etta Viola Cline, b Aug 10, 1879 No 1483
3. Mary Catherine Cline, b. Feb 16, 1885 No. 1484
4. Jacob Hubert Cline, b July 29, 1888. No 1485
5. Novella Hershberger Cline, b May 25, 1895, single.
6. Ruth Virginia Cline, b Dec 2, 1899, d Dec 6, 1899
7 Earl Daniel Cline, b. Feb 7, 1904

No. 1165. Fifth Generation. 1159.

7) Frederick Cline, b. Aug 19, 1852, in Rockingham Co., Va., m. Susan Miller, b Apr. 28, 1853 Mr Cline died Mar. 17, 1922. Buried in Mill Creek cemetery. Church of the Brethren

1 Stella M Cline, b Sept 1, 1873 No 1187
2 Saylor B. Cline, b. Dec 30, 1874. No. 1488.
3 Ottie E Cline, b Dec 31, 1876 No. 1489
4 Florence A Cline, b Jan 3, 1882 No 1491.
5 Hubert Whitfield Cline, b. Nov 22, 1884, single
6 Herman M Cline, b Feb 10, 1889 No 1493

No. 1166. Fifth Generation. 1159.

8) Annie Cline, b Apr 11, 1857, in Rockingham Co, Va, m in 1875, John Good, b July 21, 1855 Address McGahesville, Va Farmer Church of the Brethren

1 Saylor Daniel Good, b Mar 12, 1876 No 1494
2 William C. Good, b. Aug 27, 1878 No. 1498

3 Dora Susan Good, b Feb 10, 1880 No 1499
4. Mertie Elizabeth Good died in infancy
5 Franklin Good died in infancy
6. Ernest Michael Good, b Nov. 11, —— No. 1501.
7 Sattie Della Good, b June —, 1890. No 1502.
8 Clarence DeWitt Good, b April ————. No 1503
9 Ollie Belle Good, b July —, 1900 No 1504.

No. 1167. Fifth Generation. 1159.

9) Jacob Cline, b Oct 13, 1861, in Rockingham Co, Va, m. (!st) ————
Risling She died soon after marriage. One child also died He married (2nd)
Laura A. Weast, May 18, 1891 She was born Mar 11, 1871. Address: Mt Sidney,
Va Farmer. United Brethren
1 Arcell L. Cline, b. Nov. 6, 1892. No. 1505.
2. Hubert S. Cline, b Nov. 18, 1894 No. 1506
3. Omega C Cline, b Dec 21, 1896 No 1507.
4. Arline M. Cline, b July 4, 1899 No. 1508.
5 Clarence E Cline, b. Aug. 14, 1901 No 1509.
6 Leonard D Cline, b Oct 3, 1903 No 1510
7. Bessie V. Cline, b. Sept. 23, 1905 No 1511.
8 Raymond A Cline, b. July 31, 1908 No. 1512

No. 1168. Fifth Generation. 1159.

10) Sue Cline, b April 18, 1864, in Rockingham Co, Va, d Aug 23, 1931
She had married Dec 12, 1882, John Wampler, b May 12, 1862. He died Feb
23, 1925 Farmer at Port Republic, Va Church of the Brethren
1. Maud Wampler, b Nov 28, 1884 No 1513
2 Mollie Wampler, b July 8, 1886. No 1516.
3 Whitfield E Wampler, b Nov. 28, 1888 No 1517.
4. Nina Wampler, b April 25, 1895 No. 1520.
5. Lillie Pearl Wampler, b Oct 1, 1891, d Nov 5, 1897
6 Fleta Wampler, b. Aug 3, 1897, No 1521
7. Charles M Wampler, b Nov 1, 1899, d Mar 19, 1925
8. Alfred R Wampler, b Sept 27, 1903
9 Eula Kathryn Wampler, b. Dec. 6, 1905 No 1522

No. 1169. Fifth Generation. 1159.

11) Joseph Cline, b Sept 29, 1866, in Rockingham Co, Va, d Feb 1, 1910,
buried in Zion Mennonite Church cemetery in Rockingham Co., Va He married
Mary M Heatwole, b Jan 9, 1867, d. Dec 17, 1938 Farmer Mennonites
1. Sallie L Cline, b Nov 14, 1889. No. 1170.
2 Edgar J Cline, b Jan 26, 1897 No. 1171

No. 1170. Sixth Generation. 1169.

1) Sallie Cline, b Nov 14, 1889, near Broadway, Va, m Robert Neff, b Jan
8, 1879 No issue

No. 1171. Sixth Generation. 1169.

2) Edgar J Cline, b Jan 26, 1897, near Broadway, Va, m. July 9, 1919, Mattie V Brunk, b Jan 13, 1889 Address Broadway, Va Farmer and poultryman
Mennonite.
1 Mary Kathryn Cline, b Dec 23, 1920
2 Pauline Virginia Cline, b Mar 3, 1922

No. 1172. Third Generation. 5.

1) Samuel Landes, b. June 10, 1801, in Pendleton Co , W. Va , d. in July, 1884, at Decatur, Ia He married May 2, 1822, Mary Magdalena Siple, b. May 13, 1803 She died in 1886 in Iowa Both are buried at Decatur, Ia. They moved in Sept., 1837, to Putnam Co , Ind , taking father Landes with them. Samuel Landes was a merchant at Greencastle, Ind , until March, 1885, when he moved to Clark Co , Ia He kept a country store and grinding mill at Westerville, Decatur Co., Ia. Samuel Landes was one of the founders of Simpson College, now Depauw University.

1. Diana Landes, b Feb 10, 1823, d. Feb. 21, 1823.
2. Margaret Landes, b June 7, 1824 No 2191
3. Annanias Landes, b May 15, 1826 No 2200
4 James Madison Landes, b Feb 8, 1830 No 2216
5 John Franklin Landes, b. Oct. 26, 1831. No. 2229.
6 Mary Magdalene Landes, b May 3, 1834 No 2240.
7. Samuel Louis Landes, b Dec. 15, 1835. No 2245
8 Frances Agnes Landes, b Apr 7, 1838 No. 2250
9. Henry Jacques Landes, b Sept 9, 1842 No 2252

No. 1173. Third Generation. 5.

2) John Landes, Jr , b Apr 1, 1803, in Pendleton Co , W Va , d July 14, 1882, in Augusta Co , Va. He married Nancy Griffith, b about 1798, d May 15, 1867. Buried in the Salem cemetery near Mt. Sidney, Va Farmer. Lutherans.

1 Frances Landes, b Apr 24, 1826 No 1975
2. Marion Landes, b Aug 6, 1827, d Oct 12, 1911, single
3 Magdalena Landes, b. Jan. 14, 1829, d Feb. 11, 1847.
4 Erastus Landes, b Jan 6, 1831 No 1988
5 William Landes, b Dec 20, 1833 No 2027
6 Sallie Landes, b Mar 24, 1835, d July 19, 1904.
7. Nancy Belle Landes, b Oct 20, 1839, d Feb 4, 1840

No. 1174. Third Generation. 5.

3) Abraham Landes, b ———, 1813, in Va., d ——————, in Ind He married Hannah M.chael, born in Va , ——————, died in Ind. They were married in Augusta Co , Va., in 1830 In 1839 they moved to Putnam Co , Ind , where they settled on a farm of 192 acres Here they lived until their death This farm was located near Hamrick station In Putnam Co , their granddaughter Mrs Leota O'Hair still owns the same farm

1. Adaline E. Landes, b. Oct 20, 1833, single, not living
2. Benjamin Frankl n Landes, b Sept 29, 1835, not living
3. Sarah Rachel Landes, b Sept 19, 1837. No 2339
4 Mary Landes, b. Feb 27, 1840 No 2330
5 John Wesley Landes, b Sept 6, 1843 No 2336.

No. 1175. Third Generation. 5.

4) Susanna Landes, b ——————, m Lewis Keller, b ——————— They lived in Putnam Co , Ind

1 Samuel Keller, b ——————
2 Hiram Keller, b. ——————
3 John Keller, b. ——————
4 Frances Keller, b ——————

No. 1176. Third Generation. 5.

5) Nancy Landes, b ——————, m William Bittle, b ——————— They lived in Putnam Co , Ind.

1 Joseph Bittle, b ————.
2 John Bittle, b ————.
3. Silas Bittle, b ————.
4 William Bittle, b ————.

No. 1177. Third Generation. 5.

6) Hannah Landes, b ————, m. John William Wilson, b. ————.
They lived in Putnam Co., Ind
   1 William Henry Wilson, b ————. No 2284.
   2. Martha Jane Wilson, b ————. No. 2285.
   3. Sarah Frances Wilson, b ———— No. 2290.
   4 Elizabeth Wilson, b ————, d at 67 years, single
   5 Charles Wilson, b ————, d at 4 years.
   6 John Franklin Wilson, b ———— No 2292
   Charles died at Hopeville, Ia.

No. 1178. Third Generation. 5.

7) Christian Landes, b. April 5, 1814, in Augusta Co., Va, d Mar. 16, 1893, in Putnam Co, Ind On Oct. 1, 1840, he married Elizabeth A Hillis, b Jan. 18, 1823; she died Dec 25, 1891 Both were buried at Greencastle, Ind. Address. Greencastle, Ind
   1 Mary Joanne Landes, b April 27, 1843 No 1542
   2 William H Landes, b Mar 11, 1845, d. Feb, 1894
   3 Samuel E Landes, b May 22, 1847 No 1543
   4 Sarah Ellen Landes, b Sept 16, 1849 No 1544
   5 Laura E Landes, b June 2, 1852. No 1545.
   6 Katie Alice Landes, b. Apr. 1, 1855. No. 1546.
   7 Albert P Landes, b Nov. 12, 1857 No 1547
   8 Flora Florence Landes, b. May 22, 1860 No. 1550.
   9 Abram G Landes, b May 7, 1867.
  10 George Landes, b Nov 10, 1870 No 1553

No. 1178½. Third Generation. 5.

8) Catherine Landes, b Mar 10, 1810, in Va, m May 13, 1832, in Virginia, by the Rev. Rhodes, Conrad Siple, b June 4, 1811, d Jan 13, 1891, she died May 13, 1872 Both died at Hopeville, Ia, and were buried in the Gregg cemetery.
   1. Eliza Jane S ple, b Feb 21, 1833 No 2296
   2 Louis Henry Siple, b July 7, 1834, d Sept 11, 1860, in Civil War.
   3. Frances Siple, b Mar 20, 1836. No. 2317
   4 Son Siple, b. Sept 11, 1847, lived 11 hours.
   5 Charles Siple, b May 10, 1851. No 2324

No. 1179. Third Generation. 5.

9) Henry Landes, b ————, 1819, in Va, d in Putnam Co, Ind, in Jan, 1876, he married Oct 26, 1849, Ella Reeves They lived in Putnam Co, Ind
   1 Charles Wesley Landes, b ———— No. 3361.
   2 James Albert Landes, b. ————
   3 Sall e Olive Landes, b. ————
   4 Frank Lee Landes, b ————.

No. 1180. Third Generation. 7.

2) Barbara Brannaman, b Feb 14, 1806, near Edom, Va, d. in 1891 She married Peter Baker at Danville, O Farmer at Danville, O Barbara Baker was possessed with a rare voice as a vocal singer and retained her strong voice until

her later years. Mr. Baker was buried at Danville, O., and Mrs Baker was buried at Delaware, O.

    1. Sarah Baker, b. May 7, 1826 No. 1655
2. Adaline Baker, b. Nov. 13, 1827, d. Dec. 15, 1915, single.
3. Mary Baker, b. Nov 23, 1829 No. 1673
4 Susanna Baker, b. Feb. 12, 1832. No. 1665.
5. Oren Baker, b. June 11, 1835 No. 1674
6. Leroy Baker, b. —————, d. in Civil War, buried in Tenn
7 Anna Elizabeth Baker, b. Oct 11, 1843 No. 1679.
8. Daniel Baker, b. —————, d. single
9. Russell Baker, b —————, separated from his wife; can not be located
10 Melville Quincy Baker, b Oct 10, 1849 No 1681

No. 1181. Third Generation. 7.

    3) Susan Brannaman, b. —————, 1809, near Edom, Va, d. —————, 1893, in Ind She married Upton Shaw, 1810, and died in 1875 in Ind. Susan came with her parents from Rockingham Co, Va, to near Danville, O, in 1920 We have not been able to find when she migrated to Ind, but they lived in Putnam Co., Ind, where they died in the vicinity of Cloverdale Methodist. Buried in Cloverdale cemetery. Farmer Moved from Wooster, O, in covered wagon, in July, 1848

    1. Leonard Shaw, b. —————, 1831. No 1689
2. Lillyman Shaw, b. —————, 1833. No. 1690
3. Hester A. Shaw, b —————, 1835 No 1691
4 Lewis Shaw, b. —————, 1838. No. 1692.
5 Oliver Shaw, b —————, 1840. No 1693
6. Adaline Shaw, b —————, 1842 No 1694
7 Amelia Shaw, b —————, 1848 No 1695
8 Mary E. Shaw, b May 30, 1852 No 1696

No. 1182. Third Generation. 7.

    4) Ann Brannaman, b Feb. 10, 1814, near Edom, Va, d Oct 8. 1908, near Louisville, Ky. Ann came with her parents from Virginia to near Danville, O. where she later married on Mar 5, 1837, John Christian Theiss (Tice), born Feb 9, 1804. He died July 25, 1855, near Louisville, Ky Teacher Methodists. Ann Brannaman Theiss was a remarkable woman physically, spiritually, and mentally. She was left a widow when her youngest child was a year old and her oldest daughter was 14 years of age She raised and educated five children, three of whom became prominent teachers, and all highly respected citizens She made several trips to California alone after the age of 80 years, and retained all of her faculties until her death at the age of 94 years She gave to her children three things, a desire for education, strong moral character, and physical stamina Buried at Hanods Creek cemetery, Old Ham Co., Ky

    1 Mary Louise Theiss, b Feb 20, 1838, d. Dec 2, 1839
2. Anna Rebecca Theiss, b Feb 8, 1841 No 1707
3 Enoch George Theiss, b Jan. 19, 1844, d Aug 6, 1844
4 Charles Henry Theiss, b. July 5, 1845 No 1712.
5 Oren Brannaman Theiss, b Jan 25, 1848 No 1713
6 John Filmore Theiss, b July 23, 1852, d Oct 7, 1872
7 Martha Amelia Theiss, b Nov. 3, 1854 No 1719

No. 1183. Third Generation. 7.

    5) Jacob Brannaman, b Sept 6, 1816, near Edom, Va, d June 3, 1865 He married Elizabeth Stillinger, b Dec 14, 1824, in Germany She died Mar 5, 1897

Farmer Methodist. In 1855 they migrated to Putnam Co, Ind, where they reared their family Their address was Cloverdale, Ind, where many of their descendants are still to be found. Buried in Cloverdale cemetery

1. Joseph Brannaman, b Dec 27, 1843 No 1722
2. Samuel Brannaman, b Mar. 25, 1845. No. 1724
3. Marillo Elizabeth Brannaman, b Mar. 14, 1847 No 1733
4. Lydia Ann Brannaman, b ————, 1848, single.
5. John Christian Tice Brannaman, b June 19, 1851 No. 1738.
6. Emily Adaline Brannaman, b April 1, 1853 No. 1746
7. William Christie Brannaman, b. Feb 15, 1855 No 1752
8. Mary Jane Brannaman died in infancy
9. Eliza Jane Brannaman and Daniel, twins, died at birth
11. Charles Albert Brannaman, b ————, 1864, d ————, 1888

No. 1184. Third Generation. 7.

6) Elizabeth Brannaman, b ————, 1819, in Rockingham Co, Va, d. Nov. 27, 1902, at Louisville, Ky In 1845 she married William H C Lukemeier, b ————, 1817. He died Feb 23, 1905, at Louisville, Ky Address was 1832 W. Market St, Louisville, Ky Housewife Methodists Burial place Eastern cemetery, Louisville, Ky

1. Mary Lukemeier, b in 1846, d in same year
2. Caroline M Lukemeier, b May 4, 1849, d Apr 19, 1920, single.
3. Julia Ann Lukemeier, b ————, 1853, d in same year.
4. Henry Adam Lukemeier, b Sept 28, 1851. No. 1759.
5. Catherine Elizabeth Lukemeier, b July 2, 1855 No 1765
6. Lydia Lukemeier, b Jan 27, 1858 No. 1766
7. Emma Lukemeier, b and d about 1860.
8. Louis Jacob Lukemeier, b Jan 9, 1862 No 1769.
9. Infant died at birth.
10. Infant died at birth.

No. 1185. Third Generation. 7.

7) Lydia Brannaman, b Oct 14, 1821, at Danville, O., d Sept 14, 1878, at Louisville, Ky She married a Mr Klipp, b ————. he died on Nov. 14, 1844 She later married Jacob Hargesheimer, b Jan 2, 1815. He died Aug 31, 1897, near Louisville, Ky Farmer Methodists Address was R 2, Sta E, Louisville, Ky Buried at Hillcrest near Louisville, Ky.

1. Daniel Klipp, b May 31, 1841, d June 19, 1855.
(Second marriage)
2. Frederick Hargesheimer, b Sept 30, 1845. No. 1776.
3. Caroline Hargesheimer, b May 9, 1848, d. Sept 8, 1848.
4. Carl Hargesheimer, b Dec 1, 1849, d July 1, 1850.
5. Susanna Hargesheimer, b April 21, 1851 No. 1785
6. Adam Hargesheimer, b July 12, 1853 No 1790
7. John Hargesheimer, b Oct 31, 1855 No 1801

No. 1186. Third Generation. 7.

8) Julia Brannaman, b May 8, 1826, in Knox Co, O, d Nov 14, 1895, at Jonesville, Ind She married in June, 1854, John H Kirkhof, b Dec 25, 1809, d Nov 10, 1868 Farmer Members of the White Creek German M E Church where they are buried Address Jonesville, Ind

1. John Henry Kirkhof, b Mar 28, 1855 No 1812
2. Daniel Frederick Kirkhof, b. May 12, 1857 No 1813
3. Mary A Kirkhof, b ————, d in infancy

No. 1199. Fifth Generation. 1189.

7) Rhoda Keagy, b April 11, 1869, in Ind., m. June 29, 1889, E. E Byrum at Grand Junction, Mich , where they lived until June 29, 1898, when they moved to Moundsville, W. Va. They later located at Anderson, Ind , where they died He was a printer by trade. He published the "Gospel Trumpet" and the "Shining Light," both weekly papers

1. Ethel Elsie Byrum, b July 1, 1890. No. 1200.
2. Berdie Ruth Byrum, b. Aug 9, 1892. No. 1201.
3. Enoch Orlo Byrum, b. Aug 1, 1894. No. 1202
4. Mabel Grace Byrum, b Mar 29, 1898. No 1203
5. Bernice Mariva Byrum, b Dec. 27, 1900
6. Nilah Virginia Byrum, b. April 7, 1907.

No. 1200. Sixth Generation. 1199.

1) Ethel Elsie Byrum, b. July 1, 1890, in Mich., m. June 15, 1912, Frank Eugene Kimbal.

1. Rhodora Dale Kimbal, b. July 16, 1913.
2 Kieth Byrum Kimbal, b. Jan. 8, 1916.

No. 1201. Sixth Generation. 1199.

2) Birdie Ruth Byrum, b. Aug 9, 1892, in Mich , m. Oct 24, 1920, Walter Lee Greenawalt They reside in Topeka, Ind. Church of God.

1. Mariva Maxine Greenawalt, b. Sept. 10, 1921.

No. 1202. Sixth Generation. 1199.

3) Enoch Orlo Byrum, b. Aug. 1, 1894, in Mich., m Sept. 7, 1920, Lois Irene McDonald.

1. Nelda Jane Byrum, b. July 10, 1921.
2 Lois Roberta Byrum, b Oct 19, 1923
3. Rheva Ann Byrum, b April 10, 1925

No. 1203. Sixth Generation. 1199.

4) Mabel Grace Byrum, b Mar 29, 1898, in Mich , in 1920, m Odie Stevens
1 Joan Lee Stevens, b ——————.

No. 1204. Fifth Generation. 1189.

8) Esther Naomi Keagy, b Nov. 14, 1870, in Ind , on Nov 14, 1886, m. Louis N Gridley, b Nov. 19, 1861, at San Diego, Calif , moved to Butte in 1898

1 Lula Florence Gridley, b Nov. 3, 1891.
2 Claude Wallace Gridley, b April 24, 1894

No. 1205. Fifth Generation. 1189.

10) Hannah Catherine Keagy, b Nov. 3, 1875, in Ind , m Andrew Willing. They live at Anderson, Ind Church of God

1 Joseph (adopted), b April 12, 1915

No. 1206. Fifth Generation. 1189.

11) Sarah Adaline Keagy, b Sept 12, 1877, in Ind , on Nov 10, 1898, m Charles W Davidson, living at Bridgeport, O.

No. 1207. Fourth Generation. 26.

5) Susanna Keagy, b May 18, 1839, in Augusta Co , Va , and d Mar 25, 1908 She, on Mar 22, 1857, married Daniel Brenneman of Fairfield Co , O , b June 8, 1834, and d Sept 10, 1919 Both were buried at Oak Ridge cemetery, Goshen, Ind They were members of the Mennonite Church and resided in Fairfield Co , O , where Daniel was born and reared Soon after marriage yet the

same year, he was ordained to the ministry in which capacity he labored for sixty-two years. Concerning his early ministry, we quote from the Hartzler and Kauffman Mennonite Church History: "He entered upon his work at once with great vigor and soon rose to prominence, his services being called for from far and near In March, 1864, he moved to Elkhart Co., Ind., where his ministry was noted for the intense interest stirred up among the people and for his conflict with Jacob Wisler."

Wisler was the bishop of the district and a leader of the ultra-conservative element, opposing Sunday schools, English preaching, evening meetings, etc., which practice Daniel Brenneman, John F. Funk, and others maintained were essential to a more efficient propagation of the gospel. Wisler was finally silenced, and in 1871 withdrew from the church and with his few followers organized a separate branch.

Concerning this stage in the history of the church, we again quote from the above mentioned church history "As time passed on the necessity and demand for English preaching became more urgent, and the body of members became more and more convinced that this want should be supplied. About this time Daniel Brenneman a minister from Ohio appeared on the field In the eyes of many he was the man for the place He was orthodox in his views, though inclined to be radical on some questions He could handle languages excellently He was eloquent, aggressive, a good singer, and full of life. The church revived, and crowded houses greeted him wherever he went His services were demanded frequently at funerals and on other occasions "

After the separation of the ultra-conservatives, Brenneman and some others contended that still more aggressive efforts should be put forth. In fact he and John F Funk actually conducted in 1872 at Masontown, Pa, the first revival meeting in the history of the Mennonite Church in the United States It was on the issue of revival meetings, prayer and testimony meetings, etc, which the church at that time did not see fit to endorse (though they have since done so) that he was finally, in 1874, separated from the mother church, an ordeal that was painful to both parties concerned The result was a new Mennonite body, now known as the Mennonite Brethren in Christ He was the founder, in 1878 of the Gospel Banner and he was its editor for a number of years The paper was adopted and still remains to be the official church organ He served for many years as presiding elder of the Indiana-Ohio Conference

He spent the greater part of his energy and means in promoting the cause he had espoused, and to which he felt the Lord had called him While not thus engaged, he was busy with the plow, cultivator or hoe, in which occupation he also took great delight In the language of one of his neighbors, "He was the hardest working preacher I ever knew " He reached the ripe old age of 85 years and lived to see the day when the bitter feeling toward him had largely disappeared, and the most of his old brethren would invite him to preach when he visited among them, a privilege which he appreciated very much His mortal remains, with those of his companion, now lie peacefully at Oak Ridge, Goshen, Ind, there awaiting the summons from on high (By his son T H B)

1 Mary Magdalena Brenneman, b Apr 24, 1859 No 1208
2 Timothy Henry Brenneman, b Sept 20, 1860. No. 1209.
3 John Samuel Brenneman, b May 4, 1862 No 1214
4 Josiah L Brenneman, b June 28, 1864 No. 1215
5 Rhoda K. Brenneman, b July 17, 1866. No 1220
6 Martha Ann Brenneman, b July 29, 1868 No 1222
7 Naomi Susan Brenneman, b Sept 1, 1870 No 1226
8 Daniel Jacob Brenneman, b May 19, 1873 No 1227

9 Phoeba Pauline Brenneman, b Aug 31, 1875 No. 1228.
10 Mahlon Moody Brenneman, b Nov. 12, 1877 No 1229

No. 1208. Fifth Generation. 1207.

1) Mary Magdalena Brenneman, b April 24, 1859, in Ohio, m Nov. 30, 1893, John S. Sherk, b. —————————, d. May —, 1897. School teacher at Goshen, Ind. Mennonite Brethren in Christ Buried at Oak Ridge, Goshen, Ind. No children

No. 1209. Fifth Generation. 1207.

2) Timothy H. Brenneman, b. Sept 20, 1860, in Fairfield Co., O., d Mar. 24, 1935, at Goshen, Ind. On Sept. 23, 1883, he married Laura E Dakrymple, b Jan. 15, 1860 Mennonite Brethren in Christ Deacon Printer, and retired R R mail clerk. United States railway mail clerk on the N. Y Central R. R. between Chicago and Cleveland 1893-1923. Address. Goshen, Ind

1 Jesse Lamar Brenneman, b Aug. 26, 1886 No 1210.
2. Ruth Victoria Brenneman, b Sept. 10, 1888 No 1211
3 Naomi Brenneman, b Mar. 12, 1891. No. 1212.
4. Orpha Brenneman, b: May 4, 1895. No. 1213.

No. 1210. Sixth Generation. 1209.

1) Jesse Lamar Brenneman, b Aug. 26, 1886, in Elkhart Co, Ind, m. Aug. 11, 1923, Nancy E. Nysewander, b. July 11, 1887 He was graduated from Goshen High School in 1904, and from Goshen College in 1906, and from Chicago University with a B S degree in 1908 After teaching for a few years in Decatur, Ill, High School and in Westminster College, Fulton, Mo, he graduated from the University of Wisconsin with an E E degree He then taught in the electrical engineering department of the University of New Mexico until the outbreak of the World War He was drafted into the army and as conscientious objector was finally sent to Fort Leavenworth for a period of fifteen years He was liberated at the close of the War After the War he taught for some time in the Oklahoma School of Mines. Since 1922 he has been connected with the electrical engineering department of Kansas State College, Manhattan, Kans He is the author of a college textbook, "Direct Current Machinery" Mennonite Brethren in Christ

1. Elwin Donald Brenneman (adopted). b Dec 11, 1929
2 Margaret Zoe Brenneman (adopted), b Jan 3, 1930

No. 1211. Sixth Generation. 1209.

2) Ruth Victoria Brenneman, b. Sept 10, 1888, in Elkhart Co, Ind She graduated from Goshen, Ind., High School in 1910, and from Bradley Polytechnic Institute, Peoria, Ill., in 1911 She received the degrees of Bachelor of Philosophy, from the University of Chicago and Master of Arts, Columbia University She has been a teacher of home economics in the public schools of South Bend, Ind., Niles, Mich, and Eureka College, Eureka, Ill She has been a teacher of chemistry in State Teachers College, Indiana, Pa, since 1928 Mennonite Brethren in Christ Single.

No. 1212. Sixth Generation 1209.

3) Naomi Brenneman, b Mar 12, 1891, at Goshen, Ind, graduated Goshen, Ind, High School She received the Bachelor of Arts degree from Oberlin College, 1915, Master of Arts degree from University of Chicago, 1921, and Doctor of Philosophy degree from Cornell University, 1933 She has held the following positions Instructor in Olivet University 1917, 1918 Instructor in English, Goshen College, 1918, Professor of English, Bluffton College, since 1918 Mennonite Brethren in Christ Single

No. 1213. Sixth Generation. 1209.

4) Orpha Brenneman, b May 4, 1895, at Goshen, Ind, m. Mar 27, 1932, Paul C. Huber Orpha was a graduate Goshen High School, 1914, student of music at Goshen College and Bluffton College She followed the profession of bookkeeper. They reside at Goshen, Ind.

No. 1214. Fifth Generation. 1207.

3) John Samuel Brenneman, b May 4, 1862, in Fairfield Co., O. On Oct 1, 1899, he married Mary Jamison, d Mar —, 1901. On Dec 25, 1908, he married Gertrude Smith. Publisher, banker, and farmer Presbyterians. They live at Sedalia, Mo.

No. 1215. Fifth Generation. 1207.

4) Josiah Brenneman, b. June 28, 1864, at Goshen, Ind, m Rebecca Herber, b. Aug 23, 1866, d April 8, 1925 Painter by trade, also engaged in farming. In 1908 he moved to western Nebraska where he took up a homestead. He is the deacon in the home church near Lewellen, Nebr.

1 Orval Henry Brenneman, b. April 21, 1895 No 1216.
2 Herbert Claire Brenneman, b Jan 16, 1898. No 1217.
3. Mary Helen Brenneman, b. Feb 8, 1903, d April 26, 1903.
4. Phoeba Mae Brenneman, b Feb 1, 1905 No 1218.
5. Daniel Calvin Brenneman, b Sept 17, 1907. No. 1219.

No. 1216. Sixth Generation. 1215.

1) Orval Henry Brenneman, b April 21, 1895, in Elkhart Co, Ind., m April 17, 1919, Rhoda Sparks He was pastor of the Mennonite Brethren of Christ Church at Lewellen, Nebr., at the time of his death which occurred Nov. 17, 1925

1 Elizabeth Rebecca Brenneman, b. June 21, 1920.
2. David Josiah Brenneman, b. Dec. 1, 1921.
3 Orval Henry Brenneman, b. Mar 1, 1926.

No. 1217. Sixth Generation. 1215.

2) Herbert Claire Brenneman, b. Jan 16, 1898, in Elkhart, Ind., m. Nov 14, 1918. Elsie Henry They reside on a farm near Goshen, Ind Mennonite Brethren **in Christ.**

1. Ruth Eleanor Brenneman, b June 1, 1920
2. Paul Mahlon Brenneman, b Nov 11, 1921.
3 Wayne Henry Brenneman, b Oct 19, 1923
4 Verla Louis Brenneman, b Sept 8, 1926, d July 12, 1929

No. 1218. Sixth Generation. 1215.

4) Phoeba Mae Brenneman, b Feb 1, 1905, in Elkhart Co, Ind, m May 18, 1928, Rev Paul Ummel They belong to Missionaries in Nigeria, West Africa, where they reduced to writing the unwritten language of the Dakakkari tribe Mrs. Ummel has translated for them the Gospel of Mark

1 Helen Lucille Ummel, b Aug. 3, 1932

No. 1219. Sixth Generation. 1215.

5) Daniel Calvin Brenneman, b Sept 17, 1907, in Elkhart Co, Ind., m May 16, 1928, Stella Seibert They live on a farm near Goshen, Ind, R. 4

1 Howard Daniel Brenneman, b Mar 15, 1929

No. 1220. Fifth Generation. 1207.

5) Rhoda K Brenneman, b July 17, 1866, at Goshen, Ind, on May 25, 1893 she married Henry S Cressman, of Waterloo, Ont Teacher and nurse Mennonite Brethren in Christ Address Lashburn, Sask, Canada

1 Virgil Cressman, b July 17, 1895 No 1221
2. Daniel Ward Cressman, b June 30, 1899, single Contractor

No. 1221. Sixth Generation. 1220.

1) Virgil Cressman, b July 17, 1895, m April 2, 1920, Pauline May Brehaut, of Prince Edward Islands They reside on a farm near Lashburn, Sask , Canada
1. Rhoda May Cressman, b May 30, 1921.
2 Jean Marguerite Cressman, b Nov 3, 1922
3. Ruth Kathleen Cressman, b Nov 13, 1926.
4 James Headley Cressman, b. Sept 22, 1932

No. 1222. Fifth Generation. 1207.

6) Martha A Brenneman, b. July 29, 1868, at Goshen, Ind In Nov , 1894, she married Dwight Croff, b Aug 16, 1861 He died May 13, 1905. Buried at Oak Ridge cemetery Mennonite Brethren in Christ Address: 9063 Jamison Way, Haywood, Calif
1 Esther Marie Croff, b April 11, 1896. No. 1223.
2. Susan Virginia Croff, b May 27, 1900 No 1224
3 Martha Madonne Croff, b April 18, 1902 No 1225

No. 1223. Sixth Generation. 1222.

1) Esther Marie Croff, b April 11, 1896, at Goshen, Ind , m April 28, 1918, Rev Roy L Hollenback Nazarenes.
1. Miriam Esther Hollenback, b April 27, 1919
2 Chester Byron Hollenback, b. Feb 14, 1923
3 Roy Leonides Hollenback, b. Sept 9, 1926
4. David Mervin Hollenback, b Aug 9, 1928
5 Bonnie Elizabeth Hollenback, b Nov 12, 1931

No. 1224. Sixth Generation. 1222.

2) Susan Virginia Croff, b May 27, 1900, at Goshen, Ind., m. Nov. 2, 1925, to John Eccles. They reside at 9063 Jamison Way, Haywood, Calif Baptists
1 Thomas Dwight Eccles, b Aug. 31, 1925

No. 1225. Sixth Generation. 1222.

3) Martha M Croff, b April 18, 1902, at Goshen, Ind , on April 18, 1922, she married Archibold Cruse He died Jan 22, 1923, m (2nd) Custer Hawley of Orland, Calif.
1. Custer Hawley, Jr , b Oct 26, 1924.
2. Charles Dwight Hawley, b Nov. 11, 1925
3. Martha Ellen Hawley, b. Jan 23, 1929.
4 Virginia Helen Hawley, b Feb. 21, 1931

No. 1226. Fifth Generation. 1207.

7) Naomi Susan Brenneman, b Sept 1, 1870, at Goshen, Ind , d Oct 27, 1927. She married John Kane Music teacher and photographer, Los Angeles, Calif Mennonite Brethren in Christ

No. 1227. Fifth Generation. 1207.

8) Daniel Jacob Brenneman, b Mar 19, 1873, near Goshen, Ind He was united in marriage Dec 23, 1903, to Iva M Doering Minister Mennonite Brethren in Christ Later he preached for the Free Methodists Address· Crowley, Colo Daniel has filled several positions of trust he has been a teacher, bank cashier, and postmaster
1 Lida Grace Brenneman, b. Aug 14, 1906
206

2 Fernole Bonnie Brenneman, b. June 16, 1910.

3. William Doering Brenneman. b April 3, 1914

No. 1228. Fifth Generation. 1207.

9) Phoeba Pauline Brenneman, b Aug 31, 1875, at Goshen, Ind In 1908 she was united in marriage to Rev Calvin F. Snyder Address Hochow Kansee, China

Phoeba P. Brenneman, after graduating from Spring Arbor Seminary, engaged for a number of years in home mission work in various cities of Indiana and Ohio, and in 1904 entered the foreign missionary service in China under the Christian and Missionary Alliance In 1908 she was united in marriage to Rev Snyder in Shanghai, China, who was working under the same board They are still actively and successfully engaged in west China near the border of Tibet They have endured many hardships, including narrow escapes from bandits

Their only child, Albert Brenneman Snyder, b Sept 7, 1909, died at Kunston, Pa, in March, 1913, while they were home on furlough He was buried at Bethlehem, Pa.

No. 1229. Fifth Generation. 1207.

10) Mahlon Moody Brenneman, b Nov. 12, 1877, at Goshen, Ind, m Dec 12, 1903, Adaline Auxberger, b Sept 27, 1875 Address: Berne, Ind Nurseryman and apiarist. Mennonite Brethren in Christ.

1 Esther Evangeline Brenneman, b April 5, 1906

2 Annie Loreen Brenneman, b Oct 17, 1907

3 Frederick Herring Brenneman, b. Feb. 17, 1909.

No. 1230. Fourth Generation. 26.

7) Jacob Keagy, b May 21, 1844, in Augusta Co, Va, m. Emmily Forwood. His home was in St. Petersburg, Fla He was a teacher. He died in 1897 No children

No. 1231. Fourth Generation. 26.

8) Anna Keagy, b Mar 9, 1847, in Augusta Co, Va. She married Ansel M Thomas They lived at Battle Creek, Mich. Both are physicians of the Hygiene School

1 Clara May Thomas, b April 6, 1874 No 1232

No. 1232. Fifth Generation. 1231.

1) Clara May Thomas, b Apr 6, 1874, at Mt. Crawford, Va, m. June 11, 1892, George W Hall, at Battle Creek, Mich Mr Hall failing to provide for her and child, she obtained a divorce and returned to Virginia Later she married Arthur C. Miller of Dayton, Va

1 Harold Rollie Hall, b. May 24, 1893

No. 1233. Fourth Generation. 27.

1) Mariah Eversole, b Aug 13, 1830, d. June 15, 1903, m. Joseph Fawett Graham, b. Dec. 23, 1815, d Aug 5, 1889 Both were buried at Mt Tabor, 4 miles east of Lancaster, O.

1. David Eversole Graham, b Aug 1, 1849, d Aug. 2, 1862

2 Eliza Eliker Graham, b May 9, 1851, d Mar 25, 1885.

3 Reuben Wood Graham, b April 29, 1855 No 1234

4 Arthur St. Clair Graham, b. Feb 16, 1857.

5 Thomas Hamer Graham, b Feb 16, 1857 No. 1235.

6 Mary Elizabeth Graham. b Oct 31, 1860 No 1239

7 James Driver Graham, b July 31, 1863.

8. Flora Ann Graham, b. Dec. 28, 1865

9 Gertrude Graham, b. July 28, 1869

No. 1234. Fifth Generation. 1233.

3) Reuben Wood Graham, b April 29, 1853, d Jan 8, 1933, m. Dec 30, 1885, Catherine Beery, b. Oct 1, 1859 She died June 7, 1927 United Evangelical Address was Lancaster, O

1. Eva Gertrude Graham, b Oct 4, 1886

2 Anna Fern Graham, b Oct 18, 1891, d. Oct 6, 1892

No. 1235. Fifth Generation. 1233.

5) Thomas Hamer Graham, b Feb 16, 1857, m. June 27, 1890, Ida Hine, b. Sept. 9, 1868. Retired farmer. First Methodist Burial place at Mt Tabor, 4 miles east of Lancaster, O Address 1335 E Main St, Lancaster, O.

1. Arthur Roy Graham, b April 8, 1891 No 1236.

2 Viola Graham, b April 18, 1892 No 1237.

3. Reuben Neal Graham, b Sept 22, 1893 No. 1238

4. Miles Wesley Graham, b June 22, 1895

5. Mary Graham, b. Aug 20, 1896 No 1239

6 Joseph Franklin Graham, b. Dec. 29, 1897. No. 1240.

7. Thomas Harrison Graham, b May 6, 1901 No 1241.

8 James Kenneth Graham, b Oct 7, 1902 No 1242

9 Loren Kine Graham, b. Oct 3, 1905.

No. 1236. Sixth Generation. 1235.

1) Arthur Roy Graham, b April 8, 1891 On April 1, 1918, he married May Belle Streeby, b Oct 25, 1899 Address 2113 Indiana Way. N E, Canton, O

No. 1237. Sixth Generation. 1235.

2) Viola Graham, b April 18, 1892, near Lancaster, O, m Dec. 31, 1912, Raymond Marshal, b May 27, 1887 Mr Marshal died ———————— Viola is a school teacher in Fairfield Co, O Address 1335 East Main St, Lancaster, O

1. Everett Graham Marshal, b May 29, 1914

No. 1238. Sixth Generation. 1235.

3) Reuben Neal Graham, b Sept 22, 1893 In Sept, 1916, he married Burdette Keim, b. Sept 24, 1894 She died June 8, 1920 Address Canton, O

1 Donald Graham, b June 27, 1917

2. Gene Miriam Graham, b May 17, 1920

No. 1239. Sixth Generation. 1235.

5) Mary Graham, b. Aug 20, 1896, near Lancaster, O., m July 20, 1921, Edward G Miller, b Dec 29, 1886 Address Lancaster, O, R. 10.

1 Marjorie Miller, b Oct. 30, 1923.

2 Elinor Louise Miller, b July 19, 1927

No. 1240. Sixth Generation. 1235.

6) Joseph F. Graham, b Dec. 29, 1897 near Lancaster, O., m Willie Mae Spencer, Aug. 5, 1924. Address: 218 Wingate Road, Georgetown, S. C.

1. Ida Josephine Graham, b. Aug. 14, 1926

2. Joseph Franklin Graham, b Aug. 7, 1929.

No. 1241. Sixth Generation. 1235.

7) Thomas Harrison Graham, b May 6, 1901, near Lancaster, O. On Dec. 24, 1923, he married Mary Mabel Dupler, b. Aug 31, 1901 Address. East King St, Lancaster, O.

1 Richard Ellwood Graham, b Mar 1, 1925

2 Virginia Anne Graham, b Sept 17, 1928.

3. Frederick Lee Graham, b Feb 9, 1930.

No. 1242. Sixth Generation. 1235.

8) James Kenneth Graham, b Oct. 7, 1902, near Lancaster, O., m Jan. 28, 1928, Hazel Julia Spangler, b July 25, 1905. Address· 1335 E Main St., Lancaster, O

No. 1243. Fifth Generation. 1233.

6) Mary Elizabeth Graham, b Oct 31, 1860, d Mar 29, 1918 She married Filmore Beery, b Sept 22, 1856, he died Oct 26, 1910 They were married Oct. 4, 1882.

1 Flory Beery, b Sept 22, 1886, d. Aug 13, 1888.

2. Frederick Beery, b Aug 27, 1889, d April —, 1891

3 Gertrude Elizabeth Beery, b Sept 1, 1902 She is an English Teacher at Oak Harbor High School

No. 1244. Fourth Generation. 27.

3) Jacob Eversole, b June 29, 1832, d in Sept, 1914, m. Katherine Swartz, b Mar. 10, 1834, d Feb 27, 1924 Farmer Evangelical Buried at Shelbyville, Ill. Address was Westerville, Ill

1. Thomas Clinton Eversole, b ———, 1857 No 1244¼

2 John Peter Eversole, b May 3, 1859 No 1245

3 Emma Eversole, b Oct 18, 1860. No 1247

4 Ella Eversole, b Sept 13, 1863 No 1249

5 David S. Eversole, b ———, 1867. No. 1250.

6. Mattie Eversole, b April 13, 1869 No 1252

7 William Miller Eversole, b April 27, 1871 No 1254

8 Anna Eversole, b Sept 9, 1873 No 1258

9 Grant W Eversole, b May 6, 1865 No 1259

10 George Washington Eversole, b April 21, 1876 No. 1259½

No. 1244¼. Fifth Generation. 1244.

1) Thomas Clinton Eversole, b Feb 7, 1857, d May 3, 1923, at Shelbyville, Ill, m. Elizabeth Fritz, Nov 3, 1881 She was born June 6, 1862, d Aug 21, 1935. Both were buried at Shelbyville, Ill

1 Bessie Ellen Eversole, b Oct. 16, 1882, d May 22, 1903.

2. William Harvey Eversole, b Feb 2, 1884. No 2158.

3 Wilhe Mina Eversole, b Mar 9, 1891 No 2159

No. 1245. Fifth Generation. 1244.

2) John Peter Eversole, b May 3, 1859, d July 31, 1929, m. Ella Small, b. Mar 10, 1864 They were married Aug 4, 1886 Buried at Shelbyville, Ill.

1 Gertrude Pearl Eversole, b Nov 27, 1887 No 2160.

2 Orlie Lester Eversole, b May 3, 1895 No 1246.

No. 1246. Sixth Generation. 1245.

2) Orlie Lester Eversole, b May 3, 1893, m Jan 2, 1924, Emma Hendy, b. July 23, 1905. Address Westerville, Ill. Farmer

1 John Peter Eversole, b July 24, 1928

2. Joseph DeWitt Eversole, b Aug 29, 1931

No. 1247. Fifth Generation. 1244.

3) Emma Florence Eversole, b Oct 18, 1860, d Nov 6, 1934, m. Jan 26, 1882. John B. Fritz, b June 29, 1858, d Dec 25, 1914 Both were buried at Greenwood cemetery, Decatur, Ill Address 768 N Union St., Decatur, Ill.

1. Dessie Fritz, b. April 17, 1884 No 1248
2. Lloyd E. Fritz, b Oct 4, 1886, d Jan 7, 1893
3. Edgar Earl Fritz, b Mar. 28, 1888 No 2161.
4 William Lawrence Fritz, b Dec. 5, 1898 No 2162.

No. 1248. Sixth Generation. 1247.

1) Dessie Viola Fritz, b April 17, 1884, m Nov. 15, 1906, George Schilling, b. Oct 6, 1891.

No. 1249. Fifth Generation. 1244.

4) Lou Ella Eversole, b. Sept 13, 1863. On Feb 14, 1886, she married Jacob B. Small, b July 15, 1860 He died Jan 19, 1922 Farmer Methodists Address Neodesha, Kans.
1 Emory H Small, b Dec 3, 1887 No 2163.
2. Wright J Small, b Jan 29, 1890 No. 2165
3 Gertrude Wager Small, b Mar 15, 1892 No 2167.
4. Grace Irene Small, b Dec 5, 1898 No 2168.
5. Elmer Charles Small, b Sept. 10, 1903 No 2169
6 Ora Katherine Small, b Jan 2, 1907 No 2170

No. 1250. Fifth Generation. 1244.

5) David Swartz Eversole, b Apr 10, 1867, m in 1894 Hope Boyce, b Nov 30, 1871 Address: Shelbyville, Ill. Farmer.
1. Edna Elizabeth Eversole, b May 11, 1895 No 1251
2. Orrville Eversole, b July 11, 1896 No. 2174.
3. Hazel Eversole, b Sept 13, 1899, d Apr 8, 1911
4. Everett Boys Eversole, b July 29, 1906 No 2175
5 David Loren Eversole, b Feb 7, 1917, d Feb 19, 1917

No. 1251. Sixth Generation. 1250.

1) Edna Elizabeth Eversole, b May 11, 1895, m Oct 29, 1924, Otto Kindt, b Mar 3, 1899
1 Vera Elizabeth Kindt, b Dec 26, 1925
2 Mary Virginia Kindt, b Dec 18, 1932

No. 1252. Fifth Generation. 1244.

6) Mattie Eversole, b April 13, 1869, m Feb 25, 1891, Preston Hunter, b Aug. 24, 1869 Farmer at Findlay, Ill Address Findlay, Ill Evangelical Church
1 Homer Hunter, b Dec 20, 1891 No 1253

No. 1253. Sixth Generation. 1252.

1) Homer Vernon Hunter, b Dec 20, 1891, m June 4, 1913, Beatrice Workman, b Oct 28, 1891
1. Inos Workman Hunter, b April 6, 1914, d April 1, 1917.
2. James Preston Hunter, b. Jan 25, 1916
3. Robert Anderson Hunter, b July 17, 1918, twin
4. Roberta Helen Hunter, b. July 17, 1918, twin.
5. Jean Elizabeth Hunter, b. Nov. 28, 1930

No. 1254. Fifth Generation. 1244.

7) William Miller Eversole, b April 27, 1871, m Oct 27, 1902, Bertha Alice Wheatley, b Jan. 6, 1879. Mr Eversole died Sept 22, 1922 Buried at Greenwood cemetery, Moweaqua, Ill
1. Harley Wheatley Eversole, b Mar 9, 1904 No. 1255
2. James Harold Eversole, b Nov 6, 1905 No. 1256
3. Evelyn Almeda Eversole, b June 18, 1910 No. 1257.

4 Glen William Eversole, b Aug 10, 1914
5 Floyd Earl Eversole, b Nov 27, 1917.

No. 1255. Sixth Generation. 1254.

1) Harley Wheatley Eversole, b Mar. 9, 1904, m. Jan. 19, 1924, Bessie Suppes, b. May 15, 1903. Farmer at Moweaqua, Ill. Evangelical
1. Lyle Edward Eversole, b. Mar. 30, 1927.
2 Jo Ann Eversole, b April 3, 1931

No. 1256. Sixth Generation. 1254.

2) James Harold Eversole, b. Nov. 6, 1905, m. Laura Mae Pierce, Oct. 27, 1922. Address Shelbyville, Ill
1. Maurice Dwayne Eversole, b. June 22, 1924.
2 Marilyn Jean Eversole, b Aug 12, 1928.
3 Donald Lee Eversole, b June 20, 1935.

No. 1257. Sixth Generation. 1254.

3) Evelyn Almeda Eversole, b. June 18, 1910, m. Cecil Shieck, Mar. 8, 1933. Address: Palmer, Ill

No. 1258. Fifth Generation. 1244.

8) Anna Eversole, b Sept 9, 1873, m Frederick Bair, b. June 5, 1874.
1 Sidney Lynn Bair, b Aug 14, 1896. No. 2176.
2 George W. Bair, b Feb 22, 1898. No. 2177.
3. Lloyd Wallace Bair, b Jan 29, 1900 No 2178
4 Jacob M Bair, b Feb. 21, 1902 No 2179
5 Christian D. Bair, b July 23, 1911.
6 Cecile Bair, July 29, 1914.

No. 1259. Fifth Generation. 1244.

9) Grant W Eversole, b May 6, 1865, m April 14, 1897, Mattie Carr, b. Aug 18, 1869, d. July 8, 1928 Farmer Evangelical Buried at Shelbyville, Ill. Address: Westervelt, Shelby Co , Ill.
1. Edgar B. Eversole, b. Feb. 8, 1898. No 2171
2 Leverette W Eversole, b. June 4, 1902 No 2172
3 Lois C Eversole, b Oct 13, 1905. No. 2173

No. 1259½. Fifth Generation. 1244.

10) George Washington Eversole, b April 21, 1876, d Feb 22, 1920 He married on Mar 14, 1902, Anna Durkee, b June 24, 1880.
1 Dwight L Eversole, b April 14, 1906
2 Mary Belle Eversole, b Oct 14, 1909.

No. 1260. Fourth Generation. 27.

5) David Eversole, Jr , b. Mar. 12, 1838, d Oct. 4, 1911, m Susan Miesse, b. July 25, 1841, d. Dec. 15, 1879. He married (2nd) Mary Ann Price, b. Jan. 5, 1837, d Nov. 17, 1891. Buried at King cemetery near Middlepoint, O Farmer in Van Wert Co., O. United Brethren.
1. Mary E. Eversole, b Sept. 20, 1862 No 1261.
2 Minnie Lee Eversole, b Jan. 5, 1867 No. 1262
3 Abbie Eversole, b. May 13, 1871, d Dec. 5, 1878.
4. Sherman Eversole, b Jan. 17, 1865 No. 1263.
5. Luella Eversole, b. April 10, 1869. No 1264.
6. Susan Belle Eversole, b Mar 19, 1873 No. 1265.
7. Pearl D. Eversole, b May 13, 1875 No. 1266.
8. Arthur D. Eversole, b. Apr 13, 1877 No 1267.
9 Charles Foster Eversole, b. Nov 8, 1879 No 1269.

No. 1261. Fifth Generation. 1250.

1) Mary E. Eversole, b. Sept 20, 1862, m Mar 27, 1881, William H. Meyers, by Rev. Samuel Whitmore Mr Meyers died Oct. 12, 1924. She married (2nd) Albert W. Fling; he died Feb. 22, 1932.

1. Birl Eldo Meyers, b Sept 6, 1881 No. 2180.
2. Viola Kate Meyers, b April 4, 1883 No. 2181.
3. David Raymond Meyers, b. Aug 13, 1889.
4. Hazel Annie Meyers, b Mar 31, 1891

No. 1262. Fifth Generation. 1260.

2) Minnie Lee Eversole, b Jan 5, 1867, d Nov. 12, 1886, m Mar 29, 1884, G. Frank Bell.

1. Onie Philena Bell, b. Mar 15, 1885 Mrd Evans.

No. 1263. Fifth Generation. 1260.

4) Sherman W. T Eversole, b. Jan. 17, 1865, d Nov. 11, 1928, m. Alice McGowan, b. July 9, 1866 He was a railroad clerk. Methodist. Buried at Hillsdale, Mich. Address. 206 N Manning St , Hillsdale, Mich.

1 Zelma Fern Eversole, b Nov 7, 1892. No. 1263½.

No. 1263½. Sixth Generation. 1263.

1) Zelma Fern Eversole, b Nov 7, 1892, m. Aug 25, 1917, Arthur Barber. Address: Orlando, Fla.

1. Nancy Fern Barber, b. Nov. 21, 1925.
2. Barbara Ann Barber, b. Mar. 18, 1929.

No. 1264. Fifth Generation. 1260.

5) Anna Luella Eversole, b Apr 10, 1869, m. John Fry, b. May 4, 1862. Address: Haviland, O. Farmer. M E Church.

1. Harry Russel Fry, b. Jan. 14, 1897.
2. Orpha Leona Fry, b. May 18, 1903. No. 1358.

No. 1265. Fifth Generation. 1260.

6) Susan Belle Eversole, b Mar 19, 1873, m Dec 23, 1890, Noah Stiverson, b ————, 1866 Congregational Address Hudson, Mich , R. 4.

1. Frederick G. Stiverson, b ————, 1891. No. 1351.
2. Iva M. Stiverson, b ————, 1893 No 1352.
3. Joel David Stiverson, b ————, 1895. No. 1353.
4. Ola May Stiverson, b ————, 1897. No 1354.
5. Geneva L. Stiverson, b. ————, 1899. No. 1355.
6. Ada Armetha Stiverson, b ————, 1901 No 1356.
7. Elmer A. Stiverson, b ————, 1903. No 1357.
8. Susan Leona Stiverson, b ————, 1906
9. Dorothy E Stiverson, b ————, 1908
10. Vola Belle Stiverson, b ————, 1910.
11. Nolan Dorr Stiverson, b ————, 1915.

No. 1266. Fifth Generation. 1250.

7) Pearl D. Eversole, b May 13, 1875, d in 1917, married Lula Thatcher. Address: Middlepoint, O

1. Doyt Eversole died young.
2 Miles Lawton Eversole, b. ——————. No. 2182.

No. 1267. Fifth Generation. 1260.

8) Arthur Graham Eversole, b. April 13, 1877, d. Nov. 17, 1918, m. June 7, 1903, Ida Keirns, b. Oct. 4, 1881   Address· Delphos, O , R 4. Farmer. United Brethren.

   1. Harold Eugene Eversole, b June 3, 1904. No. 1268.
   2. Martha Lodena Eversole, b Jan. 26, 1908.
   3. Milo Ross Eversole, b. July 13, 1915.
   4. Ilo Lucille Eversole, b. Mar 7, 1918.

No. 1268. Sixth Generation. 1257.

1) Harold Eugene Eversole, b June 3, 1904, m. Feb 10, 1922, Pauline Clark, b. April 27, 1904. Address: Delphos, O., R. 4. Farmer. Methodists.

   1. Robert Eugene Eversole, b. June 30, 1922.
   2. Harold Richard Eversole, b. Aug. 2, 1923.

No. 1269. Fifth Generation. 1260.

9) Charles Foster Eversole, b Nov 8, 1879, d. Sept. 30, 1937; m. Sept. 10, 1905, Estella Tabler, b. April 14, 1880. Furniture dealer at Middlepoint, O. Mr. Eversole was a teacher of music for sixteen years, but on account of failing health gave up this vocation for his present business. To the time of his death he served as choir director for the Presbyterian Church. He had taught piano, voice, and theory of music. No children.

No. 1270. Fourth Generation. 27.

6) Lydia Eversole, b Aug 1, 1840, d Jan 10, 1933, m. in 1857 to Newton Peters, b ————, 1829, d ————, 1919 Address was 148 West 6th Ave., Lancaster, O.

   1. Preston Peters, b ————, 1858 No. 1271.
   2. Charles Felton Peters, b. ————, 1859. No 1272.
   3. Lizzie Peters, b. ————, 1864. No. 1273.
   4 Robison Jones Peters, b. ————, 1867. No. 1274
   5. Martha Peters, b. ————, 1869. No. 1275.
   6 Gaylor Clark Peters, b ————, 1871. No 1276.
   7 Jessie Peters, b ————, 1881 No 1277

No. 1271. Fifth Generation. 1270.

1) Preston Peters, b. ————, 1858, m in 1880 to Katherine Groom, b. ————, 1850. Address. Commercial Point, O Banker.

   1. Grace Peters, b ————, 1881 No 1278.
   2 Charles Peters, b ————, 1882 No 1279
   3. Albert Peters, b ————, 1884 No. 1280
   4. Flora Peters, b ————, 1886 No 1281.
   5. Newton S. Peters, b ————, 1893 No. 1283.
   6 Edwin M. Peters, b ————, 1893, d. ————, 1904.

No. 1272. Fifth Generation. 1270.

2) Charles Felton Peters, b ————, 1859, d. in 1913, m. in 1887 Nannie Trimble, b ————, 1861. Address. 122½ Broad Street, Lancaster, O.

   1. Agnes Olivia Peters, b ————, 1889. No 1284.
   2 Charles Wesley Peters, b. ————, 1900. No. 1285

No. 1273. Fifth Generation. 1270.

3) Lizzie Peters, b ————, 1864, m in 1883 to James C. Claypool, b. ————, 1850, d. ————, 1927 Address· 148 West 6th Ave., Lancaster, O.

   1. Carl P. Claypool, b ————,' 1884. No. 1286.
   2. Clark W. Claypool, b ————, 1891 No. 1287.

No. 1274. Fifth Generation. 1270.

4) Robinson Jones Peters, b ———, 1867, m in 1898 to Ida Estella Compton, b. ———, 1874. Address 1810 Pine Street, Boulder, Colo.

1 Ralph C. Peters, b. ———, 1899.

His address: 270 Trement Ave , Kenmore, N Y

No. 1275. Fifth Generation. 1270.

5) Martha Peters, b ———, 1869, m in 1921, James A Beery, b ———, 1866 Address 1850 Oak St., Columbus, O No children.

No. 1276. Fifth Generation. 1270.

6) Gaylord Clark Peters, b ———, 1871, m in 1901 Nellie Timbers, b. ———, 1876. Address: 271 E 5th Ave , Lancaster, O.

1. Genevieve Peters, b ———, 1902 No 1288
2. Margaret Martha Peters, b. ———, 1914

No. 1277. Fifth Generation. 1270.

7) Jessie Peters, b ———, 1881, m in 1911, William Chalmers Jones, b ———, 1874 Address 115 16th Ave , Columbus, O

1 Marjorie Jones, b. ———, 1912.
2. Helen Louise Jones, b ———, 1916
3. William Chalmers Jones, Jr , b ———, 1920

No. 1278. Sixth Generation. 1271.

1) Grace Peters, b ———, 1881, m. in 1923 George H. Hartman, b. ———, 1872 Address: New London, O.

No. 1279. Sixth Generation. 1271.

2) Charles Peters, b. ———, 1882, m in 1909, Florence Orders, b. ———, 1890 Address· Ashville, O No children

No. 1280. Sixth Generation. 1271.

3) Albert Peters, b ———, 1884, m in 1908 Rom A Cline, b ———, 1889. Address: Louckbourne, O

1. Evelyn Peters, b ———, 1911.
2 Everett Peters, b. ———, 1915

No. 1281. Sixth Generation. 1271.

4) Flora Peters, b ———, 1886, m in 1908 John C. Brossman, b. ———, 1887 Address: Summitt Station, O.

1. Catherine E Brossman, b ———, 1909 No 1282
2. Pella L. Brossman, b. ———, 1912
3 Rollan J. Brossman, b. ———, 1917.

No. 1282. Seventh Generation. 1281.

1) Catherine E Brossman, b ———, 1909, m in 1928 Joseph Raymond Roby, b. ———, 1899 Address: Summitt Station, O

1. Lou Ann Roby, b ———, 1929

No. 1283. Sixth Generation. 1271.

5) Newton S Peters, b ———, 1890, m. in 1913 Isa Trego, b. ———, 1895. Address: Commercial Point, O

1 Betty Ann Peters, b ———, 1917.

No. 1284. Sixth Generation. 1272.

1) Agnes Olivia Peters, b ———, 1889, m in 1922 Frank Simon Hooker, b. ———, 1863. Address 829 East Main St , Lancaster, O.

214

No. 1285. Sixth Generation. 1272.

2) Charles Wesley Peters, b. ———, 1900, m. in 1918 Edith Taggert, b ———, 1904 Address 140 Amelia St , Zanesville, O

No. 1286. Sixth Generation. 1273.

1) Carl P. Claypool, b July 21, 1884, m Aug 5, 1919, Ethel Phelps, b. Nov. 16, 1888. Address· Box 372, R. 9, Fresno, Calif
1 Alden Keith Claypool, b Dec 17, 1928
2. Lois Elizabeth Claypool, b May 24, 1933.

No. 1287. Sixth Generation. 1273.

2) Clark W Claypool, b ———, 1891, m. in 1920 Prudence Jackson, b ———, 1893. Address Cedar Hill Road, Lancaster, O., R. D.
1. Dorothy Claypool, b ———, 1921
2. James R. Claypool, b. ———, 1923
3. Donald Clark Claypool, b. ———, 1925

No. 1288. Sixth Generation. 1276.

1) Genevieve Peters, b. ———, 1902, m in 1924 Overton Melitis Cowden, b. ———, 1901. Address. 7893 Rogers Ave , Rogers Park, Chicago, Ill.

No. 1289. Fourth Generation. 27.

8) Emmanuel Eversole, b Dec. 28, 1842, d. Aug 13, 1917, m. Sept. 16, 1869, Sarah Elizabeth Artz, b June 30, 1850 Address Thawville, Ill Farmer Methodists. Buried at Onorga cemetery, Onorga, Ill
1. Hardy A. Eversole, b Feb. 2, 1871 No 2183.
2. George A. Eversole, b Aug 25, 1872 No 2184.
3. Mary G Eversole, b Mar 6, 1874 No 2185.
4. Clara E Eversole, b. Nov 13, 1876 No 2188
5 Hazel A. Eversole, b July 22, 1885. No 2189.
6 John Logan Eversole, b May 21, 1887 No 2190

No. 1290. Fourth Generation. 27.

9) John P Eversole, b Feb 10, 1845 In June, 1914, Mr Eversole visited friends near Harrisonburg, Va , and exclaimed "that their old home farm is worth $50,000 and that is the most beautiful country he had ever seen." He married Abbie Brown. They lived at Bremen, O No children.

No. 1291. Fourth Generation. 27.

10) Nancy Eversole, b Sept 13, 1847, d June 2, 1909. On Aug. 30, 1866, she married Abraham B. Turner, b Jan 3, 1840. He died Nov. 20, 1932. Farmer Evangelical They moved from Fairfield Co , O , in 1847 to El Paso, Ill., where they are buried in the Evergreen cemetery, El Paso, Ill.
1. David Turner, b June 20, 1867, d. Mar. 12, 1868
2 George Thomas Turner, b Jan 3, 1869, d Oct. 25, 1903.
3. Alvin Perry Turner, b Jan. 5, 1871. No. 1292.
4 Martha Elizabeth Turner, b Dec 27, 1872. No. 1300.
5. Cora Alice Turner, b Mar 31, 1875. No· 1295.
6. Ira Benton Turner, b July 14, 1877, d April 27, 1905
7 Carrie R Turner, b. July 8, 1880 No. 1296.
8 Frank Eversole Turner, b May 31, 1883 No. 1297.
9 Anna Marie Turner, b Mar 22, 1886. No. 1300.

No. 1292. Fifth Generation. 1291.

3) Alvin Perry Turner, b Jan 5, 1871, d Jan 21, 1904, m Sarah A Yambert. Farmer.

1. A. Lucille Turner, b June 1, 1898 No 1293.

2 Wayne Y Turner, b. Mar. 28, 1901, is a Civil Engineer at San Francisco, Calif.

No. 1293. Sixth Generation. 1292.

1) A Lucille Turner, b June, 1898, m a Mr. Cullem. Mrs. Cullem was an osteopath doctor and trained nurse at Merced, Calif.

No. 1295. Fifth Generation. 1291.

5) Cora Alice Turner, b. Mar. 31, 1875, m. Dec. 31, 1903, Joseph W. Crout. Farmer at El Paso, Ill

1 George T. Crout, b ——————, single, M.D., St. Francis Hospital, Evanston, Ill.

2. Neele Crout, b ——————, single, nurse at Presbyterian Hospital, Chicago, Ill.

3. Mary Crout, b ——————

4. Carl T. Crout, b ——————.

5 Dorothy M Crout, b. ——————.

6. Barbara Crout, b. ——————.

7. Alice Crout, b. ——————

No. 1295. Fifth Generation. 1291.

7) Carrie Rebecca Turner, b July 8, 1880, m Joseph H. Martin, deceased, to whom two sons were born, both deceased. She married (2nd) Otto Grieser. They reside at St. Paul, Nebr.

No. 1297. Fifth Generation. 1291.

8) Frank Eversole Turner, b May 31, 1883, married and has two sons

1. Weldon M Turner, b. —————— No 1298.

2 R Maurice Turner, b —————— Maurice is married and lives at Dallas, Tex , N. F. R.

No. 1298. Sixth Generation. 1297.

1) Weldon M. Turner, b. ——————, m ——————, and has two children Address: Gary, Ind.

1. Weldon Eugene Turner, b. ——————.

2 Bettie Joan Turner, b. ——————.

No. 1300. Fifth Generation. 1291.

9) Annie Marie Turner, b Mar 22, 1886 Single She remained at home to care for her mother who passed away Nov 20, 1932, at El Paso, Ill. Her sister, Martha Elizabeth Turner, the fourth child of the family, is a Christian worker. She was for thirteen years a boys' matron and teacher.

No. 1301. Fourth Generation. 27.

11) Martha Eversole, b. Dec. 27, 1850. On June 4, 1878, she married Jacob Lewis Tidd, b. Feb. 11, 1851, d June 10, 1925 Merchant at Lancaster, O. Evangelical. Buried at Forest Rose cemetery, near Lancaster, O.

1. Hazel Tidd, b. Nov. 19, 1883. No 1302.

2. Jessie Tidd, b. Jan. 28, 1885 No 1303

3 Winfred Tidd, b. April 2, 1886. No. 1304.

4 Clyde Carlton Tidd, b. Nov. 14, 1888. No. 1305.

No. 1302. Fifth Generation. 1301.

1) Hazel Tidd, b. Nov 19, 1883, m Jan 15, 1898, Joseph Dunfee, b Aug 15, 1866. Hazel Tidd Dunfee is professionally known as Josephine Dunfee. She is a noted orchestra and concert singer having appeared with many famous orchestras

including the New York Symphony and Boston Symphony. She was soloist with Sousa's Band and Patrick Conway's Band for many seasons. She also appeared in many operas. Her vocal studio is in Lancaster, O. Address: Dunfee's Vocal Studio, Lancaster, O. Cathol.cs.

1. Margaret Martha Dunfee, b Dec. 2, 1906. Miss Dunfee is her mother's accompanist. She is also a poet and writer.

No. 1303. Fifth Generation. 1301.
2) Jessie Tidd, b Jan 28, 1885, m Dr Robert G Owen, b. Mar. 3, 1883 Address: Walled Lake, Mich. Offices in Detroit, Mich. Unitarians.

No. 1304. Fifth Generation. 1301.
3) Winfred Tidd, b April 2, 1886, m. April 5, 1914, Edward Clark, b Dec. 4, 1884 The above is Mr Clark's theatrical name, his maternal name is Michael Capita, born in San Felice near Naples, Italy Catholic. Theatrical profession Address: 732 Madison Ave , Lancaster, O
1. Minnie Martha Clark, b. Aug. 1, 1918
2 John Jacob Clark, b June 24, 1921

No. 1305. Fifth Generation. 1301.
4) Clyde Carlton Tidd, b Nov 14, 1888, at Lancaster, O., m. June 15, 1910, Flora Marie ——————, b Dec 3, 1891 Address: Maderia, O., Box 55. Clerk for railway express Presbyterians.
1 Helen Grace Tidd, b Feb. 18, 1912 No 1350.
2 Mary Martha Tidd, b Nov 20, 1915
3. Virginia Margurite Tidd, b Aug 8, 1918
4 Clyde Robert Tidd, b June 5, 1922
5 William Frederick Tidd, b. Jan 4, 1926

No. 1306. Fourth Generation. 28.
1) Marie A. Miller, b. ——————, m Rev. T G Clewell of Cleveland, O.
1 George Clewell, b ——————
2. Lilly Clewell, b ——————
3 Howard Clewell, b ——————
4 Clara Clewell, b ——————
5. Grace Clewell, b ——————

No. 1307. Fourth Generation. 23.
2) Mary Elizabeth Miller, b Feb 22, 1839, m June 27, 1858, J. B. Turner, b. Aug. 19, 1835 She died Feb 14, 1895
1 George E. Turner, b Aug 8, 1859
2. Albert F. Turner, b. Aug. 13, 1861.
3 John Mason Turner, b. Aug 15, 1863.
4 William S. Turner, b April 15, 1865
5 Charles N Turner, b. Feb. 4, 1867.
6. Walter F Turner, b Nov 3, 1868
7 Paul DeWitt Turner, b Sept 13, 1873
8. Mary R. Turner, b. Aug 20, 1875.
9 Martha E Turner, b. Feb. 7, 1878, d Jan 17, 1888
10 James A Turner, b April 14, 1880

No. 1308. Fourth Generation. 23.
3) Michael C. Miller. b about 1811, m. Emma Reed, b —————— Mr Miller was for two terms county treasurer at Lancaster, O.
1. Stella Miller, b Aug 8, 1866 No 1308¼.
2 Robert Miller, b. ——————.

No. 1308¼. Fifth Generation. 1308.

1) Stella Miller, b. Aug. 8, 1866, near Bern, O , m Nov 8, 1894, James A. Beery, b Sept. 1, 1866, near Bern, O Address 594 East Rich St., Columbus, O. Presbyterians.

    1. Kennell Beery, b. ————, 1898

    2 Irene Beery, b. ————, 1902.

No. 1309. Fourth Generation. 27.

2) Henry Eversole, b Oct 2, 1831, d Dec 11, 1909, m Oct. 2, 1858, Sarah Jane Work, b. Oct. 10, 1836. She died Aug 8, 1919 Farmer. Christian Church Address. Hudsboro, Ill Buried at Greary Point, Ill.

    1. Lula L. Eversole, b Jan 16, 1860, d Sept 29, 1920

    2 McClellen Eversole, b Aug 25, 1861 No 1310.

    3. Henley Eversole, b July 31, 1863. No 1311

    4 John Henry Eversole, b Feb 17, 1867 No 1312

    5 Berta Eversole, b Nov 30, 1872, d Sept 17, 1873

No. 1310. Fifth Generation. 1309.

2) McClellen Eversole, b Aug 25, 1861, m Nov 30, 1893, Jennie Eversole, b Sept 21, 1867, d Feb 13, 1930 Address Arcola, Ill Insurance and real estate Christian

    1. Selma A Eversole, b. Nov 20, 1894 No 1359

    2 Miriam Grace Eversole, b Feb 16, 1900. No 1360.

    3 McClellen Eversole, Jr , b Oct 27, 1902, single.

    4 Mary Etta Eversole, b. July 14, 1905 No 1362.

No. 1311. Fifth Generation. 1309.

3) Henley Eversole, b July 31, 1863, m Mar 26, 1895, Orpha Olive Wagner, b Mar. 8, 1873, of Newman, Ill Address Newman, Ill Farmer Inventor Historian Merchant

    1. John Henley Eversole, b Sept. 13, 1909.

    2 William Eversole, b ————

    3. Mary Eversole, b ————

John Henley graduated from the Culver Military Academy; William and Mary, at Williamsburg, Va., College

No. 1312. Fifth Generation. 1309.

4) John Henry Eversole, b Feb 17, 1867, at Lancaster, O., m Sept. 16, 1896, Elizabeth Moyer, b. Jan. 23, 1870 She died Jan 11, 1931. Retired grain dealer and farmer. Champaign, Ill Christian Church.

    1 Lenore Eversole, b April 13, 1900 No 1363.

    2 Mildred Eversole, b. Nov. 4, 1902, at home.

No. 1313. Fourth Generation. 28.

4) John E. Miller, b Oct 14, 1844, m Nov. 7, 1867, Catherine Sites, b. Jan 15, 1849 She died May 7, 1928 Address: 751 East Main St., Lancaster, O. Buried in Lancaster Mausoleum.

    1 Orrin W. Miller, b. Oct. 25, 1872.

    2 Grace Viola Miller, b June 29, 1879, d Aug. 11, 1879.

No. 1314. Fourth Generation. 28.

6) David E Miller, b. ————, m. Mary Bowers, b ———— He was buried at Lancaster, O. Mrs. Miller was buried at Arcola, Ill

    1 Charles B. Miller, b April 4, 1878, twin No 1315.

    2. Harry G Miller, b April 4, 1878, twin. No 1317.

No. 1315. Fifth Generation. 1314.

1) Charles B. Miller, b. April 4, 1878, m Feb. 16, 1901, Iva McGee, b. Jan. 25, 1883. Building and loan secretary. Christian Address: Brocton, Ill., Box 86.

1. Lucille Miller, b. Oct. 13, 1902 No 1316
2. Charles W. Miller, b Sept 25, 1920.

No. 1316. Sixth Generation. 1315.

1) Lucille Miller, b Oct 13, 1902, m Aug. 5, 1920, John Kerfoot Jones, b June 23, 1900. Address· 105 Michigan Ave., Hobart, Ind. Burial at Arcola, Ill.

1. Janet Kirfoot Jones, b July 16, 1928.

No. 1317. Fifth Generation. 1314.

2) Harry G Miller, b April 4, 1878, m Grace ———— Miller Address Brocton, Ill , Box 86 No children.

No. 1318. Fourth Generation. 28.

7) Franklin Pierce Miller, b Mar 2, 1853, m. Jan. 5, 1875, Sarah E. Hempy, b Jan. 4, 1853 Retired farmer Evangelical Place of burial, Mt. Tabor, O. Address: Pleasantville, O.

1. Harvey Ray Miller died in infancy
2 Arlie M. Miller, b April 15, 1878
3 James F Miller, b Sept. 1, 1879

No. 1319. Fourth Generation. 24.

7) Daniel Showalter, b Dec 21, 1839, d Mar 17, 1887, m. Jan 8, 1863, Mary Heatwole, b Jan. 3, 1842, d. Feb 6, 1932 Address Broadway, Va Farmers Mennonites. Burial at Trissels.

1. Emma Elizabeth Showalter, b Nov. 5, 1863 No 1320.
2 Margaret Anna Showalter, b April 21, 1865 No 1328.
3. Frances Virginia Showalter, b. May 12, 1867, d Feb. 5, 1888
4 Gabriel DeWitt Showalter, b Oct 20, 1869 No 1331
5 Infant died April 4, 1872
6 Sallie Belle Showalter, b Feb 21, 1873, d Mar 11, 1876
7 Mary Magdalene Showalter, b Aug. 3, 1875
8 Bertie Ollie Showalter, b Oct 22, 1877 No 1332
9 Albert Alvin Showalter, b Jan 12, 1880
10 Howard Daniel H. Showalter, b. Sept 29, 1882. No. 1333.

No. 1320. Fifth Generation. 1319.

1) Emma Elizabeth Showalter, b Nov 5, 1863, m Nov. 27, 1884, Joseph Shank, b. July 3, 1857 Farmer Mennonite minister, ordained Jan. 1, 1905 Address Broadway, Va

1. Daniel David Shank, b July 27, 1886. No. 1321
2. Mary Catherine Shank, b. Dec 17, 1887. No. 1322
3. Sallie Elizabeth Shank, b Oct. 30, 1890 No. 1323
4 Samuel Aaron Shank. b April 6, 1893. No 1324
5 Infant Shank, b and d Nov 28, 1895.
6 Emma Frances Shank, b Nov 5, 1896 No 1325
7 Anna Mae Shank, b Sept 3. 1899 No 1326
8 Ezra Abram Shank, b Nov 17, 1902 No 1327.
9. Sarah Rebecca Shank, b Nov. 5, 1905
10. Ruth Virginia Shank, b Sept 23, 1908.

No. 1321. Sixth Generation. 1320.

1) Daniel David Shank, b. July 27, 1886, in Rockingham Co, Va, m. Nov. 4, 1908, Abbie C Lahman, b. Mar 8, 1886 Farmer. Mennonites Related, see No. 863 for family report. Both died three hours apart of pneumonia, Feb. 17, 1920

No. 1322. Sixth Generation. 1320.

2) Mary Catherine Shank, b Dec 17, 1889, in Rockingham Co, Va., m. Jan. 27, 1916, Noah Wilmer Geil, b. May 24, 1889, near Broadway, Va. Farmer. Mennonites. He was ordained to the ministry, Jan. 5, 1922, at the Lindale Church. Address: Broadway, Va.

1 Maude Elizabeth Geil, b Sept 9, 1918
2. Mary Rebecca Geil, b Nov. 13, 1919
3. Ethel Virginia Geil, b June 3, 1924

No. 1323. Sixth Generation. 1320.

3) Salle Elizabeth Shank, b Oct 30, 1890, in Va, m. June 8, 1916, Irvin D Showalter, b June 3, 1891 Address Linville, Va Farmer Mennonite.

1. Clayton Daniel Showalter, b Dec 1, 1917.
2. David Ezra Showalter, b Nov. 27, 1918.
3. Alma Mae Showalter, b July 12, 1920
4 Eula Marie Showalter, b. Aug 9, 1922
5. Vada Elizabeth Showalter, b. Sept. 3, 1926.
6 Arlene Catherine Showalter, b. Feb. 19, 1930.

No. 1324. Sixth Generation. 1320.

4) Samuel Aaron Shank, b April 6, 1893, in Rockingham Co, Va, m. June 7, 1916, Mary Catherine Geil, b July 26, 1891, near Broadway, Va Farmer Mennonites He was ordained to the ministry, Mar 24, 1928, at the Lindale Church Address: Broadway, Va

1 Joseph Geil Shank, b April 14, 1917
2 Catherine Frances Shank, b. Mar. 26, 1919
3 Samuel Aaron Shank, b Nov 20, 1920
4 Robert Edwin Shank, b Feb. 26, 1925, d Nov 10, 1926
5 Lois Anna Shank, b Nov 25, 1927.

No. 1325. Sixth Generation. 1320.

6) Emma Frances Shank, b. Nov 5, 1896, in Rockingham Co, Va, m. Dec 12, 1918, Abner F Weaver, b June 28, 1894, near Waynesboro, Va Farmer. Mennonites Address: Waynesboro, Va.

1. Infant daughter, b. and d Jan. 2, 1920
2. Mary McNeil Weaver, b. June 29, 1922
3 Paul Abner Weaver, b Sept. 26, 1924.
4 Raymond Shank Weaver, b Nov 23, 1928.

No. 1326. Sixth Generation. 1320.

7) Annie Mae Shank, b Sept 3, 1899, in Rockingham Co, Va, m. Nov. 1, 1922, Peter W Blosser, b Nov 16. 1893 Address· Harrisonburg, Va Farmer Mennonites

1. Alice Virginia Blosser, b Sept 16, 1924
2 James DeWitt Blosser, b Aug 31, 1930

No. 1327. Sixth Generation. 1320.

8) Ezra Abram Shank, b. Nov 17, 1902, in Rockingham Co, Va, m. June 12, 1926, Blanche Marie Layman, b Oct 27, 1904, at Davidsville, Pa. He was ordained to the ministry at the Canton, O, Mennonite Mission

1 Junior Lee Shank, b July 2, 1928.

No. 1328. Fifth Generation. 1319.

2) Margaret Anna Showalter, b April 21, 1865, m. Oct. 13, 1887, Charles T. Meyers. Mrs. Meyers died Nov 5, 1901, and was buried at the Trissels Church.

1 Bertha G Meyers, b. Dec 24, 1888 No. 1329

2 Paul S. Meyers, b. May 18, 1891. No. 1330

No. 1329. Sixth Generation. 1328.

1) Bertha G. Meyers, b. Dec 24, 1888, m Oct. 8, 1914, Henry W. Lambertson, b. Mar 15, 1877. Address Pocomoke City, Md Mrs. Lambertson is a Mennonite.

1. Mary Elizabeth Lambertson, b Mar. 6, 1916.

2 Margaret Anna Lambertson, b. Oct. 28, 1926.

No. 1330. Sixth Generation. 1328.

2) Paul S Meyers, b. May 18, 1891, m Aug., 1928, Jannet Whitmore. Address: North River, Va Mennonite.

1. Anna Elizabeth Meyers, b April 29, 1930.

No. 1331. Fifth Generation. 1319.

4) Gabriel Dewitt Showalter, b. Oct 20, 1869, m. Kathryn Mullany of Washington, D C He died Aug 21, 1904. Buried at Trissels Church

No. 1332. Fifth Generation. 1319.

8) Bertie Ollie Showalter, b. Oct 22, 1877, m David Eiman, of Wellman, Ia., Aug. 17, 1910 Address Wellman, Ia Farmer Mennonites.

1. Mary Virgnia Eimen, b. May 2, 1911.

2. Martha Elizabeth Eimen, b Sept 10, 1912.

3. Paul Howard Eimen, b July 16, 1914.

4 Erma Mae Eimen, b May 2, 1916

5. Anna Ruth Eimen, b July 23, 1918

No. 1333. Fifth Generation. 1319.

10) Howard D. H Showalter, b Sept. 29, 1882, m. Oct. 28, 1908, Flora May Grove, b May 2, 1886 Address Broadway, Va Farmer. Mennonites.

1. Carl Grove Showalter, b Mar. 15, 1911.

2. Mary Emma Showalter, b. Feb. 24, 1913

3. Howard DeWitt Showalter, b July 30, 1914.

4 Jacob Daniel Showalter, b Feb. 15, 1916.

5. Owen Franklin Showalter, b. Aug. 23, 1918.

6 Kathryn Virginia Showalter, b Aug 20, 1920.

7. James Edwin Showalter, b. Jan. 5, 1925.

8. Doris Jean Showalter, b Aug 2, 1927

No. 1334. Fourth Generation. 24.

8) Joseph Showalter, b June 5, 1833, near Broadway, Va., m. Elizabeth (Kit) Cline, b Sept 15, 1828 They lived at Broadway, Va Farmer Mennonites. Buried at Linville cemetery

1 Elizabeth Showalter, b Aug 19, 1855 No 1335

2 Frederick Showalter, b Jan 1, 1857, d Dec 28, 1862

3 John F Showalter, b Jan 1, 1859 No. 1336

4 Joseph Daniel Showalter, b July 1, 1861 No 1337

No. 1335. Fifth Generation. 1334.

1) Elizabeth Showalter, b Aug 19, 1855, d. July 12, 1884, m ——— Spitzer.

1 Mary Ann Spitzer, b ——————— No 1339

2. Charles E. Spitzer, b April —, 1881. No. 1341
3. Laura Spitzer, b. and d 1884.

No. 1336. Fifth Generation. 1334.
3) John F. Showalter, b Jan 1, 1859, m ——————.
1. Daisy C. Showalter, b Jan 31, 1878 No 1342.
2. Ada F. Showalter, b. Sept. 25, 1879 No 1343.
3. Minnie M. Showalter, b Aug. 2, 1883
4. Sidney L. Showalter, b. Feb. 5, 1886. No 1344

No. 1337. Fifth Generation. 1334.
4) Joseph Daniel Showalter, b. July 1, 1861, d Dec 28, 1888 He was married and had one daughter.
1 Mary Showalter, b ————— No. 1338

No. 1338. Sixth Generation. 1337.
Mary Showalter, b —————, m ——— Gilbert, b ———
1. Orville Gilbert, b —————.
2. Ivan Gilbert, b. ———
3 Ethel Gilbert, b. —————.

No. 1339. Sixth Generation. 1335.
1) Mary Ann Spitzer, b. —————, m ——— Martz, b. ———
1. Casper Martz, b. ———, 1893.
2. Maud Martz, b. ————— No 1340
3. Fannie Martz, b. —————
4. Walter Martz, b. —————
5. Bertha Martz, b. —————
6 Dannie Martz, b —————

No. 1340. Seventh Generation. 1339.
2) Maud Martz, b. —————, m ——— Hall, b ———
1 Opel Hall, b —————
2. Elna Hall, b —————
3. Harold Hall, b. —————
4 Alice Hall, b —————.
5 Galen Hall, b —————.

No. 1341. Sixth Generation. 1335.
2) Charles E Spitzer, b April —, 1881 He was married and has four children
1. Cathleen Spitzer, b —————.
2. Elnor Spitzer, b —————
3. Frances Spitzer, b —————.
4 Charles Spitzer, Jr., b —————

No. 1342. Sixth Generation. 1336.
1) Dasie C Showalter, b Jan 31, 1878, in Va. m Orrville Layman, b

1 Mabel V Layman, b Nov —, 1901 No 1349
2 Lewis Clinton Layman, b July 2, 1903
3. Willard A Layman, b April —, 1905, d Sept 1. 1932
4. Bernard Layman, b July 30, 1907
5 Sidney L Layman, b —————, 1908
6 Alice Layman, b Feb —, 1910. d Nov —, 1910
7. Edith Layman, b Aug 27, 1912, d July 1, 1922
8 Hazel Layman, b —————, 1914.

9. Slemp Layman, b ———, 1916
10. Charlena Layman, b. Aug —, 1918
11 Shelva Layman, b Jan —, 1922

No. 1343. Sixth Generation. 1336.
2) Ada F Showalter, b Sept 25, 1879, m Alden Hilliard.
1. Estella Hilliard, b Oct. 7, 1901 No 1345
2 Nina Hilliard, b Sept. 23, 1903 No 1346
3 Treva Hilliard, b Aug 25, 1905 No. 1347
4 Eva Hilliard, b Aug 24, 1907 No 1348

No. 1344. Sixth Generation. 1336.
4) Sidney L Showalter, b Feb 5, 1886, m Lessie Rhodes.
1. Margaret Rhodes Showalter, b ———, 1914

No. 1345. Seventh Generation. 1343.
1) Estella Hilliard, b Oct 7, 1901, m Russell Stern.

No. 1346. Seventh Generation. 1343.
2) Nina Hilliard, b Sept 23, 1903, m Earl Simmers

No. 1347. Seventh Generation. 1343.
3) Treva Hilliard, b Aug 25, 1905, m Raymond Holsinger.
1 Bertie Lee Holsinger, b Sept —, 1929.

No. 1348. Seventh Generation. 1343.
4) Eva Hilliard, b Aug. 24, 1907, m Galen V Wampler.
1. Everett Wampler, b ———

No. 1349. Seventh Generation. 1342.
1) Mabel V Layman, b Nov —, 1901, m ——— Shank.

No. 1350. Sixth Generation. 1305.
1) Helen Grace Tidd, b Feb 18, 1912, m. Gerald Grate, Sept 1, 1928.
1 Thomas Carlton Grate, b Sept. 25, 1930.

No. 1351. Sixth Generation. 1265.
1) Fred Garner Stiverson, b 1891, m. Julia Pritchard
1. Eva Marie Stiverson, b. ———.
2. Ola Arlene Stiverson, b ———.
3 Fred Stiverson, Jr., b. ———.

No. 1352. Sixth Generation. 1265.
2) Iva Merle Stiverson, b. ———, 1893, m. (1st) ——— Thompson, m.
(2nd) Albert Gould, b ———.
1. Charles Thompson, b ———
2. Franklin Gould, b ———.
3 Rodger Gould, b ———
4 Sarah Belle Gould, b ———

No. 1353. Sixth Generation. 1265.
3) Joel David Stiverson, b ———, 1895, m Maude Lamb.
1 A. Dale Stiverson, b ———.
2 Naomi Stiverson, b ———
3 Joyce Stiverson, b ———
4 Opal Charlene Stiverson, b ———.

223

No. 1354. Sixth Generation. 1265.
4) Ola May Stiverson, b ———, 1897, m J. L. Meddaugh
1. Leona Patricia Meddaugh, b. ———.

No. 1355. Sixth Generation. 1265.
5) Geneva Lula Stiverson, b ———, 1899, m Harry J. Crisp, b. ———
1. Rex William Crisp, b. ———
2. Clara Belle Crisp, b ———
3 Elizabeth June Crisp, b. ———.

No. 1356. Sixth Generation. 1265.
6) Ada Armetha Stiverson, b ———, 1901, m Ferris D Clouse.
1. Luther E Clouse, b ———.
2 Ferris E Clouse, b ———

No. 1357. Sixth Generation. 1265.
7) Elmer Arthur Stiverson, b ———, 1903, m. Katherine Hawley
1 Elmer Eugene Stiverson, b ———

No. 1358. Sixth Generation. 1264.
3) Orpha Leona Fry, b. May 18, 1903, m Bryan Bowman, April 12, 1923 Address Continental, O

No. 1359. Sixth Generation. 1310.
1) Selma A. Eversole, b. Nov. 20, 1894, m Thomas E Henley, June 8. 1924 Address· Angola, Ill, R. D
1 Robert Samuel Henley, b June 5, 1927
2 Roger Philip Henley, b. July 30, 1930.

No. 1360. Sixth Generation. 1310.
2) Miriam Grace Eversole, b Feb 16, 1900, m. June 10, 1922, Ralph Byron Boyer. Dairy and ice cream Paris, Ill

No. 1362. Sixth Generation. 1310.
4) Mary Etta Eversole, b July 14, 1905, m William Burten Henley, Dec 19, 1925. Illinois Central traveling inspector. Address: 2229 E 7th St., Chicago, Ill.
1 Richard Burten Henley, b Oct 5, 1933

No. 1363. Sixth Generation. 1312.
1) Lenore Eversole, b. April 13, 1900, m June 4, 1923, Richard Stoner Fisher, b. Dec 22, 1900. Address: 927 N. Main St., Fostoria, O. Housewife Christian Church
1. Eugene Albert Fisher, b April 7, 1927

No. 1364. Fourth Generation. 30.
1) Jacob Breneman, b. Jan. 29, 1824, near Edom, Va. He died Nov. 18, 1908 He married Catherine Shank, b April 7, 1823, near Broadway, Va. She died Oct, 1894, both are buried in the Weaver cemetery near Oronogo, Mo Mennonites. They lived in Joplin, Mo
1 Samuel Breneman, b Dec 2, 1846 No 1365
2 Anna Breneman, b. Aug 18, 1851. No. 1366.
3. Mary M Breneman, b Dec 17, 1853, single
4 Bettie Breneman, b Nov 16, 1857. No 1367.
5 Sophiah Breneman, b July 17, 1860. No. 1368.
6 Sarah C Breneman, b Mar 13, 1865 No 1369
7 Abraham Daniel Breneman, b. and d. in infancy.
Mary M Breneman lives at Purcell, Mo Baptist

No. 1365. Fifth Generation. 1364.

1) Samuel S. Breneman, b. Dec. 2, 1846, in Rockingham Co, Va, m. June 29, 1879, Kate Haycraft. Samuel died Dec. 25, 1908. Gardener at Webb City, Mo. Methodists No children.

No. 1366. Fifth Generation. 1364.

2) Anna Breneman, b Aug 18, 1851, in Rockingham Co., Va., m. Oct. 25, 1874, Joseph G Good. Farmers in active life at Oronogo, Mo., but now retired and living at Hesston, Kans Mennonites He is a deacon.

1 Jay Good, b Sept 11, 1875. No 1402
2 Oliver Good, b. Jan. 11, 1878. No. 1404.
3 Elias Good, b Feb 23, 1880, d Aug 16, 1881
4 Leroy Good, b. June 15, 1882. No. 1405.
5. Amos Good, b. Nov. 18, 1884. No. 1406.
6. Sarah C. Good, b Oct 1, 1887 No. 1407
7 Mary E Good, b Jan 29, 1890, single.
8 Mark Good, b Nov 18, 1892. No 1408

Mary Esther Good has been many years a teacher at Hesston College, now at Golden, Colo. Her permanent address is Hesston, Kans.

No. 1367. Fifth Generation. 1364.

4) Bettie Breneman, b Nov 16, 1857, in Rockingham Co, Va., m. William Olsen, b May 22, 1853 Address. Carl Junction, Mo Methodists.

1 Leslie L Olsen, b Oct 18, 1889 No 1411.
2. Emory H. Olsen, b Aug 24, 1891, single

No. 1368. Fifth Generation. 1364.

5) Sophiah Breneman, b July 17, 1860, in Va, d Oct 5, 1921, m. Sept 21, 1884, William Jordon Farmer at Wray, Colo Buried in Grandview cemetery, Wray, Colo

1 Leonard Jordon, b. Sept. 6, 1886
2 Florence Jordon, b Feb 22, 1891 No 1428
3 Clark Jordon, b April 19, 1894. No 1429
4 Edith Jordon, b Feb 7, 1896

No. 1369. Fifth Generation. 1364.

6) Sarah C Breneman, b Mar 13, 1865, m Aug 24, 1892, William Gunning, he died in 1926 He operated a flour mill at Webb City, Mo

1 Fern E. Gunning, b. June 23, 1893. No. 1412.
2 Latta E. Gunning, b Aug 9, 1898. No. 1413.
3 Treva C Gunning, b ——————, single

No. 1370. Fourth Generation. 30.

2) Daniel Breneman, b. ——————, 1826, near Edom, Va., m. Catherine Hoover, b ——————, 1840 He died in 1902 and she died in 1906. Buried in the Oak Grove cemetery in Rockingham Co, Va.

1. Anna L Breneman, b April 10, 1872 No 1371
2 Abram D Breneman, b Jan 3, 1874. No. 1372
3 John R. Breneman, b Feb 28, 1876 No. 1373
4 Syram R Breneman, b July 3, 1879 No 1374
5 David E Breneman, b April 3, 1883 No 1375

No. 1371. Fifth Generation. 1370.

1) Annie Breneman, b April 10, 1872, m Frank Caldwell Address Fulks Run, Va No issue

No. 1372. Fifth Generation. 1370.

2) Abram D. Breneman, b Jan. 3, 1874, m Clara Cline Turner Address: Genoa, Va No issue

No. 1373. Fifth Generation. 1370.

3) John R Breneman, b Feb. 28, 1876, m Emma Turner Address Cootes Store, Va Merchant. No issue.

No. 1374. Fifth Generation. 1370.

4) Syram R. Breneman. b July 3, 1879, in Rockingham Co, Va Single Railway mail clerk Address 914 Mass Ave, N W, Washington, D. C

No. 1375. Fifth Generation. 1370.

5) David E. Breneman, b April 3, 1883, in Rockingham Co, Va, m Sibert Noon Address. Kenasha, Wis, Sibert Room Staunton 2320 Rosevelt Rd No issue

No. 1376. Fourth Generation. 30.

3) Elizabeth Breneman, b. Mar, 1830, near Edom, Va, d July 5, 1893, m. David Baker, b. Nov. 6, 1830, d. Mar 16, 1895. They moved from Rockingham Co, Va, to Milford, Kans, in 1866, where they died and were buried. Address was Milford, Kans.

1. Abraham William Baker, b Mar 20, 1852, single No 1430
2. Hannah Mary Baker, b Jan. 15, 1857 No 1431
3. John Riley Baker, b Jan 7, 1859 No 1437
4 Edward Baker, b Dec. 9, 1865 No. 1438

No. 1377. Fourth Generation. 30.

4) Sophiah Breneman, b April 2, 1840, near Edom, Va, d. May 15, 1919, m John Fawley, b. Aug 1, 1834, d Nov. 1, 1917. They moved from Rockingham Co, Va., to Milford, Kans, in 1866, where they lived and died Buried at Milford, Kans., which was their address. Farmers

1. Abraham Fawley, b April 21, 1859, never married No 1439.
2 Ashby Fawley, b. Oct 27, 1861. No 1440.

No. 1378. Fourth Generation. 30.

5) Anna Breneman, b. Jan. 22, 1832, near Edom, Va, d. Dec. 13, 1902; she married Joseph Mitchael, b ————. Address was Cherry Grove, Va. Buried in the Reedy cemetery.

1. Jacob Mitchael, b. ————. No. 1381.
2. Perry Mitchael, b. ————. No 1382.
3. Mary Catherine Mitchael, b. Aug. 14, 1853. No. 1383.

No. 1379. Fourth Generation. 30.

6) Abraham Breneman, Jr, b Mar. 3, 1835, near Edom, Va, d. May 14, 1894, m. Mary Hoover, b. Dec 9, 1837, d ————, 1896 Both were buried at the Trissels Church. Mennonites.

1. David M. Breneman, b Mar. 23, 1858 No. 1426.
2. John William Breneman, b. Dec 20, 1859. No 1392.
3. Hannah V. Breneman, b Feb. 13, 1862, never married
4. Delilah C. Breneman, b June 3, 1865 No 1394
5 Mary E. Breneman, b. Jan. 26, 1867, never married.
6. Abraham H. Breneman, b Jan. 27, 1869 No 1396
7. Jacob R. Breneman, b Aug 7, 1872 No 1399
8 Dasie Ellen Breneman, b Dec 19, 1874 No 1401

No. 1380. Fourth Generation. 30.

7) Mary Breneman, b —————, m Calvin Sprinkle, b. ————— No issue.

No. 1381. Fifth Generation. 1378.

1) Jacob Mitchell, b —————, m Susan Click, b. ————— They lived in Rockingham Co, Va

1. Viola Mitchell, b. —————
2. Charles Mitchell, b —————.

No. 1382. Fifth Generation. 1378.

2) Perry Mitchell, b —————, m ————— He separated from his wife and moved west They had issue

No. 1383. Fifth Generation. 1378.

3) Mary Catherine Mitchell, b Aug 14, 1853, m. Franklin Monroe Stinespring, b. Nov 11, 1848 Mary died Dec. 13, 1902 Franklin died Sept 13, 1925 They were buried in Linville Creek cemetery.

1 Joseph M. Stinespring, b. Aug 22, 1873 No 1384.
2. Curtis Price Stinespring, b. Mar 7, 1877. No. 1386
3 Anna Myrtle Stinespring, b Oct. 7, 1879 No 1387
4 Louella Stinespring, b Aug 25, 1881 No 1388
5 John Stinespring, b Feb 18, 1883. No. 1389
6. Berlin Stinespring, b Oct 1, 1886 No. 1390
7 Daphna Stinespring, b Dec 27, 1894 No 1391

No. 1384. Sixth Generation. 1383.

1) Joseph M. Stinespring, b Aug. 22, 1873, m Sept 14, 1898, Emma R Ritchie. Address: Harrisonburg, Va, 264 W Market St Merchant. United Brethren Church

1 William F Stinespring, b Sept. 24, 1901. No 1385.

No. 1385. Seventh Generation. 1384.

1) William F. Stinespring, b Sept 24, 1901, m Mary F. Albright.

Mr. Stinespring was a student at the Virginia University and the Yale University where he received his B A degrees. He expected to sail June 22, 1932, for a year's research work in Palestine on a fellowship by Yale University, where he will be granted his Ph.D. degree, with headquarters at Jerusalem While there he will visit and study excavation work now in progress at Tel Beit Mirsim in southern Palestine, Jerash in east Jordan, and Antioch in Syria.

1 William Forest Stinespring, b Mar 16, 1929.

No. 1386. Sixth Generation. 1383.

2) Curtis Price Stinespring, b Mar. 7, 1877, m April 23, 1910, Mary Green, b Nov 15, 1888 Druggist. United Brethren Address: Cornelia, Habersam Co, Ga

1 Curtis Price Stinespring, Jr, b Oct 29, 1915
2 John Franklin Stinespring, b. May 23, 1918.
3 Ruth Cannon Stinespring, b April 10, 1922
4 Mary Sue Stinespring, b Mar 25, 1925
5. Elizabeth Ann Stinespring, b. Mar 25, 1929

No. 1387. Sixth Generation. 1383.

3) Anna Myrtle Stinespring, b. Oct 7, 1879, m Russell Fristae Farmer Methodists Address· Sharon, Md

1 Monroe Fristae, b —————.

2. Joseph Fristae, **b.** ——————.
3. Headley Fristae, **b.** ——————.
4. Mitchell Fristae, b ——————.
5. Everett Fristae, b ——————.
6 Louise Fristae, b ——————.
7 Minnie Fristae, b ——————.
8. Anna May Fristae, b ——————

No. 1388. Sixth Generation. 1383.

4) Louella Stinespring, b Aug 25, 1881, m Frederick Black Address: Staunton, Va. Farmer.

1. Archibold Black, b ——————
2 John Roy Black, b ——————.
3 Frederick Black, Jr., b. ——————.
4. Daphna Black, b. ——————.
5 Mary Jean Black, b ——————.

No. 1389. Sixth Generation. 1383.

5) John Stinespring, b Feb 18, 1883 He died Aug. 31, 1923, m. Katherine Miller, b ——————. One baby died in infancy

No. 1390. Sixth Generation. 1383.

6) Berlin Stinespring, b. Oct 1, 1886, m Irene ——————. Insurance agent. Address: Huntington, W. Va., General Delivery.

1. Berlin Stinespring, Jr., b. ——————.

No. 1391. Sixth Generation. 1383.

7) Daphna Stinespring, b Dec 27, 1894, m Jan 17, 1917, John Walker Chenault, b. June 3, 1893. Railroad agent, post master, merchant. United Brethren and Baptist. Address: Daphna, Va Burial place Linville Creek cemetery.

1. Dorothy Elizabeth Chenault, b. May 9, 1921.

No. 1392. Fifth Generation. 1379.

2) John William Breneman, b Dec 20, 1859, m. (1st) Mary Wine, b ——————. She died. He married (2nd) Belle Turner, b. ——————. Address Broadway, Va.

1. Lizzie Ellen Breneman, b. Oct. 24, 1885, died in her teens.
   (From second marriage)
2 Katherine Rebecca Breneman, b Mar 12, 1895. No. 1393.
3 Howard Calvin Breneman, b. Sept. 2, 1901, d. Sept. 22, 1903.
4. Spencer Clarence Breneman, b Mar 12, 1903
5. Wilson Raymond Breneman, b. Sept. 17, 1914.

No. 1393. Sixth Generation. 1392.

2) Katherine Rebecca Breneman, b Mar 12, 1895, m Noah Spitzer Address Broadway, Va.

No. 1394. Fifth Generation. 1379.

4) Delilah C. Breneman, b June 3, 1865, m Aug. 16, 1884, Benjamin F Weaver, b May 29, 1862 He died Dec 9, 1918 Related, see No 389.

1 Willie A Weaver, b April 8, 1886 No 1395

No. 1395. Sixth Generation. 1394.

1) Willie A Weaver, b April 8, 1886, m Cora A Wilson, b April 13, 1891 They were married Nov. 20, 1910 Address Oronogo, Mo Farmer

No. 1396. Fifth Generation. 1379.

6) Abraham H. Breneman, b. Jan 27, 1869, in Va., m. Mar. 13, 1889, Mary V. Weaver, b. July 28, 1866, in Va. Abraham died May 13, 1893. Buried at Weaver cemetery near Oronogo, Mo Address was Oronogo, Mo. Farmer. Mennonites. Related.

1. Bessie E Breneman, b Dec. 13, 1889. No. 399.
2. Zaidee Alice Breneman, b Jan. 11, 1892 No. 400

No. 1399. Fifth Generation. 1379.

8) Jacob R. Breneman, b Aug 7, 1872, in Va, m Dorcas Aubry Address: Fulks Run, Va

1. Mae Zella Breneman, b May 6, 1903 No. 1400.

No. 1400. Sixth Generation. 1399.

1) Mae Zella Breneman, b May 6, 1903, m Robert Liskey

No. 1401. Fifth Generation. 1379.

8). Daisy Ellen Breneman, b Dec 19, 1878, d. Jan 26, 1928, m. July 11, 1904, Irvin C. Kutz, b. June 28, 1883 Address· Oronogo, Mo. Farmer Methodists

1 Mary Catherine Kutz, b April 18, 1905. No 1409.
2. Vera Adaline Kutz, b. May 24, 1907. No. 1410
3 Charles Jacob Kutz, b Jan 20, 1909
4 Alfred William Kutz, b June 7, 1915

No. 1402. Sixth Generation. 1365.

1) Jay Good, b. Sept 11, 1875. in Jasper Co., Mo., m. Oct, 1903, Myrtle Roloson, b. ———, 1879 She died May 8, 1920. Buried at Mt Hope cemetery, Webb City, Mo Address Doniphan, Mo Lumber dealer. Methodists

1. Ruth Good, b May 2, 1904 No. 1403.
2 Earl R Good, b Feb 5, 1910
3 Anetta Good, b May 9, 1914

No. 1403. Seventh Generation. 1402.

1) Ruth Good, b May 2, 1904, in Jasper Co, Mo., m ——— Walmer. They live in St Louis, Mo, 4265 Russell Ave. No issue.

No. 1404. Sixth Generation. 1366.

2) Oliver Good, b Jan 11, 1878, in Jasper Co, Mo, m. Anna Wilson. Address: Oronogo, Mo. No children.

No. 1405. Sixth Generation. 1365.

4) Leroy Good, b. June 15, 1882, at Oronogo, Mo, m Oct. 20, 1921, Mary Nunamaker, b Jan. 25, 1884. Address: Sterling, Ill. Farmer. Mennonites.

1 Frances Arlene Good, b. Sept. 5, 1924

No. 1406. Sixth Generation. 1366.

5) Amos Good, b Nov 18, 1884, at Oronogo, Mo, m Oct 28, 1926, Lula May Miller, b. Nov 27, 1886 Address 118 El Medio St, Ventura, Calif Shoe cobbler. Presbyterian

1. Gene Frances Good, b Oct. 21, 1927

No. 1407. Sixth Generation. 1366.

6) Sarah C. Good. b. Oct. 1, 1887, at Oronogo, Mo., m. Oct. 11, 1908, A. L. Downs, b. April 23, 1888 Address Lake Charles, La Mechanic Mennonites

1. Lester Downs, b. ———.
2 Andrew Downs, b. ———

229

No. 1408. Sixth Generation. 1366.

8) Mark Good, b. Nov. 18, 1892, at Oronogo, Mo., m. Jan. 7, 1917, Viola Tweedy, b. Aug. 16, 1896. Oronogo, Mo , R 1 Carpenter. Mennonites.

1. Lucille Ketureh Good, b. May 2, 1920.
2. Lawrena Milford Good, b Sept. 29, 1921
3. Leland Leslie Good, b. Sept. 9, 1925.

No. 1409. Sixth Generation. 1401.

1) Mary Catherine Kutz, b April 18, 1905, at Oronogo, Mo., m. Mar. 4, 1929, Gerald Hovey, of Alba, Mo. Address· Oronogo, Mo.

1. Lois Marie Hovey, b. Sept. 15, 1930.
2 Charles Eugene Hovey, b. June 12, 1932

No. 1410. Sixth Generation. 1401.

2) Vera Adaline Kutz, b. May 24, 1907, at Oronogo, Mo , m J. H. Smith of Jasper, Mo , Nov. 7, 1929.

1. Lloyd Edward Smith, b. July 28, 1933.

No. 1411. Sixth Generation. 1367.

1) Leslie Leland Olson, b Oct 18, 1889, near Oronogo, Mo , m. April 14, 1920, Rose M. Walker, b Aug 22, 1894, d. Mar 14, 1932 Life insurance agent Address: Carl Junction, Mo. Burial place at Kennett, Mo No children

No. 1412. Sixth Generation. 1369.

1) Fern Gunning, b June 23, 1893, near Oronogo, Mo., m Lawrence E Vaughn Dairy farmer at Oronogo, Mo.

1. William M. Vaughn, b. April 21, 1914.
2 Catherine R. Vaughn, b ————
3. Lawrence E Vaughn, b July 16, 1918
4. Mildred L Vaughn, b Aug. 14, 1921

No. 1413. Sixth Generation. 1369.

2) Latta E. Gunning, b Aug. 9, 1898, near Oronogo, Mo , m Charles A Holden, an attorney at Tulsa, Okla

No. 1414. Fourth Generation. 31.

1) Emmanuel Grove, b. ————, 1838, d ————, 1925, m. Eliza Young. No children Buried in Newcomers cemetery, Darke Co., O

No. 1415. Fourth Generation. 31.

2) David Grove, b. Mar. 23, 1837, near Edom, Va. During the Civil War he with his brother Emmanuel, came to Darke Co., O , to escape services in the Southern army. Here he married Hannah Miller of Trotwood, O., b. Sept. 8, 1846. She died in 1896. He later married in 1897 Lydia Sease at Arcanum, O. No issue to this union David died Oct 10, 1929, at the age of over 92 years His second companion died in 1931 All were buried in Newcomers cemetery, Darke Co., O.

1. Elizabeth Grove, b. 1864, d 1880.
2. David Grove, Jr., b. June 30, 1865 No. 1416
3. Levi Grove, b. April 7, 1867. No. 1417.
4. Samuel Grove, b Sept. 8, 1869 No 1422.
5 Edwin Grove, b Nov 23, 1875 No. 1425.

No. 1416. Fifth Generation. 1415.

2) David Grove, Jr , b. June 30, 1865, in Darke Co , O , m. Emma Swanson, b Dec 21, 1875, in Sweden They were married at Long Beach, Calif., where

they still reside. Christian Church   Address. 334 E. 21st St , Long Beach, Calif. No children.

No. 1417. Fifth Generation. 1415.

3) Levi Grove, b April 7, 1867, in Darke Co , O., m. Elmira Hooker in 1888 in Darke Co She died in 1920 Address. Arcanum, O. Old German Baptist. Buried in Darke Co. Farmer.

1. Perry Grove, b. ————, 1889 No 1418.
2 Elsie Grove, b Sept. 8, 1891 No 1419.
3. Anna Grove, b Feb 17, 1898 No 1420
4 Mary Grove, b ————, 1905. No. 1421.

No. 1418. Sixth Generation. 1417.

1) Perry Grove, b ————, 1889, in Darke Co , O , m. ————

No. 1419. Sixth Generation. 1417.

2) Elsie Grove, b Sept 8, 1891, in Darke Co , O., m. in 1911, Harry Stichter, b Aug. 21, 1889 Address. Arcanum, O Farmer Old German Baptist.

1 Ralph Stichter, b Feb 13, 1915.
2 Treva Stichter, b Nov 30, 1916
3 Roy Stichter, b May 7, 1920
4 Ruth Stichter, b April 4, 1922.

No. 1420. Sixth Generation. 1417.

3) Anna Grove, b Feb 17, 1898, in Darke Co , O., m. April 19, 1919, Willis Denlinger, b June 10, 1897 Farmer.

1 Robert Denlinger, b Nov. 10, 1919

No. 1421. Sixth Generation. 1417.

4) Mary Grove, b ————, 1905, in Darke Co., O., m. Jacob Bowman, b.

No. 1422. Fifth Generation. 1415.

4) Samuel Grove, b Sept 8, 1869, in Darke Co , O , m in 1891 Nora Ann Daniels, b Feb 26, 1873. Address Laura, O Farmer.

1. Ambert Grove, b Aug. 8, 1891. No. 1423.
2. Ruby Elizabeth Grove, b July 14, 1898. No. 1424.

No. 1423. Sixth Generation. 1422.

1) Ambert Grove, b. Aug 8, 1891, in Darke Co , O , m. Mar. 26, 1916, Clara Ellen Stickley, b Feb. 24, 1891 Address Laura, O , R. 1. Farmer.

1 Freda Grove, b Jan 23, 1920

No. 1424. Sixth Generation. 1422.

2) Ruby Elizabeth Grove, b July 14, 1898, in Darke Co , O., m. June 8, 1917, Charles Ray Cross, b Aug. 13, 1898 Shop workman. Christian Church.

1 Jean Ellen Cross, b. Feb 6, 1918
2 June Elizabeth Cross, b Oct. 8, 1920

No. 1425. Fifth Generation. 1415.

5) Edwin Grove, b Nov. 23, 1875, in Darke Co , O., m in 1897, May Etter, of Covington, O , b June 12, 1878 Railroader Christian Church Address: East Smithfield St , Bradford, O No children

No. 1426. Fifth Generation. 1379.

1) David Millard Breneman, b Mar 23, 1858, in Va , m. Anna Isabelle Hale, b May 10, 1864 They were married April 11, 1888 Ranching in S. Dak Address Wessington Springs, S Dak Methodists

1. Walter Hale Breneman, b. Aug 5, 1890. No. 1427.
2. Howard David Breneman, b. June 7, 1896.

No. 1427. Sixth Generation. 1426.

1) Walter Hale Breneman, b Aug. 5, 1890, m. June 15, 1915, Edith Levina Eagle, b. ———— She died April 29, 1923 Address: Wessington Springs, S. Dak.
1. Edith Ann Breneman, b April 19, 1917
2. Emogene Breneman, b. Sept. 2, 1918.

No. 1428. Sixth Generation. 1368.

2) Florence Jordon, b Feb. 22, 1891, near Oronogo, Mo , m. July, 1908, Raymond Clarence Goodwin, b. May 27, 1887 Address· 330 6th Ave., N. Wausau, Wis. Dealer in h.gh grade granite
1. Lelia Mary Goodwin, b. Mar 7, 1909.
2 Lloyd Raymond Goodwin, b Dec. 19, 1910
3 Everett E. Goodwin, b. July 11, 1913.
4 Catherine Goodwin, b Aug 3, 1915.
5. Floy Agnes Goodwin, b. July 30, 1916.
6. Luella Sophiah Goodwin, b April 1, 1918.
7. Harry Leroy Goodwin, b. May 31, 1924.

No. 1429. Sixth Generation. 1368.

3) Clark James Jordon, b April 19, 1894, near Oronogo, Mo., m. Oct. 10, 1916, Cleta Edith Price, b Mar. 22, 1898. Address: Wray, Colo Farmer. Methodists.
1 Erma Ruth Jordon, b. May 7, 1919.

No. 1430. Fifth Generation. 1376.

1) Abraham William Baker, b. Mar 20, 18£2, in Rockingham Co , Va , went with his parents from Va. to Milford, Kans , in 1866 where the elder Bakers lived and died. Sometime later Abraham went to Kansas City where it is reported he became pretty well provided with money and possessions. It seems he never married.

No. 1431. Fifth Generation. 1376.

2) Hannah Mary Baker, b Jan 15, 1857, in Va., m. Jan. 15, 1882, John Emmett Denver, b. June 20, ——. Address: Milford, Kans Carpenter. Congregational. Burial ground at Milford, Kans.
1. Linnie Denver, b Dec. 7, 1883. No. 1432.
2. Esther Denver, b. Dec. 11, 1885 No. 1434.
3. Marvin Denver, b Jan. 7, 1893. No. 1435.
4 E. J. Denver, b. July 29, 1895. No. 1436

No. 1432. Sixth Generation. 1431.

1) Linnie Denver, b Dec. 7, 1883, at Milford, Kans., m. ———— Nixon, b. ————.
1. Juanita Nixon, b. ————.
2 Delephone Nixon, b ————.
3. Donald Nixon, b ————
4. Mabel Nixon, b. ————, said to be married.

No. 1434. Sixth Generation. 1431.

2) Esther Denver, b Dec 11, 1885, at Milford, Kans., m. Harry Steinfort, b ————.
1. Marvin Steinfort, b ————, d ————.

2 Helen Steinfort, b ————————.
3 Chester Steinfort, b. ————————

No. 1435. Sixth Generation. 1431.
3) Marvin Denver, b Jan 7, 1893, at Milford, Kans., m. Mazie Steinfort, b. ————————.
   1. Mary Ellen Denver, b ————————, d. ————————.
   2. Alice Mazie Denver, b. ————————

No. 1436. Sixth Generation. 1431.
4) E. J Denver, b July 29, 1895, at Milford, Kans, m. Kate Mellinger. Address: Junction City, Kans. No children.

No. 1437. Fifth Generation. 1376.
3) John Riley Baker, b. Jan 7, 1859, in Rockingham Co, Va, m Ella Florida. No children Address· 3110 Grand Ave, Apartment 102, Kansas City, Mo.

No. 1438. Fifth Generation. 1376.
4) Edson B Baker, b Dec 9, 1865, in Rockingham Co., Va., m. Lucy Neil, b. ———————— He is said to live in Kansas City and have one child.

No. 1439. Fifth Generation. 1377.
1) Abraham Fawley, b April 21, 1859, in Rockingham Co, Va. Unmarried. He lives at Milford, Kans., occupied in farming and stock raising, also in the merchandise business. He is president of the Milford State Bank He and his brother, it is said, own two sections of land near Milford, Kans.

No. 1440. Fifth Generation. 1377.
2) Ashby Fawley, b Oct 16, 1861, in Rockingham Co, Va., m. Feb., 1893, Cornelia Brown, b April 21, 1874, d May 22, 1908. Farmer and stock raiser at Milford, Kans. He is also a director in the bank of which his brother is its president Burial at Milford, Kans. Congregational
   1. John Howard Fawley, b Mar 17, 1902, d May 25, 1921.

No. 1441. Sixth Generation. 1162.
1) Annie E. Lam, b Aug 15, 1869, m Dec 25, 1890, J. C. Armstrong, b Jan. 25, 1869 Address Penn Laird, Va Housekeeper. Methodist Burial ground at McGaheysville, Va.
   1. Wilmer L. Armstrong, b. Sept. 20, 1891. No. 1442.
   2. Loa T. Armstrong, b. Mar 23, 1897 No. 1443.
   3. Ruth E. Armstrong, b Oct 21, 1899 No. 1444
   4. Naomi J. Armstrong, b Aug 3, 1903, d. Mar. 26, 1906

No. 1442. Seventh Generation. 1441.
1) Wilmer L Armstrong, b Sept. 20, 1891, m. Nov 19, 1913, Bertie A Hoover, b Oct 19, 1892. Address Penn Laird, Va. Farmer. Methodists Burial place McGaheysville, Va.
   1. Annie Jane Armstrong, b April 28, 1916, died same day.
   2. Jennings Armstrong, b Oct 5, 1918.
   3. Marion J. Armstrong, b. Mar 19, 1920.
   4. Nellie Armstrong, b. June 23, 1926, d. Jan. 23, 1931.
   5. Helen Armstrong, b. Mar 16, 1928.

No. 1443. Seventh Generation. 1441.
2) Loa T. Armstrong, b. Mar. 23, 1897, m. Aug. 31, 1918, Lida Liskey, b. June 7, 1898 Address· Penn Laird, Va. Carpenter. Methodists.
   1. Nelson Armstrong, b Mar. 24, 1927

No. 1444. Seventh Generation. 1441.

3) Ruth E. Armstrong, b Oct 21, 1899, m Dec 11, 1918, Merle Kisling, b Feb 4, 1894 Address Penn Laird, Va Farmer Methodists Burial ground at McGaheysville, Va

1. Dorothy Kisling, b and d May 5, 1925
2 Nancy Kisling, b April 24, 1926

No. 1445. Sixth Generation. 1162.

2) Laura C Lam, b July 22, 1872, d April 11, 1922, m in 1899, Robert S Crawn, b April 6, 1873, he died July 29, 1927 Farmer Church of the Brethren Address. North River, Va Burial in Mill Creek cemetery

1 Refa V. Crawn, b Aug 17, 1902. No 1446
2 Nellie C. Crawn, b Sept 8, 1905. No 1447
3. Warren S Crawn, b. Jan 23, 1908.

No. 1446. Seventh Generation. 1445.

1) Refa V. Crawn, b. Aug 17, 1902, m ——————, —————— Liskey

No. 1447. Seventh Generation. 1445.

2) Nellie C. Crawn, b. Sept 8, 1905, m Oct. 21, 1924, Frank M. Cline, b Oct. 19, 1899. Address: Weyers Cave, Va Farmer Church of the Brethren

1. Lois C. Cline, b. Nov 12, 1925.
2. Welty C. Cline, b. Feb 17, 1927.
3. Lawrence R. Cline, b. Dec. 25, 1931.

No. 1448. Sixth Generation. 1162.

4) Ada Susan Lam, b. Feb 28, 1877, m Dec 28, 1904, Winfred Baker, b in 1880 Address: Mt Crawford, Va. Farmer Methodists

1. Nellie Arvetta Baker, b ——————, 1915

No. 1449. Sixth Generation. 1162.

5) John W Lam, b. Oct 8, 1879, m Aug 16, 1903, Nora H. Lineweaver, b. Mar —, 1879 Address. McGaheysville, Va Painter. Methodists

1 Mabel Evins Lam, b. ——————, 1905.
2 Ethel J. Lam, b. ——————, 1907
3. Lucille Lam, b. ——————. 1909.
4. Alda Lam, b. ——————, 1911

No. 1450. Sixth Generation. 1162.

8) Sattie E. Lam, b Jan. 1, 1889, m May 8, 1909, Ernest C. Long, b April 12, 1889. Address: West Point, Va Church of the Brethren

1. Ethel C. Long, b July 15, 1914.

No. 1451. Sixth Generation. 1161.

1) Walter Adam Cline, b. Aug 17, 1870, near Versailles, Mo, m. Laura Harrison, b. Mar. 8, 1877, d May 11, 1928 Address: Versailles, Mo Farmer. Methodist Burial in Glenstead cemetery. No children

No. 1452. Sixth Generation. 1161.

2) John Samuel Cline, b. Oct 11, 1874, near Versailles, Mo., d July 16, 1928, m. Jan. 16, 1920, Bessie Gerlb Address· Versailles, Mo Farmer. Methodists Burial in Prairie View cemetery.

1. Aubry D Cline, b. ——————, 1920
2. Sadie Bernice Cline, b. ——————, 1922.
3 William Paul Cline, b ——————, 1925
4. John Stanley Cline, b. ——————, 1926

No. 1453. Sixth Generation. 1161.

3) Sophia Kate Cline, b Mar 8, 1877, near Versailles, Mo., m Dec. 23, 1910, W. Stanley Eyeman, b Dec 7, 1870 Address Versailles, Mo Farmer. Church of the Brethren. Burial place in Prairie View cemetery.

1 Ruth Claudria Eyeman, b April 15, 1912. No 1454.

2 Myrl Katherine Eyeman, b. Sept 5, 1914.

3. Ruby Benson Eyeman, b Sept 15, 1917.

4 Thomas Daniel Eyeman, b June 23, 1919, d. July 21, 1919.

No. 1454. Seventh Generation. 1453.

1) Ruth Claudria Eyeman, b April 15, 1912, near Versailles, Mo., m Aschol Ferguson, Feb. 4, 1930

1 Don C Ferguson, b Nov. 23, 1930.

No. 1455. Sixth Generation. 1160.

1) Mary Elizabeth Cline, b. ——————, m J. H. Hinkle, b ——————.

1. Charles M. Hinkle, b. ——————

2. Walter Hinkle, b. ——————

3 Edgar Hinkle, b. ——————. No. 1456.

4 Lena Hinkle, b ——————. No. 1457.

5. Clarence Hinkle, b. ——————

6. Ruth Hinkle, b. ——————. No 1458

7. Nellie Hinkle, b. —————— No 1459.

8. Pauline Hinkle, b ——————. No 1460.

9 William Hinkle, b ——————.

No. 1456. Seventh Generation. 1455.

3) Edgar Hinkle, b ——————, m ——————

1. Marvin Hinkle, b. ——————

2. Helen Hinkle, b ——————

3. John Hinkle, b. ——————.

4. Ruth Hinkle, b ——————

5 Earl Hinkle, b ——————

6 Paul Hinkle, b ——————.

7. Infant Hinkle, b ——————.

No. 1457. Seventh Generation. 1455.

4) Lena Hinkle, b ——————, m —————— Moore, b. ——————

1. Nancy Moore, b. ——————.

2. Elizabeth Moore, b ——————.

3. Bobby Moore, b ——————.

No. 1458. Seventh Generation. 1455.

6) Ruth Hinkle, b. ——————, m —————— Kooutz, b ——————.

1 Geraldine Kooutz, b ——————

No. 1459. Seventh Generation. 1455.

7) Nellie Hinkle, b ——————, m. —————— Hensley, b. ——————.

1. Welty Hensley, b. ——————

No. 1460. Seventh Generation. 1455.

8) Pauline Hinkle, b. ——————, m. —————— Rodgers, b ——————. No issue.

No. 1461. Sixth Generation. 1160.

2) Lucy E. Cline, b. ——————, m B F Werner, b —————— Address· Alexandria, Va.

1. Wilmer Werner, b ——————. No 1462
2. Ollie K. Werner, b ————— No 1463
3. Infant died —————.
4. Leon Werner, b. —————. No 1464
5. Alvin Werner, b ————.
6 Clara Werner, b ————.

No. 1462. Seventh Generation. 1461.

1) Wilmer Werner, b. —————, m. —————.
1. Wilmer Werner, Jr., b. —————.

No. 1463. Seventh Generation. 1461.

2) Ollie K. Werner, b. —————, m. ——— Sutler, b. —————.
1. Mildred Sutler, b —————
2. Houston Sutler, b. —————.

No. 1464. Seventh Generation. 1451.

4) Leon Werner, b. —————, m —————.
1. James F. Werner, b. —————.

No. 1465. Sixth Generation. 1160.

4) Laura F. Cline, b —————, m. David Layman, b —————. Address: Harrisonburg, Va.
1. Zenith Layman, b. —————.

No. 1466. Sixth Generation. 1160.

5) Thomas F. Cline, b —————, m Ollie Lineweaver, b —————.
Address: McGaheysville, Va
1. Everett Cline, b —————
2. Hensel Cline, b. —————.

No. 1467. Sixth Generation. 1160.

6) Charles D. Cline, b —————, m Mar. 22, 1910, Myrtle Cox, b. Mar. 14, 1881. Address. McGaheysville, Va Farmer. Church of the Brethren.
1. Nancy Grace Cline, b April 13, 1914
2. Wendall Ivan Cline, b. Nov. 14, 1917

No. 1468. Sixth Generation. 1160.

7) Emma Cline, b. —————, m Edward Vernon, b. —————. Address: Pirkey, Va.
1. Carroll Vernon, b. —————.
2 Valley Vernon, b. —————.
3 Reba Vernon, b. —————. No 1469.
4. Marie Vernon, b —————
5. Ralph Vernon, b —————.

No. 1469. Seventh Generation. 1468.

3) Reba Vernon, b —————, m ——— Shifflette.
1. Sylvia Shifflette, b —————.
2. Mildred Shifflette, b. —————.
3. Samuel Shifflette, b. —————.

No. 1470. Sixth Generation. 1160.

8) William E. Cline, b. —————, m Ola Garber, b. —————. Address: Ft. Defiance, Va.
1. Phyllis Cline, b. —————.
2. Elton Cline, b. —————.

3. Quenton Cline, b ————.
4 Paul Cline, b ————

No. 1471. Sixth Generation. 1160.

10) Hattie Cline, b. ————, m George F. Bateman, b. ————.
Formerly of North Platte, Nebr. Address: McGaheysville, Va.
1. Lloyd Bateman, b. ————. No. 1472.
2. Frances Bateman, b ————.

No. 1472. Seventh Generation. 1471.

1) Lloyd Bateman, b ————, m. ————.
1. Connie Bateman, b. ————.

No. 1473. Sixth Generation. 1160.

11) Fleeta V. Cline, b. ————, m Joseph Crickenberger, b. ————.
Address: New Hope, Va.
1. Catherine Crickenberger, b. ————.
2. Orrville Crickenberger, b ————.
3. Isaac Crickenberger, b. ————.

No. 1474. Sixth Generation. 1163.

1) Nellie M. Wampler, b. Aug. 22, 1881, m. ———— Hartman, b. ————.
1. Reba Hartman, b. Aug 12, 1910.
2. Cecil Hartman, b July 13, 1912.

No. 1475. Sixth Generation. 1163.

2) Mamie E. Wampler, b. Feb. 23, 1884, m ———— Rodeffer, b. ————.
1. Leah Rodeffer, b. Aug 21, 1910.
2. William Rodeffer, b Dec. 22, 1912
3. Dorothy Rodeffer, b. Aug 4, 1918.
4. David Rodeffer, b Nov 9, 1924

No. 1476. Sixth Generation. 1163.

3) Lititia J. Wampler, b Dec. 18, 1886, m Charles S Mundy, b. ————.
Address: Harrisonburg, Va., R. 6.
1. Theodore Mundy, b. Feb. 18, 1907. No 1477.
2. Nellie Mundy, b April 23, 1909. No. 3552.
3. D Clement Mundy, b. Jan 4, 1911. No. 3553.
4 Avis Mundy, b Jan 21, 1914. No. 3554.

No. 1477. Seventh Generation. 1476.

1) Theodore Wampler Mundy, b. Feb. 18, 1907, m. Aug. 3, 1930, Arline Margaret Marshal, b Dec. 21, 1908. Address: Harrisonburg, Va. Church of the Brethren.
1. Maxine Margaret Mundy, b Aug 10, 1933.

No. 1478. Sixth Generation. 1163.

5) Leonard Wampler, b. Mar. 30, 1892, m. Thelma Jane Hutton. Address: Warrenton, Va.
1. Norman Wampler, b. Nov. 15, 1921.
2. Leonard S. Wampler, Jr, b. Aug. 16, 1923.

No. 1479. Sixth Generation. 1163.

6) Clinton I. Wampler, b. Jan 13, 1895, m. Lillian Garber, b Aug. 23, 1898.
Address: Port Republic, Va.
1. Stanley Wampler, b June 2, 1917.
2. Julius Wampler, b. Mar. 26, 1922.

237

3. Deyerley Belle Wampler, b Aug 21, 1924
4. Gene Milton Wampler, b Aug. 24, 1937.

No. 1480. Sixth Generation. 1163.

7) Clarence S. Wampler, b Feb. 9, 1899, m Willie Bond, b ————.
Address: McGaheysville, Va
1. Richard Wampler, b Feb. 22, 1930

No. 1481. Sixth Generation. 1164.

1) Florence Elizabeth Cline, b. Sept. 9, 1877, m Dec. 26, 1899, Jacob M.
Rodeffer, b. Mar 20, 1878 Address· Grottoes, Va. Farmer. Church of the Brethren Burial place in Mill Creek cemetery.
1. Justice Rodeffer, b Mar 28, 1901, d Mar. 30, 1901.
2. Charles Ceophus Rodeffer, b. Nov. 4, 1902. No. 1482.
3. Selch Frances Rodeffer, b Mar. 29, 1906
4. Mary Elizabeth Rodeffer, b. Feb. 3, 1915.
5 Paul Ervin Rodeffer, b April 1, 1919

No. 1482. Seventh Generation. 1481.

2) Charles Ceophus Rodeffer, b Nov 4, 1902, m. Jan. 1, 1932, ————
in Texas Address: Mowen, N. C

No. 1483. Sixth Generation. 1164.

2) Etta Viola Cline, b Aug 10, 1879, m Dec 21, 1904, Isaac Jackson Long,
b. July 10, 1881 Address Port Republic, Va. Farmer Church of the Brethren No children.

No. 1484. Sixth Generation. 1164.

3) Mary Catherine Cline, b Feb 16, 1885, m Nov 18, 1914, William W Cox,
b. Aug 10, 1888 Address Fairfax, Va. Farmer Church of the Brethren
1. Dorothy Eliza Cox, b Jan 27, 1917.
2. Frances Geneva Cox, b July 27, 1919
3. Norman S. Cox, b June 14, 1924

No. 1485. Sixth Generation. 1164.

4) Jacob Hubert Cline, b July 29, 1888, m Oct 9, 1912, Edna C Mundy, b.
Aug 7, 1888. Farmer. Church of the Brethren No children

No. 1436. Sixth Generation. 1164.

7) Earl Daniel Cline, b Feb 7, 1904, m Sept 18, 1928, Mary N Diehl, b.
———— Employe of wholesale house at Harrisonburg, Va., which is his address.
1. Nancy Jean Cline, b. April 30, 1933.

No. 1487. Sixth Generation. 1165.

1) Stella M. Cline, b Sept. 1, 1873, d Dec. 13, 1929. She married William
Trobaugh. Address: North River, Va
1. Ray Trobaugh, b ————.

No. 1488. Sixth Generation. 1165.

2) Saylor B. Cline, b. Dec. 30, 1874, d. May —, 1917, m. Odie Trobaugh
Address: North River, Va No children

No. 1489. Sixth Generation. 1165.

3) Ottie E. Cline, b. Dec. 31, 1876, m Dec. 28, 1904, Marvin B Hartman,
b. Feb. 22, 1880. Address· North River, Va Farmer Brethren Burial in Mill
Creek cemetery in Rockingham Co , Va.

1. Virginia C. Hartman, b Sept 7, 1903. No. 1490
2 Russell I Hartman, b June 14, 1907.

No. 1490. Seventh Generation. 1489.

1) Virginia C Hartman, b Sept 7, 1903, m. Sept 8, 1929, Theodore C Crawn, b April 12, 1905
1 Elnora Virginia Crawn, b June 8, 1931

No. 1491. Sixth Generation. 1165.

4) Florence A. Cline, b Jan 3, 1882, m. Newton Mundy. Address: Fort Republic, Va.
1 Margaret Mundy, b. ——————— No 1492
2 Bessie Mundy, b. ———————.
3 Wilber Mundy, b ———————.

No. 1492. Seventh Generation. 1491.

1) Margaret Mundy, b ———————, m Paul Simmers, b. ———————
1 Bettie May Simmers, b ———————
2 Harry Lee Simmers, b ———————.

No. 1493. Sixth Generation. 1165.

6) Herman M. Cline, b Feb 10, 1889, m Ethel Cline, b ——————— No children.

No. 1494. Sixth Generation. 1166.

1) Saylor Daniel Good, b Mar 12, 1876, m Dec 30, 1900, Sallie K Sniteman, b July 29, 1876, at South English, Ia Address 21 S Webster St, Naperville, Ill Cabinetmaker Brethren
1 John Jay Good, b. Oct. 2, 1901 No 1495.
2 Eva Fern Good, b Nov 7, 1902 No 1496
3 Harry William Good, b Oct. 25, 1909. No 1497

No. 1495. Seventh Generation. 1494.

1) John Jay Good, b Oct 2, 1901, m Frances Youngman, b Oct 25, 1905
1 John Jay Good, Jr, b. Oct. 24, 1926.
2 Robert Youngman Good, b Oct 6, 1928
3 Caryl Marie Good, b April 6, 1930.

No. 1496. Seventh Generation. 1494.

2) Eva Fern Good, b Nov. 7, 1902, m Paul Malenberg
1 J. Edward Malenberg. b Aug 16, 1933

No. 1497. Seventh Generation. 1494.

3) Harry William Good, b Oct 25, 1909, m Mary Louise Eckert
1. Sallie Lu Good, b. July 15, 1933

No. 1498. Sixth Generation. 1166.

2) William Cowan Good, b Aug 27, 1878, m (1st) Grace Early (deceased), m (2nd) Ethel Crickenberger.
1. Mary Good, b. ———————
2. Welty Good, b ———————.
3. Lois Good, b. ———————.
4 Naomi Good, b ———————, d ———————
   (From second wife)
5. Isaac Good, b. ———————.
6 John M. Good, b ———————.
7 Lawrence Good, b. ———————.

8. Marguerite Good, b. ————————.

9 Lorraine Good, b. ————————.

No. 1499. Sixth Generation. 1166.

3) Dora Susan Good, b. Feb. 10, 1880, in Va., m. Jan. 3, 1905, Benjamin S. Rodeffer, b July 9, 1881 Address: Port Republic, Va Farmer. Church of the Brethren.

1. Theresa C Rodeffer, b. Aug. 12, 1907.

2. Fravel D Rodeffer, b. Sept 9, 1908. No. 1500

3 M Kathleen Rodeffer, b May 5, 1914.

No. 1500. Seventh Generation. 1499

2) Fravel D Rodeffer, b Sept. 9, 1908, m. Laura Showers, May 27, 1935. Address: 143 N. Chestnut St., Palmyra, Pa

No. 1501. Sixth Generation. 1166.

4) Ernest Michael Good, b Nov 11, ——, d. in 1929, m. Vada Rodeffer, b. ————————.

1. Clifford Good, b. ————————.

2. Vera Good, b. ————————.

3 Orville Good, b. ————————.

4. Sylvia Good, b. ————————.

5. Edsel Good, b ————————.

No. 1502. Sixth Generation. 1166.

5) Sattie Della Good, b June —, 1890, m Claude Mundy, b. ————————

1. Thersa Mundy, b. ————————.

2. Leon Mundy, b. ————————.

3. Marie Mundy, b. ————————.

4 Mildred Mundy, b. ————————.

5. Claude Mundy, Jr., b ————————.

No. 1503. Sixth Generation. 1166.

6) Clarence D. Good, b May 12, 1896, m July 9, 1899, Fern Collier, b. May 9, 1899 Address· Earlville, Ill. Laborer. Church of the Brethren.

1. Collier Myers Good, b June 9, 1920.

2. Fay Ann Good, b. July 15, 1922.

3 Clarence DeWitt Good, Jr, b. Nov. 2, 1925.

No. 1504. Sixth Generation. 1166.

7) Ollie Belle Good, b July —, 1900, m George Nicholes.

1. Odessa Nicholes, b ————————.   ·

2 Billie Nicholes, b. ————————, d ————————.

3. Bobby Nicholes, b ————————

4. Edsel Nicholes, b ————————.

No. 1505. Sixth Generation. 1167.

1) Ercell L. Cline, b Nov 6, 1892, m G. B Howell Address: Woodville, Pa., care of Pa. State Hospital.

1. H. H. Howell, b ————————.

2. Lillian Howell, b ————————.

3. Gladys Howell, b ————————

No. 1506. Sixth Generation. 1167.

2) Hubert S. Cline, b. Nov 18, 1894, m June 5, 1919, Irma L Harman, b. Apr. 28, 1898 Address: Mt Sidney, Va Postmaster United Brethren.

1 H Carroll Cline, b Mar 29, 1920
2 Charline W Cline, b Mar 25, 1923
3 JaNelle F A Cline, b July 9, 1928

No. 1507. Sixth Generation. 1167.

3) Omega C Cline, b Dec 21, 1896, m F E Landes Address. Lebanon, Pa
1. Lester Landes, b ————————
2. Cleo Landes, b ————————
3 Dorris Landes, b ————————
4 Charmaine Landes, b ————————.

No. 1508. Sixth Generation. 1167.

4) Arline M Cline, b July 5, 1899, m B F Reed. Address: Lebanon, Pa.
1. Charlotte Reed, b ————————.
2. Everett Reed, b ————————.
3. Phyllis Reed, b ————————
4 Carson Reed, b ————————
5. Johnnie Reed, b. ————————
6 Geraldine Reed, b ————————

No. 1509. Sixth Generation. 1167.

5) Clarence E Cline, b Aug 14, 1901, m Hazel Sheets Address: Rolla, Va.
1 Gay Cline, b ————————
2 Melvin Cline, b ————————
3 Helen Cline, b ————————.
4. Clarence E Cline, Jr, b ————————
5. Shirley Cline, b ————————

No. 1510. Sixth Generation. 1167.

6) Leonard D Cline, b Oct 3, 1903, m ———————— Address: Dayton, Va.
1. Raymond Cline, b ————————.
2 Leona Cline, b ————————.

No. 1511. Sixth Generation. 1167.

7) Bessie V Cline, b Sept 23, 1905, m. Aug 1, 1924, Chester M Dilks. Address Renova, Pa.
1 Charles Raymond Dilks, b June 16, 1933

No. 1512. Sixth Generation. 1167.

8) Raymond A Cline, b July 31, 1908, m ————————. Address: Jenkinstown, Pa
1 Josephine Cline, b ————————

No. 1513. Sixth Generation. 1568.

1) Maud Wampler, b Nov 28, 1884, m. John Diehl Address. West Wolf St., Harrisonburg, Va Laborer Brethren
1. Marie Diehl, b May 9, 1909. No 1514
2. Oliver Diehl, b Aug. 29, 1910
3 Mabel Diehl, b Nov 9, 1911
4. Fay Diehl, b Oct 28, 1914. No 1515
5 Doyd Diehl, b July 8, 1917

No. 1514. Seventh Generation. 1513.

1) Marie Diehl, b May 9, 1909, m ———— Quick.
1 Dorothy Maxine Quick, b July 9, 1929

No. 1515. Seventh Generation. 1513.
4) Fay Diehl, b Oct 28, 1914, m ———— Milstead
1. Roland Milstead, b May 2, 1933.

No. 1516. Sixth Generation. 1168.
2) Mollie Wampler, b July 8, 1886, m John Martz Address Reezletown,
Va. Farmer. Brethren.
1. Mervil Martz, b Sept 13, 1908
2. Raymond Martz, b Mar 11, 1910
3. Carlton Martz, b Oct 30, 1912.
4 Everett Martz, b May 15, 1916.
5. Jay Martz, b Jan 18, 1919
6. Galen Martz, b Feb 14, 1923

No. 1517. Sixth Generation. 1168.
3) Whitfield E Wampler, b Mar 28, 1889, m Aug 4, 1908, Nora B Riddle,
b. Mar. 4, 1891. Address Pottstown, Pa Farming Brethren.
1. Francis Marion Wampler, b Oct 6, 1910. No 1518.
2. Dee Franklin Wampler, b Mar 25, 1911 No 1519
3. Mildred Leanna Wampler, b. Oct. 22, 1916
4. Lucille Susan Wampler, b July 6, 1919
5. Whitfield E. Wampler, Jr., b June 23, 1924.
6. Lillian Naomi Wampler, b July 5, 1909, d Nov. 20, 1909.

No. 1518. Seventh Generation. 1517.
1) Francis Marion Wampler, b Oct 6, 1910, m Grace Bealer, Aug. 3, 1932
1. Francis Marion, Jr , b ————————

No. 1519. Seventh Generation. 1517.
2) Dee Franklin Wampler, b Mar 25, 1911, m Cloris Miller
1. Deloris Ann Wampler, b ————————

No. 1520. Sixth Generation. 1168.
4) Nina Wampler, b. April 25, 1893, m Ernest Martz, b ———————— Address: 122 N. Chestnut St , Palmyra, Pa. Carpenter. Brethren.
1. Kathryn Martz, b Oct. 19, 1915.

No. 1521. Sixth Generation. 1168.
6) Fleeta Wampler, b Aug 3, 1897, m Dec 24, 1925, Roy F Cline, b Jan.
22, 1894. Address: Linville, Va Farmer Brethren. No issue.

No. 1522. Sixth Generation. 1168.
9) Eula Kathryn Wampler, b Dec 6, 1905, m Benjamin Yeigh Address.
639 Franklin St , Reading, Pa

No. 1523. Fifth Generation. 1039.
1) Annie Laura Bowers, b Nov. 23, 1864, d June 30, 1929, m. Dec 1, 1889,
Samuel J. Hott, b. Feb 8, 1861 Address Channing, Tex Postmaster. Methodists. Burial at Channing, Tex
1. Gladys Maurine Hott, b Oct 24, 1890 No 1524

No. 1524. Sixth Generation. 1523.
1) Gladys Maurine Hott, b Oct 24, 1890, m Aug 28, 1918, Robert A DeFee,
b. Mar 10, 1883 Address Channing, Tex County judge Methodists
1. Robert A DeFee, Jr., b. Oct. 8, 1919
2. William DeFee, b. Sept 5, 1921
3. Dorothy Anne DeFee, b May 2, 1932.

No. 1525. Fifth Generation. 1039.

2) John H. Bowers, b. Oct 25, 1866, d Sept. 9, 1933, m Dec. 1, 1889, Willie M Womack, b. Nov. 22, 1868 Address. 4027 Michaux St, Houston, Tex. Merchant. Methodists. Burial at Hereford, Tex.

1. Doris Elizabeth Bowers, b. Oct. 4, 1893. No 1526
2 Robert Womack Bowers, b. Nov 18, 1896 No 1527
3 John Wayne Bowers, b. Aug 31, 1908.
4. James Clifford Bowers, b Jan 14, 1913, d. Feb 25, 1913.

No. 1526. Sixth Generation. 1525.

1) Doris Elizabeth Bowers, b. Oct 4, 1893, m. Jan. 1, 1917, Walter E. Dunlap, b. Feb. 25, 1892. Real estate and insurance. Methodists. Burial ground at Hereford, Tex. Address: Hereford, Tex

1. Walter E. Dunlap, Jr., b Nov. 12, 1917, died same day
2. William Dean Dunlap, b. July 27, 1921.
3 Elizabeth Ann Dunlap, b July 9, 1926.

No. 1527. Sixth Generation. 1525.

2) Robert Womack Bowers, b Nov 18, 1896, m Feb 17, 1917, Maggie Ray Stanley, b. Oct. 30, 1896. Address Alvin, Tex Grocery merchant Baptists.

1. Margaret Elizabeth Bowers, b Nov 7, 1920
2 Robert Stanley Bowers, b April 8, 1922

No. 1528. Fifth Generation. 1039.

3) Thomas Edward Bowers, b May 30, 1869, m. April 12, 1899, Daisy Bellah, b Jan 11, 1879 Address 5741 Goliad Ave, Dallas, Tex Retired Presbyterians.

1 Douglas Bowers, b Feb 2, 1900
2 Dorothy Bowers, b. Nov 6, 1906 No 1529
3 Elizabeth Bowers, b. Sept 3. 1909

No. 1529. Sixth Generation. 1528.

2) Dorothy Bowers, b. Nov 6, 1906, m April 12, 1930, Dr J. M Lyle, b. Feb. 9, 1896 Physician and surgeon Address 2421 Stadium Drive, Fort Worth, Tex Methodists

1 Barbara Lyle, b. Sept 29, 1931
2. Winfred Lyle, b Sept 13, 1934

No. 1530. Fifth Generation. 1039.

4) Mollie Virginia Bowers, b Aug 20, 1871, m April 26, 1899, Samuel C. Raney, b Nov 29, 1862 Cumberland Presbyterians Address Alvord, Tex. Stock farmer. Burial at Alvord. Tex

1 Ione Virginia Raney, b Feb 16, 1900 No 1531
2. Joe Bowers Raney, b. Sept 13, 1901.
3 Frances Inez Raney, b Nov 29. 1902, d July 13, 1913
4 Jack Raney, b May 28, 1904
5. Annie Laura Raney, b Dec 22, 1905 No 1532.
6 Henry Clay Raney, b. Sept 18, 1907.
7. Hazel Louise Raney, b Dec 19, 1909. No 1533
8 Naomi Elizabeth Raney, b Dec 15, 1911, d Oct. 26, 1920.
9 Clyde Arthur Raney, b Nov 22, 1913

No. 1531. Sixth Generation. 1530.

1) Ione Virginia Raney, b Feb 16, 1900, m Nov. 22, 1924, Josh N. Whitaker, b Oct 2, 1895. Dairy Farmer Address Alvord, Tex Church of Christ

1. Daisy Ann Whitaker, b Dec. 12, 1925

No. 1532. Sixth Generation. 1530.

5) Annie Laura Raney, b Dec. 22, 1905, m Jan 17, 1933, Lloyd Strange, b. Feb 23, 1901. Presbyterians Address: Marquez, Tex., R 2. Magnolia Petroleum Co.

No. 1533. Sixth Generation. 1530.

7) Hazel Louise Raney, b Dec. 19, 1909, m June 24, 1934, Clyde W. Thomas, b. Sept. 11, 1909. Address Nocona, Tex. Tailor Baptists.

No. 1534. Fifth Generation. 1089.

7) Joseph Richard Bowers, b Jan 22, 1878, m Oct. 11, 1905, Ethel Bellah, b. Aug. 21, 1880, d April 27, 1931 Address: Denton, Tex. Banking Presbyterians Burial place at Mountain Park cemetery, Saint Joe, Tex.

1 William Herman Bowers, b. Aug. 23, 1908 No. 1535.

No. 1535. Sixth Generation. 1534.

1) William Herman Bowers, b Aug 23, 1908, m. June 9, 1934, Elaine Griggs, b. Feb. 8, 1911. Government employe Presbyterians. Address· 1511 Franklin St., N. E., Washington, D. C.

1. William Joseph Bowers, b. May 17, 1935.

No. 1536. Fifth Generation. 1089.

8) Pearl Elva Bowers, b. April 27, 1880, m Nov 1, 1900, Theodore A. Ross, b. April 24, 1873 Presbyterians Address 601 Ave D , N. W , Childress, Tex Stock farmer.

1. Agnes N. Ross, b April 24, 1902 No. 1537.
2. William T. Ross, b. Feb. 19, 1906. No. 1538.

No. 1537. Sixth Generation. 1536.

1) Agnes N. Ross, b April 24, 1902, m Oct 25, 1927, Herman Smith, b. May 26, 1893. Presbyterian and Baptist Address 311 3rd St , N E , Childress, Tex Ford agency.

1 Herman Ross Smith, b Feb 13, 1929
2. Nellora Ruth Smith, b Mar 10, 1933

No. 1538. Sixth Generation. 1536.

2) William T. Ross, b Feb 19, 1906, m Nov 18, 1933, Ivie Helm, b Mar 19, 1911 Presbyterian and Methodist Address Childress, Tex. Banking

No. 1539. Fifth Generation. 1089.

9) Robert Ashby Bowers, b July 31, 1882, m July 14, 1909, Nannie Peery, b July 20, 1888 Presbyterians Address: Childress, Tex Banking.

1 Charlene Bowers, b. July 25, 1913.
2. Roberta Bowers, b July 1, 1918

No. 1540. Fifth Generation. 1089.

10) Edna Lee Bowers, b July 13, 1885, m Nov. 30, 1905, T. J. Cothren, b. Nov. 27, 1883. Housewife Presbyterian Address: 3144 Mt. View Drive, San Diego, Calif

1. Isla Cothren, b. Nov. 7, 1906. No. 1541
2. Edward Henry Cothren, b Dec. 10, 1908

No. 1541. Sixth Generation. 1540.

1) Isla Cothren, b Nov 7, 1906, m Mar. 15, 1929, Mason M. Ham, b Nov. 28, 1908. Salesman Baptist. Address: 3152 Mt View Drive, San Diego, Calif

1. Joy Isla Ham, b Nov. 5, 1930.
2. Mary Joan Ham, b. Feb 2, 1932
3. Barbara Jean Ham, b Sept 29, 1933

No. 1542. Fourth Generation. 1178.

1) Mary Joanna Landes, b April 27, 1843, d May 11, 1923, m June 8, 1878, William D. Butler. They lived at Greencastle, Ind, where they are buried.

    1. Betty Butler, b ————. No 1542¼

No. 1542¼. Fifth Generation. 1542.

1) Betty Butler, b ————, m. Elbert Mintou They live in Mo.

    1. Mary Joanna Mintou, b ———— No 1542½.

    2. Percy Mintou, b. ————. No. 1542¾

No. 1542½. Sixth Generation. 1542¼.

1) Mary Joanna Mintou, b ————, m. William Brooks, b. ————. Address. 329 S. Oak Park Ave., Oak Park, Ill

No. 1542¾. Sixth Generation. 1542¼.

2) Percy Mintou, b ————, m Vesper Winkler, b. ————. Address: Oak Park, Ill.

    1. Lois Marie Winkler, b ————.

No. 1543. Fourth Generation. 1178.

3) Samuel E. Landes, b. May 22, 1847, d May 6, 1919, m. Jennie Turner, d. ————. They lived at Greencastle, Ind, where they were also buried.

    1. Harry Landes, b. ————, d. ————

    2 Anna Landes, b ————. No 1543¼.

No. 1543¼. Fifth Generation. 1543.

2) Anna Landes, b ————, Greencastle, Ind, m. C I. Frohman. Address 8th St., Columbus, Ind.

    1 Charles Edward Frohman, b. ————, 1922

No. 1544. Fourth Generation. 1178.

4) Sarah Ellen Landes, b Sept 16, 1849, d Mar 2, 1930, m April 3, 1882 S. P. Bowen. Buried at Greencastle, Ind.

    1 Nellie Bowen, b ————, single, d ————

No. 1545. Fourth Generation. 1178.

5) Laura E Landes, b June 2, 1852, d May —, 1901, m. Simpson Stoner, June 23, 1873, at Greencastle, Ind.

    1. Christian E Stoner, b ————. No 1545¼

    2 Edith Stoner, b ————. No. 1545½.

No. 1545¼. Fifth Generation. 1545.

1) Christian E. Stoner, b ————, m Nellie Koessler.

    1. Simpson Stoner, b ————, single at Greencastle, Ind.

    2. Katherine Stoner, b. ————. No. 1545¾.

No. 1545½. Fifth Generation. 1545.

2) Edith Stoner, b ————, d ————, m A A Houck, b. ————, d. ————

    1 Russell Allen Houck, b ————, Unionville, Mo

    2. Hugh Houck, b. ————, St Louis, Mo

    3. Laura Houck, b ————, St. Louis, Mo.

    4 John Houck, b. ————, Indianapolis, Ind

No. 1545¾. Sixth Generation. 1545¼.

2) Katherine Stoner, b ————, m Robert Botorff. Address. 2241 Jackson, San Francisco, Calif.

No. 1546. Fourth Generation. 1178.

6) Katie Alice Landes, b. April 1, 1855, d April 25, 1931, m Jan. 6, 1876, Johnathan Houck, b May 31, 1852, d Jan 10, 1932 Both were buried at Greencastle, Ind. Farmer. Methodists

1 Laura Florence Houck, b Oct. 8, 1883, d May 25, 1899
2 Lloyd Landes Houck, b Oct 12, 1885 No 1552

No. 1547. Fourth Generation. 1178.

7) Albert P. Landes, b. Nov 12, 1857, m Mar 25, 1891, Mary Louise Ellis, b Aug 21, 1867. Painter and decorator. Methodists Address 204 Spring Ave, Greencastle, Ind.

1 Herbert Ellis Landes, b Oct 5, 1894 No 1548
2 Ruth Elizabeth Landes, b July 1, 1896 No 1549

No. 1548. Fifth Generation. 1547.

1) Herbert Ellis Landes, b Oct 5, 1894, m Sept 4, 1919, Wyota Ewing Address 8th S Michigan Ave., Chicago, Ill.

1 Mary Lou Landes, b. Feb 4, 1922
2 John Landes, b May 5, 1923

No. 1549. Fifth Generation. 1547.

2) Ruth Elizabeth Landes, b July 1, 1896, m. W C Ruddell, Oct 15, 1923 Address 2010 7th Ave, Oakland, Calif

No. 1550. Fourth Generation. 1178.

8) Flora Frances Landes, b May 22, 1860, m Dec 21, 1882, James Edgar Houck, at Greencastle, Ind Address Greencastle, Ind Farmer Methodists

1 David Worth Houck, b Jan 13, 1894 No 1551

No. 1551. Fifth Generation. 1550.

1) David Worth Houck, b Jan 13, 1894, m Sept 12, 1920, Norris McPheron, b Aug 3, 1894 Address Greencastle, Ind, R 2 Farmer. Methodists

1 James McPheron Houck, b. Sept 22, 1921

No. 1552. Fifth Generation. 1546.

2) Lloyd Landes Houck, b Oct 12, 1885, m Dec 26, 1920, Marie Houck, b Sept 2, 1897 Address Reelsville, Ind

1 Jonathan Wilson Houck, b May 31, 1923

No. 1553. Fourth Generation. 1178.

10) George Landes, b. Nov 10, 1870, m Mar. 25, 1909, Florence L Greiner, b. Jan. 22, 1868 Address· 126 E Washington St, Greencastle. Ind Fire insurance. Methodists.

1 Mary Florence Landes, b. Feb 26, 1915

No. 1554. Fourth Generation. 33.

1) Ira H. Hildebrand, b June 17, 1869, m Sept 4, 1894, Laura B. Stern, b Aug 12, 1873. Farmer. Christian Church Address Noblesville, Ind, R 6

Note —This being the only posterity of Henry Hildebrand son of Anna Barbara Breneman the posterity of this family ceases with this family record at his death

No. 1555. Fourth Generation. 34.

1) Jacob A Rhodes, b Oct 17, 1831, in Rockingham Co, Va, d Dec —, 1924, m. in 1854 Nellie Snyder, b ————, 1831 They were buried at Santa Barbara, Calif. Christian.

1. David F Rhodes, b ————, 1855 No 1556
2 Mollie Rhodes, b ————, 1857

3 Maggie Rhodes, b ——————, 1860.
4 Perry Rhodes, b. ——————, 1864.
5 Albert Rhodes, b ——————, 1867, d at three days old

No. 1556. Fifth Generation. 1555.
1) David F. Rhodes, b ——————, 1855, m in 1877, Emma Stoner, b. ——————, 1859, d. Jan. 29, 1929 Address: Fort Landersdale, Fla. Mrs Rhodes was a member of the Christian Church; Mr. Rhodes was a Christian Scientist.
   1. C. G. Rhodes, b ——————, 1879, single
   2. Lita Rhodes, b. ——————, 1882 No 1557.
   3. Nora Rhodes, b. ——————, 1887 No 1558
   4 Vera Rhodes, b. ——————, 1890 No 1559.
   5. Ava Rhodes, b ——————, 1892 No 1560

No. 1557. Sixth Generation. 1556.
2) Litha Rhodes, b ——————, 1882, m J D Bryan. Christian Science.
1. Virginia Bryan, b ——————.

No. 1558. Sixth Generation. 1556.
3) Nora Rhodes, b ——————, 1887, m H H Temple, b. ——————. Christian Science.
   1. Constance Temple, b. ——————

No. 1559. Sixth Generation. 1556.
4) Vera Rhodes, b ——————, 1890, m D D Sparks, b ——————. Christian Science
   1. Dean Sparks, b. ——————
   2. Marion Sparks, b ——————.

No. 1560. Sixth Generation. 1556.
5) Ava Rhodes, b ——————, 1892, m F O Davis No children. Christian Science.

No. 1561. Fourth Generation. 34.
2) Henry E Rhodes, b Dec 30, 1833, in Rockingham Co., Va , m (1st) Anna Heatwole, b Mar 9, 1835, d 1867, m (2nd) Julia Hildebrand, b ——————, d ——————, 1929 Anne was buried at Keokuk, Ia , and Julia was buried at Smith Center, Kans. Barber.
   1. Maggie F. Rhodes, b Jan 27, 1856 No 1562
   2 Martin B Rhodes, b ——————, 1858 No. 1563.
   3 Aljernon F Rhodes, b ——————, 1860 No 1564.
   4 David H Rhodes, b ——————, 1862 No 1565
   5 Samuel R Rhodes, b. ——————, 1864 No 1566
   6. Jennie Rhodes, b ——————, 1866 No 1567
     (Second wife)
   7 Henry E. Rhodes, b. Sept 2, 1873 No 1568
   8 Alice B. Rhodes, b Oct 11, 1878 No 1569

No. 1562. Fifth Generation. 1561.
1) Maggie F Rhodes, b Jan 27, 1856, m Joseph Barnett, b ——————, d. —————— She married (2nd) ———— Lowe. They lived at 315 N. 9th, Council Bluffs, Ia She had five children from first marriage, and one son from second marriage. No further report

No. 1563. Fifth Generation. 1561.
2) Martin B Rhodes, b. Dec 24, 1857, m Blanche Wolf, Dec 24, 1896, at Ottawa, Ia Address: Kansas City, Kans., R. 1 It is said that they have three children

247

No. 1564. Fifth Generation. 1561.

3) Algernon F Rhodes, b Dec. 3, 1859, m Kate Chandler. Five children

No. 1565. Fifth Generation. 1561.

4) David H. Rhodes, b Feb 9, 1862, m Clara A Salsgiver, in 1891, at Clarinda, Ia Buried at Wymers, Nebr. Two children

No. 1566. Fifth Generation. 1561.

5) Samuel R. Rhodes, b Feb 2, 1864, d in 1901, m Effie Corbon Buried at Montrose, Mo. Two sons

No. 1567. Fifth Generation. 1561.

6) Jennie E. Rhodes, b. July 27, 1866, d Dec 28, 1925, m A L Davenny Buried at Smith Center, Kans.

No. 1568. Fifth Generation. 1561.

7) Henry E. Rhodes, Jr., b Sept 2, 1873, m Nora Perry, about 1897. Three daughters

No. 1569. Fifth Generation. 1561.

8) Alice B Rhodes, b Oct. 11, 1878, m Charles Weltmer in 1897 He is not living She married (2nd) a Mr. Kimmel in 1930 Three children from first union.

No. 1570. Fourth Generation. 34.

4) Peter Swope Rhodes, b Nov 25, 1838, d Mar 20, 1924, m Isabelle Lawler, b. ——————, d Feb 26, 1910 Mrs Rhodes was buried at Wayne, Mich ; Mr. Rhodes, at Roanoke, Va. Minister in the Christian Church
1. Joseph Samuel Rhodes, b and d in infancy
2 John Ashburn Rhodes, b Dec 24, 1866 No 1571.
3. Medora Elizabeth Rhodes, b Oct 13, 1868 No 1572.
4. Ella Belle Rhodes, b Jan 7, 1870 No 1573.
5. Ernest Benton Rhodes, b and d in infancy
6. William Edmund Rhodes, b Nov 9, 1875. No 1574
7. Alberta Virginia Rhodes, b. May 7, 1877 No 1577
8 Florence F. Rhodes, b. June 3, 1879 No 1579.
9 Mabel S Rhodes, b. 1881, d. 1882.

No. 1571. Fifth Generation. 1570.

2) John Ashburn Rhodes, b Dec 24, 1866, m. Sept 21, 1887, Lillian C Chevry, b. June 14, 1867 Address Athens, Ga Methodist.
1. Henry Cherry Rhodes, b. June 28, 1888, d Oct. 7, 1913.
2. Mattie Ashburn Rhodes, b June 6, 1891

No. 1572. Fifth Generation. 1570.

3) Medora Elizabeth Rhodes, b. Oct. 13, 1868, m. Sept. 14, 1887, Clarence S. Sikes, at Edinburg, Ind. Address: 2353 Walton Way, Augusta, Ga Three children.

No. 1573. Fifth Generation. 1570.

4) Ella Belle Rhodes, b Jan 7, 1870, m. Jan 12, 1899, John Easten Alexander, b June 11, 1873. Address: Gordon, Wis. Christian Church
1. Wanda Alexander, b. July 14, 1900, d April 16, 1909
2 Karle Alexander, b. Dec. 28, 1901, d. Oct 5, 1909
3. Earl Alexander, b. June 10, 1907.
4. Dale Alexander, b May 3, 1910, d July 1, 1911.
5. Merle Alexander, b. Oct. 28, 1916.

No. 1574. Fifth Generation. 1570.

6) William Edmund Rhodes, b. Nov 9, 1873, m. Florence Lula Green, b. Sept. 1, 1881 (separated). He married May 13, 1912, Edith Stump, b. Mar. 12, 1878 District life insurance manager Address· 14 Cullumber St., Watsonville, Calif.

1. Fern Rhodes, b. May 13, 1897 No. 1575
2. May Luella Rhodes, b July 4, 1898 No 1576
   (From second wife)
3. Wilma E. Rhodes, b Jan 1, 1914.
4. Lelia E. Rhodes, b. Oct. 7, 1915.
5. William Rhodes, Jr., b. Sept 28, 1917.
6 Edwin Rhodes, b July 16, 1920.

No. 1575. Sixth Generation. 1574.

1) Fern Isabelle Rhodes, b May 13, 1897, m. Aug 16, 1920, Donald T. Hampton, b July 14, 1890 Address 125-38th St., San Francisco, Calif. Presser in tailor shop. Christian Church

1. Donald William Hampton, b Jan. 1, 1923
2 Verla May Hampton, b Aug. 7, 1925
3 Fre Bert Hampton, b Aug. 19, 1928

No. 1576. Sixth Generation. 1574.

2) May Luella Rhodes, b July 4, 1898, m ———— Gallup. Address 1310 Stout St., Denver, Colo

No. 1577. Fifth Generation. 1570.

7) Alberta Virginia Rhodes, b May 7, 1877, d Dec. 10, 1934, m. June 16, 1901, at St Paul, Minn., James D. Boyle, b. May 14, 1872, at Blenham, Ont., Canada, d. July 16, 1937 Address Pine City, Minn. Disciples of Christ.

1 Lorilla James Boyle, b. Aug 18, 1902. No. 1578
2 Carrie Edell Boyle, b Feb 29, 1904
3 Mary Belle Boyle, b July 3, 1911

No. 1578. Sixth Generation. 1577.

1) Lorilla James Boyle, b Aug 18, 1902, married July 9, 1929, Norma Elizabeth Blish, at Hannibal, Mo Address 100/ 8th St., Fargo, N. Dak.

1. Bruce James Boyle, b. Aug. 31, 1931
2 Mary Carolyn Boyle, b Sept 24, 1936.

No. 1579. Fifth Generation. 1570.

8) Florence Fidelia Rhodes, b June 3, 1879, m. April 2, 1901, Floyd Heon Cary, b. April 17, 1880; m (2nd) Edward Edson Freske, b. Mar., 1878; were married July 22, 1912 Mrs Freske is a Christian and Mr Freske is a Lutheran Mr. Cary was a Methodist Address: Brownston, Minn.

1 Darrell Bruce Cary, b Sept. 22, 1904. No 1580
2. Inez Mae Cary, b. Aug 9, 1906. No. 1581.
   (Second union)
3 Ida Belle Freske, b June 13, 1913 No 3471.
4 Edell Freske, b April 29, 1915. No 3472

No. 1580. Sixth Generation. 1579.

1) Darrell Bruce Cary, b Sept 22, 1904 Twice married. Address. 350 Morrison St., Portland, Oreg

No. 1581. Sixth Generation. 1579.

2) Inez Mae Cary, b Aug 9, 1906, m Chester Holzborn. Address. 8125 W Fessender, Portland, Oreg.
1. Norma Mae Holzborn, b. April 25, 1929
2 Ralph Holzborn, b Mar. 5, 1931.
3. Doren Bruce Holzborn, b. July 10, 1933.
4 Owen Clifford Holzborn, b. Dec 4, 1936

No. 1582. Fourth Generation. 34.

6) John L. Rhodes, b Jan 1, 1842, in Rockingham Co., Va , d. Jan. 4, 1932, m Mar 27, 1871, Belle I Wilson, b Aug. 27, 1850 She died Oct 30, 1929. Address: Beatrice, Nebr. Farmer. Teacher. Minister. Christian Church.
1. Lois Wilson Rhodes, b. Dec. 1, 1875. No 1583
2 Charles Porter Rhodes, b Mar 1, 1878 No. 1585
3. Arthur A Rhodes, b July 29, 1880 No 1586
4. Clara Rhodes, b. Dec 3, 1883, single, R N at Beatrice, Nebr , Hospital

No. 1583. Fifth Generation. 1582.

1) Lois Wilson Rhodes, b Dec 1, 1875, d. Aug. 22, 1913, m June 4, 1902, Dr Oliver C Diehl, b. Dec 25, 1872. Address Dillen, Nebr Teacher. Christian Church
1 Oliver R Diehl, b April 8, 1905
2 Eleanor R Diehl, b. June 13, 1907 No 1584

No. 1584. Sixth Generation. 1583.

2) Eleanor R. Diehl, b June 13, 1907, m W C Steffensmeyer. Address: Lincoln, Nebr

No. 1585. Fifth Generation. 1582.

2) Charles Porter Rhodes, b Mar. 1, 1878, m Ruth Evans Address Edmonton, Alta., Canada. Produce manager Christian Church.
1 Robert Rhodes, b. Dec. 9, 1916.

No. 1586. Fifth Generation. 1582.

3) Arthur A. Rhodes, b July 29, 1880, m Feb 12, 1908, Anna Merrill, b. Nov 11, 1880 Address. Beatrice, Nebr. Farmer. Christian Church.
1. John S Rhodes, b. July 18, 1909.

No. 1587. Fourth Generation. 34.

7) Daniel H Rhodes, b June 5, 1844, in Rockingham Co., Va , m. Sept. 20, 1890, Cora V. Spiker, b June 11, 1865 Minister of Church of Christ. Address. Toms Brook, Shenandoah Co., Va Burial at Bank Church, in Rockingham Co., Va
1. Ruth M. Rhodes, b July 2, 1892. No. 1645.
2. Paul E. Rhodes, b Sept. 10, 1893, twin No. 1647
3. Pauline E. Rhodes, b. Sept 10, 1893, twin. No. 1646
4. W. Irving Rhodes, b Dec —, 1895 No. 1648.

No. 1588. Fourth Generation. 34.

8) Joseph W Rhodes, b Oct. 9, 1846, in Rockingham Co, Va , d. May 30, 1926, m Mariah Jane Whitmer, b April 29, 1845, d April 8, 1878, married (2nd) April 15, 1879, Civilia Susan Whitmer, b Oct. 7, 1857, d April 18, 1881, married (3rd) Dec. 22, 1881, Ella Pollard, b Oct 8, 1856 Clerk in auditing department of Norfolk and Western Railway. Address: 417 Wellington Ave , Roanoke, Va
(From first wife)

1. Luther Aldine Rhodes, b. April 21, 1867. No. 1641.
2. Dora Magdalene Rhodes, b July 1, 1871, d. Feb. 21, 1872.
3. Arthur Curry Rhodes, b Jan. 21, 1873, d. Dec. —, 1929.
   (From second wife)
4. Otho Lucas Rhodes, b. Nov 24, 1880, d. Oct. 31, 1884.
   (From third wife)
5. Edna Rhodes, b. Sept. 7, 1883, d. Sept. 20, 1884.
6 Herbert Pollard Rhodes, b. Sept 20, 1885. No. 1644.
7. Frank Spencer Rhodes, b Dec 4, 1889, d. Feb. 28, 1890.
8. Ella May Rhodes, b May 21, 1892, single.
9 Harry Rhodes, b April 9, 1894, d Jan. 17, 1896.

No. 1589. Fourth Generation. 34.

12) Levi C Rhodes, b Nov 22, 1853, in Rockingham Co, Va., d. June 14. 1929, m. Bettie ————, d ———————— No issue. He married (2nd) Effie C ————————, Dec 7, 1910 Building contractor. Christian Church. Address: Roanoke, Va.

1 Lois Rhodes, b May 21, 1912
2 Helen Rhodes, b. Oct 2, 1918.

No. 1590. Fourth Generation. 35.

1) Frances Hildebrand, b Sept 14, 1841, near Waynesboro, Va., d. June 4, 1927, m Dec. 20, 1860, David Kennedy, b Oct. 25, 1828. He died Jan. 23, 1902. Buried at Madrid, Augusta Co, Va They lived near Madrid, Va. Mennonites.

1. Mary M. Kennedy, b Mar. 5, 1863. No. 1591.
2. Emma Catherine Kennedy, b. June 27, 1865 No. 1599.
3. Elizabeth Jane Kennedy, b May 7, 1868. No. 1603
4. Cenia F. Kennedy, b Sept. 28, 1870 No. 1608.
5 Jacob Samuel Kennedy, b Mar 27, 1875, single.

No. 1591. Fifth Generation. 1590.

1) Mary M Kennedy, b Mar. 5, 1863, near Madrid, Va., m. in 1887 John E Craig, b Mar. 18, 1864 . Address: Waynesboro, Augusta Co, Va. Mennonites.

1 Walter D. Craig, b. Oct 2, 1888 No. 1592
2. Eliza F. Craig, b Mar 6, 1890 No 1593
3 Bessie F. Craig, b Oct 18, 1891 No 1594
4. Ernest E Craig, b. July 25, 1894 No 1595.
5. Arthur C. Craig, b April 26, 1896 No. 1596.
6. Ada E. Craig, b. July 12, 1898 No 1597
7 Mary A Craig, b April 26, 1901 No. 1598
8 Jacob C P Craig, b Dec 10, 1903, single

No. 1592. Sixth Generation. 1591.

1) Walter D. Craig, b Oct 2, 1888, near Waynesboro, Va, m. Sept. 5, 1915. near New Hope, Va, Lottie A Matthew, b. in 1890. Church of the Brethren Address: Waynesboro, Va Burial in Hildebrands cemetery.

1. Mary Sue Craig, b ————, 1916
2. Helen Louise Craig, b ————, 1917.

No. 1593. Sixth Generation. 1591.

2) Eliza F. Craig, b Mar 6, 1890, near Waynesboro, Va., m. Jan. 26, 1916, at New Hope, Va., Samuel C. Blosser, b Nov 26, 1891. Farmer. Mennonites. Address: Crimora, Va. Burial in Hildebrands cemetery

1 Carl E. Blosser, b. Nov 14, 1916, d April 1, 1927.
2. Glen H. Blosser, b. Feb 19, 1918

3. Irvin F. Blosser, b May 5, 1919.
4. Ray C. Blosser, b. Mar. 23, 1921.
5. Vance L. Blosser, b Feb. 4, 1924.
6. Marvin D Blosser, b Mar. 9, 1925.
7. Eva Mae Blosser, b. Sept. 24, 1926.
8. Callie B. Blosser, b. May 15, 1930
9. William C. Blosser, b Sept 13, 1931
10. Sylvia M Blosser, b Dec. 31, 1932

No. 1594. Sixth Generation. 1591.

3) Bessie F Craig, b Oct. 18, 1891, near Waynesboro, Va, m. May —, 1916, Everett Frazier, b Sept 12, 1888 Address Waynesboro, Va Laborer in factory. Mennonites Burial in Hildebrands cemetery
1. Clifton E. Frazier, b. Jan. 22, 1919.
2 Gracie M S. Frazier, b Jan. 29, 1920

No. 1595. Sixth Generation. 1591.

4) Ernest E Craig, b July 25, 1894, near Waynesboro, Va, m Jan. 5, 1921, at Staunton, Va, Addie B Smiley, b Sept 17. 1896 Stationary engineer Mennonites Address Newport News, Va Burial in Hildebrands cemetery.
1. Edith Hope Craig, b Dec 21, 1921.
2 Robert Edward Craig, b Aug. 22, 1924.

No. 1596. Sixth Generation. 1591.

5) Arthur C Craig, b April 26, 1896, near Waynesboro, Va., m Nov. 19, 1924, at Clifton Forge, Va, Sadie Hostetler, b in 1897 Address: 5927 Nelson St, Staunton, Va Mennonites. No issue.

No. 1597. Sixth Generation. 1591.

6) Ada E Craig, b July 12, 1898, near Waynesboro, Va., m. Dec 23, 1920, at Hermitage, Va, William C Smiley, b Aug 10, 1894. Mennonites. Burial in Hildebrands cemetery Address. 421 Baltimore Ave, Staunton, Va
1. Woodrow Penelton Smiley, b April 10, 1927, d same day.
2 Mary Ann Smiley, b. April 6, 1930.
3 Peggy Jane Smiley, b. Jan. 13, 1935.

No. 1598. Sixth Generation. 1591.

7) Mary A. Craig, b April 26, 1901, near Waynesboro, Va, m. April 12, 1921, at Waynesboro, Va John D. Martin, b ———, 1898 Address: Waynesboro, Va., R 2. Farmer. Mennonites. Burial in Springdale Mennonite cemetery.
1. Clinton E Martin, b ———, 1923.
2 Roy D Martin, b ———, 1924
3. Thelma G. Martin, b. ———, 1929.
4. Mary Frances Martin, b. ———, 1933.

No. 1599. Fifth Generation. 1590.

2) Emma Catherine Kennedy, b June 27, 1865, near Madrid, Va, m June 5, 1887, Kasper Newton Swartzel, b Nov 28, 1858 He died Nov. 28, 1924 Emmanuel Lutheran Church Address 520 Clark St, Bluefield, W Va.
1 Charles David Swartzel, b May 4, 1888. No 1600
2. George Lee Swartzel, b. Sept. 8, 1891.
3. Irving Frank Swartzel, b. Mar 31, 1897
4 Virginia Eve Swartzel, b Feb 19, 1900 No 1601
5. Fannie Pearl Swartzel, b Nov 10, 1889 No 1602

No. 1600. Sixth Generation. 1599.
1) Charles David Swartzel, b May 4, 1888, m. Aug. 7, 1916, at Havre, Mont., Charlotte Grenley. Address· Bluefield, W. Va.

No. 1601. Sixth Generation. 1599.
4) Virginia Eve Swartzel, b Feb. 19, 1900, m. June 1, 1922, Arthur Edward Shumaker, at Bluefield, W Va. Address. Box 67, Mabscott, W. Va.

No. 1602. Sixth Generation. 1599.
5) Fannie Pearl Swartzel, b Nov 10, 1889, d Dec. 4, 1918, m. April 5, 1910, at Bristol, Va, Alexander Herbert Sloane. Address. Morgantown, W. Va. Buried at Bluefield, W. Va. Fam.ly living at 324 Maple Ave, Morgantown, W. Va.
1. Earl Vance Sloane, b. —————.
2. Thelma Louise Sloane, b. —————.
3 Charles Everett Sloane, b. —————.

No. 1603. Fifth Generation. 1590.
3) Elizabeth Jane Kennedy, b. May 7, 1868, in Augusta Co., Va., m. July 11, 1888, Ashby M. Hanger, b. Jan 23, 1867, he died June 23, 1917 Buried at Madrid, Va., Presbyterians Address: Waynesboro, Va
1. Harry Lee Hanger, b Sept. 19, 1889. No 1604.
2. Clarence Emory Hanger, b June 21, 1891.
3. Grover Cleveland Hanger, b Nov. 6, 1892 No. 1605.
4. Fannie Pearl Hanger, b Dec 22, 1895 No 1607.
5. Elsie Catherine Hanger, b. Sept 5, 1900 No 1606.
6. Emmet Newton Hanger, b Oct 5, 1904

No. 1604. Sixth Generation. 1603.
1) Harry Lee Hanger, b Sept 19, 1889, m Dec 24, 1913, Effie M. Doorus, b. Aug 31, 1889. Address. Waynesboro, Va. Presbyterians.
1. Hansford M. Hanger, b. Mar. 28, 1918.
2. Ruth Elizabeth Hanger, b April 22, 1926.
3 Nelson LeRoy Hanger, b. Feb 24, 1928.

No. 1605. Sixth Generation. 1603.
3) Grover Cleveland Hanger, b. Nov 6, 1892, m. Dec. 25, 1927, at Waynesboro, Va., Edith E. Gochenour, b July 18, 1895 Methodists. Carpenter. Address: Waynesboro, Va, R. 1
1 Charlotta May Hanger, b. Nov. 11, 1920.

No. 1606. Sixth Generation. 1603.
5) Elsie Catherine Hanger, b Sept 5, 1900, m. June 16, 1918, at Rockville, Md, William H. Snow, b. Nov 3, 1899. Address: Waynesboro, Va.
1 Charlotte Arline Snow, b Jan. 18, 1919, d. July 20, 1919.

No. 1607. Sixth Generation. 1603.
4) Fannie Pearl Hanger, b. Dec. 22, 1895, m. April 28, 1920, at Waynesboro, Va., Frank D Brown, b July 7, 1901 Housewife. Presbyterians Address: Waynesboro, Va, R 1 No issue Burial place at Mt Zion Lutheran Church, Va

No. 1608. Fifth Generation. 1590.
4) Cenia F Kennedy, b Sept 28, 1870, in Augusta Co, Va, m. 1904 Frank E Weaver, b Dec 22, 1862, in Lancaster Co, Pa., d Nov. 28, 1910. Buried at Springdale Church. Address. Waynesboro, Va Mennonites
1 Margaret A. Weaver, b. Nov. 9, 1904. No. 1609.
2 Ada F Weaver, b May 20, 1906 No 1610

3. Walter K. Weaver, b Dec 13, 1907 No 1611.

4 Franklin E. Weaver, b Oct 28, 1910 No. 1612

No. 1609. Sixth Generation. 1608.

1) Margaret A. Weaver, b Nov. 9, 1904, m June 1, 1924, Charles Vangundy Address: Waynesboro, Va.

1. Frances Irene Vangundy, b Aug 5, 1925
2. Edith Mae Vangundy, b Sept. 21, 1930
3. David Earl Vangundy, b Jan 3, 1931.

No. 1610. Sixth Generation. 1608.

2) Ada F. Weaver, b May 20, 1906, m. Aug 26, 1925, Harry Arnold Address Waynesboro, Va.

1. Evelyn Virginia Arnold, b. June 18, 1926.
2 Floyd David Arnold, b Mar 22, 1928
3. Mary Elizabeth Arnold, b May 8, 1931.
4 Wallace Lee Arnold, b. Mar 13, 1932.

No. 1611. Sixth Generation. 1608.

3) Walter K. Weaver, b Dec 13, 1907, m. April 14, 1926, Tracil Mae Simmons. Address: Waynesboro, Va.

1. Wilson Floyd Weaver, b. Sept 16, 1927.
2 James Edward Weaver, b. Dec. 31, 1928.
3. Lester Ralph Weaver, b June 15, 1930, d Aug 5, 1930
4. Ethel Louise Weaver, b June 2, 1931.
5 Ray Houston Weaver, b June 11, 1933

No. 1612. Sixth Generation. 1608.

4) Franklin E. Weaver, b Oct 28, 1910, m July 6, 1929, Katie Grove Address: Waynesboro, Va.

1 Marion Clayton Weaver, b. Oct. 2, 1930.
2 Oliver Grove Weaver, b. April 7, 1933.

No. 1613. Fourth Generation. 35.

2) Samuel Hildebrand, b Jan 11, 1845, near Waynesboro, Va, m. Nov. 19, 1874, Fannie Williams, b 1850 Address Waynesboro, Va Burial near Waynesboro, Va.

1. George H. Hildebrand, b Oct 20, 1875, d Aug. 18, 1901
2 Hubert N Hildebrand, b. May 22, 1885, d July 25, 1901
3. Arthur J Hildebrand, b Dec. 28, 1876. No. 1614.
4. Frank W. Hildebrand, b May 14, 1878. No. 1618.

No. 1614. Fifth Generation. 1613.

3) Arthur Jacob Hildebrand, b. Dec. 28, 1876, m. in 1899, Nettie Belle Philips, b. Jan 14, 1877 Address: 738 Panco St., Baltimore, Md. Automobile business. Lutheran.

1. Percy C. Hildebrand, b ————, 1899
2. Fay B Hildebrand, b ————, 1901 No 1615.
3. Violet Hildebrand, b ————, 1904. No. 1616
4 Phyllis Hildebrand, b. ————, 1911. No. 1617.

No. 1615. Sixth Generation. 1614.

2) Fay B. Hildebrand, b ————, 1901, m in 1924, Dolly Baker Address 700 S. Panco St, Baltimore, Md

No. 1616. Sixth Generation. 1614.

3) Violet Hildebrand, b ————, 1904, m in 1917, Ira Blackman Address. Bocaraton, Fla.

No. 1617. Sixth Generation. 1614.

4) Phyllis Hildebrand, b. ————, 1911, m in 1928, Lewis B. Williams. Address: 738 S. Panco St , Baltimore, Md

No. 1618. Fifth Generation. 1613.

4) William Frank Hildebrand, b May 14, 1878, m in 1903 at Staunton, Va., Minnie V. Sheets, b. Mar 29, 1878 Millwright Lutheran Address 735 Panco St., Baltimore, Md.

No. 1619. Fourth Generation. 35.

3) Jacob L Hildebrand, b Aug 11, 1848, near Waynesboro, Va., d. Mar. 6, 1927, m April 9, 1872, Annie R Beery, b. Nov 24, 1845, d. Jan. 19, 1895 He married a second wife, Emma Hildebrand. She died Feb 9, 1907. All were buried at the Hildebrands Church in Augusta Co , Va They lived near Waynesboro, Va

1 John Samuel Hildebrand, b July 6, 1873, never married.
2. Susan Magdalene Hildebrand, b Dec 12, 1874 No. 1620.
3 Sarah Virginia Hildebrand, b Jan 27, 1877 No. 1628
4 David Henry Hildebrand, b April 1, 1878. No. 1630
5 William Treavy Hildebrand, b Dec. 25, 1879, d. June 21, 1882.
6 Annie Belle Hildebrand, b Nov 28, 1881 No. 1632.
7 James Jacob Hildebrand, b. Jan 18, 1884 No. 1633.
8 Harry Davis Hildebrand, b. April 7, 1886. No 1635.
9 Clara Mae Hildebrand, b Feb. 10, 1888 No. 1636
10. Guy Estell Hildebrand, b. Dec 18, 1890 No 1637.
   (From second wife)
11 Russell A Hildebrand, b Mar. 22, 1898. No 1638.
12. Nellie Elizabeth Hildebrand, b. Aug 14, 1899. No. 1639.
13. Mary Glen Hildebrand, b Mar. 3, 1901, single.
14 Emma Ruth Hildebrand, b Dec. 15, 1902. No. 1640.

No. 1620. Fifth Generation. 1619.

2) Susan Magdalene Hildebrand, b Dec. 12, 1874, near Waynesboro, Va., m. Feb 17, 1897, Homer A Wine, b Sept. 10, 1875. Address Waynesboro, Va. Housewife Lutheran.

1 Jacob Earl Wine, b Nov 30, 1897 No. 1621.
2. Raymond Edward Wine, b. Feb 13, 1899. No 1622
3 Annie Kathrine Wine, b Feb 15, 1901 No 1623.
4 Lettie Belle Wine, b Jan 12, 1903. No 1624
5 Blanche Tyne Wine, b July 30, 1904 No 1625.
6. Hazel Lee Wine, b Mar 24, 1906. No. 1626.
7 Ethel May Wine, b May 5, 1909 No 1627.
8 Carthon A Wine, b Nov. 13, 1911.

No. 1621. Sixth Generation. 1620.

1) Jacob Earl Wine, b Nov 30, 1897, m. April 28, 1926, Edna Snow, b ———————— Address· Waynesboro, Va.

No. 1622. Sixth Generation. 1620.

2) Raymond Edward Wine, b Feb 13, 1899, m Dec. 17, 1919, at Hagerstown, Md , Eunice Townsend Address· Waynesboro, Va.

No. 1623. Sixth Generation. 1620.

3) Anna Katherine Wine, b. Feb. 15, 1901, m. John Bowman Kennedy, b April 18, 1901, m Dec. 21, 1920. Address: Crimora, Va. Farmer. Methodists
1. John Wallace Kennedy, b Mar. 23, 1922
2. Glen Calvin Kennedy, b Sept 17, 1924
3. Gladys Isabell Kennedy, b Feb 15, 1929
4 Lois Catherine Kennedy, b Dec 25, 1934

No. 1624. Sixth Generation. 1620.

4) Lettie Belle Wine, b. Jan. 12, 1903, m. June 6, 1923. Benjamin Carnigie Bowling. Address 2243 Adams Ave , Huntington, W Va

No. 1625. Sixth Generation. 1620.

5) Blanche Tyne Wine, b July 30, 1904, m Dec 27, 1927, at Verona, Va , Raymond H Riddle Address Thomasville, Pa. R 1 Farmer Methodists
1. Raymond Hennes Riddle, b. Oct 3, 1928
2. Nancy Jane Riddle, b Mar 23, 1930
3 Lois Jean Riddle, b Aug 5, 1933

No. 1626. Sixth Generation. 1620.

6) Hazel Lee Wine, b Mar 24, 1906, m June 12, 1926. at Richmond Va , Howard Montgomery. b Mar 23, 1902 Address Reidsville. N C Laborer Methodists
1. Cora Lee Montgomery, b Nov 24, 1929
2 Margaret Ann Montgomery, b Oct 24, 1931
3 Pauline Elizabeth Montgomery, b. Dec. 3, 1933.

No. 1627. Sixth Generation. 1620.

7) Ethel May Wine, b May 5, 1909. m Jan 25, 1928, at Frederick, Md , Albert L Freed, b Jan. 30, 1907 Address Crozet, Va Barber Presbyterians
1 Virginia Magdalena Freed, b April 27, 1929

No. 1628. Fifth Generation. 1619.

3) Sarah Virginia Hildebrand, b Jan 27, 1877. m 1901, Finley H Rosen, b May 16, 1872, at Madrid. Va Address Middlebrook. Va , R 1 United Brethren
1 Ethel G Rosen, b ———, 1901 No 1629.
2 Evelyn G. Rosen, b Aug 18, 1907
3 Irvin T Rosen, b Oct. 29, 1915

No. 1629. Sixth Generation. 1628.

1) Ethel G Rosen, b. ———, 1901, m. ———, 1922, at Middlebrook. Va , Bryan Reed Address Swoope, Va

No. 1630. Fifth Generation. 1619.

4) David Henry Hildebrand, b. April 1, 1878, m. 1901, to Edna B Obaugh, b June 29, 1881 Address Bridgewater, Va Carpenter and cabinetmaker Brethren Church Related, see No 1840
1. Mary R Hildebrand, b Sept 23, 1902 No 1841
2 Earl D Hildebrand, b Nov 1, 1914, d Dec 1, 1914
3. Roy J Hildebrand, b July 26, 1916

No. 1632. Fifth Generation. 1619.

6) Anna Belle Hildebrand, b Nov 28, 1884, m 1909, William Alexander Homan, b June 26, 1881, at Ft Defiance, Va Housekeeper Presbyterians Address: Waynesboro, Pa, R 4
1 Hansford H Homan, b Sept 15, 1910

No. 1633. Fifth Generation. 1619.

7) James Jacob Hildebrand, b Jan. 18, 1884, m. in 1907, at Staunton, Va., Sadie C. Hahn, b. Sept. 27, 1883. Carpenter. Presbyterians. Address: 6325 Page Ave, St Louis, Mo

1 Mabel B. Hildebrand, b ————, 1908 No 1634.
2. Julius E Hildebrand, b ————, 1911
3 Franklin R Hildebrand, b. ————, 1915.
4. Agnes M. Hildebrand, b. ————, 1917, d. same year.
5. Louis R Hildebrand, b ————, 1919
6 Maynard W. Hildebrand, b ————, 1922.
7 Donald K. Hildebrand, b ————, 1926
8. Gloria J Hildebrand, b ————, 1928

No. 1634. Sixth Generation. 1633.

1) Mabel B Hildebrand. b ————, 1908, d 1930, m. Feb 8, 1930, at St Charles. Mo, H L Wilson Buried at Mt View, Va Address 6325 Page Ave, St Louis, Mo

No. 1635. Fifth Generation. 1619.

8) Harry Davis Hildebrand, b April 7, 1886, m Sept 5, 1923, at Washington, D. C., Mary A Meyers, b May 1, 1904, at Edom, Va Railway postal clerk Address. 1008 Hamilton Blvd, Hagerstown, Md. Presbyterians

1 Ann Elizabeth Hildebrand. b Oct 31, 1925

No. 1636. Fifth Generation. 1619.

9) Clara Mae Hildebrand, b Feb 10, 1888, m Mar 26, 1918, at Staunton, Va, Herman B Bruffey, b Jan 4, 1892, at Grottoes, Va Housewife Methodists. South Address 2608 4th St, Washington, D C No issue

No. 1637. Fifth Generation. 1619.

10) Guy Estell Hildebrand, b. Dec. 18, 1890, m. April 5, 1915, at Ft Defiance, Va, Leona E Reed, b. Feb. 2, 1891, at Weyers Cave, Va Salesman Presbyterians Address 306 N New, Staunton, Va

1. Cleveland L Hildebrand, b. Dec 17, 1916.
2 Hilda Christine Hildebrand. b May 20, 1920

No. 1638. Fifth Generation. 1619.

11) Russell Abram Hildebrand. b Mar. 22, 1898, m. Nov 8, 1917, at Hagers town, Md, Bertie Esther Roadcap. b Mar —, 1900, at Weyers Cave, Va Address. Waynesboro, Va Tinner Methodists

1 Louise Hildebrand, b. June —, 1918.
2 Gladys Hildebrand, b Oct —, 1920
3 Jacob Hildebrand, b May —, 1923
4 Georgia Hildebrand, b. Oct. —, 1925

No. 1639. Fifth Generation. 1619.

12) Nellie Elizabeth Hildebrand, b Aug 14, 1899, m 1923 at Waynesboro, Va, Herman E Gochenour. b April 8, 1903 Housewife Mt Vernon M E, South Address· 2745 4th St, N E, Washington, D C

1 Jean Elizabeth Gochenour, b May 23, 1924
2 Helen Joyce Gochenour, b Dec 25, 1925

No. 1640. Fifth Generation. 1619.

14) Emma Ruth Hildebrand. b Dec 15, 1902, m Sept, 1922. at Washington. D C, Aldo F Kite, b. Aug 11, 1903 Address Waynesboro, Va

1 Charlotte Lee Kite, b Sept 6, 1923

2 Audry Mae Kite, b July 1, 1926
3 Emma Gene Kite, b. ————————.

No. 1641. Fifth Generation. 1588.
1) Luther Aldine Rhodes, b April 21, 1867, m Mary Beulah DeVier.
1. Mary Lillian Rhodes, b ——————— No 1642
2 Helen Magdalena Rhodes, b. ——————. No. 1643

No. 1642. Sixth Generation. 1641.
1) Mary Lillian Rhodes, b. ——————, m ———— Snapp
1 Alfred Jackson Snapp, b ——————

No. 1643. Sixth Generation. 1641.
2) Helen Magdalena Rhodes, b ——————, m ———— Bliss, b ——————.
1 Mary Jane Bliss, b ——————.
2 Verne Fairbanks Bliss, b ——————

No. 1644. Fifth Generation. 1588.
6) Herbert Pollard Rhodes, b. Sept 20, 1885, d. April 18, 1927, m Bertha
Mae Gray, b. ———————— Their son is living with his mother at Detroit, Mich.
1. Ralph Jackson Rhodes, b Mar 18, 1920

No. 1645. Fifth Generation. 1587.
1) Ruth M Rhodes, b. July 2, 1892, m July 9, 1913, Earl R. Miley, b Aug.
23, 1889. Address. Toms Brook, Va Homemaker Christian Church Burial
ground at Toms Brook, Va
1 Virginia Lee Miley, b. Mar. 9, 1919
2. Earl Miley, Jr , b. Feb 7, 1922.
3 Richard Miley, b Dec 1, 1925, d same day
4 Elizabeth Ann Miley, b Dec. 11, 1927.

No. 1646. Fifth Generation. 1587.
3) Pauline E. Rhodes, b. Sept. 10, 1893, m Mar. 1, 1917, Harry Keller, b
May 9, 1895. Homemaker. Christian Church Burial at Toms Brook, Va. Address: Toms Brook, Va.
1. Paul Rhodes Keller, b. Jan. 23, 1918
2. Milfred Ann Keller, b Oct 2, 1919, d. Mar. 31, 1921.
3. Genevieve Keller, b Mar. 26, 1925.
4. Kenneth Daniel Keller, b. Mar. 13, 1933.

No. 1647. Fifth Generation. 1587.
2) Paul E. Rhodes, b. Sept. 10, 1893, m. Feb. 11, 1923, Mary Virginia Haran.
Mr. Rhodes belongs to the Christian Church, and Mrs. Rhodes to the Lutheran
Church. No children.

No. 1648. Fifth Generation. 1587.
4) W. Irving Rhodes, b Dec. —, 1895, m. Aug., 1929, Mary Evelyn Boyle
Address: Petersburg, W Va
1. Irving Richard Rhodes, b. July 5, 1930.
2 Joann Frances Rhodes, b. April 1, 1932

No. 1649. Fourth Generation. 35.
4) Magdalena Hildebrand, b. Oct 16, 1853, d. Jan 2, 1906, m Aug 27, 1876,
Lindsley Swartzel, b. Nov. 4, 1852, d April 27, 1915. Farmer Buried at Madrid,
Va Address was Waynesboro, Va.
1. Bettie F Swartzel, b Sept. 17, 1878 No 1650
2. Ida F Swartzel, b April 21, 1881 No. 1651.

3. Cornelia A. Swartzel, b. Oct. 2, 1883, single.

4. Emma J. Swartzel, b. Dec 11, 1886, d Mar 2, 1887

5. Frederick S. Swartzel, b Oct 6, 1888. No 1652.

No. 1650. Fifth Generation. 1649.

1) Bettie F Swartzel, b Sept 17, 1878, m. Lacy Via, b. ———— Address: Waynesboro, Va.

No. 1651. Fifth Generation. 1649.

2) Ida Florence Swartzel, b April 21, 1881, m Dec 23, 1915, at Staunton, Va., John W Nutty, b May 28, 1888 Housekeeper Church of the Brethren Address. Staunton, Va.

1 Eva Magdalene Nutty, b. Feb. 5, 1917

2 Edith Mae Nutty, b. Oct 19, 1918

3. Robert Linsy Nutty, b Oct 23, 1920.

4. Dorothy Lee Nutty, b Nov 19, 1922, d Feb 5, 1924.

5 Fay Christian Nutty, b April 9, 1924

No. 1652. Fifth Generation. 1649.

5) Frederick S. Swartzel, b Oct 6, 1888, m. Mar 31, 1915, Mabel M Benson, b. April 28, 1884, d Feb 5, 1933 Farmer. Methodists Address Waynesboro, Va. Burial at Hildebrands Church

1. Ray C Swartzel, b Oct 18, 1916

2 Walter J Swartzel, b Nov 7, 1917.

3 Anna May Swartzel, b Dec 3, 1918, d April 26, 1920

4 Elsie M. Swartzel, b Nov 8, 1919

5 Harry Lee Swartzel, b Feb 20, 1921, d Sept 4, 1927

6 Dorothy G. Swartzel, b April 26, 1922

7 Edna J Swartzel, b Sept 8, 1924.

8 Howard E Swartzel, b Sept 3, 1926.

9 Thelma F. Swartzel, b Aug 20, 1928.

No. 1653. Fourth Generation. 35.

5) Mary E. Hildebrand, b. Aug. 5, 1856, m. Dec. 18, 1889, at home, James N. Merrett, b. Aug. 9, 1850 Homemaker Methodists Burial ground at Hildebrands Church. Address: Waynesboro, Va.

1. Mattie J. Merrett, b ————, 1892, single.

2 Jacob William Merrett, b ————, 1894. No 1654

No. 1654. Fifth Generation. 1653.

2) Jacob William Merrett, b ————, 1894, m 1917, Athalie M Gochenour, at Staunton, Va. Address Waynesboro, Va.

1. Evelyn V. Merrett, b ————.

2 James Conrad Merrett, b ————.

3 Herbert C. Merrett, b. ————.

No. 1655. Fourth Generation. 1180.

1) Sarah Baker, b May 7, 1826, d Aug —, 1897, m Calvin Sapp, b Dec. 21, 1821, d. Feb 27, 1881 Buried at Gambier, O They had lived at Omaha, Nebr, where Mr. Sapp practiced medicine

1. Joseph Sapp, b ————.

2 Clinton Sapp, b ————. No 1656

3. Laura Sapp, b ———— No. 1657

4 Dora Barbara Sapp, b Dec. 28, 1860. No 1658

5 Florence Victoria Sapp, b ————, 1865 No 1661

6. Louetta S Sapp, b. April 6, 1867. No. 1663.

No. 1656. Fifth Generation. 1655.

2) Clinton Sapp, b. ——————, was never married. He was a practicing physician at Omaha, Nebr. Buried in South Omaha, Nebr

No. 1657. Fifth Generation. 1655.

3) Laura Sapp, b. ——————, m Dr E W Whitney Address 8155 Fairview Ave, La Mesa, Calif

No. 1658. Fifth Generation. 1655.

4) Dora Barbara Sapp, b Dec. 28, 1860, m July 27, 1885, Albert W Hayward, b Dec 9, 1861. Address· 1217 Cornell Drive, Dayton, O
1. Dorothy Hayward, b Dec 4, 1900 No 1659.
2 Robert Clinton Hayward, b July 13, 1905. No 1660

No. 1659. Sixth Generation. 1658.

1) Dorothy Hayward, b. Dec. 4, 1900, m. Nov. 30, 1925, Robert Ely Paysell.
1 Barbara Paysell, b. Aug 30, 1931.

No. 1660. Sixth Generation. 1658.

2) Robert Clinton Hayward, b July 13, 1905, m. Ada Braemer, b ——————.

No. 1661. Fifth Generation. 1655.

5) Florence Victoria Sapp, b ——————, 1865, m. Edward Denmore Miller, at Garden City, Kans Homemaker Congregational Address 8073 Lemon Ave, La Mesa, Calif. Burial ground at Gambier, O
1. Maude Anita Miller, b. —————— No 1662

No. 1662. Sixth Generation. 1661.

1) Maude Anita Miller, b ——————, m Albert J. Howell, b ——————.

No. 1663. Fifth Generation. 1655.

6) Louetta S Sapp, b April 6. 1867, m. Mar 30, 1890, Prof William H Miller, b. Feb. —, 1853, d April 4, 1921. Telegrapher Methodists Address· 2221 Yale Ave., North, Seattle, Wash
1 William Clinton Miller, b Oct. 21, 1891. No 1664.

No. 1664. Sixth Generation. 1663.

1) William Clinton Miller, b Oct 21, 1891, m. Annatta Clara Jenkins, b April 17, 1901 Address: Cresswell, Oreg, R. 1 No children

No. 1665. Fourth Generation. 1180.

4) Susanna Baker, b. Feb 12, 1832, d Dec 10, 1919, m. William J. Smith, b Feb. 7, 1831, d Aug. 5, 1904 Address: Gambier, O Farmer Methodists Buried in Hopewell cemetery near Gambier, O
1. Addie Belle Smith, b. July 15, 1859. No 1666
2 Leroy Smith, b June 13, 1860, d Mar 28, 1862
3 Olive Leona Smith, b Jan. 25, 1862, single.
4. Harry Judson Smith, b Oct 24, 1865, d Dec 27, 1938
5. Walter Eugene Smith, b Feb 25, 1870, single
6 Lura Estella Smith, b. Mar 31, 1872 No. 1671
Olive, Harry, and Walter reside together on a farm 2½ miles from Gambier, R 2, O.

No. 1666. Fifth Generation. 1665.

1) Addie Belle Smith, b July 15, 1859, m Nov 6, 1879, Rolla Dyer, b Sept. 21, 1851. Housewife. Methodists Buried at Gambier, O
1 Addie Avanelle Dyer, b Nov 4, 1880 No 1667.

No. 1667. Sixth Generation. 1666.

1) Addie Avanelle Dyer, b Nov 4, 1880, m. July 6, 1905, Lewis Akers, b Aug. 25, 1881. Housewife Methodists Mr. Akers is a Methodist minister. He was for many years president of the Asbury Methodist College near Louisville, Ky., but on account of failing health he asked for a relief, after which he was given a charge at Orrville, O , where he served for two years after which he was transferred to Canton, O (now 1937) Mr Akers is an unusually able speaker, and his services are much called for Address 1919 7th St , S W., Canton, O

1 William Gerald Akers, b June 25, 1906 No 1668
2 Lewis Robeson Akers, Jr , b Dec 19, 1907 No 1669
3. Dorothy Dyer Akers, b Mar 26, 1909. No. 1670
4 Richard Lawrence Akers, b Oct 20, 1919

No. 1668. Seventh Generation. 1667.

1) William Gerald Akers, b June 25, 1906, m Ruth Elizabeth Fountaine, b. June 14, 1904 Mr Akers is professor of modern language at William and Mary College in Virginia

1 Lois Avanella Akers, b May 16, 1933

No. 1669. Seventh Generation. 1667.

2) Lewis Robeson Akers, Jr , b Dec 19, 1907, m Mary Ellen Baker, b June 28, 1909 Minister in the Methodist Church

1 Martha Carolyn Akers, b April 21, 1934

No. 1670. Seventh Generation. 1667.

3) Dorothy Dyer Akers, b Mar 26, 1909, m. James Gilmour Ranch, b Aug. 26, 1911 Mr Ranch is extension secretary of Board of Temperance, Washington, D. C Mrs Ranch is professor in art at Asbury College, Wilmore, Ky.

No. 1671. Fifth Generation. 1665.

6) Lura Estella Smith, b Mar. 31, 1872, m Sept 19, 1894, Thurman L. Eley, b. Aug. 30, 1867 Mr Eley is a physician at Gambier, O Methodists Address Gambier, O

1 Forest Wayland Eley, b Aug 19, 1895. No. 1672.

No. 1672. Sixth Generation. 1671.

1) Forest Wayland Eley, b. Aug. 19, 1895, m. Aug. 19, 1916, Jennie Stahl, of Newark, O Address: 444 Mt. Vernon Rd , Newark, O.

1 Margaret Virginia Eley, b June 22, 1917.
2 Clifton Eley, b. Mar 8, 1924

No. 1673. Fourth Generation. 1180.

3) Mary Baker, b. Nov 23, 1829, d Nov. 2, 1868, m William Sturgeon, b Jan. 24, 1824, d Dec 15, 1899 Mary Baker was buried at Danville, O , and Mr Sturgeon was buried at Newark, O

1. Clifford Leroy Sturgeon, b Oct 21, 1855 No 1818
2 Melville Sumner Sturgeon, b Mar 2, 1857, single
3 Clara Victoria Sturgeon, b Jan 24, 1859 No. 1820
4 Eva Adaline Sturgeon, b. July 3, 1860. No. 1823.
5 Elmer Elsworth Sturgeon, b Aug 21, 1862 No 1826
6 Lizzie Ione Sturgeon, b Aug. 2, 1864 No 1827
7 Charles William Sturgeon, b Nov 12, 1866 No 1828

No. 1674. Fourth Generation. 1180.

5) Oren M Baker, b June 11, 1835, d June 11, 1878, m Oct 4, 1868, Tibitha Alexander, b Aug. 27, 1843, d April 15, 1875 Physician Church of Christ and Methodist. Burial at Danville, O.

1 Curtis Leroy Baker, b Dec 25, 1869 No 1675
2. Mary Ellen Baker, b Aug 17, 1874 No 1678.
3. ———— Baker, b. ——————, d. —————.

No. 1675. Fifth Generation. 1674.

1) Curtis Leroy Baker, b Dec 25, 1869, m Nov 26, 1902, Jennie Knowles, b. June 1, 1872 Mr Baker is a member of the Church of Christ, Mrs Baker, Methodist Church Physician Address· Marion, O , R 4 Burial place at Marion, O.

1 Donn Murry Baker, b Aug. 31, 1903. No 1676
2 Martha Jane Baker, b Jan 29, 1909 No 1677

No. 1676. Sixth Generation. 1675.

1) Donn Murry Baker, b Aug 31, 1903, m Mary Wait, of Cleveland, O , Apr. 29, 1929. Address· 4432 W. 60th St., Cleveland, O. Church of Christ.
1. Curtis Lee Baker, b Nov 30, 1933 Burial place at Marion, O

No. 1677. Sixth Generation. 1675.

2) Martha Jane Baker, b Jan 29, 1909, m Aug 15, 1928, James Carter Beard, of Republic, O. Burial place at Republic, O Methodists Address: Republic, O
1. Janet Ann Beard, b July 24, 1932

No. 1678. Fifth Generation. 1674.

2) Mary Ellen Baker, b Aug. 17, 1874, m Nov 15, 1915, Herbert M. Brooks, b Aug. 31, 1881. Farmer Church of Christ Burial ground at Marion, O. Address Marion, O., R. 4. No children

No. 1679. Fourth Generation. 1180.

7) Anna Elizabeth Baker, b. Oct. 11, 1843, d 1888, m. in 1870, Joel E. Sears, b. ———, 1841, d. in 1876 Merchant Methodists Burial at Delaware, O. Address was Newark, O.
1. Clifton W. Sears, b Oct 11, 1871. No. 1680

No. 1680. Fifth Generation. 1679.

1) Clifton W. Sears, b. Oct. 11, 1871, m in 1893, Etta L———, b July 30, 1872. Address: 1860 Homewood Drive, Pasadena, Calif. Dealer in oil and gas. Methodists. Burial place at Forest Lawn, Glendale, Calif
1 Helen Adaline Sears, b. Mar 11, 1909.

No. 1681. Fourth Generation. 1180.

9) Mellville Quincy Baker, b. Oct. 12, 1849, d. Mar 15, 1930, m Alice Josephine Strain, b Aug. 10, 1859. Buried at Newark, O.
1. Robert Quincy Baker, b. Sept 14, 1883 No. 1682.
2. Marguerite Baker, b Mar. 9, 1884

No. 1682. Fifth Generation. 1681.

1) Robert Quincy Baker, b Sept. 14, 1883, m Feb 23, 1909, Margaret Swindell, b. July 12, 1886 Address 1 Sheridan Rd, Coshocton, O Banker Episcopalian. Burial ground at Newark, O.
1. Robert Quincy Baker, Jr , b June 15, 1910.
2. William Pearce Baker, b Mar 17, 1917

No. 1689. Fourth Generation. 1181.
1) Leonard Shaw, b ———, 1831, d ———, 1876, m Amanda Walbaco, b. ———

1 James Shaw, b ———.
2 Mary Shaw, b ———
3 Billy Shaw, b ———
4. Eliza Shaw, b ———.
5 Etta Shaw, b. ———

No. 1690. Fourth Generation. 1181.
2) Lillyman Shaw, b ———, 1833, d ———, 1913, m Cassie Dicks, b

1 Maggie, b. ———.
2 Emery, b ———
3 Billy, b ———
4 Ethel, b. ———
5 Emma, b ———
6 Nora, b ———.
7 Cora, b ———
8 Martha, b ———
9 Bertha, b ———
10 Frank, b ———
11 Olla, b. ———.
12 George, b ———

No. 1691. Fourth Generation. 1181.
3) Hester Shaw, b ———, 1835, d. ———, 1914, m. William Cummings, b ———.

1 Billy Cummings, b. ———.
2 Louise Cummings, b ———.
3. Anna Cummings, b. ———
4 Charles Cummings, b. ———
5 Etta Cummings, b. ———.
6 Ezra Cummings, b. ———.
7. Pearl Cummings, b. ———

No. 1692. Fourth Generation. 1181.
4) Lewis Shaw, b. ———, 1838, d. Feb —, 1922, m. Julia Stringer, b. ——— Lived at Cloverdale, Ind.

1 Clara Shaw, b ———

No. 1693. Fourth Generation. 1181.
5) Oliver Shaw, b ———, 1840, d ———, 1912, m Mahala Runion, b. ——— Address Cloverdale, Ind

1 Florence Shaw, b ———
2 Upton Shaw, b ———

No. 1694. Fourth Generation. 1181.
6) Adaline Shaw, b. ———, 1842, d. ———, 1869, m John R. Butler, b ——— Lived at Cloverdale, Ind

1 Sarah Butler, b ———, m ———. Farmer Cloverdale, Ind., R 1.

No. 1695. Fourth Generation. 1181.
7) Amelia Shaw, b. ———, 1848, d Aug 6. 1932, m William Larkin, b ——— Address. Cloverdale, Ind

1 Reason Larkin, b ———

2. Charles Larkin, b ───────
3 Olla Larkin, b. ───────.
4. Lillie Larkin, b. ───────.

No. 1696. Fourth Generation. 1181.

8) Mary E. Shaw, b May 30, 1852, d ───────, m. Samuel B. Wright,
b. ───────, 1847, d ───────, 1925. They were married in 1871. Housewife.
Missionary, Baptist Address: Putnamville, Ind
1. Clarence Wright, b. Nov. 24, 1872 No 1697.
2. Ida J. Wright, b Sept. 10, 1876. No. 1702.
3. Joseph B. Wright, b. Dec 22, 1878. No. 1703
4. E. P. Wright, b. Mar. 7, 1881 No. 1704.
5. Guy T. Wright, b Mar 25, 1888 No. 1705
6 Emmons Wright, b Jan 16, 1893. No 1706

No. 1697. Fifth Generation. 1696.

1) Clarence Wright, b. Nov. 24, 1872, at Putnamville. Ind , m in 1896 Rosa
Ressler Address· Center Point, Ind Farmer
1. Veneta Wright, b Dec. 1, 1897 No 1698
2. Roy Wright, b Aug 28, 1899 No 1699
3. Clarence Wright, Jr., b. Nov 10, 1903. No. 1700.
4 Marie Wright, b. May 28, 1909. No. 1701.

No. 1698. Sixth Generation. 1697.

1) Veneta Wright. b Dec 1. 1897, m Roy Shultz, b Sept 24, 1897 Address:
Center Point, Ind
1. Donald Shultz, b. Sept. 8, 1920.
2 Mary Jane Shultz, b Nov 13, 1921

No. 1699. Sixth Generation. 1697.

2) Roy Wright, b. Aug. 28, 1899, m Mary K Brothers. b July 7, 1905 Address: Center Point, Ind.

No. 1700. Sixth Generation. 1697.

3) Clarence Wright. Jr , b. Nov 10, 1903, m Lorene Kaiser. b Mar 1, 1909.
Address: Center Point, Ind
1. Geraldine Wright, b May 7, 1920.
2 Shirley Ann Wright, b. Feb 15, 1936

No. 1701. Sixth Generation. 1697.

4) Marie Wright, b May 28, 1908, m Ernest Kiser, b Mar. 11, 1907. Address Center Point, Ind

No. 1702. Fifth Generation. 1696.

2) Ida J. Wright, b Sept 10, 1876, at Putnamville, Ind., m in 1900, Charles
A Heath, b ───────, 1872 Address Reevesville, Ind. Farmer Christian
Church
1. Loren Heath, b June —, 1901
2. Eula Clay Heath, b Feb 19, 1905
3. Charles Arthur Heath, b. April 7, 1907.

No. 1703. Fifth Generation. 1696.

3) Joseph B. Wright, b Dec. 22, 1878, at Putnamville, Ind , m 1909, to Lois
Brackney Christian Church Address Putnamville, Ind Farmer
1 Joseph Oakley Wright, b ───────, 1914.

No. 1704. Fifth Generation. 1696.

4) E. P. Wright, b Mar 7, 1881, at Putnamville, Ind., m 1921, Marjorie Leslie Physician. Presbyterian Address 1222 State, Belvidere, Ill.

No. 1705. Fifth Generation. 1696.

5) Guy T. Wright, b. Mar. 25, 1888, at Putnamville, Ind., m 1910, to Tuna Smitheson. Address: Greencastle, Ind. Road contractor.

1. Adopted child, Barbara Jean Wright, b ——————.

No. 1706. Fifth Generation. 1696.

6) Emmons Wright, b Jan. 16, 1893, at Putnamville, Ind , m. Losa Huffman, b. ————, 1892. They were married in 1913. Farmer Reevesville, Ind. No issue

No. 1707. Fourth Generation. 1182.

2) Ann Rebecca Theiss, b Feb 8, 1841, d Dec 5, 1907, m in 1867 James Harrison Capito, b April 12, 1843, d Aug 21, 1911. Housewife. Methodist. Address: Los Angeles, Calif Burial in Rosedale cemetery, Los Angeles, Calif.

1. Charles Everett Capito, b. Sept 18, 1868 No 1708
2. James Oren Capito, b May 9, 1871. No. 1710.
3 John Theiss Capito, b April 11, 1874. No. 1711.

No. 1708. Fifth Generation. 1707.

1) Charles Everett Capito, b Sept. 18, 1868, d Aug 26, 1932, m Nov 23, 1895, Lula E Gates, b. July 31, 1868. Salesman. Methodists Burial in Inglewood cemetery, Los Angeles, Calif Address: Los Angeles, Calif

1. Bessie Ruth Capito, b Aug 26, 1901
2 Charles Everett Capito, Jr , b May 5, 1906. No. 1709

No. 1709. Sixth Generation. 1708.

2) Charles Everett Capito, Jr , b May 5, 1906. m June 11, 1932, Leona Heletha Honifield Address Wasco, Calif

No. 1710. Fifth Generation. 1707.

2) James Oren Capito, b May 9, 1871, m —————————, and lives at Los Angeles, Calif

No. 1711. Fifth Generation. 1707.

3) John Theiss Capito, b April 11. 1874, m Hettie ———— He died Sept 9, 1924, leaving no children

No. 1712. Fourth Generation. 1182.

4) Charles Henry Theiss, b July 5, 1845, d Dec. 31, 1925, m. in 1878, Nellie Higgins Charles Henry moved to California as a young man and there changed his name to Charles Meredith due to the hard spelling of his birth name. He was a brill ant mathematician and educator He was an outstanding student all his life, his best position was superintendent of schools of California, after which he held several executive positions at different places in California, and last at Elsiner, Calif , was principal of the high school; his personality was outstanding to such an extent that most of his pupils used him as an example and revered his memory

He died at his home in Elsiner, Calif , his body was cremated and his ashes were buried in his mother's grave at Harrods Creek cemetery in Oldham Co , Ky.

1 Ethel Meredith Theiss, b Mar 17, 1878. Ethel is living somewhere in New York City or some of its suburbs She was an actress and her stage name was Jane Meredith.

No. 1713. Fourth Generation. 1182.

5) Oren Brannaman Theiss, b Jan 25, 1848, m April 25, 1878, Mary Greenwood Haydon, b Dec 13, 1860 Newsboy Druggist Doctor Teacher Farmer

They were members of the Methodist Church Mr. Theiss was first a newsboy for the "Louisville Courier Journal" After graduating from the male high school, he studied medicine and practiced just a short time He left the profession and became a pharmacist for John Newman at 5th and Chestnut Sts, Louisville, Ky From this place he went to teaching at Talmuth, Ky, and thence to Frankfort, Ky. From the last named place he was secured as principal of the 17th and Duncan Street public schools, Louisville, Ky., and remained there for 22 years. Having purchased a farm in Oldham Co, Ky, from his savings, he took up this work in 1898 and still owns it. He has increased its size to 300 acres It is now one of the good producing dairy farms of the country.

Professor Theiss is a thorough student of English grammar, having written a book on English history and literature He is a chess player of considerable note, an honorary member of the Louisville Club, having served as its first secretary and at one time champion of Louisville In addition to being a self-made educated, cultured gentleman, he is a man of strong personality whose honesty and morals have never been questioned by any one His children and grandchildren and friends will always remember his humor, and love of poetry He is today, Feb. 17, 1939, in good health (written by his son Oren B. Theiss, Jr) Address: Prospect, Oldham Co, Ky Place of burial, Harrods Creek, Oldham Co, Ky

    1. Charles Hayden Theiss, b Sept. 23, 1879, d May —, 1908
    2 Coral Theiss, b Jan 30, 1882. No 1714
    3. Oren Brannaman Theiss, Jr, b Aug 3, 1887 No 1716
    4. John Greenwood Theiss, b Jan 24, 1890 No 1717.
    5. Chester Blanchard Theiss, b Sept 15, 1902 No 1718

No. 1714. Fifth Generation. 1713.

2) Coral Theiss, b Jan 30, 1882, in Ky, m A H Clore County school trustee Address: Skylight, Ky Episcopal and Christian Churches
    1 Arthur Hayden Clore, b Aug 7, 1905 No 1715
    2 Oren Brannaman Clore, b April 25, 1909
    3 Robert Hodge Clore, b Oct 30, 1912
    4 John Greenwood Clore, b July 30, 1919

No. 1715. Sixth Generation. 1714.

1) Arthur Hayden Clore, b. Aug 7, 1905, m Dec 19, 1931, Dessie Adcock, b. Feb. 13, 1907. Address: Skylight, Ky. Farmer. Christian Church
    1 Oren Brannaman Clore, b. Aug 20, 1933

No. 1716. Fifth Generation. 1713.

3) Oren Brannaman Theiss, Jr, b Aug. 3, 1887, in Ky, m June 2, 1920, Katherine Miller Greenfield, b. Nov 4, 1898, divorced June 30, 1932 Automobile salesman. Address Buechel, Ky, or 849 S 3rd St, Louisville, Ky. Episcopal Church.
    1 William Nelson Theiss, b Jan 16, 1923.

No. 1717. Fifth Generation. 1713.

4) John Greenwood Theiss, b Jan 24, 1890, d. Dec 4, 1918, in Sallie Lee Hawley, b June 12, 1889. Farmer Christian Church Address Prospect, Ky.
    1. Mary Christine Theiss, b Mar 15, 1913

No. 1718. Fifth Generation. 1713.

5) Chester Blanchard Theiss, b Sept. 15, 1892, in Ky, m Mar, 1916, Roberta Williams, b. Nov 18, 1893 Farmer. Christian Church. Address: Prospect, Ky.
    1. Robert Bowling Theiss, b Jan 14, 1917

2. Chester Blanchard Theiss, Jr., b April 17, 1924
3 Charles Howard Theiss, b. Dec. 19, 1926.

No. 1719. Fourth Generation. 1182.

7) Martha Amelia Theiss, b. Nov. 3, 1854, d. April 2, 1934, m. April 29, 1878, John T. English, b. June 24, 1848, d. June 10, 1931. Teacher and farmer. Address was Prospect, Ky , now Buechel, Ky.
1. Herbert T. English, b. July 16, 1879. No. 1720.
2. Orena Brannaman English, b. Nov 10, 1883. No. 1721.

No. 1720. Fifth Generation. 1719.

1) Herbert T English, b. July 16, 1879, m. Edith Pearson Ourn, Aug. 19, 1929 No children

No. 1721. Fifth Generation. 1719.

2) Orena Brannaman English, b. Nov 10, 1883, m. Harvey Clifton Shanks, Jan. 4, 1905, d April 9, 1928. She later married John Chandler Bourne Oct. 29, 1930. Address: Buechel, Ky.

No. 1722. Fourth Generation. 1183.

1) Joseph Brannaman, b Dec. 27, 1843, d July 14, 1868, m. Sarah Kayler, b. May 18, 1848. They lived at Cloverdale, Ind He died at an early age and his widow married his brother Samuel.
1. Almeda C Brannaman, b Sept 11, 1868 No. 1723.

No. 1723. Fifth Generation. 1722.

1) Almeda C. Brannaman, b Sept 11, 1868, in Ind , m Joseph McKamey. Address: Cloverdale, Ind
1 Bertha G McKamey, b. Dec 2, 1895.
2. Ira C. McKamey, b. Feb. 19, 1897
3. Ona M. McKamey, b Aug. 30, 1898
4. Nettie F. McKamey, b April 11, 1900
5. Lenna V. McKamey, b. Sept. 20, 1901.
6. Arley E. McKamey, b. April 27, 1903.
7 James S McKamey, b Feb. 15, 1905, d. April 28, 1910.
8. Paul McKamey, b. Aug. 18, 1907, d same day
9. Lola D. McKamey, b. Dec. 27, 1910.

No. 1724. Fourth Generation. 1183.

2) Samuel Brannaman, b Mar. 25, 1845, d. Sept. 3, 1887, m Sarah Kayler Brannaman, b May 18, 1848, d Feb 19, 1938. Address Cloverdale, Ind
1. Henry Clifford Brannaman, b June 22, 1871 No. 1725.
2. Clinton Frederick Brannaman, b. May 7, 1873 No. 1727.
3. John Wilford Brannaman, b July 18, 1876 No. 1728.
4. James Wesley Brannaman, b. Dec 15, 1878. No. 1729.
5. Clara Belle Brannaman, b. Mar. 29, 1881. No. 1730.
6 Ida Mae Brannaman, b. June 1, 1883. No. 1731.
7. Ralph S. Brannaman, b. May 29, 1886. No. 1732.

No. 1725. Fifth Generation. 1724.

1) Henry Clifford Brannaman, b June 22, 1871, m. Hester Hood Address: Cloverdale, Ind.
1 Mary Brannaman, b. —————. No. 1726.

No. 1726. Sixth Generation. 1725.

1) Mary Brannaman, b. —————, she died and left issue, m. Frank Cash, b. —————.
1. Catherine Cash, b. ————— No 1726¼.

No. 1726¼. Seventh Generation. 1726.

1 Catherine Cash, b ——————, m Harold Goble. Address. Cloverdale, Ind.

No. 1727. Fifth Generation. 1724.

2) Clinton Frederick Brannaman, b May 7, 1873, d Dec 29, 1920, m Rena Frazer. No issue.

No. 1728. Fifth Generation. 1724.

3) John Wilford Brannaman, b July 18, 1876, m. Annie McCamey, b. ——————, m. (2nd) Lida Wilson.
1. Roxey Brannaman, b. ——————.
2. Leonard Brannaman, b. ——————.
(From second wife)
3. Laura Opel Brannaman, b ——————.

No. 1729. Fifth Generation. 1724.

4) James Wesley Brannaman, b Dec 15, 1878, m. Rosa Akens, b. ——————.
1. Eugene Brannaman, b. ——————.
2. Evelyn Brannaman, b. ——————.
3. Glenden Brannaman, b ——————.
4. Gilbert Brannaman, b. ——————
5 Charles Brannaman, b. ——————.

No. 1730. Fifth Generation. 1724.

5) Clara Belle Brannaman, b. Mar 29, 1881, m. James A. Shumaker.
1. Jay Shumaker, b ——————.
2. Ernest Shumaker, b. ——————.
3. Emmitt Shumaker, b. ——————.

No. 1731. Fifth Generation. 1724.

6) Ida Mae Brannaman, b. June 1, 1883, m Everett Leonard. They live in Florida and have a family. N. F. R.

No. 1732. Fifth Generation. 1724.

7) Ralph S Brannaman, b May 29, 1886, m Della O Conner, b ——————. Address: Cloverdale, Ind.
1. Jewel K Brannaman, b Jan. 21, 1910. No. 3655.
2. Basil B Brannaman, b. Sept. 17, 1917.

No. 1733. Fourth Generation. 1183.

3) Marillo Elizabeth Brannaman, b. Mar 14, 1847, d. Dec 3, 1896, m. Frederick Wander, b. ——————.
1. Archie E. Wander, b. ——————. No 1734.
2 Clara W Wander, b ——————. No 1735.

No. 1734. Fifth Generation. 1733.

1) Archie E Wander, b ——————, m Dora Wander, b ——————. Address: Columbus, O. Have issue. N. F. R.

No. 1735. Fifth Generation. 1733.

2) Clara W. Wander, b ——————, m. John Linnville Address· Cloverdale, Ind.
1. Jessie Linnville, b ——————. No 1736
2 Mary Lee Linnville, b ——————
3. Frederick Linnville, b —————— No. 1737.

268

4 Bert Sackett Linnville, b ——————.
5 John A Linnville, b. ——————.

No. 1736. Sixth Generation. 1735.

1) Jessie Linnville, b. ——————, m Birch McCamey, b. ——————.
1. —————— McCamey, b. ——————.
2. —————— McCamey, b. ——————.
3. —————— McCamey, b. ——————.
4. —————— McCamey, b. ——————.

No. 1737. Sixth Generation. 1735.

3) Frederick Linnville, b. ——————, m Ola ——————.
1. —————— Linnville, b. ——————.

No. 1738. Fourth Generation. 1183.

5) John Tice C. Brannaman, b. June 19, 1851, d Oct. 1, 1923, m. Oct. 25, 1877, Teletha C. Davis, b. Oct. 26, 1854, d. Jan. 9, 1926. Farmer. Church of Christ. Burial at Cloverdale, Ind. Address: Cloverdale, Ind.
1 Retha Etta Brannaman, b Aug 4, 1878. No 1739.
2. Cora Annis Brannaman, b Mar 12, 1880. No. 1740.
3 Hattie Jane Brannaman, b. June 12, 1882. No. 1741.
4. Oren R Brannaman, b Mar. 10, 1885. No. 1742.
5. Flossie Brannaman, b Dec. 12, 1886. No. 1743.
6. Ezra Brannaman, b Jan 14, 1888, d Feb 23, 1889
7 Clarence Brannaman, b Dec. 15, 1889. No. 1744.
8. Hazel Brannaman, b July 8, 1893 No. 1745.

No. 1739. Fifth Generation. 1738.

1) Retha Etta Brannaman, b Aug 4, 1878, d. Dec. 9, 1916, m. Jan. 24, 1906, Verley Greenlee, b Aug 19, 1881. Address Cloverdale, Ind. Farmer. Church of Christ. Burial place at Cloverdale, Ind.
1 Delbert P. Greenlee, b Jan 24, 1908, d Feb 5, 1927.
2 Archie P Greenlee, b. July 20, 1911.
3. Telithia E Greenlee, b June 12, 1914

No. 1740. Fifth Generation. 1738.

2) Cora Annis Brannaman, b Mar. 12, 1880, m Nov 25, 1911, William R. Walker, b. April 30, 1880. Address Cloverdale, Ind Farmer. Church of Christ. Burial place at Cloverdale, Ind
1 Donna Mae Walker, b. Oct 14, 1912
2 John W Walker, b Sept 29, 1913
3. Austin E. Walker, b Dec 10, 1914.
4 Bessie Fern Walker, b. Nov. 4, 1916.
5. Kenneth E. Walker, b July 25, 1918.
6 Russell Walker, b Sept 6, 1920
7. Emerson Walker, b. Oct. 5, 1921.
8. Martha Rose Walker, b Dec 26, 1924, d. Mar. 2, 1926.

No. 1741. Fifth Generation. 1738.

3) Hattie Jane Brannaman, b June 12, 1882, d Feb. 19, 1907, m. Mar. 25, 1902, H. C. Bradstreet. Farmer. Church of Christ.
1. Infant, stillborn.
2. Alta Fern Bradstreet, b. ——————.
3. Glacia Bradstreet, b ——————
All died in infancy.

No. 1742. Fifth Generation. 1738.

4) Oren R Brannaman, b. Mar. 10, 1885, m Mar 10, 1907, Bonnie Mae Rule, b Aug. 28, 1886. Address Cloverdale, Ind Farmer Church of Christ Burial at Cloverdale, Ind.

1 Wayne R. Brannaman, b Mar 20, 1913

No. 1743. Fifth Generation. 1738.

5) Flossie Brannaman, b Dec 12, 1886, d Mar. 12, 1923, m Nov 20, 1907, Velta O Mann, b Nov 17, 1884 Address· Cloverdale, Ind Farming Church of Christ.

1. Gernie E Mann, b Aug 20, 1908, d May 29, 1916
2. Dennie Lee Mann, b. Nov. 9, 1913, d April 20, 1918
3 Vernon Doyle Mann, b. Feb. 20, 1921.

No. 1744. Fifth Generation. 1738.

7) Clarence Brannaman, b Dec. 15, 1889, m Oct 2, 1915, Loue E Wright, b. Dec. 21, 1896. Address Cloverdale, Ind. Farmer. Church of Christ

1. Tulta Farrell Brannaman, b Oct. 19, 1916, d Jan 13, 1917
2. Clarence Cleon Brannaman, b Feb 24, 1918.
3. John Olen Brannaman, b Nov. 27, 1925

No. 1745. Fifth Generation. 1738.

8) Hazel Brannaman, b July 8, 1893, m Jan 6, 1918, Everall Wallace, b July 7, 1897 Address: Cloverdale, Ind. Farmer Church of Christ.

1. Daphne Pearl Wallace, b Jan 23, 1919
2. Helen Louise Wallace, b Oct. 11, 1921
3. Irvin B. Wallace, b. April 4, 1924

No. 1746. Fourth Generation. 1183.

6) Emily Adaline Brannaman, b. April 1, 1853, m Dec , 1870, William Henry Sackett, b. Nov. 13, 1846, d. June 1, 1880. Address: Ramona, Calif.

1. Samuel Albert Sackett, b Feb 23, 1872 No. 1747.
2 Ida Mae Sackett, b. July 21, 1873, d. May 26, 1903
3 Homer Eddy Sackett, b Mar. 5, 1875 No 1749.
4. Leroy Walter Sackett, b Dec 14, 1876 No. 1751.
5. Jennie Sackett, b Nov. 27, 1878, d Oct. 8, 1883

No. 1747. Fifth Generation. 1746.

1) Samuel Albert Sackett, b Feb 23, 1872, d Dec 24, 1935, m. June 1, 1904, Agnes Klingelhoffer, b. April 6, 1878 Address 4000 Hastings St., El Paso, Tex. Lawyer. Christian Church.

1 Forrest Victor Sackett, b. Sept. 9, 1905. No. 1747¼.
2. Arlien Sackett, b. Oct. 10, 1907. No. 1748
3. Albert Klingelhoffer Sackett, b. Mar. 2, 1909 No 1748½.
4. Hazel Agnes Sackett, b July 1, 1920.

No. 1747¼. Sixth Generation. 1747.

1) Forrest Victor Sackett, b Sept 9, 1907, m Dec 20, 1935, Bernice Mitchel. Address: 4000 Hastings St., El Paso, Tex.

No. 1748. Sixth Generation. 1747.

2) Arlien Sackett, b. Oct 10, 1907, m Sept 24, 1925, Travis Leslie Irby, b. Nov. —, 1901.

1. Travis Leslie Irby, Jr., b. April 4, 1928.
2. Albert Ray Irby, b. July 10, 1931.

No. 1748½. Sixth Generation. 1747.

3) Albert Klingelhoffer Sackett, b Mar 2, 1909, m Mollie Lawler.

No. 1749. Fifth Generation. 1746.

3) Homer Eddy Sackett, b. Mar 5, 1875, m Nov. 18, 1903, Verona Ella Heck, b. Feb. 15, 1878 Attorney at law Christians Judge of U S Supreme Court. Address. 753 Tyler St, Gary, Ind.
1. Henry Richmond Sackett, b Mar 9, 1907. No. 1750

No. 1750. Sixth Generation. 1749.

1) Henry Richmond Sackett, b Mar 9, 1907, m. Aug. 12, 1931, Dorothy Shannon. Address. Gary, Ind Attorney at law with his father.
1. Susanna Dorothy Sackett, b May 27, 1934
2. James Homer Sackett, b Jan 25, 1936

No. 1751. Fifth Generation. 1746.

4) Leroy Walter Sackett, b Dec 14, 1876, m Aug., 1904, Emily Whistler Engaged in Y work. Address. 2002 Fairview, Houston, Tex. No children

No. 1752. Fourth Generation. 1183.

7) William Christie Brannaman, b Feb 15, 1855, m. Nov. 3, 1877, Emily Jane Brown, b. Oct 11, 1854, d April 6, 1921 Carpenter Christian Church. Burial place at Crown Hill cemetery, Indianapolis, Ind. Address. 1154 Congress Ave., Indianapolis, Ind
1 Lorena Estella Brannaman, b Sept 12, 1878 No. 1755.
2 Ethel Ora Ida Brannaman, b Feb 17, 1880, d. Dec. 12, 1885.
3. Jessie A. Brannaman, b Sept 8, 1883. No. 1753.
4 Erna May Brannaman, b Aug 22, 1886 No 1756.
5 Grace Cecil Brannaman, b Sept 22, 1889, d. Aug. 10, 1908.
6 Walter Scott Brannaman, b. Jan. 28, 1892.
7. Delbert Wallace Brannaman, b May 25, 1895.

No. 1753. Fifth Generation. 1752.

3) Jessie A. Brannaman, b. Sept 8, 1883, m Sept 19, 1906, Frederick Fly, b Mar 8, 1884 Rug cleaner Christian Church Address: 1154 Congress Ave., Indianapolis, Ind.
1 William Lawrence Fly, b Dec 11, 1907. No. 1754

No. 1754. Sixth Generation. 1753.

1) William Lawrence Fly, b Dec 11, 1907, m Helen M Wakefield. Address: 13th & Penna Sts, Indianapolis, Ind.

No. 1755. Fifth Generation. 1752.

1) Lorena Estella Brannaman, b Sept. 12, 1878, d. July 8, 1901, m Charles F Brown No issue

No. 1756. Fifth Generation. 1752.

4) Erna May Brannaman, b Aug 22, 1886, m Harry L. Busselle. Erna and her daughter Elzabeth Marie lost their lives in the Graystone Apartment Hotel fire in Indianapolis, Ind, on Nov. 12, 1927, there being twelve lives lost in the fire.
1. Elizabeth Marie Busselle, b ——————, d. Nov. 12, 1927.
2. Arthur E Busselle, b. ——————. No. 1757

No. 1757. Sixth Generation. 1756.

2) Arthur E. Busselle, b ——————, m Josephine McNamee, b. ——————.
Address 1226 Cook Ave, Cleveland, O.

No. 1759. Fourth Generation. 1184.

4) Henry Adam Lukemeier, b Sept. 28, 1851, d. Oct 14, 1932, m. Sept. 8, 1881, Emma C. Kleiber, b. Jan 31, 1857. He was foreman in a trunk factory. Methodists. Address: 1817 Grant Line Road, New Albany, Ind. Burial place at New Albany, Ind.
1. Louis Henry Lukemeier, b Sept. 11, 1882. No 1760
2. Lorenzo Lukemeier, b. Oct 30, 1886. No. 1761
3. Bertha Katherine Lukemeier, b Mar 10, 1884. No 1762
4 William Frederick Lukemeier, b Oct 3, 1889 No 1763.
5. Erwin Clarence Lukemeier, b. Oct 29, 1895. No. 1764.

No. 1760. Fifth Generation. 1759.

1) Louis Henry Lukemeier, b. Sept 11, 1882, m. Mar. 3, 1926, Hazel Basham, b. May 13, 1907. Address: Grant Line Road & S St, New Albany, Ind. Taxi cab business Methodists
1. Ruth Hazel Lukemeier, b Dec 7, 1926
2. Louis Henry Lukemeier, Jr, b. Oct 18, 1930

No. 1761. Fifth Generation. 1759.

2) Lorenza Lukemeier, b. Oct 30, 1886, m. April 20, 1911, Kate Hope, b. Nov. 26, 1891. Moulder by trade. Evangelical. Address: 124 Cabel St, Louisville, Ky.
1. Katherine Lucile Lukemeier, b. Nov. 22, 1913

No. 1762. Fifth Generation. 1759.

3) Bertha Katherine Lukemeier, b Mar. 10, 1884; never married. She was a registered nurse. Methodist. She lived in New Albany, Ind Address: 1817 Grant Line Rd., New Albany, Ind.

No. 1763. Fifth Generation. 1759.

4) William Frederick Lukemeier, b. Oct 3, 1889, m Nellie ————. Foreman Peerless Mfg. Co., Louisville, Ky. Methodists
1. Infant b. and d. ————.
2 William Lukemeier, b ————.
3. Emily Louise Lukemeier, b. ————.

No. 1764. Fifth Generation. 1759.

5) Erwin Clarence Lukemeier, b. Oct 29, 1895, m. June 24, 1919, Henrietta Speier, b. May 10, 1896. Machinist. Methodists. Burial at New Albany, Ind. Address: 1817 Grant Line Rd, New Albany, Ind
1. Louise Emily Lukemeier, b Jan 16, 1921
2. Henry Irvin Lukemeier, b May 29, 1922
3. Bertha Mae Lukemeier, b. Sept. 26, 1926, twin.
4. Eleanor Jean Lukemeier, b Sept. 26, 1926, twin.
5. Henrietta Lukemeier, b. Feb 12, 1932

No. 1765. Fourth Generation. 1184.

5) Catherine Lukemeier, b. July 2, 1855, d. Dec. 1, 1923. Never married. Seamstress. Methodist. Address: 1832 W. Market St, Louisville, Ky. Buried in Eastern Cemetery, Louisville, Ky.

No. 1766. Fourth Generation. 1184.

6) Lydia Lukemeier, b. Jan 27, 1858, m. Henry Schoppenhorst, b. Aug. 23, 1857, d. Dec. 1, 1923. Address: 4147 West Broadway, Louisville, Ky.
1. Frederick William Schoppenhorst, b Nov. 13, 1887, d July 10, 1908.
2 Edgar Allen Schoppenhorst, b ————, 1884, d. ————, 1888.

3. Ruby Schoppenhorst, b Feb 3, 1885, d. Mar 22, 1935, single
4. Henry Schoppenhorst, b ———, 1887, d ———, 1891
5 Ada Lee Schoppenhorst, b ———, 1889, d ———, 1890.
6. Elmer Givin Schoppenhorst, b Dec. 11, 1891. No. 1767.
7. Louis Schoppenhorst, b. ———, 1895, d. ———, 1899
8 Edward H. Schoppenhorst, b. ———, 1893, d ———, 1895
9 John Victor Schoppenhorst, b Dec. 22, 1897, d same day
10 Charles Wesley Schoppenhorst, b Aug. 6, 1900. No. 1768.

No. 1767 Fifth Generation. 1766.

6) Elmer Givin Schoppenhorst, b Dec. 11, 1891, d Aug. 21, 1921, m. Oct 24, 1914, Florence Gray, b Nov. 20, 1892. Undertaker and embalmer. Address 4147 W. Broadway St , Louisville, Ky
   1 Virginia Schoppenhorst, b Mar 20, 1921

No. 1768. Fifth Generation. 1766.

10) Charles Wesley Schoppenhorst, b Aug 6, 1900, m Oct. 14, 1926, May Bert, b. July 16, 1901 Undertaker and embalmer. Christian Church Address· 652 S 42nd St , Louisville, Ky
   1 Dorothy Bert Schoppenhorst, b Feb 19, 1929.

No. 1769. Fourth Generation. 1184.

8) Louis Jacob Lukemeier, b Jan 9, 1862, d July 21, 1934, m. Aug. 1, 1889, Add e Franck, b. Sept 8, 1864 Night watchman Methodist. Burial in Eastern cemetery, Louisville, Ky Address 1105 Whitney, Louisville, Ky.
   1. John Franck Lukemeier, b July 16, 1890. No 1770
   2 Zelda Annie Lukemeier, b Nov 15, 1891 No 1771
   3 Elizabeth Caroline Lukemeier, b April 12, 1896 No 1772
   4 Lydia Lukemeier, b Sept 28, 1899 No 1773
   5 Albert Louis Lukemeier, b May 9, 1902 No 1774
   6 Gladys Catherine Lukemeier, b Sept. 8, 1904 No 1775.

No. 1770. Fifth Generation. 1769.

1) John Franck Lukemeier, b July 16, 1890, m Mar. 27, 1913, Minnie Scarbrough, b Sept. 17, 1892, d Mar 25, 1925 Woodworker Methodists Burial in Evergreen cemetery, Louisville, Ky Address 3555 Taylor Blvd , Louisville, Ky.
   1 Ruth Geneva Lukemeier, b Aug 25, 1916
   2. John Albert Lukemeier, b June 7, 1919.
   3 Alice May Lukemeier, b Jan 4, 1925, d Jan 6, 1925.

No. 1771. Fifth Generation. 1769.

2) Zelda Annie Lukemeier, b Nov 15, 1891, m. Aug 28, 1918, Earl Humphry, b. Nov 2, 1889, d Aug 14, 1920 Mrs Humphry is now a cook in a wealthy home. Methodist. Cave Hill cemetery, Louisville, Ky Address 1105 Whitney, Louisville, Ky No children.

No. 1772. Fifth Generation. 1769.

3) Elizabeth Caroline Lukemeier, b April 12, 1896, d Nov 29, 1929, m. Silas Payton Meyer, b. May 13, 1895, m Nov —, 1919. Housekeeper. Methodist. Burial in Cave Hill cemetery, Louisville, Ky Address 4375 Taylor Blvd., Louisville, Ky.
   1. Carol Louise Meyer, b Nov 19, 1921
   2 Alice Elizabeth Meyer, b May 22, 1925.
   3. Frances Rhea Meyer, b Mar 16, 1929.

0

No. 1773. Fifth Generation. 1769.

4) Lydia Emily Lukemeier, b Sept 28, 1899, m Dec 2, 1920, Curtis Rhodes, b. April 27, 1899. Address· 2632 Duncan St, Louisville, Ky Housekeeper. Methodist.

1. Wanda Elizabeth Rhodes, b Aug. 13, 1934.

No. 1774. Fifth Generation. 1769.

5) Albert Louis Lukemeier, b May 9, 1902, m. Sept 10, 1924, Catherine Helm, b. July 23, 1908. Address 2652 Griffith Ave, Louisville, Ky. Laborer.

1. Alberta Marie Lukemeier, b. July 30, 1925.
2. Betty Addilyn Lukemeier, b Nov. 28, 1928

No. 1775. Fifth Generation. 1769.

6) Gladys Catherine Lukemeier, b Sept 8, 1904, m. July 6, 1928, Herman Betz, b July 31, 1904. Address. 1105 Whitney, Louisville, Ky Housekeeper Method st. Burial in Schardein cemetery, Louisville, Ky

1. Elizabeth Ann Betz (stillborn), Jan. 3, 1930.
2 Herman Betz, Jr, b. Mar. 20, 1931

No. 1776. Fourth Generation. 1185.

1) Frederick Hargesheimer, b Sept. 30, 1845, d. Nov. 13, 1905, m Aug. 25, 1869, Lavania Balmer, b. Dec. 23, 1850, d Aug 28, 1904 Grocery clerk Methodists. Burial in Cave Hill cemetery, Louisville, Ky Address· Louisville, Ky

1. Lydia E. Hargesheimer, b. Dec 19, 1870 No 1777.
2. Mary E Hargesheimer, b Mar 5, 1873, d Oct 25, 1873.
3. Charles F Hargesheimer, b Aug 21, 1874. No 1778.
4 Florence E Hargesheimer, b April 9, 1879 No 1780.
5. Arthur L. Hargesheimer, b. Oct 10, 1880 No 1783
6 Clifford Hargesheimer, b. Mar 29, 1886. No. 1784.
7. Henry C Hargesheimer, b Dec 9, 1890, d. April 14, 1925.

No. 1777. Fifth Generation. 1776.

1) Lydia F. Hargesheimer, b Dec 19, 1870, m. April 22, 1890, John W. Tilden, b Sept. 28, 1864 Address 2507 Darmesnil, Louisville, Ky. Printer by trade. Burial at St. Louis, Mo Cathol.cs.

1. Infant daughter, b April 17, 1892, d. same day.
2 Infant son, b Sept 13, 1894, lived three days.

No. 1778. Fifth Generation. 1776.

3) Charles F. Hargesheimer, b Aug 21, 1874, m. 1896, Alice Haas, b July 14, 1872. Address: Chicago, Ill. Watchcase maker. Methodists.

1. Earl Hargesheimer, b ————— No 1779.

No. 1779. Sixth Generation. 1778.

1) Earl Hargesheimer, b. —————, m. Lillie —————. **They live in** Chicago, Ill.

1. Marvin Hargesheimer, b —————, 1924
2. Jeanne Hargesheimer, b —————, 1927.

No. 1780. Fifth Generation. 1776.

4) Florence E. Hargesheimer, b April 9, 1879, m Sept. 22, 1897, John Akers, b. May 31, 1875. Address: 1521 Anderson St, Louisville, Ky. Grocer Baptists. Burial place Cave Hill cemetery, Louisville, Ky

1. Charles F. Akers, b Oct 2, 1898 No. 1781.
2. Harlan J. Akers, b. Nov. 4, 1906.
3. Virginia M. Akers, b May 27, 1914 No. 1782.

No. 1781. Sixth Generation. 1780.

1) Charles F. Akers, b. Oct 2, 1898, m. Dec. 25, 1917, Leona Ballman, b. May 22, 1898. Address· Louisville, Ky. Clerk Presbyterians. Burial place at Cave Hill cemetery, Louisville, Ky.

1 Charles Marlen Akers, b. Nov. 1, 1919.

No. 1782. Sixth Generation. 1780.

3) Virginia M. Akers, b May 27, 1914, m Aug. 12, 1931, John Moore, b. Oct. 2, 1910. Address: 1521 Anderson St, Louisville, Ky. Ford employe. Baptist.

1. Virginia May Moore, b. Aug 11, 1932.

No. 1783. Fifth Generation. 1776.

5) Arthur L Hargesheimer, b. Oct 10, 1880, m. 1924, Minnie Brown, b. July 14, 1888. Service station manager. Methodists. Address: Louisville, Ky. Burial place in Cave Hill cemetery, Louisville, Ky.

No. 1784. Fifth Generation. 1776.

6) Clifford Hargesheimer, b Mar 29, 1886, m. in 1917 Ruby Conrad Address: Louisville, Ky. Clerk Methodists

1. Maxine Hargesheimer, b. Feb. 14, 1927.

No. 1785. Fourth Generation. 1185.

5) Susanna Hargesheimer, b April 21, 1851, d. June 3, 1908, m. Mathias Kurtz, b Mar. 31, 1843, d in 1913 Farmer Methodists Burial at Hillcrest, Louisville, Ky. Address: Louisville, Ky

1. John E. Kurtz, b Jan. 12, 1872. No. 1786.

2 Edward Kurtz, b. Jan 31, 1874, d Dec 22, 1902.

3 Jacob Kurtz, b Oct. 22, 1877. No. 1788.

4. William Kurtz, b Oct. 9, 1883.

No. 1786. Fifth Generation. 1785.

1) John E. Kurtz, b Jan 12, 1872, m Mar 15, 1892, Lula W. Quillman, b. Sept. 22, 1870, d April 9, 1903 Steam engineer. Reformed Church. Address: Hotel Victoria, 10th Broadway, Louisville, Ky Burial at Hillcrest, Manilick Rd., Louisville, Ky.

1. Emma Soph a Kurtz, b Dec 17, 1892, d June 30, 1894.

2. John Ernest Kurtz, b June 12, 1896, d. May 4, 1931.

3. Anna May Kurtz, b Jan 1, 1899 No 1787.

4. Ruth Julia Kurtz, b ————, 1902, d at nine months.

No. 1787. Sixth Generation. 1786.

3) Anna May Kurtz, b. Jan. 1, 1899, m. Oct. 4, 1922, Benjamin F. McAdams, b. May 6, 1899. Address· Valley Station, Ky. Machinist. Baptists.

1. James Ernest McAdams, b and d at birth.

2. Benjamin F. McAdams, Jr., b June 2, 1926.

3 Norman Kenneth McAdams, b July 24, 1932.

No. 1788. Fifth Generation. 1785.

3) Jacob Kurs (or Kurtz), b Oct. 22, 1877, m. Jan. 16, 1908, Catherine Drexler, b. April 10, 1877, d Aug 9, 1923 Restaurant Address: 1439 Christy Ave., Louisville, Ky.

1 Catherine Kurtz, b Oct 9, 1909 No. 1789

2. Louise Kurtz, b Sept 30, 1911

3. Mary Kurtz, b April 10, 1914

4. Jacob Kurtz, Jr, b Aug 28, 1915.

5. Robert Kurtz, b. Jan 2, 1918

No. 1789. Sixth Generation. 1788.

1) Catherine Kurtz, b Oct 9, 1909, m Frank Kreamer, Sept. 4, 1933.

No. 1790. Fourth Generation. 1185.

✱ 6) John Adam Hargesheimer, b July 12, 1853, d June 8, 1930, m. Sophiah Driedoppel, b. Dec. 5, 1858, d Jan 24, 1879, m. (2nd) Martha Stephens, b Aug. 31, 1852, d. June 13, 1920 They lived in Jefferson Co., Ky., near Louisville. Farmer. Presbyterians

1. Kate Hargesheimer, b. Nov 15, 1878 No 1791.
   (From second wife)
2. Leroy Hargesheimer, b. Dec. 28, 1880, single.
3. Alice Oriana Hargesheimer, b Aug. 24, 1885. No 1795.
4 Oren John Hargesheimer, b. Mar 20, 1889 No 1799.
5. Henrietta Hargesheimer, b. June 16, 1892, d. Sept —, 1894.

No. 1791. Fifth Generation. 1790.

1) Kate Hargesheimer, b Nov 15, 1878, m. June 22, 1899, John H. Cooper, b. Mar. 31, 1880. Address: 1793 W. Hill St., Louisville, Ky. Methodist. Burial place at Hillcrest cemetery, Louisville, Ky

1. Esther Leona Cooper, b Sept 2, 1900.
2. Ralph Chester Cooper, b. Jan. 31, 1903. No. 1792.
3. Mary Alice Cooper, b. Oct. 1, 1905. No. 1793.
4. Charles Adam Cooper, b April 26, 1908. No 1794.
5. Oren Henry Cooper, b. Oct. 19, 1910.
6. Leroy Ivan Cooper, b. June 20, 1913.

No. 1792. Sixth Generation. 1791.

2) Ralph Chester Cooper, b Jan. 31, 1903, m. Sept. 16, 1933, Pyrrha Hargesheimer, b. May 22, 1906. Address: Valley Station, Ky.

No. 1793. Sixth Generation. 1791.

3) Mary Alice Cooper, b. Jan. 31, 1905, m Oct. 26, 1929, Lawrence W. Richeson.

No. 1794. Sixth Generation. 1791.

4) Charles Adam Cooper, b April 26, 1908, m. Feb. 10, 1931, Angle Lee Mahony, b. ———————.

1. Delores June Cooper, b Jan. 11, 1932.
2. Charles Adam Cooper, Jr , b. Sept. 30, 1933.

No. 1795. Fifth Generation. 1790.

✱ 3) Alice Oriana Hargesheimer, b. Aug. 24, 1883, m. Sept. 27, 1906, Frederick J. Weihe (Wy), b. July 16, 1878 Produce dealer Baptists. Address: 1734 W. Hill St., Louisville, Ky.

1. Frederick A. Weihe, b. June 27, 1907. No. 1796.
2. Vernon I. Weihe, b. Mar. 3, 1909. No 1797.
3. Atwell Weihe, b. Dec. 6, 1911. No 1798
4. Ruth Weihe, b. Jan. 7, 1914.
5. Leora Weihe, b. Aug. 15, 1915, d. Sept. 3, 1915.
6. Robert Weihe, b. Nov. 15, 1917, twin.
7. Raymond Weihe, b. Nov 15, 1917, twin.
8. Edgar Weihe, b. Jan. 6, 1922.

No. 1796. Sixth Generation. 1795.

✗ 1) Frederick A. Weihe, b June 27, 1907, m 1929, Marie Foster, b. July 10, 1907. Address: 1734 W. Hill St , Louisville, Ky Transfer business.

276

1 Donaly Weihe, b. ———, 1930 — *Burial Hillcrest*
2 George Weihe, b May 29, 1933 *— Burial at Hebron*
Fred M Weihe — 1944

No. 1797. Sixth Generation. 1795.

2) Vernon J. Weihe, b. Mar. 3, 1909, m. 1932, Euva Blarark, b. April 4, 1908. Address: Louisville, Ky. Radio announcer.

No. 1798. Sixth Generation. 1795.

3) Atwell Weihe, b. Dec. 6, 1911, m. in 1933, Kathleen Jones, b. April 10, 1910. Tobacco worker. Address: 1734 W. Hill St., Louisville, Ky.

No. 1799. Fifth Generation. 1790.

4) John Ernest Hargesheimer, b. Mar. 20, 1889, m. Mar. 22, 1915, Mrs. Lillian McFadzen, b. Mar. 1, 1887. Address. Valley Station, near Louisville, Ky. Actor. Methodists.

1. Adopted daughter, Pyrrha Hargesheimer, b. May 22, 1906. No. 1792.

No. 1800. Sixth Generation. 1799.

1) Pyrrha Hargesheimer, b. May 22, 1906, m. Sept. 16, 1933, Ralph Chester Cooper, b. Jan. 31, 1903. Come in two ways, see No. 1792.

No. 1801 Fourth Generation. 1185.

7) John Hargesheimer, b. Oct 31, 1855, d Nov. 5, 1912, m. May 3, 1881, Wilhelmina Quillman, b. Mar. 21, 1862, d. Dec 17, 1909. Farmer. Methodists. Address. Louisville, Ky., R 2, Station E Burial in Hillcrest cemetery, Louisville, Ky.

1. George Hargesheimer, b Jan. 14, 1883. No 1802.
2. Charles S Hargesheimer, b Sept. 27, 1885. No. 1803.
3. Carrie Hargesheimer, b. Oct. 8, 1887 No 1806
4. John E. Hargesheimer, b Mar. 2, 1890. No. 1808.
5. Sall e B. Hargesheimer, b. Sept. 28, 1892, d. Jan. 6, 1916.
6. Wilhelmina Isabella Hargesheimer, b Mar. 2, 1896 No. 1809.
7. Elizabeth Isabella Hargesheimer, b April 11, 1899.
8 Raymond C. Hargesheimer, b April 26, 1902. No. 1810.
9 Edward E Hargesheimer, b Jan 11, 1905. No. 1811.

No. 1802. Fifth Generation. 1801.

1) George Hargesheimer, b. Jan. 14, 1883, m. Oct. 3, 1906, Carolina Gutermuth, b. May 15, 1873 Address. R 2, Station E, Louisville, Ky. Carpenter. No children Reformed Church.

No. 1803. Fifth Generation. 1801.

2) Charles S Hargesheimer, b. Sept 27, 1885, m Oct. 9, 1906, Mamie Gutermuth, b Mar. 14, 1887. Farmer Reformed Church Burial in Hillcrest cemetery, Louisville, Ky. Address R. 2, Station E, Louisville, Ky.

1. Elmer Hargesheimer, b July 31, 1908. No. 1804.
2 Stella Hargesheimer, b. Dec 2, 1910. No 1805.
3. Ernest Hargesheimer, b. Sept 4, 1912, d Oct. 6, 1912.
4. Clyde Hargesheimer, b Dec 22, 1914.
5 Clarence Hargesheimer, b Oct. 2, 1917.

No. 1804. Sixth Generation. 1803.

1) Elmer Hargesheimer, b July 31, 1908, m. Mar 13, 1925, Mary Henry, b. July 31, 1906. Park employe Methodists Address: Louisville, Ky.

1. Charles E. Hargesheimer, b. Nov. 8, 1927.
2. Lois Marie Hargesheimer, b. Nov. 11, 1929.
3. Stanley R. Hargesheimer, b. Nov. 12, 1930. *Hillcrest*

George D. Weihe, b. May 29, 1933. D. 11/15/2015
Married Joann Geeing - Aug 3/1957
1. Jeffrey A. Weihe - b. 2/29/60 - d. 9/23/80 - Hillcrest
2. Joel A Weihe - b. Sept 5, 1962
3. Jerry A Weihe - b Oct 11, 1964

No. 1805. Sixth Generation. 1803.

2) Stella Hargesheimer, b Dec 2, 1910, d Oct. 13, 1932, m. Jan. 3, 1931, Sylvester McGaren, b. Feb. 4, 1911 Address R. 2, Station E, Louisville, Ky. Laborer. Burial in Hillcrest cemetery, Louisville, Ky. Reformed Church.

1 Doris Jean McGaren, b. Aug. 5, 1931.
2. David Lee McGaren, b. Oct 10, 1932.

No. 1806. Fifth Generation. 1801.

3) Carrie Hargesheimer, b Oct 8, 1887, m. Dec 15, 1908, Richard Whitworth, b. April 1, 1879, d. July 1, 1915 Farmer. Church of God Address: Shively, Ky. Burial in Hillcrest cemetery, Louisville, Ky.

1. Viola W. Whitworth, b Nov. 28, 1909. No. 1807.
2. Margaret Whitworth, b Jan 2, 1916

No. 1807. Sixth Generation. 1806.

1) Viola W. Whitworth, b Nov 28, 1909, m Nov. 30, 1929, Vernon Whitmore Lile, b. Nov. 30, 1908. Railroad shop laborer. Church of God Address: Shively, Ky. No issue.

No. 1808. Fifth Generation. 1801.

4) John E. Hargesheimer, b Mar 2, 1890, m Mar 1, 1919, Mamie Stephens, b. Dec 1, 1897. Farmer. Reformed Church Address: R. 2, Station E, Louisville, Ky.

1. Evelyn Hargesheimer, b. Nov. 4, 1919.

No. 1809. Fifth Generation. 1801.

6) Wilhelmina L. Hargesheimer, b Mar 2, 1896, m April 4, 1923, Frank Davis, b. Sept. 8, 1896 Address Tacoma, Wash City fireman. Methodist.

No. 1810. Fifth Generation. 1801.

8) Raymond Hargesheimer, b April 26, 1902, m April 28, 1923, Anna M. Schoenbachler, b. Aug 15, 1904 Address 4115 La Salle Ave, Louisville, Ky. Gas laborer Methodists Burial in Hillcrest cemetery, Louisville, Ky.

1. Blanche La Verne Hargesheimer, b. Feb 6, 1924
2 Vera Jean Hargesheimer (adopted), b Sept 27, 1927

No. 1811. Fifth Generation. 1801.

9) Edward E. Hargesheimer, b. Jan 11, 1905, m Oct 9, 1927, Eliza L. Henry, b. Feb. 17, 1904. Laborer. Reformed Church Burial in Hillcrest cemetery, Louisville, Ky. Address: R 2, Station E, Louisville, Ky.

1. Edward J Hargesheimer, b. Jan. 23, 1927.
2. Robert L. Hargesheimer, b Mar 19, 1928
3 Helen E. Hargesheimer, b. Mar. 26, 1930

No. 1812. Fourth Generation. 1186.

1) John Henry Kirkhof, b. Mar. 28, 1855, m. June 5, 1877, Emeline H. Badgley, b. May 13, 1857. Address 410 Sherman St, Healdsburg, Calif. Farmer.

1. William Herbert Kirkhof, b. Aug. 11, 1878, d Feb 5, 1886.
2 Sarah Ellen Kirkhof, b Feb 15, 1880, twin. No 1972
3. Julia Etta Kirkhof, b. Feb 15, 1880, twin. No. 1973.
4. John Edwin Kirkhof, b May 15, 1885. No. 1974.
5. Frederick Henry Kirkhof, b May 15, 1885, d. Aug. 20, 1885.
6. George Orin Kirkhof, b April 15, 1891, d Aug 20, 1891.

No. 1813. Fourth Generation. 1186.

2) Daniel Frederick Kirkhof, b. May 12, 1857, d July 1, 1882, m. Dec. 25, 1880, Mary Cobb, b. Oct. 15, 1863, d June 6, 1932. Railroader. German Methodist. Burial at Hayden, Ind.

1 Hugo F. Kirkhof, b. Feb. 10, 1882 No. 1814.

No. 1814. Fifth Generation. 1813.

1) Hugo Frederick Kirkhof, b. Feb. 10, 1882, m. June 7, 1906, Nellie Holmes, b. July 7, 1887. Address Indianapolis, Ind., R. 1, Box 269 Laborer. Methodists.

1. Harriett M Kirkhof, b April 9, 1913
2. Dorothy C. Kirkhof, b. Aug. 16, 1914
3. Jack H. Kirkhof, b. July 2, 1919.

No. 1815. Fourth Generation. 1186.

4) Louis Frank Kirkhof, b Sept 1, 1861, m. Sept. 3, 1882, Orpha L. Erwin, b. Sept. 12, 1864 Address: 1120 Gayden Ave., Norfolk, Va. Merchant. Methodists.

1. Vernon M. Kirkhof, b April 13, 1886. No 1816
2. Julia H. Kirkhof, b. Feb 9, 1888.

No. 1816. Fifth Generation. 1815.

1) Vernon M. Kirkhof, b April 13, 1886, m Nov. 1, 1922, Sallie Conover
1. Franklin D Kirkhof, b. —————.

No. 1817. Fourth Generation. 1186.

5) Adaline Kirkhof, b Sept 23, 1863, m. Benjamin F. Major. When last heard from, they lived at Quapaw, Okla

1. ————— Major, b. —————.
2 ————— Major, b —————.
3. ————— Major, b. —————.
4. ————— Major, b —————.
5. ————— Major, b. —————.
6 ————— Major, b. —————.

No. 1818. Fifth Generation. 1673.

1) Clifford Leroy Sturgeon, b Oct 21, 1855, d —————, 1912, m. Sept. 26, 1894, Anna Smith, b. —————.

1. Mary Katherine Sturgeon, b Dec. 20, 1895. No. 1819
2 Clifford Benjamin Sturgeon, b June 29, ——.

No. 1819. Sixth Generation. 1818.

1) Mary Katherine Sturgeon, b Dec 20, 1895, m Aug 19, 1918, Rannell E Duncan.

No. 1820. Fifth Generation. 1673.

3) Clara Victoria Sturgeon, b Jan 24, 1859, m. Jan. 6, 1885, Wallace Milton Rank, b —————. Address 111 N. 6th St., Newark, Ohio.

1. Mary Louise Rank, b Mar 12, 1886. No 1821.
2 Melville Leroy Rank, b. Sept 28, 1889 No. 1822.

No. 1821. Sixth Generation. 1820.

1) Mary Louise Rank, b Mar 12, 1886, m Grover Foor Hart, June 21, 1917. Address: 552 Stanton Ave, Springfield, O. Teacher and homemaker. Methodists.

1 Robert David Hart. b. May 3, 1919.
2 William Mellville Hart, b. Nov. 6, 1921

No. 1822. Sixth Generation. 1820.

2) Mellvılle Leroy Rank, b Sept 28, 1889, m. Sept. 1, 1919, Blanche Ellis, b. Sept. 1, 1894. Address: 113 Chester Parkway, Duluth, Minn M L. Rank enlisted in the U S Navy April 13, 1917. Honorably discharged April 30, 1919, as electrician's Mate, 1st class He now holds the position of Lieutenant (J. G.) in the U. S. Naval Reserve

1 Logene Clair Rank, b. May 25, 1923.

2 Donald Wallace Rank, b Sept. 5, 1929

No. 1823. Fifth Generation. 1673.

4) Eva Adaline Sturgeon, b July 3, 1860, m. Jan 6, 1886, Joseph L. Gafford, b. June 7, 1858. He is president of Iowa Grain Produce Company at Burlington, Ia Presbyterians. Address: 112 Clay St , Burlington, Ia.

1. Gertrude G Gafford, b Nov. 1, 1888 No 1824

2. Helen M. Gafford, b. Oct. 23, 1890. No. 1825.

3. Eugene J. Gafford, b June 25, 1896 No 3637.

No. 1824. Sixth Generation. 1823.

1) Gertrude G Gafford, b Nov 1, 1888, m June 3, 1913, T. Emory Patterson. Address: 21 Woodcrest Ave , Dayton, O.

1. Virginia Adaline Patterson, b July 23, 1919

2. Nancy Jane Patterson, b. April 5, 1929

No. 1825. Sixth Generation. 1823.

2) Helen M Gafford, b Oct 23, 1890, m April 28, 1917, Clıfford W L. Day.

No. 1826. Fifth Generation. 1673.

5) Elmer Ellsworth Sturgeon, b. Aug 21, 1862, m. Dec. 4, 1901, Sarah Emma Parrish, b. Mar 24, 1880. Mr Sturgeon is a rancher at Hay Sprıngs, Nebr. He was one of the first settlers ın Sherıdan Co , Nebr., having come here in May, 1884, and homesteaded along the Nıobrara River, seventeen mıles southeast of the present site of Hay Sprıngs At that tıme there were no roads or towns in this part of Nebraska Address Hay Sprıngs, Nebr Methodısts

1. Evelyn Elızabeth Sturgeon, b Mar. 11, 1913

2. Myrtle Maxine Sturgeon, b. Mar. 20, 1921.

No. 1827. Fifth Generation. 1673.

6) Lizzie Ione Sturgeon, b Aug 2, 1864, m. Nov. 20, 1888, Charles Israel, b. Dec. 13, 1860 Merchandıze broker. Congregational Address: 5003 Capital, Omaha, Nebr.

1. Donald Israel, b. Mar 14, 1890, d. Nov 5, 1890.

2. Harold Ellsworth Israel, b. May 4, 1892, single.

3. Russell Wıllıam Israel, b Nov. 1, 1893, single.

No. 1828. Fifth Generation. 1673.

7) Charles William Sturgeon, b Nov. 22, 1866, m. Sept. 26, 1888, Bertha Bogan, b. Nov. 30, 1866 Real estate broker Methodıst Church. Address: Melbourne, Fla., Box 602.

1. Evelyn Sturgeon, b Jan 23, 1893 No. 1829.

No. 1829. Sixth Generation. 1828.

1) Evelyn Sturgeon, b Jan. 23, 1893, m C. P. Plummer, of 120 Veshıng Blvd., Cheyenne, Wyo.

No. 1830. Fourth Generation. 36.

1) Samuel E Walton, b ——————, m Mary Kiracofe, b. ——————.

No. 1831. Fourth Generation. 36.
2) Mary Walton, b ——————, m. Dennis Michael, b. —————.

No. 1832. Fourth Generation. 36.
3) Catherine Walton, b. ——————, m. Chapman Walton, b. —————.

No. 1833. Fourth Generation. 35.
4) George W. Walton, b Nov. 24, 1857, in Augusta Co., Va , m. in 1877, Martha Moyer, b. April 21, 1851. Address: Elkton, Va.

   1. Nettie F. Walton, b. ——————, m. C. W. McGuire of Elkton, Va.

No. 1834. Fourth Generation. 37.
1) Samuel Harrison Obaugh, b May 18, 1848, d Dec. 20, 1925, m. Caroline Propes, b. Dec. 29, 185—, d May 8, 1922. Address: Staunton, Va Burial at Staunton, Va.

   1. Ida Obaugh, b Nov. 13, 1872, d. Jan 27, 1877.
   2. David L. Obaugh, b Jan. 10, 1875
   3 Ella Obaugh, b. Feb 10, 1877.
   4. Myrtle Obaugh, b Nov. 8, 1879.
   5 William B Obaugh, b Dec. 6, 1892
   6. Arthur Obaugh, b ——————.
   7 Asa Obaugh, b. ——————.

No. 1835. Fourth Generation. 37.
2) Sarah Obaugh, b ——————, m John Rawley, b. ————— Buried at Mt. Olivet Church

   1. James Rawley, b. ——————.
   2. Charles Rawley, b ——————
   3. Nell e Rawley, b —————
   4 Daisy Rawley, b. ——————.
   5. Dyche Rawley, b. ——————.

No. 1836. Fourth Generation. 37.
3) James A Obaugh, b Mar. 26, 1854, at Mt Solon, Va., d. Sept. 22, 1902, m. Mary Jane Propes, b 1856, d. 1924 Burial at Barren Ridge, Va., which was their address.

   1. Edna Blanche Obaugh, b June 29, 1881. No 1840
   2. Owen Blaine Obaugh, b. May 4, 1884. No 3479.
   3. Roxie Belle Obaugh, b. Jan 6, 1886.
   4. Elizabeth Beatrice Obaugh, b. Mar. 23, 1890 No 3480.
   5. Mary Beulah Obaugh, b Jan 22, 1897 No 3481.

No. 1837. Fourth Generation. 37.
4) William Albert Obaugh, b Dec 24, 1856, m Sept 12, 1880, Mary Belle Hoffman, b. Aug 22, 1858 Justice of the Peace. United Brethren. Address: Mt. Solon, Va.

   1. Bliss Everett Obaugh, b Sept 18, 1881. No. 1838
   2. Frederick H. Obaugh, b Jan. 28, 1883 No 1839.

No. 1838. Fifth Generation. 1837.
1) Bliss Everett Obaugh, b Sept. 18, 1881, m June 13, 1909, Ella Hedrick. Address: 120 C St , Senate Court, Washington, D C

No. 1839. Fifth Generation. 1837.
2) Frederick H Obaugh, b Jan 28, 1883, m Oct 11, 1919, Myrtle Virginia Armstrong Address Mt. Solon, Va No children.

No. 1840. Fifth Generation. 1836.

1) Edna Blanche Obaugh, b. June 29, 1881, at Mt Solon, Va., m. 1901 to David Henry Hildebrand, b. April 1, 1878. Church of the Brethren. Housekeeper. Address: Bridgewater, Va Burial at Hildebrands Church.

1. Mary R. Hildebrand, b Sept 23, 1902. No. 1841.
2. Earl D. Hildebrand, b. Nov 1, 1914, d. Dec 1, 1914.
3. Ray J. Hildebrand, b. July 26, 1916

No. 1841. Sixth Generation. 1840.

1) Mary R. Hildebrand, b Sept. 23, 1902, m. at Hagerstown, Md, 1923, C. B. Meadows. Address: Waynesboro, Va.

1. ——— Meadows, b. ———————.
2. ——— Meadows, b. ———————.

No. 1842. Fourth Generation. 38.

2) William Watson Brenaman, b ———, 1854, d. Dec 23, 1908, m. Dec. 16, 1886, Lillie G. Patterson, b ———————. Watson was a newspaper editor at Staunton, Va. Presbyterians. Buried at Staunton, Va.

1. Homer Patterson Brenaman, b. Aug 29, 1889. No. 1842½
2. William Watson Brenaman, b Mar 10, 1895, his address is Kainelle, W. Va.

No. 1842½. Fifth Generation. 1842.

1) Homer Patterson Brenaman, b Aug 29, 1889, at Staunton, Va, m. Sept. 5, 1921, Myrtle Mabel Shoemaker, b Sept. —, 1900. Address: Box 32, Athens, W. Va. Bookkeeper. Presbyterians.

1. Elsie Myrtle Brenaman, b. July 27, 1923
2. Robert Lee Brenaman, b April 5, 1928.
3. Homer Patterson Brenaman, Jr., b April 5, 1930.

No. 1843. Fourth Generation. 38.

3) Bettie Brenaman, b. Sept. 29, 1857, at Mt Solon, Va., m. Sept. 25, 1884, Robert M. Houff, b. Mar. 17, 1857. Mrs Houff died Mar. 5, 1931; Mr. Houff died in 1903. Both were buried at the Mt. Pisgah cemetery in Augusta Co., Va. Mrs. Houff was educated at the Dayton Seminary and at the state normal school after which she taught school for several years in Rockingham and Augusta counties before marriage. They belonged to the Methodist Church.

1. Santa Houff, b. Oct. 8, 1885. No. 1844.
2. Edna Houff, b. Sept. 1, 1887. No. 1845.
3. Roy Augusta Houff, b. Oct. 11, 1889, d. July, 1914.
4) Ruth Houff, b. Oct. 3, 1891. No. 1846.

No. 1844. Fifth Generation. 1843.

1) Santa Houff, b. Oct. 8, 1885, at Mt Sidney, Va., m. Mar. 18, 1905, Emmitt Cline, b. Sept 17, 1882, at Long Glade. Housewife. Methodists. Burial at Parnassus, Va. Address: Mt. Solon, Va.

1. Ralph M. Cline, b. Mar 19, 1906, d. May 12, 1927.
2 Leroy S Cline, b. July 21, 1914.
3. Edna Ruth Cline, b. Dec. 15, 1919.

No. 1845. Fifth Generation. 1843.

2) Edna Houff, b Sept 1, 1887, she was run down and killed by an automobile in front of her home Feb 5, 1935. She married Emmitt L Wilberger, Sept. 20, 1908, at Mt Sidney, Va Address: Mt. Solon, Va.

1. Katherine Bancroft Wilberger, b. Mar. 9, 1916.
2 Mildred Montgomery Wilberger, b July 8, 1919.
3 Bettie Wayne Wilberger, b. Oct. 4, 1922.

No. 1846. Fifth Generation. 1843.

4) Ruth Houff, b. Oct 3, 1891, at Mt. Sidney, Va., m. Nov. 18, 1918, Hugh B. Bell, at Mt. Solon, Va. Address: Mt. Solon, Va.

1. Helen Brenaman Bell, b. Aug. 24, 1920.
2. Bettie Eleanor Bell, b. July 7, 1930.

No. 1847. Fourth Generation. 38.

7) Buena Brenaman, b. Feb. 23, 1865, at Mt. Zion, Va., m. Charles Gladwell, b. May 5, 1875, at McDowell, Va. Housekeeper. Burial place in Parnassus M. E. cemetery, Va. Address: 115½ E. Washington St , Greensboro, N. C.

1. Gooch Vawn Gladwell, b. Aug. 20, 1901. No. 1848.
2. Robert Trevy Gladwell, b. Oct. 30, 1903. No. 1849.

No. 1848. Fifth Generation. 1847.

1) Gooch Vawn Gladwell, b Aug. 20, 1901, m. Nov. 17, 1920, at Staunton, Va., Louretta M. Armentrout. Manager storage garage Methodists. Address. 912 Omaha St., Greensboro, N. C.

1. Juniatti Layne Gladwell, b. Aug. 18, 1921.
2. Gooch Vawn Gladwell, Jr , b May 6, 1923
3. Ellwood Yates Gladwell, b. Aug. 10, 1925.
4. Vista Adaline Gladwell, b. April 26, 1927.
5. Jack Oneil Gladwell, b. Nov. 15, 1929, d Jan. 8, 1930.
6 Charles Calvin Gladwell, b. Jan. 4, 1931.

No. 1849. Fifth Generation. 1847.

2) Robert Trevy Gladwell, b Oct. 30, 1903, m Dec. 24, 1929, Carma Alexander, b. July 14, 1907, at Pleasant Darden, N. C Plater. Methodists. Address· 1223 Randolph, Greensboro, N. C.

1. Robert Trevy Gladwell, Jr., b. July 24, 1934.

No. 1850. Fourth Generation. 38.

8) Margaret Brenaman, b. Sept. 7, 1867, at Mt. Solon, Va., m. Sept. 17, 1896, at Mossy Creek, Va., Charles Reid, b. Feb. 1, 1864, at Shenandoah, Va. He died Mar. 8, 1910. Housekeeper. Methodists. Burial at Mossy Creek.

1. Everett Bell Reid, b. Dec 8, 1897 No. 1851.
2. Ethel Elizabeth Reid, b. April 6, 1900
3. Robert Glen Reid, b. Dec. 8, 1901
4. Elsie Grace Reid, b Feb 18, 1903. No. 1850¾.
5. Kenny Kathleen Reid, b Oct. 3, 1905.
6. Sidney Boxley Reid, b. Jan. 22, 1908.

No. 1850¾. Fifth Generation. 1850.

4) Elsie Grace Reid, b Feb. 18, 1903, m ——— Moyers.

1 Charles Moyers, b June 20, 1932, d. Aug 26, 1934.
2 Bettie Joe Moyers, b Oct. 22, 1935

No. 1851. Fifth Generation. 1850.

1) Everett Bell Reid, b Dec 8, 1897. m. Ada Virginia Simmons. Address Staunton, Va.

1 Phillis Katherine Reid, b. Jan. 14, 1929.
2 Charlotte Ann Reid, b May 28, 1932

No. 1852. Fourth Generation. 38.

9) Samuel Harrison Brenaman, b. Nov. 30, 1869, m. 1917 to Nancy Belle Hamrick, b. Aug. 23, 1889. Presbyterians at Mossy Creek Church. Farmer and commissioner of revenue of North River district Address Mt Solon, Va.

1. Charlotte Hamrick Brenaman, b Oct 9, 1918.
2. Elizabeth Sprinkle Brenaman, b Nov 28, 1919.
3. Margaret Harrison Brenaman, b Mar 1, 1923
4. Samuel Hugh Brenaman, b. Feb. 9, 1934.

No. 1853. Fourth Generation. 3º.

10) Charles L. Brenaman, b ————, 1873, m. in 1895 to Salena Gladwell, b. ————, 1873. Traveling salesman Presbyterians Burial place at Mt. Zion Church, Augusta Co., Va Address 1128 W Grass St, Richmond, Va.

1 Hugh C Brenaman, b. Dec. 6, 1898 No 1854.
2 Annie Lee Brenaman, b ————, 1900 No 3644
3. Robert S. Brenaman, b ————, 1903 No 3645.
4 Mary Brenaman, b ————, 1911 No 3646

No. 1854. Fifth Generation. 1853.

1) Hugh Crawford Brenaman, b Dec 6, 1898, m. June 11, 1927, Miriam Boykin Normant, b Nov 11, 1903, at Richmond, Va Presbyterians. Director of Athletics at St. Christopher's School Address St Christopher's School, Richmond, Va., R 2

1 Anne Normant Brenaman, b. Feb 20, 1929.
2 Julia Blair Brenaman, b Mar 7, 1933.

No. 1855. Fourth Generation. 39.

1) John Abraham Thuma, b Dec. 16, 1851, in Augusta Co, Va, m April 15, 1875, to Jennie H Clark, b Mar. 12, 1855, in same county She died July 24, 1925. Mr. Thuma died Jan. 12, 1931 Both were buried in the Silver Creek cemetery at Jamestown, O They moved to Jamestown in 1884 He was an active member of the Methodist Church as long as his health would permit He was a member of the official board and president of the trustees at various times, also superintendent of the Sunday school He was a successful business man and was for many years connected with the Adams-Thuma Lumber Co He was its president and manager up to the time of his death His two oldest children were born in Virginia, and the last one was born in Ohio Address· Jamestown, O.

1 Charles Ernest Thuma, b Feb. 4, 1876. No 1856
2. Clara Edna Thuma, b Oct 11, 1879 No 1857.
3 Mabel Grace Thuma, b Mar 18, 1885. No 1860

No. 1856. Fifth Generation. 1855.

1) Charles Ernest Thuma, b Feb 4, 1876, in Augusta Co, Va., m. July 14, 1904, Bertha E Gregg, b Mar 21, 1884, at Washington C H, O Lumber dealer. Methodists Address· Jamestown, O., Box 90

1. Robert Ernest Thuma, b. Aug. 8, 1905, d. Aug 22, 1906.
2 Willard Gregg Thuma, b May 24, 1907
3. Lela Marshall Thuma, b July 24, 1912

No. 1857. Fifth Generation. 1855.

2) Clara Edna Thuma, b Oct 11, 1879, in Augusta Co, Va, m. in 1900 to George Eckerle, b. Mar 12, 1875, at Xen a, O. Address 225 E Main St, Xenia, O

1. Catherine Eckerle, b. ————, 1903. No 1858
2 Clark Eckerle, b ————, 1905. No 1859

No. 1858. Sixth Generation. 1857.

1) Catherine Eckerle, b ————, 1903, m Raymond Tobias Address: R 3, Xenia, O.

1. Richard Clark Tobias, b. ————

2. Donald Philip Tobias, b ———————.
3 Robert Marvin Tobias, b ————————

No. 1859. Sixth Generation. 1857.

2) Clark Eckerle, b ————, 1905, m. Pauline Nash. Address: Xenia, O.
1 Elaine Eckerle, b. Aug. 24, 1938, in Xenia, O.

No. 1860. Fifth Generation. 1855.

3) Mabel Grace Thuma, b. Mar 18, 1885, at Jamestown, O., m. in 1906 to Ora Frances Reeves, b. May 13, 1878 Address: Jamestown, O. Methodists. Clothier business
1. Frances Elizabeth Reeves, b. ————, 1907.
2. Alice Virginia Reeves, b. Jan. 2, 1910 No 3288.
3 Robert John Reeves, b ————, 1915.
4 Helen Lucile Reeves, b ————, 1918
   Frances is a teacher, Alice is a registered nurse

No. 1861. Fourth Generation. 39.

2) Thomas Newton Thuma, b Dec 29, 1853, d Jan. —, 1935, married (1st) Belle Murry; married (2nd) Ida Riggleman
1 Mary Thuma, b. ——————— No. 1862

No. 1862. Fifth Generation. 1861.

1) Mary Thuma, b ——————, m Jackson Waters.
1 Mary Thuma Waters, b ——————— No 1863.

No. 1863. Sixth Generation. 1862.

1) Mary Thuma Waters, b ——————, m Irvin Byrum.
1. ——————— Byrum, b. ———————

No. 1864. Fourth Generation. 39.

3) Fannie Elizabeth Thuma, b ————, 1860, in Augusta Co , Va , m. Jacob Shobe, b. June 16, 1854, near Elida, O , where they lived for a number of years. She died Feb 24, 1887, and was buried at Saratoga, Ind. Mr Shobe was buried in California
1. Virginia Alvina Shobe, b July 13, 1883. No. 1865.
2. Laverno Thuma Shobe, b. ————. No. 1870.

No. 1865. Fifth Generation. 1864.

1) Virginia Alvina Shobe, b. July 13, 1883, m Jan. 6, 1900, Arthur Delbert Staup, b Oct. 7, 1873 Address 118 Harrison Ave , Lima, O.
1. Lewis Prescott Staup, b Dec 5, 1900 No. 1866.
2 Harold Edgar Staup, b June 27, 1903 No. 1867.
3 Nancy Reba Staup, b July 27, 1906 No 1868
4. Claire Eugene Staup, b Feb 13, 1909 No 1869
5 Marion Delbert Staup, b Aug 23, 1911
6 Clyde Laverno Staup, b June 27, 1914.
7 Paul Franklin Staup, b. Jan 6, 1917.
8 Carl Wesley Staup, b. Sept 1, 1918
9 Lawrence Sylvester Staup, b. April 26, 1921.

No. 1866 Sixth Generation. 1865.

1) Lewis Prescott Staup, b Dec. 5, 1900, m. Bessie Halliday. Address: 1717 Fairfax Rd., Toledo, O

No. 1867. Sixth Generation. 1865.

2) Harold Edgar Staup, b. June 27, 1903, m. Cleta Hallenbacher.
1. —————— Staup, b. ——————.
2. —————— Staup, b. ——————.

No. 1868. Sixth Generation. 1865.

3) Nancy Reba Staup, b. July 27, 1906, m. Carl Leo Ellis. Address. 721 S. Pine St., Lima, O.
1. Gene Marie Ellis, b. May 26, 1926.

No. 1869. Sixth Generation. 1865.

4) Claire Eugene Staup, b. Feb. 13, 1909, m. Retha Gassard Address: Box 474, R. 3, Toledo, O.
1. —————— Staup, b. ——————.
2. —————— Staup, b ——————.

No. 1870. Fifth Generation. 1864.

2) Laverne Thuma Shobe, b. ——————, near Elida, O., m. Julia Fasnaught of Elida, O. Mrs Shobe and her children live at 722 Railroad Ave, Mt. Vernon, Wash.
1. Bernerd Shobe, b ——————. No 1871
2 Pauline Shobe, b. ——————.

No. 1871. Sixth Generation. 1870.

1) Bernerd G Shobe, b. ——————, m. —————— Spott, b ——————. Address· 722 Railroad Ave, Mt. Vernon, Wash

No. 1872. Fourth Generation. 39.

4) Sallie Florence Crum, b Sept 14, 1868, at Saratoga, Ind, m April 27, 1887, C. M. Shireling, b Nov. 7, 1865. Address Saratoga, Ind Housekeeper. United Brethren.
1. Roy E. Shireling, b. Nov. 15, 1888 No 1873.
2. Marjor.e Shireling, b. ——————. No. 1874
3. Reva G. Shireling, b. ——————. No. 1875.

No. 1873. Fifth Generation. 1872.

1) Roy E Shireling, b. Nov 13, 1888, m. L. Simmons. Address: Union City, Ind.
1 Bettie Jean Shireling, b. ——————

No. 1874. Fifth Generation. 1872.

2) Marjorie Shireling, b ——————, m. Ersnel Richtert, Jan 1, 1918. Address: 446 Oak St., Dayton, O.
1. Stanley Morris Richtert, b ——————

No. 1875. Fifth Generation. 1872.

3) Reva G. Shireling, b ——————, m Harold S Brown, Dec 31, 1928 Address: 208 Bruce St., Eaton, O.
1. —————— Brown, b. ——————.

No. 1876. Fourth Generation. 40.

1) Margaret Elizabeth Kiracofe, b. April 12, 1851, in Augusta Co., Va, d Feb. 1, 1919, at her home near Allentown, O She married William Shock, b. Aug. 22, 1850, d Aug 20, 1933 Address: Elida, O Farmer. Buried at Allentown, O. United Brethren
1. John Wesley Shock, b. Feb. 14, 1873 No. 1877
2. Clinton A Shock, b. Mar 13, 1875. No 1882

3. James Stewart Shock, b Nov 25, 1876. No. 1884.
4 Aravilla Jane Shock, b Sept 16, 1878. No 1885
5 Charles Shock, b. Aug. 30, 1880, d. Oct. 26, 1884.
6. Harley Otterbein Shock, b. Jan 19, 1882. No. 1886.
7. Reuben Roy Shock, b. Nov 4, 1884. No. 1887.
8. Myrta Belle Shock, b. Jan. 25, 1887. No. 1889.
9. Mary Mal nda Shock, b. April 8, 1889. No. 1890.
10. Samuel Ira Shock, b. Nov. 14, 1890. No. 1891.
11. Elva Lenora Shock, b July 2, 1893. No. 1892.
12. Infant son, b. July 9, 1895, d next day.
13. Luther Pearl Shock, b. Jan 1, 1897. No. 1893.
14. Infant daughter, stillborn.

No. 1877. Fifth Generation. 1876.

1) John Wesley Shock, b. Feb 14, 1873, in Allen Co, O, m. July 13, 1895, Ida M. Cary, b April 11, 1876, at Kemp, O. United Brethren minister Address: 1604 Homestead St, Toledo, O.
1. Harold William Shock, b Mar. 10, 1896 No. 1878.
2. Edna May Shock, b. Oct 13, 1897. No. 1879.
3. Lucile Lillian Shock, b Dec. 1, 1899 No. 1880.
4. Margaret Rebecca Shock, b. Oct. 9, 1902, d same day.
5. Clarice Irene Shock, b April 9, 1904 No. 1881.
6. Evelyn Katherine Shock, b. June 20, 1910, d Jan. 19, 1930.

No. 1878. Sixth Generation. 1877.

1) Harold William Shock, b Mar. 10, 1896, m. Dec. 25, 1917, Erma Davis. Address: Nevada, O.
1. Harold William Shock, b. —————.
2. Helena Shock, b ————.
3. Edna Catherine Shock, b. —————.
4. Luella Shock, b. —————
5 ————— Shock, b. —————.
6. John Shock, b. —————.
7. ————— Shock, b. —————.

No. 1879. Sixth Generation. 1877.

2) Edna May Shock, b Oct 13, 1897, m. Nov. 28, 1918, Harry Hull. Address: Carey, O

No. 1880. Sixth Generation. 1877.

3) Lucile Lillian Shock, b. Dec. 1, 1899, m. Bertsel Fruchey, Aug. 1, 1920, at Columbus Grove, O Address· Napoleon, O.
1 ————— Fruchey, b —————.
2. ————— Fruchey, b. —————
3 ————— Fruchey, b. —————

No. 1881. Sixth Generation. 1877.

5) Clarice Irene Shock, b April 9, 1904, m. Dec. 25, 1925, R. C. Wirt at North Baltimore, O Address North Baltimore, O

No. 1882. Fifth Generation. 1876.

2) Clinton Albirtus Shock, b Mar. 13, 1875, near Elida, O, m. Dec. 24, 1898, Tirzah Aravilla John, b June 23, 1876, of Elida, O. Methodists. Vice president and manager of Northern Texas Telephone Co, at Sherman, Tex. Address: Box 179, Sherman, Tex.
1. Chadwick Emerson Shock, b. Nov 1, 1903. No. 1883

2. Flarion Karl Shock, b Sept. 24, 1910 No 1894
3 Donald Clinton Shock, b. Oct. 20, 1919.

No. 1883. Sixth Generation. 1882.

1) Chadwick Emerson Shock, b Nov. 1, 1903, m Oct 30, 1926, at Sherman, Tex., Winnifred Blake, b. Dec 24, 1902, at Gainesville, Tex. Address Garland, Tex. Telephone exchange manager. Methodist.
1. Beverley Gene Shock, b. Oct. 9, 1927.
2. Donna Carolyn Shock, b. July 15, 1935.

No. 1884. Fifth Generation. 1876.

3) James Stewart Shock, b Nov 25, 1876, near Elida, O, m May 11, 1902, Alvena Royer, b July 9, 1882 Address Shannon St., Van Wert, O United Brethren.
1. Dolph Shock, b Sept 13, 1903 No 1895.
2 Max Shock, b Mar 3, 1912
3 Francis Shock, b Aug 22, 1914
4 Ardith Shock, b Oct 16, 1916, d Oct. 14, 1920
5 James Shock, b June 1, 1919

No. 1885. Fifth Generation. 1876.

4) Aravilla Jane Shock, b Sept 16, 1878, m Samuel Cary, b ——————,
d. —————— She m (2nd) Dec 30, 1922, Richard Jones, b. ——, 1881. Address 734 S Elizabeth St, Lima, O Methodists
1. Cleta Cary, b Sept 4, 1904 No 1896.
2 Dearl Cary, b June 19, 1910, d. Nov. —, 1926.

No. 1886. Fifth Generation. 1876.

6) Harley Otterbein Shock, b Jan 19, 1882, near Elida, O, m Lillie Potts Address: Lima, O, R. 4. United Brethren.
1 Horace Shock, b ——————— No 1897

No. 1887. Fifth Generation. 1876.

7) Reuben Roy Shock, b Nov 4, 1884, near Elida, O, m June 26, 1909, Blanche E Clouser, b Nov 14, 1889 Address Lima, O, R 6 Farmer International Bible Student.
1 Rodney Roy Shock, b Oct 21, 1910 No 1888.
2. Rasamond Oliva Shock, b April 26, 1918 No 3643.
3 Lillian Blanche Shock, b. Oct. 18, 1921.

No. 1888. Sixth Generation. 1887.

1) Rodney Roy Shock, b Oct 21, 1910, m Oct. 17, 1932, Dora Gertrude Locker Address: Lima, O., R. 6.

No. 1889 Fifth Generation. 1876.

8) Myrta Belle Shock, b Jan 25, 1887, near Elida, O, m Mar 7, 1907, Jesse Dershem, b July 22, 1883 Farmer United Brethren. Address Spencerville, O, R. 3 Burial place at Allentown, O
1. Russell Dwight Dershem, b Jan 28, 1908, d Feb 22, 1909.
2 Wilda Odessa Dershem, b Oct 9, 1909
3 Everett Emerson Dershem, b Aug 16, 1911
4 Ross Franklin Dershem, b. Oct 28, 1913
5 Ilo Louise Dershem, b June 11, 1918
6 Gerald Eugene Dershem, b Sept 24, 1922
7 Ivan Wallace Dershem. b May 22, 1925

8 Adrian Deloss Dershem, b Nov. 28, 1927
9. Erma Arline Dershem, b. July 27, 1932.

No. 1890. Fifth Generation. 1876.

9) Mary Malinda Shock, b April 8, 1889, near Elida, O., m Verna Bowers Address Waynesfield, O, R 2 Methodist Protestant
1 Ronald Bowers, b ——————.
2 Richard Bowers, b ——————
3. Helen Bowers, b ——————
4 Mary Bowers, b ——————
5 Eleanor Bowers, b ——————
6 Kathleen Bowers, b ——————.
7 William Bowers, b. ——————.

No. 1891. Fifth Generation. 1876.

10) Samuel Ira Shock, b Nov 14, 1890, near Elida, O, m. Pearl Gould Address: Sapulpa, Okla Oil pumper. Methodists.
1 Lorenze Shock, b ——————
2 Cleon Shock, b ——————.
3. Vernon Leil Shock, b ——————.
4 Adelia Dean Shock, b. ——————.

No. 1892. Fifth Generation. 1876.

11) Elva Lenora Shock, b July 2, 1893, near Elida, O, m Nov. 29, 1911, C F Shinabery, b April 8, 1890 Housewife United Brethren. Mr Shinabery is foreman at Locomotive shops in Lima Address 524 S Central Ave, Lima, O
1 Margaret E Shinabery, b Mar 25, 1914 No 1899
2. Bernard C. Shinabery, b July 2, 1916
3 Helen Petite Shinabery, b Nov 3, 1919
4 Gene Edward Shinabery, b. Oct. 2, 1929.

No. 1893 Fifth Generation. 1876.

13) Lutie Pearl Shock, b Jan 1, 1897, near Elida, O, m M O. Sowers Address Convoy, O. United Brethren
1 Garnett Sowers, b ——————.
2 William Sowers, b. ——————.

No. 1894. Sixth Generation. 1882.

2) Flarion Karl Shock, b Sept 24, 1910, m Dec 24, 1934, Eugenia Fern Graham, b Aug 4, 1915. Address: Garland, Tex. Telephone Methodists

No. 1895. Sixth Generation. 1884.

1) Dolph Shock, b Sept 13, 1903, m April 9. 1929. Dorothy Runnion Address· Van Wert, O, R. 5.

No. 1896. Sixth Generation. 1885.

1) Cleta Cary, b Sept 4, 1904, m July 3, 1922, Ellwood Ridenour. Address Lima, O, R 6 Farmer Lutherans

No. 1897. Sixth Generation. 1886.

1) Horace Shock, b ——————, m Eunice Martin

No. 1898. Sixth Generation. 1890.

3) Helen Bowers, b ——————, m Eugene Miller Address· Elida, O, R 2
1 Earl Gene Miller, b Sept —, 1934

No. 1899. Sixth Generation. 1892.

1) Margaret E Shinabery, b. Mar 25, 1914, m. Richard Davisson, b July 11, 1911. Address: 524 S. Central Ave , Lima, O.

1. Richard Clinton Davisson, b. July 11, 1934.

No. 1900. Fourth Generation. 40.

2) Sarah J. Kiracofe, b Nov. 12, 1852, in Augusta Co , Va., m. Levi Baxter, b. Feb. 26, 1854, d. —————. Address. Delphos, O , R. 2. Farmer. United Brethren.

1. Alpha Baxter, b Jan. 25, 1890 No 1901
2. William R Baxter, b. July 23, 1895. No. 1903.

No. 1901. Fifth Generation. 1900.

1) Alpha Baxter, b Jan 25, 1890, in Allen Co , O., m. Ralph DeLong, b. Aug. 23, 1886. Address: Spencerville, O.

1. Grace DeLong, b. Mar. 4, 1908 No. 1902.
2. Evelyn Fay DeLong, b. Aug. 23, 1916.
3. Cecil May DeLong, b Nov 4, 1919.
4. Dorothy Louise DeLong, b. Sept 30, 1924.

No. 1902. Sixth Generation. 1901.

1) Grace DeLong, b Mar 4, 1908, m. Burdette Purdy.

1. Ralph Eugene Purdy, b April 27, 1930.

No. 1903. Fifth Generation. 1900.

2) William R. Baxter, b. July 23, 1895, near Elida, O , m. Lula Long, b. —————, 1904. Address: 4434 E. Blvd , Cleveland, O.

1. Eleanor Ruth Baxter, b. Nov. 8, 1919.
2 Jean Baxter, b. May 6, 1923.
3 William Robert Baxter, b. Dec. 20, 1924.
4. Chad Baxter, b. Aug. 27, 1928.

No. 1904. Fourth Generation. 40.

3) John L. D. Kiracofe, b. Feb 15, 1854, d. Feb. 2, 1926, m. Martha McBride, b. —————, d —————. He later married Fannie Mapes.

1. Lillie Kiracofe, b. —————, m. and had a daughter.
2. Alta Kiracofe, b. —————, m. a Mr. Taylor and had issue
3. Jacob Kiracofe, b. —————, d. —————.
4. Lesta Otterbein Kiracofe, b —————, m N. F. R.
5. Vernie Kiracofe, b. —————, d. —————.
   (From second wife)
6. Fay Kiracofe, b. —————, m. a Mr. Wallace.
7. June Kiracofe, b June 25, 1897. No. 1910.
8. Thelma Kiracofe, b —————, m. a Mr. Coburn.
9. William Robert Kiracofe, b. —————, m.
10. John Kiracofe, Jr., b. —————, m.
11. Wilbur Kiracofe, b. —————, m.

No. 1910. Fifth Generation. 1904.

7) June Kiracofe, b. June 25, 1897, m Mar. —, 1916, Montie F Weaver, b Mar. 2, 1896 Address: Maumee, O., R. 2 Housewife. Methodists.

1. Crystal Weaver, b —————, 1917.
2. Alice Belle Weaver, b —————, 1919
3 Robert Weaver, b. —————, 1920
4 Max Weaver, b. —————, 1924.

5. Bettie Jane Weaver, b. ————, 1926.
6. Sarah Weaver, b. ————, 1929.

No. 1915. Fourth Generation. 40.

5) Samuel Henry Kiracofe, b. April 2, 1859, d Nov. 26, 1887, m Ella Foster. Burial place at Allentown, O.

1. Lewis A. Kiracofe, b. Sept. 3, 1880. No. 1916.
2. Samuel William Kiracofe, b June 16, 1887. No. 1917.

No. 1916. Fifth Generation. 1915.

1) Lewis A. Kiracofe, b Sept 3, 1880, d. Feb. 13, 1933, m. Oct. 19, 1907, Aliene Gleason, b. April 10, 1884. They were married at Independence, Mo. Painter. Address: 629 7th St., Eureka, Kans. Buried at Eureka, Kans. Freemason.

1 Harriett Isabelle Kiracofe, b. Oct. 12, 1917, d. Aug 26, 1934
2. Ella Thadene Kiracofe, b. Jan 29, 1922.
3. Regena Lau Kiracofe, b. Sept. 10, 1924.
4 Lewis Lee Kiracofe, b. April 30, 1930

No. 1917. Fifth Generation. 1915.

2) Samuel William Kiracofe, b. June 16, 1887, m. Jan. 2, 1923, Mrs. Elma A. Jones (nee Marthy), b June 3, 1892. Deputy Sheriff, Los Angeles, Calif., now Sergeant criminal Div Address: 1310 S Catalina Ave., Redonda, Calif. No issue.

No. 1918. Fourth Generation. 40.

6) Elnora Malinda Kiracofe, b Sept. 24, 1864, m. William R. Hullinger, b. May 9, 1863. Address Lima, O , R 6 Methodist Protestant. Mrs Hullinger is not living.

1. Infant, b. Mar. 2, 1886, d.
2. Mildred Leota Hullinger, b. May 18, 1902. No. 1919.

No. 1919. Fifth Generation. 1918.

2) Mildred Leota Hullinger, b. May 18, 1902, m. Rev. Paul H. Cramer, b. April 5, 1902 Address: New Hampshire, O. Housewife. Methodists.

No. 1920. Fourth Generation. 40.

7) Charles W. Kiracofe, b Dec 7, 1865, d. Feb. 19, 1926, m. Anna Hileman, b. Feb. 5, 1871. Burial place in Linwood cemetery, Ft. Wayne, Ind. Address: 910 Lincoln Ave., Ft. Wayne, Ind

1. R. Glen Kiracofe, b. Aug. 20, 1892. No 1921.
2. Valry M. Kiracofe, b. ————, 1894 No. 1922.
3. Archie R. Kiracofe, b ————, m N. F R.
4. Daisy Pearl Kiracofe, b. ————. No. 1924
5. Huber R Kiracofe, b. ———— No. 1925.
6 Clifford W Kiracofe, b Feb. 1, 1905, N. F. R.

No. 1921. Fifth Generation. 1920.

1) R. Glen Kiracofe, b Aug 20, 1892, m. April 7, 1917, Hazel D. Davidson. Engineer. United Brethren No issue Address: 2910 S. Anthony Blvd., Ft. . Wayne, Ind

No. 1922. Fifth Generation. 1920.

2) Valry M. Kiracofe, b. ————, 1894, d. Nov 12, 1937, m. Doyl Smith. United Brethren. Address: 734 W 3rd St, Ft Wayne, Ind.

No. 1924. Fifth Generation. 1920.

4) Daisy Pearl Kiracofe, b. ————, m. Todd Morrisson. United Brethren. Address· 1002 Hilbourne Ave , Milwaukee, Wis.

No. 1925. Fifth Generation. 1920.

5) Huber R. Kiracofe, b. —————, m. Address: 1124 Sinclair St., Ft. Wayne, Ind. U. B. Church.

No. 1927. Fourth Generation. 40.

8) Newton Irvin Kiracofe, b May 24, 1867, m April 26, 1888, Catherine Frys.nger, b. Jan 24, 1866 Farmer United Brethren Address: Wren, O Burial place at Wren, O.

1. John B. Kiracofe, b Nov. 6, 1889. No. 1928.
2. Anise Maud Kiracofe, b June 2, 1890 No 1929
3. Fannie Kiracofe, b Aug 4, 1893 No. 1930 .
4. Lloyd L. Kiracofe, b Feb 14, 1895. No 1931
5 Edna D. Kiracofe, b. Dec 24, 1903. No 1931½

No. 1928. Fifth Generation. 1927.

1) John B. Kiracofe, b. Nov. 6, 1889, m. 1911, to Maude Wood, b Sept. 12, 1890. Address: Dixon, Mont. Teacher. Methodists.

1. Juanita E Kiracofe, b —————, 1912.

No. 1929. Fifth Generation. 1927.

2) Anise Kiracofe, b June 2, 1891, m Mar 22, 1911, M. C. Cully, b. April 9, 1884. Address: Ohio City, O. Farmer. U. B. Church.

1. Mildred Cully, b. Dec 19, 1911
2 Robert Cully, b. Dec. 18, 1915

No. 1930. Fifth Generation. 1927.

3) Fanny Kiracofe, b Aug 4, 1892, on Mar 24, 1915, m O. C Fegley, b Sept 27, 1891. Address Wren, O , R. 1 Farmer U B. Church.

1. Chester Fegley, b Feb. 19, 1916.
2. Carl Fegley, b Sept. 30, 1917.

No. 1931. Fifth Generation. 1927.

4) Lloyd L. Kiracofe, b. Feb. 14, 1895, m Feb. 27, 1919, Madaline A. Mosier, b. Feb. 25, 1897. Address: Willshire, O , R 2 Farmer. U. B. Church

1. Lloyd L. Kiracofe, Jr., b. April 9, 1923.
2. Richard Kiracofe, b. June 27, 1925.
3. Gloria June Kiracofe, b Jan 4, 1927.

No. 1931½. Fifth Generation. 1927.

5) Edna D. Kiracofe, b. Dec. 24, 1903, m Harry Bowen.

1. Charles Bowen, b. —————.
2. Glen Bowen, b —————.

No. 1933. Fourth Generation. 40.

9) Lockey A. Kiracofe, b. Feb. 22, 1870, near Elida, O., m Dec. 4, 1909, John W. Strayer, b. Jan. 3, 1861, of Elida, d. Dec 4, 1922. Weaver of rugs. Methodists Address Elida, O., R. 2. Buried in Allentown cemetery.

1. Rolla J Strayer, b July 17, 1911. No. 3662

No. 1934. Fourth Generation. 40.

10) James Stewart Kiracofe, b. Nov. 23, 1873, near Elida, O., m June 17, 1897, Mary Emma Taylor, b. Jan 9, 1875. Farmer. United Brethren. Burial at Wren, O. Address: Convoy, O , R 3.

1 Esta Maude Kiracofe, b. Feb.' 15, 1898, single.
2. Albert Clinton Kiracofe, b. Jan. 16, 1900, d May 17, 1916
3 Thomas Stewart Kiracofe, b. April 16, 1903. No. 1935.

4. Harlan Howard Kiracofe, b. Feb 2, 1906 No. 1936.

5 Dellas Marion Kiracofe, b Jan 28, 1909. No. 1937.

No. 1935. Fifth Generation. 1934.

3) Thomas Stewart Kiracofe, b. April 16, 1903, m Feb., 1927, Cleo Irene Richard, b. Feb. 5, 1910. Address Convoy, O , R 3. Farmer. United Brethren.

1. Betty Jean Kiracofe, b. July 20, 1929.

2 Billy Dean Kiracofe, b. Nov. 13, 1930.

No. 1936. Fifth Generation. 1934.

4) Harlan Howard Kiracofe, b Feb. 2, 1906, m Mar. 16, 1929, Margaret Bolenbaugh, b Dec. 28, 1910 Address Willshire, O., R 2. United Brethren. Laborer.

1 Margie Joan Kiracofe, b. Mar 26, 1930

No. 1937. Fifth Generation. 1934.

5) Dellas Marion Kiracofe, b Jan. 28, 1909, m Dec. 28, 1929, Edith Florence, b. April 24, 1911. Laborer. United Brethren Address: Convoy, O., R. 3.

1. Son Kiracofe, b ————.

No. 1938. Sixth Generation. 372.

1) Annie E. Brunk, b. July 9, 1866, in Rockingham Co., Va., m. Joseph H. Brunk, of Linville, Va , July 27, 1913 Mr. Brunk was born Feb 23, 1851. Farmer. Mennonites Address. Linville Depot, Va.

No. 1939. Sixth Generation. 372.

3) John D. Brunk, b. Mar. 13, 1872, in Rockingham Co., Va , was united in marriage Sept 2, 1897, to Mary Kate Martin, b May 29, 1875 Mr. Brunk was a prominent teacher of music and writer of hymns and assisted in compiling a number of church hymnals and writing sacred songs Their years were spent at Goshen College, Goshen, Ind , where he taught music in the school. Mennonites. He died Feb. 6, 1926, and was buried in the Prairie Street cemetery at Elkhart, Ind.

1 Salome Brunk, b June 10, 1898, d same day.

2 Harry Samuel Brunk, b. Oct 31, 1899, d. Nov 18, 1902.

3. Carreno Brunk, b Jan 18, 1901 No 1940.

4. Hermione Brunk, b Mar. 19, 1903 No 1941.

5. John Milton Brunk, b. Nov 14, 1904. No. 1942.

6. Neiman Artler Brunk, b. Oct. 28, 1906, single.

7 Fannie Susan Brunk, b. Sept. 24, 1908 No 1943.

8. Mary Elizabeth Brunk, b. May 4, 1913, single.

No. 1940. Seventh Generation. 1939.

3) Carreno Brunk, b Jan. 18, 1901, in Rockingham Co , Va., m. Dec. 24, 1924, John Howard Brown, b May 10, 1900 Address: Goshen, Ind. No children

No. 1941. Seventh Generation. 1939.

4) Hermione Brunk, b. Mar 19, 1903, in Rockingham Co., Va , m. June 16, 1929, Dorsa Yoder, b Oct. 19, 1896.

1. John Menly Yoder, b. Oct. 4, 1931.

2 William Dorsa Yoder, b Jan 5, 1935

No. 1942. Seventh Generation. 1939.

5) John Milton Brunk, b Nov 14, 1904, in Rockingham Co., Va., m June 7, 1931, Elsie Yoder, b Oct. 7, 1905, in Logan Co , O Address: Goshen, Ind

1 Catherine Ann Brunk, b Nov 6, 1932.

No. 1943. Seventh Generation. 1939.

7) Fannie Susan Brunk, b. Sept. 24, 1908, m. Nov. 25, 1934, Henry Wismer Leatherman, b. Jan. 12, 1911. Address: ————, Tex.

No. 1944. Sixth Generation. 372.

4) Laura E. Brunk, b. Oct 10, 1877, near Harrisonburg, Va., m. Dr. DeWitt R. Good, Sept. 25, 1900. She died Aug. 8, 1901.

No. 1945. Sixth Generation. 374.

1) Adaline Virginia Brunk, b. Sept. 10, 1872, d Dec. 11, 1907, and was buried at Hadjin, Turkey, in Asia Minor, where she was a missionary to the natives of Hadjin, Turkey. Never married.

No. 1946. Sixth Generation. 374.

2) Verda Ellen Brunk, b. July 5, 1875, m. Nov. 29, 1899, Thomas Woods, b ————, d. Sept. 22, 1924.
1. William Woods, b. Nov. 6, 1900.
2. Harry Woods, b. Mar. 19, 1902, disappeared about the year 1920 and probably not living now.

Verda Ellen married (2nd) Mar. 31, 1928, to Daniel S. Weldy. Oil station attendant. Mennonite Brethren in Christ. Address· 508 Garfield Ave., Elkhart, Ind.

No. 1947. Sixth Generation. 374.

3) John Kreider Brunk, b. Dec 26, 1876, m June 4, 1902, Mae Belle Caiger, b. Mar. 14, 1880. Address: Lawrenceburg, Ky. Jeweler.
1. Ruth Beryl Brunk, b. May 13, 1910. No. 1948.

No. 1948. Seventh Generation. 1947.

1) Ruth Beryl Brunk, b May 13, 1910, m Melbourne Hawkins, July 19, 1929. Address: Lawrenceburg, Ky.
1. Betty Beryl Hawkins, b. July 12, 1930.
2. John Melbourne Hawkins, b. Sept. 4, 1933.
3. Joe Kelly Hawkins, b. Mar. 18, 1935.

No. 1949. Sixth Generation. 374.

4) Anna Barbara Brunk, b Dec. 11, 1878, m. May 5, 1900, Edgar E. Brode Draftsman.
1. Geraldine Beatrice Brode, b. ————. No. 1950.

No. 1950. Seventh Generation. 1949.

1) Geraldine Beatrice Brode, b. ————, m. Dr. Leland Stanford Evans. Address: Detroit, Mich.
1. Leland Stanford Evans, Jr., b. May 27, 1932.

No. 1951. Sixth Generation. 375.

2) Ida C. Brunk, b. Aug. 28, 1877, m. Dec. 20, 1900, Walter C. Roudabush, b. June 12, 1878. Address: 230 N. Lewis, Staunton, Va. Housekeeper Mennonite
1. Laura C. Roudabush, b. Nov. 23, 1901. No. 2058.
2. Louise C. Roudabush, b. Nov. 2, 1903 No. 2059.

No. 1952. Sixth Generation. 375.

3) Charles Clifford Brunk, b. Jan. 14, 1879, m. May 13, 1903, Anna Jane Swink, b. Nov. 27, 1881. Address: Waynesboro, Va. Rural mail carrier. Presbyterians. Burial ground in River View cemetery, Waynesboro, Va.
1. Mary Moore Brunk, b. Mar. 31, 1904. No. 2060.

No. 1953. Sixth Generation. 375.

4) Hershey Waldo Brunk, b. Jan. 30, 1881, m Nov., 1914, Addie V. Shifflett, b. June 7, 1889. Government worker. Church of God, River View cemetery, Waynesboro, Va. Address: Fairfax, Va.

1. Earle Douglas Brunk, b. Oct. 21, 1915.
2. Owen Kendal Brunk, b Feb. 3, 1917.
3. Sylvia Frances Brunk, b. Mar. 17, 1918.
4. Ruth Lillian Brunk, b. June 13, 1925.

No. 1954. Sixth Generation. 375.

5) William M. Brunk, b. Feb. 1, 1888, m. Dec. 24, 1908, Orpha Metzler, b. Nov. 29, 1889, d. April 13, 1933 Address. Columbiana, O., R. 1. Farmer. Mennonites. Burial in Midway Mennonite cemetery.

1. Letha Marie Brunk, b. Dec. 7, 1909. No. 1954½.

No. 1954½. Seventh Generation. 1954.

1) Letha Marie Brunk, b. Dec. 7, 1909, m. June 23, 1935, David A. Wenger, b. July 8, 1911. Address. Columbiana, O. Farmer. Mennonite.

1. Jean Wenger, b. ————.

No. 1955. Sixth Generation. 376.

1) Rawley C. Rhodes, b. Mar. 28, 1880, m. Sept. 29, 1901, Rhoda E. Wenger, b. Dec. 15, 1876 Farmer. Mennonites. Address: Dayton, Va. Burial at Weavers Church.

1 Mary V. Rhodes, b Jan. 13, 1903. No. 2061.
2. Dee I. Rhodes, b Oct. 17, 1904. No. 2062.
3. William L. Rhodes, b. Aug 24, 1907. No. 2063.
4. Mabel V. Rhodes, b. Sept. 28, 1912. No. 2064.

No. 1956. Sixth Generation. 376.

2) Ina Susan Rhodes, b. Nov. 15, 1885, m. Jacob Hurst, b. ————. Address: East Earl, Pa.

No. 1957. Sixth Generation. 376.

3) Verna V. Rhodes, b. Jan. 25, 1891, m. May 30, 1912, George William Wenger, b. Oct. 16, 1886 Address. Dayton, Va. Farmer. Bible student.

1. Edith E. Wenger, b. Aug. 10, 1913.
2. Naomi E. Wenger, b. April 6, 1916.
3. Martin L. Wenger, b. Dec. 15, 1922.

No. 1953. Sixth Generation. 376.

4) Samuel L. Rhodes, b. Jan. 27, 1896, m. Oct 16, 1919, Ella Amelia Rohrer, b. Mar. 14, 1898. Address: Dayton, Va. Related, for family see mother's line, No. 621.

No. 1959. Sixth Generation. 378.

1) Minnie F. Brunk, b. Sept. 24, 1885, m. Sept. 12, 1915, Jesse H. Heishman, b. Dec. 26, 1885. Mennonites. Address: Harrisonburg, Va., R. 1. Truck driver.

1. Nancy K. Heishman, b. June 23, 1916.
2. Jessie May Heishman, b. April 3, 1920.
   A foster son taken Mar. 26, 1930, name Melvin C. Day Heishman, b. Mar. 5, 1929.

No. 1960. Sixth Generation. 378.

2) Annie Josie Brunk, b. Aug. 20, 1887, m May 8, 1912, Charles C. Branner, b. May 11, 1886 Railroad work Mennonites Burial in Lindale cemetery. Address· Broadway, Va.

1. Ollie Frances Branner, b. Aug. 20, 1913 No. 2065.

2. John Robert Branner, b. Jan. 17, 1917.
3. Phoeba Charlene Branner, b. Dec 3, 1925.

No. 1961 Sixth Generation. 1092.

1) Frank G. Krohn, b. Mar 17, 1900, m Lillian Hilty, b ——————. Mr. Krohn belongs to the Missionary Church and Mrs Krohn is a Mennonite Address: Pandora, O. Farmer
1. Caroline Keith Krohn b. ——————.
2. Charles Krohn, b. ——————.

No. 1962. Fifth Generation. 1090.

4) Benjamin F. Frank, b. Mar. 23, 1874, m Nov. 16, 1916, Ivie Andes, b. Oct. 31, 1882. Mr. Frank is a Presbyterian and Mrs. Frank is a member of the Christian Church
1. Lester Benjamin Frank, b. July 15, 1917
2. Alfred Levi Frank, b. Mar. 28, 1921.

No. 1963. Fifth Generation. 1090.

5) Edward B. Frank, b Mar. 7, 1876, m. Edna Staly, b. —————— Baptists.
1. Emma Frank, b July —, 1905. No. 1964
2 Bessie Frank, b Oct 5, 1909. No. 1965.

No. 1964. Sixth Generation. 1963.

1) Emma Frank, b. July —, 1905, m June 10, 1929, R Gordon Sharp. They live at St. Joseph, Mo. Baptists
1 William Sharp, b. Oct. 1, 1930.

No. 1965. Sixth Generation. 1963.

2) Bessie Frank, b Oct 5, 1909, m Nov. 28, 1928, Claude Kennerly They reside at Wichita, Kans.
1 Bettie LaVon Kennerly, b. ——————, 1930

No. 1966. Sixth Generation. 1093.

1) Clarence Baldwin Frank, b. Nov. 4, 1902, m. Edna Brown Address. Mt. Clinton, Va. United Brethren.

No. 1967. Sixth Generation. 1093.

2) Carl Frank, b April 28, 1905, m. June 10, 1930, Laura Brown Address: Mt Clinton, Va. United Brethren.

No. 1968. Fifth Generation. 1090.

7) Addie P. Frank, b July 11, 1881, m. Roscoe C Welsh, Oct. 25, 1913. He died Mar 5, 1923. She resides at Bellevue, Ky. Presbyterian No children

No. 1969. Fifth Generation. 1090.

9) John S. Frank, b Jan. 30, 1887, m Nov. 5, 1914, Grace Waite. Address: Oklahoma City, Okla. Presbyterians
1. Richard Frank, b Aug. 20, 1915.
2. Harold Frank, b. April 26, 1917.
3. Charles Frank, b. Nov. 7, 1929.

No. 1970. Fifth Generation. 1090.

10) Joseph C. Frank, b Feb. 10, 1890, m. Cassaranda Blardel, Dec. 25, 1920. Address: Oklahoma City, Okla
1. Mary Evelyn Frank, b. Mar. 10, 1923.

No. 1971. Sixth Generation. 1078.

2) Miriam Beery, b Feb 8, 1903, at Lancaster, O , m. Nov. 16, 1926, to John Frederick Farnas Insurance broker at Lancaster, O.

1 John Frederick Farnas, Jr , b. Mar. 25, 1928.

No. 1972. Fifth Generation. 1812.

2) Sarah Ellen Kirkhof, b Feb. 15, 1880, m Arthur G. Houck Address: Grants Pass, Oreg.

1. Henry Calvin Houck, b. Mar. 23, 1902. No. 3638.
2 Eugene Levi Houck, b Feb 2, 1904, d May 5, 1925.
3. Arthur Everett Houck, b. July 30, 1908.
4. Lowell Edwin Houck, b July 4, 1911, d. Aug. 21, 1931.

No. 1973. Fifth Generation. 1812.

3) Julia Etta Kirkhof, b Feb 15, 1880, twin, m Miles McIntyre Address 410 Sherman St , Healdsburg, Calif.

1. Miles August McIntyre, b Aug 24, 1915, d. Sept. 6, 1915.

No. 1974. Fifth Generation. 1812.

4) John Edwin Kirkhof, b May 15, 1885, d Aug 22, 1924, m Hazel Andrews At present she is Mrs Bob Knight, Portola, Calif.

1 Edna Pearl Kirkhof, b. Oct. 21, 1917.

No. 1975. Fourth Generation. 1173.

1) Frances Landes, b April 24, 1826, in Augusta Co , Va , d May 13, 1871, m. Samuel Craun, b Mar 15, 1821 He died June 5, 1864. Buried in the Salem Lutheran cemetery in Va Address Centerville, Va Farmer Lutherans

1. John W. Craun, b Oct. 27, 1848 No 1976
2. Ellen Craun, b. ———, 1852 No 1981
3. George Craun, b Aug 3, 1851 No 1982
4. Alice Craun, b. Dec 14, 1856 No 1983
5. Granville Craun, b Dec 22, 1852. No 1984
6. Julia Craun, b. ——— No 1985.
7. Eddie Craun, b. Mar 23, 1860 No 1986
8. Emma Craun, b. Dec 15, 1863 No 1987
9. Sarah Craun, b Dec 10, 1855, d April 19, 1857.
10. Joseph Craun, b. Jan 6, 1858, d Aug. 6, 1860

No. 1976. Fifth Generation. 1975.

1) John W. Craun, b. Oct. 27, 1848, d May 22, 1908, m. Dec. 24, 1873, Barbara Landes, b Oct 14, 1854, d Dec 6, 1895 Buried in the Salem Lutheran cemetery. Address: Mt Sidney, Va Machinist. Lutheran.

1 Fannie Craun, b Oct 25, 1874 No. 1977.
2. Walter Craun, b. July 28, 1879, d April 6, 1915.

No. 1977. Sixth Generation. 1976.

1) Fannie Craun, b Oct. 25, 1874, m Sept. 11, 1895, Henry C. Coffman, b. June 30, 1869. Address Mt. Sidney, Va.

1. Edith Coffman, b. ———. No. 1978.
2. Helen Coffman, b. April 29, 1903, d Sept. 8, 1929.
3 John Coffman, b. July 18, 1904. No. 1979.
4. Rachel Coffman, b. Jan. 4, 1909 No. 1980.
5. Barbara Coffman, b. Nov. 27, 1911.
6. Henry Clay Coffman, Jr , b Sept 11, 1914
7. Ralph Coffman, b May 12, 1916

No. 1978. Seventh Generation. 1977.

1) Edith Coffman, b ————————, m Lee C Pence, Nov. 11, 1919.
1 Frances Pence, b Dec 7, 1920

No. 1979. Seventh Generation. 1977.

3) John Coffman, b July 18, 1904, m. Lottie Early Shaver, June 25, 1928

No. 1980. Seventh Generation. 1977.

4) Rachel Coffman, b Jan 4, 1909, m. Harold S Adams, Sept. 19, 1931
1 Mary Helen Adams, b Nov 23, 1932.

No. 1981. Fifth Generation. 1975.

2) Nancy Ellen Craun, b. ————————, 1852, d April 18, 1919, m in 1867 Joseph M. Jordon, b. May 25, 1842, d July 12, 1929 Farmer. Lutherans. Burial at Salem Church in Augusta Co., Va. Address: Staunton, Va.
1. James S. Jordon, b. Feb. 1, 1869. No 2056.
2. Wm. C. Jordon, b. Aug. —, 1871, d Aug —, 1924, Tahona, Okla.
3. Joseph B. Jordon, b Mar. —, 1873, d. Oct —, 1878
4 Jacob M. Jordon, b May —, 1875, Peak, Kans.
5. Frances M. Jordon, b. Aug —, 1877, Dodge City, Kans.
6. Lewis G. Jordon, b. May —, 1879, Hutchinson, Kans.
7. Luella M. Jordon, b. Oct —, 1883, Bloom, Kans
8. Zade C. Jordon, b. June —, 1892, Mt. Hope, Kans.
9. Zeke L. Jordon, b. Sept. —, 1895, Hutchinson, Kans
10. Elsie Jordon, b ———————, Rock, Kans.
11. Alma E. Jordon, b. ———————, Cincinnati, O.
12. Lavina B. Jordon, b. ———————, Augusta, Kans.
13. Johnnie Jordon, b. ———————, d young.
14. Everett Jordon, b. ———————, d. young.

No. 1982. Fifth Generation. 1975.

3) George Craun, b. Aug. 3, 1851, d May 22, 1908, m Martha Simmons.
1. ———— Craun, b. ————————
2. ———— Craun, b ————————
3. ———— Craun, b. ————————.
4. ———— Craun, b. ————————.
5. ———— Craun, b. ————————.

No. 1983. Fifth Generation. 1975.

4) Alice Craun, b Dec. 14, 1856, d ————————, 1926, m. Feb., 1881, Link Houff, b. Dec. 2, 1857, d 1916 Farmer. Lutheran. Burial in Pleasant Valley Lutheran cemetery. Address: Staunton, Va, R. 4.
1. Eddie Bell Houff, b. ————————, 1882, d ————————, 1885
2. Anne Houff, b. ————————, 1884. No. 2036.
3. Elsie Houff, b ————————, 1886 No 2038.
4. Emmett Houff, b. ————————, 1887. No. 2039.
5. Elmer Houff, b ————————, 1888 No 2040
6. Myrtle Houff, b ————————, 1895. No 2041.
7. James Houff, b. ————————, 1897. No. 2042
8. Loey Houff, b. ————————, 1901. No 2043

No. 1984. Fifth Generation. 1975.

5) Granville Craun, b. Dec 22, 1852, d April 2, 1913, m Etta Early, b.

————————.

1. ———— Craun, b. ————————.

298

2. ———— Craun, b ————.
3. ———— Craun, b. ————.
4. ———— Craun, b. ————.
5 ———— Craun, b ————.
6 ———— Craun, b. ————.

No. 1985. Fifth Generation. 1975.
6) Julia Craun, b ————, m. ———— Cauady.
1. Evelyn Lena Cauady, b. ————; married a Mr. Whitehead.
2. Evert Cauady, b. ————.

No. 1986. Fifth Generation. 1975.
7) Eddie M. Craun, b. Mar 23, 1860, d Oct. 18, 1935, m. Jan 28, 1886, J. Clark Ruff, b. Oct. 4, 1858, d June 22, 1909. Farmer Lutheran and Mennonite. Burial in Salem Lutheran cemetery, Mt. Sidney, Va., which was their address also.
1. Wilmer C. Ruff, b. Oct. 26, 1886 No. 2045.
2. John Miner Ruff, b. Dec. 26, 1887 No. 2046.
3. Edgar Paul Ruff, b Jan. 10, 1890, d. Sept. 1, 1933.
4 Evalena Ruff, b Mar. 29, 1892 No 2047.
5. Samuel K. Ruff, b May 14, 1894, d Sept 26, 1931.
6 Margaret Ruff, b Nov. 16, 1898 No. 2048.
7. Daniel H. Ruff, b. June 20, 1902 No 2049.
8 Owen F Ruff, b Aug 15, 1908, d Aug. 20, 1927.

No. 1987. Fifth Generation. 1975.
8) Emma Craun, b Dec 15, 1863, d June 4, 1932, m. in 1883 Charles Houff, b May 20, 1863. He died July 20, 1903 Merchant. Presbyterians. Burial in Mt Carmel cemetery. Address· Raphine, Va
1. Edna Pearl Houff, b Jan 21, 1887. No. 2050
2. Charles Clarence Houff, b Aug 12, 1889. No. 2051.
3 Mary Alma Houff, b. July 25, 1892 No 2052.

No. 1988. Fourth Generation. 1173.
4) Erastus Landes, b Jan 6, 1831, in Augusta Co , Va , d Jan 20, 1904, was married Oct 20, 1854, by Rev. Daniel Brower, to Lydia M Landes, b. April 5, 1834, d Oct 18, 1903. Burial in the Salem cemetery, Augusta Co , Va. Farmer. Lutheran. Address· Stonewall, Augusta Co., Va
1 John Samuel Landes, b Jan. 13, 1856 No. 1989.
2. William Newton Landes, b Dec. 2, 1857. No. 1990.
3. George Washington Landes, b Dec 14, 1859 No. 1992.
4. Nancy Elizabeth Landes, b Mar 11, 1862 No. 1998.
5. David Hamilton Landes, b. Aug. 6, 1864. No. 1999
6. Henry Lee Landes, b Jan 6, 1867 No. 2012.
7. Emma Jane Landes, b July 6, 1869. No. 2015.
8. Nettie Florence Landes, b. May 29, 1873, d June 29, 1876.
9. Ida Margaret Landes, b. Aug. 3, 1875. No 2019.

No. 1989. Fifth Generation. 1938.
1) John Samuel Landes, b Jan. 13, 1856, d. Jan. 6, 1933, m. Jan. 13, 1878, Ida C. Craun, b Oct. 8, 1860. Farmer. Lutherans. Burial in Salem cemetery, Va. Address: Weyers Cave, Va.
1. Mary Margaret Landes, b. June 1, 1879, d. Nov. 30, 1914.
2. Nettie A. Landes, b Mar. 5, 1882, d. Jan. 10, 1892
3 Turner Ashby Landes, b May 20, 1885

No. 1990. Fifth Generation. 1938.

2) William Newton Landes, b. Dec 2, 1857, d. Jan 23, 1883, m. Jan 25, 1880, Elizabeth D. Cook, b. Mar. 30, 1859, d Jan 23, 1883 Farmer. Burial in Salem cemetery. Address: Stonewall, Augusta Co., Va

1. Florence C. Landes, b. Oct. 16, 1880, d. Dec. 28, 1902.
2. Willie Kate Landes, b Oct. 10, 1882. No. 1991.

No. 1991. Sixth Generation. 1990.

2) Willie Kate Landes, b. Oct 10, 1882, d. Nov. 10, 1934, m. Walter Parrish. They lived at Mt. Sidney, Va. Both are dead, burial in the Salem cemetery. No living issue.

No. 1992. Fifth Generation. 1938.

3) George Washington Landes, b. Dec. 14, 1859, d. Dec. 9, 1920, m Jan. 22, 1885, Fannie Craun, b. ———, 1863. Farmer. Lutherans. Burial in Salem cemetery, Mt. Sidney, Va. Address: Weyers Cave, Va.

1. Eugene C. Landes, b. Dec 25, 1885. No. 1993.
2. Teretha F. Landes, b. Dec. 11, 1887, d. June 8, 1894.
3. Zula M. Landes, b Dec. 19, 1890. No 1994.
4. Frank E. Landes, b. Nov 9, 1893. No 1995.
5. Cleta M. Landes, b. Oct 30, 1895. No 1996
6. Clifton D. Landes, b. Oct. 2, 1898 No. 1997.

No. 1993. Sixth Generation. 1992.

1) Eugene C. Landes, b. Dec 25, 1885, m. Oct. 20, 1910, Pearl Wilberger Address. Harrisonburg, Va No children

No. 1994. Sixth Generation. 1992.

3) Zula M. Landes, b. Dec 19, 1890, m. M. B Wilberger, Jan. 3, 1909. Address: Weyers Cave, Va

1. ——— Wilberger, b. ———
2. ——— Wilberger, b. ———.
3. ——— Wilberger, b. ———.
4. ——— Wilberger, b. ———
5. ——— Wilberger, b ———.
6. ——— Wilberger, b. ———.
7. ——— Wilberger, b. ———.

No. 1995. Sixth Generation. 1992.

4) Frank E. Landes, b. Nov 9, 1893, m Jan. 24, 1915, Amiga L. Lin, b. ———. Address: Harrisburg, Pa.

1. ——— Landes, b. ———.
2. ——— Landes, b ———.
3. ——— Landes, b ———.
4 ——— Landes, b. ———.

No. 1995. Sixth Generation. 1992.

5) Cleta M. Landes, b. Oct. 30, 1895, m. Jan. 13, 1918, J. C Eddins Address: Weyers Cave, Va.

1. ——— Eddins, b. ———.

No. 1997. Sixth Generation. 1992.

6) Clifton D. Landes, b Oct. 2, 1898, m Aug. 31, 1931, Virginia Early. Address: 18 High St., Staunton, Va.

1. ——— Landes, b. ———.

4) Nancy Elizabeth Landes, b Mar. 11, 1862, d. Mar. 1, 1897, m. William Franklin Fry, b. —————, d Sept. 9, 1917.

1. Walter Emmette Fry, b. —————. No. 2006.
2. Archie Lee Fry, b. Jan. 6, 1884 No. 2007.
3. Stuart William Fry, b. Oct. 30, 1886. No. 2008.
4. Marion Marvin Fry, b Mar. 18, 1888. No. 2009.
5. Charles Wilson Fry, b. Feb. 2, 1890 No. 2010.
6. Carletta Pearl Fry, b. Aug 30, 1893. No. 2011

No. 1999. Fifth Generation. 1988.

5) David Hamilton Landes, b. Aug 6, 1864, d. Sept. 6, 1912. On Dec. 19, 1886, he married Margaret M. Fifer, b Feb. 23, 1804; she died Jan. 31, 1918. Lutherans. Burial in Salem cemetery Address. Mt Sidney, Va.

1 Melvin E. Landes, b. Oct. 8, 1887, d. 1891
2 Lillie M. Landes, b. June 2, 1889 No. 2000.
3. William H. Landes, b Sept 17, 1891. No. 2001.
4. Carletta B Landes, b. April 1, 1894. No. 2002.
5. Bertha L. Landes, b Oct 28, 1896 No 2003.
6. Mary L. Landes, b. April 13, 1901. No 2004.
7. Charles W. Landes, b. Sept. 18, 1903. No 2005.

No. 2000. Sixth Generation. 1999.

2) Lill e M Landes, b June 2, 1889, m. Feb 21, 1908, Charles S. Cook, b Nov. 25, 1885, d. Dec. 12, 1921. Seamstress. St. James Lutheran Church. Burial in Salem cemetery. Address: Mt Sidney, Va.

1 Helen M Cook, b Nov. 9, 1911.

No. 2001. Sixth Generation. 1999.

3) William H. Landes, b Sept. 17, 1891, d. —————, 1930, m. Georgia L. Shifflett Address. Dayton, Va

No. 2002. Sixth Generation. 1999.

4) Charletta B Landes, b. April 1, 1894, m. May 4, 1913, Harry E Byers, b. Aug. 9, 1893. Lutherans Mt Sidney, Va Burial in Salem cemetery, Augusta Co., Va.

1. David W Byers, b Sept. 23, 1914
2 Samuel F. Byers, b April 17, 1918.
3 Ed th M. Byers, b Sept 28, 1920, d Nov 5, 1920.
4 Harry Lee Byers, b. Oct 2, 1922

No. 2003. Sixth Generation. 1999.

5) Bertha L Landes, b Oct 28, 1896, m Karl H. Eddins. Address: 213 Delaware Ave., Brunswick, Md

No. 2004. Sixth Generation. 1999.

6) Mary L. Landes, b April 13, 1901, m. April 5, 1933, Frederick C Lickliter, b Aug 3, 1897. Lutherans Address Churchville, Va Housekeeper.

1 Howard Craig Lickliter, b. Jan 27, 1934.

No. 2005. Sixth Generation. 1999.

7) Charles W. Landes, b. Sept. 18, 1903, m Catherine Odin. Address: 29 East D St., Brunswick, Md.

No. 2006. Sixth Generation. 1998.

1) Walter Emmette Fry, b. —————, 1882, m Clara Belle Brown. Address: Harrisonburg, Va., R. 5.

No. 2007. Sixth Generation. 1998.

2) Archie Lee Fry, b Jan. 6, 1884, d instantly May 11, 1933, from falling off a roof. He married Nov 1, 1911, Myrtle V. Baylor, b June 30, 1887. Contractor. United Brethren. Burial at Jerusalem Chapel near Churchville, Va Address: Harrisonburg, Va.

1. Edith Nirine Fry, b June 6, 1914.
2. Anna Lee Fry, b. Dec. 24, 1918.
3 Robert Sylvester Fry, b. Aug 22, 1920, d Dec 12, 1924

No. 2008. Sixth Generation. 1993.

3) Stuart William Fry, b Oct 30, 1886, m April 10, 1910, Lottie Lee Lambert, b Aug 14, 1886 Central Methodists Carpenter and farmer Burial in Salem cemetery, Mt. Sidney, Va Address: Churchville, Va.

1 Clara Pauline Fry, b. June 21, 1912. No. 2025.
2 Marie Louise Fry, b May 27, 1913 No. 2026.

No. 2009. Sixth Generation. 1998.

4) Marion Marvin Fry, b. Mar 18, 1888, m. Sept 24, 1914, Nora Baylor, b. May 25, 1893 United Brethren Carpenter Address. Churchville, Va Burial at Jerusalem Chapel.

1 James Eugene Fry, b April 7, 1920
2. Walter Aldeen Fry, b Oct 3, 1922
3. Russell Lee Fry, b. Dec. 24, 1925.
4. Harold Baylor Fry, b Sept 22, 1931.

No. 2010. Sixth Generation. 1993.

5) Charles Wilson Fry, b Feb 2, 1890, m April 15, 1915, Bertha Bolik, b Dec. 16, 1894 Reformed Church. Brick mason Address: Mt. Crawford, Va Burial in Salem cemetery, Augusta Co.

1 Raymond Franklin Fry, b Jan 13, 1916
2. Gladys Virginia Fry, b Sept 23, 1917, d Feb 13, 1920.
3 George Henry Fry, b. Mar 16, 1919, d Feb 10, 1920.
4. Irene Elaine Fry, b Sept 15, 1928

No. 2011. Sixth Generation. 1998.

6) Carletta Pearl Fry, b Aug 30, 1893, m. Feb. 25, 1913, Stuart Roudabush, b. Feb. 15, 1891. Farmer Presbyterians Address King Ferry, N Y Burial in Salem cemetery, Va.

1. Marion W Roudabush, b Sept 9, 1914
2. Margaret Virginia Roudabush, b. June 22, 1916.
3. Mary Elizabeth Roudabush, b Mar 8, 1919.
4. Whanetia W. Roudabush, b. Dec 5, 1920
5 Edith Marie Roudabush, b. May 5, 1924.
6. Helen Pauline Roudabush, b. Dec 12, 1926.
7. Anna Belle Roudabush, b Aug 12, 1928.
8. Marcia Elaine Roudabush, b Aug 24, 1932.

No. 2012. Fifth Generation. 1928.

6) Henry Lee Landes, b Jan 6, 1867, m Oct. 1, 1891, Sallie M. Lutwiler, b. July 11, 1869, d. June 7, 1923. Burial place in Salem Church cemetery, Augusta Co., Va. Address: Mt Sidney, Va. Carpenter Lutherans

1. Junie L. Landes, b. June 3, 1892. No 2013.
2. Stella L Landes, b Nov 7, 1894 No 2014

No. 2013. Sixth Generation. 2012.

1) Junie L. Landes, b June 3, 1892, m Oct 14, 1914, Earl Carver, b. Aug. 13, 1890.
1. Nelson E. Carver, b Feb 5, 1916.
2. Fillmore L. Carver, b. July 16, 1917.
3. Elvin L Carver, b. Jan 2, 1919.

No. 2014. Sixth Generation. 2012.

2) Stella L. Landes, b Nov 7, 1894, m. Oct 27, 1915, Jessie Barth Wine, b. Dec. 8, 1893.
1. Winston B. Wine, b. Sept. 21, 1916
2. Charlotte F. Wine, b. May 28, 1918.
3. Maxine Harding Wine, b Nov 2, 1920.
4. Margaret Bernice Wine, b April 17, 1923
5. Ellen Landes Wine, b Aug. 2, 1928

No. 2015. Fifth Generation. 1908.

7) Emma Jane Landes, b July 6, 1869, m Sept 15, 1896, by Rev. D. P. T. Crickebberger, to J. Samuel Huffman, b April 18, 1869. Address Mt. Sidney, Va. Teacher and farmer. Lutherans Burial ground in Salem cemetery, Augusta Co., Va.
1. Bertha Agnes Huffman, b Oct. 3, 1897. No. 2016.
2. Ethel Pauline Huffman, b Feb 25, 1902 No 2017.
3. Leslie Sylvester Huffman, b Sept. 9, 1904. No 2018

No. 2016. Sixth Generation. 2015.

1) Bertha Agnes Huffman, b Oct 3, 1897, d. Aug 18, 1929, m. July 30, 1927, C. Leslie Cudney Clerk. Methodist Burial, Middletown, N Y No issue.

No. 2017. Sixth Generation. 2015.

2) Ethel Pauline Huffman, b Feb. 25, 1902, d April 13, 1931, m Feb. 26, 1923, Virgil P Gwin. Burial in Salem cemetery, Augusta Co, Va Address: Massanutten Academy, Woodstock, Va.
1. Norma Jane Gwin, b Nov 15, 1927. Norma lives with her grandparents, Mr. and Mrs. I. Samuel Huffman

No. 2018. Sixth Generation. 2015.

3) Leslie Sylvester Huffman, b. Sept 9, 1904, m. May 8, 1930, G Kathleen Anderson, b. Mar. 14, 1907. Chauffeur Presbyterians No children Address: 15 Dolson Ave, Middletown, N. Y.

No. 2019. Fifth Generation. 1988.

9) Ida Margaret Landes, b Aug 3, 1875, m George C Fifer. Address: Weyers Cave, Va.
1. Usher Lee Fifer, b —————. No 2020.
2. Dorothy Fifer, b —————. No. 2021.
3. Leslie P. Fifer, b ————— No 2022
4. Virginia Fifer, b. ————— No 2023
5. Mabel Fifer, b. —————. No 2024
6. Ward H. Fifer, b. —————.

No. 2020. Sixth Generation. 2019.

1) Usher Lee Fifer, b. —————, m Mary Shumate, b. ————— Address: 555 N. Main St, Harrisonburg, Va.
1. ————— Fifer, b —————.

2. ——— Fifer, b ———.

3. ——— Fifer, b. ———.

No. 2021. Sixth Generation. 2019.

2) Dorothy Fifer, b ———, m Lee A. Landes, b. ———. Address: Fort Defiance, Va

1. ——— Landes, b. ———.

No. 2022. Sixth Generation. 2019.

3) Leslie P. Fifer, b. ———, m Gurney Boyers, b ———. Address: Fort Defiance, Va

1. ——— Fifer, b. ———.

2. ——— Fifer, b. ———.

3. ——— Fifer, b. ———.

No. 2023. Sixth Generation. 2019.

4) Virgnia Fifer, b ———, m. Emery Craun, b ———. Address: Mt. Crawford, Va.

1. ——— Craun, b. ———.

No. 2024. Sixth Generation. 2019.

5) Mabel Fifer, b Aug 8, 1907, m. Dec 29, 1928, Otis Baker, b Oct. 7, 1909. Burial ground at Dayton, Va. Address: Dayton, Va. Laborer. Methodists.

1. Sheldon Baker, b. Dec. 15, 1929.

2 Ivan Baker, b July 31, 1931.

No. 2025. Seventh Generation. 2008.

1) Clara Pauline Fry, b. June 21, 1912, m. Franklin Faught Address Churchville, Va.

No. 2026. Seventh Generation. 2008.

2) Marie Louise Fry, b May 27, 1913. m Tony B. Lamb. Address: Churchville, Va, R. 1.

1. Lorine Elizabeth Lamb, b ———.

No. 2027. Fourth Generation. 1173.

5) William Landes, b Dec 20, 1833, d. Oct 27, 1907, m. in 1860, Delilah Ellen Alexander, b Mar 26, 1844, d Oct. 28, 1912 Farmer Mennonite and Lutheran. Address: Mt. Sidney, Va Burial in Salem cemetery.

1. Laura Frances Landes, b June —, 1861. No 2028.

2. Nancy Margaret Landes, b. Feb 14, 1864. No. 2029.

3. Sarah Jane Landes, b. Aug. 27, 1866 No. 2030.

4. John Alexander Landes, b Nov. 21, 1868 No. 2031.

5. Martha Florence Landes, b July 30, 1872. No. 2032

6. Rebecca Ellen Landes, b. Feb. 28, 1875. No 2035.

7. William Kenny Landes, b. Oct. 19, 1878, died an infant.

8. Charles Stewart Landes, b. Jan. 10, 1881. No. 2033.

9. Wallace Payton Landes, b. Dec 3, 1884. No. 2034.

No. 2028. Fifth Generation. 2027.

1) Laura Frances Landes, b. June —, 1861, m. Dec 22, 1880, M. Luther Link, b. Mar. 17, 1857. Farmer Lutherans Burial place in Salem Lutheran cemetery. Address: Mt. Sidney, Va.

1. Daniel William Link, b. Sept. 23, 1881. No 3427.

2 Elzabeth Catherine Link, b Feb. 15, 1884. No 3430

3. Clara Ellen Link, b. July 10, 1888 No 3435.

4 Mary Martin Link, b May 17, 1893. No 3437.

No. 2029. Fifth Generation. 2027.

2) Nancy Margaret Landes, b. Feb 14, 1864, d 1930, m. in 1894 John P. Simmons. Christian Church Address· Mason City, Ia. Burial at same place.

1 Ruth Simmons, b. —————
2 Carl Simmons, b. —————.

No. 2030. Fifth Generation. 2027.

3) Sarah Jane Landes, b Aug 27, 1866, m. William Simmons.

1. ————— Simmons, b. —————
2 ————— Simmons, b —————.

No. 2031. Fifth Generation. 2027.

4) John Alexander Landes, b Nov 27, 1868, m Lula M Moore, b. —————

1. ————— Landes, b —————
2 ————— Landes, b —————
3 ————— Landes, b. —————.
4. ————— Landes, b —————
5. ————— Landes, b —————
6 ————— Landes, b —————
7 ————— Landes, b —————
8 ————— Landes, b —————
9 ————— Landes, b —————.

No. 2032. Fifth Generation. 2027.

5) Martha Florence Landes. b July 30, 1872, m in 1889 L H Reed. Farmer. Lutherans. Burial in Salem cemetery near Mt Sidney, Va Address: Church-ville, Va

1. Mamie A Reed, b July 1, 1890
2. William C. Reed, b Dec 18, 1892
· 3. Hallah F. Reed, b Oct. 28, 1894
4 Santa P Reed, b Oct 8, 1896
5 Earnest G Reed, b Nov. 28, 1898.
6. Wallace B Reed, b April 4, 1900
7 Sheton L. Reed, b July 17, 1902
8. Alma S. Reed, b July 12, 1904.
9 Syrena C Reed, b Sept 20, 1906
10 Blair H Reed, b Jan 10, 1909
11 Frances E Reed, b Dec 25, 1911
12 Evelyn S Reed, b Jan 12, 1913.

No. 2033 Fifth Generation. 2027.

7) Charles Steward Landes, b Jan 10, 1881, m April 17, 1929, Norma L Rimel, b July 14, 1900 Address Weyers Cave, Va Farmer Lutheran. Burial in Salem cemetery

1 Janet Page Landes, b April 4, 1930
2 Lesley Ross Landes, b Sept 11, 1932
3 Sarah Ellen Landes. b June 20, 1935

No. 2034. Fifth Generation. 2027.

8) Wallace Peyton Landes, b Dec 3. 1884, m Sadie F Byers

1 ————— Landes, b —————
2 ————— Landes, b —————
3 ————— Landes, b —————
4 ————— Landes, b —————
5 ————— Landes, b —————.

6) Rebecca Ellen Landes, b. Feb. 28, 1875, m Sept 18, 1901, D. G. Baylor, b. April 12, 1873. Address 315 Sherwood Ave, Staunton, Va Cabinetmaker Presbyterians.

1. Helen Baylor, b Aug 12, 1902 No. 2053.
2. Margaret Page Baylor, b. April 6, 1905.
3. William Marshal Baylor, b. April 2, 1907
4. Alita Baylor, b. Jan. 27, 1909.
5. Jessie Ellen Baylor, b. Feb. 26, 1912
6. David Julian Baylor, b Sept 8, 1914

No. 2036. Sixth Generation. 1933.

2) Annie Elizabeth Houff, b Feb 12, 1884, m Dec 12, 1906, G Vernie Link, b. Aug 14, 1884 Farmer. Lutheran Address Staunton, Va, R 4.

1. Helen Leora Link, b ————, 1908 No 2037.
2 Mary Elizabeth Link, b ————, 1919.
3. Mal Vernie Link, b ————, 1925

No. 2037. Seventh Generation. 2036.

1) Helen Leora Link, b ————, 1908, m. Dec. 16, 1926, Golden Smith Address· Staunton, Va., R. 4.

1. Wilfred Link Smith, b ————, 1930

No. 2038. Sixth Generation. 1933.

3) Elsie Houff, b. ————, 1886, m —————— Address· Bloom, Kans
1. Harold Houff, b. ————.

No. 2039. Sixth Generation. 1933.

4) Emmett Houff, b ————, 1887, m Pearl Howell Address: Bloom, Kans.
1. Floyd Houff, b. ————.

No. 2040. Sixth Generation. 1983.

5) Elmer Houff, b ————, 1888, m Violet Wallace They live in California No children.

No. 2041. Sixth Generation. 1933.

6) Myrtle Houff, b ————, 1895, m O Jay Meyerhoeffer Address Staunton, Va, R. 1.

1 Alphadine Meyerhoeffer, b ——————

No. 2042. Sixth Generation. 1983.

7) James Houff, b ————, 1897, m Loma Moore Address: Staunton, Va., R. 2.

1. James Houff, Jr., b. ——————.
2. Reginald Houff, b. ——————

No. 2043. Sixth Generation. 1983.

8) Loey Houff, b ————, 1901, m Dess Davis. Address. Akron, O
1 Master Eddie Houff, b ————.

No. 2045. Sixth Generation. 1986.

1) Wilmer C Ruff, b Oct 26, 1886, m Eva Carpenter, of Durham, N C Address 401 23rd St, Washington, D C No children

No. 2046. Sixth Generation. 1936.

2) John Miner Ruff, b Dec 26, 1887, m Jean Sell. Address. 3000 Walnut Ave., Altoona, Pa.
1 Freda Ruff, b ————, 1925.

No. 2047. Sixth Generation. 1986.

4) Evelena Ruff, b Mar 29, 1892, m. E. Pursell Quick   Address. Staunton, Va.

1. —————— Quick, b —————————.
2. —————— Quick, b. —————————.
3. —————— Quick, b —————————.

No. 2048. Sixth Generation. 1986.

6) Margaret Ruff, b Nov 16, 1898, m. E A Kersh   Address: Harrisonburg, Va.

1 Edgar Orlin Kersh, b Nov. 7, 1921.
2. Charles Lenfred Kersh, b June 2, 1927.
3. Hildred Kerah Kersh, b. Nov 12, 1918, d Aug 23, 1926.

No. 2049. Sixth Generation. 1986.

7) Daniel Ruff, b June 20, 1902, m. Margie Stein   Address: 4123 Gray Ave, Detroit, Mich.

1. —————— Ruff, b —————————

No. 2050. Sixth Generation. 1987.

1) Edna Pearl Houff, b Jan 21, 1887, m Erma R McCormick   Address: 246 W. High St, Elkton, Md

1 Erma Gwendolyn McCormick, b. ——————————
2 Jane McCormick, b ——————————

No. 2051. Sixth Generation. 1937.

2) Charles Clarence Houff, b Aug. 12, 1889, m Mary Lydia Coyner
1. Charles Houff, b ——————, 1933

No. 2052. Sixth Generation. 1987.

3) Mary Alma Houff, b July 25, 1892, m Nov 22, 1911, Raymond Campbell, b. Mar 21, 1891. Farmer Presbyterians Burial at Mt Carmel, Va. Address: Raphine, Va., R 2.

1. Molton Leonard Campbell, b June 27, 1913.
2. Lester Edward Campbell, b Nov 18, 1915.
3 Frederick Newton Campbell, b. Dec 20, 1918
4 Mary Margaret Campbell, b Sept 10, 1920.
5. Charles Franklin Campbell, b July 19, 1922
6 Ruth Helen Campbell, b. July 22, 1928.

No. 2053. Sixth Generation. 2035.

1) Helen Baylor, b Aug 12, 1902, m —————— Henderson, b. —————————.

No. 2056. Sixth Generation. 1981.

1) James S Jordon, b. Feb 1, 1869, m Oct 1, 1894, Maggie P. Byers, b. Feb 23, 1878. Mining and farming Presbyterians Address: Staunton, Va., R. 4.
1 Margaret E Jordon, b July 7, 1899 No 2057.

No. 2057. Seventh Generation. 2056.

1) Margaret E Jordon, b July 7, 1895, m —————— Carroll

No. 2058. Seventh Generation. 1951.

1) Laura C. Roudabush, b Nov 23, 1901, m Oct. 10, 1922, William W. Smalls, b. July 20, 1884 Address Staunton, Va No children Housewife Baptists.

No. 2059. Seventh Generation. 1951.

2) Louise C. Roudabush, b. Nov. 2, 1903, m Feb 14, 1924, Walter E Cohen, b June 14, 1888 Address N Coulter St, Staunton, Va Housewife Baptists. No children

No. 2060. Seventh Generation. 1952.

1) Mary Moore Brunk, b Mar 31, 1904, m Oct. 1, 1924, Charles Frederick Jones, b. Oct 8, 1903 No children

No. 2061. Seventh Generation. 1955.

1) Mary V. Rhodes, b. Jan 13, 1903, m. Feb 11, 1923, Wilmer Shank, b. —————. Address Harrisonburg, Va.

1 Mabel L. Shank, b. Jan 2, 1924
2. Floyd C. Shank, b Feb 27, 1925.
3. Norman R Shank, b. Dec 14, 1926
4. Gladys L. Shank, b Dec 2, 1928
5. Rawley J Shank, b. June 10, 1931.

No. 2062. Seventh Generation. 1955.

2) Dee I. Rhodes, b Oct 17, 1904, m. Aug 10, 1934, Catherine Van Pelt Address: Dayton, Va

No. 2063. Seventh Generation. 1955.

3) William R Rhodes, b Aug 24, 1907, m Sadie Rhodes, Mar. 20, 1929 Address: Dayton, Va.

1. Glen W. Rhodes, b April 6, 1930
2. Don L Rhodes, b Feb 5, 1935.

No. 2064. Seventh Generation. 1955.

4) Mabel V Rhodes, b Sept 28, 1912, m Oliver Kiser, Dec 21, 1935 Address: Dayton, Va.

No. 2065. Seventh Generation. 1960.

1) Ollie Frances Branner, b Aug 20, 1913, m. Lloyd Rhodes, Feb 11, 1933. Address 307 W Market St, Harrisonburg, Va

No. 2056. Fifth Generation. 237.

1) Samuel H. Blosser, b Oct 3, 1855, m May 30, 1876, Emma C Shifflett, b. Jan. 2, 1856, d Mar. 15, 1930 Address· Dayton, Va Poultryman. Mennonites.

1. Lydia A. Blosser, b April 19, 1877. No 2067.
2. Amos H Blosser, b July 12, 1879. No 2072
3. Earnest D Blosser, b Feb 27, 1881 No 2079
4. Magdalena Blosser, b Feb. 22, 1883 No 2082.
5. Emma E. Blosser, b. Feb 26, 1885 No 2088
6. Peter Blosser, b Aug 6, 1887. No 2090.
7. Ida S. Blosser, b 1889, d 1892.
8 Samuel O Blosser, b. Nov. 26, 1891. No. 2091.
9. Fannie R. Blosser, b Mar 10, 1894 No 2092
10. Katie L Blosser, b Oct 10, 1896 No. 2094.
11. Jonas E Blosser, b. —————, 1898 No 2095
12. Frederick Blosser, b Jan 25, 1900. No. 2096.
13. Priscilla R. Blosser, b Jan. 23, 1903 No. 2097.

No. 2057. Sixth Generation. 2066.

1) Lydia A. Blosser, b April 19, 1877, near Dayton, Va, m. William J. Keyton, b. Nov. 7, 1863 Address: Harrisonburg, Va Farmer. Mennonites

1. Samuel J. Keyton, b Oct 22, 1898 No 2068

2. Forest H Keyton, b. July 29, 1900 No. 2069.

3. Wilmer F. Keyton, b ————————

4 Edna V Keyton, b Feb 25, 1906 No. 2070.

5. Evangeline F. Keyton, b. Nov. 28, 1908 No. 2071

6 Virgil L. Keyton, b Sept 25, 1911.

7 Walter B. Keyton, b Aug 10, 1914

8. Mary E. Keyton, b Mar. 17, 1917

9. Catherine L. Keyton, b. May 18, 1920.

No. 2068. Seventh Generation. 2057.

1) Samuel J Keyton, b Oct 22, 1898, m Lillian Helm, b. ————————, 1901
Address. Elkridge, Ind

1. Lloyd S. Keyton, b June 10, 1922, d April 2, 1928.

2. Harold J Keyton, b. June 15, 1925

3. Charles W. Keyton, b. Feb. 22, 1927.

4 James L. Keyton, b June 6, 1929

5. Mildred E Keyton, b Aug. 15, 1931.

No. 2069. Seventh Generation. 2057.

2) Forest H. Keyton, b July 29, 1900, m Lillian Huffman, b Sept 15, 1899.
Address Harrisonburg, Va

1 Jannita Huffman, b Jan 1, 1922

2 Malile Keyton Huffman, b. Mar 8, 1924.

No. 2070. Seventh Generation. 2067.

4) Edna V. Keyton, b Feb 25, 1906, m Lester E Oliver, b. Mar. 30, 1903
Address McGaheysville, Va

1. Nelson L. Oliver, b. Nov 27, 1924.

2. Lorrene V. Oliver, b Aug 14, 1926

3. Agnes R Oliver, b Jan 19, 1928, d. Dec 19, 1930

4 Evelyn P. Oliver, b Nov 29, 1930

5 Floyd R. Oliver, b Dec 31, 1932.

No. 2071. Seventh Generation. 2067.

5) Evangeline F Keyton, b Nov 28, 1908, m Jan 25, 1925, Dwane F Hopkins, b. Jan 3, 1906

1. Eunice A Hopkins, b May 5, 1926

2. Margie Ann Hopkins, b Aug 8, 1928

3. Jennings A. Hopkins, b Jan 17, 1932

4 Ivan DeWitt Hopkins, b June 27, 1935

No. 2072. Sixth Generation. 2065.

2) Amos H Blosser, b July 12, 1879, near Dayton, Va , m. Ada M. Suter, b. Mar. 14, 1887, d May 27, 1907. He married (2nd) Lucy May Wyant, b. Nov 1, 1884. Employe of Blosser Hatchery, Harrisonburg, Va. Address. Harrisonburg, Va. Mennonites.

1. Vada M. Blosser, b May 17, 1907 No 2073
   (From second marriage)

2 Walter H. Blosser, b Aug. 6, 1908 No. 2074

3. Effie May Blosser, b May 30, 1910 No 2075

4 Russell Amos Blosser, b. Oct 25, 1911 No. 2076

5. Virgil Randolph Blosser, b Nov 13, 1912 No 2077.

6. Roy Lee Blosser, b April 27, 1917. No 2078

7 Alice Virginia Blosser, b April 15, 1919, d. same day.

8. Evelyn Pauline Blosser, b Feb. 27, 1922

9. Lottie Frances Blosser, b. May 30, 1923
10. George Ralph Blosser, b Aug 20, 1926

No. 2073. Seventh Generation. 2072.

1) Vada M. Blosser, b. May 17, 1907, d Sept 20, 1931, m Nov. 24, 1926, George Ira Sandridge, b June 13, 1904.
1. Morris Lynwood Sandridge, b. Oct 7, 1927
2. Millard Suter Sandridge, b. May 7, 1929.
3. Bettie Lee Sandridge, b July 6, 1930, d Oct 29, 1930
4. Shirley Wilson Sandridge, b Sept 5, 1931.

No. 2074. Seventh Generation. 2072.

2) Walter Henry Blosser, b Aug 6, 1908, m Sept 3, 1927, Rosalyn E. Dutrow, of Elkton, Va, b Dec 26, 1910 Address: Harrisonburg, Va. Employee of Daly Shoe Co.
1. Walter Henry Blosser, Jr, b. Nov 16, 1928, d May 2, 1930
2. Wanda Elizabeth Blosser, b Jan 9, 1931
3. Mary Alice Blosser, b. Dec. 17, 1932
4. Dorothy Marie Blosser, b Nov 23, 1934

No. 2075. Seventh Generation. 2072.

3) Effie May Blosser, b May 30, 1910, m Cletis Life, b Aug. 22, 1909, of McGaheysville, Va.
1. Marcella Virginia Life, b Dec. 6, 1927.
2. Vernon Talmadge Life, b. April 20, 1929
3. Charles Amos Life, b April 26, 1930

No. 2076. Seventh Generation. 2072.

4) Russell Amos Blosser, b. Oct 25, 1911, m May 18, 1935, Virginia Lee Grady, b Oct. 18, 1918 Truck driver

No. 2077. Seventh Generation. 2072.

5) Virgil Randolph Blosser, b Nov. 13, 1912, m. Minnie Velma Jameson, b April 22, 1913, of Harrisonburg, Va Employee of Campbell Shoe Co.
1. Catherine Ann Blosser, b Mar. 11, 1932.

No. 2078. Seventh Generation. 2072.

6) Roy Lee Blosser, b April 27, 1917, m Aug. 3, 1935, Ida Alice Mitchell, b. Dec. 10, 1918, of Cross Keys, Va.

No. 2079. Sixth Generation. 2065.

3) Ernest David Blosser, b. Feb. 27, 1881, near Dayton, Va, m. Bertie Alice Brown, b. Oct. 20, 1879 Farmer. Church of God in Christ Mennonite Address: Archbold, O.
1. Paul Franklin Blosser, b Nov. 11, 1902. No. 2080.
2. Lewis David Blosser, b Feb 11, 1904, d Nov. 12, 1923.
3. Martin Samuel Blosser, b Mar. 5, 1905, d. Mar. 12, 1905.
4. Nettie Jane Blosser, b Sept. 10, 1906 No. 2081.
5. Willie James Blosser, b April 14, 1908, d same day.
6 John Reuben Blosser, b Mar 1, 1909, d April 3, 1910.
7. Rebecca Ruth Blosser, b May 21, 1910.
8. Homer Lee Blosser, b Mar. 10, 1912, d Nov. 9, 1934.
9. Emma Mae Blosser, b May 26, 1913.
10. Owen Henry Blosser, b. Oct 15, 1915
11. Perry Timothy Blosser, b Oct 10, 1917, d Aug 21, 1928.

12. Noah Christian Blosser, b May 24, 1919
13. Charles Daniel Blosser, b. Oct. 6, 1920.

No. 2080. Seventh Generation. 2079.

1) Paul Franklin Blosser, b Nov. 11, 1902, m. June 4, 1923, Cora Wendendorth, b April 27, 1908 Laborer in steel mills Address· Youngstown, O.
1. Pauline Louise Blosser, b Mar 20, 1924.
2. Howard Lee Blosser, b. Mar. 18, 1927.
3 Betty Lou Blosser, b. Feb 8, 1929.

No. 2081. Seventh Generation. 2079.

4) Nettie Jane Blosser, b Sept 10, 1906, m. Nov. 30, 1924, Ira Buerge, b. Jan. 16, 1896. Laborer in hatchery. Church of God in Christ Mennonite. Address: Wauseon, O.
1. Vada Ruth Buerge, b July 12, 1926
2. Edith Mar Buerge, b Mar. 17, 1928.
3. Harold Gene Buerge, b. July 26, 1934.

No. 2082. Sixth Generation. 2066.

4) Magdalena Blosser, b. Feb. 22, 1883, at Dayton, Va., m. Emmanuel Hartman. Address: Archbold, O. Mennonites.
1. Lucy Virginia Hartman, b Nov. 29, 1905. No. 2083.
2. Emma Irene Hartman, b Jan. 3, 1907 No 2084.
3. Herman E. Hartman, b Aug 23, 1908 No. 2085.
4. Wayland Samuel Hartman, b. Dec 6, 1910 No. 2086.
5. Elias John Hartman, b Dec 25, 1911. No 2087.
6 DeWitt Blosser Hartman, b Sept 6, 1915.
7. David Paul Hartman, b and d. Nov 8, 1918.
8. Sarah Ruth Hartman, b Nov 15, 1920.

No. 2083. Seventh Generation. 2082.

1) Lucy Virginia Hartman, b. Nov. 29, 1905, m. Feb 26, 1925, Horace Thievry, b. Jan. 18, 1895 Farmer Address Fayette, O.
1. Paul Henry Thievry, b Oct 27, 1925
2. Carl Herbert Thievry, b July 12, 1929.

No. 2084. Seventh Generation. 2082.

2) Emma Irene Hartman, b. Jan. 3, 1907, m Jan. 3, 1929, Louis Poorman, b. Feb 22, 1904 Factory employee Address: Swanton, O.
1. Betty Louise Poorman, b. July 4, 1933.

No. 2085. Seventh Generation. 2082.

3) Herman E. Hartman, b. Aug 23, 1908, m. Sept 27, 1927, Clara E. Hoplinger, b Sept 27, 1909 Address Archbold, O Farmer.
1. Robert Lowell Hartman, b Oct 31, 1929.
2. William Emmanuel Hartman, b Nov. 27, 1932.

No. 2086. Seventh Generation. 2082.

4) Wayland Samuel Hartman, b Dec. 6, 1910, m Feb. 1, 1934, Wilma Elnora Kuszmaul, b May 23, 1914 Address. Archbold, O Filling station employee.
1. Betty Elnora Hartman, b. Dec. 12, 1934.

No. 2087. Seventh Generation. 2082.

5) Elias John Hartman, b Dec. 25, 1911, m June 2, 1935, Doris E. Rebean, b. Jan. 6, 1914 Address. Wauseon, O Railroad employee

No. 2088. Sixth Generation. 2066.

5) Emma Elizabeth Blosser, b Feb. 26, 1885, near Dayton, Va , m Jan. 24, 1909, Christian Kulp, b April 27, 1876 Address· Nappanee, Ind. Mennonites

1 Samuel Kulp, b Aug 17, 1910 No. 2089.
2. Susanna Kulp, b Aug 5, 1912, d April 19, 1915.
3. Joseph Kulp, b June 13, 1914
4 Mary Kulp, b. Nov 29, 1915.
5. Martha Kulp, b Mar. 7, 1918
6 Ernest Kulp, b. Feb. 25, 1920.
7. Christian Kulp, Jr , b. May 4, 1922
8. Emma Kulp, b Feb 12, 1924
9. Barbara Kulp, b May 18, 1926
10 Isaac Kulp, b July 29, 1927

No. 2089. Seventh Generation. 2088.

1) Samuel Kulp, b Aug 17, 1910, m Sept. 19, 1931, Louella M. King, b. June 21, 1908 Address Archbold, O

1 Richard Allen Kulp, b Sept 3, 1932.
2 Virginia Ruth Kulp, b May 21, 1934.

No. 2090. Sixth Generation. 2066.

6) Peter Blosser, b Aug 3, 1887, near Dayton, Va , m Myrtle Naomi Mc-Dorman, b Dec 3, 1893. Hatchery and poultryman. Address: Wauseon, O

1. Lois Cleda Blosser, b. Nov 3, 1917.
2. Robert M. Blosser, b. Dec 29, 1922
3. Marquis D Ray Blosser, b. Jan 26, 1925.
4. Helen Lou Blosser, b Dec. 30, 1929

No. 2091. Sixth Generation. 2065.

8) Samuel O Blosser, b Nov. 26, 1891, near Dayton, Va , m Jan 26, 1916, Fannie Craig, b Mar 6, 1890 Farmer Mennonites Address: Crimora, Va

1. Carl Edward Blosser, b Nov 14, 1916, d April 1, 1927
2. Glen Harvey Blosser, b. Feb 19, 1918
3. Irvin Pendleton Blosser, b. May 5, 1919
4 Roy Clifton Blosser, b Mar 23, 1921
5 Vance Lee Blosser, b Feb 4, 1924
6. Marvin David Blosser, b. Mar 9, 1925
7. Eva May Blosser, b Sept 24, 1926
8 Calis Bowman Blosser, b. May 15, 1930
9. William Clyde Blosser, b Sept 13, 1931
10. Sylvia Marie Blosser, b Dec 31, 1932.

No. 2092. Sixth Generation. 2066.

9) Frances R Blosser, b Mar 10, 1894, near Dayton, Va , d Oct 10, 1918, m. Leslie K. Lehman Farmer. Address Dayton, Va

1. Charlotte C. Lehman, b. June 29, 1914. No 2093.

No. 2093. Seventh Generation. 2092.

1) Charlotte C Lehman, b June 29, 1914, m Otho Shull, June 30, 1935.

No. 2094. Sixth Generation. 2066.

10) Katie L Blosser, b. Feb 10, 1896, near Dayton, Va., m Oct 12, 1913, Ephraim Lehman, b. Mar. 19, 1890 Address: Dayton, Va Blacksmith Mennonites.

1. Wilmer D. Lehman, b. Mar. 23, 1915.

2. John D. Lehman, b Sept. 6, 1918.
3. Lester F. Lehman, b. July 8, 1921, d Dec 28, 1930.
4. Roy Henry Lehman, b. Mar. 18, 1923.
5. Ruth C. Lehman, b. Sept. 23, 1925
6. Emma C. Lehman, b. July 15, 1929
7. Charlotte Rebecca Lehman, b June 12, 1934.

No. 2095. Sixth Generation. 2066.
11) Jonas E Blosser, b. ————, 1898, near Dayton, Va., m. Myra McDorman. They live at Dayton, Va

No. 2096. Sixth Generation. 2066.
12) Frederick P. Blosser, b Jan 25, 1900, near Dayton, Va., m. Retta Bible, b. Sept 12, 1894, d. Mar. 29, 1917 He married (2nd) Catherine F. Heatwole, b. July 27, 1919, of Hinton, Va.
1. Della Ruth Blosser, b Mar 21, 1917
   (From second marriage)
2 Frederick P. Blosser, Jr., b. Feb. 7, 1920
3. Ethlyn C. Blosser, b. Aug. 18, 1921

No. 2097. Sixth Generation. 2066.
13) Priscilla R Blosser, b. Jan 23, 1903, near Dayton, Va , m. Marvin Shull They live at Dayton, Va.
1. Earl A. Shull, b. May 8, 1923.
2. Ethel R. Shull, b July 18, 1924
3 Harry Lee Shull, b Dec 6, 1925

No. 2093. Fifth Generation. 237.
2) Ann e F. Blosser, b June 7, 1857, near Harrisonburg, Va., m. in 1883 Joseph Metzler, b April 6, 1853, d Oct 21, 1938. Address: North Lima, O. Farmer. Mennonites. Buried in cemetery at Midway Church.
1. Elmer Daniel Metzler, b May 19, 1887. No 2099.
2 Elsie Maud Metzler, b. Jan 31, 1890. No. 2100
3. Mabel Grace Metzler, b Aug 12, 1897. No. 2101
4 Mary Elizabeth Metzler, b June 27, 1899. No. 2102

No. 2099. Sixth Generation. 2093.
1) Elmer Daniel Metzler, b. May 19, 1887, m Mattie Eddy. Address: 1493 Gutry Ave , Long Beach, Calif
1 Marelda Metzler, b ————, 1910

No. 2100. Sixth Generation. 2093.
2) Elsie Maud Metzler, b Jan. 31, 1890, m Ivan J Lehman, b. Feb 10, 1885 They were married Aug. 1, 1912 Address: Columbiana, O Farmer. Mennonites
1. Kathryn Elvada Lehman, b Jan 31, 1917
2 Galen Jay Lehman, b Dec 5, 1922

No. 2101. Sixth Generation. 2098.
3) Mabel Grace Metzler, b Aug. 12, 1897, m Sept 28, 1929, Adin Miller. Address Columbiana, O Farmer Mennonites.
1. Donald Bruce Miller, b Sept 7, 1930.
2 Edward George Miller, b Mar 29, 1934

No. 2102. Sixth Generation. 2098.
4) Mary Elizabeth Metzler, b June 27, 1899, m Nov. 2, 1929, as his second wife, Albert J Steiner Mr Steiner is bishop of the Mennonite congregations of Mahoning Co , O Address North Lima, O. Farmer and minister.

No. 2103. Fifth Generation. 237.

3) Margaret S Blosser, b. Nov. 9, 1858, near Harrisonburg, Va , d. in Augusta Co., Va., Dec 28, 1917, m. to Jacob Martin, a Mennonite minister, of Augusta Co., Va. No children.

No. 2104. Fifth Generation. 237.

7) Mary M. Blosser, b Dec. 16, 1867, near Harrisonburg, Va., d. May 6, 1899, m. April 7, 1892, Abraham F Grove, b Dec 9, 1864 Farmer Mennonites Address: Waynesboro, Va
1. Homer A. Grove, b Sept 6, 1893. No. 2105

No. 2105. Sixth Generation. 2104.

1) Homer A Grove, b Sept 6, 1893, m April 22, 1916, Minnie I Moore. Farmer. Methodists. Address South English, Ia
1. Mary L Grove, b. Oct. 15, 1916.
2. Harry L. Grove, b June 19, 1920
3. Twin to Harry died at birth.

No. 2106. Fifth Generation. 237.

9) Rudolph P. Blosser, b Jan 27, 1873, near Harrisonburg, Va , m in 1894 Elsie V Ralston, b April 25, 1873, d Nov 2, 1895, m (2nd) Dec 29, 1898, Annie C. Wyant, b Mar. 10, 1876
1. Sallie D. Blosser, b Feb 24, 1895, single.
   (From second wife)
2. Ressie P. Blosser, b Feb. 25, 1900 No 2107.
3. Ward W Blosser, b May 19, 1901. No. 2108.
4 Mary M Blosser, b April 7, 1903 No. 2109.
5. Ruby D Blosser, b July 16, 1905 No 2110.
6. Anna L. Blosser, b Feb 24, 1907 No 2111
7. Margaret G. Blosser, b Mar 1, 1909 No 2112.
8 Alma May Blosser, b. May 21, 1911.
9. Rudolph P. Blosser, Jr , b. April 21, 1915.
10. Harold T Blosser, b. Nov 19, 1918.

No. 2107. Sixth Generation. 2106.

2) Ressie P. Blosser, b. Feb 25, 1900, m July 9, 1921, Paul Buchwalter, b. Aug. 15, 1897. Auto mechanic.
1 Ruth Buchwalter, b. May 12, 1923, lived 4 days
2 Ruby Buchwalter, b. April 24, 1925.
3. Erlis Buchwalter, b. Dec 19, 1926.
4. Leah Buchwalter, b. Jan. 20, 1932

No. 2108. Sixth Generation. 2106.

3) Ward Wyant Blosser, b. May 19, 1901, d Dec 19, 1925, m April 11, 1925, Lavina Sibert.

No. 2109. Sixth Generation. 2106.

4) Mary M Blosser, b April 7, 1903, m June 7, 1923, Carl Lehman, b Dec. 19, 1899. Mechanic
1. Carl Lehman, Jr., b. Sept 24, 1924.
2 Marjorie Lehman, b. Jan. 24, 1929.

No. 2110. Sixth Generation. 2106.

5) Ruby D. Blosser, b. July 16, 1905, m May 15, 1926, Elwood Forney, b Oct. 22, 1904. Cabinetmaker in furniture factory
1. Robert Forney, b. Jan 9, 1927.
2. Virginia Forney, b Feb 29, 1928.

3. Richard Forney, b. June 3, 1929, d April 19, 1933.
4. Frederick Forney, b Oct 5, 1935

No. 2111. Sixth Generation. 2106.
6) Annie L. Blosser, b. Feb 24, 1907, m. July 6, 1929, Henry Brown, b. April 1, 1896. Auto mechanic.
1. Betty Lou Brown, b. Sept. 17, 1935

No. 2112. Sixth Generation. 2106.
7) Margaret G Blosser, b. Mar 1, 1909, m June 6, 1932, Daniel Good, b. Jan. 13, 1910. Laborer.
1. Dorothy Good, b. Mar 19, 1933.
2. Carol Margaret Good, b Dec. 14, 1935.

No. 2113. Fifth Generation. 238.
1) Sarah Ann Early, b. —————, m. Archibold VanPelt.
1. Willie VanPelt, b —————. No. 2114.
2. Edward VanPelt, b —————. No 2115.
3. Ward VanPelt, b —————. No 2116
4. Maud VanPelt, b ————— No 2117.

No. 2114. Sixth Generation. 2113.
1) Willie VanPelt, b —————, m Irene Grecy.
1 Katherine Ann VanPelt, b —————

No. 2115. Sixth Generation. 2113.
2) Edward VanPelt, b —————, m Alice Fairchild.
1. Stanley VanPelt, b —————.
2. Avis VanPelt, b. —————.
3. Velma VanPelt, b. —————.

No. 2116. Sixth Generation. 2113.
3) Ward VanPelt, b. —————, m. Alice Eavy
1. Eugene VanPelt, b —————.
2. Ethel VanPelt, b —————.
3. Ward VanPelt, Jr., b —————.
4. Paul VanPelt, b —————
5. Katherine VanPelt, b. —————.
6 Nancy VanPelt, b. —————.

No. 2117. Sixth Generation. 2113.
4) Maud VanPelt, b —————, m (1st) Wright Garber, b. —————;
m. (2nd) Henry Cox, b. —————.
1. Evelyn Garber, b. —————.
2. Helen Garber, b. —————
3 Lilly Cox, b —————.
4. Katherine Cox, b —————.
5. Robert Cox, b. —————
6. Joseph Cox, b —————.

No. 2118. Fifth Generation. 238.
3) David Early, b. —————, m. Della Rankins.
1. Harry Early, b. ————— No. 2119.
2. H. F. Early, b ————— No 2120.
3. Wade Early, b. ————— No 2121
4 Willis Early, b ————— No. 2122

No. 2119. Sixth Generation. 2118.

1) Harry Early, b. —————, m. Grace Cary.
1. Harry Early, Jr., b —————.
2. Frances Early, b. —————.
3 David Early, b —————
4. John Early, b. —————
5. Walter Early, b. —————.

No. 2120. Sixth Generation. 2118.

2) H. F. Early, b ————— , m Esther Lee Smith
1. H. F. Early, Jr., b —————
2. Donald F. Early, b. —————
3. William S. Early, b. —————
4. Agnes Early, b. —————.
5. David Early, b —————
6. John Early, b. —————.
7. Robert Early, b. —————.

No. 2121. Sixth Generation. 2118.

3) Wade R Early, b. ————— , m Helen Miller
1. Margaret C. Early, b. —————.
2 Nell W Early, b. —————.
3 Jiles Early, b —————.

No. 2122. Sixth Generation. 2118.

4) Willis Early, b. ————— , m Elizabeth Rose, b —————.
1. Willis George Early, b —————.
2. Conway Early, b. —————.
3. Jasper Early, b. —————
4. Ransome Early, b. —————.
5 Kenneth Early, b —————.
6 Clyde E. Early, b —————.

No. 2123. Fifth Generation. 238.

4) Joseph Early, b ————— , m Fannie Houff, b. —————. No children.

No. 2124. Fifth Generation. 238.

5) Lucy Early, b. ————— , m. Preston Arey, b —————.
1 Cleda Arey, b —————. No. 2125.

No. 2125. Sixth Generation. 2124.

1) Cleda Arey, b. ————— , m Basil Coffman, b —————.
1. Carr Coffman, b —————.
2. Doris Coffman, b —————.
3. Richard Coffman, b —————.

No. 2126. Fifth Generation. 238.

6) Charles Early, b ————— , m. Lizzie McCutchen, b —————.
1 Anna Belle Early, b —————
2 Irene Early, b —————. No. 2127.

No. 2127. Sixth Generation. 2126.

2) Irene Early, b ————— , m Walter Bottles, b —————
1. Delbert Bottles, b. —————.

316

2) Sallie M Early, b July 6, 1872, m Feb. 23, 1893, Charles A. Myres, b. April 21, 1870.

1. Dessie F. Myres, b Aug. 20, 1894. No. 2129.
2. Frances E. Myres, b. Mar. 17, 1897. No. 2130
3. E. Elmer Myres, b. July 17, 1902 No. 2131.
4. Mary E. Myres, b. Oct. 31, 1905. No. 2132.
5. Charles Myres, b Feb. 15, 1908, d. Feb. 29, 1908.
6 Hazel E. Myres, b Dec 15, 1911, single.

No. 2129. Sixth Generation. 2128.

1) Dessie F. Myers, b Aug 20, 1894, m. Dewey D. Fleishman, Sept. 27, 1921
1. Dolle D. Fleishman, b. Oct 13, 1923
2 Melva R Fleishman, b. Aug 25, 1925.
3 Allen M Fleishman, b Nov. 19, 1929.

No. 2130. Sixth Generation. 2128.

2) Frances E Myers, b. Mar. 17, 1897, m. Jan 28, 1917, Atlee F. McNeet, b Jan. 7, 1896. Address: Dayton, Va. Farmer.
1. Roland M. NcNeet, b June 13, 1922
2 Mary Lee McNeet, b Feb 16, 1924.
3. Kathleen F. McNeet, b Jan. 26, 1926, d. Aug 2, 1927.
4 Glenna W. McNeet, b Feb. 26, 1927.
5. Harold F. McNeet, b Aug. 10, 1928
6 Norman D McNeet, b. June 9, 1929.
7. Carl N. McNeet, b May 16, 1934

No. 2131. Sixth Generation. 2128.

3) G Elmer Myers, b. July 17, 1902, m June 17, 1931, Lillian Miller, b Sept. 28, 1906.
1. Joan R Myers, b Mar 11, 1933, twin.
2 Joyce E Myers, b Mar 11, 1933, twin.
3 Dorthy Lee Myers, b. Sept. 5, 1934

No. 2132. Sixth Generation. 2128.

4) Mary E. Myers, b. Oct 31, 1905, m. June 6, 1928, Wilbur S. Wright, b. Feb 28, 1900
1 Dennis D Wright, b. Oct 27, 1929
2 Owen Lee Wright, b Mar 29, 1933.

No. 2133. Fifth Generation. 239.

3) Frank W Early, b May 31, 1876, m in 1901 Emma F Glick, b. April 10, 1880
1 Ruth E Early, b Nov 3, 1903 No 2134
2 Irene V. Early, b July 3, 1906 No 2135

No. 2134. Sixth Generation. 2133.

1) Ruth E Early, b Nov 3, 1903, m Aug 31, 1929, Buffin Kiser, b Aug 3, 1902
1 Jeanne F Kiser, b Mar 27, 1930
2 Norlyn E Kiser, b Jan 5, 1933

No. 2135. Sixth Generation. 2133.

2) Irene V Early, b July 3, 1906, m Sept 3, 1929, Ray F Wright, b Dec 24, 1901

No. 2136. Fifth Generation. 239.

4) J. Roy Early, b. Mar. 13, 1879, m Dec. 21, 1904, Ida E. Showalter, b. April 20, 1881. Address: Dayton, Va Farmer and thresher. Dunkards. Related. For family see mother's line, No. 977.

1. Vera M. Early, b. Feb. 5, 1906. No. 978.
2. Naomi V. Early, b. Dec 9, 1908 No. 979.
3. Samuel S. Early, b. Sept. 7, 1912. No. 2139
4. Byard D. Early, b. April 29, 1917.
5. Mary O. Early, b. Oct. 24, 1919.

No. 2139. Sixth Generation. 2136.

3) Samuel S. Early, b Sept 7, 1912, m. Sept. 23, 1933, Nellie F. Heatwole, b. Dec. 19, 1911. No children.

No. 2140. Fifth Generation. 239.

5) Octava V. Early, b. Mar. 13, 1879 (twin), m April, 1913, Solomon G Miller, b. July 1, 1876. He died April 17, 1935.

1. Elizabeth F. Miller, b. Mar 16, 1915.

No. 2141. Fifth Generation. 240.

1) John Samuel Rhodes, b Aug. 26, 1857, near Hinton, Va., m Annie Landes.
1. Otho Lee Rhodes, b. ——————, died single.
2. Bertha Rhodes, b ——————, married but no F. R.
3. Pearl Rhodes, b. ——————, married, no further record.
4. Turner Rhodes, b. ——————, single.

No. 2142. Fifth Generation. 240.

2) Lucy Ella Rhodes, b June 3, 1859, d. July 5, 1936, m May 18, 1887, Charles Douglas Whitmer.

1. Ira Newton Whitmer, b. May 26, 1888 No. 2143.
2. Claude Clarence Whitmer, b. Jan 20, 1890. No 2144.
3. Vernie Landes Whitmer, b. July 24, 1891. No. 2145.
4. Nettie Irene Whitmer, b. Sept. 4, 1892 No. 2146.
5. Charles Samuel Whitmer, b. Mar. 23, 1895. No. 2147.
6. Mary Susan Whitmer, b. April 10, 1897. No. 2148.
7. Nina Belle Whitmer, b Sept 24, 1899 No 2149.
8. Nora Hermian Whitmer, b. Oct. 26, 1902.

No. 2143. Sixth Generation. 2142.

1) Ira Newton Whitmer, b May 26, 1888, m July 12, 1911, Jennie Virginia Beasley.

1. Frederick Wilson Whitmer, b. Dec. 22, 1912.

No. 2144. Sixth Generation. 2142.

2) Claude Clarence Whitmer, b Jan. 20, 1890, m. Dec 31, 1919, Mary Virginia Ritchie.

1. Eugene Ritchie Whitmer, b. Mar. 13, 1928

No. 2145. Sixth Generation. 2142.

3) Vernie Landes Whitmer, b July 24, 1891, d Aug. 26, 1926, m. June 11, 1913, Herman L Bell

1. Theodore R Bell, b. Dec 7, 1914, d July 27, 1918
2 James Rudolph Bell, b ——————, 1916
3 Clara Elizabeth Bell, b. May 8, 1918
4. Warren Coolridge Bell, b April 19, 1920
5. Dorthy Virginia Bell, b. ——————.

6 William Crawford Bell, b April 1, 1923.

7. George W. Bell, b. Feb 22, 1925

8. Jessie Fay Bell, b July 12, 1926, d. Sept 28, 1926, twin.

9. Bessie May Bell, b July 12, 1926, d. Oct. 14, 1926, twin.

No. 2146. Sixth Generation. 2142.

4) Nettie Irene Whitmer, b Sept. 4, 1892, m. Oct 14, 1914, Luther I. Shull. Address: Staunton, Va.

1. Mervin Conrad Shull, b Oct 27, 1915.

2. Ward Clayton Shull, b Nov. 12, 1917.

3. Ella Katherine Shull, b. Nov. 29, 1919.

4. Elizabeth Moline Shull, b. Aug 2, 1922.

5 David McGellis Shull, b. Nov. 4, 1925, d. May 9, 1927.

No. 2147. Sixth Generation. 2142.

5) Charles Samuel Whitmer, b Mar. 23, 1896, m. Feb. 23, 1921, Wilda P. Wheelbarger, daughter of Joseph and Fannie Wheelbarger.

1 Donald Fremont Whitmer, b. April 28, 1923, d. May 3, 1923.

2 Elnora Lorrain Whitmer, b July 31, 1927.

3 Howard Douglas Whitmer, b. Oct 10, 1931

4 Charles Marcus Whitmer, b. Sept 19, 1935.

No. 2148. Sixth Generation. 2142.

6) Mary Susan Whitmer, b April 10, 1897, d. Feb 26, 1933, m. Dec. 24, 1917, Clarence L. Fulton.

1. Frances Catherine Fulton, b Nov. 28, 1918.

2 Helen Louise Fulton, b. Nov. 18, 1919.

3. Charlotte Elizabeth Fulton, b Jan. 26, 1921.

4. Edith Norwood Fulton, b. Jan 25, 1923.

5. Norma Utilla Fulton, b. Jan. 22, 1926

6. Jennings Homer Fulton, b. Feb. 9, 1930.

7 Ferne Avilla Fulton, b. Feb. 17, 1933.

No. 2149. Sixth Generation. 2142.

7) Nina Belle Whitmer, b Sept. 24, 1899, m. Sept. 24, 1918, Virgil Lamar Wheelbarger, b. Dec. 17, 1897.

1. Christina Maxine Wheelbarger, b Oct. 18, 1919.

2. Roland Lamar Wheelbarger, b Aug. 14, 1921.

3. Arnold Guayle Wheelbarger, b. Sept. 13, 1923.

4. Chester Stanley Wheelbarger, b. May 5, 1926.

No. 2150. Sixth Generation. 595.

2) Bessie E. Zepp, b. July 5, 1902, m Kervin Lippy. Address: Hanover, Pa. No children.

No. 2151. Sixth Generation. 595.

3) Nellie Agnes Zepp, b. Nov 23, 1905, m. Joshua Brown. Address: Ft. Wayne, Ind

1. Joshua William (Billy) Brown, b ——————.

No. 2152. Sixth Generation. 596.

1) Percy S. Rhodes, b Mar 18, 1900, m. Sept. 8, 1926, Mary Arey, b May 27, 1899 They live in Harrisonburg, Va Bank teller.

1. Doris Jean Rhodes, b. July 26, 1927.

2 Harold Arey Rhodes, b. Aug. 23, 1931.

No. 2153. Sixth Generation. 595.

3) Harley E Rhodes, b Dec 2, 1907, m Feb 24, 1934, Alta Sophiah Wengei, b Oct. 26, 1906 Address: Hinton, Va. Bank teller.

1 James Edward Rhodes, b. Nov. 20, 1934.

No. 2154. Sixth Generation. 597.

1) Mary Naomi Rhodes, b Mar 16, 1899, m Earl W. Horst, b. Sept 3, 1898 Farmer. Mennonites. Address: Dayton, Va.

1. Naomi V. Horst, b Oct. 19, 1924
2 Fannie Mae Horst, b. Feb 18, 1925.
3. Alfred F Horst, b April 11, 1930
4. Mark R Horst, b July 4, 1931

No. 2155. Sixth Generation. 597.

2) Minnie Susan Rhodes, b May 24, 1901, m Phares M Whitmer, b Feb 9, 1894.

1 Ruth Nettie Whitmer, b Feb 3, 1924
2 Paul Reuben Whitmer, b April 14, 1926
3. Mary Elizabeth Whitmer, b Oct 13, 1927
4 John Henry Whitmer, b Aug 27, 1930
5 David Rhodes Whitmer, b Nov 7, 1932
6 Joseph Daniel Whitmer, b Jan 29, 1936

No. 2156. Sixth Generation. 597.

3) Annie Catherine Rhodes, b Mar 1, 1903, m Merle M Whitmer, b May 7, 1900. Address Dayton, Va

1 Walter Emmanuel Whitmer, b May 16, 1926
2 Daniel Rhodes Whitmer, b June 5, 1928
3. Elsie Marie Whitmer, b Sept. 14, 1930
4 Martha Frances Whitmer, b. April 20, 1932
5 Amos Henry Whitmer, b July 25, 1933
6 Harry Alfred Whitmer, b Feb 12, 1935

No. 2157. Sixth Generation. 597.

4) Fannie Rebecca Rhodes, b June 25, 1906, m Walter R Royer, b Oct 7, 1903

1 Marcus H. Royer, b Feb 1, 1933
2 Grace E Royer, b Dec 21, 1934.

No. 2158. Sixth Generation. 1244¼.

2) William Harvey Eversole, b Feb 2, 1884, m Feb 21, 1909, Nellie Cheetham, b. Oct. 2, 1890.

1 Katheryn Barbara Eversole, b Nov 27, 1910
2 Herbert Earl Eversole, b. Nov. 28, 1912

No. 2159 Sixth Generation. 1244¼.

3) Wilhe Mina Eversole, b Mar 9, 1891, m Bert Comley, b ——————— Not living

1. Dorothy Delores Comley, b Sept. 21, 1913
2 Herbert Harold Comley, b Oct 28, 1927

No. 2160. Sixth Generation. 1245.

1) Gertrude Pearl Eversole, b Nov 27, 1887, m June 9, 1909, Nelson DeWitt Boys, b Oct 3, 1886 Live at Shelbyville, Ill

1. Ella June Boys, b. Mar. 10, 1919.

No. 2161. Sixth Generation. 1247.

3) Edgar Earl Fritz, b Mar 28, 1888, m July 20, 1914, Edna Ripley, b Oct. 6, 1891. No children

No. 2162. Sixth Generation. 1247.

4) William Lawrence Fritz, b Dec 5, 1898, m Nov 24, 1923, Mary Troster, b April 30, 1900.

1. James Sherwood Fritz, b. July 20, 1924.

No. 2163. Sixth Generation. 1249.

1) Emory Aaron Small, b Dec 3, 1887, m Addie Reeves, Feb. 10, 1912
1 Melvin Aaron Small, b April 9, 1913 No. 2164
2 Clarence Adion Small, b. Nov 22, 1915.
3 Harold Everett Small, b Nov 18, 1925

No. 2164. Seventh Generation. 2163.

1) Melvin Aaron Small, b April 9, 1913, m Alice Johnson, Sept 9, 1934

No. 2165. Sixth Generation. 1249.

2) Wright J Small, b Jan 29, 1890, m Hazel Mae Wager, Mar 23, 1912
1 Earl J Small, b Sept 4, 1913 No 2166
2 Gwendolyn Small, b Sept 6, 1915

No. 2166. Seventh Generation. 2165.

1) Earl J Small, b Sept 4, 1913, m Dorothy Bert, Feb 14, 1935

No. 2167. Sixth Generation. 1249.

3) Gertrude E Small, b Mar. 15, 1892, m Frank Wager, Sept 12, 1914.
1 William Wade Wager, b Feb 28, 1916

No. 2168. Sixth Generation. 1249.

4) Grace Irene Small, b. Dec 5, 1898, m Frank Jensen, June 1, 1922.
1 Dorothy Lee Jensen, b May 11, 1923.
2. Loren Thomas Jensen, b May 17, 1925.
3 Billy Irwin Jensen, b Mar 5, 1928.

No. 2169. Sixth Generation. 1249.

5) Elmer Charles Small, b Sept 10, 1903, m Ruth Lindslow, June 10, 1928

No. 2170. Sixth Generation. 1249.

6) Ora Katherine Small, b Jan 2, 1907, m Gladner Brewster, Oct 26, 1929
1 Beverly Dene Brewster, b April 20, 1931

No. 2171. Sixth Generation. 1259.

1) Edgar Eversole, b Feb 8, 1898, m Eula Fry, Dec 8, 1928.
1 James Eversole, b Oct 2, 1929

No. 2172. Sixth Generation. 1259.

2) Leverette Eversole, b Jan 4, 1902, m June, 1930, Arlie Antone, b 1902
1 Nancy Ann Antone, b Aug 13, 193—

No. 2173. Sixth Generation. 1529.

3) Lois Eversole, b Oct 13, 1905, m June 1, 1935, Vincent Shaw

No. 2174. Sixth Generation. 1250.

2) Orrville Eversole, b July 11, 1896, m Dec 25, 1924, Ruby Price, b April 29, 1904
1 David Eugene Eversole, b Dec 21, 1925
2 Paul Eversole, b Jan 14, 1927

3. Hazel Eversole, b. Aug. 9, 1928.
4. Susan Anne Eversole, b. Nov 11, 1933.

No. 2175. Sixth Generation. 1250.

4) Everette Boys Eversole, b July 29, 1906, m Oct 13, 1929, Lucelle Weakley, b. 1906.

No. 2176. Sixth Generation. 1258.

1) Sidney Lynn Bair, b. Aug 14, 1896, m. Ethel Corley.
1. Florence Arloa Bair, b May 11, 1918.
2. Lynn Bair, b. Aug. 9, 1920

No. 2177. Sixth Generation. 1258.

2) George W. Bair, b Feb 22, 1898, m Myrl Corley, b Nov 23, 1900.
1. Joan Arloa Bair,, b. Feb 10, 1932
2 James Richard Bair, b. June 11, 1933.

No. 2178. Sixth Generation. 1258.

3) Lloyd Wallace Bair, b. Jan 29, 1900, m Blossom Wigand, b April 5, 1908.

No. 2179. Sixth Generation. 1258.

4) Jacob M. Bair, b. Feb. 21, 1902, m Erma Hendricks, b June 13, 1905.

No. 2180. Sixth Generation. 1261.

1) Birl Eldo Myers, b Sept. 6, 1881, m Dessie White Albert, b. Aug 26, 1878

No. 2181. Sixth Generation. 1261.

2) Vola Kate Myers, b. April 4, 1883, m Hall Chambers, b Nov. 11, 1885.
1. Helen Lenore Chambers, b Oct 25, 1907.
2. Richard William Chambers, b Jan 29, 1910

No. 2182. Sixth Generation. 1266.

2) Miles Lawton Eversole, b. —————, m Goldie ————— They lived near Middlepoint, O.
1. Elizabeth Eversole, b —————

No. 2183. Fifth Generation. 1289.

1) Hardy Atkin Eversole, b Feb. 2, 1871, m Feb. 15, 1898, Catherine Walsh. They live in Delrey, Ill. He farms his mother's farm
1. Mildred Eversole, b. Dec 31, 1900, lives at home.
2. Marion Eversole, b. June 24, 1905, d. Jan 9, 1923.

No. 2184. Fifth Generation. 1289.

2) George Artz Eversole, b. Aug. 25, 1872, d. April 10, 1907, m. Mary Schultze. They had two children but both died in infancy.

No. 2185. Fifth Generation. 1289.

3) Mary Gabriella Eversole, b Mar. 6, 1874, m Hugh Conn.
1. Merle Conn, b. —————; m. Raymond Maddin, and had a daughter Marilyn Maddin, b. —————.
2. Vena Conn, b. —————; m. Louis Shoon

No. 2188. Fifth Generation. 1289.

4) Clara Elizabeth Eversole, b. Nov. 13, 1876, m. Ulysses Daughorthy, Feb 12, 1896 They live at Ottawa, Kans
1. Edna Daughorthy, b —————
2. Ethel Daughorthy, b. —————.
3. Ruth Daughorthy, b. —————

4. Winifred Daughorthy, b. —————.
5. Erma Daughorthy, b —————.
6. Ila Daughorthy, b —————.
7 Lois Daughorthy, b —————
8. Lester Daughorthy, b. —————.
9. Lloyd Daughorthy, b ————— .
10. Beverly Daughorthy, b. —————.
11. Gordon Daughorthy, b. —————.
12. Raymond Daughorthy, b. —————.

No. 2189. Fifth Generation. 1289.

5) Hazel Anna Eversole, b. July 22, 1885, m Mar 12, 1913, John Stephens. They farm at Onarga, Ill. No children

No. 2190. Fifth Generation. 1289.

6) John Logan Eversole, b. May 21, 1888, m. Jan. 28, 1915, Hulda Harthe, b. Sept 8, 1887. Address: Onarga, Ill
1 John Wayne Eversole, b July 13, 1925.

No. 2191. Fourth Generation. 1172.

2) Margaret Landes, b June 7, 1824, in Augusta Co, Va., d. Jan. 1, 1908, at Topeka, Kans, m. William Riley Griffith of Tippecanoe Co., Ind., b. June 8, 1820. They were married Dec 23, 1847, at Greencastle, Ind. Mr. Griffith took an active part in the early border troubles of Kansas. He was a delegate to the Wyandote convention which framed and adopted the constitution of the state of Kansas, and one of the signers of the constitution which is still in effect in Kansas He was elected superintendent of public instruction on the first state ticket, and died while in office He died Mar. 12, 1862, at Topeka, Kans, where he lived.
1. William Roscoe Griffith, b. Oct. 7, 1848. No. 2192.
2 Mary Agnes Griffith, b May 9, 1850. No 2193
3. Margaret Alice Griffith, b June 19, 1852 No. 2194.
4. Harriett Magdalena Griffith, b. Mar 22, 1856. No. 2197.
5 Augusta Virginia Griffith, b Jan 24, 1858. No 2198
6 Annie Laura Griffith, b May 20, 1860 No. 2199

No. 2192. Fifth Generation. 2191.

1) William Roscoe Griffith, b Oct 7, 1848, at Westerville, O, d Mar 21, 1921, at Emporia, Kans, m Sept 27, 1877, to Olive McFadden, b. April 18, 1857. Mr. Griffith entered the hardware business in 1869 at Emporia and remained at that for thirty years, after which he took an active part in politics and served as county treasurer of Lynn Co, Kans.
1. Harvard Lee Griffith, b. July 30, 1879. No. 2192¼.
2. Nellie Griffith, b Sept 9, 1881 at Emporia, Kans She succeeded her father as treasurer of Lynn Co., Kans., and served two years She now has a position of trust with the largest bank in Emporia.

No. 2192¼. Sixth Generation. 2192.

1) Howard Lee Griffith, b July 30, 1879, in Emporia, Kans, m. Jan. 10, 1912, Agusta Kuhlman. Both lived in Emporia, Kans He is a traveling salesman

No. 2193. Fifth Generation. 2191.

2) Mary Agnes Griffith, b June 19, 1850, at Topeka, Kans, m Jan 27, 1871, Oliver Hawkins He died April, 1872. No children.

No. 2194. Fifth Generation. 2191.

3) Alice Margaret Griffith, b June 19, 1852, d. Dec 11, 1908, in Washington, D. C. She married George Sidney Chase, a prominent attorney of Topeka, Kans, in July, 1876 They moved to Washington, D C, where he practiced until his death in 1911 They were buried in Washington, D. C.

1 George Sidney Chase, Jr, b. Oct. 10, 1877. No. 2195.

2. Enoch Aquilla Chase, b Aug. 13, 1880 No. 2196

No. 2195. Sixth Generation. 2194.

1) George Sidney Chase, Jr, b Oct 10, 1877, at Topeka, Kans, m Josephine Brandon, of St. Louis, Mo No issue He was former vice president of the St. Louis, Mo, Trust Company, St Louis, Mo He has retired on account of ill health. They live in St. Louis, Mo.

No. 2196. Sixth Generation. 2194.

2) Enoch Aquilla Chase, b Aug 13, 1880, at Topeka, Kans, m Evelyn Jessie Oliver, of New York City Like his father he is practicing law at Washington, D. C.

1 Norman Oliver Chase, b Sept 4, 1909.

2. Edgar Griffith Chase, b. Sept. 12, 1910.

3 Enoch Dunlap Chase, b Aug 4, 1914.

4 Evelyn Chase, b Oct 24, 1915

All born in Washington, D. C.

No. 2197. Fifth Generation. 2191.

4) Harriett Magdalena Griffith, b Mar. 22. 1856, m. June 7, 1876, Henry Leonard No children They lived at Topeka, Kans.

No. 2198. Fifth Generation. 2191.

5) Augusta Virginia Griffith, b. Jan. 24, 1858, m. Morris Bowers They live in Denver, Colo.

1. Virginia Bowers, b. ——————.

2. Hazel Bowers, b. ——————.

No. 2199. Fifth Generation. 2191.

6) Annie Laura Griffith, b May 20, 1860, m. Henry Leonard, her brother-in-law, a successful life insurance organizer and former president of the Manhattan Life Insurance Company of Manhattan, Kans, which he organized, until 1934, when he resigned on account of old age. He was the former manager of the Home Life Insurance Co., of St Louis, Mo.

No. 2200. Fourth Generation. 1172.

3) Ananias Landes, b May 15, 1826, d. Aug. 12, 1878. As a youth he went with his parents from Augusta Co, Va, to Putnam Co, Ind., where they settled near Greencastle Later he engaged in the mercantile business with his father until 1856 when they moved to Bloomfield, Doris Co, Ia., and later moved to near Hopeville, Clark Co., Ia, in 1875, where he resided until his death He married Anchor Boyd of Greencastle, Ind, Feb 14, 1850 She was born Oct 12, 1834, and died July 26, 1889 Both were buried in the Gregg cemetery four miles from Hopeville, Ia They were Presbyterians.

1. John Henry Landes, b Oct. 6, 1850. No 2201.

2. Margaret Agnes Landes, b Mar 11, 1852. No. 2208.

3 Albert Cary Landes, b Sept 3, 1854 No. 2209

4. Robert Samuel Landes, b Feb. 28, 1862. No. 2213.

5 Augusta Anker Landes, b. Nov 9, 1864. No 2214.

6 Emma Magdalene Landes, b. July 8, 1870 No 2215

No. 2201. Fifth Generation. 2200.

1) John Henry Landes, b. Oct. 6, 1850, near Greencastle, Ind, d. Feb 19, 1933, at Keosauqua, Ia, where he lived. He married Caldone Josephine Cunningham. She died Aug. 14, 1906 He married (2nd) Mrs Laura Davis Watkins. He was an educator, writer, and newspaper owner Congregational Church

1. Don Henry Landes, b May 20, 1884, twin. No. 2202
2. Carl Cunningham Landes, b. May 20, 1884, twin No. 2203.
3 Gene Boyd Landes, b Mar 28, 1887 No 2204
4 Magdalena Landes, b Oct 13, 1890. No. 2205
5. Bates Edward Landes, b May 15, 1895. No. 2206.
(From second marriage)
6 Laura Landes, b ——————— No 2207

No. 2202. Sixth Generation. 2201.

1) Don Henry Landes, b May 20, 1884, at Keosauqua, Ia, m. at Douglas, Ariz, to Nell Klein of Ft Wayne, Ind Merchant. No children.

No. 2203. Sixth Generation. 2201.

2) Carl Cunningham Landes, b May 20, 1884, at Keosauqua, Ia, d in 1935 at Los Angeles, Calif He married Edna Burrell. She died in 1936.

1 Burrell Landes, b Oct. 9, 1914, at Los Angeles, Calif.

No. 2204. Sixth Generation. 2201.

3) Gene Boyd Landes, b Mar 28, 1887, at Keosauqua, Ia, m. Julia Day at Ottumwa, Ia They lived for some time at Charleston, W. Va They now reside in New York. Mr Landes has been a successful manager and overseer of several chemical compounds owned by a New York firm and has been located at different places Their present address is 10 Cambr.dge Court, Larchmont, New York City

1. Mary Jane Landes, b. Aug 19, 1922.
2. Dorothy Ann Landes, b Mar 29, 1924

No. 2205. Sixth Generation. 2201.

4) Magdalena Landes, b. Oct. 13, 1890, at Keosauqua, Ia, m. Sept. 10, 1913, at Spring River, Nebr, to Bates Miller Manning He was b June 3, 1888

1. Betty Josephine Manning, b. Sept. 2, 1918
2. John Albert Mann ng, b June 18, 1921.
3 Frances Jean Manning, b. Aug. 27, 1923.

No. 2206. Sixth Generation. 2201.

5) Bates Edward Landes, b May 15, 189-, at Keosauqua, Ia, m. Gladys Rebecca Workman, at Fairfield, Ia., Sept. 1, 1921.

1 James Edward Landes, b July 20, 1928 at Des Moines, Ia.

No. 2207. Sixth Generation. 2201.

6) Laura Landes, b ——————, at Keosauqua, Ia, m Lawrence E. Daugherty

No. 2208. Fifth Generation. 2200.

2) Margaret Agnes Landes, b Mar 11, 1852, at Greencastle, Ind, m Feb 3, 1870, Oliver Cromwell Macy, near Bloomfield, Ia He died Mar. 26, 1935, at Olathie, Kans Address. Olathie, Kans Methodists Farmer and banker.

1 Mary Anker Macy, b. July 13, 1871. No. 2210.
2 John Riley Macy, b July 24, 1873, single
3 Amanda Caldone Macy, b Feb 12, 1875, d. Nov. 11, 1898.
4 Ulysses Samuel Macy, b Jan 3, 1877. No 2211.
5 Arthur Landes Macy, b. Nov. 8, 1881 No 2212.
6 Callie Macy, b ——————, d at 18 years

No. 2209. Fifth Generation. 2200.

3) Albert Cary Landes, b Aug 3, 1854, at Greencastle, Ind , d. at Brooklyn, Ia., April 1, 1923. He married Lola G. Burns, of Keokuk, Ia., born in 1863 in Chicago, Ill. Mrs. Landes is a talented choir singer. Albert Cary Landes was a successful physician and surgeon at Brooklyn, Ia., and as he was a successful financier, he left an estate, valued at over two hundred thousand dollars, to his wife at the time of his death. At his request his wife purchased the ground and built a park which she presented to the city of Brooklyn, Ia , at a cost of over ten thousand dollars which was dedicated as the Landes Park No children

No. 2210. Sixth Generation. 2208.

1) Mary Anker Macy, b July 13, 1871, at Bloomfield, Ia., m. James Ward Carter, b Mar. 16, 1871, at Browning, Mo They were married at Laclede, Mo., Oct 7, 1895. He was a railway conductor, he died Nov 17, 1929, at Colorado Springs, Colo., and was buried at Denver, Colo., where the family reside
1. Mary Carter, b July 3, 1899 No 2210¼
2. Verna Agnes Carter, b. Oct 6, 1902. No 2210½
3. Jennis Ward Carter, b. Jan. 22, 1910, d. Oct 6, 1910.

No. 2210¼. Seventh Generation. 2210.

1) Mary Carter, b. July 3, 1899, at Laclede, Mo , m. Dick Hill. He was a railroad engineer. They live at Denver, Colo.
1. Doris Hill, b. Feb. 12, 1921.
2. Donald Hill, b. April 25, 1926
3 Dixie Lee Hill, b Sept 26, 1933.

No. 2210½. Seventh Generation. 2210.

2) Verna Agnes Carter, b Oct. 6, 1902, m Sept 3, 1926, Glade Jameson, of Denver, Colo. He is a real estate man.

No. 2211. Sixth Generation. 2208.

4) Ulysses Samuel Macy, b Jan 3, 1877, at Mt Moriah, Mo., d. Sept. 17, 1917, at Los Animas Government Hospital, Colo. He was buried at Laclede, Mo. He married Miriam Grant of San Diego, Calif , in New York City. She was a daughter of Duet Grant, and granddaughter of Ulysses S. Grant. Ulysses S Macy entered the Naval Academy at Annapolis, Md., in 1892, and graduated April 4, 1898 Four months ahead of his graduation he entered the Spanish American War. He was on board the Ashley's flag ship during one of the engagements in Cuban waters, having charge of the center magazine in the battle of Santiago, July 3, 1898. The table in his room was splintered This was all the damage done during the engagement After the war he served on land and sea. He was advanced to the position of Lieutenant Commander and lived at San Diego, Calif , until his death.

No. 2212. Sixth Generation. 2208.

5) Arthur Landes Macy, b Nov 8, 1881, at Mt. Moriah, Mo , m Jessic Young, July 12, 1910, at DeLague, Colo. Merchant at Branch, Colo.
1. Ardis Landes Macy, b Mar 18, 1921.
2. Donald Landes Macy, b. Dec. 24, 1926.

No. 2213. Fifth Generation. 2200.

4) Robert Samuel Landes, b Feb 28, 1862, at Bloomfield, Ia , m Susan Estella Stanley, of Grand River, Ia. She died Nov 11, 1890, at Grand River He married later Martha Tabitha Rogers May 10, 1893. He lived at Grand River and later at Lacona, Ia.
1. Alice Landes, b. Mar 24, 1887, single

2. Effie Landes, b Mar. 5, 1889 No 2264
   (From second marriage)
3. Gussie Mae Landes, b. May 5, 1896 No. 2265.
4. Mary Isabella Landes, b. Nov 28, 1897. No. 2266.
5. Robert Samuel Landes, Jr, b Jan. 5, 1900. No. 2268.
6. Helen Olive Landes, b Sept. 14, 1901.
7 Martha Margaret Landes, b. Oct. 2, 1904. No. 2269.

No. 2214. Fifth Generation. 2200.

5) Augusta Anker Landes, b Nov 9, 1864, at Bloomfield, Ia., m. Sept 1, 1890, William Edward Bruffey, b Oct 31, 1861, at Attica, Ia. Mrs. Augusta Bruffey is a professional artist, having been awarded medals for portraits. She specializes in animal paintings, her work having been exhibited at St. Louis, Mo., World's Fair in 1903, Portland, Oreg, in 1904, and various other places. She resides at Searcy, Ark. No children At the age of twenty Mr Bruffey became interested in railway construction work, and for a number of years was associated with the Cary Brothers and Co, contractors He also served the Cleveland administration as chief clerk of the R. M. S and for a period assistant manager and cashier of the Walter A Wood Harvester Co, at Omaha, Nebr. Later he entered the hardware, saddling, and implement business at Springdale, Ark., in 1894. He retired from active business in 1914 to Crestline Ranch, his home, where he lived until his death Jan. 5, 1935. Buried at Mountain Grove, Mo, in the Hill Creek cemetery in the family burying ground

No. 2215. Fifth Generation. 2200.

6) Emma Magdalene Landes, b July 8, 1870, at Bloomfield, Ia, m at Springdale, Ark, June 3, 1898, John D Pope, b at Trion, Ga, Nov. 26, 1865. They live at Searcy, Ark, where he is a successful piano dealer.
1. Margaret Pope, b. June 23, 1903.

No. 2216. Fourth Generation. 1172.

4) James Madison Landes, b Feb 8, 1830, in Augusta Co., Va., m. Mar. 2, 1854, Elizabeth Frances Miles, b June 22, 1838, at Crawfordsville, Ind. Divorced at St. Joe, Mo, in 1874: m. (2nd) Pauline Hart at Kirksville, Mo Address: Kirksville, Mo. Farmer.
1. Martha Magdalena Landes, b Dec 14, 1855. No 2217.
2. Walter Girard Landes, b July 8, 1857. No. 2222.
3. John Edwin Landes, b. Feb 2, 1859. No. 2224.
4. Samuel Reuben Landes, b Feb 28, 1861. No. 2225.
5. Virginia Agnes Landes, b. Mar. 2, 1863 No. 2226.
6. Henry Ellsworth Landes, b. ————— No. 2227.
7. William Sherman Landes, b —————. No 2228
8 Lydia A. Landes, b Nov. 9, 1869, d. young.
   (From second marriage)
9 Arthur Landes, b Dec. 28, 1879.

No. 2217. Fifth Generation. 2216.

1) Martha Magdalena Landes, b Dec 14, 1855, m. James C. Barnhardt, b —————, d. ————— She married (2nd) Charles Wemple, in St Joe, Mo, 1886.
1. Daisy Barnhardt, b —————, 1874. No. 2218
2 Myrtle Barnhardt, b —————, 1876, d. —————, 1900.
3 Lon Barnhardt, b —————, 1878. No. 2219.
4 Sadie Barnhardt, b —————, 1880 No 2220
   (From second marriage)

5 Fannie Wemple, b ————, 1887, d. ————, 1889.
6 Walter O Wemple, b ————, 1889 No 2221.
7. Harry B. Wemple, b ————, 1891 No. 2221¼.
8. Anna Wemple, b ————, 1893. No 2221½.

No. 2218. Sixth Generation. 2217.

1) Daisy Barnhardt, b. ————, 1874, m Jacob Lorne They live in Lewistown, Ida.
1 ———— Lorne, b. ————.

No. 2219. Sixth Generation. 2217.

3) Lon Barnhardt, b. ————, 1878, m Mary McClain No children

No. 2220. Sixth Generation. 2217.

4) Sadie Barnhardt, b. ————, 1880, d. in 1926, m. Henry Jacobs.

No. 2221. Sixth Generation. 2217.

6) Walter O. Wemple, b. ————, 1889, in St. Joe, Mo , m ———— Briggs, at West Pla ns, Mo , d in 1911, m second wife in 1913.
1. Norman Wemple, b. ————.
2. ———— Wemple, b ————
(From second union)
3. Gladys Wemple, b ————.

No. 2221¼. Sixth Generation. 2217.

7) Harry B. Wemple, b. ————, 1891, m ————
1. Daughter Wemple, b ————

No. 2221½. Sixth Generation. 2217.

8) Anna Wemple, b ————, 1893, m ———— Richardson
1 Daughter Richardson, b. ————

No. 2222. Fifth Generation. 2216.

2) Walter Girard Landes, b July 8, 1857, m Feb 22, 1883, Martha Ellen Starr, b Feb. 22, 1861, d Jan. 6, 1926, at Kirksville, Mo
1. John Roy Landes, b Feb. 8, 1884
2 Ray Starr Landes, b. July 13, 1886
3. Mauns Ellen Landes, b Nov 16, 1887. No 2223

No. 2223. Sixth Generation. 2222.

3) Mauns Ellen Landes, b. Nov 16, 1887, m Morris Duff, Feb. 22, 1909 She later divorced Duff and married Dr. Joseph Beebe, of Kansas City, Mo
1. John Landes Duff, b April 22, 1910, at Kirksville, Mo.
John Duff married Loucille Whitacre at Kansas City, Mo

No. 2224. Fifth Generation. 2216.

3) John Edwin Landes, b. Feb 2, 1859, at Elk Creek, Ia , d Dec 21, 1926, at Kirksville, Mo , m Dec 21, 1886, Nancy Adaline Elliott She died in 1924. They lived at Kirksville, Mo
1 Helen Landes, b ————, 1895, is a practicing physician in Florida (osteopath)
2. John Orin Landes, b ————, 1890, is a talented musician, and band player, he plays in large shows

No. 2225. Fifth Generation. 2216.

4) Samuel Reuben Landes, b. Feb 28, 1861, at Elk Creek, Ia , m May Casby, at Salt Lake City, Utah Both Mr and Mrs. Landes were osteopath doc-

tors Mrs. Landes died in 1900 Samuel later married at Grand Rapids, Mich., May Turner, where he lived. He died in 1932 at Grand Rapids, Mich. No children.

No. 2226. Fifth Generation. 2216.

5) Virginia Agnes Landes, b Mar 2, 1863, single, is a practicing osteopath physician in Chicago, Ill

No. 2227. Fifth Generation. 2216.

6) Henry Ellsworth Landes, b ——————— (single), is a practicing (osteopath) physic.an in Florida

No. 2228. Fifth Generation. 2216.

7) William Sherman Landes, b. ———————, m Maud Crenshaw.
1. Elmer Landes, b ———————

No. 2229. Fourth Generation. 1172.

5) John Franklin Landes, b. Oct 26, 1831, at Greencastle, Ind., d. April 16, 1920, at Leon, Ia., m. Dec. 14, 1865, Emma Johnson at Hopeville, Ia. She died in 1871. Merchant and farmer, admitted to the bar at Princeton, Ind., in 1855. He moved to Iowa and was elected to the Iowa Legislature from Clark Co., before the Civil War. He enlisted in the War July 28, 1862, at Hopeville in the 18th Infantry, and was promoted to Captain of Company A, where he served until the close of the War. Coming to Hopeville he engaged in the mercantile business. Thence he moved to Leon, Ia., where he became a large land holder. John Franklin marr.ed (2nd) Frances Elizabeth Trower of Westerville, Ia., June 29, 1876. She died Mar. 14, 1918, at Leon, Ia.
1. Lucius Johnson Landes, b Mar. 23, 1869. No. 2230.
   (Second marriage)
2. Mary Magdalene Landes, b. Mar 26, 1877. No. 2231.
3. Harry Lincoln Landes, b. April 27, 1879. No 2234.
4. Medora Leah Landes, b Oct 1, 1884. No 2235.
5. Estella Landes, b July 9, 1893. No 2239.

No. 2230. Fifth Generation. 2229.

1) Lucius Johnson Landes, b. Mar. 23, 1869, at Hopeville, Ia., d. Nov. 5, 1915, at Grand River, Ia. He married Rose DeKalb of DeKalb, Ia. He left one daughter, who lives with her mother at Iowa City, Ia.
1. Emma Margaret Landes, b. ———————.

No. 2231. Fifth Generation. 2229.

2) Mary Magdalena Landes, b Mar. 26, 1877, at Westerville, Ia., m. Elmer Harris, Nov. 29, 1900, in Va Mr. Harris is a dealer in monuments at Leon, Ia., and is also owner of 2,200 acres of land near Leon, Ia. Methodists.
1. Norborn Harris, b Aug 23, 1901. No. 2232.
2. John Raymond Harris, b Dec. 28, 1903 No. 2233.
3. Leah June Harris, b April 9, 1906; she is a teacher in New York City.

No. 2232. Sixth Generation. 2231.

1) Norborn Harris, b Aug 23, 1901, at Leon, Ia., m. Jan. 6, 1923, Pearl Van Pelt. He is engaged in the monument business with his father at Leon.
1. Marjorie N. VanPelt Harris, b. ———————.

No. 2233. Sixth Generation. 2231.

2) John Raymond Harris, b. Dec. 28, 1903, at Leon, Ia., m. Aug. 28, 1933, Doris Blaine.

3) Harry Lincoln Landes, b. April 27, 1879, m Nellie West, Oct. 9, 1906 No children.

4) Medora Leah Landes, b Oct 1, 1884, m Mar 1, 1908, at Leon, Ia, Warren Day.
1. Ethel Dale Day, b. —————. No. 2236
2. Frances Day, b —————. No. 2237.
3 Margaret Day, b. —————. No. 2238.
4. Alice Day, b. —————, d, age 17 years.

1) Ethel Dale Day, b. —————, m Harold Gilroth

2) Frances Day, b —————, m Everett Boles.

3) Margaret Day, b. —————, m. Oren Harnard.

5) Estella Landes, b. July 9, 1893, at Leon, Ia, m. Bruce Reasoner.
1. Frances Reasoner, b. ———, 1920.
2 Mescal Mauris Reasoner, b. ———, 1925.

6) Mary Magdalene Landes, b May 3, 1834, in Augusta Co., Va, m. James Thompson Embree, a prominent and wealthy attorney and citizen of Princeton, Ind. He was a lieutenant colonel in the 58th Regiment of the Civil War from Ind. He died four years after the war closed His wife died young also, their four children were reared by their Grandmother Embree.
1. Lucius Embree, b. ————— No 2241
2. Jesse Fremont Embree, b —————, d. at 7 years.
3. Samuel Landes Embree, b. —————.
4. Elisha Robb Embree, b —————, never married.
Note.—Samuel Landes Embree was an excellent Pianist and entertainer, and at one time headed a comedy of his own, with 21 specialists touring the middle west We have no further record of him.

2) Lucius Embree, b. —————, m. Luella Casey, b —————. He like his father was an attorney at Princeton, Ind.
1. James Casey Embree, b. —————. No. 2242.
2. Morton Casey Embree, b ————— No 2243.
3. Louise Embree, b. ———, 1884, writer and author.
4 Clotilda Embree, b ————— No 2244.

1) James Casey Embree, b —————, at Princeton, Ind, m Laura Coburn He lives in Seattle, Wash. Civil engineer
1. Howard Charles Embree, b. —————
2 John Lucius Embree, b. —————.

2) Morton Casey Embree, b. —————, at Princeton, Ind, m. Mary Ione Schenley Attorney at Princeton, Ind.

1. Mirian Lisette Embree, b ————.
2. Morton Thomas Embree, b. ————.
3. Barbara Lou Embree, b. ————.
4. Jackson Schenley Embree, b ————.

No. 2244. Sixth Generation. 2241.
4) Clotilda Embree, b ————, m. Claude Douglas Funk. Mrs. Funk was an artist. Address: Indianapolis, Ind.
1. Lucia Funk, b. ————.

No. 2245. Fourth Generation. 1172.
7) Samuel Louis Landes, b Dec. 15, 1835, in Augusta Co, Va., d Aug. 1, 1920, at San Diego, Calif., married at Hopeville, Ia., June 19, 1886, to Elizabeth Emery, daughter of Dr. Jesse Emery Samuel L Landes was a physician in California, and lke his other relatives in the medical profession became very wealthy.
1. Jessie Embree Landes, b. April 12, 1867. No. 2246.
2. Samuel Edwin Landes, b Jan. 1, 1873 No. 2247.
3. Bertha M Landes, b July 11, 1876 No. 2248.

No. 2246. Fifth Generation. 2245.
1) Jessie Embree Landes, b April 12, 1867, at Hopeville, Ia., d. Aug., 1931, at Julian, Calif., m at Murry, Ia, Edith Briley of Ill He was a druggist.
1 Florence Landes, b. Jan 15, 1899 No. 2246¼

No. 2246¼. Sixth Generation. 2246.
1) Florence Landes, b Jan 15, 1899, m Estella Coleman. They live at San Diego, Calif No children

No. 2247. Fifth Generation. 2245.
2) Samuel Edwin Landes, b Jan 1, 1873, at Hopeville, Ia, d. May 30, 1932, m Ellen Jameson of Glenwood, Ia , m (2nd) Beatrice Jones, b Feb. 28, 1889, at San Diego, Calif. Druggist at San Diego, Calif
1. Millicent Landes, b Oct 16, 1915.
2. Jack H. Landes, b Oct. 17, 1924.
3 Richard E. Landes, b. Sept 1, 1926.

No. 2248. Fifth Generation. 2245.
3) Bertha M Landes, b July 11, 1876, at Hopeville, Ia , m. David George Jamison, Council Bluffs, Ia He was from a pioneer Scotch family, b. July 14, 1858, at Glenwood, Ia , where he was a leading citizen and financier He died Jan. 14, 1930, at San Diego, Calif.
1. Margaret Elizabeth Jamison, b Feb 3, 1903. No 2249

No. 2249. Sixth Generation. 2248.
1) Margaret E Jamison, b. Feb. 3, 1903, m. Alton Harpst, of Meadville, Pa., Oct. 1, 1927, at San Diego, Calif
1 Natilie Gene Harpst, b June 25, 1928.
2 Beverly Anna Harpst, b. June 9, 1931.
L.ve at San Diego, Calif

No. 2250. Fourth Generation. 1172.
8) Frances Agnes Landes, b Sept. 19, 1838, near Greencastle, Ind , d. Oct. 25, 1912, in St Clair Co., Mo She married Mar. 12, 1862, Benjamin Newland Prier, of Hopeville, Ia. Buried in Kidds cemetery. Presbyterians Mr. Prier was b. April 25, 1840, in Edgar Co , Ill , and died in Mo , Aug. 21, 1920. He was a Civil War veteran, enlisted in Co. B, 18th Iowa infantry, as 3rd sergeant, July 12, 1862.

1. Mary Magdalene Prier, b Nov 30, 1862 No 2251
2 Samuel Edward Prier, b Mar 13, 1865 No 2271
3. Florence Prier, b June 20, 1866, d Sept 19, 1873
4. Frank Loren Prier, b April 19, 1872 No 2274
5 Maud Lola Prier, b Aug 2, 1880 No 2275.

No. 2251. Fifth Generation. 2250.
1) Mary Magdalena Prier, b Nov 30, 1862, at Hopeville, Ia , m. William Frazer, Nov 2, 1883, of Mo
1. Jessie Frazer, b. Sept 16, 1888. No. 2280.

No. 2252. Fourth Generation. 1172.
9) Henry Jacques Landes, b. Sept. 19, 1842, at Greencastle, Ind , d. in 1910, m. Minerva Jane R ley, June, 1851, at Hopeville, Ia They lived at Leon, Ia Merchant and farmer. Methodists
1. Laura Agnes Landes, b June 9, 1870. No. 2253.
2 Franklin Henry Landes, b Mar. 14, 1872 No 2262.
3. Samuel Riley Landes, b Sept 27, 1875. No. 2262¼.

No. 2253. Fifth Generation. 2252.
1) Laura Agnes Landes, b. June 9, 1870, m. Thomas Roberts, an Englishman, at Westerville, Ia. Miller and large landholder Address· Westerville, Ia
1. Blanche Roberts, b ——————. No 2254.
2. Ralph Roberts, b. ——————. No 2255
3 Frank Roberts, b ——————, lives in Denver, Colo
4. Grace Roberts, b —————— No 2257.
5. Bernice Roberts, b —————— No. 2258.
6. Mildred Roberts, b ——————. No. 2259.
7. Clarence Roberts, b ——————, single, Leon, Ia.
8. Ruth Roberts, b. —————— No 2261.

No. 2254. Sixth Generation. 2253.
1) Blanche Roberts, b. ——————, m Borin Tulis Address· Decatur, Ia

No. 2255. Sixth Generation. 2253.
2) Ralph Roberts, b ——————, m Grace Lape

No. 2257. Sixth Generation. 2253.
4) Grace Roberts, b ——————, m Paul Chastain. Address: Leon, Ia
1 Daughter Chastain, b. ——————.

No. 2253. Sixth Generation. 2253.
5) Bernice R. Roberts, b. ——————, m Frank Hoskinsmith Address: Des Moines, Ia

No. 2259. Sixth Generation. 2253.
6) Mildred Roberts, b ——————, m William Alley.

No. 2261. Sixth Generation. 2253.
8) Ruth Roberts, b. ——————, m Eldon Studebaker.
1. Daughter Studebaker, b ——————.

No. 2262. Fifth Generation. 2252.
2) Franklin Henry Landes, b. Mar 14, 1872, m Delphine Hourland Medical doctor at Mt Ayr, Ia.
1. Beatrice Landes, b —————— No. 2263.
2 Helen Louise Landes, b. ——————, is teaching at Independence, Ia

No. 2262¼. Fifth Generation. 2252.

3) Samuel Riley Landes, b Sept. 27, 1875, m Eva Bolt, of Union, Ia. Samuel was engaged in insular service in the Philippine Islands, being private secretary to General McArthur After his return to the United States, he was General State Agent for an Insurance Co He died Jan., 1936 Interred in National cemetery at Casper, Wyo His widow is in Oklahoma City, Okla.

No. 2253. Sixth Generation. 2252.

1) Beatrice Landes, b ——————, m August Luyben. Address Omaha, Nebr.

No. 2254. Sixth Generation. 2213.

2) Effie Landes, b Mar 5, 1889, at Grand River, Ia , m. T. C Watkins, of Lacona, Ia , b Dec 9, 1885 They l ve at Charlton, Ia.
1. Alice Watkins, b July 19, 1896, Lacona, Ia.
2 Margaret Stella Watkins, b July 11, 1916, at Charlton, Ia.

No. 2265. Sixth Generation. 2213.

3) Gussie Mae Landes, b May 5, 1896, at Lacona, Ia., m. Oct. 6, 1916, at Charlton, Ia., Paul Raymond Poling
1 Bernice Irene Poling, b April 7, 1917, twin   No. 2270
2 Thelma Ilene Poling, b April 7, 1917, twin
3. Helen Pauline Poling, b. July 14, 1920
4. Landes Raymond Poling, b. Nov 23, 1923.
5 Marvin James Pol.ng, b June 6, 1925

No. 2265. Sixth Generation. 2213.

4) Mary Isabelle Landes, b Nov 28, 1897, at Lacona, Ia., m Jan. 9, 1914 Jesse Pearl Freeman; he died Jan 6, 1933
1 Vivian Freeman, b Jan. 5, 1915   No 2267
2 Mabel Irene Freeman, b. Oct. 17, 1916.
3. Robert Edward Freeman, b June 8, 1918
4. Guy Richard Freeman, b Nov. 25, 1920.
5. Frances Cecilia Freeman, b Jan. 16, 1923.
6. Mary Pearl Freeman, b Aug. 19, 1925.
7. Esther Maxine Freeman, b April 2, 1928
8 Laronna Jeanne Freeman, b Feb 6, 1933

No. 2267. Seventh Generation. 2265.

1) Vivian Freeman, b Jan 5, 1915, at Lacona, Ia , m. Rex Conner, b Dec. 29, 1912, at Charlton, Ia
1. Everett Wayne Conner, b Nov 21, 1935
2. Carol Marie Conner, b Sept 8, 1936

No. 2268. Sixth Generation. 2213.

5) Robert Samuel Landes, Jr , b Jan 5, 1900, at Lacona, Ia , m July 6, 1921, Esther Janise Willis.
1. Wilma Irene Landes, b. May 15, 1922.

No. 2259. Sixth Generation. 2213.

7) Martha Margaret Landes, b Oct 2, 1904, at Lacona, Ia , m. July 2, 1924, Harry Beeler, b Mar. 3, 1900
1 Carl G. Beeler, b July 24, 1925, Lacona, Ia
2. Allen S. Beeler, b May 26, 1927, Lacona, Ia.
3. Marion Gene Beeler, b. Feb 14, 1930, Lacona, Ia.
4. Margaret Helen Beeler, b Jan 29, 1932, Gary, Ind.

5. Daniel King Beeler, b. April 13, 1934, Gary, Ind
6. Janise Irene Beeler, b July 14, 1936, Gary, Ind

No. 2270. Seventh Generation. 2255.

1) Bernice Irene Poling, b April 7, 1917, m Dec 13, 1933, at Charlton, Ia., Raymond Galloway Higbee, b Jan 6, 1913, at Pleasantville, Ia.
1. Phyllis Marie Higbee, b. June 10, 1934

No. 2271. Fifth Generation. 2250.

2) Samuel Edward Prier, b Mar. 3, 1865, at Hopeville, Ia , m Oct 21, 1906, Delia Hutton, at Osceola, Mo.
1. Carl Edward Prier, b. July 19, 1904.
2 Varlah Lowerie Prier, b. Aug 4, 1908. No. 2272.
3 Benjamin Taylor Prier, b Nov 30, 1910 No. 2273
4. Ralph Emerson Prier, b. Oct 14, 1912
5. Reno Alonzo Prier, b. June 14, 1914.
6 Dormon Crawford Prier, b. June 18, 1916
7. Dorothy Fleet Prier, b. Feb. 10, 1918
8 Junita Dew Prier, b Oct 31, 1922.

No. 2272. Sixth Generation. 2271.

2) Varlah Lowerie Prier, b. Aug 4, 1908, m July 14, 1930, Lloyd Warren, of Clinton, Mo.
1. Lloyd Eugene Warren, b Mar 23, 1934
2. Winona Lucile Warren, b. July 19, 1936

No. 2273. Sixth Generation. 2271.

3) Benjamin Taylor Prier, b. Nov 30, 1910, m Bina Lee Parks, b Jan 1, 1936, of Osceola, Mo.

No. 2274. Fifth Generation. 2250.

4) Frank Loren Prier, b April 10, 1872, at Hopeville, Ia., m Jan 30, 1904, Emma Cable Mr. Prier died Dec 19, 1930, buried at Kidds Chapel cemetery, St. Clair Co , Mo. No children.

No. 2275. Fifth Generation. 2250.

5) Maud Lola Prier, b. Aug 2, 1880, at Hopeville, Ia., m Hezekiah Murphy, Sept. 9, 1896 Divorced She married (2nd) Thomas Coleman Gibbens, Nov 29, 1903; he died Oct. 20, 1909; m (3rd) Felix Delbert Branson, April 14, 1925.
1. Frederick Murphy, b Aug 28, 1897. No. 2276
2. Benjamin Forest Gibbens, b Nov 9, 1904 No 2277
3. Maud Pauline Gibbens, b. Mar. 16, 1907 No. 2278.
4 Coleman St. Clair Gibbens, b Mar. 14, 1909 No 2279

No. 2276. Sixth Generation. 2275.

1) Frederick Murphy, b. Aug 28, 1897, m. Josie Shoemaker, Dec 3, 1917. Divorced He married (2nd) Lelia Lemons Divorced He married (3rd) Wilma Bause, Jan. 1, 1934.
1. Lelia Mae Murphy, b April 19, 1935

No. 2277. Sixth Generation. 2275.

2) Benjamin Forest Gibbens, b. Nov 9, 1904, m Feb 13, 1930, Fern Keyes
1. Norma Jane Gibbens, b Jan 26, 1932.
2. Frank Loren Gibbens, b. Aug 10, 1935.

No. 2278. Sixth Generation. 2275.

3) Maud Pauline Gibbens, b. Mar 16, 1907, m Aug 3, 1928, Clarence Dody
1. Billy Lee Dody, b Mar. 10, 1930
2 Betty Joe Dody, b April 14, 1932.

No. 2279. Sixth Generation. 2275.

4) Coleman St. Clair Gibbens, b. Mar. 14, 1909, m. Dec 28, 1932, Lena Hally.
1. Jackie Coleman Gibbens, b. Jan 8, 1935.

No. 2280. Sixth Generation. 2251.

1) Jessie Frazer, b. Sept 16, 1888, m. Burley Long, Dec. 9, 1901.
1. Harvard Higgins Long, b May 9, 1903. No 2281.
2. Harry E. Long, b. Oct 13, 1906 No 2282.
3. Guy Russell Long, b Sept. 28, 1912. No. 2283.
4. Nellie Alma Long, b. Sept. 28, 1914, d. Jan. 9, 1922.
5. Elton James Long, b. July 5, 1922

No. 2281. Seventh Generation. 2280.

1) Harvard Higgins Long, b May 9, 1903, m Mar 9, 1924, Alma May Robinson.
1. Ray B Long, b Nov. 16, 1924.
2. Baby Lee Long, b. Oct 28, 1926, d. Nov 1, 1926
3. Glen D. Long, b April 18, 1929.
4 Junita Louise Long, b. Mar 5, 1932.
5. Shirley Mae Long, b. Dec. 20, 1933
6. Billy Burl Long, b July 12, 1936.

No. 2282. Seventh Generation. 2280.

2) Harry E Long, b. Oct. 13, 1906, m. Oct. 21, 1925, Maud Biles; m. (2nd) Maud Eckla Ledleiter, Dec 9, 1932
1. Jerry Lee Long, b April 29, 1935

No. 2283. Seventh Generation. 2280.

3) Guy Russell Long, b Sept 28, 1912, m. Ruby Pauline Queen, April 25, 1930 No children.

No. 2284. Fourth Generation. 1177.

1) William Henry Wilson, b. ————————, d at 35 years of age Buried at Oak Hill cemetery, Union Co , Ia. He was never married

No. 2285. Fourth Generation. 1177.

2) Martha Jane Wilson, b ————————, in Augusta Co , Va , d at the age of 80 years; m Samuel Stark at Hopeville, Ia
1 Wilbert Stark, b ———————— No 2286.
2 Jessie Stark, b ———————— No 2287.
3. Eva Stark, b ————————. No 2288.
4. Mary Stark, b ———————— No 2289

No. 2286. Fifth Generation. 2285.

1) Wilbert Stark, b. ————————, m ———————— Lashball They lived at Hopeville, Ia.
1 William Stark, b ————————

No. 2287. Fifth Generation. 2285.

2) Jesse Stark, b. ————————, m. Irene Jackson, at Murry, Ia., d. at Grand River, Ia.
1. Wendal Stark, b ————————, at Hopeville, Ia.
2. Ethel Stark, b. ————————, at Hopeville, Ia.

No. 2288. Fifth Generation. 2285.

3) Eva Stark, b ————————, m Vern Chapman, at Hopeville, Ia.
1. Gussie Chapman, b. ————————.

335

No. 2289. Fifth Generation. 2285.

4) Mary Stark, b ————————, d. ————————, m Allie Palmer, b.
———————, d ————————
1. Glen Palmer, b. ————————
2 Dorothy Palmer, b. ————————.
3. Mabel Palmer, b. ————————.
4 Mary Palmer, b ————————

No. 2290. Fourth Generation. 1177.

3) Sarah Frances Wilson, b ————————, m Eli Stark at Hopeville, Ia.
1. John Stark, b. ————————. No 2291.
2. Bert Stark, b. ————————, d. young.

No. 2291. Fifth Generation. 2290.

1) John Stark, b. ————————, m. Esther Cole.

No. 2292. Fourth Generation. 1177.

5) John Franklin Wilson, b. ————————, near Greencastle, Ind., m. Etta
Palmer, b. ———————— Deceased They moved to Hopeville, Ia., where he
resided.
1. Albunes Wilson, b. ————————, d ten days old.
2. Erma Wilson, b. ———————— No 2293
3. Alta Wilson, b. ———————— No 2294.
4 Beulah Wilson, b ———————— No 2295

No. 2293. Fifth Generation. 2292.

2) Erma Wilson, b. ————————, at Hopeville, Ia , m Roscoe Johnson.
1. Gerald Wilson, b ————————.

No. 2294. Fifth Generation. 2292.

3) Alta Wilson, b ————————, at Hopeville, Ia , m Albert Strubhan, at
Hopeville, Ia.
1. Harold Strubhan, b. ————————, Hopeville, Ia
2. Olive Strubhan, b. ————————, Hopeville, Ia
3. Merrill Strubhan, b ————————, Hopeville, Ia

No. 2295. Fifth Generation. 2292.

4) Beulah Wilson, b ————————, at Hopeville, Ia., m. Harry Strubhan.
Address: Hopeville, Ia.
1. Lester Strubhan, b. ————————.
2. Thelma Strubhan, b. ————————.

No. 2296. Fourth Generation. 1178½.

1) Eliza Jane Siple, b Feb 21, 1833, in Pendleton Co., Va., d Jan. 14, 1898,
in Benton Co., Ia., m. ———————— Ogle, in Putnam Co , Ind He died and was buried
in Ind., Feb. 12, 1855. She married Thomas Sherrill b in 1828 in Putnam Co., Ind.
He died at Ellinsville, N Dak. Buried at Benton, Ia.
1. Lawrence Ogly, b Dec 12, 1851, in Ind No. 2297.
2. Catherine Ogly, b. Sept. 19, 1853, in Ind No 2310.
3. Samuel Webb Sherrill, b. Dec 17, 1856. No. 2311.
4. Mary Sherrill, b. Oct. 4, 1858. No. 2312
5. John Sherrill, b. June 11, 1860, d. in infancy.
6. Nancy Sherrll, b. June 10, 1862. No. 2313
7. William Sherrill, b. June 28, 1864. No record
8. Jessie Sherrill, b Mar ––, 1866 No. 2314

336

9　Emma Sherrill, b July 31, 1869　No. 2315

10　Olive Sherrill, b July 1, 1871　No 2316

No. 2297. Fifth Generation. 2296.

1) Lawrence Ogly, b Dec 12, 1851, near Greencastle, Ind., d Mar. 30, 1900, near Blockton, Ia　He married April 19, 1873, Eliza Turner Carter, b. Feb. 5, 1856　She died Nov. 27, 1931, at Mt. Ayr, Ia　Both were buried at Mt. Ayr, Ia

1　Clyde Ogly, b Mar 19, 1874. No 2298

2　John T Ogly, b 1876, d. 1879

3. Maud Ogly, b July 26, 1878. No 2299

4　Mae Ogly, b. Sept 7, 1880　No 2305

5. Daughter, b. 1882, d 1884

6. Lawrence Leonard Ogly, b Sept. 23, 1884, d April 1898

7　Phoeba Priscilla Ogly, b Dec 15, 1886　No. 2307

8　Earl Raymond Ogly, b April 26, 1894

9　Guy Clifford Ogly, b April 14, 1895　No 2308.

10　Clay B Ogly, b Oct 15, 1898　No 2309

No. 2298. Sixth Generation. 2297.

1) Clyde Ogly, b Mar 19, 1874, in Ringold Co., Ia , m Sept. 29, 1897, Laura Spencer, deceased　Clyde died Oct 20, 1897, buried in Hickory Grove cemetery, Benton, Ia

No. 2299. Sixth Generation. 2297.

3) Maud Ogly, b July 26, 1878, m Sept 8, 1897, William Poor, b July 13, 1876. They live in Mt Ayr, Ia

1. John Poor, b Feb 3, 1899　No 2300

2　Esta Poor, b Oct 1, 1900　No 2301

3　Marguerite Poor, b Oct 22, 1902　No 2302

4　Nelle Poor, b Dec 20, 1906. No 2303

5　Homer Poor, b Jan 21, 1912

6　Eloise Poor, b Oct 29, 1916　No 2304

7　Mary Elaine Poor, b July 15, 1921

No. 2300. Seventh Generation. 2299.

1) John Poor, b Feb 3, 1899, m May 10, 1931, Edna Hillis, b Oct 31, 1903, at Greencastle, Ind　They live in Greencastle, Ind.

1　James Hillis Poor, b July 2, 1932 at Chanute, Kans.

2　Robert Poor, b Dec 5, 1934, at Greencastle, Ind.

No. 2301. Seventh Generation. 2299.

2) Esta Poor, b. Oct 1, 1900, m April, 1925, to Leslie Torrence, at St. Charles, Ia , b June 7, 1901　They are living at Milton Jc., Kans.

1　John William Torrence, b June 26, 1927

2　James Leslie Torrence, b July 3, 1932.

No. 2302. Seventh Generation. 2299.

3) Marguerite Poor, b Oct 22, 1902, m. Oct. 27, 1922, at Creston, Ia., Herman Oleson, b Jan 22, 1900　They live at Mt Ayr, Ia

1　Betty Oleson, b May 17, 1923

2　Jean Oleson, b. Jan 7, 1925

No. 2303. Seventh Generation. 2299.

4) Nellie Poor, b Dec 20, 1906, at Mt Ayr, Ia , m Sept 12, 1928, Joseph Middleton, b Sept 28, 1907　Address Mt Ayr, Ia

1　William Robert Middleton, b Jan 26, 1930

No. 2304. Seventh Generation. 2299.

6) Eloise Poor, b Oct 29, 1916, at Mt Ayr, Ia , m Aug 29, 1935, in Des Moines, Ia., Victor Anderson

No. 2305. Sixth Generation. 2297.

4) Mae Ogly, b Sept 9, 1880, in Ringold Co , Ia , m. Carl E Drake, b. April 15, 1882. He d.ed Nov 11, 1930 Buried at Blockton, Ia. Mae lives at Temple, Tex., with her daughter.
1. Mardale Drake, b April 1, 1906. No. 2306

No. 2306. Seventh Generation. 2305.

1) Mardale Drake, b April 1, 1906, m July 4, 1926, in Colo , to Lloyd Wilson. They live at Temple, Tex

No. 2307. Sixth Generation. 2297.

7) Phoeba Priscilla Ogly, b. Dec. 15, 1886, m Dec., 1908, John Boorman They live at Long Beach, Calif.
1. Ivan Boorman, b. ————.
2. Inez Boorman, b. ————.
3. Clark Boorman, b. ————.
4. John Boorman, b ————.

No. 2308. Sixth Generation. 2297.

9) Guy Clifford Ogly, b. April 26, 1895, m Mona Keenan, in Des Moines, Ia. They live at Blockton, Ia.
1. Marie Ogly, b Dec. 23, 1920
2. John Paul Ogly, b. June —, 1929

No. 2309. Sixth Generation. 2297.

10) Clay Bemont Ogly, b Oct 15, 1898, m at Alliance, Nebr , to Medro ————. They live in Hyannis, Nebr.
1. David Ogly, b July —, 1931.
2. Cecilia Ogly, b ————, 1935

No. 2310. Fifth Generation. 2296.

2) Catherine Ogly, b Sept 19, 1853, at Greencastle, Ind , m David McNelty (deceased) Mrs. McNelty is living at Centralia, Wash.
1. Oscar McNelty, b ————.
2. Lawrence McNelty, b ————
3. Jessie McNelty, b. ————, d. ————.
4. Robert McNelty, b ————.
5. Frank McNelty, b. ————.
Oscar and Robert are living in Centralia, Wash ; Lawrence, at Fargo, N. Dak.; Frank, at Spokane, Wash

No. 2311. Fifth Generation. 2296.

3) Samuel Webb Sherrill, b. Dec. 17, 1856, d in N Dak. Buried at Creston, Ia. He married Deel Morrisson near Creston, Ia They had a daughter, Dona Sherrill She is married and lives in Little Rock, Ark

No. 2312. Fifth Generation. 2295.

4) Mary Sherrill, b Oct 4, 1858, m to a Mr Homer He is dead. They had a son, Joseph Homer, that married and lives in Council Bluffs, Ia. Mary married (2nd) Josh Rush (deceased). Later she married a man by the name of King and had five children The author failed to get the names

No. 2313. Fifth Generation. 2296.

6) Nancy Sherrill, b. June 10, 1862, d in Calif, and is buried there; m. Henry Massey (deceased).
1. Henry Massey, Jr, b. ——————.
2. Lido Massey, b. ——————.
3. Mary Massey, b. ——————

No. 2314. Fifth Generation. 2295.

8) Jessie Sherrill, b. Mar —, 1866, m. Frank Scott. They live in Creston, Ia.
1. Earl Scott, b ——————, marr.ed and lives in Council Bluffs, Ia.

No. 2315. Fifth Generation. 2296.

9) Emma Sherrill, b July 31, 1869, m James Bane They live in Wauseca, Minn.
1 Esther Bane, b ——————, m and lives in Long Beach, Calif. No further record.

No. 2316. Fifth Generation. 2296.

10) Olive Sherr.ll, b. July 1, 1871, m C W. Welsher. They live in Iowa City, Ia
1. Eber Welsher, b. ——————, m. and lives in Iowa City, Ia.
2 Donna Welsher, b. ——————
3. Lynn Welsher, b ——————.

No. 2317. Fourth Generation. 1178½.

3) Frances Siple, b. Mar 20, 1836, near Greencastle, Ind, m. Felix Prier, Hopeville, Ia, Dec. 28, 1860 He d.ed May 3, 1883 Frances died Sept. 29, 1892. Both were buried at Appleton City, Mo
1 John Landes Prier, b Oct 29, 1861, d. Sept 27, 1865.
2. Katy Prier, b June 17, 1866 No 2318.
3. Albert Prier, b Nov 16, 1867. No 2319.
4 Eliza Prier, b. Dec. 16, 1870 No. 2320.

No. 2318. Fifth Generation. 2317.

2) Katy Prier, b. June 17, 1866, m William Hinkley. He died at Kansas City, Mo, Oct, 1929.

No. 2319. Fifth Generation. 2317.

3) Albert Prier, b Nov 16, 1867, d Nov. 28, 1892, m Augusta Bennett.
1 Gaevney Prier, b May 23, 1892

No. 2320. Fifth Generation. 2317.

4) Eliza Prier, b Dec 16, 1870, m Edwin Kennedy He died Sept. 7, 1899. She married (2nd) James Calton, June 11, 1903.
1. Lee Kennedy, b Sept 9, 1895 No 2321
2. Merle Kennedy, b Mar 26, 1897. No 2322
(From second marriage)
3. James Calton, Jr, b Feb 8, 1905, twin
4 Lawrence Calton, b Feb 8, 1905, twin No. 2323.

No. 2321. Sixth Generation. 2320.

1) Lee Kennedy, b Sept 9, 1895, m April 1, 1923, Delia Bulle
1. Bonnie Jean Kennedy, b Oct 20, 1926

No. 2322. Sixth Generation. 2320.

2) Merle Kennedy, b Mar 26, 1897, m Ethel Collins, June 1, 1920 She died Mar 6, 1921.

339

No. 2323. Sixth Generation. 2320.

4) Lawrence Calton, b. Feb 8, 1905, m Darline Furry, Dec. 24, 1930.
1 Lyone Calton, b. Nov 17, 1931.
2. Lawrence Calton, Jr., b Feb 23, 1935.

No. 2324. Fourth Generation. 1178½.

5) Charles Siple, b May 10, 1851, d Feb —, 1923, m Anna Elizabeth Chew at Hopeville, Ia She died in 1885 Buried in Gregg cemetery, Clark Co., Ia
1. William Henry Siple, b Oct 31, 1871 No 2325.
2. Louis Albert Siple, b July 1, 1874. No 2326
3. Katherine Jane Siple, b July 29, 1877 No 2328.
4. Lossen Siple, b ————, 1880. No. 2329.
5. Emma Faye Siple, b ——————, died and buried at Kellerton, Ia.

No. 2325. Fifth Generation. 2324.

1) William Henry Siple, b Oct. 31, 1871, d Oct 4, 1933, buried at Kellerton. Ia. He married Aury Wilson, b June 23, 1868 She is living in Kellerton, Ia
1. Avary Siple, b Dec —, 1898, d. Feb —, 1919
2. Lavan Siple, b. Sept. 30, 1900.

No. 2326. Fifth Generation. 2324.

2) Louis Albert Siple, b July 1, 1874, at Hopeville, Ia , d. Nov. 29, 1928, at Mt. Ayr, Ia. Buried at Hopeville, Ia He married Sept 2, 1905, at Osceola, Ia., Bessie Smith, b. May 25, 1882, at Hopeville, Ia She is living in Mt Ayr, Ia
1 Louise Siple, b Oct. 29, 1907 at Thayer, Ia No. 2327
2 Lucile Siple, b Sept 4, 1918

No. 2327. Sixth Generation. 2326.

1) Louise Siple, b. Oct 29, 1907, at Thayer, Ia., m. Feb. 26, 1922, Leslie Ballau, b Mar. 23, 1906 Address. Kellerton, Ia
1. Baby daughter died in infancy
2. Duane Ballau, b. July 1, 1928
3. Montella Ballau, b. Sept 29, 1935

No. 2328. Fifth Generation. 2324.

3) Katherine Siple, b July 29, 1877, m Bert Whitson, Sept 24, 1896 Mrs Whitson died at Kansas City, Mo , July 24, 1919 Buried at Kellerton, Ia
1. Edna Whitson, b Oct. 27, 1898 No 2328¼.
2. Lela Whitson, b Aug 29, 1900 No 2328½
3. Helen Whitson, b. July 31, 1906. No 2328¾

No. 2328¼. Sixth Generation. 2328.

1) Edna Whitson, b Oct 27, 1898, m George Rex. They live in Detroit, Mich
1. Elaine Rex, b ————.

No. 2328½. Sixth Generation. 2328.

2) Lela Whitson, b Aug 29, 1900, m Oct 31, 1917, Floyd Creveling
1. Valeria Creveling, b ————. No 2328⅞.

No. 2328¾. Sixth Generation. 2328.

3) Helen Whitson, b. July 31, 1906, m Floyd Greliland, Feb. 28, 1923
1. Virginia Mae Greliland, b Oct 31, 1923

No. 2328⅞. Seventh Generation. 2328½.

1) Valeria Creveling, b —— ————, m Eden Steward

4) Lossen S Siple, b ————, 1880, near Hopeville, Ia., m Eva Hewlett, d. and buried at Kellerton, Ia He married (2nd) in Kansas City, Mo, Elsie ————. She died in Los Angeles, Calif, where Mr Siple resides.

    1. Earl L. Siple, b May 18, 1908
      (From second marriage)
    2 Betty Jean Siple, b. Sept —, 1929

No. 2330. Fourth Generation. 1774.

4) Mary Landes, b Feb 27, 1840, d Dec. 4, 1900. She was buried at Hamrick, Ind, m William C Gilmore, b. April 8, 1840. He died May 30, 1926; he was buried at Greenwood, Ia In early life they lived at Hamrick, Ind., where Mrs. Gilmore died Mr Gilmore later moved to Greenwood, Ia., where he reared his family

    1. Mabel Clair Gilmore, b Nov. 27, 1868 No 2331.
    2. Walter Clayton G lmore, b May 7, 1870 No. 2332.
    3 Benjamin Franklin Gilmore, b Aug —, 1872, d. ————, 1877
    4 Abraham Alexander Gilmore, b ————, 1874. No. 2333
    5. Edith Gertrude Gilmore, b July 25, 1882 No 2334.
    6 Ethel Landes Gilmore, b June 19, 1884 No 2335

No. 2331. Fifth Generation. 2330.

1) Mabel Claire Gilmore, b Nov 27, 1868, m Charles R Buffington, b in 1864. They live at Glenwood, Ia Methodists Burial place at Glenwood, Ia.

    1 Mary Adaline Buffington, b Mar 5, 1913.

No. 2332. Fifth Generation. 2330.

2) Walter Clayton Gilmore, b May 7, 1870, m Elizabeth Houston. No issue

No. 2333. Fifth Generation. 2330.

4) Abraham Alexander Gilmore, b ————, 1874, m. Helen Hunt
    1 Leonard Hunt Gilmore, b ————.
    2 Mabel Gilmore, b ————
    3 Wayne Clayton Gilmore, b ————.
    4 Walter Gilmore, b ————.
    5 Harry Gilmore, b ————.

No. 2334. Fifth Generation. 2330.

5) Edith Gertrude Gilmore, b July 25, 1882, m Madison C. Warren
    1 Merrill Gilmore Warren, b ————
    2 Charles Rollan Warren, b ————
    3 Clyde Clayton Warren, b ————.

No. 2335. Fifth Generation. 2330.

6) Ethel Landes Gilmore, b June 19, 1884, m Charles C Staehling.
    1 Donna Marie Staehling, b ————.
    2. Dorothy Anna Staehling, b. ————.

No. 2336. Fourth Generation. 1174.

5) John Wesley Landes, b Sept 6, 1843, d Feb. 6, 1905, m Laura J Boone, n 1878. She died Nov 3, 1935 Both were buried at Hamrick Station, Hutchison Co., Ind.

    1 Lena Leota Landes, b July 23, 1879 No 2337
    2. Abbie Landes, b ————, 1881, d at four months.

No. 2337. Fifth Generation. 2336.

1) Lena Leota Landes, b. July 23, 1879, m June 18, 1902, Cyrus M. O'Hair, b. Dec 11, 1874. Farmer. Methodists Burial ground at Brick Chapel, Ind Address: Greencastle, Ind , R 3.

    1. Durban Landes O'Hair, b Sept 14, 1903. No 2338.

    2. Madonna O'Hair, b. Nov. 15, 1909

No. 2338. Sixth Generation. 2337.

1) Durban Landes O'Hair, b Sept 14, 1903, m Margaret Mary Kelly, Sept. 4, 1936.

No. 2339. Fourth Generation. 1174.

3) Sarah Rachel Landes, b Sept 19, 1837, d Nov 22, 1891, m. Nov. 22, 1855, Aaron Lewis, b. Nov 30, 1829. He d Feb 25, 1916 Farmer. Christian Church. Buried at Glenwood, Ia Address: Glenwood, Ia

    1. Laura Louise Lewis, b. Aug 9, 1856, d Nov 19, 1862.

    2. Abraham Alexander Lewis, b. May 27, 1859, d. Nov. 7, 1862

    3. Mary Adaline Lewis, b Feb 25, 1861, d Nov 22, 1862

    4. Ida Edith Lewis, b. Aug 31, 1862 No. 3357.

    5. John Franklin Lewis, b April 7, 1864, d Nov 16, 1932 No 3364.

    6. Sarah Almeda Lewis, b Mar 16, 1867. No. 3360.

    7. Lena Leota Lewis, b Jan. 12, 1869, d Nov 5, 1870

    8. Aaron Zimro Lewis, b. Mar. 6, 1874 No 3362.

    9. Ira Earl Lewis, b Feb 18, 1878, d Mar 3, 1885

No. 2340. Fourth Generation. 42.

1) Joseph Brenneman, b April 13, 1838, in Fairfield Co., O , d. in Allen Co., O., Oct 20, 1917. He married Feb 16, 1860, Nancy Hilyard, b. May 13, 1842, d. Dec. 8, 1877. He married (2nd) Catherine Kreider (nee Musser) Feb. 15, 1880. She d. Nov. 17, 1900 He married (3rd) Sarah F Berry (nee Landes) Jan. 31, 1907. She died Feb 19, 1914 Burial in Salem cemetery near Elida, O

    1. Daniel H. Brenneman, b April 10, 1861 No 2341

    2. Mary M. Brenneman, b April 27, 1863 No. 2350.

    3. Lydia A Brenneman, b Feb 20, 1865 No 2360.

    4. Simeon Brenneman, b Feb. 18, 1867, d Dec 18, 1872.

    5. Malinda Brenneman, b Jan 20, 1869, d. Dec 17, 1872.

    6 Margaret F Brenneman, b Feb 20, 1871. No. 2366.

    7. Noah H Brenneman, b July 20, 1873. No. 2381.

    8. Infant (stillborn), Jan. 21, 1875

    (From second wife)

    9. Emma C. Brenneman, b. Nov. 17, 1880 No 2376.

    10. Susanna A Brenneman, b Oct 2, 1883 No. 2378.

No. 2341. Fifth Generation. 2340.

1) Daniel H. Brenneman, b Apr.l 10, 1861, near Elida, O., m Josephine Kiester, b. —————, d Nov. 10, 1906, m. (2nd) Ida Shook, d 1929 Daniel died June —, 1926. They lived in Allen Co , O Buried in Pike cemetery.

    1. Aldine J. Brenneman, b. June 8, 1883 No. 2342.

    2. John A Brenneman, b July 6, 1884, d. Nov. 3, 1903.

    3 Myrtle A. Brenneman, b Aug 22, 1885 No 2347.

    4. James C. Brenneman, b. Feb. 13, 1887 No 2349

    5. Lydia A Brenneman, b Feb. 10, 1888

    6. Infant son, b and d Aug. 20, 1888

    7. Edith R Brenneman, b Jan 10, 1891, d Aug 19, 1891.

    8. Otto Glen Brenneman, b. April 15, 1892 No. 2348

    9. Infant son, b. Aug. 27, 1893, d. Sept. 14, 1893

No. 2342. Sixth Generation. 2341.

1) Aldine J Brenneman, b. June 8, 1883, m Lydia McMillan. Address. 1027 Holmes, L ma, O.
1. Opal Brenneman, b Aug 13, 1904. No. 2342¼.
2. Infant son died at birth
3. Mildred Brenneman, b Aug 23, 1907. No. 2344.
4. Virgil A Brenneman, b. Mar 20, 1912. No. 2343.
5. Lillian Brenneman, b. Dec. 12, 1910. No. 2345.
6. Lucile Brenneman, b Aug 9, 1914 No 2346.
7. Dale Brenneman, b July 27, 1917.
8. Geneva Brenneman, b Nov 26, 1919.
9. Robert Brenneman, b April 20, 1922.
10. Marvin Brenneman, b. Aug 2, 1925
11. Violet Brenneman, b Jan. 12, 1928.
12. Cletus Eugene Brenneman, b. Jan. 14, 1932.

No. 2342¼. Seventh Generation. 2342.

1) Opal Brenneman, b Aug 13, 1904, in Lima, O , m. Albert Ketler. Address 1713 S. Main, Lima, O.
1. June Ketler, b ——————.
2. James Ketler, b. ——————.

No. 2343. Seventh Generation. 2342.

4) Virg 1 A. Brenneman, b Mar 20, 1912, in Lima, O., m. May 29, 1929, Beulah Grace Lewis, b April 17, 1910 Address: Delphos, O.
1. Gaynella Mae Brenneman, b April 11, 1930.
2 Carolyn Joyce Brenneman, b Mar 11, 1934.
3. Virgil Aldine Brenneman, Jr , b Mar. 17, 1936
4. Iama Jane Brenneman, b July 8, 1937.
5. Ronald Lee Brenneman, b. Sept 4, 1938.

No. 2344. Seventh Generation. 2342.

3) Mildred Brenneman, b Aug 23, 1907, in Lima, O , m. Don Kocher of Elida, O. Address· Lima, O , Lost Creek addition.
1 Patricia Louise Kocher, b Apr.l 25, 1930.
2 George Thomas Kocher, b Aug 25, 1932

No. 2345. Seventh Generation. 2342.

5) Lillian Brenneman, b Dec 12, 1907, m. Charles Blue Address: N. West St , Lima, O
1. Rosemary Margaret Blue, b May 7, 1931
2. Betty Catherine Blue, b Nov. 16, 1933
3 Robert Glen Blue, b Mar. 14, 1937.

No. 2346. Seventh Generation. 2342.

6) Lucille Brenneman, b Aug 9, 1914, m Kent Hamilton, of Lima, O. Address. 410 West High St , Lima, O.
1 Robert Bruce Hamilton, b. June 11, 1937

No. 2347. Sixth Generation. 2341.

3) Myrtle Brenneman, b Aug 22, 1885, m Amos Miller. Address· Venedocia, O.
1. Iva Mae Miller, b April 18, 1908 No 2355.
2 Mabel Miller, b. Jan 22, 1910, twin.
3. Hazel Miller, b. Jan 22, 1910, twin, died.

4. Robert Miller, b ————————

5 Lester Miller, b ————————

No. 2348. Sixth Generation. 2341.

8) Otto Glen Brenneman, b April 15, 1892, m Elizabeth R Brunk, b Jan 29, 1889. Lives in La Fontaine, Ind.

1. Jannette Brenneman, b. June 13, 1913

2 Wilma Brenneman, b June 1, 1925, d Sept 19, 1928

No. 2349. Sixth Generation. 2341.

4) James C Brenneman, b Feb 13, 1887, m Lodelia G Ellis, b. June 6, 1883, were married May 6, 1913 They live at Fruita, Colo., their present address

1. Ralph Brenneman, b. Dec. 15, 1913, d Dec 25, 1913, twin.

2. Raymond Brenneman, b Dec. 15, 1913, d. Mar 27, 1914, twin

3 James Morris Brenneman, b Aug. 29, 1915

4. Garth Andrew Brenneman, b Oct 14, 1917

5. Edith Rae Brenneman, b Dec 4, 1923

No. 2350. Fifth Generation. 2340.

2) Mary M Brenneman, b April 27, 1863, near Elida, O , m Sept 18, 1883, George H D. Ross, of Rockingham Co , Va , b Feb 29, 1860, d Aug 23, 1936 Buried in the Salem cemetery near Elida, O They lived near Elida, O , most of their lives except a few years that they lived at La Junta, Colo. Address· Elida, O. Mennonites Minister Farmer.

1. Jennie M. Ross, b Oct 18, 1884 No 2351

2. Onie O. Ross, b Mar 17, 1888 No 2352

3. Nora B Ross, b. Sept 30, 1892 No 2356

4 Lottie E Ross, b ————————, d Nov. 24, 1895

5. Julia A Ross, b. ————————, d Aug 11, 1898

6 Robert R Ross, b. July 17, 1901. No 2358

7. J. Mark Ross, b July 25, 1904 No 2359

No. 2351. Sixth Generation. 2350.

1) Jennie M Ross, b Oct 18, 1884, near Elida, O , m. Nov 20, 1911, Bruce R. Jackson, b Feb. 26, 1883 He is Santa Fe accountant Presbyterians. Address 505 E Palmer, Glendale, Calif

1 Melba Lorrain Jackson, b Jan 25, 1914

2 Margaret Lucile Jackson, b Feb 11, 1918.

3. Bruce Ross Jackson, b July 8, 1920

No. 2352. Sixth Generation. 2350.

2) Onie O Ross, b Mar 17, 1888, near Elida, O., m William Slater, b. June 2, 1885; m. (2nd) Charles M Drury, b Aug 15, 1888, m. (3rd) Carl Nelson.

1 Julia Marzelle Slater, b Aug 27, 1907. No. 2353.

2. George Wade Slater, b Aug 18, 1909. No 2354.

No. 2353. Seventh Generation. 2352.

1) Julia Marzelle Slater, b Aug 27, 1907, m. Nov. 8, 1926, Henry G. Leidsen, b. May 25, 1904 Accountant. Presbyterians. Address. 1454 E. 36th St., Oakland, Calif.

1. Kathryn Joyce Leidsen, b July 10, 1927.

No. 2354. Seventh Generation. 2352.

2) George Wade Slater, b Aug 18, 1909, m Agda Peterson Address: Piedmont, Calif.

No. 2355. Seventh Generation. 2347.

1) Iva Mae Miller, b April 18, 1908, d ————————, m Jacob McConahay. Address· Venedocia, O

No. 2356. Sixth Generation. 2350.

3) Nora Belle Ross, b Sept 30, 1892, near Elida, O , m Mar. 4, 1922, Ralph Frances Webb, b. Oct 7, 1895 Interurban operator United Brethren Address: 858 E. High St., Lima, O.

1 Mary Beth Ross, b. Feb 1, 1914 No 2357

No. 2357. Seventh Generation. 2356.

1) Mary Beth Ross, b. Feb. 1, 1914, near Elida, O., m. Feb. 1, 1934, James Howard Cook, b Jan 4, 1913 Recreation supervisor public schools, Lima, O Address. 853 E. High St , Lima, O United Brethren

1 Carl Robert Cook, b June 5, 1935

No. 2358. Sixth Generation. 2350.

5) Robert Rex Ross, b June 17, 1901, near Elida, O , m Clara Good, b. May 24, 1902 Address. Delphos, O , R 2 Farmer. Mennonites.

1. Myron Ellis Ross, b May 10, 1927.
2 Helen Julia Ross, b Oct. 15, 1928
3 Wilfred Mark Ross, b Jan 22, 1933
4. Robert Dean Ross, b May 8, 1936

No. 2359. Sixth Generation. 2350.

6) J Mark Ross, b July 25, 1904, near Elida, O , m June 23, 1929, Eliza E Brenneman, b Nov. 8, 1904 Farmer Mennonites Address Kalona, Ia

1 Beula Fern Ross Adopted child, b Oct 16, 1932

No. 2360. Fifth Generation. 2340.

3) Lydia A Brenneman, b Feb 20, 1865, near Elida, O , m. Aug. 9, 1888, Samuel S. Diller, b July 2, 1868 Address Elida, O , R 1 Farmer. Mennonites. Burial place in Salem cemetery near Elida, O.

1 Bertha Frances Diller, b Sept 7, 1889 No 2361
2. Infant son, died at birth, Jan 26, 1892
3 Joseph B Diller, b Feb 25, 1893 No 2363.
4. Nancy C Diller, b Feb 24, 1896 No 2364
5. Infant son died at birth, April 19, 1898.
6 Mary A Diller, b July 27, 1899 No 2365

No. 2361. Sixth Generation. 2360.

1) Bertha Frances Diller, b Sept 7, 1889, near Elida, O , m. Feb. 22, 1911, Ansil Showalter. b Sept 1, 1882, in Va Address La Junta, Colo Farmer Mennonites

1. Helen Margaret Showalter, b Jan 10, 1912 No 2362
2. Alta Mae Showalter, b Oct 7, 1913 No 3640
3 Ralph D Showalter, b July 30, 1916. d April 15, 1917
4. Robert Dale Showalter, b Mar 23, 1918
5 Jay Willard Showalter, b Mar 11, 1923
6 Ernest Dean Showalter, b Mar 16, 1929
7 Norma Jean Showalter, b Aug 19, 1931

No. 2362. Seventh Generation. 2361.

1) Helen Margaret Showalter, b Jan 10, 1912, m Nov. 27, 1930, Maurice E Buerge, living in Santa Monica, Calif

1 Helen Elizabeth Buerge, b May 18, 1933

No. 2363. Sixth Generation. 2360.

3) Joseph B. Diller, b. Feb 25, 1893, near Elida, O , m Nov 18, 1917, Barbara Greider, b May 19, 1897. Joseph was killed in an automobile accident, Dec. 19, 1926. Address: Elida, O., R. 1 Farmer Mennonites

1. Norman Jacob Diller, b June 13, 1918.
2. Hermon Samuel Diller, b. Nov. 26, 1919.
3. Mary Kathryn Diller, b June 5, 1921
4. Lydia Esther Diller, b. May 12, 1923.
5 Martha Salena Diller, b Dec 1, 1925.

No. 2364. Sixth Generation. 2350.

4) Nancy Catherine Diller, b. Feb 21, 1896, near Elida, O , m. Feb. 22, 1917, Samuel R. Blosser, b May 11, 1893 Address. Elida, O , R 1. Laborer. Mennonites.

1. Samuel Diller Blosser, b June 5, 1919.
2. Ray Edward Blosser, b Nov 19, 1922
3. Lydia Ann Blosser, b Feb 7, 1924
4. Mary Jane Blosser, b Mar. 8, 1927
5 Betty Jean Blosser, b. Feb 6, 1932
6 Roy Dean Blosser, b Dec 14, 1933.

No. 2365. Sixth Generation. 2360.

6) Mary Ann Diller, b July 27, 1899, near Elida, O , m. Orlo S Bixel, b Nov 11, 1899. Farmer and trapper. Mennonites Address· Comins, Mich.

1 Bertha Lucile Bixel, b April 25, 1920
2 Joseph S Bixel, b. Feb. 26, 1923.
3. Dorothy Gene Bixel, b Oct. 4, 1926

No. 2366. Fifth Generation. 2340.

6) Margaret F. Brenneman, b Feb 20, 1871, near Elida, O., m. Aug. 7, 1889, Charles Keller, b. Nov 22, 1866 Address Mt Sidney, Va Laborer. Mennonites. Burial place at Pike Church, Rockingham Co., Va.

1. Sylvester F Keller, b Mar 27, 1891 No 2367.
2. Joseph E Keller, b Dec 8, 1892 No. 2368.
3 Noah W. Keller, b Feb. 8, 1895 No 2371
4 Mary M. Keller, b. Mar. 30, 1887, d Jan 10, 1898
5 Anna M. Keller, b Jan. 28, 1899 No. 2372.
6. George E. Keller, b. July 20, 1901 No. 2373.
7. Sarah L. Keller, b Sept. 12, 1903. No. 2374.
8. Fanny I. Keller, b. April 2, 1906. No. 2375
9 Harry L. C. Keller, b June 5, 1908, d. May 31, 1925.

No. 2367. Sixth Generation. 2366.

1) Sylvester F Keller, b. Mar 27, 1891, m Dec 24, 1915, Emma Roberts, b. April 10, 1892 Address: Mt Sidney, Va. Machinist. No children

No. 2368. Sixth Generation. 2365.

2) Joseph E Keller, b Dec 8, 1892, m. Jan 24, 1914, Della Morris Address: Forsythe, Mont Railroader.

1. Wilda Keller, b. Jan. 4, 1915. No. 2369.
2. Ethel Keller, b. July 5, 1917. No. 2370.
3. Helen Keller, b. Sept. 24, 1920.
4. Lois Keller, b. Dec. 10, 1922
5. Infant son (stillborn), b. Sept. 20, 1928

No. 2369. Seventh Generation. 2368.

1) Wilda Margaret Keller, b Jan. 4, 1915, m. (1st) —————— Koski; m. (2nd) July 25, 1936, Robert J Marlotte, b Oct. 18, 1906. Address: 2700 4th Ave., Seattle, Wash. Truck driver Catholic

1 Hugo Andrew Koski, b May 31, 1933.

No. 2370. Seventh Generation. 2368.

2) Ethel Keller, b July 5, 1916, m Mar. 7, 1932, Virgil Satherwaitte, b. May 31, 1907. Address: Forsythe, Mont. Housewife.

1. Joseph Edward Satherwaitte, b. June 27, 1932.
2. Ernest Henry Satherwaitte, b June 12, 1933.
3 James Earl Satherwaitte, b. Jan. 13, 1935, d. at four days.
4 George Raymond Satherwaitte, b Oct. 17, 1936

No. 2371. Sixth Generation. 2366.

3) Noah W Keller, b. Feb. 8, 1895, m. Eva —————, d. —————. Miner. Lives in California. Address Los Angeles, Calif. No children.

No. 2372. Sixth Generation. 2366.

5) Anna M. Keller, b Jan 28, 1899, m. Feb 19, 1917, Guy M. Hulvey, b Oct. 26, 1899 Address. Harrisonburg, Va , R. 1. Housewife Presbyterians.

1 Stanley B Hulvey, b May 12, 1919
2. Marvin A Hulvey, b Nov. 25, 1921
3. Martin D Hulvey, b. Aug. 10, 1926.
4 Theressa M Hulvey, b April 19, 1928

No. 2373. Sixth Generation. 2366.

6) George E Keller, b July 20, 1901, m Alice M Adkins. Address: Fisherville, Va Machinist

1. Steward W. Keller, b —————
2. Dwight Keller, b. - —————.

No. 2374. Sixth Generation. 2366.

7) Sarah L. Keller, b Sept 18, 1903, m. Dec. 20, 1919, George E. Robertson, b. May 10, 1887, d Jan 7, 1935. Address Mt. Sidney, Va. Railroader. Methodists. Burial in Woodbine cemetery, Harrisonburg, Va

1 Charles E Robertson, b Aug. 6, 1921.
2. Margaret L Robertson, b July 31, 1924
3. Thomas D Robertson, b. Mar 18, 1927
4. Mary E Robertson, b. Sept. 3, 1931.
5. James W. Robertson, b April 16, 1935

No. 2375. Sixth Generation. 2356.

8) Fanny I. Keller, b April 2, 1906, d Sept. 25, 1930, m. May 27, 1930, Cecil Shehan Presbyterian Buried in Woodbine cemetery, Harrisonburg, Va.

No. 2376. Fifth Generation. 2340.

9) Emma C Brenneman, b Nov 17, 1880, near Elida, O , d. Mar. 17, 1914, of a rare disease caused by eating raw uncooked pork She married Mar 2, 1902, Joseph Heatwole, b Sept 4, 1876 Address Elida, O. Mennonite

1. Orpha Heatwole, b Sept 26, 1902 No. 2376¼
2. Susanna Heatwole, b Mar. 14, 1904 No 303
3. Warren Heatwole, b June 15, 1906
4. Milton Heatwole, b June 30, 1908
5. John Heatwole, b. Sept 14, 1910.

6. Mary Heatwole, b. Dec 13, 1912 No. 325½
7 Mark Heatwole, b July 8, 1915. No. 2377¾

No. 2376¼. Sixth Generation. 2376.

1) Orpha Heatwole, b Sept 26, 1902, m Sept 19, 1936, Lee Dryden Address: Phoenix, Ariz.

No. 2377. Sixth Generation. 2376.

2) Susanna Heatwole, b. Mar 14, 1904, m in Allen Co, O , Elmo F. Showalter, b Nov 27, 1898, in Va Address· Roscoe, Calif Manufacturer. Mennonites Related. For family, see No 1145

No. 2377¾. Sixth Generation. 2376.

7) Mark Heatwole, b. July 8, 1915, m Dorothy Davidson of near Elida, O.
They live in Lima, O.

No. 2378. Fifth Generation. 2340.

10) Susanna A Brenneman, b Oct 2, 1883, m Nov 23, 1905, Perry Smith, b. Mar. 3, 1884. Farmer Mennonites He is a deacon Address· Lima, O , R 3 Burial place in Salem cemetery near Elida, O
1 Emma Catherine Smith, b Oct 15, 1906
2. Norman Olver Smith, b Aug 30, 1908 No 2379
3 Arthur Cletus Smith, b Sept. 15, 1910 No 2380
4 Clara Alberta Smith, b Nov 4, 1912
5 Nelson Dwight Smith, b Mar 29, 1915, d Jan 9, 1916
6 Esther Lucile Smith, b Sept 14, 1917
7 Ruth Elizabeth Smith, b Nov 24, 1919

No. 2379. Sixth Generation. 2373.

2) Norman Oliver Smith, b Aug 30, 1908, m Oct 5, 1930, Clara Berry, b Sept 16, 1911 Farmer Mennonites Address Elida, O , R. 1
1 Marjorie Louise Smith, b Nov. 18, 1937

No. 2380. Sixth Generation. 2378.

3) Arthur Cletus Smith, b Sept 15, 1910, m in 1936, Mary Elizabeth Tucker, b June 27, 1917 Laborer Mennonites Address Elida, O , R 1.

No. 2381. Fifth Generation. 2340.

7) Noah H Brenneman, b July 20, 1873, m Sallie S Heatwole, b. Jan 27, 1878, near Harrisonburg, Va Farmer. Mennonites Address. Elida, O , R 1 Related, and come in two ways. For further record see Nos 548 to 552 inclusive

No. 2382. Fourth Generation. 42.

2) Susanna Brenneman, b Nov 5, 1839, in Fairfield Co, O , d in the home of her daughter, Mrs Mary C Breneman, near Elida, O , Aug. 15, 1924 She married Christian B Brenneman, of Orrville, O , June 2, 1863 He was born April 21, 1842, and died Oct. 21, 1927, at the home of his daughter Mrs Sophiah E Shenk, near Elida, O Both were buried in the Salem cemetery Early in life he was a farmer, but after middle life he worked at the cabinet trade until he retired from active work Mennonites of which he was a minister having been ordained in 1869 in Allen Co, O He was a successful evangelist having conducted evangelistic meetings in eleven states He was a great friend to children Address was Elida, O
1. Sophiah E. Brenneman, b May 24, 1864 No 2383
2 Lydia M. Brenneman, b Dec. 14, 1865, d Feb 3, 1873
3 Mary Catherine Brenneman, b Oct 29, 1867. No. 2384

No. 2383. Fifth Generation. 2382.

1) Sophiah E Brenneman, b May 24, 1864, in Wayne Co, O, m Isaac S Shank, b. Feb 24, 1863, in Va Farmer near Elida, O Related, for family see Nos 693 to 705 inclusive and 327

No. 2384. Fifth Generation. 2382.

3) Mary Catherine Brenneman, b Oct 29, 1867, in Wayne Co, O., m Dec. 4, 1886, Charles D Breneman, b near Singers Glen, Va. Lived near Elida, O., nearly all of their lives. Address Elida, O Farmer Mennonites Burial place in Salem cemetery near Elida, O Related, for family records see Nos. 162 to 172¼ inclusive. Two sons live near Elida, O Their three daughters and youngest son live in Orrville, O

No. 2385. Fourth Generation. 42.

3) Lydia Brenneman, b April 21, 1841, in Fairfield Co, O, d May 30, 1921 On Nov 7, 1867, she married Isaac B Stemen, b Dec 22, 1843, d April 20, 1931. Both were buried in the Salem cemetery near Elida, O Farmer Carpenter Mennonites. Address Lima, O, R 3

1 John M Stemen, b Aug 7, 1868, d Dec 23, 1872
2 Samuel E. Stemen, b April 7, 1870 No 2386
3 Anna B. Stemen, b Dec 19, 1871 No 2393
4. Amanda J Stemen, b Dec 17, 1873. No. 2404.
5 George W Stemen, b. Dec 14, 1875 No. 2408
6 Simeon B Stemen, b Nov 28, 1877 No 2413
7. Rhoda E. Stemen, b Dec 31, 1879. No 2317.
8. Lydia C. Stemen, b Sept 22, 1881. No 2424
9. Martha M Stemen, b Sept 7, 1883 No 2425.

No. 2384. Fifth Generation. 2382.

2) Samuel E Stemen, b April 7, 1870, near Elida, O, d. May 26, 1906, m. Mary E Heatwole, b April 3, 1868, d June 8, 1923 Both were buried in the Salem cemetery. Samuel came to his death by attempting to save his oldest son from drowning while they had gone fishing His son Clifford had fallen into deep water and the father jumped into the water being a good swimmer but for some reason sank to the bottom of the stream, while his son made his escape. He lived near Elida, O Farmer Mennonites.

1 Clifford O Stemen, b Sept 10, 1894 No 2387.
2 Robert M Stemen, b Dec. 10, 1895 No 2388.
3. Alma V Stemen, b Feb 16, 1897 No 3482.
4. Gabriel I Stemen, b. Aug. 16, 1898 No 2389.
5 Marie E Stemen, b Feb 6, 1901 No 2391
6 Lydia Ann Stemen, b Oct 11, 1902. No 2390
7 John Milton Stemen, b May 14, 1905. No 2392

No. 2387. Sixth Generation. 2386.

1) Clifford O Stemen, b Sept 10, 1894, m May 18, 1936, Marjorie Gwinn

No. 2388. Sixth Generation. 2386.

2) Robert M Stemen, b Dec 10, 1895, m Dec 28, 1930, Marguerite Franks, b Sept 12, 1906 Address Goshen, Ind Restaurant operator. Mennonites
1 Mary Ann Stemen, b Dec 15, 1931
2 Jane Stemen, b May 29, 1934, d same day.
3 James Arthur Stemen, b ————

349

No. 2389. Sixth Generation. 2386.

4) Gabriel L. Stemen, b Aug 16, 1898, m Fern Gardner Restaurant operator. Address: Iowa City, Ia.

1. Alice Marie Stemen, b ——————.

No. 2390. Sixth Generation. 2386.

6) Lydia Ann Stemen, b. Oct. 11, 1902, m Sept 25, 1927, Guy Smoker, b. Nov. 24, 1902 Clerk in post office Mennonites Address· Osceola, Ind, R. 1.

1. David Eugene Smoker, b Jan 22, 1930
2. James Samuel Smoker, b Aug 31, 1932
3. Diane Elizabeth Smoker, b June 4, 1936

No. 2391. Sixth Generation. 2386.

5) Elsie Marie Stemen, b Feb. 6, 1901, m May 17, 1930, Fred Stone Thurston, b. Sept 4, 1896. Address 5005 Ferdinand St, Chicago, Ill Housewife Mennonite.

1. Fred Stone Thurston, Jr, b April 1, 1931
2 Dolores Ellen Thurston, b Jan. 17, 1933.

No. 2392. Sixth Generation. 2386.

7) John Milton Stemen, b May 14, 1905, m May 28, 1927, Adeline L Higgins, b. July 17, 1904. Restaurant waiter Mennonites Address: 101 Lawndale, Goshen, Ind

1. Mary Carolyn Stemen, b July 30, 1928
2. John Roger Stemen, b July 27, 1931

No. 2393. Fifth Generation. 2335.

3) Anna B. Stemen, b. Dec 19, 1871, near Elida, O , m. Jan. 25, 1894, John S Ross, b. April 26, 1870, d. Feb 21, 1935 Address Gulfport, Miss Farmer. Mennonites. Buried in Gulfport Evergreen cemetery.

1. Edith Amanda Ross, b April 3, 1895. No 2394
2. Ernest Allen Ross, b June 17, 1896. No. 2395.
3. Lydia Amelia Ross, b Dec. 17, 1897. No 2396
4. Justus Isaac Ross, b. Oct. 8, 1899. No 2397.
5. Beulah Ann Ross, b. Oct 7, 1901 No. 2398.
6. J. Sherman Ross, b Dec 28, 1902. No 2399
7. Howard Stemen Ross, b. April 29, 1904, single
8. George Willis Ross, b Dec 7, 1907. No 2400.
9. Myron Elliott Ross, b Nov 15, 1908. No. 2401.
10. Vernon Steiner Ross, b. May 1, 1910, twin. No. 3586.
11. Virgil Franklin Ross, b. May 1, 1910, twin No. 2302.
12. Geneva Catherine Ross, b. Nov. 11, 1912. No. 2403

No. 2394. Sixth Generation. 2393.

1) Edith Amanda Ross, b April 3, 1895, m April 24, 1922, Russell B Wenger, b. April 24, 1890. Address. Gulfport, Miss. Farmer. Mennonite

1. Ruby Lee Wenger, b Feb 3, 1923.
2. Edna Mae Wenger, b Mar. 16, 1926

No. 2395. Sixth Generation. 2393.

2) Ernest Allen Ross, b June 17, 1896, m. Feb 13, 1921, Ethel Pears, b July 17, 1901. Sh.pbuilder and trapper at Anchorage, Alaska From his biography the following is taken· Heroic efforts of his wife who sped with him over Alaskan trails by dog team were made to save the life of Ernest A Ross, a native of Lima, O., and a World War veteran, according to word received here Ross who was

a trapper in the Susitna Valley near Anchorage, Alaska, became ill about two weeks before his death while making his rounds of his trap lines His wife lashed him to a sled and traveled a full day to reach an Indian runner who dashed all night to a telephone by which an airplane was summoned Despite the efforts he died before medical aid was obtained Military funeral services were held Monday on the Motorship Discoverer, in Cook Inlet. Attending the funeral were 50 American Legion members, the widow and son Ernest. He was buried at sea. The widow's address is Anchorage, Alaska He d Mar. 23, 1935.

    1. Ernest Allen Ross, Jr , b Sept 23, 1923

No. 2396. Sixth Generation. 2393.

    3) Lydia Amelia Ross, b. Dec. 17, 1897, m Oct. 22, 1917, Stephen S. Vercoe, b. Oct. 12, 1897. Address Gulfport, Miss Mechanic and plumber. Mennonites.

    1. Ross Sherman Vercoe, b April 26, 1919.
    2 Amy Eileen Vercoe, b Nov 14, 1921.
    3. Edith Elaine Vercoe, b. Nov. 18, 1922.
    4. Doris Marie Vercoe, b Dec. 26, 1924.
    5. John Stephen Vercoe, b Aug 28, 1926

No. 2397. Sixth Generation. 2393.

    4) Justus Isaac Ross, b. Oct. 8, 1899, m Oct. 12. 1923, Etta M. Davis, b. Oct. 16, 1901. Address: Gulfport, Miss. Plumber Mennonites.

    1. Douglas Wayne Ross, b Aug. 4, 1926.
    2 Nera Anita Ross, b Mar. 11, 1935

No. 2398. Sixth Generation. 2393.

    5) Beulah Ann Ross, b Oct 7, 1901, m. Oct. 24, 1921, in Portland, Oreg., Harvard C. Speakman Address: 1126 W. Arch St , Shamokin, Pa. Methodists. Electric welder

    1. Harvard J. Speakman, Jr., b May 31, 1923.

No. 2399. Sixth Generation. 2393.

    6) John Sherman Ross, b Dec 28, 1902, m. Jan. 21, 1928, Rita Wenger, b. Nov. 23, 1908 Address· Gulfport, Miss. Hotel manager. Mennonite.

    1. Richard Sherman Ross, b Oct. 21, 1929.
    2. Don Owen Ross, b. Sept. 13, 1930.

No. 2400. Sixth Generation. 2393.

    8) George Willis Ross, b Dec. 7, 1907, m. Mary V. Hoover, b. Nov. 1, 1909. They live in Toledo, O , R. 3.

    1. Reta Carolyn Ross, b May 6, 1934.
    2. Elaine Marie Ross, b Aug 31, 1936.

No. 2401. Sixth Generation. 2393.

    9) Myron Elliott Ross, b Nov. 15, 1908, m. April 1, 1935, Margaret E. Vick, b Jan 20, 1918 Address· Gulfport, Miss. Mennonite Musician.

    1. Gordon Conrad Ross, b Feb 29, 1936.

No. 2402. Sixth Generation. 2393.

    11) Virgil F. Ross, b. May 1, 1910, m Nov 1, 1934, Nellie Bauer. Address: Mobile, Ala. Mill worker Mennonites

No. 2403. Sixth Generation. 2393.

    12) Geneva Catherine Ross, b Nov 11, 1912, m. May 16, 1933, Dennis W Sheehan. Mechanic Mennonites

    1. Ronald D Sheehan, b April 2, 1934
    2. John Charles Sheehan, b Dec 31, 1937.

No. 2404. Fifth Generation. 2385.

4) Amanda Jane Stemen, b Dec. 17, 1873, near Elida, O , m Jan. 25, 1894, Henry B. D.ller, b. April 21, 1866, d June 18, 1916. Farmer. Mennonites. Address: Lima O., R. 3 Buried in Salem cemetery.
1. Lela Pauline Diller, b Dec 8, 1894 No 2405
2. Harry Stemen Diller, b. Mar 20, 1900 No. 2406.
3. Lois Elizabeth Diller, b Mar 31, 1903, single
4. Vernon Samuel Diller, b Nov. 20, 1908. No 2407.
5. Grace Amanda Diller, b July 10, 1911, d. Feb 14, 1927

No. 2405. Sixth Generation. 2404.

1) Lela Pauline Diller, b Dec 8, 1894, near Elida, O , m Feb 14, 1914, Emery Edwin Layman, b May 12, 1892 Address Lima, O , R 4 Carpenter Mennonites
1. Henry Edwin Layman, b Feb 9, 1916 No. 3483
2. Dorothy Mabel Layman, b April 29, 1918.
3 Ernest Diller Layman, b April 13, 1920
4. Oliver Wayne Layman, b Feb 9, 1922
5. Mary Alice Layman, b June 12, 1924.
6. Carl Emerson Layman, b June 22, 1927
7. Grace Irene Layman, b. July 4, 1930

No. 2406. Sixth Generation. 2404.

2) Harry Stemen Diller, b Mar 20, 1899, near Elida, O , m April 20, 1922, Nellie Lantz, b Feb. 16, 1903 Address Elida, O , R 2 Stock dealer and farmer Mennonites.
1. Kenneth Samuel Diller, b Mar 5, 1923
2 Doris Pauline Diller, b Oct 14, 1926
3. Helen Lois Diller, b Mar 23, 1938.

No. 2407. Sixth Generation. 2404.

4) Vernon Samuel Diller, b Nov 20, 1907, near Elida, O., m Sept 3, 1932, Beulah Glade Wagner, b Nov 12, 1910. Address Cummins, Mich Farmer Mennonite
1. Wayne William Diller, b Jan 28, 1934
2 Paul Henry Diller, b Oct 4, 1936

No. 2408. Fifth Generation. 2385.

4) George W Stemen, b Dec 14, 1875, near Elida, O , d Nov. —, 1922, m April 6, 1902, Bertha M. Hartzler, b Oct 31, 1879 Railway mail clerk Mrs Stemen's address: Lima, O , R 4 Buried in Salem cemetery near Elida, O
1. Lawrence Stemen, b Feb 6, 1904 No 2409.
2. Wanda Stemen, b Dec 5, 1905 No 2410
3. Edith Stemen, b Aug. 31, 1907 No 2411.
4 Wayne S Stemen, b July 15, 1909 No 2412
5 Bertha Stemen, b Mar 2, 1915 No 3587
6. Dorothy Stemen, b Jan 27, 1917 No 3588
7 Gerald Stemen, b. Aug 27, 1920

No. 2409. Sixth Generation. 2408.

1) Lawrence Stemen, b Feb 6, 1904, m June 15, 1927, Helen McAllister, b. July 16, 1904, d ——————— Address. Lamontier Ave , Cleveland, O. Street-car conductor No children He married (2nd) ——————, she died, he married (3rd) Mary Koren, in 1937.

No. 2410. Sixth Generation. 2408.

2) Wanda Stemen, b Dec 5, 1905, m July 4, 1924, Allen Neely, b Jan 28, 1902. Painter Address. Lima, O., R. 7.
1 Norman Neely, b April 12, 1926.
2 Milton Neely, b. Nov 10, 1927.
3 Marilyn Neely, b Mar 22, 1931
4 Larry Neely, b May 14, 1932

No. 2411. Sixth Generation. 2408.

3) Edith Stemen, b Aug 31, 1907, m Mat Weiman Address· Lima, O. Machinist.
1 Bettie Weiman, b Feb 11, 1926
2. Virginia Weiman, b Aug 30, 1927.

No. 2412. Sixth Generation. 2408.

4) Wayne S. Stemen, b July 15, 1909, m June 15, 1933, Velma Deffendeffin, b June 26, 1912. Motorman on Cleveland St Railway. Address· 13606 Union Ave., Cleveland, O Methodist
1 Barbara Ann Stemen, b June 16, 1936

No. 2413. Fifth Generation. 2385.

6) Simeon B Stemen, b Nov 28, 1877, m Oct 21, 1899, Mary Brenneman, b Mar. 20, 1881 Rural mail carrier from Elida, O Mennonites Address Lima, O, R 3
1 Una Irene Stemen, b May 16, 1901 No 2414
2 Lewis Isaac Stemen, b July 22, 1904 No 2415
3 Martha L Stemen, b Sept 4, 1915 No 2416
4. Amanda S Stemen, b Dec 17, 1919.

No. 2414. Sixth Generation. 2413.

1) Una Irene Stemen, b May 16, 1901, m Nov 26, 1919, Benjamin Hoover, b. Mar 23, 1895 Address Lima, O, R 4. Machinist
1. Virgil Hoover, b Sept 9, 1920.
2 Eileen Hoover, b Nov 7, 1923

No. 2415. Sixth Generation. 2413.

2) Lewis Isaac Stemen, b July 22, 1904, m Sept 6, 1929, Grace Lantz, b Mar 5, 1910 Address Elida, O, R 2 Farmer Mennonites
1 Chester Lewis Stemen, b Jan 2, 1938.

No. 2416. Sixth Generation. 2413.

3) Martha L Stemen, b Sept 4, 1915, m John Swartz, b Oct 17, 1911. Address Delphos, O, R 2
1. Dennis Swartz, b May 31, 1937.

No. 2417. Fifth Generation. 2385.

7) Rhoda E Stemen, b Dec 31, 1879, near Elida, O, m Oct 21, 1899, Andrew S Shenk, b July 29, 1878 Address. Elida, O, where they reside Mennonites.
1. Menno Wilson Shenk, b Nov 16, 1900 No 2418
2 Carol W Shenk, b May 20, 1902 No. 2419
3. Oliver W Shenk, b Nov 2, 1903. No 2420
4 Edgar Shenk, b July 28, 1906 No. 2421
5 Rhoda Shenk, b June 24, 1908 No 2422
6 Margaret Shenk, b May 26, 1910 No 2423

7. Roland Shenk, b Dec 22, 1911.

8. Louis Shenk, b. June 30, 1915. No. 166¼.

No. 2418. Sixth Generation. 2417.

1) Menno Wilson Shenk, b Nov 16, 1900, m May 18, 1926, Doris Dale, b Sept 30, 1903. Address: Lima, O Railroad fireman No issue.

No. 2419. Sixth Generation. 2417.

2) Carol W. Shenk, b May 20, 1902, m Aug 30, 1931, Olive Irene Comps, b. June 29, 1907. Address Lima, O , R 3 Mail carrier. Mennonites.

1. Marjorie Sue Shenk, b Jan. 16, 1934.
2. Ruby Janelle Shenk, b Oct 7, 1935
3. Stanley Jon Shenk, b Dec 28, 1936

No. 2420. Sixth Generation. 2417.

3) Oliver W Shenk, b. Nov. 2, 1903, m April 12, 1936, Vita Davis, b. —————————. Address: 21 Winetta Lane, New York City, N. Y.

An adopted son, James Andrew Shenk, b July 13, 1935

1 Brian Elizabeth Shenk, b Jan 3, 1937

No. 2421. Sixth Generation. 2417.

4) Edgar Shenk, b. July 28, 1906, m. Mar , 1931, May Bennett, of Goshen, Ind. Address: Pittsburgh, Pa Greyhound bus driver. No issue.

No. 2422. Sixth Generation. 2417.

5) Rhoda Shenk, b June 24, 1908, m Mar 3, 1932, Jeffrey A. Hatton. Mill worker. Methodists. Address: Lima, O., R. 4.

1. Margaret Lillian Hatton, b. Dec 4, 1932.
2. William Wilson Hatton, b. Jan. 18, 1935.

No. 2423. Sixth Generation. 2417.

6) Margaret Shenk, b. May 26, 1910, m. May 31, 1931, Menno E. Yoder, b. Sept. 17, 1905. Assembly of God. Minister. Address: 208 Hall St , Orrville, O. Laborer.

1. J. Wallace Yoder, b. Mar 26, 1932.
2. David Winston Yoder, b. Dec 22, 1933.
3. Rhoda Eilene Yoder, b. May 8, 1935.
4. Gerald Andrew Yoder, b Sept. 6, 1936

No. 2424. Fifth Generation. 2385.

7) Lydia C. Stemen, b. Sept 22, 1881, near Elida, O , m. April 21, 1909, C. Sherman Swartz, b. Aug. 3, 1881, in Va. Address Elida, O., R. 1. Farmer and mechanic Mennonites. Burial in Salem cemetery near Elida, O. Related, come in two ways. See No 326 for family.

No. 2425. Fifth Generation. 2385.

8) Martha M. Stemen, b Sept 7, 1883, near Elida, O., m Ami Messinger of near Bluffton, O. Address: Elida, O.

Adopted son, Ronald Messinger, b ——————

No. 2426. Fourth Generation. 42.

4) Anna Brenneman, b. April 1, 1842, in Fairfield Co., O , d May 9, 1930, near Elida, O She married Rev. Christian Good of Mole Hill in Rockingham Co , Va., Nov. 9, 1892, where she lived until his death in Feb , 1916, and where he was buried. Shortly after his death she returned to her former home in Allen Co , O , where she lived until her death, and was buried in the Salem cemetery near Elida, O. Her earlier life before marriage was spent in caring for her parents No issue

No. 2427. Fourth Generation. 42.

5) Henry A. Brenneman, b. Sept. 7, 1844, in Fairfield Co., O., m Mary Virginia Rhodes, b. May 31, 1848, in Rockingham Co, Va She died Nov. 10, 1925, and was buried in Va. Henry was instantly killed by lightning Aug 28, 1872 while assisting a neighbor in measuring up some wheat in his barn. They lived near Elida, O., and he was buried in the Salem cemetery at that place They were related. For full history see No. 251.

1. Timothy H. Brenneman, b. July 14, 1871, d. Jan 28, 1905

No. 2428. Fourth Generation. 42.

6) Moses Brenneman, b. May 4, 1846, in Fairfield Co., O., d Jan. 22, 1923 On Oct. 1, 1870, he married Mary A Stemen, of Elida, O , b. Aug. 20, 1850. She died Aug 5, 1925. Both were buried in the Salem cemetery near Elida, O. Mennonites. At the age of nine years he came with his parents from Franklin Co, to Sugar Creek Twp., Allen Co , O , where he grew to manhood on the 175 acre farm that his father had purchased soon after settling in this county Soon after his marriage he purchased 74 acres of the old homestead from his father which he improved and lived on until his death Mr. Brenneman was a model farmer of his day, and a respected citizen in the community where he lived. At the age of twenty years he united with the Mennonite Church in Allen Co., and on the 10th of Sept., 1885, was ordained to the ministry in which he served faithfully until his death. He was naturally of a strong spiritual disposition, and by some was thought inclined to look on the serious side of life, yet always of a cheerful nature even when under severe trials In the church he stood firm in his convictions, yet could yield to others when he found himself in the wrong Address. Lima, O , R. 3.

1. Infant son, b July 24, 1872, d same day.
2. Menno Brenneman, b Sept 27, 1873, d Oct 24, 1873.
3. Andrew J. Brenneman, b Feb. 7, 1875 No. 2429.
4 John M Brenneman, b Mar. 31, 1877. No 2433.
5. Simeon Brenneman, b Mar 4, 1879 No 2436.
6 Moses Brenneman, Jr , b Mar 31, 1881 No. 2437.
7. Rudy R Brenneman, b Feb 28, 1883. No. 2438
8 Adam S Brenneman, b. Oct 3, 1884. No. 2439.
9 Martha J Brenneman, b Jan 19, 1887 No 2439¼
10 Alpheus N Brenneman, b April 22, 1892. No. 2440.
11 Mary Ellen Brenneman, b July 23, 1894 Teacher.

No. 2429. Fifth Generation. 2428.

3) Andrew Brenneman, b Feb 7, 1875, near Elida, O , m Sarah Elizabeth Durr, b April 9, 1879, she died from the accidental explosion of oil in a coal stove May 21, 1935 Burial in the Salem cemetery near Elida Farmer. Mennonites On May 21, 1905, he was ordained to the ministry at the Pike Church near Elida. O. A few years later he moved with his family to Plainview, Tex , where he served as pastor for a few years, after which he returned to his former home at Elida, O. He has served as pastor of the Central Mennonite Church at Elida since 1925. Address Elida, O., R 1

1. John D. Brenneman, b Sept 5, 1901 No 2430
2 Paul E Brenneman, b Feb 10, 1904 No 2431.
3 Timothy H. Brenneman, b. Oct 7, 1905. No. 2432
4. Mary Esther Brenneman, b Nov 30, 1908 No. 3706.
5 Ruth Elizabeth Brenneman, b Jan 27, 1912
6 Moses Sampson Brenneman, b Sept. 29, 1915

No. 2430. Sixth Generation. 2429.

1) John D Brenneman, b Sept. 5, 1901, m June 30, 1934, Alma Miller, of near Lima, O Church of the Brethren Address 1340 Grand Blvd, Detroit, Mich. Mercantile business.

1 John Lynwood Brenneman, b. Aug 3, 1935

No. 2431. Sixth Generation. 2429.

2) Paul E. Brenneman, b Feb 10, 1904, m Dec 26, 1931, Mildred Purdy, b Dec 5, 1908 Both are teaching school Methodists Address· Olton Route, Plainview, Tex

1 Richard Purdy Brenneman, b Dec 17, 1932

No. 2432. Sixth Generation. 2429.

3) Timothy H Brenneman, b Oct 7, 1905, m May, 1928, Rowena J Leedy, b July 24, 1906 Related, see No 336 Mennonites Ordained for missionary to South America Sept 11, 1938, at Central Mennonite Church, Elida, O Address. Pehuajo, F C O, Buenos Aires, S A

1 Patricia Ann Brenneman, b Aug 24, 1931
2 Donald Leedy Brenneman, b Feb 19, 1934

No. 2433. Fifth Generation. 2423.

4) John M. Brenneman, b Mar 31, 1877, near Elida, O, m Anna G. Good, b Sept 9, 1885 They were married Dec 25, 1904 Farmer. Mennonites Burial place in Salem cemetery near Elida, O Address· Elida, O, R 1

1 Eva Blanche Brenneman, b. Nov 5, 1905, single
2 Victor Laverne Brenneman, b Jan 5, 1908 No 2434
3 Walter Ray Brenneman, b June 8, 1911 No 2435
4 Ralph Alpheus Brenneman, b April 5, 1913
5 Anna Grace Brenneman, b Sept 23, 1914
6 Frederick Ernest Brenneman, b May 15, 1917
7 Clara Elizabeth Brenneman, b July 13, 1919
8 Simon Peter Brenneman, b June 11, 1923.
9. John M Brenneman, Jr, b Mar 6, 1925.
10 B Andrew Brenneman, b Sept 5, 1928
11 Luella May Brenneman, b May 21, 1933.

No. 2434. Sixth Generation. 2433.

2) Victor Laverne Brenneman, b Jan 5, 1908, d. Mar 19, 1937, m Mar 1, 1929, Maxine Ashton, b. June 27, 1906 Address. Elida, O, R 1 Electrician

1 Victor L. Brenneman, Jr, b Aug 26, 1929
2 Walter A Brenneman, b. Mar 9, 1931

No. 2435. Sixth Generation. 2433.

3) Walter Ray Brenneman, b June 8, 1911, m April 1, 1934, Martha Musselman, b Feb. 11, 1915 Address Lima, O Mechanic

No. 2436. Fifth Generation. 2423.

5) Simeon Brenneman, b Mar 4, 1879, near Elida, O, m Jan 1, 1908, Lillie A. Burkholder, b. April 27, 1883, near Dale Enterprise, Va Farmer Mennonites Address Elida, O, R 1 Related, see No 605

1 Edwin S. Brenneman, b Dec 9, 1908
2 Mary Evelyn Brenneman, b Mar 11, 1913
3 Robert E. Brenneman, b Jan 28, 1915

No. 2437. Fifth Generation. 2428.

6) Moses H Brenneman, Jr., b Mar 31, 1881, near Elida, O., m Oct 12, 1910, Lillie Mae Geiger, b Sept 18, 1883. Address. Elida, O., R. 1 Farmer Mennonites.

1. Geneva Elizabeth Brenneman, b April 24, 1914
2 Mary Gladys Brenneman, b June 11, 1917.

No. 2438. Fifth Generation. 2428.

7) Rudy R Brenneman, b Feb. 28, 1883, near Elida, O, m. Feb 15, 1911, Elnora Hilty, b Oct 5, 1884, near New Stark, O Farmer and poultryman. Mennonites Address Lima, O, R 3 Burial ground in Salem cemetery, Sugar Creek Twp., Allen Co, O

1 Leland H. Brenneman, b July 31, 1912
2 Mary Florence Brenneman, b April 8, 1918
3 John M Brenneman, b Feb 19, 1921
4 Marjorie June Brenneman, b June 12, 1925.

No. 2439. Fifth Generation. 2428.

8) Adam S Brenneman, b Oct 3, 1884, near Elida, O, m. Mar 18, 1914, Lessie Elizabeth Diller, b July 15, 1892 Address Elida, O Dry cleaner at Lima, O Mennonites

1 Richard L Brenneman, b April 5, 1916
2 Paul William Brenneman, b Mar 2, 1921, d. July 8, 1934
3 Alice Ann Brenneman, b July 28, 1926

No. 2439¼. Fifth Generation. 2428.

9) Martha J Brenneman, b July 19, 1887, near Elida, O Martha remained at home and cared for her parents until they died Her sister Mary Ellen was a schoolteacher for several years after wh ch they resided on the old home with their youngest brother until 1936, when he married, after which they moved into their present home two miles north of Elida, O Address Elida, O, R 1 Mennonites

No. 2440. Fifth Generation. 2428.

10) Alpheus N Brenneman, b April 22, 1892, near Elida, O, m June 2, 1936, Ellen B Landes, of Lititz, Pa, b Sept. 9, 1890 They live on the old homestead where Alpheus was born and lived all h.s life Address Lima O, R 3 Farmer Mennonites No issue.

No. 2441. Fourth Generation. 42.

8) Catherine Brenneman, b Dec 10, 1849, in Fairfield Co, O, d at Gulfport, Miss, Nov. 19, 1926, m Daniel S Brunk, b Feb 8, 1857, near Harrisonburg, Va Farmer Mennonites Mr Brunk was ordained to the ministry at the Salem Church near Elida, O, July 1, 1888 He lives at Harrisonburg, Va. Mrs Brunk was buried in the Salem cemetery near Elida, O

1. Jacob B Brunk, b Sept 24, 1877 No 2442
2 John M Brunk, b Oct 15, 1879 No 2445
3 Annie R Brunk, b June 30, 1881 No 2446
4 Jesse H Brunk, b Dec 2, 1884 No 2449
5. Infant daughter (stillborn) in 1878

No. 2442. Fifth Generation. 2441.

1) Jacob B Brunk, b Sept 24, 1877, near Elida, O, m April 21, 1901, Ada V Shank, b. June 27, 1871, near Versailles, Mo Schoolteacher until 1931 Minister in the Mennonite Church until 1927 when he changed his membership to the Church of God Address 523 Matthews St, Sikeston, Mo

1. Esther Marie Brunk, b. Mar. 30, 1902 Single A missionary in Argentina, South America
2. Ruth Minerva Brunk, b. June 15, 1904.
3. Sharon Daniel Brunk, b May 1, 1907. No 2443
4. Geneva Kathryn Brunk, b May 1, 1912. No. 2444

No. 2443. Sixth Generation. 2442.

3) Sharon Daniel Brunk, b May 1, 1907, m June 17, 1933, Cleo Elma Cook, b. Sept. 9, 1907. Address: 607 N Fairview, Lansing, Mich Laborer Mennonites.
1. Bonnie Lucille Brunk, b April 9, 1934

No. 2444. Sixth Generation. 2442.

4) Geneva Kathryn Brunk, b May 1, 1912, m Feb 14, 1936, Joe S Montague at Anderson, Ind

No. 2445. Fifth Generation. 2441.

2) John M. Brunk, b Oct. 15, 1879, near Elida, O , d at Gulfport, Miss., Nov. 12, 1930 He married Sept 9, 1900, Annie E. Rhodes, b. Mar. 13, 1876, in Va. Farmer. Carpenter. Mennonites. He was a minister Buried at Gulfport, Miss
1. Wilmer S. Brunk, b July 14, 1901.
2 Zela K. Brunk, b July 10, 1903, d June 21, 1908.
3. Grace A. Brunk, b. April 16, 1906
4. Orvin S. Brunk, b. Aug 16, 1908.
5. Gladys V. Brunk, b. Aug. 26, 1911
6. Ada Mae Brunk, b July 14, 1916, d July 16, 1916

No. 2445. Fifth Generation. 2441.

3) Anna R Brunk, b June 30, 1881, near New Stark, O., m. Feb 14, 1901, Amos W. Rhodes, b. Nov 23, 1873, in Va Farmer Mennonites Mr. Rhodes is a deacon in the Mennonite Church Address La Junta, Colo Burial place in La Junta cemetery.
1. Marvin D. Rhodes, b. July 30, 1903 No. 2447.
2 John E. Rhodes, b. Dec 31, 1904. No. 2448.
3. Edna C. Rhodes, b. July 29, 1910, d April 13, 1932
4. Vernon S. Rhodes, b Jan 10, 1920
(Adopted) son Paul James Rhodes, b July 18, 1926.

No. 2447. Sixth Generation. 2446.

1) Marvin D. Rhodes, b July 30, 1903, near La Junta, Colo , m Dec 12, 1932, Hazel C. Schertz. Farmer Mennonites. Address. La Junta, Colo., R. 1

No. 2448. Sixth Generation. 2446.

2) John E. Rhodes, b Dec. 31, 1904, near La Junta, Colo , m Mar 6, 1926. Grace Edith Snyder. Address La Junta, Colo Farmer Mennonites
1. Leland C. Rhodes, b. Dec 26, 1927.
2. John Edward Rhodes, Jr., b Jan 1, 1931

No. 2449. Fifth Generation. 2441.

4) Jesse H Brunk, b. Dec 2, 1884, near New Stark, O , m. Nov. 29, 1906, Myrtie C Berry, b. May 29, 1885, near Harrisonburg, Va. Farmer Mennonites Jesse died Mar. 11, 1916, near Hesston, Kans Buried at the Pennsylvania Church near Hesston.
1. Olive Marie Brunk, b. Mar 15, 1908 No 2450.
2. Mary Kathryn Brunk, b. May 8, 1911 No 2451
3. Zelma Virginia Brunk, b April 20, 1915

No. 2450. Sixth Generation. 2449.

1) Olive Marie Brunk, b Mar. 15, 1908, m June 16, 1929, Lewis W. Geil, b Dec. 4, 1907. Address Gulfport, Miss, R 1 Laborer. Mennonites.

1. Robert Gordon Geil, b. Sept. 5, 1930.

No. 2451. Sixth Generation. 2449.

2) Mary Kathryn Brunk, b. May 8, 1911, m. July 9, 1932, Paul L. Yoder, b. Sept 30, 1909. Broom manufacturer Address: Lyman, Miss.

1 Paul Kenneth Yoder, b. ————, 1933.

No. 2452. Fourth Generation. 42.

9) Levi Brenneman, b July 27, 1851, in Fairfield Co, O., d. Nov 13, 1905, m. Emma Coyle, b Feb 19, 1850, of DeKalb Co, Ind She died April 4, 1917. Both were buried in the Salem cemetery near Elida, O. Farmer. Mennonites Address: Lima, O, R 3 No children

No. 2453. Fourth Generation. 42.

12) Magdalena Brenneman, b June 30, 1857, near Elida, O, m Dec 26, 1876, John Blosser, b Aug 5, 1855, near Bluffton, O, d July 28, 1921. In 1869 he with his mother and family moved to near New Stark, O, where he has since resided Farmer. Mennonites He was ordained to the ministry in 1891 and to the office of bishop in 1905 He regarded these calls to service and responsibility with great seriousness and never spared himself to fulfill his obligations in this work. In his earlier work of the ministry he spent much t.me, and often with great personal sacrifice, in evangelistic work of the Mennonite Church, with a marked degree of success He had for many years been especially interested in the educational welfare of our young people in his own church He was for a number of years president of the Mennonite Board of Education, and a warm supporter of Goshen College He was for a number of years an ardent supporter of the Book and Tract Society of the church, of which he was president He did not live to a great age, but he lived rapidly and much, and his life was filled to an unusual degree with a full measure of difficulty and success, its joys and sorrows, its love and service and sacrifices He was laid to rest in the Hassen cemetery near New Stark, O, his home community.

1. Katherine Blosser, b. Nov. 9, 1878 No. 2454.
2. Christian B. Blosser, b Aug. 9, 1880 No 2455
3. Naomi Blosser, b. Dec 13, 1882, d July —, 1937, single
4. Lessie Blosser, b. Sept. 3, 1885. No. 2458.
5 Timothy Henry Blosser, b. July 27, 1888. No. 2459.
6. John Marcus Blosser, b June 23, 1890. No. 2460
7 Mary Magdalene Blosser, b. Jan. 13, 1897. No. 2461.

No. 2454. Fifth Generation. 2453.

1) Katherine Blosser, b Nov 9, 1878, near New Stark, O., m May 30, 1912, John Andrew Hilty, b Jan 17, 1878 They served at the Orphans' Home at West Liberty, O, for several years as superintendent and matron and assisted in the Los Angeles Mennonite Mission for several years. Later they united with the community church at their present address 121 Wilder Ave, Goshen, Ind.

1. John Maurice Hilty, b Aug. 16, 1913
2 James David Hilty, b Nov. 21, 1916

No. 2455. Fifth Generation. 2453.

2) Christian B. Blosser, b Aug. 9, 1880, near New Stark, O, m June 20, 1906, Carrie Mae Yoder, b Aug 10, 1882 He taught public school for several years after which he taught for several years in the Goshen College where he also

served as its dean for awhile Because of failing health he resigned and served for years as county agent for the farm bureau of Elkhart Co , Ind. Mennonites. Address: 1013 S. 11th St., Goshen, Ind.

1. Ralph Yoder Blosser, b. Mar. 22, 1907. No. 2456.
2. Christine Janet Blosser, b. Dec. 13, 1910 No. 2457.
3. James Richard Blosser, b. Oct. 9, 1915
4. Sara Magdalene Blosser, b. April 3, 1918
5 Henry Franklin Blosser, b Aug. 31, 1924.

No. 2456. Sixth Generation. 2455.

1) Ralph Yoder Blosser, b Mar. 22, 1907, m Aug. 28, 1935, Elizabeth Habeggar, of Berne, Ind. Ralph is teaching school Address. Pine Ridge, Ky.

No. 2457. Sixth Generation. 2455.

2) Christine J. Blosser, b Dec 13, 1910, m Dec 23, 1934, John E Hartzler, Jr. Address Jeromesville, O Teaching.

No. 2458. Fifth Generation. 2453.

4) Lessie Blosser, b Sept. 3, 1885, near New Stark, O , m June 16, 1914, Joseph D Yoder, b Jan 14, 1886. He is a chemical engineer Address: 4 Cliff Way, Larchmont, N Y.

1 Joseph Yoder, Jr , b Sept. 28, 1916
2. John Blosser Yoder, b. April 21, 1920.
3 Mary Louise Yoder, b Nov 14, 1924.

No. 2459. Fifth Generation. 2453.

5) Timothy H. Blosser, b. July 27, 1888, near New Stark, O , m June 4, 1913, Iva E. Stahly, b. Aug. 11, 1888 Farmer Mennonites Mr Blosser is a lover of fine Holstein cows Burial place is at Union (Twp) Center, Elkhart Co., Ind Address. Nappanee, Ind.

1. John Robert Blosser, b. April 11, 1914
2. Timothy Hofert Blosser, b. Jan 7, 1920.
3. George Edgar Blosser, b Nov 23, 1925

No. 2460. Fifth Generation. 2453.

6) John Marcus Blosser, b June 23, 1891, near New Stark, O., m Mar 15, 1916, Ella Mabel Breckbill, b Sept. 3, 1891. Produce dealer Mennonite Brethren in Christ. Address: 402 N. Ind Ave., Goshen, Ind.

1. Paul Marcus Blosser, b Mar. 5, 1917
2. Fred Breckbill Blosser, b Sept. 21, 1919
3. John Henry Blosser, b Nov 11, 1921.
4 Bettie Marie Blosser, b Dec 26, 1929
5. Rosemary Elaine Blosser, b. Mar 8, 1933.

No. 2461. Fifth Generation. 2453.

7) Mary M Blosser, b. Jan. 13, 1898, near New Stark, O., m June 14, 1922, Orie Benjamin Gerig, b Jan 18, 1894 Mr Gerig was sent to France in Near East Relief work during the World War, and after the war closed was appointed by the United States government in the League of Nations, and sent to Geneva, Switzerland where they still are located (1939) Member of Society of Friends Address 23 Ave , Pierre Odier, Geneva, Switzerland

1 Carolyn Janet Gerig, b Dec 23, 1924
2. John Sebastian Gerig, b. Nov. 29, 1930

No. 2462. Fourth Generation. 44.

2) Catherine Brenneman, b Mar 20, 1843, in Fairfield Co , O., d. in Putnam Co., O , Oct 10, 1881, m Christian N Shank, b Dec 6, 1840. Farmer. Mennonites. Address: Oakwood, O

1 Samantha A. Shank, b Mar 13, 1871. No 2463.
2 George B. Shank, b Dec 22, 1872. No. 2464.
3 Catherine Shank, b Nov 27, 1874 No 2465.
4 Marion M. Shank, b Dec. 6, 1876, twin, d Feb 13, 1905
5 Mary M Shank, b Dec 6, 1876, twin No. 2478
6. Samuel C. Shank, b Mar. 28, 1879, single.
7 Infant, b Sept 10, 1881, d same day.

No. 2463. Fifth Generation. 2462.

1) Samantha S Shank, b Mar 13, 1871, m. Mar. 6, 1891, Edward C. Warden, b. Sept 2, 1867. Telegraph operator at Dupont, O. Methodists.

1. Luella Warden, b May 22, 1907 No 3596.
2. Carl E Warden, b Aug. 6, 1911

No. 2464. Fifth Generation. 2462.

2) George B Shank, b. Dec. 22, 1872, m. Dec 22, 1896, Ivy Campbell, b. Dec 22, 1876. Address Danville, O Farmer U B Church.

1. Russell N. Shank, b Jan 16, 1898
2. Ellen D. Shank, b. April 4, 1900.
3. Ralph B Shank, b June 30, 1902

No. 2465. Fifth Generation. 2462.

3) Catherine Shank, b Nov. 27, 1874, m July 19, 1896, L C Reynolds, b. April 9, 1875. Farmer Address Cont nental, O.

1. George O Reynolds, b Sept. 5, 1897.
2 Goldie M. Reynolds, b Feb 7, 1899
3 Frederick L Reynolds, b Aug 13, 1901
4 Albert N Reynolds, b April 4, 1904

No. 2466. Fourth Generation. 44.

3) Lydia Brenneman, b Feb 17, 1845, in Fairfield Co , O , m. Amos Schmidt, Dec 1, 1870 Mrs Schmidt died April 23, 1881 Buried in Salem cemetery near Elida, O. Farmer. Mennonites.

1 Sarah Schmidt, b Oct 2, 1871, single.
2 Anna Schmidt, b July 22, 1873, single
3 Henry Schmidt, b Feb. 18, 1875, single.
4. Samuel Schmidt, b Dec 22, 1876. No 2467.
5. Mary Schmidt, b May 11, 1878, d Aug. 27, 1879.
6. Lydia B Schmidt, b Sept 20, 1880. No 2468

No. 2467. Fifth Generation. 2466.

4) Samuel Smith, b Dec 22, 1876, m Jan 28, 1904, Alice Shupe, b May 5, 1884. Farmer. Mennonites Address Harper, Kans , R. 1.

1. Mary Laura Smith, b. Feb 21, 1907
2. Ruth Alice Smith, b. April 24, 1910
3. Vernon Henry Smith, b Mar 24, 1912.
4. Clyde Earl Smith, b. Feb 13, 1920
5. Edna Irene Smith, b. Oct. 17, 1921.

No. 2468. Fifth Generation. 2466.

6) Lydia Schmidt, b. Sept 20, 1880, m April 25, 1914, Joseph Miller, b May 25, 1885. Mennonites Address Bremen. O Oil field worker.

1 Emma Miller, b April 12, 1915
2. Edna Miller, b Aug 8, 1916
3 Cora Miller, b Feb 9, 1920

No. 2469. Fourth Generation. 44.

4) Nancy Brenneman, b Mar 6, 1847, in Fairfield Co , O , d ————, 1936.
She married Adam R. Hartman He died April 8, 1912 Address Nappanee, Ind.
Farmer. Mennon tes.
1 Anna Hartman, b Aug. 26, 1871, d. June 1, 1897.
2. Amanda Hartman, b Sept. 23, 1873. No 2470.
3. George Hartman, b. Nov. 18, 1876.
4. Cora Hartman, b Oct 30, 1878. No. 2471
5 Franklin Hartman, b. Feb. 1, 1881. No 2472.

No. 2470. Fifth Generation. 2469.

2) Amanda Hartman, b Sept 23, 1873, m. Jan. 6, 1895, Amos Weldy. Farmer.
Mennonites Address: Wakarusa, Ind.
1. Cora Weldy, b Mar 6, 1896
2 Ray Weldy, b ————, 1898.

No. 2471. Fifth Generation. 2469.

4) Cora Hartman, b. Oct. 30, 1878, m. William Shaum.

No. 2472. Fifth Generation. 2469.

5) Franklin Hartman, b Feb. 1, 1881, m. Feb 24, 1902, Anna Mary Weldy,
b Sept 21, 1878. Franklin was ordained minister in the Mennonite Church in
1899. Address: 421 Clossen Court, Ludlow, Ky.
1. Esther Marle Hartman, b Dec 19, 1904 No 2473.
2. Frank Talmadge Hartman, b Feb 25, 1906. No 2474.
3. Dorothy Virginia Hartman, b Aug. 29, 1912
4 Lokata Jeannette Hartman, b Aug 3, 1914.
5. Ruth Edna Hartman, b May 11, 1918

No. 2473. Sixth Generation. 2472.

1) Esther Marie Hartman, b Dec 19, 1904, m Dec 30, 1925, George T.
Howard, b. Sept. 24, 1904 Address 1922 S 48th Court, Cicero, Ill Budget expert.
1 Gene T. Howard, b Nov. 2, 1926
2 Emery Howard, b. Dec 11, 1928

No. 2474. Sixth Generation. 2472.

2) Frank Talmadge Hartman, b Feb. 25, 1906, m. Ruby ————. They
were married Mar 6, 1929. Address. Swarth, Tenn Traveling salesman.

No. 2475. Fourth Generation. 44.

5) Henry Brenneman, b. April 7, 1851, in Allen Co , O He was killed by a
train Sept 18, 1913 He married Dec 4, 1876, Elizabeth Shank, b. Jan 15, 1847
Farmer. Mennon tes Address Ottawa, O
1 Genetta Brenneman, b. Sept 2, 1871 No. 2476
2 Ida Mae Brenneman, b Nov 5, 1872 No 2483.
3. Emma Brenneman, b. Feb 3, 1874, d Dec. 21, 1874
4. Artimens Brenneman, b Oct 26, 1875, d same day
5. Adam Brenneman, b. June 27, 1877. No 2484
6. Margaret Brenneman, b Jan 31, 1880. No. 2486
7. Harry Brenneman, b. Nov 4, 1881 No 3659
8 Delilah Brenneman, b. Dec 20, 1884. No. 3660.
9. Roy Adrian Brenneman, b July 9, 1886 No 2487.

No. 2476. Fifth Generation. 2475.

1) Gennette Brenneman, b. Sept 2, 1871, m Oct 8, 1892, Samuel Clevenger, b April 23, 1870. Address: Stanton, Mich Farmer.

1. Reuben Ambrose Clevenger, b. July 18, 1893, d. July 31, 1918.
2. Belle Esther Clevenger, b April 14, 1895. No. 2477.
3. Clarence Henry Clevenger, b April 1, 1897. No. 2479.
4. Sylvester Clevenger, b. April 19, 1899. No. 2480.
5. Albert Clevenger, b. Oct. 28, 1901. No. 2481.
6. Alvin Clevenger, b. Feb 25, 1904. No. 2482.
7. Samuel Everett Clevenger, b. July 1, 1908.

Note.—Reuben A Clevenger was wounded and placed in the hospital that was bombed by the Germans, where he died He entered service Sept. 19, 1917, and went to France with Company C, 49th infantry.

No. 2477. Sixth Generation. 2476.

2) Belle Esther Clevenger, b April 14, 1895, m. 1918, Emerson Swift, b. Oct. 23, 1897. Address: Vestaburg, Mich. Mechanic

1. Ilah Belle Swift, b. June 1, 1919.
2. Reuben Emerson Swift, b April 24, 1921
3. Gennette Marcella Swift, b Oct. 14, 1922
4. Bettie Marie Swift, b April 20, 1924.
5. Dorlah Mae Swift, b. June 9, 1926.
6. Teddy Everette Swift, b July 18, 1927.
7. Leona Lou Swift, b. Oct 10, 1929.

No. 2478. Fifth Generation. 2462.

5) Mary M Shank, b Dec 6, 1876, m. June 25, 1898, Clyde Ritchie, b. Feb. 12, 1878. Farmer. Evangelical Address Scott, Van Wert Co, O
1. Evaline B. Ritchie, b. May 11, 1899

No. 2479. Sixth Generation. 2476.

3) Clarence Henry Clevenger, b. April 7, 1897, m June 13, 1920, Tressie Buskirk, b Aug 29, 1899. Address: Stanton, Mich., R. 2. Farmer.

1 Dorothy Catherine Clevenger, b Nov 11, 1921
2. Nile Clarence Clevenger, b. Sept 4, 1924.

No. 2480. Sixth Generation. 2476.

3) Sylvester Aden Clevenger, b. April 9, 1899, m Sept. 8, 1929, Ermah Marie Brown, b. Feb 4, 1911. Address. Stanton, Mich. Gas station and garage owner.

No. 2481. Sixth Generation. 2476.

4) Albert Clevenger, b. Oct 28, 1901, m Aug. 10, 1923, Nellie Black, b. Jan. 12, 1905. Rawleigh salesman. Address: Pioneer, O.

1. Wayne Albert Clevenger, b Aug 31, 1924.
2. Kenneth Waldo Clevenger, b April 8, 1927.
3. Cecil Ray Clevenger, b. Aug 8, 1928.
4. Stanley J. Clevenger, b. Mar 30, 1930.

No. 2482. Sixth Generation. 2476.

5) Alvin Clevenger, b Feb 25, 1904, m June 5, 1927, Eunice M. Daniel, b. April 5, 1908. Address: 832 Barry Ave, Chicago, Ill. Elevator operator.

1 Walter Roy Clevenger, b. April 4, 1928
2. Caroline Marie Clevenger, b Dec 11, 1929.

No. 2483. Fifth Generation. 2475.

2) Ida Mae Brenneman, b Nov 3, 1872, m Aug 29, 1891, George W Moore, b. April 1, 1869 Address Rushmore, O Farmer. United Brethren.

1. Flossie Moore, b Mar 20, 1893, d Mar 23, 1893.
2. Beulah Moore, b Mar 8, 1895
3. Infant Moore, b Feb 3, 1897, d same day
4. Ida Moore, b Mar 8, 1898, d next day

No. 2484. Fifth Generation. 2475.

5) Adam Brenneman, b June 27, 1877, m July 22, 1905, Susie Herring, b. Sept 26, 1887 Address. Cloverdale, O , R 2.

1. Waldo Brenneman, b Mar. 3, 1906 No 2485.
2. Paul Orlando Brenneman, b April 8, 1909 No. 3661
3. Myron Brenneman, b. Aug 5, 1910
4. George Henry Brenneman, b Sept. 14, 1912.
5. Ruth Brenneman, b. Oct 14, 1914 No 3658
6. Beulah Brenneman, b Aug 10, 1916
7. Oscar Brenneman, b Sept 20, 1918
8. Leonice Brenneman, b Feb 17, 1921
9. Della Brenneman, b Jan 14, 1923.

No. 2485. Sixth Generation. 2484.

1) Harry Waldo Brenneman, b Mar. 3, 1906, m Dec 24, 1929, Ethel Galliver, b Dec 24, 1909 She is a schoolteacher Address 817½ Elm St., Toledo, O. Baker

1. Ronald Leroy Brenneman, b Nov 6, 1930
2. Lewis Eugene Brenneman, b ——————.
3. Frederick Earl Brenneman, b. ——————
4. Betty June Brenneman, b ——————

No. 2486. Fifth Generation. 2475.

6) Margaret Brenneman, b Jan 31, 1880, m. Nov 15, 1902, George Basinger, b. July 21, 1883, killed on railroad Aug 10, 1916 Address Columbus Grove, O Engineer on railroad.

1. Zeulah Laoma Basinger, b Sept 6, 1905.
2. Illa Marcella Basinger, b. Aug. 22, 1910

No. 2487. Fifth Generation. 2475.

7) Roy Adrian Brenneman, b July 9, 1886, m May 21, 1907, Edith Belle Strite, b June 13, 1883. Address Tekonsha, Mich Farmer.

1. Marie Brenneman, b. Nov. 4, 1911
2. Blanche Brenneman, b. July 28, 1915.
3. Raymond Brenneman, b July 21, 1918.
4. Effie Idell Brenneman, b. Sept 29, 1920
5. Ima Mae Brenneman, b June 10, 1923
6. Harold Adrian Brenneman, b. Mar. 3, 1925.

No. 2488. Fourth Generation. 44.

6) Sarah Brenneman, b Sept 25, 1853, in Putnam Co , O., d Nov. 24, 1934, m. Feb. 3, 1876, Jacob D Brenneman, b May 5, 1852, near Elida, O. He died Mar. 12, 1924 They lived near El da, O , which was their address. Farmer. Mennonites Related. Buried in Salem cemetery.

1. Anna Brenneman, b Dec. 26, 1876 No. 2489.
2. Elizabeth Brenneman, b Jan. 7, 1879 No. 2492
3. Ada Brenneman, b Oct 28, 1880. No. 2493.
4. Effie Brenneman, b. May 27, 1883. No. 2494

5. Jacob A Brenneman, b Sept 22, 1885 No 2495
6 Twin daughters (stillborn), Sept 7, 1893
7 Samuel A Brenneman, b. Feb 25, 1897 No 2499.

No. 2489. Fifth Generation. 2488.
1) Anna Brenneman, b Dec 26, 1876, in Putnam Co, O, m Nov. 28, 1896, William F. Cotner, b. June 2, 1871, d May 4, 1936. Farmer and schoolteacher. Methodists. Address: Pueblo, Colo.
1 Sarah Ada Cotner, b April 6, 1901. No 2490
2. Zelma Cotner, b Nov. 14, 1904 No 2491.
3. Effie Lorine Cotner, b Sept 19, 1908. No 3686.
4 Harold William Cotner, b. Jan 28, 1911.
5 Lucile Cotner, b Mar. 5, 1915. No 3687

No. 2490. Sixth Generation. 2489.
1) Sarah Ada Cotner, b April 6, 1901, near Pueblo, Colo., m. Sept 3, 1927, Cecil E Wade, b. Oct 23, 1900 On Jan 9, 1932, Sarah married (2nd) Robert William Sumey, b Dec 14, 1893, at Uniontown, Pa. Methodist. Address· Pueblo, Colo.
1 Robert William Sumey, Jr, b Aug 30, 1938, twin.
2 Mary Ann Sumey, b Aug 30, 1938, twin

No. 2491. Sixth Generation. 2489.
2) Zelma Cotner, b Nov 14, 1904, near Pueblo, Colo, m Mar 3, 1928, Dallas L Cooper, b Dec. 3, 1904, in Red Willow Co, Cedar Bluff, Kans Farmer. Salesman Methodist
1. Sherley Ann Cooper, b May 4, 1934

No. 2492. Fifth Generation. 2488
2) El zabeth Brenneman, b Jan 7, 1879, in Putnam Co, O, d May 27, 1919, m. April 6, 1904, Charles E Rusler, b Jan 9, 1884 Address: Pueblo, Colo. Methodists No children.

No. 2493. Fifth Generation. 2488.
3) Ada Brenneman, b Oct 28, 1880, in Putnam Co, O, m July 18, 1916, Mose D. Miller, b Dec 28, 1877 Address Delphos, O, R 2. Farmer Mennonites

4) Effie Brenneman, b May 27, 1883, in Putnam Co, O, m Nov 12, 1918, Joseph E Heatwole, as second wife. He was born Sept 4, 1876, in Va. Farmer Mennonites No children Address Elida, O.

No. 2494. Fifth Generation. 2488.
5) Jacob A Brenneman, b Sept 22, 1885, in Putnam Co, O, m Aug 22, 1907, Anna V. Swartz, b. April 3, 1889, in Va Address Elida, O, R 1 Farmer. Mennonites.

No. 2495. Fifth Generation. 2488.
1. Edna Irene Brenneman, b Aug 2, 1908 No 2496
2. William Oral Brenneman, b. Dec 29, 1912. No 2497.
3. Freda Estella Brenneman, b Feb. 4, 1915 No. 2498
4. Elizabeth Grace Brenneman, b Jan. 10, 1919

No. 2496. Sixth Generation. 2495.
1) Edna Irene Brenneman, b. Aug 2, 1908, m. June 1, 1927, Merle G Stemen, b. Aug. 28, 1904. Related Address Elida, O Laborer Mennonites
1 Dale A Stemen, b Aug 24, 1928
2. Warren Lee Stemen, b. Sept. 17, 1930.
3. Marian Elizabeth Stemen, b Mar. 16, 1932.

4 Anna Margaret Stemen, b. June 13, 1934.

5 John Jacob Stemen, b. Jan. 4, 1936.

No. 2497. Sixth Generation. 2495.

2) William Oral Brenneman, b. Dec 29, 1912, m Oct. 6, 1935, Mabel Esther Smith, b. Jan. 28, 1913. Address Elida, O.

No. 2498. Sixth Generation. 2495.

3) Freda Estella Brenneman, b. Feb. 4, 1915, m Paul Wesley Smith, b Jan. 14, 1911. They were married in 1934 Address Elida, O. Mennonites

1. Wendal Paul Smith, b. Aug 26, 1934

2 Carol R Smith, b. April 2, 1937.

No. 2499. Fifth Generation. 2488.

7) Samuel A. Brenneman, b Feb. 25, 1897, near Elida, O., m Dec 4, 1919, Elizabeth Powell, b June 7, 1886 Address Elida, O , R 1. Farmer. Mennonites.

1. Clifford Brenneman, b Oct 25, 1920

2. Beulah Brenneman, b Oct. 19, 1921, d Jan. 6, 1924.

3. Florence Brenneman, b April 22, 1925.

4. David Brenneman, b. June 20, 1927.

5. Harold Brenneman, b Jan 19, 1930.

No. 2500. Fourth Generation. 44.

7) Samuel Brenneman, b. July 26, 1857, in Putnam Co , O , d. June 4, 1930, m. Oct. 6, 1881, Catherine Stemen, b. Feb. 2, 1858 Farmer Mennonite Burial in the Salem cemetery near Elida, O Lived in Van Wert Co , O. Address. Middlepoint, O.

1. Irvin Brenneman, b Sept. 15, 1882

2. Amanda Brenneman, b. Aug 9, 1884

3 Verna M. Brenneman, b. Nov 12, 1886. No. 2501

4. Myrtle Brenneman, b Sept 15, 1889.

5. Franklin Brenneman, b. June 21, 1893 No 2503.

6 Mary Goldie Brenneman, b Sept 20, 1897.

No. 2501. Fifth Generation. 2500.

3) Verna M. Brenneman, b Nov 12, 1886, in Van Wert Co., O , m Dec 20, 1906, John Good, b. July 15, 1886, near Elida, O Address: Lima, O , R 4 Laborer. Mennonites.

1. Waldo C. Good b Dec 11, 1907, d Aug. 3, 1915, by drowning

2. Carl B. Good, b. June 28, 1909, d Dec. 27, 1909.

3. Kenneth G. Good, b. Nov. 15, 1910. No. 2502

4. Mildred C. Good, b. Jan 10, 1913.

No. 2502. Sixth Generation. 2501.

3) Kenneth G. Good, b. Nov. 15, 1910, near Elida, O., m Aug 2, 1932, Kathryn E. Brunk, b. Mar. 6, 1910 in Va. Address Harrisonburg, Va.

1. Nolan Kenneth Good, b June 2, 1933.

No. 2503. Fifth Generation. 2500.

5) Franklin Brenneman, b June 21, 1893, in Van Wert Co , O., m Dec 16, 1917, Hazel Opelt, b. Dec. 8, 1892 Address· Middlepoint, O. Farmer.

No. 2504. Fourth Generation. 44.

8) George G. Brenneman, b. Sept. 14, 1862, near Rushmore, O , m. Aug 12, 1883, Lena Kehr, b. Mar 19, 1861. Address· Milford, Ind. Farmer. Mennonites.

1. Edward D Brenneman, b April 28, 1884. No. 2505

2 Ella S. Brenneman, b Sept 18, 1885 No. 2507.

3. Clyde G. Brenneman, b Oct 26, 1892 No 2510

4 Florence Brenneman, b Dec 26, 1896, d Feb 19, 1897.

No. 2505. Fifth Generation. 2504.

1) Edward D Brenneman, b April 28, 1884, near Wakarusa, Ind., m. Nov. 11, 1905, Nellie Kehr, b. Aug 21, 1887 Address: Wakarusa, Ind Thresher. Mennonites.

1. Hazel Brenneman, b Aug 15, 1907. No. 2506
2. George Brenneman, b. Sept. 12, 1911
3. Ethel Brenneman, b July 7, 1914
4. Evelyn Brenneman, b. Aug. 30, 1916.
5. Walter Brenneman, b. Jan. 15, 1919.
6 Fern Brenneman, b July 13, 1921.
7. Paul Brenneman, b Aug 18, 1924.
8 Harold Brenneman, b Dec. 14, 1927.

No. 2506. Sixth Generation. 2505.

1) Hazel Brenneman, b Aug. 15, 1907, m. Mar. 16, 1927, Maynard Metzler, b. Dec. 23, 1905. Laborer. Mennonites. Address· 1015 Maple Row, Elkhart, Ind.

1. Donald E. Metzler, b Oct. 17, 1927
2. Norma Jean Metzler, b. Jan. 16, 1930.

No. 2507. Fifth Generation. 2504.

2) Ella S Brenneman, b Sept 18, 1885, near Wakarusa, Ind , m Oct 30, 1904, Timothy Weldy, b Jan 28, 1886 Address Nappanee, Ind Farmer Mennonites.

1 Orphy C. Weldy, b. Oct. 11, 1905 No. 2508
2 Floyd M. Weldy, b Apr.l 14, 1908 No. 2509
3 Rubedean Weldy, b. June 16, 1910
4 Florence Weldy, b. April 14, 1913
5 Maxine Weldy, b June 17, 1915.
6. Robert Weldy, b Feb 24, 1921.
7 Francis Weldy, b May 25, 1924.

No. 2503. Sixth Generation. 2507.

1) Orphy C Weldy, b Oct 11, 1905, m June 11, 1927, Harvey Weaver, b. June 21, 1904 Address Wakarusa, Ind Farmer Mennonites

No. 2509. Sixth Generation. 2507.

2) Floyd M Weldy, b. April 14, 1908, m Sept 15, 1928, Marian Schrock, b. April 24, 1908. Address Nappanee, Ind. Farmer Mennonites.

No. 2510. Fifth Generation. 2504.

3) Clyde G. Brenneman, b Oct 24, 1892, m Mar 21, 1912, Rubedene Holdeman, b Mar 20, 1894. Address· Wakarusa, Ind Elevator employee

1 Theron Brenneman, b Feb. 17, 1914.
2 Clifford Brenneman, b Oct 19, 1921.

No. 2511. Fourth Generation. 45.

1) Jacob B. Huber, b Dec. 1, 1844, in Perry Co., O., d June 2, 1925, near Elida, O. He married Elizabeth C Good, b. Jan 3, 1847, in Rockingham Co., Va., d. Mar. 31, 1931 Both were buried in the Salem cemetery near Elida, O. Farmer and carpenter. Mennonite Church, of which he was a deacon. Address: Elida, O.

1. Rebecca F. Huber, b Mar 10, 1867 No. 2512.
2 John F Huber, b. July 26, 1868 No 2513
3. Anna E. Huber, b Jan 4, 1870

4. Mary C. Huber, b Jan 26, 1872. No. 2521
5 Barbara M Huber, b. Aug. 1, 1873 No 2528
6. Abraham P. Huber, b Aug 12, 1876. No. 2531
7. Simon G. Huber, b Nov. 22, 1878 No 2533
8. Joseph E. Huber, b Dec 8, 1880. No 2534
9 Lydia C. Huber, b May 5, 1883 No 2535
10 Jacob T. Huber, b Aug. 23, 1885. No. 2536.
11. Henry A. Huber, b. Nov 26, 1887. No 2537

No. 2512. Fifth Generation. 2511.

1) Rebecca F. Huber, b Mar 10, 1867, m June 28, 1908, Jacob J. Yoder, b May 11, 1861. She was the second wife They live near Elida, O., which is their address Farmer. Mennonites. No children.

No. 2513. Fifth Generation. 2511.

2) John F. Huber, b July 26, 1868, in Putnam Co , O , m April 1, 1897, Lucy J. Irons, b April 1, 1872. They live in Lima, O Mennonites
1 Elizabeth M. Huber, b Sept 15, 1898 No. 2514.
2. Christine L Huber, b. Oct 10, 1899 No 2515
3 Rebecca Ruth Huber, b Jan. 8, 1901, m. Arthur J Leis
4. Anna M. Huber, b Sept. 7, 1902, m Joseph Mitchell.
5 Clara E. Huber, b June 20, 1904, m. Robert H. Vose.
6 Frances W. Huber, b ——————, m. Earl Gaskel.
7. Florence N. Huber, b. ——————, m Charles Leigh.
8 Esther M Huber, b ——————, m. Clayton Markley
9. Jacob W. Huber, b. ——————
10. J Frank Huber, b. ——————.
11. Christ'an B Huber, b ——————, No 2515½
12 Infant Huber, b April 24, 1916, d July 28, 1916

No. 2514. Sixth Generation. 2513.

1) Elizabeth Margaret Huber, b Sept 15, 1898, m Orvil D. Bame Address: Lima, O., R. 3.
1 Rosemary Bame, b ——————
2 Virlin Bame, b ——————.
3. Orvil Bame, b. ——————.
4. Harvey Bame, b. ——————.

No. 2515. Sixth Generation. 2513.

2) Christine L. Huber, b Oct. 10, 1899, d. ——————, m. Marion Green.
1 Robert Green, b ——————, d. July 7, 1937.
2. Dav'd Green, b. ——————.
3. Stephen Green, b. ——————.
4. Rosella Green, b. ——————.
5. Eugene Green, b. ——————.
6. John Green, b. ——————.
7. Daniel Green, b ——————
8. Ruth Naomi Green, b. ——————.

No. 2515½. Sixth Generation. 2513.

11) Christian B. Huber, b ——————, m. Margaret McMillan, Lima, O.
1. Patricia Huber, b. Feb 9, 1938.

No. 2521. Fifth Generation. 2511.

4) Mary C. Huber, b. Jan. 26, 1876, near Versailles, Mo., d. Sept. 3, 1897. She married Dec 21, 1893, Andrew Diller Address: Lima, O , R. 3 Mennonites

1 Clarence S. Diller, b Dec 10, 1894 No 2526
2 Mary Elizabeth Diller, b May 13, 1897. No. 2527.

No. 2526. Sixth Generation. 2521.
1) Clarence S. Diller, b Dec. 10, 1894, near Elida, O., d. Jan. 14, 1934 He married Ella Greider, b April 8, 1897. Address· New Carlisle, O Mennonites. He was a deacon.
1. Richard Ray Diller, b Sept 5, 1920.
2 Victor Virgil Diller, b July 17, 1921.
3. Edwin Ernest Diller, b Aug 29, 1923
4. Mary Elizabeth Diller, b Dec. 23, 1924.
5. Clarence Charles Diller, b. Aug 29, 1926.
6 Paul Franklin Diller, b. May 30, 1929.

No. 2527. Sixth Generation. 2521.
2) Mary E Diller, b May 13, 1897, near Elida, O., m Aug. 16, 1923, Henry S Hartman, b April 9, 1897, in Va Address Elida, O, R 1. Mennonites House-wife.
1 Richard E. Hartman, b. June 23, 1924.
2. Paul G Hartman, b May 17, 1927

No. 2528. Fifth Generation. 2511.
5) Barbara M. Huber, b Aug 1, 1873, near Versailles, Mo, m. Dec 30, 1894, Daniel G King, of West Liberty, O Address. Elida, O., R 1. Poultryman. Mennonites
1 Edward M. King, b Dec. 21, 1895. No. 2529.
2. Hattie M King, b. Aug 24, 1897. No 2530.
3 Della E King, b July 7, 1899, single.

No. 2529. Sixth Generation. 2523.
1) Edward M King, b Dec 21, 1895, near West Liberty, O, m. Dec 31, 1916, Elizabeth Auxberger, b July 4, 1894 Address Elida, O, R 1 Bus driver for the Greyhound Co
1 John Franklin King, b Nov 9, 1918
2 Paul Oliver King, b Dec 21, 1921.
3 Freda Mae King, b May 26, 1923.
4 Clara Belle King, b Dec 8, 1924
5 Betty Ann King, b April 19, 1926
6 Robert Lee King, b Aug 31, 1930

No. 2530. Sixth Generation. 2528.
2) Hattie M King, b Aug 24, 1897, near West Liberty, O, m. Feb 16, 1917, Otho B Shenk, b April 22, 1894 Address: Elida, O, R. 1 Farmer. Mennonites. Minister.
1. Mark Shenk, b Dec 19, 1917
2 Louella Shenk, b May 6, 1923.
3 Paul David Shenk, b. July 10, 1932.

No. 2531. Fifth Generation. 2511.
6) Abraham P Huber, b Aug 12, 1876, in Putnam Co, O, m. Nov. 24, 1904, Hattie Mae Snyder, b. June 30, 1875. Address. Goshen, Ind Carpenter Mennonite Brethren in Christ.
1. Paul C. Huber, b Oct. 28, 1905 No 2532
2. David R Huber, b Sept 28, 1907.
3 J. Luke Huber, b. Jan. 13, 1913
4 J Mark Huber, b Nov 2, 1914

No. 2532. Sixth Generation. 2531.

1) Paul C. Huber, b Oct 28, 1905, m Mar 27, 1932, Orpha Brenneman, b May 4, 1895. They reside in Goshen, Ind Address Goshen, Ind Related, see No. 1213.

No. 2533. Fifth Generation. 2511.

7) Simon G Huber, b Nov 22, 1878, in Allen Co, O., m Nov 24, 1901, Amanda Bontrager, of Logan Co, O, b Jan 7, 1876 She died Nov. 16, 1937. Address. Harrisonburg, Va Mennonites Deacon
1. Clarence W. Huber, b Aug 30, 1902 No 3469
2. Mary Huber, b. Sept —, 1906
3. Ira J. Huber, b Sept —, 1915. No. 3470

No. 2534. Fifth Generation. 2511.

8) Joseph E Huber, b Dec. 8, 1880, Putnam Co, O, m Oct. 20, 1907, Emma L. Burkholder, b July 9, 1883, near Harrisonburg, Va Carpenter and farmer Mennonites Address: Delphos, O, R 2 Related, for family see No 828

No. 2535. Fifth Generation. 2511.

9) Lydia C Huber, b May 5, 1883, in Putnam Co, O, m Lewis J Lehman He is a minister in the Mennonite Brethren in Christ Church Address Goshen, Ind.
1. Louella Lehman, b. ————————.
2. Ray Lehman, b. ——————.
3. Huber Lehman, b ——————.

No. 2535. Fifth Generation. 2511.

10) Jacob T Huber, b Aug 23, 1885, in Putnam Co, O, d Nov 8, 1928, by driving his truck on the railroad He married Mar 12, 1909, Martha R Jones, b. May 15, 1888. Address Elida, O Burial at Salem cemetery
1. Fern M Huber, b May 26, 1910, m Dale Wilcons
2. Lawrence J Huber, b Jan 5, 1912, m Eilene Faust
3. Ralph F. Huber, b May 25, 1914, m Laura Belle Red
4. Grace E. Huber, b. April 11, 1916
5. Sarah Huber, b Feb 19, 1918
6. Arthur W Huber, b Mar 14, 1920
7. Alma Huber, b July 28, 1922
8. Hermen E. Huber, b Aug 15, 1924
9. Mildred H Huber, b Nov 8, 1926

No. 2537. Fifth Generation. 2511.

11) Henry A. Huber, b Nov 26, 1887, in Putnam Co, O, m Feb. 24, 1909, Luella E Lehman, b Oct 19, 1886 Address Sturgis, Mich Carpenter Burial in Oaklawn cemetery, Sturgis, Mich
1. Rhoda Elizabeth Huber, b. Jan 6, 1910 No 3374.
2. Mary Henrietta Huber, b Nov 18, 1911, twin No 3375
3. Marion Henry Huber, b Nov 18, 1911, twin
4. Lehman Good Huber, b. Sept 1, 1913
5. Robert Sherman Huber, b June 21, 1915
6. Fred Warren Huber, b April 10, 1917
7. Luella Dorine Huber, b Oct 18, 1919, d Oct. 11, 1925.
8. James Huber, b. July 16, 1922, d same day.

No. 2538. Fourth Generation. 45.

3) Henry Huber, b Mar 10, 1849, in Fairfield Co, O, d ——————, m. Elizabeth Myers, b. May 4, 1851 Brethren Address: Wakarusa, Ind.

1. Isaac Huber, b June 12, 1871, d. Dec. 5, 1871.
2 John M Huber, b Oct 19, 1872 No. 2539
3. Sarah C. Huber, b Mar 12, 1875, d. April 12, 1875.
4 Daniel S Huber, b. May —, 1876, d. Sept 23, 1877.
5 Christian P. Huber, b. Aug 8, 1878 No. 2543.
6 Urbannus Huber, b June 22, 1881. No. 2544.
7. Emma S Huber, b. May 23, 1884. No. 2547
8. Hattie A. Huber, b Jan 11, 1890 No. 2549.

No. 2539. Fifth Generation. 2533.

2) John M. Huber, b Oct. 19, 1872, Putnam Co, O, m. Nov. 23, 1893, Mary E. Kelchner, b. July 20, 1874. Church of the Brethren. Burial place in Yellow Creek cemetery near Goshen, Ind Address: Goshen, Ind, R. 3.
1. Elizabeth Mae Huber, b Sept 25, 1894 No. 2540.
2. Henry Samuel Huber, b Oct 28. 1896 No. 2541.
3 Anna Amelia Huber, b Oct 8, 1904. No. 2542.
4. Mabel Blanche Huber, b Dec. 9, 1907, d. Oct 17, 1908.

No. 2540. Sixth Generation. 2539.

1) Elizabeth Mae Huber, b Sept. 25, 1894, m Dec. 29, 1924, H C. Stover. Address Dow, N Dak.
1 Carl Richard Stover, b May 28, 1926
2 George Wesley Stover, b. Jan. 28, 1928

No. 2541. Sixth Generation. 2539.

2) Henry Samuel Huber, b Oct 28, 1896, m. Alva Huntsberger, Sept 14, 1918. Address. Bremen, Ind.
1. Edwin Devon Huber, b Aug 4, 1919
2 Kenneth Lamar Huber, b. Jan 11, 1922.
3. Esther Maxine Huber, b Mar 5, 1925
4 Eleanor Joy Huber, b Mar 30, 1929.
5. Mary Ellen Huber, b. April 29, 1933.

No. 2542. Sixth Generation. 2539.

3) Anna Amelia Huber, b Oct 8, 1904, m Mar 24, 1923, Maynord E. Bechtol, at Elkhart, Ind
1 Margaret Elzabeth Bechtol, b Sept 29, 1923
2 Evelyn Marcelle Bechtol, b Feb 22, 1925
3. Earl Edgar Bechtol, b April 16, 1927
4 Paul Virgil Bechtol, b Mar 20, 1920
5. Lowell Huber Bechtol, b Jan 17, 1931
6 Barbara Ann Bechtol, b Feb 1, 1933

No. 2543. Fifth Generation. 2533.

5) Christian Huber, b Aug 8, 1878, m Dec 24, 1908, Minnie Leota Kreider, b. Nov 27, 1889 Address Goshen, Ind, R 5 Farmer. Church of the Brethren.
1 Frank Henry Huber, b Nov 11, 1909
2 Goldie Elizabeth Huber, b Mar 25, 1914
3 John Wilbert Huber, b May 28, 1916.

No. 2544. Fifth Generation. 2533.

6) Urbannus Huber, b June 22, 1881, m Dec 22, 1906, Lula Barringer, b. Oct, 1889, d. Mar. 10, 1926 He married (2nd) Edith Weybright, b. Aug. 20, 1892. Burial at Yellow Creek, near Goshen, Ind Address Goshen, Ind.
1. Vernon Edith Huber, b Aug 16, 1909 No 2545
2. Chester A Huber, b Mar 17, 1913 No 2546

No. 2545. Sixth Generation. 2544.

1) Vernon Edith Huber, b Aug 16, 1909, m Alva Culp
1. Carl Ray, b Feb 28, 1933.

No. 2546. Sixth Generation. 2544.

2) Chester A Huber, b Mar. 17, 1913, m Fern Sechrist, Dec. 31, 1932

No. 2547. Fifth Generation. 2533.

7) Emma S. Huber, b May 23, 1884, m Sept 15, 1906, William H Anglemyer, b Dec. 23, 1885. Farmer Address Wakarusa, Ind. Church of the Brethren.
1. Walter V. Anglemyer, b Aug 12, 1907 No 2548
2. Levi H. Anglemyer, b Nov 25, 1909
3 Roy M. Anglemyer, b. May 12, 1912
4. Elmer H Anglemyer, b Jan 2, 1915
5. Leona M. Anglemyer, b April 12, 1917.
6. George U. Anglemyer, b Dec 4, 1922.

No. 2548. Sixth Generation. 2547.

1) Walter V Anglemyer, b Aug. 12, 1907, m Dec 31, 1928, Sobrina Collins, b. Feb. 20, 1910. Address. Bremen, Ind, R 2 Farmer.
1. William G. Anglemyer, b ——————
2 Emma A Anglemyer, b ——————.

No. 2549. Fifth. Generation. 2538.

8) Hattie Amelia Huber, b Jan 11, 1890, m Feb 27, 1909, Mino Stauffer, b. Dec. 23, 1886 Farmer. Church of the Brethren Address: New Paris, Ind.
1. Dorothy Mae Stauffer, b Mar 25, 1910 No. 2550
2. Clarence Christian Stauffer, b. Jan 4, 1913
3. Ethel Armeda Stauffer, b. July 9, 1915.

No. 2550. Sixth Generation. 2549.

1) Dorothy Mae Stauffer, b Mar 25, 1910, m Harvey Ebersole, Mar 25, 1929.
1. Clarence Henry Ebersole, b Feb. 17, 1930

No. 2551. Fourth Generation. 45.

4) Barbara Huber, b. June 24, 1851, in Fairfield Co, O, m. Nov 20, 1873, John S. Bixler Farmer Mennonites Address Wakarusa, Ind
1. John H. Bixler, b Dec 20, 1874, d Nov. 21, 1878.
2 Jacob K. Bixler, b Sept 5, 1877 No 2552
3. Anna J. Bixler, b Nov 29, 1879, single.
4. E. Matilda Bixler, b Jan 27, 1882 No 2553
5 Frederick E Bixler, b May 7, 1885, single.

No. 2552. Fifth Generation. 2551.

2) Jacob K. Bixler, b Sept 5, 1877, m Dec 22, 1904, Susie J. Bailey, b Jan 21, 1876, at Cullom, Ill. He was ordained to the ministry April 29, 1894, and to the office of bishop Nov. 3, 1907 Mennonites Address· 2752 Prairie St, Elkhart, Ind.
1. Esther May Bixler, b. Mar 30, 1910

No. 2553. Fifth Generation. 2551.

4) E Matilda Bixler, b Jan 27, 1882, m. Lloyd I Hershberger, Sept 12, 1908. Address: Wakarusa, Ind.
1. Gladys B. Hershberger, b June 21, 1909, d Mar. 23, 1910.

No. 2554. Fourth Generation. 45.

5) George Huber, b Sept 24, 1853, in Putnam Co, O, m Sarah Swickard, Jan. 23, 1876 Methodists Address Coldwater, Mich Farmer and milling business. No children Both died at Wakarusa, Ind

No. 2555. Fourth Generation. 45.

6) Matilda Huber, b. June 16, 1858, in Putnam Co., O., m. June 16, 1876, Eliphas B. Reedy, b Mar. 15, 1853, in Mifflin Co, Pa, d. Sept. 25, 1912. Methodists. Address: Belleville, Wis Present address: Niles, Calif.

1 John H Reedy, b Oct 24, 1876 No. 3385
2. George W. Reedy, b Jan. 22, 1879 No. 3386.
3. Jacob B Reedy, b. Nov. 13, 1881. No 3387
4. Anna E Reedy, b April 26, 1884, d May 28, 1884
5. Barbara J. Reedy, b Dec. 9, 1885 No 3388.
6 Christian E Reedy, b Aug 25, 1891
7. Ira F. Reedy, b Nov 21, 1895. No 3389
8 Ethel Reedy, b. June 18, 1898 No. 3390.

No. 2556. Fourth Generation. 45.

10) Emma Huber, b Feb 20, 1867, in Putnam Co, O. (deceased), m. July 19, 1888, Peter B Yoder, as his second wife He was born Sept. 17, 1855. Mennonites. Farmer Address Wakarusa, Ind

1. Harvey N Yoder, b May 5, 1889 No 3367.
2 Jacob Oscar Yoder, b Nov 22, 1890, d Jan. 2, 1891
3 Anna E Yoder, b Nov 17, 1891, d April 26, 1892
4 George V Yoder, b Aug 12, 1893 No 3369.
5 Forest A Yoder, b Oct 3, 1895 No 3370
6 Clarence E Yoder, b Nov 21, 1897 No 3371.
7. Mary N. Yoder, b Oct 24, 1900. No 3372.
8 Huber A. Yoder, b July 14, 1903 No. 3373.

No. 2557. Fourth Generation. 46.

1) Susan Mumaw, b Mar 15, 1847, in Holmes Co., O, d. April 10, 1936, m Feb 18, 1869, John K Weldy. He died April 12, 1912 Address: Wakarusa, Ind

1. George Weldy, b Nov 21, 1869 No 2558.
2 Jacob I. Weldy, b Dec. 31, 1871 No 2565.
3. Daniel S Weldy, b Dec 19, 1873, d. July 11, 1938 No. 2570
4 Amos B Weldy, b Jan 11, 1876 No 2573.
5. Silas L Weldy, b Nov 27, 1877 No. 2576.
6. Martin D. Weldy, b Mar 2, 1879 No 2578
7 Ira Weldy, b. Mar 8, 1881 No. 2579
8. Homer R Weldy, b Sept 22, 1883 No 2582.
9. Walter Weldy, b Dec. 28, 1885 No. 2584
10 Elmer Weldy, b Dec 10, 1887 No. 2585.
11 Ruth A Weldy, b Mar 29, 1890 No 2586

No. 2558. Fifth Generation. 2557.

1) George Weldy, b Nov 21, 1869, m Jan 18, 1891, Lucretia J. Witmer, b June 2, 1871, at Wakarusa, by George Lambert Farmer Mennonites Address Wakarusa, Ind

1 Nelson E Weldy, b Jan 14, 1892 No 2559.
2 Samuel R Weldy, b Jan 15, 1894 No. 2561.
3 Walter E Weldy, b May 18, 1898, d Oct. 12, 1900
4. Daniel G Weldy, b Aug 12, 1900, d Aug 31, 1903.
5 Mary S Weldy, b Feb 23, 1906 No 2562

, 6 G Glen Weldy, b Oct 27, 1908 No 2563.

7. L Edna Weldy, b July 24, 1912. No 2564

No. 2559. Sixth Generation. 2558.

1) Nelson E Weldy, b Jan 14, 1892, m Dec 16, 1913, Wilma Metzler, of Nappanee, Ind

1. Catherine Ocalo Weldy, b Dec. 28, 1914. No 2560

2 Curtis Orvill Weldy, b April 6, 1917

No. 2560. Seventh Generation. 2559.

1) Catherine Ocalo Weldy, b Dec 28, 1914, m Elon Beck, June 17, 1934

No. 2561. Sixth Generation. 2558.

2) Samuel Weldy, b Jan 15, 1894, m May 15, 1915, Alva E. Loucks, of Wakarusa, Ind.

1. Maurice L. Weldy, b. Oct. 30, 1915

2. Mirian R. Weldy, b July 26, 1921

3. Dale D Weldy, b June 11, 1929

4. Keith E Weldy, b. May 2, 1933

No. 2562. Sixth Generation. 2558.

5) Mary S. Weldy, b Feb 23, 1906, m Aug. 24, 1929, Elmer B. Hilty, of Marshallville, O Address. Marshallville, O Mennonites Farmer

1. Beatrice Joan Hilty, b. Oct 5, 1932.

2. James Edward Hilty, b. Dec. 17, 1934.

No. 2563. Sixth Generation. 2558.

6) G. Glen Weldy, b Oct 27, 1908, m Mar 9, 1929, Blanche E. Bleile, of Nappanee, Ind.

No. 2564. Sixth Generation. 2558.

7) L. Edna Weldy, b July 24, 1912, m Oct 7, 1933, Raymond D. Yoder, of Middlebury, Ind

No. 2565. Fifth Generation. 2557.

2) Jacob I Weldy, b. Dec 31, 1871, m Sept 21, 1895, Rhoda Priscilla Landes, b. Jan. 8, 1876, near Wakarusa, Ind Farmer Mennonites. Burial at Olive, Elkhart Co, Ind. Address· Wakarusa, Ind.

1. Arthur Willis Weldy, b June 26, 1896. No. 2566

2 Bertha Violet Weldy, b April 2, 1900. No 2567.

3. Eldon Joseph Weldy, b June 1, 1906. No. 2568

4. Myron Demas Weldy, b. June 7, 1910 No. 2569

5. Dwight Eugene Weldy, b Jan. 10, 1918

No. 2566. Sixth Generation. 2565.

1) Arthur Willis Weldy, b June 26, 1896, m April 14, 1917, Martha Catherine Holdeman, b Mar. 2, 1900 Farmers Mennonites

1 Lois Fern Weldy, b. Feb 17, 1918.

2. Vivian Lucille Weldy, b. Dec. 15, 1919.

3. Mearl Clayton Weldy, b. Mar 15, 1922.

4 Verna Faye Weldy, b. June 1, 1926

No. 2567. Sixth Generation. 2565.

2) Bertha Violet Weldy, b. April 2, 1900, m Sept 6, 1919, Earl C. Harter, b. Oct. 5, 1897. Farmer.

1. Miriam Rosetta Harter, b July 1, 1920

2. Violet Vernice Harter, b June 26, 1922

3. Letha Marie Harter, b July 26, 1924

4 Wayne Eugene Harter, b Nov 19, 1932

No. 2568. Sixth Generation. 2535.

3) Eldon Joseph Weldy, b June 1, 1906, m Oct 14, 1928, Lucille L. Martin, b. June 23, 1911. Eldon has been teaching school since 1925.

1. Norma Jean Weldy, b Aug. 26, 1929

2. Theron Jay Weldy, b Oct 16, 1934.

No. 2569. Sixth Generation. 2565.

4) Myron Demas Weldy, b June 7, 1910, m. June 10, 1934, Cleo Frances Weaver, b Nov 11, 1911 Myron has taught school since 1929.

No. 2570. Fifth Generation. 2557.

3) Daniel S Weldy, b Dec 19, 1873, d. July 11, 1928, m Dec. 20, 1896, Ada C. Shaum, b. Nov 11, 1874, d Feb 27, 1927 He married (2nd) Verda Ellen Brunk b. July 5, 1875 They were married Mar. 30, 1928. Manager gas station. Mennonites. Address. 508 Garfield Ave , Elkhart, Ind. Burial in Prairie St. cemetery, Elkhart, Ind

1. Gladys Ruth Weldy, b. Nov 15, 1898. No 2571.

2. Clifford Emerson Weldy, b May 23, 1904. No. 2572

No. 2571. Sixth Generation. 2570.

1) Gladys Ruth Weldy, b Nov 15, 1898, m Aug 10, 1923, John R. Piatt.

1. John J. Piatt, b Dec 10, 1925.

2. Mary Ann Piatt, b. Jan 29, 1928.

No. 2572. Sixth Generation. 2570.

2) Clifford Emerson Weldy, b May 23, 1904, m June 26, 1931, Gladys Robbins, Greensburg, Ind

1. Catherine Ellen Weldy, b Sept 15, 1934

No. 2573. Fifth Generation. 2557.

4) Amos B Weldy, b Jan 11, 1876, m Jan 2, 1898, Sarah E Blosser, b. Oct. 1, 1878 Address Nappanee, Ind Farmer

1. Bernice B Weldy, b Oct. 16, 1902. No. 2574

2. Paul J Weldy, b Oct 14, 1907 No 2575

3 Twila Lucile Weldy, b June 1, 1912

No. 2574. Sixth Generation. 2573.

1) Bernice B Weldy, b Oct 16, 1902, m Cephas Yoder, Mar 3, 1923

1 Jay Earl Yoder, b June 10, 1924

2 Helen Marie Yoder, b Mar 29, 1927.

3. Allen Keith Yoder, b May 20, 1935

No. 2575. Sixth Generation. 2573.

2) Paul Jay Weldy, b Oct 14, 1907, m Mary Bleile, Feb 27, 1932

1 Samuel Jay Weldy, b Nov 3, 1935

No. 2576. Fifth Generation. 2557.

5) Silas L Weldy, b Nov. 27, 1877, m Oct 8, 1899, Elnora Metzler, b Jan 10, 1880. Mennonite Minister Address. Wakarusa, Ind Burial ground at Olive Church.

1 Warren Maynard Weldy, b Aug 6, 1903 No 2577

They have an orphan boy name Walter Wayne Weaver, b April 27, 1914.

No. 2577. Sixth Generation. 2576.

1) Warren Maynard Weldy, b. Aug. 6, 1905, m July 12, 1930, Edna May Weaver, of Wakarusa, Ind.

1 Loren Maynard Weldy, b. Feb. 17, 1932.
2. Paul Edward Weldy, b July 29, 1933.

No. 2578. Fifth Generation. 2557.

6) Martin D. Weldy, b Mar 2, 1879, m. Mar. 12, 1904, Mary Welty, b. Nov. 18, 1882 Address· Elkhart, Ind Salesman. Mennonites.

1 Forrest M. Weldy, b. ——, 1904, d ——, 1914.
2. Donald L. Weldy, b. Sept 26, 1925

No. 2579. Fifth Generation. 2557.

1) Ira Weldy, b Mar 8, 1881, m Dec 6, 1903, Minerva Welty, b. Sept 4, 1880. Address: Wakarusa, Ind Farmer. Mennonites.

1. Grace M. Weldy, b. Dec. 6, 1905   No 2580
2. Ethel N. Weldy, b Dec 6, 1909. No 2581.
3. John W. Weldy, b April 12, 1916

No. 2580. Sixth Generation. 2579.

1) Grace M Weldy, b Dec 6, 1905, m Harold Metzler

No. 2581. Sixth Generation. 2579.

2) Ethel N. Weldy, b Dec 6, 1909, m Dec 6, 1934, Walter Miller, of Elkhart, Ind., by Silas L Weldy, uncle of the bride

1. Wayne N. Miller b Oct 5, 1936

No. 2582. Fifth Generation. 2557.

8) Homer R Weldy, b Sept 22, 1883, m Dec 3, 1904, Chloe M. Miller, b. May 24, 1886 Address· Nappanee, Ind Farmer Church of the Brethren. Burial place in Union Center cemetery.

1. Kenneth C. Weldy, b May 31, 1905, d Nov. 12, 1905.
2 Florence M Weldy, b Mar 24, 1907.
3. Veda F Weldy, b Oct 23, 1909 No 2583

No. 2583. Sixth Generation. 2582.

3) Veda F. Weldy, b Oct. 23, 1909, m Feb 16, 1936, Lorenzo A. Pellett. They are living at 1609 Florine Court, South Bend, Ind

No. 2584. Fifth Generation. 2557.

9) Walter Weldy, b. Dec 28, 1885, d. in 1934, m. Rosa Miller. Address: Wakarusa, Ind.

1. Virgil Weldy, b. Nov. 2, 1909
2. Kenneth Weldy, b. Dec. 26, 1913

No. 2585. Fifth Generation. 2557.

10) Elmer L. Weldy, b Dec 10, 1887, m. Feb 29, 1908, Minnie V. Strope, b. May 10, 1888. Farmer. Mennonites. Address: Wakarusa, Ind.

1. Evelyn Virginia Weldy, b Oct. 26, 1914

No. 2586. Fifth Generation. 2557.

11) Ruth A. Weldy, b. Mar 29, 1890, m. Jan 20, 1912, Alvin J Yoder. Address: Nappanee, Ind Farmers. Mennonites.

1. Herschel Yoder, b. ——.
2. Leonard Yoder, b ——.

376

No. 2587. Fourth Generation. 46.

2) Henry A. Mumaw, b Jan. 27, 1850, near Winesburg, O., d April 1, 1908, m. June 27, 1872, Malinda Blosser of Ohio, b. Dec. 27, 1852. She d. May 11, 1935. Both were buried in the Prairie St cemetery, Elkhart, Ind. Soon after marriage they settled in Elkhart, Ind , and he engaged in the printing business for 14 years, after which he attended medical college at Chicago, Ill., from which place he graduated in 1886, for the practice of homeopathic medicine, practicing in Nappanee, Ind., and Orrville, O , and later in Elkhart, Ind. In 1894 he founded Elkhart Institute, which passed into other hands a few years later and is now known as Goshen College, located at Goshen, Ind

1. Phoebe Mumaw, b. Sept. 4, 1873. No. 2588
2. Andrew Mumaw, b June 15, 1877, d Oct. 11, 1918.
3. Clara Mumaw, b. Feb 12, 1880 No 2589

No. 2588. Fifth Generation. 2587.

1) Phoebe Mumaw, b Sept 4, 1873, in Elkhart, Ind , m Aaron Kolb, b. Dec 7, 1871, of Kitchener, Ont. where they resided Mr. Kolb was a correspondent and had charge of the Book Department of the Mennonite Publishing Co., at Elkhart, Ind , for many years Later he was postmaster and connected with the Labor Department of the Canadian Government Church worker and Musician He served also as secretary of the Home and Foreign Relief Commission, organized in 1896 He d. May 15, 1937.

1 Elmeda M. Kolb, b April 20, 1913.

No. 2589. Fifth Generation. 2587.

3) Clara Mumaw, b. Feb 12, 1880, d Nov 15, 1932, m Glenn G Unsicker They lived in Elkhart, Ind Clara was a bank employee for 20 years.

No. 2590. Fourth Generation. 46.

3) Amos Mumaw, b June 27, 1852, near Winesburg, O , d in Wayne Co., O., May 15, 1906 He married Aug 24, 1876, Catherine Shaum, b June 13, 1856, near Wooster, O. After marriage they lived for a few years in Allen Co., 14½ years in Elkhart Co., Ind , and later in Wayne Co , O., where he died He was a minister in the Mennonite Church Farmer Burial in the Martins cemetery near Orrville, O

1. George S Mumaw, b Sept 6, 1877 No 2591
2 Levi Mumaw, b Nov 16, 1879, d June 4, 1935 No 2594
3. Amos B Mumaw, b Aug 1, 1882 No. 2595
4 Harry Mumaw, b Aug 30, 1884 No 2598.
5. Infant son (stillborn), Mar. 1, 1887.
6 Adam Henry Mumaw, b July 11, 1888 No. 2599.
7 Mary Catherine Mumaw, b Oct 15, 1890, d Jan. 3, 1891.
8. Martha Ellen Mumaw, b. Dec 23, 1891, single. No. 2599½.
9 Anna Naomi Mumaw, b Dec 22, 1894, single No 2599½.
10. Daniel W Mumaw, b May 15, 1900 No 2600
11 John Rudy Mumaw, b Mar 11, 1904 No 2601.

No. 2591. Fifth Generation. 2590.

1) George S Mumaw, b. Sept 6, 1877, m Sept 14, 1907, Lucy E. Wilson, b April 13, 1878 Farmer and carpenter Address Salem, O Mennonite

1. Catherine Esther Mumaw, b June 16, 1908 No 2592
2. George Wilson Mumaw, b June 12, 1909
3 Marion Edward Mumaw, b April 19, 1911. No 2593.
4 Dorothy A Mumaw, b Aug 30, 1912, d same day.
5 Byron E. Mumaw, b Jan 7, 1914. No. 3608.

No. 2592. Sixth Generation. 2591.

1) Catherine Esther Mumaw, b June 16, 1908, m July 4, 1933, Perce King. Address· Salem, O.

No. 2593. Sixth Generation. 2591.

3) Marion Edward Mumaw, b April 19, 1911, m Aug 26, 1932, Mary Eagleton. They reside in Salem, O.

1. Phyllis Marie Mumaw, b ——————.
2. Harold Edward Mumaw, b ——————.
3 Delores Ann Mumaw, b. ——————

No. 2594. Fifth Generation. 2590.

2) Levi Mumaw, b Nov. 11, 1879, near Winesburg, O., d. June 4, 1935, m Fannie E. Shoemaker, June 9, 1903, daughter of J S Shoemaker, of Dakota, Ill She was b. Oct. 14, 1881, d Jan 9, 1921. Levi was for a number of years secretary-treasurer of the Mennonite Publishing House at Scottdale, Pa , where he lived He married Aug. 8, 1923, Alice Hershey, b Dec. 24, 1883 He and his first wife were buried in the Martins cemetery near Orrville, O , with both of their children.

1. Russell J Mumaw, b. Sept 8, 1905, d July 14, 1927
2. Infant daughter, b Mar 23, 1908, d next day

No. 2595. Fifth Generation. 2590.

3) Amos B Mumaw, b. Aug 1, 1882, near Elida, O , m Mar 27, 1906, Emma F. Rohrer, b Mar. 23, 1881, of Orrville, O Farmer Mennonites Burial place in Martins cemetery. Address: Dalton, O

1. Stanford R. Mumaw, b April 3, 1907. No. 2596.
2. Homer A Mumaw, b Jan 13, 1909. No 2597.
3 Ralph Wayne Mumaw, b. Sept 17, 1911 No 3607
4 Infant daughter, b Jan 29, 1915, d Feb 1, 1915
5. Irvin Richard Mumaw, b Jan 1, 1916.
6 Clare Laverne Mumaw, b. May 20, 1917.

No. 2596. Sixth Generation. 2595.

1) Stanford R Mumaw, b April 3, 1907, m Aug. 1, 1933, Lavina Hilty, of near Orrville, O. Mennonites He was ordained to the ministry Aug. 17, 1930, at the Martins Church near Orrville, O Address Dalton, O.

1. Maxine Lois Mumaw, b. April 4, 1937

No. 2597. Sixth Generation. 2595.

2) Homer A Mumaw, b. Jan 13, 1909, m Sept 2, 1933, Katherine Keener.
1 Russell Amos Mumaw, b. Jan. 23, 1938.

No. 2598. Fifth Generation. 2590.

4) Harry Mumaw, b Aug. 30, 1884, near Elkhart, Ind., m Jan 30, 1913, Minnie Hostetler, b. Feb 23, 1883. Farmer Mennonite Deacon. Address: Wooster, O.

1. Gladys C. Mumaw, b Dec. 26, 1913.
2 Mark David Mumaw, b. April 22, 1916
3 Ethel May Mumaw, b. April 13, 1924.

No. 2599. Fifth Generation. 2590.

6) Adam Henry Mumaw, b July 11, 1888, near Elkhart, Ind , m Dec 16, 1917, Clara Belle Zook, b. April 1, 1891 Address· Wooster, O Farmer Mennonites.

1 Harvey David Mumaw, b Jan. 21, 1919
2 Walter Jay Mumaw, b Dec. 10, 1921.
3 Floyd Ellis Mumaw, b Aug. 15, 1923

No. 2599½. Fifth Generation. 2590.

8) Martha Ellen Mumaw, b Dec. 23, 1891 Single. Linotypist at the Mennonite Publishing House, Scottdale, Pa

Anna Naomi Mumaw, b Dec 22, 1894. Single. Book department of the Mennonite Publishing House, Scottdale, Pa.

No. 2600. Fifth Generation. 2590.

10) Daniel W. Mumaw, b May 15, 1900, near Wooster, O., m. Feb. 7, 1923, Estella Anna King, b. Nov. 8, 1900 Address: Weilersville, O.

1. Mary Catherine Mumaw, b. Dec 26, 1924.
2. Carl Edward Mumaw, b May 10, 1927.
3. Virgil Robert Mumaw, b May 18, 1931
4. Ward Daniel Mumaw, b. May 30, 1938

No. 2501. Fifth Generation. 2590.

11) John Rudy Mumaw, b. Mar 12, 1904, near Wooster, O., m. May 27, 1928, Esther Mosemann, b July 24, 1905, of Lancaster, Pa Mennonites and teacher. Mr. Mumaw is located at Harrisonburg, Va, and is a teacher in the Eastern Mennonite School at that place. He was ordained to the ministry Mar. 24, 1928. Address: Harrisonburg, Va

1. Helen Elizabeth Mumaw, b April 2, 1929
2. Grace Naomi Mumaw, b Dec 22, 1930.
3. Catherine Ruth Mumaw, b July 22, 1932.
4. Lois Esther Mumaw, b. May 3, 1934
5 Miriam Louise Mumaw, b. Jan 14, 1938

No. 2602. Fourth Generation. 45.

6) John Mumaw, b. Jan 31, 1862, near Winesburg, Holmes Co., O., m. Mar. 9, 1893, Lydia A Good, b Feb 28, 1866 Address: Elkhart, Ind. Farmer. Mennonites.

1. Enos Mumaw, b Nov. 13, 1894 No. 2603.
2. Henry Mumaw, b June 1, 1898.
3. Cora Mumaw, b Dec 16, 1899 No. 2604.
4 Ira Mumaw, b. Jan 28, 1902. No 2606.
5. Aaron Mumaw, b Jan 17, 1904 No. 2605.
6. Clara Mumaw, b Dec. 26, 1905

No. 2603. Fifth Generation. 2502.

1) Enos Mumaw, b Nov. 13, 1894, m Feb. 19, 1919, Ruth E. Lehman, b Nov 19, 1896 Address Elkhart, Ind, R 5 Salesman Mennonites.

1. Kathryn Louise Mumaw, b Dec. 3, 1920.
2. Winifred Elizabeth Mumaw, b. Oct 7, 1925.
3 Frances Rebecca Mumaw, b Jan. 1, 1931.

No. 2504. Fifth Generation. 2502.

3) Cora Mumaw, b Nov 16, 1899, m Nov 24, 1921, Elmer D. Tyson, b Feb 11, 1899 Address Goshen, Ind. R 3 Farmer Mennonites

1 Raymond Lamar Tyson, b Dec 4, 1922
2 Harold DeVon Tyson, b Mar. 30, 1925
3. Merl Henry Tyson, b Oct 1, 1926
4 Evelyn May Tyson, b Aug 2, 1929
5. John Herbert Tyson, b Dec 3, 1933

No. 2605. Fifth Generation. 2602.

5) Aaron Mumaw, b Jan 17, 1904, m Sept 4, 1926, Florence Loucks, b. May 18, 1907 Address· Goshen, Ind Carpenter and farmer. Mennonites.

1. Erma Loraine Mumaw, b. Sept 21, 1927.
2. Melba Berdine Mumaw, b April 24, 1930.
3. Elnora Kay Mumaw, b Sept 26, 1935.
4. Arlene Fay Mumaw, b. Nov. 20, 1937

No. 2606. Fifth Generation. 2602.

4) Ira Mumaw, b Jan. 20, 1902, d June 14, 1937, m. Feb 11, 1923, Martha Weaver, of Wakarusa, Ind., b. Nov. 3, 1900
1. Lowell Mumaw, b April 18, 1924
2. Mary Louise Mumaw, b Nov. 26, 1926
3. Gladys Mumaw, b. Aug 28, 1928.

No. 2607. Fourth Generation. 49.

2) Abraham L Funk, b Oct 22, 1863, m June 5, 1911, Mary Winslow Wetherell. Christian Science practitioner. First Church of Christ, Boston, Mass, with branch membership, Fourth Church of Christ, Scientists, San Francisco, Cal

No. 2608. Fourth Generation. 49.

3) Elizabeth Ann Funk, b July 23, 1865, m Oct. 24, 1888, Oswell Schmick, b. Feb. 19, 1859. Painter and decorator Presbyterians Address 411 Delaware St, Hiawatha, Kans.
1. Laura Bell Schmick, b Dec. 25, 1889. No. 2609.

No. 2609. Fifth Generation. 2608.

1) Laura Bell Schmick, b Dec 25, 1889, m Sept 29, 1915, Claude E Hoffman, b. Sept 1, 1887. Address 528 Wochtel Ave., Petoskey, Mich. Christian Church.
1. Helen Elizabeth Hoffman, b. Mar 31, 1919.

No. 2610. Fourth Generation. 49.

3) Lydia M Funk, b Mar 7, 1868, m Mar 13, 1889, Edmund Sohn, b April 2, 1857, d. Sept. 5, 1918. Buried at Oneida, Kans Christian Church. Address: Oneida, Kans
1 Norma S Sohn, b Sept 19, 1892, single, Christian.
2 Mary E. Sohn, b. Mar. 4, 1897. No 2611
3 Nellie M. Sohn, b. May 24, 1903 No. 2612.

No. 2611. Fifth Generation. 2610.

2) Mary E Sohn, b. Mar. 4, 1897, m Aug 29, 1918, Harry F Huff, b. Sept. 12, 1897 Address: One da, Kans Christian Church.
1. Melba May Huff, b June 21, 1919

No. 2612. Fifth Generation. 2610.

2) Nellie M Sohn, b May 21, 1903, m Dec, 1921, Wayne F. Anderson, b Oct 19, 1902, d Jan 2, 1930 Mrs Anderson died Jan. 9, 1927 Christian Church. Address Oneida, Kans Burial at same place
1 William Robert Anderson, b ─────────.
2 Lucille Marie Anderson, b ─────────.

No. 2613. Fourth Generation. 49.

6) James E Funk, b Mar 7, 1872, m Nov 8, 1905, Jennie L Marvin, b. Oct 2, 1878, at Stroudsburg, Pa Retired farmer Methodists Burial at Seneca, Kans Address: 313 N 6th St, Seneca, Kans.
1. Omer Marvin Funk, b Nov 26, 1912.

No. 2614. Fourth Generation. 49.

7) Eva Odell Funk, b. Feb 28, 1874, m Mar., 1906, Byron L. Graves. She died Nov. 8, 1925 Farmer Christian Church Burial in Oneida cemetery, Oneida, Kans., which was their address.

No. 2615. Fourth Generation. 49.

8) Fred W. Funk, b Aug 20, 1878, d April 5, 1931, m. Feb. 28, 1904, Maude Graham, b. Nov. 2, 1877. Farmer. Christian Church. Buried at Seneca, Kans. Address Seneca, Kans.
  1. Clifford E. G. Funk, b Nov 10, 1907.
  2 Marguerite Louise Funk, b Dec. 18, 1914
  Fred W. Funk was a good citizen and neighbor.

No. 2616. Fourth Generation. 50.

1) Anna M. Funk, b Sept 30, 1838, near Rushville, Rockingham Co., Va., d. April —, 1900, m. Aug 23, 1863, James C Heltzel They lived near Mt. Clinton, Va Mennonites.
  1. Fann e J Heltzel, b April 29, 1865. No 2617.
  2. Charles H Heltzel, b Aug 6, 1867 No 2619
  3. Hettie L. Heltzel, b May 14, 1869 No 2620.
  4. Samuel Clinton Heltzel, b Oct 14, 1871 No 2621.
  5 R. T D. Heltzel, b Sept 27, 1873 No 2622.
  6 Kemper L Heltzel, b Mar 25, 1875, d. June 9, 1876.
  7 Anna May Heltzel, b Dec 2, 1876, d July 2, 1900.
  8 Wade H Heltzel, b. —————, d at age of 14 years.
  9. Mattie Heltzel, b Mar, 1880, d —————, 1880.

No. 2617. Fifth Generation. 2616.

1) Fannie J Heltzel, b April 29, 1865, near Mt. Clinton, Va, d Jan. 6, 1910, m May 15, 1883, C B Cline Farmer. Presbyterians. Address: Mt. Clinton, Va.
  1. Kemper P. Cline, b Mar 6, 1885 No. 3313.
  2 James Neff Cline, b June 18, 1886 No 3314.
  3. Lester L. Cline, b Oct 6, 1887. No. 3315.
  4. Anna P. Cline, b. July 10, 1889 No. 3316
  5. Arthur Boyd Cline, b April 18, 1891. No. 3317
  6 DeWitt T. Cline, b Dec 28, 1892. No 3319.
  7 William Warren Cline, b Aug 11, 1893. No. 3320
  8. Lula Frances Cline, b Sept 3, 1899 No. 3322.
  9. Rawley Ruff Cline, b Sept 22, 1905. No. 3321.

No. 2619. Fifth Generation. 2616.

2) Charles H. Heltzel, b. Aug 6, 1867, m. Nov 6, 1904, Laura Beidler. Farmer Presbyterians Address. Harrisonburg, Va
  1 Mary M Heltzel, b Nov 18, 1909
  2 Albert Beidler Heltzel, b July 22, 1911
  3 Grace Virginia Heltzel, b May 9, 1914. No 3323.

No. 2620. Fifth Generation. 2616.

3) Hettie L Heltzel, b Oct 14, 1869, m Jan 29, 1907, R. J. Swope. Presbyterians Address· Singers Glen, Va No children

No. 2621. Fifth Generation. 2616.

4) Samuel Clinton Heltzel, b Oct 14, 1871, near Mt. Clinton, Va., m. Nov. 15, 1894, Sallie Barbara Heatwole, b Nov 14, 1874, daughter of Henry S Heatwole Presbyterians. Farmer Address: Spring Creek, Va

1. Turner Isaac Heltzel, b Sept 23, 1895, d May 1, 1899.
2. Infant daughter, b. Dec 6, 1896, d same day.
3. Anna Rosella Heltzel, b Oct. 14, 1898. No. 3324.
4. Esther Lillian Heltzel, b Dec. 20, 1900. No 3325
5. Hunter Putnam Heltzel, b Oct 9, 1902. No. 3326
6. Ruby Elizabeth Heltzel, b. Feb 6, 1905 No 3327.
7. Rachel Katherine Heltzel, b Aug 23, 1908 No 3328.
8. Irene Rebecca Heltzel, b April 11, 1910
9. Samuel Clinton Heltzel, Jr, b Oct 4, 1912
10. Massey Mott Heltzel, b April 4, 1915
11. Lula Henrietta Heltzel, b. Oct. 10, 1918
12 Infant daughter, b Mar 3, 1922, d next day
Note.—Massey Mott Heltzel is preparing for the ministry.

No. 2522. Fifth Generation. 2616.

5) R. T. D. Heltzel, b. Sept. 27, 1873, m Oct 4, 1904, Minnie Showalter, b.
——————, d ————— He married (2nd) Sadie Hopkins. Mail carrier and farmer. Address: Mt Clinton, Va Presbyterians No children

No. 2523. Fourth Generation. 50.

2) Susan Funk, b. Jan 11, 1842, near Rushville, Va., m Mar. 28, 1867, Jacob H. Whissen Farmer. Address Broadway, Va
1. Elizabeth Whissen, b June 14, 1868 No 2624
2. Dorothy Frances Whissen, b June 20, 1870 No 2625.
3. Annie C Whissen, b. May 28, 1872 No 2626
4. Ella S. Whissen, b Nov 23, 1873 No 2627
5 John F Whissen, b Nov 11, 1875 No 2628
6. Hettie V. Whissen, b. Mar 19, 1878 No. 2629
7. Ida M. Whissen, b Feb 25, 1880 No 2630
8. Susan J Whissen, b Feb. 7, 1882 No 2631

No. 2524. Fifth Generation. 2523.

1) Elizabeth A Whissen, b June 14, 1868, near Broadway, Va., m William Flick, in 1893 Address· 155 15th St, Richmond, Calif
1. Sherer Gilbert Flick, b ————— Died in infancy.

No. 2625. Fifth Generation. 2523.

2) Dorothy Frances Whissen, b. June 20, 1870, near Broadway, Va., d Feb 27, 1913, m C. Newton Donovan. Address Dover, Pa.
1. Grantville Donovan, b —————
2. Arnold Donovan, b —————.
3. Pauline Donovan, b ————— No 3289
4. Susie Donovan, b —————. No. 3290
5. Dorothy F Donovan, b Feb 11, 1913. No 3291.

No. 2525. Fifth Generation. 2523.

3) Annie C Whissen, b May 28, 1872, near Broadway, Va., m Frank Good Address. Broadway, Va., R. 2
1. Carl Milton Good, b Dec 25, 1906 No 2626¼
2. Haler W. Good, b —————. Single, his address is Santa Barbara, Calif

No. 2526¼. Sixth Generation. 2626.

1) Carl Milton Good, b Dec 25, 1906, near Broadway, Va., m April 25, 1930, Effie May Tailor, b April 25, 1912. Address 365 W Market St, Harrisonburg, Va.

1. Wayne Milton Good, b Jan 13, 1935
2 Joyce Ann Good, b Aug 19, 1936

No. 2527. Fifth Generation. 2623.

4) Ella S. Whissen, b Nov 25, 1873, near Broadway, Va , m. Aldine Spitzer. They live in Pa
1. Paul G. Spitzer, b. ——————
2. James Spitzer, b ——————, d. ——————.
3 Robert Spitzer, b. ——————.
4. Mabel Spitzer, b ——————, d. ——————.
5. Laco Spitzer, b ——————.
6. Jessie Spitzer, b. ——————
7. Nina Spitzer, b. ——————.

No. 2623. Fifth Generation. 2623.

5) John F. Whissen, b Nov 11, 1875, near Broadway, Va., m. Carrie Donovan. Address: Wray, Colo., Box 692.
1. Raymond Whissen, b. ——————.
2. Elizabeth Whissen, b ——————
3. Grace Whissen, b. ——————.
4. Callie Whissen, b. ——————.
5. Gladys Whissen, b. ——————.
6 Anna Whissen, b. ——————.

No. 2529. Fifth Generation. 2623.

6) Hettie V Whissen, b Mar 19, 1878, near Broadway, Va., m. Ira Moore, b. April 8, 1873. They were married Jan. 23, 1903 Address: Harrisonburg, Va. Farmer.
1. Iva May Moore, b. May 4, 1904. No 3292.
2. James Howard Moore, b. July 8, 1905, d July 15, 1927.
3 Ira Whissen Moore, b May 13, 1908 No. 3293.
4 Beulah Virginia Moore, b. Feb. 24, 1910. No. 3294.
5. Wilkie Ruth Moore, b. Oct. 13, 1912. No. 3295.
6. Edward Moore, b. Sept 2, 1914, twin.
7. Elsie Moore, b. Sept. 2, 1914, twin. No 3296.
8. Albert David Moore, b. Oct. 8, 1916.
9. Martin Wilson Moore, b. Oct. 9, 1918.

No. 2530. Fifth Generation. 2623.

7) Ida M. Whissen, b. Feb 25, 1880, near Broadway, Va., m. J. Frank Shoemaker.
1. F. Whissen Shoemaker, b May 1, 1911 No. 3297.
2. Harold M. Shoemaker, b April 18, 1912
3. Virginia R. Shoemaker, b July 5, 1914.
4. R. Ellwood Shoemaker, b. Dec 8, 1916.
5. Lucille A Shoemaker, b Aug. 27, 1919.

No. 2631. Fifth Generation. 2623.

8) Susie J. Whissen, b Feb 7, 1882, near Broadway, Va., m. Dec. 29, 1910, William Frank Simmers, b Feb 29, 1881 Address· Dayton, Va., R. 1. Farmer
1 Paul J Simmers, b Feb 17, 1911
2. Ira F. Simmers, b Feb 25, 1914.
3. John S. Simmers, b June 23, 1916
4 Roy O Simmers, b Aug 15, 1921.

No. 2632. Fourth Generation. 50.

3) Samuel C. Funk, b Oct. 30, 1845, near Rushville, Va, m Dec 19, 1867, Elizabeth Anna Adams. Address Ottobine, Va Machinist United Brethren.

1. Viola F. Funk, b. Mar. 28, 1869. No. 2633
2. Katie Lula Funk, b July 17, 1871. No. 2634
3. Ida R. Funk, b Nov 19, 1873. No 2635
4. Bertha J. Funk, b July 2, 1876. No. 2636
5. Effie E Funk, b Nov 4, 1878. No 2637
6. Infant Funk, b —————, d Oct 25, 1881
7. Infant, b. —————, d Mar 10, 1883.
8. Arabella Gertrude Funk, b April 24, 1884, d —————, 1897
9. Edna H. Funk, b May 1, 1888, d. Jan 3, 1889

No. 2633. Fifth Generation. 2632.

1) Viola F. Funk, b. Mar 28, 1869, near Ottobine, Va, m May 17, 1888, John H. Brunk. Farmer United Brethren Address Rushville, Va

1. Beulah Brunk, b June 25, 1890, d. Aug 18, 1890.
2. Welby Leo Brunk, b Sept 8, 1891 No 3304.
3. Edgar R Brunk, b Aug 16, 1893 No 3305
4. Leona E. Brunk, b June 9, 1895 No. 3306.
5. Joseph A. Brunk, b Nov 15, 1897 No 3307.
6 Infant daughter, b Mar 5, 1900, lived 10 days
7. Horace C. Brunk, b Feb 23, 1901, d. Oct 7, 1906
8. Bayard F. Brunk, b April 29, 1902 No 3308
9 Dwight F. Brunk, b Dec 10, 1904 No 3309.
10 Helen V. Brunk, b Feb 2, 1907, d June 29, 1907
11 Virginia Glen Brunk, b ————— No 3310.
12. Marguerite Brunk, b ————— No 3311.
13. Dorothy Brunk, b ————— No. 3312.

No. 2634. Fifth Generation. 2632.

2) Katie Lula Funk, b. July 17, 1871, near Ottobine, Va, m Franklin E. Bowman.

1 Arlie S Bowman, b. June 21, 1895 No 3298.
2 Gertrude A Bowman, b Oct. 20, 1896 No 3299
3 Irene V Bowman, b Sept 17, 1898 No 3300.

No. 2635. Fifth Generation. 2632.

3) Ida R Funk, b Nov. 19, 1873, near Ottobine, Va, m Oct. 15, 1896, Walter E. Chapman

1. Goldie Chapman, b May 30, 1901. No 3301.
2. Paul Chapman, b Feb 29, 1904. No 3302
3. Tracy O Chapman, b Aug 24, 1898 No 3303
4 Francis Chapman, b. Sept 8, 1907 No 3303¼
5. Rosalie Virginia Chapman, b Jan 26, 1919.

No. 2636. Fifth Generation. 2632.

4) Bertha J Funk, b July 2, 1876, near Ottobine, Va, m. Phares Hinkle No children.

No. 2637. Fifth Generation. 2632.

5) Effie E Funk, b. Nov 4, 1878, near Ottobine, Va, m J Herbert Skelton.

1. Edna Merle Skelton, b —————, 1906 No 2637¼
2 Ralph H. Skelton, b ——————, 1909.
3. Herald Skelton, b. —————, 1916.
4 Joan Elizabeth Skelton, b ——————, 1920

No. 2637¼. Sixth Generation. 2637.

1) Edna Merle Skelton, b ————, 1906, m Erwin Ansminger

1. Anna E Ansminger, b. ————, 1928

No. 2638. Fourth Generation. 50.

4) Esther H Funk, b Jan. 2, 1848, near Rushville, Va., m William Gladwell. Address Mt. Clinton, Va No children.

No. 2639. Fourth Generation. 50.

5) Martin D Funk, b Aug 14, 1851, near Rushville, Va., m Frances M Jordon, Oct 20, 1875. She was b May 6, 1849 He died Oct 13, 1926 Mrs Funk died July 25, 1931 Brick manufacturer. Mrs. Funk was a Presbyterian. Address Wray, Colo. Burial at Wray, Colo

1 Amy Gertrude Funk, b Feb 1, 1882, d Aug 16, 1883.

2 Daniel Christian Funk, b Mar 6, 1884. No 2640

3. Howard Charles Funk, b Oct. 3, 1885 No 2641.

4 Ernest Martin Funk, b July 8, 1890 No. 2642.

5. Walter Harold Funk, b May 1, 1895, d. in 1910

No. 2640. Fifth Generation. 2639.

2) Daniel Christian Funk, b Mar 6, 1884, m Maude A McGee, b. Nov 23, 18— General contractor Presbyterians Address· Wray, Colo

1 Harold Nathan Funk, b Feb 28, 1912

2. Benjamin Ivan Funk, b. April 21, 1913

No. 2641. Fifth Generation. 2639.

3) Howard Charles Funk, b Oct. 3, 1885, m Nov 23, 1913, Clora Noffsinger, b. June 2, 1895 Address Wray, Colo

1 James Martin Funk, b Dec 21, 1914

2. Frances Funk, b June 2, 1916

3 Thelma Funk, b Sept 18, 1917

No. 2642. Fifth Generation. 2639.

4) Ernest Martin Funk, b July 8, 1890, m Aug 23, 1919, Rose Jameson, b Mar. 9, 1893 Physician Presbyterians Address· 7122 Marconi St, Huntington Park, Calif

1 Jameson Ernest Funk, b July 13, 1920.

2 Paul Martin Funk, b Feb 17, 1921

3. Margaret Ernestine Funk, b Nov 16, 1930

4 Ellen Frances Funk, b Jan 17, 1932.

No. 2643. Fourth Generation. 50.

6) Abraham B Funk, b Dec 12, 1853, near Rushville, Va, m Ella L Ringold She died and was buried at Ellison, N Dak Mr Funk died ————, and was buried at Yoder, Colo They lived at Ellison, N Dak, at time of his wife's death.

1. Daisy Funk, b April 10, 1881 No 3329

2 Mollie Funk, b Sept 14, 1882 No 3333

3 Ruth Funk, b Mar 26, 1893 No 3334

No. 2644. Fourth Generation. 50.

7) James N. Funk, b May 21, 1856, near Rushville, Va, m June 8, 1890, Henrietta Morris, b Feb 24, 1861 Address. Wray, Colo Brick manufacturer

1 Edna Pearl Funk, b Oct. 13, 1894 No 2645.

2 Walter Herschel Funk, b Mar 26, 1896 No 2646

No. 2745. Fifth Generation. 2544.

1) Edna Pearl Funk, b. Oct 13, 1894, m June 8, 1919, Charles B. Noffsinger
Address: Wray, Colo. Farmer

1. Paul James Noffsinger, b. April 10, 1920
2. Warren Herschel Noffsinger, b Feb 21, 1921
3. Delbert Earl Noffsinger, b. June 28, 1922
4. Leona Maxine Noffsinger, b May 9, 1926
5. Charline Edna Noffsinger, b April 13, 1928
6. Helen Leora Noffsinger, b Dec 13, 1931

No. 2646. Fifth Generation. 2644.

2) Walter Herschel Funk, b Mar 26, 1896, m in 1920, Helen H Sigmiller.
Address: Wray, Colo

1. Stewart Wayne Funk, b April 28, 1923
2. Keith Ardell Funk, b Nov 27, 1925
3. Mary Margarite Funk, b Sept 20, 1928

No. 2647. Fourth Generation. 51.

1) Ann Elizabeth Ridenour, b Feb 10, 1850, in Va, d Feb. 27, 1875, at
Monroeville, Ind. She married Louis F Niezer, b April 14, 1840, d Oct 8, 1925.
Both were buried at Monroeville, Ind Catholic

1. Mary M. Niezer, b. Sept 8, 1872, single
2. Louis B Niezer, b. Feb. 22, 1875, single

No. 2548. Fourth Generation. 51.

2) Adam Pierce Ridenour, b Mar 3, 1853, in Va, d. in Stephens Co., Kans.,
July 28, 1928. He married Aug. 13, 1877, Angeline Sheets, at Van Wert, O. She
was b. Dec. 13, 1857, d Jan. 15, 1928 They were buried in Hugoton, Stephens
Co., Kans.

1. John Calhoun Ridenour, b. May 10, 1878. No. 2649
2. Nelle Irene Ridenour, b. Sept. 4, 1879 No. 2650
3. Herman J. Ridenour, b Feb. 9, 1881, d April 21, 1894.
4. Adam Otto H. Ridenour, b. Jan. 31, 1883. No 2651.
5. Cleveland H. Ridenour, b. June 30, 1884, d. Mar. 20, 1887.

No. 2649. Fifth Generation. 2548.

1) John Calhoun Ridenour, b May 10, 1878, m Beatrice M Hawley, Jan. 13,
1913. Address: Klaber, Wash

1. Jean Louise, b April 15, 1925 (adopted).

No. 2650. Fifth Generation. 2648.

2) Nellie Irene Ridenour, b Sept 4, 1879, m William Lampe, Feb. 3, 1909.
Both were buried at Yakima, Wash

1. Frances Eleanor Lampe, b April 9, 1910
2. Henry Adam Lampe, b May 4, 1912, d ————, 1935.
3. William John Lampe, b Nov 6, 1913
4. Nellie Beatrice Lampe, b. June 23, 1915
5. Angeline Lampe, b Feb 17, 1917.
6. Mary Catherine Lampe, b July 23, 1918
7. Helen Genevieve Lampe, b. Dec 15, 1920
8. Fred Lampe, b Sept 29, 1923, d next day.

No. 2551. Fifth Generation. 2548.

4) Adam Otto Ridenour, b Jan 31, 1883, m Aug 25, 1915 Irene Elma Wear, b. Jan. 31, 1892. Farmer and rancher Address Moscow, Kans. Methodists. Burial place, Hugoton, Kans.

1. Adam Otto Ridenour, Jr, b May 29, 1916
2. Walter Loren Ridenour, b Aug 2. 1919.
3. Rosalie Anna Ridenour, b. Sept 29, 1921
4 Richard Lynn Ridenour, b July 9, 1923.
5 Gladys Grace R denour, b June 14, 1925.
6 Donald Victor Ridenour, b. April 17, 1929
7 Paul Eldon Ridenour, b July 8, 1930
8. John Robert Ridenour, b May 30, 1932

No. 2652. Fourth Generation. 51.

3) Lydia Margaret Ridenour, b ———, 1855, d. ———, 1875, m Valentine Shaffer, b Jan 4, 1852, d Nov 11, 1930 School teacher. Address: Monroeville, Ind. Both were buried at Monroeville, Ind

1 Lydia Esther Shaffer, b. ———, 1875 No. 2656.

No. 2553. Fourth Generation. 51.

4) Ephraim B Ridenour, b Nov 14, 1878, d April 5, 1920, m. Catherine Hayse. Deceased They lived at Monroeville, Ind

1. Evelyn G. Ridenour, b ————, m, Peter Krock 1 child
2 Emelyn R Ridenour, b ————, deceased.

No. 2554. Fourth Generation. 51.

5) Catherine Ridenour, b April 11, 1861, d July 28, 1933, m. Dec. 21, 1882, Charles Wickwire, b Sept 1, 1858, d April 25, 1929. Farmer. Church of Christ Scientists. Address· 403 East Broad St, Angola, Ind

1. Ethel Wave Wickwire, b Nov 1, 1883, teacher.
2 Virginia Esther Wickwire, b Mar. 8, 1885, teacher.
3 Rebecca Ruth Wickwire, b. June 20, 1893, d. Feb —, 1894.
4. George Charles Wickwire, b Feb 7, 1895, teacher.

Note.—The members of this family are all single and are teaching When they have their vacation, they still maintain their home at 403 East Broad St., Angola, Ind

No. 2555. Fourth Generation. 51.

6) Sarah Ridenour, b June 29, 1863, d Mar 22, 1917, m. Nov. 24, 1887, Edwin Albert Walborn, b. Mar 21, 1860 Address Van Wert, O., R 2. Farmer Lutherans Burial in Woodlawn cemetery, Van Wert, O.

1 Lewis Earl Walborn, b Mar 10, 1890 No 2660.
2 Edwin Herschel Walborn, b June 18, 1892, d. Aug. 5, 1900.
3 Beulah Walborn, b Jan 15, 1898. No 2661
4 Walter Ivan Walborn, b Jan 27, 1899 No 2662.
5. Cecil Roscoe Walborn, b. Dec 4, 1901, d Mar 5, 1903.

No. 2556. Fifth Generation. 2552.

1) Lydia Esther Shaffer, b ———, 1875, m Dec. 25, 1895, Newton Brown, b ———, 1874 Esther died in 1911 Buried at Monroeville. Address· Monroeville, Ind. Farmer Methodists

1. Ivan Shaffer Brown, b Aug 13, 1906 No 2657.
2. Guy Kenneth Brown, b Mar 31, 1908 No 2658
3 Ferol Esther Brown, b April 7, 1910 No 2659

No. 2657. Sixth Generation. 2656.

1) Ivan Shaffer Brown, b. Aug 13, 1906, m in 1932, Betty Freewald. Address: 118 E. Kildare, Lima, O

No. 2658. Sixth Generation. 2656.

2) Guy Kenneth Brown, b Mar 31, 1908, m Aug 17, 1929, Mary Jane Klinker. Address 2320 E. Pontiac St , Ft. Wayne, Ind.
1 Betty Lou Brown, b May 18, 1930

No. 2659. Sixth Generation. 2656.

3) Ferol Esther Brown, b April 7, 1910, m Mar 17, 1928, Edward DeFrain. Living at Petersburg, Fla No issue

No. 2660. Fifth Generation. 2655.

1) Lewis Earl Walborn, b Mar. 10, 1890, m in 1921, Helen E Hillburgh, of Pittsburgh, Pa They live at 744 E 2nd St., Tucson, Ariz
1. Eloise Eleanore Walborn, b July —, 1922

No. 2661. Fifth Generation. 2655.

3) Beulah Walborn, b Jan. 15, 1898, near Van Wert, O , m. Aug. 25, 1925, Dewey W. Zipperer Lutherans Mr Zipperer is a Lutheran minister and is located at Waynesboro, Va., at present No children

No. 2662. Fifth Generation. 2655.

4) Walter Ivan Walborn, b Jan 27, 1899, m in 1924, Lucile Shadle of Wheatridge, Colo. They live in Wheatridge, Colo. (near Denver).

No. 2663. Fourth Generation. 52.

1) Michael Brunk, b Oct 4, 1844, near Edom, Va , d. April 1, 1921, at Knoxville, Tenn. He married Rebecca J. Hogan, b Dec 26, 1846, d. Sept. 24, 1891. He married April 20, 1893, Mrs. Lessie Shank (nee Smith). Mr. Brunk is a Christian and Mrs Brunk is a Mennonite Farmer and carpenter. He lived in Missouri until after his second marriage when he moved to near Knoxville, Tenn. He and his first wife were buried at Jerico Springs, Mo His last wife was buried at Knoxville, Tenn. She died Dec 28, 1935 His first marriage took place Mar. 1, 1865.
1. Charles Christian Brunk, b. Jan 17, 1868, unmarried.
2. William W. Brunk, b. Feb 22, 1870 No 2664
3. Annie E. Brunk, b. Oct. 30, 1872, twin No 2669
4. Maggie C. Brunk, b. Oct 30, 1872, twin No 2665
5. Ervin Edward Brunk, b. Sept. 20, 1875. No 2671.
6 Miller Michael Brunk, b. July 19, 1878. No. 2672.
7. Ella R. Brunk, b June 14, 1884 No 2673

No. 2664. Fifth Generation. 2663.

2) William Washington Brunk, b Feb. 22, 1870, m Addie Battle, at Nashville, Tenn., in 1899.
1. Lilian Brunk, b ——————, m a Mr Stevens and lives at Rutherford, N. J.
2. Alfred Brunk, b ——————, lives in Ohio
3. Clifford Brunk, b. ——————, lives in New York City

No. 2665. Fifth Generation. 2663.

3) Maggie Catherine Brunk, b Oct 30, 1872, m Dec 25, 1895, John W Clemmens, b Dec 25, 1872 Farmer and carpenter Brethren Address: Parsons, Kans

1 Lyman Brunk Clemmens, b June 29, 1897. No. 2666.

2. Leta Clemmens, b. Feb 25, 1899 No 2667

3 Leona Clemmens, b Sept. 16, 1905 No. 2668.

No. 2666. Sixth Generation. 2665.

1) Lyman Brunk Clemmens, b June 29, 1897, m in April, 1927, Lenora Cook, of Parsons, Kans No issue.

No. 2667. Sixth Generation. 2665.

2) Leta Clemmens, b Feb 25, 1899, m Sept 7, 1919, Samuel Elijah Sparks They live at Melrose, N Mex

1. Kathryn Sparks, b. July 9, 1922.

2 Samuel Harlan Sparks, b. Feb. 10, 1924.

No. 2658. Sixth Generation. 2665.

3) Leona Clemmens, b Sept 16, 1905, m Sept , 1924, George Allison, b. Nov. 13, 1888, in Texas.

1. Robert Neal Allison, b Feb 13, 1920

No. 2669. Fifth Generation. 2663.

4) Annie E. Brunk, b Oct. 30, 1872, m in 1896, William Lones, at Knoxville, Tenn. Three children of six survive.

1 Lessie Lones, b ——————. No. 2670.

2 Mam e Lones, b ——————.

3 Virginia Lones, b ——————

No. 2670. Sixth Generation. 2669.

1) Lessie Lones, b ——————, m William Dukes, of Knoxville, Tenn

No. 2671. Fifth Generation. 2663.

5) Ervin Edward Brunk, b. Sept 20, 1875, m. Aug , 1901, Cora Sandy, of Mo They reside at Rochester, N. Y.

1. Margaret Brunk, b. Aug. 26, 1903

2 Marian Brunk, b. May 18, 1906.

3 Russell Brunk, b. Sept 20, 1907

4. Kathryn Brunk, b April 1, 1913.

5 Curtis Brunk, b July 20, 1919

No. 2672. Fifth Generation. 2663.

6) Miller Michael Brunk, b July 19, 1878, m. Feb. 13, 1900, Susan Sandy of Mo They reside at Sebring, Fla.

1. Nina Marie Brunk, b Sept 28, 1902, m. A White of Boston, Mass.

2. Lloyd S Brunk, b Sept 12, 1905, of Columbia, S. C.

3 Max Edwin Brunk, b Sept 12, 1914, of Sebring, Fla

No. 2673. Fifth Generation. 2663.

7) Ella R Brunk, b June 14, 1885, m. L E Smith of Elon College, of North Carolina. Address: Elon College, N. C.

1. Rebecca Smith, b ——————

2. L. E Smith, Jr., b. ——————.

No. 2674. Fourth Generation. 52.

2) Annie Elizabeth Brunk, b July 15, 1846, in Va , m Feb. 21, 1866, DeWitt Coffman Beery, b. Feb. 27, 1846, in Va They lived at Jerico Springs, Mo. Farmer. Methodists. Buried at Jerico Springs, Mo

1 Joseph William Beery, b June 9, 1867. No. 2675.

2 Gunning Christian Beery, b. Mar 1, 1869 No 2678.

3. Maggie Olive Beery, b Nov 1, 1870. No 2680.
4 DeWitt A. Beery, b July 9, 1872. No 2684
5 Anna Belle Beery, b Feb 4, 1874, d. Nov 18, 1874.
6. Viola May Beery, b Mar 25, 1876 No 2685
7. John K. Beery, b Mar 31, 1878
8 Ivy Frances Beery, b April 4, 1880. No 2689.
9. Ethel Cleo Beery, b. Nov 24, 1882 No 2690
10 Elsie Sidney Beery, b April 28, 1885. No. 2691.
11. Jessie Lee Beery, b July 31, 1887. No 2692.

No. 2675. Fifth Generation. 2674.

1) Joseph William Beery, b June 9, 1867, at Edom, Va , m Sarah Sanders, May 9, 1897, now living at Atwood, Colo. Mercantile business

1. Bernis Lydia Beery, b Mar 12, 1898 No. 2676.
2 Harley Newman Beery, b. Sept 27, 1906. No 2677.

No. 2376. Sixth Generation. 2675.

1) Bernis Lydia Beery, b. Mar 12, 1898, m May 26, 1920, Edward Kline An electric engineer. Address 36 W Nevada Place, Denver, Colo.

1. Vincent Murry Kline, b May 22, 1921.
2 Joseph Vernon Kline, b. Feb 10, 1923
3 Kathleen May Kline, b Feb. 12, 1926
4. Hugh Francis Kline, b Dec. 10, 1928

No. 2377. Sixth Generation. 2675.

2) Harley Newman Beery, b Sept 27, 1906, m Oct. 29, 1927, Lucille Ruth Propst. Auto salesman His hobby is music Address Atwood, Colo

1 Sarah Ruth Beery, b. Mar. 3, 1929
2. Harley Eugene Beery, b June 12, 1931

No. 2678. Fifth Generation. 2574.

2) Gunning Christian Beery, b Mar. 1, 1869, m. Aug. 9, 1904, Rachel Trask, b. Nov. 20, 1883, of Deer Lodge, Mont Address: 1113 Paguin St., Columbia, Mo.

1. Dorcas Augusta Beery, b Sept 10, 1905. No 2679.
2. Monri DeWitt Beery, b Feb 16, 1907
3. Evelyn Claire Beery. b. Mar. 26, 1915.
4. Gunning Trask Beery, b Jan. 16, 1921.

No. 2679. Sixth Generation. 2578.

1) Dorcas Augusta Beery, b Sept. 10, 1905, at Deer Lodge, Mont , m Strickney Stark. They live at Louisiana, Mo.

1. Lloyd Strickney Stark, b Feb. 28, 1930
2 Margaret Stark, b Mar. 2, 1933.

No. 2680. Fifth Generation. 2574.

3) Maggie Olive Beery, b Nov 1, 1870, m Aug. 14, 1893, Benjamin H. Anderson, b. Mar. 18, 1868 Farmer. Methodists Address 434 S Mill St , Bolivar, Mo

1. Lola B. Anderson, b May 11, 1894, teacher in the school of journalism at Columbia, Mo. Single
2. B Herschel Anderson, b July 11, 1900 No 2681
3. DeWitt M Anderson, b Mar. 2, 1904. No. 2682.
4. Wilbur F. Anderson, b Nov 13, 1906 No 2683
5 Robert Finis Anderson, b Sept. 17, 1908

No. 2581. Sixth Generation. 2580.

2) Benjamin Herschel Anderson, b July 11, 1900, m. Dec 8, 1921, Dixie Grant, b April 23, 1905 Address· Fair Play, Mo , R 3. Farmer. Methodists. Burial place in Slagel cemetery.

1. Benjamin Herschel Anderson, Jr , b. May 9, 1922.
2 Robert Grant Anderson, b July 23, 1926
3. William Howard Anderson, b Aug. 4, 1928.
4. James Anderson, b. Sept 10, 1935, d same day.

No. 2582. Sixth Generation. 2680.

3) DeWitt M. Anderson, b Mar. 2, 1904, m. April 26, 1924, Mildred White, b. Feb. 14, 1903 Address: Lebanon, Mo Mail carrier.

1. Mary Louise Anderson, b May 27, 1929

No. 2683. Sixth Generation. 2680.

4) Wilbur F. Anderson, b. Nov. 13, 1906, m. Aug 8, 1928, Glee Huffman, b. April 6. 1909. Address Jerico Springs, Mo Farmer. Methodists

1 Francis Lee Anderson, b Aug 11, 1930.

No. 2584. Fifth Generation. 2574.

4) DeWitt A Beery, b July 9, 1872, m. Aug 23, 1898, Jennie Slavens. Minister. M. E. Church

1. Bethel Beery, b May 25, 1899
2 Ruth Beery, b May 18, 1901

No. 2585. Fifth Generation. 2674.

6) Viola May Beery, b Mar. 23, 1876, m June 18, 1896, S. E. Yokley, b. Jan. 29, 1874, d Aug 23, 1903 She married (2nd) Jan. 23, 1913, G. W. Frieze. Farmer. Methodists, South Burial place at Jerico Springs, Mo Address: Jerico Springs, Mo.

1. Katie Delpha Yokley, b July 31, 1897. No. 2686.
2. Gladys Anna Yokley, b Aug. 19, 1899, d. Oct. 2, 1903
3. Garland Alexander Yokley, b June 21, 1901 No. 2687.
4. Samuel Lovel Yokley, b July 9, 1903 No. 2688.
5. Lois Lamoyne Yokley, b. Nov. 14, 1914, d Sept. 3, 1931.

No. 2586. Sixth Generation. 2585.

1) Katie Delpha Yokley, b July 31, 1897, m July 12, 1928, C. I Griffin, a railroad carrier from Stockton, Mo She was a schoolteacher for seventeen years. She graduated from Springfield College. No children.

No. 2587. Sixth Generation. 2585.

3) Garland Alexander Yokley, b June 21, 1901, m. Dec , 1922, Hazel Deiffenderfer, of Jerico Springs, Mo Farmer near Jerico Springs, Mo.

1. Lloyd Lee Yokley, b Nov 11, 1922.
2. Samuel Afton Yokley, b Sept. 20, 1924
3. Garland Junior Yokley, b. April 20, 1928
4. Darrel Amos Yokley, b April 27, 1931
5. Franklin Dale Yokley, b Mar. 5, 1933

No. 2688. Sixth Generation. 2685.

4) Samuel Lovel Yokley, b July 9, 1903, m. Dorothy Kranz, of Chicago, Ill., where they live He works in a bakery

1 Dorothy Dolores Yokley, b April 26, 1928.

No. 2689. Fifth Generation. 2674.

8) Iva Frances Beery, b April 4, 1880, m. Aug 20, 1907, Ben F. Melcher, b. Mar. 1, 1873 Address. 109 W North St , Warrensburg, Mo. Merchant. Methodists.
1. Lucile Frances Melcher, b Aug. 1, 1908, d July 23, 1911.
2. Ben Beery Melcher, b. Dec. 26, 1909.
3. Mildred Irene Melcher, b. Oct. 16, 1912.
4. Beatrice Pauline Melcher, b May 27, 1917

No. 2690. Fifth Generation. 2674.

9) Ethel Cleo Beery, b. Nov 24, 1882, m in 1913 A. Clyde Thurman They live on a ranch in western Wash.ngton. Address Mt Vernon, Wash , R 2.
1. Myron Beery Thurman, b April 19, 1914, is in school at Washington university, Seattle, Wash.
2. Alberta Ruth Thurman, b Dec 9, 1915, is in her second year college work (1936) at Mt Vernon, Wash

No. 2691. Fifth Generation. 2674.

10) Elsie Sidney Beery, b April 28, 1885, m Aug 17, 1904, Robert Allen Ryan, b May 3, 1884 Both were born near Cedarville, Mo They moved in spring of 1905 to Gallatin Co , Mont , and for the last 22 years have lived in Sweet Grass Co , Mont. He followed ranch farming, until in 1937 Mr. Ryan became service manager for the International Harvester Co Evangelical. Address Big Timber, Mont.
1. Ralph Wesley Ryan, b. Mar. 4, 1906, single
2 Viola Blanche Ryan, b Jan 5, 1910, is nursing
3 Louis Elizabeth Ryan, b Nov. 11, 1911, teaching school
4 Bonnie Jean Ryan, b Dec 11, 1913.
5. Raymond Donald Ryan, b Feb 7, 1922

No. 2692. Fifth Generation. 2674.

11) Jessie Lee Beery, b July 31, 1887, m in 1919 Paul J Lester Accountant Methodists Address· 1972 N. Clay St , Springfield, Mo.
1. David Beery Lester, b. Sept 12, 1925

No. 2693. Fourth Generation. 52.

4) Joseph H. Brunk, b Feb 23, 1851, near Edom, Va , m. Catherine V. Geil, b. July 6, 1853, d Jan , 1911. Mr. Brunk married (2nd) wife Annie E Brunk, daughter of Samuel and Susan Hartman Brunk, July 27, 1913 Mennonites Address: Linville Depot, Va Farmer
1 Ada May Brunk, b. Jan. 4, 1877. No. 2694

No. 2694. Fifth Generation. 2693.

1) Ada May Brunk, b Jan 4, 1877, near Edom, Va , m May 8, 1913, Crawford J. Neff, b Feb 4, 1874 Address: Linville, Va Farmer. Presbyterians No children

No. 2695. Fourth Generation. 52.

5) Noah C Brunk, b Dec 30, 1852, near Edom, Va , m Carrie Hite, b ——————, d. ——————— Mr. Brunk is living in Calif. No issue reported

No. 2696. Fourth Generation. 52.

6) Fannie R. Brunk, b April 29, 1855, near Edom, Va., m in 1878, Jacob H Stauffer. They lived at Aberdeen, S Dak , and are now living at Winchester, Va
1. Clinton Stauffer, b ——————— No. 3365
2. Harry Stauffer, b ———————. No. 3366.
3. Bessie Stauffer, b ———————, single.

No. 2697. Fourth Generation. 52.

9) Frank T. Brunk, b Sept. 18, 1862, near Edom, Va., m. Nellie Foos, in 1866 Hardware business at Eau Claire, Wis., which is their address.

1. Joyce Brunk, b ——————, was married and had one child. She drowned in a river near her home.

No. 2638. Fourth Generation. 53.

2) Anthony A Brenneman, b Feb 14, 1852, near Edom, Va., m. Feb. 8, 1876, Lucretia A Winger, b. May 8, 1852, and d Aug. 22, 1933. Farmer. Baptists. Burial in Rose Hill Park, Oklahoma City, Okla, Lot 96, Block No. 10. Address: Waurika, Okla.

1. John L Brenneman, b. Nov. 28, 1876. No 2699
2. Oscar H. Brenneman, b. Dec 22, 1880. No 2700.
3 Myrtle M. Brenneman, b. Jan 20, 1882, d. Nov 18, 1883.
4. Mollie M. Brenneman, b Oct 29, 1883 No 2703

No. 2699. Fifth Generation. 2698.

1) John L Brenneman, b Nov 28, 1876, in Mo, m June 12, 1901, Ora Aultman, b. Jan. 7, 1880. Farmer Baptists Burial place at Oklahoma City, Okla. Address: Harlington, Tex. No children

No. 2700. Fifth Generation. 2698.

2) Oscar H Brenneman, b Dec. 22, 1880, in Mo., m Jan. 28, 1903, Linnie D Aultman, b Dec 25, 1882. They separated in 1923 In 1933 Oscar married (2nd) Charlotte Dufour Children are from first marriage Address: 621 Dakota Ave., Medford, Oreg.

1. Kenneth S. Brenneman, b Mar. 3, 1904. No. 2701.
2. Audree A Brenneman, b Aug 16, 1911 No 2702.

No. 2701. Sixth Generation. 2700.

1) Kenneth S Brenneman, b Mar. 3, 1904, in Mo, m. Jan 28, 1923, Evelyn Brazelton, b May 8, 1907 Mechanic. Christian Science Address: 2840 Hellen St., Oakland, Calif. No issue

No. 2702. Sixth Generation. 2700.

2) Audree A Brenneman, b. Aug 16, 1911, m. Dec. 11, 1929, Herbert Gustave Kraft, b 1906 They soon separated and she married Dec. 3, 1934, Kenneth Edward Kessler, b. in 1899 Occupation protection. Christian Science. Business address. 503 Central Bank Building, Oakland, Calif. No children. Residence: 116 Greenback Ave, Piedmont, Calif.

No. 2703. Fifth Generation. 2638.

4) Mollie M. Brenneman, b Oct 29, 1883, m. May 3, 1904, Gettis E. Evans, b. Oct 12, 1878 Farmer Baptist Address: Waurika, Okla. Burial ground, Waurika, Okla.

1. Anthony Sevier Evans, b. April 5, 1905. No. 2704.
2. Irvin H. Evans, b July 15, 1908 No 2705

No. 2704. Sixth Generation. 2703.

1) Anthony Sevier Evans, b April 5, 1905, m. Mar. 11, 1926, Ona Kriskil, b Feb. 14, 1906. Rural mail carrier. Baptist and Christian. Address: Waurika, Okla. Burial, same place.

1. Alice Myrl Evans, b. July 2, 1929.

No. 2705. Sixth Generation. 2703.

2) Irvin H. Evans, b Jan 15, 1908, m Aug 28, 1932, Mary Ann Sheffield, b. May 29, 1914 Filling station operator Baptists Address Waurika, Okla No issue.

No. 2705. Fourth Generation. 53.

3) Jacob H Brenneman, b Mar 29, 1854, near Edom, Va, d April 3, 1920, m. Feb 9, 1876, Marie Emaline Evans, b May 7, 1857, d Jan. 5, 1914 Buried in Plano cemetery Stafford Co, Kans, where they had settled in 1880. Farmer. Baptists Address: St. John, Kans.

1. Daisy L. Brenneman, b Sept 29, 1877 No 2707
2 Ella M Brenneman, b May 31, 1879 No 2709
3. William L Brenneman, b Nov. 17, 1881, d Sept. 15, 1900.
4 Ethel M. Brenneman, b. Nov. 19, 1884 No 2712
5 Henry D Brenneman, b Aug 23, 1886 No 2716
6 Blanche M Brenneman, b Sept 10, 1893 No 2718
7. Jennie M. Brenneman, b Dec 9, 1895 No 2719
8 Carl E Brenneman, b April 15, 1898, d. May 31, 1899

No. 2707. Fifth Generation. 2706.

1) Daisy L Brenneman, b Sept 29, 1877, m Nov 15, 1899, Lester A. Henry, b. Oct. 1, 1876 They lived together a few years, then separated. Daisy on June 2, 1906, marr.ed Claude L. Martin He was a painter and paper hanger Address: Garden City, Kans. Baptist.

1. Auletha Aurela Henry, b Feb 8, 1901 No 2708

No. 2703. Sixth Generation. 2707.

1) Auletha Aurela Henry, b Feb 8, 1901, m in 1920 Glen Cadman Address: Walsenburg, Colo

1 Gunnison Glen Cadman, b Feb 27, 1924

No. 2709. Fifth Generation. 2706.

2) Ella M Brenneman, b May 31, 1879, d Nov 8, 1925, m Feb 9, 1902, Edward H. Hawley, b Dec 31, 1874 Address St John, Kans Mail carrier Burial at St. John, Kans.

1. Edna May Hawley, b. Nov 22, 1902, d Mar 3, 1903
2 Minnie Mabel Hawley, b May 31, 1904 No 2710
3 Ervin Dale Hawley, b. Dec. 24, 1911. No 2711
4 Opal Irene Hawley, b April 11, 1913, d Aug. 12, 1913
5 Jessie Emaline Hawley, b Oct 9, 1920, is in Catholic Convent at Kansas City, Kans.

No. 2710. Sixth Generation. 2709.

2) Minnie Mabel Hawley, b May 31, 1904, m Aug 15, 1923, Robert Wesley Clowers, b April 4, 1899 Farmers Housewife Baptists Burial at St John, Kans Address· Elkhart, Kans

1 Robert Wesley Clowers, Jr, b Nov 6, 1924, d Nov 14, 1924
2. Wanda May Clowers, b Jan 21, 1927
3. Bobby Lee Clowers, b July 20, 1929
4 Bettie Lou Clowers, b April 30, 1931
5. Nancy Ann Clowers, b July 16, 1933

No. 2711. Sixth Generation. 2709.

2) Ervin Dale Hawley, b Dec 25, 1911, at St John, Kans, m July 21, 1933, Gold e Pansy Heale, b June 21, 1913, at Stillwater, Okla Street commissioner at White Water, Kans Address: White Water, Kans, Box 116

1. Ervin Dale Hawley, b Feb 10, 1934, at White Water, Kans.

No. 2712. Fifth Generation. 2706.

4) Ethel M. Brenneman, b. Nov 19, 1884, m Dec 24, 1901, Francis A Ira, b Oct. 14, 1883 Baptist and Nazarene Address: Dodge City, Kans. Railway employee

1. Cecil C. Ira, b April 28, 1903 No 2713.
2. Irma Irene Ira, b. Nov 14, 1905. No. 2714
3. Leo Elmer Ira, b Sept 3, 1910. No 2715.
4 Melvin R. Ira, b Sept 20, 1913
5. Winfred Lee Ira, b Aug 18, 1917.
6 Alfred Lawrence Ira, b Nov 17, 1919
7 Donald Gene Ira, b April 6, 1924.

No. 2713. Sixth Generation. 2712.

1) Cec l Carl Ira, b April 28, 1903, m. in 1925, Florence Haines. Laborer. Address 2608 James St, Bellingham, Wash. No issue

No. 2714. Sixth Generation. 2712.

2) Erma Irene Ira, b Nov 14, 1905, m June 20, 1922, Charles L. Burnett. Farmer Baptists Address. Dodge City, Kans

1. Lawrence L Burnett, b July 16, 1925
2. Betty Lou Burnett, b Aug 10, 1926
3 Irma Gene Burnett, b Dec 13, 1932

No. 2715. Sixth Generation. 2712.

3) Leo Elmer Ira, b Sept 3, 1910, m Blanche Bricker Construction worker. Address Dodge City, Kans

1 Leo Dean Ira, b July 18, 1930
2 Willard Dale Ira, b July 20, 1931

No. 2716. Fifth Generation. 2706.

5) Henry D Brenneman, b Aug 23, 1886, m Jan 8, 1908, Maggie A Donner, b Jan 30, 1888 Insurance Baptists Burial place in Plano cemetery, Stafford Co, Kans Address 306 El zabeth St, Ft Collins, Colo.

1 Baby daughter, b Dec 23, 1908, d Dec 30, 1908
2 Floyd Brenneman, b Aug 27, 1910 No 2717
3 Virgil O Brenneman, b Oct 13, 1914

No. 2717. Sixth Generation. 2716.

2) Floyd Brenneman, b Aug 27, 1910, m Aug 8, 1932, Lavona E Karmey, b Sept 16, 1910 Sergeant at armory Address: Fort Collins, Colo Baptists

1. Beverly Ann Brenneman, b Dec 9, 1933
2. Janet Lee Brenneman, b May 6, 1935.

No. 2718. Fifth Generation. 2706.

6) Blanche M Brenneman, b Sept 10, 1893, m Oct 14, 1910, Ozy Taylor, b Jan 4, 1886. Salesman Christian Church Address: Knisely, Kans.

1. Melvin L Taylor, b April 13, 1913
2 Marvin F Taylor, b Aug 4, 1915
3. Beulah M. Taylor, b. Mar 29, 1917.
4. Clayton W. Taylor, b April 28, 1918
5. Bettie Lou Taylor, b Mar 2, 1924
6. Billy Taylor, Jr, b July 25, 1931

No. 2719. Fifth Generation. 2706.

7) Jennie M Brenneman, b Dec 9, 1895, m. Mar 30, 1919, Vern Nevins, b. Sept. 19, 1898 Mechanic Church of Christ Address 817 Remington St, Ft. Collins, Colo

1. Emma Eileen Nevins, b July 9, 1920
2. Marion Carl Nevins, b. June 1, 1923
3. Bonnie Joyce Nevins, b June 20, 1931

No. 2720. Fourth Generation. 53.

4) Fannie A Brenneman, b. Sept. 4, 1856, near Edom, Va., m Dec 26, 1876, Edward M. Winger, b Jan 23, 1855. Address. Elmira, Mo Farmer Baptists.
1 Martin D. Winger, b. Dec. 17, 1877, d Dec 3, 1896
2. William H. Winger, b. Oct. 20, 1879 No 2721.
3 Maud M Winger, b Nov. 27, 1880, d Feb 27, 1881
4. Ira L Winger, b April 15, 1884, d. Dec 3, 1884
5. Ernest G. Winger, b. May 30, 1886, d Sept. 21, 1886
6. Charles E. Winger, b Oct. 3, 1887, d Mar 1, 1888.
7. Lula M. Winger, b Sept 23, 1892 No. 2724.

No. 2721. Fifth Generation. 2720.

2) William H Winger, b Oct 20, 1879, m Dec. 24, 1902, Jennie Easton. Telegraph operator. Mrs. Winger is a Christian Address. 1612 Washington St., Kansas City, Mo.
1 Gladys Sarah Winger, b. Dec. 7, 1903 No 2722
2 Opal May Winger, b Nov. 23, 1905 No 2723
Note.—This home was finally broken up and the parents separated William H. Winger married on Dec. 25, 1924, Lula Marie Mullen, b May 27, 188—, and is at present in the secondhand furniture business He resides at same place as at first

No. 2722. Sixth Generation. 2721.

1) Gladys Sarah Winger, b Dec 7, 1903, m Aug 23, 1929, Jack Bullard. Salesman Episcopalian Address 4052 Bettimore, Kansas City, Mo No issue.

No. 2723. Sixth Generation. 2721.

2) Opal May Winger, b Nov 23, 1905, m July 19, 1926, Caline Boone Address. 1492 Chestnut St., Long Beach, Calif No issue

No. 2724. Fifth Generation. 2720.

7) Lula M Winger, b. Sept 23, 1892, m Jan 10, 1915, William M. James, b. May 10, 1891. Garage mechanic Baptists Address. Elmira, Mo
1. Roberta Maxine James, b. Oct 8, 1918

No. 2725. Fourth Generation. 53.

5) Virginia M Brenneman, b Oct 13, 1858, near Edom, Va, d Jan 5, 1934, m. Nov. 28, 1878, William K Strope, b Dec 13, 1855, d May 13, 1929 Farmers. Christian Church. Address Cameron, Mo Burial at Mirabile, Mo
1. George W Strope, b May 26, 1880 No 2726
2 Martin Luther Strope, b Nov. 6, 1881 No 2727.
3. Minnie M. Strope, b Oct 24, 1883 No 2730
4 Jennie May Strope, b Mar 3, 1885. No 2733

No. 2726. Fifth Generation. 2725.

1) George W Strope, b May 26, 1880, m June 15, 1902, Hattie M Bassett Farmer and carpenter. Burial place at Mirabile cemetery, Mirabile, Mo. Address· Cameron, Mo These folks soon separated early in life. Mr Strope never married again, and lives on his father's old homestead 9 miles southeast of Cameron, Mo, where he patiently cared for his parents in their declining years until their death.

No. 2727. Fifth Generation. 2725.

2) Martin Luther Strope, b Nov 6, 1881, m April 26, 1910, Anna Gardner, b. Sept. 7, 1878 Address: 1510 S 10th St, St. Joseph, Mo. Night watchman.

1. Jennie Anna Strope, b July 28, 1910 No 2728.
2. Luther Karns Strope, b Nov 2, 1912. No 2729.
3 Edna May Strope, b June 28, 1917.

No. 2728. Sixth Generation. 2727.

1) Jenn e Anna Strope, b July 28, 1910, m May 1, 1926, Clifton Luellen. Address Turney, Mo.

1. Clifton Luther Luellen, b April 21, 1927.
2 Darn Dean Luellen, b. July 23, 1929.
3. Bobby Luellen, b. June 20, 1931
4 Joe Ann Luellen, b. Oct 2, 1934.

No. 2729. Sixth Generation. 2727.

2) Luther Kearns Strope, b Nov 2, 1912, m Aug 3, 1935, Lena Grace Richardson Address: 1502 S 10th St, St Joseph, Mo No issue

No. 2730. Fifth Generation. 2725.

3) Minnie M Strope, b Oct 24, 1883, m. May 20, 1906, John Burton Gordon. Address· Turney, Mo Farmer

1 Maggie Christina Gordon, b Sept 21, 1907. No 2731.
2 Anna May Gordon, b May 28, 1910. No. 2732
3 John Burton Gordon, b April 24, 1912, d. July 14, 1914
4 George William Gordon, b Nov. 7, 1920

These parents did not agree very well and they got a divorce Minnie married a man by the name of William Alexander of Dumont, Ia.

No. 2731. Sixth Generation. 2730.

1) Maggie Christina Gordon, b Sept 21, 1907, m Glen Walker. They live in Oklahoma somewhere and have two children.

No. 2732. Sixth Generation. 2730.

2) Anna May Gordon, b May 28, 1910, m Phil Thatcher They live in California and have two children

No. 2733. Fifth Generation. 2725.

4) Jennie May Strope, b Mar 3, 1885, m Jan 1, 1906, William S Henderson, b. Feb 10, 1884 Address 614 Broad St, Warrensburg, Mo Nursing Christian

1. Alfred K Henderson, b Feb 8, 1907 Single Barber
2 Dolly Virginia Henderson, b July 7, 1908 No 2734.

No. 2734. Sixth Generation. 2733.

2) Dolly Virginia Henderson, b July 7, 1908, m May 18, 1935, Carl Angel Farmer. Address: Warrensburg, Mo

1. William Alford Angel, b April 23, 1936

No. 2735. Fourth Generation. 53.

6) Hettie C. Brenneman, b. Oct 4, 1860, near Edom, Va., m. Feb. 4, 1886, John B. Hardman, b Feb 4, 1859 Address· Polo, Caldwell Co, Mo Farmer Brethren Burial ground in Oak Grove cemetery, near Polo, Mo.

1 Olin Orrel Hardman, b April 10, 1887 No 2736

No. 2736. Fifth Generation. 2735.

1) Olin Orrel Hardman, b April 10, 1887, d. in 1917, m May 29, 1910, Rose Green. Farmer and miller Brethren Address Polo, Mo. Burial place in Oak Grove cemetery.

1 Paul Ivan Hardman, b Oct 11, 1912, single He is a traveling salesman for wholesale automobile accessories at 3618 College Ave., Kansas City, Mo.

No. 2737. Fourth Generation. 53.

7) Martin D Brenneman, b Mar 19, 1863, near Edom, Va , d Sept 5, 1886, at Polo, Mo , m Sept 29, 1884, Esther O Bosserman, b Oct 21, 1859, d Dec. 5, 1935. Martin was buried at Kingston, Mo Esther was buried at Kenilworth, Pa. Address was Polo, Mo. Farmer. Brethren

1 Leo Leslie Brenneman, b. July 18, 1885 No. 2738.

No. 2738. Fifth Generation. 2737.

1) Leo Lesl'e Brenneman, b July 18, 1885, m. Sept 25, 1915, Eulessa Bien, b. May 25, 1891 Insurance broker Presbyterian. Address: 100 East 42nd St., New York City, N. Y.

1. Mayre Louese Brenneman, b. Nov 2, 1916
2. Margery Ann Brenneman, b. Jan 22, 1921.

No. 2739. Fourth Generation. 53.

8) Emma S. Brenneman, b Feb 16, 1865, near Edom, Va , m May 1, 1887, Charles H. Smart, b July 20, 1862. Address Polo, Mo Carpenter Methodists.

1 Edna E Smart, b Aug 23, 1889 No 2740
2 Blanche B. Smart, b April 27, 1891 No 2741

No. 2740. Fifth Generation. 2739.

1) Edna Earl Smart, b. Aug 23, 1889, m Nov 6, 1910, Forrest Lee Meredith, b. Nov 4, 1888 Railroad agent C M St P Methodist Address Conroy, Ia.

1. Twins not named, b April 27, 1912, d. same day.
2. Lois Elaine Meredith, b Nov 25, 1920, d Feb 8, 1922
3. Dorothea John Meredith, b June 27, 1924, d same day.
4 Loretta Lea Meredith, b May 14, 1929

No. 2741. Fifth Generation. 2739.

2) Blanche Bell Smart, b April 27, 1891, m. June 20, 1920, Audrian Swartz White, b May 16, 1891 Methodist. Address 2177 East 46th, Kansas City, Mo. Furnace salesman. No issue.

No. 2742. Fourth Generation. 53.

9) Minnie H. Brenneman, b May 6, 1867, near Edom, Va., m. Nov 3, 1898, Jesse A. Moyer, b. Mar 22, 1875 She died Feb 1, 1900 Farmers Brethren. Address. Millville, Ray Co , Mo Burial in Oak Grove cemetery near Polo, Mo

1. Minnie M. Moyer, b. Jan. 21, 1900 No 2743.

No. 2743. Fifth Generation. 2742.

1) Minnie M. Moyer, b. Jan. 21, 1900, m Feb 26, 1918, Walter Clarida, b. July 29, 1880. Farmer and telephone operator Christian Union. Address: Richmond, Mo., R. 1. Burial in New Hope cemetery, Ray Co , Mo

1. Infant son (stillborn), April 12, 1920.
2 Infant son (stillborn), Feb 22, 1921.
3. Louise Faye Clarida, b. May 12, 1924
4. Walter Grover Clarida, b. Jan 10, 1928.

10) Mary E. Brennenen, b. Sept 5, 1869, in Mo., m Nov 23, 1898, Christifer C. Brewen They lived near Cowgill, Caldwell Co., Mo. After the death of her husband, she married Joseph T Brewen, a furniture dealer and undertaker at Cowgill, Mo After his death she married Grant Jones, a Baptist preacher and still lives at Cowgill No issue.

No. 2745. Fourth Generation. 54.

1) Anna Wenger, b July 1, 1849, near Edom, Va., m. Jan. 7, 1878, David F. Senger of Sengersville, Augusta Co., Va They lived near Linville Station, Rockingham Co., Va Dunkards

1. Isaac C. Senger, b Jan 25, 1882 No 2763

No. 2745. Fourth Generation. 54.

2) Joseph Wenger, b Oct. 28, 1850, near Edom, Va., d. Sept. 26, 1908, m. Anna Rhodes, his first wife, who died May 17, 1896; m Feb 10, 1898, Mrs. Etta M. Lutholtz.

1. Clara A. Wenger, b Oct 19, 1872 No. 2747
2. Charles R. Wenger, b Sept 16, 1874 No. 2749
3 Joseph L Wenger, b April 19, 1876. No. 2750.
4 Byrd W. Wenger, b Sept 29, 1877, single
5. Emma C Wenger, b Aug 21, 1880 No 2751.
6. Isaac Howard Wenger, b Oct 21, 1882, d Feb 24, 1899
7. Infant son, b. Dec 30, 1883, d Feb 2, 1884
8 Anna Pearl Wenger, b Aug 4, 1886 No 3502
9 Owen Jacob Wenger, b Jan. 31, 1889. No. 3504
   (From second marriage)
10. Ivan M Wenger, b Dec. 22, 1898 No 3505.
11. Josie Pauline Wenger, b Feb 22, 1901 No 3506.
12 Burtrom Brown Wenger, b April 16, 1903. No. 3507.
13 Wilson Dodd Wenger, b May 10, 1905, single.

No. 2747. Fifth Generation. 2745.

1) Clara A Wenger, b Oct 19, 1872, near Edom, Va., m Oct 8, 1890, David S Geil, b Nov 25, 1862 They moved with their family to near South English, Ia. A few years later they moved to Lyman, Miss Their children were born in Va Mennonites. Address Lyman, Miss

1 Joseph Earl Geil, b Jan 17, 1892 No 3484
2 Abraham Ward Geil, b Sept. 7, 1894 No 3485
3 David Paul Geil, b April 13, 1898 No 3486
4 Jacob Clarence Geil, b Aug 1, 1900 No 3487.
5 Annie E Geil, b Oct 16, 1901 No 3488
6 Maida Pearl Geil, b Feb 25, 1904 No 3489.
7. Lewis Wenger Geil, b Dec 4, 1907. No. 2748.

No. 2743. Sixth Generation. 2747.

7) Lewis Wenger Geil, b Dec 4, 1907, in Va., m June 16, 1929, Olive Marie Brunk, b Mar. 15, 1908 Address Gulfport, Miss Laborer. Mennonites.

1 Robert Gordon Geil, b Sept 5, 1930
2. James Lewis Geil, b. Aug 5, 1933

No. 2749. Fifth Generation. 2745.

2) Charles R Wenger, b Sept. 16, 1874, near Edom, Va., m Oct 18, 1898, Emma C Fulk, b Dec 23, 1878 They moved to near Brooklyn, Ia., in 1902.

1. Paul Byron Wenger, b Nov 9, 1899 No 3490

2. Virgil Merl Wenger, b May 25, 1902. No 3491.
3. Lester R. Wenger, b Sept 26, 1904, single at Milford, Ind
4. Rita Pearl Wenger, b Nov. 23, 1908 No 3492
5. Viola Mae Wenger, b. Sept 4, 1918. No 3493

No. 2750. Fifth Generation. 2745.

3) Joseph T. Wenger, b April 19, 1876, near Linville, Va., m Olive Zirkle, in 1899. Farmer but now retired Address· West 8th St , Harper, Kans
1. Russell B. Wenger, b April 24, 1900. No 3494
2. Glen Z. Wenger, b. Dec 24, 1902, single. Barber at Pasadena, Calif , 3583 Brandon St. Born at Brooklyn, Ia
3. Roy G. Wenger, b. Nov 19, 1906 No. 3495
4. Lois V. Wenger, b. April 4, 1911 No. 3496.
5. Elmer J. Wenger, b Oct. 14, 1912, twin, single Gulfport, Miss.
6 Elver F Wenger, b. Oct 14, 1912, twin, single Merchant, Harper, Kans.
7. Mabel A Wenger, b Feb 6, 1914. No 3497.

No. 2751. Fifth Generation. 2746.

5) Emma Katherine Wenger, b Aug 21, 1880, near Cowan, Va., m Aug 20, 1902, Martin Ulysses Dutro, at Atkinson, Ill Distributor of O K. Welding machines in eastern Iowa and Illinois. He also operates his own tire shop at Muscatine, Ia Address: Muscatine, Ia United Brethren.
1. James Harold Dutro, b Oct 5, 1903 No. 3498.
2. Edna Muriel Dutro, b Jan 2, 1907. No. 3499
3. Martin Lloyd Dutro, b. May 9, 1908 No 3500.
4. Emma Florence Dutro, b July 5, 1911, twin No 3501.
5 Emery Lawrence Dutro, b July 5, 1911, twin, single, is living in Muscatine, Ia. U. B. Church.

No. 2752. Fourth Generation. 54.

3) Jacob C. Wenger, b. Jan 19, 1853, near Edom, Va , d Mar. 22, 1927, m. Dec. 21, 1879, Susanna Virginia Suter, b Nov 26, 1859. Address Linville Depot, Va. Mennonites.
1. Oscar Emmanuel Wenger, b June 19, 1881 No 3556
2. Mary Elizabeth Wenger, b July 28, 1882
3. Lydia Florence Wenger, b. Aug. 15, 1883.
4. Isaac Luther Wenger, b Oct. 4, 1885. No. 3558.
5. Homer David Wenger, b Dec 10, 1886 No. 3564.
6. Margaret Virginia Wenger, b May 4, 1888.
7. Laura Rebecca Wenger, b Aug. 23, 1889. No 2765.
8. Anna Suter Wenger, b. Dec. 30, 1890 No. 2766.
9. Sarah Jane Wenger, b. Mar. 20, 1892 No 2767.
10. Lillie Frances Wenger, b Aug. 23, 1893. No 2768
11. Perry Gabriel Wenger, b. Nov 18, 1894 No 3560.
12. John Robert Wenger, b Feb. 2, 1896 No 3561.
13. Clara Alma Wenger, b July 21, 1899 No 3562
14. Katie Ethel Wenger, b. Nov. 22, 1900
15. Lucy Wenger, b. Nov. 4, 1902 No. 3563.

No. 2753. Fourth Generation. 54.

4) Henry H. Wenger, b Feb. 14, 1856, near Edom, Va., ————, m. Dec 20, 1882, Sallie R. Swope, b. Nov 26, 1855, d Sept 10, 1919. Address: Linville Depot, Va. Mennonites.
1. Franklin Wenger, b Oct. 19, 1883. No 2769.

2. Mattie Wenger, b Nov 25, 1884. No. 2770.
3. Henry Wenger, Jr, b April 23, 1886 No. 3569.
4. Elizabeth Wenger, b Aug. 2, 1887.
5 John D. Wenger, b. Mar. 2, 1889. No. 3565.
6 Benjamin Wenger, b June 4, 1890. No. 2771.
7. Jacob C. Wenger, b. Dec. 20, 1893. No. 3570.

No. 2754. Fourth Generation. 54.

6) Isaac B. Wenger, b. Oct. 10, 1860, near Edom, Va., m. June 4, 1895, Mary Lula Beery, b July 2, 1868 Address: Linville, Va. Farmer.
1. Isaac Beery Wenger, b May 30, 1896 at Newark, N. J.
2. Clarence Windham Wenger, b. Jan 24, 1899 at Dallas, Tex.
3. Reno Lawrence Wenger, b. Aug. 21, 1900 at Staunton, Va.

No. 2755. Fourth Generation. 54.

7) David Wenger, b April 20, 1863, near Edom, Va., d. Sept. 29, 1933, m. Nov. 14, 1895, Dora B. Rhodes Milling, at Linville Depot, Va.
1. Barbara Magdalena Wenger, b. Aug 27, 1896.
2. DeWitt Wenger, b. Oct. 1, 1897.
3. William Roy Wenger, b Mar. 4, 1899
4. Cora Elizabeth Wenger, b. Jan 2, 1904, d Sept 25, 1904.
5. Charles Edgar Wenger, b. Jan. 5, 1905, d. July 16, 1905.
6. and 7. Stillborn twins
8. Minnie Wenger, b. ————, 1910.

No. 2756. Fourth Generation. 54.

8) Minnie C Wenger, b Mar 12, 1865, near Edom, Va., m. Dec. 20, 1882, Jacob S. Geil, b May 11, 1859, d May, 1932. Farmer. Clerk in store, and mining employee for the last 14 years of his life Mrs. Geil's address is 516 Lee Ave., Harrisonburg, Va. Mennonites
1. Gertrude Ola Geil, b. Nov. 17, 1883. No 2757.
2. Isaac Abraham Geil, b. June 2, 1885. No 2758.
3. Sadie May Geil, b June 29, 1887. No 2759.
4. Lydia Elizabeth Geil, b Mar 5, 1889. No 3440.
5. Lula Maude Geil, b. Jan. 11, 1891, R.N , single.
6. Jacob Clark Geil, b Jan. 27, 1893. No. 3441.
7. Minnie Ethel Geil, b Mar. 9, 1895 No 2760
8. Clinton Wenger Geil, b. Feb 9, 1897 No. 3442
9. David Newton Geil, b. Dec 12, 1898 No 3443.
10. Orien Golden Geil, b Nov 24, 1900, single.
11. Steward Franklin Geil, b. Sept 24, 1902 No. 3444.
12. Iva Rosa Geil, b. July 3, 1904 No 3445.
13. Edna Geil, b. Sept. 17, 1906, single, R N , at Harrisonburg, Va.

No. 2757. Fifth Generation. 2756.

1) Gertrude Ola Geil, b Nov. 17, 1883, near Linville, Va , m. June 28, 1905, Walter E. Rhodes, b. Aug 18, 1875 He died April 6, 1936. He was depot agent at Linville station for over thirty years. Address: Linville, Va.
1. Weltie Eugene Rhodes, b. Aug 1, 1906 No. 3446
2. Alma Gertrude Rhodes, b. Sept. 20, 1907.
3. Marie Catherine Rhodes, b Mar 29, 1910.
4. Harold Franklin Rhodes, b Dec. 8, 1911.
5 David James Rhodes, b May 16, 1913. No 3447
6 Ethel Elizabeth Rhodes, b Dec. 25, 1915
7. Mildred Geil Rhodes, b Aug 12, 1917.

8. Jacob Clark Rhodes, b. Dec. 8, 1918
9 Charles William Rhodes, b. Feb 18, 1920.
10. Gilbert Newton Rhodes, b. Jan 1, 1925.

No. 2758. Fifth Generation. 2756.

2) Isaac Abraham Geil, b June 2, 1885, m July 13, 1912, Nellie O Harra, b. May 24, 1889 Address: Missoula, Mont.

1. Donald Geil, b. Oct 1, 1913.
2 Helen Geil, b June 1, 1916
3. James (Bud) Geil, b Nov. 17, 1917.
4. Mickey Geil, b. Sept 15, 1922
5. Patricia Geil, b. Mar 23, 1934.

No. 2759. Fifth Generation. 2756.

3) Sadie May Geil, b June 29, 1887, m Dec 25, 1912, Edward Clarence Rhodes, b. Sept 6, 1881. Address: 267 S High St, Harrisonburg, Va

1. Eleanor Geil Rhodes, b. June 16, 1917. No 3669.
2. Paul Edward Rhodes, b Jan 17, 1929.

No. 2760. Fifth Generation. 2756.

7) Minnie Ethel Geil, b. Mar 9, 1895, m April 18, 1917, Hersie B McCauley, b. Feb., 1886. Address 320 Franklin St, Harrisonburg, Va.

1. Beverly Joan McCauley, b July 19, 1920, d next day
2. Hersie B. McCauley, Jr, b April 9, 1922

No. 2761. Fourth Generation. 54.

9) John J. Wenger, b Nov 16, 1866, near Edom, Va, m. Aug 23, 1899, Isa Nellie Beery, b April 26, 1875 Address. Linville Depot, Va Farmer. Mennonites. No children

No. 2762. Fourth Generation. 54.

10) William H Wenger, b Aug 25, 1869, near Edom, Va., d. Jan. 27, 1936, m. Nov 25, 1896, Florence Leona Moore, of Baltimore, Md Physician Address: 1506 N. Capital St, Washington, D C Mrs. Wenger died in Feb., 1929

1. Florence Irma Wenger, b Oct 25, 1897. No 2762¼.

No. 2762¼. Fifth Generation. 2762.

1) Florence Irma Wenger, b Oct 25, 1897, d in June, 1929, m William Grandlund, of Washington, D. C.

1. Paul Grandlund, b. —————.

No. 2763. Fifth Generation. 2745.

1) Isaac C. Senger, b Jan. 25, 1882, m Dec 8, 1909, Annie C. Rhodes, of near Broadway, Va No children.

No. 2765. Fifth Generation. 2752.

7) Laura Rebecca Wenger, b. Aug 23, 1889, m Jan 20, 1914, Lewis A Burkholder, b. Nov. 24, 1889 Address Denbigh, Va. Dairyman and poultryman. Mennonites.

1. James D. Burkholder, b Oct 24, 1914.
2. Nelson D. Burkholder, b Mar 24, 1916
3. June E. Burkholder, b June 9, 1920.
4. Frances V. Burkholder, b Feb 21, 1925.
5. Lewis A Burkholder, Jr., b Feb 8, 1927.

402

8) Anna Suter Wenger, b Dec 30, 1890, m. June 1, 1915, Perry S. Martin, b. Mar. 5, 1890. Perry is president of the Shenandoah Mfg. Co., Harrisonburg, Va. Mennonites.

1. Robert Wenger Martin, b April 23, 1917.
2. Jacob Weldon Martin, b. Nov. 30, 1918
3. May Elizabeth Martin, b Mar. 23, 1922
4 Virginia May Martin, b. May 26, 1924.
5. Ruth Fern Martin, b. April 16, 1927.
6. John Richard Martin, b Sept 2, 1928.
7. Margaret Rhodes Martin, b. June 13, 1930
8. Perry Sanford Martin, b. Sept 2, 1931
9. Ralph Edward Martin, b. June 24, 1933

No. 2767. Fifth Generation. 2752.

9) Sarah Jane Wenger, b. Mar 20, 1892, m Jan 19, 1915, Henry D. Weaver, b. Jan. 6, 1890, at Waynesboro, Va Mennonites Merchant and business manager of the Eastern Mennonite School at Harrisonburg, Va

1. Virg'nia Marie Weaver, b. Jan. 25, 1917.
2. Richard Samuel Weaver, b. Nov 2. 1919
3. Cleo Wenger Weaver, b. June 30, 1921.
4. Janet Elizabeth Weaver, b Jan 19. 1926
5. Henry David Weaver, b May 5, 1928

No. 2763. Fifth Generation. 2752.

10) Lillie Frances Wenger, b Aug 23, 1893, m June 25, 1914. Albert Moffett Faught, b Mar 10, 1895 Methodists. Farmer. Address: Edom, Va.

1. Rachel Wenger Faught, b. Sept. 26, 1917. No. 3566.
2. Charles Marvin Faught, b Nov. 29, 1921.
3. Shardene Jane Faught, b Oct 9, 1924
4. Dan La Mar Faught, b. Oct 5, 1933.

No. 2769. Fifth Generation. 2753.

1) Franklin I. Wenger, b Oct 19, 1883, m Sept 13, 1911, Bertie Pearl Shank, b. Feb 24, 1884, d Feb 26, 1931 Address. Waynesboro, Va. Farmer. Mennonites No children He married June 7, 1933, (2nd) Beulah Swope, b. May 26, 1896. Frank d April 11, 1935. Buried in Spr.ngdale cemetery

No. 2770. Fifth Generation. 2753.

2) Mattie R Wenger, b Nov 25, 1884, m Mar 15, 1910, John Hill, b. May 18, 1884. Address Perkasie, Pa
1 Leona Fay Hill, b Aug 18, 1912 No. 3567
2 Mildred Maxine Hill, b June 1, 1914

No. 2771. Fifth Generation. 2753.

6) Benjamin B. Wenger, b June 4, 1890, m Oct 29, 1914, Cora Mohler, b. Feb. 5, 1893. Address· Telford, Pa Lutheran

1. Lawrence Wenger, b Sept 29, 1915 No. 3568.
2. Howard Wenger, b. May 6, 1918

No. 2772. Fourth Generation. 55.

2) Barbara Wenger, b May 17, 1855, near Greenmount, Va., m Nov. 13, 1877, Jacob A. Andes. He died Dec. 15, 1915 Address: Cave Station, Va Christian Church.

1. Alfred Wellows Andes, b. Nov. 19, 1880. No. 2773
2. Iva Della Andes, b. Oct 31, 1882 No 2774.

403

3. Emmet Wenger Andes, b. Mar 20, 1887, single
4. Owen Wade Andes, b Feb 27, 1891. No 3555.

No. 2773. Fifth Generation. 2772.

1) Alfred Wellows Andes, b Nov. 19, 1880, d June 23, 1936, m. Dec 26, 1912, Minnie E. Bowman, b. Mar. 27, 1887 Minister in Christian Church. He was very able and active in his duties Address· Harrisonburg, Va
1. William Jacob Andes, b. Mar 19, 1915
2. Roy Harold Andes, b. Oct. 18, 1916.
3. Raymond Nelson Andes, b Sept 12, 1918.
4. Clarene Evelyn Andes, b. Oct. 2, 1921
5. Mark Winston Andes, b June 3, 1923

No. 2774. Fifth Generation. 2772.

2) Iva Della Andes, b Oct 31, 1882, m Nov. 9, 1916, Benjamin Franklin Frank, b. Mar. 23, 1874. Presbyterians They were married Nov 9, 1916 Farmer. Address: Harrisonburg, Va.
1. Lester Benjamin Frank, b. July 15, 1917.
2. Alfred Leon Frank, b. Mar. 28, 1921.

No. 2775. Fourth Generation. 55.

3) Solomon B. Wenger, b Jan 7, 1857, near Greenmount, Va., m Sallie J. Beery, b. Aug. 30, 1855, in Va, d at South English, Ia , Sept. 30, 1883. On April 13, 1886, he married Belle Irene Gruey, b. Sept. 22, 1857. She died Aug 29. 1916. His first wife was a Dunkard, second wife, a Mennonite On Nov. 2, 1918, he married Mrs. Minnie Wampler Miller, b Dec 25, 1866, in Va. Both are Mennonites. Address: South English, Ia. Ch ldren all from second wife.
1. Edith G Wenger, b Jan 30, 1888 No 2776
2. Clark A. Wenger, b Sept 20, 1889 No 2777.
3. Arthur J. Wenger, b Aug 29, 1893, d Mar 3, 1936
4. Emery B. Wenger, b. May 16, 1896, d April 12, 1908.
5 Milo E. Wenger, b Aug 16, 1900 No 2778

No. 2775. Fifth Generation. 2775.

1) Edith G Wenger, b Jan 30, 1888, m Nov 2, 1919, C E. Morgan Address: Richland, Ia.
1. Owen Morgan, b June 24, 1922
2. Allen Morgan, b Sept 1, 1928

No. 2777. Fifth Generation. 2775.

2) Clark A Wenger, b Sept 20, 1889, m Mamie Cook, of South English, Ia. Address: South English, Ia
1. Paul Wenger, b. Jan 5, 1916
2. Dale Wenger, b. July 21, 1917
3. Dyerl Wenger, b. Jan 16, 1925.

No. 2778. Fifth Generation. 2775.

5) Milo E. Wenger, b. Aug 16, 1900, m Margaret Noppsinger, of South English, Ia Milo was killed by accident Nov 30, 1934, by the falling of a garage door where he worked.
1. Elizabeth Wenger, b. Jan 18, 1929.

No. 2779. Fourth Generation. 55.

4) Anna Wenger, b Oct 7, 1858, near Greenmount, Va., d Jan. 5, 1934, m Jan. 29, 1885, Benjamin Brenneman, b Sept 27, 1855, of near Elida, O He died

Feb. 8, 1918. Address· Denbigh, Warwick Co., Va. Farmer. Mennonite. Deacon. Both were buried in Warwick River cemetery.

1. Amos Brenneman, b Nov 6, 1885. No. 2780
2. Hannah M. Brenneman, b Dec. 4, 1886, trained nurse, single.
3. Susanna Brenneman, b. Nov 2, 1888, d. Feb. 22, 1892.
4. Hettie Brenneman, b. Jan. 6, 1890.
5. Timothy Brenneman, b. Aug. 11, 1891, d. Nov., 1892.
6. John W. Brenneman, b Jan. 30, 1893. No. 2781.
7. Aldine Brenneman, b Dec 14, 1894, twin. No 2842.
8. Alfred Brenneman, b. Dec. 14, 1894, twin. No. 2843.
9. Benjamin Brenneman, Jr., b Nov. 25, 1897. No. 2844.
10. Anna Brenneman, b. Feb 3, 1899.
11. Irvin Brenneman, b. Dec 17, 1904, d. Mar. 18, 1913.

No. 2780. Fifth Generation. 2779.

1) Amos Brenneman, b Nov. 6, 1885, m Jan. 17, 1932, Magdalena Frances Showalter, b. Sept 6, 1892, in Va Address Denbigh, Va Dairyman Mennonite.

1 George R. Brenneman, b. Jan. 21, 1934.

No. 2781. Fifth Generation. 2779.

6) John W. Brenneman, b Jan. 30, 1893, m Dec. 24, 1926, Pearl E. Shank, b. Jan. 6, 1905. Address: Denbigh, Va Mennonite Mechanic.

1. Bettie Jane Brenneman, b Feb 8, 1928.
2. John Henry Brenneman, b Oct 22, 1929.
3. Bertha Frances Brenneman, b Dec. 14, 1932.

No. 2782. Fourth Generation. 55.

5) Lydia Wenger, b. May 10, 1860, near Greenmount, Va., m. Nov. 13, 1883, Cyrus B. Showalter, b Oct. 14, 1857, near Singers Glen, Va , d. Aug. 20, 1937. Farmer. Mennonites. Address Conway, Kans Related.

1. Edward W. Showalter, b Sept 8, 1884. No 1107.
2. Elizabeth O Showalter, b Dec 17, 1885. No 1108.
3. Hannah B. Showalter, b Nov 13, 1887 No 1110.
4. Oliver B. Showalter, b Sept 15, 1889 No 1111.
5. Amos M. Showalter, b Dec. 15, 1891 No. 1112.
6 Ada May Showalter, b. Feb 4, 1894 No 1113
7. John L. Showalter, b April 23, 1896 No. 1114.
8. Nellie Kate Showalter, b Mar. 20, 1898 No. 1115.
9. Clara M Showalter, b Nov. 1, 1900. No. 1116.

No. 2783. Fourth Generation. 55.

6) Adam Wenger, b Feb. 9, 1862, near Greenmount, Va., m. Nov., 1888, Amanda Rohrer, b. Dec 27, 1865 Address: Salem, O., R. 5. Mennonites. Farmer.

1. Mattie R. Wenger, b April 19, 1890 No. 3335.
2. Israel Rohrer Wenger, b Nov. 30, 1891. No 3336.
3. Abraham Jacob Wenger, b Feb. 15, 1893. No. 3337.
4 Lena Susan Wenger, b Oct. 18, 1895. No. 3338.
5. Amos Daniel Wenger, b Aug 11, 1897. No. 3339.
6. Stella Virginia Wenger, b. June 10, 1899. No. 3340
7. Hannah B. Wenger, b. Dec. 23, 1901. No. 3341.
8. Joseph H. Wenger, b. July 26, 1903, Salem, O
9. Edith Wenger, b Feb 24, 1905. No. 3342.

405

10. Anna May Wenger, b. Jan —, 1907, Salem, O.
11. David Adam Wenger, b July 8, 1910. No. 3343

No. 2784. Fourth Generation. 55.

7) Timothy J. Wenger, b. Feb. 18, 1864, near Greenmount, Va, m Nov. 30, 1886, Mary Powell. Teacher and farmer Mennonites Address: Stuarts Draft, Augusta Co., Va.

1. Anna Belle Wenger, b. June 6, 1888 No 2785.
2. Lessie May Wenger, b Jan 2, 1890 No 3598.
3. Hannah Etta Wenger, b Jan. 6, 1892 No. 3599.
4. Mary Magdalene Wenger, b Aug 8, 1893. No. 2786.
5. Lula Fannie Wenger, b. July 1, 1895.
6. Ida Wenger, b. April 13, 1898 No 3600
7. Roy Wenger, b. Mar. 30, 1900 No 3601.
8. Katie Wenger, b Feb. 11, 1903 No 3602
9. Powell Wenger, b June 5, 1905. No. 3603

No. 2785. Fifth Generation. 2784.

1) Anna Belle Wenger, b June 6, 1888, m. Dec, 1912, Moses Hertzler. Address: Denbigh, Va.

No. 2786. Fifth Generation. 2784.

4) Mary Magdalena Wenger, b Aug 8, 1893, m Jan 3, 1915, Samuel H Brunk, b. May 7, 1892. Mennonite Minister Address. Fentress, Va

1. Ida Mae Brunk, b Mar 14, 1916 No 3604
2. George Franklin Brunk, b. Nov 12, 1918
3. Daniel Wenger Brunk, b June 11, 1920
4 Edith Mollie Brunk, b Mar 19, 1922
5. Samuel Henry Brunk, Jr, b Oct 31, 1926

No. 2787. Fourth Generation. 55.

8) Amos Daniel Wenger, b. Nov 25, 1867, near Greenmount, Va., the son of Jacob and Hannah Breneman Wenger He was of a quiet unassuming disposition. He grew to manhood in Virginia He was reared on the homestead and taught the customary methods of farming, along with the practice of thrift and economy As a young man his life was spent mostly at work on the farm. In early life he was already religiously inclined, with a desire for an education. He united with the Mennonite Church in Allen Co, O., in 1889 He was baptized by Bishop John M. Shenk He taught school in Keokuk Co., Ia., in 1890 and 1891, after which he attended the state normal at Warrensburg, Mo, for several years, and later spent one year in Penn College at Oskaloosa, Ia. While in Missouri he was ordained to the ministry in Bethel Church, Cass Co., Mo, by Bishop Daniel Kauffman, after which several years were spent in evangelistic work mostly in Pennsylvania, where on July 1, 1897, he was married to Mary Hostetler of Millersville, Pa She died July 14, 1898 On January 1, 1899, he started on a tour around the world. He spent six months in Bible lands and wrote a book of his travels entitled "Six Months in Bible Lands, and Around the World in Fourteen Months," which was read with much interest by many people. In March, 1900, he was married to Anna M Lehman, Millersville, Pa. They located on a farm near Fentress, Norfolk Co., Va. For the last fifteen years of his life he served as president of the Eastern Mennonite School at Harrisonburg, Va It may truthfully be said of him that almost his entire life was spent in the interest of the church of which he was a devoted member —Written by his brother S. B. Wenger.

On Oct. 5, 1935, he arose and ate his breakfast at the dining room table. Soon after he lapsed into unconsciousness. A.d was summoned but in the face of all efforts he never regained consciousness, but peacefully passed away without uttering a word. He was buried in the cemetery near the Mt. Pleasant Church near Fentress, Va. Address: Fentress, Norfolk Co., Va.

1. Mary Magdalene Wenger, b. Jan. 14, 1903. No. 2788.
2. Anna May Wenger, b. May 27, 1904. No. 2789.
3. Amos Daniel Wenger, Jr , b. Mar. 29, 1906. No. 2790.
4. Ralph Lehman Wenger, b. Feb 9, 1908, d. May 16, 1909.
5. Paul Lehman Wenger, b. Oct 1, 1909. No. 2791.
6. Ruth Hannah Wenger, b Apr. 15, 1911.
7. Rhoda Elizabeth Wenger, b. Aug 6, 1913.
8. Chester Lehman Wenger, b. Apr. 10, 1918.

No. 2783. Fifth Generation. 2787.

1) Mary Magdalena Wenger, b Jan 14, 1903, m. Aug. 28, 1929, Leonard Ellwood Martin, b. Apr. 17, 1905 He died June 12, 1930. She married July 12, 1932, Warren Alderfer Kratz, b Dec. 11, 1899

1. Joanne Esther Kratz, b. Nov. 21, 1935.

No. 2789. Fifth Generation. 2787.

2) Anna May Wenger, b May 27, 1904, m June 5, 1930, John Faye Garber, b. Feb. 25, 1905

1. Leonard W lbur Garber, b May 10, 1931.
2 Rhoda Elizabeth Garber, b Dec 24, 1932.
3. Stanley David Garber, b Nov 9, 1934.
4. Phebe Ruth Garber, b Oct. 5, 1936.

No. 2790. Fifth Generation. 2787.

3) Amos Daniel Wenger, Jr , b Mar 29, 1906, m Oct. 25, 1931, Lenora Mildred Harkins, b May 15, 1906

1 Amos Daniel Wenger, Jr , b Aug 19, 1932.
2. John Ralph Wenger, b June —, 1936.
3 Mary Rachel Wenger, b Oct 20, 1937

No. 2791. Fifth Generation. 2787.

5) Paul Lehman Wenger, b Oct 1, 1909, m. June 22, 1934, Martha Driver, b. Aug 2, 1912, daughter of Joseph R. Driver and Lizzie Weaver.

No. 2792. Fourth Generation. 55.

10) Magdalena Wenger, b Oct 24, 1872, near Greenmount, Va , m. Mar. 12, 1891, John J. Brunk, b Nov 24, 1862, near Broadway, Va. He died Sept. 9, 1900. Farmer. Mennonites Address Greenmount, Va

1 Menno Jacob Brunk, b. Oct 3, 1892
2 Kate Amanda Brunk, b Oct 15, 1893, d. Jan., 1933.
3 Lew.s Samuel Brunk, b Oct. 30, 1895. No 2793.
4 Mary Edith Brunk, b July 22, 1897. No 3605.
5 Anna Barbara Brunk, b June 6, 1899

No. 2793. Fifth Generation. 2792.

3) Lewis Samuel Brunk, b Oct. 30, 1895, m Nov 3, 1915, Eva M. Liskey Farmer. Brethren.

11) Catherine E. (Katy) Wenger, b Mar 25, 1875, near Greenmount, Va., m July 15, 1900, George R. Brunk, b Dec 31, 1871, in McPherson Co, Kans He lived on the farm while in Kansas until 1910 when he migrated to Warwick Co , Va., where he devoted much of his time to the orchard industry. Both were members of the Mennonite Church Mr. Brunk was ordained to the ministry Oct 1, 1893, in McPherson Co , Kans , and on Oct 23, 1898, to the office of bishop in Harvey Co., Kans , where he served the church until 1910, when he took up his residence in Warwick Co., Va He served this district until his death April 30, 1938. He held a number of other places of trust in the Church. He assisted in organizing the Eastern Mennonite School, serving on the Board of Trustees, Faculty Committee, etc He was editor of the "Sword and Trumpet" published by himself, and author of "Ready Scriptural Reasons " Address· Denbigh, Va.

1. Truman H. Brunk, b. Dec. 22, 1902. No. 3344.
2. Stella Victoria Brunk, b Jan 15, 1905. No 3345.
3. Edna Frances Brunk, b. Jan 20, 1907 No 3346
4 Menno Simon Brunk, b Aug. 9, 1909 No. 3347.
5. George Rowland Brunk, b. Nov. 18, 1911 No. 3348
6. Katie Florence Brunk, b. May 3, 1913. No 3349.
7. Ruth Wenger Brunk, b. Mar. 15, 1915
8. Lawrence Burkhart Brunk, b. Feb. 23, 1917 No 3702.

No. 2795. Fourth Generation. 56.

2) Henry Tilman Brenneman, b. Sept. 8, 1858, near Edom, Va., m. in 1881, Eliza Keister, b. Apr. 15, 1856, in Va. Soon after their marriage near Elida, O , they moved to near North Manchester, Ind , where they now reside Farmer. Old Order Dunkard Church Burial place at North Manchester, Ind Address North Manchester, Ind.

1. Edward Brenneman, b June 8, 1882, d at five years.
2. Elmer Brenneman, b. Nov. 26, 1884, d. at three years.
3. Orley Brenneman, b Feb. 21, 1886. No. 2796.
4. Elizabeth Brenneman, b. Feb. 7, 1887 No 2798.
5. Lanie Brenneman, b. July 13, 1888 No. 2801
6 Philoma Brenneman, b. May 13, 1892. No. 2802.

No. 2796. Fifth Generation. 2795.

3) Orley Brenneman, b. Feb. 21, 1886, m Lydia Karns. He married (2nd) Lydia Gripe. Address North Manchester, Ind Issue from first wife.

1. Annie Brenneman, b. —————. No. 2797

No. 2797. Sixth Generation. 2795.

1) Annie Brenneman, b —————, near North Manchester, Ind , m. Jacob Larance. No children

No. 2798. Fifth Generation. 2795.

4) Elizabeth Brenneman, b Feb 7, 1887, near North Manchester, Ind , m Abraham Metzler.

1. Ralph Metzler, b. —————. No 2799.
2 Carman Metzler, b. ————— No 2800
3. Carl Metzler, b —————, single and is in Calif

No. 2799. Sixth Generation. 2798.

1) Ralph Metzler, b —————, m Orlean Grosnickle.

1. ——— Metzler, b —————

2. ——— Metzler, b. ———.
3. ——— Metzler, b. ———.

No. 2800. Sixth Generation. 2793.

2) Carman Metzler, b. ————, m Wane Rittenhause, of Liberty Mills, Ind. No issue.

No. 2801. Fifth Generation. 2795.

5) Lanie Brenneman, b. July 13, 1888, near North Manchester, Ind., m. Clarence Spoon. She later married Thurman Isley They live at Wabash, Ind., and have no children

No. 2802. Fifth Generation. 2795.

6) Philoma Brenneman, b May 13, 1892, near North Manchester, Ind., m ———Reniker. They live at North Manchester and have no children.

No. 2803. Fourth Generation. 56.

3) Jesse P. Brenneman, b. Oct. 11, 1860, near Edom, Va., m. Feb. 28, 1888, Jerusha Wenger, b. Oct. 11, 1865, in Mahoning Co., O. They lived at different places in Ohio until 1892 when they settled near Newton, Kans., where they have lived ever since. Burial ground at Pennsylvania Church near Hesston, Kans. Address: Newton, Kans Farmer. Mennonites

1. Lula Pearl Brenneman, b. Oct 11, 1890. No. 2804.
2 Naomi Esther Brenneman, b. Aug 16, 1896, was a foreign missionary to Central Province, India
3. Noah Jasper Brenneman, b. July 27, 1898, d Dec. 24, 1918.
4. Sarah Ruth Brenneman, b Feb. 24, 1901, single, teacher.
5. Eunice Frances Brenneman, b. June 17, 1902 No. 2805.
6. Amos Joseph Brenneman, b Mar 25, 1906. No. 2806.
7 Jessie Pauline Brenneman, b June 2, 1907.

No. 2804. Fifth Generation. 2803.

1) Lula Pearl Brenneman, b. Oct. 11, 1890, m Feb 8, 1911, Peter Jantz. Farmer. Mennonites Address: Newton, Kans, R 2.

1 Estella Elizabeth Jantz, b Apr 5, 1912.
2 Mary Evelyn Jantz, b Dec. 20, 1913.
3. Leota Ethel Jantz, b. Sept. 25, 1915.
4 Ephraim B. Jantz, b Sept. 14, 1917.
5 Charles Amos Jantz, b Nov. 3, 1919.
6 Arthur Abraham Jantz, b Dec. 22, 1920, deceased.
7. Naomi Ruth Jantz, b Mar. 18, 1922.
8 Lawrence Ezra Jantz, b May 8, 1925.
9. Baby born Mar. 16, 1933, d. same day.

No. 2805. Fifth Generation. 2803.

5) Eunice Frances Brenneman, b June 17, 1902, m. Aug. 8, 1923, Abram E Zook They are missionaries in the Congo Belge, West Africa District.

1. John Edwin Zook, b Oct. 3, 1924
2. Ruth Elizabeth Zook, b. Aug. 20, 1927, in Africa.

No. 2806. Fifth Generation. 2803.

6) Amos Joseph Brenneman, b. Mar. 25, 1906, m. June 13, 1931, Gladys Lucille Zeller.

1. Martha Louise Brenneman, b. July 5, 1932.
2. Lloyd Joseph Brenneman, b. July 1, 1934.

7) Jessie Pauline Brenneman, b June 2, 1907, m. May 11, 1930, Alvin P. Stahly.

1. Robert Dean Stahly, b June 5, 1932.

No. 2803. Fourth Generation. 55.

4) Fannie Brenneman, b ————————, near Edom, Va , m ———— Frantz. Address: North Manchester, Ind.

1. Daughter Frantz, b ————————, N. F R

No. 2809. Fourth Generation. 56.

7) Lyd a E Brenneman, b. Dec 16, 1869, near Edom, Va., m June 19, 1890, Peter Sheets. He died Oct 1, 1905 Address: Reeds, Mo , R. 1. Farmer. Mennonites.

1. Clara L. Sheets, b. Feb 23, 1892, d Jan 16, 1893.
2. John W. Sheets, b Aug. 29, 1894 No 2810
3. Paul E. Sheets, b. May 22, 1904. No 2811

Mrs. Lydia E Sheets later married a man by name of Kahl. They live at Reeds, Mo

No. 2810. Fifth Generation. 2809.

2) John W. Sheets, b Aug 29, 1894, m Louise Paul Address: Newton, Kans.

1. Stanley Sheets, b. ————————.
2 Yoeta Sheets, b. ————————.
3 Donald Sheets, b. ————————.

No. 2811. Fifth Generation. 2809.

3) Paul E Sheets, b May 22, 1904, m Alpha White Address: Reeds, Mo., R. 1.

1. Carl E Sheets, b Jan 13, 1935.

No. 2812. Fourth Generation. 56.

8) George Brenneman, b ————, 1871, near Edom, Va , m. Dec 24, 1908, May Brown Farmer Mennonites Address: Newton, Kans.

1 Lawrence Brenneman, b Nov. 3, 1911.
2. Roy Brenneman, b Dec 23, 1920
3 Jessie Brenneman, b. April 13, 1923
4. Marie Brenneman, b. Sept. 8, 1925

No. 2813. Fourth Generation. 56.

9) Joseph W. Brenneman, b ————, 1873, near Edom, Va , m Elizabeth C. Lehman, b ————, 1873. Carpenter Brethren Church. Address: Newton, Kans., R. 1.

1. Daniel J Brenneman, b ————, 1897 No 2814.
2 Grace E Brenneman, b. ————, 1900 No. 2815

No. 2814. Fifth Generation. 2813.

1) Daniel J Brenneman, b ————, 1897, m Fern Nichols, b. ————, 1904 Address: Newton, Kans

1. Dorma Louis Brenneman, b. ————, 1925
2. Rex D. Brenneman, b. ————, 1927
3. Richard J. Brenneman, b. ————, 1930.

No. 2815. Fifth Generation. 2813.

2) Grace E Brenneman, b ————, 1900, m Charles E Monroe

No. 2816. Fourth Generation. 56.

10) Annie Brenneman, b. July 15, 1875, near Edom, Va., m. Dec. 25, 1901, T. C. Mackey, b Aug. 7, 1863, d July 7, 1922. Address: 1738 S. Main St., Carthage, Mo. Farmer Mennonites Burial place at Avilla, Mo.
1. Clarence Mackey, b. Oct. 6, 1909.
2. Andy Mackey, b Dec 18, 1915.

No. 2317. Fourth Generation. 56.

11) Jennie Brenneman, b Sept 22, 1879, near Edom, Va., m. Dec. 24, 1908, Lossen P. Major, b Jan. 6, 1878 Address: Reeds, Mo., R. 1. Farmer. Mennonites
1. Paul E. Major, b. June 5, 1916
2. John P Major, b Mar 27, 1920

No. 2818. Fourth Generation. 58.

1) Elizabeth Blosser, b Dec. 21, 1837, near Elida, O., m. Thomas Bowers, b. ————, 1835 Christian Church Farmer. Address: Van Wert, O. Burial at Convoy, O
1 Magdalena Bowers, b July 20, 1858. No. 3401.
2. George Bowers, b Mar 26, 1860 No. 3403
3 Jane Bowers, b Oct 20, 1861. No 3407
4. Etta Bowers, b Sept 20, 1863. No 3413.

No. 2319. Fourth Generation. 53.

2) Mary Blosser, b Oct 19, 1839, near Elida, O , d Aug. 8, 1913 Buried at Convoy, O. After the death of her sister, Elizabeth, she married Thomas Bowers in 1865. Address: Van Wert, O
1 Ellen Bowers, b. June 10, 1867 No 3419.
2. David Wesley Bowers, b Jan 13, 1869. No 3420.
3 William Bowers, b May 20, 1871, single, railroader
4. Henry A. Bowers, b Dec. 18, 1873, d. Oct 6, 1894
5 Cora Bowers, b Dec 28, 1874 No 3421.
6 Albert Bowers, b Jan 12, 1878. No 3424.

No. 2820. Fourth Generation. 58.

3) John Blosser, b. Aug 21, 1841, near Allentown, O , m. Mary Plumber
1. James Blosser, b. ————

No. 2521. Fourth Generation. 58.

4) David Blosser, b April 27, 1843, near Allentown, O., m. Lila Lumy.
1. William Blosser, b. ————
2 Lydia Blosser, b ————.
3. Nancy Blosser, b ————
4. Lula Blosser, b ————.
5. Effie Blosser, b. ————.
6. Emma Blosser, b. ————.

No. 2822. Fourth Generation. 58.

5) George W Blosser, Jr , b June 22, 1845, near Allentown, O , d. April 17, 1938, Pasadena, Calif, m Mina Newton, b Feb. 25, 1846, d. Nov. 26, 1885, m Ollie Johnson, b April 13, 1864, d April 5, 1910 Children from first wife Address· 400 S Marengo Ave , Pasadena, Calif Buried at Pasadena, Calif.
1. Lester Blosser, b. July 15, 1883 No 2823
2. Ruby C. Blosser, b Dec 2, 1892. No. 2825.
3 Helen Blosser, b Dec 12, 1903 No. 2826

No. 2823. Fifth Generation. 2822.

1) Lester Blosser, b. July 15, 1883, m Hazel Cole. Address· 327 E. Delmar St., Pasadena, Calif Electrician.

   1. George C. Blosser, b. Oct 25, 1905. No. 2824

No. 2324. Sixth Generation. 2823.

1) George C. Blosser, b. Oct 25, 1905, m. Elsie Haifley, b. Nov. 11, 1905. Address. Lone Pine, Calif.·

No. 2825. Fifth Generation. 2322.

2) Ruby C. Blosser, b. Dec. 2, 1892, m Jesse P. Powell, b Dec. 23, 1892. Merchant. Address: 400 S. Marengo Ave , Pasadena, Calif

   1. Richard M. Powell, b ————, 1923.

   2. Janice E. Powell, b ————, 1927.

No. 2826. Fifth Generation. 2822.

3) Helen Blosser, b. Dec 12, 1903, m Rev Irye Townsend Address. Sweetwater, Tex. One child

No. 2827. Fourth Generation. 58.

7) Henry Blosser, b. Oct 1, 1849, near Allentown, O , d. Aug. 17, 1934, m. Mary E Bolander, b. Oct , 1853, d Jan 7, 1927. Contractor. Address: 407 S West St , Lima, O. Buried in Woodlawn cemetery, Lima, O.

   1. Stephen Albertus Blosser, b Dec 1, 1875 No. 2828

   2. Emma Blosser, b May 4, 1878 No. 2831.

   3. Eugene Franklin Blosser, b Jan 19, 1880. No. 2832.

No. 2823. Fifth Generation. 2827.

1) Stephen Albertus Blosser, b Dec 1, 1875, d Oct 5, 1934, m Ada H. Engle, b April 19, 1881 Mr Blosser was placed in the family mausoleum at St. Johns cemetery, Catholic, Lima, O. Address: Lima, O Salesman Catholic.

   1. Marzella C. Blosser, b July 18, 1905 No. 2829

   2. James Cavil Blosser, b. Aug 11, 1910. No 2830

No. 2829. Sixth Generation. 2828.

1) Marzella C. Blosser, b July 18, 1905, m Robert Cornelius, Lima, O. No issue.

No. 2830. Sixth Generation. 2828.

2) James Kavil Blosser, b. Aug 11, 1910, m Zetta Fern Diehl, b. May 7, 1910, m. June 29, 1929 Address: Lima, O.

   1. Sherely Jene Blosser, b Mar. 21, 1934.

No. 2331. Fifth Generation. 2827.

2) Emma Blosser, b May 4, 1878, in Lima, O , m. Charles W. Crown, b. 1872. They live at 325 N. Shore Drive, Lima, O. Filling station operator.

   1. Frederick Crown, b. June 18, 1907.

No. 2832. Fifth Generation. 2827.

3) Eugene Franklin Blosser, b. Jan 19, 1880, in Lima, O , m. Bessie M. Rumbaugh, b. Nov. —, 1879 Pumper at solar refinery. Address: 728 Holly St , Lima, O.

   1. Francis William Blosser, b. May 13, 1903. No 2833

   2. Mary Alice Blosser, b Aug 17, 1905, d. Nov 16, 1906

   3. Evelyn Y. Blosser, b Mar 30, 1907.

4 Eugene Dale Blosser, b. May 4, 1911.
5. Don Wilson Blosser, b. June 25, 1913.
6. Mabel Charelien Blosser, b May 10, 1918

No. 2833. Sixth Generation. 2832.
1) Francis William Blosser, b. May 13, 1903, in Lima, O., m. Lucille Rasor.
1. Mary Jane Blosser, b. Nov. 11, 1926
2. Thomas Henry Blosser, b Mar. 1, 1930.

No. 2834. Fourth Generation. 58.
9) Lewis Blosser, b Oct 9, 1853, near Allentown, O., m. Retta Barnes, b. 1860, d. 1886; m. (2nd) Sarah A. Berchard, b. 1862, d. 1928. Address: 445 N. E. Floral Place, Portland, Oreg Children from first wife
1 Berta Blosser, b ————, 1880, d ————, 1881.
2 Wardie Blosser, b ————, 1882, d ————, 1885.
3. Lela Blosser, b ————, 1884, d. ————, 1924.
4 Gerald Blosser, b ————, 1889, d ————, 1930.
5 Harold L. Blosser, b ————, 1898, and is married to Anna Heysick. He is a physician at Portland, Oreg., and has a son, born in 1930.

No. 2835. Fourth Generation. 58.
10) Martin Blosser, b. Dec. 6, 1855, m Nov 26, 1885, Barbara F. Seifert, b. Nov. 1, 1859, d. Sept 11, 1925 Address· W Wayne St., Lima, O. Retired.
1 Hazel Blosser, b. April 13, 1887. No. 2836

No. 2836. Fifth Generation. 2835.
1) Hazel Blosser, b. April 13, 1887, m. Nov. 6, 1906, Orman Justice, b. Feb. 1, 1887, in Lima, O. They live in Lima, O.
1. Ruth Justice, b. June 19, 1908
2. Amelia Justice, b Mar. 5, 1910, d Jan , 1937.
3 Ralph Justice, b Aug. 8, 1914, d. Sept , 1935.

No. 2837. Fourth Generation. 58.
11) Nancy Blosser, b. Mar 22, 1860, near Allentown, O., d. Mar. 13, 1888, m William Alonza Bechtel, b. April 25, 1849. He died Mar. 3, 1911. He was buried at Greenlawn cemetery near Elida, O Address: Elida, O.
1. Earl Bechtel, b 1880, d Feb. 11, 1888.
2 Mina Bechtel, b Sept. 18, 1883. No. 2838.
3. Grover Bechtel, b ————, 1884, d. May 31, 1887.
4 Hazel Bechtel, b July 24, 1886. No. 2839.

No. 2838. Fifth Generation. 2837.
2) Mina Bechtel, b Sept 18, 1883, m. June 8, 1906, Willis Huffer, b. Sept. 19, 1881. Address Elida, O Oil pumper Methodists. No issue.

No. 2839. Fifth Generation. 2837.
4) Hazel Bechtel, b July 24, 1886, m June 14, 1905, George L. Brunk, b Dec. 2, 1882. Dentist at Lima, O Related, see No 435 Address: 621 W Elm St., Lima, O
1 Carl Brunk, b Feb 11, 1906 No 436
2 Wilford Brunk, b Mar 21, 1910 No 3284
3 Ruth Brunk, b June 4, 1915

No. 2840. Fourth Generation. 58.
12) Lydia Blosser, b Oct 30, 1860, near Allentown, O , m Jacob Staver, b. Sept 14, 1862. Address: Lima, O., Lafayette Rd. No issue.

No. 2841. Fourth Generation. 59.

2) Benjamin Brenneman, b. Sept. 27, 1855, near Elida, O , d. Feb. 8, 1918, m. Jan. 29, 1885, Anna Wenger, b Oct. 7, 1858, near Greenmount, Va. Farmer and carpenter Mennonites. He was a deacon in the church Related, see No. 2779. Anna died Jan 5, 1934 Address: Denbigh, Va.

1. Amos Brenneman, b Nov. 6, 1885 No. 2780.
2 Hannah Brenneman, b. Dec. 4, 1886, R N., single.
3. Susanna Brenneman, b Nov. 2, 1888.
4. Hettie Brenneman, b Jan 6, 1890.
5 Timothy Brenneman, b. Aug. 11, 1891, d Nov. 2, 1892.
6. John W Brenneman, b Jan. 30, 1893. No. 2781.
7. Aldine Brenneman, b. Dec. 14, 1894, twin. No 2842.
8 Alfred Brenneman, b. Dec 14, 1894, twin No 2843.
9 Benjamin Brenneman, b Nov 25, 1897 No 2844
10 Anna Brenneman, b. Feb. 3, 1899.
11. Irvin Brenneman, b. Dec 17, 1903, d. Mar 18, 1913.

No. 2842. Fifth Generation. 2841.

7) Aldine Brenneman, b. Dec 14, 1894, near Elida, O., m Dec 9, 1920, Sallie A. Hartman, b. Jan. 11, 1900, in Va Address. Harrisonburg, Va. Mennonites.

1. Rosalyn Mae Brenneman, b May 28, 1925
2 Merna Ruth Brenneman, b. April 5, 1930.

No. 2843. Fifth Generation. 2841.

8) Alfred Brenneman, b. Dec. 14, 1894, near Elida, O , m Sept 25, 1925, Verda Hershberger, b. near Walnut Creek, O , June 18, 1903 They live at Denbigh, Va. Mennonites.

1. Alfred Glen Brenneman, b. May 4, 1927.
2 Anna Mae Brenneman, b. Dec 10, 1931.

No. 2844. Fifth Generation. 2841.

9) Benjamin Brenneman, b. Nov 25, 1897, near Elida, O , m June 9, 1926, Salome Bechtel, b. near Springs, Pa., Feb 19, 1905. Address· Harrisonburg, Va. Mennonites.

1. Esther Brenneman, b. April 17, 1927.
2. Francis Brenneman, b. Dec 15, 1929.
3. Naomi Brenneman, b. July 26, 1932, d. Oct 28, 1933
4. Louise Brenneman, b Sept. 2, 1934
5 Charles Brenneman, b. Sept. 4, 1936

No. 2845. Fourth Generation. 59.

3) Nancy E Brenneman, b. Mar 16, 1858, near Elida, O., d. ———, 1921, m. Mar. 5, 1896, Jacob B Welty, of Nappanee, Ind. She was the second wife. Mennonites. No issue.

No. 2846. Fourth Generation. 59.

4) John I Brenneman, b. Feb 12, 1859, near Elida, O , m Feb 19, 1907, Rebecca Frances Breneman, b Feb 16, 1870, in Va. Address: Elida, O. Related, see No 163 No issue

No. 2847. Fourth Generation. 59.

5) Susanna Brenneman, b July 12, 1867, near Elida, O , m. Nov 27, 1902, Homer C Brown, of Va. Mennonite She died in Fulton Co , O

1. Nancy Jane Brown, b Oct. 1, 1903. No 3350
2 Clara Alice Brown, b April 15, 1907.
3 Arthur Paul Brown, b Oct. 26, 1910.

No. 2843. Fourth Generation. 60.

1) Lydia Brenneman, b April 14, 1850, in Fairfield Co., O , d. Dec. 2, 1935, m. Jan 28, 1869, Henry Chandler, b Dec 17, 1840 He died June 8, 1925 Farmer. United Brethren. Buried in the Salem cemetery near Elida, O. Address· Rushmore, O.

1. Lucinda Chandler, b. Nov. 1, 1870 No. 2849.
2. Leah Chandler, b Aug. 9, 1872 No 2850.
3. Orpha Ruth Chandler, b Mar 13, 1873. No. 2852.

No. 2849. Fifth Generaticn. 2848.

1) Lucinda Chandler, b Nov 1, 1870, near Rushmore, O , m. Dec. 22, 1892, Joseph Wilson, 1860-1932 They lived at Rushmore, O Address: Rushmore, O. United Brethren. Buried at the Salem cemetery. No issue

No. 2850. Fifth Generation. 2848.

2) Leah Chandler, b Aug 9, 1872, near Rushmore, O , d. in 1910, m. Nov. 25, 1897, John W. Unland, b. ————— They lived near Rushmore, O United Brethren. Address Rushmore, O. Farmer.

1. Elpha Mae Unland, b Oct 17, 1898. No 2851.

No. 2851. Sixth Generation. 2850.

1) Elpha Mae Unland, b Oct 17, 1898, near Rushmore, O , m. April 12, 1922, Manford M. Shank, b July 14, 1881, d ————, 1935. Address: Mt. Cory, O. Farmer.

1. Leah Lucinda Shank, b. Jan. 4, 1923.
2 Bertha Lucile Shank, b. May 4, 1925.
3. Joseph David Shank, b Feb 20, 1927, d. in infancy
4. Manford Melroy Shank, Jr., b. Feb. 17, 1928.
5. Alta Mae Shank, b Feb. 26, 1929.

No. 2852. Fifth Generation. 2848.

3) Orpha Ruth Chandler, b Mar 13, 1873, near Rushmore, O., m. Sept. 15, 1898, Elias Howard. Farmer United Brethren. Address: Ft. Jennings, O.

1 Connie Irene Howard, b July 27, 1899. No 2853.
2. Rosetta Howard, b Jan. 2, 1901 No. 2854.

No. 2853. Sixth Generation. 2852.

1) Connie Irene Howard, b July 27, 1899. m. June, 1919, Everett Evans, b. Oct. 29, 1893. Address: Columbus Grove, O. Farmer.

1. Lloyd Evans, b. Oct. 20, 1918.
2. Roy Evans, b. May 12, 1921.
3. Mary Ruth Evans, b April 25, 1922, d. Aug. 14, 1930.
4. Howard Evans, b Aug 22, 1923.
5. Dorris Evans, b. Mar. 11, 1924
6 Rosetta Jane Evans, b Mar 2, 1926.
7. Verda Evans, b Feb 18, 1927
8 Josephine Evans, b. Feb. 22, 1928.

No. 2854. Sixth Generation. 2852.

2) Rosetta Howard, b. Jan. 2, 1901, m. Edward Samuel.

1. William Dennis Samuel, b June 16, 1920.

No. 2855. Fourth Generation. 60.

3) Elizabeth Brenneman, b Dec 3, 1854, near Delphos, O , d. Aug. 27, 1931, m. Aug 13, 1878, Perry E Heidelbaugh, b. Mar 22, 1856, d Nov. 29, 1936. Buried in Greenlawn cemetery near Elida, O., in their mausoleum. Address: Delphos, O.

1. Infant daughter, b. June 12, 1879 died same day.
2. Marion B. Heidelbaugh, b. June 3, 1880 No. 2856.
3. Leah Olive Heidelbaugh, b Nov. 20, 1882 No 2858.

No. 2856. Fifth Generation. 2855.

2) Marion B. Heidelbaugh, b June 3, 1880, near Delphos, O , m. Aug. 27, 1903, Goldie Red, b. May 17, 1885 Address. Delphos, O Farmer. Methodists.
1. William Heidelbaugh, b June 13, 1904.
2. Breta Heidelbaugh, b. May 15, 1906. No. 2857.
3. Albert Heidelbaugh, b. June 20, 1917.
4. Audrey Heidelbaugh, b. Dec 27, 1921.
5. Alma Jean Heidelbaugh, b. Mar. 24, 1926

No. 2857. Sixth Generation. 2856.

2) Breta Heidelbaugh, b. May 15, 1906, near Delphos, O., m. June 2, 1929, Charles Buckles. Address. Delphos, O.
1. Marion Edwin Buckles, b July 4, 1930
2. Donald Lee Buckles, b. Feb. 20, 1934.

No. 2858. Fifth Generation. 2855.

3) Leah Olive Heidelbaugh, b. Nov. 20, 1882, m. Jan. 23, 1906, Ephraim Howard, b. Jan. 26, 1883.
1. Roy Howard, b. Jan. 14, 1907.
2. Perry Howard, b Feb. 16, 1909.
3. Myron Eugene Howard, b Oct 7, 1917.

No. 2859. Fourth Generation. 60.

4) Samuel Stemen Brenneman, b July 5, 1859, near Delphos, O , m. Feb. 8, 1883, Elizabeth Stemen, b. Oct 6, 1861, near Elida, O. Address. Delphos, O., R. 2. Farmer. Methodists. Mr Brenneman after the death of his parents purchased the old homestead where he has lived his entire life, and has become one of the influential citizens of his community.
1. Ira Brenneman, b. Dec 1, 1883. No. 2860
2. Herschel Brenneman, b. Sept. 2, 1888. No. 2861.

No. 2860. Fifth Generation. 2859.

1) Ira Brenneman, b Dec. 1, 1883, near Delphos, O , m. Sept. 15, 1909, Anna Ritchie, b. Sept. 16, 1887. Farmer Methodists He resides on his father's farm. Address: Delphos, O., R. 2.
1. Oren Bryce Brenneman, b. July 22, 1910.
2. Richard Norman Brenneman, b. July 2, 1913.
3. Nile Merton Brenneman, b. July 16, 1914.
4. Leah Esther Brenneman, b Mar 20, 1918
5. Betty Jane Brenneman, b. Dec 31, 1923.
6. Ruth Belle Brenneman, b Jan 14, 1925, d Oct. 6, 1925
7. Catherine Viola Brenneman, b Aug 27, 1926.
8. Carrie Lenore Brenneman, b June 12, 1928.

No. 2861. Fifth Generation. 2859.

2) Herschel Brenneman, b Sept 2, 1888, near Delphos, O , m. Feb 22, 1917, Edna Rebecca Good, daughter of Jacob and Malinda Good, b. June 10, 1897, d. Mar. 30, 1919. Herschel married (2nd) Mary Good, daughter of Simon and Barbara Good, April 4, 1926, b. Aug. 1, 1891, near Elida, O. Farmer. Mennonites. Address: Delphos, O , R. 2 Place of burial in Salem cemetery near Elida, O.

1. Carroll Edwin Brenneman, b. Dec. 5, 1917.
   (From second union)
2. Jeanette Thelma Brenneman, b. Mar. 12, 1927.
3. Joan Elizabeth Brenneman, b Aug 2, 1928.
4. Charlotte Jane Brenneman, b. Jan. 20, 1930

No. 2862. Fourth Generation. 61.

1) John B. Stemen, b Feb. 28, 1854, Fairfield Co., O., d. Mar. 16, 1930, m. Dec. 8, 1878, Jennie Mauger, b. Sept. 28, 1859, d. July 29, 1908. Both are buried in the Violet cemetery near Pickerington, O. Address: Pickerington, Fairfield Co., O. Farmer. Methodists.
1. Ezra M. Stemen, b. ——————.
2. Samuel B Stemen, b ——————.
3. Jessie Stemen, b. ——————.
4. Maude Stemen, b ——————.
5. Lydia Stemen, b. ——————.

No. 2863. Fourth Generation. 61.

2) Nancy Stemen, b. June 6, 1855, in Fairfield Co., O., d. Mar. 11, 1936, m Nov. 2, 1882, Wesley Mosier, b. May 1, 1850. Farmer. Davids Reformed. Burial in Violet cemetery, Pickerington, O. Address: Pickerington, O.
1. Emma Mosier, b Nov. 3, 1883, m. Bish.
2. Cora Mosier, b. Oct. 26, 1885, m. Axline.
3. Lydia Mosier, b. May 14, 1889.
4 Ollie Mosier, b. May 4, 1893, m. Kistler.
5. Florence Mosier, b. April 25, 1898, m Welch.

No. 2864. Fourth Generation. 61.

3) Lewis H. Stemen, b Mar. 21, 1862, in Fairfield Co., O., d. May 11, 1930, m. Dec. 22, 1892, Lydia Fenstermaker, b. Mar. 9, 1866. Farmer. United Brethren. Burial in Violet cemetery. Address: Pickerington, O.
1. Charles Stemen, b Nov 24, 1893.
2. Dessie Stemen, b July 12, 1898, m. Haynes.

No. 2865. Fourth Generation. 61.

4) William W. Stemen, b Oct 4, 1864, in Fairfield Co., O., m. Mar. 1, 1899, Martha J. Wright, b. Jan. 30, 1876. Address. Pickerington, O. Retired farmer. Methodists. Burial place in Violet cemetery.
1. Ella Mae Stemen, b. May 23, 1902.

No. 2856. Fourth Generation. 61.

5) Emma Stemen, b. Jan. 26, 1868, in Fairfield Co., O., m. Feb. 18, 1899, Thomas Longstroth, b. June 1, 1868, he died May 17, 1927. Farmer. Methodists. Place of burial in Violet cemetery, Pickerington, O. Address: Pickerington, O.
1. Stella Mae Longstroth, b July 3, 1899, d. in 1900.

No. 2867. Fourth Generation. 62.

1) Henry S. Brenneman, b. Mar. 7, 1859, in Fairfield Co., O., m Feb. 26, 1885, Mary Martin Mr Brenneman d. Sept 17, 1932. Address: Canal Winchester, O.
1. Wilfred M. Brenneman, b. Feb. 11, 1896. No. 2868.

No. 2868. Fifth Generation. 2867.

1) Wilfred M. Brenneman, b. Feb. 11, 1896, near Canal Winchester, O., m. Nov. 26, 1914, Mary Harris. Address: Canal Winchester, O
1. Donald H Brenneman, b June 28, 1915

3) Malinda Brenneman, b. June 28, 1862, in Fairfield Co , O , m. Andrew Guisinger. Address: Pickerington, O

1. Noah B. Guisinger, b. Jan 27, 1890 No. 2870.
2. Mary M. Guisinger, b Feb 17, 1892 No 2871
3 Vernon A Guisinger, b. May 2, 1894, d July 25, 1912.
4. Emma J. Guisinger, b. Dec. 17, 1899. No. 2872.
5. Walter L. Guisinger, b May 5, 1903 No 2873.
6. Henry N Guisinger, b May 13, 1906 No 2874.
7. Catherine Z. Guisinger, b. June 7, 1909 No 2875.

No. 2870. Fifth Generation. 2369.

1) Noah B. Guisinger, b Jan 27, 1890, near Pickerington, O , m. Helen Wood in 1923. She died in 1935 He married (2nd) Laura Ramsey in 1936 No issue. Address: 1340 E 20th Ave., Columbus, O.

No. 2371. Fifth Generation. 2369.

2) Mary M. Guisinger, b Feb. 17, 1892, near Pickerington, O., m Charles Smith, Aug. 20, 1923. Mary M died July 21, 1935. Address: Canal Winchester, O.

1. Doris Mae Smith, b. Jan 7, 1925.

No. 2872. Fifth Generation. 2369.

4) Emma J. Guisinger, b Dec 17, 1899, near Van Wert, O., m. Loren Hawbecker, in Dec., 1922 Address. Patascola, O.

1. Donna Hawbecker, b. July 16, 1926

No. 2873. Fifth Generation. 2369.

5) Walter L. Guisinger, b. May 5, 1903, near Van Wert, O , m. Phyllis Wells. Address: Brice, O.

1. One daughter, Alice Mae d. at birth.
2. Adopted daughter Martha, b Dec 27, 1934.

No. 2374. Fifth Generation. 2869.

6) Henry N. Guisinger, b. May 13, 1906, near Van Wert, O , m. Lillian Raver, Sept. 5, 1925. Address: Basil, O

1. Kenneth Guisinger, b June 7, 1926.

No. 2875. Fifth Generation. 2869.

7) Catherine Z. Guisinger, b June 7, 1909, near Pickerington, O., m. Arnold Switzer, June 19, 1934. Address: Pickerington, O.

1. Janet Ann Switzer, b. Aug. 5, 1935.

No. 2376. Fourth Generation. 63.

1) Nancy Jane Brenneman, b. April 26, 1858, near Elida, O., d. Oct. 22, 1937, at Craigville, Ind., m John David Griffith, b ————, d. Aug. 28, 1881 She married (2nd) William Gahman, b. Mar. 24, 1861, d. April 21, 1933, at Craigville, Ind. Address: Craigville, Ind. Farmer. Burial in Salem cemetery, near Elida, O.

1. Thomas Griffith, b. ————. No. 2880.
   (From second union)
2. Lesta Gahman, b. ————. No. 2881.
3. Martin Gahman, b. ———— No 2882
4. Ottomar Gahman, b. ————, 1890. No. 2883
5. Elda Gahman, b ————, 1892. No 2884
6. Floyd Gahman, b. ————. No. 2885

7. Anna Gahman, b. Nov. 5, 1896. No 2886
8. Breta Gahman, b. May 7, 1899 No 2887.
9. John N. Gahman, b. ——————, d at 3 months.

No. 2880. Fifth Generation. 2876.

1) Thomas Griffith, b. July 3, 1881, m Elizabeth Barger, b. ——————.
Address Decatur, Ind.
1. William Griffith, b ——————.
2. Herman Griffith, b. ——————.
3. Leah Griffith, b. ——————.
4. Glen Griffith, b ——————.

No. 2881. Fifth Generation. 2876.

2) Lesta Gahman, b. ——————, m Frank Bright. Address: Tocsin, Ind
1. Martin Bright, b. ——————.
2. Wallace Bright, b. ——————.
3. Merea Bright, b. ——————.
4. Ruth Bright, b ——————.
5. Rethal Bright, b. ——————.
6. Gerald Bright, b ——————.

No. 2382. Fifth Generation. 2876.

3) Martin Gahman, b ——————, m Ethel Warthman Address: Craigville, Ind.
1. Robert Gahman, b. ——————.
2. Arthur Gahman, b. ——————
3. Alice Gahman, b. ——————.
4. Vera Gahman, b. ——————

No. 2883. Fifth Generation. 2876.

4) Ottomar Gahman, b ——————, 1890, m Ada Elliott. Address: 4081 Lawrence Ave, Detroit, Mich.
1. Evelyn Gahman, b. ——————.
2. Thomas Gahman, b. ——————.
3. Roscanna Gahman, b. ——————.
4. Paul Gahman, b. ——————.

No. 2884. Fifth Generation. 2876.

5) Elda Gahman, b ——————, 1892, m. Charles R. Hogg. Address: Bluffton,
Ind. No children.

No. 2885. Fifth Generation. 2876.

6) Floyd Gahman, b ——————, m. Ruth Leyse Address: 550 Riverside
Drive, New York City, N. Y.
1. Phyllis Gahman, b ——————.

No. 2886. Fifth Generation. 2876.

7) Anna Gahman, b Nov. 5, 1896, m. Jan. 10, 1917, Clarence Abbott, b. Sept.
3, 1896. Address. Van Wert, O Farmer. United Brethren.
1. Walter Neal Abbott, b Dec 6, 1917.
2. Cora Irene Abbott, b Jan. 1, 1920.
3. Esther Jane Abbott, b. May 22, 1922.
4. Roscoe Earl Abbott, b April 29, 1930.

No. 2887. Fifth Generation. 2876.

8) Breta Aravilla Gahman, b May 7, 1899, m. May 29, 1926, Omer Clare Odell, b. Dec 17, 1897. Address: 1027 W Elm St., Lima, O. Methodists.

1. Richard Earle Odell, b July 31, 1927.

No. 2888. Fourth Generation. 63.

2) Mary Brenneman, b May 12, 1860, near Elida, O , d. April 3, 1938, m. May 20, 1875, William P. Furry, b. Nov 28, 1855, d. Dec. 17, 1920. Address: Elida, O. Farmer and mason Methodists Burial in Salem cemetery near Elida, O.

1. Charles A. Furry, b. Mar. 15, 1877. No. 2889
2. John W. Furry, b. Aug 20, 1879. No 2892
3. Iona May Furry, b. 1881, d. Sept 8, 1884
4. Cloyd M. Furry, b. Dec 9, 1883 No 2893.
5. Earl Furry, b. Mar. 29, 1886 No. 2895
6. Lena A. Furry, b. May 11, 1888 No. 2897
7. Roy C. Furry, b. Sept 18, 1890 No 2898.
8. Elsie E. Furry, b. Feb 3, 1893. No. 2899.
9. Harry C. Furry, b. Mar 29, 1895. No 2900
10. Myrtle L. Furry, b. May 14, 1898 No. 2901.
11. William P. Furry, Jr , b. Dec 12, 1900 No. 2902.
12. Robert V. Furry, b Dec. 24, 1904 No. 2903.

No. 2889. Fifth Generation. 2888.

1) Charles A Furry, b Mar. 15, 1877, near Elida, O., killed by accident at Lima Locomotive Shop, Dec. 17, 1923 He married April 26, 1900, Nora Parker, b. Oct. 26, 1877, d. Dec 14, 1920 Buried in Salem cemetery near Elida, O. Mechanic. Methodists. Address: Lima, O.

1. Ira W. Furry, b. Nov. 18, 1900 No 2890.
2. Frank Furry, b. Jan. 28, 1903. No. 3590.
3. Margaret Furry, b Mar. 3, 1905. No. 2891
4. Parker Furry, b. July 17, 1907 No 3591.
5. Zoe Furry, b. Oct. 22, 1910. No 3592
6. Betty Furry, b. Nov. 14, 1920.

No. 2890. Sixth Generation. 2889.

1) Ira W. Furry, b. Nov. 18, 1900, m. April, 1922, Elsie Bressler, b. Oct. 3, 1902. Methodists. Druggist. Address: 384 S Pine St., Lima, O.

1. Charles Wilber Furry, b Jan. 7, 1926.

No. 2891. Sixth Generation. 2889.

3) Margaret Furry, b. Mar. 3, 1905, near Elida, O., m. June 21, 1924, Herbert Stump, b. Jan. 11, 1902. They live in Lima, O. Salesman. Methodists.

1. Gene Stump, b. Nov. 1, 1925.
2. Frederick Stump, b. Oct. 3, 1931.
3. Janice Stump, b. May 5, 1934.

No. 2892. Fifth Generation. 2888.

2) John W. Furry, b. Aug. 20, 1879, near Elida, O., m Jan., 1910, Goldie W. Bell, b. April —, 1891. Address: Elida, O. Lineman. United Brethren.

1. Donald L. Furry, b. Sept. 20, 1910. No. 3579.
2 Bettie Lee Furry, b. Nov 28, 1923.

No. 2893. Fifth Generation. 2888.

4) Cloyd M. Furry, b Dec. 9, 1883, near Elida, O., m. Dec. 23, 1908, Mary Stewart, b Sept. 18, 1887. Address: Lima, O., R 4 Machinist. United Brethren.
1. John Furry b. Nov. 9, 1910. No. 2894.

No. 2894. Sixth Generation. 2893.

1) John Furry, b Nov 9, 1910, m. Oct. 2, 1933, Winona Miller, b. Dec. 7, 1912. Church of the Brethren Address: Lima, O. Machinist.

No. 2895. Fifth Generation. 2888.

5) Earl Furry, b. Mar. 28, 1886, near Elida, O , d. by accident at Lima Loco-motive Shop, Jan. 27, 1917 He married Dec. 25, 1910, Edna Lyberger, b. Nov. 1, 1889. Address: Harrod, O. Shop worker. Brethren. Burial in the Salem cemetery near Elida, O.
1. Edgar W. Furry, b May 4, 1914. No. 2896
2. Clifford E. Furry, b Feb. 9, 1917.

No. 2896. Sixth Generation. 2895.

1) Edgar W Furry, b May 4, 1914, m. Aug. 21, 1933, Corda Stubbs, b. May 18, 1914 Address: Harrod, O. Salesman Brethren.
1. Thomas Earl Furry, b. Dec. 1, 1934.

No. 2897. Fifth Generation. 2888.

6) Lena A Furry, b May 11, 1888, near Elida, O., m. ————, 1924, Robert D Berryman Address State Hospital, Lima, O No children.

No. 2898. Fifth Generation. 2888.

7) Roy Clayton Furry, b. Sept. 18, 1890, near Elida, O., d. April 16, 1937, m. Dec. 24, 1911, Bessie Brenneman, b Oct 20, 1892. Farmer. Methodists. Address. Elida, O. Burial in Salem cemetery near Elida, O.
1. Dorothy Mary Furry, b. Nov. 20, 1912
2. Marion Clayton Furry, b. Oct. 16, 1916.
3 Helen May Furry, b. May 11, 1921.
4 Arthur Earl Furry, b June 27, 1925.
5. La Donna Grace Furry, b. Feb. 22, 1931.

No. 2899. Fifth Generation. 2888.

8) Elsie E. Furry, b. Feb. 3, 1893, near El.da, O., m. May 21, 1914, Jerome Basinger, b Mar. 27, 1878. Address: Lima, O. Salesman. Methodists.
1. Ruth E. Basinger, b. Feb. 16, 1915. No. 3285.
2. Lois J. Basinger, b. Dec 23, 1917.

No. 2900. Fifth Generation. 2888.

9) Harry C. Furry, b Mar. 29, 1895, near Elida, O., m. in 1923, Waive Sphar. They live at Wren, O. Lineman.
1 Louany Furry, b. May 8, 1925, d ————, 1928.

No. 2901. Fifth Generation. 2888.

10) Myrtle L. Furry, b. May 14, 1898, near Elida, O., m. May 24, 1917, Howard Hoag. Musician. Address: Ionia, State Hospital, Mich.

No. 2902. Fifth Generation. 2888.

11) William P. Furry, Jr., b Dec. 12, 1900, near Elida, O , m April 21, 1924, Pauline Copeland, b. Aug 25, 1907 Address: Elida, O. Laborer. United Brethren
1 Eileen Furry b. Oct. 25, 1925
2 Billy L Furry, b Dec 14, 1930

No. 2903. Fifth Generation. 2888.

12) Robert V. Furry, b Dec 24, 1904, near Elida, O., m. June 12, 1925, Naomi Stettler, b. Feb. 5, 1907. Address: Delphos, O Mechanic. Methodists

1. Mary Louise Furry, b. Dec. 29, 1925.
2. Evelyn Lee Furry, b. Aug. 9, 1930
3. Phyllis Jean Furry, b. May 14, 1932.
4. Robert Earl Furry, b. June 8, 1935.

No. 2904. Fourth Generation. 63.

3) John H. Brenneman, b June 21, 1862, near Elida, O , m. Oct. 30, 1884, Anna Guterba, b. May 28, 1865, d. ——————. Address: Elida, O. R 1. Farmer. Lutherans. Burial in Salem cemetery near Elida, O.

1. Offa B. Brenneman, b. Sept. 7, 1885 No 2905
2. Zoa Brenneman, b. Mar 7, 1891, d. Oct 22, 1895
3. Forest A Brenneman, b April 22, 1895. No 2906
4. Eula Viola Brenneman, b. Jan. 12, 1897 No 2907
5. John Rowland Brenneman, b Dec. 23, 1901 No 2908.
6 An adopted daughter, Mildred Brenneman, b April 3, 1905. No 2909

No. 2905. Fifth Generation. 2904.

1) Offa B. Brenneman, b. Sept 7, 1885, near Elida, O., m July 15, 1908, Margaret Jones of Gomer, O., b Feb. 20, 1884 Address: Lima, O , R 3. Farmer. Congregational.

1. Dorothy Brenneman, b Oct 30, 1911

No. 2905. Fifth Generation. 2904.

3) Forest A. Brenneman, b April 22, 1895, near Elida, O , m Mar 4, 1920, Ed.th Stemen, b ——————, daughter of Samson and Kate Stemen. Address: Elida, O., R. 1. No issue.

No. 2907. Fifth Generation. 2904.

4) Eula Viola Brenneman, b Jan 12, 1897, near Elida, O., m Nov. 14, 1916, Emerald Irvin. They live at Harley, Ida. Painter

1. Irene Irvin, b April 17, 1919.
2. June Irvin, b. June 12, 1925.

No. 2908. Fifth Generation. 2904.

5) John Rowland Brenneman, b. Dec. 23, 1901, near Elida, O., m Aug. 21, 1929, Freda Johnson, b Nov , 1904. They live in Delphos, O Mechanic.

1. Maryl.n Brenneman, b. ——————, 1931
2. John Brenneman, b ——————, 1935.

No. 2909. Fifth Generation. 2904.

6) Mildred Brenneman, b April 3, 1905 (adopted), m. Feb 22, 1925, George Hoover. Address· Elida, O Farmer.

1. John Hoover, b. Mar. —, 1929, d. young.
2. Anna Mary Hoover, b April —, 1930

No. 2910. Fourth Generation. 63.

5) Lydia Brenneman, b Mar 13, 1867, near Elida, O , m. Aug 3, 1889, Enos Huffer, b Dec. 10, 1866, d Jan 25, 1939 Farmer Address· Elida, O , R 1

1. Merlin Huffer, b. Jan 17, 1887 No 2911
2. Odessa Huffer, b July 5, 1890 No 2912

No. 2911. Fifth Generation. 2910.

1) Merlin Huffer, b Jan 17, 1887, m Dec 18, 1898, Fay Taflinger, of Lima, O. Address: Elida, O., R 1 Farmer.

1. Margaret Huffer, b. June 26, 1924.

No. 2912. Fifth Generation. 2910.

2) Odessa Huffer, b July 5, 1890, m. Ambrose Basinger. Divorced. She married (2nd) Lang Raymond She married (3rd) Robert Reynold.

1. Ilo Basinger, b Dec 18, 1918

No. 2913. Fourth Generation. 63.

6) Sarah Elizabeth Brenneman, b Sept 24, 1872, near Elida, O., d. ————, 1914, m William Laman Address: Lima, O

1. Harold Laman, b ————, m Canelle Langtrake.
2. Otis Laman, b ————, m. Helen Crackenberger.
3. Virgil Laman, b. ————, m Maxine Buti

No. 2914. Fourth Generation. 64.

1) John B. Diller, b Dec 16, 1856, near Elida, O., d. Nov. 27, 1916, m. Caroline E. Brenneman, b. May 1, 1858. Address: Elida, O. Farmer and carpenter. Mennonites Burial place in Salem cemetery, Elida, O

1 Mintie A. Diller, b June 7, 1879 No. 2915.
2. Ervin O Diller, b April 2, 1884 No 2916
3 Samuel O Diller, b Dec 29, 1887. No. 2920.

No. 2915. Fifth Generation. 2914.

1) Mintie A. Diller, b June 7, 1879, near Elida, O , m April 2, 1901, Simeon Huber. Farmer and carpenter Burial ground in Salem cemetery near Elida, O. Address: Elida, O , R. 1 Mennonites

1. Alvin Edwin Huber, b June 15, 1902, d May 3, 1934.
2. Lestie Irene Huber, b Feb 24, 1905, d Aug 20, 1919.
3. Infant, b. Feb 25, 1911, d. same day.
4. Effie Lucele Huber, b. Oct. 3, 1912.
5. Edna Caroline Huber, b. Oct 9, 1914.
6. Reuben Lee Huber, b. Feb. 23, 1919

No. 2916. Fifth Generation. 2914.

2) Ervin O. Diller, b April 2, 1884, m. May 24, 1908, Susanna R. Shenk, b. Dec 2, 1886. Mennonite Laborer and farmer Address: Elida, O., R. 1.

1. Ira A. Diller, b. May 29, 1909. No 2917.
2. Clara A Diller, b Aug 18, 1910. No 2918.
3. Ralph H. Diller, b Nov. 24, 1914. No 2919.
4. Martha A Diller, b. Aug 24, 1922.

No. 2917. Sixth Generation. 2916.

1) Ira A. Diller, b May 29, 1909, m Beulah Brenner of near Orrville, O. Address: Elida, O , R 1 Truck driver. Mennonites.

1. May E. Diller, b. May 21, 1935.

No. 2918. Sixth Generation. 2916.

2) Clara A Diller, b Aug 18, 1910, m. Harold Good, b. Mar. 12, 1912, near Elida, O. Address: Elida, O , R 2. Farmer Mennonites.

No. 2919. Sixth Generation. 2916.

3) Ralph H Diller, b Nov 24, 1914, m Esther Good, b. Dec. 24, 1909 Address Elida, O , R. 1 Mennonites Farmer.

No. 2920. Fifth Generation. 2914.

3) Samuel O. Diller, b. Dec. 29, 1887, m in 1909 Elsie Leona Huber, b. Nov. 9, 1891. Address: Delphos, O., R. 2. Oil pumper. Mennonite.

1. Cleo Fern Diller, b. Oct 12, 1913. No 2921.
2. Irene Mildred Diller, b. Jan 8, 1917, died.
3. Chester Alton Diller, b. July 21, 1918.
4. Doyle J. Diller, b. Dec 11, 1921, twin, d
5. Dale J. Diller, b. Dec 11, 1921, twin, d.
6. Ursel Richard Diller, b Sept 1, 1924
7. Melvin Carl Diller, b Sept. 13, 1926.

No. 2921. Sixth Generation. 2920.

1) Cleo Fern Diller, b. Oct. 12, 1913, m. April 4, 1932, Garner Gales, b. Oct. 2, 1910. Address: Spencerville, O.

1. Laverne Samuel Gales, b Feb. 15, 1933.
2. Elsie Leona Gales, b. Sept. 24, 1934

No. 2922. Fourth Generation. 64.

4) George Diller, b. Mar. 23, 1861, m. Nov. 21, 1885, Lydia F Brenneman, b. Aug. 16, 1863. She died Aug 24, 1932 He d.ed ————, 1935. Address. Elida, O., R. 1. Farmer. Mennonites. Burial in Salem cemetery near Elida, O

1. Lesta M. Diller, b. Jan. 1, 1887. No 2923.

No. 2923. Fifth Generation. 2922.

1) Lesta M. Diller, b. Jan. 1, 1887, near Elida, O., m. Jan. 7, 1909, Amandus Brubaker, b Oct. 25, 1883 Address: Lima, O , R 3. Farmer Mennonites.

1. Harney Brubaker b April 1, 1910, d. same date.
2. Erma Louella Brubaker, b June 17, 1911
3. Clara Esther Brubaker, b. Sept 22, 1912.
4. Harold Adrian Brubaker, b. Oct. 16, 1914 No. 3647.

No. 2924. Fourth Generation. 64.

5) Barbara Diller, b Jan 28, 1864, near Elida, O., d. May 4, 1922, m Dec. 25, 1884, John Powell, of Va. He died May 12, 1897 Farmer. Mennonites. She married (2nd) Abram D. Weaver. Burial in Salem cemetery near Elida O. Address was Elida, O.

1. Elizabeth Powell, b. June 7, 1886. No. 2925.
2. Dora Powell, b. June 5, 1888, twin No 2926
3. Cora Powell, b. June 5, 1888, twin. No. 2927.
4. Samuel Powell, b. Mar. 23, 1892 No. 2928.
5. Anna Powell. b. Sept. —, 1897. No. 2930.

No. 2925. Fifth Generation. 2924.

1) Elizabeth Powell, b June 7, 1886, near Elida, O , m Dec. 4, 1919, Samuel A. Brenneman, b. Feb. 25, 1897 Burial place in Salem cemetery. Farmer. Mennonites. Address: Elida, O , R 1

1. Clifford Brenneman, b Oct 25, 1920
2. Beulah Brenneman, b. Oct. 19, 1921, d Jan. 6, 1924.
3. Florence Brenneman, b. April 22, 1925.
4. David Brenneman, b June 20, 1927.

No. 2926. Fifth Generation. 2924.

2) Dora Powell, b. June 5, 1888, near Elida, O , m Oct. 1, 1908, William Heatwole, b. Nov. 23, 1882, of Va. Burial place in Salem cemetery. Address: Elida, O., R. 2. Farmer. Mennonites.

1. Virgil Heatwole, b. Nov. 27, 1909.
2. Alma Heatwole, b. Sept. 13, 1911.
3. Raymond Heatwole, b. July 10, 1913.
4. Grace Heatwole, b. Aug. 26, 1916.
5. Lewis Heatwole, b Aug. 29, 1918.
6. Vernon Heatwole, b. June 15, 1927.

No. 2927. Fifth Generation. 2924.
3) Cora Powell, b June 5, 1888, near Elida, O., m. ——————, Roy Greeg Barnt, b. —————— Address. Delphos, O , R. 2. Farmer. Mennonites.
1. Carl Barnt, b. ——————.
2. Ruth Barnt, b. ——————.
3. Ray Barnt, b. ——————.
4. Irene Barnt, b. ——————.
5. Vera Barnt, b. ——————.
6. Richard Barnt, b. ——————.

No. 2928. Fifth Generation. 2924.
4) Samuel J. Powell, b. Mar. 23, 1892, near Elida, O., m. April 30, 1913, Laura A. Shenk, b. June 8, 1892 Address. Elida, O., R. 1. Farmer. Mennonites.
1. Mabel E. Powell, b. Mar. 23, 1892.
2. John K. Powell, b Aug 15, 1915 No. 2929.
3. Dorothy M Powell, b. April 6, 1917 No. 3702.
4. Betty M. Powell, b. Nov. 23, 1921, d. Jan. 16, 1928.
5. Samuel J. Powell, Jr., b. Feb. 23, 1923.

No. 2929. Sixth Generation. 2928.
2) John K Powell, b Aug. 15, 1915, m. Ethel Lahman. Address· Elida, O., R. 1. Laborer. Mennonites.
1. Donna Lou Powell, b. Sept 20, 1936.

No. 2930. Fifth Generation. 2924.
5) Anna Marie Powell, b Sept 14, 1897, near Elida, O., m Nov. 15, 1916, William Franklin Hartman, b. Sept 22, 1892, of Va Farmer and mechanic. Mennonites.
1. Marvin D. Hartman, b. Aug. 11, 1918
2. Clara I. Hartman, b. June 26, 1921.
3. Edwin S. Hartman, b. May 31, 1926.
4. Robert M. Hartman, b. Nov. 15, 1928.

No. 2931. Fourth Generation. 64.
6) Henry B. Diller, b April 21, 1866, near Elida, O., d. June 18, 1916, m. Jan. 25, 1894, Amanda Jane Stemen, b Dec. 17, 1873. Burial in Salem cemetery near Elida, O. Address: Lima, O , R. 3 Farmer. Mennonites. Related
1. Lela Pauline Diller, b. Dec 8, 1894. No. 2405.
2. Harry Stemen Diller, b. Mar. 20, 1900. No 2406.
3. Lois Elizabeth Diller, b. Mar. 31, 1903, single.
4. Vernon Samuel Diller, b. Nov. 20, 1908. No. 2407.
5. Grace Amanda Diller, b. July 10, 1911, d. Feb. 14, 1927.

No. 2932. Fourth Generation. 64.
7) Samuel S. Diller, b. July 2, 1868, near Elida, O., m. Aug 9, 1888, Lydia A. Brenneman, b. Feb. 20, 1865. Burial place in Salem cemetery, near Elida, O. Address: Elida, O , R. 1. Farmer Mennonites. Related

1 Bertha Frances Diller, b Sept 7, 1889 No 2361

2. Infant son, b. Feb. 25, 1892, d same day.

3. Joseph B. Diller, b Feb. 25, 1893. No. 2363.

4. Nancy C. Diller, b Feb 24, 1896 No 2364.

5. Infant son, b. April 19, 1898, d. same day.

6 Mary A. Diller, b July 27, 1899 No. 2365.

No. 2933. Fourth Generation. 64.

8) William Diller, b May 31, 1870, near Elida, O , d. July 11, 1928, m. June 28, 1891, Anna R. Shank, b. Nov. 9, 1872, near Versailles, Mo., d. Mar 7, 1933. Burial in Salem cemetery near El da, O Address· Elida, O. Farmer Mennonites.

1. Lessie Elizabeth Diller, b. July 15, 1892. No 2934.

2. Arthur D. Diller, b. Oct 10, 1895. No 2935.

3. Laura Sarah Diller, b Nov 2, 1898, d Dec 10, 1908.

4. Clara Esther Diller, b. Oct 22, 1901. No 2936.

5. Wilmer S. Diller, b. Oct 21, 1904. No. 2937.

6. Osie Irene Diller, b Dec 22, 1908, d. Jan. 16, 1933.

7. Vera Mae Diller, b. Sept —, 1910, d Jan 5, 1913.

8. Della Barbara Diller, b Sept 21, 1913

No. 2934. Fifth Generation. 2933.

1) Lessie Elizabeth D.ller, b July 15, 1892, near Elida, O , m Mar. 18, 1914, Adam S Brenneman, b. Oct. 3, 1884 Burial place in Salem cemetery near Elida, O. Address: Elida, O. Dry cleaner Mennonites.

1. Richard L. Brenneman, b. April 5, 1916.

2. Paul William Brenneman, b Mar 2, 1921, d July 8, 1934

3. Alice Ann Brenneman, b. July 28, 1926

No. 2935. Fifth Generation. 2933.

2) Arthur D. Diller, b Oct 10, 1895, near Elida, O , m Dec 27, 1923, Malinda K Bevington, b. Feb 25, 1901 H gh-school teacher Methodists. Address: 3722 Wyckliffe Parkway, Toledo, O

1. David B. Diller, b. May 29, 1925.

2. Jacqueline A. Diller, b July 7, 1928.

No. 2936. Fifth Generation. 2933.

4) Clara Esther Diller, b. Oct 22, 1901, near Elida, O., m Oct. 16, 1927, Carlton R. Wyse, b Feb. 25, 1907. Laborer and mechanic. Defenseless Mennonite Address: Archbold, O.

1. William Russell Wyse, b Sept. 13, 1928

2. James Wyse, b ———, 1937.

No. 2937. Fifth Generation. 2933.

5) Wilmer S D ller, b Oct 21, 1904, near Elida, O , m July 2, 1932, Mary A. Schosker, b Feb. 25, 1907 Barber by trade Mr Diller is a Methodist and Mrs. Diller is a Catholic. Address. 301 S. Main St , Delphos, O.

1. Marylin Emily Diller, b May 7, 1936

No. 2933. Fourth Generation. 64.

9) Andrew Diller, b. May 1, 1873, near Elida, O , m Dec. 21, 1893, Mary C. Huber, b. Jan. 26, 1876, d. Sept. 3, 1897 He married (2nd) Oct. 25, 1898, Nancy C. Brenneman, b. May 7, 1867, she died June 2, 1937. Burial place in Salem cemetery near El da, O Address Elida, O , R 1 Farmer Mennonites. Related.

1. Clarence S. Diller, b. Dec 10, 1894 No. 2526.

2. Mary E. Diller, b May 13, 1897. No 2527
   (From second union)
3. Harvey Andrew Diller, b. Aug. 30, 1899, d. July 25, 1900.
4. Esther Ada Diller, b. July 14, 1901. No. 369
5. Florence Edna Diller, b Oct 23, 1902. No. 434.
6. Rudy Harold Diller, b Oct 29, 1909. No. 371.

No. 2939. Fourth Generation. 65.

1) William Henry Brenneman, b. Jan. 10, 1862, near Elida, O., m. (1st) Della Pease, b. ——————. She died ——————. He married (2nd) Mariah Poling, b. Feb. 5, 1869. William H. Brenneman d May 16, 1890. Methodist. Buried in Salem cemetery near Elida, O.
   1. Ida Brenneman, b Jan 6, 1889. No 2940.

No. 2940. Fifth Generation. 2939.

1) Ida Brenneman, b Jan 6, 1889, m April 14, 1910, Walter Dieterich, b. May 31, 1888. Address 2 Pinehurst Ave., Dayton, O.
   1. Martha V. Dieterich, b Nov 23, 1914. No. 3287.
   2. Robert W. Dieterich, b. Sept 23, 1916. No. 3656.

No. 2941. Fourth Generation. 65.

2) John Franklin Brenneman, b Oct 6, 1863, near Elida, O, d. Nov. 13, 1925, m Oct. 6, 1890, Elsie Miller, b Jan 6, 1871 Carpenter. Methodists. Burial in Woodlawn cemetery, L ma, O Address South Metcalf St., Lima, O.
   1. Verla May Brenneman, b Oct. 31, 1890. No. 2942.
   2 Forest B. Brenneman, b. July 11, 1892
   3. Grace Brenneman, b Nov 7, 1894
   4. Osa Laonne Brenneman, b May 18, 1900 No. 2943.

No. 2942. Fifth Generation. 2941.

1) Verla M Brenneman, b Oct 31, 1890, in Lima, O , m. Sept 18, 1912, H. P. Allen, b Feb 17, 1891 Methodists. Address 500 S. Metcalf St , Lima, O. Machinist.
   1. Cahleene Allen, b Aug 11, 1913, twin.
   2 Geraldine Allen, b Aug 11, 1913, twin.

No. 2943. Fifth Generation. 2941.

4) Osa Laonne Brenneman, b May 18, 1900, in Lima, O., m. April 9, 1921, Walter Henry Howard, b. Nov. 9, 1896 Address· 423 Rice St , Springfield, O. Methodists.
   1 Walter Henry Howard, Jr., b Sept. 1, 1924.
   2. Marianna Howard, b Sept. 27, 1928

No. 2944. Fourth Generation. 65.

3) Benonia S. Brenneman, b Dec 6, 1864, near Elida, O., d. Jan. 10, 1937, m. Dec 5, 1891, Caddie McBride, b June 25, 1871. Carpenter. Presbyterians. Address: 709 W. Kibby St , Lima, O.
   1. Herschel Clayton Brenneman, b Nov. 18, 1892, single.
   2. Ralph E Brenneman, b. Aug 8, 1899 No 3286

No. 2945. Fourth Generation. 65.

4) George W. Brenneman, b. Oct. 6, 1866, near Elida, O , m. Dec 17, 1887, Viola Thomas, b Oct. 31, 1870 Address. Elida, O., R. 2. Farmer. Methodists.
   1 Esther Pearl Brenneman, b. Oct 6, 1891. No 2946
   2. Treva Evangene Brenneman, b. Sept. 2, 1907.

No. 2946. Fifth Generation. 2945.

1) Esther Pearl Brenneman, b Oct 6, 1891, m Henry J Brunk, b Jan 23, 1888. Address. Otto Lake, Mich Dentist. Related, see No 439.

1. William H Brunk, b. June 23, 1916

No. 2947. Fourth Generation. 65.

6) Nancy Brenneman, b. Dec 14, 1869, near Elida, O., m. Mar. 31, 1888, Delbert McBride, b Nov. 28, 1866 and d. Jan. 4, 1931. Elevator operator. Methodists She married (2nd) July 3, 1938, Dr William Roush, b ———, 1866. Address: 499 N Jameson Ave., Lima, O

1. Ira McBride, b. Aug. 4, 1889 No. 2948.
2. Ray McBride, b July 7, 1893, d. Jan. 4, 1914.

No. 2948. Fifth Generation. 2947.

1) Ira McBride, b. Aug 4, 1889, m Dec 25, 1915, Mabel Myers, b. in 1888. Ticket agent at the interurban station, Lima, O.

No. 2949. Fourth Generation. 65.

7) Daniel L. Brenneman, b Jan 1, 1871, near Elida, O., m. Jan. 31, 1893, Mary E. Davidson, b. July 28, 1878 Address Elida, O., R 1. Farmer. Methodists.

1 Edith E. Brenneman, b. Aug. 3, 1894. No 2950.
2. John W. Brenneman, b. Aug. 21, 1896 No 2951.
3. Wallace D. Brenneman, b. Sept 15, 1917 No 3580

No. 2950. Fifth Generation. 2949.

1) Ed.th Estella Brenneman, b Aug 3, 1894, near Elida, O , m Dec. 23, 1915, Russell Wolf, b July 22, 1890 Address Bluffton, R 2, O. Farmer. Methodists.

1. Helen Elizabeth Wolf, b Sept 6, 1916
2 Lois Marie Wolf, b. Oct 27, 1922

No. 2951. Fifth Generation. 2949.

2) John W. Brenneman, b Aug 2, 1896, near Elida, O., m. July 13, 1929, Gertrude I. Lacey, b. Aug. 4, 1904. Mechanic foreman Methodists Address: 1222 Leland Ave., Lima, O.

1. Philip David Brenneman, b Feb. 17, 1938

No. 2952. Fourth Generation. 65.

8) Samuel S. Brenneman, b Oct 2, 1874, near Elida, O., m. Sept. 22, 1901, Elizabeth Mos.er, b Aug. 4, 1875, d June 17, 1930. Buried in Salem cemetery. Farmer. Mennonites. Address: Elida, O.

1 Ansel Brenneman, b. Sept. 4, 1902, d. Oct 3, 1902.
2. Velma May Brenneman, b. July 7, 1904. No. 2953.
3. Clarence Henry Brenneman, b Nov 19, 1907 No 2954
4. Ray John Brenneman, b. Aug 3, 1910. No. 2955.
5. Orvin Cless Brenneman, b Aug 19, 1912. No. 2956.

No. 2953. Fifth Generation. 2952.

2) Velma May Brenneman, b. July 7, 1904, m. Lester McCullough. Address: Kenton, O Methodists.

1. Margaret McCullough, b. ————
2. Ida McCullough, b. ————.
3. Daniel McCullough, b ————.
4. Anna Ruth McCullough, b ————.

No. 2954. Fifth Generation. 2952.

3) Clarence Henry Brenneman, b Nov 19, 1907, m Laura Good Address·
Logan, O. Mennonites Farmer

1. ———— Brenneman, b. ————.

No. 2955. Fifth Generation. 2952.

4) Roy John Brenneman, b Aug 3, 1910, m. Bertha McCandish. Address:
Bremen, O. No children.

No. 2956. Fifth Generation. 2952.

5) Orvin Cless Brenneman, b. Aug 19, 1912, m Zoe Foust Address: Delphos, O., R. 2.

No. 2957. Fourth Generation. 65.

9) Anna Margaret Brenneman, b June 10, 1877, d. Mar. 11, 1911, m April
28, 1901, Amos Miller, b Mar 18, 1873 Address: Elida, O., R. 2. Farmer. Christian Church Burial in Walnut Grove cemetery near Delphos, O No children.

No. 2958. Fourth Generation. 65.

10) James Alexander Brenneman, b April 29, 1879, near Elida, O , d. Nov.
24, 1936, m. Aug. 24, 1921, Dora E. Culbertson, b. Jan 3, 1884. United Brethren.
Mr Brenneman early in life accepted Christ as his Saviour after which he entered school in Otterbein College at Westerville, O., for the purpose of better
fitting himself for service for his Saviour. In 1915 he graduated from that institution and then taught school for a time When the United States entered the
World War, he enlisted in the Y M. C. A and was sent to France Upon his
return he entered the Bonebrake Seminary graduating in 1921, after which he
served several different congregations as pastor In July of 1936 he was stricken
with a malady which caused his death Funeral services were held both at Clay
City, Ind , and at the United Brethren Church in Elida, O , after which he was
taken for burial in the Salem cemetery near Elida, O. No children.

No. 2959. Fourth Generation. 65.

11) Osa Augusta Brenneman, b Nov 22, 1884, near Elida, O , d May 5,
1921, m Charles Clifford Plikard, b Mar 4, 1880 They live at Spencerville, O
Christian Church Burial in the Walnut Grove cemetery, four miles east of
Delphos, O.

1 Olive Ruth Plikard, b Dec 8, 1908 No. 2960
2. Esther Marie Plikard, b Sept 9, 1910, single Her present address: 439
College Ave , Fostoria, O

No. 2960. Fifth Generation. 2959.

1) Olive Ruth Plikard, b. Dec. 8, 1908, m May 25, 1929, Stephen A Tarbell,
b Dec. 25, 1904 Salesman Baptists Address 648 North Pearl St , Albany, N. Y.

No. 2961. Fourth Generation. 66.

1) Maude May Brenneman, b Sept 25, 1873, m. George M. Sandy. Address:
123 N. Carrie St., McPherson, Kans

1 Ethel Sandy, b. Feb. 22, 1892 No. 2962
2. Orpha V. Sandy, b April 4, 1895. No. 2963.
3. Lillian E. Sandy, b Jan. 6, 1900

No. 2962. Fifth Generation. 2961.

1) Ethel Sandy, b Feb. 22, 1892, m. David Fulkerson.
1. Harold David Fulkerson, b. April 24, 1919.

No. 2953. Fifth Generation. 2951.

2) Orpha V. Sandy, b April 4, 1895, m John B Leyda

1. John B. Leyda, Jr., b Feb. 7, 1919.

No. 2964. Fourth Generation. 66.

2) John Ernest Brenneman, b May 31, 1876, m Jan. 1, 1903, Annie Peeler. Address: Norborne, Mo

1. Helen Brenneman, b. Dec. 5, 1903, d. Nov. 3, 1905.
2. Elmira Brenneman, b Dec 10, 1905 No 2965
3. Virgin a Brenneman, b Mar 19, 1908. No 2966.
4. Elwin Brenneman, b Dec. 31, 1910
5. Henry Brenneman, Jr., b. April 7, 1914, twin.
6. Allen Brenneman, b April 7, 1914, twin
7. Julia Brenneman, b Oct. 3, 1917.

No. 2955. Fifth Generation. 2964.

2) Elmira Brenneman, b. Dec 10, 1905, m Roy Hogan.

1. ———— Hogan, b ————————.
2. ———— Hogan, b. ————————.

No. 2966. Fifth Generation. 2964.

3) Virginia Brenneman, b. Mar 19, 1908, m Harold Rhodabaugh

No. 2957. Fourth Generation. 66.

3) Bertha Viola Brenneman, b Feb 4, 1878, m George Armentrout. Address: Norborne, Mo.

1. Viola Armentrout, b. June 4, 1897, d Oct 12, 1915.
2. Floyd Armentrout, b. Nov. 11, 1907, d Nov 18, 1915.
3. Glenn Armentrout, b June 20, 1911. No. 2968.
4 Carl Armentrout, b. Sept 16, 1919

No. 2968. Fifth Generation. 2967.

3) Glenn Armentrout, b June 20, 1911, m ————————.

1. ———— Armentrout, b. ————————.
2. ———— Armentrout, b. ————————.

No. 2969. Fourth Generation. 66.

4) Leona Anna Brenneman, b. May 12, 1880, d July 1, 1926, m. May 12, 1898, James E. Lindsey. Address. Pullman, Wash.

1. Oliver Ernest Lindsey, b. Jan. 6, 1900. No. 3694.
2. Ruth Lindsey, b. Mar. 3, 1901 No. 3695.
3. Lois Lindsey, b. Feb. 12, 1904. No. 3696.
4. Elizabeth Lindsey, b. April 16, 1905 No. 3697
5. James Leonard Lindsey, b July 24, 1907 No. 3698.
6. Martha Lindsey, b. Mar. 9, 1909. No 3668
7. Mark Rex Lindsey, b Jan. 2, 1911. No. 3699.
8. Leona Lindsey, b Aug 2, 1912 No 3692

No. 2970. Fourth Generation. 65.

6) Elma Elizabeth Brenneman, b Jan. 19, 1891, m. James W. Redd, Dec. 7, 1911. Address: Ada, O. Farmer.

1. Orville K. Redd, b. Sept. 20, 1912.
2. Loren H. Redd, b. May 18, 1915.
3. Eldred T. Redd, b. Aug. 16, 1918.
4. Ruth E. Redd, b. Mar. 9, 1920

5 Leona E Redd, b Sept 6, 1922.

6 J Warren Redd, b Sept. 4, 1925

7 Anita F. Redd, b Nov. 3, 1929

No. 2971. Fourth Generation. 67.

1) John B Culp, b June 11, 1862, near Elida, O., m. Anna Stemen, b Oct. 1, 1863 They live in Elida, O. Laborer. United Brethren

1. Lester Culp, b. Feb 26, 1887. No. 2972.

2 Fae Culp, b. Mar 22, 1890 No. 2973.

3 Agnes Culp, b. Feb. 20, 1896 No 2974.

4. John Culp, Jr., b Feb. 16, 1898, twin, single

5 Andrew Culp, b Feb 16, 1898, twin No 2975

6 Lloyd Culp, b. Dec. 29, 1902 No 2976.

No. 2972. Fifth Generation. 2971.

1) Lester S Culp, b Feb 26, 1887, m Feb 27, 1907, Eva V. Irvin, b Dec. 4, 1885, d Sept. 7, 1937 Salesman for Adlera Music Co United Brethren. Address: 1011 Cedar St., La Grande, Oreg

1. Edward Henry Culp, b Aug 30, 1909

2 Mary Evelyn Culp, b July 4, 1911.

3. Lester Donald Culp, b July 29, 1915.

No. 2973. Fifth Generation. 2971.

2) Fae Culp, b Mar 22, 1890, m James D. Sodders, b Jan. 13, 1894. Address: Elida, O.

1 Everett Sodders, b Dec 2, 1917

2. Ilene Sodders, b. Oct 5, 1926

3. Theodore Sodders, b Jan 30, 1929, twin

4 Edward Sodders, b Jan 30, 1929, twin

No. 2974. Fifth Generation. 2971.

3) Agnes Culp, b Feb. 20, 1896, m Aug. 19, 1922, Foster Samuel Irvin, b. Oct 16, 1898. Address Lima, O., R 3 Farmer Methodists.

1. Charles Foster Irvin, b Oct 28, 1923

2. Thelma Faye Irvin, b. Oct 25, 1925.

No. 2975. Fifth Generation. 2971.

5) Andrew Culp, b Feb 16, 1898, m Irene Nixon They live in Elida, O. Laborer

1 Harold Culp, b Feb 13, 1923

2 Lois Culp, b Dec 10, 1926.

3. Clyde Culp, b Feb 23, 1929

No. 2976. Fifth Generation. 2971.

6) Lloyd Culp, b Dec 29, 1902, m Marcella Morea Address Delphos, O. Laborer

1. Gene Culp, b. —————

2. Genette Culp, b —————.

3. Renald William Culp, b —————.

No. 2977. Fourth Generation. 67.

3) Emma J Culp, b Oct 8, 1866, d June 19, 1937, m Dec. 2, 1886, Samuel G. Moore, b Jan. 10, 1865 He died June 29, 1919 Blacksmith shop. She was a Mennonite No children. They lived in Elida, O.

4) Nancy C. Culp, b. Feb 10, 1869, m. Mar. 8, 1888, Moses D. Evers, b Jan. 17, 1867. Farmer. Mennonites. Address: Elmira, Lane Co., Oreg. Burial in Inmans cemetery.

1. John David Evers, b. Jan 9, 1889, d. Sept. 22, 1889.
2. Dorothy M. Evers, b. Oct. 16, 1890 No. 2979.
3. Cora C. Evers, b June 22, 1895 No. 2981.
4. Ira Samuel Evers, b. Mar 29, 1898. No 2982.
5. Laura Ann Evers, b. Aug 2, 1900. No 2983
6. Nancy Jane Evers, b. Aug. 14, 1903. No. 2984.
7. Irvin D. Evers, b. Mar. 28, 1906, d Sept. 27, 1925.
8. Roy Daniel Evers, b. Nov. 16, 1910. No. 2985.

No. 2979. Fifth Generation. 2978.

2) Dorothy M. Evers, b Oct. 16, 1890, m Dec 1, 1909, William Bond, b. Nov. 20, 1882. Address. Hubbard, Oreg Farmer and minister. Mennonites. Burial place at Hopewell Mennonite Church.

1. Nancy Bond, b. Oct. 2, 1910. No. 2980
2. Charles D. Bond, b. Nov. 4, 1911
3. Cora J. Bond, b. Oct. 17, 1914
4. Mary M. Bond, b Dec 26, 1915.
5. Ella M. Bond, b. June 11, 1919
6. George E. Bond, b Jan. 4, 1922
7. Alice I. Bond, b. Jan 10, 1925.
8. Ira J Bond, b. Sept. 29, 1926, d Dec 29, 1927.
9. Frances D. Bond, b Dec. 16, 1928
10. Laura R Bond, b. Oct. 9, 1931.

No. 2980. Sixth Generation. 2979.

1) Nancy C. Bond, b. Oct. 2, 1910, m Mar. 19, 1933, Elmer Glick, b. Dec. 30, 1898. Address: Brownsville, Oreg., R. 1. Farmer. Mennonites

No. 2981. Fifth Generation. 2978.

3) Cora C. Evers, b. June 22, 1893, m July 17, 1917, Michael Wagler, b. Mar. 20, 1891. Address: Beaver Creek, Oreg Farmer and laborer. Mennonites.

1. Lena Nancy Wagler, b. Sept. 3, 1918.
2. Menno Jacob Wagler, b Mar. 4, 1920.
3. Mabel Catherine Wagler, b. July 17, 1922, d Dec. 30, 1922.
4. Paul Daniel Wagler, b. Aug. 29, 1924.
5. John Samuel Wagler, b April 19, 1927, d Nov. 2, 1927.
6. Ruth Katie Wagler, b. Nov. 7, 1928.
7. Ruby Aldine Wagler, b Oct. 19, 1931, d. May 15, 1933.
8. Ray David Wagler, b. Mar 6, 1934.

No. 2982. Fifth Generation. 2978.

4) Ira Samuel Evers, b. Mar. 29, 1898, m. April 11, 1920, Leah C. Hamilton, b. Aug. 13, 1899. Address: Sheridan, Oreg Laborer. Mennonites. Burial at Hopewell, Oreg.

1. Clyde Wayne Evers, b Nov. 7, 1921.
2. Ralph John Evers, b. Feb. 2, 1924, d. May 18, 1924.
3. Ruth Mary Evers, b. Mar. 16, 1925, d. Aug. 23, 1925.
4. Lois Catherine Evers, b. Mar. 14, 1927.
5. Viola Louise Evers, b. Dec 9, 1928.

6. Iris Jean Evers, b. Oct. 27, 1931.

7. Ira Samuel Evers, Jr., b. June 14, 1933.

No. 2933. Fifth Generation. 2978.

5) Laura A. Evers, b. Aug 2, 1900, m. April 3, 1921, John S. Weaver, b. Aug. 11, 1897. Farmer Mennonite. Burial place Albany, Oreg. Address: Sheridan, Oreg.

1. Roy Dan'el Weaver, b. Nov. 18, 1921.

2. Wilma Ruth Weaver, b. Aug 9, 1924.

3. Betty Jean Weaver, b Nov. 2, 1926, d Nov. 10, 1929.

4. Verna Louise Weaver, b. Mar. 24, 1928.

5. Clarence Donald Weaver, b. July 20, 1930.

No. 2934. Fifth Generation. 2978.

6) Nancy Jane Evers, b Aug. 14, 1903, m. Nov. 6, 1927, Herbert Emmanuel Widmer, b. Sept. 5, 1899. They were married in the American Church in Jerusalem, Palestine After a brief visit in Palestine and Syria they located in Jerusalem, and later in Hiafa, near Mt Carmel They enjoyed their work among the Jews as missionaries, but on account of Mrs Widmer's health they returned to America On Nov. 19, 1933, Mr Widmer accepted a call to fill a vacancy of the Zion Mennonite Church at 207 Jefferson St., Dallas, Oreg. Burial place at Albany, Oreg Address 207 Jefferson St, Dallas, Oreg.

1. Grace Evelyn Widmer, b Aug. 5, 1929

2. David and Daniel Widmer, b April 16, 1931, d. July 29, 1933.

4 Nathan Wayne Widmer, b Aug 23, 1932

5 Jonathan Lee Widmer, b Jan 26, 1934

Note.—David and Daniel (twins) wandered away and were killed at the same time on the railroad track by a train.

No. 2985. Fifth Generation. 2978.

8) Roy Daniel Evers, b Nov 16, 1910, m July 3, 1933, Velma Miller, b. Oct. 9, 1909. Laborer in furniture factory. Mennonites Address Hoquiam, Wash.

No. 2936. Fourth Generation. 67.

5) Malinda A Culp, b Aug 26, 1872, m. Jan 22, 1898, William Stinbuck, b. July 25, 1873. Oil pumper. Mennonite and United Brethren. Burial in Salem cemetery, near Elida, O. Address· Elida, O., R 1.

1. Lawrence W. Stinebuck, b. April 25, 1899. No. 2987.

2 Clara M. Stinebuck, b Oct. 19, 1902 No. 2988.

3 Boyd C. Stinebuck, b Mar. 20, 1904 No. 2989

4 Goldie I. Stinebuck, b. July 26, 1906, d April 3, 1907.

5. Albert W. Stinebuck, b April 25, 1908 No. 2990

6. Harold N. Stinebuck, b Oct 22, 1911, d Dec. 3, 1913

7. Zelma E. Stinebuck, b May 25, 1914.

No. 2937. Fifth Generation. 2986.

1) Lawrence W. Stinebuck, b April 25, 1899, m May 15, 1920, Susie M. Martin, b. Mar. 23, 1900. Address: Harlegin, Tex. Oil field worker.

1. Charles F. Stinebuck, b. May 19, 1921.

No. 2938. Fifth Generation. 2986.

2) Clara M. Stinebuck, b Oct 19, 1902, m. May 28, 1923, Frank R Cunningham, b. April 28, 1894; m. (2nd) Ernest D East, Jan , 1937. Address: Elida, O. Baptist.

1. Cecil B. Cunningham, b Dec 26, 1923, d April 3, 1936.
2 Virgin a J Cunningham, b May 21, 1926, d. June 18, 1927.

No. 2989. Fifth Generation. 2936.
3) Boyd C Stinebuck, b Mar 20, 1904, m Mar 28, 1923, Violet M. Wallis
Oil field worker. Address Bowden, Okla
1 Boyd W Stinebuck, b Aug 11, 1926.
2 Elsie J Stinebuck, b Dec. 4, 1928

No. 2990. Fifth Generation. 2936.
5) Albert W. Stinebuck, b April 25, 1908, m Feb 19, 1927, Emma H Dorland.
Address: Sapulpa, Okla Oil pumper
1 Charles W Stinebuck, b Oct 4, 1927
2. Albert W St.nebuck, Jr, b Mar. 16, 1928.

No. 2991. Fourth Generation. 67.
6) Christian L Culp, b Nov 14, 1873, near Elida, O, m Laura Showalter,
b. Sept. 13, 1878, Pleasant Valley, Va Address Harrisonburg, Va.
1 Lloyd Culp, b. Dec 27, 1901 No. 2992.
2. Cloyd Culp, b and d in infancy.
3. Leroy Culp, b Nov 12, 1914.

No. 2992. Fifth Generation. 2991.
1) Lloyd Culp, b Dec 27, 1901, near Harrisonburg, Va, m Florence Butter-
ford, b April 15, 1896 Address Harrisonburg, Va.
1. Frances Culp, b. May 18, 1922, d in infancy.
2. Helen Culp, b. May 29, 1923.

No. 2993. Fourth Generation. 67.
8) Cora Mae Culp, b May 22, 1878, m Thomas S Glass, b Dec 10, 1878,
d. Oct. 21, 1929 Address Elida, O Laborer United Brethren.
1 David Glass, b April 4, 1901 No 2994.
2 Amanda Glass, b May 1, 1910 No. 2995.
3. Bern ce Glass, b. June 16, 1921.

No. 2994. Fifth Generation. 2993.
1) David Glass, b April 4, 1901, m Florence Laman Cannery operator
Address. Elida, O.
1. Marian Glass, b Mar. 21, 1923.

No. 2995. Fifth Generation. 2993.
2) Amanda Glass, b. May 1, 1910, m Emerson Coolridge. They live in
Elida, O Laborer United Brethren.
1 Thomas Coolridge, b April —, 1936

No. 2996. Fourth Generation. 67.
9) Martha Magdalene Culp, b Mar 3, 1881, m Dec. 2, 1899, Thomas Stinebuck. Laborer United Brethren They l ve in Elida, O
1. Orlo Stinebuck, b and d in infancy
2. Bernard Stinebuck, b Sept 2, 1914

No. 2997. Fourth Generation. 67.
10) Sarah Evelyn Culp, b Sept 9, 1883, m Jan. 31, 1901, Burdette LaRue,
b. Oct. 23, 1875 Laborer Toledo, O
1. Lena LaRue, b April 11, 1904 No 2998.
2. Clifford LaRue, b. April 10, 1908 No 2999.

434

3. Irene LaRue, b May 29, 1910
4. Wilbur LaRue, b Feb 9, 1912.

No. 2993. Fifth Generation. 2997.

1) Lena LaRue, b April 11, 1904, m Mar 20, 1923, Robert Meyers. They live in Toledo, O Laborer
1. Elaine Meyers, b Feb 25, 1929

No. 2999. Fifth Generation. 2997.

2) Clifford LaRue, b April 10, 1908, m. April 25, 1928, Frances Lee. Laborer. Address: Toledo, O.
1. Dollie LaRue, b Jan 9, 1929

No. 3000. Fourth Generation. 63.

1) Ollie M. Brenneman, b. Aug 1, 1873, m April 15, 1905, Bruce Glaze, b. Jan. 17, 1880. Manufacturer Lutherans Address· Andrews, Ind. No issue.

No. 3001. Fourth Generation. 68.

2) Orpha A Brenneman, b Oct 31, 1875, near Van Wert, O , m. Oct. 4, 1894, John Thurman, b Jan 10, 1873 Farmer Lutherans. Orpha died Mar. 23, 1918 Address· Hudson, Mich
1 William Herbert Thurman, b Dec , 1895, d Mar 27, 1896
2 Estella M Thurman, b. Jan. 2, 1898 No 3002.
3 Harold D Thurman, b. Feb 24, 1903 No 3003.
4 Lucille Thurman, b June 28, 1905. No 3004

No. 3002. Fifth Generation. 3001.

2) Estella M. Thurman, b Jan 2, 1898, m Nov 2, 1918, Oren B. Foster, b. July 14, 1897. Congregational Address Hudson, Mich , R 1. Farmer.
1 J. Richard Foster, b June 1, 1920
2 Alan D. Foster, b Sept 15, 1926

No. 3003. Fifth Generation. 3001.

3) Harold Thurman, b June 28, 1905, m July 11, 1931, Grace E Tucker, b. July 9, 1909 Bus driver Lutherans Address. 511 Soule Blvd., Ann Arbor, Mich

No. 3004. Fifth Generation. 3001.

4) Lucille Thurman, b June 28, 1905, m Sept 12, 1925, Leroy Maples, b. Oct. 20, 1903. Address: Rollin, Mich Farmer Methodist.
1. Norma Jean Maples, b July 11, 1926

No. 3005. Fourth Generation. 68.

3) David Willison Brenneman, b April 15, 1878, m May 9, 1904, Edith Thompson, b. Aug 10, 1881. Address Van Wert, O , R 1 Farmer. Lutherans.
1 Dale Brenneman, b. Feb 18, 1905 No 3006
2 George Brenneman, b Feb 27, 1910 No 3007.

No. 3005. Fifth Generation. 3005.

1) Dale Brenneman, b Feb 18, 1905, m July 30, 1927, Essie Washburn, b. May 7, 1907. Address Van Wert, O , R 1 Farmer Methodist.
1 John W Brenneman, b May 16, 1931

No. 3007. Fifth Generation. 3005.

2) George Brenneman, b Feb 27, 1910, m Oct 28, 1930, Helen Le Valley, b. Jan. 26, 1910 Address 608 High St., Van Wert, O Painter Contractor.

No. 3008. Fourth Generation. 68.

4) Loy S. Brenneman, b. Feb. 8, 1880, m. April 28, 1907, Alice Strack, b Feb 2, 1885. Address: Waterloo, Ind , R. 2 Farmer Methodist.

1. Paul M. Brenneman, b July 12, 1908. No. 3009.

No. 3009. Fifth Generation. 3008.

1) Paul M. Brenneman, b. July 12, 1908, m. Sept. 28, 1929, Helen Deetz, b. Nov. 12, 1906. Teaching. Methodists. Address: Ashley, Ind.

1 Dean M. Brenneman, b. Oct. 16, 1932

No. 3010. Fourth Generation. 68.

5) Oscar E. Brenneman, b. April 27, 1885, in Allen Co., Ind., m April 18, 1908, Ethel Bracken, b Feb 4, 1886, in Marion Co , Ind. Painter. Christian Church. Address: Indianapolis, Ind , R. 16.

1. William Brenneman, b Feb 21, 1909, is a florist. Address: Indianapolis, Ind., R. 16, Box 189.

No. 3011. Fourth Generation. 68.

6) Harold D. Brenneman, b. Aug. 13, 1890, m. June 30, 1920, Hazel Ellison, b. Oct. 18, 1890. Salesman. Congregational. Christian Church. Address: 505 E. Oregon St., Urbana, Ill.

1. Marjorie A. Brenneman, b. Sept. 6, 1922
2. George Bruce Brenneman, b. Sept. 6, 1924.

No. 3012. Fourth Generation. 69.

2) Sarah E. Brenneman, b. May 21, 1850, near Elida, O , d. Dec. 24, 1915, m. Aug. 20, 1874, Christian H. Mosier, b Aug. 4, 1854. Laborer and contractor. Mennonites. Address: Elida, O. Burial in Salem cemetery near Elida, O.

1. Elizabeth Mosier, b. Aug 11, 1875 No. 3013.
2. Ella Mosier, b. April 18, 1877. No. 3014.
3. Ida Mosier, b. Sept. 24, 1879. No. 3020.
4. John L. Mosier, b. Nov. 5, 1881. No. 3021.
5. Dora C. Mosier, b. Aug. 13, 1883. No. 3022
6. Jacob Cless Mosier, b. May 10, 1889. No. 3023.

No. 3013. Fifth Generation. 3012.

1) Elizabeth Mosier, b. Aug. 11, 1875, d. June 17, 1930, m. Sept. 22, 1901, Samuel S. Brenneman, b Oct. 2, 1874 Farmer. Mennonites. Address: Elida, O. Related. Burial in Salem cemetery near Elida, O.

1. Ansel Brenneman, b. Sept. 4, 1902, d. Oct. 3, 1902.
2. Velma May Brenneman, b. July 7, 1904. No. 2953.
3. Clarence Henry Brenneman, b. Nov. 19, 1907. No. 2954.
4. Ray John Brenneman, b. Aug. 3, 1910. No. 2955.
5. Orvin Cless Brenneman, b. Aug. 19, 1912. No. 2956

No. 3014. Fifth Generation. 3012.

2) Ella A. Mosier, b. April 18, 1877, m Aug 11, 1897, Roy Tucker, b. Aug. 30, 1874. Well driller and laborer. Address: Elida, O., R 2. Mennonite.

1. Henry Edgar Tucker, b. May 24, 1898. No. 3015.
2. Harry Oscar Tucker, b Feb 15, 1900. No. 3016.
3. Sarah Alice Tucker, b Dec. 14, 1901, single.
4. Etta Lucille Tucker, b. Oct 8, 1907. No. 3017.
5. Frank Chester Tucker, b. Jan. 25, 1912 No. 3018.
6. Mary Elizabeth Tucker, b June 27, 1917 No. 3019.

No. 3015. Sixth Generation. 3014.

1) Henry Edgar Tucker, b May 24, 1898, near Elida, O., m. Feb. 22, 1919, Lucy Frances Stemen, b. July 13, 1893. Address: Elida, O.

1. Harold Riley Tucker, b Oct 12, 1919, d. Oct 6, 1926.
2. Gerald Everett Tucker, b. Mar. 5, 1921.
3. Mildred Floretta Tucker, b. April 14, 1923.
4. Dorothy Margaret Tucker, b. Sept 20, 1925.
5. Luella Wavelene Tucker, b. Jan 7, 1927.
6. Dale Russell Tucker, b Aug. 19, 1928.

No. 3016. Sixth Generation. 3014.

2) Harry Oscar Tucker, b. Feb. 15, 1900, near Elida, O., m. Sept. 29, 1923, Helen Ruth Allmeier, b. Aug. 22, 1903 Address: Delphos, O.

1. Harry Oscar Tucker, Jr., b. Sept. 7, 1924.

No. 3017. Sixth Generation. 3014.

4) Etta Lucille Tucker, b. Oct. 8, 1907, near Elida, O., m. May 24, 1930, Lloyd Raymond Sroufe, b. Aug. 14, 1905. Address: 100 (block) N. Union St., Lima, O.

1. Nelda Louise Sroufe, b. Oct. 26, 1930.
2. Sarah Lucille Sroufe, b. Aug. 15, 1937.

No. 3018. Sixth Generation. 3014.

5) Frank Chester Tucker, b Jan 25, 1912, near Elida, O., m. June 19, 1934, Vera Verdean Wagner, b. Aug 8, 1914 Address: Elida, O.

1. Duane Franklin Tucker, b. June 3, 1935.
2. Walter Leroy Tucker, b. June 27, 1936.

No. 3019. Sixth Generation. 3014.

6) Mary Elizabeth Tucker, b. June 27, 1917, near Elida, O , m. Aug. 15, 1936, Arthur Cletus Smith, b. Sept. 15, 1910. Address: Elida, O. Laborer. Mennonites.

No. 3020. Fifth Generation. 3012.

3) Ida Mosier, b Sept 24, 1879, near Elida, O , d July 29, 1916, m. Mar. 8, 1901, Abraham Good, b Mar 13, 1880. Farmer. Mennonites. Burial in Salem cemetery. No issue.

No. 3021. Fifth Generation. 3012.

4) John L. Mos er, b. Nov. 5, 1881. near Elida, O., m. Sept. 24, 1903, Jennie Miller, b. Oct. 5, 1882. Address. Bremen. O. Oil pumper.

1. John Harold Mosier, b. Oct. 16, 1904.
2. Edwin Mosier, b ——————.
3. Walter Mosier, b ——————
4. William Mosier, b. ——————.

No. 3022. Fifth Generation. 3012.

5) Dora C Mosier, b Aug. 13, 1883, near Elida, O., m Oct. 16, 1904, Gabriel Brunk, b. Mar. 4, 1883, of near Elida, O. Farmer. Mennonite. Minister. Related, see No. 428. Burial in Salem cemetery.

1. Marie Agnes Brunk, b July 4, 1905, d. July 27, 1905.
2. Rudy Brunk, b. July 14, 1906 No. 433.
3. Vera V. Brunk, b Jan 3, 1910. No. 782.
4. Lois Brunk, b. Nov. 15, 1911. No. 783.
5. Esther Brunk, b. Nov. 21, 1913 No. 784.
6. Ida May Brunk, b. Dec 22, 1915.

7. Mary Brunk, b Feb 20, 1918, twin
8. Martha Brunk, b. Feb. 20, 1918, twin
9. Dora Brunk, b. May 15, 1922
10. Norman Brunk, b July 22, 1924

No. 3023. Fifth Generation. 3012.

6) Jacob Cless Mosier, b. May 10, 1889, near Elida, O., d Oct. 18, 1918, m. June 2, 1914, Naomi Harrington, d Aug, 1935.

1 Norma Mosier, b July 15, 1917, m Aug 4, 1935, to Glen Harrison. Present address Colorado Springs, Colo.

No. 3024. Fourth Generation. 69.

3) Jacob D Brenneman, b. May 5, 1852, near Elida, O, d Mar. 12, 1924, m. Feb 3, 1876, Sarah Brenneman, b. Sept. 25, 1853, d Nov 24, 1934. Farmer. Mennonites Address: Elida, O, R 1 Related, for family see No. 2488

No. 3025. Fourth Generation. 69.

4) George J. Brenneman, b April 7, 1854, near Elida, O, m Anna H. Ashbaugh, Aug 19, 1875 She died ————, 1933 He married (2nd) wife, Malinda Sheets (nee Diltz), in 1934 Farmer and carpenter Address Elida, O, R 1.

1. Mary E. Brenneman, b Sept 5, 1876. No 3026
2 Clara Brenneman, b. Oct 13, 1878 No. 3027
3 Hulda H. Brenneman, b Feb 7, 1881 No 3028
4. Alfred Brenneman, b Feb 12, 1884 No 3030
5. Henry G. Brenneman, b April 17, 1887. No 3031
6 Pearl May Brenneman, b June 13, 1890 No 3032
7. William E Brenneman, b April 27, 1893, d Mar. 6, 1895
8. Abraham K Brenneman, b Nov 28, 1895 No 3034.
9. Merlin O. Brenneman, b Mar 22, 1898 No 3035
10 Evert C Brenneman, b Nov 16, 1902, d young.

No. 3026. Fifth Generation. 3025.

1) Mary E Brenneman, b Sept 5, 1876, m April 21, 1896, Charles Friesner. She died Dec 4, 1896 Issue (stillborn).

No. 3027. Fifth Generation. 3025.

2) Clara Brenneman, b. Nov 13, 1878, m Dec 22, 1904, Irvin Stemen, b. June 9, 1877. Address El da, O, R. 1. Carpenter
1. Viola Stemen, b Jan 21, 1914 No 3036

No. 3028. Fifth Generation. 3025.

3) Hulda H. Brenneman, b Feb 7, 1881, m Mar 12, 1902, John H Hughs. Salesman. Address: Lima, O.
1. Verda Bell Hughs, b Oct. 20, 1903. No 3029.
2. Velma May Hughs, b Oct 7, 1904.

No. 3029. Sixth Generation. 3028.

1) Verda Bell Hughs, b. Oct 20, 1903, m Howard Spellman
1. Joan Marie Spellman, b. ————, 1930
2. John Spellman, b. ————, 1934.

No. 3030. Fifth Generation. 3025.

4) Alfred Brenneman, b Feb 12, 1884, m June 13, 1910, Lula M. Cook, b. Dec. 16, 1887. Laborer. Address· 806 E Bradford St, Marion, Ind.
1 Claude W. Brenneman, b Sept 26, 1911

2. Gladys R. Brenneman, b June 19, 1913
3 Myra L. Brenneman, b. Dec 22, 1915.
4 George A. Brenneman, b April 13, 1917
5 Lael O Brenneman, b July 11, 1920
6. Arlo A. Brenneman, b Feb 20, 1922
7 Donald J. Brenneman, b Dec 18, 1924
8. Derald E Brenneman, b May 20, 1926

No. 3031. Fifth Generation. 3025.

5) Henry G. Brenneman, b Apr.l 17, 1887, m June 12, 1907, Clara J. Morris, b. in 1888. Address. Elida, O , R 1. Farmer Congregational.
1. Twin boys, b. Mar 23, 1920, d same day
3. June M Brenneman, b Jan 10, 1923, twin.
4. Jean M. Brenneman, b Jan 10, 1923, twin.
5. Ronald H Brenneman, b Aug. 15, 1931.

No. 3032. Fifth Generation. 3025.

6) Pearl May Brenneman, b June 13, 1890, m. Oct 28, 1908, Earl V. Reedy, b. June 11, 1887. Address. 621 N Beville Ave , Indianapolis, Ind. Salesman.
1 Leota B. Reedy, b Dec. 3, 1910 No 3033.

No. 3033. Sixth Generation. 3032.

1) Leota B Reedy, b Dec 3, 1910, m June 13, 1929, Charles Meadows, b. Dec. 18, 1909. Clerk on Big Four railway Address 621 N Beville Ave , Indianapolis, Ind.

No. 3034. Fifth Generation. 3025.

8) Abraham K Brenneman, b Nov 28, 1895, m Mar. 14, 1917, Mary Miller, b. June 17, 1894, d Dec 27, 1927 He married (2nd) Jan 5, 1931, Carena Smith, b. July 16, 1899, m Cleveland. O Address Delphos, O , R. 2.
1. Marilyn Jane Brenneman, b June 22, 1926

No. 3035. Fifth Generation. 3025.

9) Merlin O Brenneman, b Mar 22, 1898, m Mar 14, 1917, Theo Reedy, b Mar 11, 1899 Mechanic Address 277 N Mount St , Indianapolis, Ind.
1. Mary Louise Brenneman, b Mar 18, 1918.
2 Thelma Irene Brenneman, b Nov 17, 1919
3. Leona Idella Brenneman, b June 16, 1922.

No. 3036. Sixth Generation. 3027.

1) Viola Stemen, b Jan 21, 1914, m Franklin Musser, of Elida, O. They live in Lima, O
1. Joyce Ann Musser, b Oct 15, 1936

No. 3037. Fourth Generation. 69.

5) Lewis B Brenneman, b July 10, 1856, near Elida, O , d Dec 6, 1922, m Mar 25, 1880, Martha Huber, of Perry Co , O , b Jan 27, 1860, d Mar 5, 1918. Both were buried in Salem cemetery near Elida, O. Address: Elida, O., R 1 Farmer Mennonites.
1. Mary E Brenneman, b Mar 20, 1881 No 3038
2. Perry F Brenneman, b April 28, 1882 No 3039.
3. Cora F Brenneman, b Feb 22, 1885 No 3040
4 Jesse B Brenneman, b. Mar 8, 1890 No 3041
5. Sarah S Brenneman, b June 15, 1895. No. 3043.

No. 3038. Fifth Generation. 3037.

1) Mary E. Brenneman, b. Mar. 20, 1881, near Elida, O., m. Oct. 21, 1899, Simeon B. Stemen, b. Nov. 28, 1877 Related Address· Lima, O., R. 3. Mail carrier. Mennonites.
1. Una Irene Stemen, b May 16, 1901. No. 2414
2. Lewis Isaac Stemen, b. July 22, 1904. No 2415.
3. Martha L. Stemen, b. Sept 4, 1915 No 2416.
4. Amanda S. Stemen, b Dec. 17, 1919.

No. 3039. Fifth Generation. 3037.

2) Perry F. Brenneman, b April 28, 1882, m Oct, 1905, Mollie Flisher, b. Sept. 30, 1886. Perry for some reason refused to live with his wife and a few years later married another, and he now lives somewhere in Virginia Mollie and daughter live at La Junta, Colo.
1 Velma Brenneman, b. Sept 25, 1906 No 3039½.

No. 3039½. Sixth Generation. 3039.

1) Velma Brenneman, b Sept 25, 1906, m Dec. 25, 1936, Daniel Lapp of Roseland, Nebr. He is a high-school teacher at La Junta while she is a registered nurse at the same place Mennonites. Address: 800 (block) San Juan St., La Junta, Colo.

No. 3040. Fifth Generation. 3037.

3) Cora Frances Brenneman, b Feb 22, 1885, m Oct 1, 1905, Henry Good of South Boston, Va, m Oct 12, 1882 Address South Boston, Va Farming. Mennonites.
1. Beulah Irene Good, b Dec 23, 1906.
2. Elizabeth S. Good, b Nov 3, 1908 No 3264
3. Louis Henry Good, b Feb 3, 1911 No 782.
4. Ina Marie Good, b. Aug 16, 1912 No. 3265
5. Dorothy Ellen Good, b. April 8, 1914.
6. Ira Keith Good, b. Sept. 29, 1918
7. Mary Kathryn Good, b. Sept 21, 1920
8. Ruth Naomi Good, b. Oct. 19, 1924.
9. Lena Frances Good, b. Dec 20, 1927

No. 3041. Fifth Generation. 3037.

4) Jesse B. Brenneman, b Mar. 8, 1890, near Elida, O., m May 18, 1909, Bessie Hoover, b. May 5, 1891, in Va Address: Elida, O., R. 2 Farmer. Mennonites.
1. Eva Martha Brenneman b. June 22, 1912 No. 3042.
2. Hiram Brenneman, b. April 8, 1919.
3. Kathryn Brenneman, b. Mar. 8, 1921.
4. Bettie Brenneman, b. Nov. 28, 1929.

No. 3042. Sixth Generation. 3041.

1) Eva Martha Brenneman, b. June 22, 1912, m July 31, 1932, Edward M. Stalter, b. Jan. 2, 1909 Farmer. Mennonites.
1. Mary Catherine Stalter, b Oct. 31, 1932.

No. 3043. Fifth Generation. 3037.

5) Sarah S. Brenneman, b June 15, 1895, near Elida, O , m Mar. 19, 1914, Cloyd Sherrick, b Nov. 8, 1891 Address: Elida, O. Laborer.
1. Martha Leona Sherrick, b. Aug. 15, 1915
2. Harry Oscar Sherrick, b. May 20, 1918

3. Clara Marie Sherrick, b. Mar 12, 1922, d. May 21, 1924.

4. La Verne Otto Sherrick, b June 26, 1923.

No. 3044. Fourth Generation. 69.

6) Caroline E. Brenneman, b. May 1, 1858, near Elida, O., m. June 4, 1878, John B. Diller, b Dec. 18, 1856, same place. He died Nov. 27, 1916 Buried in Salem cemetery near Elida, O Address: Elida, O., R. 1. Farmer. Mennonites. Related.

1. Mintie A. Diller, b. June 7, 1879. No. 2915.
2. Ervin O. Diller, b. April 2, 1884. No. 2916.
3. Samuel O. Diller, b. Dec. 29, 1887. No. 2920.

No. 3045. Fourth Generation. 69.

7) Barbara Brenneman, b. Feb. 24, 1861, near Elida, O., d. Jan. 20, 1931, m. Oct. 4, 1888, David A. Evers, b June 17, 1863, near Harrisonburg, Va. Burial in Salem cemetery. Address. Elida, O , R 2. Farmer. Mennonites.

1. Nora Frances Evers, b. Aug 21, 1889. No 3046.
2. John Daniel Evers, b. Aug. 4, 1891 No 3047.
3. Irvin Samuel Evers, b Jan 22, 1894, d Dec 23, 1912.
4. Charles Oscar Evers, b. Jan 16, 1897. No. 3048.
5. Mary Magdalena Evers, b. Jan. 21, 1899. No. 3049.

Irvin lost his life by attempting to board a moving freight train.

No. 3046. Fifth Generation. 3045.

1) Nora Frances Evers, b. Aug. 21, 1889, m. July 14, 1909, Andrew J. Burtchin, b. July 2, 1878 Address: Lima, O , R. 4. Farmer. Christian Union.

1. Edna M. Burtchin,. b. Sept. 9, 1912
2. Charles Clinton Burtchin, b. April 13, 1915.
3. Ruth E. Burtchin, b. April 30, 1917.
4. Ada Alvena Burtchin, b. Aug. 15, 1925.

No. 3047. Fifth Generation. 3045.

2) John Daniel Evers, b. Aug. 4, 1891, m. July 3, 1919, Loretta Butler, b. Dec 22, 1901. Address: Elida, O. Trucking.

1. Martha Jane Evers, b April 10, 1921.
2. George David Evers, b Aug. 7, 1922.
3. Gale Eugene Evers, b. Oct. —, 1924.
4. Cloyd Ernest Evers, b. Mar. 12, 1930.

No. 3048. Fifth Generation. 3045.

4) Charles Oscar Evers, b. Jan. 18, 1897, m. April 2, 1924, Daisy Kuhns, b June 18, 1903. Address: Continental, O. Railway mail clerk.

1 Dorothy Marie Evers, b Jan 27, 1925.
2. Oscar Herbert Evers, b. Mar. 10, 1929.
3. Glen Osman Evers, b. Dec. 5, 1937.

No. 3049. Fifth Generation. 3045.

5) Mary Magdalene Evers, b. Jan. 21, 1899, m. Aug. 21, 1923, Joseph Elmer Rutledge, b. April 2, 1883. Address· 609 S. Clay St , Delphos, O. Salesman. Methodist.

1. Edgar Roy Rutledge, b. May 25, 1924.
2. Clara Marie Rutledge, b. Mar. 24, 1926.
3. Richard Lee Rutledge, b. April 17, 1935

8) Lydia F. Brenneman, b Aug 16, 1863, near Elida, O , d. Aug 24, 1932, m. Nov. 21, 1885, George B. Diller, b Mar 23, 1861, of same place. d. Feb. 10, 1936. Farmer. Mennonites. Related Burial in Salem cemetery. Address: Elida, O., R. 1.

1. Lesta M. Diller, b. Jan. 1, 1887. No 2923

No. 3051. Fourth Generation. 69.

9) Elizabeth M. Brenneman, b Jan. 5, 1865, near Elida, O., d. May 13, 1934, m. Oct. 7, 1886, John D. Good, b Mar. 3, 1863 He d May 6, 1894. Farmer. Mennonites. El zabeth married late in life Rev. Yost C Miller, of Lagrange, Ind John and El zabeth are buried in the Salem cemetery near Elida, O. They lived near Elida, O.

1. David A. Good, b. Aug 6, 1888 No 3052.
2 Henry L. Good, b Dec 1, 1890 No 3053.
3. John D Good, b. July 28, 1894. No 3054

No. 3052. Fifth Generation. 3051.

1) David A Good, b Aug 6, 1888, m Oct 26, 1913, Ressie Berry, b Dec 8, 1894. Farmer. Mennonite minister No issue. Address. Nampa, Ida.

No. 3053. Fifth Generation. 3051.

2) Henry L Good, b. Dec 1, 1890, m June, 1917, Ila Woods Separated.
1. Dan el D. Good, b. Feb 8, 1921
2. Robert Lee Good, b. Sept 18, 1922.

No. 3054. Fifth Generation. 3051.

3) John D. Good, b July 28, 1894, m Oct 14, 1917, Ruth Berry, b Mar. 18, 1897. Address: Elida, O , R 2. Truck huckster Mennonites.
1. Grace E. Good, b. Nov 8, 1919
2. Ira D. Good, b Feb. 9, 1923
3. Vernon A. Good, b. Aug. 20, 1925.

No. 3055. Fourth Generation. 69.

10) Nancy C Brenneman, b May 7, 1867, near Elida, O., d June 2, 1937, m. Dec. 6, 1891, Andrew Diller, b. May 1, 1873, same place Burial in Salem cemetery. Address. Elida, O., R 1. Farmer. Mennonites.
1. Harvey Andrew Diller, b Aug 30, 1899, d July 25, 1900.
2. Esther Ada Diller, b. July 14, 1901. No. 369.
3. Florence Edna Diller, b. Oct 23, 1902. No. 434.
4. Rudy Harold Diller, b. Oct 29, 1909 No. 371.

No. 3056. Fourth Generation. 69.

11) Abraham J. Brenneman, b July 21, 1870, near Elida, O., d. ————, 1934, m. Dec 6, 1891, Nancy C. Showalter, b Mar 3, 1858. She died ————, 1929. Abraham marr.ed (2nd) ———— ———— at Mansfield, O. She died ————————. All were buried in the Salem cemetery near Elida, O. Address: Mansfield, O. Truck driver. Issue from first wife
1. Bessie L. Brenneman, b. Oct. 20, 1892 No. 3057.
2. Leona F. Brenneman, b Oct. 20, 1893, twin, d May 12, 1918.
3. Viola M. Brenneman, b. Oct. 20, 1893, twin No 3058.
4. Beulah A. Brenneman, b. Dec 14, 1894, d Aug. 9, 1895
5. Menno A. Brenneman, b. May 13, 1896. No. 3059.
6. Earl J. Brenneman, b Mar. 4, 1900. No. 3060.
7. Arthur W. Brenneman, b. Mar. 27, 1902 No. 3061.

No. 3057. Fifth Generation. 3056.

1) Bessie L Brenneman, b Oct 20, 1892, m Dec 24, 1911, Roy Clayton Furry, b. Sept. 18, 1890 He died April 16, 1937. Address: Elida, O., R 1. Farmer. Methodists. Burial in Salem cemetery near Elida, O

1. Dorothy Mary Furry, b. Nov. 20, 1912.
2. Marion Clay Furry, b Oct 16, 1916
3 Helen May Furry, b May 11, 1921.
4. Arthur Earl Furry, b June 27, 1925.
5. La Donna Grace Furry, b. Feb 22, 1931.

No. 3053. Fifth Generation. 3055.

3) Viola M. Brenneman, b. Oct 20, 1893, m. June 1, 1914, Blake Moorman, b. Dec 4, 1890 Address Lima, O. Farmer. Methodists

1. Audry Moorman, b. Feb. 8, 1915
2. Vera Moorman, b Aug 26, 1917.
3. Donna Moorman, b June 6, 1926, twin
4. Datha Moorman, b June 6, 1926, twin.

No. 3059. Fifth Generation. 3055.

5) Menno A Brenneman, b May 13, 1896, m May 22, 1931, Myrtle Talbert, b. May 3, 1909 Address Mansfield, O Shopworker.

1. Herald A Brenneman, b June 1, 1931.
2. Fay O. Brenneman, b Mar. 17, 1933.

No. 3060. Fifth Generation. 3055.

6) Earl John Brenneman, b Mar 4, 1900, m. Aug 28, 1930, Lola Simpson, b. Feb 6, 1889 Address. Shelby, O , R 1 Cycle worker. Church of Christ.

No. 3051. Fifth Generation. 3056.

7) Arthur Wilber Brenneman, b Mar. 27, 1902, m. Nov. 2, 1925, Ada Kelley, b. June 22, 1909. Address. 13 Armstrong Ave , Mansfield, O. Steel worker.

1 Rowland Arthur Brenneman, b Nov 21, 1926.
2. Jackie Lee Brenneman, b Oct 6, 1928
3. Nancy June Brenneman, b. Aug 9, 1930.

No. 3053. Fourth Generation. 3062.

1) Frank P. Brenneman, b Feb 2, 1854, at Lancaster, O., d. ————, 1916, m. June 25, 1903, Catherine Horch, b. Feb 27, 1867. Merchant—Books, etc. Address: 141 W. Wheeling St., Lancaster, O Lutherans

1. George Abram Brenneman, b. June 15, 1904.

No. 3054. Fourth Generation. 71.

1) Jacob B Keller, b Oct. 27, 1846, near Elida, O , d Sept., 1914, m. Oct 22, 1868, Susan M. Blacksten, b Dec 8, 1848, in Indiana. She died June 26, 1903 They farmed awhile, then entered the grocery business, after which he operated a restaurant Address: Bronson, Mich , R. 4.

1. Ida May Keller, b Aug 23, 1869 No 3065.
2. John Franklin Keller, b July 31, 1872 No 3066
3. James Elmer Keller, b Mar 7, 1878 No 3067.

No. 3055. Fifth Generation. 3054.

1) Ida May Keller, b Aug 23, 1869, near Bronson, Mich , m. April 27, 1886, Elmer Wilber. Address. Bronson, Mich , R. 4 Farmer.

1 Jay Wilber, b. June 3, 1887.

No. 3066. Fifth Generation. 3064.

2) John Franklin Keller, b July 31, 1872, near Bronson, Mich., m. Lottie E. George, Dec. 24, 1891. It is said that Mr. Keller weighed 300 pounds. Address: Bronson, Mich., R. 4.

1. Erma Keller, b. Feb. 3, 1893
2. Lavern Keller, b. Jan. 18, 1898.

No. 3057. Fifth Generation. 3064.

3) James Elmer Keller, b. Mar. 7, 1878, near Bronson, M.ch. Mr. Keller is the largest descendant we have had reported in the Brenneman family, weighing 378 pounds. He has been on exhibition at Chicago, Milwaukee, New York, and Boston. Traveling salesman.

No. 3058. Fourth Generation. 71.

2) Abraham P. Keller, b. Jan 12, 1850, near Elida, O., m. Rebecca Thomas, in 1880. Farmer and fruit grower. Later in life these folks separated. Address: Whitehall, M ch.

1. Jennie May Keller, b. June 18, 1882
2. John W Keller, b. Feb. 8, 1884.
3. Rhoda B. Keller, b. July 6, 1892, d Nov. 19, 1892.
4. Hezzie Keller, b Mar. 31, 1894.
5. Mary Marie Keller, b. Jan. 8, 1901.

No. 3059. Fourth Generation. 71.

3) Mary C. Keller, b. Jan 29, 1851, near Elida, O., d Sept. 17, 1910, at Burr Oak, Mich., m. June 21, 1868, Abraham Eicher, b Aug 9, 1840, d. April 20, 1917. Burial in Pleasant Hill cemetery, Branch Co , Mich Address: Burr Oak, Mich Farmer. Methodists.

1. Barbara F. Eicher, b. Mar. 12, 1872 No. 3070.
2 Huldah M Eicher, b. Dec 21, 1875 No. 3072.

No. 3070. Fifth Generation. 3069.

1) Barbara F. Eicher, b. Mar. 12, 1872, m. Oct. 31, 1888, Asher D. Kesler, b. June 15, 1869 Traveling salesman. Address 530 N. Allen St., South Bend, Ind. Methodists.

1. L. D. Kesler, b. Aug. 18, 1893. No. 3071.

No. 3071. Sixth Generation. 3070.

1) L. D. Kesler, b. Aug. 18, 1893, m Mary Louise Birdwell. Address: 8133 Bennett Ave., Chicago, Ill.

1. Rosemary V. Kesler, b April 18, 1921.
2. L. D. Kesler, Jr., b. Nov. 6, 1924.

No. 3072. Fifth Generation. 3069.

2) Huldah May Eicher, b. Dec. 21, 1875, d. Sept. 3, 1933, m. Jan. 24, 1894, Henry D. Keller, b. June —, 1874, d. Aug. 17, 1926 Farmer. Methodists. Buried at Burr Oak, Mich.

1. Harold Keller, b. Sept. 12, 1905. No. 3073.
2. Harry Keller, b. Dec. 15, 1910.

No. 3073. Sixth Generation. 3072.

1) Harold Keller, b. Sept. 12, 1905, Bronson, Mich., m. Viola Hoard.

1. L. D. Keller, b. May —, 1931.

444

4) Isaac Keller, b May 24, 1852, near Elida, O., d Jan. 24, 1934, m. Feb. 14, 1876, Ella Lupold. They lived at Noble, Mich.

1. Edna B. Keller, b July 27, 1886. No. 3075
2. Miles H. Keller, b Dec. 1, 1889. No 3076.

No. 3075. Fifth Generation. 3074.

1) Edna B. Keller, b July 27, 1886, m. July 30, 1904, M. T. Russell.

No. 3076. Fifth Generation. 3074.

2) Miles H. Keller, b. Dec. 1, 1889, m. Anna Davis, Oct. 14, 1902.

No. 3077. Fourth Generation. 71.

5) Caroline Keller, b Aug 21, 1855, near Elida, O , m. in 1877, A. A. Miller. Address: Bronson, Mich. Farmer.

No. 3078. Fourth Generation. 71.

6) George W Keller, b Jan 31, 1858, near Elida, O , d ——————, m. May 4, 1882, Lodema A. Bowdish, b. May 6, 1862, d June 5, 1903 They lived in Clackamas Co., Oreg , where he was a farmer, stock raiser, and U. S. Mail carrier. Address: Dodge, Oreg.

1. John E. Keller, b. Mar 1, 1883 No 3079.
2 Jessie Keller, b. Mar. 8, 1885, d April 6, 1886
3. Cora Keller, b. Feb. 5, 1887 No 3080
4 Ethel Keller, b. Aug. 21, 1889.
5. Mabel I. Keller, b. Mar 5, 1898

No. 3079. Fifth Generation. 3078.

1) John E. Keller, b Mar 1, 1883, in Mich , m. Dec. 28, 1904, Nina C. Laecy.

No. 3080. Fifth Generation. 3078.

3) Cora Keller, b. Feb 5, 1887, in Oreg., m. Jan , 1907, William Kaske.

No. 3081. Fourth Generation. 71.

7) Sarah A. Keller, b. April 25, 1859, near Elida, O., m. in 1878 Charles Ruthruff of Blanchard, Mich. They moved to Oregon in 1905. Farmer. Both are dead.

1. Bernice Ruthruff, b. Aug. 27, 1880. No. 3082.
2. Maude Ruthruff, b. Jan. 8, 1882. No. 3083.
3. Blanche Ruthruff, b. April 23, 1891
4. Clifford Ruthruff, b. Oct. 29, 1895.

No. 3082. Fifth Generation. 3081.

1) Bernice Ruthruff, b Aug 27, 1880, m Mar. 4, 1903, Conral Ellis

No. 3083. Fifth Generation. 3081.

2) Maude Ruthruff, b Jan 8, 1882, m. Nov 17, 1902, Frederick Berry

No. 3084. Fourth Generation. 71.

8) Nancy J. Keller, b July 7, 1860, near Elida, O., m Mar. 19, 1882, Charles W. Brooks Teacher. Address: 524 Oak St., Kalamazoo, Mich. Methodists.

1. Barbara E. Brooks, b Dec 26, 1883. No. 3085.
2. Kernie O Brooks, b. Jan 20, 1888. No 3086.
3. Neva M. Brooks, b Jan 20, 1895 No 3087.

No. 3035. Fifth Generation. 3024.

1) Barbara E. Brooks, b Dec 26, 1883, m. Dec. 20, 1905, George W Markham.

No. 3086. Fifth Generation. 3024.

2) Kernie O. Brooks, b Jan 20, 1888, m Feb 25, 1908, Henry G. Warner. Separated in 1911. She married Joseph C Palmer Sept. 25, 1915. Born of first union Leland Glen Warner, b. April 20, 1909, adopted by Joseph C Palmer and now goes by the name of Palmer.

1. Leland Glen Palmer, b April 20, 1909. No 3089

No. 3037. Fifth Generation. 3024.

3) Neva M. Brooks, b Jan 20, 1893, m Jan 20, 1912, Floyd V. Aldrich; he died June 20, 1930 Address: Kalamazoo, M,ch Burial in Riverside cemetery. She married (2nd) Nov. 18, 1931, Fay E Pierson

1. June O. Aldrich, b June 2, 1913 No. 3088
2. Barbara L Aldrich, b. July 25, 1920.
3. Lawrence D. Aldrich, b Oct 10, 1927

No. 3038. Sixth Generation. 3037.

1) June O. Aldrich, b. June 2, 1913, m. Jan 7, 1931, John Van Ingen.

No. 3039. Sixth Generation. 3086.

1) Leland Glen Palmer, b April 20, 1909, m July 16, 1930, Marion J. Peckham

No. 3090. Fourth Generation. 71.

10) Joseph H. Keller, b April 23, 1863, near Elida, O , m Dec. 9, 1883, Emma Engle, b May 25, 1867, in Lagrange Co, Ind. They moved to Clackamas Co., Oreg, in 1900. Farmer at Aurora, Oreg.

1. Mary Keller, b. July 15, 1885.
2. Izola Keller, b Feb 17, 1888.
3. Laura M. Keller, b. June 12, 1890
4. Blanche E Keller, b. June 6, 1892
5. Asher B Keller, b Nov. 23, 1898
6. William E Keller, b Nov. 15, 1901, in Oregon

No. 3091. Fourth Generation. 71.

11) Rebecca Keller, b. Jan 5, 1865, near Elida, O , m. June 4, 1881, Levi Kreider, b. Nov. 13, 1857, in Lagrange Co , Ind Cabinet maker. Minister in the Mennonite Brethren in Christ Church Mrs Kreider died July 2, 1927. Buried in Pleasant Hill cemetery. Address: Bronson, Mich , R. 5

1. Lyd.a E. Kreider, b. June 27, 1882 No 3092

No. 3092. Fifth Generation. 3091.

1) Lydia E Kreider, b June 27, 1882, m. Feb. 15, 1903, Orrin M. Good, b Aug. 17, 1879 Farmer Mennonites She died April 21, 1932. Burial in Pleasant Hill cemetery. Address: Bronson, Mich.

1 Ruth I. Good, b. Dec. 24, 1903.
2. Lola M Good, b April 18, 1914.

No. 3093. Fourth Generation. 71.

12) Lydia F. Keller, b. Feb 9, 1867, near Bronson, Mich , m. Dec. 14, 1884, Noah T. Mast, b. July 26, 1860, d Nov 3, 1920. She married (2nd) Aug. 2, 1925, Joseph A. Keller, after which she lived at 648 Emerold Ave., Toledo, O Evangelical. He died in 1936

1. Avery C Mast, b June 4, 1891, d Sept 18, 1891.

No. 3094. Fourth Generation. 72.

2) Mary Elizabeth Brenneman, b April 15, 1855, Lancaster, O., m Nov. 12, 1875, M. H. Halladay, who died Oct 25, 1896 They lived at Kirksville, Mo. No issue

No. 3095. Fourth Generation. 72.

4) George D Brenneman, b July 19, 1860, Lancaster, O , deceased, m. April 13, 1891, Della Bookout Widow and daughter live in Toledo, O Harnessmaker. Address was· Kirksv lle, Mo.

1. Ruth Helen Brenneman, b. Aug 23, 1894.

No. 3095. Fourth Generation. 72.

5) Samuel S Brenneman, b at Lancaster, O , Oct 21, 1863, m Ida Knudson, April 20, 1892 Traveling salesman Address St Louis, Mo. No issue.

No. 3097. Fourth Generation. 73.

1) Emma Ellis, b about 1858, d in Texas, m ———— Miller. Catholic. She lived in Texas and had five children N. F R

No. 3098. Fourth Generation. 73.

3) Caroline Friesner, b Oct. 3, 1864, d Mar 10, 1927, m. Frederick Olmstead. 1 Maurine Olmstead, b ————————, was m and had a son named Dale.

No. 3099. Fourth Generation. 73.

4) Jacob Friesner, b Sept 24, 1865, d Sept. 11, 1893, m. Mary Imhoff.
1. Earl Friesner, b. ————————, d in infancy.
2. Roy Friesner, b. ———————— No 3100.

No. 3100. Fifth Generation. 3099.

2) Roy Friesner, b. ————————, m. Gennie Willard. They live at Burr Oak, Mich.
1. Allen Friesner, b. ————————.
2. Leslie Friesner, b. ————————.

No. 3101. Fourth Generation. 73.

5) Daniel Friesner, b. Feb 26, 1867, m. Dec. 1, 1889, Nettie E. Denman, b. Oct. 10, 1871. He worked on the Pennsylvania Railroad, now retired. Address: Middlepoint, O. Lutheran. Burial in Kings cemetery, Middlepoint, O.
1. Ray E. Friesner, b July 10, 1890. No. 3102.
2. Guy C Friesner, b. Aug. 2, 1892. No. 3103.
3. Clarence D. Friesner, b Feb 25, 1894, d. July 20, 1894.
4. Karl E Friesner, b Oct. 14, 1895. No. 3104.
5. Ethel Leona Friesner, b Sept 26, 1897 No. 3106
6. Luther E. Friesner, b. July 6, 1902 No. 3107.
7. Herold Friesner, b Jan 11, 1904, d Aug. 26, 1904.
8. Edna Leah Friesner, b June 11, 1905 No. 3108
9. Mary El zabeth Friesner, b Jan. 23, 1907. No. 3109.
10. Arthur E Friesner, b June 25, 1913
11 Richard E Friesner, b June 25, 1915 No 3129.

No. 3102. Fifth Generation. 3101.

1) Ray E. Friesner, b July 10, 1890, m Sept 25, 1915, Chrystal Mathers, b. Dec 29, 1893 They live in Toledo, O Timekeeper Lutherans.
1. Montabell Friesner, b April 11, 1916
2 Wava Friesner, b April 21, 1918.

2) Guy C. Friesner, b Aug. 2, 1892, m. Aug 25, 1913, Pauline Hogrefe, b Mar. 21, 1893 Address: Toledo, O. Trucker. Lutherans.

1. Walter E. Friesner, b Sept. 22, 1914.
2. Donald Friesner, b Nov. 11, 1923.
3. Ruth Friesner, b. Dec. 13, 1924.
4. Ruby Friesner, b. July 18, 1930.

No. 3104. Fifth Generation. 3101.

4) Karl E. Friesner, b. Oct. 14, 1895, m Nov. 11, 1916, Bertha Bruant, b. Aug. 28, 1898, d. May 30, 1931 Address: Toledo, O Pattern maker. Lutherans.

1. Madilene Friesner b. May 2, 1917. No. 3105
2. Esther Friesner, b July 18, 1918.
3. Marie Friesner, b. July 12, 1920.
4. John Friesner, b. Feb. 8, 1922.
5. Lawrence Friesner, b. May 21, 1923, d. Aug. 2, 1923.
6. Elmer Friesner, b. May 25, 1924.
7. Harold Friesner, b. July 7, 1925, d April 18, 1926.
8. Harry Friesner, b. Dec 28, 1927.
9 Louis Friesner, b. June 5, 1930.

No. 3105. Sixth Generation. 3104.

1) Madilene Friesner, b. May 2, 1917, m. Feb 8, 1936, Oscar Truex.

No. 3106. Fifth Generation. 3101.

5) Ethel Leona Friesner, b. Sept. 26, 1897, d. Feb 1, 1920, m. Dec. 14, 1915, Ernest Belch, b. Jan. 28, 1896. Millbury, O. Railroad conductor. Methodists

1. Katherine Belch, b. May 18, 1917.

No. 3107. Fifth Generation. 3101.

6) Luther E. Friesner, b. July 6, 1902, m. Dec. 17, 1921, Fayne Armstrong, b. June 9, 1902. Address: Middlepoint, O Bus driver. Lutherans

1. Luther E. Friesner, Jr., b. July 10, 1922
2. Doris Mae Friesner, b. Sept. 2, 1923, twin.
3. Evelyn Fae Friesner, b Sept. 2, 1923, twin

No. 3108. Fifth Generation. 3101.

8) Edna Leah Friesner, b. June 11, 1905, m. Aug. 7, 1922, Richard Keller, b. May 5, 1904. Address: Toledo, O. Machinist. Lutherans.

1. Naomi Louise Keller, b. April 24, 1924.
2. Helen Lorine Keller, b. Dec. 26, 1925.

No. 3109. Fifth Generation. 3101.

9) Mary Elizabeth Friesner, b. Jan. 23, 1908, m. July 2, 1929, Carl Miller, b. Jan. 31, 1906. Address: Toledo, O. Sheet metal worker. Lutherans No issue

No. 3110. Fourth Generation. 73.

6) Lydia Ann Friesner, b. July 3, 1869, d. Aug. 9, 1924, m Frank Hogmire, of Sturgis, Mich.

1. Leland Hogmire, b. ———, 1896, at Sturgis, Mich.
2. Ernest Hogmire, b. ———, at Mildred, Mont.
3. Rena Hogmire, b. Aug. 11, 1912, at Mildred, Mont.

No. 3111. Fourth Generation. 73.

7) David Keckler, b. ——————, m ——————. Address: Sturgis, Mich.
1. Dallas Keckler, b. ——————, m., has no children.
2 Edith Keckler, b. ——————, m., has two children.

No. 3112. Fourth Generation. 73.

8) Mary Keckler, b. ——————, d April 30, 1937, m. William Mellinger. Address: Burr Oak, Mich.
1. Ross Mellinger, b. ——————, m.
2. Margaret Mellinger, b. ——————.
3. Juanita Mellinger, b. ——————

No. 3113. Fourth Generation. 73.

9) Myrtle Keckler, b. ——————, m Hope Finney
1. Theran Finney, b. ——————.
2. Thelma Finney, b. ——————.
3. Catherine Finney, b ——————.

No. 3114. Fourth Generation. 73.

10) Barbara M. Keckler, b. Aug 23, 1880, m Jan. 9, 1898, Carlton E. Mathews, b. Aug. 30, 1873. Address. Sturgis, Mich., R. 3. Farmer. Methodists.
1. Stanley LaVerne Mathews, b. July 23, 1899. No. 3115.
2. Edith Winona Mathews, b. July 13, 1911. No 3116.

No. 3115. Fifth Generation. 3114.

1) Stanley LaVerne Mathews, b. July 23, 1899, m. July 17, 1919, Ruth Albertha Haack.
1. Robert Carlton Mathews, b. Sept. 22, 1920.

No. 3116. Fifth Generation. 3114.

2) Edith Winona Mathews, b. July 13, 1911, m. Oct. 12, 1927, Edward Sheldon Crego.

No. 3117. Fourth Generation. 74.

1) Laura Albina Brenneman, b. Oct 10, 1867, near Elida, O., m. April 11, 1889, David Henry Williams, b. June 21, 1859. Address: Grover Hill, O. Farmer. Methodists.
1. Gwen Lenora Williams, b Feb 20, 1890. No. 3118.
2. William David Williams, b. Jan. 4, 1893. No. 3119.
3. Anna Corris Williams, b. Aug. 18, 1894. No. 3120.
4. Wesley Walter Williams, b. Oct. 10, 1896. No. 3121.
5. Irvin Hugh Williams, b. Mar. 9, 1902. No. 3122.
6 Olwen Luella Williams, b. Nov. 29, 1903. No. 3122¼.

No. 3118. Fifth Generation. 3117.

1) Gwen Lenora Williams, b. Feb 20, 1890, m. Jan. 18, 1917, John Edgar Morgan. Gwen was a teacher in the industrial school at Chicago, Ill., for three years. Address: Venadocia, O. Presbyterians. Farmer.
1. Edgar Lowell Morgan, b. Oct. 15, 1917.
2. Mildred Gwen Morgan, b. May 13, 1920.

No. 3119. Fifth Generation. 3117.

2) William David Williams, b Jan. 4, 1893, m. Nov. 27, 1919, Jessie Amber Jones. Methodists. Address: Ohio City, O. Teacher and laborer.
1. David Gordon Williams, b. Aug 5, 1920.

2 Glen Morgan Williams, b. Mar 5, 1923
3 Don Roger Williams, b. Mar. 13, 1938.

No. 3120. Fifth Generation. 3117.
3) Anna Corris Williams, b Aug 18, 1894, m May 5, 1927, Frederick Simin-
dinger. Address· Delphos, O , R. 4. Methodists Farmer. No issue.

No. 3121. Fifth Generation. 3117.
4) Wesley Walter Williams, b Oct 10, 1896, m April 5, 1923, Pauline Olive
Kohn Address: Rockford, O Clothier
1. Luanna Gwen Williams, b Feb. 10, 1931

No. 3122. Fifth Generation. 3117.
5) Irvin Hugh Williams, b Mar 9, 1902, m June 7, 1927, Bonita Eutsler
Railway mail clerk. Presbyterians Address Acton, Ind , Box 100
1 Robert Irvin Williams, b Jan 10, 1929
2 David Ross Williams, b June 29, 1931
3. Conrad Rex Williams, b Sept 13, 1932

No. 3122¼. Fifth Generation. 3117.
6) Olwen Luella Williams, b Nov 29, 1903, m Mar. 30, 1935, Homer N.
Allen. Automobile mechanic Address· 887 N Washington St , Van Wert, O.
Methodists. Olwen was a schoolteacher for several years.

No. 3123. Fourth Generation. 74.
2) Irvin E Brenneman, b Aug 28, 1869, near Elida, O , m. July 7, 1893,
Ollie Kiracofe, b. June 16, 1873 Address· Elida, O , R 1. Farmer. Methodists
They had an adopted daughter Opal Fair. She married ————————

No. 3124. Fourth Generation. 74.
3) Sarah E. Brenneman, b. July 19, 1871, d. in 1921, m. J Albert Morris, b.
1869, d. 1928 Both were buried in the Greenlawn cemetery near Elida, O.
1. Walter N Morris, b April 28, 1898. No. 3125.
2. Harold Morris, b. Nov. —, 1900
3. Theo Claribel Morris, b. Jan 17, 1906.
4. Clarence Thomas Morris, b. May 25, 1908. No. 3126.

No. 3125. Fifth Generation. 3124.
1) Walter N. Morris, b. April 28, 1898, near Elida, O , m. Nellie Burkholder,
b. Feb. 18, 1897. Methodists. Address 904 N. Jameson Ave., Lima, O. Silk
spotter.
1. Donald N. Morris, b Mar. 6, 1926.

No. 3126. Fifth Generation. 3124.
4) Clarence Thomas Morris, b. May 25, 1908, near Elida, O., m. Helen Carnes.
1. Phillis Morris, b. Feb —, 1934

No. 3127. Fourth Generation. 74.
4) Stephen A. Brenneman, b Nov. 8, 1873, near Elida, O., m Ina Sawmiller,
b. Oct. 7, 1877. Separated. On June 20, 1910, he married Pauline M. John, of
Elida, O Address: Elida, O., R. 1. Farmer Methodists
1. Edna Ellouise Brenneman, b. Jan 5, 1899. No 3128.

No. 3128. Fifth Generation. 3127.
1) Edna Ellouise Brenneman, b Jan 5, 1899, m Nov. 14, 1917, Arthur Robert
Griggs, b. Mar 22, 1894 Address Avant, Okla , Box 97 Oil field employee.
Methodists

1. Edna Elene Griggs, b Aug 22, 1918
2. Burl Raymond Griggs, b Mar 17, 1920
3. Bonnie Lou Griggs, b Apr.l 9, 1926
4. Ina Jane Griggs, b. Aug 7, 1931
5. Jesse Leon Griggs, b Nov 28, 1934.

No. 3129. Fifth Generation. 3101.

11) Richard E. Friesner, b June 25, 1915, m Oct 3, 1936, Eileen Mauchly, b. ————, 1917.

No. 3130. Fourth Generation. 76.

1) Caroline Beery, b Mar. 12, 1866, in Noble Twp, Branch Co, Mich., m. Dec. 7, 1889, Loren A Root, b Oct 24, 1861, in Steuber Co., Ind.
1. Earl Root b. June 25, 1890 No 3131
2. Hazel Root, b Aug. 9, 1891 No. 3132.
3. Madge Root, b April 18, 1893. No. 3135.
4. Vera Root, b Dec. 21, 1895 No. 3136
5. Elsie Root, b. Sept 3, 1897. No. 3137.

No. 3131. Fifth Generation. 3130.

1) Earl Root, b June 25, 1890, in Branch Co, Mich, m. Oct. 25, 1916, Carrie Louise Wilkins, b Nov 8, 1896. Address: Bryan, O.
1. Marian Elizabeth Root, b Aug 7, 1919
2 Barbara Wauneta Root, b Feb 7, 1923.

No. 3132. Fifth Generation. 3130.

2) Hazel Root, b Aug 9, 1891, in Garrett, Mich, m Nov. 28, 1912, Harry J. Knauss, b. Oct 18, 1885, in Branch Co, Mich.
1. Nellie Marjorie Knauss, b Mar 4, 1914 No. 3133.
2. Elzie Madge Knauss, b Oct 2, 1917 No 3134.
3. Mary Caroline Knauss, b Dec. 10, 1922.
4. Margaret Aileen Knauss, b Mar. 30, 1931.

No. 3133. Sixth Generation. 3132.

1) Nellie Marjorie Knauss, b Mar 4, 1914, m Mar. 23, 1934, Robert R. Pierson, of Elkhart, Ind
1. Ruth Joan Pierson, b Sept 23, 1935.

No. 3134. Sixth Generation. 3132.

2) Elzie Madge Knauss, b Oct. 2, 1917, m Sept. 22, 1934, Ward C Shaffer, b. May 13, 1908.
1. Loren Dale Shaffer, b Nov 13, 1935.
2. Della Bernice Shaffer, b. Oct 9, 1936

No. 3135. Fifth Generation. 3130.

3) Madge Root, b. April 18, 1893, in Garrett, Ind, m Feb. 11, 1922, Jay H. Crow, b May 16, 1889, in Branch Co, Mich Address Coldwater, Mich.
1. Robert Jay Crow, b Feb 22, 1925, d May 21, 1933
2 George Henry Crow, b Aug 9, 1931.

No. 3136. Fifth Generation. 3130.

4) Vera Root, b Dec 21, 1895, in Garrett, Ind, m April 13, 1920, Lela G. Hilyerd, b May 31, 1898, Branch Co, M ch, d Jan 18, 1925. Vera married (2nd) Lula E. Shearer, b June 24, 1907, in Plainview, Mich
1. Leta Lucille Root, b Oct 12, 1922

2. L. J. Root, b. Mar. 23, 1927.
3. Elizabeth Mae Root, b. Oct. 13, 1928.

No. 3137. Fifth Generation. 3130.

5) Elzie Root, b. Sept 3, 1897, in Milgrove, Ind., m. Dec. 3, 1922, Estell S. Hammon, b. July 26, 1899, in Branch Co, Mich.
1. LaVern Charles Hammon, b. Mar. 9, 1924.
2. Katherine June Hammon, b. June 28, 1926
3. Reah Jean Hammon, b. Jan. 6, 1928.

No. 3138. Fourth Generation. 76.

3) Abraham Beery, b. April 19, 1869, at Bronson, Mich., m. Sept. 2, 1893, Fannie French. She d. July, 1895. He married (2nd) Jan. 9, 1896, May Ganger who died July 26, 1896 He married (3rd) April 19, 1897, Nannie May Oberholser who died Jan. 11, 1929. Mr. Beery married (4th) April 2, 1931, Laura Morrill.
1. Ruth Beery, b. Aug. 1, 1894 from first union.
Two adopted children that he and Nannie Oberholser raised:
1. Son L. D. Beery.
2. Daughter Lucile Beery, m Clarence Walters They have two children, Lillian May and Clarence Walters, Jr

No. 3139. Fourth Generation. 76.

5) William Franklin Beery, b Jan. 5, 1872, m. Jan 5, 1895, Laura Moffett, b. Oct. 17, 1878, d. April 13, 1905. He married (2nd) Blanche Fair, Jan. 17, 1907, b. April 27, 1885. Farmer at Branch, Mich. Burial in Pleasant Hill cemetery, Branch, Mich
1. Lloyd Beery, b April 11, 1896. No. 3140.
2. Ethel May Beery, b. Feb 15, 1899. No 3141
3. William Frank Beery, b. Dec. 2, 1915. No. 3142.

No. 3140. Fifth Generation. 3139.

1) Lloyd Beery, b April 11, 1896, d. Mar. 6, 1927, m. April 11, 1917, Erma Fair, b. Nov. 21, 1897. Farmer. Burial in Pleasant Hill cemetery. Address: Bronson, Mich.
1. Leo Irvin Beery, b. Dec 9, 1917.
2. Laura Maurine Beery, b. Nov. 16, 1919.
3. J. D. Beery (stillborn).
4. Vera Belle Beery, b. Feb. 11, 1923.
5. Bernetta Fern Beery, b. April 10, 1926.

No. 3141. Fifth Generation. 3139.

2) Ethel May Beery, b. Feb. 15, 1899, m. Nov. 18, 1915, Roy Emerson Dean, b. Nov. 18, 1897. Farmer. No issue. Address: Bronson, Mich., R. 1.

No. 3142. Fifth Generation. 3139.

3) William Frank Beery, Jr., b. Dec. 2, 1915, m. Dec. 31, 1933, Bertha Modert, b. June 10, 1915. Address: Bronson, Mich., R. 2 Farmer. No issue.

No. 3143. Fourth Generation. 76.

8) Harvey F. Beery, b. Mar. 5, 1878, d. May 20, 1903, m. Oct. 23, 1901, Cecil Swift, b. April 5, 1885.
1. Reah Beery, b. Feb. 12, 1904. No. 3144.

No. 3144. Fifth Generation. 3143.

1) Reah Beery, b. Feb. 12, 1904, m. June 5, 1920, Roy Fellers. Address: Coldwater, Mich.

1. Eloice Ruth Fellers, b. April 6, 1922.

No. 3145. Fourth Generation. 76.

9) Matilda Beery, b. April 13, 1880, m. Mar. 24, 1900, Stephen Swift, of Bronson, Mich.

1. Ivan J. Swift, b. Feb. 2, 1901. No. 3146.
2. Fabian D. Swift, b. Feb. 6, 1905. No. 3147.
3. Erma L Swift, b. Oct. 15, 1906. No. 3148.
4. Letha H. Swift, b. Nov. 25, 1907. No. 3149.
5. Merlin A. Swift, b. Jan. 11, 1913, d. Mar. 18, 1915.
6. Boka Angella Swift, b. Aug 21, 1917. No. 3150.
7. Ethen Arthur Swift, b. Oct. 9, 1924.

No. 3145. Fifth Generation. 3145.

1) Ivan J. Swift, b Feb. 2, 1901, m June 3, 1922, Ina Stewart.

1. Arnold A. Swift, b Mar 10, 1923
2 Galen Ivan Swift, b Feb 3, 1925
3. Wayne Donald Swift, b. April 29, 1927.
4. Stanley Lamar Swift, b. Aug 26, 1929.
5 Irvin Dean Swift, b Aug 17, 1931.
6 Ellen Marie Swift, b. Sept 26, 1933
7. Ilene Mae Swift, b April 29, 1936.

No. 3147. Fifth Generation. 3145.

2) Fabian D. Swift, b. Feb 6, 1905, m June 16, 1926, Alice Myrtle McCullough.

1. Melvin Neil Swift, b Sept. 6, 1927
2. Glen D. Swift, b. Feb 22, 1930.
3. Edward Allen Swift, b. Mar. 16, 1935.
4. Jerry Ellis Swift, b. Oct. 26, 1936.

No. 3148. Fifth Generation. 3145.

3) Erma L. Swift, b. Oct. 15, 1906, m. Nov. 8, 1924, Burr Howland.

1. Wilma Eleota Howland, b. Jan. 31, 1926.
2. Irene Mae Howland, b. Feb. 9, 1928.

No. 3149. Fifth Generation. 3145.

4) Letha Belle Swift, b. Nov. 25, 1907, m. Oct. 8, 1928, Worthy Fair.
1. Donna Belle Fair, b. Sept. 24, 1930.
2. Sherly Ann Fair, b. Aug. 3, 1935.

No. 3150. Fifth Generation. 3145.

6) Boka Angella Swift, b. Aug. 21, 1917, m. Mar. 23, 1935, Kenneth Hopkins.
1. Norman Lee Hopkins, b. July 7, 1936, d. same day.

No. 3151. Fourth Generation. 76.

10) Elizabeth Beery, b May 9, 1882, m. Nov. 6, 1906, Thomas Fair.
1. Son b. in 1907, d. at birth.
2. Bernetta Fair, b. Aug. 15, 1908. No. 3152.

No. 3152. Fifth Generation. 3151.

2) Bernetta Fair, b Aug 15, 1908, m Nov. 15, 1930, Bertrand Ranch.

No. 3153. Fourth Generation. 76.

11) Arthur Beery, b April 4, 1885, m Jan. 1, 1908, Mildred Beery. She died Aug. 14, 1937.

No. 3154. Fourth Generation. 76.

12) Irvin Beery, b. Feb. 6, 1889, m Oct 14, 1911, Gula Calhoun

No. 3155. Fourth Generation. 77.

1) Fanny Stemen, b —— about 1870, m. Warren Morrison. Address: Grover Hill, O.
  1. Myrtle Sarah Morrison, b. July 5, 1887, d Dec. 10, 1887.
  2 William Thomas Morrison, b. June 23, 1888 No 3156.
  3. Laura Eva Morrison, b Sept 6, 1889. No. 3157
  4 Charles Glen Morrison, b. July 5, 1892, d Dec 25, 1898.
  5 Alfred James Morrison, b April 20, 1894 No 3158
  6 Mary May Morrison, b. Nov 17, 1896. No. 3159

No. 3156. Fifth Generation. 3155.

2) William Thomas Morrison, b June 23, 1888, m Mary Clark Address. Hillsdale, Mich.
  1. Lloyd George Morrison, b ——————, twin.
  2 Floyd Warren Morrison, b. ——————, twin.
  3. Laura May Morrison, b. ——————.
  4. Anna Lucille Morrison, b. ——————
  5 Leonard Morrison, b ——————
  6 Lois Marie Morrison, b ——————
  7. Ruth Morrison, b ——————.
  8. Edna Belle Morrison, b ——————.
  9. John Morrison, b. ——————.
  10. Martha Morrison, b. ——————.

No. 3157. Fifth Generation. 3155.

3) Laura Eva Morrison, b ——————, m. William Price Address: Lima, O. No children.

No. 3158. Fifth Generation. 3155.

5) Alfred James Morrison, b. ——————, m Ethel Reed. Address: Detroit, Mich
  1. Alpha Morrison, b. ——————.
  2. Homer Morrison, b ——————.

No. 3159. Fifth Generation. 3155.

6) Mary May Morrison, b ——————, m. John Butcher. Address: Spencerville, O. No children.

No. 3160. Fourth Generation. 77.

2) James Wisher, b ——————, 1874, m. Blanche Pease. Address: Menden, Mich.
  1. Inez Wisher, b ——————, deceased, was married and had two sons and a daughter.
  2. Ottie Wisher, b ——————, m. and has four children. They live in Mich.
  3. Walter Wisher, b. ——————. No. 3161
  4. Florence Wisher, b. ——————, m, has 2 children
  5. Thomas Wisher, b ——————, m, has 2 children.

3) Walter Wisher, b ——————, m Zula Swartz. Address: Grover Hill, O.

1. Max Wisher, b ——————, twin.

2. Rex Wisher, b. ——————, twin

No. 3162. Fourth Generation. 77.

3) Charles Wisher, b Jan. 30, 1876, m. 1897, Flora B Wolford, b. Jan. 15, 1876 Address Spencerville, O, R 2.

1. Thomas O Wisher, b. Oct 16, 1897. No. 3163.

2 Edna B Wisher, b Oct. 4, 1899 No 3164.

3. Ora C Wisher, b. May 19, 1901. No 3165.

4 Ray A. Wisher, b Feb 26, 1903. No 3166.

5. Zelma Fae Wisher, b Feb 4, 1905 No. 3167.

6 George W Wisher, b May 5, 1907 No. 3168.

7. Kathryn Wisher, b Aug 6, 1908. No. 3169.

8 David V Wisher, b Jan 19, 1913.

No. 3163. Fifth Generation. 3162.

1) Thomas O Wisher, b Oct 16, 1897, m in 1923 Ruth Hirtzel. Address: Tampa, Fla.

1 Charles D Wisher, b. Feb 1, 1926.

2 Dorothy Elaine Wisher, b June 2, 1928, d Nov. 7, 1934.

3. Doris Virginia Wisher, b Dec 26, 1929, d. Feb 26, 1930.

4 Thomas Robert Wisher, b Aug. 9, 1932.

No. 3164. Fifth Generation. 3162.

2) Edna B. Wisher, b Oct 4, 1899, m. in 1921 Robert McTone. Address: 622 Hoffman St, Ft. Wayne, Ind.

1. Charles Robert McTone, b Feb 1, 1922

2. Elizabeth Anna McTone, b Sept. 5, 1925.

3. Ruth Irene McTone, b July 31, 1929

No. 3165. Fifth Generation. 3162.

3) Ora C. Wisher, b May 19, 1901, m. in 1935, Henrietta Faring. Address: Spencerville, O.

1. Phyllis Marie Wisher, b Sept. 11, 1936.

2. Charles Richard Wisher, b. Jan. 30, 1938.

No. 3166. Fifth Generation. 3162.

4) Ray A Wisher, b. Feb. 26, 1903, m in 1926 Glenna Shaffer. Address: West Toledo, O

1. Retha Fern Wisher, b Mar. 30, 1927.

2. Howard Ray Wisher, b. April 6, 1930.

3. Carolyn Jean Wisher, b. Dec 31, 1932

No. 3167. Fifth Generation. 3162.

5) Zelma Fae Wisher, b Feb. 4, 1905, m. in 1927 Daniel Davis. Address: West Toledo, O.

1. Donna Jean Davis, b Mar. 17, 1931

2 Jannet Lee Davis, b Sept. 13, 1934

No. 3168. Fifth Generation. 3162.

6) George W Wisher, b. May 5, 1907, m in 1932, Bernice Smith. Address: Spencerville, O, R. 2.

1. Donald William Wisher, b June 2, 1934

2. Georgia May Wisher, b. Mar. 8, 1936.

3. Garold Eugene Wisher, b. Nov. 22, 1937.

No. 3169. Fifth Generation. 3162.

7) Kathryn A. Wisher, b. Aug. 6, 1908, m. Pryce Hagerman, 1929, b. Jan. 24, 1904, d. by accident, Aug. 30, 1937. Address: Spencerville, O. Three children: 2 stillborn; 1 died soon after birth.

No. 3170. Fourth Generation. 77.

4) William Wisher, b. ————, 1878, m. Daisy Wolford. No children. Address: Spencerville, O., R. 2.

No. 3171. Fourth Generation. 77.

5) Daisy Mae Wisher, b. Sept 22, 1880, m June 7, 1901, J. Franklin Dunlap. Address: Grover Hill, O.

1. David Franklin Dunlap, b. May 3, 1902. No. 3172.
2. Charles Emmet Dunlap, b. Sept 28, 1903. No. 3173.
3. Walter Alva Dunlap, b. May 20, 1905. No. 3174.
4. Thomas Lawrence Dunlap, b. Mar. 24, 1907. No. 3175.
5. Edna Marie Dunlap, b. Mar. 24, 1909, d at 22 months.
6. Ray Allen Dunlap, b. Oct. 29, 1910. No. 3176.
7. Harry Elvin Dunlap, b. Oct. 31, 1912.
8. Velma Leota Dunlap, b. Oct. 17, 1914.
9. Mary Ruth Dunlap, b Jan. 19, 1919.

No. 3172. Fifth Generation. 3171.

1) David Franklin Dunlap, b. May 3, 1902, m. Leona Ballman
1. Richard Eugene Dunlap, b. ——————.
2. Charles David Dunlap, b. ——————.

No. 3173. Fifth Generation. 3171.

2) Charles Emmett Dunlap, b. Sept. 28, 1903, m. Ruth Vetter.
1. Robert Eugene Dunlap, b. ——————.

No. 3174. Fifth Generation. 3171.

3) Walter Alva Dunlap, b. May 20, 1905, m. Almeda Ulrich.

No. 3175. Fifth Generation. 3171.

4) Thomas Lawrence Dunlap, b Mar. 24, 1907, m. Ida Bianchs.

No. 3176. Fifth Generation. 3171.

6) Ray Allen Dunlap, b. Oct. 29, 1910, m. Mary Montague.

No. 3177. Fourth Generation. 77.

6) Jennie Wisher, b Jan 15, 1883, m. Aug. 16, 1902, David Dunlap, b. ——————. Address: Jackson, Mich.

1. Ruth Dunlap, b. ——————. No. 3178.
2. Bessie Dunlap, b. ——————. No. 3179.
3. Verna Dunlap, b. ——————.
4. Roy Dunlap, b. ——————.
5. Nellie Dunlap, b. ——————.
6. Marcile Dunlap, b. ——————. No. 3180.
7. Harold Dunlap, b. ——————.
8. Mildred Dunlap, b. ——————.
9. Marie Dunlap, b. ——————.
10. Ward Dunlap, b. ——————.

No. 3178. Fifth Generation. 3177.

1) Ruth Dunlap, b ————————, m John Gotschall.
1. Wilmer Gotschall, b. ————————
2. David Gotschall, b ————————.

No. 3179. Fifth Generation. 3177.

2) Bessie Dunlap, b. ————————, m. Louis Rose.
1. Wayne Rose, b ————————
2 Betty Rose, b. ————————.

No. 3180. Fifth Generation. 3177.

6) Marcile Dunlap, b ————————, m Archie Gregory.
1 Edwin Gregory, b ————————.
2. Robert Gregory, b. ————————
3. Mickel Gregory, b. ————————
4 Marcilene Gregory, b ————————.

No. 3181. Fourth Generation. 77.

8) Elsie Wisher, b. ————————, m. Lester Johnson.
1. Viva Johnson, b. ————————, m , has no children.
2. Lloyd Johnson, b. ————————, m., has no children.
3. Charles Johnson, b ————————, m , has one child.
4. Freda Johnson, b ————————, m , has one child.

No. 3182. Fourth Generation. 77.

9) Mary Wisher, b. ————————, m. Henry Miller.
1. Ruby Miller, b. ————————, d in infancy
2. Margaret Miller, b ————————
3 Nellie Miller, b ———————— No 3183
4. Carl Miller, b. ————————
5 Paul Miller, b. ————————.
6 Richard Miller, b ————————

No. 3183. Fifth Generation. 3182.

3) Nellie Miller, b ————————, m. Wendall Adams.
1 Gary Dean Adams, b ————————.

No. 3184. Fourth Generation. 78.

1) Edna Lee Brenneman, b Sept. 20, 1881, m William Anderson Painter.
Address 1228 3rd St., 715 Conrad Dept , Washington, D. C.
1. Gladys Anderson, b Aug 20, 1899 No. 3185.
2 Francis B Anderson, b July 26, 1905. No. 3185¼
3. Carl Edwin Anderson, b. Jan 21, 1908 No. 3185½.

No. 3185. Fifth Generation. 3184.

1) Gladys Anderson, b Aug. 20, 1881, m Doyle Duff. Address: Washington,
D. C No children.

No. 3185¼. Fifth Generation. 3184.

2) Francis B Anderson, b July 26, 1905, m. at Detroit, Mich., Evelyn
Peddycard Address: 1531 Mt Pleasant St , Washington, D. C

No. 3185½. Fifth Generation. 3184.

3) Carl Edwin Anderson, b Jan. 21, 1908, m Esther Snyder Address:
Washington, D. C

No. 3186. Fourth Generation. 79.

1) William J. Brenneman, b April 10, 1878, near Elida, O, m Lula May, b. —————, m. in 1902 He married (2nd), 1933, Mary Ellen Forsythe. Address: Lake View, O.

    1 Glenna May Brenneman, b April 30, 1903, d. April 19, 1908.
    2. Breta Pearl Brenneman, b Sept 27, 1908
    3. William Wallace Brenneman, b Dec 15, 1909 No. 3285.
    4. Elizabeth Louise Brenneman, b. Mar 29, 1912. No 3187

No. 3187. Fifth Generation. 3186.

4) Elizabeth Louise Brenneman, b Mar. 29, 1912, m. John Hill Address: Lima, O Methodists

No. 3183. Fourth Generation. 79.

2) Merlin Brenneman, b Nov 14, 1879, near Elida, O, d April 19, 1938, m. Oct. 24, 1904, Boka Kem Rumbaugh, b July 5, 1885. Worked in Budget office for state of Ohio. Burial in West Union cemetery, Columbus, O Address: 2771 Arlington Ave., Columbus, O Methodists.

    1. Howard Merlin Brenneman, b. Mar. 20, 1907 No. 3189.
    2. Henrietta Elzabeth Brenneman, b. July 11, 1911 No. 3190.

No. 3189. Fifth Generation. 3183.

1) Howard Merlin Brenneman, b Mar 20, 1907, m. Feb 11, 1933, Thelma Quinley. Auditor for General Electric Address. Schenectady, N. Y.

No. 3190. Fifth Generation. 3188.

2) Henrietta Elizabeth Brenneman, b July 11, 1911, m Robert Scott Peoples, Aug 18, 1934. Address 1120 Virgin a Ave, Columbus, O.

No. 3191. Fourth Generation. 79.

3) Abner Brenneman, b June 12, 1882, near Elida, O, m. June 14, 1906, Mabel Crites, b July 1, 1883, in El da, O Address El da, O Bank cashier. Methodists. Burial place in Greenlawn cemetery near Elida, O.

    1. James Robert Brenneman, b April 2, 1909
    2. Helen Crites Brenneman, b Jan 23, 1915

No. 3192. Fourth Generation. 79½.

3) Myrtle Leona Brenneman, b Aug 7, 1893, m Dec. 29, 1913, Harry W. Maxwell, b. Nov 8, 1889, in Lagrange Co, Ind Address Burr Oak, Mich., R. 2.

    1 Virgil Barry Maxwell, b Dec 25, 1914.
    2 Cleo Maxine Maxwell, b. April 4, 1918
    3 Audry Lou Maxwell, b June 4, 1928
    4. Warren Lee Maxwell, b Oct. 18, 1929

No. 3193. Fourth Generation. 79½.

4) Lee Jacob Brenneman, b Mar 12, 1895, at Cedar Springs, Mich, m Ruth Luc le Knowles, May 14, 1919, born in Toledo, O, Mar 13, 1898 Address: 2826 116th St, Toledo, O

    1. Robert Lee Brenneman, b Aug 26, 1921, in Toledo
    2. Richard Dean Brenneman, b July 2, 1929, in Toledo

No. 3194. Fourth Generation. 80.

2) Mary M Funk, b July 5, 1855, m Feb 17, 1881, George Crook They lived at Bremen, O

    1. Frances E Crook, b Jan 3, 1883

4) Rebecca Funk, b. Aug. 24, 1859, m Henry Cummins.
1. Roy Cummins, b. May 9, 1890, d Oct , 1890.
2. Elizabeth Cummins, b April 18, 1892.
3. Clarence Cummins, b June 14, 1897.

No. 3196. Fourth Generation. 80.

7) Elizabeth Funk, b. Sept 14, 1864, m. Thomas Newman.
1. Charles E Newman, b and d in infancy.

No. 3197. Fourth Generation. 81.

3) Mary Beery, b. April 8, 1849, near Bremen, O , m. Dec. 11, 1877, David A. Shatzer, he died Sept 29, 1879 Mary married (2nd) Samuel Blosser, April 19, 1891. Address· Bremen, O. Mennonites
1. Mary Jane Shatzer, b Nov 2, 1878. No 3198.
   (From second union)
2. Samuel R Blosser, b May 11, 1893 No 2364.

No. 3193. Fifth Generation. 3197.

1) Mary Jane Shatzer, b Nov 2, 1878, m Oct. 8, 1897, E Thomas Brown. Presbyterians. Address Bremen, O , R 1 Mr. Brown died ——————.
1. Martha F Brown, b Oct 8, 1898 No. 3279
2. William L. Brown, b Mar 9, 1900. No 3280
3 Harba Dell Brown, b Aug 27, 1902 No 3281.
4. David Samuel Brown, b Sept 16, 1904 No. 3282
5 Ernest C Brown, b Sept 9, 1907 No 3283.
6 Carlton Brown, b. April 9, 1909, d Aug 27, 1930
7. Fern Brown, b. Dec 2?, 1911

No. 3199. Fourth Generation. 81.

5) Lydia Beery, b Nov 29, 1855, near Bremen, O , m Benjamin Senger. Later divorced She marr ed (2nd) James D Llewellyn, b Mar. 7, 1852, d Dec. 9, 1936. Brick mason Church of God Burial in Salem cemetery near Elida, O. Address. Continental, O
1. Preston Senger, b. ————, 1881 No 3376
2. Mary E. Senger, b Feb 23, 1883 No 3377
3 Bertie Senger, b Jan 14, 1885 No 3378
4 Harry Senger, b. July 26, 1887 No 3379
5 Viola Belle Llewellyn, b June 21, 1890 No 3380
6 Hazel Verl Llewellyn, b Oct 21. 1892 No. 3382.
7. Elnora Llewellyn, b Jan. 15, 1897. No 3384.

No. 3200. Fourth Generation. 81.

6) Sarah E Beery, b. April 23, 1861, near Bremen, O , m. Samuel Mills, Jan. 6, 1881, b April 14, 1849, d Jan 17, 1914 She died June 12, 1935. Farmer. Methodists. Address: R mer, O.
1 Abraham E Mills, b Mar 24, 1882, single
2 Alonzo Ernest Mills, b May 28, 1884 No 3201.
3. Lorena M Mills, b. Feb 15, 1887 No 3202
4 Tressie J Mills, b Mar 17, 1889 No 3205
5 Herbert E Mills, b Mar 7, 1900 No 3206

2) Alonzo Ernest Mills, b May 28, 1884, m in 1906 Iva E Deffenbaugh, b. Feb. 8, 1884, in Putnam Co., O. Deputy clerk probate office Lima, O Address: 751 Brice Ave., Lima, O. Methodists.

1 Ruth M. Mills, b. ————, 1907.
2. Lester E. Mills, b. ————, 1909.
3. Cloren E. Mills, b. ————, 1916.
4. Helen E. Mills, b. ————, 1918
5. Nelda L Mills, b Sept. 10, 1925.

No. 3202. Fifth Generation. 3200.

3) Lorena Mae Mills, b. Feb. 15, 1887, m. Dec. 9, 1906, Thomas G. Thomas, b. July 27, 1886. Farmer. Ottawa River Christian Church. Address: Ft Jennings, O., R. 1.

1. Ray Gordon Thomas, b. Nov. 28, 1908 No. 3203.
2. Mildred Alma Thomas, b. April 9, 1914 No. 3204.

No. 3203. Sixth Generation. 3202.

1) Ray Gordon Thomas, b Nov. 28, 1908, m. June 23, 1929, Myrtle Mae Seitz, b. Oct. 15, 1908 Glass blower. Christian Church. Address: 1614 N. Tacoma Ave, Indianapolis, Ind.

1. Betty Jean Thomas, b. Jan. 15, 1932.
2. Marlene June Thomas, b Aug. 30, 1935.

No. 3204. Sixth Generation. 3202.

2) Mildred Alma Thomas, b April 9, 1914, m Jan. 1, 1934, Carlyle T Price, b. April 26, 1912. Glass blower. Christian Church Address. 4151 Lewis Ave., Toledo, O.

No. 3205. Fifth Generation. 3200.

4) Tressie Jane Mills, b. Mar 17, 1889, m Jan 7, 1914, Russell Rohrer, b. Oct. 27, 1887. Farmer. Christian Church. Address: Columbus Grove, O., R. 3. Burial place in Ottawa River Church cemetery.

1. Marjorie Rohrer, b Oct 31, 1914.
2. Paul Rohrer, b. Aug. 30, 1917.
3. Donna Gene Rohrer, b July 18, 1923.

No. 3206. Fifth Generation. 3200.

5) Herbert E. Mills, b. Mar 7, 1900, m 1919, Lelah Hughs, b 1902. Designer. Christian Church.

1. Vernon Mills, b. Jan. 21, 1923.

No. 3207. Fifth Generation. 3197.

2) Samuel R Blosser, b. May 11, 1893, m Feb 22, 1917, Nancy Catherine Diller. Laborer. Mennonites. Address: Elida, O., R. 1. Related, for family see No. 2364.

No. 3208. Fourth Generation. 82.

1) John W. Beery, b July 15, 1856, in Fairfield Co., O., m. Oct. 25, 1883, Clara Gunsaulia. Concrete builder Mennonites. Address: Wadsworth, O

1. Raymond W. Beery, b July 1, 1886, d July 1, 1888.
2. Stanley C. Beery, b Mar. 7, 1890.
3. Sophiah M. Beery, b Dec. 14, 1892

No. 3209. Fourth Generation. 82.

2) Abraham H. Beery, b. Mar. 25, 1858, m Dec 30, 1886, Fannie L. Lehman Farmer. Caledonia, Mich.

1 Floyd A Beery, b July 25, 1887, d Dec. 25, 1898.

No. 3210. Fourth Generation. 82.

3) Mary C. Beery, b. Mar. 23, 1861, m. Oct. 27, 1881, Orlando Swainhart. He died Sept. 20, 1902 Farmer. Baptists Address: West Salem, O

1. Bert B. Swainhart, b Feb 7, 1883 No. 3703.
2. Christian C. Swainhart, b Nov 27, 1884. No. 3211.

No. 3211. Fifth Generation. 3210.

2) Chr'stian C. Swainhart, b. Nov. 27, 1884, m Feb 5, 1905, Minnie Sechrist. Farmer. Address: West Salem, O.

No. 3212. Fourth Generation. 82.

5) Lydia Beery, b July 13, 1864, m Abraham Leatherman June 27, 1888 Carpenter. Address: Muskegon, Mich

1 Orr Leatherman, b July 31, 1892
2. Dottie Leatherman, b Feb 6, 1894

No. 3213. Fourth Generation. 82.

8) Malinda M. Beery, b Jan 24, 1871, d Mar 18, 1905, m. John Nogle, July 3, 1889. He d July, 1905 Mason by trade Address· Dighton, Osceola Co , Mich.

1. Harold Nogle, b. Aug 10, 1892, d Feb 11, 1893
2. Hazel A Nogle, b Oct 9, 1894.
3 Leonard L. Nogle, b Nov 10, 1895
4. Henry L. Nogle, b Nov. 28, 1896, d Dec 12, 1896.
5. Horace L. Nogle, b Dec 27, 1897, d. Feb 9, 1898.
6. Ruby A. Nogle, b. Mar. 2, 1899.
7. Dennis A. Nogle, b. May 25, 1901
8. Theodore C. Nogle, b. Dec 17, 1903
9. Fannie B. Nogle, b. Jan 26, 1905.

No. 3214. Fourth Generation. 85.

2) William C Brenneman, b. Nov 20, 1860, near Cairo, O , m Dec. 25, 1884, Mary I. Berryhill, b. June 18, 1865 Mr. Brenneman lived for many years on his 183-acre farm a few miles north of L.ma, O , until in 1918 he sold his farm for 225 dollars per acre. Since that time he has lived at 1038 West Elm St , Lima, O. He is one of the directors in the Central Building and Loan Association. They are members of the Christian Church

1. Joshua Brenneman, b Mar 4, 1886. Single, and resides with his parents. He is a printer by trade
2. Beryl Y. Brenneman, b. Jan 13, 1888 No 3215.

No. 3215. Fifth Generation. 3214.

2) Beryl Y. Brenneman, b Jan. 13, 1888, m Aug. 21, 1907, J. H. McBride. Address: 1038 W. Elm St., Lima, O.

1. William B. McBride, b. Nov. 29, 1908

No. 3216. Fourth Generation. 85.

3) Mary Brenneman, b. Feb. 2, 1863, near Cairo, O , d Aug 25, 1931, m. James Goodman, b. June 30, 1859, d May 8, 1921. Farmer. Christian Church. Mrs. Goodman since her husband's death has lived in Cairo, O , and has left the farm of 160 acres to the care of her children. Burial at Cairo, O Address: Cairo, O.

1. Vernie E. Goodman, b Oct 14, 1899. No 3217
2. Harvey A. Goodman, b May 31, 1901 No 3218.
3. Lottie May Goodman, b June 3, 1905 No 3219

No. 3217. Fifth Generation. 3216.

1) Vernie E. Goodman, b. Oct. 14, 1899, m Frederick Beam Farmer near Lima, O. Mr. Beam d Dec. 12, 1934. Address. 714 N St , Lima, O. No children. She married (2nd) G. A. Boyer, April 11, 1936

No. 3218. Fifth Generation. 3216.

2) Harvey A Goodman, b May 31, 1901, m Esther Loverage, b Mar. 29, 1907. Address. Lima, O , R. 5.
1 Merlyn Duane Goodman, b. July 19, 1927.
2. Donald Leroy Goodman, b. Jan. 19, 1929

No. 3219. Fifth Generation. 3216.

3) Lottie May Goodman, b June 3, 1905, d April 12, 1925, m. Charles Sandy

No. 3220. Fourth Generation. 85.

5) Sarah A. Brenneman, b July 20, 1867, near Cairo, O., m Mar. 8, 1891, Benjamin F. Myers, b. Mar 20, 1870, near Greenmount, Va. Farmer. They live near Cairo, O , on a farm of 320 acres Address Lima, O , R 3
1 Alvin A Myers, b. Jan. 21, 1894
2 Charles Myers, b Feb 3, 1900
3 Ada Eliza Myers, b Dec 1, 1908
These children are all unmarried and reside at home

No. 3221. Fourth Generation. 85.

7) Benton Brenneman, b. Aug 19, 1872, near Cairo, O , m Sept., 1893, Sarah Mell, b Oct 24, 1876 He owns and operates his farm of 171 acres a few miles north of Ca ro, O. Christian Church Address. Cairo, O.
1. Nellie Brenneman, b July 30, 1894 No 3222
2 Treva Brenneman, b. Oct. 7, 1899 No 3223
3 Gail A Brenneman, b Dec 6, 1902 No 3224
4. Clarence B. Brenneman, b Dec 27, 1912 No 3639.

No. 3222. Fifth Generation. 3221.

1) Nellie Brenneman, b July 30, 1894, m Reuben Valentine Address· Cairo, O.
1 Ralph Valentine, b. Feb 29, 1912.
2. Richard Valentine, b. Nov. 9, 1917
3. Betty May Valentine, b. Oct 21, 1921

No. 3223. Fifth Generation. 3221.

2) Treva Brenneman, b. Oct. 7, 1899, m. Paul Williams.
1. Louise May Will ams, b. Nov 9, 1922
2. Paul Wilber Williams, b Mar. 17, 1935

No. 3224. Fifth Generation. 3221.

3) Gail A. Brenneman, b. Dec 6, 1902, m Florence Hofferbert, b July 22, 1905.
1. Helen Louise Brenneman, b Jan. 13, 1928.
2 Gail Brenneman, Jr , b April 24, 1930

No. 3225. Fourth Generation. 85.

8) Frank Brenneman, b Dec 23, 1874, near Cairo, O , m. Sarah Wenger, b. May 24, 1874, in Rockingham Co , Va She died Mar. 2, 1921. Buried in the Sugar Creek cemetery near L ma, O He married (2nd) Ella Morgan, b Nov 7, 1885. Mr Brenneman is a successful farmer owning 345 acres a few miles north of Lima Address: Lima, O , R. 5.

1 Joseph Earl Brenneman, b Aug 5, 1901. No. 3226.
2. Dasie Mae Brenneman, b Dec 15, 1902 No 3227.
3. Chrystal Ruth Brenneman, b Aug 8, 1904 No 3228.
4. Mary Eliza Brenneman, b April 27, 1908 No 3229.
5 Paul Abraham Brenneman, b Sept 11, 1916
6 Frank Martin Brenneman, b Feb 28, 1921, d June 14, 1921.
 Children all from first union.

No. 3226. Fifth Generation. 3225.

1) Joseph Earl Brenneman, b Aug 5, 1901, m Erma Lamb, b Jan 6, 1913 Address: L ma, O., R. 3

1 Bobbie Joe Brenneman, b April 20. 1930
2 Don Lee Brenneman, b Aug 5, 1932
3. James Roger Brenneman, b June 9, 1934.

No. 3227. Fifth Generation. 3225.

2) Dasie Mae Brenneman, b Dec 15, 1902, m Wayne Solomon. Laborer.
1. Frank Albert Solomon, b Nov 19, 1922

No. 3228. Fifth Generation. 3225.

3) Chrystal Ruth Brenneman, b Aug 8, 1904, m Clarence Brant. Automobile mechanic Address Cairo, O.

1 Marjorie Leota Brant, b Jan 21, 1927, d Jan. 29. 1927.
2. Melva Irene Brant, b Nov 27, 1928, d Dec 3, 1928.
3 Kenneth Brant, b June 19, 1930.
4 Chrystal Ardeth Brant, b Sept 23, 1933.
5. Darrel Kay Brant, b Dec 7, 1936

No. 3229. Fifth Generation. 3225.

4) Mary Eliza Brenneman, b April 27, 1908, m Ralph Joseph
1 Richard Franklin Joseph, b July 13, 1927.
2 Lela Ruth Joseph, b Sept 3, 1929
3 Carl Dewey Joseph, b May 19, 1931.
4. Betty Lou Joseph, b Mar 21, 1933

No. 3230. Fourth Generation. 87.

1) George Brenneman, b Jan 10, 1859, near Cairo, O , d Sept 16, 1899, m Elizabeth Peters, b. Jan 4, 1854, d Nov 11, 1894 They lived near Cairo, O. Buried in the Wesley Chapel cemetery near Cairo, O

1. Mary A Brenneman, b June 4, 1883, d Nov 14, 1894
2. Esther Brenneman, b Sept 4, 1887. No. 3231.

No. 3231. Fifth Generation. 3230.

2) Esther Brenneman, b Sept 4, 1887, near Cairo, O., d. Feb 18, 1913, m. Alexander Watts Address was Lima, O Lutheran

1 Robert B Watts, b Sept 3, 1910
2. Charles Watts, b Oct 15, 1912
 Robert and Charles live at 64 W Perrin Ave , Springfield, O.

2) Lewis Brenneman, b Feb. 9, 1861, near Cairo, O., d. by accident on railroad, Sept. 14, 1897 He married Marcella Mosier, b. Nov 13, 1863. No children

3) Mary Brenneman, b. July 27, 1864, near Cairo, O., m. Charles Blaine, b. April 2, 1864. He is supposed to have died by accident in St. Louis, Mo. She married (2nd) Albert Allen, b April 2, 1864 They live near Waynesfield, O.

1. Schyler C. Blaine, b. Feb 13, 1886, d. July 28, 1886.
2. Grover C. Blaine, b. Oct. 5, 1888, d Aug. 10, 1890.
3. Charles Elmer Blaine, b Aug. 3, 1887. No. 3234.
4. Calvin R Blaine, b Mar. 26, 1890 No 3235
5. Earl Cecil Allen, b Jan 9, 1907. No. 3236.

3) Charles Elmer Blaine, b. Aug 3, 1887, m. Eva Ballau, b. in Chicago, Ill.

1. Calvin Blaine, b. ——————.
2. Elmer Blaine, b. ——————.
3 Grace Blaine, b ——————
4. Rabella Blaine, b. ——————.
5. Helen Blaine, b. ——————.
6 Paul Blaine, b. ——————.

4) Calvin R. Blaine, b. Mar. 26, 1890, m. Iona Davis, Mar. 22, 1913

1. Stewart Blaine, b. ——————.
2. Grace Blaine, b. ——————.

5) Earl Cecil Allen, b Jan 9, 1907, m June 15, 1930, Alice McName, b May 12, 1908. Address: Waynesfield, O.

1) Jacob Ward, b. Dec. 15, 1859, near Cairo, O., d. Sept. 5, 1900, m Alice Tigner, b. Dec. 25, 1861. They live in Lima, O.

1. Ida May Ward, b. May 24, 1886. No. 3238.
2 Oscar Ward, b July 24, 1891. No. 3239.
3. Ruth Esther Ward, b. June 29, 1895 No 3240.
4. Pearl Ward, b. June 11, 1897. No 3241.
5 Arthur Ward, b. Dec. 3, 1898. No 3242
6 Jacob Ward, Jr., b May 4, 1901, d. Mar. 20, 1908

1) Ida May Ward, b May 24, 1886, m. Ray Armstrong. Address· 37 Laville St., Dayton, O.

1. Charity Armstrong, b. ——————.
2. Leroy Armstrong, b ——————.
3. Oscar Armstrong, b. ——————.
4. Mary Armstrong, b. ——————.
5. James Armstrong, b. ——————.
6. Walter Armstrong, b ——————.
7. Verna Armstrong, b ——————.
8. Rebecca Armstrong, b. ——————.

No. 3239. Fifth Generation. 3237.
2) Oscar Ward, b April 24, 1891, m Eva Burgner, b April 24, 1896. Address: N. Union St , Lima, O
1 Fannie Alvia Ward, b. Mar. 4, 1927.

No. 3240. Fifth Generation. 3237.
3) Ruth Esther Ward, b. June 29, 1895, m Joseph Postrack.
Two adopted children

No. 3241. Fifth Generation. 3237.
4) Pearl Ward, b. June 11, 1897, m Florence Rowan.
1. Alice Rowan, b in 1922.

No. 3242. Fifth Generation. 3237.
5) Arthur Ward, b. Dec. 3, 1898, m. Flossie Duff. No issue

No. 3243. Fourth Generation. 88.
2) Benjamin F Ward, b Nov 4, 1864, near Cairo, O , m. Almina E. Waters, b. June 19, 1871, in St Marys, O She d ed June 27, 1925. Address: 701 Hendricks St., St. Marys, O.
1. Clarence G. Ward, b May 27, 1890 No 3244
2. Ernest R Ward, b Nov. 25, 1893
3 Maudie May Ward, b Feb 4, 1896

No. 3244. Fifth Generation. 3243.
1) Clarence G Ward, b. May 27, 1890, m Lillian Ruth Linton, b. May 23, 1897.
1. Lester Harold Ward, b Mar 26, 1914.
2. Helen Bernice Ward, b. Sept 9, 1916.
3. John Benjamin Ward, b Feb 17, 1919

No. 3245. Fourth Generation. 88.
4) Hugh O. Ward, b Mar 10, 1866, near Cairo, O , m. Amelia Gahman, b. Mar. 13, 1871, d July 23, 1895. Hugh d June 9, 1925. They lived in Elida, O
1. Hazel Odessa Ward, b Sept 17, 1890. No 3246.

No. 3245. Fifth Generation. 3245.
1) Hazel Odessa Ward, b Sept 17, 1890, m Evan H. Jones, b. Dec. 22, 1884. Address: Elida, O R 1.
1. Blanche Amel a Jones, b. Nov. 30, 1913.
2 Dorothy Elizabeth Jones, b April 15, 1915.
3. Ralph Donald Jones, b. Dec. 1, 1917.
4. Floyd Edwin Jones, b. Nov. 7, 1919
5. Evan Hugh Jones, b. Dec. 27, 1921.
6 Kenneth Warren Jones, b. Feb 27, 1923
7. Mary Lois Jones, b June 5, 1925.

No. 3247. Fourth Generation. 83.
6) Frank C. Ward, b. June 1, 1873, near Cairo, O , m. Sept. 15, 1897, Mary A. McDorman, b. July 24, 1880 She died Jan 2, 1918. Laborer. United Brethren. Address: Elida, O., R 1
1. Levi Glenwood Ward, b Oct 13, 1898. No. 3571.
2. Infant, b. and d July 24, 1900.
3 Nellie Rebecca Ward, b. Oct 15, 1901
4 Ethel Lucille Ward, b July 17, 1903, d Feb 11, 1918.

5 Ralph Franklin Ward, b Oct 1, 1904, died by accidental electrocution Jan. 17, 1930

6 William Walter Ward, b Jan 17, 1908 No. 3572

7 Jessie Irene Ward, b Oct. 7, 1909. No 3573.

No. 3248. Fourth Generation. 89.

1) Mary Meyers, b ————, 1858, m. Aug 15, 1880, Levi Weaver, d. Sept., 1934. She m. (2nd) Oct 2, 1883, John Faught

1. Walter Weaver, b. ————.
2. Ida Faught, b ————.
3. William Faught, b ————.
4 Franklin Faught, b. ————.
5. Bessie Faught, b. ————, deceased.

No. 3249. Fourth Generation. 89.

2) Jennie Meyers, b May 23, 1860, m May, 1888, John W. Dorman
1. Bessie Dorman, b ———— Address Mt. Forest, Mich.

No. 3250. Fourth Generation. 89.

3) Charles Fremont Meyers, b Nov. 18, 1862, m Dec 5, 1897, Lydia C. Kimmel Address: 1932 East Roy St, Ft Wayne, Ind.

1. Ethel Meyers, b. ————.
2. Gladys Meyers, b ————.
3. Mae Meyers, b ————
4. Goldie Meyers, b. ————
5. Nellie Meyers, b. ————.
6 Melvin Meyers, b ————.
7. Dorothy Meyers, b. ————.
8. Mildred Meyers, b. ————.
9. Treva Meyers, b ————
10. Clarence Meyers, b. ————.

No. 3251. Fourth Generation. 89.

4) Emma Meyers, b Oct 12, 1864, m Feb 11, 1883, George W Beck. Address Ft Wayne, Ind , R. 4.

1. Minnie Beck, b. ————
2. Anna Beck, b. ————, deceased.
3. Charles Beck, b. ————.
4. William Beck, b ————, deceased
5. George Beck, b. ————.
6 Edward Beck, b. ————.
7. Martha Beck, b. ————.
8. Harry Beck, b. ————.
9. Catherine Beck, b. ————.
10. Samuel Beck, b. ————.
11. Carl Beck, b. ————.
12. Theodore Beck, b. ————.
13. Paul Beck, b. ————, twin.
14. Pauline Beck, b. ————, twin.

No. 3252. Fourth Generation. 92.

2) Ora Brenneman, b Mar 26, 1870, d ————, m. Frank W. Snyder, b. Feb. 24, 1859.

1 Bonnie May Snyder, b July 6, 1890, d July 12, 1897.

2 May Elizabeth Snyder, b Feb. 11, 1893. No 3253.

No. 3253. Fifth Generation. 3252.

2) May Elizabeth Snyder, b Feb. 11, 1893, d. Mar , 1938, m. Glen G. Roberts, b. Jan. 14, 1891. They reside at 326 N. Charles St , Lima, O.

1. May Elizabeth Roberts, b Sept 30, 1922, d. Oct 2, 1922.
2. Martha Jane Roberts, b Oct 12, 1924.
3. Ruth Ellen Roberts, b Oct 15, 1929.

No. 3254. Fourth Generation. 92.

3) Amos Sylvester Brenneman, b Nov. 10, 1872, near Cairo, O , m. (1st) Rose Snyder, he married (2nd) Anna Eicher They lived near Cairo, O.

No. 3256. Fourth Generation. 93.

1) Jesse Austin Brenneman, b July 3, 1883, near Cairo, O., m. Lena Olt, b in 1888, d. in May, 1921. Address· Cairo, O

1. Jesse Raymond Brenneman, b in 1908.
2. Frances Cathryn Brenneman, b July 31, 1913.
3. Emma Brenneman, b Sept 1, 1916.
4 Clarence Edwin Brenneman, b Dec 15, 1911, d at two days.
5. Virgil Edward Brenneman, b April 30, 1920.

No. 3257. Fourth Generation. 93.

2) Esta Rebecca Brenneman, b Nov 28, 1884, near Cairo, O , m. Delton C. Watters Address Cairo, O. No children

No. 3258. Fourth Generation. 93.

3) James Sheldon Brenneman, b Aug 3, 1886, near Cairo, O., m Mary Best, b Apr l 9, 1916. Address: Cairo, O. Vault builder

1. Mary Ellen Brenneman, b. Mar 20, 1936

No. 3259. Fourth Generation. 93.

4) Mattie Orfa Brenneman, b June 3, 1888, m. Leslie Harbert, b. 1887, d. April 21, 1938. They live in Elida, O. No issue.

No. 3261. Fourth Generation. 93.

6) Charles Sherman Brenneman, b April 29, 1898, near Cairo, O , m. Nov. 17, 1931, Lena Fuller, b April, 1913. They live in Elida, O Laborer. United Brethren

1. Junior Brenneman, b Mar. —, 1934
2 Mary Brenneman, b —————

No. 3261½. Fourth Generation. 93.

7) Oscar Harold Brenneman, b. Feb 12, 1904, near Cairo, O , m. Margaret Kingsley. They live in Delphos, O , 226 4th St.

1. Betty Jean Brenneman, b. June 24, 1924.

No. 3262. Fourth Generation. 94.

1) Ethel Brenneman, b Sept 16, 1875, near Cairo, O., m. John Marsh, b. Jan. 15, 1863, d. June 4, 1930 Address. Buckland, O.

1. Llewena Marsh, b. Aug. 11, 1901. No. 3262¼.
2. Irene Marsh, b Aug 21, 1905. No 3262½.
   Two infants died at birth

No. 3262¼. Fifth Generation. 3262.

1) Llewena L. Marsh, b Aug 11, 1901, near Buckland, O., m June 27, 1937, Samuel H. Chrismer, b. Oct. 5, 1897 Mrs Chrismer was a schoolteacher for 17 years Congregational Christian Address· Buckland, O.

No. 3262½. Fifth Generation. 3262.

2) Irene A. Marsh, b Aug 21, 1905, near Buckland, O , m. June 27, 1936, James D. Eisley, b Oct 26, 1904. Mrs Eisley was a schoolteacher for 10 years Congregational Christian. Address· Buckland, O.

1. John Jacob Eisley, b Feb 21, 1938

No. 3253. Fourth Generation. 95.

1) Minnie Elva Belch, b Mar 24, 1874, near Cairo, O , m F. Sherman Miller, b. Nov. 9, 1870 Address. Cairo, O No children

No. 3264. Sixth Generation. 3040.

2) Elizabeth S Good, b Nov. 3, 1908, m July 8, 1933, Arthur S Brunk, b. Jan. 25, 1911. Farmer Mennonites Address: South Boston, Va. Related

No. 3255. Sixth Generation. 3040.

4) Ina Marie Good, b. Aug 16, 1912, m Sept. 10, 1933, Henry C. Stalter Address. South Boston, Va Mennonites.

1. Freda M. Stalter, b. Aug 21, 1934
2. Louise V. Stalter, b Sept 19, 1936

No. 3266. Seventh Generation. 586.

1) Russell DeWitt Cline, b July 7, 1902, m Feb 15, 1928, Mabel Rebecca Rohrer.

1. Glen Rohrer Cline, b Aug 17, 1929
2 Marie Elizabeth Cline, b Mar 2, 1931
3. Stanley Robert Cline, b May 12, 1932
4. Joseph Russell Cline, b. Jan 2, 1934
5. James Rohrer Cline, b Dec 26, 1936

No. 3257. Seventh Generation. 586.

2) Emery Turner Cline, b June 25, 1904, m Sept 27, 1926, Pauline Werner.

1. Phyllis Louise Cline, b. July 29, 1927
2. Kirkley Wallace Cline, b Jan 11, 1929
3 Rosa Lee Cline, b. Aug 10, 1933

No. 3263. Seventh Generation. 587.

1) Roy DeWitt Burkholder, b Jan. 24, 1908, m Sept 1, 1931, Mary Rebecca Rhodes, daughter of John H and Emma (Martin) Rhodes, b. Sept. 21, 1904.

1. Roy DeWitt Burkholder, Jr , b. Aug. 27, 1933.
2. Oliver Atlee Burkholder, b. May 13, 1935

No. 3269. Seventh Generation. 587.

2) John Samuel Burkholder, b. July 13, 1909, m. Feb 14, 1929, Vernie Magdalena Knisely, daughter of Fielding K. and Maggie Wenger Knisely

1. Sadie Lee Burkholder, b Jan. 1, 1930.
2. Wilda May Burkholder, b. May 4, 1931
3. Beulah Frances Burkholder, b Mar. 28, 1933.
4. Warl Pennybacher Burkholder, b Aug. 30, 1934.

No. 3270. Seventh Generation. 587.

3) Esther Larue Burkholder, b Mar. 12, 1911, m. Rhodes Beery Landes, b. Mar. 21, 1916, son of Miner W and Ida Rhodes Landes.

1 Ralph Elburn Landes, b Mar. 15, 1937.

No. 3271. Seventh Generation. 587.

5) Paul Marvin Burkholder, b. Jan. 5, 1915, m Elizabeth Frances Wenger, daughter of Abram D. and Eva Lena (Harper) Wenger, b. Nov. 16, 1916.

No. 3272. Sixth Generation. 584.

4) Andrew L. Burkholder, son of Caleb W. and Mary Etta Heatwole, b. Nov. 30, 1889, m. Mar. 6, 1910, Anna B Hoover, b. Oct. 20, 1889 Address: New Holland, Pa , R. 1.

1. Aaron Caleb Burkholder, b. Jan 11, 1911. No. 3273.
2. Esther M. Burkholder, b. June 28, 1916 No. 3274.
3. Paul H. Burkholder, b. Sept. 18, 1917
4. John A. Burkholder, b. Dec. 26, 1918.
5. Benjamin Burkholder, b Nov. 1, 1922

No. 3273. Seventh Generation. 3272.

1) Aaron Caleb Burkholder, b. Jan 11, 1911, m. Alta Burkholder, daughter of Frank and Minnie (Witmer) Burkholder. Address: Blue Ball, Pa.

1. Ruth Burkholder, b. ————

No. 3274. Seventh Generation. 3272.

2) Esther M Burkholder, b June 28, 1916, m Lester Groff. Address: Blue Ball, Pa.

No. 3275. Fourth Generation. 83.

1) George W. Beery, b Oct. 27, 1857, near Bremen, O., m Feb. 1, 1879, Hannah E. Roley, b. Feb 3, 1857, d. July 2, 1932 Mr. Beery practiced medicine for 20 years in Hocking Co , O , and in 1909 he located in Lancaster, O., at which place he practiced up to the present time (1939) but he has now retired usually spending his winters in the South with his daughters. Not affiliated with any church. Address: 768 East Main St , Lancaster, O Burial in Forest Rose cemetery, Lancaster, O.

1. Blanche B Beery, b. April 7, 1880 No 3276
2. Bessie B. Beery, b Mar 9, 1882, twin No. 3277.
3 Jesse Beery, b Mar 9, 1882, twin No 3278.

No. 3276. Fifth Generation. 3275.

1) Blanche B Beery, b April 7, 1880, in Hocking Co., O., m Samuel S Stille Address: Mobile, Ala

1 George C. Stille, b. ————

No. 3277. Fifth Generation. 3275.

2) Bessie B Beery, b Mar 9, 1882, in Hocking Co , O , m Edward C. Oliver. Address· Magnolia Springs, Ala

1 ———— Oliver, b ————
2 ———— Oliver, b ————, both died in infancy

No. 3278. Fifth Generation. 3275.

3) Jesse Beery, b Mar 9, 1882, in Hocking Co , O., m. Minnie Fulk Address. Cincinnati, O

1. Georgie Beery, b ————
2 Gene Wallace Beery, b. ————

469

No. 3279. Sixth Generation. 3193.

1) Martha F. Brown, b. Oct. 8, 1898, m. Dec. 24, 1921, Louis R. Wood, b. Dec. 25, 1896. Laborer Christian Church. Address: Columbus Grove, O., R. 3.
1. Mary M. Wood, b. Mar. 17, 1923.
2. Vada K. Wood, b. Nov. 11, 1926.

No. 3280. Sixth Generation. 3198.

2) William L. Brown, b. Mar 9, 1900, m Maud Robison. Address: Fostoria, O. Laborer. Methodists.
1. Ida L Brown, b May 11, 1928.
2. William Brown, Jr., b. Sept. 16, 1930

No. 3281. Sixth Generation. 3198.

3) Harba Belle Brown, b Aug 27, 1902, m Nov., 1922, Wilmer Cooper. Laborer Methodists. Address: Forest, O
1. Thomas Cooper, b June 3, 1923.
2. Donald Cooper, b. Aug 11, 1924
3 Thelma Cooper, b. May 9, 1926.
4 Pauline Cooper, b ——————
5. Marien Cooper, b. ——————.
6. Mauna Ruth Cooper, b Jan. 29, 1931.

No. 3282. Sixth Generation. 3198.

4) David Samuel Brown, b Sept. 16, 1904, m Zelma Chadwick. Address: Fostoria, O. Laborer. Methodists.
1. Ivolene Brown, b Feb. —, 1928
2. Anna Belle Brown, b. ——————, 1930

No. 3283. Sixth Generation. 3198.

5) Ernest C. Brown, b Sept. 9, 1907, d Dec 20, 1936, m. Eva ——————. Address: Lancaster, O Groceryman Methodists
1. Edna J. Brown, b ——————
2. Martha J. Brown, b. ——————.

No. 3284. Seventh Generation. 435.

2) Wilford Brunk, b Mar. 21, 1910, m Sept 7, 1932, Martha Yingling of Lima, O Address: 815 College Ave, Lima, O. Dentist.

No. 3285. Fifth Generation. 3186.

3) William Wallace Brenneman, b Dec 15, 1909, m. April 25, 1937, Ruth E. Basinger, b. Feb. 16, 1915 Address: Springfield, O Related, see No. 2899.

No. 3286. Fifth Generation. 2944.

2) Ralph E. Brenneman, b. Aug. 8, 1899, in Lima, O., m. Elnor R. Hicks. B. O. freight office. Presbyterians. Address· 709 West Kibby St, Lima, O.

No. 3287. Sixth Generation. 2940.

1) Martha V. Dieterich, b Nov 23, 1914, at Dayton, O., m June 27, 1936, William Hangen, b Jan 11, 1909.

No. 3283. Sixth Generation. 1860.

2) Alice Virginia Reeves, b. Jan 2, 1910, m Nov 9, 1935, Dr. Edwin J. Steden, b. May 29, 1896 Address 2504 Sherwood Road, Columbus, O. Catholic Burial place at Jamestown, O
1. Edwin Joseph Steden, Jr., b Oct 7, 1936
2. Elizabeth Ann Steden, b. Mar 7, 1938.

No. 3289. Sixth Generation. 2525.
3) Pauline Donovan, b ——————, m George Baer.

No. 3290. Sixth Generation. 2625.
4) Susie Donovan, b. —————, m. ——— Yankey.

No. 3291. Sixth Generation. 2525.
5) Dorothy F. Donovan, b Feb 11, 1913, m. Mar. 30, 1934, Warren W. Keller, b. Mar. 26, 1913. Address: Dayton, Va.
1. William Richard Keller, b. Nov. 3, 1935.

No. 3292. Sixth Generation. 2629.
1) Iva May Moore, b May 4, 1914, m Ward E Showalter, b. July 19, 1902. Address: Timberville, Va No issue

No. 3293. Sixth Generation. 2629.
3) Ira Whissen Moore, b May 13, 1908, m. June 15, 1931, Pauline Reedy.

No. 3294. Sixth Generation. 2623.
4) Beulah Virginia Moore, b Feb 24, 1910, m. Aug. 28, 1932, Joseph W. Neff.
1. Janet A. Neff, b April 24, 1933

No. 3295. Sixth Generation. 2529.
5) Wilkie Ruth Moore, b Oct 13, 1912, m. Mar. 28, 1934, Glen W. Miller.
1. Donald William Miller, b Mar. 16, 1935.
2. Jean Moore Miller, b July 20, 1936.

No. 3296. Sixth Generation. 2529.
7) Elsie Moore, b. Sept 2, 1914, m. Sept 5, 1936, Edwin O. Good.

No. 3297. Sixth Generation. 2530.
1) F. Whissen Shoemaker, b. May 1, 1911, m. Ora L Shoemaker, b. June 11, 1914.
1. Delos N. Shoemaker, b May 17, 1934
2. Sidney M Shoemaker, b April 21, 1936

No. 3298. Sixth Generation. 2534.
1) Arlie S. Bowman, b June 21, 1895, m Louise Wilson of Morgantown, N. C., Nov. 15, 1928.

No. 3299. Sixth Generation. 2634.
2) Gertrude A Bowman, b Oct 20, 1896, m Solon Arland Hausenpluck, Oct 22, 1919.
1. Solon Arland Hausenpluck, Jr, b Jan. 17, 1923.

No. 3300. Sixth Generation. 2534.
3) Irene Vesta Bowman, b. Sept 17, 1898, m. Everett Willard Cole, of Richmond, Va, Aug 27, 1920

No. 3301. Sixth Generation. 2535.
1) Golden Chapman, b. May 30, 1901, m. Edna ———————
1. Dwight Leon Chapman, b April 1, 1925
2 Hilda May Chapman, b Sept. 9, 1928

No. 3302. Sixth Generation. 2635.
2) Paul Chapman, b. Feb 29, 1904, m Anna Fadeley.
1. Phyllis Mae Chapman, b Nov. 23, 1925, twin
2. Bernice Fay Chapman, b. Nov 23, 1925, twin.

3. Maxine Virginia Chapman, b Jan 31, 1928.
4 Jennings Leo Chapman, b Feb. 22, 1930.

No. 3303. Sixth Generation. 2635.
3) Tracy O. Chapman, b Aug. 24, 1898, m. Luther L. Bear
1. Norma June Bear, b. April 15, 1923.
2. Edwin Edgar Bear, b. Feb 16, 1928

No. 3303¼. Sixth Generation. 2635.
4) Francis Chapman, b. Sept 9, 1907, m Ada Householder.
1. Roger Lee Chapman, b Oct. 26, 1927.
2. Garlan Eugene Chapman, b April 22, 1930

No. 3304. Sixth Generation. 2633.
2) Welby L. Brunk, b Sept. 8, 1891, m Mae ————.
1. John Leo Brunk, b. ————
2. Roy Scott Brunk, b. ————.

No. 3305. Sixth Generation. 2633.
3) Edgar R Brunk, b Aug 16, 1893, m Jessie Chessire. No children.

No. 3306. Sixth Generation. 2533.
4) Leona E. Brunk, b June 9, 1895, m. Raymond W. Stewart.
1. Raymond W. Stewart, Jr, b ————.
2. Kenneth Stewart, b. ————.

No. 3307. Sixth Generation. 2533.
5) Joseph A. Brunk, b Nov 15, 1897, m Mary ———— They have a family.

No. 3308. Sixth Generation. 2533.
8) Bayard F. Brunk, b. April 29, 1902, m Marie ————.
1. Harold Brunk, b. ————.

No. 3309. Sixth Generation. 2633.
9) Dwight F. Brunk, b. Dec 10, 1904, m. Naomi ————
1. ———— Brunk, b. ————.
2. ———— Brunk, b. ————.

No. 3310. Sixth Generation. 2633.
11) Virginia Glen Brunk, b ————, m George Raynolds Hallida. No children.

No. 3311. Sixth Generation. 2633.
12) Marguerite Brunk, b. ————, m Samuel Landes.

No. 3312. Sixth Generation. 2633.
13) Dorothy Brunk, b. ————, m. Willard Bruce Michael.

No. 3313. Sixth Generation. 2617.
1) Kemper Price Cline, b Mar 6, 1885, near Mt. Clinton, Va., m. Oct. 3, 1931, at Cumberland, Md, Irene Neff, of Piedmont, W. Va. Address: Clarksburg, W. Va.
1. Paul Charles Cline, b. Dec 26, 1933
2. Kemper Price Cline, Jr, b. Mar. 22, 1936

No. 3314. Sixth Generation. 2617.
2) James Neff Cline, b June 18, 1886, near Mt. Clinton, Va, m Sallie Anna Deputy.

1. James M. Cline, b. Oct. 2, 1923.
2. Frances Gene Cline, b. Nov. 18, 1925.
3. Bettie Anna Cline, b. June 30, 1926.
4. William Deputy Cline, b. Oct 28, 1928.

No. 3315. Sixth Generation. 2617.

3) Lester Lloyd Cline, b. Oct 6, 1887, near Mt. Clinton, Va., m. Reatha Rodeffer.
1. Mary Frances Cline, b ————, m Melvin Stiffey.
2. Charles Newton Cline, b ————.
3. Evelyn Reatha Cline, b. ————.
4. Helen Marie Cline, b. ————
5. Lester Lloyd Cline, Jr., b. ————.
6. Dorothy Lillian Cline, b. ————.
7. Janet Christine Cline, b ————.
8 Mildred Julia Cline, b. ————.

No. 3316. Sixth Generation. 2517.

4) Anna Pauline Cline, b July 10, 1889, near Mt. Clinton, Va , m. Winton L. Earman, Oct 17, 1906.
1. Mary Virginia Earman, b. Feb 1, 1921

No. 3317. Sixth Generation. 2617.

5) Arthur Boyd Cline, b April 18, 1891, near Mt. Clinton, Va., m. Ola Amanda Swope, b. Mar. 10, 1894 Address. Mt. Clinton, Va.
1. Frankie Elizabeth Cline, b July 24, 1913, d Aug. 9, 1913.
2. Harold Joseph Cline, b July 30, 1914. No 3318.
3. Edith Virginia Cline, b May 18, 1917.
4. Charles Wilson Cline, b Aug 4, 1919
5 Erma Catherine Cline, b. July 15, 1921

No. 3318. Seventh Generation. 3317.

2) Harold Joseph Cline, b July 30, 1914, m Goldie Larain ————, b. Mar. 1, 1913.
1. Kenneth Edwin Cline, b July 16, 1936.

No. 3319. Sixth Generation. 2617.

6) DeWitt Talmadge Cline, b Dec 28, 1892, m. Nora Strickler Showalter, b. April 15, 1895, m. Dec 24, 1917.
1. Dale L. Cline, b. Jan 17, 1919.
2 Marion Roscoe Cline, b. Sept. 28, 1920.
3. Fannie Jane Cline, b. Jan. 7, 1924.
4. Margaret Elizabeth Cline, b Nov 19, 1925.
5. Galen DeWitt Cline, b. July 16, 1928.
6. Stanley Talmadge Cline, b. April 7, 1930
7. Richard Aaron Cline, b Oct. 13, 1931.
8. Andrew Daniel Cline, b Aug. 27, 1932, twin
9. Amos Samuel Cline, b. Aug. 27, 1932, twin.
10. Franklin R Cline, b Mar. 21, 1934

No. 3320. Sixth Generation. 2617.

7) William Warren Cline, b Aug 11, 1893, near Mt. Clinton, Va., m. Hazel
————.

No. 3321. Sixth Generation. 2617.
8) Rawley Ruff Cline, b. Sept. 22, 1905, near Mt Clinton, Va., m Frances Cristine Gilbert, Nov. 11, 1929.

No. 3322. Sixth Generation. 2517.
9) Frances Lula Cline, b Sept 13, 1899, near Mt. Clinton, Va , m. Julian Cline Driver, b Dec. 22, 1923, of New Market, Va. Address: Cumberland, Md.
1. Dorlas Jacob Driver, b. Oct. 21, 1924.
2. Julian Wayne Driver, b. Jan. 6, 1926.
3. Betty Lucille Driver, b. Dec 11, 1929.

No. 3323. Sixth Generation. 2619.
3) Grace Virginia Heltzel, b May 9, 1914, m Dec. 4, 1936, Michael Roller. Address: Harrisonburg, Va

No. 3324. Sixth Generation. 2621.
3) Anna Rosella Heltzel, b Oct. 14, 1898, m Edward Warren Wright, Oct. 14, 1920.
1. Kathleen Eugen a Wright, b. Sept 28, 1926.

No. 3325. Sixth Generation. 2521.
4) Ester Lilian Heltzel, b Dec. 20, 1900, m. April 22, 1920, Raymond Bryan Miller.
1. Robert Eugene Miller, b May 11, 1921.
2. Marvin Bryan Miller, b. Aug. 11, 1924.
3. Barbara Mae Miller, b July 8, 1933
4 Daniel Ward Miller, b. Mar. 1, 1935.

No. 3326. Sixth Generation. 2521.
5) Hunter Putnam Heltzel, b. Oct. 9, 1902, m Katherine Elizabeth Ralston, Dec. 3, 1932.
1. Hunter Putnam Heltzel, Jr., b. Sept 9, 1934.

No. 3327. Sixth Generation. 2621.
6) Ruby Elizabeth Heltzel, b Feb. 6, 1905, m. Hensel Dorsey Riddleberger, Oct. 28, 1927.
1. Hensel Dorsey Riddleberger, Jr., b Aug. 1, 1928.
2. Mary Lou Riddleberger, b Feb. 27, 1930.

No. 3328. Sixth Generation. 2521.
7) Rachel Katherine Heltzel, b. Aug. 23, 1908, m. Aug. 13, 1932, Raymond Warren Snow. No issue.

No. 3329. Fifth Generation. 2643.
1) Daisy Funk, b April 10, 1881, m. Dec. 24, 1902, Thomas Arey. Cook and housekeeper. Church of the Brethren. Address: 519 E. Pikes Peak, Colorado Springs, Colo.
1. Ernestine B. Arey, b July 17, 1904. No 3330
2. Nina R. Arey, b. Oct. 29, 1908. No. 3331
3. A. Grace Arey, b. April 2, 1914. No 3332.

No. 3330. Sixth Generation. 3329.
1) Ernestine B. Arey, b. July 17, 1904, m. June 12, 1923, George Wagoner.
1. Paul A. Wagoner, b. Mar. 8, 1924. -
2. Dorothy Ruth Wagoner, b. May 3, 1928.
3. Phyllis Wagoner, b. July 29, 1931

No. 3331. Sixth Generation. 3329.

2) Nina R. Arey, b. Oct. 29, 1908, m Sept. 28, 1929, Donald J. Hylton.
1. Jessie Ruth Hylton, b July 4, 1930.
2. Lois E. Hylton, b. Jan. 23, 1932.

No. 3332. Sixth Generation. 3329.

3) A. Grace Arey, b. April 2, 1914, m June 30, 1931, Jacob Braum.

No. 3333. Fifth Generation. 2643.

2) Mollie Funk, b. Sept. 14, 1881, d Jan. 11, 1935, m. Arthur Sponaugle, b. Jan. 14, 1874, in Circleville, W. Va They were married Mar. 18, 1903. After marriage they lived for a number of years at Cando, N. Dak., where he owned 800 acres of land. Later he sold his farm and went to Wisconsin, and later to Rich Hill, Mo., where his wife died and was buried in Greenlawn cemetery, Rich Hill, Mo. Address: Rich Hill, Mo They belong to the Reorganized Church of Christ of Latter Day Saints.
1 Louise D Sponaugle, b Feb. 2, 1905 No. 3574.
2. Marion C. Sponaugle, b. May 31, 1906 No. 3575.
3. Frances A. Sponaugle, b Oct. 3, 1907. No. 3576.
4. Arthur N. Sponaugle, b. Oct. —, 1908.
5. Myrtle V. Sponaugle, b. Feb 7, 1910. No 3577.
6. Minn e Irene Sponaugle, b Mar 8, 1911. No. 3578.
7. Porter W. Sponaugle, b April 9, 1913, d. ———, 1915.
8. Charles L. Sponaugle, b Dec. 10, 1916.
9. Elmer E. E. Sponaugle, b April 26, 1919.
10. Ralph F. Sponaugle, b. Mar. 8, 1922
11. August W. Sponaugle, b. Aug. 9, 1923.

No. 3334. Fifth Generation. 2643.

3) Ruth Funk, b. Mar. 26, 1893, m. John Clark. Address: Irricana, Alta., Can.
1. Paul Clark, b. —————.
2. Nael Clark, b. —————.

No. 3335. Fifth Generation. 2783.

1) Mattie R Wenger, b April 19, 1890, m. William Ziegler. Address: Salem, O.
1. Ralph W. Ziegler, b. Jan. 22, 1917.
2. Esther M. Ziegler, b Feb. 11, 1923
3. Kenneth W. Ziegler, b. Aug. 1, 1926.
4. Lois V. Ziegler, b Sept. 7, 1930.

No. 3336. Fifth Generation. 2783.

2) Israel Rohrer Wenger, b. Nov. 30, 1891, Rockingham Co., Va., m. Vesta Gearig in Fulton Co, O., where they lived Israel was instantly killed Nov 4, 1927. Address: Wauseon, O.
1. Mildred A. Wenger, b. Dec. 19, 1921.
2. Violet M. Wenger, b. Feb 8, 1923
3. Marjorie P. Wenger, b July 30, 1926.

No. 3337. Fifth Generation. 2783.

3) Abraham Jacob Wenger, b. Feb 15, 1893, m. Esther Yoder. They live at Fentress, Va
1 Charlotte I. Wenger, b Jan 20, 1920.
2. John D. Wenger, b April 14, 1921.

3. Mary E. Wenger, b. July 22, 1923.
4. Homer A. Wenger, b July 14, 1925.
5. Melvin I. Wenger, b Sept. 21, 1929.
6. Ruth A Wenger, b. Nov 17, 1930.
7. Herbert Wenger, b. Mar. 15, 1933.

No. 3338. Fifth Generation. 2783.

4) Lena Susan Wenger, b. Oct 18, 1895, m Edwin Weaver   Address: Columbiana, O.
1. Alma M Weaver, b. Jan. 30, 1919.
2. Edith A. Weaver, b. July 21, 1920.
3. Paul W. Weaver, b. Feb. 23, 1922.
4. David A. Weaver, b. June 29, 1923.
5. Howard E. Weaver, b Jan 3, 1926
6. Sarah A. Weaver, b. April 1, 1928
7. Mary E. Weaver, b. Aug. 24, 1931.
8 Anna K. Weaver, b Sept. 8, 1935

No. 3339. Fifth Generation. 2783.

5) Amos Daniel Wenger, b Aug 11, 1897, m Mary E Wenger. Address: Harrisonburg, Va.
1. Joseph H. Wenger, b. Sept. 11, 1926.
2. Miriam F. Wenger, b Oct 29, 1927
3. Reba G Wenger, b June 3, 1929
4 Eunice A Wenger, b. Nov 4, 1931.
5 Ruth E Wenger, b. Mar. 8, 1936.

No. 3340. Fifth Generation. 2783.

6) Stella Virginia Wenger, b. June 10, 1899, m. Frank R. Good   Address: Dayton, Va.
1. Mary G Good, b April 11, 1925
2 Irene A. Good, b Oct. 13, 1926
3. Margaret E. Good, b. Oct. 16, 1928
4 Lewis E. Good, b. Mar. 29, 1930
5 Edith M. Good, b. Jan. 12, 1933.

No. 3341. Fifth Generation. 2783.

7) Hannah B. Wenger, b. Dec. 23, 1901, m Enos L. Witmer. Address: Columbiana, O.
1. J. Elmer Witmer, b. June 12, 1927.
2. Daniel A. Witmer, b Dec. 10, 1928.
3. Stella V. Witmer, b. Feb. 1, 1935.
4 Vesta M. Witmer, b. Dec. 9, 1934.
5 Enos J. Witmer, b Oct 1, 1936

No. 3342. Fifth Generation. 2783.

9) Edith Wenger, b Feb. 24, 1905, m. John R Martin. Address Dalton, O.
1. Emory D. Martin, b. May 1, 1932.
2 Amanda M Martin, b. June 6, 1934.

No. 3343. Fifth Generation. 2783.

11) David Adam Wenger, b. July 8, 1910, m. Letha M. Brunk. Address: Columbiana, O.
1. Jean L Wenger, b. —————.

No. 3344. Fifth Generation. 2794.
1) Truman H. Brunk, b. Dec 22, 1902, m. Jan. 16, 1923, Ruth M. Smith, b. May 10, 1903. Mr Brunk was ordained minister in Mennonite Church in Va., July 22, 1934. Address Denbigh, Va. Mennonites
  1. Evelyn Nada Brunk, b April 19, 1927.
  2. Truman Harold Brunk, Jr., b. May 19, 1931.
  3. Margaret Kathleen Brunk, b. Nov. 19, 1932.

No. 3345. Fifth Generation. 2794.
2) Stella Victoria Brunk, b Jan 15, 1905, m June 15, 1927, J. Ward Shank, b. July 30, 1904
  1 Rowland Ward Shank, b. June 21, 1929
  2 Audrey May Shank, b. May 7, 1932.

No. 3346. Fifth Generation. 2794.
3) Edna Frances Brunk, b Jan 20, 1907, m Aug 1, 1932, Arthur Virgil Hertzler, b. Feb. 9, 1907.
  1 Robert Allen Hertzler, b Oct 15, 1933

No. 3347. Fifth Generation. 2794.
4) Menno Simon Brunk, b Aug 9, 1909, m Mar 22, 1932, Seba Ernestine Harmon, b. May 7, 1909. Address· Denbigh, Va.
  1. David Jones Brunk, b Nov. 10, 1933
  2. Marie Frances Brunk, b Feb. 20, 1936

No. 3343. Fifth Generation. 2794.
5) George Rowland Brunk, b Nov. 18, 1911, m Sept. 20, 1932, Margaret Grace Suter, b. Mar 12, 1911 Mennonites. He was ordained minister in the Mennonite Church in Va , July 22, 1934 Address: Denbigh, Va.
  1. Gerald Robert Brunk, b. Mar. 17, 1937.

No. 3349. Fifth Generation. 2794.
6) Katie Florence Brunk, b May 3, 1913, m Dec. 12, 1935, John F. Shank, b. Feb 19, 1911.

No. 3350. Fifth Generation. 2847.
1) Nancy Jane Brown, b Oct. 1, 1903, m. Raymond Nair of Rockingham Co., Va Address: Broadway, Va.

No. 3351. Fifth Generation. 1159.
3) John Cline, b. Dec 27, 1852, in Rockingham Co., Va , m. Susan Flory at Mill Creek, Va She died in about a year after their marriage and was buried at Mill Creek. After her death he went west and married Sarah Garber and located at McPherson, Kans , where he and his last wife are both buried. He was a minister in the Church of the Brethren at McPherson, Kans.
  1. Elizabeth Cline, b. Jan 9, 1875. No 3352.
     (From second union)
  2. Harvey Cline, b ——————.
  3 Samuel Cline, b. ——————.
  4 John Cline, b. ——————
  5 Mary Cline, b ——————, m Wichael.
  6. Gertrude Cline, b. ——————, m. Adams.
  7. Eva Cline, b. ——————.
  8. Ruth Cline, b. ——————
  9 Susan Cline, b ——————

10. Zelma Cline, b. —————.
11. Bertha Cline, b. —————.

Note.—Mr. Cline died in May, 1911. His first wife was born May 19, 1855, d. Jan. 20, 1875. He married first time Oct. 26, 1873. Elizabeth has given her family report in full but all efforts to get any response from the other members have failed to be respected, so the author is clear of them not being represented in the records

No. 3352. Sixth Generation. 3351.

1) Elizabeth Cline, b. Jan 9, 1875, in Rockingham Co., Va., m. Oct. 25, 1893, Roy L. Pittman, b. Oct. 29, 1868, d. April 15, 1924. He is buried at the Mill Creek Church of the Brethren cemetery. Housewife. Church of the Brethren. Address: 432 East Elizabeth St, Harrisonburg, Va.

1. Mary Rebecca Pittman, b. April 3, 1897, d Aug. 29, 1900.
2. Barbara Susan Pittman, b. Jan 12, 1902 No. 3353.
3. George Cline Pittman, b. Aug. 14, 1905. No. 3354
4. Infant daughter, b. April 4, 1900, d same day.
5. Annie Belle Pittman, b Mar. 18, 1908. No. 3355.
6. Infant daughter, b. Feb 22, 1911, d. two days later.
7. Minnie Ruth Pittman, b. Oct. 15, 1912. No. 3356
8. Infant son, b. July 10, 1915, d same day.

No. 3353. Seventh Generation. 3352.

2) Barbara Susan Pittman, b Jan 12, 1902, m. Dec 22, 1923, Howard S. Gordon.

1. Ray Samuel Gordon, b. Dec. 21, 1924.
2. Elizabeth Ann Gordon, b. Jan. 23, 1927.

No. 3354. Seventh Generation. 3352.

3) George Cline Pittman, b. Aug 14, 1905, m. Jan. 22, 1932, Helen Louise Bartley.

No. 3355. Seventh Generation. 3352.

5) Annie Belle Pittman, b. Mar. 18, 1908, m Jan 22, 1932, Maynard M. Knisely.

No. 3356. Seventh Generation. 3352.

7) Minnie Ruth Pittman, b Oct. 15, 1912, m. Oct 23, 1931, Roy L. Fitzwater.

1. Lois Pittman Fitzwater, b Nov. 28, 1934.

No. 3357. Fifth Generation. 2339.

4) Ida Edith Lewis, b Aug 31, 1862, d Nov. 25, 1889, m. Feb. 22, 1888, at Pacific Junction, Ia., to Charles P. S. Brown, b Jan. 5, 1853, d. May 8, 1927 Burial at Glenwood, Ia. Christian Church. Address: Glenwood, Ia.

1. Ida Almeda Brown, b. Nov 16, 1889. No 3358.
2. Twin brother b. as above d same day

No. 3358. Sixth Generation. 3357.

1) Ida Almeda Brown, b. Nov 16, 1889, m June 4, 1906, at Merriam, Kans., Earl Carson Smith, b May 13, 1885. They were divorced later but he died. She later married William Fouster Jacobs at Ottawa Lake, Mich., m. April 14, 1877. They were married Oct. 19, 1933. Burial place in Lakeview cemetery, Ottawa, Mich. Address: Ottawa Lake, Mich., Box 54

1. Desdemona Lewis Smith, b Jan 26, 1908 No. 3359

No. 3359. Seventh Generation. 3358.

1) Desdemona Lewis Smith, b. Jan. 26, 1908, m. Feb. 22, 1933, at Sylvania, O., John David Rosenbrock, b April 7, 1911. They live at Riga, Mich , which is their address.

1. David Earl Rosenbrock, b. Aug 12, 1936.

No. 3350. Fifth Generation. 2339.

6) Sarah Almeda Lewis, b. Mar 16, 1867, m. Feb. 25, 1890, Stacy Moore Lee, b. ——————, d June 26, 1911. Address: Pacific Junction, Ia.

1. Lewis Arle Lee, b. Jan. 10, 1891.
2. Cecil Lorey Lee, b Nov. 23, 1892.
3. Sarah Madge Lee, b. Aug 31, 1897.
4. Theodore Stacy Lee, b. June 4, 1904.
5. Kenneth Eugene Lee, b Sept. 26, 1907.

No. 3361. Fourth Generation. 1179.

1) Charles Wesley Landes, b ——————, m. Oct. 17, 1877, Lillie Root.
1. Nellie Landes, b —————, m. Dove
2. Hallie Landes, b ——————, m. Pittinger, at Albany, Ind.

No. 3362. Fifth Generation. 2339.

8) Aaron Zimri Lewis, b Mar 6, 1874, m. Effie Ryckman, b. Feb. 27, 1876. They live at Council Bluffs, Ia. Address: 2000 Madison Ave., Council Bluffs, Ia.

1. Alberta Lewis, b. Nov 29, 1903   No. 3363.
2. Pauline Lewis, b. Mar. 6, 1907.

No. 3363. Sixth Generation. 3362.

1) Alberta Lewis, b. Nov. 29, 1903, Council Bluffs, Ia., m. Louis C. Kelly.
1. Betty Lou Kelley, b. July 12, 1927.
2. Louis Kelley, Jr., b. June 2, 1931.

No. 3364. Fifth Generation. 2339.

5) John Franklin Lewis, b. April 7, 1864, d. Nov. 16, 1932, m. Aug., 1928, Mrs Mary (McGovern) Burgess. No children.

No. 3365. Fifth Generation. 2796.

1) Clinton Stauffer, b. ——————, m. Pacy Humpston. They live in Winchester, Va.

1. Ashly Stauffer, b. ——————.
2. —————— Stauffer, b. ——————.

No. 3366. Fifth Generation. 2693.

2) Harry Stauffer, b ——————, m Jane Grey. Address: Front Royal, Va.

No. 3367. Fifth Generation. 2555.

1) Harvey Nicholis Yoder, b May 5, 1889, m Nov 23, 1910, Eliza Newcomer, b. Dec. 17, 1888. Farmer and teacher. Mennonites   Address: Elkhart, Ind. Burial place at Olive Church near Wakarusa, Ind.

1. Paul Emerson Yoder, b June 4, 1914. No. 3368.
2. Merrell Jay Yoder, b June 4, 1916
3. Emma Elizabeth Yoder, b. Oct. 10, 1917.
4. David Willis Yoder, b. Mar 23, 1920
5. Ivan Bernet Yoder, b Dec 26, 1921.
6 Earl Lamar Yoder, b. Mar 13, 1925.

479

7. Miriam Naomi Yoder, b Oct. 26, 1927.
8. Carl Edward Yoder, b. Jan 11, 1932.

No. 3368. Sixth Generation. 3367.
1) Paul Emerson Yoder, b. June 4, 1914, m. Dec. 31, 1935, Ruth Burkholder.

No. 3369. Fifth Generation. 2556.
4) George V. Yoder, b. Aug. 12, 1893, d. Feb. 1, 1922, m. in 1914, Florence Mary Enders, b. Aug. 14, 1896   Mennonites.
1. Charles Leonard Yoder, b June 10, 1915.
2. Harold Devon Yoder, b Aug. 13, 1917.

No. 3370. Fifth Generation. 2556.
5) Forrest Anson Yoder, b. Oct. 3, 1895, m Feb. 27, 1919, Florence Bollinger, b. Aug. 30, 1899. Address. Mishawaka, Ind. Farmer.

No. 3371. Fifth Generation. 2555.
6) Clarence Earl Yoder, b Nov. 21, 1897, m Mar. 4, 1937, Alma Louise ————. Address: Yreka, Calif

No. 3372. Fifth Generation. 2556.
7) Mary Naomi Yoder, b. Oct. 24, 1900, m. Oct. 4, 1928, Clarence Smeltzer. Address: Wakarusa, Ind. Farmer. Mennonites.
1. Dale Eugene Smeltzer, b Aug. 25, 1930.
2. James Owen Smeltzer, b Mar. 17, 1932, d. next day.
3. Ralph Jay Smeltzer, b Aug. 2, 1933, d. May 4, 1937.
4. Glen Keith Smeltzer, b. May 26, 1935.
5. Malba Fay Smeltzer, b Oct 31, 1936

No. 3373. Fifth Generation. 2556.
8) Huber Austin Yoder, b July 14, 1903, m. Aug. 20, 1925, Laura Edith Thompson. Teacher. Mennonites. Address. Cleveland Ave., Elkhart, Ind
1. Wayne LaMar Yoder, b July 1, 1927.
2. Marjorie Eilene Yoder, b. Nov. 11, 1930.
3. Lorene Marie Yoder, b. April 18, 1933

No. 3374. Sixth Generation. 2537.
1) Rhoda Elizabeth Huber, b. Jan. 6, 1910, m. Oct. 6, 1934, Alpha Davis, at Goshen, Ind. Address: Terre Haute, Ind. Brethren Church.
1. Charles Norman Davis, b. Aug 19, 1935.
2. Sanford K. Davis, b. Sept. 19, 1937.

No. 3375. Sixth Generation. 2537.
2) Mary Henrietta Huber, b. Nov. 18, 1911, m. Dec. 1, 1933, Kenneth A. Miller, at Sturgis, Mich   Address: Detroit, Mich.
1. Robert William Miller, b. Jan. 25, 1935.

No. 3376. Fifth Generation. 3199.
1) Preston Senger, b ————, 1881, m. Lottie Armentrout. Address: Continental, O.
1. Verle Senger, b. ——————.
2. Alice Senger, b. ——————.
3. Walter Senger, b. ——————.
4. Homer Senger, b. ——————.
5. Marie Senger, b. ——————.

6. Wilber Senger, b. ———————
7. Lola Senger, b. ———————.
8. David Senger, b. ———————.

No. 3377. Fifth Generation. 3199.

2) Mary E Senger, b Feb. 23, 1883, m. Lawrence Prowant. Address: Flint, Mich., R. F. D , Beecher Rd
1. Ernest Prowant, b. ———————.
2. Alice Prowant, b. ———————.
3. Katie Prowant, b ———————.
4. Vernie Prowant, b. ———————.
5. Harvey Prowant, b. ———————.
6. Naomi Prowant, b. ———————.

No. 3378. Fifth Generation. 3199.

3) Bertie Senger, b. Jan 14, 1885, m. Anna McBee Address: Corlamas, Calif.
1. Anie Senger, b. ———————.
2. Lydia Senger, b. ———————.
3. Wilber Senger, b. ———————.
4. Retta Senger, b ———————

No. 3379. Fifth Generation. 3199.

4) Harry Senger, b July 26, 1887, m Mary James, who died. He was twice married afterwards. Address: Lawrenceville, Ill Children from first union.
1. Dorman Senger, b. ———————.
2. Raymond Senger, b. ———————.
3. Marie Senger, b. ———————.
4 Erma Senger, b ———————
5. Kenneth Senger, b. ———————.
6. Imogene Senger, b ———————.
7. Harry Senger, Jr , b. ———————.
8 Blanche Senger, b ———————.

No. 3380. Fifth Generation. 3199.

5) Viola Belle Llewellyn, b. June 21, 1890, m (1st) Runkle Barnhart. Separated. She married (2nd) Frederick Barnhart, brother of her first husband. Children from first husband
1. Forrest Barnhart, b ———————. No. 3381
2. Everett Barnhart, b. ———————.

No. 3381. Sixth Generation. 3380.

1) Forrest Barnhart, b ———————, m Ada ———————.
1. Donnie Barnhart, b ———————

No. 3382. Fifth Generation. 3199.

6) Hazel Verl Llewellyn, b. Oct 21, 1892, m. Frank Shaffer, b. Sept. 21, 1897. Divorced. She married (2nd) Cornelius Weagley, b. April 5, 1894. Address: 222 1st St., Lima, O. Burial in Salem cemetery near Elida, O. Issue from first union.
1. Noble Raymond Shaffer, b. 1910, d. Mar. 25, 1933.
2. Norma Josie Shaffer, b 1912, d July 24, 1933.
3. Beulah Alberta Shaffer, b July 13, 1914. No. 3383

No. 3383. Sixth Generation. 3392.

3) Beulah Alberta Shaffer, b July 13, 1914, m Howard Knapp. Address: Deshler, O.

1. Dickey Wayne Knapp, b Feb. 25, 1931.
2. Marjorie Dianna Knapp, b. Dec. 23, 1934.
3. Nancy Sue Knapp, b. Aug. 22, 1936

No. 3384. Fifth Generation. 3199.

7) Elnora Llewellyn, b Jan. 15, 1897, m Frederick Taylor. Address: Ft Wayne, Ind   No children

No. 3385. Fifth Generation. 2555.

1) John Henry Reedy, b. Oct 24, 1878, d. Aug 31, 1910, m. Sept. 27, 1906, Mabel C. Philips.

1. Charles B Reedy, b. July 2, 1907, d 1908
2. Elizabeth Reedy, b June 18, 1909.
3. Henry Calvin Reedy, b Mar. 15, 1911.

No. 3386. Fifth Generation. 2555.

2) George W. Reedy, b Jan 22, 1879, m. Dec. 11, 1920, Florence Brown.

1. Marguerite E. Reedy, b Oct. 6, 1921.
2. Ethel M. Reedy, b. May 6, 1923.
3. George F. Reedy, b Feb 24, 1925.
4. Edward H. Reedy, b Sept. 5, 1927.
5. Harry L. Reedy, b. Aug 9, 1929.
6. Harold F. Reedy, b. April 20, 1932.

No. 3387. Fifth Generation. 2555.

3) Jacob B. Reedy, b. Nov. 13, 1881, m. Oct. 8, 1913, Lillian Longsworth. No issue.

No. 3388. Fifth Generation. 2555.

5) Barbara F. Reedy, b. Dec. 9, 1885, m. Jan. 8, 1918, Bascome Montgomery. He died Feb. 2, 1931. Barbara married Sept. 26, 1931, Clarence L. Anderson. No issue reported.

No. 3389. Fifth Generation. 2555.

7) Ira F. Reedy, b. Nov. 21, 1895, m. July 1, 1921, Virginia Lincoln. Lieutenant on police force, Oakland, Calif.

1. Frances V. Reedy, b. April 8, 1922
2. Irene F. Reedy, b. Oct. 26, 1923.

No. 3390. Fifth Generation. 2555.

8) Ethel M. Reedy, b. June 18, 1898, m. Sept. 6, 1933, Charles L. Williams

1. Charles Williams, Jr., b. Aug. 31, 1934.
2. John K. Williams, b. Jan 1, 1936

No. 3391. Seventh Generation. 864.

2) Ruby Frances Brunk, b Dec. 12, 1911, Harrisonburg, Va., m. Jan. 27, 1935, Elmer R. Martin, of Greencastle, Pa   Mennonites.

No. 3392. Sixth Generation. 664.

3) Perry Elmer Shank, b Dec 15, 1882, m. Oct. 19, 1907, Loma Hostetler, b. Nov. 22, 1883, d. Mar 19, 1938 Address. Denbigh, Va   Orchardist. Mennonites.

1. Elvin Shank, b Sept 6, 1909   No. 3393
2 Malinda Catherine Shank, b. Sept. 22, 1914

No. 3393. Seventh Generation. 3392.

1) Elvin Shank, b. Sept. 6, 1909, m. Feb. 23, 1935, Blanche Rector, of Washington, D. C. They reside in Washington, D. C.

No. 3394. Sixth Generation. 654.

5) Cora E. Shank, b Mar. 13, 1887, m Feb. 2, 1912, Irvin King, b. Nov. 13, 1885. Address: Royersford, Pa Farmer Mennonites.
  1. Leona M. King, b. Jan 4, 1913, d. Jan. 10, 1925.
  2. Myron A. King, b. May 11, 1915.
  3. Tillman R. King, b July 24, 1917, d Oct. 12, 1931.
  4. Evelyn E King, b Nov. 28, 1919
  5. Aaron M. King, b June 26, 1922.
  6. Cora E. King, b May 15, 1925, twin.
  7. Clara E. King, b May 15, 1925, twin.
  8. Laura E King, b Feb 6, 1928
  9. Almeda E. King, b July 23, 1931.

No. 3395. Sixth Generation. 654.

7) Lewis D. Shank, b Mar. 25, 1894, m April 6, 1927, Thelma Lewis, b. May 10, 1906. Address: Brentwood, Md.
  1 Ronald Lewis Shank, b. Mar. 5, 1934.

No. 3396. Sixth Generation. 652.

11) Mary Virginia Shenk, b Dec 2, 1900, m. Dec. 5, 1936, Joseph Longacher. Address Oyster Point, Va
  1. Son, b Sept. —, 1938.

No. 3397. Seventh Generation. 665.

2) John Mark Shank, b. —————, m. Reba Heatwole of Harrisonburg, Va. Address: Reading, Pa.

No. 3393. Seventh Generation. 665.

3) Naomi Ruth Shank, b. —————, m. Jack Lawson of Hampton, Va. Address: Hampton, Va.
  1. Daughter, b in 1935

No. 3399. Seventh Generation. 665.

4) Ralph M. Shank, b —————, m. June 4, 1937, Bessie McCasky. They are under appointment as missionaries to Africa Reading, Pa., is their home address.

No. 3400. Sixth Generation. 670.

8) Martha May Shenk, b May 15, 1909, m. Aug. 13, 1935, Ralph E. Palmer, b June 24, 1903. Address: Denbigh, Va Railway employee. Mennonites.
  1. Margaret Louise Palmer, b. Mar. 17, 1935.

No. 3401. Fifth Generation. 2818.

1) Magdalena Bowers, b July 20, 1856, near Allentown, O., d. at Rockford, O., Nov 27, 1884 She married Albert Miller in 1878. They lived at Rockford, O.
  1. Ida Miller, b. 1880, d. 1903, at Rockford, O
  2. Earl Miller, b 1884 No. 3402.

No. 3402. Sixth Generation. 3401.

2) Earl Miller, b in 1884 at Rockford, O, m. Edith Brookhart. He lives at Albuquerque, New Mexico, where their children were all born.

1. Maxwell Miller, b. —————.
2. Kenneth Miller, b. —————.
3. Rowena Miller, b —————.
4. Helen Miller, b —————
5. June Miller, b. —————.
6 Floyd Miller, b. —————
7. Stanley Miller, b. —————.

No. 3403. Fifth Generation. 2818.

2) George W. Bowers, b Mar. 26, 1860, in Allen Co , O , m. in 1881 Annie E. Webb, b. Nov. 22, 1863, in Fayette Co., O Address: Convoy, O. Farmer in Van Wert Co., O , and Farmers Insurance Company Director. He resided in Van Wert Co., nearly all his life. Methodists
1. Jesse W. Bowers, b. Oct 15, 1882 No. 3404

No. 3404. Sixth Generation. 3403.

1) Jesse W Bowers, b. Oct. 15, 1882, in Van Wert Co , O , m Dec 20, 1903, Alby Leola Beck, b. Nov 30, 1885, in Van Wert Co., O Methodists Dr. Jesse W. Bowers, A.B., Sc.D , M D., is a surgeon He has been President of Indiana State Medical Board for fifteen years, President of Federation of State Medical Boards of the United States, Trustee of John Fletcher College, Ex-President of National Electric Medical Association, Commanding Officer, Lieutenant, Colonel Surgical Hospital No 30 United States Army Reserve He resides at Ft Wayne, Ind. Address: 418 to 426 Citizens Trust Building, Ft Wayne, Ind
1 Gah Theodore Bowers, b. May 20, 1905 No. 3405.
2 Ferne Bowers, b. Jan. 9, 1908. No. 3406

No. 3405. Seventh Generation. 3404.

1) Gah Theodore Bowers, b. May 20, 1905, in Van Wert Co., O , m May 4, 1930 Margaret A. Thurman, b. June 27, 1905, at Milton, Ind. Methodists Gah T. Bowers, B.S., M.D. Surgeon. He graduated from Electric Medical College, M.D., in 1928; he graduated from Ohio Northern University, B S , 1928; he graduated from Indiana University, M D., in 1929, he graduated from Indiana University, M.D., Cum Laude in 1930. Miss Thurman, his companion, graduated from Indianapolis, Ind. Methodist School for Nursing, Indianapolis, Ind Office address: 418-426 Citizens Trust Building, Ft Wayne, Ind.
1. George Wilbert Bowers, b. Feb 14, 1932, Ft Wayne, Ind.
2. Barbara Jean Bowers, b Oct 3, 1934, Ft. Wayne, Ind.

No. 3406. Seventh Generation. 3404.

2) Ferne Bowers, b. Jan 9, 1908, at Cincinnati, O., m. May 31, 1930, George A. McDowell, of Logansport, Ind., b Mar. 24, 1905 Ferne is a graduate of Mus. B. of Depauw University School of Music Mr McDowell is a graduate of Indiana University, B S., 1927, of Indiana University Medical Department, M D , 1930, and of Indiana University, Cum Laude, M D , 1931 He specialized in obstetrics and pediatrics. He resides in Ft Wayne, Ind Methodists. Office address 418-426 Citizens Trust Building, Ft. Wayne, Ind.
1. Richard Bowers McDowell, b April 8, 1931, Ft Wayne, Ind
2. Ann McDowell, b July, 1934, Ft Wayne, Ind

No. 3407. Fifth Generation. 2818.

3) Martha Jane Bowers, b Oct 20, 1861, at Convoy, O , m Oct 18, 1883, Peter E. Webb Address. Convoy, O.

484

1. Bess e C. Webb, b. April 29, 1884 No 3408.
2. Goldie C. Webb, b. Oct. 22, 1886. No. 3412.

No. 3408. Sixth Generation. 3407.
1) Bessie C. Webb, b. April 29, 1884, at Convoy, O., m. 1906, Jay Lare. Farmer at Convoy, O.
1. Eva Lare, b Aug 26, 1906 No 3409
2. Catherine Lare, b Aug 20, 1909 No. 3410
3. Donald Lare, b. Sept 9, 1913. No 3411.

No. 3409. Seventh Generation. 3408.
1) Eva Lare, b. Aug 26, 1906, Van Wert, O , m Feb. 13, 1925, Byron Showalter. Address. Van Wert, O , R 3.
1 Richard Showalter, b May 27, 1926, at Van Wert, O.
2 Byron Wayne Showalter, b Oct 24, 1930, at Van Wert, O.
3 Vivian Showalter, b Sept 5, 1931, at Van Wert, O.

No. 3410. Seventh Generation. 3408.
2) Catherine Lare, b. Aug 20, 1909, at Convoy, O , m June 30, 1928, Richard Wherry. Mechanic. Address Convoy, O.
1 Harold Wherry, b. Dec 22, 1931.

No. 3411. Seventh Generation. 3408.
3) Donald Lare, b. Sept. 9, 1913, at Convoy, O , m. Jan. 13, 1934, Rudy Fensler. Address: Convoy, O

No. 3412. Sixth Generation. 3407.
2) Goldie C. Webb, b Oct 22, 1886, at Convoy, O , m. John Van Gundy of Convoy, O. Address Albuquerque, New Mexico. Methodist Minister.
1. Gerald Van Gundy, b July 13, 1908
2 Carl Van Gundy, b. Oct 23, 1911. No. 3412¼.
3. Garnet Van Gundy, b July 30, 1914. No. 3412½.
4 Delmar Van Gundy, b Jan. 22, 1916

No. 3412¼. Seventh Generation. 3412.
2) Carl Van Gundy, b Oct 23, 1911, m in 1934, Margaret Russell. Address: Albuquerque, New Mexico.

No. 3412½. Seventh Generation. 3412.
3) Garnet Van Gundy, b. July 30, 1914, m Dec. 25, 1933, Delbert Jameson. Address: Albuquerque, New Mexico.

No. 3413. Fifth Generation. 2818.
4) Etta Bowers, b Sept. 20, 1863, near Van Wert, O , m. Ruell Putnam, b. Oct. 2, 1861. Address Rockford, O   Farmer.
1. Orvie Putnam, b Aug 8, 1888. No 3414
2. Ocie Putnam, b Nov. 18, 1890 No 3415.
3 Otie Putnam, b Nov 23, 1892 No. 3416

No. 3414. Sixth Generation. 3413.
1) Orvie Putnam, b Aug. 8, 1888, at Rockford, O , m June 10, 1920, Grace Baroff, b. July 29, 1893. Address Van Wert, O
1 Harold Robert Putnam, b. Nov. 4, 1921, Van Wert, O

No. 3415. Sixth Generation. 3413.
2) Ocie Putnam, b Nov 18, 1890, at Rockford, O , m. May 17, 1913, Carl Tracy. Address: Convoy, O. Salesman.

No. 3416. Sixth Generation. 3413.

3) Otie Putnam, b. Nov. 23, 1892, at Rockford, O , m Mar. 1, 1910, Chauncy Kilgore. Address: Convoy, O. Mechanic.

1. Altha Kilgore, b. Sept 29, 1912 No. 3417.
2. Marlın Kilgore, b. June 25, 1914. No. 3418

No. 3417. Seventh Generation. 3416.

1) Altha Kilgore, b. Sept 29, 1912, at Plymouth, Ind , was a graduate nurse at the Methodıst Hospıtal, Ft. Wayne, Ind She marrıed George Landes, assıstant manager, Vitreous Steel Corporation, Nappanee, Ind.

No. 3418. Seventh Generation. 3416.

2) Marlin K lgore, b June 25, 1914, at Convoy, O., m. Feb 19, 1934, Helen Gehres, of Convoy, O
1. Sondra Ann Kilgore, b. Jan 26, 1935.

No. 3419. Fifth Generation. 2819.

1) Ellen Bowers, b. June 10, 1867, Van Wert Co , O., m. May 17, 1930, Lewis Roebuck, of Columbia City, Ind No issue.

No. 3420. Fifth Generation. 2819.

2) Davıd Wesley Bowers, b. Jan 13, 1869, Van Wert Co., O , m Sept. 1, 1897, Louvilla E Jones, of Convoy, O Farmer and engineer.

1. Beatrıce Irene Bowers, b Nov. 12, 1899 Music teacher.
2. Harold Wert Bowers, b. Oct. 14, 1909. School teacher.

No. 3421. Fifth Generation. 2819.

5) Cora Bowers, b. Dec 28, 1874, Van Wert Co., O , m. Sept , 1897, Leo Wert. He died July 20, 1918, m.nıster ın the Chrıstian Church Address: La Fayette, O.

1. Ward Wert, b July, 1906. No. 3422.
2. Harold Wert, b. Oct 14, 1909 No. 3423

No. 3422. Sixth Generation. 3421.

1) Ward Wert, b. July, 1906, m. Helen Kromm
1. Wilma Jeane Wert, b Mar. 4, 1920
2. Mary Lou Wert, b Oct 29, 1922
3. Donna B. Wert, b. Oct. 12, 1928.

No. 3423. Sixth Generation. 3421.

2) Harold Wert, b Oct. 14, 1909, Van Wert Co., O., m. 1930, Florence Hicks. Address: Continental, O.

1. William Wert, b. ————, 1931.
2. Robert Wert, b. ————, 1933.
3. Marlyn Wert, b. ————, 1935.

No. 3424. Fifth Generation. 2819.

6) Albert Bowers, b. Jan. 12, 1878, Van Wert Co , O., m. Ethel Crites, of Convoy, O. They reside ın Lansıng, Mich.

1. Gertrude Bowers, b. Dec. 8, 1901 No. 3425.
2. Ralph Bowers, b Nov. 20, 1903.
3. Doyt Bowers, b. Aprıl 12, 1910. No. 3426

No. 3425. Sixth Generation. 3424.

1) Gertrude Bowers, b. Dec. 8, 1901, Van Wert Co., O , m. Aaron Watters. Address: Lansıng, Mıch. Mechanic.

1. Rodney Watters, b June —, 1920
2. Robert Watters, b. July —, 1922.
3. Doris Watters, b. Jan 3, 1923.

No. 3426. Sixth Generation. 3424.
3) Doyt Bowers, b. April 12, 1910, Van Wert Co., O., m. July 3, 1936, Marian Bowers. Mechanic at Lansing, Mich.

No. 3427. Sixth Generation. 2028.
1) Daniel William Link, b. Sept. 23, 1881, Augusta Co., Va., m. Aug. 23, 1903, Martha Jane Sheets, b Mar. 10, 1885 Address: Mt. Sidney, Va. Farmer. U. B. Church, Mt. P.sgah.
1. Angeline Catherine Link, b Dec. 31, 1905. No. 3428.
2. Elwood Ralph Link, b July 3, 1909. No 3429.
3. Irene Frances Link, b Oct 27, 1913

No. 3428. Seventh Generation. 3427.
1) Angeline Catherine Link, b. Dec. 31, 1905, m. Aug. 8, 1928, Joseph Lewis Wenger. Address: Staunton, Va.
1. Robert Lewis Wenger, b Jan 27, 1931.
2. Jennie Ellen Wenger, b. May 28, 1933.

No. 3429. Seventh Generation. 3427.
2) Elwood Ralph Link, b. July 3, 1909, m June 2, 1932, Mary Alexander. Address: Stuarts Draft, Va
1. Anna Jane Link, b. Mar. 15, 1933.
2. Bettie Lou Link, b June 7, 1934.
3. Joan Link, b. May 10, 1936.

No. 3430. Sixth Generation. 2028.
2) Elizabeth Catherine Link, b. Feb. 15, 1884, m. April 30, 1902, William E. Huffman. Address: Haymarket, Va.
1. Drusilla B. Huffman, b Feb 9, 1903. No. 3431.
2. Joseph Theodore Huffman, b. Nov. 27, 1906. No. 3432.
3. Frances Elaine Huffman, b. Aug. 22, 1909. No. 3433.
4. Hildreel Hawthorne Huffman, b. April 12, 1912. No. 3434.
5. Eunice Margaret Huffman, b. Dec 5, 1914.
6. Virginia Carroll Huffman, b. July 17, 1917.

No. 3431. Seventh Generation. 3430.
1) Drusilla B. Huffman, b Feb. 9, 1903, m. June 11, 1925, Warren E. Wright

No. 3432. Seventh Generation. 3430.
2) Joseph Theodore Huffman, b. Nov 27, 1906, m. Eva Perry, Sept. 12, 1931.
1. Bobby W.llis Huffman, b. Nov. 9, ——.

No. 3433. Seventh Generation. 3430.
3) Frances Elaine Huffman, b. Aug 22, 1909, m Clinton Dodd, Jan. 1, 1936.

No. 3434. Seventh Generation. 3430.
4) Hildreel Hawthorne Huffman, b April 12, 1912, m. July, 1931, Garfield Dawson
1. Jacquillin Dawson, b. —————.

No. 3435. Sixth Generation. 2028.
3) Clara Ellen Link, b. July 10, 1888, m. June 10, 1913, Charles W. Good. Address: Mt. Sidney, Va.

1. Martin Luther Good, b Mar. 17, 1915. No. 3436.
2. Daniel Good, b. Nov. 8, 1918.
3. Agnes Good, b. Nov. 8, 1925.
4. Charles Ivan Good, b. July 31, 1927.
5 Adele Good, b. June 13, 1929.

No. 3436. Seventh Generation. 3435.

1) Martin Luther Good, b. Mar. 17, 1915, m. Nov. 4, 1933, Martha Alice Alexander.

No. 3437. Sixth Generation. 2028.

4) Mary Martin Link, b May 17, 1893, m. Oct., 1913, Robert E. Hicklin. Address: Stuarts Draft, Va.
1. Sylvia Edward Hicklin, b Dec. 24, 1915

No. 3438. Seventh Generation. 1108.

2) Oliver D. Showalter, b. April 6, 1914, m Frances Miller, April 5, 1936 Address: Broadway, Va. Miller. Mennonites.
1. Gerald Wesley Showalter, b. Mar. 18, 1937.

No. 3439. Seventh Generation. 1108.

3) George A. Showalter, b. Sept 20, 1915, m. Nov. 23, 1935, Neva C. Payne, b. Oct. 26, 1916. Address: 2006 N. 13th St , Kansas City, Kans Armour Co., employee.

No. 3440. Fifth Generation. 2756.

4) Lydia E. Geil, b. Mar. 5, 1889, Rockingham Co , Va., m. Jan. 16, 1916, Warner J. Stearn, b. Nov 9, 1889. Address: Linville, Va. No children

No. 3441. Fifth Generation. 2756.

6) Jacob Clark Geil, b Jan 27, 1893, Rockingham Co., Va., m. Feb 7, 1923, Elsie Shobbrook, b Sept 20, 1901 Address: Hinsdale, Mont
1. Allen Newton Geil, b. Nov. 20, 1924.
2. Jackson Clark Geil, b Feb. 14, 1926.
3. Virginia Ruth Geil, b Mar. 10, 1927.
4. Laura Jean Geil, b. April 7, 1930.
5. Thomas Dick Geil, b. Sept. 24, 1933.

No. 3442. Fifth Generation. 2756.

8) Clinton Wenger Geil, b Feb 9, 1897, Rockingham Co , Va., m. April 10, 1919, Mary B. Bayliss, b in Lestershire, England, Feb 29, 1896. Address: Anaconda, Mont.
1 Billie Clinton Geil, b Jan. 16, 1928.
2. Philip Bayliss Geil, b. Nov. 14, 1930.
3. Mariam Geil, b. Dec. 23, 1933.

No. 3443. Fifth Generation. 2756.

9) David Newton Geil, b. Dec 12, 1898, Rockingham Co., Va , m. June 8, 1925, Frances Virginia Bazzel, b Oct 9, 1906. Address: Harrisonburg, Va.
1. Charles Stuart Geil, b. Jan. 6, 1928.
2. Robert Lyman Geil, b Nov. 30, 1935.

No. 3444. Fifth Generation. 2756.

11) Stuart Franklin Geil, b. Nov 24, 1900, m. May 11, 1935, Anna Pauline Liskey, b. Aug. 31, 1907. Address: Harrisonburg, Va.
1. Polly Stuart Geil, b Dec 30, 1936.

No. 3445. Fifth Generation. 2756.

12) Iva Rosa Geil, b. June 3, 1904, m Dec 21, 1930, George Hillis Bovington. Address: Seattle, Wash.

1. George Geil Bovington, b Aug 9, 1934.
2. Nancy Elizabeth Bovington, b April 9, 1937.

No. 3446. Sixth Generation. 2757.

1) Weltie Eugene Rhodes, b. Aug. 1, 1906, m. June 14, 1932, Minnie Pearl Deavers, b April 14, 1907.

1. Neancy Jean Deavers, b. June 8, 1934
2 Margie Lee Deavers, b. April 9, 1937.

No. 3447. Sixth Generation. 2757.

5) David James Rhodes, b May 16, 1913, m. Nov. 28, 1936, Mary Ellen Roadcap, b. Oct. 6, 1916

No. 3448. Sixth Generation. 188.

1) Eva Magdalena Breneman, b. May 4, 1905, m Oct 16, 1930, James Heighton Benson, b. Mar. 27, 1906

1. Katherine Luvernie Benson, b Oct. 16, 1933 (stillborn).
2. Phillis Douglas Benson, b. Sept 8, 1934.
3. Sylvia June Benson, b. Mar. 25, 1936
4. Virginia Mae Benson, b May 14, 1937.

No. 3449. Sixth Generation. 191.

1) Mary Elizabeth Crawn, b. Oct. 31, 1906, m Aug. 29, 1935, Rev. W. Boyd Bryant. Methodists.

No. 3450. Sixth Generation. 191.

2) Ruby Louise Crawn, b April 25, 1908, m. Jan. 16, 1937, Lawrence T. Hendrick.

No. 3451. Seventh Generation. 526.

1) Mildred Virginia Heatwole, b Feb. 26, 1913, m. Wade A. Kiracofe.
1. Lois Jean Kiracofe, b Sept 29, 1930.

No. 3452. Seventh Generation. 526.

2) Glen Owen Heatwole, b Feb. 28, 1914, m. Margaret V. Shiflett.

No. 3453. Seventh Generation. 526.

3) Hubert Alvin Heatwole, b Aug. 24, 1915, m. Blanche E. Boose of Pa.
1. Joyce Elizabeth Heatwole, b. June 19, 1936.

No. 3454. Seventh Generation. 574.

1) Grace Larue Good, b Mar 22, 1897, m. Dec. 4, 1919, Lewis Samuel Hartman, b. June 18, 1898. Address Dayton, Va

1. Harold Franklin Hartman, b. Dec. 21, 1921.
2. Ruth Louise Hartman, b Oct. 29, 1923.
3. Lewis Perry Hartman, b Oct. 28, 1925
4. Paul Samuel Hartman, b. Dec. 15, 1927.
5. Anna May Hartman, b. Dec. 29, 1931.
6. Rosalie Grace Hartman, b. Nov. 6, 1934.

No. 3455. Seventh Generation. 574.

2) Frank Rush Good, b. Dec. 16, 1899, m. Dec. 12, 1923, Stella Virginia Wenger, b. June 10, 1899, at Waynesboro, Va. Address: Dayton, Va.

1. Mary Grace Good, b. April 11, 1925.
2. Irene Amanda Good, b. Oct. 13, 1926

3. Margaret Evelyn Good, b Oct 16, 1928
4. Lewis Edwin Good, b. Mar. 29, 1930
5. Edith Marie Good, b Jan 12, 1933.

No. 3456. Seventh Generation. 574.

3) Oliver Lewis Good, b. Nov. 25, 1903, m June 3, 1927, Arline Rohrer, b. Sept. 16, 1908, near Dayton, Va. Address: Harrisonburg, Va.
1. Eunice Arline Good, b. Mar. 1, 1928.
2. Joseph Henry Good, b. Feb. 13, 1930.
3. Alice Grace Good, b. Jan. 30, 1932
4. Martha Anne Good, b April 28, 1934.
5. John Oliver Good, b. May 17, 1936.

No. 3457. Seventh Generation. 574.

4) Josie Irene Good, b. Oct. 7, 1907, m. Oct 7, 1930, Daniel W. Koogler, b. Sept. 12, 1906. Address: Harrisonburg, Va
1. Louise Katherine Koogler, b. Oct. 29, 1931.
2. Charles Good Koogler, b. Jan. 8, 1936.

No. 3458. Seventh Generation. 574.

5) Marion Samuel Good, b Feb. 27, 1913, m. Dec 18, 1935, Esther Martin, b. Jan. 27, 1915, at Dalton, O Address: Dayton, Va.
1. Howard Samuel Good, b. Oct. 16, 1936

No. 3459. Seventh Generation. 575.

2) Louetta J. Knisely, b. May 3, 1898, m. Nov. 17, 1925 John E. Koogler, b. Dec. 15, 1902. Address. Harrisonburg, Va., R. 1.
1. Rosella E Koogler, b. Nov. 1, 1927.
2. Ruth L. Koogler, b. Dec. 17, 1930.
3. Ervin L. Koogler, b. Dec. 15, 1934.

No. 3460. Seventh Generation. 575.

3) DeWitt F. Knisely, b. Aug 15, 1902, m. Feb. 18, 1933, Alda Shank, b. Feb. 22, 1906. Address: Dayton, Va.
1. Charles D. Knisely, b Jan. 31, 1934.
2. Anna Lee Knisely, b. June 23, 1935.
3. James L. Knisely, b. Jan. 30, 1937

No. 3451. Seventh Generation. 575.

4) Leonard F. Knisely, b. Dec 13, 1904, m June 20, 1934, Ruth Shank, b. June 9, 1912. Address. Hinton, Va.
1. Mary E Knisely, b. June 16, 1935.
2. Josie V. Knisely, b. Oct 3, 1936.

No. 3452. Seventh Generation. 575.

5) Lewis S. Knisely, b. Aug. 28, 1907, m Sept. 4, 1929, Elizabeth Koogler, b. Mar. 21, 1907. Address: Harrisonburg, Va.
1. Orpha A. Knisely, b. June 18, 1930.
2. Ellen R. Knisely, b. May 5, 1932.
3. Amos S. Knisely, b Jan 31, 1934.
4. Wilda G. Knisely, b Aug. 23, 1935.
5. Byard E. Knisely, b. June 18, 1937.

No. 3453. Seventh Generation. 575.

6) John R. Knisely, b. Sept 18, 1909, m. Feb 17, 1937, Amy Martin, b Sept. 3, 1911. Address: Dayton, Va

No. 3464. Seventh Generation. 576.

1) Irene M. Jones, b. Aug 12, 1902, m. Jan. 26, 1922, Robert R. Swartz. Address: Dayton, Va., R. 2.
1. Dwight F. Swartz, b. Jan. 14, 1924.
2. Mildred E. Swartz, b. Dec. 22, 1927.

No. 3455. Seventh Generation. 576.

2) Edna R. Jones, b Sept 2, 1906, m. May 7, 1930, John Harmon.
1. Shirley Belle Harmon, b. June 29, 1931.
2. Merlin David Harmon, b. Aug. 6, 1933.

No. 3466. Seventh Generation. 576.

3) Vada A. Jones, b. Aug 14, 1909, m. May 7, 1930, James T. Shank, b. Oct. 6, 1908. Mennonite. Minister Address: Mt. Crawford, Va.
1. James L. Shank, b. Jan 17, 1933.
2. Charles F. Shank, b Jan. 10, 1936.

No. 3457. Seventh Generation. 578.

1) Alma Marie Rhodes, b Dec 12, 1901, m June 5, 1935, Raymond Barnhart Shank. Address: Harrisonburg, Va.
1. Mildred Lorene Shank, b June 10, 1937.

No. 3468. Seventh Generation. 578.

2) Reuben Franklin Rhodes, b. July 14, 1913, m. Dec 26, 1935, Esther Priscilla Wenger. Address: Dayton, Va.
1 Elva Irene Rhodes, b. Nov. 5, 1936.

No. 3469. Sixth Generation. 2533.

1) Clarence W. Huber, b Aug. 30, 1902, m Mar. 1, 1925, Violet Ida Baker, b. Dec. 7, 1902. Address: South Boston, Va. Farmer. Mennonites.
1. Elizabeth Catherine Huber, b. Feb. 9, 1926.
2. Martha May Huber, b May 20, 1927.
3. Gertrude Viola Huber, b. Nov. 29, 1928
4. George Amos Huber, b. Dec. 27, 1929.
5. John Samuel Huber, b. Sept. 20, 1931.
6. Florence Esther Huber, b. Nov 2, 1933.
7. Lois Violet Huber, b July 19, 1935, d May 27, 1937.

No. 3470. Sixth Generation. 2533.

3) Ira J. Huber, b. Sept. —, 1915, m Nov. 8, 1936, Hannah Marie Heatwole. Address: Mt. Crawford, Va Mennonites

No. 3471. Sixth Generation. 1579.

3) Ida Belle Freske, b June 13, 1913, m. Sept., 1932, John Fritz Johnson, of Minneapolis, Minn He died Nov. 12, 1933. She married July 5, 1934, Orthyl Hildus Anderson, at Hudson, Wis. Address: Brownston, Minn.
1. Robert Edward Johnson, b. Oct. 10, 1933
   (From second union)
2. Joan Carol Anderson, b. Nov. 5, 1935.

No. 3472. Sixth Generation. 1579.

4) Stella Edell Freske, b April 29, 1915, m. Oct. 16, 1934, George Leroy Miller. Address· 1210½ 6th St., W. Minneapolis, Minn.
1. Florence Jeane Miller, b. Sept. 21, 1935.

No. 3473. Seventh Generation. 950.

1) Raymond Ercil Campbell, b. Aug 12, 1908, m June 8, 1932, Sarah Elizabeth Coffman, b. Sept 24, 1909, by Lewis Shank. Address Dayton, Va Farmer. Mennonites.

1. Raymond Ercil Campbell, Jr , b Mar 22, 1933.
2 Heber Coffman Campbell, b April 28, 1937.

No. 3474. Seventh Generation. 950.

2) Herman Samuel Campbell, b Mar 5, 1910, m June 30, 1931, Grace Mariah Shank, b. May 25, 1908, by Bishop Lewis Shank Address· Dayton, Va., R. 2. Mennonites.

1. Beverley Nell Campbell, b. April 16, 1933.

No. 3475. Seventh Generation. 950.

3) Edna Elizabeth Campbell, b Oct 7, 1911, m Nov. 26, 1929, Marvin Turner Kiser, by A. P. Heatwole Address· Stuarts Draft, Va. Mennonites.

1. Ray Daniel Kiser, b. Oct. 12, 1930.
2. Orvin Herman Kiser, b. May 17, 1932.

No. 3476. Seventh Generation. 950.

4) Thelma Frances Campbell, b Mar 1, 1913, m April 26, 1933, Oren Shank Kiser, b June 24, 1911, m. by Joseph R Driver. Address: Waynesboro, Va. Mennonites.

1. Melba Frances Kiser, b. Aug. 13, 1934
2 Norman Campbell Kiser, b Nov 25, 1935

No. 3477. Seventh Generation. 949.

3) Lola Elizabeth Parrot, b Aug 9, 1907, m Feb 9, 1927, Harvey Hill Smith.
1. Bettie Ann Smith, b Sept 28, 1928
2 Harvey Hill Smith, Jr., b April 1, 1935

No. 3478. Seventh Generation. 949.

4) Carl G Parrot, b Sept 20, 1912, m Jan. 2, 1932, Anna Newton Fielding
1. Margaret Elizabeth Parrot, b July 5, 1936.

No. 3479. Fifth Generation. 1836.

2) Owen Blaine Obaugh, b May 4, 1884, m April 23, 1906, Etha Williams.

No. 3480. Fifth Generation. 1836.

4) Elizabeth Beatrice Obaugh, b Mar 23, 1890, m May, 1909, Bell M. Harris.

No. 3431. Fifth Generation. 1836.

5) Mary Beulah Obaugh, b Jan 22, 1897, m. 1920, Ernest M East

No. 3482. Sixth Generation. 2386.

3) Alma V. Stemen, b. Feb. 16, 1897, near Elida, O , m. Goldie Holp.

No. 3483. Seventh Generation. 2405.

1) Henry Edwin Layman, b Feb 9, 1916, m June 30, 1937, Verdie Sheller, of Iowa.

No. 3484. Sixth Generation. 2747.

1) Joseph Earl Geil, b Jan. 17, 1892, near Edom, Va , m Ruth E Bauslog, of South English, Ia. Address: Gulfport, Miss. Mennonites

1. Dorothy Mae Geil, b Jan., 1920, at Nashville, Tenn.
2. Maida Allene Geil, b. Feb 12, 1926, at Gulfport, Miss.
3. J. Earlin Geil, b. Mar. 18, 1928, at Gulfport, Miss.

492

No. 3485. Sixth Generation. 2747.

2) Abraham Ward Geil, b Sept. 7, 1894, near Harrisonburg, Va, m. Nellie E. Smith, Sept. 10, 1919, of South English, Ia He died Nov. 2, 1933 Address· Gulfport, Miss. Mennonites.

1 Floyd Edwin Geil, b Sept. 3, 1920, Harper, Kans.
2. Beulah Fern Geil, b. Feb. 23, 1922, Gulfport, Miss.
3. Joseph Ward Geil, b. Mar. 9, 1925, Gulfport, Miss.
4. Ethel Darline Geil, b. Jan. 17, 1927, Gulfport, Miss.

No. 3486. Sixth Generation. 2747.

3) David Paul Geil, b. April 13, 1898, near Daphna, Va., m. Dec. 3, 1919, Cara E. White, at South English, Ia. Address: Gulfport, Miss. Mennonites

1. Clarence Wayne Geil, b. Sept. 10, 1921, Lyman, Miss.
2 David Paul Geil, Jr, b Mar 8, 1927, Hansboro, Miss.

No. 3487. Sixth Generation. 2747.

4) Jacob Clarence Geil, b Aug. 1, 1900, Broadway, Va, m. June 26, 1932, Beulah Nix, of Gulfport, Miss Address Gulfport, Miss. Mennonites

1. Jerry Lyman Geil, b. May 13, 1936, Gulfport, Miss.
2. Barbara Ann Geil, b July 6, 1937, Gulfport, Miss.

No. 3488. Sixth Generation. 2747.

5) Annie E Geil, b Oct 16, 1901, Harrisonburg, Va., m. Jan 1, 1923, Isaac E. Hershey, of La Junta, Colo. Address: Gulfport, Miss Mennonites.

1. Ralph Geil Hershey, b. Oct. 26, 1924, Gulfport, Miss.

No. 3489. Sixth Generation. 2747.

6) Maide Pearl Geil, b Feb 25, 1904, Harrisonburg, Va., m. April 8, 1923, Earl Carr of Zenda, Kans. Address Gulfport, Miss. Mennonites.

1. Gean David Carr, b Jan. 6, 1924, Hansford, Miss.
2 Bettie Earline Carr, b Aug 28, 1925, Gulfport, Miss.
3. Ruth Marie Carr, b Dec. 27, 1926, Gulfport, Miss.
4. Carol Louise Carr, b June 23, 1928, Gulfport, Miss.
5. Clara Ann Carr, b. Jan 1, 1931, Gulfport, Miss.
6 Virginia Pearl Carr, b. April 6, 1936, Gulfport, Miss.

No. 3490. Sixth Generation. 2749.

1) Paul Byron Wenger, b Nov 9, 1899, near Edom, Va., m. Bessie King, b Sept 3, 1907, of Gulfport, Miss Address Gulfport, Miss

1 Paul Byron Wenger, Jr, b June 2, 1929
2 Bettie Lou Wenger, b Nov. 8, 1931.
3. Charles Payton Wenger, b Oct 13, 1934, d Dec. 5, 1934
4. Catherine Rose Wenger, b April 30, 1935.

No. 3491. Sixth Generation. 2749.

2) Virgil Merl Wenger, b May 25, 1902, near Edom, Va., m Oct 25, 1922, Fielden Powers. Address Gray Eagle, Minn

1. Everett Morris Powers, b May 16, 1926
2. Gail Lorraine Powers, b July 15, 1930

No. 3492. Sixth Generation. 2749.

4) Rita Pearl Wenger, b Nov 23, 1908, at Brooklyn, Ia, m Jan 21, 1929, John Sherman Ross, b Dec 28, 1902 Address· Gulfport, Miss Mennonites

1. Richard Sherman Ross, b Oct. 21, 1929
2. Don Owen Ross, b Sept. 13, 1930.

No. 3493. Sixth Generation. 2749.

5) Viola Mae Wenger, b. Sept. 4, 1918, Genoa, Colo , m. Oct. 26, 1936, Milton E. Berkey.

1. Vera Ellen Berkey, b. Mar. 12, 1937.

No. 3494. Sixth Generation. 2750.

1) Russell B. Wenger, b April 24, 1900, Linville, Va , m. April 24, 1922, Edith Ross, b April 3, 1895 Address: Gulfport, Miss. Farmer. Mennonites.

1. Ruby Lee Wenger, b. Feb. 3, 1923.
2. Edna Mae Wenger, b. Mar. 16, 1926

No. 3495. Sixth Generation. 2750.

3) Roy G. Wenger, b. Nov 19, 1906, at Brooklyn, Ia., m 1930, Thelma Palmer. He is with the Skelly Oil Co , Harper, Kans

1. Barbara Dean Wenger, b. Dec. 23, 1931.
2 Virginia Lee Wenger, b. Sept 3, 1932.
3. Betty Lou Wenger, b May 20, 1934

No. 3495. Sixth Generation. 2750.

4) Lois V. Wenger, b April 4, 1911, at Brooklyn, Ia., m. 1932, Leland Bowden, of Gulfport, Miss. Address: Harper, Kans.

1. Roy Leland Bowden, b Jan. 2, 1934

No. 3497. Sixth Generation. 2750.

7) Mabel A. Wenger, b. Feb. 6, 1914, at Brooklyn, Ia., m 1935, Ira Morgan, at Harper, Kans Address: Waldron, Kans.

No. 3498. Sixth Generation. 2751.

1) James Harold Dutro, b. Oct 5, 1903, at Brooklyn, Ia., m. June 1, 1924, Vanetia Alice Meeker. He is distributor for the O K. Rubber Welding Machine in Idaho, Oregon, and Washington. He also operates his own tire shop at 115-14 Ave., South, Nampa, Ida Church of Christ.

1. Phillis Anetia Dutro, b. June 24, 1926, d. Dec. —, 1936.
2. Rollin Lloyd Dutro, b. Aug 19, 1928.
3 Rodney Leland Dutro, b. May 19, 1930

No. 3499. Sixth Generation. 2751.

2) Edna Muriel Dutro, b. Jan. 2, 1907, at Brooklyn, Ia., m. April 18, 1926, John Nelson Hauson. They are both ministers and are living at 228 N. Frout St., Mankato, Minn.

1. Fern Rae Hauson, b Jan. 9, 1927.
2. Harold Franklyn Hauson, b Jan. 22, 1929.

No. 3500. Sixth Generation. 2751.

3) Martin Lloyd Dutro, b May 9, 1908, at Brooklyn, Ia , m Mar. 10, 1928, Erma Ernesta Chapman, at Muscatine, Ia He is United Brethren Minister, living at Olin, Ia. No children.

No. 3501. Sixth Generation. 2751.

4) Emma Florence Dutro, b July 5, 1911, Brooklyn, Ia., m. Jan. 9, 1932, Frederick William Lange, at Muscatine, Ia. United Brethren.

1. Donna Delores Lange, b. Aug 25, 1932

No. 3502. Fifth Generation. 2746.

8) Anna Pearl Wenger, b Aug. 4, 1886, near Daphna, Va , m Dec 20, 1911, Bernard E. Sheets. Address. Mt Sidney, Va United Brethren.

1. Joseph Howard Sheets, b Nov. 11, 1912. No. 3503.
2. Bernard Claude Sheets, b. July 13, 1914.
3. Laura Pearl Sheets, b. Feb. 5, 1917.
4. Lois Virginia Sheets, b. July 25, 1919.
5. Charlotte May Sheets, b. Oct. 1, 1923.
6. Evelyn Wenger Sheets, b. May 22, 1926
7. Beulah Chloe Sheets, b. Aug. 29, 1928.

No. 3503. Sixth Generation. 3502.

1) Joseph Howard Sheets, b. Nov. 11, 1912, near Mt. Sidney, Va., m. Nov. 10, 1936, Pauletta How. Address: Bayard, W. Va. United Brethren Minister.

No. 3504. Fifth Generation. 2745.

9) Owen Jacob Wenger, b. Jan. 31, 1888, near Daphna, Va., d. Feb. 27, 1926, at Brooklyn, Ia , m. Minnie M Doty, b May 28, 1889, in Brooklyn, Ia.   He was married Aug. 16, 1910.
1 Alvin R. Wenger, b. Dec. 25, 1911
2. Owen D. Wenger, b. May 20, 1914
3. Laura E. Wenger, b Jan 31, 1919.
4 Ruth A. Wenger, b. Sept 21, 1922.

No. 3505. Fifth Generation. 2746.

10) Ivan Marion Wenger, b Dec. 22, 1898, Daphna, Va , m. Nannie Ray Pence.
1 Joe Lynwood Wenger, b Aug. 16, 1926.

No. 3506. Fifth Generation. 2745.

11) Josie Pauline Wenger, b Feb. 22, 1901, Daphna, Va., m. 1922, Wilson Penn ngton. He died O:t., 1923.
1. Edith Loraine Pennington, b Aug 16, 1923.

No. 3507. Fifth Generation. 2746.

12) Burtrom Brown Wenger, b. April 16, 1903, Daphna, Va., m. June 23, 1933, Bertha Carnell Shifflett, b. Sept. 17, 1910
1. Howard William Wenger, b. July 8, 1934.
2. Nancy Jane Wenger, b. Jan. 29, 1937.

No. 3503. Sixth Generation. 1573.

3) Earl Barton Alexander, b. June 10, 1907, m. Aug. 17, 1936, Madelyn Martha Williksen, of Dell Rapids, S Dak Address. Gordon, Wis.
1 Wanda Marie Alexander, b July 19, 1937, at Ashland, Wis.

No. 3509. Fourth Generation. 41.

1) El,zabeth Ann Woodell, b Oct. 19, 1853, near Sangersville, Va., d. Aug. 29, 1934, m Dec. 30, 1874, at their home near Sangersville, Va , Samuel Dalhouse Jones, b May 15, 1869, d June 4, 1924 Buried in the Cuba, Ill., cemetery. United Brethren and Methodist They live at Cuba, Ill.
1. William Howard Jones, b. Nov. 24, 1875 No 3510.
2 Sarah E. (Bessie) Jones, b Dec 15, 1877, d Oct. 17, 1886.
3. Minnie Louella Jones, b Aug 16, 1879. No 3513.
4. Alice Virginia Jones, b. June 18, 1881. No 3516
5. Rheba Marie Jones, b. Mar. 14, 1894. No. 3521.

No. 3510. Fifth Generation. 3509.

1) William Howard Jones, b Nov 24, 1875, m. Dec 29, 1898, at Ipava, Ill., Sadie Hammond, b. Feb. 10, 1878 Address: Lewistown, Ill, R F. D.

1. Harold Dwayne Jones, b. Feb. 8, 1900. No 3511
2. Ila Olive Jones, b. April 6, 1902. No. 3512.
3. Maurice Howard Jones, b. Mar. 18, 1910.

No. 3511. Sixth Generation. 3510.

1) Harold Dwayne Jones, b Feb. 8, 1900, m. Peoria, Ill, April 8, 1927, Vada Carver, b. June 10, 1900. Mr. Jones died June 14, 1934; Mrs. Jones d. Aug. 1, 1934.

No. 3512. Sixth Generation. 3510.

2) Ila Olive Jones, b. April 6, 1902, m Sept 24, 1922, at Carthage, Ill., to Floyd Danner, b Dec. 24, 1901. Address. 345 Thompson Court, Canton, Ill.
1. Richard Lee Danner, b May 11, 1929

No. 3513. Fifth Generation. 3509.

3) Minnie Louella Jones, b. Aug 16, 1879, d Oct 17, 1935, m. April 8, 1903, Abraham Lincoln Yarnell. He died Nov. 30, 1934.
1. Irma Virginia Yarnell, b. Jan. 19, 1907. No. 3514.
2. Mildred Bernadine Yarnell, b Oct. 8, 1913. No 3515.

No. 3514. Sixth Generation. 3513.

1) Irma Virginia Yarnell, b. Jan. 19, 1879, m. Sept. 1, 1926, at Pekin, Ill., Voyle Johnathan Petri, b. Aug. 26, 1907. Address: 1201 S. 5th St., Pekin, Ill.

No. 3515. Sixth Generation. 3513.

2) Mildred Bernadine Yarnell, b Oct. 8, 1913, m Jan., 1935, Fretz Hugo Simon, b. May, 1911. Address: 6th St , Pekin, Ill

No. 3516. Fifth Generation. 3509.

4) Alice Virginia Jones, b. June 18, 1881, at Parnassus, Va., m. Jan. 28, 1903, Alvin Smith, b. Feb. 10, 1873 Address: 1042 East Center St., Bellflower, Calif.
1. Esther Elizabeth Smith, b. Oct 19, 1903. No. 3517.
2. Ruth Marie Smith, b. Jan. 15, 1905. No. 3518.
3. Mina Louella Smith, b July 27, 1906.
4. Alma Virginia Smith, b June 3, 1908. No. 3519.
5. Barbara Mae Smith, b May 25, 1910. No. 3520.
6. Howard Alvin Smith, b. June 17, 1912.
7. Maralee Smith, b. June 13, 1914
8. Earl Dwayne Smith, b. Aug 30, 1918.

No. 3517. Sixth Generation. 3516.

1) Esther Elizabeth Smith, b. Oct 19, 1903, m. Gerald Woods, b Feb. 27, 1902. Address: 675 Moline Ave., Long Beach, Calif.
1. Barbara Jean Woods, b. —————.

No. 3518. Sixth Generation. 3516.

2) Ruth Marie Smith, b. Jan. 15, 1905, m. Glen O. Pease.
1. Janet Virginia Pease, b. April 22, 1936.

No. 3519. Sixth Generation. 3516.

4) Alma Virginia Smith, b. June 3, 1908, m at Albuquerque, New Mexico, Robert C. Hopkins, Nov 11, 1933.

No. 3520. Sixth Generation. 3516.

5) Barbara Mae Smith, b. May 25, 1910, m Arthur Loew

No. 3521. Fifth Generation. 3509.

5) Reba Marie Jones, b Mar. 14, 1894, m Sept 15, 1918, Charles William Chaplan, b. Aug 18, 1896 Address. Lewistown, Ill.

1. Iris Onalee Chaplan, b. Feb. 10, 1925.

No. 3522. Fourth Generation. 41.

2) Stewart Irvin Woodell, b Dec 28, 1855, near Mt. Solon, Va., d. Nov. 26, 1926, m Emma Swearinger Farmer. United Brethren. Burial in Greenwood cemetery, Canton, Ill

1. Elgin Bruce Woodell, b ——————— No. 3523
2. Marvin Earl Woodell, b ——————— No 3524
3. Artie Fern Woodell, b. ——————— No 3525
4. Byron Mead Woodell, b ———————.
5. Lois Esther Woodell, b ———————, deceased.
6 Maud Evelyn Woodell, b ——————— No 3525¼.
7. Leathe Mildred Woodell, b. ———————. No 3526
8 Paul Kenneth Woodell, b ———————. No 3527.
9 Hugh Harrison Woodell, b ———————
10. Frances Pearl Woodell, b ——————— No. 3528.

No. 3523. Fifth Generation. 3522.

1) Elgin Bruce Woodell, b ———————, m. Mabel ———————. Address: Cuba, Ill

1. Lois Woodell, b ———————
2 Milburn Woodell, b ———————
3. Rose Woodell, b ———————
4. Doris Woodell, b ———————
5. Lucile Woodell, b ———————.
6. Junior Woodell, b ———————.

No. 3524. Fifth Generation. 3522.

2) Marvin Earl Woodell, b ———————, m Sadie Bishop. Address 4241 Ravenwood Ave., St Louis, Mo

No. 3525. Fifth Generation. 3522.

3) Artie Fern Woodell, b ———————, m Philip Burgett Address: 303 N 7th Ave., Canton, Ill.

No. 3525¼. Fifth Generation. 3522.

6) Maude Evelyn Woodell, b. ———————, m Cecil Bruce Shryock.

1. Dennis William Shryock, b ———————
2. Leland Byron Shryock, b ———————

No. 3526. Fifth Generation. 3522.

7) Leathe Mildred Woodell, b ———————, m ——————— Mills.

1. Bettie Lee Mills, b. ———————.
2. Betty Mills, b ———————
3. Leathe Mills, b ———————.

No. 3527. Fifth Generation. 3522.

8) Paul Kenneth Woodell, b ———————, m ——————— They have two children.

No. 3528. Fifth Generation. 3522.

10) Frances Pearl Woodell, b ———————, m (1st) ——————— Slack; m. (2nd) ——————— Randall. They have two children

3) Margaret Jane Woodell, b. April 11, 1857, at Mt. Solon, Va , d. Oct 21, 1913, buried at Cuba, Ill , m George Caddell Bruce, b. in Edinburg, Scotland, Jan. 22, 1829. They lived at Staunton, Va Mr Bruce was buried in Hebron cemetery, Staunton, Va.

    1. Kenny Irvin Bruce, b. —————— No 3530
    2. George Caddell Bruce, b Oct 9, 1895 No 3532
    3. Ada Bruce, b. Sept 1, 1887, Staunton, Va. No. 3533.
    4. Reba Bruce, b. July 3, 1894, Staunton, Va. No. 3534
    5. Irma Bruce, b. Nov. 3, 1898 No. 3535.

No. 3530. Fifth Generation. 3529.

1) Kenny Irvin Bruce, b ——————, m Gordie West Dever   Address: Akron, O.

    1. Joselin Dever, b. ——————. No. 3531.
    2. Clyde West Dever, b ——————, m , has a child
    3. Elizabeth Dever, b. ——————
    4. Ruth Dever, b. ——————
    5. Denver Dever, b ——————.

No. 3531. Sixth Generation. 3530.

1) Joselin Dever, b. ——————, m. Bingham Blovis
    1. Juanita Blovis, b. ——————.
    2. Gwendlyn Blovis, b. ——————.

No. 3532. Fifth Generation. 3529.

2) George Caddell Bruce, Jr , b Oct 9, 1895, Staunton, Va , m Jane Ellen Ricker, b. Nov. 14, 1895, Bideford, Me. Address. 508 Park Ave., West Princeton, Ill. Jeweler and watchmaker. Burial at Princeton, Ill

    1. Elliott Robert Bruce, b Aug. 21, 1918, Pontiac, Ill
    2. George Caddell Bruce, Jr , b. April 6, 1921, Pontiac, Ill
    3. Laura Jane Bruce, b Feb 27, 1927, d. April 29, 1930.

No. 3533. Fifth Generation. 3529.

3) Ada Bruce, b at Staunton, Va., Sept 1, 1887, d. Jan. 28, 1920. Buried at Cuba, Ill She married Edd Shotts They lived in Chicago, Ill.

No. 3534. Fifth Generation. 3529.

4) Reba Bruce, b. July 3, 1894, at Staunton, Va , m. Charles M. Browning, June 19, 1910, Richwood, W Va Presbyterians Registered Nurse. Address: 1529 3rd Ave., Apt. 2, Huntington, W. Va

    1. James Ralph Browning, b Aug. 6, 1914.
    2. Bruce Browning, b. Nov. 5, 1916. Catholic.

No. 3535. Fifth Generation. 3529.

5) Irma Bruce, b. Nov. 3, 1898, at Staunton, Va., m. Karl Joseph Lamoreaux. Address: 923 N. Grant St., Bay City, Mich.

    1. George Ward Lamoreaux, b. ——————.
    2. Karl Joseph Lamoreaux, Jr., b. ——————.

No. 3536. Fourth Generation. 41.

4) John Baldwin Woodell, b Feb. 18, 1861, at Mt Solon, Va , m. Minnie Quindora Troyer, b. Dec. 21, 1873 They were m. Nov. 19, 1891, at Hebron Church school, Augusta Co., Va. Address: 1001 Hamilton St , Pekin, Ill. Civil engineer.

1. Ethel Virginia Woodell, b Feb 15, 1893 No. 3537
2. Willa Clark Woodell, b Jan. 15, 1895 No 3538
3. Halla Baldwin Woodell, b Nov 12, 1896 No 3539.
4. Lena Elizabeth Woodell, b May 18, 1898. No. 3540.

No. 3537. Fifth Generation. 3536.

1) Ethel Virginia Woodell, b Feb. 15, 1893, Staunton, Va , m. at Pekin, Ill., Aug 3, 1920, Herbert Haslem, b. June 4, 1894, at Langshire, England. Address: 304 W. Main St., Havanna, Ill

1. Beverly June Haslem, b. June 20, 1929.
2. John Robert Haslem, b. June 20, 1930

No. 3538. Fifth Generation. 3536.

2) Willa Clark Woodell, b Jan. 15, 1895, Plunketsville, Va , m. at Beverly Hills, Chicago, by Rev. Carpenter, Feb. 18, 1930, Noah Herbert Ricker, b. Feb. 18, 1897, at Boston, Mass. Address: 1208 N. Main, Pontiac, Ill.

No. 3539. Fifth Generation. 3536.

3) Halla Baldwin Woodell, b Nov 12, 1896, at Peoria, Ill , by Rev. Shaw, First M. E. Church, Rowena Margarette Butler, b. Aug. 22, 1897 Address: 1109 South 6th St , Pekin, Ill.

1 Edward Butler Woodell, b Mar. 9, 1921, Manita, Ill
2 Phyllis Jean Woodell, b Dec 26, 1923, Pekin, Ill.
3 Robert Howell Woodell, b Feb 19, 1925, Pekin, Ill.

No. 3540. Fifth Generation. 3536.

4) Lena Elizabeth Woodell, b. May 18, 1898, m. at Ottawa, Ill , June 28, 1922, Von Eertmoed, b July 2, 1900, at Pekin, Ill Address: 201 Amanda St., Pekin, Ill

1 Lenora Mae Eertmoed, b May 3, 1923, Pekin, Ill.

No. 3541. Fourth Generation. 41.

5) Mary Catherine Woodell, b Nov 22, 1863, Mt Solon, Va , m Sept. 7, 1893, at Bridgewater, Va , by Rev John Click, Robert H Harris, b April 5, 1863. Address Lewistown, Ill Christian Science. No issue

No. 3542. Fourth Generation. 41.

6) William Howard Lee Woodell, b Aug 4, 1866, Mt Solon, Va , m. Lula Rusmisel, b ————————. Farmer and minister Address: Mt. Solon, Va.

1. Elmer Woodell, b ——————— No 3543
2. William I Woodell, b. —————— No 3544
3. Marie Woodell, b ——————— No. 3545
4 Clara Woodell, b ———————. No. 3546.
5. Edgar Woodell, b ———————.
6. Paul Woodell, b ———————
7. Samuel Woodell, b ———————.
8. Mary Woodell, b ———————.
9. Earl Woodell, b. ———————.
10 Wright Woodell, b. ———————.

No. 3543. Fifth Generation. 3542.

1) Elmer Woodell, b ————————, m ———————— Address: Mt Solon, Va.
1 Eldon Woodell, b ——————
2 Irvin Woodell, b ———————.

499

No. 3544. Fifth Generation. 3542.

2) William I. Woodell, b ————, m Gladys ————. Address· Mt Solon, Va.
   1. William Woodell, Jr, b. ————

No. 3545. Fifth Generation. 3542.

3) Marie Woodell, b ————, m Oliver Tombs. Address: Mt. Solon, Va
   1. Olin Tombs, b ————
   2. Leroy Tombs, b ————.

No. 3546. Fifth Generation. 3542.

4) Clara Woodell, b. ————, m Charles Nelson. Address Mt Solon, Va.

No. 3547. Fourth Generation. 41.

7) James Harrison Woodell, b. Sept 11, 1869, Mt Solon, Va, m Frances Burr in N. C. He is president and director of Wisconsin College of Music Address: Stowel Ave., Milwaukee, Wis. Christian Science.
   1. Charles Burr Woodell, b. ————.

No. 3543. Fourth Generation. 41.

8) Virginia Ida Woodell, b. Mar 2, 1874, Mt. Solon, Va, m. Aug 9, 1894, at their home in Augusta Co, Va, William Dent Clark, b Feb. 12, 1867. Farmer. Methodists. Address· Cuba, Ill., R. 1. Burial place at Cuba, Ill.
   1. Lavell Clark, b. June 26, 1895, d Sept 22, 1901
   2. Odessa Orlean Clark, b Oct. 18, 1896 No 3549.
   3. Alvin Howard Clark, b Jan 16, 1899. No 3550
   4. Oren Earl Clark, b April 25, 1903 No. 3551.

No. 3549. Fifth Generation. 3548.

2) Odessa Orlean Clark, b Oct 18, 1896, at Lewistown, Ill., m. at Beardston, Ill., Aug 31, 1916, M. E Church by Rev Byron, Guy Philip Taylor, b. Aug 25, 1895. Address: Center, Ill., R. 6.
   1. Charles Edward Taylor, b April 8, 1898, d same day.
   2. Alberta Mae Taylor, b Oct 18, 1926, at Canton, Ill

No. 3550. Fifth Generation. 3543.

3) Alvin Howard Clark, b. Jan. 16, 1899, at Lewistown, Ill., m. April 5, 1931, at Beverly Hills, Chicago, Ill, by Rev Carpenter, Marion Katherine Burmaster, b. June 14, 1907. Medical doctor at Elmwood, Ill
   1. William Roger Clark, b Aug. 4, 1932, Canton, Ill.

No. 3551. Fifth Generation. 3548.

4) Oren Earl Clark, b April 25, 1903, at Cuba, Ill, m Sept 17, 1925, at Carthage, Ill, Marjorie Louise Thomas, b Aug. 12, 1907, at Canton, Ill. Address: Cuba, Ill.
   1. Lawrence Kent Clark, b. Oct 24, 1926, Canton, Ill.

No. 3552. Seventh Generation. 1476.

2) Nellie Elizabeth Mundy, b April 13, 1909, m June 21, 1931, Mark Raymond Wampler, b. Sept 12, 1907 Address: Harrisonburg, Va. Merchant. Church of the Brethren.
   1. Jerry Mundy Wampler, b May 21, 1937.

No. 3553. Seventh Generation. 1476.

3) D Clement Mundy, b June 4, 1911, m Jan. 1, 1934, Leona Frances Miller, b. Nov. 22, 1913. Address Harrisonburg, Va Church of the Brethren. Laborer.
1. DeWayne Page Mundy, b April 16, 1935.

No. 3554. Seventh Generation. 1476.

4) Avis Rosaline Mundy, b Jan. 21, 1914, m. Sept 2, 1936, George Wilson Swartz, b. Mar 21, 1914 Teacher Church of the Brethren. Address: Harrisonburg, Va.

No. 3555. Fifth Generation. 2772.

4) Owen Wade Andes, b Feb. 27, 1891, m. Aug. 30, 1922, Carrie A. Senger, b. Mar. 29, 1891. Address. Harrisonburg, Va Mechanic. Christian Church.
1. Earline Evelyn Andes, b. Aug 20, 1925
2. Garnet Senger Andes, b April 5, 1927.

No. 3556. Fifth Generation. 2752.

1) Oscar E. Wenger, b June 19, 1881, near Edom, Va, m. Nov. 9, 1905, Bessie P. Heatwole, b July 7, 1881 Address· Linville, Va. Farmer Mail carrier. Mennonites.
1. Raymond H Wenger, b Feb 2, 1907 No 3557
2. Marvin I. Wenger, b Mar 23, 1911, d same day
3 Linden M. Wenger, b Dec 26, 1912
4. Mildred G. Wenger, b Sept 21, 1916
5. Edith V. Wenger, b April 2, 1919

No. 3557. Sixth Generation. 3556.

1) Raymond H. Wenger, b Feb 2, 1907, m. June 25, 1932, Fannie Harkins, b. Oct. 2, 1904, near Lancaster, Pa.
1. Elizabeth Ann Wenger, b Jan. 28, 1934.

No. 3558. Fifth Generation. 2752.

4) Isaac Luther Wenger, b. Oct 4, 1885, near Edom, Va., m. Mae Areheart of Timberville, Va Presbyterians. Farmer and retired mail carrier.
1. Helen Virginia Wenger, b ——————.
2. Marjorie Elizabeth Wenger, b ——————. No. 3559.
3. Isaac Luther Wenger, Jr, b. ——————.
4. Dorsey Robert Wenger, b. ——————.
5. Owen Panton Wenger, b. ——————, d. at three months.

No. 3559. Sixth Generation. 3558.

2) Marjorie Wenger, b ——————, m. Heath Woolworth.

No. 3560. Fifth Generation. 2752.

11) Perry Gabriel Wenger, b. Nov. 18, 1894, near Edom, Va., m. Nov. 9, 1910, Chloe Mae Logan, b Dec 1, 1900. He is business manager of the Shenandoah Mfg Co., at Harrisonburg, Va Brethren. Address: Harrisonburg, Va.
1. George Logan Wenger, b Dec. 5, 1929.
2. Charles Logan Wenger, b July 18, 1935.

No. 3561. Fifth Generation. 2752.

12) John Robert Wenger, b. Feb 2, 1896, near Edom, Va, m. May 22, 1921, Berthy M. Eby, b Dec 10, 1897, d. Mar 2, 1922. Buried at Lindale Mennonite Church He married (2nd) April 21, 1928, Dorothy Mellinger, b. Sept 21, 1903. He is a farmer and lives on the Old Homestead near Edom, Va. Address: Linville, Va. Mennonites.

1. Evelyn Mellinger Wenger, b. June 9, 1929.
2. John Robert Wenger, Jr., b. Mar. 1, 1931.
3. Joanna Elizabeth Wenger, b Sept 22, 1933.
4. Margaret Alice Wenger, b April 11, 1935.
5. Emily Susanna Wenger, b. Feb. 20, 1937.

No. 3562. Fifth Generation. 2752.

13) Clara Alma Wenger, b. July 21, 1899, near Edom, Va., m. Aug 24, 1924, Raymond J. Shenk, b July 31, 1896. Carpenter Mennonite Minister. Address: 5 Calvin St., Brentwood, Md.
1. Doris Jean Shenk, b Jan 14, 1926
2. Raymond Jacob Shenk, b Nov 30, 1927.
3. Harold Leon Shenk, b. Dec. 14, 1928
4. Clarene Virginia Shenk, b July 5, 1932

No. 3563. Fifth Generation. 2752.

15) Lucy Blanche Wenger, b. Nov 4, 1902, near Edom, Va , m. Dec 8, 1926, Jacob Andrew Shenk, b Feb 17, 1900 Poultryman Owner of Shenk Electric Hatchery at Harrisonburg, Va.
1. Jacob Paul Shenk, b Jan 7, 1931
2. James Allen Shenk, b. Mar 3, 1934.

No. 3564. Fifth Generation. 2752.

5) Homer David Wenger, b. Dec. 10, 1886, near Edom, Va , m. Dec. 8, 1914, Velma Effie Cook, b April 4, 1891 Farmer Mennonites. Address: South English, Ia.
1. Harry Jacob Wenger, b Jan 2, 1916.
2. Wayne Justein Wenger, b Oct 21, 1919.
3. Wilma Elene Wenger, b Mar 11, 1924.

No. 3565. Fifth Generation. 2753.

5) John David Wenger, b Mar 2, 1889, near Edom, Va., m. April 12, 1916, Nora Elizabeth Bowman, b. Feb 7, 1886 Address: Glidden, Ia Farmer.
1. Harold Everett Wenger, b. April 3, 1917

No. 3566. Sixth Generation. 2768.

1) Rachel Wenger Faught, b Sept 26, 1917, m. May 27, 1933, David A. Reed. Methodist and Lutheran.
1. Stanley David Reed, b. Nov. 14, 1935.
2. Ellen Dale Reed, b. Aug. 23, 1937.

No. 3567. Sixth Generation. 2770.

1) Leona Fay Hill, b Aug 18, 1912, m. April 7, 1933, William Moyer.
1. Shirley Mae Moyer, b Sept 4, 1934

No. 3568. Sixth Generation. 2771.

1) Lawrence Wenger, b Sept. 29, 1915, m. Oct 27, 1934, Viola Willis, b. Feb. 19, 1917. Lutherans.
1. Loretta Jean Wenger, b. Oct. 11, 1935.

No. 3569. Fifth Generation. 2753.

3) Henry S. Wenger, b. Aug 23, 1886, m June 16, 1920, Amy Heatwole, b. July 13, 1894. Address. Waynesboro, Va Mennonites.
1. Lillian Gertrude Wenger, b. Oct. 31, 1921
2. Clarice Joan Wenger, b. April 18, 1928.

No. 3570. Fifth Generation. 2753.

7) Jacob C. Wenger, b. Dec 20, 1893, m Oct. 8, 1921, Mary E. Kulp, b. Sept. 24, 1895. Address: Souderton, Pa. Mennonites.

1. Ray William Wenger, b. Jan 11, 1923
2. Doris Arlene Wenger, b. Mar. 25, 1927.
3. Carl Robert Wenger, b Oct. 8, 1930.
4. Floyd Kulp Wenger, b May 2, 1932.

No. 3571. Fifth Generation. 3247.

1) Levi Glenwood Ward, b Oct 13, 1898, m. Nellie Brown, in 1932. Address: 815 Frey St., Jackson, Mich. No issue

No. 3572. Fifth Generation. 3247.

6) William Walter Ward, b Jan 17, 1908, m. Laura Moyer in 1931. Address: Lima, O., R. 4.

1. Ralph Ward, b. —————, 1933.
2. Margaret Ward, b. —————, 1935

No. 3573. Fifth Generation. 3247.

7) Jessie Irene Ward, b. Oct 7, 1909, m. Kenneth Layland. Address: 600 block, S. Metcalf St., Lima, O. No issue.

No. 3574. Sixth Generation. 3333.

1) Louise D. Sponaugle, b Feb. 2, 1905, m. in 1930 at Independence, Mo., Stanley Johnston. Address Smithville, Mo

1. Fern Johnston, b. and d Dec, 1930.
2. Peggy A. Johnston, b Mar, 1932
3. James G. Johnston, b Mar, 1934

No. 3575. Sixth Generation. 3333.

2) Marion C. Sponaugle, b May 31, 1906, m. in 1930, Elsie Ziebarth. Address: North Redwood, Minn.

1. Dorlene F. Sponaugle, b. Aug., 1931.

No. 3576. Sixth Generation. 3333.

3) Frances A. Sponaugle, b Oct 3, 1907, m. in May, 1927, W. G. Cutsforth at Chetek, Wis.

1. Marjean Cutsforth, b. April, 1930.
2. Russell D. Cutsforth, b. Aug, 1931.
3. Eilene Cutsforth, b. Aug, 1932
4. Carroll G. Cutsforth, b Sept, 1934
5. Ellen G. Cutsforth, b Jan, 1936

No. 3577. Sixth Generation. 3333.

5) Myrtle V. Sponaugle, b Feb 7, 1910, m. May, 1930, Theodore Crowls, at Independence, Mo. Address. Rich Hill, Mo.

1. Claude C. Crowls, b —————, 1931.
2. Ronald G Crowls, b. —————, 1932
3. Joan M. Crowls, b. —————, 1935.
4. Diana B. Crowls, b. —————, 1936

No. 3578. Sixth Generation. 3333.

6) Minnie Irene Sponaugle, b. Mar 8, 1911, m. Sept., 1933, Kermit Williams, of Napoleon, Mo. Address: Rich Hill, Mo.

1. Harold M. Williams, b. —————, 1935.

No. 3579. Sixth Generation. 2892.

1) Donald L. Furry, b Sept 20, 1910, m June 3, 1937, Ruth Sunderland, b June 18, 1910. They live in Elida, O

No. 3580. Fifth Generation. 2949.

3) Wallace D. Brenneman, b Sept 15, 1917, near Elida, O., m. Jane Gillispie, b. Mar. 19, 1917, m July 24, 1937. Draftsman Methodist.

No. 3581. Sixth Generation. 1075.

1) Edith V. Driver, b Oct 17, 1894, near Versailles, Mo, m Richard Fulton, Feb., 1930, b. Nov 12, 1890 Address· Los Angeles, Calif. Mechanic. Presbyterians. Mrs. Fulton is a Registered Nurse

No. 3582. Sixth Generation. 1075.

2) David K Driver, b Mar. 8, 1897, near Versailles, Mo, m. July 4, 1908, Sadie Eleanor Stockton, b July 12, 1897 Address. LaJunta, Colo Baptists.

1. David Stockton Driver, b Nov 4, 1919.
2. Lydia Eleanor Driver, b Feb 26, 1921.
3. Dorothy Myrne Driver, b Nov 12, 1926

No. 3583. Sixth Generation. 1075.

3) Alice I Driver, b. April 6, 1899, near Versailles, Mo, m. Charles C. Snyder, b. Mar. 4, 1895. Address Cheraw, Colo Mennonites.

1. Marjorie Louise Snyder, b Oct 17, 1932.

No. 3584. Seventh Generation. 655.

4) Rowena Stemen, b Jan 16, 1909, near Elida, O, m Kenneth Yoder. Address: Denbigh, Va. Mennonites

No. 3585. Seventh Generation. 655.

5) Nina Stemen, b May 25, 1911, near Elida, O, m Loren Yoder. Address: Denbigh, Va Mennonites.

1. Connie Rae Yoder, b July 26, 1937.

No. 3586. Sixth Generation. 2393.

10) Vernon Steiner Ross, b May 1, 1910, m. in 1937 Verna Childer of Anchorage, Alaska, where they now reside

No. 3587. Sixth Generation. 2408.

5) Bertha Stemen, b Mar 2, 1915, m Roy Brewer, Mar 30, 1937

No. 3588. Sixth Generation. 2408.

6) Dorothy Stemen, b. Jan 27, 1917, m Oct 10, 1936, Kenneth Shaw. They live in Cleveland, O.

1. David Kenneth Shaw, b. Aug. 5, 1937.

No. 3589. Seventh Generation. 427.

3) Charles Clayton Brunk, b April 8, 1912, m Marcella Miller. Address: Elida, O.

1. John M Brunk, b ————, 1937, only lived a short time

No. 3590. Sixth Generation. 2389.

2) Frank Furry, b Jan. 28, 1903, m Feb 14, 1935, Margaret Brennen, b. April 13, 1902 Distributor Methodist and Catholic Address: 18 Superior Court, Lima, O.

1. Sallie Jo Furry, b. Mar. 8, 1936.

No. 3591. Sixth Generation. 2889.

4) Parker Furry, b July 17, 1907, m. May —, 1936, Fern Dray. Address: 135½ East Spring St., Lima, O. Methodists No children.

No. 3592. Sixth Generation. 2889.

5) Zoe Furry, b Oct. 22, 1910, m. May —, 1934, Emerson Paul. They live at 22 Superior Court Clerk at Gulf refinery Methodist and Lutheran.

No. 3593. Seventh Generation. 645.

2) Irene D. Shenk, b. Mar 17, 1903, m Albert Smith. They live in Dayton, O., in the 1100 block, North Main Street.
1. Kenney Smith, b ——————.

No. 3594. Seventh Generation. 645.

3) Paul C. Shenk, b. ——————, 1907, m. Sept. 17, 1932, Catherine Lydia Miller, b. Aug 20, 1912. Address. 204 East O'Conner St., Lima, O.

No. 3595. Seventh Generation. 645.

4) Merl Shenk, b ——————, 1911, m. Thelma ——————. They live in Toledo, O. No children.

No. 3596. Sixth Generation. 2463.

1) Luella Lone Warden, b. May 22, 1907, m. Aug. 16, 1925, Hugh M. Brown, b. June 5, 1901. Address. Defiance, O. Dentist Methodists.
1. Robert Hugh Brown, b Oct. 22, 1927.
2. Merilyn Ann Brown, b. Feb 12, 1931.

No. 3597. Sixth Generation. 528.

6) Maud Irene Tutwiler, b. ——————, m. (1st) Blanchford Argenbright; m (2nd) Weldon Linhoss; m. (3rd) William Laws.
1. Lucille Argenbright, b ——————, deceased.
2. Helen Argenbright, b ——————.
3. John Linhoss, b. ——————.
4. Roy Linhoss, b ——————.
5. Phillis Linhoss, b ——————.
6. Peggy Ann Laws, b. ——————.

No. 3598. Fifth Generation. 2784.

2) Lessie May Wenger, b Jan. 2, 1890, m Aug. 23, 1923, Abram W. Hershberger, b Feb. 11, 1875. Address: Harrisonburg, Va., R. 4
1. Beatrice Hershberger, b Mar. 12, 1925
2. Mildred Hershberger, b. April 26, 1927.
3. Abram Wenger Hershberger, b. May 9, 1928
4. Ruth Marie Hershberger, b. Dec 27, 1930

No. 3599. Fifth Generation. 2784.

3) Hannah Etta Wenger, b Jan 6, 1892, m. Dec. 27, 1932, Ernest H. Miller, b. Aug. 18, 1889. Address. Fentress, Va. Mennonites. Farmer.
1. Harvey Wenger Miller, b. Jan. 23, 1934.

No. 3600. Fifth Generation. 2784.

6) Ida Wenger, b. April 13, 1898, m. Oct. 28, 1929, Abram G. Shaddinger, b. Feb. 17, 1901. Address· Fentress, Va Truck driver Mennonites.
1. Laura Mae Shaddinger, b. July 28, 1931.
2. Gladys Marie Shaddinger, b Aug. 12, 1934.

No. 3501. Fifth Generation. 2784.

7) Roy Gordon Wenger, b Mar 30, 1900, m April 16, 1927, Marian K. Rosenberger, b Feb. 22, 1906 Address. Fentress, Va Dairyman. Mennonites. Deacon.

1. Roy Gordon Wenger, Jr., b Sept 3, 1929
2. Donald Paul Wenger, b. Feb. 10, 1931.
3. Ruth Marie Wenger, b Dec 28, 1935.

No. 3602. Fifth Generation. 2784.

8) Katie Wenger, b. Feb 11, 1903, d Aug. 6, 1933, m. Oct 12, 1928, Marvin E. Miller, b. Aug. 7, 1898 Address Fentress, Va Farmer and clerk Mennonites.

1. Merlin Robert Miller, b. July 16, 1929
2 Mildred Elizabeth Miller, b May 27, 1932

No. 3603. Fifth Generation. 2784.

9) Powell Oliver Wenger, b. June 5, 1905, m Dec 6, 1933, Hazel Virginia Swope, b. July 22, 1911. Address· Fentress, Va Farmer. Mennonites.

1. Dorothy Pearl Wenger, b. Feb 9, 1935
2. Carl Everett Wenger, b Sept 11, 1938

No. 3604. Sixth Generation. 2786.

1) Ida Mae Brunk, b Mar. 14, 1916, m Oct 11, 1936, Richard W. Leatherman, b. Mar. 22, 1913. Address: Fentress, Va. Mennonites

1. Betty Jean Leatherman, b. Oct. 13, 1937

No. 3605. Fifth Generation. 2792.

4) Mary Edith Brunk, b. July 22, 1897, m Alfred Hartman. No issue.

No. 3606. Sixth Generation. 1075.

6) Harvey Allen Driver, b. Mar 13, 1906, m. Dec 24, 1936, Priscilla Irene Liechty, b. Aug. 21, 1906, R.N. Address: La Junta, Colo. Mennonites.

No. 3507. Sixth Generation. 2595.

3) Ralph Wayne Mumaw, b. Sept. 17, 1911, m June 28, 1936, Mildred Schrock, b May 21, 1913. Farmer. Mennonites Address: Smithville, O.

1. Janet Sue Mumaw, b. May 31, 1937.
2. Mary Jane Mumaw, b. Nov. 7, 1938.

No. 3608. Sixth Generation. 2591.

5) Byron E. Mumaw, b. Jan. 7, 1914, m. ————. Address: Salem, O.

1. Patricia Ann Mumaw, b. ————, 1937.

No. 3609. Sixth Generation. 270.

8) Emmanuel J. Burkholder, b. May 23, 1891, near Harrisonburg, Va., m. Sept. 8, 1915, Ella Virginia Weaver, of Waynesboro, Va. Address: Harrisonburg, Va., R. 1. Salesman. Mennonites.

1. Austin Beidler Burkholder, b. July 19, 1916.
2. Edith Marie Burkholder, b. Nov. 18, 1918

No. 3610. Sixth Generation. 270.

9) Amos H. Burkholder, b July 30, 1893, near Harrisonburg, Va., m. Josephine Esther Weaver, b Feb. 13, 1896, m. Oct. 27, 1915 Piano tuner and salesman. Mennonites. Address: Harrisonburg, Va.

1. Margaret Esther Burkholder, b Aug. 12, 1916. No. 3614.
2. Lydia May Burkholder, b. May 14, 1920. Mennonite.
3. Noland Dwight Burkholder, b Oct. 23, 1927

No. 3611. Sixth Generation. 270.

10) Ella D. Burkholder, b. April 4, 1897, near Harrisonburg, Va., m. Leon Davis, b. Jan. 11, 1892. Now retired. Christian. Address: Salem, O.

1. Owen Paul Burkholder Martin, b. May 17, 1917. Mennonite. P. O. Elkhart, Ind.
2. Delamore W. Davis, b. Jan. 29, 1923.
3. Charles L. Davis, b. June 2, 1924.
4. Robert N. Davis, b. April 3, 1926.

No. 3612. Seventh Generation. 275.

1) Esther C. Good, b. Dec. 12, 1906, m. Dec. 25, 1933, Mahlon C. Lapp, b. Jan. 27, 1903. Address. Sterling, Ill. Farmer. Mennonites.

No. 3513. Seventh Generation. 275.

2) Lloyd D. Good, b. Dec. 3, 1912, m. Dec. 25, 1933, Cora B Lapp, b. Sept. 14, 1912. Address: Sterling, Ill. Electrician. Mennonites.

1. Lois Ann Good, b. Oct. 20, 1934.

No. 3614. Seventh Generation. 3610.

1) Margaret Esther Burkholder, b. Aug. 12, 1916, m Oct. 22, 1937, James M. Coakley, b. April 1, 1913 Both are silk mill employees. Mennonites. Address. Dayton, Va.

No. 3615. Seventh Generation. 993.

5) Mary E. Burkholder, b Mar. 3, 1911, near Harrisonburg, Va., m Dec. 8, 1935, Lloyd Martin. Address. Columbiana, O Mennonites.

1. Shirley Martin, b April 12, 1937.

No. 3616. Seventh Generation. 993.

6) Joseph A. Burkholder, Jr., b. Sept. 8, 1913, near Harrisonburg, Va., m. May 29, 1937, Faye Lehman Address: Columbiana, O. Mennonites.

No. 3517. Seventh Generation. 273.

2) Lettie E. Burkholder, b. June 15, 1908, m. Oct. 7, 1936, Robert H. Graves, of Vesuvius, Va. Address: Waynesboro, Va Factory employee. Mennonite and Methodist.

No. 3618. Seventh Generation. 273.

3) Roy A. Burkholder, b. April 9, 1912, m Aug. 7, 1931, Anna Nasetka of East Vandergrift, Pa She is of Catholic parentage; Roy is a Mennonite. They live in Philadelphia, Pa.

1. Roy Burkholder, Jr., b. Aug. 11, 1932.

No. 3619. Seventh Generation. 273.

4) Nelson R Burkholder, b Nov. 6, 1915, m. April 15, 1936, Ruth Sandridge, of Harpster, O Address: Waynesboro, Va. Factory employee. Mennonite and Methodist.

No. 3620. Seventh Generation. 272.

1) Bertha Catherine Burkholder, b Sept. 11, 1896, m. Paul Bender. Address: Goshen, Ind. Mennonite Professor in Goshen College, Goshen, Ind.

No. 3621. Seventh Generation. 272.

2) Nellie A. Burkholder, b. Mar. 2, 1899, m. Newton S. Weber, b. Oct. 10, 1897. Mennonite. Minister at Ft. Wayne, Ind., Mission, 1209 St. Marys Ave.

1. Naomi Catherine Weber, b April 15, 1924.
2. Ruth Marie Weber, b. May 20, 1926.

3. Rhoda Elizabeth Weber, b Jan. 20, 1929
4. John Newton Weber, b Dec 6, 1931

No. 3622. Seventh Generation. 272.

3) Lena Gertrude Burkholder, b. Dec. 12, 1900, m. Harry Anthony Brunk, b. —————. Address. Harrisonburg, Va Mennonites
1. James Robert Brunk, b. —————.
2. David Christian Brunk, b. —————.
3 Samuel Frederick Brunk, b —————.

No. 3623. Sixth Generation. 176.

5) Alvin Samuel Breneman, b Feb 6, 1914, m Aug 8, 1936, Phillis Brown.

No. 3624. Seventh Generation. 519.

4) David Roy Eberly, b Mar 10, 1914, near Orrville, O., m Dec. 21, 1937, Mabel Yoder of Orrville, O , b. April 7, 1910 Address Orrville, O. Mennonites. Laborer.

No. 3625. Seventh Generation. 271.

1) Ira B. Swope, b June 23, 1892, near Harrisonburg, Va., m. Dec. 7, 1911, Emma F. Pullen of Va , d Nov 23, 1931, m. (2nd) Selina G. Jennings, Dec. 13, 1933. She was b. July 22, 1903 Address: Sterling, Ill , R 1 Farmer. Mennonites.
1. Ward Joseph Swope, b Nov 1, 1912 No 3635.
2 Esther Elizabeth Swope, b Sept 9, 1915. No. 3634.
3 Earl Harding Swope, b. Aug 12, 1923

No. 3626. Seventh Generation. 271.

2) Mary Edna Swope, b Dec 3, 1893, near Harrisonburg, Va , m. Dec. 3, 1916, Cleophas N Steiner. Address· Sterling, Ill.
1. Arlene Frances Steiner, b. Sept 16, 1917.
2. Harold David Steiner, b. May 17, 1924.

No. 3627. Seventh Generation. 271.

3) John Abraham Swope, b. Sept. 11, 1896, near Harrisonburg, Va , m. Aug. 13, 1919, Mabel M. Basinger. Address North Lima, O.
1 James Wilford Swope, b. April 1, 1921
2 Martha Jean Swope, b June 6, 1929.

No. 3623. Seventh Generation. 271.

4) Oliver David Swope, b. Aug 21, 1898, near Harrisonburg, Va., m. Nov. 10, 1923, Helen McGhee Address: 417-18th Ave., R V , Beaver Falls, Pa.

No. 3629. Seventh Generation. 271.

5) Herman F Swope, b. Dec. 12, 1900, near Harrisonburg, Va., m. Feb. 3, 1923, Mabel Detrow, b. Aug 31, 1903 Address: Leetonia, O. Farmer Mennonites.
1 Wilmer D Swope, b Dec. 16, 1925.
2 Carolyn Marie Swope, b Feb. 10, 1930.

No. 3630. Seventh Generation. 271.

6) Nannie Elizabeth Swope, b Jan. 6, 1902, m Feb 14, 1925, Arden M Lehman. Address: Greenford, O
1 Helen Irene Lehman, b Nov. 20, 1928
2 Dorothy Mae Lehman, b May 31, 1934

No. 3631. Seventh Generation. 271.

7) Joseph Weaver Swope, b Feb. 29, 1904, m. June 15, 1935, Mary E. Hertzler. Address: Belleville, Pa
1. Stanly Wallace Swope, b. July 9, 1938.

No. 3632. Seventh Generation. 271.

8) Paul Showalter Swope, b April 24, 1905, m. Aug., 1936, Lois McFerren. Address: North Lima, O
1 Verna Marie Swope, b. Nov. 20, 1937

No. 3633. Seventh Generation. 271.

9) Emmanuel Jacob Swope, b. June 24, 1907, m. June 24, 1933, Nola Leinbach Address North Lima, O
1 Palmer Ray Swope, b. Aug. 17, 1935.

No. 3634. Eighth Generation. 3625.

2) Esther Elizabeth Swope, b Sept. 9, 1915, m Dec 13, 1933, Lester Martin of Kouts, Ind. Address. Kouts, Ind.
1. Kenneth Ira Martin, b. Sept. 29, 1934.
2. Samuel William Martin, b. Oct. 6, 1935.

No. 3635. Eighth Generation. 3625.

1) Ward Joseph Swope, b. Nov 1, 1912, m. April 14, 1937, Irene Hayen of Sterling, Ill. Address: Sterling, Ill.

No. 3636. Seventh Generation. 454.

1) Ivan W. Brunk, b July 29, 1915, in Va., m. Jan. 6, 1938, Anna Naomi Jennings of Concord, Tenn. They live at Seattle, Wash. Mennonites.

No. 3637. Sixth Generation. 1823.

3) Eugene J Gafford, b June 25, 1896, m. Jan. 23, 1937, Gladys Gertrude Griffith, b. Oct. 29, 1902 Address· Burlington, Ia.

No. 3638. Sixth Generation. 1972.

1) Henry Calvin Houck, b Mar. 23, 1902, m. June 6, 1936, June Maclean. Address: Grants Pass, Oreg.

No. 3639. Fifth Generation. 3221.

5) Clarence B. Brenneman, b Dec. 27, 1912, near Cairo, O , m. Sept. 27, 1936, Neva E. Tucker, b. Nov. 15, 1915. Address: Lima, O., R. 5. Farmer near Cairo, O. Congregational Christian Church. Burial in Memorial Park cemetery, Lima, O

No. 3640. Seventh Generation. 2361.

2) Alta Mae Showalter, b. Oct. 7, 1913, near La Junta, Colo., m. Jan. 25, 1938, Nick Augimari. They live in Los Angeles, Calif.

No. 3641. Seventh Generation. 888.

2) Norma Virginia Shank, b Sept 3, 1920, near Harrisonburg, Va., m. Mar. 15, 1938, John J Deputy, of near Harrisonburg, Va Mennonite They were married by Bishop S H Rhodes

No. 3642. Seventh Generation. 297.

2) Reba Virginia Driver, b Oct 11, 1917, near Waynesboro, Va , daughter of Rhodes Homer, and Annie M (Weaver) Driver, m Feb 8, 1938, Alvin Weaver of Waynesboro, Va Mennonite They were married by Bishop Joseph R Driver

No. 3643. Sixth Generation. 1887.

2) Rosamond Oliva Shock, b. April 26, 1918, near Lima, O , m. Robert Marshal. They live on Harrison Ave., Lima, O.

1. Courtney Allen Marshal, b. Feb. —, 1938.

No. 3644. Fifth Generation. 1853.

2) Anna Lee Brenaman, b. Nov. 18, 1900, in Richmond, Va., m. Lewis Orien Wrenn, b. Nov. 15, 1897.

1. Hugh Orien Wrenn, b. Oct. 16, 1925.

No. 3645. Fifth Generation. 1853.

3) Robert S. Brenaman, b Mar. 4, 1903, in Richmond, Va., m. Josephine Saunders, b. Dec. 20, 1903. They live at 211 N 7th St , Richmond, Va.

1. Mary S. Brenaman, b. Aug 18, 1932.
2. Carter Braxton Brenaman, b. Nov. 18, 1936

No. 3646. Fifth Generation. 1853.

4) Mary Charles Brenaman, b ————, 1911, in Richmond, Va., m E N. Earman. They live at 1128 N. Grace St., Richmond, Va

No. 3647. Sixth Generation. 2923.

4) Harold Adrian Brubaker, b. Oct. 16, 1914, near Lima, O., m. May 5, 1938, Eva R. Burkholder, b ————————, of Waynesboro, Va , by Bishop Joseph R. Driver of the same place. Mennonites. Address: Lima, O., R. 3. Farmer.

No. 3648. Seventh Generation. 1035.

4) Mary Frances Driver, b. Feb 16, 1917, near Waynesboro, Va , m. May 7, 1938, Alva Henry Showalter, b ————————, near Waynesboro, Va., by Joseph R. Driver, father of the bride. Mennonites. Address: Waynesboro, Va.

No. 3649. Fifth Generation. 173.

8) Frank Breneman, b May 30, 1889, near Brooklyn, Ia.; m June 2, 1938, Alice Fryer, b Dec. 3, 1901.

No. 3650. Sixth Generation. 177.

4) Bruce Bucknam, b Oct 7, 1911, in Council Bluffs, Ia , m April 17, 1938, Marjorie Fox, b. Jan. 27, 1917.

No. 3651. Sixth Generation. 177.

2) Marjorie Louise Bucknam, b Jan. 29, 1905, in Council Bluffs, Ia , m. July 25, 1938, James Alexander, b. May 30, 1893. Address: 1247 Fairmont Ave , Council Bluffs, Ia.

No. 3652. Sixth Generation. 177.

3) Edith Barbara Bucknam, b. July 2, 1908, in Council Bluffs, Ia , m Sept. —, 1932, Hugh Reedy McAlexander Both died together July 11, 1937, when their home burned down from some unknown cause No issue They lived at Council Bluffs, Ia.

No. 3653. Seventh Generation. 672.

1) Fannie V. Shenk, b Oct. 7, 1918, near Fentress, Va , m. June 12, 1938, Andrew Hartzler of West Liberty, O , by George R Brunk Mennonites Address· Fentress, Va.

No. 3654. Seventh Generation. 633.

4) Wilber D. Shenk, b Aug 19, 1905, near Elida, O , m June 26, 1938, Bertie Lee Baer, b. Sept. 3, 1914, daughter of Adam and Bertie Baer of Hagerstown, Md. Schoolteacher. Mennonites Address· Philadelphia, Pa.

No. 3655. Sixth Generation. 1732.

1) Jewel K. Brannaman, b Jan. 21, 1910, near Cloverdale, Ind., m. Eugenia Goble. Address: Cloverdale, Ind.

1. Barbra Lou Brannaman, b. Nov. 14, 1938.

No. 3656. Sixth Generation. 2940.

2) Robert W. Dieterich, b. Sept. 23, 1916, m June 4, 1938, Bettie Steinhagon, b. Aug 19, 1916. Clerk. Congregational Christian Church. Address: 2 Pinehurst Ave., Dayton, O.

No. 3657. Seventh Generation. 399.

1) Ethel Marie Ebersole, b Sept 20, 1913, at Elkhart, Ind, m June 5, 1938, at the Prairie St, Mennonite Church, Elkhart, Ind., Ivan R Lind of Tangent, Oreg, by Bishop Sanford C. Yoder, President of Goshen College. They will reside at Hesston, Kans, where Mr. Lind will teach Bible and Commerce at Hesston College. Mennonites.

No. 3558. Sixth Generation. 2480.

5) Ruth Brenneman, b Oct 14, 1914, near Spencerville, O, m. Oct 10, 1935, John Gaskill, b. Jan. 14, 1913. Address: Spencerville, O., R 2 Baptists.

1. Merle Gene Gaskill, b. Feb. 19, 1936, twin.
2 Earl Dean Gaskill, b. Feb 19, 1936, twin

No. 3659. Fifth Generation. 2475.

7) Harry Brenneman, b Nov. 4, 1881, near Ottawa, O., m. ————————, Emma Spitnale, b. ————————, d ————————, m. (2nd) Florence Brown, b. ————————. Address: Ottawa, O., R 5.

1. Mary Brenneman, b. ————————, d ————————.
2. Martha Brenneman, b. ————————, d ————————.
   (From second union)
3 Sophiah Brenneman, b. ————————.

No. 3660. Fifth Generation. 2475.

8) Delilah Brenneman, b. Dec 20, 1884, m. ————————, Willard Elkins, b. Aug. 18, 1877. Address: Cloverdale, O., R. 2.

1. Cecil Chester Elkins, b. ————————.
2. Dorothy Rosama Elkins, b. ————————.

No. 3661. Sixth Generation. 2484.

2) Paul Orlando Brenneman, b. April 8, 1909, near Spencerville, O., m. Ruth Cosnaux (French by birth) in Toledo, O Address: 1233 Mich. Ave, Toledo, O.

1. Barbara Ann Brenneman, b. ————————.
2. Donald Otto Brenneman, b. ————————.

No. 3662. Fifth Generation. 1933.

1) Rolla J. Strayer, b July 17, 1911, near Elida, O., m. Aug. 26, 1938, Mabel M. Russell of Delphos, O Address: Elida, O, R 2 Employee.

No. 3663. Sixth Generation. 1884.

2) Max Shock, b. Mar. 3, 1912, in Van Wert, O., m. Sept 1, 1934, Florence Mankin. Salesman. United Brethren. Address: Van Wert, O

No. 3664. Sixth Generation. 1884.

3) Frances Shock, b Aug 22, 1914, in Van Wert, O, m May 1, 1936, Madge Angevine of same place. Address Van Wert, O. Grocery clerk. Lutherans.

No. 3665. Sixth Generation. 652.

14) John H. Shenk, b. April 19, 1910, near Denbigh, Va , m. June 26, 1938, Emily Brackbill, daughter of Milton Brackbill of Paoli, Pa   Address. Denbigh, Va

No. 3666. Seventh Generation. 304.

4) Naoma M. Heatwole, b Nov 26, 1912, near Dayton, Va , m. May 25, 1938, Lester Campbell of near Waynesboro, Va , by Bishop S. H. Rhodes.

No. 3667. Seventh Generation. 293.

5) Ruth M Weaver, b. Oct. 6, 1914, near Dayton, Va , m June 4, 1938, Timothy Deputy of near Dale Enterprise, Va , by Bishop S. H. Rhodes.

No. 3658. Fifth Generation. 2969.

6) Martha Lindsey, b. Mar. 9, 1909, m July 14, 1935, William S. Bruckner, b. April 10, 1891. Hotel manager. Address. 1611 S. E. Belmont, Portland, Oreg

No. 3669. Sixth Generation. 2759.

1) Eleanor Geil Rhodes, b. June 16, 1917, in Harrisonburg, Va., m. May 4, 1938, L. Harold Lee, b. Nov. 13, 1911. Address: Harrisonburg, Va. Methodists.

No. 3670. Seventh Generation. 902.

1) Helen Hempy, b. Feb. 2, 1901, near Rushsylvania, O., m. ——————. Three children.

No. 3671. Seventh Generation. 902.

2) Myron G. Hempy, b Aug. 27, 1905, near Rushsylvania, O., m ——————. Address: Rushsylvania, O. Road contractor.

No. 3672. Sixth Generation. 910.

1) Stella Good, b. Mar. 4, 1884, Columbus, O., m. Charles Trout. Farmer. Address: Van Buren, O.
1. Richard Charles Trout, b Dec. 24, 1911 No. 3688.
2 Robert Good Trout, b. Mar 10, 1910. No. 3689.
3. Van Abraham Trout, b Aug. 21, 1915. No 3690.
4. Dorothy Trout, b Nov. 20, 1918

No. 3673. Sixth Generation. 910.

3) Harry N. Good, b April 29, 1890, Columbus, O , m. Nellie Nichols of Chardon, O. Address: Jefferson, O., R. 5.
1. James Warren Good, b ——————.
2. Harry Neal Good, Jr., b ——————.

No. 3674. Sixth Generation. 911.

1) Ralph Spence, b. Nov. 18, 1889, Delaware, O., m. Florence Thompson, b. Feb. 14, 1898, d. Mar. 17, 1921, m. (2nd) Maud Isabelle Donovon   Insurance Agent of 257 S. Sandusky St , Delaware, O   Methodists.
1. Lucile Spence, b. Dec. —, 1919, d. same day.
2. Ruthella Florence Spence, b Jan 18, 1921.

No. 3675. Sixth Generation. 911.

2) Pauline Spence, b. April 18, 1891, at Delaware, O , m Frederick Hyer. Address. Powell, O. Farmer.
1. Willard Hyer, b. ——————, deceased.

No. 3676. Sixth Generation. 911.

3) Anna Spence, b. Nov 22, 1893, Delaware, O , m. Verne Hecker. Address: 460 Midgard Rd., Columbus, O   Architect.

No. 3677. Sixth Generation. 911.

4) Paul Spence, b Aug 29, 1895, Delaware, O , m. Florence Norman. Address: 181 Clinton St , Columbus, O He was a World War veteran. Engineer Methodist

1. Annabelle Spence, b ————, 1922
2. Norma Spence, b ————, 1928.
3. Martha Jane Spence, b ————, deceased.

No. 3678. Sixth Generation. 912.

1) Mary H. Bunn, b Oct 16, 1891, Springfield, O , m. Sept. 1, 1913, Harold Bagford, b. Nov. 8, 1890, at Troy, O County surveyor. Baptists Address: 419 W. Race St., Troy, O.

1. Donald Elbert Bagford, b. ————.
2. Dorothy Bagford, b ————.

No. 3679. Sixth Generation. 912.

2) Lenora Freed Bunn, b. Mar. 7, 1905, Springfield, O., m. Jan. 22, 1934, Randall E. Riley, of New York City Accountant. Episcopal. Address: 343 E. 55th St , Apt. 20, New York City, N. Y.

No. 3680. Sixth Generation. 913.

1) Vivian Helen Bailey, b. Dec. 9, 1894, Columbus, O., m. Nelson Hickman, a farmer at Reynoldsburg, O Methodists Mrs. Hickman is a graduate of the Ohio State University. Address: Reynoldsburg, O.

1. Seymore Hickman, b. ————.

No. 3681. Sixth Generation. 913.

2) Stanley Bailey, b. Oct 17, 1896, Columbus, O , m. ————. Address not given.

1. Son, b. ————.

No. 3682. Sixth Generation. 913.

3) Frances Bailey, b Oct 22, 1903, Columbus, O., m. Prof. Theodore Fitzgerald of Ohio State University Address: 879 College Ave., Bexley, O.

No. 3683. Sixth Generation. 915.

1) Harold V. Freed, b Nov. 1, 1895, near Lancaster, O , m. Lucile Turner Address: Basil, O. Farmer and stock raiser with his father.

No. 3684. Sixth Generation. 915.

2) Lola G. Freed, b Jan 28, 1901, near Lancaster, O., m. Carl Menson They live in Columbus, O.

No. 3685. Sixth Generation. 915.

3) Dorothy Freed, b May 13, 1903, near Lancaster, O , m Ivan Gundy Address: Canal Winchester, O.

No. 3686. Sixth Generation. 2489.

3) Effie Lorine Cotner, b. Sept. 19, 1908, near Pueblo, Colo., m. Richard Cooper, b April 12, 1908, an attorney of Pueblo, Colo. They live in Kansas Methodists.

1. James Arlen Cooper, b Oct. 23, 1935

No. 3687. Sixth Generation. 2489.

5) Lucile Cotner, b Mar 5, 1915, near Pueblo, Colo., m. June 17, 1937, Charles Wobbie, b. June 24, 1906, at Youngstown, Kans. Farmer near Pueblo, Colo Methodists.

513

No. 3688. Seventh Generation. 3672.

1) Richard Charles Trout, b. Dec. 24, 1911, Van Buren, O , m. April 10, 1935, Constance Cooper, daughter of Venus Cooper of North Baltimore, O. He is a member of the "Marion Star" staff. Address 747 Davids St., Marion, O

1. James Warren Trout, b. July 13, 1938.

No. 3689. Seventh Generation. 3672.

2) Robert Good Trout, b Mar. 10, 1913, Van Buren, O., m Marie Zeisloft, of West of Findlay, O , daughter of Ray Zeisloft of Liberty Twp They were married Dec. 24, 1936. Address: Thornsville, O. Schoolteacher.

No. 3690. Seventh Generation. 3672.

3) Van Abraham Trout, b Aug. 21, 1915, Van Buren, O , m Aug. 21, 1938. Virginia Dreisbach, daughter of O C Dreisbach of Findlay, O. Address Pandora, O. Schoolteacher.

No. 3691. Seventh Generation. 327.

3) Isaac S. Shenk, b. July 8, 1913, near Elida, O , m. Grace Setzler, b Nov 4, 1916. Address: Springs, Pa.

1. Norma Jean Shenk, b. Dec. 28, 1936.

No. 3692. Fifth Generation. 2969.

8) Leona Lindsey, b. Aug. 2, 1912, m. Mar. 3, 1934, Hilling Clifford Nelson, b. ——————. Address. 118 W. Richmond Ave , Dayton, Wash. Teacher.

1. Clifford Leon Nelson, b. Mar. 3, 1936.

No. 3693. Seventh Generation. 519.

1) Barbara Frances Eberly, b. Dec. 25, 1909, m. June 1, 1938, Paul Martin, b. ——————. Address: Orrville, O Farmer. Mennonites.

No. 3694. Fifth Generation. 2969.

1) Oliver Ernest Lindsey, b. Jan. 6, 1900, m. Winifred Simpson. No children. Address: Tacoma, Wash.

No. 3695. Fifth Generation. 2969.

2) Ruth Lindsey, b. Mar. 3, 1901, m Daniel James Crowley. Address: Long Beach, Wash.

1. Eugene James Crowley, b. ——————
2. Eilene Ruth Crowley, b ——————.
3. Roseanne Crowley, b. ——————.
4. Eva Jean Crowley, b. ——————.
5. Donella Crowley, b. ——————.
6. Lee Paul Crowley, b. ——————.

No. 3695. Fifth Generation. 2969.

4) Lois Lindsey, b. Feb. 12, 1904, m. Riley S. Johnston. Address: Spokane, Wash.

1. Riley Lindsey Johnston, b. ——————.

No. 3697. Fifth Generation. 2969.

5) Elizabeth Lindsey, b April 16, 1905, m. Floyd A. Allington. They live in Calif. No children.

No. 3698. Fifth Generation. 2969.

6) James Leonard Lindsey, b. July 24, 1907, m. Edith Begerow. They live in Calif.

514

1. Leona Lindsey, b. ————.
2. George Lindsey, b. ————.

No. 3699. Fifth Generation. 2969.

8) Mark Rex Lindsey, b Jan. 2, 1911, m. Edna Morrison They live at Seattle, Wash. No children.

No. 3700. Sixth Generation. 409.

1) Harold M. Weaver, b Feb. 25, 1905, in Jasper Co., Mo., m. Ruby Jantz. Address: Oronogo, Mo. One child.

No. 3701. Seventh Generation. 698.

3) Dorothy M Powel, b April 6, 1917, near Elida, O., m. Lawrence B. Brunk, b. Feb. 23, 1917, son of George and Katy Wenger Brunk of Denbigh, Va. Address: Denbigh, Va.

No. 3702. Fifth Generation. 3210.

1) Bert B. Swinehart, b. Feb 7, 1883, near West Salem, O , m. Pearl ————. Address: Wadsworth, O., N. Limon St.
    1. Clifford Swinehart, b. Aug —, 1916, married
    2. Leland Swinehart, b. ————, 1923, single.

No. 3703. Seventh Generation. 825.

1) Clifford A Burkholder, b. Oct. 31, 1897, near Harrisonburg, Va., m Jan. 16, 1935, Marie Goard, b. Sept. 14, 1906 of Sibbling, Minn. Address: 105 Pershing Ave , Brentwood, Md.
    1 Joan Marie Burkholder, b. Sept. 2, 1938.

No. 3704. Sixth Generation. 154.

8) Mae S Turner, b. Dec 15, 1912, near Broadway, Va., m. Claude Turner. Mennonites. Address. Broadway, Va.

No. 3705. Seventh Generation. 628.

3) Lydia F. Shenk, b June 13, 1899 near Elida, O , m. Jan 28, 1939 at the home of Mary Burkhard, Goshen, Ind , by M C Lehman, Charles L Shank, b. May 22, 1886 near Versailles, Mo , son of Lewis H and Mary E. Wenger Shank. Lydia was formerly a teacher at Goshen College, Goshen, Ind Charles was formerly a missionary at Dhamtari, C P , India, but for several years was employed by the Hoover Sweeper Co , at Canton, O , as an architect Address North Canton, O , R 6.

No. 3706. Sixth Generation. 2429.

4) Mary Esther Brenneman, b Nov 30, 1908, near Elida, O., m Jan. 6, 1939, Durbin T. Yoder of North Dakota Esther is a R N. Mr. Yoder is a medical physician. They are located at 1136 S. W., Fifth St., Miami, Fla. Mennonites.

No. 3707. Seventh Generation. 628.

5) Elsie R. Shenk, b. July 31, 1903, near Elida, O., m. June 8, 1933, Ira Stoltzfus, of Pa. Address: Martinsburg, Pa Farmer. Mennonite.
    1. Victor Ezra Stoltzfus, b. Mar. 24, 1934.
    2. Virginia Mae Stoltzfus, b. Apr. 24, 1938.

INDEX

517

518

6	Blosser, Annie L., Henry Brown	2111
6	Blosser, Amos H., Ada M. Suter & Lucy May Wyant	2072
7	Blosser, Aquilla H., Mabel A. Frey	856
6	Blosser, Benjamin, Jerucia Head	955
5	Blosser, Christian B., Carrie May Yoder	2455
6	Bosser, Christina J., John E. Hartzler	2457
6	B'osser, Daniel J., Grace P. Heatwole	1141
4	Blosser, David, Lila Luma	2821
7	B osser, Effie May, Curtis Life	2075
6	Blosser, Elizabeth, John Philips	958
4	Blosser, Elizabeth, Thomas Bowers	2818
5	B'osser, Emma, Charles W. Crown	2831
6	Blosser, Emma Elizabeth, Christian Kulp	2088
6	B!osser, Ernest David, Bertie Alice Brown	2079
5	Blosser, Eugene Franklin, Bessie M. Rumbaugh	2832
6	Blosser, Frances, Frederick Philips	959
6	Blosser, Frances R., Leslie K. Lehman	2092
6	Blosser, Francis William, Lucile Rasor	2833
6	Blosser, Frederick P., Rettie Bible & Catherine F. Heatwole	2096
4	Blosser, George, Mina Newton & Ollie Johnson	2822
6	B'osser, George C., Elsie Haifley	2824
5	Blosser, Helen, Rev. Irve Townsend	2826
4	B'osser, Henry, Mary E. Bolander	2827
5	B'osser, Hazel, Orman Justice	2836
6	B'osser, Jacob, Minerva Showalter	954
6	Blosser, James Kavil, Zetta Fern Diehl	2830
6	Blosser, Jonas F., Myra McDorman	2095
5	Blosser, John Marcus, Ella Mabel Brackbill	2460
6	Blosser, Joseph, Effie Whilbarger	956
4	B'osser, John, Mary Plumber	2820
6	Blosser, Katie L., Enhraim Lehman	2094
5	Blosser, Katherine, John Andrew Hilty	2454
5	Blosser, Lessie, Joseph D. Yoder	2458
5	Blosser, Lester, Hazel Cole	2823
4	B'osser, Lewis, Retta Barnes & Sarah A. Berchard	2834
6	B'osser, Lydia A., William J. Keyton	2067
4	B'osser, Lydia, Jacob Staver	2840
6	Blosser, Mahlon L., Pauline S. Heatwole	1143
6	Blosser, Magdalena, Emmanuel Hartman	2082
5	B'osser, Margaret S., Jacob Martin	2103
6	Blosser, Margaret G., Daniel Good	2112
4	B'osser, Martin, Barbara F. Seibert	2835
6	B'osser, Marzella C., Robert Cornelious	2829
5	B'osser, Mary M., Abraham F. Grove	2104
6	B'osser, Mary M., Carl Lehman	2109
5	Blosser, Mary M., Benjamin Gerig	2461
4	Blosser, Mary, Thomas Bowers	2819
6	B'osser, Michael O., Fannie M. Good	1142
6	Blosser, Nannie E., Elmer R. Brunk	1139
6	Blosser, N Pearl J. Early Suter	1138
4	B'osser, Nancy, William Alonzo Bechtel	2837
7	B'osser, Nettie Jane, Ira Buerge	2081
7	Blosser, Oren D., Emily Slaubaugh	856½
6	B'osser, Orpha V., Homer R. Suter	1140
7	Blosser, Paul Franklin, Cora Weldendorth	2080
6	B'osser, Peter Myrtle Naomi McDorman	2090
6	B'osser, Priscilla R., Mervin Shull	2097
6	B'osser, Ralph Yoder, Elizabeth Habeggar	2456
6	Blosser, Ressie P., Paul Buchwalter	2107
7	B'osser Roy Lee, Ida Alice Mitchell	2078
5	B'osser, Ruby C., Jesse P. Powell	2825
6	B'osser, Rudy D., Elwood Forrer	2110
5	Blosser, Rudolph P., Elsie V. Ralston & Annie C. Wyant	2106
7	Blosser, Russell Amos, Virginia Lee Grady	2076
5	Blosser, Samuel H., Emma C. Shifflett	2066
6	Blosser, Samuel O., Fannie Craigg	2091
5	Blosser, Samuel R., Nancy Catherine Diller	3207
5	Blosser, Stephen Albertus, Ada H. Engle	2828
5	Blosser, Timothy H., Iva E. Stahly	2459
7	Blosser, Vada M., George Ira Sandridge	2073
7	B'osser, Virgil Randolph, Minnie Velma Jameson	2077
7	B'osser, Walter Henry, Rosalyn E. Dutrow	2074
6	Blosser, Ward Wrant, Lavina Sibert	2108
6	Bond, Nancy C., Elmer Glick	2980
6	Bowers, Albert, Ethel Crites	3424
5	Bowers, Annie Laura, Samuel J. Hott	1523

519

523

527

6	Bunn, Mary H., Harold Bagford	3678
7	Burkholder, Aaron Caleb, Alta Burkholder	3273
6	Burkholder, Ada F., John S. Click	601
6	Burkholder, Aldine C., Annie May Blanks	599
6	Burkholder, Amos H., Josephine Esther Weaver	3610
6	Burkholder, Annie C., Henry S. Alderfer	823
6	Burkholder, Andrew L., Anna B. Hoover	3272
7	Burkholder, Bertha Catherine, Paul Bender	3620
7	Burkholder, Clifford A., Ava Marie Goard	3703
6	Burkholder, Effie A., Perry Cline	586
6	Burkholder, Ella D., Leon Davis	3611
6	Burkholder, Ellis W., Alice V. Heatwole	603
7	Burkholder, Elizabeth Marie, Melvin Hostetler	1000
6	Burkholder, Emma L., Joseph E. Huber	828
6	Burkholder, Emmanuel J., Ella Virginia Weaver	3609
7	Burkholder, Esther Larue, Rhodes Beery Landes	3270
7	Burkholder, Esther M., Lester Groff	3274
7	Burkholder, Harry C., Goldie Stauffer	999
6	Burkholder, Herman F., Anna V. Good	829
6	Burkholder, John D., Dora Humbert	272
7	Burkholder, John D., Jr., Marjorie V. Heatwole	928
7	Burkholder, John S., Vernie M. Knisely	3269
6	Burkholder, Joseph A., Fannie Showalter	274
7	Burkholder, Joseph A., Jr., Faye Lehman	3616
6	Burkholder, Lewis A., Laura R. Wenger	830
7	Burkholder, Lena Gertrude, Harry Anthony Brunk	3622
7	Burkholder, Lettie E., Robert H. Graves	3617
6	Burkholder, Lillie A., Simeon Brenneman	605
6	Burkholder, Maggie F., Emmanuel J. Swope	271
7	Burkholder, Margaret Esther, James M. Coakley	3614
7	Burkholder, Mary E., Lloyd Martin	3615
6	Burkholder, Martin L., Etta M. Swartz	825
7	Burkholder, Marion D., Eva C. Moyers	827
6	Burkholder, Minnie M., Jacob Kiser	585
6	Burkholder, Nannie C., Daniel W. Good	275
7	Burkholder, Nellie A., Newton S. Weber	3621
7	Burkholder, Nelson R., Ruth Sandridge	3619
6	Burkholder, Oliver A., Anna G. Showalter	587
7	Burkholder, Paul Marvin, Elizabeth F. Wenger	3271
7	Burkholder, Raymond A., Elizabeth M. Smith	604
7	Burkholder, Roy A., Anna Nasetka	3618
7	Burkholder, Roy DeWitt, Mary Rebecca Rhodes	3268
6	Burkholder, Reuben S., Effie V. Grove	273
6	Burkholder, Sophiah M., Otho O. Rhodes	826
6	Burkholder, Walter O., Anna Belle Fulk	600
6	Buselle, Arthur E., Josephine McNamee	1757
5	Butler, Betty, Elbert Mintou	1542¼
6	Byrum, Birdie Ruth, Walter Lee Greenawalt	1201
6	Byrum, Enoch Arlo, Lois Irene McDonald	1202
6	Byrum, Ethel Elsie, Frank Eugene Kimball	1200
6	Byrum, Mabel Grace, Odie E. Stevens	1203
6	Calton, Lawrence, Darline Furry	2323
7	Campbell, Edna Elizabeth, Marvin Turner Kiser	3475
7	Campbell, Herman Samuel, Grace Mariah Shank	3474
7	Campbell, Raymond Ercil, Sarah Elizabeth Coffman	3473
7	Campbell, Thelma Frances, Joseph R. Driver	3476
5	Capita, Charles Everett, Lula F. Gates	1708
6	Capita, Charles Everett, Jr., Leona H. Homfald	1709
5	Capita, James Oren, married	1710
5	Capita, John Theiss, Hattie ——	1711
7	Carter, Mary, Dick Hill	2210¼
7	Carter, Verna Agness, Glade Jameson	2210½
6	Cary, Cleta, Ellwood Ridenour	1896
6	Cary, Darrell Bruce,	1580
6	Cary, Inez Mae, Chester Holzborn	1581
7	Cash, Catherine, Harold Goble	1726¼
6	Cauady, Evelena, —— Whitehead	2204
5	Chandler, Leah, John W. Unland	2850
5	Chandler, Lucinda, Joseph Wilson	2849
5	Chandler, Orpha Ruth, Elias Howard	2852
6	Chapman, Francis, Ada Householder	3303¼
6	Chapman, Golden, Edna M. Fadeley	3301
6	Chapman, Paul, Anna Fadeley	3302
6	Chapman, Tracy O., Luther L. Bear	3303
6	Chase, Enoch Aquilla, Evelyn Jessie Oliver	2196

6	Frank, Carl, Laura Brown	1967
5	Frank, Charles Michael, Jane G. Christman	1087
6	Frank, Clarence Baldwin, Edna Brown	1966
5	Frank, Edward B., Edna Staly	1963
6	Frank, Emma. R. Gordon Sharp	1964
5	Frank, John S., Grace Waite	1969
5	Frank, Joseph C., Cassaranda Blardell	1970
5	Frank, Laura Belle. John W. Daugherty	1091
5	Frank, Loisa Bell, John F. Swank	1088
5	Frank, Susan M., William H. Whistler	1083
5	Frank, William Henry, Lenna Baldwin	1093
6	Frazer, Jessie, Burley Long	2280
4	Freed, Abraham, Susan Harmon	893
5	Freed, Alva T., Myrtle Freed	915
5	Freed, Charles L., Ida Stuart	914
5	Freed, Clara S., Michael Krause	894
6	Freed, Dorothy, Ivan Gundy	3685
5	Freed, Ella M., James Spence	911
5	Freed, Emma P., S. E. Bunn	912
5	Freed, Etta A., H. S. Bailey	913
5	Freed, Frances Elizabeth, Charles D. Clemant	909
6	Freed, Harold V., Lucile Turner	3683
5	Freed, Lydia, Abram Good	910
6	Freed, Lala G., Carl Menson	3684
5	Freed, Mary M., John Hemky	901
5	Freed, Stella B., Robert Rutter	916
7	Freeman. Vivian, Rex Conner	2267
6	Freske, Ida Belle, John Fritz	3471
6	Freske, Stella Edell, George Leroy Miller	3472
4	Friesner, Caroline. Frederick Olmstead	3098
4	Friesner, Daniel, Nettie E. Denman	3101
5	Friesner, Edna Leah, Richard Keller	3108
5	Friesner, Ethel Leona. Ernest Belsh	3106
5	Friesner, Guy C., Pauline Hogrefe	3103
4	Friesner, Jacob. Mary Imhoff	3099
5	Friesner, Karl E., Bertha Bruant	3104
5	Friesner, Luther E. Fayne Armstrong	3107
4	Friesner, Lydia Ann, Frank Hogmire	3110
6	Friesner, Madilene. Oscar Truax	3105
5	Friesner, Mary Elizabeth, Carl Miller	3109
5	Friesner, Richard E., Eileen Mauchly	3129
5	Friesner, Ray E., Chrystal Mathers	3102
5	Friesner. Roy, Gennie Willard	3100
6	Fritz, Dessie, George Schilling	1248
6	Fritz. Edgar Earl, Edna Ripley	2161
6	Fritz, William Lawrence. Mary Troster	2162
6	Fry, Archie Lee. Myrtle V. Baylor	2007
6	Fry, Charletta Pearl, Stewart Roudabush	2011
6	Fry, Charles Wilson. Bertha Bolik	2010
7	Fry, Clara Pauline, Ward Franklin Faught	2025
6	Fry, Esther Marie, Henry E. Stahl	181
4	Fry, Maggie. Ashbury Menefee Hamrick	224
7	Fry, Marie Louise. Tony B. Lamb	2026
6	Fry, Marion Marvin, Nora Baylor	2009
6	Fry. Orpha Leona, Bryan Bowman	1358
6	Fry, Paul Raymond, Cecilia Keenan	180
6	Fry, Stewart William, Lottie Lambert	2008
6	Fry. Walter Emmette. Clara Belle Brown	2006
5	Fulk, Abraham Breneman, Martha Susan Howes	207
5	Fulk, Ada Susan. Robert Shifflett	204
5	Fulk, Anna Belle. Walter O. Burkholder	201
5	Fulk, David I., May B. Hopkins	202
5	Fulk, Effie Frances. Ollie G. Warner	203
5	Fulk, John Edward, Beulah Warner	205
5	Fulk, Josiah Franklin, Emma May	200
5	Fulk, Lesta Pearl. Byrl C. Skelton	206
4	Funk, Abraham L., Mary Winslow Wetherall	2607
4	Funk, Abraham B., Ella L. Ringold	2643
4	Funk, Anna M., James C. Heltzel	2616
5	Funk, Bertha J., Phares Hinkle	2636
5	Funk, Daisy, Thomas Arey	3329
5	Funk, Daniel Christian, Maude McGee	2640
5	Funk, Edna Pearl. Charles E. Noffsinger	2645
5	Funk, Effie E., J. Herbert Skelton	2637
4	Funk, Elizabeth Ann. Oswell Schmick	2608
4	Funk, Elizabeth, Thomas Newman	3196

5	Morrison, William Thomas, Mary Clark	3156
5	Mosier, Dora C., Gabriel Brunk	3022
5	Mosier, Elizabeth, Samuel S. Brenneman	3013
5	Mosier, Ella A., Roy Tucker	3014
5	Mosier, Ida, Abraham Good	3020
5	Mosier, John L., Jennie Miller	3021
5	Mosier, Jacob Cless, Naomi Anderson	3023
7	Mouse, Harry F., Pearl Mechum	5291¼
7	Mouse, Lillian M., Guy Flint & J. H. L. Meyers	5291½
5	Moyer, Minnie M., Walter Clarida	2743
5	Mumaw, Aaron, Florence Loucks	2605
5	Mumaw, Adam Henry, Clara Belle Zook	2599
4	Mumaw, Amos, Catherine Shaum	2590
5	Mumaw, Amos B., Emma F. Rohrer	2595
6	Mumaw, Byron E.	3608
6	Mumaw, Catherine Esther, Perce King	2592
5	Mumaw, Clara, Glenn G. Unsicker	2589
5	Mumaw, Cora, Elmer D. Tyson	2604
5	Mumaw, Daniel W., Estella Anna King	2600
5	Mumaw, Enos, Ruth E. Lehman	2603
5	Mumaw, George S., Lucy E. Wilson	2591
5	Mumaw, Harry, Minnie Hostetler	2598
4	Mumaw, Henry A., Malinda Blosser	2587
6	Mumaw, Homer A., Katherine Keener	2597
5	Mumaw, Ira, Martha Weaver	2606
4	Mumaw, John, Lydia A. Good	2602
5	Mumaw, John Rudy, Esther Mosemann	2601
5	Mumaw, Levi, Fannie Shoemaker & Alice Hershey	2594
6	Mumaw, Marion Edward, Mary Eagleton	2593
5	Mumaw, Martha E. & Anna Naomi	2599½
5	Mumaw, Phoebe, Aaron Kolb	2588
6	Mumaw, Ralph Wayne, Mildred Schrock	3607
6	Mumaw, Stanford R., Lavina Hilty	2596
4	Mumaw, Susan, John K. Weldy	2557
7	Mundy, Avis Rosaline, George Wilson Swartz	3554
7	Mundy, D. Clement, Leona Frances Miller	3553
7	Mundy, Margaret, Paul Simmers	1492
7	Mundy, Nellie Elizabeth, Mark Raymond Wampler	3552
7	Mundy, Theodore, Arline Margaret Marshall	1477
6	Murphy, Frederick, Josie Shoemaker & Lelia Lemon & Wilma Bause	2276
5	Obaugh, Bliss Everett, Ella Hedrick	1838
5	Obaugh, Edna Blanche, David Henry Hildebrand	1840
5	Obaugh, Elizabeth Beatrice, Bell M. Harris	3480
5	Obaugh, Frederick H., Myrtle Virginia Armstrong	1839
4	Obaugh, James A., Mary Jane Propes	1836
5	Obaugh, Mary Beulah, Ernest M. East	3481
5	Obaugh, Owen Blaine, Etha Williams	3479
4	Obaugh, Samuel H., Caroline Propes	1834
4	Obaugh, Sarah, John Rawley	1835
4	Obaugh, William Albert, Mary Belle Hoffman	1837
5	Ogly, Catherine, David McNelty	2310
6	Ogly, Clay Bemont, Medro ————	2309
6	Ogly, Clyde, Laura Spencer	2298
6	Ogly, Guy Clifford, Mona Keenan	2308
5	Ogly, Lawrence, Eliza Turner Carter	2297
6	Ogly, Mae, Carl E. Drake	2305
6	Ogly, Maud, William Poor	2299
6	Ogly, Phoeba Priscilla, John Boorman	2307
6	OHair, Durban Landes, Margaret Mary Keller	2338
6	OHalleran, Ethel Laverne, Rowland Bohnsack	178
6	OHalleran, Robert Charles, Eva Beery	179
6	Olson, Leslie Leland, Rose M. Walker	1411
6	Palmer, Leland Glen, Marion J. Peckham	3089
6	Parrett, Martin L., Margaret Catherine Brooks	949
6	Parrett, Mary F., Herman T. Campbell	950
7	Parrot, Lola Elizabeth, Harvey Hill Smith	3477
7	Parrot, Carl G., Anna Newton Fielding	3478
5	Pence, Edd, Cora Early	572
6	Peters, Agnes Olivia, Frank Simon Hooker	1284
6	Peters, Albert, Rom A. Cline	1280
5	Peters, Charles Felton, Nannie Trimble	1272
6	Peters, Charles, Florence Orders	1279
6	Peters, Charles Wesley, Edith Taggart	1285
6	Peters, Flora, John G. Brossman	1281